C000181507

The Mustard BOOK

ROSAMOND MAN & ROBIN WEIR

GRUB STREET • LONDON

For Keith, with love – r.m.
To Elizabeth, Charlotte and Matthew – r.w.

This edition published in 2010 by
Grub Street
4 Rainham Close
London
SW11 6SS
Email: food@grubstreet.co.uk
Web: www.grubstreet.co.uk

First published in Great Britain 1988
by Constable and Company Limited as *The Compleat Mustard*

Copyright © 1988, 2010 by Rosamond Man and Robin Weir

A CIP record for this title is available from The British Library
ISBN 978-1-906502-59-1

All rights reserved. No part of this book may be reproduced or transmitted in any form or by any means, electronic or mechanical, including photocopying, recording or any information storage and retrieval system, without permission in writing from the publisher.

Printed and bound in Slovenia

Contents

Mustard jars from *Essai sur l'Histoire de la Moutarde de Dijon*,
E. Jobard (undated)

Foreword

Moustarde apres disner
After meat comes mustard.

OLD FRENCH PROVERB

Venice, for centuries, was queen of the ancient spice trade. How fitting, then, that she should give birth to the idea of a book on mustard. After pepper, mustard is the world's second most important spice. Yet, unlike other spices, mustard has caused no wars: it grows so obligingly easily that it has always been there, ready to be gathered when wanted. Man has used it, since time immemorial, in countless ways. As with any ingredient which becomes familiar in many countries, it took on many personalities, and its appearance was sometimes highly unexpected. Venice was the scene of one very original marriage.

Dining at the pretty La Colomba restaurant, Robin Weir was presented with a pudding – and a challenge. Could he guess the secret ingredient? If so, the dessert was on the house. Creamy in colour and texture, its appearance gave no clue. The first mouthful revealed a sweetness, a hint of pears and a slight, but definite, bite. Three helpings later the secret was still unrevealed. But the old proverb was apt, for the vital spice was indeed mustard – in the form of the wonderful Mostarda di Venezia, quinces preserved in a sugar syrup spiced with white mustard seed. Similar to the better known Mostarda de Cremona (traditionally served with cold meats) though in purée form rather than with whole fruits, the Mostarda, in Venice, is served with a dollop of the rich creamy cheese, *mascarpone*, to produce that elusive-tasting dessert.

The idea was born, and soon it was mustard in everything; mustard soups, mustard sauces, mustard ice cream, mustard biscuits. Sacks of mustard seed sat in all corners of our kitchens, jars of mustard lined our shelves. And the more we experimented, the more endless seemed the possibilities.

The research began. The problem was not, as so many had asked, whether there was enough to write a book on mustard, but to know how, and when, to stop.

History turned up fascinating, and often tantalizing, details. Prehistoric man had supposedly chewed mustard seeds. A bag of seed, ready for sowing, had been found at the Mycenaean site of Marmariani in Greece, and mustard had been discovered in a Bronze Age lake dwelling of Morigin at Lake Bienne.

From India, where the plant's early flowering signifies the first sign of spring, came many folk tales, none so charming as that of the grower going to sleep at night, a mustard seed and a drop of water in the palm of his hand. By morning, a large plant had grown.

France had other, less complimentary tales. Their picturesque phrase to describe a vain and stupid man, '*Il est le premier moutardier du Pape*', dates back to medieval times. When Cardinal Jacques Duèse was installed as Pope John XXII at Avignon in 1316, his relatives wasted no time in asking for jobs. One distant cousin from Dijon knew only about mustard, and since the Pope was reputedly mad about the stuff, he was rewarded with his title (another cousin jumping on the bandwagon as 'second mustarder'), and a pretty uniform: pale apple green, a mustard pot slung over his shoulder and the motto 'I tickle the palate and excite the nose'.

Monasteries were large consumers of mustard. The accounts of the Cathedral Saint Etienne, near Dijon, for 1447 show that: 'Firstly, the 5th day of September for the day of Clement 7 pints of mustard were made.' The mustard maker returned on 16 October, 2 December and 30 January to replenish the well-used pot.

France inveigled her culture, and her mustard, into Thomas Jefferson's life. On his return home, he adopted many French habits, planted mustard seed in his garden and ordered the condiment (some 5 lbs each, of two types, in 1790) from a Paris grocer. Some seventy years later, wild mustard greens were to provide precious nourishment for many during the Civil War.

We were surprised to learn how high in nutrients mustard is: 25 per cent protein, 29 per cent fat, salts of calcium, phosphorus, magnesium and sulphur, plus Vitamin B – though you would need to eat more than the stomach could cope with, to benefit. Its uses in medicine were ancient and legion, though we doubt its efficacy as an aphrodisiac, especially one eighteenth-century recommendation to apply poultices to the affected area.

Also somewhat surprising was Argentina's love of mustard. Perhaps in view of the magnificent local beef, and the large Anglo community, it is logical. Interestingly both English and Latin tastes are catered for, as not only is the mild condiment Savora (first marketed by Colman's in 1999) very popular but also the fiery English brand. Indeed Colman's largest factory in South America is located in the Argentine. The rest of that vast continent largely ignores mustard, except high in the mountains of Colombia, where it appears in various local dishes.

Mountainous regions would seem to be good for mustard: the tiny country of Nepal grows a staggering 79,000 tonnes a year, making her the world's third largest producer, most of it going to India.

Over half the world's made mustard still comes from the French town of Dijon, although no longer does any one firm list, as in 1780, over eighty different varieties. While we may not have quite that range today, we are again becoming more conscious of mustard's many guises. No longer are we limited to just English or French on the supermarket shelf. There are whole grain mustards, smooth mustards, herby mustards, sweet mustards, mild and hot mustards (though none so hot as the Japanese), mustards made with champagne, mustards made with ale – an age-old combination this, for ale used to be spiced with mustard seed to prevent undue fermentation.

We have tried to paint as complete a portrait of this fiery little plant as space allowed. The journey has been long, sometimes frustrating, occasionally fraught. But it has always been interesting, often exciting and, gastronomically, very rewarding. Mustard is primarily a stimulant. We hope that this book will stimulate you to become, like us, 'enthusiasts'.

Rosamond Man
Robin Weir

Sinapis Nigra

Mustard plant, from *Medical Botany*, 1821

Introduction

Botany and horticulture
for high purpose did the gods ordain
the mustard plant to grow beneath
the feet of mortals.

ATTRIBUTED TO MONTAIGNE (1533–92)

Mustard is a very easy plant to grow. It epitomizes the old country saying, 'One year's seed: seven years' weed' – one species in particular can lie dormant for a hundred years in the soil, only to flourish again given the right conditions.

This habit of self-seeding has often made mustard an unconscious recorder of history. In California, for instance, it is easy to trace the steps of one of the early missionaries, Father Junipero Serra. Accompanying the Spanish military on their colonization of Upper California, he set out, in 1768, with Captain Gaspar de Portolá: 'The route of his walk is today the route of the main north - south highway, and it is vividly marked in the spring by the blossoming mustard whose seeds the friar scattered as he went.' (Alastair Cooke, *America*.) Thus was the first network of 'bible-trails' marked out, an ingenious and fool-proof method of map-drawing.

By nature, the plant is a biennial, sown one year to produce its flower and seed the next, but as man started to cultivate it in earnest, new annual strains were evolved. It is extraordinarily obliging in its reproduction – indeed for the Hindus it is the symbol of fertility – and a pound of white seed (approximately 70,000 seeds) can produce 55 million seeds by the second generation. A mere twelve ounces of the much smaller black seed produces some 500 million offspring within two seasons – roughly 3,400 'grandchildren' for every seed.

Mustard comes from a very large family – the Cruciferae – and among its relations are the cresses, radishes, turnips, and horseradish. Although a fiery strain runs through much of the family, it is nevertheless friendly to man, no known member being poisonous. Three species can be classified as mustard and they all belong to the cabbage branch of the family, the *Brassicas*. The white, or yellow, mustard once so familiar to the English countryside is *Brassica alba* (Boiss), *Brassica hirta* or – in its Greek guise – *Sinapis alba* (giving the medical name for the mustard plaster, sinapism). It is the smallest of the species.

Sinapis alba was probably introduced to England by the Romans: it is certainly native to the Mediterranean region, while black mustard grew further east, round what we now call Iran. The mustard found growing wild today in Gloucestershire is the white, and Tewkesbury was the earliest known centre of English mustard making. Black mustard was another import, again probably with the Romans, though maybe at a later date, but by the nineteenth century it had been known as a 'wild' plant for at least one hundred years.

Until the early Tudors, the growing of mustard, as indeed of all herbs, had been the province of the monasteries. That mustard was important can be seen from the fact that they had a 'mustardarius' – someone in charge of growing and distributing the mustard. Then came the rise of Tewkesbury mustard, followed by Mrs Clements of Durham in 1720, and finally Jeremiah Colman. Although few know his exact recipe we do know that Colman's made use of both white and black seeds, very carefully selected, as were the growers. Indeed today, Colman's supply their growers with the seed for growing; the new crop is all delivered to Colman's who again select the seed and return it to the farmers for the next season's sowing. For the last thirty years, though, black mustard has played no part in the famous table mustard.

Black, or true, mustard, *Brassica nigra* (Koch), was known to the Greeks – Hippocrates refers to it – decades before Alexander the Great had conquered the plant's native land. Legend has it that Darius, the Persian king, sent Alexander a bag of sesame seed, to illustrate the large numbers of his army. Alexander returned a bag of mustard seed - not only greater numbers in his army, but a greater fieriness. What colour were those seeds? White mustard seed is nearly twice as large as the black; the black is smaller than sesame, and indigenous to the area. We can only suppose ...

The black seed probably came to Europe via the early Arab spice traders, being shipped from Alexandria. Certainly mustard flourished in Egypt: great quantities were found in the XIIth Dynasty (1991–1786 BC) tomb of Dira Abu'n-Nega, near Thebes, and there are specimens from the New Kingdom Age (1567–1085 BC) at the Dokki Agricultural Museum in Cairo. The largest of the species, it grows 8-12 ft tall, though its seeds are half the size of its white relative and – confusingly – not black, but a reddish-brown. Nowadays the growers of black mustard are few and far between: England has cultivated none since the Second World War. Only in areas where labour is plentiful and cheap (Sicily, Southern Italy, Ethiopia) is the seed deliberately sown, for *B. nigra* must be gathered by hand. It is all too apt, when shaken, to scatter those minuscule seeds.

Brassica juncea (Coss), brown or Indian mustard, grows 4-6 ft high and presents no problems in harvesting: the monstrous machines that are the pickers of today can easily scoop millions of the seeds in one greedy mouthful. It hails from the Himalayas, spreading westward to the Crimea and eastward to China, and has always been significant in that vast sub-continent – as a seasoning spice, of course, and, before the discovery of chillies in the New World, presumably even more desirable for its pungency than for the nuttiness it gives to so many dishes today. Almost more important was the oil obtained from the seed, particularly favoured for culinary use in Bengal. The leaves are popular as a vegetable in Northern India and also in China (where they are called *Bak-Choi*, much loved fresh and pickled).

Samples found at Channu–Daro Sind in Lower India dating from 3000 BC are almost certainly from the brown species, although there is conflict. One writer says these are *B. nigra*, but all the authorities agree that this is not native to India. Mustard greens are without doubt *B. juncea*, and as the plant's native terrain lies within western China, it is probably the brown seed that is listed in the ancient herbal of Shen Nung, emperor some 5,000 years ago. Pottery vessels containing mustard were also found at Ban Po Village, North Xyan in Shenxi Province, dating back to 5000-4000 BC, so the Chinese were certainly among the earliest cultivators of the plant, if not the first.

Today Canada is the world's largest producer, with 122,317 metric tons produced in 2003, accounting for 43 per cent of world production. Like Colman's suppliers, the farmers are given the seed, told how many acres to sow, and are paid cash for the crop. It is a thriving business, and some 250,000 acres annually go under mustard cultivation in South Alberta and Saskatchewan, half growing *B. juncea* and half *Sinapis alba*. Most of the white goes across the border into the United States, the world's biggest importer of mustard. Some of the brown goes westward to Japan, where they enjoy a very hot mustard as a table condiment, often mixed with *wasabi* (horseradish) to enliven it further, but the largest importer of Canada's brown seed is France, which grows only about half its mustard seed requirements.

Close behind is Russia; they have extensive areas under cultivation at Sarepta in Southern Russia, where the plant is indigenous. Little appears in the West about Russians and their mustard. They make a great deal of oil from it, which they appreciate highly, using it much as we use the best olive oil. In 1986 letters to the editor of *Literaturnaya Gazeta (The Literary Gazette)*, complaining that mustard could only be bought in 3-litre jars, were at first thought to be a hoax. But eventually it was discovered that 'a factory in the Ukraine had decided to make the change to cut its workload, by reducing from 10,000 to 333 the number of jars produced from each ton of pungent Soviet mustard' (80,000 metric tons in 2003, the most recent figure we have). 'The magazine concluded, with a note of despair, that as a result mustard in the giant jars would soon go off, forcing every family to throw it away. Then, once again, there would be another mustard deficit' (*The Times*, 3 February 1986).

Mustard, together with vines, was introduced into the Dijon area of Gaul by the Romans, whose use of the condiment is well documented by Marcus Gabius Apicius. Living during the heyday of the Roman Empire (80-40 BC), he was fascinated by food. He was also very rich, and spent most of his fortune on his obsession. He left a fascinating record of Roman eating and cooking habits in which mustard is often mentioned – as a preservative, in sauces, with meat, with fish, with vegetables, as a vegetable (still enjoyed as such in a few remote areas of the south). The Romans obviously liked their mustard, though Plautus, 150 years earlier, had so disliked it that he mentions it in two of his plays particularly disparagingly.

Interestingly, almost the entire Arab world has ignored the condiment, although charlock, mustard's wild cousin, is sometimes eaten in Turkey as a young salad leaf, and there is one delightful tale from an English traveller in sixteenth-century Byzantium of the procession through Constantinople of all the traders, including 300 Bulgarian mustard makers. Other than that, the seed hardly appears on the Arab table.

On a more sinister note, mustard has lent its name to another product which employs the same irritant qualities as those produced by mustard oil. Athenas said of mustard that it hurt the eyes because of irritation caused by the pungency of the smell. Mustard gas is much more dramatic. It causes acute conjunctivitis (often followed by temporary blindness), choking, and burning of the skin (Hitler suffered from English mustard gas shells in Belgium four days before Armistice was declared – 'a few hours later my eyes had turned into burning coals, it had grown dark around me'). However, the Chinese in the fourth century BC, according to Joseph Needham (*Science and Civilization in China, Vol. IV, Part 2*), were actually using mustard precisely for that purpose. 'It is clear that . . . it was customary to use toxic smokes made by burning balls of dried mustard . . . in stoves, the smoke being directed against troops attacking cities, or blown into the openings of enemy sap tunnels.' Once again, the Chinese seem to have been pioneers in the field, but today the gas – dichlorethyl sulphide – is made by adding chlorine to ethyl sulphate, and its effects, unlike those of mustard, are only destructive. Thankfully, mustard seed ends its days more usually in the mustard pot.

Original mustard plasters, c. 1880

MUSTARD & MEDICINE

I got home at half-past ten,
And mustard-poulticed and barley-
watered myself tremendously.

CHARLES DICKENS, LETTER TO MISS HOGARTH, 18 AUGUST 1858

Both these remedies, barley water to soothe and revive, a mustard poultice to stimulate the blood vessels and guard against chill, were highly popular with the Victorians – indeed barley water is still seen today on many a hospital bedside table. But it was the heyday especially of the mustard poultice and plaster. The poultice was the milder though both were similarly made by mixing mustard with wheat flour (or linseed meal) to a thick paste with water, the proportions depending on the strength required. Spread on to brown paper, or linen, covered with gauze, the poultice was then applied to the appropriate area – though not left for too long, or blisters could ensue. Ten minutes was the recommended time for people 'with delicate skins . . . ¾ hour for those with very tough, insensitive skins', at the end of which the area would be bright red due to the irritant factor of the mustard on the skin. This caused the blood vessels to open, promoting an increased circulation – hence the redness.

The human body's efficiency in producing a counter-irritant response to mustard being slapped on the skin – a speeding up of the blood circulation – was no doubt largely responsible for the reduction of inflammation. With congestion removed, the nervous pressure is relieved, and thus the pain. Hence, for many years, mustard had also been recommended for rheumatism, which is often distressingly painful, as old Jeremiah Colman well knew. In his will he ordered that mustard oil should be given free to those who asked for it, but when 10,000 people applied following an article in *Truth* magazine Colman's started to sell it through chemists and grocers.

The essential oil of mustard had been noted some two centuries before, by Nicolas Le Febvre, though it was not until 1819 that another chemist, Thibierge, noticed that one of its constituents was the beneficial sulphur. Nonetheless, even without this sophisticated chemical knowledge, the ancients had long preached the virtues of mustard.

For the Greeks, the word came from the Gods. Aesculapius, the Greek god-physician himself, proclaimed the benefits of preparations made from the green plants, and Pythagoras prescribed mustard as an aid to improved memory, and as an antidote to scorpion and serpent bites. Hippocrates (c. 460-377 BC), the 'Father of Medicine', wrote extensively about mustard and was one of the first

† 1 *Sinapi ſativum.*
Garden Muſtard.

† 3 *Sinapi ſativum alterum, Dod.*
Field Muſtard.

‡ 4 *Sinapi album.*
White Muſtard.

† 5 *Sinapi ſylveſtre minus.*
Small wilde Muſtard.

¶ The

Mustard plants in *Gerard's Herbal*, 1597

to be specific. White mustard was a great cleanser of the alimentary system – both as an emetic, and as a laxative. Crushed, the seed could be drunk in a hot sweet-sharp solution (presumably a sweetened vinegar), or with hyssop as mustard and cress, in warm honey and water.

Dioscorides, writing his *De Materia Medica* in the first century, added that mustard was 'virtuous in ridding one of the superfluous moods of the brain' and also that it was efficacious in removing deafness and a buzzing of the ears. Athenas, in contemporary Rome, echoed these views, adding that Cyprus mustard was the best. The Romans also used mustard to combat stiffness, mixing it with olive oil and rubbing it into the affected parts.

In India, mustard oil has for centuries been used to anoint and massage the body, to soothe and invigorate. Susruta the Elder, the fourth-century physician, also advised that the bed linen and room of the sick should be fumigated with mustard to drive away malignant spirits.

As a native of Asia, brown mustard seed appears also in Chinese medicine, being highly recommended in a sixth-century herbal. One hundred years later, it was specified for treating carbuncles and swellings, in the form of a mustard plaster. Recently, the Chinese have been experimenting again with mustard, this time the white seed. In the case of chronic bronchitis, they have treated approximately 300 patients with a 10-20 per cent solution injected into various acupuncture points, achieving an 80 per cent success rate.

Western medicine owed much in its early days to the Arab physicians and the Moorish conquest of Spain. And mustard, though hardly cared for as a condiment by the Arabs, had an ancient medicinal history. It is mentioned in several of the great Arabic treatises, particularly that of Al-Biruni (c. AD 1050) who gives its name in various languages and states that 'It is used as a curative in dyspepsia and flatulence.'

Here we would seem to have one of the first specific references to mustard as an aid to digestion. True, Pliny had said that it was wholesome for the body and Hippocrates mentions it as a great internal cleanser. In fact, the same quality of mustard – its irritant ability – is at work in both cases, though of different degrees. For the English herbalists and physicians from Tudor times onward, this gastronomic benefit was to assume as great an importance as its medicinal virtues.

John Gerard praised mustard on both accounts in his herbal of 1597. Not only was it good for the digestion, provoking appetite and warming the stomach, but 'It helpeth the Sciatica, or ache in the hip or huckle bone . . . It also appeaseth the toothache being chewed in the mouth. It helpeth those that have their hair pulled off, it taketh away the blue and black marks that comes out of bruisings.' Interestingly, centuries later, when we went to the Mustard Shop in Norwich, Don Hoffman (the then manager) told us he could remember his grandmother using mustard to alleviate bruising.

Dr Thomas Cogan attributed even greater powers to mustard in *The Haven of*

Mustard bath advertisement from the *Tatler*, 1927

Health (1605): 'The force of the seed is perceived by eating mustard, for if it is good in making to weep we are straightway taken by the nose and provoked to sneeze, which plainly declareth that it soon pierceth the brain. Wherefore as it is a good sauce and procureth appetite, so it is profitable for the pulse, and for such students as be heavy-headed and drowsy, as if they would fall asleep with meat in their mouths. And if any be given to music, and would fain have clear voices, let them take mustard-seed in powder, work the same with honey into little balls, of which they must swallow one or two down every morning fasting, and in a short time they shall have very clear voices.' A Dublin receipt of 1778 suggests standing 'garlic and ½ oz of mustard in a quart of white wine for a week, then drink as much as you wish' as a remedy against asthma, and in the nineteenth and early twentieth centuries mustard was being much advised in the treatment of bronchitis, pleurisy and pneumonia. It had long been used for coughs (hiccoughs, too, a pinch of mustard in cold water) – Culpeper mentions mustard mixed with honey as 'good for old coughs', while another ancient remedy has the seed boiled with dried figs in strong ale.

Despite mustard's great helpfulness to the stomach's digestive powers, taken in too large a quantity, it is one of nature's most efficient laxatives (particularly the white seed). It is also a powerful emetic. Indeed it is one of the few emetics which also act as a stimulant, and is therefore extremely useful in cases of poisoning where there is also breathing or heart failure (but we must stress that while a solution of mustard in warm water will, in an emergency, act quickly as an emetic, it is *not* a substitute for a doctor).

On a less dramatic level, mustard baths are still a useful, and relaxing, remedy for stiffness after extreme physical exertion, although for a long soak we would suggest half of one of Colman's packets of specially prepared Bath Mustard, unless you wish to emerge looking like a lobster! For unbroken chilblains, a foot bath is similarly efficacious; mustard ointment was the great eighteenth-century treatment for this unpleasant complaint, both in England and in France. Mustard baths were also advised for those seeking a fine complexion, and since mustard does open the pores, thus allowing the skin to be thoroughly cleansed, it is a reasonable theory.

Today, mustard is not much used in medicine except by the homeopaths, who use mainly the black seed, for ear, nose and throat complaints, though also for colic and urinary problems. The white seed is used for problems with the oesophagus and the middle ear.

Sinapis nigra. Black Mustard. ☉

C. Mathews. Del. & Sc.   Pub.d by W. Baxter, Botanic Garden, Oxford 1839.

COMMERCIAL MUSTARD MAKERS:

DIJON

Il n'est ville se nom Dijon
Il n'est moustarde que à Dijon.

FOURTEENTH–CENTURY FRENCH PROVERB

The first reference to mustard in the Dijon archives occurs in 1336, when a whole cask was consumed at a banquet. Mustard mills, mortars for making mustard, and pots of mustard are frequently mentioned in wills and inventories, and in 1347, we find in the town records a sum of '12 francs' for sending mustard to the Queen. Dijon mustard was obviously considered the finest: in 1354, the Receiver-General of Burgundy bought mustard seed and vinegar to make 200 lb of mustard, sent in four barrels to King Jean.

The first ordinance relating to the vinegar-mustard makers of Dijon was drawn up in 1390. The date, and use of the word 'mustard', must dispel the myth, beloved by Dijon, of the word's origin. For it had only been nine years since Charles VI had rewarded the city, and his uncle, Philip the Bold, for sending 1,000 men to the ever-continuing fight against Flanders. The reward was a coat of arms with the motto *Mout me tarde*, I ardently desire, on a banner underneath. The story goes that the Dijonnaise were linguistically careless. The middle word *me* had appeared below the other two on the loop of the banner, and was subsequently dropped, producing a new motto – *Mout tarde*, much burning, not inappropriate to the town's main claim to fame. The more usual derivation is from the Latin, *must* (much) or *mustum* (the newly fermented wine juice) and *ardens* (burning). Or maybe the Celts gave us the word with their *mwstertt* (to give off a strong odour).

The specifications of the ordinance were almost identical to the instructions given some thirteen and a half centuries earlier by Columella of Gades in his *De Re Rustica* (AD 42): 'Clean the mustard seed with great care, sift and swill with cold water . . . leave to soak in water for two hours then stir, and after squeezing the seeds in one's hands, throw them into a mortar . . . and crush with the pestle. When well ground, stir the paste towards the middle and flatten same with the hand. When well compressed, form grooves in the paste and pour nitrated water on hot coal previously placed in the grooves so as to rid the grain of all

PHILIPPE·LE·HARDI

Philippe le Hardi, Duke of Burgundy 1364-1408.
It was in 1390 that the first ordinance was drawn up
relating to mustard and vinegar makers in Dijon.

Coat of arms of *Moutardiers*, 1634. Granted in 1634 by Louis XIV

its bitterness and to preserve it from mould. Heat slightly so that the humidity disappears completely and pour strong white vinegar on the mustard stirring the mixture with the pestle and pass through a sieve.' The principles are still startlingly similar. The use of hot coals is especially interesting – for it is not so much bitterness that is removed by the heat as pungency. For all of Dijon's mustard starts life as '*extra forte*' (extra hot or strong). It is not extra pressings that make some mustards hot, but heating (for one tenth of a second at 130°C, on the pasteurization principle) that makes some mustards mild.

1407 (according to Garnier, *Essai sur l'Histoire de la Moutarde de Dijon*) saw a further edict: 'it was forbidden to use anything other than good mustard seed, and only to soak it in good vinegar from the vines, without adding sour wine (*vin aigre*) or the verjuice of apples.' Verjuice was traditionally taken to mean sour grape juice (i.e. from unripe grapes) but crab apple juice was often used instead, particularly where grapes were scarce. Interesting is the distinction between good wine vinegar, properly acetified, and wine that was sour simply through having gone bad. Despite the heavy penalties for using rotten vinegar, or wine, the rules continued to be broken. In 1443, there was an edict concerning the use of weights and measures in the selling of mustard, and a body of inspectors was set up.

Dijon's honour remained intact, despite the plethora of mustard sellers who had taken advantage of the new portable mill which appeared at the beginning of the century. This enabled many newcomers to enter the trade, primarily gro-

Mustard seller, eighteenth century (Nicholas de Larmessin)

Techniques for vinegar and mustard making from
Encyclopaedia Panckouke (eighteenth century)

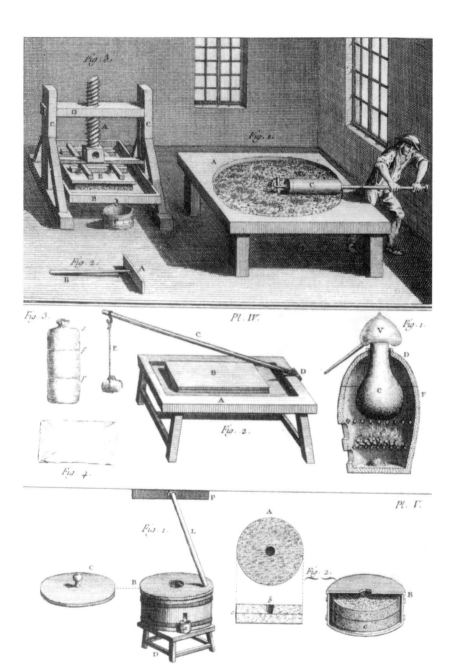

cers, candlemakers (long associated in Paris with mustard making) and apothecaries (long associated in Dijon with mustard). It was an apothecary who was ordered 'to make mustard for the said King our sire and Madame the Queen' in 1477. The said King was Louis XI, and he had just annexed Burgundy into his kingdom. Legend has it that 'he was as devoted to mustard as much as to the leaden figure of the Virgin which decorated his velvet cap' and he undoubtedly had a good supply. For the apothecary had taken three days to grind 4 lb of mustard seed into mustard which filled two small casks.

In 1634, the vinegar and mustard makers decided to unite into one corporation in an attempt to regulate the profession. New rules covered the inspection of utensils and standards of hygiene; no master could have more than one shop and one apprentice at a time. Louis XIV granted them their own arms, azure with a funnel of silver, which were proudly displayed on banners and engraved on numerous seals. In 1712 even stricter statutes were drawn up – for the first time, the word '*moutardiers*' appears. Among the signatories was François Naigeon, father of the founder of one of Dijon's greatest mustard houses.

François Naigeon had become a master vinegar maker in 1703 and soon became a major force in the mustard market. His goods were well known to Parisian gourmets: no doubt his passionate concern for quality played a large part in his meteoric rise. His son Jean-Baptiste (usually referred to simply as Jean Naigeon) instituted a small but revolutionary change in mustard making. In about 1756, the date usually given as the founding of the house, he decided to substitute verjuice for vinegar in the making of his mustard. Although verjuice had been known and used in Roman times, it had been ignored by the French mustard makers for centuries. Yet with Dijon surrounded by vineyards, what could be more logical? With such a choice to hand, Jean was able to specify which grape variety he wanted and exactly when they should be picked. Unripe grapes produce a very pure, sour juice, with no sugar or acetic acid present. Mustard made with verjuice is thus very fine, slightly less acidic or pungent than that made with vinegar. Naigeon's mustard was a roaring success. Imitations abounded but mustard from the house of Naigeon was, for many years, considered far and away the finest. Jean's son continued the business until 1808 when the firm was taken over by another Dijon mustard maker, Fremiet. Thereafter a succession of well-known Dijon names appeared over the doorway in Rue St Jean – Piron, Pierrot, Bizouard – until the firm was absorbed by Amora S.A. in 1977.

Dijon, of course, had many other mustard makers. In 1856 Denis Bornier was registered as a maker of the famous Dijon gingerbread, *pain d'épices*, which not unnaturally is spiced with mustard. Two years later he applied to the Mayor for permission to inscribe over his doorway '*Usine à vapeur, fabrique de chocolat de moutarde Bornier-Cery*' (his wife's name). He was jumping on the bandwagon created three years earlier by the invention of a man whose name today is synonymous with Dijon mustard. The words '*usine à vapeur*' (steam mill) give the game away.

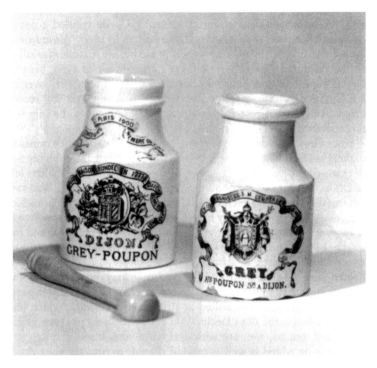

Grey Poupon jar 1875, and Grey Jar 1865: Post- and pre-merger

Until 1853, mustard seed had always been ground in hand-operated mills. Then Maurice Grey, who in 1843 had taken over the firm of Demartelet (founded originally around 1769 by Forey), invented a new machine. It was simple but it could crush, grind to a fine powder, then sieve the seed virtually all in one operation. Whereas previously one man could manufacture 16-17 kg of mustard a day, now the same man could produce 50 kg in a day. Everyone was clamouring for the new machine, advertising its proud possession not only above their doorways but also on their pots.

Maurice Grey was awarded two medals in 1855, one for his mustard, the other for his machine, and in 1860 he became the first Dijon mustard maker to be honoured by a royal appointment. In 1866 he was joined by Auguste Poupon. Although Grey obviously hoped his son, Anatole, would come into the business – he entitled a paper covering all aspects of mustard making, written in 1867, 'Moutarde, à mon fils' (Mustard, to my son) – it was not to be, for Anatole was killed at the Battle of Champigny in 1870. The House of Grey became Grey-Poupon, and remained so until 1970 when it was taken over by S.E.G.M.A.[1] Maille. Happily the name Grey-Poupon is still recognized all over the world as Dijon

---

[1] Société d'Exploitation des Grandes Marques Alimentaires

The Maille shop in Dijon today

mustard, and head of the ship is a direct descendant of Auguste, Henry Poupon.

Since Grey's heyday, in 1865, when there were thirty-nine mustard makers in Dijon, the industry has seen the decline, or the gobbling up, of many of the great houses. By 1911, there were only ten makers left in Dijon, four in the surrounding districts. The First World War saw the numbers diminish even further and by the early thirties firms like Amora were well on the way to becoming huge conglomerates.

In 1937 the regulations governing the making of mustard, and the seed to be used, finally became law. Specifically forbidden is the use of white seed – except in Alsace-Lorraine. Otherwise, only black or brown seed – or a mixture of the two – may be used, and the 'denomination of mustard from Dijon is reserved for mustard in paste made with crushed, and bolted to sifted seed'. Verjuice, which had been specified in the 1853 Declaration of the Academy of Dijon, is still permitted, but so, too, are wine and wine vinegar. Salt, spices and water can be added as well as sulphur dioxide to preserve the colour, but anything else – be it but a grain of white seed, a pinch of flour – and the paste can no longer be called mustard. It then has to be labelled 'condiment'. Seed selection is very carefully controlled. Cleared of all impurities and any bad grain, it is thoroughly washed and moistened, causing the grain to swell. It is then sent to the mill to be ground with the vinegar, verjuice or wine, salt and spices. The grinding is a fine art, the mills must be tuned with great precision so as to merely break the brown husks without crushing them so they can easily be sieved without leaving any bran to adulterate the bright yellow kernel. The paste is then pumped into huge oak casks and left to mature for five to eight days, vast wooden spatulas occasionally stirring the mixture. Only then is it ready to be bottled and labelled with those prized words '*Moutarde de Dijon*'. For Dijon was also granted in 1937 the right – like wines – to an Appellation Contrôlée. The mustard need not have come from the area of Dijon, it need only be made in the manner prescribed for it to be called Dijon mustard. Nonetheless nearly all the mustard so called is in fact from Dijon or its environs.

Sadly, today the makers are few. The Second World War saw the demise of most of the small family concerns. Now, despite an annual production of approximately 59,000 tonnes of mustard, 80 per cent of the market is controlled by Amora and S.E.G.M.A. (the latter a conglomeration of Maille/Grey Poupon and Parizot, another nineteenth-century Dijon maker) with Bocquet-Moutarde de France the biggest independent enterprise. For 85 per cent of the French, Dijon's mustard is their preferred variety, for the rest of the world, Dijon's name is synonymous with the finest mustard you can buy. But for the exotic mustards, so favoured today, we must turn to Paris.

Amora globe mustard pot, *c.*1930

COMMERCIAL MUSTARD MAKERS:
PARIS AND THE PROVINCES

It is not such a bad trade, Savalette and Le Comte have made a fortune . . .

SEBASTIEN MERCIER, LE TABLEAU DE PARIS, 1782–1788

Long before those two gentlemen were making mustard their fortunes, the plant was providing a regular income for the monastery of the Abbey St-Germain-des-Prés at the time of Charlemagne the Great (c. AD 800). Some two hundred years later, a monk from the Benedictine Abbey de Saint-Gall also mentions mustard – as one of the food items figuring prominently on their table. Perhaps because the monasteries were such great consumers of mustard, the trade in its early years was always associated with the tallow makers. Then the '*vinaigriers*' entered the arena and in 1254 they too were permitted to make mustard. Yet mustard makers as such were not mentioned in The Book of Trades for that year. Officially they still fell under the aegis of the chandlers, although undoubtedly specialists were emerging – the tax register of 1292 lists ten '*moutardiers*'. In 1417, the *moutardiers* were included in the 15 Articles which detailed precisely how vinegar and sauce makers should run their business. At the end of the century, in 1494, they were at last formed into a corporation, although adulterations persisted and Rabelais accused the mustard men of 'pissing in their pots'.

A new law in 1567 urged the mustard makers to insist on the cleanliness of their utensils. It was also forbidden for any one master to buy up all the mustard seed available in the market on any one day. The laws grew ever tighter and in 1658 Louis XIV drew up forty-three new articles: the mustard makers were now thoroughly protected. They, and only they, were allowed to sell mustard 'under pain of 100 pounds fine and seeing their illicit merchandise thrown into the river'. It was time for the fortunes to be made.

Savalette, an established maker of fine vinegars, decided in the middle of the century to launch a series of 'fine and aromatic mustards'. He was soon supplying Louis XIV and his court. The riches flowed in, and mustard became a profession 'with a house of its own'.

Around 1665, a group of gourmets and gastronomes formed themselves into the Société Vert-Pré, their ideals 'to renew the formulas of ancient French cuisine'. Among their products was mustard – a mustard which survived until 1960, when Amora absorbed the company. It was the eighteenth century, though, that

Amora bulk dispenser for shops, 1930s to 1960s.
These are still in use in parts of France today.

was to become the age of new mustards, and rivalling mustard makers.

In 1742, M. Le Comte invented a new white vinegar, which earned him the appointment of 'Vinaigrier Ordinaire' to the King. His pupil Capitaine, who succeeded him in 1769, had on his list over 150 vinegars (for toilette, medicinal and gastronomic use) and more than thirty mustards, including, as he proudly boasted, 'that in powder from England'. Nonetheless, he was overshadowed by two even greater names: Maille and Bordin.

Antoine Maille had registered as a master in 1742 and within five years was well established. He used sandstone vessels for distilling, thus avoiding the intrusive flavour of copper, and offered his clients – including Madame de Pompadour – nearly a hundred varieties of vinegar, both for the toilette and the table. His mustards numbered twenty-four and although not all were of his invention (capers and anchovies, for instance, had been launched by Le Comte), the quality was recognized as superb. Tarragon, red with three fruits, garlic, nasturtium, Chartreuse, lemon peel, lemon juice, yarrow, mushrooms, truffles, sixberries, were among the most popular. In 1769, on the death of Le Comte, Maille took over as 'Vinegar-Distiller to the King and their Imperial Majesties'.

He had already amassed great riches, and soon put them to good use. He was a philanthropist and in 1771 gave enormous quantities of vinegar to the city of Moscow, where plague was raging. His reward was another title, Vinaigrier to Her Imperial Majesty, Catherine the Great. He was no less generous to his own

Mustard seller's costume, 1835

Bornibus jars 1950s and 1858-1930

countrymen. Every Monday morning, mustard was given away to the poor of Paris and outlying rural parishes – but to cure their chilblains.

The French Revolution, meanwhile, was about to cause upheaval in Paris, and in the life of Maille's successor, André-Arnoult Acloque. Born into the brewing business, he had made himself a small fortune with an establishment in the Paris suburbs. He also gained a less welcome reputation by defending the King when he was mobbed in 1792. In 1800 he bought the house of Maille, which he ran until his death two years later. In his short reign Acloque added many new mustards – chive, gherkin, shallot, morille (a type of mushroom), tomato, black (with olives), sweet mustard, green with fine herbs, and four-berries (good against chilblains and a 'superlative' condiment). Sadly, his son displayed not a jot of interest in mustard, and in 1819 signed a contract with the young Maille. Within the next seven years, Maille had recaptured the whole business.

François Bordin meanwhile had set up in Rue Simon le France, a 'wretched street, one of the most squalid quarters of Saint Martin' wrote Grimod de la Reynière. Here he flourished for twenty-three years, before moving 'to a magnificent locale in the Rue Saint Martin'. De la Reynière continues: 'It is there displayed with all pomp, this mustard of health and fragrance, which has earned such honour from the Louvre, and the Faculty – who have judged it for the last twenty-five years as favourable to the health as a mustard can be. The make of Bordin, one of the best and most celebrated of Paris, is now known to the two ends of Europe. The Russians eat his mustard like jam.'

In 1803 Bordin created a new mustard – Champagne – 'which has a flavour, a bouquet, an aroma easier to rejoice at than describe'. Two years later, he surpassed himself with his Moutarde Impériale, created in honour of Napoleon and 'superior to all others being made today, with much more aroma . . .' Despite the wonderful mustard, Napoleon ignored him. But royal patronage returned with Charles X, his successor Louis-Philippe, and the Emperor Napoleon III.

Together with Bordin, the house of Maille dominated the Paris market for most of the century, but in its closing years Maille began to decline. By 1930, the last direct descendant was dead. In 1963, the Dijon firms of Grey Poupon and André Ricard bought it out, forming, in 1970, the conglomeration of S.E.G.M.A. Maille. So the name lives, though with only eight of the original twenty-four mustards.

In the middle of the nineteenth century a Burgundian by the name of Bornibus decided to try his luck in the capital. He quickly made a spectacular name for himself, particularly for his so-called 'ladies' mustard', and he was a constant medal winner – thirty-five in 1890. His heirs kept up the tradition of fine mustards and by 1988 it was the only firm in Paris (as Grey Poupon in Dijon) still run by a direct descendant, Madame Hélène Boutet, who operates from the original premises at 60 Boulevard de la Villette.

Mustard making was not confined to Paris and Dijon. Saint-Maixent seems to have enjoyed early fame, and Orléans had its own corporation of vinegar and mustard makers. Besançon produced a dry powder, which did not find much favour, and Angers made a mustard paste, sold in small barrels. Better were the mustards of Châlons – stronger than Dijon; Reims – highly thought of among connoisseurs; and Saint-Brieuc (in Brittany), created by Le Maout, who later did well in Paris.

The town of Meaux produced a successful whole grain mustard, made by the monks since the early seventeenth century. In 1760, it was given to the Pommery family, who continued producing it according to the old formula, and in 1826 it received the accolade of Brillat-Savarin's recommendation. For that philosopher in the kitchen, Dijon's mustard did not take first place; '*Il n'est moutarde que de Meaux*' was his firm opinion.

In 1825 Louit was founded in Bordeaux. Their sensation came in 1845 with a new Moutarde Diaphane which soon sold a million pots a year. The firm was eventually absorbed by Amora. Bordeaux's success encouraged others. Small factories were set up in Avallon, Beaune, Brive, Cambrai, Coulommiers, Le Havre, Lille, Montmirail, Nancy, Nantes, Rouen, Strasbourg . . . It seemed as if all France was making its own mustard – except in the south, where garlic, pimentoes and pepper still took precedence.

1 2 3 4 5 6 7 8

ERÝSIMUM CHEIRANTHOÍDES. TREACLE-MUSTARD. 2⟋

I. Russell Del.   C. Mathews Sc

COMMERCIAL MUSTARD MAKERS:
ENGLAND AND THE UNITED STATES

He a good wit? Hang him baboon! His wit is as thick as Tewkesbury mustard!

FALSTAFF, HENRY IV, PART II, WILLIAM SHAKESPEARE

In medieval times, mustard making in England fell mainly within the province of the monasteries, with a few street-sellers in the large towns. Otherwise it tended to be made at home. In the sixteenth century one town suddenly emerged as a great mustard centre: Tewkesbury, in Gloucestershire. Its mustard was thick in texture, pungently hot in taste and came to be used, in all sorts of phrases, to mean one who was stupid and peppery.

By 1657, however, it was being highly praised. The herbalist Coles said, 'In Gloucestershire about Tewkesbury they grind mustard seed and make it up into balls which are brought to London and other remote places as being the best that the world affords.' Two factors gave Tewkesbury mustard its individuality: the infusion of horseradish which gave added pungency, and the manner in which it was sold. The seed, once washed and pounded in a mortar, or with a large cannon ball, was sifted; the flour was mixed with a cold infusion of horseradish and 'well beaten or stirred up for the space of at least an hour'. The mixture was then formed into large balls and dried. It was thus most convenient for transporting around the country, to sell at the local markets. The mustard ball could be kept until needed, when it would be reconstituted with vinegar, verjuice, cider, red wine, buttermilk or cherry juice, sometimes with honey or sugar added. It was extremely hot. Strangely, today in Tewkesbury there is no record of the business which made the town so famous: it must have been very much a cottage industry, and it vanished as dramatically as it had first appeared.

In 1720 'it occurred to an old woman of the name of Clements, resident at Durham, to grind the seed in a mill and to pass the meal through the various processes which are resorted to in making flour from wheat. The secret she kept for many years to herself, and in the period of her exclusive possession of it, sup-

THE NATIONAL CONDIMENT.

MEDALS.
—o—
LONDON.
PARIS.
PHILADELPHIA.
MOSCOW.

KEEN'S MUSTARD

1st PRIZE, SYDNEY, 1880.

SHAKSPERE

Shows that MUSTARD was in use
300 years ago.

KEEN'S MUSTARD

FACTORY ESTABLISHED.
A.D. 1742.

Was first Manufactured 125 years after
Shakspere's death.

Keen's advertisment 1880

plied the principal parts of the kingdom, and in particular the metropolis, with this article; and George the First stamped it with fashion by his approval' (*The Gentlemen's Magazine*, September 1807).

Mrs Clements' mustard flour took England by storm, and competitors soon appeared. Within three years, the *London Journal* was carrying an advertisement: 'To all families, etc. – The Royal Flower of Mustard Seed is now used and esteemed by most of the Quality and Gentry. It will keep good in the Flower as

Keen's mustard pot, 1870s, and mustard ointment, 1920s

long as in the seed, and one spoonful of the Mustard made of it will go as far as three of that sold at chandlers's shops, and is much wholesomer.' Manufacturers continued to spring up throughout the century, and by the latter years Newcastle and Gateshead also boasted their own makers.

In Durham itself, with Mrs Clements presumably long since dead, the business seems to have been dominated by the Ainsley family. They claimed to have been established in 1692, and probably were – but as flour rather than mustard millers. By 1900, the only maker left was Simpson and Willan, who set up in 1888 and did not stay in business for long into the new century. In truth, Durham had enjoyed its heyday with Mrs Clements, for already in 1810 *Bailey's Agricultural Durham* was stating, 'This plant (mustard) was formerly much grown in this county, and *Durham Mustard* was proverbial for its excellence. At present a crop of mustard is rarely met with.' It was not to be met with again, and Durham's mustard, if it is remembered at all, lives on only in the phrase a 'Durham man': 'a knock-kneed man was so called, and was said to grind mustard between his knees', (Neasham's *North Country Sketches*). Mustard manufacturing had one more move to make – and this time it was not going to be ousted.

Before we turn to the Norfolk miller, we should perhaps remember the origins of a saying still in common use today – 'as keen as mustard'.

In 1742, in Garlick Hill, London, Messrs Keen & Sons set up in the mustard business. They were well placed to provide the city taverns with the condiment

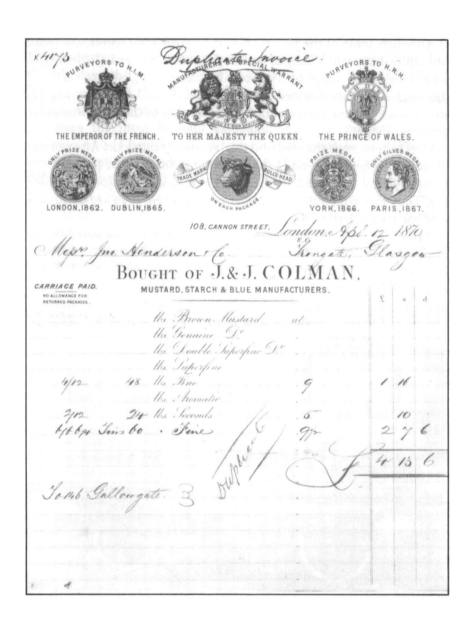

Colman's invoice, 1870

so necessary to the chop house customers and were hugely successful, their name quickly becoming synonymous with mustard. A century later, despite the competition from Jeremiah Colman, Keen's (by now Keen Robinson & Belville) were still flourishing, and their product found great favour in Australia. In 1903 however, like so many of their French contemporaries, they were taken over. Mr Colman's competition had proved too much.

In 1804 Jeremiah Colman bought a windmill standing by Magdalen Gate in Norwich and set up in the business that he already knew – flour milling. Success brought expansion ten years later, when he took over a mill at Stoke Holy Cross, four miles to the south of the city.

Stoke Mill was a flour and mustard mill. Jeremiah, a cautious man, thought long and hard, and finally decided to continue making mustard. A wise decision: in 1856, the business had grown so much it had to move again. New premises were bought just outside Norwich, at Carrow on the River Wensum. As the factory expanded, so did the city for now Colman's works are officially in Norwich.

Although some of the process is still a tightly kept secret, the basic principles have not changed much. Fine quality seed (brown and white) – now all supplied by specially selected English growers – is thoroughly examined, tested for quality and cleaned. After drying, it is stored until needed, then blended so the quality of the final product is always constant.

Steel rollers crush the seed and steel sieves sift the flour. 'After a final blending of the brown and white flours it is ready to be put into the famous yellow labelled tins, themselves made in the adjoining building. The remaining husks

Colman's covered box wagon, 1911

What *is* this Mustard Club?

★ *In response to numerous enquiries, we have pleasure in making public the following brief account of the origin and aims of the Mustard Club.*

THE Mustard Club (1926) has been founded under the Presidency of the Baron de Beef, of Porterhouse College, Cambridge. It is a Sporting Club, because its members are always there for the meat. It is a Political Club, because members find that a liberal use of Mustard saves labour in digestion and is conservative of health. It is a Card Club, but Members are only allowed to play for small steaks.

The motto of the Mustard Club is "Mustard Makyth Methuselahs," because Mustard keeps the digestion young. The Password of the Mustard Club is "Pass the Mustard, please!"

Where is the Mustard Club?

There are more than ten million branches of the Mustard Club—in fact, wherever a few people are mustered together at dinner, there you have a meeting of the Mustard Club. Every home where people respect their digestion is a branch of the Mustard Club.

The Café Royal, Simpsons in the Strand, and all restaurants where good food is enjoyed, are frequented by members of the Mustard Club. Harley Street is a stronghold of the Mustard Club because doctors know the value of Mustard in the proper assimilation of food.

The Objects of the Mustard Club.

To enrol all Grumblers, Curmudgeons, and such other persons who by omitting the use of Mustard have suffered in their digestions, and to bring such persons to a joyous frame of mind and healthy habit of body by the liberal use of Mustard.

To encourage the use of Mustard, not only with Beef and Bacon, but to show how it improves the flavour of Mutton, Fish, Cheese and Macaroni.

To teach the younger generation that the true foundation of health and good digestion is the Mustard-pot.

RULES of the Mustard Club

1. Every member shall on all proper occasions eat Mustard to improve his appetite and strengthen his digestion.
2. Every member when physically exhausted or threatened with a cold, shall take refuge in a Mustard Bath.
3. Every member shall once at least during every meal make the secret sign of the Mustard Club by placing the mustard-pot six inches from his neighbour's plate.
4. Every member who asks for a sandwich and finds that it contains no Mustard shall publicly refuse to eat same.
5. Every member shall see that the Mustard is freshly made, and no member shall tip a waiter who forgets to put Mustard on the table.
6. Each member shall instruct his children to "keep that schoolboy digestion" by forming the habit of eating Mustard.

OFFICERS OF THE MUSTARD CLUB.

Mustard Club poster, *Daily Mirror*, 29 October 1926

have their oil extracted, then are dried and sold for animal feed.

It sounds simple, but Jeremiah spent a great deal of time and thought perfecting his mustard flour. The public responded magnificently; the big bull trademark and the name of Colman's were very quickly established. In 1866 Queen Victoria rewarded him with a royal appointment, the Prince of Wales following suit two years later and King Victor Emanuel of Italy added his seal of approval in 1869. Business expanded so quickly that often four trains were required to take away one day's production. The trains were Colman's own, with their emblem emblazoned on the sides of the cars. The army were supplied with a daily ration of mustard; Captain Scott took some to the Antarctic – efficacious against frost-bite; it was requisite in the luggage of every colonial; and a letter, from some far-flung part, with merely a drawing of a large bull's head above the word England, was safely delivered to Norwich.

No little part of this phenomenal success was due to marketing. In the early days, the advertisements were very simple – a mustard yellow background, with the words Colman's Mustard in huge letters, or perhaps just the lugubrious bull image.

Perhaps the most brilliant campaign was that thought up for Colman's by S H Benson, Ltd, the advertising agents, in 1926. Posters went up on all the London buses – 'Has Father Joined the Mustard Club?' Interest aroused, a 'prospectus' was published for the share issue. When a badge was offered, 2,000 applications were made; every day. Colman's had to open a special department with ten girls to deal with the influx. The success was beyond Benson's – and Colman's – wildest dreams. A card game was produced; eight Mustard Club songs were published; the club motto 'Mustard makyth Methuselahs' and the armorial bearings appeared all over the place on menus and postcards. The campaign continued for another seven years.

Today, the product that is so uniquely English mustard, with its bright yellow colour (turmeric added for vibrancy) and its pungent flavour (the careful blending of white and brown seeds) is still the favoured brand of some 85–90 per cent of the British market.

In the United States, they also have bright yellow mustard but it is much milder in flavour. As recently as 1904, the Americans were not great mustard buyers. Despite R. T. French's claim, in 1885, to be 'the largest manufacturer of mustard in western New York State', sales were far from high. Robert French thought he knew the answer: 'a new kind of prepared mustard; one that is mild and has a true mustard flavour, and yet is light and creamy in consistency and color . . . It must be mild, for I believe that these hot mustards are used sparingly not because they are hot, but because people do not like them.'

French passed the problem over to his plant superintendent, George Dunn, who for some months experimented with different formulae. And then one day, Dunn came up with the solution. A cable was sent to Francis, 'Eureka!'. 'Eureka WHAT?' wired Francis in return – his specification long since forgotten. The

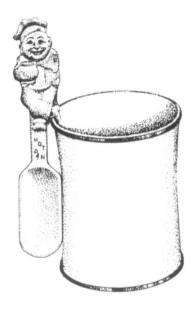

Hod Dan, the Mustard Man was the basis of French's
advertising during their growth in the early 1950s

excitement was a golden-yellow condiment, marketed as French's Cream Salad
Brand – a little cream added to the mustard had changed its character dramatically, making it suitable especially as a salad dressing. It changed the company's
fortune, and by 1915, sales topped one million dollars. In 1926 the family decided to sell out: Colman's was now the biggest manufacturer of mustard on both
sides of the Atlantic.

Despite the continuing popularity of both the hot English and the mild
American mustards, recent times have seen a revival of many small independent
mustard makers in both countries.

In the United States, there are now hundreds of brands of American 'speciality' mustards. Some are Dijon-style, others based on Colman's mustard flour,
while Biggi sells mustards in the 'Russian style (hot and sweet), Chinese style
(extra hot), English style (smooth and somewhat hot) and German style (hot,
smooth and horseradishy)'. In Canada, Stone County produce the wonderful
Honeycup Mustard – well worth looking for.

In Britain, Gordons started by making a mustard using their English wine for
flavouring and soon added to the range. Taylors, established in fact since the time
of William IV, continued making their extra hot mustard while Wiltshire
Tracklements became one of the success stories of the latter twentieth century,
starting with a pot of homemade mustard on sale in the local pub. There is also,
interestingly, a company – Boize – who have revived the ancient English tradition of flavouring their horseradish sauce with mustard.

MAKING MUSTARD
AT HOME

For our ancestors, making mustard in the home was very much a labour of love, despite Hannah Woolley's simple-sounding instructions: 'Dry well your seed, then beat it little by little at a time in a Mortar, and sift it, then put the powder in a Gally Pot[2], and wet it with vinegar very well, then put in a whole Onion pilled but not cut, a little Pepper beaten, a little Salt, and a lump of Stone sugar' (*The Queen-Like Closet*, 1670). Even with a quern (a pair of stones, one convex, the other concave, between which mustard seed was easily crushed, the 'flour' being pushed up the sides) rather than a mortar in the kitchen, this required patience, time and a strong wrist. The sifting especially was problematical – you really did have to grind the seed very fine to be able to sieve it satisfactorily.

That magic innovation, the food processor, would have been a prized possession: with this, making mustard is easy. What you cannot do is grind the *dry* seed in the food processor. There is insufficient friction – they bounce around and ultimately change the container from transparent to opaque (sadly, proven . . .). So always soak the seed first, for *at least* 24-36 hours, checking from time to time to see if more liquid is needed to immerse the seed completely. Absorption capacity varies enormously depending on the age of the mustard seed – the longer it has been stored, the drier it will be. *Never* seal the jar when soaking

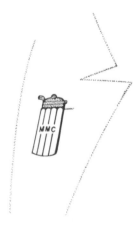

Mustard Club lapel badge, 1920s

---

[2] A small earthenware pot, much used by apothecaries for putting ointments in

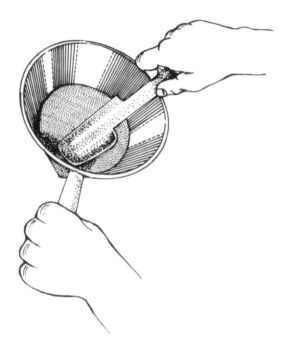

The technique for removing the husks

mustard seed. It expands beyond belief and if sealed may well explode!

Vinegar is the age-old recommended liquid – and it will produce a milder mustard because the (dried) ground seeds release an enzyme (allyl senevol), some of which is dissipated in the soaking. If, however, further vinegar is used in the mixing, then the mustard can become quite pungent: again variation is enormous depending to a great extent on the vinegar used. Grape juice, 'must' (for the wine makers who wish to experiment with mustard) and water can also be used for the soaking, though water alone we found gives a rather bland flavour. It is more usual to add water as a 'mixer' to dilute a strong vinegar, despite John Evelyn's recommendation for 'water only, or the Broth of powder'd Beef' to be added to the 'stamp'd' seed. However, he then also added 'verjuice, Sugar, Claret-wine and Juice of Limon', thereby supplying flavour to this 'excellent sauce to any sort of Flesh or Fish'.

Once the seed is well soaked, it will break up quickly in the food processor – always use the metal blade. It then only remains to remove the husks (in Dijon, these are fed to the pigs: in a Bordeaux mustard, some of the crushed hulls are left in the mustard). This is a simple, although fairly time-consuming, procedure – and, like tying one's shoelaces, far easier to do than describe (see illustration, above). You will need a plastic spatula with a curved blade, and two conical sieves, both preferably metal; certainly, the final sieving *must* be through a metal sieve as the mesh has to be extremely fine and large nylon sieves are too coarse in texture.

Rotating the spatula with the tip in the palm of your hand, 'wind' it round and round the sieve, the curved part of the blade forcing the mustard paste through the mesh, the husks remaining behind. The process is repeated using a second, finer sieve to obtain a completely husk-free mustard, though it may occasionally be necessary to dilute the paste a little if it is too thick to sieve easily. Resist the temptation to dilute it too much, though, or you'll have a liquid on your hands. Home-made mustard does tend to be a little thinner than the commercially made product, since the centrifuges can remove all the husks with greater ease.

Your mustard is now ready for spicing. Here is where the fun begins, but do have some yoghurt at hand when tasting, also plain water biscuits and/or Cheddar cheese to give a bland background. Remember too Eliza Acton's advice. She was talking of the making of forcemeats but it applies equally well to the making of mustards and is as relevant now as in 1845: 'No particular herb or spice should be allowed to predominate powerfully in these compositions, but the whole of the seasonings should be taken in such quantity only as will produce an agreeable savour when they are blended together' (*Modern Cookery for Private Families*).

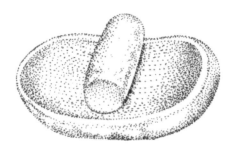

Saddle quern used for grinding mustard, c. 1500

Sisymbrium Irio London Rocket ☉

I.R.Del.   Pub.d by W.Baxter, Botanic Garden, Oxford. 1835.   C. Mathews, Sc.

DIJON MUSTARD

The result of *many* experiments, this produces a mild Dijon-style mustard – not quite so brightly yellow as Dijon's Dijon, but very good. The addition of the spices seems to darken the colour (though of course commercial Dijons also vary enormously – from a pale grey to lurid chrome yellow), and the seed itself obviously influences this. One can make a brighter, more pungent mustard by substituting cider or wine vinegar for grape juice and merely adding allspice, cinnamon, nutmeg and ground cloves, but the lack of herbs does make for a slightly less subtle mustard.

175 g/6 oz brown mustard seed
300 ml/½ pint unsweetened grape juice
3 cloves, ground in a spice grinder
15 peppercorns, crushed in a mortar
½ teaspoon ground ginger
2 tablespoons dried chervil
½ teaspoon ground nutmeg
¼ teaspoon dried thyme
1 teaspoon ground cinnamon
2 garlic cloves, chopped
2 teaspoons dried tarragon
3 bay leaves
1 teaspoon Maldon salt

Soak the mustard seed in the grape juice, mixing in the herbs thoroughly. Leave for 36-48 hours, topping up with a little extra liquid if necessary – the seeds should be just covered. Cover the jar or bowl but don't seal tightly.

Place in the food processor and whizz for 3 minutes, using the metal blade, then leave to stand for 3 hours. Reprocess for 5 minutes. Pour into a conical strainer (mesh size approximately 15 per inch/6 per cm) and with a plastic spatula work the paste through the strainer. Transfer the paste to a finer strainer (mesh size approximately 30 per inch/12 per cm), and repeat the process.

Spoon the mustard into small jars and store, out of direct light, for at least 2 weeks before using, preferably a month. We have found the flavour good for up to 4-5 months, but without the colour-reserving sulphur dioxide it goes dark quite quickly. Small jars help to reduce the oxidation. Makes 300-450 ml/½-¾ pint, depending on the swelling powers of the seed, and the fineness of the sieve.

Now you have made your Dijon mustard, the world is your mustard pot, so to speak. You could, of course, cheat and use a bought Dijon to begin with.

To 300 ml/½ pint Dijon mustard, add for the following mustards:
Tarragon: 6-8 small sprigs (5 cm/2 in) fresh tarragon, finely chopped
Five-herb: 1 teaspoon each, finely chopped – parsley, chervil, tarragon, chives, shallots
Green pepper: 2-3 tablespoons green peppercorns, thoroughly drained from brine
Garlic-parsley: 2-3 garlic cloves, finely chopped, 2 tablespoons parsley, finely

chopped

Three-fruits red: 3 tablespoons fresh tomato purée, 1 tablespoon strawberry purée, 1 teaspoon cassis (it may sound mad, but it's a traditional mustard and very good)

Mint: 2-3 tablespoons fresh mint, very finely chopped

Orange and clove: replace half the soaking liquid with concentrated frozen orange juice, add ½ teaspoon finely ground cloves

Paprika: another traditional mustard – 2-3 tablespoons sweet paprika, but do know your paprika (in Hungary, there are six strengths, few of them available outside that country. Frequently it's either very hot or very sweet!).

Other exotic combinations are often on sale, such as banana and pimento mustard, pineapple mustard, blueberry mustard. We leave you in the kitchen ...

ANCHOVY MUSTARD

Excellent with steaks and fish, or in salad, cream or yoghurt dressings. You can use either home-made Dijon as the base or, for a punchier mustard, Dijon's extra strong.

300 ml/½ pint Dijon mustard
15-20 anchovy fillets, drained and
  pounded

2 eggs

Put the mustard, anchovy fillets and eggs into the food processor and blend, using the metal blade, for 1-1½ minutes. Very, very good. Makes about 400 ml/ 14 fl oz.

DILL MUSTARD

Excellent without the egg yolks – even better with them.

75 ml/3 fl oz Dijon mustard
3 tablespoons sugar
4 teaspoons dried dillweed
1 teaspoon Maldon salt

freshly ground black pepper
1 teaspoon vinegar
2 egg yolks

Put everything in the food processor and blend thoroughly. Can be used straight away, though it improves with a week's keeping. Makes about 2 small jars.

Type 1 A 1738-1775

Type 1 B 1775-1820

Type 2 A 1820-1830

Type 2 B
Inscription manuscrite
Type 2 C
Inscription au pochoir

Type 3 A 1810-1845
Type 3 B 1840-1850
Encadrement à la roulette

Type 4 A 1845-1885
Type 4 B 1845-1885
Encadrement à la roulette

Type 5 A 1850-1920
Type 5 B après 1900

Type 6 après 1908

Development of French jar shapes from 1738 to 1908.
The shapes developed as a result of the need to seal the pots and
of better pottery manufacturing techniques.

LENORMAND MUSTARD

The mustard maker's bible, *Manuel du Moutardier* by Julia de Fontenelle, still used in France today, was published in 1887 by Manuels-Roret. We found this mustard in it, remarkably similar to a Bordeaux despite a thorough sieving. Good with frankfurters and sausages of that ilk.

175 g/6 oz brown mustard seed
300 ml/½ pint red or white wine or cider vinegar
1 tablespoon fresh, chopped parsley
½ tablespoon celery seed
1 tablespoon fresh, chopped chervil
1 tablespoon fresh, chopped tarragon
1 garlic clove, chopped
3 anchovy fillets, drained but not washed of their oil
½ teaspoon Maldon salt

Mix everything together and leave to soak for 36-48 hours, topping up with more vinegar as necessary to keep the seeds just immersed.

Place in a food processor and process in short, sharp bursts, using the metal blade, until the mixture turns the colour of coarse-grained mustard, i.e. brown with bright flecks of yellow. This will probably take about 2 minutes. Leave to rest for 2 hours, then reprocess for 4-5 minutes until the colour is more evenly yellow/brown. Sieve on the Dijon principle, using the larger meshed sieve first, then the very fine one. Put in small jars and store for 2-3 weeks before using. Makes about 2-3 small mustard jars.

MOUTARDE SOYER

As well as running (and redesigning) the Reform Club kitchens, writing books for the poor (and the rich), rushing out to Crimea to organize food for the Army, going to the opera and cooking dinner for his friends, Alexis Soyer also found time to invent, and patent, various sauces. His Aromatic Mustard was particularly popular: this recipe, published in the *Manuel du Moutardier* and attributed to Soyer, may, or may not, be the patented version. But it is good.

175 g/6 oz brown mustard seed
300 ml/½ pint white wine vinegar
4 teaspoons fresh, chopped parsley
2 teaspoons dried chervil
4 teaspoons fresh chives, chopped
3 garlic cloves, chopped
1 teaspoon celery seed
¼ teaspoon four-spice mixture (see below)
½ teaspoon dried thyme
½ teaspoon ground cinnamon
1 teaspoon dried tarragon
2 teaspoons Maldon salt
2 tablespoons olive oil

Combine all the ingredients except the oil, and leave to stand for 36–48 hours. Process in a food processor for 3 minutes, leave to rest for 3 hours, then whizz again for 4–5 minutes. Add the oil and blend for 1 minute, in short, sharp bursts. Pass through two sieves as described for Dijon mustard, then bottle in small jars and keep for 1–2 weeks to mature. Makes 2–2½ small jars.

Note: Four-spice mixture is made with equal quantities of ground cinnamon, cloves, nutmeg and Jamaican pepper or allspice as it is now known.

MOUTARDE À L'ANCIENNE

Pommery's Moutarde de Meaux must be the most famous of the old coarse-grained mustards – mild, nutty and encased in lovely stoneware jars with red wax tops (now sadly often replaced by plastic). A good relation this, nice for cooking or as a table mustard.

75 g/3 oz brown mustard seed
175 ml/6 fl oz cider vinegar, or a mixture of white wine, water and vinegar
a good pinch of Maldon salt
freshly ground black pepper
1 teaspoon finely chopped fresh tarragon
½ teaspoon ground coriander
3 cardamom pods, seeds removed and ground
½ teaspoon sweet red pepper flakes, ground
pinch of ground bayleaf
¼ teaspoon fresh thyme, finely chopped
½ teaspoon very finely chopped fresh fennel
2–3 pinches ground cinnamon
2–3 pinches ground cloves

Soak the seed in the vinegar for 36–48 hours. Put in the food processor, add salt and the spices, then blend for 1 minute. Leave for 2–3 hours, then blend for 1–2 minutes. Don't overprocess or you may break up too much of the mustard meal, releasing more volatile oil and making too pungent a mustard. The point of this one is a pleasantly nutty flavour without too much potency. Leave for 2–3 weeks before using – the longer it matures, the mellower it will be. Makes about 4–5 small jars.

SESAME MUSTARD

A beautiful mustard: not too strong and exquisitely nutty. Particularly good for bringing out the full flavour of chicken.

175 g/6 oz brown mustard seed
450 ml/¾ pint unsweetened white grape juice
140 g/4½ oz (white) sesame seed
1 teaspoon Maldon salt

Soak the mustard seed in 350 ml/12 fl oz of the grape juice for 36-48 hours. Add the remaining juice, the sesame seed and salt and leave for another 12 hours. Then whizz, briefly, to lightly break up the seeds and thoroughly blend. Add a little more grape juice if the mixture seems too thick. Leave for a week or two to mature. Makes about 6–8 small jars.

ROMAN MUSTARD

A coarse-grained mustard, based on Apicius's combination of pine kernels and almonds blended with mustard seed. Quite pungent, deliciously nutty . . .

275 g/10 oz brown mustard seed
225 ml/8 fl oz red wine vinegar
350 ml/12 fl oz red unsweetened
  grape juice
3 teaspoons Maldon salt

2 teaspoons cumin seeds, finely
  ground
50 g/2 oz flaked almonds
75 g/3 oz pine kernels, unroasted
  (roasted nuts give too over-
  whelming a flavour)

Soak the mustard seed in the vinegar and grape juice, mixing in the salt and cumin seeds. Leave, covered but not sealed, for 36-48 hours. Put in the food processor and whizz for 1-2 minutes until coarsely ground, then add the almonds and pine kernels and run very briefly until they are completely broken up – don't overprocess. Makes about 700-800 ml/1¼-1⅓ pints.

GUINNESS MUSTARD

This is a stout mustard indeed – good at any barbecue, transforms bangers and mash.

275 g/10 oz brown mustard seed
450 ml/¼ pint Guinness
225 ml/8 fl oz red wine vinegar
1 teaspoon four-spice mixture (p. 52)

3 teaspoons Maldon salt
1 teaspoon black pepper, freshly
  ground

Soak the seed in the Guinness and vinegar, having mixed in all the spices, for 36-48 hours. Place in the food processor and run briefly – just until the seed is coarsely ground and the whole nicely blended. Makes about 700 ml/1¼ pints.

LEMON MUSTARD

This is quite tangy, and good for cooking, but if you want to tone it down substitute unsweetened grape juice for the vinegar.

40 g/1½ oz white mustard seed
40 g/1½ oz brown mustard seed
175 ml/6 fl oz cider vinegar
1 teaspoon Maldon salt

3 tablespoons lemon juice
grated zest of 1 small lemon
2 teaspoons clear honey
pinch of ground cinnamon

Soak the mustard seed in the vinegar for 36–48 hours, adding a little extra vinegar if necessary. Blend in the food processor for 1 minute, add the remaining ingredients and leave to stand for 2 hours, then whizz again for 2–3 minutes. Pot up and leave for at least a month. Makes 4 small jars.

TEWKESBURY MUSTARD

It is, of course, difficult to know exactly what the Tewkesbury mustard of our ancestors tasted like. This, though, makes an interestingly pungent mustard – good with roast beef, even better with the Yorkshire pudding and a dollop of rich gravy.

175 g/6 oz brown and white mustard seed, roughly half and half
300 ml/½ pint cider vinegar

¼ teaspoon Maldon salt
freshly grated horseradish

Soak the seed in the vinegar for 36–48 hours, adding extra vinegar if necessary to cover, then stir in the salt and blend in the food processor for 2 minutes. Leave for 2 hours. Add freshly grated horseradish – start with 1–2 tablespoons, but the quantity will depend on the pungency of the radish, the mustard seed and your tastes. Whizz again for 2 minutes, then taste – remembering that the mustard will mellow somewhat with time. Add extra horseradish if wished, whizz quickly just to blend in. Leave for at least 2 weeks. Makes 5–6 small mustard jars.

HOT JAPANESE MUSTARD

This *is* hot – be warned. In Japan, you are often given a small dish of made-up mustard, another of fresh grated horseradish, and chopsticks to mix the two together in the proportions you want. Based on that idea, this invention is particularly good for cooking.

75 g/3 oz brown mustard seed

150 ml/¼ pint water

1 teaspoon fresh grated horseradish

1 teaspoon Japanese plum vinegar

Soak the seed in water for 36-48 hours, then blend for 2 minutes in the processor. Leave for 1 hour, add the horseradish and vinegar and leave for another hour. Blend again very briefly. Pot up and let it mature for 2-3 weeks. Makes 3-4 small jars.

MATTHEW'S MUSTARD

Matthew is eleven. He is an expert on mustard, with a fine palate, and this is the mustard with his seal of approval.

175 g/6 oz brown mustard seed

225 ml/8 fl oz white grape juice

125 ml/4 fl oz cider vinegar

good pinch of four-spice mixture
(p. 52)

¼ teaspoon Maldon salt

thick honey

Soak the seed and spices in the juice and vinegar for 36-48 hours. Blend for 2 minutes, then leave for 2-3 hours. Blend again for 1-5 minutes – the longer time will give a hotter mustard – then strain through a *coarse* sieve, just to remove the biggest hulls, still leaving the mustard slightly gritty. Or, for a really coarse-grained mustard, don't sieve at all.

Measure the volume of the mustard and melt half that volume of thick honey (runny honey gives too liquid a result). Pour into the mustard and mix well. Leave for a day then taste. If you would like the mustard sweeter, then melt a little more honey and add. The proportions vary between 1:2 and 2:3 of honey to mustard, depending on the seed, how long you have blended it, the sweetness of the honey, and your palate. Leave for a week. Makes 4-7 small jars, depending on the sieving and the amount of honey added.

MOSTARDA DI CREMONA (1)

Mostarda in Italian indicates their mustard-flavoured fruit relishes, *senapa* being the word for mustard. The Cremona relish is probably the most famous – and certainly the most readily obtained, both in Italy and abroad. Its traditional usage is as an accompaniment to roast eel, or *bollito misto*, that beautiful dish of boiled meats.

We give here two recipes out of the multitude available. The first, kindly sent to us by Enrico Dondi from Cremona (the family famous for their *mostardas*), dates from 1678 and is from *Practica de Speciali*, published in Venice and written by Father Domenico Avda, Capo Speciale dell'Archiopedale di Santo Spirito di Roma. It takes the form of a dialogue:

Q: How do you make Mostarda di Cremona?

A: Take a good quantity of black grapes, half a donkey panierful [these vary in size enormously, making a guess at quantity virtually impossible!], and make it into a pulp, then put it to cook in a zinc-lined pan that is completely dry, stir constantly with a stick – do not use a metal stick – take care that it does not burn. Cook until the grape skins come off.

Then with a mixer [what sort of contraption was this, in 1678?] pass through a double-skinned strainer, then cook again, continuously stirring until pulp takes on body. While it is cooking add bitter orange peel, seasoned with honey and cut into small chunks 5-6 lbs, then take off stove and when cold put back on again adding half a pound of cinnamon well pestled. Take one pound of mustard ground, put it to soften with boiling water so it becomes a paste, after 24 hours add pulp and it becomes a noble thing. Add more or less mustard depending if you like it strong or weak.

The original Mostarda di Cremona recipe, in the possession of the Dondi family in Cremona, c. 1678

1 kg/2¼ lb grapes (seedless if you
 want to keep your sanity)
mustard powder
ground cinnamon

zest of 1 Seville orange, all pith
 removed, very finely chopped
3 tablespoons thick honey

Put the honey in a small, heavy-based pan and melt gently, then add the chopped orange skin and simmer for 20 minutes, adding more honey if in danger of burning the pan. Remove the peel from the pan and leave to drain.

Meanwhile, wash the grapes, take off the stalks, and blanch the grapes in boiling water for 60 seconds. Then peel – the easiest way is to squeeze them as you open up the scar from the stalk: the skin should then easily slip away. Dragoon children or kind friends to help, and do the whole operation over a bowl to catch all the juices.

Using an enamel pan – the acidity of the grapes will turn aluminium (and the grapes) black – bring the fruit, with the juice, slowly to simmering point, then very gently continue to simmer until reduced to the consistency of marmalade, adding extra grape juice if absolutely necessary to prevent burning. Add the cinnamon and leave to cool, then stir in the crystallized orange zest.

Make the mustard into a paste with boiling water, then stir into the grapes once cooled. Reheat, stirring constantly, and simmer very gently until hot right through. Pot in sterilized jars and seal once cool. Makes about 4-5 small jars.

MOSTARDA DI CREMONA (2)

This is the modern recipe, using crystallized fruit. Fruits in all the *mostardas* vary enormously depending on what is in season, what looks good in the market, how you feel . . .

450 g/1 lb assorted crystallized
 fruits (pear, orange, cherry,
 pumpkin, quince etc)
250 g/9 oz caster sugar

6 tablespoons brown mustard seed
pinch of Maldon salt
¼ teaspoon dried red pepper flakes

Dissolve the sugar in 150 ml/¼ pint water, add the mustard seed, salt and pepper flakes and simmer gently for 10 minutes. Allow to cool then stand for 24 hours. Return to the pan, bring to the boil, then strain through a metal strainer and again return to the pan with the crystallized fruit. Simmer for 10–15 minutes, gently, then remove the fruit to sterilized jars and pack tightly. Pour over the syrup, cool and then cover. If the sugar/mustard syrup crystallizes, it has been reduced too much so reboil with a little extra water added. Makes about 700 g/1½ lb.

MOSTARDA DI VENEZIA

This is traditionally made with quinces, although some recipes use a mixture of quince and pears. Since quinces can be hard to come by, and their flavour is very full, do this if necessary. But if you can get those sweet-smelling, golden fruit (and some enterprising greengrocers do stock them now, though only in season, in the early autumn) you will be rewarded. Keep them until the aroma is fully developed, then they are ready for use. Wipe off the soft down before peeling, and don't throw away peel and cores – they can be used to flavour apple pies, purées, jellies.

2 kg/4¼ lb quinces, or a mixture of quince and pears
juice and grated zest of 1 lemon

200 g/7 oz caster sugar
4 tablespoons mustard powder

Peel, core and chop the quinces, putting them into a saucepan with about 600 ml/1 pint water and the lemon zest and juice to prevent discolouration. Add enough water just to cover the fruit, stir in half the sugar and bring to a simmer. Cook until the fruit is soft (about 45 minutes for quinces, 5-10 minutes for pears). Remove from the pan with a slotted spoon and place in the food processor. Add the remaining sugar and the mustard, dissolved in a little boiling water to a paste, to the pan. Stir, then simmer gently until the liquid is reduced by about half and of a good syrupy consistency. Add a little to the fruit in the processor and blend. If the purée is too thick, add more liquid – the final consistency should be similar to apple sauce, and it will slightly thicken in the cooling. Bottle in sterilized jars, cool, then seal. Leave for 3-4 weeks. Makes about 1.4 kg/3 lbs.

Eighteenth century Italian Mostarda de Fruita jar from
Palais des Ducs Museum, Dijon

MOSTARDA DI FRUITA

A cross between Mostarda di Venezia and Mostarda di Cremona. As with the Cremona relish, it is excellent with cold meats, spiced beef, tongue or a large ham on the bone.

500 g/18 oz quinces, prepared weight (approx 700 g/1½ lb whole quinces)

500 g/18 oz under-ripe pears, prepared weight (approx 700 g/ 1½ lb whole pears)

150 g/5 oz pumpkin flesh from near the skin (start with a 275 g/10 oz slice)

200 g/7 oz dried figs, stalks removed

juice and grated peel of 1 lemon

700 g/1½ lb caster sugar

375 ml/13 fl oz white wine

4 tablespoons mustard powder

Peel and core the quinces and pears, chopping them into walnut-sized pieces and dropping them into a bowl acidulated with the lemon juice to prevent discolouration. Chop the pumpkin flesh into similar-sized chunks; prick the figs with a skewer 10-12 times but don't cut them up. Put all the fruit into a large pan, just cover with fresh water, add 100 g/3½ oz sugar and the lemon peel and simmer gently until the fruit is slightly tender. Check regularly with a fork after about 5 minutes; the quince will take about 20 minutes, the rest of the fruit 5-10 minutes. Remove the fruit as it is cooked and leave to dry, discarding the water at the finish.

Mix about three-quarters of the wine with the remaining sugar and heat gently, stirring constantly to avoid burning. Add more wine if necessary and reduce until it is nicely thick, the consistency of golden syrup. Add the mustard, dissolved in a little boiling water to a paste. Stir well, then simmer for another minute.

Pack the fruit into jars and pour over the hot syrup. Leave to cool, then seal. Mature for at least a week; if possible, resist temptation for a month. Makes 1.8-2.3 kg/4-5 lbs.

MOSTARDA ALL'USO TOSCANO

Pellegrino Artusi was one of the most famous Italian cookery writers of the nineteenth century, elegantly combining the traditional with the imaginative. We have not found reference to a Tuscan *mostarda* elsewhere, but curiously it is not dissimilar to a *mostarda* found in Carpi, in the province of Modena, the other side of the Apennine Mountains.

350 g/12 oz black grapes, seedless if possible

650 g/1 lb 6 oz white grapes

500 g/1 lb 2 oz apples, pink-fleshed if possible

1 large pear

125 ml/4 fl oz white wine
50 g/2 oz candied lemon peel,
  very finely chopped

25 g/1 oz mustard powder
powdered cinnamon

Peel, seed (if necessary) and mash the grapes with their juice. Peel, core and chop the apples and pear, then bring to the boil with the wine and simmer until the fruit is soft, 10-15 minutes. Add the grapes and continue simmering, stirring frequently, until the whole is a tender pulp.

Blend in the food processor, return to the heat and reduce until it is the consistency of jam. Leave to cool, stir in the mustard mixed with a little extra wine, and the candied peel. Pot in sterilized jars, sprinkle a little ground cinnamon on top and seal. Leave for at least 2 weeks. Makes 1.1-1.4 kg/2½-3 lbs.

SPICY ITALIAN VINEGAR WITH MUSTARD (ACETO PICANTE ALLA SENAPE)

A traditional Tuscan recipe – every family has its own variation. It is good as a sauce on its own, in salad dressings, and for making mustard. The quantities of herbs are for fresh ingredients. If you have to use dried, halve the amount, and in any case always use fresh parsley: dried is a travesty.

2 litres/3½ pints red wine vinegar
  (white wine or cider vinegar
  can be used, but the red gives a
  lovely warm colour)
2 teaspoons thyme
2 teaspoons marjoram
4 teaspoons oregano
4 teaspoons basil
4 teaspoons rosemary needles
  stripped from the stalk
4 bay leaves
good bunch of flat parsley, finely
  chopped

10 garlic cloves, chopped
4 small onions, finely chopped
10 cloves
2 teaspoons black pepper
2 teaspoons freshly grated nutmeg
2 teaspoons Maldon salt
150 ml/¼ pint olive oil
5 cinnamon sticks, totalling about
  37.5 cm/15 in in length, broken
  into small pieces
2 tablespoons mustard powder

Put all the ingredients except the oil and mustard into a large jar. Seal and shake once a day for the first week, then twice a week for the next two weeks. After about three weeks remove the cinnamon bark, and add the olive oil and mustard powder. (Make sure all the cinnamon is removed – it doesn't soften and will cause havoc with the food processor.)

Blend in a food processor in small batches, for 2-3 minutes at a time. Strain through a fine meshed sieve and discard any small pieces of herbs and spices.

Return to the jar and leave for at least another week before using. It will separate naturally, so needs to be shaken before use. Makes about 2 litres/3½ pints.

MRS BEETON'S HORSERADISH VINEGAR

Some of Isabella Beeton's recipes are distinctly odd: her 'Indian Mustard, an excellent Relish to Bread and Butter, or any cold Meat' is anything but. This horseradish vinegar, though, is excellent. We always make it up in the quantities she gave – and always seem to be needing more.

125 g/4 oz freshly grated horserad-   a pinch of cayenne pepper
    ish   1.1 litres/2 pints red wine vinegar
1 small shallot, very finely chopped

'Put all the ingredients into a bottle, which shake well every day for a fortnight. When it is thoroughly steeped, strain and bottle, and it will be fit for use immediately. This will be found an agreeable relish to cold beef, & c. *Seasonable.* – This vinegar should be made either in October or November, as horseradish is then in its highest perfection.' Makes about 1.1 litres/2 pints.

TARTAR MUSTARD

Eliza Acton, from whom this recipe comes, states, 'This is an exceedingly pungent compound, but has many approvers.' Indeed so.

'Rub four ounces of the best Durham mustard very smooth with a full teaspoonful of salt, and wet it by degrees with strong horseradish vinegar, a dessertspoonful of cayenne, or of chilli vinegar, and one or two of tarragon vinegar when its flavour is not disliked. A quarter-pint of vinegar poured boiling upon an ounce of scraped horseradish, and left for one night, closely covered, will be ready to use for this mustard, but it will be better for two or three days.

'Durham mustard, 4 oz [125 g]★; salt, large teaspoonful; cayenne or chilli vinegar, 1 dessertspoonful [2 teaspoons]; horseradish vinegar, quarter-pint [150 ml].'

★Use any good English mustard powder or mustard flour – and divide the quantities by four.

ENGLISH MUSTARD

Since (we feel) only a masochist would want to grind, by hand, in a mortar, so finely as to be able to sift it easily, the correct proportions of brown and white mustard seed (which are a closely guarded secret), we have spared you the intricacies of a recipe for making English mustard from scratch. Messrs Colman spend every day making, and marketing, various mustard powders – including one with no wheat flour for those on a gluten-free diet. But it is worth remembering their advice when wishing to turn mustard powder into mustard (and it is surprising how many think it unimportant): always use *cold* water. The reason for this is strictly chemical. The addition of cold water to ground mustard seed produces a chemical reaction between the enzyme myrosin and the glucosides sinigrin, (in black mustard seed) and sinalbin (in white mustard seed). Acting as a catalyst, the water enables the myrosin to ferment the sinigrin, breaking it up into the essential oil of mustard (allyl isothiocyanate), potassium salt and sugar, producing a pungent odour and sharp taste. On the sinalbin, the myrosin acts to produce sulpho-cyanate of acrinyl, sulphate of sinapine and sugar, unaromatic and less acrid in taste. The combination of all these is the clean, sharp taste of English mustard!

If you use tepid or boiling water, the formulae are lost. It is often said that it is the pungency that is destroyed: in fact, the burning sensation remains but with a slight bitterness and an absolute lack of any flavour. If you cook the mustard, the pungent overtones *are* lost, and very often any taste too though that will depend on the length of the cooking. In many cases, what happens is that the mustard vastly heightens the flavour of the base ingredient of the dish while leaving no trace of itself. But for the Englishman, and his roast beef, or slice of ham off the bone, the mustard must be mixed with cold water, left to stand for ten minutes, and then consumed.

Sauces

Woe was his cook but if his sauce were poynaunt and sharpe . . .

THE FRANKLYN, FROM THE PROLOGUE TO CHAUCER'S CANTERBURY TALES

The Franklyn, as a Knight of the Shire, was an important man, ever prepared for a multitude of visitors, and his cook had to get things right. In Chaucer's day, the palate demanded highly spiced and, to our taste, somewhat sharp sauces. Vinegar was often used alone, particularly with salted fish; sweetly spiced with cinnamon and ginger it would accompany roasted eels and lamprey, while with mustard and sugar it was especially served with brawn. That particular trio crops up in early manuscripts again and again (and again – in 1914 the *Daily Mail* recommended 'the simplest sauce for boiled bacon – a teaspoon of mustard and vinegar and pepper and sugar').

Most sauces went to the other extreme, being a complicated amalgam of many herbs and spices, and there were definite rules as to what sauce went with what. Brawn, beef and salt mutton had mustard; lamb, suckling pig, kid or fawn had ginger sauce; veal and bacon had verjuice (crab apple). Besides these, there were other, more specialized sauces such as chaudron for swan, camelyne for wild fowl, gaunt-cel for goose, peverade for venison, gelatine for water fowl and egurdouce for fish.

Many of these sauces were uncooked (unless they contained the innards, blood or fat of the animal they were to accompany) and they were usually very thick – almost a paste – and served on little saucers beside the main dish. The Roman influence is easily discernible: Apicius's recipes were mostly complex, with a multitude of herbs and spices as well as dates, figs, nuts, honey, oil, must, broth, wine – and mustard.

One must remember that in medieval days much meat was past its prime, or heavily salted. And, as there were no forks, dishes were either reduced to a pulp (no doubt losing much of their flavour) or had to be served in a form easily edible in one's fingers (and were therefore often rather tasteless and dry). Either way, a sharp sauce to enliven the dish must have been a welcome relief. The Harleian manu-

The Franklyn, a modern Chaucerian figure from
a series made by the Rye pottery

script of 1450 has a sauce for roasted crane which minces the liver of the bird
before mixing it with 'pouder' of ginger, vinegar and mustard. This principle
remained a favourite for several decades, and in Stere Hit Well, the Pepysian Library
manuscript 1047, there is a 'Sauce for a Pyke' almost identical in its making.

Meanwhile, in Paris, the *sauciers* had their own guilds, officially authorizing them
to sell their sauces (as did the vinegar makers) on the streets. The narrow thorough-
fares were thronged with men shouting out their wares, '*Sauce à la moutarde*', '*Sauce
à l'aillée*', '*Sauce verte*'. It must have been very convenient for the cook – you could
just pop outside when the vendors were in your street and buy not only mustard,
vinegar or oil, but bread, flour, milk, butter, cheeses or pâtés. Often the children
were sent on these errands: Goodman of Paris wrote that the 'little children sang
at night while going for wine or mustard'. By 1650, there were some 600 'walking *mustardiers*'. London too had her street peddlers, some selling sauces though
more favoured actual provisions: garlic, interestingly, was widely sold.

The English sauces at this time were remarkably similar to the French. Both kitchens now saw a gradual change from the highly spiced, thick medieval sauce to smoother, subtler recipes, so that by the mid-seventeenth century many were merely unthickened gravies, judiciously flavoured with a few herbs and spices – though the permutations on this were enormous.

Vinegar however was still popular in England as a sauce: alone (particularly on salads), with mustard and also with horseradish. John Gerard's *Herball* of 1597 states: 'the horseradish, stamped with a little vinegar put thereto, is commonly used for sauce to eate fish with and such like meates as we do mustarde.' Horseradish and mustard were also associated together. Tewkesbury mustard was spiced with the root and Evelyn recommends steeping it in vinegar for a 'sallet' dressing (p.67-8) – though by now oil had made a comeback to the salad. For, despite the English predilection for vinegar alone, there is a recipe for 'salat' in the *Forme of Curye* which firmly states, after instructions to wash and pick over the herbs, 'pluk hem small with thyn hond and myng hem well with rawe oile. Lay on vynegar and salt and serve it forth.'

Mustard was also used in horseradish sauces, though to lightly colour rather than flavour them. Quite what effect it had in this recipe from *Dorset Dishes of the Eighteenth Century* is hard to imagine: 'Crate very fine 8 large sticks of horse-radish and put into it three tablespoonfuls of white chile vinegar, a teaspoonful of mixed mustard and a gill of good cream, a gill of good white sauce seasoned with a little cayenne, some salt and very little white sugar. Then freeze the sauce as ice cream and serve.'

By this time, there was a clear division in sauce making. Catsups (from the Chinese *koe-chiap* meaning a relish or pickled fish sauce) were in fashion. Some included mustard, and many were combined in complicated mixtures. But also appearing were new recipes for very simple sauces. A mixture of butter, vinegar and mustard is frequently cited, not just for pork and fish dishes, but also for simpler fare such as 'sodde Eggs', hard-boiled eggs quartered, then fried in butter before being seasoned with vinegar and mustard.

From Germany, presumably with the Hanoverian Elector, had come sauces for brawn and boar's head which introduced as the sweet element port or red-currant jelly. The variations on this were many, most notably the sauce we now consider indisputably English: Cumberland.

By the time of George IV, with Carême installed in the palm-tree-columned kitchens of Brighton Pavilion, an incredible number of sauces – taking days to make – were appearing on the royal table, including Sauce Ravigote à l'Ancienne: with onions, Chablis, consommé, lemon juice, garlic, shallot, gherkins, capers, herbs simmered, then added to a Sauce Espagnole, strained, 1 teaspoon mustard added, strained again then a little butter added just before serving – one wonders whether the mustard would have been noticed by its absence.

More obviously noticeable was mustard's inclusion in the many salad dressings that abounded. Richard Dolby, who had made the Thatched House Tavern in St

James's Street so fashionable a venue for the Regency bucks, created a dressing, clearly similar to a rémoulade (p.69); while Dr Kitchiner in his pompously titled *Apicius Redivivus, The Cook's Oracle* has a salad dressing which became popular as Dr Kitchiner's Salad Cream. A mixture of eggs (hard-boiled), cream, vinegar and mustard, this appears throughout the century in slightly varying guises to become universally known as English Salad Cream. Well made, it is very good, though the commercial travesties today do little to recommend its appearance on the table.

Mustard is used in these salad dressings, and often in mayonnaise, not just for its flavour. For one of mustard's great properties is that it acts as an emulsifier, thickening the sauce by 'holding' together the droplets of oil and vinegar. It is thus very useful in the making, too, of somewhat tricky sauces, such as hollandaise, since it minimizes the threat of curdling. Chemically, this is due to its absorption powers: the powdered seed absorbs up to one and a half times its own weight of oil, and twice of vinegar.

Today, once more, we have veered toward simpler sauces though with a certain amount of misplaced enthusiasm for odd combinations. There are some occasions when even mustard cannot come to the rescue, in spite of this suggestion in a recent American book: 'If lobster and blueberries or duck livers and kiwi fruit must be combined, mustard in a light cream sauce can give them togetherness.' This is to abuse both our digestions and mustard.

MUSTARD VINAIGRETTE

The basic recipe for vinaigrette has hardly changed in 300 years. The English name – French dressing – recognizes the French influence in the addition of oil to the dressing. Previously, we had swamped our salads – and much else – with little but vinegar and sugar, much to the astonishment, and complaint, of foreign visitors. John Evelyn, with memories of vinegar and sugar being 'the constant vehicles', devised a perfect 'sallet dressing': 'Take of clear, and perfectly good *Oyl-Olive*, three Parts; of sharpest *Vinegar* (sweetest of all *Condiments* – for so some pronounce it, perhaps for that it incites Appetite, and causes Hunger, which is the best Sauce), *Limon*, or Juice of *Orange*, one Part, and therein let steep some Slices of *Horse-Radish*, with a little *Salt*; Some in a separate *Vinegar*, gently bruise a *Pod* of *Guinny-Pepper* [cayenne pepper], straining both the *Vinegars* apart, to make use of Either, or One alone, or of both, as they best like; then add as much *Tewksbury*, or other dry *Mustard* grated, as will lie upon an Half-Crown Piece: Beat, and mingle all these very together; but pour not on the *Oyl* and *Vinegar*, ''till immediately before the *Sallet* is ready to be eaten: And then with the *Yolk* of two new-laid *Eggs* (boyl'd and prepar'd, as before is taught) squash, and bruise them all into mash with a Spoon; and lastly, pour it all upon the *Herbs*.'

With minor changes, that is the recipe we give here, and it is commonly used today. We do add sugar, despite Evelyn's comment that it 'is almost wholly banished from all, except the more effeminate palates', and, for this basic vinaigrette, we omit the egg yolks – though they make for a deliciously creamy dressing, the beginnings of a rémoulade in fact. Remembering his note 'That the *Liquids* may be made more, or less *Acid*, as is most agreeable to your Taste', you can of course change the proportions of oil to vinegar. Many writers recommend a one to five, or one to six ratio: much will depend on the vinegar, the mustard, the salad to be dressed. Your palate, of course, is the final arbiter.

½ teaspoon sugar
1 teaspoon Dijon mustard
1 tablespoon wine, cider or
   Horseradish vinegar (p. 61)

3 tablespoons best olive oil
Maldon salt
freshly ground black pepper

Mix the sugar, mustard and vinegar of your choice to a paste. Beat in the oil to make a thick liaison, then season – lightly – with salt and freshly ground black pepper. Taste and adjust the proportions, if wished, accordingly. Makes enough dressing for a salad for 4-6

Punch cartoon, 28 June 1856. Gun toting was just as common in the United States in those days

YELLOW SAUCE

In Spain, a dash of mustard powder is often added to vinaigrettes – one of the very few appearances of mustard in the Spanish kitchen. In this yellow sauce – Salsa Amarilla – it is blended with Madeira and stock, and is very reminiscent of Apicius with his 'wine, oil, broth, vinegar, mustard and pepper' combinations. We tried it with a good boiling fowl, cold pork and beef: excellent in all cases.

125 g/4 oz freshly grated   a pinch of cayenne pepper
  horseradish   1.1 litres/2 pints red wine vinegar
1 small shallot, very finely chopped

Separate the egg whites from the yolks, pressing the former through a fine sieve and reserving. Mash the yolks, then stir in the Madeira to make a thick paste. Beat in the oil drop by drop, whisking well all the time, then add a good pinch of salt. Warm the stock until just beginning to melt and beat, slowly and thoroughly, into the mixture. Add the vinegar, mustard and pepper. In Spain they use mustard powder but the Dijon gives a smoother sauce. Lastly, stir in the egg whites. Makes about 300 ml/½ pint.

SAUCE RÉMOULADE

There is a certain amount of entanglement historically between the sauces rémoulade and tartare. Rémoulade was probably invented during the eighteenth century, along with so many other classic sauces. Certainly, Menon, the prolific French writer of the 1740s and 1750s, mentions it. His recipe is fairly simple, basically a vinaigrette with shallots, garlic, capers, anchovies, parsley and mustard added. By the nineteenth century, hard-boiled egg yolks – occasionally also a raw egg yolk – have made their appearance. At the close of the century, it seems firmly established that sheltering under the name of rémoulade are two, significantly different, versions of the sauce. The household recipe is based on hard-boiled egg yolks, with seasonings and oil added: the restaurant version has mayonnaise as the foundation – giving what many people today would recognize as Sauce Tartare. Curnonsky, in *Bons Plats, Bons Vins* (1949), gives both varieties of the rémoulade – though several pages apart and with no comment on either. To add to the confusion, his Sauce Tartare is very similar to the (household) rémoulade, but with an interesting note that the liaison will not hold very long so should be made at the last moment. If necessary though, one can substitute a raw egg yolk for one of the hard-boiled yolks 'but it is no longer a true Sauce Tartare'. We have now come full circle to today's generally accepted method of making Sauce Rémoulade. It is creamier, less heavy and rich than the mayonnaise-based sauce (though both are indisputably good) and is often given as the alternative foundation to mayonnaise for making Sauce Tartare. So, if you should be given a sauce by another name that you thought was tartare (or rémoulade) it is perhaps comforting to know that neither you, nor the chef, has gone mad.

2 hard-boiled egg yolks
1 raw egg yolk
1 teaspoon wine or cider vinegar
1 teaspoon Dijon mustard
Maldon salt
freshly ground black pepper
150 ml/¼ pint best olive oil

1 teaspoon finely chopped tarragon
1 teaspoon finely snipped chives
1 teaspoon chervil
1 teaspoon drained, chopped
  capers
1 teaspoon anchovy paste

Mash the hard-boiled egg yolks with the vinegar to a smooth paste, then beat in the raw egg yolk. Add the mustard with a touch of salt and pepper, then whisk in the oil slowly, as when making mayonnaise. When it is thick and smooth, stir in the chopped herbs, capers and, finally, the anchovy paste. Serves 4

MUSTARD MAYONNAISE

Mayonnaise is perhaps the classic summer sauce. Thick, rich and gleaming gold-en yellow, home-made mayonnaise is instantly distinguishable from its commer-cial cousins. Sadly, its making seems to inspire terror in many, though with the electric blender – provided all the ingredients are at room temperature, and a stern patience is adhered to in the initial pouring of the oil – it is magically simple. Room temperature, incidentally, does not mean the kitchen in a New Orleans house on a June day – the oil should be clear but not hot: cooks in the tropics usually have to cool it a little on ice before proceeding. Should you want, how-ever, to make the sauce on a cold winter's day, you may have to stand the oil – if it is at all cloudy – in a warm room for a few hours, or put it in a bowl of warm water, until it is crystal clear. If the bowl is very cold, rinse that in warm water too, then dry very thoroughly. With a mustard mayonnaise, of course, the prob-lems are slightly eased by the fact that the mustard itself acts as an emulsifier.

2-3 egg yolks
1 tablespoon Dijon mustard
½ teaspoon Maldon salt

1 teaspoon wine or cider vinegar
  or juice of ½ lemon
300 ml/ ½ pint olive oil

Whisk the egg yolks thoroughly in a large bowl. Many advocate a wooden spoon for the beating but a whisk is easier and quite satisfactory. Add the mustard and salt and a few splashes of vinegar and whisk again. Then pour a few drops of oil into the bowl – it is best to have the oil in a jug for easy control. Whisking all the time, add a few more drops of oil only after the last have been absorbed by the eggs. As the liaison thickens you can pour the oil in a slow stream but in the beginning do go slowly. Whisk until really thick and the mayonnaise falls with a 'plop', then add a few more drops of vinegar (or lemon juice) to sharpen lightly. Should disaster strike and the sauce curdle, start again with another egg yolk in a clean bowl, adding the curdled mixture drop by drop as before. The mayonnaise will keep in an airtight jar in the fridge for 1-2 weeks, through if the sauce does not come to the top of the jar, you may have to skim off the surface skin. Until experience makes a confident 'mayonnaiser' of you, start with 3 egg yolks; after that you will find that you need only 2. You can also, of course, experiment with different mustards to vary the flavour subtly. Serves 6

AVOCADO, ANCHOVY AND MUSTARD MAYONNAISE

A perfect combination: you can alter the balance of ingredients to taste, and according to the dish it is to accompany.

300 ml/½ pint mayonnaise (p. 70, made without the mustard or with only ¼ teaspoon added)
1 medium-sized, ripe avocado

1¼ anchovy fillets, drained and soaked in milk for 10 minutes
1 teaspoon Dijon mustard

Mash the avocado thoroughly, pound the anchovy fillets, then stir into the mayonnaise and add the mustard. Beat or whisk very briskly to completely meld everything together. With these quantities, no flavour is too overpowering – if you want to heighten one of them, then add more avocado, anchovy or mustard, but don't overdo it: the harmony must not be too disturbed. Serves 6-8

THE POET'S RECEIPT FOR SALAD

The Reverend Sydney Smith was a charmer. An esteemed gourmet, a noted wit, an intellectual, he was friend to the great. Banished to the country by the Church for his liberal views, he continued to amuse, to condole, to advise, in never-ending correspondence. His recipe for salad, delightfully written in verse, was well known amongst his friends but appeared for the first time in print in Eliza Acton's *Modern Cookery for Private Families*. She makes an interesting point: 'We could not venture to deviate by a word from the original, but we would suggest, that the mixture forms almost a substitute for salad, instead of a mere dressing.' Her 'suggestion' is certainly correct – it is a delicious potato salad (albeit mashed), and the last line of the poem, 'Fate cannot harm me – I have dined today', is surely indicative of this. The mistaken allusion to it as a dressing was obviously as prevalent in Miss Acton's time as it is today. Perhaps the confusion arose with the alternative version of the poem, which only differs in four lines and which appeared in Lady Holland's *Memoirs of the Reverend Sydney Smith*, published, ten years after Eliza Acton, in 1855. Perhaps he had taken to serving the potato salad on a bed of greenery. In any event, here is the salad (with both endings). Exceeding good, as Miss Acton would have said, with pickled herrings, or any smoked fish, or chicken.

> Two large potatoes, passed through kitchen sieve
> Unwonted softness to the salad give;
> Of mordent mustard, add a single spoon,
> Distrust the condiment which bites so soon;
> But deem it not, thou man of herbs, a fault,
> To add a double quantity of salt;
> Three times the spoon with oil of Lucca crown,
> And once with vinegar, procured from town;
> True flavour needs it, and your poet begs
> The pounded yellow of two well-boiled eggs;
> Let onion atoms lurk within the bowl,
> And, scarce suspected, animate the whole;
> And lastly, in the flavoured compound toss
> A magic teaspoon of anchovy sauce:
> Then, though green turtle fail, though venison's tough,
> And ham and turkey are not boiled enough,
> Serenely full, the epicure may say –
> Fate cannot harm me – I have dined today.

Lady Holland's version has four spoons of oil and two of vinegar, and continues after 'anchovy sauce':

> Oh, green and glorious! Oh, herbaceous treat!
> Twould tempt the dying anchorite to eat;
> Back to the world he'd turn his fleeting soul,
> And plunge his fingers in the salad-bowl!

Stick to the Acton quantities, using teaspoons for the mustard and salt (very scant for the salt), tablespoons for the oil and vinegar, and about half a small onion, extremely finely chopped. Serves 2

MUSTARD BUTTER

Very simple, and keeps well in fridge or freezer. Cut in slices and serve on fish, steak, lamb cutlets, vegetables.

225 g/8 oz unsalted butter
2-3 tablespoons Dijon or other
   mustard of your choice

freshly ground white pepper
   (optional)
dash of lemon juice (optional)

Have the butter quite soft but not melting, then beat in the mustard, distributing it evenly throughout. Season with a grinding of white pepper and a splash of lemon juice if wished, then form into a 'sausage'. Chill until required, then cut into slices and put on your dish just before serving. Serves 8.

   A particularly good variant of this is to fry 2-3 tablespoons black mustard seed in ½ tablespoon oil until they start to splutter (cover the pan or they will be all over the kitchen). Drain and mix into the butter. This gives a nutty butter rather than a mustardy one – you can, of course, add a bit of both seed and mustard for another variation.

SAUCE DIJONNAISE

There are countless sauces under the Dijon flag – all naturally with mustard in them. Here are two old classics, one cold (similar to, but much simpler than, a rémoulade) and one hot – a mousseline, akin to hollandaise but easier to make.

4 hard-boiled egg yolks
4 teaspoons Dijon mustard
juice of 1 lemon

150-300 ml/¼-½ pint olive oil
Maldon salt
freshly ground black pepper

Sieve the egg yolks, then mash to a paste with the mustard. Thin with lemon juice, briskly whisking, then add the oil, drop by drop at first, in a slow but steady stream as the sauce thickens. After adding the first quarter-pint, continue until the sauce is as thick as you like it, then season lightly with salt and freshly ground pepper. Serves 6

SAUCE MOUSSELINE DIJONNAISE

3 egg yolks
juice of 1 lemon
Maldon salt
freshly ground black pepper

1 teaspoon cold water
175 g/6 oz unsalted butter
2 tablespoons Dijon mustard

Whisk the eggs in a bowl, add the lemon, salt, pepper and water and whisk again. Cut the butter into small pieces, put in the bowl with the mustard and place over a pan of simmering water. Now whisk constantly and at a steady pace until the whole is light, frothy and all the butter melted. Use a large bowl or it will splash all over you, the kitchen, the cooker. And be warned, it does take 15-20 minutes. Worth it. Serves 6

BEURRE BLANC À LA MOUTARDE
WHITE BUTTER WITH MUSTARD

One of the simplest – as far as ingredients are concerned – and subtlest of sauces. That 'Prince of Gastronomes', Curnonsky, said: 'It is a sauce of exquisite finesse and lightness, discreetly seasoned with Angevin shallots … Remember that the shallot must be, so to speak, volatilized in the vinegar, and that it should be no more than a remote presence... Many gastronomes hold that there is a sort of sleight of hand in making this sauce,...see if you can give them the lie' (*A l'infortune de pot*, 1946). The trick – if there is one – in making this sauce successfully is not to let the butter actually melt – it must soften and appear to be *about* to melt, before the next piece is added. Then you will have the white creamy perfection that is *beurre blanc*. Bearing in mind the requisite remoteness of the shallots, it is an ideal sauce for spicing with mustard. A hint of mustard. A mild Dijon is good or, more delicately, very finely chopped mustard leaf seedlings. Here is Curnonsky's basic recipe.

4 shallots, very, very finely chopped
125 ml/4 fl oz white wine vinegar
250 g/9 oz unsalted butter, cut
   into small dice
freshly ground black pepper

Additional spicing: 1 scant teaspoon mild Dijon mustard, herb-flavoured if wished, or 2 tablespoons finely chopped mustard seedlings

The shallots must be chopped so finely they are almost mashed. Place in a small saucepan – preferably heavy-bottomed as this will not transmit the heat so fiercely – with the wine vinegar. Cook gently until the shallots are quite soft, the vinegar almost completely evaporated.

Take the pan off the heat and whisk in the butter – piece by piece, adding each knob after the last has quite softened and almost melted – until the sauce is thick and creamy. That is the 'princely' method: many people find it easier to cool the shallot mixture, then whisk in the butter over a very low heat, lifting the pan off every few seconds – and instantly if the butter appears to be actually melting. Once it starts running, the sauce is lost, and you may well need to make it a few times to get it right. Try it in quarter-quantities at first, and remember the whole process should be quick – two minutes at the most. When it is ready, give 2-3 grindings of the pepper mill and stir in the mustard, or leaves, quickly. Serve at once, with fish, chicken or tiny, young, steamed vegetables. Serves 6

MUSTARD CREAM SAUCE

Another supremely simple sauce, and one of the most sublime, perfect with practically anything.

125 g/4 oz unsalted butter
125 ml/4 fl oz double cream
dash of lemon juice

1-2 teaspoons Dijon or other
mustard of your choice

Melt the butter in a wide pan (this helps the quick thickening of the cream), when just about to sizzle pour in the cream, stir and bubble fairly hard for a minute or so until it has lightly thickened. Add a squeeze of lemon juice and stir in the mustard. Start with 1 teaspoon, then taste and add accordingly. Serve immediately with fish, flesh, fowl, vegetables. There are many variations – adding herbs, a combination of mustards, anchovies, a few soft roes, whatever is suited to your dish. The delicately green cream sauce from the Îles Chausey is a sophisticated variation with shallots and garlic sautéed in the butter, more mustard and a splash of vinegar instead of lemon, then cream and a couple of spoonfuls of finely chopped parsley and tarragon stirred in. Superb with cod, even more so with mackerel.

SAUCE MESSINE

From Lorraine, this delicious concoction is perfect with the fine fat trout that hail from the River Moselle – or indeed any beautifully fresh fish.

few sprigs chervil, leaves very finely chopped
few sprigs parsley, very finely chopped
few sprigs tarragon, leaves stripped off the stalks and very finely chopped
2 tablespoons finely chopped shallots

1 tablespoon finely grated lemon peel
50 g/2 oz butter, softened
1 teaspoon flour
1½-2 teaspoons Dijon mustard
2 egg yolks
300 ml/½ pint single cream
juice of 1 small lemon

Mix the herbs, shallots and lemon peel together. Mash the butter and flour until the butter is quite soft, then add the mustard, mixing well, and blend in the egg yolks, lastly the cream. Put into a saucepan with the herb mixture and beat with the pan standing in another containing hot (not boiling) water. Stir continually until the sauce is thickening and the cream *almost* about to come to the boil. On no account must it ever actually boil or that lovely smooth velvetiness will be lost. Just before serving, squeeze in the lemon juice. Serves 4

CORIANDER AND MUSTARD SAUCE

Coriander seeds are sweet and orangey, the leaves pungent and slightly peppery. Lovely together.

125 g/4 oz unsalted butter
1½ tablespoons coriander seeds, crushed (do not use pre-ground coriander; it is quite different)
125 ml/4 fl oz double cream
squeeze of lemon juice

squeeze of orange juice or tangerine juice if possible (about 2 segments, crushed and sieved)
1 teaspoon Dijon mustard
small bunch fresh coriander leaves, very finely chopped

Melt the butter, add the coriander seeds and cook gently until the aroma starts to give – about a minute, but watch the butter doesn't brown. Add the cream, bubble hard for 2-3 minutes until thickening, then add a squirt of orange juice, and lemon to sharpen. Finally stir in the mustard and, off the stove, the coriander leaves. For fish, chicken, lamb or veal. Serves 6

SAUCE SAINT-MALO

Excellent with all kinds of fish, particularly shellfish.

75 g/3 oz unsalted butter
25 g/1 oz flour
400 ml/14 fl oz fish stock
2 shallots, very finely chopped

100 ml/3½ fl oz dry white wine
3 anchovy fillets, soaked in milk, drained and pounded
1 tablespoon Dijon mustard

Melt 25 g/1 oz of the butter, sprinkle in the flour and stir thoroughly to make a smooth roux. Gradually add the fish stock, stirring all the time, until well amalgamated and the sauce starts to thin down. Keep stirring until it thickens again, then simmer on a very low heat for about 10 minutes.

Meanwhile, put the shallots and the wine in another pan and heat until the wine has completely reduced. Stir in the pounded anchovy fillets and the remaining butter and cook, still stirring, until all is well blended. Now sieve it into a bowl. Give the velouté sauce a stir, making sure there are no lumps, then – off the fire – whisk in the anchovy and shallot butter. Stir in the mustard and serve at once. Serves 4-6

RUSSIAN SAUCE

From Carême, probably one of the greatest exponents of sauce making, comes this simple sauce 'for large cuts of roast beef'.

1 slightly heaped tablespoon unsalted butter
1 slightly heaped tablespoon flour
350 ml/12 fl oz home-made beef stock (or you could use leftover gravy, slightly thinned down)
1 tablespoon finely chopped parsley

1 tablespoon finely chopped chervil
1 tablespoon finely chopped tarragon
1 teaspoon Dijon mustard
½ teaspoon sugar
pinch 'of fine pepper'
juice of 1 small lemon

Melt the butter in a pan and stir in the flour briskly to make a smooth roux. Cook gently for 4–5 minutes until it is lightly nutty brown, then very gradually pour in the stock, stirring all the time to prevent lumps. Cook for about 8 minutes, continually stirring, until it is just starting to thicken. Meanwhile, have another pan with boiling water at the ready. Put the chopped herbs into a sieve, dip into the water and blanch for 30 seconds. Shake off excess water and add the herbs to the velouté. Stir for another few minutes until the sauce thickens to about single cream consistency. Take off the heat, add the mustard, sugar, a grinding of black pepper and the strained juice of a lemon. Serves 4

Note: There is another Russian sauce, mayonnaise-based, with sieved caviare and the coral and tomalley of a lobster stirred in. Larousse states, 'Add mustard'; others omit it.

SAUCE ROBERT

A sauce of great antiquity and, although the French may lay claim to it and say that it was named after their great Norman duke, it is, according to E. S. Dallas – who is usually very reliable – in fact English. 'The French had their *brouet de chevreuil*; and the English had their Roebroth and Roebrewert, for which there were a number of varying receipts. One of these receipts the French picked up; and with that glorious faculty of altering names which has never failed them since they appear in history, they thought its name must be the same as that of their famous Norman duke, and they called it Robert' (Kettner's *Book of the Table*, 1877). Its age is not in dispute: Taillevent, the great medieval chef, writes of it and by the sixteenth century it was so prevalent that Rabelais says it must accompany 'ducks, rabbits, roasts, fresh pork, poached eggs, salt hake, and a thousand other viands'. Today the sauce is usually an accompaniment to roast pork though it is excellent too with goose.

2 tablespoons unsalted butter
3-4 large onions, very finely
    chopped
1 generous tablespoon flour
300 ml/½ pint good light stock

splash of cider vinegar
1 tablespoon Dijon mustard
Maldon salt
freshly ground white pepper

Melt the butter, then add the onions (the amount varies enormously from authority to authority). Cook gently, stirring occasionally, until they are nicely golden, then sprinkle with the flour, stir and cook a few moments longer. Gradually pour in the stock (you can substitute a few tablespoons medium-dry white wine for some of the stock if you wish), stirring all the while, then simmer gently for a further 15 minutes. Add a splash of vinegar, then stir in the mustard. Lightly season and serve. Serves 4–6

HORSERADISH SAUCE

It seems to be an ancient English practice to stir a little mustard into horseradish sauce – not to season it, for it would be difficult to add to such a powerful flavour, but to colour it a gentle yellow: a sensible idea, for grated horseradish quickly discolours to grey or, even more unappetizingly, pale brown.

3-5 tablespoons grated horseradish
    (the lesser amount for the fresh-
    ly pulled and grated root – well
    scrubbed and peeled, of course)
1 tablespoon white wine or cider
    vinegar

1 teaspoon caster sugar
150 ml/¼ pint double cream,
    whipped to the soft peak stage
1 teaspoon made English mustard

Mix the grated root with the vinegar and sugar and leave for 5 minutes. Then stir into the cream, lightly but thoroughly, and lastly add the mustard. You can add a bit more if liked to heighten the colour. A must with roast beef – nice too with pork and chunky lamb chops. Serves 4-6

BENTON SAUCE

Despite the title of her book, *A New System of Domestic Cookery* (published 1806), Maria Rundell is reflecting an age old combination in this recipe for a sauce very similar to the medieval dipping sauces. It is very good.

50 g/2 oz fresh horseradish, very finely grated

4 tablespoons wine or cider vinegar

1 teaspoon made English mustard

2 teaspoons caster sugar

Grate the horseradish into the vinegar, add the mustard then the sugar. Whisk briskly until the sugar is dissolved then leave to stand for at least 2 hours. Particularly good as a piquant antidote to the richer cuts of pork. Serves 4

Colman's Mustard shop in Norwich opened in 1973, the 150th anniversary of the company

CUMBERLAND SAUCE

One of the best of the English cold sauces – except that its origins are probably not English. Certainly it does not hail from the county of Cumberland. Legend has it that it was named after Ernest, Duke of Cumberland (brother of the Prince Regent, later the last Elector of Hanover). Undoubtedly, in Hanover we are nearer its true birthplace for it is very similar to a 'Hanoverian' sauce given by Elizabeth Ayrton for boar's head in *The Cookery of England* and to a sauce said by Soyer in his *Gastronomic Regenerator* to be the German accompaniment to the same dish (still made today in many Bavarian households).

2 Seville oranges (or 1 sweet orange and 1 large lemon)	Maldon salt
	freshly ground black pepper
6 tablespoons redcurrant jelly	sprinkling of ground ginger
1-1½ teaspoons Dijon mustard	8 tablespoons port

Pare the rind from the oranges (or orange and lemon) being careful to keep them pith-free. Cut into matchstick strips and blanch in boiling water for 5 minutes. Drain and reserve.

Meanwhile, melt the jelly, preferably in a bain-marie, add the mustard, stirring until smoothly amalgamated, then add the orange strips and strained juice, a good grinding of pepper, a little salt and a pinch of ground ginger. Stir for a further minute, pour in the port and cook for another 5 minutes. Pour into a small bowl and let cool – the sauce will thicken as it cools. It is not meant to be thickly set so do not add gelatine or cornflour as advocated in some recipes – this destroys the delicate texture and clear flavour. Serves 4

THOMAS JEFFERSON'S
SAUCE FOR 'STEW MADE OF COLD MEAT'

Before leaving Washington for Monticello, Jefferson always sent ahead of him a list of provisions to be put in store. Mustard makes frequent appearances, on one occasion '6 bottles of mustard' being called for. However, Jefferson knew when little was best: its contribution here is small in amount, significant in flavour. A sauce good for leftover game and roast beef, preferably fairly rare to begin with so as not to be thoroughly overdone in the recooking.

40 g/1½ oz unsalted butter	¼ teaspoon freshly ground black pepper
2 tablespoons walnut ketchup	
2 tablespoons redcurrant jelly	Maldon salt
1 teaspoon Dijon mustard	

Heat the butter, ketchup and jelly with 2 tablespoons water, stirring until the jelly is melted and the sauce nicely blended. Add the mustard, pepper and salt to taste and simmer gently. Lay your slices of meat in the sauce and cook for 2-3 minutes to heat through. Serves 2

'SAUCE FOR A MAWLERD (ROSTED)'

Among the papers in Samuel Pepys' library was the manuscript *Stere Hit Well*, dating it seems from the late fifteenth century and mainly concerned with cookery. This sauce for roast duck is an exemplary lesson in how to make perfect gravy – before cornflour and other sundry devices arrived on the culinary scene, with such devastating results. It can be applied to almost any joint, with the substitution of an appropriate liquid for ale (wine, port, cider, brandy or other liqueur, even orange, apple or grape juice) and a mustard suitable to the meat being roasted.

> Take onyons And mense them Wele
> Put sum yn thy mawlerd so have ye Sele [good luck]
> And mynce mo[re] Onyons I the[e] ken [tell]
> With the grece of the malwerd seth [boil] hit then
> Put ale musterd And hony ther to
> Boyle all to gedy tyll hit be enowe.

2 medium onions	1 teaspoon Dijon mustard (or mustard of your choice)
1 tablespoon of fat from the roasting juices	1-2 teaspoons clear honey
3-4 tablespoons ale or other alcohol or fruit juice	Maldon salt (optional) freshly ground black pepper

Chop one onion coarsely and put in, or under the joint (good luck is always welcome – and so is the flavour the onion gives to the meat), then roast in the usual manner. When the meat is done, strain off the pan juices, putting one tablespoon of fat in a small pan, skimming off the rest.

Grate an onion into the hot fat and cook for 5 minutes until softened. Mix in the mustard, then stir in the ale and the honey. Bring to the boil, add the reserved, skimmed meat juices, then cook, stirring, for 2–3 minutes until the honey is dissolved. Season with salt if necessary, and a good grinding of black pepper, then taste. Depending on the ale used, you may need a little more honey. If port, or a sweetish liqueur or fruit juice was the liquid, it may need a little sharpening – a squeeze of lemon should be sufficient. Serve very hot. Serves 4–6

AMBROSE HEATH'S SAUCE FOR GOOSE OR DUCK

Very simple, very good.

2 tablespoons made mustard
the juice of 1 lemon

2 tablespoons port
sprinkling of cayenne pepper

Whisk everything together in a small saucepan, bring to the boil and serve hot.
Serves 2-3

SEVILLE MUSTARD SAUCE

If you are a habitual maker of fine sauces – Espagnole or demi-glace, for example – they will give a fine base for this. For most of us lesser mortals, a good,
strongly reduced chicken or beef stock, or even leftover gravies from such joints,
will do admirably.

300 ml/½ pint good chicken or
    beef gravy (not a stock cube in
    sight) or 600 ml/1 pint chicken
    or beef stock reduced by half
1 Seville orange

1 tablespoon brandy, whisky,
    kirsch, etc or red or port wine
1 teaspoon Dijon mustard
½ teaspoon Matthew's mustard (p.55)
pinch of cayenne

Bring the gravy or stock to a simmer. Meanwhile, peel the orange (no pith to
be taken with the zest), cut into matchsticks and blanch for a minutes in boiling water. Drain and chop finely, add to the gravy, then squeeze in the juice
through a strainer. Add the alcohol and boil for 1 minute, then turn off the heat
and stir in the mustards. Stir for a good minute before adding a dusting of
cayenne. Serve in a hot sauceboat with steak, chicken breasts or legs. Oddly
enough, it is good with pork too. Serves 3-4

MUSTARD AND GINGER SOUR CREAM SAUCE

Sharp, with a nice bite, and good with cold fish, chicken or lobster.

150 ml/¼ pint sour cream
5 cm/2 inch piece fresh root gin-
    ger, peeled and grated
1-2 teaspoons Dijon mustard
1-2 tablespoons olive oil

juice of 1 lemon
freshly ground white pepper
freshly ground allspice
few sprigs salad burnet, very fine-
    ly chopped (optional)

Chill the sour cream. Add the ginger and mustard (start with 1 teaspoon and adjust to taste). Stir in the oil, half the lemon juice and a generous grinding each of white pepper and allspice. Taste, adding more oil or lemon accordingly, then stir in the salad burnet just before serving. If you can't beg, borrow or steal some of this heavenly herb, don't try and substitute anything else. Nothing tastes the same. Serves 6

ORANGE, MUSTARD AND YOGHURT SAUCE

Very refreshing, with a hint of piquancy. Particularly good with smoked chicken or turkey: or thin it down with extra orange, add some olive oil and use as a salad dressing.

1 sweet orange
1 teaspoon Matthew's mustard
   (p. 55)
150 ml/¼ pint thick natural
   yoghurt

splash of Spicy Italian vinegar
   (p.60)
3-4 cardamom pods, seeds
   removed and crushed
sprinkling of cinnamon

Very finely grate about a quarter of the orange zest into a bowl. Squeeze the juice, strain and add with the mustard. Stir in the yogurt, add a dash of vinegar, then sprinkle over the cardamom seeds and a touch of cinnamon. Chill lightly. Serves 4-6

VERY SUPERIOR BREAD SAUCE

Very unorthodox but very good. Like many inventions, it happened by accident.

25 g/1 oz butter
3-4 spring onion bulbs, finely
    chopped
2 garlic cloves, thinly sliced
1 heaped tablespoon flour
1 heaped teaspoon mustard powder
600 ml/1 pint milk

3-4 slices wholemeal bread
Maldon salt
freshly ground black and white
    peppers
freshly grated nutmeg
freshly ground allspice
pinch of cinnamon

Melt the butter, add the onions and garlic and sweat gently for 5 minutes to soften but not colour. Sprinkle in the flour and mustard powder, stir to make a thin, smooth paste, then gradually pour in about half the milk. Stir for 5-7 minutes until it begins to thicken, then break the bread into small pieces and whisk in. Simmer, very gently, for 20 minutes, checking occasionally and adding a little milk if need be to prevent sticking. Then add another 150 ml/¼ pint of milk and simmer for a further hour, adding the remaining milk little by little as it is absorbed. The end result should be thick and creamy. Season with a little salt, fairly generously with the peppers, nutmeg and allspice. Serves 4-6

DEVIL CHANTILLY

A slight adaptation of a recipe from Nancy Shaw's *Food For the Greedy* (published 1936) – a must for the bookshelves, and worth the search.

1½ teaspoons Matthew's mustard
    (p.55)
1 teaspoon Spicy Italian vinegar
    (p.60)
1 teaspoon anchovy sauce or ½
    teaspoon anchovy paste

½ teaspoon Maldon salt
¼ teaspoon freshly, and coarsely,
    ground white pepper
½ teaspoon Worcestershire sauce
150 ml/¼ pint double cream

Mix the mustard, vinegar, anchovy sauce or paste, salt, pepper and Worcestershire sauce together – thoroughly. Whip the cream until soft peaks form, then fold the mustard mixture into the cream. Chill before serving. A little grated lemon peel is a nice addition. Serves 4

GUBBINS SAUCE

The Victorian author, Edward Spencer, adopted the charming alias of Nathaniel Gubbins for his weekly humorous column in the *Daily Express* during the late nineteenth and early twentieth century. The name – and the sauce – reek of the British Empire in its heyday.

> … invaluable, especially for the sluggard. The legs and wings of fowl, turkey, pheasant, partridge or moor-hen should only be used. Have these scored across with a sharp knife, and divided at the joints. And when your grill is taken, 'hot as hot', but *not burnt*, from the fire, have poured over it the following sauce. Be very particular that your cook pours it over the grill just before it is served up. And it is of the most vital importance that the sauce should be made, and well mixed, on a plate *over hot water* – for instance, a slop-basin should be filled with boiling water and a plate placed atop.
>
> Melt on the plate a lump of butter the size of a large walnut. Stir into it, when melted, two teaspoons of made mustard, then a dessert-spoonful of vinegar, half that quantity of tarragon vinegar, and half a tablespoonful of cream – Devonshire or English. Season with salt, black pepper and cayenne, according to the (presumed) tastes and requirements of the breakfasters.
>
> (*Cakes and Ale*, Edward Spencer, 1897)

Delicious at any meal, with any sort of grilled meat – particularly tiny lamb cutlets. A double boiler for the making is easier than a plate, an ounce of butter about the right amount, and, to our tastes, a tablespoon of cream to smooth the edges. Serves 2

19th century drawing of the mustard-mill in Pandon Dean, Newcastle-upon-Tyne

ALICE B. TOKLAS'S DEVIL SAUCE

It is the eccentricity, plus of course the anecdotes about Alice Toklas and Gertrude Stein's years in France, combined with the sharp commonsense that one expects to come out of a French kitchen, that makes her *Cook Book* such irresistible reading. A very devilish sauce this (we cut the cayenne by half), which she served with some thoroughly devilled smelts.

300 ml/½ pint dry white wine
1 tablespoon white wine vinegar
1 tablespoon chopped shallots
¼ teaspoon black pepper
225 ml/8 fl oz tomato juice (or
  1½ tablespoons tomato purée
  mixed into 200 ml/7 fl oz good
  chicken stock)
1¼ tablespoons butter, softened

1¼ tablespoons flour
1 tablespoon English mustard powder
1 tablespoon Dijon mustard
½ tablespoon anchovy paste
⅛ teaspoon cayenne pepper (or
  less)
2-3 saffron filaments, crushed in 1
  tablespoon boiling water

Put 50 ml/2 fl oz wine in a pan with the vinegar, shallot and black pepper: simmer over a low heat, until reduced by half. Add the tomato juice and remaining wine and bring to the boil. Mash the flour and butter to a smooth paste, then stir into the simmering sauce, little by little, until the sauce thickens, being careful to prevent lumps forming. Mix the powdered mustard with the Dijon and the anchovy paste, stir in the cayenne and the saffron with its soaking water. Whisk into the sauce thoroughly, then simmer very gently for 10 minutes. Strain into a warmed sauceboat and serve immediately. Serves 6

GLAZES

There are many glazes with mustard for all varieties of meat. Sugar and mustard for ham is perhaps the best known: below are a few variations to start the experimental ball rolling.

FOR HAM OR GAMMON JOINTS

2 tablespoons Dijon mustard
2 tablespoons brown sugar

4 tablespoons cream

Mix all together and smear over the joint – increase the quantities proportionately for a large ham.

FOR PORK

2 tablespoons Matthew's mustard
(p.55)
1 tablespoon Dijon mustard

1 tablespoon soy sauce
1 tablespoon olive oil

FOR LAMB

2 tablespoons redcurrant jelly
(even better, crab apple jelly)
1 tablespoon Roman mustard
(p.53)

1 tablespoon olive oil
2 tablespoons red wine

FOR BEEF

2 tablespoons Anchovy mustard
(p.49)
1 tablespoon Worcestershire sauce

2 tablespoons port
2 tablespoons olive oil

FOR CHICKEN

1 tablespoon Lemon mustard
(p.54)
1 tablespoon lemon juice

1-2 garlic cloves, crushed
2 tablespoons apple jelly
1-2 tablespoons olive oil

The variations on these are infinite: marmalade is good with pork (English mustard, ginger wine and oil), mint jelly with lamb (Dijon mustard, Calvados and oil). You can spice it up, or down: you can add herbs, alcohol or sauce seasonings (Harvey's, Tabasco, chilli, etc) to suit your mood, the dish – and your store-cupboard.

DEVILLED GLAZE

2 tablespoons Dijon mustard
2 tablespoons black treacle
2 tablespoons brown sugar

3 tablespoons soy sauce
2 teaspoons anchovy paste
cayenne pepper

Dip the spoon in a flavourless oil before measuring out the treacle, which will then fall easily off the spoon. Add 1 tablespoon boiling water, then mix in the remaining ingredients. Divinely good for grilled chicken wings.

Mustard seller, 1586, France

Soups

Soup of the Evening, Beautiful Soup

ALICE'S ADVENTURES IN WONDERLAND, LEWIS CARROLL

Mustard has been used as an ingredient in soup for a long time. Theophrastus, a Greek scholar (372–287 BC) who did much research on plants, heavily praised it and grew it especially 'to use in soups'. It would seem to be the leaves he used rather than the seed, at that stage often finely ground and sprinkled on foods much as we do pepper today. At any rate, the combination had been discovered – and appreciated.

It appears next in fourteenth-century France, specifically as 'mustard soup'. Taillevent and the Goodman of Paris have almost identical recipes, only the last sentence differing slightly. It may have been a very old and well-known recipe, for the soup is a primitive one – basically an oil, water and wine bouillon, seasoned with mustard, then poured over a thick 'mess' of crumbled 'crisped bread'.

When the idea reached England, we don't know, but Michael Smith has two fine soups in his *English Cookery*. One is a delightfully simple concoction of chicken stock and cream; the other, a lovely earthy purée of mushrooms. Research turned up one or two other interesting recipes – Jerusalem artichokes and mustard, modernized with yoghurt to give lightness and a tang, while several cooks seem to have appreciated the virtues of mustard with ham stocks. Really surprising, though, and particularly pleasing, were the kitchen experiments. Day after day, as the wooden spoons stirred, so did the telephone wires buzz. Mustard was good in soup. English mustard, Dijon mustard, mustard seed, mustard oil, mustard greens . . . We had to stop. But the way was clear. Add a little mustard, and there was beautiful soup.

CREAM OF ONION AND MUSTARD SOUP

Classic French onion soup needs no addition: deeply brown and sweet, it is earthy and satisfying. Creamy onion soup is altogether different. Delicate and pale, it takes to spicings of all sorts.

2 very large onions, finely chopped
2 tablespoons unsalted butter
25 cm/1 inch piece fresh root ginger, peeled and grated
1 teaspoon sugar
freshly grated nutmeg
1.5 litres/2½ pints good chicken stock

8-10 sprigs fresh mint, preferably eau-de-Cologne
juice of ½ large lemon
Maldon or sea salt
freshly ground white pepper
150 ml/¼ pint double cream
1 tablespoon Dijon mustard

Sweat the onions with the butter in a small, deep pan – a butter paper placed on top of the onions helps keep them elegantly pale. Cover tightly and leave over the gentlest of heats for 20-30 minutes. They should be very soft and creamy coloured.

Stir in the ginger, sugar, a generous grating of nutmeg, and half a ladleful of stock, then simmer, covered, for another 5 minutes. Liquidize, with half the remaining stock, to a fine purée.

Pour the rest of the stock into a large pan, and gradually add the purée, whisking briskly all the while. Chop the mint very finely and add, with the lemon juice, to the soup. Bring to bubbling point, season with salt and a good grinding of white pepper, then stir in the cream. Let the soup be very hot but not quite boiling, then stir in the mustard and serve immediately with warm crusty bread. Serves 4-6

RED PEPPER SOUP

Strangely, the Aztec kitchen did not have soup. But once the Spanish arrived and made the introduction, it was quickly welcomed, and Mexican inventiveness soon produced a host of brightly coloured, exotically flavoured dishes. A great favourite is Elisabeth Lambert Ortiz's classic Sopa de Pimientos Morrones (to be found in her lovely book, *Latin American Cooking*). The idea that it might combine with a jar of mustard with green peppers was a good one.

1 large onion, finely chopped
2 tablespoons olive oil
3-4 large red peppers
1 litre/1¾ pints good chicken stock
Maldon or sea salt
freshly ground black pepper

1 mace blade, crumbled
300 ml/½ pint natural yoghurt
1-2 tablespoons mustard with green peppers
handful finely chopped fresh coriander leaves

Heat the onion very gently in the oil until well softened but hardly coloured. Meanwhile, split the peppers in half, remove the seeds and put under a very hot grill until the skin is quite charred. When they are really blackened, wrap in a damp cloth and leave for 5 minutes. Then peel off the skins, rubbing any charred flesh clean under warm running water. Chop the peppers and purée with the onions.

Return to the pan, and whisk in the stock. Season lightly, add the mace and bring to the boil before simmering, covered, for about 20 minutes. Taste, adding more salt and pepper if need be, then mix the yoghurt with the mustard, and beat into the soup, off the heat. Serve sprinkled with the chopped coriander. An excellent luncheon soup, especially chilled. Serves 6

FENNEL SOUP WITH CINNAMON STICKS

We tend to think of fennel as an odd, foreign vegetable. Yet it was one of the nine holy herbs in Anglo-Saxon times and one of the four 'hot' herbs of the medieval garden, where it was much grown by monks. A good blend with mustard, too.

2 large bulbs of Florence fennel, finely sliced, and green fronds reserved, finely chopped
3 tablespoons olive oil
1 litre/1¼ pints veal or good chicken stock
½ teaspoon ground cinnamon

50 ml/2 fl oz crème fraîche
50 ml/2 fl oz double cream
1 tablespoon Roman mustard (p.53)
Maldon or sea salt
freshly ground black pepper
4 cinnamon sticks

Warm the oil in a large pan, then add the fennel and sauté gently for about 10 minutes, turning occasionally. Add the chicken stock and ground cinnamon, bring almost to the boil, then simmer very gently, covered, for 30 minutes until the fennel is soft.

Liquidize and return the soup to the heat, bringing it very slowly to simmering point. Whisk the crème fraîche, double cream and mustard together, then beat in all but 30 ml/2 tablespoons. Add salt and black pepper, then whisk the soup until lightly frothy.

Pour into warmed soup bowls, drizzle a little of the reserved cream/mustard mixture over each, garnish with the chopped fronds, and pop in a cinnamon stick, for each person to stir and flavour their soup. Warmed sesame bread and chilled butter make a particularly good accompaniment. Serves 4

PUMPKIN AND PRAWN SOUP

In America pumpkin means pumpkin pie and Thanksgiving, in England we hollow them out for Hallowe'en, and in the Middle East they eat many a bowl of the nutty seeds. From the Caribbean comes perhaps the best way of dealing with this giant. Squash soups of all sorts are popular there, but pumpkin has the sweetest, fullest flavour. We added the mustard and prawns. And, if they haven't all been nibbled away, add a garnish of the seeds to heighten the pumpkin taste.

1 kg/2¼ lb pumpkin
450 g/1 lb unshelled, boiled
   prawns
½ lemon
3 sprigs parsley
1 mace blade
1 small onions, unpeeled and cut
   in half
2 tablespoons unsalted butter

2 large onions, finely chopped
1 large garlic clove, crushed
2 tablespoons mustard powder
Maldon or sea salt
freshly ground black and white
   pepper
lemon juice (optional)
150 ml/¼ pint single cream
mustard and cress, to garnish

If you want the seeds (which you should), start the day before. Scrape them out of the pumpkin (wrap that in clingfilm and keep chilled), then wash them very thoroughly of all fibres, dry and lay out on a baking sheet. Leave them for at least 12, preferably 24 hours in a very low oven. When they are quite dry and slightly shrivelled, rub off the casings and lightly toast them. They can be stored in an airtight jar.

Peel the prawns, putting the heads, shells and roes, if any, into a large pan with the half lemon, parsley, mace blade and small onion. Cover with 1.1 litres/2 pints cold water and bring to the boil, then simmer, uncovered, for about 30-45 minutes. Strain and reserve the stock.

Sweat the chopped onions and garlic clove in the butter until nicely softened, then sprinkle over the mustard powder. Stir and cook for a further few minutes, while peeling and chopping the pumpkin. Add that to the pan and turn around until lightly golden all over, then pour in the stock. Simmer for 30 minutes until the pumpkin is tender, then liquidize.

Return the purée to the pan, add the prawns and a good seasoning of salt, black and white peppers, then simmer for 10 minutes.

Taste, and add a little lemon juice if the flavour needs heightening – this will depend on your pumpkin, for even home-grown ones vary in their intensity of taste. Stir in the cream and garnish with some chopped mustard and cress. Serve hot but not blazingly so – this is a subtle soup and excessive heat kills it. Serves 6

GAMMON AND GRUYÈRE SOUP

Two classic combinations – ham and cheese, gammon stock and mustard – marry here to give a soup that can be as gutsy or as delicate as you wish. For a starter, light but with some substance, everything should be very finely chopped. For a warming supper soup, the ham can be left quite chunky and beaten egg whisked in at the finish. Either way it is very good.

1 gammon knuckle, soaked in cold water for 1 hour
1 tablespoon sunflower oil
3 shallots, finely chopped
1 leek, finely sliced
1 carrot, finely sliced lengthways
1 onion skin
2 cloves
1 tablespoon brown mustard seed
1 small sprig fresh sage
300 ml/½ pint dry white wine or dry cider

1 tablespoon walnut ketchup
freshly ground green pepper (green peppercorns are available freeze-dried – corns in brine are not suitable. Use black if necessary)
lime juice
1 tablespoon Dijon mustard
2 large eggs, beaten (optional)
handful of fresh parsley, very finely chopped
125 g/4 oz Gruyère cheese, minutely diced

Place the gammon knuckle in a pan of fresh cold water and bring to a lively simmer, then let it bubble for 5 minutes before discarding the water. Keep the knuckle aside and heat the oil in the pan, add the mustard seeds and leave for a minute until they start to pop. Add the shallots, leek and carrot and sauté gently for 5 minutes, then add the onion skin, cloves, sage and white wine. Cook on a fierce heat for 2 minutes, then pour in 1.1 litres/2 pints cold water and immerse the knuckle. Bring the liquid to the boil quickly, then simmer, very gently, for about an hour, with the pan half-covered.

Remove the knuckle and strain the stock – preferably into a tall jug. Stand this in a basin of cold water to speed up the cooling process, and the fat can then easily be skimmed off the top. (Or start the day before, chilling the stock overnight, if you wish.) Skin and defat the knuckle, cut off all the meat and chop either very finely or coarsely as you prefer.

Return the stock and the meat to the pan and heat until simmering. Season with the walnut ketchup, a good grinding of pepper (it shouldn't need salt, but check), and a squeezing of lime juice, then take a small ladleful of stock and mix with the mustard in a bowl.

If you want a 'supper' soup, let the liquid boil hard for 30 seconds, then drop in the beaten eggs, whisking briskly as you pour. Turn off the heat, add the parsley, tip in the cheese, and stir in the mustard/stock mixture. Serve at once. If you're not adding the eggs, then simply stir in the parsley and cheese, stirring for about 20 seconds, then add the mustard and again, serve immediately. Melba toast or crusty bread and chilled butter to accompany. Serves 4-6

MUSHROOM AND BLOOD ORANGE SOUP

Mushrooms and mustard are good together. This clear soup is lightly sweetened with the deep red juice of a blood orange. Or you can blend it to give a fine tweedy texture – ideal when the night is cold, and one's spirits are down.

350 g/12 oz small button mushrooms, wiped with a damp cloth
75 g/3 oz unsalted butter
3 tablespoons dry Madeira or dry
   sherry

freshly ground allspice
1.1 litres/2 pints chicken stock
juice of 1½ blood oranges
1½ teaspoons Dijon mustard

Cut the mushrooms in half through the stalk, then slice crossways very finely. Melt the butter in a wide pan until frothy and slightly 'nutty', then add the mushrooms and cook for 2-3 minutes, stirring, adding extra butter if need be. Pour in the Madeira and bubble for a minute over a high heat, then grind over lots of allspice. Pour in the stock and bring quickly to the boil. Add salt to taste – pepper, for once, is superfluous.

Mix the orange juice with the mustard, then, with the pan off the heat, briskly whisk into the soup. Serve with thin, thin slices of good wholemeal bread. Serves 6

STILTON AND ALMOND SOUP

Stilton makes wonderful soup – even stale end pieces, provided you soak them in a little milk first. And it combines well with nuts of all sorts. We have made this with walnuts and hazelnuts as well as almonds – these give the most delicate flavour, hazels being slightly sweeter and walnuts intensely nutty.

75 g/3 oz Stilton, crumbled
125 g/4 oz flaked almonds
1 lime
freshly grated nutmeg
75 ml/3 fl oz Greek yoghurt,
   thinned with a little milk to single cream consistency

1.1 litres/2 pints chicken stock
Maldon or sea salt
freshly ground black pepper
1 tablespoon Matthew's mustard
   (p.55)

Put the Stilton with three-quarters of the almonds in a blender. Grate the lime zest and reserve, then squeeze the juice into the blender, and add 300 ml/½ pint of the stock. Liquidize to a thick purée, add another 300 ml/½ pint stock and blend again, then transfer to a pan and gradually beat in the rest of the stock over a low heat.

Simmer for 5-10 minutes and toast the remaining almonds meanwhile until deeply golden. Stir the yoghurt into the soup, then season – lightly with salt, well with pepper. Take a ladleful out of the pan and mix in a bowl with the mustard, then pour back into the soup. Mix well and serve at once, garnished with grated lime zest and toasted almonds. Good with very hot, crusty rolls. Serves 4

FISH SOUP

Fish soups are strangely neglected in England, which is a pity for they are very good and infinitely versatile. For a heartier dish you could add a couple of red mullet, quickly sautéed in mustard oil, then roughly chopped, and perhaps a few prawns. Variations are endless, depending only on your tastes – and what happens to looks good on the fishmonger's slab.

350 g/12 oz cod fillet
1.1 litres/2 pints veal stock or
   light beef broth
1 teaspoon brown mustard seed
freshly grated nutmeg
pinch of cayenne pepper
2 teaspoons lemon juice

150 ml/¼ pint medium dry white
   wine
1 box mustard and cress
1 teaspoon arrowroot
Maldon or sea salt
croûtons (preferably fried in mustard oil), to serve

Bring the stock to the boil, then turn to a low simmer, add the fish and poach for 3-4 minutes until beginning to firm up, then remove from the stock, skin and flake it, taking out as many bones as possible.

Add the mustard seed, a generous grating of nutmeg and a pinch (or two) of cayenne pepper to the stock and simmer for 15 minutes before returning the fish to the pan. Simmer for another 2-3 minutes, then add the lemon juice, white wine and the mustard and cress, finely chopped. Cook for no more than 3 minutes, raising the heat slightly so the stock is not quite boiling.

Mix the arrowroot with a little cold water, stir into the soup and whisk lightly until it is slightly thickened. Season with salt to taste, then serve immediately, with the croûtons in a bowl on the table. Serves 4-5

DEEP-FRIED GREENS SOUP

Deep-fried seaweed has long been a favourite on Chinese menus. When we discovered that the 'seaweed' was not seaweed at all but *bak choi*, often called mustard greens, the dish became a firm favourite at home too. Spring greens, cabbage or even broccoli leaves are all good substitutes. Fine shredding is of the essence, and mustard oil for that extra 'bite' – almost imperceptible, until you taste the greens cooked in another oil. As a vegetable, they can accompany chicken, pork or fish. Alone they make an unusual starter, especially with prawn crackers – also fried in mustard oil. Dropped into boiling hot consommé, they make a wonderfully sizzling soup.

1.5 litres/2½ pints good beef consommé
150 ml/¼ pint dry sherry
1 small head fresh spring greens or about 150 g/5 oz *bak choi*, shredded as finely as possible (preferably using the slicing blade in a food processor)

lemon juice
freshly ground white pepper
mustard oil, for deep-frying
1 fat garlic clove, very finely chopped

Pour the consommé into a large pan with the sherry, a good squeeze of lemon juice and a generous grinding of white pepper. Bring to the boil, then simmer gently.

In another large, deep pan heat a good 25 mm/1 inch of mustard oil until nearly smoking. Standing well back from the pan, tip in the shredded greens – they will splutter enormously for a few seconds. Once the sizzling has died down, you can stir the greens, with a chopstick ideally, until they are deeply brown all over. Watch carefully, for the dividing line between nicely charred and inedibly burnt is very fine – about 2-2½ minutes usually does them perfectly. Then immediately remove with a large slotted spoon and pile on to a dish.

Quickly pour about a tablespoon of the hot oil into a small pan, add the garlic and stir-fry for a minute until crispy and golden, then scatter over the greens. Bring the soup to the boil, pour into individual soup plates and drop a good handful of greens into the centre of each. Eat instantly. Serves 4-6

Note: Once the oil has cooled, strain it through muslin then pour into a clean bottle and keep for re-use.

IN COMMEMORATION OF HER MAJESTY'S JUBILEE

KEEN'S

1742 AND 1887

THE MOST EXALTED ORDER OF THE STAR OF INDIA

MUSTARD

FIRST MANUFACTURED 1742
IN THE REIGN OF GEORGE II.

Starters

Now good digestion wait on appetite,
And health on both.

MACBETH, WILLIAM SHAKESPEARE

Perhaps mustard should have been on Macbeth's table as an aid to both appetite and digestion. A touch of it in sauces, in marinades, or as a condiment will increase the salivation rate as much as eightfold. This not only sets in motion the digestive processes (to give good and efficient appetite) but it also heightens the awareness of the taste buds to such an extent that it brings out the flavour of all foods subsequently eaten at the same meal – whether or not they also contain mustard.

So what more ideal place in a meal for mustard, than at the beginning? History shows that it used to be so – after the first remove, soup, came brawn with mustard sauce as the second remove. The brawn could be any cold cooked meat, not necessarily brawn as we know it today, but the point was that it always appeared before the main set pieces were put on the table. Certainly Gerard knew that 'mustard makes an excellent sauce good to be eaten with gross meats, whether fish or flesh, because it doth help indigestion, warmeth the stomach and provoketh appetite.' And it is interesting that until the introduction of the Russian service by Carême in the nineteenth century, all the main dishes, roast fish and meats, were placed on the table simultaneously after the second remove of brawn and mustard sauce had been served *alone*. With the new order of service, the meal became a matter of courses. The idea of having ten or more set pieces on the table all at once disappeared very rapidly – and so did mustard's place at the start of the meal. Even with the advent of salads and cold starters, an idea which came from America at the beginning of this century, mustard did not regain its former position, although the dishes involved were admirably suited to the spice.

A few isolated exceptions exist of course: Scandinavia has her Gravlax with mustard and dill sauce (p. 115) – although often it is served as a dish on its own for festive occasions rather than as a mere introduction. Burgundy has a wider repertoire, principally involving eggs, to give some beautiful and stimulating appetizers. And yet the scope is so much greater. Simple salads, such as finely sliced sweet tomatoes and shredded raw leeks, are enhanced with a mustard vinaigrette; a plate of charcuterie will often benefit from an accompaniment of mustard (Germany knows this, and rarely will cold meats arrive without their mild and sweet mustard pot), while crudités, the classic pre-dinner nibble, definitely need a spicy dip.

Pasta takes to mustard very nicely – ribbons or bows in a plain mustard cream sauce, perhaps with a little tuna or salmon (smoked or fresh), make a good beginning to a light meal.

Britain has many traditional supper dishes that, in smaller portions, make unusually good beginnings; little cheese soufflés, small strips of Welsh Rarebit among others. Even the classic smoked salmon is enhanced by a little mustard – as one wartime airman, stuck in Scotland and utterly fed up with the prize fish in all its forms, discovered. It became a habit he adhered to for the rest of his life. Lunching at Wilton's in London one day, he asked for the mustard. 'With smoked salmon!' exclaimed the horrified waiter. 'You bring the mustard, I'm paying the bill.' The Colman's was brought.

The potential is vast but suit your starter to the menu. If the next course is delicate, keep the mustard touch light. With gutsier dishes to follow, one can be bolder, but never forget that fine dividing line between a mild stimulation and highlighting of flavours, and mustard's more powerful role as irritant.

SOUFFLÉ OMELETTE WITH MUSTARD AND TOMATO SAUCE

In Burgundy, where they may be said to know about mustard, omelettes flavoured with the condiment are a favourite: sometimes as a light lunch with a good, well-dressed green salad, and often as a starter, to whet one's taste buds for the many courses to follow.

2 large, ripe but firm tomatoes	40–50 g/1½-2 oz unsalted butter
3 large eggs	4 tablespoons double cream
1 large egg white	1 teaspoon Dijon mustard
Maldon salt	lemon juice
freshly ground black pepper	

Blanch the tomatoes in boiling water, then peel. Chop one very finely, discarding the seeds and juices. Liquidize and then sieve the other to make a smooth purée.

Beat the eggs until frothy, season with salt and pepper, then whisk the white until stiff and fold lightly but thoroughly into the eggs. Melt a knob of butter in a heavy frying pan over a high heat and when sizzling pour in the eggs. Put the remaining butter in another pan, ideally wide and shallow. Melt quickly, add the tomato purée, and whisk it once or twice, then leave to simmer. By this time the bottom of the omelette should have started to set. Lift the edges up gently with a palette knife and swirl the unset eggs to the edge of the pan. Scatter over the chopped tomato, and keep swirling the eggs until they are almost completely set, just slightly moist in the middle still. Fold in half and slide on to a hot plate. Now you have to work fast, adding the cream to the sauce and bubbling over a fierce heat for about 30 seconds, whisking briskly. Stir in the mustard and a squeeze of lemon juice, pour over the omelette and serve at once. Since omelettes have to be quickly made, and instantly eaten, this is probably best for you and one other. Or just pamper yourself. Serves 2

MUSTARD KIPPER SALAD

Kippers are something one should be pedantic about. Buy the best and buy them whole. Frozen or canned fillets are useless. Mallaig, Loch Fyne and Isle of Man are the place names to look out for, and are worth the search. Particularly when, as here, you are serving the kippers raw.

2 large kippers
about 150 ml/¼ pint yoghurt, depending on thickness
½-1 teaspoon lemon mustard (p.54)

1 small, sweet onion, very finely chopped
fresh dillweed, very finely chopped
lemon juice
freshly ground white pepper

Skin the kippers, cut off the heads and tails, then pull out the large bone, bringing out as many side bones as possible with it. Now comes the boring bit – using tweezers if you wish, pull out *all* the small bones remaining in the kipper. It is tedious, it is time-consuming, but it must be done. Chop the kipper flesh fairly finely, put in a bowl and add the remaining ingredients. Half a dozen sprigs of dill should be enough (at a pinch dried will do, about 1 teaspoon) and be sure to snip it finely – it's surprising how like a fish bone a long piece can seem. Add just enough mustard and lemon to taste, chill for about 20 minutes, then serve surrounded by triangles of bread fried until crisp in butter. An excellent dish. Serves 6-8

CHICKEN WINGS WITH MUSTARD AND LIME

In the Middle Eastern kitchen chicken wings are always cut off, to be cooked separately in a variety of ways, then served as a mezze. It is a habit worth copying. The wings are too good not to enjoy on their own – and the mustard seeds add a nutty dimension to the traditional Arab marinade of lime or lemon juice.

6 chicken wings
juice of 2-3 limes
1 garlic clove, very finely chopped
3 tablespoons brown mustard seed

3 tablespoons mustard oil
pinch of sugar (optional)
25 mm/1 inch piece ginger root, very finely chopped

Marinate the wings in a shallow bowl with the lime juice and garlic clove. Turn several times and leave for at least 30 minutes and up to 6 hours.

Place the chicken, with the marinade, in a pan, preferably in one layer, then add a little water to just cover. Simmer very gently, uncovered, for about 20-30 minutes until the meat is tender. Meanwhile, fry the mustard seeds in the oil until they start to splutter. Remove them, add the ginger to the pan and fry for about a minute until golden and crispy. Keep aside with the mustard seeds.

Turn the heat up under the chicken, taste the sauce, adding a pinch of sugar if needed, and cook fiercely for a minute to lightly reduce the cooking juices. Stir in the mustard seeds and ginger, then pile into a dish and serve with warm bread to mop up the juices. Serves 3-6

SMOKED SALMON, AVOCADO AND MOZZARELLA SALAD

A simple variation on that Italian classic, tomato and mozzarella salad. The sauce is also excellent served with plain smoked salmon if one is feeling extravagant.

1 small crisp lettuce, such as Cos or Romaine, finely shredded
225g/8 oz smoked salmon, cut into 6 thin slices
250 g/9 oz mozzarella cheese, finely sliced
3 small avocados
freshly ground black pepper
cayenne pepper

For the dressing
lemon juice
2 tablespoons Matthew's mustard (p.55)
150 ml/¼ pint olive oil
3 thin spring onions, green tops only, very finely snipped
small posy fresh dillweed, very finely snipped
2-3 drops Tabasco sauce

Divide the shredded lettuce between six plates. Lay the salmon down one side of each, then the slices of cheese in the middle. Leave the avocado until just before serving or it will discolour.

To make the dressing, stir the juice of half a lemon into the mustard, then gradually add the oil, whisking constantly until it is thick and well emulsified. Beat in the chopped onion, and dillweed, then taste and add extra lemon if needed, before stirring in a few drops of Tabasco – there should be a bite not searing hotness. At the last minute, cut the avocados in half, peel and stone them, then slice very finely. Arrange the slices on the plates, then grind over a little black pepper – not too finely – and sprinkle a pinch of cayenne on the salmon. Pour over the dressing and serve with thin, thin slices of brown bread, lightly buttered. Serves 6

SMOKED HADDOCK WITH HORSERADISH DRESSING

Among the many things Colman's Mustard Club produced was a highly entertaining little booklet, *Mustard Uses Mustered*, written by the founder, Baron de Beef. Full of fascinating snippets of information, it includes a suggestion for mock smoked salmon sandwiches: mustard-buttered brown bread enveloping thin slices of smoked haddock fillet. An intriguing thought – but why not? Raw kipper is good, smoked salmon, of course, very good; and we decided that smoked haddock is excellent. Particularly with this Victorian-inspired dressing in which the mustard acts as a flavour enhancer for the horseradish rather than exuding its own taste.

3 tail pieces smoked haddock fillet, about 175 g/6 oz each in weight	6 tablespoons fresh breadcrumbs, soaked in water
For the dressing	2 tablespoons milk
4 tablespoons freshly grated horse-radish	1 teaspoon Dijon mustard
	pinch of salt
juice of 2 oranges	pinch of sugar
6 tablespoons olive oil	

Blend the horseradish and orange juice together, add the oil and blend again. Squeeze the breadcrumbs of as much water as possible, then heat, very gently, with the milk, stirring frequently until the mixture is quite dry without being browned. Cool slightly, then add to the dressing with the mustard, salt and sugar and blend well. Pour into a bowl.

Slice the haddock very thinly, on the diagonal as one would smoked salmon. You won't get such long slices as the flesh of haddock is coarser grained, but this doesn't matter as long as the pieces are small and neat. Arrange on individual serving plates and accompany with the sauce and thin brown bread and butter – rye bread is good. Serves 6

DEVILLED HAM PASTE

The travesties produced under the label 'paste' make many shudder. Serve them up as 'pâté' and you have welcome thanks. Which, as Elizabeth David says, is both 'comical and misleading'. Fish and meat pastes are not only delicious but have a perfectly respectable heritage in the English kitchen. Pâtés are equally good but quite different – the raw ingredients are mixed together *before* cooking. So let's be proud of our traditions and serve such dishes as Potted Beef, Sardine Butter and Ham Paste under their rightful titles.

175 g/6 oz ham, off the bone, chopped coarsely
125 g/4 oz curd cheese
juice of ½ blood orange
1 teaspoon lemon mustard (p.54)

¼-½ tablespoon Matthew's mustard (p.55)
¼ teaspoon coriander seeds
cayenne pepper
clarified butter

Chop the ham in a food processor until quite fine, then add the remaining ingredients except the coriander seeds, cayenne and butter. Dry fry the coriander for a minute or so until the aroma is pungent, then crush lightly in a mortar and pestle and add to the ham. Whizz until the mixture is quite pasty. Taste, adding extra Matthew's mustard if need be, and a pinch of cayenne: blend again. Pack into a small pot, pressing well down to exclude all air, then cover with melted clarified butter and chill until ready to serve. Provided you have put a good layer of butter on – at least 15 mm/½ inch – it will keep for 2-3 days. Serve with Melba toast or crunchy warm bread. Serves 4-6

POTTED SMOKED OYSTERS

Cans of smoked oysters are a wonderful store-cupboard standby – extremely versatile and ridiculously cheap.

175 g/6 oz canned smoked oysters, drained and rinsed
175 g/6 oz fromage blanc
1-2 tablespoons Matthew's mustard (p.55)

cayenne pepper
small posy salad burnet, very finely chopped
lemon juice
clarified butter

Chop the oysters coarsely, then combine in a food processor with the remaining ingredients except the lemon juice and butter. Taste, adding extra mustard if necessary and a squeeze of lemon if the flavours need sharpening. Pack into small pots and cover well with clarified butter, then chill for up to 48 hours. Serve with Melba toast and lemon wedges. Serves 4-6

MUSTARD AND GINGER CRAB

A small but rich starter. If you can use fresh crab so much the better – but don't be tempted by canned artichoke hearts. They're only slightly less trouble, for a vastly inferior taste.

6 small artichokes
225 g/8 oz white crabmeat, flaked
2 tablespoons grated fresh ginger
1 small garlic clove, finely
    chopped then lightly crushed
3 tablespoons double cream
3 tablespoons light mayonnaise
few drops soy sauce

squeeze of lemon juice
½-1 tablespoon coarse-grained
    mustard
Maldon salt
freshly ground black pepper
mustard vinaigrette (p.67)
mustard and cress

Break off the artichoke stalks and discard. Cook the artichokes in a large pan of boiling water until a leaf at the bottom will pull off easily and the little 'half-moon' of flesh is tender. Drain and cool, then peel off the leaves (keep for soup or a starter the next day) and scrape out the hairy chokes to leave the hearts. Trim their bottoms if necessary so they stand upright, then marinate in the mustard vinaigrette while preparing the crab.

   Combine the flesh in a bowl with the remaining ingredients except the mustard and cress, mixing thoroughly and adjusting the balance of flavours to taste. Drain the artichoke hearts, put on individual plates, and pile a little crab on top of each. Surround with chopped mustard and cress and serve, lightly chilled, with brown bread and butter. Serves 6

Taylor's of Newport Pagnell, founded in the reign of William IV, is the only other independent mustard maker in England dating from the nineteenth century.

MUSTARD CRUMBLES

Sweet crumbles are a classic of the English kitchen – yet rarely does a savoury crumble feature. One day, at Rudland and Stubbs in Smithfield market, there appeared on the menu fish crumble. We have added a mustard sauce and spiced the crumble.

350 g/12 oz fish, a combination of smoked and plain haddock is good
125 g/4 oz potted shrimps
700 ml/1¼ pints milk
60 g/2½ oz unsalted butter
scant 4 tablespoons flour
1 teaspoon Dijon mustard
2-3 tablespoons double cream
freshly ground white pepper

Maldon salt (optional)
For the crumble
150 g/5 oz flour, half and half wholemeal to white
75 g/3 oz unsalted butter, chilled, then cut into small pieces
2 teaspoons coarse-grained mustard powder (now marketed by several firms)
Maldon salt

Cook the fish in the milk for 10 minutes, then stir in the potted shrimps (butter and all). As soon as the butter has melted, remove the fish and shrimps. Skin, bone and flake the fish then mix with the shrimps in a bowl. Keep aside.

Strain the milk and keep warm. For the sauce, melt the butter, then stir in the flour and cook for 2 minutes, stirring vigorously to make a smooth roux. Off the heat, gradually add the milk, constantly stirring to avoid lumps. Return to the heat and bring to a bubble, gently and still stirring all the while, until the sauce has thickened. Add the Dijon mustard, then pour half to three-quarters over the fish, mixing well. The fish should be generously coated without swimming in sauce. Pile into small ovenproof dishes.

Mix the flour with the mustard powder and a pinch of salt then rub in the butter until the mixture resembles fine breadcrumbs – or simply whizz in a food processor for a couple of minutes. Sprinkle over the fish and bake in the oven at 200°C/400°F/Gas Mark 6 for 25-35 minutes until the crumble is golden and lightly crisp on top. Mix the remaining sauce with the cream, heat (stirring to prevent lumps) until bubbling then pour into a small jug and serve with the crumbles. Serves 6

MUSTARD PRAWN PUFFS

Beignets – little deep-fried choux pastry puffs – terrify many home cooks. But they are not difficult to make: speed and good elbow power are the main requisites. Let imagination do the rest, for many ingredients can be folded into your basic choux mixture to give these wonderfully airy *bonnes bouches*.

75 g/3 oz unsalted butter
125 g/4 oz flour
3 large eggs
½ teaspoon mustard powder
275 g/10 oz boiled prawns (generous half-pint)
tarragon mustard
½ firm but ripe avocado

3 spring onions, green tops only, very finely snipped
peanut oil, for deep-frying
Maldon salt
lemon juice
a big bunch of parsley, very finely chopped

Put 225 ml/8 fl oz cold water into a smallish pan with the butter and bring to the boil. Take the pan off the heat and throw in all the flour at once, then beat quickly and vigorously until you have a thick, very glossy paste. Cover and chill for an hour. Beat in the eggs one at a time, whisking extremely hard between each addition. The glossier the mixture looks, the better. Sprinkle in the mustard powder and a squeeze of lemon juice. Peel the prawns (keep the shells for stock), then chop them finely and mix with a little tarragon mustard, about a teaspoonful. Peel the avocado and chop into tiny dice, mix with the prawns then carefully fold into the paste. Finally add the chopped green onion tops.

Fill a large pan about one-third full of oil and heat until a cube of stale bread turns gold in 60 seconds (180°C/350°F for those equipped with a fat thermometer). Taking up a tablespoon of batter at a time, smoothing the top with another spoon, drop it gently into the pan and cook, five or six at a time so they have room to swirl around, for 4-5 minutes until beautifully golden and puffed up. Drain well on absorbent paper, cook the rest the same way, then pile on to a bed of chopped parsley. Sprinkle with a little lemon juice and Maldon salt and eat instantly. Makes about 35

Savourez la
SAVORA

Fish

And they gave him a piece of broiled fish and of an honeycomb.

ST LUKE, 24:42

What a wonderful image that verse conjures up – a fish fresh from the sea that morning, grilled no doubt with the local olive oil, perhaps a squeeze of fresh lemon, followed with newly baked bread and honey made from the powerful thyme that covers the hillsides around Jerusalem. Mustard undoubtedly was not there for, despite the parable of the mustard seed, it is doubtful whether the plant Christ referred to was *Brassica nigra* – botanists have been arguing for centuries over that. Mrs Grieve in her *Modern Herbal* suggests that it was confused with a type of tree, abundant by the Sea of Galilee, similar in looks to the mustard plant, possibly *Salvadora persicoria*. Other scholars have simply stated there was a confusion in the translation from the early Greek. Whichever, it seems certain that it was not mustard.

Many early writings suggest fish as a partner to mustard, and it was a common idea in medieval times. Just how widely mustard was used with fish we can clearly see from the papers of Isabella of Portugal. Married to Philip the Good, Duke of Burgundy, she kept a comprehensive domestic record from the year of her marriage, 1430, until three years before her retirement from court in 1457. In particular it covers, in detail, the foods bought on a daily basis, and notes whether it was a fast day or not and when a banquet was given. Fascinatingly, while it clearly shows a greater consumption of mustard on both such days, this was highest on fast days, when fish was the prime dish. The expenditure on vinegar and verjuice too (both of course used in the making of mustard) was also greater. Undoubtedly, piquant sauces, in great variety, were used to render changes in the menu, for even though there was a wide selection of fish available – bream, mackerel, salmon, carp, shrimp (also much favoured on meat-eating days), mussels, perch and herrings – with three fast days every week, much ingenuity was needed to avoid a dull diet. Saffron, cumin, caraway and pepper were all bought in greater quantity besides mustard. Sadly, the Duchess's papers relate only to expenditure – would that she had had her chef record his trans-formations of the ingredients so carefully listed.

Today, we have a much smaller repertoire, though in Dijon they still serve salmon with mustard – deliciously combined in La Toison d'Or restaurant where the fish is pasted with mustard and served on a tomato and cheese sauce. Sweden has her Gravlax, and herrings are traditionally served in Britain with a mustard sauce. But there it seems to stop. (Salt fish, since antiquity a natural partner to mustard – and one of the few dishes where mustard is recommended in the Middle Eastern kitchen, by Al-Baghdadi in the thirteenth century – has almost entirely disappeared from the modern table.) The field is wide open for exper-imentation.

Fresh tuna would be nicely enlivened by a little mustard, though again that is not a new idea. The Romans knew it well, and it has been suggested that mus-tard was an ingredient in the fermented sauce, *garum*, highly prized – and expen-sive – at the close of the Roman Empire. (This included pickled tuna intestines, possibly also anchovies, though the exact recipe is unknown.) We do know that mustard was popular with shellfish, both for poaching and in sauces. Apicius has a sauce for spiny lobster with chopped sautéed onions, pepper, lovage, caraway, cumin, figdates, honey, vinegar, wine, broth, oil, reduced must, and, 'while boil-ing add mustard'! Raw smoked fish proved a highly successful partner, and Japan serves a hot, hot mustard dip with raw fish.

Of all the ingredients we tried with mustard, fish, perhaps, has the most potential. The variety of fish is so endless, and our stock of old recipes so small. But whatever fish you are cooking – with or without mustard – you cannot fail to thank mustard afterwards: a spoonful mixed with cold water as a rinse for the pots, pans and plates will dispel any unpleasant fishy odours.

MARINATED HADDOCK FILLET WITH ORANGE AND MUSTARD

Blood orange juice is the secret to this very simple but elegant and delicious dish. Buy plenty of the oranges in season, and freeze the juice in ice cube con-tainers for use throughout the summer.

700 g/1½ lb haddock fillet, skinned	125 ml/4 fl oz double cream
juice of 1 large lemon	Maldon salt
juice of 2 blood oranges	freshly ground black pepper
4 tablespoons butter	1 tablespoon Dijon mustard

Put the fish in a shallow dish and pour over the lemon and orange juices. Leave for at least 30 minutes, preferably 2-3 hours, turning once or twice. (Unless the kitchen is very hot it is best not to chill the fish while marinating as this dulls the flavours.)

Melt the butter in a large frying pan. Take the fish out of the marinade and pat lightly dry then add to the pan and sauté for 2-3 minutes. Turn and sauté the other side for 1-2 minutes – the fish should be just done right through but not overcooked. Remove and keep on a warmed serving platter.

Add the marinade to the pan and bubble for 2½-3 minutes, then stir in the cream and boil hard for a further 2-3 minutes, until lightly thickened. Season, not too heavily, with salt and pepper, then stir in the mustard and cook for another 30 seconds. Pour immediately over the fish and serve. Good with thin, steamed leeks for dipping, on the asparagus principle, into the sauce. For a summer extravaganza, the recipe is gorgeous with fillets of fresh salmon. And asparagus, of course. Serves 4-6

MACKEREL IN BLACK TREACLE AND MUSTARD

Victor Gordon's unusual and stimulating *English Cookbook* provided the inspiration for this unlikely combination. While we were trying his recipe for Blackerel, improvisation was necessary due to an unusually empty store-cupboard. Of mustard there was no lack. The end result was dark, spicy – and very good.

4 mackerel, very fresh, cleaned and split
200 ml/7 fl oz cider vinegar
1 teaspoon brown mustard seed
¼ teaspoon black peppercorns
2 cloves
25 mm/1 inch piece cinnamon bark
4 spring onions, finely chopped
1 tablespoon mustard oil
1 tablespoon unsalted butter, plus extra for finishing the sauce

1 large onion, finely chopped
1 tablespoon soft, dark brown sugar
150 ml/¼ pint fish stock
1 tablespoon black treacle
½ teaspoon walnut ketchup
pinch of cayenne pepper
pinch of ground ginger
¼ teaspoon powdered mustard
lime juice
1-2 tablespoons chopped walnuts
finely chopped parsley

Simmer the vinegar for 5 minutes with the mustard seed, black peppercorns, cloves and cinnamon bark. Cool until barely tepid, then pour over the fish in a shallow dish, sprinkle on the chopped spring onion, and leave for at least 2 hours, turning occasionally. (If you have some home-made pickled walnuts, use their vinegar as does the original recipe. Do not use vinegar from bought pickled walnuts as this tends to be malt vinegar and is far too overpowering.)

Remove the fish from the marinade and pat dry. To make the sauce, melt the mustard oil and butter until foaming, then add the chopped onion and cook until soft and darkly coloured, about 15 minutes. Stir in the sugar and caramelize over a gentle heat, then pour in half the marinade and bubble hard for 2-3 minutes. Add the rest of the marinade, the fish stock and the treacle. Stir well, then lower the heat again, add the walnut ketchup and simmer while cooking the fish.

Mix together the cayenne pepper, ground ginger and powdered mustard, then sprinkle on both sides of each mackerel. Put under a medium hot grill, flesh side upwards, and cook for about 15 minutes, until quite blackened – but not burnt.

Turn the heat up under the sauce, whisk in a small knob of butter to gloss and lightly thicken then add a squirt of fresh lime juice. Serve the fish sprinkled with chopped walnuts and lots of parsley with the sauce handed round separately. A good green salad and crusty bread, to mop up the sauce, are the only accompaniments needed. Serves 4

MACKEREL STEWED WITH WINE

'No red wine with fish' is one of those taboos made to be broken. In the Loire, for instance, freshly caught salmon are delectably cooked in the local red wine (and incidentally, fresh mint – another English rule quietly ignored!). Mackerel, with its strong flavour, is a good candidate for unconventional treatment and we idly wondered whether red wine and mustard would make up a happy trio. Of course, it had already been done – by Eliza Acton. As she herself wrote, very good. One can do no better than reproduce her recipe.

> Work very smoothly together a large teaspoonful of flour with two ounces of butter, put them into a stewpan, and stir or shake them round over the fire until the butter is dissolved; add a quarter of a teaspoonful of mace, twice as much salt, and some cayenne; pour in by slow degrees three glasses of claret; and when the sauce boils, lay in a couple of fine mackerel well cleaned, and wiped quite dry; stew them very softly from fifteen to twenty minutes, and turn them when half done; lift them out, and dish them carefully; stir a teaspoonful of made mustard to the sauce, give it a boil, and pour it over the fish. When more convenient, substitute port wine and a little lemon-juice for the claret.
>
> Mackerel, 2: flour, 1 teaspoonful; butter, 2 oz [50 g]; seasoning of salt, mace, and cayenne; claret, 3 wine-glassesful [300 ml/½ pint]; made mustard, 1 teaspoonful; 15 to 20 minutes.

Note: Made mustard refers to freshly made powdered English mustard, but Dijon mustard can be used with equal success. Serves 2

HERRINGS IN OATMEAL WITH MUSTARD

Herrings, being one of the oily fish, have always called for a mustard accompaniment though occasionally freshly grated horseradish root was used instead. Salted herrings, despite being a winter staple for the poor (especially in the North), were also considered a delicacy and often replaced the 'brawn' course of a great feast on 'lean' days. This is beautifully illustrated in a fascinating document written in the 1420s by a Master Chiquart, cook to Amadeus VIII, Count-Duke of Savoy. For the banquet celebrating the marriage of his master to Marie, daughter of the Duke of Burgundy, which took place on a 'lean' day, he instructed: 'Get big salt fish such as salt mullets … with several other salt fish … then, with this, get herrings and set them out in another fine dish by themselves; for all that has just been mentioned there is no other sauce needed but mustard.' It is still the finest sauce, and the traditional Scottish method of dipping the fish in oatmeal adds a welcome texture.

6 plump fresh herrings, filleted
75 g/3 oz medium-coarse oatmeal
75 g/3 oz unsalted butter
Maldon or sea salt
freshly ground white pepper

For the sauce
1 tablespoon lemon juice
75 g/3 oz unsalted butter, cut into
  small pieces
1-2 teaspoons Dijon mustard

Rinse the herrings quickly, then dry well. Be careful not to dislodge the roes – or, if that's impossible, keep them whole and cook separately. Cover the fish all over with oatmeal, pressing well in. Melt the butter and when it is foaming add the herrings (you'll probably have to use two frying pans, otherwise use a large roasting pan over two hotplates). Cook for 3–5 minutes each side until crispy and browned, then transfer on to hot serving plates, and keep warm.

For the sauce, bubble the lemon juice in a small pan until reduced by half, then add a piece of butter. Whisking constantly over a medium heat, add more butter once the first piece has melted. The sauce should be pale in colour and creamy in consistency. Never stop whisking; if it should become too hot and seem in danger of curdling, lift the pan high off the heat until cooled slightly. (It's a good idea to have a bowl of iced water by the cooker, into which you can dip the bottom of the pan and quickly reduce the temperature.) As soon as the last piece of butter has melted, whisk in the mustard, pour the sauce into a jug and serve immediately.

Note: Traditionally, in Scotland, they use bacon fat to fry the fish. Delicious if you have some. Serves 6

COD STEAKS WITH WALNUT AND MUSTARD SAUCE

In the Middle East, nut sauces of all kinds are popular. Walnuts are favoured for fish, and they marry well with mustard to make a fine sauce for cod steaks – firm in flesh but often bland in flavour. If you can buy inshore cod, do. The difference in taste is startling.

4 cod steaks
300 ml/½ pint dry white wine
2 parsley sprigs
6 white peppercorns, lightly
  crushed
1 thyme sprig
1 bay leaf
5 cm/2 inch piece lemon zest, or
  Seville orange zest

finely chopped parsley
1 lime, cut into quarters
For the sauce
175 g/6 oz walnuts
juice of 1-2 limes
3-4 tablespoons olive oil
1 teaspoon Dijon or Roman mustard (pp.48 and 53)
Maldon or sea salt

Put the wine, parsley sprigs, peppercorns, thyme, bay leaf and lemon or orange zest into a pan with 300 ml/½ pint water. Bring quickly to the boil, then simmer gently for 25 minutes. Leave to cool.

Place the cod steaks in a wide shallow pan, cover with the cooled bouillon, then bring slowly to the boil. Just before it boils, turn the heat very low and cook the steaks, the liquid barely bubbling, for about 15 minutes until they are just done. Take off the heat and leave them to cool in the stock. When they are tepid, transfer to a serving plate and cover loosely with foil. Do not chill unless you absolutely have to – in which case bring to room temperature before serving.

Return the stock to the heat and bubble furiously until it has reduced to no more than 3-4 tablespoons.

Make the sauce by grinding the nuts, in a coffee grinder in small batches, to a fine powder. Whisk with the lime juice, then add the oil, a little at a time, to make a thick emulsion. Stir in the mustard, then a little salt and finally some of the reduced stock to thin the sauce down slightly and soften the flavour. How much you add is very much a matter of taste – and mood. Serve the fish, sprinkled thickly with chopped parsley, accompanied by lime quarters, and let people help themselves to sauce. Serves 4

TIMES-BAKED TROUT

One of the finest ways to cook trout, or indeed any whole fish, keeping it moist and succulent, firm yet tender. Beloved of Victorian anglers, the method was no surprise to M. Henry Poupon, President of S.E.G.M.A. Maille. For French fishermen, he said, it was the only way to cook trout. *We* use *The Sunday Times,* one whole sheet being just the right size to envelop one fish. For lovers of pink trout, the choice of newspaper needs no comment ... By one of those curious quirks of coincidence, the greatest users of mustard also happen to be readers of those venerable organs.

6 fresh trout, cleaned, heads and
   tails left on
6 tablespoons Roman mustard (p53)
50 g/2 oz pine nuts

Maldon or sea salt
freshly ground black pepper
6 pages of *The Sunday Times*

Wipe the trout with a damp cloth. Mix the mustard with the pine nuts, lightly crushing a few of the nuts to release their oil. Season lightly with salt and black pepper, then spread the paste thickly on the inside of each fish. Skewer the fish closed with cocktail sticks then wrap each in a sheet of newspaper, turning down the ends to make a neat parcel. Soak under the cold tap until quite wet, then bake in the oven at 180°C/350°F/Gas Mark 4 for 10-25 minutes, until the paper is almost dried out. The discrepancy in time depends on the size of your fish and on your oven – convector ovens dry the paper more quickly. Fish over 700 g/1½ lb will probably need about 30-35 minutes, while a really big one (say 1.5

kg/generous 3 lb) will need an hour. To serve hot, peel the paper off – the skin should come cleanly, too, to give you a perfectly done trout. Cold, it is equally delicious: simply leave to cool in the paper, then peel away. Small new potatoes and fresh peas or baby broad beans complete the perfect summer dish. Serves 6

MUSTARD AND HONEYED SALMON FILLET

In medieval times, fish was often cooked with sweetness and spices: reminiscent of Apicius in ancient Rome with his blend of herbs, honey, nuts, raisins and mustard. For salmon, it would be too much of a good thing, but mustard and honey give a delicate sweet-sharp flavour.

1.1-1.4 kg/2½-3 lb salmon, skinned and boned to leave 2 large fillets
4 tablespoons clear honey
125 g/4 oz unsalted butter, softened
4 tablespoons Five-herb mustard (p.48)

Maldon or sea salt
freshly ground white pepper
4 x 5 cm/2 inch very thin slices of fresh, peeled ginger
lemon wedges, to serve

Lightly season the salmon with salt and freshly ground pepper. Heat the honey until runny, then brush all over the salmon, on both sides, being careful when turning the fillets.

Mash the butter with the mustard, then spread the paste over the fish, again on all sides, putting a thicker layer in the middle to sandwich the fillets together. Place the fish on a large sheet of foil, then tuck two of the slices of ginger underneath the fish, and put two on the top. Fold the foil into a loose parcel, sealing the edges tightly, and cook in the oven at 220°C/425°F/Gas Mark 7 for about 20 minutes until the fish is just done. Transfer to a serving dish, in the foil, unwrapping at the table so everyone can enjoy the wonderful smell. Have lemon wedges on the table, and lots of good bread to mop up the buttery juices. A herb salad, delicately dressed, and as good a white wine as one can afford are the only other requisites. Serves 4-6.

GRAVLAX WITH MUSTARD SAUCE

One of the world's great classics, hailing from Scandinavia where it is traditionally served on Walpurgis Night (30 April) to herald the arrival of spring and the return of the salmon. It is an ideal way to treat a tailpiece – though these are no longer the bargain they once were. Kinder on the purse, and equally good for the dish, is Canadian frozen salmon. Herrings, and kippers particularly, also benefit wonderfully from being 'buried' in the pickle (*gravlax* literally means 'grave salmon'), thus obliging us with a year-round treat. The principle is the same but you will need four small herrings or two large kippers.

700-900 g/1½-2 lb tailpiece salmon

1½ tablespoons Maldon salt, lightly crushed

1 tablespoon sugar

1 tablespoon black peppercorns, crushed

small posy fresh dillweed, finely chopped

For the sauce

3 tablespoons Dijon mustard

1½ tablespoons caster sugar

1 tablespoon white wine vinegar

100 ml/3½ fl oz peanut oil

100 ml/3½ fl oz soured cream

small posy fresh dillweed, finely chopped

Maldon salt

freshly ground white pepper

First, bone the salmon. Cover the fish with a tea towel, roll it gently on a hard surface to loosen up the bones; then insert a thin-bladed knife right along the spine, before easing it down to the side, pressing as close to the bone as possible. Slit through the skin (this stays on during the pickling process), and repeat the operation on the other side of the spine, then turn the fish over and repeat again. Now you can lift off the flesh into two kite-shaped pieces. The whole process takes little longer than reading how to do it!

Mix together the salt, sugar and crushed peppercorns, then sprinkle a good layer of dill in the bottom of a dish into which the fish will fit snugly. Add a layer of the salt/sugar mixture, put in the fish, skin side down. Scatter over a layer of dillweed and pickle mixture. Place the second piece of fish, flesh side down, on top, again covering with dill, salt and sugar.

Cover with kitchen foil and a heavy weight (a couple of large tins are fine). Chill for at least 24 hours, not more than 5 days, then slice the fish, very thinly on the diagonal (like smoked salmon), and serve with lightly buttered rye bread and the mustard sauce.

This takes minutes to make but the flavour is vastly improved if it is left to stand for 2-3 hours. Whisk the mustard and sugar together, beat in the vinegar, then add the oil, whisking very briskly. It thickens quickly to a very solid vinaigrette – indeed many books suggest a vinaigrette-type sauce, and some a mayonnaise, but in Norway they serve a soured cream sauce, which is perhaps the nicest. So, add the soured cream, then the dill and season to taste with salt and pepper. Serve chilled. Serves 6-8

MONKFISH WITH MUSTARD SEEDS AND LIME

Monkfish used to be one of those glorious finds at the fishmonger that was delicious – and cheap. Now, since *nouvelle cuisine,* it has been turned into a star fish, at twice the price. Still, it is exquisite in flavour and there is little wastage. Milky in colour, rather solid in texture, it is one of the few fish where bigger is better – the large steaks across the middle or a good-sized tailpiece are the prime parts. Tailpieces in particular are easy to fillet, and attractive to serve.

1.1-1.4 kg/2½-3 lb tailpiece
    monkfish
2 tablespoons mustard oil
3 tablespoons brown mustard seed
2 tablespoons flour
75 g/3 oz unsalted butter
2 tablespoons sunflower oil

Maldon salt
freshly ground black pepper
3 tablespoons cognac
juice of 2-3 limes
125 ml/4 fl oz fish stock
¼ teaspoon Dijon mustard

Monkfish is usually sold skinned, so it merely needs filleting by slipping a long, thin-bladed knife in beside the central cartilaginous bone at the thicker end of the tailpiece, then gently cutting through the flesh to the sides down to the tip. Repeat on the other side of the bone, separating the top fillet from the bone as you do so. Lift off the top piece, then remove the bone from the bottom – you should now have two neat triangles of fish which can be sliced lengthways into three long, narrow fillets.

Heat the mustard oil in a small, deep pan until nearly smoking, then add the mustard seeds and cook, covered, for about a minute until they start to pop. Drain, discarding the oil. Mix the seeds with the flour, then coat the fillets lightly. Melt the butter with the sunflower oil; when just starting to sizzle add the fish and cook for 3-4 minutes on both sides until just cooked through. Sprinkle with a little salt and black pepper, then flame with the cognac (a slight warming in a ladle helps ensure quick ignition). Remove the fish and keep warm on a serving platter. Add the juice of 2 limes and bubble the sauce hard, then add the fish stock and return to the boil. Taste, adding the extra lime juice if necessary, then reduce slightly until lightly glazed. Stir in the mustard, pour over the fish and serve at once. Serves 6

ROAST TURBOT WITH MUSTARD, CORIANDER AND CIDER

Rarely does one see turbot at the fishmonger's nowadays, especially whole turbot. Yet our ancestors knew it well. Those extravagantly huge, diamond-shaped copper pans that adorn country house kitchen walls were specifically for the monster fish – often up to 3 feet in length, and weighing in at 20 kg/45 lb. With its large, flattened snout and knobbly-skinned back it is a daunting creature to look at, but its flesh is sweet, firm, very white – and superb in flavour. Hannah Glasse in the *Art of Cookery made Plain and Easy* (1747) bakes turbot with fresh horseradish. That led the way to mustard. Thankfully, the more manageable chicken turbot – a modest 1-1.8 kg/2¼-4 lb in size – is equally good in flavour.

1 chicken turbot, about 1.6 kg/3½ lb, cleaned but left whole
50 g/2 oz butter, plus extra for greasing
1-2 tablespoons Dijon mustard
1 tablespoon coriander seeds
Maldon or sea salt
freshly ground black pepper

freshly grated nutmeg
600 ml/1 pint dry cider
lemon juice
small posy fresh coriander leaves, finely chopped
1 teaspoon arrowroot
½-1 teaspoon Dijon mustard, to finish the sauce

Make a slight incision on the dark side of the fish from head to tail down the centre bone to prevent the fish curling up during cooking, then lay it in a large, well-buttered roasting pan and rub the mustard well into the top side of the turbot. Sprinkle over the coriander seeds, a little salt, lots of black pepper and nutmeg. Flake the butter all over the fish, then pour in the cider around the sides, drizzling just a tablespoon or two over the flesh.

Cook in the oven at 170°C/325°F/Gas Mark 3 for 40-50 minutes until the flesh is white and firm when tested with the tip of a knife. Very carefully lift out on to a warmed serving dish and rest in the turned-off oven while finishing the sauce.

Pour the cooking liquor into a small pan, reduce by fast boiling by about a third, then add a squirt of lemon juice, the fresh coriander leaves and the arrowroot mixed with a little water. Stir over a medium-low heat until slightly thickened, add the mustard, just to sharpen the sauce – it should not be overtly mustard in taste. Pour into a gravy boat and serve at once with the roast fish. Serves 6

MUSTARD GRILLED LOBSTER

Despite Apicius, lobster with mustard is not a combination that instantly springs to mind. And indeed, cold with a mustard mayonnaise it was horrid – that elusively beautiful flavour killed in an instant. Hot, with a mustard cream sauce, or as spiced soup, it was less than delightful. Then that gem of a book, *The Gentle Art of Cookery* by Mrs Leyel, gave it to us: 'Open a lobster and break its claws. Sprinkle it when open with dry mustard, pepper and salt, and cover with little pieces of butter.' One of the best ways of cooking the noble crustacean. For the lobster's sake, blanch it first. Death is instantaneous, and it is easier to scoop out the flesh. Ready cooked lobster is not suitable for the recipe since the extra grilling will toughen and dry it out.

1 live lobster, about 700 g/1½ lb in weight
50 g/2 oz unsalted butter, plus extra for greasing
dried, home-made breadcrumbs
½ teaspoon mustard powder
Maldon salt
freshly ground black pepper

For the sauce
25 g/1 oz unsalted butter
lemon juice
small bunch parsley, finely chopped
Maldon salt
freshly ground white pepper
½ teaspoon English mustard

Bring a large pan of lightly salted water to a rapid boil, then plunge in the lobster, head first. Boil for 1 minute, then lower the heat and simmer for 5 minutes – this will almost cook the lobster (normally you would allow 5 minutes to the pound). Take out and leave until just cool enough to handle.

Lie the lobster on its back and, with a sharp blow of a cleaver or large-bladed knife, divide it into two lengthways. Remove the stomach (a little dark sac confusingly near the head), then scoop out the body meat, discarding the dark vein running through the lobster. Do not discard the soft, creamy greenish meat – this is the liver (tomalley) and extremely delicious. Neither should you discard the other delicacy – the roe, or coral, present under the tail in a female lobster. Put them into separate bowls and keep aside. Now crack the large claws and carefully pull out the flesh – try and keep the pink tip intact if you can. Clean the shells and dry them, then lightly grease the insides with butter. Sprinkle with breadcrumbs, shaking off the excess, and refill with the meat, cut into chunks, leaving a gap in the middle to pile in the liver and roe.

Sprinkle with the powdered mustard, a little salt and black pepper, dot with the butter, and put under a fierce grill for 4-5 minutes. Quickly melt the butter for the sauce, whisk in the juice of a small lemon, the parsley, a little salt and pepper and then, off the heat, beat in the mustard. Serve at once with the lobster, accompanied by thinly sliced brown bread. Delicious. The sauce, incidentally, is also extremely good with tiny new potatoes – preferably steamed. Serves 2

Chicken and Turkey

And when we meet, with champagne and a chicken, at last.

LADY MARY WORTLEY MONTAGU, THE LOVER

Chicken was, until recently, a luxury. It appeared late as a food in the Western world, and seems first to have been appreciated by the islanders of Cos around the third century BC. Before that the birds were apparently kept only for their eggs. The Romans learnt quickly from the Greeks and by 175 BC it was frequently being mentioned in the records of Pompeii.

The Middle Ages continued to regard it highly, and we learn from Isabella of Portugal that fowls formed the greatest expense when her kitchen was preparing for a banquet. By the eighteenth century, when Lady Mary Wortley Montagu was writing, chicken was the epitome of a luxurious dinner for the lovers.

Today we are more blasé about chicken, now one of the cheapest of meats. This is a shame, for it is also one of the healthiest to eat. We should treat it with respect and enjoy it, for a little judicious cooking – and mustard – can work wonders on even the cheapest frozen varieties. We experimented by smearing them all over with a little Dijon mustard before roasting in a chicken brick. Every time there were comments on how intense the chicken flavour was – not a hint of the little hot seed, merely a return to the forgotten taste of chickens reared freely in the fresh air.

When we went to Colman's at Norwich, John Hemingway – who knows more about mustard than man has forgotten – told us an enchanting story of some delicious chicken once served in Nyasaland. The hostess enquired the recipe of the cook, to be told that he had merely used a little of the special poultry spice she had given him. Puzzled, she trooped her guests to the kitchen where the proud cook delightedly pointed to a packet of Poultry Mustard. This was one of Colman's most successful lines at the beginning of the last century – but for feeding to the chickens. One teaspoon per six chickens mixed in with their morning mash proved startlingly efficacious in improving their egg-laying capabilities, their strength of fertilization and their general stamina.

Interestingly, we found few recipes in the ancients for chicken with mustard. Apicius has two, then there is silence until we reach Taillevent, chef (legend has it) to Charles VI in the late fourteenth century. According to Dumas, the King, after a hard day fighting the English, arrived in the little village of Sainte-Menehould. Devastated, with only half a dozen houses still standing, it could offer neither much food, nor people to cook it. However, four pig's trotters and three chickens were found and a toolmaker's wife was asked to cook them. She did not let her King down: the birds were roasted, the trotters grilled. Both had a rolling in breadcrumbs and *fines herbes* and were served with mustard. Only the bones were left by the royal party – and the King thereafter often requested Chicken à la Sainte-Menehould. To this day, those words on a menu indicate that method of cooking, more usually with pigs' feet than chicken, and the mustard will often appear in the form of a piquant sauce.

If you're lacking stuffing ingredients for your chicken, a little mustard mixed with sautéed onions, breadcrumbs and fresh herbs brings out the flavours wonderfully – you can add fried mustard seeds for extra nuttiness. A tasteless gravy is vastly improved by an added spoonful of the condiment: bubble the sauce hard for a minute or two to reduce the taste of the mustard.

Turkey, which can be uninspiring, took on new dimensions when spiced with mustard and one of the simplest and most delicious dishes we had was leftover turkey breast, steamed to heat it through, then covered lightly with the supremely easy cream and mustard sauce (p.75). Cold, both turkey and chicken are lifted with a mayonnaise flavoured with anchovy, avocado and mustard (p.71) – again the mustard not intruding itself but enhancing a peculiarly delicate and subtle combination of tastes. And if cold leftovers are not enticing, one can mince the flesh, mix it with herbs, a little egg white, a few mustard seeds (fried until beginning to splutter) and breadcrumbs, then form it into small balls. Fried until golden and crispy, they can be accompanied by a mustard sauce of your choice. They are also excellent on a bed of mixed salad leaves with a mustard vinaigrette poured over them the instant they come out of the pan. It is not difficult, with mustard, to restore chicken to a place of honour at the table.

CHICKEN DIJON WITH SPICE AND WINE

Dijon chicken, chicken Dijonnaise, Chicken Dijon – there must be as many names, and dishes, as there are mustards. This recipe comes from the Maille leaflet; superbly simple, and supremely delicious.

1.1 kg/2½ lb chicken pieces
25 g/1 oz unsalted butter
sea salt
freshly ground black pepper
1 garlic clove, crushed
1 bay leaf
¼ teaspoon dried marjoram
¼ teaspoon dried thyme
175 ml/6 fl oz chicken stock

175 ml/6 fl oz dry white wine
12 small onions, peeled but left whole
12 whole baby carrots
400 g/14 oz canned artichoke hearts
5 tablespoons Maille Dijon mustard with white wine
1 tablespoon cornflour

Lightly brown the chicken pieces in butter in a large flameproof casserole, sprinkle with a little salt and pepper, then add the garlic, bay leaf, marjoram, thyme, chicken stock and wine. Bring to a gentle simmer, cover and cook for 35 minutes, stirring occasionally.

Add the onions, carrots and drained artichokes and cook, covered, for a further 10-15 minutes until the vegetables are tender.

Transfer the chicken and vegetables to a warmed serving platter and keep warm in a low oven. Stir the mustard into the cooking liquid and bring to the boil. Mix the cornflour with a little cold water, add to the pan and stir until lightly thickened. Pour the sauce over the chicken and serve immediately. Serves 6

CHICKEN LEGS DIJONNAISE

Another variation of Chicken Dijonnaise simply makes a mustard butter which is spread all over the chicken – under the skin. It is a particularly good method for grilling chicken legs; spicy and succulent, they are delicious hot, even better cold. Ideal picnic food, although they have been known to disappear at Saturday breakfast.

6 chicken legs
Maldon salt
finely ground black pepper
a few tarragon sprigs, very finely chopped

1-2 tablespoons Dijon mustard
75 g/3 oz unsalted butter, softened
juice of 1 large lemon

Carefully using a long, thin-bladed knife, slip it under the skin and loosen all around the leg joints. Mix some salt with a good grinding of black pepper and the chopped tarragon and rub all over each leg. Leave for 30 minutes.

Mash the mustard and the butter together, then beat in the lemon juice. Spread a little of the paste – about 2 teaspoons – between the skin and the flesh of each leg, then cook under a medium grill for 15–20 minutes, turning once. Raise the heat and grill for a further 5–10 minutes (depending on the size of the legs) until deeply golden and crispy. Serves 6

STEAMED CHICKEN BREASTS WITH NETTLE MUSTARD SAUCE

Nettles have long been known for their goodness and were a prized first sign of spring in the Victorian market place. Today, they cost nothing and are widely ignored. Delicious in soups, and this delicate sauce.

6 chicken breasts, skinned and off the bone
juice of 1 large lemon
50 g/2 oz unsalted butter
2–3 garlic cloves
600 ml/1 pint nettle tops, young top springs only, gathered wearing rubber gloves
3 cloves
6 shallots, finely chopped
200 ml/7 fl oz good chicken stock
Maldon salt
freshly ground white pepper
2 teaspoons Dijon mustard or 1–2 teaspoons lemon mustard

Put the chicken on a flat dish and squeeze the lemon juice over both sides. Leave for 30 minutes. Place the breasts in a steamer, or colander, fanned out with the thickest ends in the middle, and put over a pan of gently simmering water. Cover and cook for 5–7 minutes each side, until just done in the middle. Once cooked, keep warm in the steamer – off the heat.

Meanwhile make the sauce. Melt half the butter in a large pan, add the garlic and the cloves and cook gently for 2–3 minutes then add the shallots and sweat for a further 5–6 minutes. Wash the nettle tops (still wearing rubber gloves – the sting disappears only with cooking), rinse, shake dry and add to the pan with 6–7 tablespoons of stock. Stir, then cook until the nettles are dark green and limp, about 8 minutes.

Purée the nettles with the rest of the stock, return to the pan, add salt and pepper and bring to a simmer. Whisk in the remaining butter to thicken and gloss the sauce, then stir in the mustard. Whisk for a further minute, then pour a little sauce on to serving plates. Place the breasts on top, drizzle over a little more sauce and serve immediately. Serves 6

CHICKEN BREASTS WITH TOMATO, MUSTARD AND YOGHURT SAUCE

Tomato and mustard is a particularly good combination. Fresh tomatoes give a sweeter, subtler taste, though the canned plum variety are a good substitute – add a pinch of vanilla sugar to counteract their extra acidity. A similar, though much richer, sauce was served by John Tovey at Miller Howe, with pork chops. Based on reduced cream, lightly flavoured with tomato purée and English mustard, it is very good indeed but chicken is, perhaps, more suited to the delicacy of this recipe.

6 chicken breasts, skinned and boned
freshly ground black pepper
700 g/1½ lb fresh tomatoes
1½ teaspoons Moutarde Soyer (p.51)

1½ teaspoons Maille Dijon mustard
300 ml/½ pint natural yoghurt
Maldon salt
¾ teaspoon cornflour
handful finely chopped fresh chervil, or parsley

Sprinkle the meat with freshly ground black pepper on both sides, then leave. Bring a large pan of water to the boil, drop in the tomatoes and blanch for 3-4 minutes. Take out, cool slightly, then peel and blend to a purée. Strain into a pan, stir in the mustards and put over a very gentle heat.

Meanwhile, stabilize the yoghurt (to prevent a curdled-looking sauce): whisk it in a large shallow saucepan until smooth and fairly liquid, then add the cornflour, mixed with a little water to form a thin paste, and about ¼ teaspoon salt. Place on a low heat and bring to the boil, stirring all the time with a wooden spoon *in the same direction*. When it is just about to boil, turn the heat to the lowest possible and simmer for 10 minutes until thick and smooth. *Do not cover* the pan since steam – even one tiny droplet – will undo your good work and instantly destabilize the yoghurt. It can now be cooked with impunity. Incidentally, if you make your own yoghurt from salted goat's milk, it can be used as it is since it won't curdle. Keep an eye on the tomato mixture during the stabilization process and turn off the heat if it is reducing too rapidly. About a quarter is right – and the flavours of the mustards should have melded almost completely. You are aiming for a very fresh tomato taste – with just a hint, rather than an awareness, of mustard.

Once the yoghurt has started to simmer, you can steam the chicken. Lay the pieces in a colander or steamer over a pan of barely simmering water and steam for about 12 minutes, turning once, until just cooked through to the middle. Keep warm in the steamer, covered, but off the heat, while finishing the sauce.

Whisk the yoghurt into the tomato, check the seasoning, adjusting if necessary, blend thoroughly and bring to a bubble. Put the chicken on to warmed individual plates, spoon some sauce around or over each breast and sprinkle with lots of chopped chervil. Serves 6

STIR-FRY CHICKEN WITH MUSTARD SEEDS, SATSUMAS AND WATERCRESS

China's rare use of mustard in the kitchen nearly always combines it with chicken. This Chinese-inspired dish is simple, quick and very good.

2 chicken breasts, boned and skinned
1 egg white
3 tablespoons peanut oil
½ tablespoon brown mustard seed
2 garlic cloves, finely chopped
2 spring onions, bulbs quartered, green tops finely sliced on the diagonal
4-5 raspings of dried root ginger (not ground ginger)

pinch of ground cinnamon
150 ml/¼ pint home-made chicken stock
2 satsumas
1 tablespoon English mustard powder
1 teaspoon powdered arrowroot
Maldon salt
1 bunch watercress, finely chopped

Cut the chicken breasts into long strips, then into small pieces. Lightly beat the egg white and mix into the chicken. Chill for 20 minutes.

Heat 1 tablespoon of the oil, in a wok for preference but otherwise in a heavy-based pan (in which case you may need a little more oil for the second frying, but keep it to the minimum). Add the mustard seeds and stir fry until they start popping, about a minute. Remove the seeds and drain. Wipe the pan, add another tablespoon of oil, heat, then stir in the garlic and chopped spring onion and sauté for 4-5 minutes, stirring constantly. Remove from the pan and keep aside.

Wipe the pan clean again, then add the remaining oil. When just beginning to smoke, add the chicken and stir constantly for 2-3 minutes until opaque and firming up. Sprinkle over the ginger and cinnamon, add the reserved mustard seeds and the onion mixture and pour on the stock. Grate in a little satsuma zest, then peel the satsumas, divide one into segments, add to the pan, then blend the other and strain the juice into a small jug.

While the cooking juices are coming to the boil, mix 2 tablespoons of the satsuma juice with the mustard to form a thin paste, then pour the remaining juice into the pan. Simmer for 3-4 minutes longer, then mix the arrowroot with a little water and stir into the chicken. Stir for another minute or so until the sauce is very lightly thickened. Season lightly with salt then pile on to a shallow dish. Sprinkle over the chopped watercress and eat at once, dipping every third mouthful or so into the hot mustard. Serves 2

GRILLED POUSSIN WITH TARRAGON MUSTARD SHALLOT SAUCE

Outstanding among many memorable lunches in Lyons was a simple yet spectacularly delicious young plump chicken smothered in a mustardy onion purée, crisped in breadcrumbs and served with a piquant reduction of shallots and vinegar. Adapted, and simplified, the recipe is perfect for poussin.

1 poussin, about 450 g/1 lb in weight
50 g/2 oz unsalted butter
1 tablespoon Dijon mustard
1 tablespoon finely chopped fresh tarragon

Maldon salt
freshly ground black pepper
8 shallots, finely chopped
3 tablespoons Spicy Italian vinegar (p.60)
1 bunch watercress

Ask the butcher to split the poussin down the back, or do it yourself with a heavy sharp cleaver, then flatten each half with a good blow with the side of the cleaver.

Melt the butter, stir in the mustard and tarragon then brush each half-poussin (skin side) liberally with the mixture. Season, lightly with salt, generously with pepper, and cook under a medium grill for about 10-12 minutes until they begin to turn colour. Turn the poussin over, brush with more butter and cook for 5 minutes, then turn again, baste, and cook under a fierce heat for 4-5 minutes until the skin is really crisp, the poussin cooked through. Keep warm in a low oven, covered in foil.

Scrape up the cooking juices from the grill pan, add to the melted butter remaining in the saucepan, then stir in the shallots and sweat for 5 minutes. Pour in the vinegar and cook, over a high heat, uncovered, until the vinegar has reduced to a bare tablespoon and the shallots are mushy – the sauce should taste lightly sharp but not biting. Serve at once with each poussin half laid on a bed of chopped watercress. Serves 2

GARLIC MUSTARD CHICKEN IN A BRICK

The best way to roast a chicken is in that old Roman invention, the chicken brick. Also in this day of low-fat diets, it is the obvious answer – the method needs no fat for basting, yet gives a crispy skinned, succulent joint. Not only chickens can go into the brick – lamb, pork, pheasants, partridge all emerge perfectly cooked (though the dry game birds do need added butter). This dish evolved with the arrival of the new season's garlic. We had no lamb, the chicken was already in its brick. So, shortly afterwards, was the garlic.

1 fresh chicken, about 1.6 kg/3½ lb dressed weight
4-5 heads of garlic
Maldon salt
freshly ground black pepper
2 tablespoons Dijon mustard
3 tablespoons medium dry white wine

Rinse the chicken and pat dry inside and out, then place in the brick. Peel the garlic – try and buy heads of a good size; ideally each clove should be the size of a hazelnut. Not only will the taste be better – the peeling won't drive you insane. Bring a pan of water to the boil, throw in the garlic and blanch for 1 minute. Drain and add to the chicken brick – tuck some cloves down the sides, scatter the rest all over.

Sprinkle the chicken lightly with salt, generously with freshly ground black pepper, then mix the mustard with the wine and pour over.

Cover the brick, and cook in the oven at 200°C/400°F/Gas Mark 6 for about 1½ hours until the chicken is beautifully golden and the aroma of the garlic tantalizing. Transfer the bird to a warmed serving platter, cover and keep warm.

Strain the cooking juices into a tall jug and put the garlic in a blender. After a minute or so, all the fat will have risen to the top of the jug and can be easily spooned off. Add a couple of tablespoons of the juices to the garlic and blend to a thick purée. Thin with a little more gravy if wished but this sauce should be thick – akin to bread sauce. Reheat if necessary then pile into a small bowl. Bring the gravy to the boil, add a little hot water (not too much; the taste should be concentrated) and a sprinkling of pepper, then pour into a gravy boat and serve at once with the chicken, garlic sauce, roast potatoes and a good green salad. Any other vegetable is superfluous. Serves 5–6

SMOKED CHICKEN WITH MUSTARD VINEGAR AND DILL DRESSING

Home-smoked chicken is excellent. If you haven't a home-smoker, do, please indulge. The expense is not vast: the results are incomparable. Poultry, lamb, fish and cheese are given a new look – and taste. This dish, the chicken mixed with frizzy endive, a few nasturtium leaves and flowers, fresh herbs and the blue bonnets of borage, is one of the finest summer suppers.

2 small chickens, split into quarters

1 large head frizzy endive, washed and shredded by hand

a handful small nasturtium leaves, finely chopped

6-8 nasturtium flowers, taken off the stalks, finely chopped

2-3 sprigs lovage, coarsely chopped

2-3 sprigs lemon balm, finely chopped

2 sprigs summer savory, finely chopped

2-3 sprigs golden marjoram, finely chopped

2 dozen borage flowers, pulled off the calyx

For the dressing

1 hard-boiled egg yolk

1 egg yolk

1 teaspoon Dijon mustard

2 tablespoons Spicy Italian vinegar (p.60)

about150 ml/¼ pint extra virgin olive oil

good handful fresh dill, finely chopped

Always use your smoker outside. Apart from the fire hazard, the smell, delicious wafting on the open air, is less so in the confines of the kitchen. Place the chicken pieces, skin side up, in the smoking compartment (having fuelled the smoker according to the maker's instructions) and smoke for 20-30 minutes. Remove from the smoker and cool slightly, then take all the meat off the bones and chop into bite-sized pieces.

Mix the chicken with the endive and herbs, keeping the flowers aside.

To make the dressing, mash the hard-boiled egg yolk with the raw egg, then beat in the mustard and vinegar. Gradually add the oil, drop by drop at first (as if making mayonnaise), then in a slow trickle, whisking well all the while. Stop when it is very thick and the taste suites you. Beat in the dill and pour over the salad. Toss very thoroughly until everything is gleaming. With so many herbs, extra seasoning is almost superfluous but have salt and pepper mills on the table with good crusty bread and chilled unsalted butter. Serves 6-8

TURKEY BREASTS WITH VINEGAR, MUSTARD AND GARLIC

Turkey can be very dull. But, married to this ancient Burgundian sauce – sweet-sour in flavour and a relic from the Roman occupation – it takes on new dimensions. Traditionally, this was a sauce for chicken, turkeys being unknown in Europe until the sixteenth century. Brought over from Central America by the Spanish conquistadores, they soon became popular on the Continent. For preference, buy a hen, and one that has enjoyed a free life, ranging around the farmyard. Its fullness of flavour is so different from that of mass-produced frozen creatures that even the most ardent turkey-hater has to admit it is good.

1.4 kg/3 lb boned turkey breast
1 tablespoon peanut oil
60 g/2½ oz unsalted butter
6 fat garlic cloves, unpeeled
Maldon salt
freshly ground black pepper
150 ml/¼ pint red wine vinegar

1-1½ tablespoons Dijon mustard
1 generous tablespoon tomato purée
200 ml/7 fl oz dry white
   Burgundy, or other good wine
1 tablespoon brandy
2-3 tablespoons double cream
finely chopped parsley

Cut the turkey breast, slightly on the diagonal, into 6-8 long escalopes. Put between 2 sheets of greaseproof paper or clingfilm and batter *lightly* to flatten.

Heat the oil with 50 g/2 oz butter in a very large frying pan or roasting tin. When just beginning to bubble, add the breasts, and the garlic, and sauté gently for 9-12 minutes, turning the meat once, until cooked through and lightly golden. Transfer the escalopes to a warmed serving dish, cover with foil and keep warm over a steamer.

Drain off nearly all the fat; peel the garlic. Pour the vinegar into the pan, scraping up the sediments, bubble for 30 seconds, then pour in the wine, adding the mustard and tomato purée stirred together. Whisk lightly, add the garlic and simmer for 3-4 minutes until the vinegar fumes have been driven off. Add the brandy, cream, the rest of the butter and a little parsley. Stir vigorously, mashing the garlic lightly, until the sauce has thickened a little, season, then simmer gently for another 2-3 minutes. Pour over the turkey, sprinkle generously with the remaining chopped parsley and serve at once. Serves 6-8

HONEY AND MUSTARD ROAST TURKEY BREASTS

Apicius would undoubtedly have approved of today's penchant for the honey-mustard combination. Pine nuts — another Roman favourite — add a sweet nuttiness, while the lemon zest prevents sweetness from turning into sickliness. The obvious choice of honey is rape-seed, pale and thick with a delicate flavour. Mustard honey, though good, is rare and it crystallizes very easily. It may also have a slightly bitter aroma (which does not however affect the flavour).

2 x 700 g/1½ lb turkey breasts, boned but not skinned

50 g/2 oz unsalted butter, plus extra for greasing

3 tablespoons coarse-grained mustard

2 tablespoons rape-seed or clover honey

grated zest of ½ lemon

25 g/1 oz pine nuts

Maldon salt

freshly ground black pepper

Put the turkey breasts, flesh side down, on a lightly greased foil-lined roasting tin. Melt the butter, mustard and honey until runny then paint the skins of the breasts liberally with the mixture. Sprinkle over the lemon zest, pine nuts, a little salt and lots of black pepper, then cover the tin with foil and cook in the oven at 180°C/350°F/Gas Mark 5 for 1¼-1½ hours, basting frequently, until nicely golden and the flesh is cooked through.

Serve at once with the juices poured over. Accompaniments should be simple and beautifully fresh. Serves 6-8

DEVILLED TURKEY DRUMSTICKS

Devilling, so beloved of the Victorians, is a method particularly suited to turkey: the meat is gutsy enough to withstand the treatment, and even the most frozen of creatures is vastly improved by the spiciness. For a spectacular picnic centrepiece, paint a whole capon, trebling the quantities of glaze.

6 medium-sized turkey drumsticks

2 crushed garlic cloves

6 tablespoons Dijon mustard

3 tablespoons olive oil

3 teaspoons cayenne pepper

7.5 cm/3 inches fresh root ginger, peeled and grated

1 teaspoon soft brown sugar

few dashes Worcestershire sauce

Maldon salt

freshly ground white pepper

Score the drumsticks deeply in several places, then mix the garlic with the mustard, oil, cayenne, grated ginger, sugar and Worcestershire sauce. Season lightly with salt and pepper then paint each drumstick, liberally and evenly, with the paste. Chill for at least 12 hours, bringing to room temperature before cooking.

Heat the grill to very hot, then turn it low and cook the drumsticks for about 1¼ hours, turning frequently and basting with any juices which have poured off them, until they are very dark and the meat is cooked through.

Turn the grill to high and cook for 3-4 minutes, turning them, just to warm through thoroughly and crisp up the skin. Either serve at once with sautéed potatoes or leave to cool, when they are almost more delicious. Serves 6

Maille received a royal appointment to Queen Victoria
in 1866 and to King Edward VII in 1903

STUFFED TURKEY LEGS

Perhaps the best of the turkey variations, certainly the most elegant – and turkey shows its advantage here over chicken in that the legs are large enough to make boning them simple.

3 large turkey drumsticks
6 slices streaky bacon
4 tablespoons mustard oil
For the stuffing
125 g/4 oz Parma ham, finely chopped
50 g/2 oz fresh breadcrumbs
25 g/1 oz freshly grated Parmesan

2 tablespoons Moutarde Soyer (p.51)
2 mace blades, crumbled
5 tablespoons finely chopped parsley
2 eggs, beaten
Maldon salt
freshly ground black pepper

If you don't have an obliging butcher, chop off the small knobbly end of each drumstick with a sharp cleaver, then – using a very sharp knife, with great care – make a slit through the skin and flesh down one side of each drumstick right through to the bone. Slip the knife between the flesh and bone all the way round, then pull out the bones. Lay each piece of turkey (rectangular shaped, slightly tapered at one end), skin side down, on a clean work surface.

Mix the stuffing ingredients, except the seasoning, in a bowl, then spread a little down the centre of each piece of meat, leaving a small gap at each end. Season lightly with salt, generously with pepper, then fold the pieces into sausage shapes. Flatten the bacon with the back of a knife, then wrap around each sausage, sealing the join and covering the ends – unless you buy home-butchered cured bacon, you'll need two slices per parcel. Tie round with string to secure the sausages then plump them lightly by squeezing between the palms of the hands.

Heat the oil in a flameproof casserole until nearly smoking, then sear the sausages on all sides, turning them gently. Transfer to the oven, at 180°C/350°F/Gas Mark 4, and cook for about 40-50 minutes until cooked through. Pierce gently with a sharp knife through to the turkey flesh – the juices should run clear. Remove from the oven and cool slightly for about 5 minutes, then cut away the string, carefully remove the bacon and slice thickly. Also delicious cold. Serves 4-6

TO A MEMBER OF THE
MUSTARD CLUB

COLMAN'S

Game

**Cold stomachs must be quickened;
therefore I commend the use of mustard
with Duck, Widgin, Teal, and all water Fowl;
sugar and mustard with red Deer, Crane,
Shovelar and Bustard.**

THOMAS MUFFETT, 1655

When that gem emerged from the piles of research, it threw our plans for game awry. Game is probably man's oldest form of meat and, since prehistoric man was aware of mustard seed, the combination of game and mustard is likely to be an old one. But more recent tradition has little mustard with game – *lapin moutarde* perhaps being the obvious exception. Rabbit with mustard, in many guises, is indeed good and we played with a few other game recipes, with pleasing results. But it was not a partnership that we intended to feature heavily, until we read Dr Muffett's *Health Improvements*.

He instructs that: 'temperate meats speedy of digestion', 'Mutton, Lamb, Veal, Kid, Hen, Capon, Pullet, Chicken, Rabbet, Partridge, and Pheasant', should all have 'mustard and greenswace' without which they 'would soon corrupt in our stomachs'. Apicius had already shown the way, for he has sauces, with mustard, for nearly all those species of game singled out by Dr Muffett. With the Roman influence so heavy in our kitchens even in the Middle Ages, was it likely that a whole area of cooking would really just have vanished? The answer, of course, was that it didn't.

We knew from the Harleian manuscript that roasted crane had a sauce of the liver minced 'with pouder of ginger, vinegar and mustard'. Then for pheasant, 'his sauce is to be sugar and mustard', also for partridge and coney. Venison, too, was rubbed with powder of ginger, or mustard, to stave off 'highness' in hot weather, prior to soaking in brine or milk (a good tip if venison appears to be too high for your liking). For the Elizabethans mustard and vinegar sauce was a prerequisite with stubble goose (one fattened for the last few weeks of its life on the stubble, and eaten at Michaelmas). Though long domesticated, goose was formerly considered game. Hannah Glasse has A Hare Civet, with 'mustard and a little

Elder Vinegar'. And so it went on. Mustard, vinegar and sugar were the predominant features, giving a sharp, sweet/sour flavour redolent of the Roman sauces. Often added to these were fruits: pears, grapes, nuts and quince jam in the case of goose. The stuffing was roasted with the bird then removed and made into the sauce (a Sauce Madame). A 'gauncil' or thick flour-based garlic sauce was also often served with goose, a relic of centuries past, though by 1615 the garlic seems to have been dropped. The sweet-sour balance was still prevalent however.

Venison was the game most highly prized by all, from kings to peasant poacher, and was served at all the great feasts. The best cuts appeared on the banqueting table, the 'umbels' (innards) going into pies for the servants' hall. But mustard is not mentioned in the many references to venison sauces – perhaps because the venison had been rubbed with mustard before cooking, perhaps because mustard sauce (considered the 'best' sauce for everything) was anyway on the table. One must remember that the term 'mustard sauce' indicated 'a sharp biting sauce made of small seed, bruised and mixed with vinegar': much as we know the condiment today. Since Dr Muffett particularly included red deer to be accompanied by sugar and mustard, it seems unlikely that the combination was rare. Certainly, we had found that game and mustard were more than passing acquaintances.

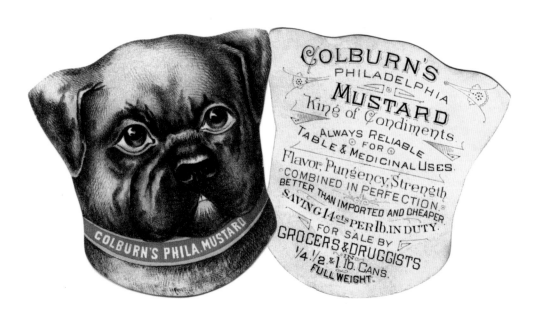

LAPIN MOUTARDE

As this is one of the classics of the French kitchen, every family has its own special recipe, but the basic components are always the same: a young rabbit, plenty of mustard (Dijon of course), cream and fresh herbs. It is simple, and quite excellent. Interestingly, the Romans (once again) knew the problems of rabbit breeding. The animals were firmly kept in *leporaria* or hare gardens, and when the Romans conquered England, they brought their rabbits with them. So well were they confined that the rabbit disappeared from the British diet along with the colonizers, and only reappeared at the end of the twelfth century, from France. Over the next 300 years large colonies of wild rabbits were established. These are gamier in flavour, though they do need to be young. Stick to the old definition of rabbit, a coney less than a year, and you will have excellent eating.

1 young rabbit or 4 rabbit hind legs
2 tablespoons unsalted butter
1 tablespoon olive oil
Maldon salt
freshly ground black pepper
4-6 tablespoons Dijon mustard
6 shallots, finely chopped

225 g/8 oz button mushrooms, finely sliced
4 tablespoons Armagnac or good brandy
300 ml/½ pint double cream
good posy parsley, very finely chopped, or a mixture of fresh chervil and chives

If using a whole rabbit, cut into joints, the two back legs, saddle split in half, and the two front legs. Melt the butter with the oil in a pan large enough, if possible, to take the rabbit pieces in one layer. Add the joints and brown lightly, then remove from the pan. Sprinkle with salt, and a good grinding of black pepper, then smear them all over with the mustard.

Add the shallots to the pan and sauté for 5 minutes, then stir in the mushrooms. Put the rabbit joints on top of the vegetables, pour over the brandy and set alight (warming the brandy first speeds the process). When the flames have died down, stir in the cream and bring to bubbling point. Cover the pan and simmer very gently for 25-30 minutes until the sauce is very thick and the meat tender. Add a little more salt and pepper if necessary then scatter over the parsley. Let it bubble, without stirring, for another 2 minutes, then serve. Serves 4

FRIED RABBIT WITH MUSTARD

Although Eliza Acton wrote in the 1840s, many of her ideas are extraordinarily up-to-date. Consider this, from her recipe for fried rabbit: 'Dish the rabbit, pour the sauce *under* it, and serve it quickly.' The original dish had no mustard, and is very good. The addition is excellent – we hope she would approve.

4 rabbit hind legs
1 large egg, beaten, or 2 egg
   whites, lightly whisked
home-made breadcrumbs, 3 days
   old and finely ground
1 tablespoon mustard powder
Maldon salt
freshly ground white pepper
300 ml/½ pint rabbit or partridge
   stock, or home-made chicken
   stock (not a cube)

2-3 strips lemon zest
75 g/3 oz unsalted butter
1 chicken liver, or rabbit liver if
   possible
1 teaspoon flour
2 tablespoons double cream
   (optional)
lemon juice
1 teaspoon lemon mustard (p.54)

Put the joints into a pan of boiling water, unsalted, and cook for 5 minutes, drain
and cool. Dip them into the beaten egg, then into the breadcrumbs previously
mixed with the mustard powder. Press the crumbs well in, then season lightly
with salt and pepper. Melt 50 g/2 oz of the butter in a large frying pan. When
it is bubbling add the pieces and gently fry for about 15 minutes, turning them
two or three times.

   Meanwhile, simmer the stock with the lemon zest, add the liver for 5 minutes, remove and mash thoroughly. Mix it with the remaining butter and the
flour to a thick paste, then add, little by little, to the stock, whisking constantly,
until the sauce thickens. Stir in the cream if wished, a squeeze of lemon juice
and the mustard. Let it bubble for a minute. When the rabbit is nicely browned
and cooked through, put on a serving dish, 'pour the sauce under it' and serve
at once. Serves 4

ROASTED HARE WITH MUSTARD, ALLSPICE AND SOURED CREAM

Hare, though highly prized by the Romans, was slightly lower on the medieval
scale than coney or rabbits. Both these appeared often on festive menus which
hare rarely did, though it figured prominently on the list of household provisions in the 1450s. By the time Henry VIII had gained the throne both were
common man's hunting – the hare usually with greyhounds and often in the
snows, when its tracks easily led its hunters straight home. Indeed, for a time,
Henry had to ban hare (and rabbit) hunting, so devastated were their numbers.
Today, hare has rightfully regained its prestige.

1 young hare, with liver reserved for the stuffing

4 large bacon rashers

125 g/4 oz butter, melted

1 teaspoon Dijon mustard

150 ml/¼ pint soured cream

freshly ground allspice (not pre-ground)

For the marinade

300 ml/½ pint red wine

3 tablespoons olive oil

1 sprig lemon thyme

Maldon salt

freshly ground black pepper

For the stuffing

1 tablespoon brown mustard seed

175 g/6 oz canned whole chest-nuts, drained and chopped

50 g/2 oz sultanas

50 g/2 oz pine nuts

5 tablespoons home-made fresh breadcrumbs

1 tablespoon white wine vinegar

2 tablespoons white wine

1 large egg, beaten

Always make sure you buy a young hare for roasting – easily distinguishable by its short neck, long joints and thin saddle. Its ears are soft and will easily tear while its older cousin will have a clearly marked cleft in the lip. The darker the meat, the longer has been the hanging – ideally 4-5 days. All hare has a bluish, thin membrane which must be removed. Fiddly rather than difficult, this is most easily accomplished by sliding a long, thin-bladed knife underneath the membrane (which is transparent), loosening it then peeling it away. Now you can put your hare in a large dish and cover with the marinade ingredients. Leave for at least 24 hours and up to 3 days – not only to tenderize but also to give flavour.

Combine all the stuffing ingredients, not forgetting to cut out any yellowish bits from the liver before chopping it finely, then season generously with black pepper and allspice. Remove the hare from the marinade (reserving the liquid), and pat dry. Place the stuffing under the front and back legs. Lay in a roasting tin then mix the mustard into the soured cream and grind in a little more allspice. Smear half the paste over the hare then cover with the bacon. Pour over the melted butter and cook in the oven, covered with foil, at 180°C/350°F/Gas mark 4 for 1½ hours, basting every 20 minutes or so. Remove the foil, dust the hare with the flour (an ancient technique called 'frothing' which facilitates the browning of the joint) and return to the oven, uncovered, for 15 minutes. Transfer the hare to a warmed serving platter, carve into joints and keep warm while finishing the sauce.

Pour the cooking juices into a pan, add the marinade and bring to the boil. Whisk in the soured cream, boil hard for a minute, adjust the seasoning if necessary, then serve at once with a little sauce poured over the joints, the rest poured into a hot sauceboat. Serves 4

CIVET OF HARE IN VINEGAR AND MUSTARD

'Harys in Cyvye' was a common medieval recipe and made its appearance again in sixteenth-century England from France where it always remained popular. It is ideal for the older hare as the long gentle stewing ensures tenderness. The ancient marinade of wine and vinegar also helps break down tough sinews – and adds a piquant flavour.

1 hare, jointed, bluish membranes removed (see previous recipe)
450 ml/¾ pint white wine (medium-dry)
150 ml/¼ pint white wine vinegar
6 cloves
2 bay leaves
2 sprigs parsley
2 sprigs thyme
2 tablespoons olive oil
4 shallots, finely chopped

1 tablespoon flour
Maldon salt
freshly ground black pepper
10 cm/4 inch strip of orange peel
225 g/8 oz tiny button mushrooms, wiped with a damp cloth and left whole
1-2 teaspoons Matthew's mustard (p.55)
25 g/1 oz unsalted butter

Put the wine, vinegar, herbs and spices into a large pan, add about 200 ml/7 fl oz water and bring to the boil. Simmer for 5 minutes, then cool and pour over the hare. Leave for 24 hours, turning the joints three or four times.

Drain the hare, patting it quite dry, and strain the marinade. Heat the oil in a large heavy-based pan, add the shallots and sweat for 5 minutes, then add the hare and brown the joints lightly. Sprinkle on the flour, stir for a minute or so, then season, lightly with salt, generously with pepper, add the orange peel and pour in the strained marinade. Bring to the boil then turn the heat to the lowest possible, cover the pan and simmer very gently for 3 hours until the flesh is meltingly tender. Add the mushrooms and cook, uncovered, for a further 15 minutes. Remove the hare and pile on to a warmed serving dish. Reduce the sauce by rapid boiling for 2 minutes, then add the mustard, adjust the seasoning if necessary and whisk in the butter to lightly glaze. Pour over the hare and serve with good crusty bread to mop up the juices. Serves 4

BRAISED WILD DUCK WITH MUSTARD AND CORIANDER

Wild duck, a rarity today, was well known to prehistoric man, providing a large part of his winter diet since it is conveniently at its best after the first frost until Candlemas (2 February). For today's tastes the bird, particularly when from the marshes, can often have an unpleasantly fishy flavour – reflecting its eating habits. Apicius had an admirable way of dealing with this by parboiling the birds in salt water, flavoured with dill. As with so many ancient ideas, this is still the best method.

2 wild ducks, hung for 10-14 days, then drawn and dressed
6 sprigs fresh dill or 2 teaspoons dried dill
75 g/3 oz unsalted butter
2 small onions, peeled but left whole
1 lemon, cut in half
1 orange, cut in half
2 x 5 cm/2 in cinnamon sticks
Maldon salt
freshly ground black pepper
2 large onions, finely sliced
2 sprigs fresh fennel or 2 dried fennel sticks

2 sprigs thyme
2 sprigs fresh savory or 1 teaspoon dried savory
1 tablespoon white mustard seed
1 tablespoon coriander seeds, lightly crushed
1 tablespoon flour
2 tablespoons Dijon mustard
4 tablespoons brandy
4 tablespoons orange juice
400 ml/14 fl oz game or good beef stock

Bring a large saucepan of salted water to the boil, then throw in the dill. Turn the heat low so the water barely simmers, then add the ducks. Leave for 5 minutes, remove, drain and dry thoroughly inside and out.

Melt the butter, when bubbling add the ducks and sear all over. Remove from the pan and stuff them each with 1 onion, half a lemon, half an orange and a cinnamon stick. Season with salt and pepper.

Add the sliced onions to the pan and sauté gently for 15 minutes, then add the fennel, thyme, savory, mustard and coriander seeds and cook, stirring until the mustard seeds start to spit. Stir in the flour and continue stirring for 3-4 minutes, then add the mustard, brandy and orange juice. Return the ducks to the pan, pour over the stock and bring quickly to the boil. Lower the heat and simmer very gently for 2-2½ hours, covered. Test for tenderness by pressing a skewer into the breast – it should slide in easily.

Remove the birds from the pan, carve to give each person half the breast and a leg (keep the carcass for stock) and keep warm. Reduce the sauce slightly, then glaze each portion with a tablespoon, serving the remainder separately. Serves 4

MUSTARDED ROAST QUAIL

Quails have been highly regarded for a very long time. They are mentioned in the Bible, when they appeared literally out of the sky and saved the fleeing Israelites along with the manna provided by the Lord. The sudden appearance of the quails is not so fanciful as it might seem for they fly until quite fatigued, often letting the wind carry them along, until they drop exhausted to the ground in flocks. The Romans condemned the birds as food as they are partial to eating hemlock and other poisonous seeds, though strangely this does not seem to affect the eater of the quail. But by medieval times they were highly popular and widely sold in the City of London. Today, they are a protected species, and our supplies are all farm-reared: less gamey than the wild creatures but still an exquisite delicacy.

12 quails	freshly ground black pepper
6 teaspoons Five-herb mustard (p.48)	6 rashers streaky bacon, beaten very thin
125 g/4 oz unsalted butter	125 ml/4 fl oz port
Maldon salt	

Quails used to be cooked undrawn in the manner of snipe and woodcock. Today, however, they are always sold drawn, and they are never hung. Spread each bird lightly with mustard and put in a roasting tin. Melt the butter and pour over the quails, season, then cover with the bacon. Cook in the oven at 200°C/400°F/Gas Mark 6 for 7-10 minutes, basting once or twice. Remove from the oven, turn the heat to 150°C/300°F/Gas mark 2 and pour off the cooking juices into a small pan. Return the birds to the oven for 2-3 minutes, meanwhile adding the port to the butter in the pan and bubbling hard. Serve the quails surrounded by triangles of fried bread, with the sauce poured over the birds. Serves 4-6

PIGEONS IN VERMOUTH, SAFFRON AND MUSTARD

Pigeons provided our ancestors with a great deal of their game; medieval manor houses had their dovecots and by Tudor times many a cottage had a small wooden pigeon house tucked on to the ends of the gables. In 1520 they cost one penny each; now they are nearer a pound. Which is amazing since most farmers are as keen as their medieval forebears to be rid of them: pigeons are not fussy as to how they fatten themselves, so long as it is on the best corn . . .

4 pigeons

2 tablespoons olive oil

2 red onions, finely chopped

300 ml/½ pint double cream

2 bay leaves

4-5 strands saffron

Maldon salt

freshly ground black pepper

4 tablespoons vermouth

300 ml/½ pint red wine

1 tablespoon Matthew's mustard
  (p.55)

Wash the pigeons inside and out. Reserve the livers if present, cutting out any yellowish bits to avoid bitterness. Heat the olive oil and sauté the onions for 15 minutes; meanwhile, very gently heat the cream in another pan with the bay leaves and saffron. Stir after 2-3 minutes to start the colour of the saffron running.

Push the onions to the side of the pan, raise the heat and lightly colour the pigeons all over, season with salt and pepper, then add the vermouth and bubble hard for 1 minute. Pour in the red wine and stew gently for 20-40 minutes, turning the birds occasionally, until they are tender. (Squabs – pigeons a month old – will need the shorter time, older birds the longer.) Remove the pigeons from the pan and carve off the breasts. Keep the carcasses for soup. Reduce the wine by boiling hard for 2-3 minutes, then strain in the cream. Return the breasts to the pan with the chopped livers and simmer gently for a further 5-10 minutes until the sauce thickens. Stir in the mustard and serve immediately with little croûtons and piles of fresh watercress. Serves 4

The original prototype Dunhill lighter in 1923 was a Colman's mustard tin

PHEASANT WITH CREMONA MUSTARD

In 1932, there appeared in Italy a rather odd cookbook – *La Cucina Futurista*, written by the famous Futurist poet (and friend of Mussolini), F. Marinetti. Obsessed with the Fascist principles of purity, virility and nationalism, the poet had earlier launched an attack on pasta – a food for the slow and docile, anti-virile and made with expensive foreign flour. There was uproar. Marinetti, undaunted, proceeded to invent the most extraordinary combinations: small blood sausages and pieces of chocolate 'swimming' in a custard sauce; fish with pineapple and bananas; roast beef surrounded by halva; fruit tart on a thin layer of chocolate, covered with tomato and spinach sauces. Some dishes, however, display historical knowledge – lamb served with stuffed dates (familiar to the Arabs) and this pheasant recipe: 'Roast a carefully cleaned pheasant, bathe it for an hour in Moscato di Siracusa [a sweet, heavy Sicilian wine] in a *bain-marie*, and for another hour in milk. To finish, stuff it with Mostarda di Cremona and candied fruit.' Overdoing it certainly, but medieval game birds had often been stuffed with grapes, pears, quinces and nuts, accompanied by a mustard and sugar sauce. And, as Elizabeth David points out, 'pheasant is very often dry, so the baths in sweet wine and milk are not such foolish ideas'.

1 brace of pheasant, giblets reserved
125 g/4 oz unsalted butter, plus a little extra, softened
5 tablespoons Mostarda di Cremona (p.55) plus 1 tablespoon extra of the syrup
Maldon salt
freshly ground black pepper

4 rashers back bacon, flattened thin
150 ml/¼ pint Muscat de Frontignan (or any good, sweetish white wine)
1 tablespoon flour
2 shallots, finely chopped
2-3 strips lemon peel
1 sprig lemon thyme
lemon juice

Pheasants are usually hung for 5-14 days so talk to your butcher when ordering them. If you buy from a supermarket, there is no choice but they are usually fairly mild. Discard any yellowish pieces from the livers, then chop them and add to the Mostarda, its fruits also chopped quite small. Mix thoroughly into the butter, pat into a sausage shape and chill until firm. Smear some plain butter underneath the skins of the pheasant breasts, then paint with a spoonful of the mustard syrup. When the stuffing mixture is quite firm, cut it in two and put one piece inside each pheasant. Season lightly with salt and pepper, then lard with the bacon.

Place the pheasants in a roasting tin, and pour over the wine. Cook in the oven at 220°C/425°F/Gas Mark 7 for 45-60 minutes – this will depend on the weight of the birds. The usual time allowed is 20 minutes to the pound plus 10 minutes extra. Baste every 10 minutes or so, then 10 minutes before the end, remove the bacon (crumble and reserve it), froth the birds with flour and return to brown the breasts. While the pheasants are cooking, make a stock with the giblets, shallots, lemon peel and thyme. Cover with cold water, bring to the boil then simmer gently. Strain and keep aside.

Once the birds are cooked, transfer them to a serving platter, carve and keep warm in the oven, covered with foil. Pour the cooking juices into the strained giblet stock and bring to the boil, add the crumbled bacon, season to taste and squeeze in a little lemon juice to offset the sweetness. Serve in a very hot sauce-boat. Serves 6-8

SALMIS OF PARTRIDGE WITH ORANGE MUSTARD SAUCE

A ginger sauce was often recommended for partridge by the medieval cook – a good idea, as its flavour can be bland compared to other game birds. It shares their tendency to dryness though, so this popular Victorian method of cooking game is ideal. The birds are part-roasted, then stewed in a highly flavoured sauce.

2 brace of partridge	juice of 1 Seville orange
50 g/2 oz unsalted butter	150 ml/¼ pint port wine
4 rashers bacon, flattened thin	1 teaspoon strong Dijon mustard
2 shallots, very finely chopped	Maldon salt
2 teaspoons white wine vinegar	freshly ground black pepper
25 mm/1 inch piece fresh root ginger, peeled and grated	1 teaspoon arrowroot

Smear the partridges liberally with butter, wrap in bacon and roast in the oven at 200°F/400°F/Gas Mark 6 for 20 minutes. Take out of the oven, remove the bacon and cut off the breasts and legs, taking off the skin. Pour the cooking juices into a small pan. Put the skin and carcasses into a pan, just cover with cold water and bring to the boil, then simmer fairly vigorously for 30 minutes, or until reduced to a good 300 ml/½ pint. Strain and reserve.

Melt the butter you poured off the roasting pan, add the shallots and stew gently for 5 minutes. If you have more than about 2 tablespoons butter, pour off the excess then deglaze the pan with the vinegar. Add the ginger, orange juice, port wine and reserved carcass stock and simmer for 10 minutes. Arrange the partridge meat in a shallow flameproof dish. Stir the mustard into the sauce, season lightly with salt and pepper, then mix the arrowroot with a little cold water and stir into the sauce, boiling for a minute to thicken. (This is not the traditional method but it gives a beautifully clear glaze.) Pour the sauce over the meat, then stew gently for a further 10 minutes or so to finish cooking the partridge. Serve from the cooking dish. Serves 4

ROAST HAUNCH OF VENISON WITH VINEGAR AND MUSTARD

Venison was the prerogative of the land-owning classes, though even they were restricted by an Act of 1671 which forbade the killing of deer by all except 'qualified persons'. Despite the harsh penalties for poaching, ways were found and venison often appeared on the menus of London coffee houses and City inns. Today we are luckier. Venison is widely farmed and though much goes to the Continent, it is increasingly available from butchers and even supermarkets. It is a lean, rich, sweet meat, ideally suited to the piquant sauces of ancient times. In the Tyrol they still finish venison with a sauce of soured cream and powdered mustard.

1.6-2 kg/3½-4½ lb haunch of
   venison
125-175 g/4-6 oz butter
2 tablespoons rowanberry or redcurrant jelly
1 tablespoon cider vinegar
2-3 teaspoons Dijon mustard
2-3 pinches ground cinnamon
1 tablespoon *beurre manié*

For the marinade
600 ml/1 pint red wine
2 tablespoons olive oil
2 tablespoons Spicy Italian vinegar
   (p.60)
2 shallots, finely sliced
2 bay leaves
1 cinnamon stick
3 sprigs thyme
Maldon salt
freshly ground black pepper

In a large dish combine the marinade ingredients, using a pinch of salt and a generous amount of black pepper. Immerse the venison, turn it several times, then leave for 1-2 days, turning regularly. Remove the meat and pat well dry. Strain and reserve the marinade.

Melt 125 g/4 oz of the butter in a roasting tin, add the venison and baste well. Cook in the oven at 180°C/350°F/Gas Mark 4 for 1-1½ hours, basting every 10 minutes. Use the extra butter if necessary — it may seem a lot but venison is a dry meat and it will absorb quite a bit. The timing depends on the size of the haunch and how pink you like the meat — test with a pointed knife gently inserted into the thickest part. The colour of the juices will indicate the doneness.

When it is cooked, transfer to a warm serving dish, cover lightly with foil and keep warm. Pour the cooking juices from the roasting tin, scraping up any sediment, into a pan. Add the strained marinade and the fruit jelly. Boil hard to reduce and melt the jelly. Add the vinegar, mustard and cinnamon and bubble for 1-2 minutes, then stir in the *beurre manié* (a mixture of equal volumes of butter and flour), whisking constantly until the sauce thickens. Serve the gravy very hot with the joint, carved thick or thin as you wish. Serves 6-8

ROAST GOOSE WITH GARLIC AND MUSTARD SAUCE

Goose is such an extravagance nowadays that to do anything beyond roasting it seems wanton. The French however still follow the medieval habit of buying their geese whole and using the neck, stuffed, to make a 'pudding'. This is delicious, and does prolong the delights of a bird which sadly does not stretch very far: a 4-4.5 kg/9-10 lb goose will really only feed six people. Keep the fat – it is delicious for frying potatoes.

1 goose, about 4.5 kg/10 lb dressed weight, with giblets if possible

Maldon salt

freshly ground black pepper

175 g/6 oz prunes, soaked in cold water overnight

3 heads of garlic, cloves peeled but left whole

150 ml/¼ pint red wine

1-2 teaspoons soft brown sugar

1 tablespoon Spicy Italian vinegar (p.60)

1-2 teaspoons coarse-grained mustard

stuffing of your choice (see below)

Remove any pin feathers from the goose, singe the wing tips, and cut away any fat near the vent. Wash inside and out, dry thoroughly then season well with salt and pepper. Lay the goose on a rack in a large roasting tin, prick the fatty bits with a fork then prick the breast skin lightly – try not to pierce the flesh. Put in the oven at 200°C/400°F/Gas Mark 6 and cook for 15 minutes, then carefully drain off any fat in the pan. Repeat this process 2-3 times to remove the excess fat which would make the prunes and garlic (to be put in later) unbearably greasy.

While this preliminary cooking is taking place, make a stock from the giblets if you have them, reserving the liver to add to your stuffing. This can be whatever you like; traditionalists go for sage and onion or you can adapt the earlier stuffings of mixed fruits, or gooseberries. Chestnuts, too, are good with goose while many like to add sausagemeat, enabling the goose to go further. Whichever you choose, make it at this point, place in a shallow buttered tin and bake for the last 45 minutes of cooking time.

After the third draining of fat, mix the drained prunes (keep the soaking water) with the garlic and stuff inside the goose. Lower the oven to 170°C/325°F/Gas Mark 3 and cook for a further 2-2½ hours, draining off the fat from the tin if it seems to be getting dangerously full. Prick the skin occasionally and turn the bird on to its breast half-way through, turning it on its back again for the last 10 minutes of cooking. The thigh joints should wiggle easily when the bird is done.

Transfer to a warmed platter, scrape out the prunes and garlic, put in a blender, and return the goose to the turned-off oven to keep warm. Add 300 ml/½ pint of giblet stock or prune soaking water to the blender and purée the mixture. Pour into a pan, add the red wine, sugar, vinegar and 1 teaspoon mustard. Bring to the boil, then simmer gently for 5 minutes – add a little more stock or prune water if the sauce is too stiff, but it should be fairly thick. Add extra mustard if you wish and adjust the seasoning, then pile into a bowl and serve very hot, with the goose, your stuffing and roast potatoes. Serves 6.

DUCK BREASTS WITH ROMAN MUSTARD

Many of Apicius's sauces for game sound an incredible hotch-potch – 'mix pepper, lovage, onion, origany, nuts, figdates, honey, broth, mustard, vinegar, oil' – until one realizes that this is basically a vinaigrette. We omitted the dates and the broth, toasted some pine nuts and made a delicious sauce to pour over grilled duck breasts.

3 large French duck breasts
50 g/2 oz pine nuts
For the sauce
handful lovage leaves, chopped
  very finely
1 small red onion, grated
freshly ground black pepper
Maldon salt

½ teaspoon finely chopped fresh
  marjoram
1-2 tablespoons Roman mustard
  (p.65)
1-2 tablespoons runny honey
50 ml/2 fl oz Spicy Italian vinegar
  (p.60)
300 ml/½ pint olive oil

Prick the duck breasts all over with a fork and put under the grill, skin side up. Cook for 7-8 minutes on a high heat then turn over and cook for a further 1-2 minutes: this will give nicely pink breasts. Well done meat will need another 3 minutes at the first grilling.

Sprinkle the pine nuts in a shallow metal dish and grill for 45 seconds-1 minute until nicely pink. Keep aside.

For the sauce, mix together the chopped lovage, grated onion, a good grinding of black pepper, a pinch of salt, the marjoram, the mustard and honey. Stir in the vinegar to make a thick paste, then gradually add the oil little by little, whisking all the time to produce a thick sauce. Taste and add more mustard, oil or vinegar as needed.

Now you need to work quickly, to keep the meat hot. Cut the breasts in half lengthways, then slice across thickly, slightly on the diagonal. Arrange on hot plates, pour over the sauce and scatter with the nuts. Serve immediately: it is very good with a warm potato salad. Serves 6

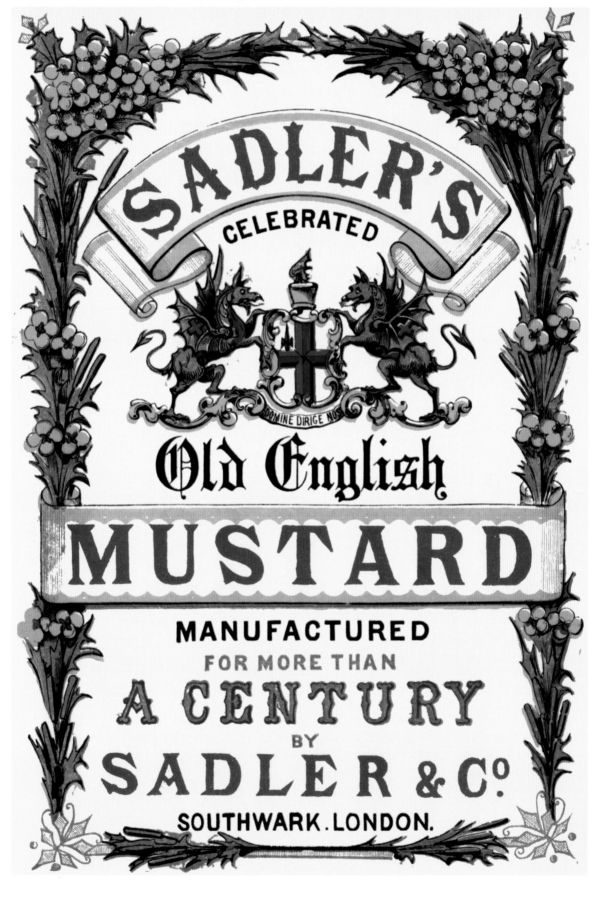

Beef

Grumio: What say you to a piece of beef and mustard?
Kate: A dish that I do love to feed upon.

THE TAMING OF THE SHREW, WILLIAM SHAKESPEARE

Although we found manufacturers strangely reticent on exact sales figures, we have established that household consumption is about 350 g/12 oz annually. A little goes along way it seems. There must be a great many homes with a pot of mustard in the store-cupboard, and we'll warrant that in most of them it only appears on the table with beef. Yet this British marriage of beef to mustard is relatively recent. Though Tudor writings often mention beef and mustard, they still continued the medieval practice of serving mustard also with brawn, salt mutton, game and fish. So why do we single out beef?

Since neolithic times it appears to have been our favourite meat. Cattle bones found in early settlements far outweigh those from any other creature and we were already exporting the beasts to the Continent before Caesar arrived. His soldiers too preferred beef, their garrisons yielding vast quantities of bones.

For much of the year beef was not eaten fresh. The difficulties and expense of keeping livestock through the winter meant that most was killed in the autumn and salted for preservation during the ensuing months. Salt beef was always served with mustard. Its value as an accompaniment was rated so highly that in the thirteenth-century Welsh manuscript, *Meddygon Myddvai*, a whole paragraph is accorded to the 'Virtues of Mustard'. It was only in the 1600s that the feeding of root crops (particularly turnips) to animals became widespread. This coincided with the introduction from Holland of vetches (clover, lucerne grass) which produced stronger and fleshier cattle, thus enabling the stock to be kept alive for fresh meat all year round. This, combined with the abolition of fast days (by Cromwell), no doubt accounts for the dramatic rise in meat consumption that then took place.

It may also explain why mustard began to be popular with beef other than in its salted state. Certainly Robert May, the great Restoration cook who published his magnificent (and, in many ways, very modern) *The Accomplisht Cook* in 1660, was recommending the combination, particularly deliciously in 'Ribs of beef with garlick, mustard, pepper, verjuice, and ginger'. No longer was mustard merely needed to disguise the rancid flavours of rotten meat; it could be appreciated as a spice in its own right. Over the next century it was more and more served with fresh meat, reaching a peak in the eighteenth century – the heyday of London's steak and chop houses.

Undoubtedly, the mustard served in Samuel Johnson's favourite eating houses would have been English, either Tewkesbury – with its fiery flavouring of horseradish – or possibly the new Durham mustard powder being hawked around by Mrs Clements. And herein is the seed of a long-running battle between the French and the English. For Dijon also reached its heyday in the eighteenth century and no Frenchman would ever consider anything other than Dijon mustard with his steak. The clean pungent taste of English mustard perhaps complements beef better than most meats, and the sharpness of Tewkesbury mustard is very good indeed with steak. What are most emphatically not good are those jars of mustard – sadly English in origin – masquerading as 'French' mustard. They have far too murky a flavour to enhance beef, or anything else for that matter.

MUSTARD COATED ROAST BEEF

'A tale without love is like beef without mustard – insipid.' So said Anatole France. And on the beef front, we absolutely agree since first using this glaze for roast beef. However succulent the joint, it is a little disappointing now without its crispy mustard coating. Good with all cuts, though large joints will need double the quantity.

1.4 kg/3 lb joint of beef, well larded
Maldon salt
freshly ground black pepper
1 tablespoon mustard powder
1 tablespoon beef dripping, lard or oil
2 tablespoons Dijon mustard

1 tablespoon Worcestershire sauce
1 tablespoon red wine vinegar
½ tablespoon soft brown sugar
1 tablespoon olive oil
150 ml/¼ pint red wine
1 tablespoon brandy
1 tablespoon redcurrant jelly

Mix a good pinch of salt with a generous grinding of black pepper and the mustard powder and rub well into the beef. Heat the dripping, then sear the beef on all sides over a high heat.

Transfer the meat on to a rack over a roasting pan. Mix together the Dijon mustard, Worcestershire sauce, vinegar, sugar and olive oil, then paint all over the beef. Cook in the oven at 230°C/450°F/Gas mark 8 for 15 minutes, then turn down to 180°C/350°F/Gas Mark 4 and roast for a further 45 minutes for very rare, 55 minutes for nicely pink, or 1¼ hours for well-done meat. Put the joint on a warmed platter and let it rest in the turned-off oven while finishing the gravy. At this stage, let us listen to the wise words of M. Boulestin: 'Do not spoil the special taste of the gravy obtained in the roasting of beef … by adding to it the classical stock which gives to all meats the same deplorable taste of soup. It is obvious that you cannot out of a joint get the sauceboat full which usually appears on the table.' Put the roasting tin over a medium heat, add the wine and brandy, scraping up all the sediment, then stir in the redcurrant jelly. Let the gravy bubble, constantly stirring until the jelly has melted. Tip into this any juices from the joint platter, then pour into a hot gravy boat. It may not be full, but the taste will be superb. Serve with tall puffs of Yorkshire pudding and that other traditional Yorkshire accompaniment, seen too little nowadays, of finely chopped onions which have been strewn with sugar and left to stand for 1 hour. Mustard on the table, of course. Serves 6

ROBERT MAY'S RIB OF BEEF

Robert May's suggestion of 'garlick, mustard, pepper, verjuice and ginger' for ribs of beef was a dish begging to be eaten. The problem in a small household is how to justify the ribs of beef – for the joint to be successful as a roast you need at least two ribs, preferably three. The answer came with Pierre Troisgros – one of the famous French restaurateur brothers. For the 'king' of Beaune has a favourite dish – one rib of beef, freshly cut off the joint (by himself, naturally) pan-fried and served with a Bordelaise sauce. Here was Robert May's chance – and we took it. A memorable dish.

1 rib of beef, nicely marbled, on the bone

5 cm/2 inch piece fresh ginger, peeled and cut into very fine slivers

2 fat garlic cloves, very finely chopped

freshly ground black pepper, ground as coarse as possible

1 tablespoon Dijon mustard

1 tablespoon olive oil

Maldon salt

25 g/1 oz unsalted butter, plus a little extra

1 tablespoon red wine vinegar

125 ml/4 fl oz good red wine

Trim any excess fat off the rib – you only want a very thin layer. Mix together the ginger, garlic, a generous grinding of black pepper, the mustard and olive oil, then smear on both sides of the beef. Leave for at least 1 hour, preferably 2-3.

Melt the butter in a large frying pan, sprinkle one side of the rib with a little salt and when the butter is bubbling add the beef. Cook over a moderate heat for 2-5 minutes, depending on how rare you like beef. Turn over, sprinkle on a little salt, add some extra butter to the pan if necessary and cook for a further

2-5 minutes. Remove the rib to a warmed serving platter and rest in a very low oven while finishing the sauce.

Pour the vinegar into the pan, scraping up all the sediment, and bubble for a minute to deglaze. Pour in the red wine and cook fiercely for 2 minutes, stirring constantly. Whisk in a tiny knob of butter if you wish to lightly glaze the sauce.

Cut the beef into slices on the diagonal, pour over the sauce and serve at once. Serves 2-3

Donald McGill postcard, 1918

MEDALLIONS OF FILLET WITH DIJON BRANDY SAUCE

The most prized part of the fillet – the 'eye' – is supremely tender, cutting like butter. It is also extremely expensive, so always buy it from a reputable butcher who will cut the pieces for you – at least 3-4 cm/1¼-1½ inches thick. Such good meat requires the simplest of cooking; this is Maille's suggested recipe.

4 medallions of fillet steak (sometimes called *filets mignons*)
Maldon salt
freshly ground black pepper
1½ tablespoons unsalted butter
3 tablespoons brandy

1 small shallot, very finely
  chopped
225 ml/8 fl oz double cream
3 tablespoons Maille Dijon mustard

Season the fillets lightly with salt and pepper. Melt the butter in a large frying pan; when bubbling add the fillets. Cook for 2-4 minutes on each side depending on the rarity wanted then pour in the brandy. Ignite and shake the pan until the flames have died down. Transfer the steaks to a hot serving platter. Stir the onion into the pan and sauté for 1 minute, then add the cream and cook over a high heat until it thickens. Stir in the mustard, bubble for another 10 seconds, then pour over the steaks and serve immediately. Serves 4

GRILLADE DES MARINIERS

Do not be fooled by the title – this is no grill but a gloriously rich stew, the meat butter-soft, the sauce thick with a heady concentration of flavours. It is a heritage from the rivermen of the Rhône – each barge would have its own version bubbling away in the galley as the great boats wound their way down to Marseilles, formerly drawn by a team of giant horses, latterly – and much less romantically – chugging away under petrol power. Do they make it still? Or have convenience foods – as in so many other areas of France – won the day?

900 g/2 lb lean rump or topside,
  cut into 6-8 slices
3 large red onions, finely sliced
4 tablespoons olive oil
Maldon salt
freshly ground black pepper
1 sprig fresh thyme, leaves
  stripped off the stalk

25 g/1 oz unsalted butter
1½ teaspoons flour
2 fat garlic cloves
3 anchovy fillets
1 tablespoon Dijon mustard
1 tablespoon red wine vinegar
4 tablespoons finely chopped parsley

An earthenware casserole is best for this. Brush 1 tablespoon of oil on the bottom, then make a layer of onions. Top with two slices of beef, then another layer of onions, meat, onions, so on: sprinkle each layer with a little salt and pepper, a few leaves of thyme, as you fill the pot. Mash together the flour and butter, cut into little pieces and strew over the top layer (which should be onions), tucking a couple of pieces down the side of the pot too. Cover with a butter paper, then a tight-fitting lid and cook in the oven at 140°C/275°F/Gas Mark 1 for about 2 hours.

Crush the garlic with the anchovy fillets, then mix in the mustard and vinegar. Lastly whisk in the remaining olive oil and the parsley. Stir into the pot, cover again with the butter paper and lid and cook for another 45 minutes–1 hour. The meat should be so tender you can cut it with a spoon – the aroma so tantalizing, you have to eat now. Serves 4-6

CARBONNADE DE BOEUF FLAMANDE

Traditionally the dark Bordeaux mustard is the mustard for this dish. Mild, sweet and dark from the husks that are left in, it has a subtle spiciness. It is not the muddy concoction that passes in England for French mustard. The name of Louit on the pot denotes authenticity, but this is hard to come by. If necessary use a good German sweet mustard.

3 tablespoons beef dripping or lard
3 large red onions, finely sliced
4 fat garlic cloves, finely sliced
900 g/2 lb stewing beef, trimmed of all gristle and fat, cut into 15 mm/½ in cubes
1 tablespoon soft brown sugar
1 tablespoon red wine vinegar
1½ tablespoons flour
Maldon salt

freshly ground black pepper
freshly grated nutmeg
1 sprig fresh thyme
3 sprigs fresh parsley
1 sprig fresh marjoram
300 ml/½ pint brown ale
150 ml/¼ pint good beef stock, or water
8-10 slices French bread
1-2 tablespoons Bordeaux mustard

Melt half the dripping in a wide, shallow casserole (essential or the bread won't fit in one layer), add the onions and sauté for 15 minutes or until nicely browned and softened, adding the garlic for the last 5 minutes. Remove the onions and keep aside. Add the rest of the dripping to the pan, put in half the meat and brown over a high heat. Remove, add the remaining meat, sear that and remove.

Sprinkle in the sugar and stir until lightly caramelized, then deglaze with the vinegar. Return the meat and onions to the pan, sprinkle over the flour and stir until all the fat is absorbed. Season – be generous with the pepper and nutmeg, light with salt, then add the herbs (use 1 teaspoon dried mixed herbs if fresh are unavailable) and pour in the ale slowly, stirring all the time. Add the stock and just enough water to cover the meat. Cover and cook in the oven at 150°C/300°F/Gas Mark 2 for about 2½-3 hours, until the meat is really tender and the sauce thickened. Smear the bread with mustard and arrange the slices over the top of the meat, mustard side down, tops just sticking out, and cook uncovered for a further 15-20 minutes until the bread is golden and crisp. Serves 4-6

BOEUF EN DAUBE DIJONNAISE

A *daube* is traditionally associated with beef, although it can encompass any large piece of meat, either left whole or chopped small, sometimes marinated, then gently braised in a stock (often wine-based) with herbs and seasonings. Ancient pots, or *daubières*, were of earthenware, stoneware, cast iron or tinned copper, usually wider than they were deep and often with a concave lid, for filling with hot embers. Although it is very much a country dish, taking its name from a word which implied a crude execution (hence our word 'daub'), and although the seasonings, herbs and stock vary from region to region, from season to season, it is certainly not slapdash. Richard Olney sums it up perfectly: '… the soul of a *daube* resides in pervasive unity – the transformation of individual qualities into a single character.'

900 g/2 lb piece of rump or topside
75 g/3 oz fresh pork back fat, cut into small narrow strips
Maldon salt
freshly ground black pepper
½ teaspoon dried mixed herbs
2 tablespoons olive oil
175 g/6 oz unsmoked streaky bacon, in one piece then cut into small cubes
125 g/4 oz fresh pork rinds, as unfatty as possible, cut into small pieces
2 onions, finely chopped
2 carrots, sliced lengthways
1 celery heart, finely chopped

For the marinade
200 ml/7 fl oz dry white Burgundy
2 tablespoons white wine vinegar
4 tablespoons brandy
2 cloves garlic, finely chopped
1 bay leaf
1 sprig fresh thyme
3 sprigs fresh parsley

To finish the sauce
2 tablespoons green peppercorns, rinsed of their brine and lightly crushed
1 tablespoon Dijon mustard
1 tablespoon unsalted butter

If you have a larding needle, lard the beef with the pieces of pork fat, then roll the joint in salt, pepper and the dried herbs. Otherwise, make small incisions all over the meat, roll the pork fat in the seasonings and press into the cuts in the joint. Put the meat in a deep bowl, add the marinade ingredients and leave for 3-6 hours, turning occasionally.

Drain and pat dry the meat. Pour the oil into your pot, then make a thin layer with half the bacon cubes and pieces of pork rind. Put in the meat, pack the chopped vegetables around it with a few on top then cover with the remaining bacon and pork rinds. Pour over the marinade and add just enough water barely to cover the meat. Cover with a tightly fitting lid and bring slowly to boiling point – this will take about 45-55 minutes, then transfer to the oven, at 150°C/300°F/Gas Mark 2, and cook for a further 1½-2 hours until the meat is exceedingly tender. Transfer the meat to a warmed platter, surround with the bacon and rind pieces and keep warm. Skim the excess fat off the sauce and pour into a pan. Add the peppercorns and mustard and bring to a hard boil. Turn to a simmer then whisk in the butter to lightly glaze. Pour over the meat and serve immediately. Serves 4-6

TEWKESBURY MUSTARD CASSEROLE

Recipes for casseroles abound – some distinctly better than others. Two requisites are paramount: a long, very gentle cooking and good seasonings. Perhaps not quite such a plethora as Hannah Glasse sometimes recommends – besides several spices, herbs and lemon peel, she has oysters, anchovy, ox palates, gherkins and mushroom powder. Eliza Acton again sums it up with beautiful simplicity in her conclusion to the recipe 'To Stew A Rump Beef': 'Grated horse-radish, mixed with some well-thickened brown gravy, a teaspoonful of mustard, and a little lemon-juice or vinegar, is a good sauce for stewed beef.' It could almost be Tewkesbury mustard casserole.

900 g/2 lb stewing steak, trimmed of fat and gristle, cubed in 15 mm/½ in pieces
5 tablespoons olive oil
4 large onions, finely sliced
6 fat garlic cloves, crushed
4 teaspoons flour
4 teaspoons mustard powder
freshly ground white pepper
4 tablespoons whisky
400 ml/14 fl oz red wine or good beef stock

4 sprigs fresh thyme
2 teaspoons fresh marjoram
3 bay leaves
12 whole allspice berries, pounded
4 cloves
2 tablespoons soft brown sugar
Maldon salt
freshly ground black pepper
1-2 tablespoons Tewkesbury mustard (p.54)
lemon juice

Heat the oil in a large, flameproof casserole until just beginning to smoke. Add the beef and sear for 2-3 minutes. Remove the meat, add the onions and garlic to the pan, stirring to coat with the oil. Cover and sweat for 10 minutes.

Sift the flour and mustard powder together, then sprinkle over the onions and stir until all the oil is absorbed. Sprinkle with freshly ground white pepper, then add the whisky and bubble for 2 minutes.

Pour in the wine, stirring all the time, then add the herbs, spices, brown sugar and stir again to mix well. Return the beef to the pan, pushing it down gently to nestle in the sauce, then cover with a tight-fitting lid and cook on the lowest possible heat for 3½-4 hours. The heat must be very gentle so use an asbestos mat if needed and check the liquid level from time to time, topping up with a little water if absolutely necessary.

Test that the meat is tender by pressing in a fork – it should go in like butter. If not, give it another 15-20 minutes, again adding a little more liquid if the sauce is too thick. Transfer the meat to a warmed dish and keep warm. Stir the Tewkesbury mustard and a squeeze of lemon into the sauce, and bubble hard for 1 minute or so until rich, concentrated and not too liquid. Season with salt and pepper then pour over the beef. Serve with mashed potatoes into which a chopped, raw onion has been stirred, and stewed mushrooms. Serves 5-6

GLAZED SALT BEEF WITH MUSTARD SAUCE

For the Tudors salt beef was still a highly regarded dish on the well-dressed table, but today it is not highly esteemed. Have we been so indoctrinated by the tales of Hanged Beef, 'it may fill the belly and cause a man to drink, but it is evil for the stone, evil of digestion,' that we are still harbouring a deep-held prejudice? The time has come for a revival of this very ancient English dish. So, find a good butcher who brines his own beef – and enjoy this.

1.6-1.8 kg/3½-4 lb salted silverside or brisket of beef, boned and rolled
1 large onion, chopped
1 leek, cut in half lengthways
1 large carrot, chopped
1 celery stick
6 white peppercorns, lightly crushed
1 bay leaf
1 parsley sprig
For the glaze
16 cloves
75 g/3 oz soft dark brown sugar
1 teaspoon powdered mustard

freshly ground allspice
1 teaspoon ground cinnamon
2 tablespoons honey
1 tablespoon orange juice
For the sauce
300 ml/½ pint medium dry cider
1 teaspoon Dijon or Tewkesbury mustard (p. 48 or p.54)
1-2 tablespoons *beurre manié* (equal volumes of flour and butter worked to a paste)
freshly ground black pepper
good posy fresh parsley, very finely chopped

Immerse the beef in cold water and soak overnight. Drain and rinse very thoroughly, then place the meat in a large pan. Strew on the vegetables, peppercorns and herbs, adding cold water to cover.

Bring slowly to boiling point, skim off any scum and taste the cooking liquid. If it is very salty, pour half away and refill – this will depend on the brine your butcher uses, but most today are fairly light. You do want the stock for the sauce though, so if at all in doubt replenish with some fresh water and bring again to the boil.

Reduce the heat to the lowest possible, cover the pan and simmer very gently until quite tender – about 3½-4 hours. Leave the meat in the liquid to cool.

Drain the meat thoroughly, patting dry the fat, then stick in the cloves all over. Put in a roasting pan. Mix together the glaze – warm the honey slightly if it is thick until easily pourable – and smear over the beef. Roast in the oven at 180°C/350°F/Gas Mark 4 for 40-50 minutes until deeply glazed. Give it the occasional baste during cooking.

About 10 minutes before serving, measure out 300 ml/½ pint of the stock (keep the rest for soup), skim off any fat and pour into a pan with the cider. Bring quickly to the boil, taste and add a little water if it is too salty, then stir in the mustard. Have the sauce at a gentle simmer and whisk in the *beurre manié*, little by little, until thickened to your liking. Add pepper and finely chopped parsley, then pour into a very hot sauceboat and serve with the salt beef cut into thin slices. Also excellent cold, with Devil Chantilly (p.84). Serves 6-8

MENU

Lamb and Mutton

*Mustard and mutton, the sign of a glutton,
Mustard and beef, the sign of a thief.*

Anon

Almost everybody we asked found this ditty familiar, yet nobody knew its origins. They sound suspiciously Victorian for, apart from the rather sanctimonious air, it seems to have been then that the partnership between mustard and mutton became frowned upon. That it was not the norm is made clear in a little book, written for Keen's in 1892 to celebrate their 150th anniversary: 'It [mustard] is, in fact, the natural piquant accompaniment to roast pork . . . and made dishes, to poultry and to some kinds of fish, and among gourmets, to *mutton*. Let the deprecator of cold mutton try a slice or two with the piquant addition of some fine mustard deftly commingled with a dash of walnut or mushroom catsup, and he will no longer despise the cold roast shoulder or the succulent boiled neck, eaten with a discreetly chosen salad.'

The interesting point is the combination of mustard and walnut catsup. It appears a century earlier in a recipe of Thomas Jefferson's for Cold Stew'd Beef and some thirty years later in the Mustard Club booklet, as a 'reader's' suggestion for Devilled Beef which states also that it is particularly good for cold mutton. Hannah Glasse mentions walnut pickle with mutton, in a hash of cold mutton and in the endpiece to a recipe, 'To Fry a Loin of Lamb': 'You do mutton the same way and add 2 spoonfuls of walnutt pickle.' Now walnuts and mutton are a particularly Arab combination, and the Romans would have known the dish. By medieval times – and right through to the Elizabethan period – mustard was the classic accompaniment to salt mutton. Some 150 years later, the nuts and the condiment were forming a *ménage à trois* with the fresh meat. Who made the link, and when? History gives us clues but not the complete answer.

Curiously, one of the very few references to mustard in the Middle Eastern kitchen combines it with lamb. The ninth-century poem by Ishaq ibn Ibrahim, quoted at the magnificent banquet given by the Caliph of Baghdad in the tenth century, has the lines: 'Last, ladle out into a thin tureen Where appetizing mustard smeared hath been, And eat with pleasure, mustarded about, this tastiest food for hurried diner-out.' A wonderfully evocative description of *sambusaks*, the glorious Arab stuffed pastries, which are still made today almost exactly as described in the poem. And, though the word used in the poem is 'meat', traditionally lamb is that meat. Mustard has disappeared from the modern recipe, nuts have made an entrance. One of the answers given to our oft-asked questions on the Arab indifference to mustard was that perhaps it was due to the area's preponderance of lamb dishes – lamb and mustard not being 'natural partners'. Yet in India there is a huge repertoire of lamb and mustard dishes: lamb baked whole, gently braised, spiced kebabs, meatballs . . .

Mustard, of course, must originally have been used to 'hot' dishes up, but many of the recipes are mild and of direct Moghul descent. And the Arab and Moghul kitchens had extremely close links. Perhaps that most influential of Arab physicians, Galen, did not appreciate mustard's virtues – though it had long been recognized as a benign influence on heavy meats.

With the second highest fat content of our animal foods (28 per cent – even with all visible fat trimmed off, the muscle itself still contains fat), lamb is indeed a heavy meat. The medievals realized that, hence their constant partnership of mustard and salt mutton. Somebody, somewhere (maybe with a knowledge of the Indian kitchen?) introduced it to the fresh meat. Glutton he may have been. But we should thank him.

BAKED LAMB CUTLETS

Lamb cutlets provide a fertile ground for experiments with mustard. If you know your cutlets come from really young, fresh lamb, simply spread them on each side with a smidgeon of mustard and olive oil, sprinkle with salt and pepper and grill – briefly. They should be pink, tender and juicy. They will not taste too much of mustard – but they will taste of lamb. For frozen cutlets, or meat of a dubious age, a slow baking will give better results.

12 lamb cutlets, trimmed of most of their fat	2 tablespoons Five-herb mustard (p.48)
3 tablespoons olive oil	lemon juice
1 bunch fresh mint	Maldon salt
300 ml/½ pint red wine	freshly ground black pepper

Sprinkle the cutlets with a little salt and black pepper. Heat the oil, and the meat and sear quickly on both sides. Make a bed of the mint in a roasting tin, place the cutlets on top – in one layer – and pour over the wine mixed with the mustard. Bake in the oven at 170°C/325°F/Gas Mark 3 for 25 minutes, then turn, baste – the liquid will have considerably reduced – and bake for another 15 minutes, by which time the juices should have almost all been absorbed. Transfer to a serving platter, squeeze over the merest hint of lemon juice and serve. Serves 4-6

DEVILLED LAMB CUTLETS

Devilling was at its most favoured during Victorian and Edwardian times, with a legion of variations and spice combinations – all subtly different. What they had in common was a reminder of the Raj kitchen and the glories of the British Empire. Note also, the walnut ketchup.

12 lamb cutlets, if possible the very thin ones sold as 'breakfast cutlets'
2 tablespoons mustard powder
2 tablespoons walnut ketchup
Maldon salt
freshly ground black pepper
50 g/2 oz unsalted butter

3 small shallots, very finely chopped
1 tablespoon soft dark brown sugar
150 ml/¼ pint red wine vinegar
1 tablespoon Worcestershire sauce
few drops Tabasco sauce
2 tablespoons mint jelly
cayenne pepper

Mix the mustard powder with 2 tablespoons cold water and the walnut ketchup to a smooth thin paste. Smear lightly on both sides of the cutlets and leave for 1 hour. Sprinkle lightly with salt and black pepper. Melt 1 tablespoon butter in a small pan, add the shallots and cook for 5 minutes. Sprinkle in the sugar and stir for 2-3 minutes until lightly caramelized, then pour in the vinegar, constantly stirring. Add the Worcester sauce, Tabasco and mint jelly and gently, gently bubble until thick and syrupy.

Meanwhile, melt the remaining butter in a large frying pan (or roasting tin). Add the cutlets and cook: 2 minutes each side is fine for thin cutlets, 3-4 minutes for thicker ones. Transfer to a warmed serving dish, pour the cooking sediments into the 'sauce' pan, stir well and pour over the meat. There will not be much sauce – but it will be very concentrated in flavour. Sprinkle with a *little* cayenne and serve at once. Serves 4-6

MUTTON CARBONADOES

Especially popular as grilled steaks in Elizabethan times were pieces of mutton fillet: 'Cut a leg of mutton in thin fillets and to make it tender: chop it on both the sides with the back of the knife so that they be not chopped through. Then salt them well and lay them, on a gridiron and broil them till they be enough, and with vinegar and minced onions serve them forth.' A little mustard completes the sauce. 'Gigot' chops have been used here (cut from across the leg of the lamb) but mutton would be equally good.

4 gigot lamb chops	150 ml/¼ pint cider vinegar
2 tablespoons olive oil	1 teaspoon sugar
Maldon salt	150 ml/¼ pint medium dry white
freshly ground black pepper	wine
2 large sweet onions, very finely	freshly ground nutmeg
chopped	1-2 teaspoons Dijon mustard

Flatten the chops lightly using a large-bladed knife, working around the bone. Brush with oil on both sides. Put the onions into a pan, deep rather than wide, add the vinegar and the sugar then simmer gently, covered, for 10 minutes. Stir, then pour in the wine and cook, covered, for a further 15 minutes until very soft. Season with plenty of nutmeg, then add the mustard (1 teaspoon) and simmer, uncovered, while cooking the chops.

Grill the chops under a medium heat for 10-15 minutes, turning once, depending upon how pink you like your lamb. Season lightly with salt and pepper then give them a further minute on each side under a high heat to brown. The onion sauce should by this time have absorbed almost all the liquid – if not, bubble hard for 1-2 minutes until it has reduced. Check the mustard, adding a little extra if necessary. It shouldn't be overpowering, but the taste should be there. Spread a little 'sauce' over each chop and serve at once. Serves 4

GRILLED SHOULDER OF LAMB

Not such an illogical idea as it might at first seem. We barbecue lamb quite happily, yet the number of people who exclaim 'Grilled roast lamb . . .' The words are almost instinctive – you have a shoulder of lamb, you have a roast lamb! Yet lamb grilled is very good, and it doesn't take long. It is not a meal for fussy eaters of thin, neat slices of meat: carve it in chunks and let the meat fall off the bone.

1 shoulder of lamb, about 1.6	2 tablespoons finely chopped
kg/3½ lb weight	mixed fresh herbs, or 1 table-
1 teaspoon mustard powder	spoon dried mixed herbs if
	absolutely necessary

4 tablespoons olive oil   Maldon salt
1 tablespoon Dijon mustard   freshly ground black pepper
150 ml/¼ pint dry white wine

Slash the meat right through to the bone, on both sides, making the gashes about 5 cm/2 inches apart. Mix the herbs with the mustard powder and rub all over the joint, pushing well into the cuts. Mix the oil, mustard and wine, pour over the joint and leave for 12-24 hours.

Drain the meat, reserving the marinade. Grill under a moderate heat (on a rack) for 5 minutes. Turn over, cook for 5 minutes then turn again. Sprinkle with a little salt and pepper, cook for a further 5 minutes then turn and repeat with the other side. Continue cooking for 20-25 minutes, turning every 5 minutes and basting with a little marinade until the outside is marvellously charred. Transfer to a hot dish, scrape up the juices from the grill pan and smear over the lamb. Eat. Serves 5-6

BAKED LAMB SHOULDER

It is strange how we get locked into culinary prejudices. Mint sauce with lamb is anathema to the Frenchman. His penchant for garlic causes English noses to wrinkle. Yet both are not merely good in taste but also have a chemical purpose. How many people though think of tomatoes and lamb as a particular partnership? The French have the edge on us: most of their *daubes* and casseroles for lamb are moistened not with stock but tomatoes. With sound reason – the acidity cuts through the fat in the meat (that, too, is why rosemary is traditionally associated with lamb – its essence performs the same function) and the sweetness adds a roundness of flavour. Mustard intensifies the taste of both the lamb and the tomatoes.

900 g/2 lb lean lamb, cubed
3 tablespoons olive oil
2 large sweet onions, chopped but
  not too finely
3 garlic cloves, cut in half
1 sprig thyme, leaves stripped
  from the stalk
3 sprigs fresh marjoram, finely
  chopped

2 sprigs fresh savory, finely chopped,
  or 1 teaspoon dried savory
400 g/14 fl oz canned plum tomatoes
Maldon salt
freshly ground black pepper
1 tablespoon Dijon mustard
150 g/5 oz Cheddar cheese,
  grated
cayenne pepper

Heat the oil, add the onions and garlic and sweat for 10 minutes. Remove from the pan. Add the lamb, lightly and quickly browning it all over. Put the onions at the bottom of an ovenproof dish, and cover with the meat. Mix the herbs together and sprinkle over. Drain the tomatoes – keeping the juice – and chop the flesh. Spread over the meat. Mix the tomato juice with salt and black pepper, then stir in the mustard. Pour over the casserole then cover with grated cheese and a light scattering of cayenne. Cook in the oven at 180°C/350°F/Gas Mark 4 for about 1¼ hours until the cheese is bubbling and golden. Serve very hot, with crusty bread to mop up the juices, and a good green salad. Serves 4-6

SADDLE OF LAMB IN MUSTARD AND PORT

Traditionally, saddle of mutton was one of the great English dishes. And from medieval to Georgian times it had a traditional stuffing – oysters. It is interesting how the idea of fish and meat was quite clearly defined: anchovies with beef, oysters with mutton, crab with lamb – each type of fish cleverly complementing its meaty partner, and not intruding with any taste of fish at all. Anchovies add piquancy and oysters a sweetness, while the crab seems to take on a delicate nuttiness. Since fresh oysters today are a wild extravagance, for this recipe use either frozen shucked oysters (beginning to be available in Britain, widely so in

America) or − for a different but equally good flavour − smoked oysters. Since saddle of mutton is almost as extravagant as oysters − and considerably harder to find − we have used a small saddle of lamb. If you have a reliable source of real mutton, treasure it, and double the quantities of the stuffing. You will of course also feed more people, say 10-12. Either way, ask the butcher to bone (but not roll or tie) the saddle for you, keeping the bones and trimmings.

1 small saddle of lamb, about 1.6 kg/3 lb boned weight, bones and trimmings reserved
2 sprigs lemon thyme
2 garlic cloves, whole but peeled
Maldon salt
freshly ground black pepper
2 tablespoons Dijon mustard
5 tablespoons port
2 tablespoons redcurrant jelly

For the stuffing
25 g/1 oz unsalted butter
1 large onion, finely chopped
225 g/8 oz shucked frozen oysters, defrosted, or 125 g/4 oz can smoked oysters, drained, plus 125 g/4 oz white crabmeat

1 bunch watercress, finely chopped
juice of 1 lemon
freshly grated allspice

For the stock
1 small onion stuck with 6 cloves
1 cinnamon stick
1 celery stick
fresh parsley
1 bay leaf
fresh chervil
small piece lemon zest
2 tablespoons white wine vinegar
½ teaspoon sugar

First, make a light stock with the reserved bones and trimmings, the stock ingredients and 1 litre/1¾ pints cold water. Bring slowly to the boil, skim off any scum then simmer gently for about 1 hour, half-covered. Simmer, uncovered, for a further 15-20 minutes until reduced to 450 ml/¾ pint. Strain, cool, skim off the fat and reserve.

To make the stuffing, melt the butter, add the onions and stew gently for 20 minutes until softened but not coloured. Remove from the heat, stir in the oysters, or smoked oysters and crabmeat, then add the watercress, lemon juice and allspice. Season well and mix thoroughly.

Place the lamb, skin side down, on a flat surface and open it out. Lay one thyme sprig and one garlic clove on each side of the saddle, then spread the stuffing evenly down both sides. Carefully turn in the outer flaps of meat, then roll together and tie securely. Place the joint, skin side up, on a roasting rack and season with salt and pepper.

Mix together the mustard and port. Gently heat the redcurrant jelly until melted − add a tablespoon of water to the pan to prevent burning. Stir into the mustard and port then smear the lamb with the paste. Cook in the oven at 200°C/400°F/Gas

Mark 6 for about 1½ hours for pink lamb (25 minutes per lb) to just over 2 hours (35 minutes per lb) for well-done meat. Baste every 30 minutes.

Remove the joint to a warmed platter, scrape up the sediments in the roasting tin, pour off any excess fat then add the stock and boil furiously for 3-4 minutes to reduce slightly and heighten the flavours. Pour into a warmed sauceboat and serve with the lamb cut into thick slices. Serves 8

LAMB RISSOLES WITH MUSTARD WINE SAUCE

One of the favourite methods of cooking lamb in the Middle East is to mince it very finely, then highly spice it, before grilling or pan-frying. Add a French sauce, and you have an excellent dish.

900 g/2 lb lean lamb, finely minced

1 large onion, grated

Maldon salt

freshly ground white pepper

3 tablespoons olive oil

1 tablespoon brown mustard seed

1 tablespoon cumin, lightly crushed

1 teaspoon powdered cinnamon

4 tablespoons finely chopped parsley

2 fat garlic cloves, crushed

For the sauce

25 g/1 oz butter

1 shallot, finely chopped

175 ml/6 fl oz red wine

2 teaspoons Dijon mustard

2 tablespoons *crème fraîche*

Put the lamb into a food processor, with the onion and a generous seasoning of salt and pepper. Heat 1 tablespoon oil, add the mustard seeds, cover the pan and cook until they start to pop – about 1 minute. Drain and add the seeds to the processor together with the cumin, cinnamon, parsley and garlic cloves. Blend until paste-like. If you don't have a processor, just mix together *very thoroughly* in a large bowl, really pounding the meat until quite smooth. With wetted hands, form into small balls. Heat the remaining oil in the wiped-out frying pan and add the meatballs – give yourself plenty of room to turn them over, so do the cooking in two batches if need be. Cook for about 6-7 minutes, turning fairly constantly until crispy and browned on the outside, still soft within. Keep warm.

Wipe out the pan with kitchen paper, add the butter and sizzle lightly. Add the shallot and sauté for 3-4 minutes, gently, then pour in the wine. Bubble hard for 2 minutes to reduce, then stir in the mustard and *crème fraîche* and cook for a further minute. Pour over the meatballs and serve immediately. Serves 6

STEAMED MARINATED MUTTON

Steamed mutton is a Moroccan favourite – there, very simply served with salt and cumin seeds sprinkled on top. But the meat is so tender it can be pulled apart in the fingers, and it is a good method for cooking English mutton, which is often of indifferent age: not mature enough to have the richness of true mutton (three to four years old) but old enough to have lost that first flush of youthful tenderness. Soy sauce, incidentally, is no newcomer to the English kitchen – it came with the first East India Company traders in the early eighteenth century.

900 g/2 lb lean lamb, cubed

2 garlic cloves, finely chopped

5 cm/2 in piece fresh root ginger, peeled and grated

½ teaspoon ground cinnamon

1 teaspoon black peppercorns, crushed

2 tablespoons Matthew's mustard (p.55)

3 tablespoons soy sauce

150 ml/¼ pint medium dry white wine

1 tablespoon syrup from Mostarda di Venezia (p. 58)

3-4 pieces of quince from Mostarda di Venezia, finely chopped

lemon juice

fresh mint sprigs, very finely chopped

Put the lamb in the bottom of a fairly wide, heatproof dish. Mix together all the ingredients except the quinces, lemon juice and mint, then pour all over the lamb. Cover the dish with greaseproof paper, tied round the top tightly, then with foil or a towel, also tied (much as one does a Christmas pudding). Put into a large pan and carefully pour in boiling water, to come two-thirds of the way up the dish. Have the water hinting at a simmer, cover the pan and cook, very gently, for about 2 hours, topping up with more boiling water as necessary.

Mix the chopped quinces with a little lemon juice to taste, then stir in the chopped mint. (Quinces with lamb was a well-known medieval partnership – again from the Arabs. Today, only the Persians – with their huge quince orchards – follow the ancient tradition, although Morocco still favours many fruit and meat stews.) Put the dip in a small bowl.

Carefully lift out the mutton dish from the pan, dry the bottom, remove the foil and paper and serve while the aroma is still drifting out of the bowl. Accompany with the quince dip. Serves 4-6

LAMB 'OVEN' CURRY

The Oxfam shop one day revealed a little treasure: a small, tatty leatherbound book, marked very firmly in red ink on the inside cover 'Property of the Colonel's Wife – PLEASE do not move, June 6th 1862.' There is no name, no mention of a place, except for one month spent visiting 'The Colonel's Aunt' in Simla. What *is* meticulously recorded though are trips to the market, what she saw, what she bought, what she paid for it and how it was cooked.

This recipe was particularly intriguing as she has noted 'especially good to be cooked in England'. Why? Because it's cooked in the oven, unlike most of her other curries? Or perhaps she has adapted it – there is no Indian title here, as with most of the other dishes. Either way, it is especially good; and it is pleasing to think the treasured book has not met such an ignominious end after all.

1.1 kg/2½ lb boned leg of lamb (about 1.8 kg/4 lb unboned weight)	1-2 garlic cloves, peeled
	Maldon salt
	juice of 2 lemons
5 cm/2 inch piece fresh root ginger, peeled and coarsely chopped	50 ml/2 fl oz mustard oil
	2 bay leaves, dried and crumbled
	1 large onion, finely sliced
1-2 green chillies, seeded and chopped	1 tablespoon mustard powder

Cut the lamb into 25 mm/1 inch cubes, trimming off any fat or gristle. In a coffee grinder, blend the ginger, chilli and garlic with a pinch of salt (this stops the chilli juices from becoming bitter). Stir the paste into half the lemon juice, and 1 tablespoon mustard oil. Pour over the lamb and leave for 2-3 hours.

Heat the remaining oil in a roasting pan, add the onions and sweat gently for 10 minutes, turning occasionally. Sprinkle over the crumbled bay leaves. Place the meat in an even layer on top of the onions, pour over the marinade and cook in the oven at 180°C/350°F/Gas Mark 4 for 45 minutes. Mix the mustard powder with 3 tablespoons cold water (there is a note in the original beside this ingredient, which is actually listed as '2 tablespoon mustard seed powdered very fine [if no cook-boy available, use COLMAN'S M.P.]'). Stir the mustard paste into the remaining lemon juice and sprinkle all over the lamb – do not turn the lamb though. Cook for a further 30 minutes then serve with a pile of pilau rice. The meat is succulently tender, the juices delicately spicy. Serves 6

THE MUSTARD CLUB AGAIN!

Pork

It is the one [animal] whose empire is the most universal, and whose qualities are the least in dispute. Without it, there would be no bacon, and consequently no cookery; without it, no ham, no sausage, no andouille, no black pudding and therefore no charcutiers ... Everything about the pig is good, what culpable lapse of memory can have transformed its name into a vulgar insult?

GRIMOD DE LA REYNIÈRE

The pig has always been the poor man's favourite meat, and it is easy to understand why. Not a drop —literally – is wasted. For the medieval peasant the great autumn slaughter was a time of high festivity and activity: the making of blood puddings, salting of sides, curing of hams, flaying of fat for lard were all part of the winter preparations. Not least was the making of Thomas Tusser's Christmas 'souse': the hind joints, ears, snout, cheeks, trotters, and, sometimes, tail were all pickled in a strong brine, often laced with ale or wine. For many a family, the pig, however preserved, was going to be their only meat for the next few months. Fortunately, it pickles and salts particularly well. Rich in fat, and succulent, it requires less salt then beef or mutton, so providing a tenderer joint. Its very richness, of course, needed offsetting, and so the range of sharp, spicy sauces – and mustard – became its natural accompaniment.

Apicius gives a mustard sauce for roast pork, and several for boiled boar. Cooked sides of pork are also pickled by him in 'mustard, vinegar, salt and honey, covering meat entirely. And when ready to use you'll be surprised.' Some 2,000 years later, the unknown author of *The Indian Cookery Book by a Thirty-Five years' Resident* – quoted by Elizabeth David in her *Spices, Salt and Aromatics in the English Kitchen* – was also using mustard as a preservative for cooked pork. Having ascertained that 'The best vindaloo is that prepared with mustard oil', he or she goes on to say that a vindaloo cooked from fat pork will keep long enough 'to be sent Home round the Cape' if stored in stone jars 'well covered with mustard oil'.

Back in medieval England, their hams and sausages saw them through the winter, and mustard had its place. With sausages so much so, according to Dumas's colourful account, that Edward III burning his way through France gave no quarter to those pleading for an end to the fiery destruction: '"Bah!" said the ferocious Plantagenet, "War without burning is sausage without mustard!"'

Ham is a natural for mustard and sugar glazes, and even with no mustard in the glaze, it is the automatic accompaniment to the meat. In the 1840s, when the first ham-sandwich sellers appeared on London streets, two of the requisites for setting up in the business were: '2d for mustard-pot and spoon' and '4d for mustard'. Colman's Mustard Club cleverly exploited the tradition with their gimmick of advertising in the provincial papers that their 'mystery man' would be 'in town' on a certain day, eating ham sandwiches. Any waiter who passed him the mustard would be given £1.

The partnership was not new, of course. Giles Rose, in the enchantingly titled *A Perfect School of Instruction for the Officers of the Mouth* (1682), finishes his recipe For A Gammon of Bacon, 'and when it is boiled raise the skin and stick it with Bays and Rosemary ... then serve it with mustard.' Apart from the Bays and Rosemary – how much nicer than the ubiquitous cloves – the recipe is most modern. And it was not just gammon that called for mustard. The Frenchman F. Misson, describing the cookshops all over London at that time, writes: 'Generally, four Spits, one over another, carry round each five or six pieces of Butcher's Meat, Beef, Mutton, Veal, Pork and Lamb: you have what Quantity you please cut off ... with this, a little Salt and Mustard upon the Side of a Plate, a Bottle of Beer and a Roll; and there is your whole Feast.' Hannah Woolley, in *The Accomplisht Lady's Delight*, a few years earlier, had recommended a sauce 'with butter, vinegar, mustard and sugar' to accompany Broyl'd Leg of Pork while in the Burgundian kitchen whole legs of pork were marinated in wine for a day, smeared with mustard and then roasted – a dish still popular today.

Italy varies her mustard accompaniment. With *zampone* (a stuffed pig's trotter), one is offered delicious fruit pickle, Mostarda di Frutta.

Since the early days when salt pork and mustard sauce opened the feasts, mustard and pork have travelled together. Without microscopes, without knowledge of the structure of meat, man's instinct has led the pig to mustard. And wisely so. For the mustard quickens the breakdown of the fatty cells, exposing a greater area of the meat fibres to the gastric juices and thereby encouraging easier and more complete assimilation.

MUSTARD SEED SAUSAGES

Thousands of tons of sausages are sold each year. Sadly, most of these are far from pleasant, yet to make one's own is not difficult. After all, if the medieval peasant, with no food processor, could do it, so can we. Skins, obtainable from any good butcher who makes his own sausages, keep well in salt, chilled, merely needing a good soaking before use. And if you haven't a sausage-filling attachment, or an obliging butcher, then you can make pretty lacy packages like the French *crépinette*, by wrapping small rounds of the mixture in softened caul fat.

700 g/1½ lb belly of pork, derinded and coarsely chopped
700 g/1½ lb lean pork, hand and
spring ideally, coarsely chopped
225 g/8 oz pork back fat
2 tablespoons brown mustard
seed, soaked for 24 hours
2 tablespoons Maldon salt
freshly ground white and black
peppers
1½ tablespoons caster sugar
2 tablespoons crushed coriander
seeds

¼ teaspoon saltpetre
2 tablespoons finely chopped fresh
parsley
1 tablespoon finely chopped fresh
thyme, or tarragon, or young
sage leaves
For the cooking
3 tablespoons olive oil
2 large onions, finely sliced
4-6 garlic cloves, sliced lengthways
150 ml/¼ pint fruity white wine
1 tablespoon Dijon mustard

Mince the pork and fat finely or whizz in a food processor. Grind the soaked mustard seed in a spice grinder – it won't pulverize completely, but sufficiently for the purpose. Add to the food processor together with the remaining ingredients and whizz again. If mixing by hand, make sure to distribute the spices evenly. Be generous with the peppers.

Fill the casings, twisting every six inches or so (a refinement only started in the early seventeenth century) and hang for 1-2 days in a dry airy place. This is not vital but greatly improves the flavour which can otherwise be a trifle bland. Half the amount will be adequate for 4-6 people, so freeze the remainder.

To cook the remainder, heat the oil in a large frying or roasting pan, add the onion and garlic and sauté gently for 10-15 minutes until soft and lightly golden. Bring some salted water to the boil, dip in the sausages for 1 minute. Drain and pat dry, then add to the onions. Brown lightly, then add the wine – mixed with the mustard – and bubble hard for 30-40 seconds. Season, lightly, reduce the heat and cook for 30-40 minutes turning the sausages frequently, until they are crisp and cooked through. Particularly good served with new potatoes, dressed while still warm in a *light* mustard vinaigrette. Green salad, of course.
Serves 4-6

PORK BALLS WITH MUSTARD-SOY DIP

A constant feature of the medieval kitchen is the dish Pommes d'Or – Golden Apples. Little balls of minced, highly spiced pork were dipped into a batter and fried until golden. Often part of the batter was mixed with a mass of finely chopped parsley, to give little green 'apples' too. With this dip, Japanese in origin, the batter is superfluous but a rolling in finely chopped parsley before frying is still a good idea.

350 g/12 oz lean pork
1 tablespoon mustard oil
1½ teaspoons brown mustard seed
freshly grated nutmeg
½ teaspoon ground caraway
5 cm/2 inch piece fresh root ginger, peeled and grated
1 small onion, grated
Maldon salt
freshly ground white and black peppers

2 teaspoons finely chopped fresh marjoram
3 tablespoons fresh parsley
1 teaspoon caster sugar
1 large egg, beaten
50 g/2 oz butter
For the sauce
2 teaspoons mustard powder
4 tablespoons light soy sauce (available at Chinese supermarkets)

Either put the pork through a mincer two or three times, or chop coarsely, then mince in a food processor.

Heat the oil in a small frying pan, add the mustard seeds, cover and fry until popping. Drain and add to the pork, together with the remaining ingredients, except the butter. Blend until thoroughly mixed and quite pasty.

With wetted hands, take a walnut-sized piece of the mixture and roll into a small ball. Test fry in a little butter until golden and crispy. Taste for seasoning, adjusting if necessary, then form the rest of the mixture into little balls. Melt the butter in a large pan, when bubbling add the meatballs and fry – in batches if necessary – until golden and cooked through. Keep warm while cooking the remainder.

Mix the mustard with 2 tablespoons cold water, then whisk in the soy sauce – adding a little more water if the sauce is too strong. Serve the pork balls with the sauce in tiny individual bowls, for people to dip into. Serves 4-6

FILLET OF PORK SEVILLE WITH MUSTARD

Although the early crusaders must have eaten sweet oranges on their travels in the Middle East, the first oranges to arrive in England were the bitter Spanish type, in the late thirteenth century. They soon found their way into the cooking pot, usually with sugar to provide those ever-present bitter-sweet sauces. The Elizabethans particularly used them with fish and chicken, but their sharp flavour also provides a good counterfoil to pork.

550 g/1¼ lb pork tenderloin, cut
   into ½ inch thick slices
Maldon salt
freshly ground black pepper
50-75 g/2-3 oz butter
juice of 2 small Seville oranges

1-2 teaspoons caster sugar
125 ml/4 fl oz chicken stock
½ teaspoon ground caraway
1 egg yolk
6 tablespoons double cream
2 teaspoons Dijon mustard

Season the meat lightly with a little salt and black pepper. Melt the butter in a large frying pan, or two, add the pork slices and sauté for 2 minutes or so until firm and opaque.

   Add the orange juice, sugar, stock and caraway, then simmer for 5-6 minutes turning the meat once. Test for doneness, giving it 1-2 minutes more if necessary. Whisk the egg yolk with the cream and mustard. Remove the meat to a warm serving dish, lower the heat and beat in the cream mixture. Heat through gently, stirring all the while until the sauce slightly thickens. Do not boil or it will curdle. Pour the sauce over, or around, as you prefer, the meat and serve. Serves 4-5

PORK FILLETS WITH MUSTARD SEEDS AND LOVAGE

Sage, which we regard as the particular herb for pork, only came into the greatest favour during the seventeenth century, although it is still the traditional flavouring for Cumberland pork sausages. Lovage, with its slight pepperiness and hint of celery, is another apt partner: the leaves for fresh cuts, the seeds good in sausages.

550 g/1¼ lb pork tenderloin cut
   into 5 cm/2 inch medallions
50 g/2 oz butter
1 tablespoon white mustard seed
10 lovage leaves, finely chopped

1 tablespoon granular mustard
3 tablespoons medium dry white
   wine
Maldon salt
freshly ground black pepper

Put the slices of pork in one layer between two sheets of greaseproof paper and flatten lightly with a meat bat. Melt half the butter, add 3-4 slices of pork so they fit neatly in one layer. Sauté for 2-3 minutes on each side until opaque and cooked right through. Remove from the pan, keep warm and cook the rest.

Add the remaining butter to the pan, and when just melted, add the mustard seeds and cook for 2 minutes until beginning to splutter. Add the lovage and cook, stirring constantly until soft and dark green.

Stir in the mustard, then pour over the wine. Raise the heat and bubble for 2 minutes, then season with a little salt and pepper. Pour over the pork fillets and serve immediately. Whatever the vegetables, keep the flavours very simple: this is a subtle and delicate dish. Serves 4

Novelty mustard containers that converted into money boxes after use

GAMMON WITH SHERRY MUSTARD SAUCE

Ham-curing methods have varied little over 2,000 years. Anne Wilson, in *Food and Drink in Britain*, describes how in Italy, c. 150 BC, 'hams had to be covered with salt and steeped in their own brine for 17 days, dried in a draught for 2, rubbed over with oil and vinegar, and then smoked for a further 2 days … Barring the oil and vinegar dressing', little has changed.

Today, in some areas the tradition of home-cured ham still persists. If you can get one of these, so much the better. If not, you could try curing a ham yourself: for the best recipes and meticulous detail – most important in home curing – turn to Jane Grigson's *Charcuterie and French Pork Cookery*. Otherwise, buy a good lean gammon joint – smoked or not as you prefer. Incidentally, Maldon salt, a staple as you will have noticed, gives excellent results if home-curing hams. Hannah Glasse on the subject: 'Yorkshire is famous for hams; and the Reason is this: Their Salt is much finer than ours in London, it is a large clear Salt, and gives the Meat a fine Flavour. I used to have it in Essex from Malding, and that Salt will make any Ham as fine as you can desire; it is by much the best Salt for salting Meat.'

1.8 kg/4 lb gammon joint, soaked overnight (even unsmoked joints benefit from a soaking; the salting process inevitably hardens the meat a little and soaking restores the succulence)

1.7 litres/3 pints bouillon (pp.186)

300 ml/½ pint amontillado sherry, plus extra if necessary

1 tablespoon light soy sauce

2 tablespoons soft dark brown sugar

freshly ground allspice

freshly ground black pepper

2 tablespoons Dijon mustard

1 tablespoon flour

1 tablespoon unsalted butter

Bring the ham to the boil in a large pan of cold water, simmer for 10 minutes then discard the water. Cover with the bouillon and bring to a good but gentle simmer. Cook for 1 hour 40 minutes – allowing 20 minutes per pound plus an extra 20.

Remove the joint from the pan and skin, then place in an ovenproof dish into which it fits snugly. Cover with the sherry and 150 ml/¼ pint of the cooking liquor. Cook in the oven at 180°C/350°F/Gas Mark 4 for 50-60 minutes, until the meat is quite tender when pierced with a fork.

Transfer the meat to a roasting tin, mix the soy sauce, sugar, allspice, pepper and mustard with 2-3 tablespoons of the sherry liquor, and smear over the ham. Raise the oven to 220°C/425°F/Gas Mark 7 and return the meat for 10-15 minutes until the glaze is melted and golden. Be careful that it doesn't burn.

Meanwhile, taste the braising liquid, adjust the seasoning if necessary, adding a little more sherry, soy, or some of the initial cooking juices if it seems too strong. (Keep the remaining stock for soup.) Stir in a touch of Dijon mustard if wished – but this sauce should be subtle – then bring to the boil, lower the heat and whisk in the flour and butter, previously mixed to a smooth paste. Beat until lightly thickened, then pour into a hot sauceboat. Serve with the ham cut into thick or thin slices as you prefer. Serves 8-10

ROMAN MUSTARD PORK CHOPS IN RED WINE

The Romans enjoyed their pigs in many guises: Virgil wrote about them, Roman soldiers took them on their marches – fresh food after the battle – and languishing banqueters had their appetites stimulated between courses by performing pigs (the Etruscans apparently trained them to march to music). Nero and his Senators preferred simply to eat the creature, pork far outstripping mutton as the favoured meat, especially salted pork, eaten with cabbage. The ancient Roman mustard, flavoured with almonds and pine kernels, goes particularly well with the fresh meat.

6 spare rib pork chops	2 rosemary sprigs
Maldon salt	2 tablespoons Roman mustard
freshly ground white pepper	(p.53)
3 garlic cloves, finely sliced	350 ml/12 fl oz red wine
lengthways	2 tablespoons olive oil
15 g/½ oz flaked almonds	25 g/1 oz pine kernels

Rub the chops all over with a little salt and black pepper, then make 4-5 slits on both sides of each chop and slide in a sliver of garlic and almond flake. Arrange on a roasting pan on top of the rosemary sprigs. Mix the mustard and wine with 1½ tablespoons of the oil and pour over.

Cook, covered, in the oven at 180°C/350°F/Gas Mark 4 for 1 hour, turning the chops once. Then uncover and cook for a further 20-30 minutes, basting every 10 minutes.

Heat the remaining oil, and sauté the pine kernels for 45 seconds until they turn pink. Scatter over the chops and serve with mashed potatoes. Serves 6

MUSTARD PORK IN MILK

This Italian method of cooking pork is unusual but excellent. Traditionally the rolled loin is used but the recipe is obligingly adaptable: loin chops, spare rib chops and belly rashers can all be substituted, the last in particular making for a very rich sauce as the melting fat combines with the milk.

6 spare rib chops
Maldon salt
freshly ground black pepper
2 tablespoons Dijon mustard
3 tablespoons olive oil
2 large onions, finely sliced
2 garlic cloves, crushed
2 thyme sprigs

1 tablespoon fresh coriander
  seeds, lightly crushed
1 tablespoon brown mustard seeds
about 600 ml/1 pint milk
350 g/12 oz fresh young broad
  beans (or frozen, if necessary)
finely chopped fresh parsley

Rub a little salt and pepper over each side of the chops, then smear both sides with mustard. Heat the oil in a large heavy-based pan (vital if the dish is not to burn), add the onions and cook for 10-15 minutes, covered, until nicely softened. Stir in the garlic, add the thyme sprigs and arrange the chops on top. Sprinkle over the seeds, a little extra salt and a good grinding of black pepper. Add the milk and bring to the boil, gently, then cover and cook, at the slowest possible simmer, for about 1 hour. Do not disturb the contents of the pan, but check after about 50 minutes that the liquid is not evaporating too quickly.

Blanch the broad beans in salted water for 2-3 minutes if young and fresh, 5-7 if frozen, then drain and add to the pan. When you lift off the lid, the milk will have formed a golden translucent veil. Stir into the meat, adding a little extra milk if need be – you don't want too much liquid but there must be enough to prevent sticking, all too easy at this stage. Cook, very gently, again covered, for a further 8-10 minutes. Sprinkle with lots of finely chopped parsley and serve. Serves 6

CRISPY ROAST PORK BELLY WITH SESAME MUSTARD

At St Faith's Fair, held annually in Norwich, the tradition was to serve crackly roast pork – with pots of mustard. The purveyors of the mustard were not always over-generous and supplies ran out very quickly. In Norfolk, if you have a near-empty mustard-pot, they still call it 'St Fay's Fair Mustard'. Well-crackled pork is not just an English tradition – the Chinese love it, especially pork belly. One word of warning: we have found gas and electric ovens very variable in their production of crackling. While this dish has never failed in a gas oven, it has proved less reliable in an electric one. If the worst comes to the worst, cut off the crackling 5 minutes before serving and crisp it under the grill. Chop it into small pieces and strew them over the pork, and disaster will be averted.

12 slices thick end pork belly, 15mm/½ inch thick

12 tablespoons Sesame mustard (p. 52)

4-5 tablespoons peanut oil

1 teaspoon sesame oil

Maldon salt

freshly ground black pepper

12 cloves

700 g/1½ lb spinach, washed, thoroughly drained and finely shredded

4 tablespoons toasted sesame seeds

Heat the oven to 200°C/400°F/Gas Mark 5 (the difference in oven temperatures is deliberate). Mix the mustard with 1½ tablespoons of the peanut oil, season lightly, then spread both sides of each pork slice with the mixture. Sprinkle over the sesame oil. Stick a clove into each slice.

Place the pork, skin upwards, in a roasting pan – put crumpled foil on either side if necessary to keep the meat upright.

Sprinkle over 12 tablespoons boiling water, then put into the oven for 40 minutes – do not baste. Turn the oven down to 140°C/275°F/Gas Mark 1, and leave for a further 15-20 minutes.

Meanwhile, heat half the remaining oil in a large pan, or wok, over a medium heat, add half the spinach and stir-fry for 5 minutes. Transfer to a warmed serving plate, then repeat with the rest of the spinach. Stir constantly while cooking. Add to the serving dish, and sprinkle with the toasted sesame seeds. Check the pork crackling, crisping under the grill if need be, then arrange the pork on top of the spinach. Sprinkle with a little extra black pepper and serve. Serves 4-6

Offal and Veal

Good husbands and huswife now chiefly be glad,
Things handsome to have as they ought to be had,
Good bread and good drinke, a good fier in the hall,
Brawne, pudding, and souse, and good mustards withal...

THOMAS TUSSER, 1557

So the poet farmer from East Anglia set the Christmas scene. It is interesting that, from very early times, offal dishes were considered great delicacies. Although originally brawn could mean any cold meat, it normally indicated leg of wild boar. By the thirteenth century, it was being made from the animal's forequarters, though all the carcass could be used except the head. This, more often than not, was boned, stuffed and highly decorated to provide the centre-piece of the main course. Brawn usually followed at the end of the banquet, either highly spiced and peppered, or sliced in sweet sauces of wine and honey, or almonds and sugar. Within the next 100 years, however, it was to gain a different companion, and move its place in the feast.

In 1387, the Bishop of Durham gave a magnificent banquet at his London palace for Richard II and the Duke of Lancaster. Among the hundreds of dishes to emerge from the ecclesiastical kitchens was a newcomer – 'Brawne with Mustard'. Sixteen years later, the dish appeared again, in the second remove, at the celebratory marriage feast of Henry IV and Joan of Navarre and by the middle of the century the combination was firmly established. 'Set forth mustard and brawne', said Russell in his *Boke of Nurture* in 1460, advice faithfully followed by George Nevill, Archbishop of York at his grand enthronement banquet in 1467. More significantly, the brawn appeared as an appetizer – 'First brawn and mustard out of course, served with malmsey', its place still sufficiently unusual to

Left: Bornibus, maker of Moutarde des Dames

cause comment. From thereon it tended always to be the opening dish, and mustard its traditional accompaniment.

By Tudor times brawn had come to be particularly associated with the Christmas table, although still occupying a high place of honour at banquets. By now it was being made from the domesticated pig as its wild cousin was extinct. The art of brawn-making started to decline in the eighteenth century, although it still appeared at Christmas, together with hogs puddings – black and white puddings or gallotines. These had been popular since Roman times, when they were served (according to Apicius) with mustard, although the recipe had been simplified over the centuries.

What had – indeed has – not changed during all those years was the traditional accompaniment: mustard. In fact, in all the ancient manuscripts, mustard was the constant companion to almost every offal dish, a point repeatedly made by Samuel Pepys. Many a dinner is described in his diary, and not only is his enjoyment obvious, so, too, is the necessity for mustard. 24 October 1662 saw him having 'a dish of tripes of my own directing covered with mustard, as I have heretofore seen them done at my Lord Crewe's'. The next day he 'Dined at home with my wife upon a good dish of neats' feet and mustard, of which I made a good meal.'

The lack of mustard in the house on 23 April 1663 had unfortunate consequences: 'At cards till late, and being at supper, my boy being sent for some mustard to a neats' tongue, the rogue stayed half an hour in the streets, it seems at a Bonfire, at which I was very angry and resolve to beat him tomorrow.' The morrow dawned, Pepys was 'up betimes, and with my salt Eele went down to the parler and there got my boy and did beat him till I was fain to take breath two or three times.'

One hundred years later, mustard was still making frequent – although less colourful – appearances in Hannah Glasse. Her recipes for Ragouts of Hogs Feet and Ears, To Fry Tripe, To Stew Tripe all have mustard, either in the cooking or as a sauce, 'Butter and Mustard in a Cup'. The association continued through to the next century although by this time much offal was considered 'lowly' food. The presence of mustard was logical: offal is often not only rich but at the same time rather bland. Some piquancy is needed to balance these qualities, as indeed it is to spice the rather delicate taste of veal. For that too, in the past, was given a sharp sauce, often of mustard.

Veal and the British have an ambivalent relationship. The Romans were partial to the meat and undoubtedly introduced it to England. Apicius has several veal recipes, including a fricassée which calls for mustard. But with the break-up of the Roman Empire, and the rise of the Anglo Saxons – who measured their wealth in cattle – veal disappeared from the menu until the Normans arrived. Probably the earliest recipe we have is in *The Forme of Curye*. Richard II must have been fond of veal for this is a simple, but delicious, dish using the leftovers in Veal Fritters. The meat appeared in many other guises, particularly on 'skuets' (small skewers) and as an Easter highlight. Along with the side of bacon (and, for the rich, milk-fed lamb) was veal pie, made from the minced meat, dried fruits, spices, wine and eggs. For the Tudors, big was beautiful, and whole legs, roasted, were the festive norm.

By the seventeenth century, the new influx of French-trained cooks were both harking back to and moving away from the medieval influences. Elegant and highly popular was the veal olive: a thin slice of meat, rolled round a spicy forcemeat, then roasted. Mustard was particularly recommended with certain veal dishes, typically breast of veal, especially when 'collared' (boned, stuffed, rolled, then roasted) or 'soused' in a strong pickling brine and boiled. An early eighteenth century manuscript, discovered by Beverly Nichols in the 1930s, is quite explicit in its directions for this dish: 'you may make sauce w[ith] butter Vinegar & mustard it w[ill] eat very well Cold.' Similar sauces appear repeatedly through the century while the repertoire of dishes is considerably widened, often to include one, or more, offals.

Veal was potted with tongue and called 'Marbled Veal', mixed with pork to make sausages (still so in Germany today, particularly *bratwurst* which is usually eaten with a coarse-grained mild mustard), or ragouted with 'a dozen veal kidneys and 2 sweetbreads' – all to be served with mustard. By this time, meat was generally of a fine quality, a fact much appreciated by the food cognoscenti, such as Samuel Johnson. Many were the gossipy suppers he enjoyed at the Mitre in Fleet Street, where he tucked into veal pies – and mustard. By now, the pies often contained the veal kidneys and sweetbreads as well as chopped meat. The association of veal with offal continued well into Victoria's reign, but with the Edwardians offal came into its own. Sweetbreads, liver and kidneys were especially favoured.

Today, the price of these delicacies is positively regal when calf is their origin, perhaps reflecting a certain snobbishness. Or perhaps it was always so: a calf's head was the vital factor in 'mock' turtle soup, a dish that graced many a grand eighteenth–century dinner table. And veal tripe in Italy is considered far superior, with a price to match, to that of the older ox.

What is sad is the turnabout in fortune of those dishes once considered fit to put before a king: the Shield of Brawne, the Hot Puddings, the Soused Collars. Dishes, which, though cheap of ingredient, reflected the care, ingenuity and skill of the cook if the right balance of texture and taste was to be achieved. Dishes which have been mustard's main companions for a very long time.

BRAWN WITH LOMBARD MUSTARD

If the thought of making brawn is daunting — let it not be. On the medieval principle of using anything *but* the head, it is indeed a simple dish. Brining is not essential but does add vastly to the flavour: if you don't have an obliging butcher to salt the meat for you, it *is* worth the little extra trouble.

900 g/2 lb hand and spring of pork, or a blade piece, on the bone
2 pig's trotters
Maldon salt
freshly ground white pepper
freshly ground allspice
lemon juice
For the brine
350 g/12 oz rock or sea salt
175 g/6 oz brown sugar
25 g/1 oz saltpetre
3 litres/5 pints of water
For the bouillon
1 large onion, coarsely chopped, some skin reserved
1 thyme sprig
3-4 parsley sprigs

1 mace blade
2 cloves
4 juniper berries, lightly crushed
nutmeg (end pieces, too small for grating, are ideal)
6 black peppercorns, lightly crushed
2 garlic cloves, peeled but left whole
1 celery stick
For the mustard sauce
2 tablespoons coarse-ground mustard powder
1½ tablespoons cider vinegar
2 teaspoons honey
2 tablespoons sweet, fortified wine – sherry, Marsala, Madeira (ginger wine is also good) – plus extra

Hand and spring joints are often pre-cut and quite large, so if you don't have a butcher who will cut it to size for you, buy a blade. To make the brine, bring all the ingredients to the boil and simmer – quite hard – for about 20 minutes, skimming off the scum occasionally. Strain and leave to cool then pour into a large earthenware crock or bowl. Add the pork joint and the trotters, making sure all are completely covered by brine, then weight them down – an old round bread board is ideal for this (it must of course be scrupulously clean) with a non-porous rock or stone on top, or else a heavy china bowl. Leave for 24 hours (longer if more convenient, but the meat may then need soaking before cooking to rid it of excessive salt).

Drain the meat, then place in a large pan, add the bouillon ingredients and plenty of cold water to cover. Bring to the boil, cover, and simmer at the gentlest of heats for 2-2½ hours. Remove the meat from the pan and cool. Strain the stock and taste. If it is quite salty, simply season – fairly highly – with freshly ground white pepper and allspice, then stir in the lemon juice –1 whole small lemon should do. If the stock is not too salty, then reduce by hard boiling, tasting every 5 minutes, to about 600 ml/1 pint, before seasoning.

Pick out all the meat from the trotters, discarding the skin and gristle. Take the meat off the main joint and chop finely. Do not be tempted to mince or chop it in a food processor – you will have a nasty mush on your hands. Taste the meat for salt, no extra should be needed, unless it was not brined. Place in a large bowl, round cake tin or loaf tin, then pour over enough seasoned stock to cover well, mixing thoroughly. Leave to cool, then cover with greaseproof paper and weight it with a plate (or another loaf tin) which will fit just inside your bowl or tin. Chill for 12-24 hours (it can be left for 2-3 days).

About one hour before serving, make the sauce (of medieval origin, taken from *The Forme of Curye*). Heat the honey, gently, with the vinegar and sweet wine. Plunge the bottom of the pan in cold water to cool quickly, then stir the mixture into the mustard powder. Leave for 30 minutes, by which time the mustard will have thickened considerably. You can either serve it as it is, or thin it down with a little extra wine as you please. Richard II's cook made 'it thynne with wyne' – we prefer it thicker, but this does depend on the powder's absorbing capacity, the time it has been left and your taste. Serves 8-10

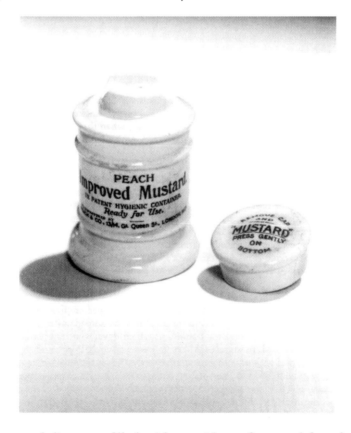

Peach's mustard dispenser filled with cartridges of mustard from below.
The scoop on top allows a knife to fit. *c.*1860s

BLACK PUDDING AND APPLE FRITTERS WITH MUSTARD AND APPLE JUICE SAUCE

In nearly all the medieval illuminated manuscripts which depict the great slaughter, there appears in the background a group of people making black puddings. These had to be made swiftly after the kill since fresh blood was of the essence – a point still agreed upon by the black-pudding makers of today.

For the best of these we have – once again – to turn to the North, to the old market towns of Bury, in Lancashire, and Barnsley, in Yorkshire, with their 'black pudding' stalls: Chadwicks, established in Bury in 1865, and Albert Hirst, their Barnsley rival – one of the few Englishmen to excel at the black pudding contests held in Mortagne-au-Perch where black puddings are serious business. Wiltshire, long famous for its pigs, has black puddings too – slender and elegant, like the puddings of the Shires rather than the fat and round shapes preferred in the North. Ireland has her own version, drisheen, similar to the French *boudin*. Unlike the French, no one on this side of the Channel marries apples to these blood sausages – despite our predilection for apple sauce and pork. Yet it is a natural partnership, the cleanness of the apple cutting through the richness of the pudding. Apple pancakes are good, so, too, simply sautéed slices of apple, but best of all are these apple fritters much loved by the medievals.

About 350 g/12 oz black pudding, sliced	¼ teaspoon arrowroot
lemon juice	*For the fritters*
For the sauce	3 small Cox's apples
100 ml/3½ fl oz mild chicken stock	1 large egg
100 ml/3½ fl oz apple juice, unsweetened	275 g/10 oz flour
	pinch of salt
2-3 teaspoons Dijon mustard	oil for frying

Squeeze a little lemon juice over the black puddings and leave aside. Heat the chicken stock and apple juice gently. Mix 2 teaspoons mustard with a little warm stock to a thin paste, then stir into the pan. Mix the arrowroot with a little cold water and reserve.

Make the batter by beating the egg with 225 ml/8 fl oz cold water until frothy, then fold in the flour whisking thoroughly until lump-free and smooth. Or simply combine the whole lot in a food processor. Core and peel the apples then slice. Pour about half the batter into a shallow dish, add the apples and turn them over several times to coat thoroughly, adding a little more batter if necessary. (Make pancakes with the leftover batter – easier than measuring half an egg!)

Pour a good inch of oil into a wide pan and heat gently until just beginning to smoke. Put the black pudding under a medium grill. When the oil is hot, add a few slices of apple – don't overcrowd the pan or they'll stick together. Cook for 2-3 minutes each side until golden and puffy. Drain on to absorbent paper and cook the rest, meanwhile turning the black pudding. Turn the heat up under the sauce, when just simmering whisk in the arrowroot to thicken very slightly (this is a thin dipping sauce). Pour into small bowls. Drain the remaining apple fritters and serve at once with the hot black pudding. Serves 4

CALVES' LIVER WITH LIME JUICE, PINE KERNELS AND MUSTARD

Calves' liver today vies with, and sometimes beats, steak in price. However it is one of the finest offals and deserves luxurious treatment. And if the price is too daunting, you can use lamb's liver (pig is a little strong in flavour for this dish) *provided* it is cut finely – almost onion-skin thin – and soaked in milk for about half an hour before cooking. Without a very obliging butcher, the best thing to do is buy the liver in a piece (about 450 g/1 lb for 4), lightly freeze, then cut it yourself.

450-550 g/1-1¼ lb calves' liver, cut very thinly
a few strips of lime zest, pith removed
juice of 2 fresh limes
1-2 teaspoons mild Dijon mustard
Maldon salt
freshly ground black pepper
50 g/2 oz unsalted butter
50 g/2 oz pine nuts
1 tablespoon sweet sherry
a little finely chopped parsley

Lightly wash the liver in cold water just to remove any blood. Shred the lime zest, blanch in boiling water for 3-4 minutes, drain and reserve. Mix together the lime juice and mustard and dip the liver slices into the juice before lightly seasoning with salt and pepper.

Melt the butter in a large heavy frying pan. When it is bubbling add the pine nuts and cook for a minute, tossing until pink. Remove with a slotted spoon and reserve.

Add the liver to the pan and cook quickly on both sides – 30-45 seconds per side will be enough if it has been finely cut. It should be just lightly pink on the inside and golden without. Put on a serving plate, add the lime juice mixture and sherry to the pan, bubble for another minute then pour over the liver. Scatter on the nuts, the lime zest and the parsley and serve immediately. This is not a dish to be kept waiting. Serves 4

VEAL KIDNEYS SAUTÉED WITH JUNIPER BERRIES, SAGE, WHITE WINE AND MUSTARD

Devilled kidneys, or steak and kidney pie, tend to be our answers to kidneys. Nothing wrong in that: they are perfectly good dishes, particularly for pig's kidneys which are stronger in flavour and better suited to such rumbustious treatment. But veal kidneys possess a certain delicacy, requiring greater subtlety.

4 small or 2 large veal kidneys	8 juniper berries, lightly crushed
25 g/1 oz unsalted butter	3 small fresh sage leaves, finely
1 tablespoon olive oil	chopped and lightly crushed
Maldon salt	150 ml/¼ pint fruity white wine
freshly ground black pepper	½ teaspoon mild Dijon mustard

Remove the fat from around the kidneys (keep it and render for future occasions) then slip off the thin outer membrane. Cut in half through the middle and snip out the fat from the 'heart'. Cut, slightly on the diagonal, into thin slices. Melt the butter with the oil in a large frying pan, *lightly* season the kidneys with salt and pepper then add to the pan and cook, flipping over the slices for about 45 seconds – they should be opaque in colour with tiny droplets of blood on the surface. Remove to a serving dish. Add the juniper berries and sage leaves, then pour in the wine. Raise the heat and bubble fiercely for 30 seconds, then whisk in the mustard. Do not be tempted to add more – it should hardly taste. Pour over the meat and serve at once. Croûtons are the classic garnish, particularly nice if dipped into finely chopped parsley when just out of the frying pan. And, in an ideal world, Gewürztraminer would be the wine used. Drink the rest of the bottle with the kidneys. Serves 4

BRAISED LAMB TONGUES

Neats' tongue (ox tongue) was a highly popular dish and tongue was also used as an ingredient in the original, and complex, mince pies. François Misson wrote about 'Christmas Pye … being eaten every-where … it is a most learned Mixture of Neats-tongues, Chicken, Eggs, Sugar, Raisins, Lemon and Orange, various Kinds of Spicery …' Not quite our taste today and, with ox tongue the price it is, rather an extravagance. Lambs' tongues, however, are economical and we can take a tip from the flavourings in that pie, for orange and lemon juices add a nice touch of sweet sharpness to the sauce.

700 g/1½ lb lambs' tongues, root
  end trimmed

Maldon salt

2 tablespoons olive oil

25 g/1 oz unsalted butter

6 leeks, cut in half lengthways

6 large carrots, quartered lengthways

24 small button onions, peeled but
  left whole

6 inner celery stalks

50 g/2 oz streaky bacon, derinded
  and cut across into thin strips

3-4 garlic cloves, peeled but left
  whole

juice of 1 large sweet orange or,
  even better, 2 blood oranges

juice of 1 small lemon

1 bay leaf

1 thyme sprig

small posy of parsley, stalks cut off
  and tied in a bundle, curly tops
  finely chopped and reserved

freshly ground black pepper

freshly ground allspice

1 tablespoon Moutarde Soyer (p.51)

½ teaspoon tomato purée

2 tablespoons *beurre manié* (equal
  volumes of flour and butter
  mashed together to a paste)

Put the tongues in a large bowl and cover with cold water, mixing in 1 table-spoon of salt to every litre/1¾ pints water. Leave overnight. This mild brining vastly improves the flavour. Drain the meat and place in a pan covered with fresh cold water. Slowly bring to the boil, skim off any scum, then cover and simmer on the lowest possible heat for about 1½ hours. Remove the meat and leave until cool enough to handle, reserving the stock.

Trim the bones and any gristle from the root end of the tongues then peel by slitting down the middle with a sharp pointed knife. The skin should then eas-ily peel away. Either cut the tongues in half through the middle or into thickish diagonal slices.

Heat the oil and butter in a large flameproof casserole, add the onions and sweat for 5 minutes, then add the leeks, carrots, celery stalks, garlic and bacon. Glaze the vegetables then make into a flat bed for the meat.

Taste the reserved stock: if it seems salty, bearing in mind that the final sauce will be reduced by a good third, measure out 300 ml/½ pint and make up to a generous 450 ml/¾ pint with water. If it is not too salty, then simply measure out the full amount. Pour over the vegetables, add the orange and lemon juices and the herbs, including the parsley stalks but not the curly tops. Bring the liq-uid to boiling point, lower the heat and lay the tongues on their bed. Season with black pepper and a little allspice, lay a buttered greaseproof paper over the tongues, then cover the pan and cook very gently for a good hour, until the meat is quite tender.

Remove the tongues from the pan, then the vegetables, arranging them on a large serving dish and placing the meat on top. Cover with foil and keep warm in a low oven.

Bring the juices in the pan to a rapid boil and reduce by about a third. Mix the mustard with the tomato purée and whisk into the sauce, then add the *beurre manié*, little by little and constantly whisking until the sauce is thickened. You may not need all the *beurre manié* – this depends both on your reduction and preference as to thickness. Pour over the tongues and scatter with the chopped parsley. Season again with a little more black pepper and freshly ground allspice. Serves 4

NOISETTES OF VEAL WITH MOSTARDA DI VENEZIA

One of the problems in buying veal is that different countries joint the animal in different ways. Properly, the noisettes, or medallions, are taken from the 'silverside' – a lengthwise-cut, small joint from the back of the leg above the knuckle. It looks very similar to the fillet in shape and size, although close comparison will reveal that the medallions have a more pronounced grain. To add to the confusion, it is often called the fillet which truly comes from the inside of the loin (like beef), although technically any boneless cut can be called a fillet. Even more confusingly, the *noix de veau* is a larger joint, also cut lengthwise, but higher up from the chump end of the loin (similar to topside of beef). This will not do for your noisettes although, if your butcher follows the traditional English cuts for veal, you are not likely to encounter that problem for the leg is usually cut *crosswise* into roasting joints. The obvious solution is to know your butcher and which method of butchering he practices, and make sure he tells you whether the medallions are from the leg or the true fillet. The latter is fine of course, but will probably be more expensive and will not need quite so long a cooking time.

6 noisettes of veal, about 2 cm/¾ inch thick	50 g/2 oz Parma ham, cut into fine dice
Maldon salt	4 tablespoons Mostarda di Venezia (p.58)
freshly ground black pepper	lemon juice
40 g/1½ oz unsalted butter	Dijon mustard (optional)
200 ml/7 fl oz white wine	

Lightly flatten the noisettes, season with a little salt and black pepper and leave aside. Melt the butter gently, and when sizzling add the veal. Cook for 1 minute each side then pour in the wine. Bubble for a minute or two, then sprinkle in the diced ham. Turn the heat low and simmer, covered, very gently for 20-25 minutes until the meat is very tender when pierced with a skewer. Meanwhile, mix the Mostarda di Venezia with a tablespoon or so of lemon juice to lightly sharpen.

Transfer the noisettes to a warmed dish, add the Mostarda to the pan and stir over a high heat until bubbling and very hot. Taste and add a touch more lemon if necessary and a spot of Dijon mustard if you wish. Serve at once. Serves 6

FRICASSÉE OF VEAL WITH FENNEL AND MUSTARD SEED

Fricassées entered our kitchens in the late sixteenth century, quite a few years before the *daube*. Since we now tend to lump the two together with ragouts and casseroles to denote any kind of stew, its earlier appearance has no apparent significance until we remember that the fork at this time was a rare, and treasured, implement of the very rich – mainly used to eat pears and ginger in syrup. And *fricasser*, from the early French, originally meant to mince, later to chop very small, thus rendering meat suitable as 'spoon' fare. Early gravies were thin, often simply highly spiced wine, reminiscent of medieval potages – though without the mustard that Apicius recommends for fricassée. By the late seventeenth century (when forks were more familiar) the meat was still chopped, though not so small, and the gravy had become a thicker sauce with more subtle flavourings.

900 g/2 lb pie veal, trimmed of any fat and gristle
2 tablespoons flour
1 tablespoon black pepper, freshly ground
1 tablespoon oregano
Maldon salt
3 tablespoons olive oil
1 tablespoon unsalted butter
3 tablespoons pine nuts
1 tablespoon white mustard seed

1 large onion, finely chopped
75 ml/3 fl oz Cinzano or dry white wine
600 ml/1 pint veal or chicken stock
3 fresh fennel stalks, feathery sprigs removed and reserved, or 2 dried fennel stalks and 5-6 sprigs fresh fennel
150 ml/¼ pint double cream
lemon juice
2-3 tablespoons Dijon mustard

Mix the flour with the pepper, oregano and a good seasoning of salt, then sprinkle all over the veal. Heat the oil, add the pine nuts and cook for a minute until pink, then remove. Add the mustard seeds to the pan and cook, covered, until they start to spit. Drain them and reserve with the pine nuts, return the oil to the pan, add the butter and, when melted, the veal. Sear lightly. Remove the meat, add the onions and sweat, gently, for 10 minutes.

Return the meat to the pan, pour in the Cinzano and bubble hard for 1 minute, then pour over the stock. Bury the fennel stalks in the meat, cover the pan and cook, the merest hint of a simmer, for 2 hours until the meat is meltingly tender. Remove the fennel stalks. Beat the cream with a squeeze of lemon juice and the mustard and stir into the pan. Cook over a highish heat for a couple of minutes until the sauce thickens slightly then pile into a tureen. Sprinkle with the reserved pine nuts and mustard seed. Chop the fennel sprigs very finely and strew on top. Serve at once. Serves 4-6

COLD LOIN OF VEAL WITH SOUR MUSTARD SAUCE

Loin of veal has always been considered one of the great or 'gross' meats: usually roasted, to be served, said Master Chiquart, with 'the proper sauce'. Often this was a Camelyne sauce – sweet, spicy and sharp, with raisins, currants, ginger, cloves and vinegar. Italy uses veal perhaps most deliciously in the glorious Vitello Tonnato – cold veal with a tunny sauce. We've adapted that principle, poaching rather than roasting the veal to ensure maximum tenderness and succulence, adding a sour cream mustard sauce, spiced with the medieval flavourings.

900 g/2 lb loin of veal, boned weight
50 g/2 oz unsalted butter
2 tablespoons olive oil
300 ml/½ pint dry white wine
1 bay leaf
1 sage sprig
2 parsley sprigs
freshly ground black pepper
Maldon salt
finely chopped chervil

For the sauce
175 ml/6 fl oz soured cream
1-2 tablespoons lemon juice
1½ teaspoons icing sugar
1 slightly heaped tablespoon Dijon mustard
¼ teaspoon four-spice mixture (p.52)
25 mm/1 in piece fresh root ginger, peeled and grated

Roll and tie the veal into a neat sausage shape, then season lightly with salt and black pepper. Melt the butter with the oil in a pan into which the meat will fit snugly. Add the veal and brown on all sides, lower the heat, add the herbs and pour in the wine. Bring to a simmer, then cook, covered, *most* gently, for 1½-2 hours until the meat is very tender. If necessary, use a heat-diffusing mat, checking the pan occasionally and adding a little water (or stock ideally) to prevent the pan from becoming dry. You don't want too much juice at the finish of cooking, but you do want 4-5 tablespoons nicely concentrated liquor.

Remove the meat from the pan and cool. Add 2-3 tablespoons water to the juices in the pan and deglaze over a high heat. Cool slightly. Mix together all the sauce ingredients, then whisk in the cooking liquor. Slice the veal thickly, arrange on a platter and pour over the sauce. Leave for at least 2 hours before serving, liberally sprinkled with finely chopped chervil. Serves 4-6

The Recipe Book of the Mustard Club

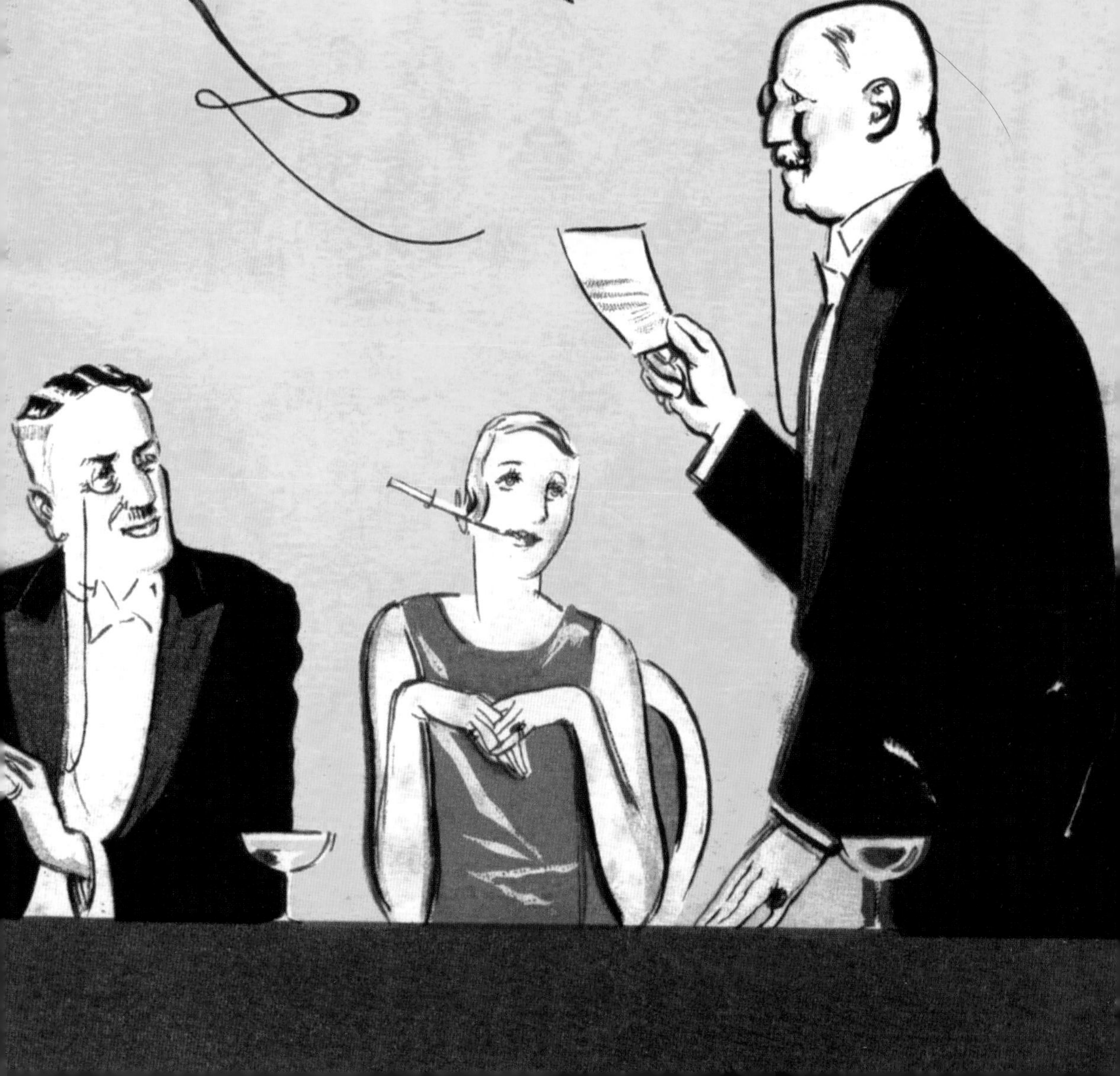

Vegetables and Pickles

'Very true,' said the Duchess: 'flamingoes and mustard both bite. And the moral of that is – " Birds of a feather flock together."'

'Only mustard isn't a bird,' Alice remarked.

'Right, as usual,' said the Duchess: 'what a clear way you have of putting things!'

'It's a mineral, I think,' said Alice.

'Of course it is,' said the Duchess, who seemed ready to agree to everything that Alice said: 'there's a large mustard-mine near here. And the moral of that is – "The more there is of mine, the less there is of yours."'

'Oh, I know!' exclaimed Alice, who had not attended to this last remark, 'it's a vegetable. It doesn't look like one, but it is.'

ALICE'S ADVENTURES IN WONDERLAND, LEWIS CARROLL

Throughout history, mustard is mentioned as being grown for its leaves, and it still is in China, India, parts of Europe, Africa and the south-eastern states of America, where considerable quantities are produced. No one knows when exactly the plant started to be cultivated for its greenery, although it was first introduced as such into Louisiana by the French. The Negro slaves soon took it into their kitchen – the peppery taste perhaps reminding them of home. It quickly became a staple and made an early – and lasting – marriage with salt pork and bacon, still a classic dish of the Black South. Nutritionally, however, it has occasionally caused problems in poor, inland communities. For mustard greens contain minute traces of 'goitrogens', which, in people on an iodine-deficient diet eating vast quantities of the leaf, can affect the thyroid's ability to use iodine, thus causing the gland to swell. The problem is rare and, for most, mustard greens are highly beneficial providing a good source of calcium, Vitamins A and C, iron and potassium. The flavour, raw, is pungently biting and a few young leaves mixed with other salad greens add a nice pep. Cooked, the flavour is less pronounced – a mildly peppery spinach would be an apt description. The Chinese – who frequently use mustard greens as a vegetable – also have a spinach salad which is dressed with mustard, sesame oil and vinegar which is remarkably similar in taste to a cooked mustard leaf salad.

The French seem first to have appreciated the mustard plant only for its vegetable qualities: Charlemagne (c. AD 800) merely states of mustard that it is a plant whose leaves can be eaten raw or cooked. There is not a mention anywhere of its use as a spicing ingredient. Centuries later, the leaf was still important in its own right. Thomas Jefferson appreciated it highly and grew it in his garden.

The precedents were ancient. Aesculapius wrote of the 'green plant' that it was a 'wholesome and agreeable herb', while Apicius has a 'dish of field vegetables' – a purée thickened with beaten eggs – which, according to some translations, contains 'green mustard' though other sources state that should read 'green peppers'. We do know, however, that the Romans pickled mustard leaves in vinegar and in AD 300 Diocletian noted that his subjects in the East ate mustard as a condiment *and* a vegetable. Far away, in China, the ancients were also pickling mustard greens. They still do, and their famous 'snow pickle' is a classic winter dish.

It is as a component in pickling, rather than as a pickle itself, that mustard has had one of its oldest and most consistent roles. The white seed in particular has highly preservative qualities, and is one of the prime ingredients in pickling spice mixes. Menandiers, around 300 BC, was pickling turnips in vinegar with mustard seed, a relish the Romans enjoyed as an appetizer: as a pickle they added mustard seed to beetroots.

Pride of place for pickles and chutneys though must go to India. The use of the seed in their pickles – hot, mild or sweet – is legion, although on fast days in certain regions only pickles without mustard seed are permitted. So, too, with the *tarkas* – a mixture of seeds fried in hot oil, often with chilli and/or garlic. Mustard seed is a prime component of these, except on a fast day, when cumin is substituted.

However, for normal pickling purposes, mustard is vital. Perhaps not in such quantities as those proposed in a charming little pamphlet probably from the twenties: 'Receipts for Cooking the Most Favourite Dishes in general use In India, Also for Preparing Chatney and India Pickle by Hadjee Allee Native of Calcutta'. Three-quarters of a pound of mustard (seed and paste) in addition to four ounces of cayenne and eleven ounces of other spices, to a mere six pints of vinegar is a trifle alarming. However, modern recipes from Bengal for vegetables with mustard are enticing. Interestingly, the combination of ground mustard and sugar — so beloved of medieval Europe — also appears here: especially in dishes of mixed vegetables, cooked in a little oil, the mustard and sugar then stirred in at the finish.

For vegetable curries, mustard oil is considered the best cooking medium, and the seeds are also used to spice many individual vegetable dishes. Moving northward, one finds the leaf — 'mustard spinach' — prominent on the table, most notably in the famous Punjabi dish, Sarson ka Saag (p.199).

If you mention mustard greens to the British, most will think of mustard and cress. Yet the greenery here is actually the cress, mustard supplying its seed. But one can also sow the seed (white) on damp absorbent paper and within a couple of days harvest a little forest of sprouts. Delicious for scattering like parsley, and perfect for delicate sandwiches.

MUSTARD GREENS IN COCONUT MILK

China, as well as the American South, combines mustard greens with salt pork in a delicious soup. And many of the Caribbean islands have a traditional soup/stew with salt pork, crab and coconut milk combined with another green leaf often called callaloo (actually from the taro plant). Crab contains iodine — the ideal nutritional partner for mustard greens — and coconut milk sweetens their peppery flavour.

450 g/1 lb mustard greens, washed and shredded finely
1.5 litres/2½ pints chicken stock
3 onions, finely chopped
3 garlic cloves, crushed
1 thyme sprig, leaves stripped off the stalk

125 g/4 oz salt belly of pork, finely diced
175 g/6 oz white crabmeat
50 g/2 oz creamed coconut
freshly ground white pepper
Maldon salt (if necessary)

Pack the greens into a large saucepan, pour over the chicken stock, then add the onions, garlic, thyme and pork belly. Bring to the boil, then simmer gently for 30 minutes until the meat and greens are tender (mustard greens will never go completely limp like chard or spinach but they shouldn't be tough and chewy).

Add the crab and the creamed coconut, raise the heat slightly and stir for a few minutes to start melting the coconut. Simmer for a further 20 minutes, stirring occasionally and checking that the coconut has completely dissolved.

Season generously with pepper, add salt if necessary — this will depend on how salty the pork was — then pour into a large tureen. Serves 4-6

MUSTARD SPINACH – SARSON KA SAAG

When India was partitioned in 1947, the displaced refugees were often given a bag of mustard seed – as a 'start in life'. Quickly and easily, the leaves provided a nutritious food, the seeds an income and next year's harvest – their oil could even be used as fuel. This dish, using the greens, is one of the Punjab's most famous though is rarely met with in the West.

900 g/2 lb mustard greens
2 turnips, finely chopped
2 celery stalks, finely chopped
3 tablespoons vegetable oil
2 large onions, finely chopped

25 mm/1 inch piece fresh root
  ginger, grated
¼ teaspoon chilli powder (or less)
Maldon salt

Wash the greens and shred finely, then shake off excess water. Pack into a large saucepan then sprinkle over the turnip and celery. Cook very gently, until softened – the greens should produce enough liquid for the cooking but check after 10 minutes and add a little water if necessary. 30-40 minutes stewing should be enough. Purée in a blender then return to the pan. Heat the oil until nearly smoking, add the onions and ginger and cook until golden. Stir in the chilli powder, then pour the mixture over the spinach purée. Season with a little salt, stir lightly and serve immediately. Serves 4

GREEN BEANS WITH MUSTARD

A curious similarity is displayed in two recipes for green beans with mustard from two kitchens many thousands of miles apart. Eastern India has a traditional dish of beans mixed with a mustard seed, garlic and green chilli paste, the whole garnished with a *tarka* of fried mustard seed and chilli powder. Apicius cooked his beans in broth, then added a paste of mustard seed, nuts, rue, honey and cumin. His garnish was a light sprinkling of vinegar. We have married the two recipes, using Roman mustard to provide the nutty element and adding cumin to the *tarka* to give an oriental flavour.

450 g/1 lb green beans, topped
  and tailed, then sliced diagonal-
  ly into 25 mm/1 inch pieces
Maldon salt
½-1 small green chilli, seeded and
  finely chopped

1 fat garlic clove, crushed
1 teaspoon Roman mustard (p.53)
2 tablespoons mustard oil
½ teaspoon brown mustard seed
½ teaspoon cumin seeds

Cook the beans in salted boiling water for 5-8 minutes, depending on their age. They should be tender but with a slight bite still. Drain them and return the empty pan to the heat with 1 tablespoon of oil.

Blend the chilli, garlic and mustard together with a pinch of salt, add to the pan and stir-fry for 30 seconds. Add the beans and stir thoroughly, over a very low heat. In another small pan, heat the remaining oil, add the mustard seed and cumin, cover, and cook until they start to splutter. Pour over the beans and serve immediately. Serves 4

BRAISED LEEKS WITH MUSTARD

Leeks, onions and garlic all display a great affinity with mustard, the spice greatly enhancing the sweetness of the Allium family. Perhaps it is not so surprising: the leaves of many of the Cruciferae contain oil of garlic, and the Alliums have certain chemical substances also found in mustard seed.

900 g/2 lb medium leeks, washed
  and trimmed
300 ml/½ pint medium dry white
  wine, dry cider or chicken stock

2 teaspoons Dijon mustard
40 g/1½ oz unsalted butter
freshly ground black pepper
Maldon salt

Cut the leeks into 4 cm/1½ inch lengths. Arrange them, standing upright, in a large, fairly shallow and preferably circular dish, packing them tightly together (see illustration below). Mix the cooking liquid of your choice with the mustard and pour over, then dot with flakes of butter. Season, generously with black pepper, very lightly with salt.

Cook in the oven at 180°C/350°F/Gas Mark 4 for 30-40 minutes until the leeks are very tender and about two-thirds of the liquid is absorbed. Should there be any leftovers, they make a heavenly soup. Serves 4

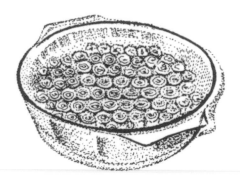

Braised leeks with mustard

STEWED RED CABBAGE WITH MUSTARD CREAM

Despite other nations' views on British vegetable cooking, we have an extraordinarily rich heritage of delicious and seemingly, nowadays, unusual vegetable recipes. Pickled red cabbage seems to be the staple today: braised with apples, sugar and vinegar the vegetable is acknowledged as a good 'foreign' accompaniment to pork or goose. Yet it was a commonplace eighteenth- and nineteenth-century dish, simply stewed in butter with peppers – black and cayenne – with either gravy or a dash of vinegar added at the finish. Eliza Acton adds cream to Savoy cabbage; we have moved the idea to red cabbage, adding juniper berries and mustard.

1 small red cabbage, core removed	freshly ground black pepper
125 g/4 oz unsalted butter	150 ml/¼ pint double cream
8 juniper berries	1½ teaspoons Dijon mustard
Maldon salt	

Shred the cabbage very finely, wash under cold water, then shake lightly. As Maria Rundell charmingly puts it in *Domestic Cookery* (1806), the cabbage needs no water 'but what hangs about it'.

Melt the butter in a large heavy-bottomed pan (essential, to prevent burning), and crush the juniper berries. When the butter begins to bubble, add the berries to the pan, then tip in the cabbage and stir thoroughly. Cover with a very well-fitting lid and cook over the lowest possible heat for 3-4 hours until the cabbage is meltingly tender. Check frequently, stirring to prevent sticking, and only add water (or a little stock) if absolutely vital. Season with salt and a good helping of freshly ground black pepper, then mix the mustard with the cream and pour into the pan.

Raise the heat and cook, stirring, until the cream is bubbling and has thoroughly coated the cabbage. Serves 4-6

STEWED CUCUMBERS IN MUSTARD CREAM

Cucumbers appeared in many guises in the eighteenth century: pickled, preserved, or in salads as today. They were also cooked – an idea we seem to have lost, but a good one, especially for those who are prone to indigestion after eating the vegetable raw. It is an excellent method for dealing with older cucumbers. Traditionally they were cooked in butter, or veal gravy, with sliced onions. Hannah Glasse added mustard – we've cut down on the butter, but added a touch of cream.

3 medium-sized cucumbers,
    peeled, seeded and cut into
    5 cm/2 inch strips
3 small onions, finely sliced
50 g/2 oz unsalted butter
3 tablespoons chicken or veal stock
1 mace blade

Maldon salt
freshly ground white pepper
100 ml/3½ fl oz double cream
lemon juice
1 teaspoon Dijon mustard
handful of finely chopped fresh
    chervil, parsley, fennel or tarragon

Melt the butter in a large pan, add the onions and sweat gently for 10 minutes. Add the cucumbers and sauté for 2 minutes, then stir in the stock, together with the mace blade, salt and a good grinding of white pepper. Cover the pan and stew gently for 6–10 minutes until the cucumber is soft but not mushy. Pour in the cream, add a squeezing of lemon juice, then stir in the mustard. Bubble for 1–2 minutes until the sauce is lightly thickened. Strew liberally with the herb of your choice and serve. Serves 6

POTATOES WITH MUSTARD SEEDS

Today there is a revival of interest in the potato: growers list varieties by the hundred, and it is once again, in many supermarkets and kitchens, being accorded the respect it received when Sir Francis Drake first brought it to England. We owe the partnership of mustard seed and potatoes to western India, where garlic, cumin, turmeric, tomatoes and chilli are also added to give a spicy bed for eggs. Here, in a much simplified recipe, they make a delicious course by themselves.

450 g/1 lb large new potatoes,
    scrubbed but not peeled
Maldon salt
1½ tablespoons peanut oil
1 small garlic clove

1 medium onion, very finely
    chopped
¼ teaspoon Dijon mustard
1 teaspoon brown mustard seed
finely chopped parsley or fresh
    coriander leaves

Boil the potatoes in salted water, drain and slice thickly. (If you must peel them, do so at this stage.)

Heat the oil in a large pan, add the onion and fry briskly until softened and golden. Crush the garlic with a pinch of salt and mix in the mustard. Add to the pan and cook for another 2 minutes to crisp the onions slightly and release the aroma of the garlic. Push to the sides of the pan. Add the mustard seeds, cover and cook until they start to spit. Add the potatoes, mixing gently so as not to break them up, then cook for a further 2 minutes until lightly browned. Pile on to a serving dish, scatter liberally with chopped parsley or coriander and serve. Serves 4-5

MUSTARD-STUFFED LOTUS ROOT

The lotus flower — so beloved of romantic writers and, floating on the lakes of Kashmir, of tourists — is more prosaically enjoyed by the orientals for its culinary qualities. The roots are used by both Indian and Chinese cooks, the latter also cooking the seeds and employing the leaves as a flavour-imparting wrapper for steamed foods. The roots are long, thin and, when cut across, reveal an intricate network of holes — ideal for stuffing as in this recipe from Elisabeth Lambert Ortiz's *Japanese Cookery*.

1 medium-sized lotus root, about 18 cm/7 inches in length (available canned from Chinese and Japanese food stores)
2 teaspoons rice vinegar
375 ml/13 fl oz light stock
¼ teaspoon soy sauce
¼ teaspoon salt
2 teaspoons mirin (Japanese rice wine)

3 tablespoons dry Japanese or English mustard
3 tablespoons white bean paste
1 teaspoon sugar
1 large egg yolk
1 small egg
50 g/2 oz flour
vegetable oil for frying

Peel the lotus root and drop into a pan of briskly boiling water and the vinegar. Simmer for 5 minutes, then drain. Return the pan to the heat, add the stock, soy sauce, salt and mirin together with the lotus root. Simmer for 5 minutes until the root is tender — there should be enough liquid to keep it covered. Remove the lotus root from the pan and cool.

Mix the mustard to a thick paste with 2-3 tablespoons hot water. Add the bean paste, sugar and egg yolk and mix until smooth. Using chopsticks and fingers, stuff the mixture into the holes running along the length of the root.

Break the egg into another bowl and whisk. Stir in 1 tablespoon of cold water, then add the flour mixing lightly with chopsticks to a batter. Coat the root with the batter.

In a heavy frying pan, heat enough oil to cover the root until bubbles form on chopsticks when they are stirred in the oil (180°C/350°F on a fat thermometer). Put the batter-coated lotus root into the pan and fry for 5 minutes, turning 2-3 times until lightly coloured. Lift out, drain on paper towels then cut into 15 mm/½ inch slices. Arrange on small plates. Serves 4

'CUCUMBERS PICKLED LIKE MANGOES'

Pickled mangoes reached Britain in the latter part of the seventeenth century and quickly attained great popularity. Since the fresh fruit was unobtainable, imitations soon appeared using cucumbers, marrows or melons as the base ingredient. The cucumber itself, although familiar to the Romans and possibly grown in English gardens during their occupation, had virtually disappeared until the fifteenth century when it was still considered a rarity. Although more widely cultivated over the next 200 years, it was still small and almost round (similar to a variety grown in Iran today) and therefore a more logical substitute than one might, at first, imagine. Oddly, when cucumbers were pickled as a preserve for the winter, there were no mustard seeds in the recipe. Only when they began to be pickled 'like mangoes' does the seed appear.

1 kg/2¼ lb small cucumbers, ideally pickling ones
2 teaspoons white mustard seed
4 large garlic cloves, very finely chopped
1 tablespoon freshly ground allspice
For the spiced vinegar
1.7 litres/3 pints white wine vinegar

2 teaspoons black peppercorns
2 tablespoons Maldon or rock salt
1 tablespoon allspice berries
5 cm/2 inch piece fresh ginger, peeled and finely sliced
2 teaspoons white mustard seed

Bring the vinegar to the boil with the pickling spices, remove from the heat and leave for 2-3 hours.

If you can get pickling cucumbers they merely need to be sliced lengthways and the seeds scooped out with an apple corer. Ordinary salad cucumbers will need to be cut into smaller lengths (to fit into the preserving jars) before deseeding. Mix together the mustard seed, garlic and freshly ground allspice, then pack into the spaces left by the seeds. Reassemble the cucumber pieces by tying two halves together with fine string and pack into sterilized jars.

Strain the vinegar, bring it again to the boil, then pour over the cucumbers. Cover the jars and leave for 24 hours. Drain off the vinegar, strain it (returning any floating spices to the jars) and heat to boiling point. Pour over the cucumbers, seal and again leave for a day. Repeat this procedure for 9 days by which time the cucumber should be 'of a good green'. You may need to add a little extra vinegar towards the end of the week. Keep for at least 3 weeks before use. Yield: about 1 kg/2¼ lb.

MANGO PICKLE

The pickled mangoes so popular with our ancestors cannot have been very hot, to judge by the cucumber/marrow recipes that abounded in imitation. Yet the traditional mango pickle of the Gujerati and Maharashtran kitchens in Western India is hot indeed – even this 'mild' version is not unpiquant, but the original recipe has 125 g/4 oz red chillies.

900 g/2 lb green mangoes
2-4 red chillies (to taste), seeded and finely chopped
2 teaspoons fenugreek seed
50 g/2 oz Maldon salt

3 tablespoons brown mustard seed
½ teaspoon ground asafoetida (available from Indian grocers)
1 tablespoon turmeric
450 ml/¾ pint vegetable oil

Cut the mangoes into quarters, slicing them away from the stone. It is almost impossible to do this job tidily, so do the best you can and place a bowl underneath to catch the juices. Chop the quarters coarsely, then scrape the remaining flesh off the stone and add to the bowl.

Blend the chillies with the fenugreek, salt and mustard seed – the mustard won't pulverize, but no matter – then mix into the asafoetida and turmeric. Bring the oil almost to boiling point and pour over the spice mixture. Stir into the mangoes, mixing quite thoroughly. Spoon the pickle into sterilized jars, making sure each has a good covering of oil. Cover and seal, then store in a cool place, shaking the jars well every day for a week. Yield: approximately 700 g/1½ lb.

BANANA, APPLE AND MUSTARD CHUTNEY

Intrigued by an Uncooked Apple and Banana Chutney in *The Apple Book* by Jane Simpson and Gill MacLennan, we added mustard and ground ginger. Very fruity, slightly piquant – extremely good.

3 medium-sized bananas, peeled and mashed
450 g/1 lb onions, peeled and chopped
450 g/1 lb cooking apples
450 g/1 lb sultanas
225 g/8 oz currants

450 g/1 lb brown sugar
300 ml/½ pint red wine vinegar
1 teaspoon Maldon salt
½ teaspoon cayenne pepper
1 teaspoon freshly grated dried ginger root
250 g/9 oz Dijon mustard

Put the bananas and onions into a large bowl. Peel, core and chop the apples – add to the bowl. Then stir in all the remaining ingredients. Mix very thoroughly, then pot in sterilized jars. Keep for at least 2 weeks before using. The authors of the original recipe state that it will keep for up to a year. With the added mustard the preserving powers should be even greater though we found that, once opened, a jar rarely lasted very long. Yield: about 2.5 kg/5½ lb.

PICCALILLI

Piccalilli is probably the most famous pickle of all – and certainly the best known mustard pickle, although it is actually turmeric which gives it that bright yellow colour. The recipe, and the name, have changed little through the years. *The Receipt Book* by A. Blencowe (1694) gives the delightful title 'To Pickle Lila – an Indian Pickle'.

900 g/2 lb cauliflower florets –
    about 1.4 kg/3 lb unprepared
    cauliflower
450 g/1 lb pickling onions, peeled
    and quartered
450 g/1 lb carrots, cut into fine
    matchsticks
450 g/1 lb white cabbage, shredded
1 large cucumber, cut into chunks
400 g/14 oz coarse rock or sea salt
1.2 litres/2 pints cider vinegar
2 tablespoons mustard powder

3 tablespoons white mustard seed
4 tablespoons brown mustard seed
3 mace blades
6 cloves
1 tablespoon turmeric
10 cm/4 inch piece fresh root ginger, peeled and grated
1 teaspoon freshly ground allspice
4 fat garlic cloves, cut into fine
    slivers
175 g/6 oz caster sugar
2 tablespoons cornflour

Place the vegetables in a very large bowl (or 2), sprinkle with the salt and leave for 24 hours. Drain off the brine, rinse the vegetables in cold water. Put the vinegar, with the remaining ingredients except the cornflour, into a preserving pan (not aluminium) and bring to the boil. Turn the heat low, add all the vegetables and simmer gently for about 15-20 minutes until they are cooked but still have a 'crunch'. Mix the cornflour to a paste with 2 tablespoons cold water, stir into the pan and boil for a couple of minutes, stirring, to lightly thicken the juices. Ladle into sterilized jars and keep for at least 1 month before using. Yield: about 2.7 kg/6 lb.

Puddings et al

I'm mad about mustard – even on custard!

OGDEN NASH

Although it was a special 'mystery' pudding that started this mustard quest, we did wonder in the beginning how mustard would fare at the meal's end. Savouries, obviously, are no stranger to the condiment, particularly those of a cheesy nature. Welsh Rarebit is famous, the Scottish, English and Buck versions perhaps less so today. Devilled dishes of sardines, herring roes, crab, kidneys or lobsters all knew mustard and were popular dinner finales in the 1930s.

Mustard is no newcomer either to baking: cheese scones and straws spring immediately to mind. Mustard bread is perhaps less obvious, but the partnership is old. Medieval and Victorian peasant alike enjoyed bread and dripping but, with no dripping to hand, the rough dark brown bread would often be enlivened with a dip into the mustard pot. In certain parts of the North of England, a pinch of mustard was – indeed still is – mixed with the dripping before it went on to the bread. And Drover's Bread (a kind of northern Cornish pasty) was made with a mustard-spiced dough, stuffed with mustard-seasoned steak. Whether Northerners would knowingly countenance mustard in their gingerbread, or parkin, is a moot point. But undoubtedly at some stage they would have consumed it, since ginger was often adulterated with mustard to ease its exorbitant price. And a conscious addition of mustard makes for a deliciously spicy gingerbread (p.212). The French equivalent, *pain d'épices*, though usually translated as gingerbread, should perhaps be rendered literally – spiced bread – since it rarely seems to contain ginger. Dijon is the centre today for most of France's *pain d'épices*, and not surprisingly mustard is often one of the spices.

Tea time can see mustard with other partners. Chocolate's flavour is considerably strengthened and coffee, too, is given a boost. Frederick the Great, an inordinate coffee drinker by all accounts, always added a pinch of mustard to his brew to bring out the flavour. It is curious, this chemical reaction that mustard has with certain flavourings and spices. Those with a bite – ginger, pepper, cayenne – are themselves heightened but also allow mustard's nip to come through. Where sweetness is of the essence – chocolate, nutmeg, cinnamon, all-spice – mustard melds into the background leaving merely the full glory of the spice concerned.

The tang of the seed in Mostarda di Venezia or Cremona is of course quite noticeable, though for those in ignorance of mustard's presence, the flavour is not definable. This led us to experiment with other fruits. Chestnuts, curiously, became quite chocolatey; mango, rhubarb and plums were intense in their fruitiness whilst pears added to a mustard blancmange (p.210) proved Ogden Nash oddly correct. But the flavour of the mustard was greatly softened, absorbed to a good degree by the bland sweetness of the fruit leaving the custard with a definite – though again indefinable – piquancy. Bananas are another fruit made intense by mustard, which is useful for making banana bread with less than very black bananas. We found an odd recommendation, made by a Mustard Club member, of mustard with Christmas pudding. Yet strangely, a little dab of mustard spread on hot Christmas puddings does bring out the full richness of the fruits.

There is a huge field here open to exploration: chocolate and rhubarb mousses – add mustard to the melting chocolate before mixing with puréed rhubarb and whipped cream; iced mousses of *mascarpone* and Mostarda di Venezia; perhaps some Mostarda di Cremona mixed into a fresh fruit salad. Most simply, one could combine the sweet and the savoury with a beautifully mature farmhouse Cheddar, a pot of Matthew's mustard (p.55) and some perfectly ripe fresh fruit. With a glass of fine port, or a lightly chilled, slightly fruity, Francken wine – what better way to end this pursuit of mustard?

Mostarda di Venezia and mascarpone served with La Colomba in Venice

LA COLOMBA'S 'MYSTERY SPECIAL'

La Colomba in Venice, home of the pud that started it all, is enchantingly decorated with paintings of doves – all originals from great artists including Braque
and de Chirico. The special dessert echoes the theme, and is served in the form
of two doves: pastry beaks and wings cleverly transform the spoonfuls of soft
cheese and quince purée into tiny little birds.

Mascarpone – the soft creamy cheese so often used in Italy for sweet dishes –
is simplicity itself to make but a thermometer is essential. Over- or under-heat-
ing will spell disaster.

450 g/1 lb Mostarda di Venezia   *For the* mascarpone
  (p.58)   1.7 litres/3 pints double cream
                                              Scant ½ teaspoon tartaric acid

To make the *mascarpone*, start the day before. Pour the cream into the top half of
a double boiler or into a bowl placed over a pan of simmering water. On a medium heat, bring the cream to a temperature of 80°C/180°F. Remove the pan
from the heat and add the tartaric acid (a vegetable acid commonly used in baking powders and fizzy drinks, available from chemists). Stir for 30 seconds, then
take the top part of the double boiler, or bowl, off the hot water. Stir for another 2 minutes, then pour the cream into a cheesecloth-lined large bowl. Leave in
a cool place, or the lowest shelf of the refrigerator, for 12 hours before using.

    To assemble the pudding, simply put 2-3 tablespoons each of the Mostarda and
the *mascarpone* on to individual serving dishes and chill lightly. Decorate if you
wish with tiny shortcrust pastry beaks and wings to make little doves. Serves 6

MUSTARD AND PEAR RING

We found the opening quote and illustration almost simultaneously. We wondered about mustard and custard, and then came upon an American recipe for
a savoury blancmange to be served with a sweet fruit pickle. The combination
did not quite work – but add pears and you have a deliciously piquant pudding.

4 eggs, beaten   ¼ teaspoon salt
225 ml/8 fl oz cold water   3 ripe pears
125 ml/4 fl oz cider vinegar   225 ml/8 fl oz double cream, plus
200 g/7 oz sugar   extra to serve (optional)
1 sachet powdered gelatine   lemon juice
1-1½ tablespoons mustard powder   borage flowers
½ teaspoon turmeric

Combine the eggs, water, vinegar, sugar, mustard, turmeric and salt in a double boiler (or place in a bowl over a pan of simmering water). Whisk constantly until the sugar is melted and everything amalgamated and slightly thickening. Sprinkle the gelatine over 2 tablespoons cold water in a small bowl, then place the bowl over another pan of simmering water and dissolve. Whisk into the custard, then leave to cool and slightly set.

Peel, core and finely chop or roughly mash one of the pears and stir into the custard. Whisk the cream until soft peaks form, and fold in. Pour into a ring mould and chill until set.

Just before serving, peel the remaining pears, slice finely and sprinkle with a little lemon juice. With a sharp pointed knife, run round the edges of the custard, dip the bottom of the ring in very hot water, put a plate over the mould, then turn over quickly – the ring should plop out neatly. Pile the sliced pears in the middle, scatter over the borage flowers and serve with extra cream – chilled – if wished. Serves 4-6

Said Brother Bill to Simple Sue,
"Let's tuck into this custard."

But when they dipped their peckers in
They found the stuff was MUSTARD!

Postcard, *c.* 1900

SPICED CHESTNUT CREAM

Strangely, mustard seems to make chestnuts taste of chocolate, rather than heightening their natural earthiness. Cacao intensifies this of course, but the effect is similar whatever the liqueur.

225 g/8 oz unsweetened chestnut purée
125 g/4 oz unsalted butter
125 g/4 oz sugar
2 teaspoons cacao
1 tablespoon mustard powder
150 ml/¼ pint double cream, whipped
175 g/6 fl oz double or single cream, chilled, to serve

Heat the purée with the butter and sugar, stirring constantly until melted. Add the cacao and mustard powder and cook for a further 2 minutes. Remove the pan from the heat and leave to cool for 30 minutes.

Whisk in the whipped cream very thoroughly, then spoon into small bowls – old-fashioned custard glasses are nice – and chill overnight. Serve with chilled cream handed round separately. Serves 4-6

MANGO AND DILL MUSTARD ICED FOOL

Lovely as a starter with a mass of very finely chopped fresh dill – and refreshing as a dessert too, with caraway seeds or eau-de-Cologne mint to garnish.

3 large or 6 medium-sized mangoes
3 tablespoons icing sugar
4 tablespoons natural yoghurt
¾ teaspoon Dill mustard (p.49)
eau-de-Cologne mint or caraway seeds, to garnish

Peel the mangoes, then slice into a food processor or blender. Add the icing sugar and purée. Blend in the yoghurt and mustard then pour into six 125 ml/4 oz dariole moulds. Freeze overnight. Unmould about 5 minutes before serving and sprinkle with caraway seeds or finely chopped mint. Serves 6

SPICED GINGERBREAD

Gingerbread has been a favourite for centuries: the medievals coloured it red with sandalwood, the Tudors black with ground liquorice. By Charles II's time, treacle was appearing on the scene and the gingerbread reputedly enjoyed by him was dark and rich with candied orange and lemon peel, spicy with ground coriander and ginger. We have kept the coriander, and added fresh ginger and mustard to make a lovely sweet-spicy bread with a bite.

50 g/2 oz butter
50 g/2 oz soft dark brown sugar
125 ml/4 fl oz treacle
2 tablespoons soured cream
1 large egg, beaten
125 g/4 oz flour
¼ teaspoon bicarbonate of soda

1 tablespoon coriander seeds, well
  crushed
1 tablespoon mustard powder
1 tablespoon ground ginger
40 mm/1½ inch piece fresh root
  ginger, peeled and grated
¼ teaspoon ground cinnamon

Heat the butter, sugar and treacle (to measure out the last, lightly oil a measuring jug and spoon – the treacle will then pour off easily), stirring until melted and well mixed together. Cool a little, then beat in the soured cream and egg, whisking very briskly. Stir in the sifted flour, bicarbonate of soda, coriander, mustard and ground ginger, then add the grated fresh ginger and cinnamon. Beat hard for 4-5 minutes, then pour into a greased 600 ml/1 pint loaf tin, or shallow ring or heart-shaped mould. Bake in the oven at 170°C/325°F/Gas Mark 3 for 35-40 minutes until it springs back when gently pressed with a finger. Cool then unmould. The bread can be iced if wished – a lemon and cinnamon glacé icing is good – but it is also excellent alone. Makes 8 slices.

MUSTARD SEED AND ALLSPICE BISCUITS

Nutty from fried mustard seeds, sweet with allspice – the only disadvantage of these biscuits is that one never seems to make enough.

225 g/8 oz butter
175 g/6 oz sugar
6 tablespoons strong coffee
2 teaspoons mustard powder
few drops pure vanilla extract

275 g/10 oz self-raising flour
2 tablespoons brown mustard seed
½ tablespoon peanut oil
freshly ground allspice

Blend the first five ingredients in a food processor, or beat well together in a large bowl. Add the sifted flour and blend well in. Fry the mustard seeds in the oil in a covered pan until they start to spit. Drain.

Break off walnut-sized knobs of dough and roll between wetted palms, then flatten and place on greased baking sheets.

Scatter some mustard seeds over each biscuit, then sprinkle generously with freshly ground allspice. Bake in the oven at 180°C/350°F/Gas Mark 4 for 15-20 minutes until lightly golden at the edges. Remove from baking sheet and cool. Makes 40-45 biscuits.

CHOCOLATE FINGERS

On our visit to Colman's we were told that mustard greatly intensifies the flavour of chocolate. Indeed it does, particularly when cocoa powder is used for baking.

225 g/8 oz unsalted butter or soft margarine
225 g/8 oz vanilla sugar
2 tablespoons natural yoghurt
2 tablespoons fresh orange juice
1 tablespoon mustard powder

7 tablespoons cocoa powder
275 g/10 oz plain flour
1 teaspoon baking powder
¼ teaspoon salt
freshly ground black pepper

Cream the butter and the sugar, either by hand or in a food processor. If you are using the latter, the remaining ingredients can then all be added at once, otherwise add one by one. Mix until thoroughly blended, then roll the dough into a long sausage shape. Place on a piece of foil or greaseproof paper, then flatten slightly – so that the biscuits will be finger-shaped. Roll and chill for at least 1 hour: although you can bake the biscuits immediately, it is more difficult to slice the dough finely. When it is chilled, very thin slices can easily be shaved off. Place on a greased baking tin, and cook in the oven at 190°C/375°F/Gas Mark 5 for 10 minutes if the slices were ⅛ inch thin, 12-13 minutes if a little thicker. For a slightly spicier biscuit, sprinkle with a little freshly ground black pepper before baking – this may sound odd, but black pepper and chocolate have met before. And it makes a deliciously piquant, very chocolatey biscuit. Any unused dough can be rewrapped and kept in the fridge for up to 2 days. Or freeze it and cut off slices with a freezer knife, giving them an extra minute or so in the cooking. Makes 55-60.

MUSTARD AND SPRING ONION BREAD

Spicy with spring onions, this bread has a lovely earthy flavour which is brought out by the mustard. It is from Gail and Mick Duff's *Food from the Country*.

1 teaspoon active dried yeast, or 2 teaspoons dried yeast, or 15 g/½ oz fresh yeast
1 teaspoon honey
150 ml/¼ pint milk, warmed

225 g/8 oz wholemeal flour
6 spring onions, finely chopped
3-4 teaspoons coarse-ground mustard powder
1 teaspoon Maldon salt

If using active dried yeast, mix all the dry ingredients together first, then stir the honey into the milk, pour into the bowl and mix thoroughly to a dough. Dried yeast will need to be scattered over the honey and milk and left to froth for 15 minutes, while fresh should be creamed with the honey and milk *before* being poured over the flour mixture. Turn the dough out on to a floured board and knead well, then return to a lightly oiled bowl, make a cross in the top and cover with a tea towel. Leave to rise for at least 1 hour until doubled in size. Knead again and form into a round, then lightly flatten. Cover with the cloth and prove for 20-30 minutes, then bake in the oven at 200°C/400°F/Gas Mark 6 for 25-30 minutes until golden. Cool on a wire rack. Serves 4-6

ROAST CHEESE

A Georgian supper dish, often served after late card games or when the master of the house returned home late. Since even the most junior in the servants' hall could easily prepare it, there was no danger of upsetting Cook by keeping her up till all hours. It is one of the many variations of the famous Welsh Rarebit which abound in English early cookery.

1 egg yolk
25 g/1 oz unsalted butter, softened
50 g/2 oz fresh white breadcrumbs
50 g/2 oz Farmhouse Lancashire
   or Cheshire cheese, finely grated
¼ teaspoon mustard powder

¼ teaspoon anchovy paste
Maldon salt
freshly ground white pepper
4 large slices of warm toast, cut
   into fingers

Mix together the egg, butter, breadcrumbs, cheese, mustard and anchovy paste, adding a little salt if using Cheshire but not with Lancashire – *real* Farmhouse Lancashire is deliciously salty on its own. Divide the mixture between four ramekins, cover with foil and bake in the oven at 180°C/350°F/Gas Mark 4 for 5-8 minutes until melted and bubbling. Remove the foil and cook for a further 2-3 minutes until very lightly browned. Serve, sprinkled with freshly ground white pepper, accompanied by toast fingers to dip into the cheese. Good port on the table, of course. Serves 4

GLAMORGAN SAUSAGES

Wales has always had fine cheeses, and made innovative use of them. Glamorgan sausages make a delicious supper or breakfast dish and fully warrant George Borrow's description, 'not a whit inferior to those of Epping'. Since the Epping sausage was noted for its meatiness, this was praise indeed.

150 g/5 oz fresh white breadcrumbs
125 g/4 oz Caerphilly cheese, grated
5 cm/2 inch piece leek, very finely chopped
2 tablespoons finely chopped parsley
½ teaspoon thyme leaves, stripped from the stalk

1 teaspoon mustard powder
Maldon salt
freshly ground black pepper
1-2 egg yolks
1 egg white
day-old breadcrumbs for coating
lard or butter for frying

Mix together the breadcrumbs, cheese, leek, herbs and mustard powder, season with a little salt and lots of black pepper then bind with 1 egg yolk. If the mixture seems a little dry, add the second yolk. Form into small, thin sausages about 5 cm/2 inches long. Lightly beat the egg white, and dip in the sausages, then roll them in the dried breadcrumbs. Fry in lard or butter until golden brown, about 5-6 minutes, turning constantly but gently. Good hot or cold. Serves 4

TRIESTE SPREAD

Tucked away, at the end of a reply to a reader's query in a back issue of *Bon Appétit*, was an intriguing comment on *mascarpone*. It stated that in the Trieste region it is mixed with gorgonzola, leek, caraway, anchovy and mustard to make a spread. Despite intensive research in Italy we found no evidence of this delicacy, however it sounded so interesting and the combination of ingredients so unlikely that we started to make it and eventually produced Trieste Spread. The name has now stuck though later we discovered in George Langs' *The Cuisine of Hungary* (where we should have looked, as Trieste was part of the Austro-Hungarian Empire until 1920) a spread called Lipto using sheep's-milk cheese. The result is delicious. A warning though: the proportions given have been arrived at after much experimenting and it is very important that the exact balance is maintained for each flavour to come out individually. Too much of this, too little of that, and the harmony is lost.

250 g/10 oz *mascarpone*, (p.210)
50 g/2 oz gorgonzola, roughly chopped
50 g/2 oz green end of a leek,

cut into 6 mm/¼ inch rings
2 anchovy fillets
2 teaspoons Dijon mustard
¼ teaspoon caraway seeds

½ teaspoon Maldon salt olive oil (optional)
freshly ground black pepper
(about ¼ teaspoon)

Blend everything, except the leek and olive oil, quickly in a food processor. The
consistency should be soft and buttery. If it is too dry or crumbly – and this will
depend largely on the ripeness and age of the gorgonzola – add a little olive oil
(not more than 2 tablespoons should be needed). Add the leek rings and whizz
again for a few seconds. Do not overprocess or the mixture will clot and become
grainy. It has always been eaten too quickly for us to test its keeping qualities.
Delicious on new potatoes or on steaks (cod as well as fillet), it is best of all
served at room temperature with black bread, thin water biscuits and a pile of
the season's first walnuts. Serves 6-8

A tango from the 1930s

Select
Bibliography

ACTON, ELIZA, *Modern Cooking for Private Families*, London, 1845

ALEE, HADJEE, *Receipts for Cooking the most Favourite Dishes in General Use in India also for Preparing Chatney and India Pickle*, Calcutta, c. 1920

APICIUS, MARCUS GABIUS, *Cooking and Dining in Imperial Rome 80 BC–AD 40*, translated Vehling, Dover, 1936

ARTUSI, PELLEGRINO, *L'Arte di Mangiar Bene*, Florence, 1950

AVADA, FATHER DOMENICO, *Practica de Speciali*, Rome, 1678

AYRTON, ELIZABETH, *The Cookery of England*, London, 1974

Baileys Agricultural Durham, 1810

BEETON, MRS, *Every Day Cookery and Housekeeping Book*, London, 1865

BENNETT, JAMES, *History of Tewkesbury*, London, 1830

BINSTEAD, RAYMOND, *Pickle and Saucemaking*, Food Trade Press, London, 1939

BLATHWAYT, RAYMOND, *As a Grain of Mustard Seed*, Colman's, Norwich, 1923

BLENCOWE, A., *The Receipt Book*, 1694

BLONDEL, MADELEINE, *Catalogue of Moutarde de Dijon Exhibition*, 1984 in Dijon

CAREME, M. A., *L'Art de la Cuisine Française*, London, 1836

CLAIBORNE, CRAIG, *Cooking with Herbs and Spices*, New York, 1970

COGAN, DR THOMAS, *Haven of Health*, 1605

COLMAN'S, *Mustard Users Mustered by Baron de Beef*, c. 1930

COLMAN'S, *Mustard Seed Crop Husbandry*, 1982

COLMAN'S, *The Advertising Art of J.J. Colman Ltd. Yellow, White and Blue*, Norwich, 1977

COLMAN'S, *History of the Mustard Pot*, c. 1920

COLUMELLA, *De Re Rustica*, AD 42

COOKE, ALASTAIR, *America*, BBC 1973

CULPEPER, NICHOLAS, *The English Physician or Herball*, London, 1653

CURNONSKY, *Bon Plats, Bon Vins*, 1949

DAVID, ELIZABETH, *Spices, Salt and Aromatics in the English Kitchen*, London, 1970

Declaration of Academy of Dijon, 1853

DECLOQUEMENT, FRANÇOISE, *Moutarde et Moutardiers*, Paris, 1982

DE FONTENELLE, JULIA, *Manuel du Moutardier, Manuels-Roret*, Paris 1827 and 1887

DENCE, *Season to Taste*, Food Trade Press London, 1985

DIGBY, SIR KENELM, *The Closet Opened, 1669*, A. McDonnell, 1910

DIOSCORIDES, *De Materia Medica*, c. AD 100

DUMAS, ALEXANDER, *Dictionary of Cuisine*, Paris, 1973

EVELYN, JOHN, *A Discourse of Sallets*, London, 1699

GERARD, JOHN, *Gerard's Herbal*, 1597

GLASSE, HANNAH, *Art of Cookery Made Plain and Easy*, 1747

'GOODMAN OF PARIS', *Le Menagier de Paris*, Paris, 1390

GORDON, VICTOR, *The English Cookbook*, London, 1985

GRIEVE, MAUD, *A Modern Herbal*, London, 1931

GRIGSON, JANE, *Charcuterie and French Pork Cookery*, 1967

HAMMER, STEPHEN, *French's Centennial*, New York, 1980

HIPPOCRATES, *Medicorum Graecorum Opus*, translated E. Littre, Paris, 1861

HOLLAND, LADY, *Memoirs of the Rev Sidney Smith*, 1855
IRELAND, ARTHUR, *The Story of the Grain of Mustard Seed,* London, 1914
JOBARD, *Essai sur L'Histoire de la Moutarde de Dijon*, (undated)
KEEN, ROBINSON AND CO., *Gossip About London City 1742 to 1892*, London 1892
KETTNER, AUGUSTE, *Book of the Table*, 1877
KIMBALL, MARIE, *Thomas Jefferson's Cook Book Virginia*, 1976
KITCHENER, WILLIAM, *Apicius Redivivus: the Cook's Oracle*, 1817
LANG, GEORGE, *The Cuisine of Hungary*, New York, 1971
LEYEL, MRS, *The Gentle Art of Cookery*, London, 1925
LIVINGSTONE, *The Book of Spices*, New York, 1969
MARINETTI, F., *La Cucina Futurista*, Rome, 1932
MAY, ROBERT, *The Accomplisht Cook*, 1660
MESSEGROVE, *Health Secrets of Plants and Herbs*, London, 1976
MISSON, FRANÇOIS, *Memoires et Observations*, 1719
MUFFETT, DR THOMAS, *Health Improvements*, 1655
NEASHAM, *North Country Sketches,* London, 1893
OCKERMAN, J., *Source Book for Food Scientists*, A.V.I., London, 1978
OLNEY, RICHARD, *Simple French Food*, London, 1981
ORTIZ, ELISABETH LAMBERT, *Japanese Cookery*, London 1986
—*Latin American Cooking*, London, 1969
PEPYSIAN LIBRARY, *Stere Hit Well*, Magdalene College, Cambridge, No. 1047
POULTNEY, S.V., *Vinegar Products*, London, 1949
REYNIERE, GRIMOD DE LA, *Almanach des Gourmands ou Calendrier Nutritif*, Paris, 1803–1810
ROSE, GILES, *A Perfect School, of Instruction for the Officers of the Mouth*, 1682
RUNDELL, MARY, *A New System of Domestic Cookery*, London, 1806
RUSSELL, J., *Boke of Nature*, 1460
SHAW, NANCY, *Food for the Greedy*, 1936
SMITH, MICHAEL, *Fine English Cookery*, London, 1973
SOYER, ALEXIS, *Gastronomic Regenerator*, London, 1846
SPENCER, EDWARD (NATHANIEL GUBBINS), *Cakes and Ale*, London, 1897
TOKLAS, ALICE B., *The Alice B. Toklas Cook Book, London*, 1954
WILSON, C. ANNE, *Food and Drink in Britain*, London, 1973
WOLLEY, HANNAH, *The Queen-Like Closet*, 1670
The Accomplisht Lady's Delight, 6th edition, 1686
YARWOOD, DOREEN, *The British Kitchen*, London, 1981

Illustrations

Mustard jars from *Essai sur l'Histoire de la Moutarde de Dijon*
Mustard plant, from *Medical Botany*, 1821
Original mustard plasters, *c. 1880* (*Photograph by Sarah Rodway*)
Mustard plants in *Gerard's Herbal*, 1597
Mustard bath advertisement from the *Tatler*, 1927
Black mustard plant, 1839
Philippe le Hardi, Duke of Burgundy 1364–1408
Coat of arms of Moutardiers, 1634 (*Drawing by Arthur Oxford*)
Mustard seller, eighteenth century
Techniques for vinegar and mustard making from the eighteenth century
Grey Poupon jar 1875, and Grey Jar 1865 (*Photograph by Sarah Rodway*)
The Maille shop in Dijon (*Drawing by Arthur Oxford*)
Amora globe mustard pot, *c. 1930* (*Drawing by Arthur Oxford*)
Amora bulk dispenser for shops (*Drawing by Arthur Oxford*)
Mustard seller's costume, 1835
Bornibus jars 1950s and 1858–1930 (*Photograph by Sarah Rodway*)
Treacle mustard plant
Keen's advertisement 1880
Keen's mustard pot ointment (*Photograph by Sarah Rodway*)
Colman's invoice, 1870
Colman's covered box wagon, 1911
Mustard Club poster, *Daily Mirror*, 29 October 1926
Hot Dan, the Mustard Man (*Drawing by Arthur Oxford*)
Mustard Club lapel badge, 1920s (*Drawing by Arthur Oxford*)
The technique for removing the husks (*Drawing by Arthur Oxford*)
Saddle quern, *c. 1500* (*Drawing by Arthur Oxford*)
London rocket plant, 1835
Development of French jar shapes from 1738 to 1908
The original Mostarda di Cremona recipe
Eighteenth century Italian Mostarda di Fruita jar (*Drawing by Arthur Oxford*)
Colman's 'Returned from Klondyke' (From an original by John Hassall, 1899)
The Franklyn (*Photograph by Michelle Garrett*)
Punch cartoon, 28 June 1856
Colman's Mustard Shop in Norwich
Postcard from Honor, Mich USA, c. 1943
The Mustard Mill in Pandon Dean, 19th Century
Mustard seller, 1586, France
Keen's Mustard, 1887
Jars from Taylor's of Newport Pagnell (*Drawing by Arthur Oxford*)
Savora advert, 1929
Colman's *John Bull* advertisement, *c. 1900*
Maille – Royal Warrant holders (*Photograph by Sarah Rodway*)
Colburn's card, front and back view
The original prototype Dunhill lighter
Sadler's Old English Mustard
Donald McGill postcard, 1918
Dijon coat of arms
Savora menu
Keen's mustard ad
Mustard Club postcard
Novelty mustard containers (*Photograph by Sarah Rodway*)
Bornibus, maker of Moutarde des Dames
Peach's mustard dispenser (*Photograph by Sarah Rodway*)
The recipe book of the Mustard Club

Braised leeks with mustard (*Drawing by Arthur Oxford*)
Colman's 'Polar Bear', c. 1920
Dessert served at La Colomba in Venice (*Drawing by Arthur Oxford*)
Mustard and custard
A tango from the 1930s

Acknowledgements

So many are the people who have helped with this book, that to list every one individually would overflow our permitted space. But to all of them we give grateful thanks.

Particularly to the National Mustard Museum, 7477 Hubbard Ave, Middleton, WI 53562, USA and Colman's Mustard Shop and Museum, 15 The Royal Arcade, Norwich NR2 1NQ; Henry Poupon, Jean-Pierre Halm, Mme Fouquet and M. Bourget of Moutarde Maille, Dijon; Hélène Boutet, Moutarde Bornibus, Paris; Françoise Turpaud, Européenne de Condiments, Dijon; Bea Slizeweski, The R.T. French Company, Rochester, New York; Dr S. A. R. Cross, Mrs Norma Walker, Don Hoffman and especially John Hemingway of Colman's, Norwich; Enrico Cinquetti Dondi, Dondi Lorenzo spa, Cremona; Giles Tullberg, Wiltshire Tracklements, Shenstone; Charles Gordon, Charles Gordon Associates, Guildford; Shreeram Vidyarthi, Books from India U.K.; K. Becker, FAO, United Nations, Rome; Amanda Courtney, British Trout Association; Lucia Godwin and Lou Powers, Thomas Jefferson Foundation, Charlottesville, Virginia; Terence Charman, Imperial War Museum; Edna Linnell, Tewkesbury Museum; Biddy Cole, Rye Pottery, Rye; W. A. L. Seaman, Archivist, Tyne & Wear County Council; D. W. Liddle, County Librarian, Gateshead; D. J. Butter, County Archivist, Durham; J. Main, Durham County Library; Paula Chesterman, Punch Publications Ltd; C. Anne Wilson, Brotherton Library, Leeds; Miriam Stead, British Museum; Nigel Hepper, Royal Botanic Gardens, Kew; J. C. Pert, Homeopathic Development Foundation; D. J. Wright, British Medical Association; and Adrian Binstead, Food Trade Press, Orpington.

Thanks, too, for permissions to reproduce, or refer to, recipes must go to Henry Poupon, SEGMA Maille, Dijon: Elisabeth Lambert Ortiz (*Japanese Cookery*, Collins, 1986); Gail and Mick Duff (*Food from the Country*, Macmillan, 1981); Victor Gordon (*The English Cook-book*, Jonathan Cape, 1985); Jane Simpson and Gill McLennan (*The Apple Book*, The Bodley Head, 1984). Thanks for permission to reproduce the illustrations on pages 21, 23, 25, 32, 50 and 88 to Madeleine Blondel, Musée de la Vie Bourguignonne; for those on pages 17, 37, 40, 41, 79 and 110 to Colman's of Norwich; and that on page 157 to Alfred Dunhill.

For specialist help of all sorts, we thank Sid Wayne of Stone County Specialities Inc, Ontario; Mike McKirdy, Cooks Books, Rottingdean; Tom Jackson of Ilkley; Jean Rosen of Dijon; Françoise Decloquement; San Firlej; Imogen Olsen; Gerry Coran and Lawrence Cooper; Pepita Aris; Maggie Black; Anna del Conte; Mrs Harold Loasby; Jill Tilsley-Benham; Dr John H. Harvey of Frome, Somerset; Marie-Pierre Moine; Caroline Schuck; Elisabeth Lambert Ortiz; Alan Davidson; and John Lyle of Sidmouth, Devon.

Very special thanks are due to Angus and Gilly Urquhart for Italian research and translations; to Heidi Lascelles and Caroline Liddell – without whose encouragement this book would never have been published; to Robin Baird-Smith for his enthusiasm, foresight and extreme patience; to Caroline Schuck, Jacqueline Korn and Scott Ewing for never-flagging encouragement; to the late James H. Weir, MD, for medical research; to Elizabeth, Charlotte and Matthew Weir for counting, mixing, tasting and helping; to the late Morgan Man for many translations from French, German and Arabic; and to Moira, Kate and Peg Man for tasting, talking and much practical help. Without them, and most especially without the constant support of Keith Perrott – who endlessly ate mustard with everything – the book would never have been written.

Index

2009

Fr**a**ce

The most in-depth campsite guides

Alan Rogers

C000219354

INSPECTED CAMPSITES & SELECTED

Compiled by: Alan Rogers Guides Ltd

Designed by: Paul Effenberg, Vine Design Ltd

Additional photography: T Lambelin, www.lambelin.com
Maps created by Customised Mapping (01769 540044)
contain background data provided by GisDATA Ltd
Maps are © Alan Rogers Guides and GisDATA Ltd 2008

© Alan Rogers Guides Ltd 2008

Published by: Alan Rogers Guides Ltd,
Spelmonden Old Oast, Goudhurst, Kent TN17 1HE
www.alanrogers.com Tel: 01580 214000

British Library Cataloguing-in-Publication Data:
A catalogue record for this book is available
from the British Library.

ISBN-978-1-906215-13-2

Printed in Great Britain by J H Haynes & Co Ltd

While every effort is taken to ensure the accuracy of the information
given in this book, no liability can be accepted by the authors or
publishers for any loss, damage or injury caused by errors in, or
omissions from, the information given.

All rights reserved. No part of this publication may be reproduced,
stored in a retrieval system or transmitted, in any form or by any means,
electronic, mechanical, photocopying, recording or otherwise, without
prior permission in writing from the publishers.

FRANCE
yes, you can

Contents

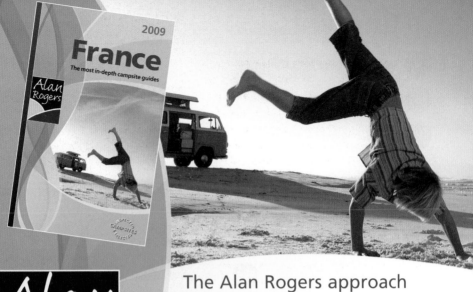

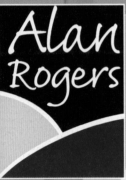

The Alan Rogers approach

Alan Rogers Guides were first published over 40 years ago. Since Alan Rogers published the first campsite guide that bore his name, the range has expanded and now covers 27 countries in five separate guides. No fewer than 20 of the campsites selected by Alan for the first guide are still featured in our 2009 editions.

There are over 11,000 campsites in France of varying quality: this guide contains impartially written reports on almost 1,000, including some of the very finest, each being individually inspected and selected. All the usual maps and indexes are also included, designed to help you find the choice of campsite that's right for you. We hope you enjoy some happy and safe travels – and some pleasurable 'armchair touring' in the meantime!

A question of quality

The criteria we use when inspecting and selecting sites are numerous, but the most important by far is the question of good quality. People want different things from their choice of campsite so we try to include a range of campsite 'styles' to cater for a wide variety of preferences: from those seeking a small peaceful campsite in the heart of the countryside, to visitors looking for an 'all singing, all dancing' site in a popular seaside resort. Those with more specific interests, such as sporting facilities, cultural events or historical attractions, are also catered for.

The size of the site, whether it's part of a chain or privately owned, makes no difference in terms of it being required to meet our exacting standards in respect of its quality and it being 'fit for purpose'. In other words, irrespective of the size of the site, or the number of facilities it offers, we consider and evaluate the welcome, the pitches, the sanitary facilities, the cleanliness, the general maintenance and even the location.

" ...the campsites included in this book have been chosen entirely on merit, and no payment of any sort is made by them for their inclusion."

Alan Rogers, 1968

INSPECTED SINCE 1968 & SELECTED

Expert opinions

We rely on our dedicated team of Site Assessors, all of whom are experienced campers, caravanners or motorcaravanners, to visit and recommend sites. Each year they travel some 100,000 miles around Europe inspecting new campsites for the guide and re-inspecting the existing ones. Our thanks are due to them for their enthusiastic efforts, their diligence and integrity.

We also appreciate the feedback we receive from many of our readers and we always make a point of following up complaints, suggestions or recommendations for possible new sites. Of course we get a few grumbles too – but it really is a few, and those we do receive usually relate to overcrowding or to poor maintenance during the peak school holiday period. Please bear in mind that, although we are interested to hear about any complaints, we have no contractual relationship with the campsites featured in our guides and are therefore not in a position to intervene in any dispute between a reader and a campsite.

Independent and honest

Whilst the content and scope of the Alan Rogers guides have expanded considerably since the early editions, our selection of campsites still employs exactly the same philosophy and criteria as defined by Alan Rogers in 1968.

'telling it how it is'

Firstly, and most importantly, our selection is based entirely on our own rigorous and independent inspection and selection process. Campsites cannot buy their way into our guides – indeed the extensive Site Report which is written by us, not by the site owner, is provided free of charge so we are free to say what we think and to provide an honest, 'warts and all' description. This is written in plain English and without the use of confusing icons or symbols.

HIGHLY RESPECTED BY SITE OWNERS AND READERS ALIKE, THERE IS NO BETTER GUIDE WHEN IT COMES TO FORMING AN INDEPENDENT VIEW OF A CAMPSITE'S QUALITY. WHEN YOU NEED TO BE CONFIDENT IN YOUR CHOICE OF CAMPSITE, YOU NEED THE ALAN ROGERS GUIDE.

- SITES ONLY INCLUDED ON MERIT
- SITES CANNOT PAY TO BE INCLUDED
- INDEPENDENTLY INSPECTED, RIGOROUSLY ASSESSED
- IMPARTIAL REVIEWS
- OVER 40 YEARS OF EXPERTISE

5

INSPECTED CAMPSITES & SELECTED

Written in plain English, our guides are exceptionally easy to use, but a few words of explanation regarding the layout and content may be helpful. Regular readers will see that our site reports are grouped into 19 'tourist regions' and then by the various départements in each of these regions in numerical order.

The Site Reports – *Example of an entry*

`Site Number` Site name

Postal address (including département)

Telephone number. Email address   alanrogers.com web address

A description of the site in which we try to give an idea of its general features – its size, its situation, its strengths and its weaknesses. This section should provide a picture of the site itself with reference to the facilities that are provided and if they impact on its appearance or character. We include details on pitch numbers, electricity (with amperage), hardstandings etc. in this section, as pitch design, planning and terracing affect the site's overall appearance. Similarly we include reference to pitches used for caravan holiday homes, chalets, and the like. Importantly at the end of this column we indicate if there are any restrictions, e.g. no tents, no children, naturist sites.

Region

Facilities

Lists more specific information on the site's facilities and amenities and, where available, the dates when these facilities are open (if not for the whole season). Off site: here we give distances to various local amenities, for example, local shops, the nearest beach, plus our featured activities (bicycle hire, fishing, horse riding, boat launching). Where we have space we list suggestions for activities and local tourist attractions.

Open: Site opening dates.

Directions

Separated from the main text in order that they may be read and assimilated more easily by a navigator en-route. Bear in mind that road improvement schemes can result in road numbers being altered. GPS: references are provided for satellite navigation systems (in degrees and minutes) as we obtain them.

Charges 2009 (or a general guide)

Regions and départements

For administrative purposes France is actually divided into 23 official regions covering the 95 départements (similar to our counties). However, these do not always coincide with the needs of tourists. For example the area we think of as the Dordogne is split between two of the official regions. We have, therefore, opted to feature our campsites within unofficial 'tourist regions', and the relevant départements are stated in our introduction to each region with their official number (eg. the département of Manche is number 50) included. We use these département numbers as the first two digits of our campsite numbers, so any campsite in the Manche département will start with the number 50, prefixed with FR.

Indexes

Our three indexes allow you to find sites by their number and name, by region and site name or by the town or village where the site is situated.

Campsite Maps

The maps relate to our tourist regions and will help you to identify the approximate position of each campsite. The colour of the campsite number indicates whether it is open all year or not. You will certainly need more detailed maps and we have found the Michelin atlas to be particularly useful.

Facilities

Toilet blocks

We assume that toilet blocks will be equipped with a reasonable amount of British style WCs, washbasins with hot and cold water and hot showers with dividers or curtains, and will have all necessary shelves, hooks, plugs and mirrors. We also assume that there will be an identified chemical toilet disposal point, and that the campsite will provide water and waste water drainage points and bin areas. If not the case, we comment. We do mention certain features that some readers find important: washbasins in cubicles, facilities for babies, facilities for those with disabilities and motorcaravan service points. Readers with disabilities are advised to contact the site of their choice to ensure that facilities are appropriate to their needs.

Shop

Basic or fully supplied, and opening dates.

Bars, restaurants, takeaway facilities and entertainment

We try hard to supply opening and closing dates (if other than the campsite opening dates) and to identify if there are discos or other entertainment.

Children's play areas

Fenced and with safety surface (e.g. sand, bark or pea-gravel).

Swimming pools

If particularly special, we cover in detail in our main campsite description but reference is always included under our Facilities listings. We will also indicate the existence of water slides, sunbathing areas and other features. Opening dates, charges and levels of supervision are provided where we have been notified. There is a regulation whereby Bermuda shorts may not be worn in swimming pools (for health reasons). It is worth ensuring that you do take 'proper' swimming trunks with you.

Leisure facilities

For example, playing fields, bicycle hire, organised activities and entertainment.

Dogs

If dogs are not accepted or restrictions apply, we state it here. Check the quick reference list at the back of the guide.

Off site

This briefly covers leisure facilities, tourist attractions, restaurants etc. nearby.

Charges

These are the latest provided to us by the sites. In those cases where 2009 prices are not given, we try to give a general guide.

Reservations

Necessary for high season (roughly mid-July to mid-August) in popular holiday areas (ie beach resorts). You can reserve many sites via our own Alan Rogers Travel Service or through other tour operators. Or be wholly independent and contact the campsite(s) of your choice direct, using the phone or e-mail numbers shown in the site reports, but please bear in mind that many sites are closed all winter.

Telephone numbers

All numbers assume that you are phoning from within France. To phone France from outside that country, prefix the number shown with the relevant International Code (00 33) and drop the first 0, shown as (0) in the numbers indicated.

Opening dates

Are those advised to us during the early autumn of the previous year – sites can, and sometimes do, alter these dates before the start of the following season, often for good reasons. If you intend to visit shortly after a published opening date, or shortly before the closing date, it is wise to check that it will actually be open at the time required. Similarly some parks operate a restricted service during the low season, only opening some of their facilities (e.g. swimming pools) during the main season; where we know about this, and have the relevant dates, we indicate it – again if you are at all doubtful it is wise to check.

Sometimes, campsite amenities may be dependent on there being enough customers on site to justify their opening and, for this reason, actual opening dates may vary from those indicated.

Some French site owners are very laid back when it comes to opening and closing dates. They may not be fully ready by their stated opening dates – grass and hedges may not all be cut or perhaps only limited sanitary facilities open. At the end of the season they also tend to close down some facilities and generally wind down prior to the closing date. Bear this in mind if you are travelling early or late in the season – it is worth phoning ahead.

The Camping Cheque low season touring system goes some way to addressing this in that many participating campsites will have all key facilities open and running by the opening date and these will remain fully operational until the closing date.

Mobile homes ⏵ page 484

Our Accommodation Section

Over recent years, more and more campsites have added high quality mobile home and chalet accommodation. In response to feedback from many of our readers, and to reflect this evolution in campsites, we have now decided to include a separate section on mobile homes and chalets. If a site offers this accommodation, it is indicated above the site report with a page reference where full details are given. We have chosen a number of sites offering some of the best accommodation available and have included full details of one or two accommodation types at these sites. Please note however that many other campsites listed in this guide may also have a selection of accommodation for rent.

Whether you're an 'old hand' in terms of camping and caravanning or are contemplating your first trip, a regular reader of our Guides or a new 'convert', we wish you well in your travels and hope we have been able to help in some way. We are, of course, also out and about ourselves, visiting sites, talking to owners and readers, and generally checking on standards and new developments.

We wish all our readers thoroughly enjoyable Camping and Caravanning in 2009 – favoured by good weather of course!

THE ALAN ROGERS TEAM

Regions

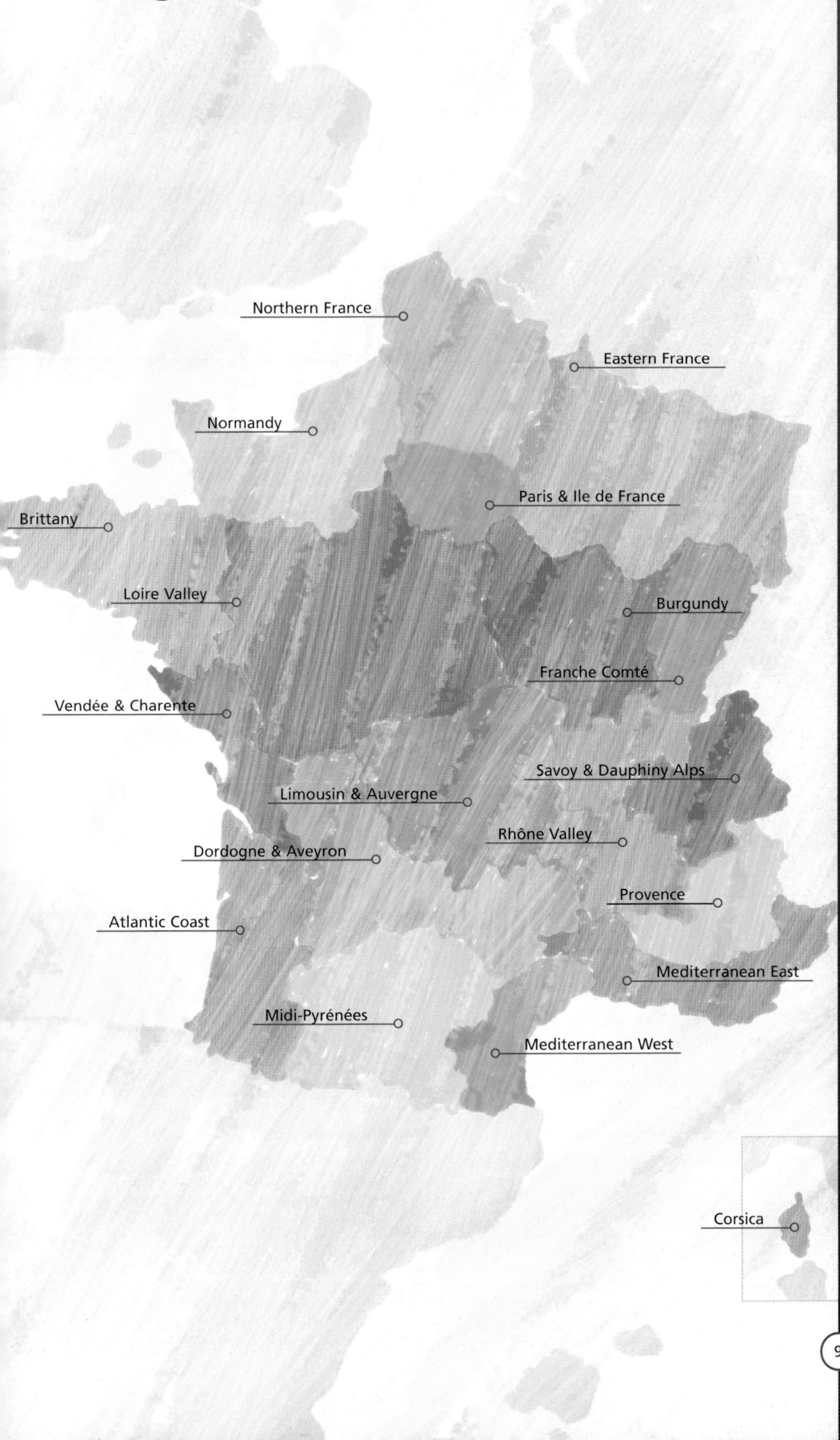

Northern France

Eastern France

Normandy

Paris & Ile de France

Brittany

Loire Valley

Burgundy

Franche Comté

Vendée & Charente

Savoy & Dauphiny Alps

Limousin & Auvergne

Rhône Valley

Dordogne & Aveyron

Provence

Atlantic Coast

Mediterranean East

Midi-Pyrénées

Mediterranean West

Corsica

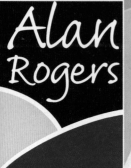

The Alan Rogers Awards

The Alan Rogers Campsite Awards were launched in 2004 and have proved a great success.

Our awards have a broad scope and before committing to our winners, we carefully consider more than 2,000 campsites featured in our guides, taking into account comments from our site assessors, our head office team and, of course, our readers.

Our award winners come from the four corners of Europe, from southern Portugal to Slovenia, and this year we are making awards to campsites in 13 different countries.

Needless to say, it's an extremely difficult task to choose our eventual winners, but we believe that we have identified a number of campsites with truly outstanding characteristics.

In each case, we have selected an outright winner, along with two highly commended runners-up.

Listed below are full details of each of our award categories and our winners for 2008.

Our warmest congratulations to all our award winners and our commiserations to all those not having won an award on this occasion.

THE ALAN ROGERS TEAM

Alan Rogers Progress Award 2008

This award reflects the hard work and commitment undertaken by particular site owners to improve and upgrade their site.

WINNER

PO8202	Turiscampo, Portugal

RUNNERS-UP

DE3202	Grav-Insel, Germany
IT60450	Marina di Venezia, Italy

Alan Rogers Welcome Award 2008

This award takes account of sites offering a particularly friendly welcome and maintaining a friendly ambience throughout reader's holidays.

WINNER

FR05000 Princes d'Orange, France

RUNNERS-UP

FR71110	Du Lac, France
DK2022	Vikær Diernæs, Denmark

Alan Rogers Active Holiday Award 2008

This award reflects sites in outstanding locations which are ideally suited for active holidays, notably walking or cycling, but which could extend to include such activities as winter sports or water sports

WINNER

FR07120 L'Ardéchois, France

RUNNERS-UP

SV4210   Sobec, Slovenia

AU0265   Park Grubhof, Austria

Alan Rogers Motorhome Award 2008

Motorhome sales are increasing and this award acknowledges sites which, in our opinion, have made outstanding efforts to welcome motorhome clients.

WINNER

UK0220   Trevornick, England

RUNNERS-UP

BE0655   De Lilse Bergen, Belgium

CZ4840   Oase Praha, Czech Republic

Alan Rogers 4 Seasons Award 2008

This award is made to outstanding sites with extended opening dates and which welcome clients to a uniformly high standard throughout the year.

WINNER

AU0440   Schluga, Austria

RUNNERS-UP

NL6520   BreeBronne, Netherlands

ES92950   Don Cactus, Spain

Alan Rogers Seaside Award 2008

This award is made for sites which we feel are outstandingly suitable for a really excellent seaside holiday.

WINNER

NL5735   Tempelhof, Netherlands

RUNNERS-UP

UK1070   Woolacombe Bay, England

CR6732   Polari, Croatia

Alan Rogers Country Award 2008

This award contrasts with our former award and acknowledges sites which are attractively located in delightful, rural locations.

WINNER

FR23030 Creuse Nature, France

RUNNERS-UP

ES90260   El Burro Blanco, Spain

IT62090   Vidor, Italy

Alan Rogers Rented Accommodation Award 2008

Given the increasing importance of rented accommodation on many campsites, we feel that it is important to acknowledge sites which have made a particular effort in creating a high quality 'rented accommodation' park.

WINNER

IT60370   Jesolo International, Italy

RUNNERS-UP

FR33300   La Jenny, France

NL5560   De Wijde Blick, Netherlands

Alan Rogers Unique Site Award 2008

This award acknowledges sites with unique, outstanding features – something which simply cannot be found elsewhere and which is an important attraction of the site.

WINNER

FR34070 Sérignan, France

RUNNERS-UP

IT60030   Pra' delle Torri, Italy

DE3182   Teutoburger Wald, Germany

Alan Rogers Family Site Award 2008

Many sites claim to be child friendly but this award acknowledges the sites we feel to be the very best in this respect.

WINNER

FR32010 Camp de Florence, France

RUNNERS-UP

ES80350   L'Amfora, Spain

IT62630   Bella Italia, Italy

Alan Rogers Readers' Award 2008

We believe our Readers' Award to be the most important. We simply invite our readers (by means of an on-line poll at **www.alanrogers.com**) to nominate the site they enjoyed most.

The outright winner for 2008 is:

WINNER

IT60200   Union Lido, Italy

Alan Rogers Special Award 2008

A special award is made to acknowledge sites which we feel have overcome a very significant setback, and have, not only returned to their former condition, but has added extra amenities and can therefore be fairly considered to be even better than before. In 2008 we acknowledged two campsites, which have undergone major problems and have made highly impressive recoveries.

UK2885   Warner Farm, England

FR32080 Le Talouch, France

The Family Selection
2009

FREE 2009 Brochure
call 01580 214000
Over 79 French campsites
hand picked for you
www.alanrogers.com/travel

Book with us
For the best holidays
on the best campsites

The Alan Rogers Travel Service was originally set up to provide a low cost booking service for readers. We pride ourselves on being able to put together a bespoke holiday, taking advantage of our experience, knowledge and contacts. Our experience is second to none and our prices are extremely competitive

Unbeatable ferry deals

At the Alan Rogers Travel Service we're always keen to find the best deals and keenest prices. There are always great savings on offer, and we're constantly negotiating new ferry rates and money-saving offers, so just call us on

01580 214000

and ask about the latest deals.
or visit www.alanrogers.com/travel

The Alan Rogers Travel Service

Whether you book on-line or book by phone, you will be allocated an experienced Personal Travel Consultant to provide you with personal advice and manage every stage of your booking. Our Personal Travel Consultants have first-hand experience of many of our campsites and access to a wealth of information. They can 'paint a picture' of individual campsites, check availability, provide a competitive price and tailor your holiday arrangements to your specific needs.

- Discuss your holiday plans with a friendly person with first-hand experience

- Let us reassure you that your holiday arrangements really are taken care of

- Tell us about your special requests and allow us to pass these on

- Benefit from advice which will save you money – the latest ferry deals and more

- Remember, our offices are in Kent not overseas and we do NOT operate a queuing system!

The aims of the Travel Service are simple

- To provide convenience - a one-stop shop to make life easier.

- To provide peace of mind - when you need it most.

- To provide a friendly, knowledgeable, efficient service – when this can be hard to find.

- To provide a low cost means of organising your holiday – when prices can be so complicated.

HOW IT WORKS

1 Choose your campsite(s) – we can book around 500 across Europe. Look for the yellow coloured campsite entries in this book. You'll find more info and images at www.alanrogers.travel.

Please note: the list of campsites we can book for you varies from time to time.

2 Choose your dates – choose when you arrive, when you leave.

3 Choose your ferry crossing – we can book most routes with most operators at extremely competitive rates.

Then just call us for an instant quote

01580 214000

or visit
www.alanrogers.com/travel

LOOK FOR A CAMPSITE ENTRY LIKE THIS TO INDICATE WHICH CAMPSITES WE CAN BOOK FOR YOU.

THE LIST IS GROWING SO PLEASE CALL FOR UP TO THE MINUTE INFORMATION.

FREE CHILD PLACES ON MANY SITES

Book the best, with the best

THIS FAMILY SELECTION IS DESIGNED TO OFFER
A HAND-PICKED RANGE OF SITES, WELL-KNOWN
TO US, WHERE YOU WILL FIND THE BEST OF
EVERYTHING THAT MAKES A GREAT HOLIDAY.

FREE BROCHURE
Pitches and mobile homes
01580 214000
www.**alanrogers**.com/travel

INSPECTED CAMPSITES & SELECTED

Leave The Hassle To Us

- All site fees paid in advance (nominal local tourist taxes may be payable on arrival).

- Your pitch or mobile home is reserved for you – travel with peace of mind.

- No endless overseas phone calls or correspondence with foreign site owners.

- No need to pay foreign currency deposits and booking fees.

- Take advantage of our expert advice and experience of camping in Europe.

Already Booked Your Ferry?

We're confident that our ferry inclusive booking service offers unbeatable value. However, if you have already booked your ferry then we can still make a pitch-only reservation for you (minimum 3 nights). Since our prices are based on our ferry inclusive service, you need to be aware that a non-ferry booking may result in slightly higher prices than if you were to book direct with the site.

It's all on-line

www.alanrogers.com is a website designed to give you everything you need to know when it comes to booking your Alan Rogers inspected and selected campsite, and your low cost ferry.

Our friendly, expert team of travel consultants is always happy to help on

01580 214000 – but they do go home sometimes!

Visit **www.alanrogers.com** and you'll find constantly updated information, latest ferry deals, special offers from campsites and much more. And you can visit it at any time of day or night!

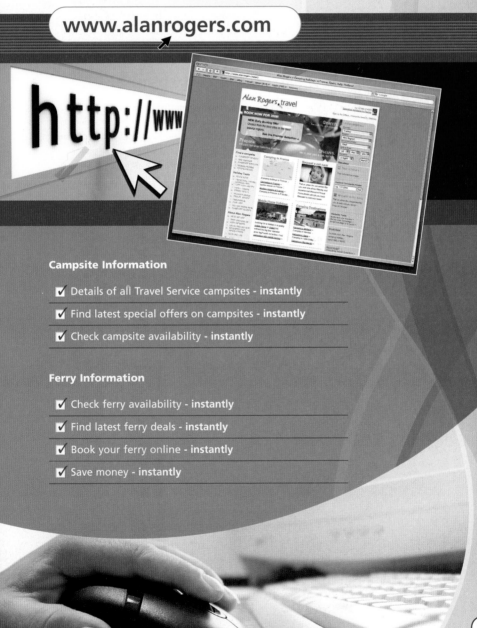

Campsite Information

- ☑ Details of all Travel Service campsites - **instantly**
- ☑ Find latest special offers on campsites - **instantly**
- ☑ Check campsite availability - **instantly**

Ferry Information

- ☑ Check ferry availability - **instantly**
- ☑ Find latest ferry deals - **instantly**
- ☑ Book your ferry online - **instantly**
- ☑ Save money - **instantly**

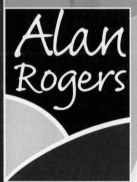

Crossing the Channel

One of the great advantages of booking your ferry-inclusive holiday with the Alan Rogers Travel Service is the tremendous value we offer. Our money-saving Ferry Deals have become legendary. As agents for all major cross-Channel operators we can book all your travel arrangements with the minimum of fuss and at the best possible rates.

Just call us for an instant quote

01580 214000

or visit
www.alanrogers.com/travel

Let us price your holiday for you
instantly!

The quickest and easiest way is to call us for advice and an instant quote. We can take details of your vehicle and party and, using our direct computer link to all the operators' reservations systems, can give you an instant price. We can even check availability for you and book a crossing while you're on the phone!

Please note we can only book ferry crossings in conjunction with a campsite holiday reservation.

MAP 1

Brittany

Rolling sandy beaches, hidden coves, pretty villages and a picturesque coastline all combine to make Brittany a very popular holiday destination. Full of Celtic culture steeped in myths and legends, Brittany is one of the most distinctive regions of France.

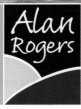

Alan Rogers

DÉPARTEMENTS: 22 CÔTES D'ARMOR, 29 FINISTÈRE, 35 ILLE-ET-VILAINE, 56 MORBIHAN, 44 LOIRE ATLANTIQUE

MAJOR CITIES: RENNES AND BREST

Brittany's 800 miles of rocky coastline offers numerous bays, busy little fishing villages and broad sandy beaches dotted with charming seaside resorts. The coastline to the north of Brittany is rugged with a maze of rocky coves, while to the south, the shore is flatter with long sandy beaches. Inland you'll find wooded valleys, rolling fields, moors and giant granite boulders, but most impressive is the wealth of prehistoric sites, notably the Carnac standing stones.

Breton culture offers a rich history of menhirs, crosses, cathedrals and castles. Strong Celtic roots provide this region with its own distinctive traditions, evident in the local Breton costume and music, traditional religious festivals and the cuisine, featuring crêpes and cider. Many castles and manor houses, countless chapels and old towns and villages provide evidence of Brittany's eventful history and wealth of traditions. The abbey fortress of Mont St-Michel on the north coast should not be missed and Concarneau in the south is a lovely walled town enclosed by granite rocks.

Places of interest

Cancale: small fishing port famous for oysters.

Carnac: 3,000 standing stones (menhirs).

Concarneau: fishing port, old walled town.

Dinan: historic walled town.

La Baule: resort with lovely, sandy bay.

Le Croisic: fishing port, Naval museum.

Guérande: historic walled town.

Perros-Guirec: leading resort of the 'Pink Granite Coast'.

Quiberon: boat service to three islands: Belle Ile (largest of the Breton islands), Houat, Hoedic.

Rennes: capital of Brittany, medieval streets, half timbered houses; Brittany Museum.

St Malo: historic walled city, fishing port.

Cuisine of the region

Fish and shellfish are commonplace; traditional *crêperies* abound and welcome visitors with a cup of local cider.

Agneau de pré-salé: leg of lamb from animals pastured in the salt marshes and meadows.

Beurre blanc: sauce for fish dishes made with shallots, wine vinegar and butter.

Cotriade: fish soup with potatoes, onions, garlic and butter.

Crêpes Bretonnes: the thinnest of pancakes with a variety of sweet fillings.

Galette: can be a biscuit, cake or pancake; with sweet or savoury fillings.

Gâteau Breton: rich cake.

Poulet blanc Breton: free-range, quality, white Breton chicken.

17

FR22010 Camping les Capucines

Kervourdon, F-22300 Tredrez-Locquémeau (Côtes d'Armor)

Tel: 02 96 35 72 28. Email: les.capucines@wanadoo.fr   www.alanrogers.com/FR22010

A warm welcome awaits at Les Capucines which is quietly situated about a kilometre from the village of Saint Michel with its good, sandy beach and also very near Locquémeau, a pretty fishing village. This attractive, family run site has 100 pitches on flat or slightly sloping ground. All are well marked out by hedges, with mature trees and with more recently planted. There are 70 pitches with electricity, water and drainage, including ten for larger units. A good value restaurant/crêperie can be found at Trédrez; others at Saint Michel. A 'Sites et Paysages' member.

Facilities

Two modern toilet blocks, clean and very well kept, include washbasins mainly in cabins, facilities for babies and disabled people. Laundry with washing machines and dryer. Small shop for essentials (bread to order). Takeaway, bar with TV and games room. New covered and heated swimming pool. Paddling pool. Playground. Tennis. Minigolf. New multisport area. Chalets and mobile homes to rent. WiFi. Off site: Beach 1 km. Fishing 1 km. Riding 2 km. Golf 15 km.

Open: 15 March - 30 September.

Directions

Turn off main D786 road northeast of St Michel where site is signed, and 1 km. to site.
GPS: N48:41.564 W03:33.398

Charges guide

Per unit incl. 2 persons incl. electiricty (7A), water and drainage	€ 14,00 - € 19,90
	€ 17,80 - € 26,60
extra person	€ 3,90 - € 5,40
child (under 7 yrs)	€ 2,80 - € 3,50

FR22030 Camping Nautic International

Route de Beau-Rivage, F-22530 Caurel (Côtes d'Armor)

Tel: 02 96 28 57 94. Email: contact@campingnautic.fr   www.alanrogers.com/FR22030

This friendly family site is on the northern shore of the Lac de Guerledan. The lake is popular for all manner of watersports and there are some pleasant walks around the shores and through the surrounding Breton countryside and forests. The site is terraced down to the lake shore and offers 100 large pitches, all with electrical connections. A number of 'super pitches' (160-200 sq.m) are also available. There is an imaginatively designed swimming pool and smaller children's pool, both heated by a wood burning stove. Small boats can be launched from the site, and other boating activities are available on the lake. A member of 'Sites et Paysages'.

Facilities

There are two toilet blocks providing adequate facilities and well placed on the site. The slopes probably make the site unsuitable for disabled people. Washing and drying machines. Small shop and takeaway (10/7-31/8). Swimming pools (15/5-25/9). Gym. Play area. Fishing. Tennis. Games room. Off site: Restaurants and crêperie nearby. Watersports. Sailing school. Riding. Canal from Nantes to Brest. Sea 50 minutes by car.

Open: 15 May - 25 September.

Directions

From N164 Rennes - Brest road, turn off between Mur-de-Bretagne and Gouarec to the village of Caurel. Site is well signed from there.
GPS: N48:12.512 W03:03.060

Charges 2009

Per person	€ 3,80 - € 6,00
child (0-7 yrs)	€ 1,90 - € 3,30
pitch incl. electricity	€ 12,40 - € 15,60

FR22040 Camping le Châtelet

Rue des Nouettes, F-22380 Saint Cast-le-Guildo (Côtes d'Armor)

Tel: 02 96 41 96 33. Email: chateletcp@aol.com   www.alanrogers.com/FR22040

Carefully developed over the years from a former quarry, Le Châtelet is pleasantly and quietly situated with lovely views over the estuary from many pitches. It is well laid out, mainly in terraces with fairly narrow access roads. There are 216 good-sized pitches separated by hedges, all with electricity and 112 with water and drainage. Some pitches are around a little lake (unfenced) which can be used for fishing. Used by three different tour operators (73 pitches). A 'green' walking area is a nice feature around the lower edge of the site and a path leads from the site directly down to a beach (about 200 m. but including steps).

Facilities

Four toilet blocks with access at different levels include washbasins in cabins and facilities for children. Three small toilet blocks on the lower levels. Motorcaravan services. Heated swimming and paddling pools. Shop for basics, takeaway, bar lounge and general room with satellite TV. Games room. Play area. Games and activities in season. Dancing (June, July and Aug). Off site: Beach 200 m. Bicycle hire, riding and golf within 1.5 km.

Open: 24 April - 9 September.

Directions

Best approach is to turn off D786 road at Matignon towards St Cast; just inside St Cast limits turn left at sign for 'campings' and follow camp signs on C90.
GPS: N48:38.234 W02:16.160

Charges guide

Per person	€ 4,30 - € 6,50
child (under 7 yrs)	€ 3,00 - € 4,30
pitch	€ 12,50 - € 20,50
electricity (6/8A)	€ 4,60 - € 5,60

Check real time availability and at-the-gate prices...

www.alanrogers.com

FR22050 Camping le Vieux Moulin

14 rue des Moulins, F-22430 Erquy (Côtes d'Armor)

Tel: 02 96 72 34 23. Email: camp.vieux.moulin@wanadoo.fr   www.alanrogers.com/FR22050

Le Vieux Moulin is a family run site, just two kilometres from the little fishing port of Erquy on Brittany's Emerald Coast on the edge of a pine forest and nature reserve. It is about 900 metres from a beach of sand and shingle. Taking its name from the old mill opposite, the site has 173 pitches all with electricity (6/9A) and some with electricity, water and drainage. One section of 39 pitches is arranged around a pond. Most pitches are of a fair size in square boxes with trees giving shade. Evening entertainment is organised and there is a friendly pizzeria.

Facilities

Two good quality toilet blocks have mostly British style toilets and plenty of individual washbasins, facilities for disabled people and babies. Washing machines and dryer. Motorcaravan service point. Shop. Pizzeria and takeaway. Bar and terrace. Heated, covered pool complex with jacuzzi and paddling pool. Play areas. Tennis. Fitness gym. TV room (with satellite) and games room. Bicycle hire. No electric barbecues. Off site: Beach 900 m. Fishing 1.2 km.

Open: 25 April - 5 September.

Directions

Site is 2 km. east of Erquy. Take minor road towards Les Hôpitaux and site is signed from junction of D786 and D34 roads. GPS: N48:38.297 W02:26.540

Charges 2009

Per person	€ 5,00 - € 6,10
child (under 7 yrs)	€ 3,50 - € 4,80
pitch incl. electricity	€ 25,00 - € 32,10
dog	€ 3,00 - € 4,00

No credit cards.

FR22060 Camping Municipal la Hallerais

4 rue de la Robardais, F-22100 Taden (Côtes d'Armor)

Tel: 02 96 39 15 93. Email: camping.la.hallerais@wanadoo.fr   www.alanrogers.com/FR22060

As well as being an attractive old medieval town, Dinan is quite a short run from the resorts of the Côte d'Armor. This useful municipal site, open for a long season, is just outside Dinan, beyond and above the little harbour on the Rance estuary. There is a pleasant riverside walk where the site slopes down towards the Rance. The 226 pitches, all with electricity (6A) and most with water and drainage, are mainly on level, shallow terraces connected by tarmac roads, with trees and hedges giving a park-like atmosphere. This is a clean, efficiently run and well organised site.

Facilities

Two traditional toilet blocks, of good quality and heated in cool weather, have some private cabins with shower and washbasin. Unit for disabled people. Laundry room. Shop. Attractive bar/restaurant with outside terrace and takeaway (all season). Swimming and paddling pools (15/5-30/9). Tennis. TV room. Playground. Fishing. Internet and WiFi. Off site: Bus in Taden, 15 minutes walk. Riding 2 km. Bicycle hire 5 km. Beach 20 km.

Open: 14 March - 1 November.

Directions

Taden is northeast of Dinan. On leaving Dinan on D766, turn right to Taden and site before reaching large bridge and N176 junction. From N176 take Taden/Dinan exit. GPS: N48:28.289 W02:01.370

Charges 2009

Per person	€ 3,25 - € 3,85
child (under 7 yrs)	€ 1,37 - € 1,67
pitch incl. electricity	€ 7,00 - € 12,10

FR22080 Yelloh! Village le Ranolien

Ploumanach, F-22700 Perros-Guirec (Côtes d'Armor)

Tel: 04 66 73 97 39. Email: info@yellohvillage-ranolien.com   www.alanrogers.com/FR22080

Le Ranolien has been attractively developed around a former Breton farm – everything here is either made from, or placed on or around the often massive pink rocks. The 520 pitches are of a variety of sizes and types, mostly large and flat, but some are quite small. Some are formally arranged in rows with hedge separators, but most are either on open ground or under trees, amongst large boulders. With many holiday caravans around the site (318 pitches), there are 100 pitches for touring units, all with electricity and some with water and drainage.

Facilities

The main toilet block is heated in cool weather and has washbasins in cabins, mostly British style WCs and good showers. Laundry. Motorcaravan services. Supermarket and gift shop. Restaurant, crêperie and bar. Indoor and outdoor pool complex. Wellness centre. Disco in high season. Minigolf. Play area. Cinema. Gym and steam room. Off site: Beach 150 m. Bicycle hire 1 km.

Open: 4 April - 13 September.

Directions

From Lannion take D788 to Perros Guirec. Follow signs to 'Centre Ville' past main harbour area and then signs to Ploumanach, La Clarté. Pass through village of La Clarté and around sharp left hand bend. Site is immediately on the right. GPS: N48:49.679 W03:28.574

Charges 2009

Per unit incl. 2 persons	€ 12,00 - € 40,00
extra person	€ 5,00 - € 8,00

www.yellohvillage.com   tel: +33 466 739 739

Check real time availability and at-the-gate prices...

www.alanrogers.com

The Travel Service
BOOK THIS SITE
CALL 01580 214000
...we'll arrange everything

FR22090 Castel Camping le Château de Galinée

La Galinée, F-22380 Saint Cast-le-Guildo (Côtes d'Armor)

Tel: 02 96 41 10 56. Email: chateaugalinee@wanadoo.fr   www.alanrogers.com/FR22090

Situated a few kilometres back from St Cast and owned and managed by the Vervel family, Galinée is in a parkland setting on level grass with numerous and varied mature trees. It has 273 pitches, all with electricity, water and drainage and separated by many mature shrubs and bushes. The top section is mostly for mobile homes. An attractive outdoor pool complex has swimming and paddling pools and two pools with a water slide and a 'magic stream'. A new indoor complex has now also been added and includes a swimming pool, bar, restaurant and large entertainment hall.

Facilities

The large modern sanitary block includes washbasins in private cabins, facilities for babies and a good unit for disabled people. Laundry room. Shop for basics, bar and excellent takeaway menu (all 1/7-26/8). Attractive heated pool complex (12/5-7/9). New covered complex with heated pool, bar, restaurant, entertainment hall and internet access. Outside terrace with large play area. Tennis. Fishing. Field for ball games. Off site: Beach and golf 3.5 km. Riding 6 km.

Open: 7 May - 12 September.

Directions

From D168 Ploubalay - Plancoet road turn onto D786 towards Matignon and St Cast. Site is very well signed 1 km. after leaving Notre Dame de Guildo. GPS: N48:35.067 W02:15.438

Charges 2009

Per person	€ 4,00 - € 6,50
child (under 7 yrs)	€ 2,50 - € 4,50
pitch with electricity	€ 13,50 - € 23,50
animal	€ 4,00

Camping Cheques accepted.

FR22100 Camping l'Abri Côtier

Ville Es Rouxel, F-22680 Etables-sur-Mer (Côtes d'Armor)

Tel: 02 96 70 61 57. Email: camping.abricotier@wanadoo.fr   www.alanrogers.com/FR22100

L'Abri Côtier is a well cared for, family run site 500 m. from a sandy beach. Small and tranquil, it is arranged in two sections separated by a lane. The pitches are marked out on part level, part sloping grass, divided by mature trees and shrubs with some in a charming walled area with a quaint, old-world atmosphere. The second section has an orchard type setting. The evening bar forms a good social centre. In total there are 140 pitches, all with electrical connections (long leads useful) and 60 fully serviced. Tim Lee and his French wife are busy with ideas for this very popular, friendly site.

Facilities

Good clean sanitary facilities, heated in low season, include some washbasins in cabins, two units for disabled visitors and a baby bath/shower. Laundry room. Well stocked shop, set menu and simple takeaway service. Bar (with TV) and outdoor terrace area. Sheltered, heated swimming pool with jacuzzi. Playground. Games room. Some entertainment in peak season. Off site: Beach 500 m. Restaurants and indoor pool in the village. Riding 1 km. Fishing 2 km. Bicycle hire 4 km. Golf 10 km.

Open: 6 May - 15 September.

Directions

From N12 (Saint Brieuc bypass) take D786 towards St Quay Portrieux. After 12 km. pass Aire de la Chapelle on the right and take second left on D47 towards Etables-sur-Mer. Take second right to site at crossroads in 100 m. GPS: N48:38.135 W02:50.128

Charges guide

Per person	€ 4,20 - € 4,70
child (under 7 yrs)	€ 2,50 - € 3,00
pitch	€ 6,50 - € 7,50
serviced pitch	€ 7,50 - € 8,50

FR22130 Camping de Port l'Epine

Venelle de Pors Garo, F-22660 Trélévern (Côtes d'Armor)

Tel: 02 96 23 71 94. Email: camping-de-port-lepine@wanadoo.fr   www.alanrogers.com/FR22130

Port L'Epine is a pretty little site in a unique situation on a promontory. There is access to the sea, therefore, on the south side of the site, with views across to Perros Guirec. The area covered by the site is not large but there are 160 grass pitches, all with electricity, which are divided by pretty hedging and trees. Some are used for mobile homes. Access is a little tight in parts. This site is ideal for families with young children (probably not for teenagers). Just outside the entrance on the north side is a further sandy bay with little boats moored and facing an archipelago of seven small islands.

Facilities

The original toilet block is well equipped and a second block has been refurbished in modern style. Shop and bar (all season) restaurant with takeaway (1/7-31/8). Small heated swimming pool and paddling pool (May - Sept). Fenced play area near the bar/restaurant. Video games. Bicycle hire. Off site: Riding or golf 15 km. Useful small supermarket up hill from site. Many coastal paths.

Open: 30 May - 11 September.

Directions

From roundabout south of Perros Guirec take D6 towards Tréguier. Pass through Louannec, take left turn for Trélévern. Go through village following camp signs – Port L'Epine is clearly marked as distinct from the municipal site. GPS: N48:48.784 W03:23.008

Charges 2009

Per pitch incl. 2 persons and electricity	€ 14,50 - € 33,00
extra person	€ 5,00 - € 7,00

The Travel Service
BOOK THIS SITE
CALL 01580 214000
...we'll arrange everything

Check real time availability and at-the-gate prices...

www.alanrogers.com

FR22110 Camping les Madières

Le Vau Madec, F-22590 Pordic (Côtes d'Armor)

Tel: 02 96 79 02 48. Email: campinglesmadieres@wanadoo.fr   www.alanrogers.com/FR22110

Les Madières is well placed for exploring the Goëlo coast with its seaside resorts of St Quay-Portrieux, Binic and Etables-sur-Mer, ports used in the past by fishing schooners and now used by pleasure boats and a few coastal fishing boats. The young and enthusiastic owners here have already made their mark on this quiet campsite. With plenty of open spaces and set in the countryside, yet near the sea (800 m), it has 93 pitches of which ten are used for mobile homes. There are no tour operators. The site has an outdoor swimming pool and some entertainment is organised in July and August by the welcoming and helpful owners. Only 800 m. away is the Vau Madec beach for swimming, fishing and collecting shellfish. This is linked to the beach at Binic by the GR34 coastal path (3 km.) where there are sandy beaches and holiday activities such as sailing, minigolf and tennis.

Facilities

Two refurbished heated toilet blocks include private cabins and facilities for disabled visitors. Laundry facilities. Motorcaravan services. Gas. Simple shop (all season). Bar, restaurant and takeaway (all season). Swimming pool (1/6-20/9). Games room. Play area. Some entertainment (high season). Mobile home rental. Caravan storage. Off site: Beach 800 m. Bus service nearby. Riding 2.5 km. Bicycle hire 3 km.

Open: 1 April - 30 October.

Directions

From St Brieuc ring-road (N12), turn north on D786 signed Paimpol (by the coast). Les Madières is at Pordic, 3 km. from the ring-road. Site is well signed from the D786. GPS: N48:34.944 W02:48.288

Charges guide

Per person	€ 4,80
child (0-10 yrs)	€ 3,00
pitch incl. electricity (10A)	€ 11,00
dog	€ 2,00

Discounts outside July and August.

- 93 pitches
- 800 m from the beach, quietly situated with shadow pitches
- Heated swimmingpool
- Heated sanitary blocks

Open from 1st April till 30th October 2008

Le Vau Madec - 22590 Pordic - Bretagne
Tel: 0033 296 790 248
www.campinglesmadieres.com

FR22140 Camping de Port la Chaine

F-22610 Pleubian (Côtes d'Armor)

Tel: 02 96 22 92 38. Email: info@portlachaine.com   www.alanrogers.com/FR22140

The Suquet family has worked hard to establish this comfortable, quiet, family site. In a beautiful location on the 'Untamed Peninsula' between Paimpol and Perros Guirec, attractive trees and shrubs provide a balance of sun and shade for the 200 pitches. There is a central road and the grassy bays or fields branch off on the gradual decline towards the bay and the sea (a sandy bay with rocks). Most of the bays have a slight slope, so those with motorcaravans will need to choose their pitch carefully. Electricity is said to be available everywhere (a long lead may be useful).

Facilities

Two traditional style toilet blocks are comfortable and fully equipped, both now completely renovated. Washbasins in cabins, British and Turkish style toilets. Cabins for families or disabled visitors. Washing machines and dryer. Bar/restaurant with terrace and takeaway (1/7-25/8). Heated swimming pool (13/6-5/9). Indoor pool planned. Play area. Games room. Pétanque. Children's entertainer in July/Aug. Beach, fishing and sailing. Off site: Bus 1 km. Village 2 km. for tennis, market, shops and restaurants. Good fishing and diving. Boat launching 1 km. Bicycle hire 2 km. Riding 6 km. Golf 18 km.

Open: 4 April - 20 September.

Directions

Leave D786 between Lézardrieux and Tréguier to go north to village of Pleubian (about 8 km). Continue on D20 towards Larmor Pleubian and site signed on left, 2 km. from Pleubian. GPS: N48:51.333 W03:07.966

Charges 2009

Per person	€ 4,30 - € 6,10
child (2-7 yrs)	€ 3,40 - € 4,00
pitch with electricity	€ 10,40 - € 14,90
dog	€ 3,00

Less 10-20% in low seasons.

BOOK THIS SITE
CALL 01580 214000
"...we'll arrange everything
The Travel Service

The Travel
Service
...we'll arrange everything
BOOK THIS SITE
CALL 01580 214000

FR22200 Camping Au Bocage du Lac

Rue du Bocage, F-22270 Jugon-les-Lacs (Côtes d'Armor)

Tel: 02 96 31 60 16   www.alanrogers.com/FR22200

This well kept former municipal site has been updated over the past few years by the current owners M. and Mme. Riviere. It is on the edge of the village beside a lake, 25 km. from the sea. It offers 181 good size pitches, all with electrical connections, set on gently sloping grass and divided by shrubs and bushes, with mature trees providing shade. Some 40 wooden chalets and mobile homes are intermingled with the touring pitches. On-site facilities include a good pool with children's section and sunbathing patio. There is also a small animal park.

Facilities

Two main sanitary blocks include facilities for disabled visitors. British and Turkish style WCs and some washbasins in cabins. Washing machine. Small shop. Bar. Swimming pool (15/6-10/9). Tennis. Football. Play area. Activity programmes July/Aug. Fishing. Bicycle hire. Off site: Supermarket in village 1 km. River 1 km.

Open: 1 April - 31 October.

Directions

From N176 (E401) Lamballe - Dinan road, about 15 km. from Lamballe take turning for Jugon-les-Lacs. Site is signed shortly after. GPS: N48:24.072 W02:19.042

Charges guide

Per person	€ 3,70 - € 4,70
child (under 7 yrs)	€ 2,70 - € 3,20
pitch	€ 13,10 - € 17,40
electricity (5A)	€ 3,00

Camping ★★★ Au Bocage du Lac
AU BOCAGE DU LAC
Hôtel de Plein Air

On the lakeside, in the pretty and historical town of Jugon Les Lacs, for both relaxation and leisure, you will find a wide range of activities : heated pool, water slide, paddling pool, childrens' mini camp, tennis, minigolf, sailing, fishing, walking. New sanitary block includes private cabins, facilities for babies. Rental of Chalets, Mobile Homes with view over the lake.
WELCOME TO BRITTANY!!
22270 Jugon les Lacs / Tél : 02.96.31.60.16
contact@campingjugon.com / www.campingjugon.com

FR22160 Camping le Neptune

Kerguistin, F-22580 Lanloup (Côtes d'Armor)

Tel: 02 96 22 33 35. Email: contact@leneptune.com   www.alanrogers.com/FR22160

Situated on the Côte de Goëlo at Lanloup, Le Neptune offers a peaceful, rural retreat for families. The friendly new owners, M. and Mme. Camard, keep the site neat and tidy and there is a regular programme of renovation. There are 84 level, grass pitches (65 for touring units) separated by trimmed hedges providing privacy and all with electricity. There are also 21 mobile homes to rent. A heated swimming pool has a retractable roof so can be open for a long season. Within walking distance is the local village, with a restaurant and shop, and sandy beaches. The site is also a good base for cycling and walking.

Facilities

The modern toilet block is of a good standard, clean and well maintained. Laundry room with washing machine and dryer. Motorcaravan services. No restaurant but good takeaway (all season). Small shop well stocked for basic needs. Bar with indoor and outdoor seating. Heated swimming pool (Easter - end Oct). Pétanque. Animation in season. New play area. Off site: Tennis 300 m. Fishing and beach 2 km. Golf 4 km. Riding 8 km. Restaurant and shop within walking distance. Beach 2.5 km.

Open: 1 April - 31 October.

Directions

From Saint Brieuc (N12) take D786 Paimpol (par la Côte). After 28 km. on approaching Lanloup, site is well signed. GPS: N48:42.490 W02:58.000

Charges guide

Per person	€ 4,00 - € 5,30
child (under 7 yrs)	€ 2,50 - € 3,40
pitch	€ 6,40 - € 8,50
electricity (6A)	€ 3,90
dog	€ 2,00 - € 2,50

Camping Cheques accepted.

Check real time availability and at-the-gate prices...
www.alanrogers.com

FR22190 Camping les Roches

Caroual Village, F-22430 Erquy (Côtes d'Armor)

Tel: **02 96 72 32 90**. Email: **info@camping-les-roches.com**   www.alanrogers.com/FR22190

Among several very good campsites in Erquy, this is a little gem. It has magnificent, panoramic views over the Bay of Erquy and is situated 900 metres from sandy beaches and two kilometres from the seaside resort of Erquy. You will receive a warm and genuine reception from the owners to their immaculately kept site. Although rather limited in amenities (no pool, restaurant or bar), nearby Erquy offers a full range of shops, restaurants and activities. The site itself offers a takeaway service in high season. Limited entertainment is also provided at that time.

Facilities

One large and two small toilet blocks are attractive and clean providing good facilities. Provision for children, babies and disabled visitors is also good. Well equipped laundry area. Small shop in reception (all season). Snack bar and takeaway (30/6-15/9), also some entertainment. Lounge area with TV. Minigolf. Play area. Off site: Erquy 2 km. Bicycle hire 100 m. Golf 2 km. Riding 5 km.

Open: 31 March - 30 September.

Directions

From the N12 southeast of Saint Brieuc take the D786 road northeast to Erquy. Site is well signed on approaching the town.
GPS: N48:36.649 W02:28.710

Charges guide

Per person	€ 3,80
child (2-7 yrs)	€ 2,80
pitch incl. car	€ 6,60
electricity (6/10A)	€ 2,80 - € 3,20

FR22210 Camping Bellevue

Route de Pléneuf Val-André, F-22430 Erquy (Côtes d'Armor)

Tel: **02 96 72 33 04**. Email: **campingbellevue@yahoo.fr**   www.alanrogers.com/FR22210

Situated a mile from the beaches between Erquy and Pléneuf Val-André, Camping Bellevue offers a quiet country retreat with easy access to the cliffs of Cap Fréhel, Sables d'Or and St Cast. There are 140 pitches of which 120 are available for touring units, most with electricity (6/10A) and 15 with water and drainage. The site also has 20 mobile homes, chalets and bungalows to rent. Children are well catered for at this campsite – there are heated swimming and paddling pools, three play areas and minigolf, pétanque and volleyball. Indoor entertainment for all includes themed evenings, Breton dancing and visits to a local cider house. There are numerous walks in the area and a vast range of aquatic sports at nearby Erquy. A 'Sites et Paysages' member.

Facilities

Two modern, unisex toilet blocks are of a high standard. Some washbasins in cubicles. Facilities for disabled visitors. Laundry facilities. Shop and bar (15/6-10/9). Restaurant and takeaway (12/6-30/9). Swimming and paddling pools (10/5-10/9). Play areas. Games room and library. Minigolf. Pétanque. Entertainment and organised activities in high season. Off site: Beach and fishing 2 km. Golf 3 km. Bicycle hire and boat launching 5 km. Riding 6 km.

Open: 15 April - 15 September.

Directions

From St Brieuc road take D786 towards Erquy. Site is adjacent to the D786 at St Pabu and is well signed.
GPS: N48:35.655 W02:29.085

Charges guide

Per unit incl. 2 persons	€ 15,50 - € 20,00
child (2-13 yrs)	free - € 4,40
extra person	€ 4,00 - € 5,00
electricity	€ 3,50 - € 4,80
dog	€ 1,30 - € 1,70

Camping Bellevue ★★★★

2 km from the beach, the campsite is situated between two seaside resorts: Erquy and Pléneuf Val André.
We offer you a family atmosphere with young children.

What make it special: 140 seperated pitches in 3-ha park with many trees and flowers. Covert heated swimming and paddling pools, beach-volleyball, miniature-golf, table tennis, playroom, billiards, table football, TV, bowling competitions, volley-ball, swimming, evening dances and karaoke.

Open from 15/04 to 15/09/07   **www.campingbellevue.fr**   **4-star comfort**

SITES & PAYSAGES DE FRANCE

Yolande et René URBAN
Camping Bellevue
Route de Pléneuf Val André
22430 ERQUY
Tél.: 00 33 2 96 72 33 04
Fax: 00 33 2 96 72 48 03
Email: campingbellevue@yahoo.fr

Check real time availability and at-the-gate prices...

www.alanrogers.com

BOOK THIS SITE
CALL 01580 214000
...we'll arrange everything
The Travel Service

FR22230 Camping Bellevue

68 boulevard du Littoral, F-22410 Saint Quay-Portrieux (Côtes d'Armor)

Tel: 02 96 70 41 84. Email: campingbellevue@free.fr   www.alanrogers.com/FR22230

With magnificent coastal views, this attractive and well cared for site lives up to its name. Family-owned for many years, it is situated on the outskirts of the popular seaside resort of St Quay-Portrieux and you will be made to feel most welcome by the owners. The 173 numbered touring pitches vary in size and 140 have 6A electricity. Some are separated by hedges, whilst others are in groups of four. Entertainment on site is limited but there is plenty to do and see around the area and a great opportunity for exploring the Goëlo coast.

Facilities	Directions
Two clean sanitary blocks provide both open and cubicled washbasins and controllable showers. Facilities for disabled visitors and babies. Laundry and dishwashing facilities. Motorcaravan service point. Shop for basics. Simple snack bar (1/7-16/9). Outdoor pool (1/6-16/9; no Bermuda shorts). Paddling pool. Volleyball. Boules. Play area. Off site: Within walking distance of St Quay-Portrieux with shops, bars, restaurants and casino. Bicycle hire 1 km. Riding 8 km. Golf 10 km.	From N12 St Brieuc by-pass, take D786 north towards Paimpol. Site is well signed northwest of St Quay-Portrieux, 13 km. from the bypass. GPS: N48:39.766 W02:50.666

Open: 26 April - 16 September.

Charges 2009

Per person (over 7 yrs)	€ 4,00 - € 5,10
child	€ 3,00 - € 3,20
pitch with 2 persons and electricity	€ 17,00 - € 21,20
dog	€ 1,50

FR22250 Camping Municipal de Cruckin

Rue de Cruckin, Kérity, F-22500 Paimpol (Côtes d'Armor)

Tel: 02 96 20 78 47. Email: contact@camping-paimpol.com   www.alanrogers.com/FR22250

A neat and well managed municipal site situated close to the historical fishing port of Cité des Islandais and within easy reach of the Ile de Bréhat. This is an ideal location for many interesting walks. The site has 130 well maintained, mostly level pitches set in both wooded and open areas and all have electricity connections (5-12A). A very large area has been provided for sports, a play area and picnic tables. Although the site does not have its own swimming pool, the beach is just a short walk away.

Facilities	Directions
One modern and heated toilet block (a second block is planned). Washbasins in cabins and showers. Facilities for babies and disabled visitors. Laundry facilities. Bread and milk (high season). Snack bar/takeaway (July/Aug). Motorcaravan service point. Large field for football. Pétanque. Fenced play area. Internet access on request. Bicycle hire. Fishing. Off site: Beach. Kérity village with shops, restaurants and cafés. Riding 2 km. Golf 10 km.	From N12 St Brieuc bypass, take D786 north towards Paimpol. Village of Kérity is 3 km. south of Paimpol. Site is signed. GPS: N48:46.180 W03:01.325

Open: 1 April - 10 October.

Charges guide

Per person	€ 2,90 - € 3,30
child (under 7 yrs)	€ 1,50 - € 2,10
pitch	€ 5,60 - € 7,10
electricity	€ 3,10 - € 3,05
dog	€ 1,10 - € 1,50

FR22280 Camping des Hautes Grées

Rue Saint-Michel, les Hôpitaux, F-22430 Erquy (Côtes d'Armor)

Tel: 02 96 72 34 78. Email: hautesgrees@wanadoo.fr   www.alanrogers.com/FR22280

This site is situated just 400 m. from the beaches and resort facilities of Erquy. You will receive a warm welcome from the owners who are keen gardeners and have created a beautiful and clean site with an abundance of flowers. There is a total of 170 grass pitches, 128 of which are for touring. They are well tended, divided by hedges and all have electricity connections. Whilst there are plenty of activities available on site including a children's club every morning in high season, it is also well positioned for fishing, diving, bathing and also for walking.

Facilities	Directions
Two toilet blocks provide modern facilities and include washbasins in cabins and pre-set showers. Laundry facilities. Motorcaravan services. Small shop (1/7-31/8). Bar and takeaway (1/7-31/8). Heated swimming and paddling pools (15/6-15/9). Small gym with good equipment. Sauna. Games room with TV. Adventure play area. Children's club. Entertainment once a week in high season. WiFi. Off site: Beach 400 m. Fishing 500 m. Bicycle hire 1 km. Golf 2 km. Riding 4 km.	From the N12, southeast of Brieuc, take the D786 to Erquy. 2 km. before Erquy, follow signs for Frehél/Matignon. At Super U roundabout follow signs for Les Hôpitaux. Site is clearly signed in village. GPS: N48:38.562 W02:25.498

Open: 1 April - 30 September.

Charges guide

Per person	€ 3,10 - € 4,90
child (under 7 yrs)	€ 1,50 - € 3,50
pitch	€ 5,60 - € 10,00
electricity (10A)	€ 2,50 - € 3,60

FR22360 Yelloh! Village les Pins

Route du Guen, le Guen, F-22430 Erquy (Côtes d'Armor)
Tel: **04 66 73 97 39**. Email: **info@yellohvillage-les-pins.com**   www.alanrogers.com/FR22360

Erquy is a pretty holiday resort nestling between two promontories. There are plenty of great sandy beaches around here, and one of the best is just 900 m. from this wooded site. Les Pins is a long-established site with many of the original facilities still in use. There are 235 touring pitches here and a further 148 pitches are occupied by mobile homes and chalets. The site boasts some impressive amenities including a top class swimming pool complex extending over 600 sq.m. with water slides, lazy river and various other water features.

Facilities	Directions
Four very old toilet blocks, all with mostly Turkish style toilets and other poor facilities. New facilities at the pools. Shop. Bar. Restaurant. Snack bar and takeaway (from 15/6). Large pool complex. Fitness centre. Sauna. Tennis. Activity and entertainment Off site: Beach 900 m. Fishing 900 m. Golf, riding and bicycle hire 2.5 km.	From St Brieuc, take the northbound D786 to Erquy. Continue through the town following signs to Cap d'Erquy and the site is well indicated. GPS: N48:38.305 W02:27.339

Open: 26 April - 13 September.

Charges guide

Per unit incl. 2 persons and electricity	€ 17,00 - € 34,00
extra person (over 1 yr)	€ 4,00 - € 5,00

www.yellohvillage.com   tel: +33 466 739 739

FR22320 Camping le Cap Horn

Port Lazo, F-22470 Plouézec (Côtes d'Armor)
Tel: **02 96 20 64 28**   www.alanrogers.com/FR22320

Le Cap Horn is in a magnificent setting with exceptional views of the Bay of Paimpol and the Ile de Bréhat. The enthusiastic new owners are keen to make visitors welcome at their site which is well positioned for exploring the Goëlo Coast, Paimpol and the Pink Granite Coast. The campsite is in two sections and slopes down to the beach. The upper section is mostly devoted to mobile homes and is reached by a road or a series of steep steps, the lower section is for tourers. There are 149 pitches with 115 good sized grass pitches for touring (90 with 6A electricity).

Facilities	Directions
Two toilet blocks including facilities for campers with disabilities but site not ideal for those with walking difficulties. Small shop. Bar, restaurant with takeaway and terrace with views over the bay (July/Aug). Heated swimming pool (1/6-15/9). Play area. Boules. Fishing. Watersports. Sports area. Bicycle hire, Organised activities (July/Aug). Internet access. Off site: Beach 100 m. Boat ramp 300 m. Riding 6 km. Golf 12 km. Shops, bars restaurant at Plouézec and Paimpol.	From Saint Brieuc take D786 north to Paimpol (par la Côte). Site is at Plouézec, south of Paimpol, well signed from D786. GPS: N48:45.588 W02:57.768

Open: 7 April - 30 September.

Charges guide

Per unit incl. 2 persons	€ 14,00 - € 21,00
incl. electricity (6A)	€ 17,00 - € 25,00
extra person	€ 4,00 - € 5,50
child (under 7 yrs)	€ 3,00 - € 5,00

FR22370 Camping la Vallée

Saint Pabu, F-22430 Erquy (Côtes d'Armor)
Tel: **02 96 72 06 22**. Email: **contact@campinglavallee.fr**   www.alanrogers.com/FR22370

This small rural site is immaculately kept by its young owners. Pitch sizes are generous, level and separated by shrubs and trees and some have shade. The amenities are all new and of a high standard. The owner is particularly proud of his sauna/relaxation room. There is little by way of entertainment on site, which makes it ideally suitable for families with very young children or couples looking for a peaceful holiday. There is a wide safe sandy beach 800 m. away. Shops and restaurants can be found nearby in Erquy, a Breton port that is picturesque and lively.

Facilities	Directions
The sanitary facilities are modern and bright with washbasins in cabins and pre-set showers. Facilities for babies and disabled visitors. Laundry facilities. Bread to order and delivered to pitch. A few basic provisions are sold in high season. Small games room. Sauna. Play area. Bicycle hire. Off site: Beach 800 m. Sand yachting. Fishing and boat launching within 1 km. Golf 4 km. Riding 10 km.	From St Brieuc travel northeast on the D786 towards Erquy. Passing turn for Pléneuf Val-Andre and site is signed on left in about 2 km. GPS: N48:36.288 W02:29.299

Open: 30 April - 7 September.

Charges guide

Per person	€ 3,60 - € 4,60
child (0-7 yrs)	free - € 2,30
pitch	€ 6,00 - € 7,70
electricity (6A)	€ 3,30

BOOK THIS SITE
CALL 01580 214000
...we'll arrange everything
Service The Travel

25

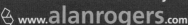

FR29020 Domaine du Saint Laurent

Kerleven, F-29940 La Forêt-Fouesnant (Finistère)

Tel: 02 98 56 97 65. Email: info@camping-du-saint-laurent.fr   www.alanrogers.com/FR29020

Saint Laurent is a well established site, situated on a sheltered wooded slope bordering one of the many attractive little inlets that typify the Brittany coastline. The site is on the coastal footpath that leads from Kerleven to Concarneau. The 260 pitches are on level terraces, under tall trees. All are of average size (100 sq.m) and divided by hedges and partly shaded, all with electricity connections. Around 50% of the pitches are occupied by tour operators or site owned mobile homes. Pitches with the best sea views tend to be adjacent to the cliff edge and may not be suitable for families with young children. Access to some places can be a little difficult, but the friendly site owners ensure that this is not a problem by offering to site any caravan using their own 4 x 4 vehicle. The swimming pool (complete with two water slides) is overlooked by the bar terrace. With organised activities and entertainment in high season, this site is an ideal choice for a lively family holiday, particularly for older children. There is direct access from the site to two small sandy bays.

Facilities

Two sanitary blocks provide combined shower and washbasin cubicles, separate washbasin cubicles, baby changing and facilities for disabled people. Washing machines, dryers and ironing. Small shop at reception (all season). Bar, snack bar and takeaway (1/7-31/8). Swimming pools. Gym and sauna. Canoe and boat hire. Two tennis courts (free). Play area. Entertainment in July/Aug. for adults and children (in English and French) with discos in the bar each evening. Bicycle hire.

Open: 5 April - 4 October.

Directions

From N165 take D70 Concarneau exit. At first roundabout take first exit D44 (Fouesnant). After 2.5 km. turn right at T-junction, follow for 2.5 km, then turn left (Port La Forêt). Continue to roundabout, straight ahead (Port La Forêt) and after 1 km. turn left (site signed here). In 400 m. left turn to site. GPS: N47:53.770 W03:57.305

Charges guide

Per unit incl. 2 persons, electricity and water	€ 17,00 - € 37,00
extra person	€ 4,60 - € 6,50
child (2-7 yrs)	€ 2,60 - € 4,50

FINISTÈRE

CAMPINGS FranceLoc

Le saint Laurent ****

Direct access to the sea.
Heated pool, paddling pool
and water slide.

Kerleven
29940, LA FORET-FOUESNANT
Tel.: +33 (0)2 98 56 97 65
Email : saintlaurent@franceloc.fr
www.camping-franceloc.fr

FR29000 Yelloh! Village les Mouettes

La Grande Grève, F-29660 Carantec (Finistère)

Tel: 04 66 73 97 39. Email: info@yellohvillage-les-mouettes.com   www.alanrogers.com/FR29000

Les Mouettes is a sheltered site on the edge of an attractive bay with access to the sea at the front of the site. In a wooded setting with many attractive trees and shrubs, the 434 pitches include just 70 for touring units, the remainder being taken by tour operators and around 131 site-owned mobile homes and tents (located together at the top of the site). The touring pitches, mostly arranged in hedged areas in the lower section, are of a good size and all have electricity. The focal point of the site is an impressive heated pool complex.

Facilities

Three clean unisex sanitary blocks. Facilities for disabled people. Laundry. Motorcaravan services. Shop (limited hours outside the main season), takeaway, bar/ crêperie, pool complex. Play area. Entertainment in main season. Dogs are not accepted after 26/6. Off site: Fishing 1 km. Golf 2 km. Riding 6 km. Bicycle hire. Beach 2 km.

Open: 16 May - 6 September.

Directions

From D58 Roscoff - Morlaix road, turn to Carantec on D173. Site is 4 km. from here on the outskirts of the village, signed to the left at roundabout after supermarket on right. GPS: N48:39.384 W03:55.484

Charges 2009

Per unit incl. 2 persons,	€ 14,00 - € 44,00

tel: +33 466 739 739 www.yellohvillage.com

yelloh! VILLAGE

Brittany

BOOK THIS SITE
CALL 01580 214000
...we'll arrange everything

The Travel
Service

Check real time availability and at-the-gate prices...

 www.alanrogers.com

Route d'Arzano, F-29310 Locunolé (Finistère)
Tel: **02 98 71 75 47**. Email: infos@camping-ty-nadan.fr

Mobile homes ▶ page 487

www.alanrogers.com/FR29010

Ty-Nadan is a well organised site set amongst wooded countryside along the bank of the River Elle. The 183 pitches for touring units are grassy, many with shade and 99 are fully serviced. The pool complex with slides and paddling pool is very popular as are the large indoor pool complex and indoor games area with a climbing wall. There is also an adventure play park and a 'Minikids' park for 5-8 year olds, not to mention tennis courts, table tennis, pool tables, archery and trampolines. This is a wonderful site for families with children. Several tour operators use the site. An exciting and varied programme of activities is offered throughout the season – canoe and sea kayaking expeditions, rock climbing, mountain biking, aquagym, paintball, riding or walking – all supervised by qualified staff. A full programme of entertainment for all ages is provided in high season including concerts, Breton evenings with pig roasts, dancing, etc. (be warned, you will be actively encouraged to join in!)

Facilities

Two older, split-level toilet blocks are of fair quality and include washbasins in cabins and baby rooms. A newer block provides easier access for disabled people. Washing machines and dryers. Restaurant, takeaway, bar and well stocked shop. Crêperie (July/Aug). Heated outdoor pool (17 x 8 m). New indoor pool. Small river beach (unfenced). Indoor badminton and rock climbing facility. Activity and entertainment programmes (high season). Bicycle hire. Boat hire. Fishing. Off site: Beaches 20 minutes by car. Golf 12 km.

Open: 3 April - 7 September.

Directions

Make for Arzano which is northeast of Quimperlé on the Pontivy road and turn off D22 just west of village at site sign. Site is about 3 km.
GPS: N47:54.284 W03:28.457

Charges guide

Per unit incl. 2 persons and electricity	€ 19,90 - € 45,90
child (under 7 yrs)	€ 1,70 - € 5,40
dog	€ 1,70 - € 5,40

Less 15-20% outside July/Aug.
Camping Cheques accepted.

Camping ★★★★ "Le Ty Nadan"

From the 3th of April

for unforgettable holidays !

www.tynadan-vacances.fr

CAMPING PLUS
LES CASTELS

BOOK THIS SITE
CALL 01580 214000
...we'll arrange everything
The Travel Service

27

FR29030 Camping du Letty

F-29950 Bénodet (Finistère)

Tel: **02 98 57 04 69**. Email: reception@campingduletty.com   www.alanrogers.com/FR29030

The Guyader family have ensured that this excellent and attractive site has plenty to offer for all the family. With a charming ambience, the site on the outskirts of the popular resort of Bénodet spreads over 22 acres with 493 pitches, all for touring units. Groups of four to eight pitches are set in cul-de-sacs with mature hedging and trees to divide each group. Most pitches have electricity, water and drainage. Although there is no swimming pool here, the site has direct access to a small sandy beach, and has provided a floating pontoon (safe bathing depends on the tides). At the attractive floral entrance, former farm buildings provide a host of facilities including an extensively equipped fitness room and new 'wellness' rooms for massage and jacuzzis. There is also a modern, purpose built nightclub and bar providing high quality live entertainment most evenings (situated well away from most pitches to avoid disturbance).

Facilities

Six well placed toilet blocks are of good quality and include mixed style WCs, washbasins in large cabins and controllable hot showers (charged). Baby rooms. Separate facility for disabled visitors. Launderette. Motorcaravan services. Well stocked shop. Extensive snack bar and takeaway (21/6-31/8). Bar with games room and night club. Reading room with four computer stations. Entertainment room with satellite TV. Fitness centre (no charge). Saunas, jacuzzi and solarium (all on payment). Tennis and squash (charged). Boules. Well equipped play area. Entertainment and activities (July/Aug).

Open: 15 June - 6 September.

Directions

From N165 take D70 Concarneau exit. At first roundabout take D44 to Fouesnant. Turn right at T-junction. After 2 km. turn left to Fouesnant (still D44). Continue through La Forêt Fouesnant and Fouesnant, picking up signs for Bénodet. Shortly before Bénodet at roundabout turn left (signed Le Letty). Turn right at next mini-roundabout and site is 500 m. on left. GPS: N47:52.020 W04:05.270

Charges 2009

Per person	€ 4,00 - € 6,50
child (1-6 yrs)	€ 2,00 - € 3,25
pitch incl. electricity	€ 12,50 - € 15,00

CAMPING Le Letty ★★★★

Direct access to the beach.
Caravans for hire.

29950 Bénodet
Finistère
Bretagne Sud

Tél. 00 33 (0)2 98 57 04 69
Fax 00 33 (0)2 98 66 22 56

www.campingduletty.com

FR29140 Siblu Camping Domaine de Kerlann

Land Rosted, F-29930 Pont-Aven (Finistère)

Tel: **02 98 06 01 77**. Email: kerlann@siblu.fr   www.alanrogers.com/FR29140

Siblu have, with careful and imaginative planning, ensured that their mobile home pitches (of which there are over 700) blend naturally into this well kept and landscaped holiday village. There are 20 touring pitches of medium size and quality, all with water and electricity. Much evening holiday camp style entertainment (with a French flavour) takes place on the bar terrace with its raised stage which overlooks the complex. The 'pièce de résistance' of the site is the superb pool complex comprising three outdoor pools with separate toboggan, attractively landscaped with sunbathing terraces, and an indoor tropical style complex complete with jacuzzi and its own toboggan.

Facilities

The main large toilet block in the centre of the park includes washbasins in cubicles. Good laundry. Mini supermarket. French style restaurant, snack restaurant, takeaway and bar. Impressive pool complex. Well equipped play areas. All weather multisport court. Tennis. Minigolf. Video games room, pool tables and satellite TV in the bar. Children's clubs. Gas barbecues are not permitted. Dogs are not accepted. Off site: Beach 5 km.

Open: 1 April - 29 October.

Directions

From Tregunc - Pont-Aven road, turn south towards Névez and site is on right.
GPS: N47:50.40 W03:47.21

Charges guide

Per pitch incl. up to 6 persons and electricity	€ 14,00 - € 40,00

Check real time availability and at-the-gate prices...

www.alanrogers.com

Château de Lanniron, F-29336 Quimper (Finistère)

Tel: **02 98 90 62 02**. Email: **camping@lanniron.com**   www.alanrogers.com/FR29050

BOOK THIS SITE
CALL 01580 214000
...we'll arrange everything
The Travel Service

L'Orangerie is a beautiful and peaceful, family site set in ten acres of a 17th-century, 42 acre country estate on the banks of the Odet river, formerly the home of the Bishops of Quimper. The site has 199 grassy pitches (156 for touring units) of three types varying in size and services. They are on flat ground laid out in rows alongside access roads with shrubs and bushes providing pleasant pitches. All have electricity and 88 have all three services. The original outbuildings have been attractively converted around a walled courtyard. With lovely walks within the grounds, the restaurant and the gardens are both open to the public and in spring the rhododendrons and azaleas are magnificent. The site is just to the south of Quimper and about 15 km. from the sea and beaches at Bénodet. The restoration of the park, including the original canal, fountains, ornamental 'Bassin de Neptune', the boathouse and the gardens is now complete. New additions are a new reception and restaurant, plus a nine-hole golf course and driving range. Used by tour operators (30 pitches).

Facilities

Excellent heated block in the courtyard and second modern block serving the top areas of the site. Facilities for disabled people and babies. Washing machines and dryers. Motorcaravan services. Shop (15/5-9/9). Gas supplies. Bar, snacks and takeaway, plus new restaurant (open daily). Swimming pool (144 sq. m) with paddling pool. Small play area. Tennis. Minigolf. Golf course (9 holes) and driving range. Fishing. Archery. Bicycle hire. General reading, games and billiards rooms. TV/video room. Karaoke. Outdoor activities. Large room for indoor activities. Pony rides and tree climbing (high season). Internet access and WiFi. Off site: Two hypermarkets 1 km. Historic town of Quimper under 3 km. Activities in the area include golf, cycling, walking, fishing, canoeing, surfing and sailing. Beach 15 km.

Open: 15 May - 15 September.

Directions

From Quimper follow Quimper Sud signs, then 'Toutes Directions' and general camping signs, finally signs for Lanniron. GPS: N47:58.630 W04:06.655

Charges guide

Per person	€ 4,25 - € 7,10
child (2-9 yrs)	€ 2,75 - € 4,50
pitch (100 sq.m)	€ 10,25 - € 17,70
incl. electricity (10A)	€ 13,25 - € 22,20
special pitch (120/150 sq.m)	
incl. water and electricity	€ 17,00 - € 27,70

Less 15% outside July/Aug.
Camping Cheques accepted.

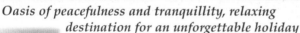

L'Orangerie de Lanniron

Castel Camping   ★★★★

Oasis of peacefulness and tranquillity, relaxing destination for an unforgettable holiday

Situated on the banks of the river Odet, this former residence of the bishops of Cornouaille welcomes you to its 90 acres botanical park where you can take advantage of several fun and sporting activities.

This is an ideal spot for discovering this part of Brittany, so rich in historical sites, monuments and folklore.

New in 2009: extraordinary heated water park (500 m² water + terrace and solarium) with 4 waterslides hidden in a rock formation, heated bath and beds, waterfall, fountains, geyser, paddling pool with water slide, Golf practice and putting green - introduction to golf.

More information or to book:
www.lanniron.com
camping@lanniron.com

Château de Lanniron Allée de Lanniron 29000 Quimper
Tel. 0033 (0) 298 90 6202 - Fax 0033 (0) 298 52 1556

 La Clef Verte   QUALITE TOURISME   ADAC 2007   CASTELS

Check real time availability and at-the-gate prices...

△ www.**alanrogers**.com

FR29040 Camping Ar Kleguer

Plage Sainte Anne, F-29250 Saint Pol-de-Léon (Finistère)

Tel: **02 98 69 18 81**. Email: **info@camping-ar-kleguer.com** www.alanrogers.com/FR29040

Ar Kleguer is located 20 minutes from the Roscoff ferry terminal in the heart of the Pays du Léon in north Finistère. The site is in two sections – one is in a quiet woodland setting which incorporates a small domestic animal and bird park. The other section is divided into several more open areas at the edge of the sea with spectacular views overlooking the Bay of Morlaix. There are 173 large and well kept pitches, all with 10A electricity connections. Of these, 125 are for touring units. This neat site is decorated with attractive flowers, shrubs and trees and there are tarmac roads. It would suit for long or short stays and is immaculately kept by the Kerbrat family. However, the real plus here is the beautiful surroundings, with the sea and beaches right on the doorstep. The friendly and helpful owners will advise on how best to enjoy this peaceful part of Brittany and suggest activities in the local area that might include walking, cycling and riding, or watersports, diving and sand-yachting.

Facilities

Three modern, tiled toilet blocks are bright, clean and heated when required. Facilities for babies, children and disabled visitors. Laundry room. Shop (July/Aug). Bar and takeaway (July/Aug). Good heated pool complex with paddling pools and slide. Tennis. Bicycle hire. Animal park. Play area. Activities for children and some entertainment in high season. Beach. Off site: Restaurant at site entrance. Sailing 800 m. Riding 3 km. Golf 5 km.

Open: Easter - 30 September.

Directions

From Roscoff take D58 to Morlaix. From Morlaix follow signs to Saint-Pol-de-Léon (centre). In the centre follow white 'campings' signs or Plage de Sainte Anne until site signs appear. GPS: N48:41.491 W03:58.030

Charges guide

Per person	€ 3,80 - € 4,90
child (2-7 yrs)	€ 2,20 - € 3,30
pitch incl. electricity	€ 8,40 - € 10,30

Camping Ar Kleguer ✶✶✶

Plage de Sainte Anne - 29250 St. Pol de Léon - Tel.: 0033 (0)2 98 69 18 81

info@camping-ar-kleguer.com - www.camping-ar-kleguer.com

FR29130 Camping des Abers

Dunes de Sainte Marguerite, F-29870 Landéda (Finistère)

Tel: **02 98 04 93 35**. Email: **camping-des-abers@wanadoo.fr** www.alanrogers.com/FR29130

The location of this delightful 12 acre site is beautiful. Almost at the tip of the Sainte Marguerite peninsula on the northwestern shores of Brittany, it is on a wide bay formed between the mouths (abers) of two rivers, L'Aber Wrac'h and L'Aber Benoit. Camping des Abers is set just back from the beach, the lower pitches sheltered from the wind by high hedges or with panoramic views of the bay from the higher places. There are 180 pitches arranged in distinct areas, many partly shaded and sheltered by mature hedges, trees and flowering shrubs, all planted and carefully tended over many years by the Le Cuff family.

Facilities

Three toilet blocks (one part of the reception building and all recently refurbished) are very clean, providing washbasins in cubicles and roomy showers (token from reception €0.80). Good facilities for disabled visitors and babies. Laundry. Motorcaravan service point. Shop stocks essentials (25/5-22/9). Simple takeaway dishes (1/7-31/8). Good play area (on sand). Games room. Breton music and dancing, cooking classes and guided walks. Splendid beach with good bathing, fishing, windsurfing and other watersports. Torch useful. Off site: Pizzeria and restaurant next door. Riding 10 km. Golf 30 km.

Open: 28 April - 30 September.

Directions

From Roscoff (D10, then D13), cross river bridge (L'Aber Wrac'h) to Lannilis. Go through town taking road to Landéda and from there signs for Dunes de Ste Marguerite, 'camping' and des Abers. GPS: N48:35.584 W04:36.183

Charges 2009

Per person	€ 3,40
child (1-7 yrs)	€ 1,90
pitch incl. electricity	€ 8,50
dog	€ 1,80
Less 10% outside 15/6-31/8.	

Brittany

The Travel Service
BOOK THIS SITE
CALL 01580 214000
...we'll arrange everything

Check real time availability and at-the-gate prices...

 www.alanrogers.com

FR29060 Flower Camping Caravaning le Pil-Koad

Route de Douarnenez, F-29100 Poullan-sur-Mer (Finistère)
Tel: 02 98 74 26 39. Email: info@pil-koad.com   www.alanrogers.com/FR29060

Pil-Koad is an attractive, family run site just back from the sea near Douarnenez in Finistère. It has 190 pitches on fairly flat ground, marked out by separating hedges and of quite good quality, though varying in size and shape. With 88 pitches used for touring units, the site also has a number of mobile homes and chalets. All pitches have electrical connections and the original trees provide shade in some areas. A large room, the 'Woodpecker Bar', is used for entertainment with discos and cabaret in July/Aug. Weekly outings and clubs for children are organised (30/6-30/8). A variety of beaches are within easy reach, with the coast offering some wonderful scenery and good walking.

www.flowercampings.com

Facilities

Two main toilet blocks in modern style include washbasins mostly in cabins and facilities for disabled visitors. Laundry facilities. Motorcaravan service point. Gas supplies. Small shop for basics (1/4-30/9). Bar, new restaurant and takeaway (all 1/6-31/8). Heated swimming and paddling pools (1/4-30/9, no Bermuda-style shorts). Tennis. Minigolf. Fishing. Bicycle hire. Playground. Off site: Restaurants in village 500 m. Riding 4 km. Nearest sandy beach 5 km. Douarnenez 6 km.

Open: 4 April - 27 September.

Directions

Site is 500 m. east from the centre of Poullan on D7 road towards Douarnenez. From Douarnenez take circular bypass route towards Audierne; if you see road for Poullan sign at roundabout, take it, otherwise there is a camping sign at turning to Poullan from the D765 road.
GPS: N48:04.560 W04:24.250

Charges 2009

Per pitch incl. 2 persons	
and electricity	€ 16,00 - € 30,80
extra person	€ 3,60 - € 5,10
child (2-7 yrs)	€ 2,30 - € 3,40
dog	€ 2,80 - € 3,50

Le Pil-Koad ★★★★
Tranquillity
Conviviality Comfort
Animations
Poullan sur Mer • 29100 DOUARNENEZ
Tel. 02 98 74 26 39 • Fax : 02 98 74 55 97 • E.mail : info@pil-koad.com •
www.pil-koad.com • Camping indépendant adhérant à la chaine Flower.

FR29160 Camping les Genets d'Or

Kermerour, Pont Kereon, F-29380 Bannalec (Finistère)
Tel: 02 98 39 54 35. Email: Enquiries@holidaybrittany.com   www.alanrogers.com/FR29160

A jewel of a small site, Les Genets d'Or is situated in a tiny country hamlet at the end of a road from Bannalec, 12 km. from Pont-Aven in Finistère. The spacious surroundings offer a safe haven for young children and a rural, tranquil environment for adults. The gently sloping, grassy site is edged with mature trees and divided into hedged glades with the odd apple tree providing shade. There are only 52 pitches (42 for touring units), all of a good size – some of over 100 sq.m. – and most pitches have electricity, each glade having a water point.

Facilities

The good quality toilet block provides all the necessary amenities and washing facilities, including a shower for disabled campers. Washing machine and dryer. Shop (15/6-30/9). Bar area. Bread delivered in season. Ice pack service. Indoor room with snooker and table tennis. Bicycle hire. Play and picnic area. Caravan storage. Off site: Riding 3 km. Beach 12 km. The village is 15 minutes walk with bars, shop, baker, etc.

Open: Easter/1 April - 30 September.

Directions

Take exit D4 from N165 towards Bannalec. In Bannalec turn right into Rue Lorec (following sign for Quimperlé) and follow site signs for 1 km.
GPS: N47:55.30 W03:41.20

Charges guide

Per unit incl. 2 persons and electricity	€ 16,00
extra person	€ 3,50
child (under 6 yrs)	€ 2,50
Less 10% for over 7 nights.	

31

The Travel Service · BOOK THIS SITE CALL 01580 214000 ...we'll arrange everything

FR29080 Camping le Panoramic

Mobile homes ▶ page 487

Route de la Plage-Penker, F-29560 Telgruc-sur-Mer (Finistère)

Tel: **02 98 27 78 41**. Email: **info@camping-panoramic.com**

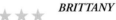

www.alanrogers.com/FR29080

This medium sized traditional site is situated on quite a steep, ten acre hillside with fine views. It is personally run by M. Jacq and his family who all speak good English. The 200 pitches are arranged on flat, shady terraces, in small groups with hedges and flowering shrubs and 20 pitches have services for motorcaravans. Divided into two parts, the main upper site is where most of the facilities are located, with the swimming pool, its terrace and a playground located with the lower pitches across the road. Some up-and-down walking is therefore necessary, but this is a small price to pay for such pleasant and comfortable surroundings. This area provides lovely coastal footpaths to enjoy. A 'Sites et Paysages' member.

Facilities

The main site has two well kept toilet blocks with another very good block opened for main season across the road. All three include British and Turkish style WCs, washbasins in cubicles, facilities for disabled people, baby baths, plus laundry facilities. Motorcaravan services. Small shop (1/7-31/8). Refurbished bar/restaurant with takeaway (1/7-31/8). Barbecue area. Heated pool, paddling pool and jacuzzi (1/6-15/9). Playground. Games and TV rooms. Tennis. Bicycle hire. WiFi. Off site: Beach and fishing 700 m. Riding 6 km. Golf 14 km. Sailing school nearby.

Open: 1 June - 15 September.

Directions

Site is just south of Telgruc-sur-Mer. On D887 pass through Ste Marie du Ménez Horn. Turn left on D208 signed Telgruc-sur-Mer. Continue straight on through town and site is on right within 1 km. GPS: N48:13.428 W04:22.382

Charges guide

Per person	€ 5,00
child (under 7 yrs)	€ 3,00
pitch	€ 12,00
electricity (6/10A)	€ 3,10 - € 4,50
dog	€ 1,60
Less 20% outside July/Aug.	

Camping LE PANORAMIC ★★★★ *BRITTANY*

On the Crozon penninsular and the Bay of Douarnenez, this is a family campsite bordering the sea, where english is spoken and everything is well-maintened. There are many holiday activities available, including a swimming pool, childrens' play area, tennis, bathing, sailing, mountain biking etc., and a further choice of cultural activities in the Armorique Regional Park - the coast, the local ports, museums and of course the richness of the Breton culture itself.

Mr et Mme JACQ
29560 Telgruc-sur-Mer - France
Tel. 0033 298 27 78 41 - Fax: 0033 298 27 36 10
Email : info@camping-panoramic.com / www.camping-panoramic.com

FR29120 Yelloh! Village le Manoir de Kerlut

F-29740 Plobannalec-Lesconil (Finistère)

Tel: **04 66 73 97 39**. Email: info@yellohvillage-manoir-de-kerlut.com

www.alanrogers.com/FR29120

Le Manoir de Kerlut is a comfortable site in the grounds of a manor house on a river estuary near Pont l'Abbe. The campsite itself has neat, modern buildings and is laid out on flat grass providing 240 pitches (90 for touring units). All have electricity connections, some also have water and drainage and around ten pitches have hardstanding. One area is rather open with separating hedges planted, the other part being amongst more mature bushes and some trees which provide shade. Site amenities are of a good quality. A 'Yelloh! Village' member.

Facilities

Toilet facilities in two good blocks (each with several rooms, not all open outside July/Aug), include washbasins all in cabins, and facilities for babies and disabled people. Laundry. Small shop. Takeaway. Large modern bar with TV (satellite) and entertainment all season. Two heated swimming pools, paddling pool and water slide. Fitness centre. Play area. Tennis. Bicycle hire. Off site: Beach 2 km. Fishing 2 km. Riding 5 km. Golf 15 km.

Open: 7 May - 20 September, with all services.

Directions

From Pont l'Abbé, on D785, take D102 road towards Lesconil. Site is signed on the left, shortly village of Plobannalec. GPS: N47:48.733 W04:13.316

Charges 2009

Per unit incl. 2 persons and 5A electricity	€ 15,00 - € 39,00
extra person	€ 5,00 - € 7,00
electricity (10A)	€ 1,00

tel: +33 466 739 739 www.yellohvillage.com

Check real time availability and at-the-gate prices...

www.**alanrogers**.com

FR29110 Yelloh! Village la Plage

F-29730 Le Guilvinec (Finistère)

Tel: **04 66 73 97 39**. Email: **info@yellohvillage-la-plage.com**   www.alanrogers.com/FR29110

La Plage is a spacious site located beside a long sandy beach between the fishing town of Le Guilvinec and the watersports beaches of Penmarc'h on the southwest tip of Brittany. It is surrounded by tall trees which provide shelter and is made up of several flat, sandy meadows. The 410 pitches (100 for touring units) are arranged on either side of sandy access roads, mostly not separated but all numbered. There is less shade in the newer areas. Electricity is available on most pitches. Like all beach-side sites, the facilities receive heavy use. Used by tour operators (176 pitches). There is plenty to occupy one at this friendly site but the bustling fishing harbour at Le Guilvinec and the watersports of Penmarc'h and Pointe de la Torche are within easy travelling distance.

Facilities

Four sanitary blocks are of differing designs but all provide modern, bright facilities including washbasins in cabins, good facilities for children and disabled people. Laundry facilities. Motorcaravan service point. Shop with gas supplies. Bright, airy well furnished bar, crêperie and takeaway. Heated swimming pool with paddling pool and slide. Sauna and fitness complex. Play area. TV room. Tennis. Minigolf. Pétanque. Giant chess/draughts. Bicycle hire. Beach. Off site: Fishing and watersports near. Riding 5 km. Golf 20 km.

Open: 4 April - 13 September, with all facilities.

Directions

Site is west of Guilvinec. From Pont l'Abbé, take the D785 road towards Penmarc'h. In Plomeur, turn left on D57 signed Guilvinec. On entering Guilvinec fork right signed Port and camping. Follow road along coast to site on left. GPS: N47:48.150 W04:18.430

Charges 2009

Per unit incl. 2 persons and 6A electricity	€ 15,00 - € 40,00
extra person	€ 5,00 - € 7,00
child (under 10 yrs)	free - € 5,00
electricity (10A)	€ 1,00
dog	€ 4,00

www.yellohvillage.com   tel: +33 466 739 739

Children's paradise

La **Plage**
Camping Village ❀❀❀

Le **Manoir** de **Kerlut**
Camping Village ❀❀❀❀

Direct access to a sandy beach

www.villagelaplage.com   www.domainemanoirdekerlut.com

29730 Le Guilvinec
Tel : 00 33 (0)2 98 58 61 90
Fax : 00 33 (0)2 98 58 89 06

29740 Lesconil
Tel : 00 33 (0)2 98 82 23 89
Fax : 00 33 (0)2 98 82 26 49

yelloh! VILLAGE

ENTERTAINMENT DURING THE WHOLE SEASON / INDOOR AND HEATED SWIMMINGPOOL / ADVENTURE PARK / TAKE ADVANTAGE OF SPECIAL OFFERS ON INTERNET
Holiday camps South Brittany France

33

BOOK THIS SITE CALL 01580 214000 ...we'll arrange everything

The Travel Service

FR29090 Camping le Raguenès-Plage

19 rue des Iles, F-29920 Névez (Finistère)

Tel: **02 98 06 80 69**. Email: **info@camping-le-raguenes-plage.com**   www.alanrogers.com/FR29090

Mme. Guyader and her family will ensure you receive a warm welcome on arrival at this well kept and pleasant site. Le Raguenès-Plage is an attractive and well laid out campsite with many shrubs and trees. The 287 pitches are a good size, flat and grassy, separated by trees and hedges. All have electricity, water and drainage. The site is used by one tour operator (60 pitches), and has 46 mobile homes of its own. A pool complex complete with water toboggan is a key feature and is close to the friendly bar, restaurant, shop and takeaway. From the far end of the campsite a delightful five minutes' walk along a path and through a cornfield takes you down to a pleasant, sandy beach looking out towards the Ile Verte and the Presqu'île de Raguenès.

Facilities

Two clean, well maintained sanitary blocks include mixed style toilets, washbasins in cabins, baby baths and facilities for disabled visitors. Laundry room. Motorcaravan service point. Small shop (from 15/5). Bar and restaurant (from 1/6) with outside terrace and takeaway. Reading and TV room. Internet access point. Heated pool with sun terrace and paddling pool. Sauna (charged). Play areas. Games room. Various activities are organised in July/Aug. Off site: Beach, fishing and watersports 300 m. Supermarket 3 km. Riding 4 km.

Open: 1 April - 30 September.

Directions

From N165 take D24 Kerampaou exit. After 3 km. turn right towards Nizon and bear right at church in village following signs to Névez (D77). Continue through Névez, following signs to Raguenès. Continue for 3 km. to site on left. GPS: N47:47.607 W03:48.040

Charges 2009

Per unit incl. 2 persons and electricity	€ 20,00 - € 36,80
extra person	€ 4,40 - € 5,70
child (under 7 yrs)	€ 2,20 - € 3,40

Le Raguenès Hotel Plage ★★★★

Direct access to the beach 300 meters

19, rue des Îles 29920 RAGUENÈZ EN NÉVEZ
Tel : 0033 298 06 80 69 Fax : 0033 298 06 89 05

✓ Heated swimming pool
✓ Water slide
✓ Direct and private access to the beach
✓ Renting of mobil-homes

Low season : 40% reduction

www.camping-le-raguenes-plage.com
info@camping-le-raguenes-plage.com

FR29170 Camping de la Piscine

B.P.12 Kerleya, Beg-Meil, F-29170 Fouesnant (Finistère)

Tel: **02 98 56 56 06**. Email: **contact@campingdelapiscine.com**   www.alanrogers.com/FR29170

There are many campsites in this area but La Piscine is notable for the care and attention to detail that contribute to the well-being of its visitors. Created by the Caradec family from an apple orchard, the 185 level, grass pitches are of generous size and are separated by an interesting variety of hedges and trees. Water, drainage and electricity points are provided, normally one stand between two pitches. A quiet site, set back from the sea, La Piscine will appeal to families looking for good quality without too many on site activities.

Facilities

Two refurbished toilet units include British and Turkish style toilets and washbasins in cabins. Facilities for disabled people. Laundry facilities. Motorcaravan service point. Shop. Takeaway (high season). Pool complex with three slides, waterfall and jacuzzi. Sauna and solarium. Play area. BMX track. Half-court tennis. TV room. Entertainment organised in high season. Off site: Beach 1 km. Bicycle hire, fishing and riding within 4 km. Golf 7 km.

Open: 15 May - 15 September.

Directions

Site is 5 km. south of Fouesnant. Turn off the N165 expressway at Coat Conq signed Concarneau and Fouesnant. At Fouesnant join D45 signed Beg Meil and shortly turn left on D145 signed Mousterlin. In 1 km. turn left and follow signs to site. GPS: N47:51.941 W04:00.932

Charges 2009

Per pitch incl. 2 persons and electricity	€ 18,80 - € 29,40
extra person	€ 3,80 - € 6,00
child (2-7 yrs)	€ 1,90 - € 3,00

Check real time availability and at-the-gate prices...

www.alanrogers.com

FR29180 Camping les Embruns

Mobile homes ▶ page 488

Rue du philosophe Alain, le Pouldu, F-29360 Clohars-Carnoët (Finistère)

Tel: 02 98 39 91 07. Email: camping-les-embruns@wanadoo.fr   www.alanrogers.com/FR29180

This site is unusual in that it is located in the heart of a village, yet is only 250 metres from a sandy cove. The entrance with its code operated barrier and wonderful floral displays, is the first indication that this is a well tended and well organised site, and the owners have won numerous regional and national awards for its superb presentation. The 180 pitches (100 occupied by mobile homes) are separated by trees, shrubs and bushes, and most have electricity (10A), water and drainage. There is a covered, heated swimming pool, a circular paddling pool and a water play pool. It is only a short walk to the village centre with all its attractions and services. It is also close to beautiful countryside and the Carnoët Forest which are good for walking and cycling.

Facilities

Two modern sanitary blocks, recently completely renewed and heated in winter, include mainly British style toilets, some washbasins in cubicles, baby baths and good facilities for disabled visitors. Family bathrooms. Laundry facilities. Motorcaravan service point. Shop and restaurant by entrance. Bar and terrace (1/7-31/8). Takeaway (20/6-5/9). Covered, heated swimming and paddling pools. Large games hall. Play area. Minigolf. Communal barbecue area. Activities for children and adults organised in July/Aug. Bicycle hire. Off site: Nearby sea and river fishing and watersports. Beach 250 m. Riding 2 km.

Open: 3 April - 19 September.

Directions

From N165 take either 'Kervidanou, Quimperlé Ouest' exit or 'Kergostiou, Quimperlé Centre, Clohars Carnoët' exit and follow D16 to Clohars Carnoët. Then take D24 for Le Pouldu and follow site signs in village. GPS: N47:46.119 W03:32.716

Charges 2009

Per unit incl. 2 persons and electricity	€ 14,50 - € 33,90
extra person	€ 3,95 - € 5,50
child (under 7 yrs)	€ 2,60 - € 3,50
animal	€ 2,00 - € 2,50

Les Embruns ★★★★

250 m from one of Brittany's sandy beaches Gwénaëlle & Gisèle welcome you in their particularly well maintained campsite where you are assured of a good holiday.
• First class facilities and amenities in a green and floral environment • Mobile homes to let
• Motorcaravan service point • Covered heated swimming pool right from the opening
• **NEW in 2009! Heated sanitary blocks**

LE POULDU - F-29360 CLOHARS-CARNOET
TEL: 0033 298 39 91 07 - FAX: 0033 298 39 97 87
www.camping-les-embruns.com
E-mail: camping-les-embruns@wanadoo.fr

FR29190 Camping les Prés Verts

B.P. 612, Kernous-Plage, F-29186 Concarneau Cedex (Finistère)

Tel: 02 98 97 09 74. Email: info@presverts.com   www.alanrogers.com/FR29190

What sets this family site apart from the many others in this region are its more unusual features – its stylish pool complex with Romanesque-style columns and statue, and its plants and flower tubs. The 150 pitches are mostly arranged on long, open, grassy areas either side of main access roads. Specimen trees, shrubs or hedges divide the site into smaller areas. There are a few individual pitches and an area towards the rear of the site where the pitches have sea views. There is direct access to the sandy beach with no roads to cross (300 m). Concarneau is just 2.5 km.

Facilities

Two toilet blocks provide unisex WCs, but separate washing facilities for ladies and men. Pre-set hot showers and washbasins in cabins for ladies, both closed 21.00-08.00 hrs. Some child-size toilets. Laundry facilities. Shop (1/7-25/8). Pizza service twice weekly. Heated swimming pool (1/6-31/8) and paddling pool. Playground (0-5 yrs). Minigolf (charged). Off site: Path to sandy/rocky beach 300 m. Coastal path. Riding 1 km. Bicycle hire 1.5 km. Supermarket 2 km. Golf 5 km.

Open: 1 May - 22 September.

Directions

Turn off C7 road, 2.5 km. north of Concarneau, where site is signed. Take third left after Hotel de l'Océan. GPS: N47:53.422 W03:56.324

Charges guide

Per unit incl. 2 persons	€ 17,50 - € 22,00
extra person	€ 5,20 - € 6,50
child (2-7 yrs)	€ 3,40 - € 4,30
electricity (2-10A)	€ 3,20 - € 7,00
dog	€ 1,30 - € 1,60

BOOK THIS SITE
CALL 01580 214000
...we'll arrange everything
The Travel Service

Check real time availability and at-the-gate prices...
www.alanrogers.com

FR29270 Camping des Dunes

67 rue Paul Langevin, F-29740 Lesconil (Finistère)

Tel: **02 98 87 81 78**   www.alanrogers.com/FR29270

On the edge of the sand dunes near the village of Lesconil, this campsite has the great advantage of providing direct access to an excellent sandy beach. The 120 sandy and grassy pitches have little shade, but are quite spacious and all have electricity. The site is only 800 m. from the village of Lesconil, a delightfully unspoilt fishing port where you can still see the little fishing fleet return each day. There is a good choice of restaurants and cafés, and a 'Centre Nautique' offering watersports.

Facilities

Two central, unisex toilet blocks have predominantly British style toilets and washbasins, both open and in cubicles. Baby area. Two toilet/shower rooms for disabled people. Laundry and dishwashing sinks. Washing machine and dryer. Baker's van visits every morning in high season. Play area for younger children. Two trampolines. Bowling alley game. Off site: Tennis nearby. Beach 100 m.

Open: 1 June - 15 September.

Directions

From Pont L'Abbé follow D102 to Lesconil. Just before village (sports stadium on right) - site signed just past stadium. Site about 1.5 km. on right, just past Camping de la Grande Plage.
GPS: N47:47.49 W04:13.42

Charges guide

Per unit incl. 2 persons and electricity	€ 23,55
extra person	€ 4,60
child (under 7 yrs)	€ 2,95

BOOK THIS SITE
CALL 01580 214000
...we'll arrange everything
The Travel Service

FR29240 Camping de Kéranterec

Route de Port la Forêt, F-29940 La Forêt-Fouesnant (Finistère)

Tel: **02 98 56 98 11.** Email: **info@camping-keranterec.com**   www.alanrogers.com/FR29240

A well established family run site with a very French ambience (unlike some of the neighbouring sites which have a much higher UK presence), Keranterec has 265 grassy pitches in two distinct areas. The upper part of the site is more open and has little shade, and is also largely taken up by private mobile homes. The lower and more mature area is predominantly for tourers, with terraced pitches set in a former orchard. Spacious and divided by mature hedging, all pitches have electrical connections (25 m. cable advised) and most also offer water and drainage.

Facilities

Two modern, fully equipped toilet blocks kept very clean include washbasins in cubicles, baby baths and facilities for disabled visitors. Laundry facilities. Small shop and bar (15/6-10/9) and takeaway (1/7-31/8). TV room with satellite. Heated swimming pool (1/6-10/9) with paddling pool, jacuzzi and three slides. There are plans for an indoor pool for 2009. Tennis. Boules. Play area. In July/August organised events and activities for the family, and a free children's club. Off site: Attractive sandy beach of Kerleven 10 minutes walk. Golf 0.8 km. Riding 2 km.

Open: 5 April - 21 September.

Directions

From N165 take D70 Concarneau exit. At first roundabout take D44 signed Fouesnant. After 2.5 km. turn right at T-junction, and follow for 2.5 km. and turn left (Port La Forêt). Continue to roundabout and take second exit (straight ahead), signed Port La Forêt. After 1 km. turn left (site signed), then in 400 m. turn left to site on left.
GPS: N47:53.930 W03:57.375

Charges 2009

Per person	€ 7,00 - € 8,50
child (1-7 yrs)	€ 3,00 - € 4,00
pitch incl. electricity	€ 13,00 - € 17,00

BOOK THIS SITE
CALL 01580 214000
...we'll arrange everything
The Travel Service

FR29260 Camping les Genêts

Rue de Gouesnac'h Nevez, F-29760 Penmarc'h (Finistère)

Tel: **02 98 58 66 93.** Email: **nohartp@wanadoo.fr**   www.alanrogers.com/FR29260

The present owners of Les Genêts, Bridgette and Pascal Rohart, bought this old, rural campsite a few years ago and have transformed it beyond recognition. The modern reception is in front of a modestly sized swimming pool that has a section for small children. The toilet block although old but adequate, is to be replaced by two new blocks. There are 100 pitches which are divided by trees and hedges and vary in both size and quality. Some in one corner of the site appear to have poor drainage. Around 40 pitches are used for mobile homes which are placed to one side of the campsite.

Facilities

One old but very clean toilet block (with no facilities for disabled visitors) has both British and Turkish style toilets, showers and wash cubicles. This is to be replaced with two new blocks. Laundry room. Bar and snack bar (July/Aug). Bread available (July/Aug). Swimming pool. Play area and trampoline. Off site: Shops and restaurants 1.5 km. Beach, fishing and boat launching 1.5 km. Riding 1.5 km. Golf 3 km.

Open: 1 April - 31 October.

Directions

From Pont l'Abbé, take the D785 southwest towards Penmarc'h. Before the town turn left eastwards on the D53 (Loc Tudy) and site is on left in about 2 km.
GPS: N47:49.05 W04:18.32

Charges guide

Per unit incl. 2 persons	€ 11,20 - € 14,60
extra person	€ 3,00 - € 3,80
child (0-7 yrs)	€ 1,80 - € 2,30
electricity (10A)	€ 2,90

FR29290 Camping Village le Grand Large

48 route du Grand Large, Mousterlin, F-29170 Fouesnant (Finistère)

Tel: **02 98 56 04 06**. Email: **grandlarge@franceloc.fr**   www.alanrogers.com/FR29290

Le Grand Large is a beach-side site situated on the Pointe de Mousterlin in natural surroundings. The site is separated from the beach by the road that follows the coast around the point. It is also protected from the wind by an earth bank with trees and a fence. There are 260 pitches with just 51 places used for tourers. Some pitches are taken by one tour operator and the site itself has tents and mobile homes to rent. Electricity is available everywhere (long leads useful) and some pitches have drainage. A small river runs through the site but it is fenced. The ground is rather sandy in places with some shrubs and mature trees. Benodet (7 km.) and Fouesnant (5 km.) are near in different directions and the sandy beach is just up the steps and across the road. A family site, Le Grand Large would also suit nature lovers in low season as it is next to a large tract of protected land, Marais de Mousterlin, ideal for walking, cycling and birdwatching. The beach itself looks over the bay towards the Isles de Glénan.

Facilities

Two neat toilet blocks, the largest only opened in high season, include plenty of washbasins in cabins. Facilities for children in the larger block, for disabled people in both. Laundry facilities. Shop. Bar overlooking the sea with attractive terrace. Crêperie/grill restaurant including takeaway. Swimming pool with paddling pool, water slides in separate pool. Tennis. Multisport court. Small play area. TV and games rooms. Bicycle hire. Off site: Beach, fishing 100 m. Golf and riding 5 km.

Open: 31 March - 16 September, with all services.

Directions

Site is 7 km. south of Fouesnant. Turn off N165 expressway at Coat Conq, signed Concarneau and Fouesnant. At Fouesnant take A45 signed Beg Meil, then follow signs to Mousterlin. In Mousterlin turn left and follow camping signs.
GPS: N47:50.520 W04:02.120

Charges guide

Per unit incl. 2 persons and 5A electricity	€ 17,00 - € 37,00
extra person	€ 5,00 - € 7,00
child (under 10 yrs)	free - € 5,00
electricity (10A)	€ 1,00

FINISTÈRE

Le grand Large****

At 2 steps away from the sea, a heated swimming pool with water slide, accommodation and animation during the season.

Mousterlin Fouesnant
29170, Route du Grd Large Pointe de Mousterlin
Tel.: +33 (0)2 98 56 04 06 • Email : grandlarge@franceloc.fr
www.camping-franceloc.fr

FR29280 La Pointe Superbe Camping

Route de Saint-Coulitz, F-29150 Châteaulin (Finistère)

Tel: **02 98 86 51 53**. Email: **lapointecamping@aol.com**   www.alanrogers.com/FR29280

La Pointe, just outside Châteaulin, has been lovingly and impressively brought back to life. Châteaulin is a bustling market town, 15 km. from the beach at Pentrez and within easy reach of Quimper, medieval Locronan and the Crozon peninsula. Although not endowed with a great deal in terms of amenities, this very tranquil site does boast particularly large, grassy pitches in a quiet valley leading down to the River Aulne. The 60 pitches all have electricity with water close by.

Facilities

The first class toilet block, kept very clean at all times, has many washbasins in cubicles. Shower cubicles are somewhat small but have full adjustable hot and cold taps. Large room with facilities for disabled visitors. Baby bathroom. Motorcaravan service point. Play area. Large activity room with basketball, badminton and children's corner. Fresh bread to order. Small shop for essentials. Off site: Châteaulin 700 m. Riding and tennis nearby. Fishing in the Aulne (permit needed). Beach 9 km.

Open: 15 March - 31 October.

Directions

Site is just southeast of Châteaulin. From the bridge over the river in town centre follow signs for St Coulitz and Quimper. Shortly turn left signed St Coulitz. Site is clearly signed at this point and is 100 m. on the right. GPS: N48:11.15 W04:05.05

Charges guide

Per unit incl. 2 persons and electricity	€ 18,50
extra person	€ 4,00
child (under 10 yrs)	€ 2,50

No credit cards. Camping Cheques accepted.

BOOK THIS SITE
CALL 01580 214000
...we'll arrange everything
The Travel Service

Check real time availability and at-the-gate prices...

www.**alanrogers**.com

The Travel Service
BOOK THIS SITE
CALL 01580 214000
...we'll arrange everything

FR29380 Yelloh! Village Port de Plaisance

7 route de Quimper, F-29950 Bénodet (Finistère)

Tel: **04 66 73 97 39**. Email: **info@yellohvillage-benodet.com**   www.alanrogers.com/FR29380

Sometimes larger campsites can lack ambiance, but it is not so with Port de Plaisance. This is a delightful, family run site with 340 pitches of which 105 are for touring campers. The pitches are mostly in two areas, where they are hedged and positioned in small groups amongst the many mature trees and flowering shrubs. Although there are five holiday tour operators on site, their presence is unobtrusive because of careful positioning amongst the trees. This is truly a campsite with something for everybody, with a wide range of entertainment and activities provided over a long season. The restaurant that overlooks the pool complex boasts a very good menu. Entertainment suitable for all ages ranges from up-to-date films to taster aquadiving lessons in the covered, heated pool. The marina at the mouth of the Odet river is 500 m. away, and from here you can enjoy a boat trip up to Quimper. The seaside town of Bénodet, with all the shops, bars and restaurants that you could wish for is just 1 km.

Facilities

Three toilet blocks, older and simple in style, include British style toilets, showers and washing cubicles. Baby room. Facilities for disabled visitors. Laundry room. Shop, bar and restaurant (all season) and takeaway (15/5-15/9). Pool complex with flumes and toboggan. Games room. Entertainment. Taster diving lessons in the pool. Multisport court. Bicycle hire. Off site: Bénodet 1 km. Fishing 1 km. Riding 2 km. Golf 3 km. Beach 1 km.

Open: 3 April - 20 September.

Directions

Take the D34 south from Quimper. Site is on the left on entering Bénodet. GPS: N47:52.924 W04:06.197

Charges 2009

Per unit incl. 2 persons and electricity (6A)	€ 15,00 - € 39,00
extra person	€ 4,00 - € 7,00
child (0-7 yrs)	free - € 4,00
dog	€ 4,00

tel: +33 466 739 739   www.yellohvillage.com

yelloh! VILLAGE

WWW.BENODET.CO.UK

Camping **Yelloh! Village**
PORT DE PLAISANCE
★ ★ ★ ★

yelloh! VILLAGE

Open from 03th of April to the 20th of September 2009.
29950 BENODET-Tél : 00 33 (0)2 98 57 02 38 fax : 00 33 (0)2 98 57 25 25 info@campingbenodet.fr

FR29340 Camping de la Côte des Légendes

B.P. 36 Keravezan, F-29890 Brignogan-Plages (Finistère)

Tel: **02 98 83 41 65**. Email: **camping-cote-des-legendes@wanadoo.fr**   www.alanrogers.com/FR29340

Located just behind a safe, sandy beach on the Bay of Brignogan and adjacent to a Centre Nautique (sailing, windsurfing, kayaking), this site is ideal for a family seaside holiday. It is a quiet site with 147 level pitches arranged in rows and protected by hedges. There are a few mobile homes and chalets for rent but no tour operators. A shop, bar and takeaway are open in high season when activities are arranged for adults and children by the helpful owner (good English is spoken). The beach of fine sand can be reached directly from the site.

Facilities

Main toilet facilities are at the rear of the site in a large block that provides washbasins in cubicles, baby baths and facilities for disabled visitors. The upper floor provides a games room with views of the sea. Further toilet facilities are at the reception building, also a laundry. Motorcaravan service point. Bar, small shop and takeaway (July/Aug). Playground and playing field. Off site: Watersports centre adjacent. Village services 700 m. Bicycle hire 1 km. Riding 6 km.

Open: Easter - 1 November.

Directions

From Roscoff take the D58 towards Morlaix and after 6 km. turn right on the D10 towards Plouescat and then Plouguerneau. Turn right on the D770 to Brignogan-Plages. In the main street go straight on following signs for site and Club Nautique. GPS: N48:40.367 W04:19.757

Charges guide

Per unit incl. 2 persons	€ 9,90 - € 12,50
extra person	€ 3,05 - € 3,75
electricity	€ 1,00 - € 3,10

Check real time availability and at-the-gate prices...
www.alanrogers.com

FR29440 Village Center Baie du Kernic

Rue de Pen An Theven, F-29430 Plouescat (Finistère)

Tel: 04 99 57 21 21. Email: contact@village-center.com

www.alanrogers.com/FR29440

This is a large site close to the beach near Plouescat and only 15 minutes from the popular beach resort of Roscoff. At present the site is in the process of complete renovation. The new owners, the Villagecenter Group, built a new bar and reception area and a pool complex in 2007 and upgrades to the rest of the site should be complete for the 2009 season, providing a good, lively site in an attractive location. There are 243 rough grass pitches separated by hedges with 143 for touring, only 45 with electricity.

Facilities

Three toilet blocks should now be refurbished. Motorcaravan services. Shop. Bar, snack bar, restaurant (July/Aug). Outdoor swimming and paddling pools, covered pool (7/4-15/9). Volleyball and basketball. Games/TV room. Organised activities (July/Aug). Internet. Off site: Fishing, beach, sailing 100 m. Bicycle hire 3 km. Golf 30 km. Tennis. Watersports. Thalassotherapy. Casino.

Open: 7 April - 15 September.

Directions

Site is on the D788 between Brignogan Plage and Roscoff, well signed from Plouescat centre. GPS: N48:39.548 W04:13.071

Charges guide

Per unit incl. 2 persons and electricity	€ 14,00 - € 29,00
extra person	€ 2,00 - € 4,50
child (under 7 yrs)	€ 1,70 - € 3,75

No credit cards.

Baie du Kernic★★

Plouescat > Brittany

• 100 m away from the beach
• Covered swimming pool and whirlpool bath

Villagecenter

BOOK YOUR HOLIDAYS
www.village-center.com
☎ +33 (0)4 99 57 21 21

FR29450 Camping le Helles

55 rue du Petit Bourg, Sainte Marine, F-29120 Combrit (Finistère)

Tel: 02 98 56 31 46. Email: contact@le-helles.com

www.alanrogers.com/FR29450

This is a delightful site with a very French feel. Out of its 130 pitches, 100 are used for touring. The pitches are grassy, level and generous in size, but with little division by hedges. Mature trees offering shade surround large open areas of numbered pitches. Mobile homes are in an area of their own. Facilities on this site are excellent and the swimming pool with surrounding terrace provides a main feature. A gate at the back of the touring area leads to the beach, which is just 300 m. away.

Facilities

Excellent sanitary facilities include washbasins in cabins and controllable showers (some also with washbasin). Baby room and facilities for disabled visitors. Laundry facilities. Bread van delivers daily. Takeaway (July/Aug). Swimming pool. Play area. Boules. Off site: Beach, fishing 300 m. Bicycle hire, riding 4 km. Golf 5 km.

Open: 1 May - 12 September.

Directions

Travelling west on D44 from Benodet turn south on to C18 signed Combrit St Marine. Site is well signed at entry to village. GPS: N47:52.08 W04:07.42

Charges 2009

Per unit incl. 2 persons and electricity	€ 19,30 - € 25,90
extra person	€ 4,10 - € 5,30
child (under 7 yrs)	€ 3,00 - € 3,50
dog	€ 2,30 - € 2,60

Check real time availability and at-the-gate prices...

www.**alanrogers**.com

FR29480 Domaine de Kervel

Kervel, F-29550 Plonevez-Porzay (Finistère)

Tel: **02 98 92 51 54**. Email: **camping.kervel@wanadoo**　　www.alanrogers.com/FR29480

This is a large, well maintained site with many mature trees providing shade and colourful landscaping with shrubs and flowers. Marked by faint lines on the ground, the grassy pitches are level and well kept. Arranged in enclosures of five to six units, each group is surrounded by trees. The excellent pool complex provides indoor and outdoor pools, sunbathing terraces, paddling pools and a slide. Nearby are a comfortable bar and separate restaurant and for youngsters on a rainy day, a large, well equipped games room. The beach of Douarnenez Bay is 1 km. and is wide, safe and popular with sailboarders. Douarnenez itself is 15 minutes by car and offers shops, bars and restaurants. There is a variety of accommodation for rent.

Facilities

One large and one small toilet block provide toilets, showers and washbasins in cabins. Baby room. Washing machines and dryers (at the large block). Bar. Restaurant. Snack bar. Shop. Swimming pools, indoor and outdoor. Games room. Multisport court. Minigolf. Off site: Beach 1 km. Douarnenez 15 minutes by car.

Open: 31 March - 30 September.

Directions

From Plonevez-Porzay travel southwest on the D107 for about 3 km. Turn west on CD107 signed Kervel and site is signed from here.
GPS: N48:06.59 W04:16.05

Charges guide

Per person	€ 4,00 - € 5,50
child (2-7 yrs)	€ 2,50 - € 3,00
pitch	€ 7,50 - € 12,50
electricity (10A)	€ 3,50

FINISTÈRE

FranceLoc

DOMAINE DE KERVEL ****

Heated outdoor swimming pools with water slides, at two steps away form the beaches of Finistère. The mobile homes are established in a green environment. **New indoor swimming pool.**

Domaine De Kervel
29550 PLONEVEZ PORZAY • Finistère - Bretagne
Tel.: +33 (0)2 98 92 51 54 • Email : camping.kervel@wanadoo.fr
www.camping-franceloc.fr

FR29470 Camping les Deux Fontaines

Feunteun Vilian, Raguenèz, F-29920 Névez (Finistère)

Tel: **02 98 06 81 91**. Email: **info@les2fontaines.fr**　　www.alanrogers.com/FR29470

Les Deux Fontaines is a large site with 288 pitches. Of these 115 are for touring, 118 are used by tour operators, and the remainder for mobile homes. The well cared for pitches are on grass, level and attractively laid out amongst mature trees and shrubs. All have 6/10A electricity connections. Trees have been carefully planted creating one area with silver birch, one with apple trees and another with palms and tropical plants. The pool complex is an excellent feature complete with chutes, flumes and waterfalls. There are numerous daytime activities for all the family to enjoy and a variety of entertainment in the evening.

Facilities

Two modern toilet blocks are of good quality and provide washbasins in cabins and pre-set showers. Separate facilities for disabled visitors. Laundry facilities. Well stocked shop. Bar. Restaurant (1/7-31/8). Takeaway (1/6-31/8). Basic motorcaravan services. Large swimming pool complex. Fitness and pamper room. Play area. Skateboard Park. 6-hole golf course. Driving range. Rollerblade hire. Off site: Fishing 1 km. Bicycle hire, riding 5 km.

Open: 15 May - 6 September.

Directions

Travel south from Nevez on the D1. The site is on the left after 3 km. and is well signed.
GPS: N47:47.57 W03:47.26

Charges guide

Per unit incl. 2 persons	€ 17,50 - € 30,40
extra person	€ 3,70 - € 5,80
child (2-7 yrs)	free - € 3,90
electricity (6A)	€ 3,50

Check real time availability and at-the-gate prices...

www.**alanrogers**.com

FR29500 Camping de la Plage

20 rue du Poulquer, F-29950 Bénodet (Finistère)

Tel: **02 98 57 00 55**. Email: **info@campingdelaplagebenodet.com**   www.alanrogers.com/FR29500

This is a large well organised site that has a rural feel, although it is only 300 m. from the beach and 800 m. from the popular seaside town of Bénodet. It has a very short season for touring. There is a great variety of shrubs and trees offering ample shade and privacy for the 300 grassy pitches. There are 190 for touring (electricity 6/10A), all attractively and informally laid out on one side of the site. Access for large units may be difficult. A further 100 pitches are used for mobile homes to rent over a longer season. A splendid pool complex has a retractable cover, flumes, a toboggan and a jacuzzi. Most of the organised entertainment takes place in the bar and on a traditional style terrace. A short walk away are the beach and promenade of Bénodet with shops, bars, restaurants and the mouth of the river Odet. There are organised river trips to the town of Quimper and the islands in the bay.

Facilities

Four large adequate toilet blocks with facilities for campers with disabilities although access is not easy. Motorcaravan services. Shop (1/7-31/8). Bar with TV and takeaway (1/7-31/8). Heated swimming and paddling pools (one can be covered), flumes, toboggan, jacuzzi (1/5-30/9)). Multisport court. Boules. Exercise bikes. Good play areas. Games room. Internet access. Miniclub and entertainment (July/Aug). Bicycle hire. Mobile homes and chalets for rent (26/4-30/9). Off site: Beach 300 m. Bénodet, bars, restaurants, shop, cinema 800 m. Boat trips. Fishing, golf, riding and bicycle hire 1 km.

Open: 1 June - 30 September (for touring).

Directions

From Fouesnant take D44 west towards Bénodet. After 10 km. take Le Letty road south. Site is well signed. GPS: N47:52.067 W04:05.850

Charges guide

Per person	€ 6,20
child (2-10 yrs)	€ 3,30
pitch incl. electricity	€ 13,30 - € 14,10
dog	€ 2,60

CAMPING DE LA PLAGE IN BENODET AND ITS STAFF ARE VERY HAPPY TO WELCOME YOU AND YOUR FAMILY ON OUR CAMPSITE IN SOUTH BRITTANY. OUR CAMPSITE IS LOCATED IN A VERY PRETTY SEASIDE RESORT CLOSE TO THE SEAFRONT (ABOUT 300M) AND FROM BENODET TOWN-CENTER (ABOUT 800 M). YOU WILL ENJOY THE OUTSTANDING NATURAL LANDSCAPE OF OUR CAMPSITE! IT IS A REAL TREAT FOR YOUR EYES! GREEN AND RELAXING CAMPSITE AS MOST OF OUR REGULAR CUSTOMERS SAY!

SPECIAL OFFER:
- 5% DISCOUNT FOR CARAVANING-TOURERS (MINIMUM 7 NIGHTS) FROM 15/6 TO 19/7 AND FROM 15/8 TO 13/9
- 5% DISCOUNT FOR 3 WEEKS' RENTAL OF A MOBIL-HOME OR CHALET

29950 Benodet - France - tel : 0033 (0)298 570 055 - fax : 0033 (0)2 98 57 12 60
e-mail : laplagebenodet@wanadoo.fr - website: www.campingdelaplagebenodet.com

FR29490 Camping de Trologot

Grève du Man, F-29250 Saint Pol-de-Leon (Finistère)

Tel: **02 98 69 06 26**. Email: **camping-trologot@wanadoo.fr**   www.alanrogers.com/FR29490

This small and attractive riverside site has a comfortable ambience and is only a short drive from the port of Roscoff. There are 100 pitches, 85 for touring, all level, grassy and hedged and with electricity (10A). Many small trees give a little shade. A comfortable bar opens onto a large terrace that surrounds the swimming and paddling pools. There is little in the way of sports provision other than table tennis and boules. Young children are catered for with an excellent play area and, for the not so young, there is entertainment in the bar during high season.

Facilities

One central toilet block includes facilities for campers with disabilities. Washing machine and dryer. Heated swimming and paddling pools (15/6-10/9). Small shop and bar (July/Aug). Play area. Boules. Billiards. Visiting food vans (July/Aug). Little organised activities (July/Aug). Off site: Pebble and sandy beaches, shell fishing and sea angling (close by). St Pol de Léon with shops, bars, restaurants 2 km. Port of Roscoff 7 km.

Open: 1 May - 30 September.

Directions

From Morlaix go north on D58 to St Pol de Léon. Follow signs for Plage/Port. Site is well signed. GPS: N48:41.600 W03:58.167

Charges guide

Per person	€ 3,50 - € 4,60
child (under 7 yrs)	€ 2,00 - € 2,80
pitch	€ 4,50 - € 6,50
electricity	€ 3,30
dog	€ 1,40 - € 2,00

Camping Cheques accepted.

41

FR29520 Camping le Cabellou Plage

Avenue du Cabellou, F-29185 Concarneau (Finistère)

Tel: **02 98 97 37 41**. Email: **info@le-cabellou-plage.com**   www.alanrogers.com/FR29520

Le Cabellou Plage is a recently developed site located close to Concarneau. The newly grassed pitches are divided by young hedges, all have 10A electricity and some also have water and drainage. Many have fine views across the estuary to the old walled town. The enthusiastic owner has tastefully landscaped many areas of the site with shrubs and flowers. A large swimming pool on site is overlooked by a terrace and bar and the beach is just 25 m. away. Le Cabellou is ideally situated for those wishing to visit Concarneau with its twice weekly market, Pont Aven and the cathedral city of Quimper.

Facilities

One modern toilet block is bright and cheerful and provides mainly open style washbasins and pre-set showers. Baby room. Facilities for disabled visitors. Laundry room. Shop planned for 2009. Bar with television and internet access. Swimming pool. Scuba lessons and water gymnastics. Bicycle hire. Off site: Bus stop outside site. Supermarkets, shops and restaurants in Concarneau 4 km. Tennis 3 km. Riding 7 km. Golf 10 km.

Open: 26 April - 20 September.

Directions

Site is just south of Concarneau. Take the D783 towards Tregunc. Turn right onto Avenue Cabellou. Site is well signed from here. GPS: N47:51.310 W03:54.313

Charges guide

Per unit incl. 2 persons	
and electricity	€ 13,00 - € 22,00
with water and drainage	€ 15,00 - € 28,00
extra person	€ 3,00 - € 6,00
child (under 10 yrs)	free - € 5,00
dog	€ 3,00

Campsite **le Cabellou Plage**   www.le-cabellou-plage.com

A peninsula in front of Concarneau

South Britany

Tél : 00 33 2 98 97 37 41

FR29510 Camping Baie de Térénez

Moulin de Térénez, F-29252 Plouézoc'h (Finistère)

Tel: **02 98 67 26 80**. Email: **campingbaiedeterenez@wanadoo.fr**   www.alanrogers.com/FR29510

There are masses of flowers and a warm welcome awaiting visitors to this site. The owners M. and Mme. Lucienne have owned this site for three years and their hard work has made it well worth visiting. There are 114 well cared for and attractive grass pitches with 98 for touring units. Separated by hedges with trees giving some shade, some are quite small. There are 50 with 8A electricity. The area is renowned for its coastal walking and scenery. Scuba diving lessons commence in the pool and afterwards in the sea. A variety of entertainment is organised in the bar, including music groups, sea shanties and traditional Breton songs.

Facilities

Two old but clean toilet blocks include facilities for campers with disabilities. Shop, bar with TV, restaurant (evenings), takeaway (all 1/7-30/8). Heated swimming and paddling pools (15/6-15/9). Minigolf. Boules. Small play area. Horse and carriage rides (high season). Off site: Fishing 1 km. Beach, sailing, boat launching 1.5 km. Riding 3 km. Bicycle hire 4 km. Golf 10 km. Town of Plouezoc'h nearby with shops, bars, restaurants. A little further is the large town of Morlaix.

Open: 1 April - 30 September.

Directions

From Morlaix take the D76 north towards Térénez. Site is well signed, on right just before village. GPS: N48:39.567 W03:50.867

Charges guide

Per person	€ 3,50 - € 5,00
child (2-7 yrs)	€ 1,00 - € 3,00
pitch	€ 4,80 - € 6,70
electricity (8A)	€ 3,00

Check real time availability and at-the-gate prices...
www.**alanrogers**.com

FR29530 Camping les Chaumières

Hameau de Kérascoet, F-29920 Névez (Finistère)

Tel: 02 98 06 73 06. Email: campingdeschaumieres@wanadoo.fr   www.alanrogers.com/FR29530

Les Chaumières is a delightful campsite, hidden away in a quiet hamlet in the Breton countryside and kept immaculate by its cheerful owner Annick. The grass pitches are well maintained, separated by hedges and provide 6 or 10A electricity. On site facilities are no more than two modern toilet blocks and two play areas for children. However, a path that divides the site leads to a safe, sandy beach. This is an ideal choice for those seeking a quiet and relaxing holiday. As the entrance to the site is very narrow, access could prove difficult for larger units.

Facilities

Two modern toilet blocks provide open washbasins and some in cabins and pre-set showers. Baby bath. Facilities for disabled visitors. Washing machine and dryer. Van for takeaway chicken and chips calls twice weekly in July/Aug. Daily bread van. Two play areas. Communal barbecue area. Torches useful. Off site: Restaurant 100 m. Fishing 1 km. Riding and bicycle hire 3 km. Nevez for shops 3 km. Pont Aven, the busy tourist town famous for impressionist painters.

Open: 15 May -15 September.

Directions

From Nevez take the D77 south. Site is well signed. GPS: N47:47.804 W03:46.466

Charges guide

Per person	€ 4,55
child (0-7 yrs)	€ 2,50
pitch	€ 6,50
electricity (6A)	€ 3,40
pet	€ 1,20

FR29540 Camping Pors Peron

F-29790 Beuzec Cap Sizun (Finistère)

Tel: 02 98 70 40 24. Email: info@campingporsperon.com   www.alanrogers.com/FR29540

This small site situated on the Cap Sizun peninsula is lovingly cared for by English owners Graham and Nikki Hatch. The site is hilly but the terrain has been terraced to provide 98 fairly level pitches. Many mature trees and shrubs provide some shade and areas of privacy. Long leads are required for the electric hook-ups. A 200 m. walk takes you to a delightful sandy bay and you can also access a coastal path. Although Pors Peron is set in a quiet and rural part of the Breton countryside, a short drive will take you to the busy port of Douarnenez.

Facilities

One central toilet block has open style washbasins and pre-set showers. Facilities for disabled visitors and babies (kept locked). Laundry facilities. No shop but bread delivered daily. Small, unfenced but safe play area with trampoline. Bicycle hire. Boules. Library and board games. WiFi. Off site: Medieval town of Pont Croix 5 km. Douarnenez for shops, market and restaurants 12 km.

Open: 1 March - 31 October.

Directions

West from Douarnenez on D7 for 12 km. Site signed on right towards Pors Peron.

Charges guide

Per person	€ 3,30 - € 3,50
child (2-7 yrs)	€ 2,00 - € 2,20
pitch	€ 3,50 - € 3,80
electricity	€ 2,50 - € 2,60

FR29550 Camping les Hortensias

La grande Allée, F-29170 Fouesnant (Finistère)

Tel: 02 98 56 52 95. Email: information@campingleshortensias.com   www.alanrogers.com/FR29550

This is a very basic but well kept site with a total of 120 pitches, 90 of which are for touring. The remaining pitches have a strong French presence for seasonal mobiles. Large trees provide shade for most and pitches are of average size, hedged and laid out in a variety of shaped areas. The owner aims to have a quiet and tranquil site. It is therefore ideal for those looking for a relaxed holiday with a very French ambience. Within a few minutes by car you can reach the town of Fouesnant, various eating places and the beaches of Beg-Meil and Cap Cos.

Facilities

The central toilet block has been refurbished to a high standard and offers vanity type washbasins in cabins and pre-set showers. Excellent facilities for disabled visitors. Baby bath. Laundry facilities. No shop but bread delivered daily. Basic play area. Off site: Nearby town of Fouesnant. Shops, restaurants, beaches, bicycle hire, riding, diving, sailing and indoor pool.

Open: 5 April - 30 September.

Directions

From Fouesnant take the D145 in the direction of Mousterlin. Site on left and well signed. GPS: N47:52.937 W04:01.136

Charges guide

Per unit incl. 2 persons	€ 12,00 - € 14,00
incl. 3 persons	€ 15,00 - € 17,00
extra person	€ 3,50
electricity (2/6A)	€ 2,50 - € 2,90

43

FR29590 Camping Tréguer Plage

Plage de Sainte Anne-la-Palud, F-29550 Plonévez-Porzay (Finistère)

Tel: **02 98 92 53 52**. Email: **camping-treguer-plage@wanadoo.fr**   www.alanrogers.com/FR29590

Set right on the dunes adjacent to a large, sandy beach on the huge sweep of Douarnenez Bay, this is apparently one of only seven campsites in Brittany with direct access to a beach, with no paths or roads to cross. It certainly is an impressive location, not manicured but on the 'wild' side, being a protected area. Tall hedges provide wind shelter, tamarisk grows in profusion and there are uninterrupted views out to sea. Some pitches nestle in the shelter of the dunes (sandier ground), others are in 'rooms' of four or eight bordered by hedging. A new pool complex opened in 2008 and the toilet block is due for modernisation. A wonderful site for those seeking a natural, maritime setting – it is officially a 'plage sauvage' and the sound of the waves comes free of charge. The owners, fairly recently arrived, are enthusiastic and have sensitive plans for updating this unique site.

Facilities

Bar, takeaway and shop (July/Aug). New swimming pool with jacuzzi, waterfall for children and paddling pool (1/6-30/9). Play area. Games room/TV. Organised entertainment (July/Aug). Direct access to beach. Off site: Restaurant 2 km. Shops 3 km. Fishing. Golf 18 km. Riding 15 km. Bicycle hire 10 km. Boat launching 3 km. Sailing 5 km. Medieval Locronan.

Open: 5 April - 27 September.

Directions

Situated on the north side of the village, it is well signed from Plonevez-Porzay.
GPS: N48:08.691 W04:16.129

Charges guide

Per person	€ 3,60 - € 5,10
child (2-7 yrs)	€ 2,60 - € 3,30
pitch	€ 2,60 - € 3,30
electricity (6A)	€ 3,40

A campsite on an untouched beach for unique holidays.

PLAGE DE TRÉGUER

Reservation on   Tél + 33 (0)2 98 92 53 52
www.camping-treguer-plage.com

FR29600 Camping de Kerleven

11, route de Port la Fôret, F-29940 La Forêt-Fouesnant (Finistère)

Tel: **02 98 56 98 83**. Email: **contact@camping-de-kerleven.com**   www.alanrogers.com/FR29600

Kerleven was established 40 years ago and enjoys an enviable location, close to the sandy Plage de Kerleven near to the pretty resort of La Fôret Fouesant. This site has been recommended by our French agent and we plan to undertake a full inspection in 2009. Pitches here are of a good size and are well shaded and separated by mature hedges. Kerleven's white sand beach is just a five minute stroll away and a good range of cafés, shops and restaurants can be found there. On-site amenities include a large swimming pool with a water slide and a separate covered pool complex which also contains a spa bath and paddling pool.

Facilities

Shop. Bar. Restaurant. Swimming pool with waterslide. Separate covered pool. Playground. Multisport pitch. Games room. Children's club and entertainment programme. Mobile homes for rent. Off site: Beach 150 m. Shops, cafés and restaurants. Port la Fôret 700 m. GR34 long distance footpath. Golf 3 km.

Open: 19 April - 30 September.

Directions

Take the D70 (Concarneau) exit from the N165 and then follow the D44 towards Fouesnant, then to Port la Fôret. After 1 km, turn left and the site is clearly signed to the left. GPS: N47:53.887 W03:57.986

Charges guide

Per unit incl. 2 persons	€ 21,00 - € 26,00
extra person	€ 6,50 - € 7,50
child (0-6 yrs)	€ 3,00 - € 4,00
electricity (5/10A)	€ 3,00 - € 4,60

Check real time availability and at-the-gate prices...
www.alanrogers.com

FR35000 Camping le Vieux Chêne

Baguer-Pican, F-35120 Dol-de-Bretagne (Ille-et-Vilaine)

Tel: 02 99 48 09 55. Email: vieux.chene@wanadoo.fr

www.alanrogers.com/FR35000

This attractive, family owned site is situated between Saint Malo and Mont Saint-Michel. Developed in the grounds of a country farmhouse dating from 1638, its young and enthusiastic owner has created a really pleasant, traditional atmosphere. In spacious, rural surroundings it offers 199 good sized pitches on gently sloping grass, most with 10A electricity, water tap and light. They are separated by bushes and flowers, with mature trees for shade. A very attractive tenting area (without electricity) is in the orchard. There are three lakes in the grounds and centrally located leisure facilities include a restaurant with a terrace overlooking an attractive pool complex. In high season, some entertainment is provided, which is free for children. The site is used by a Dutch tour operator (20 pitches).

Facilities

Three very good, unisex toilet blocks, which can be heated, include washbasins in cabins, a baby room and facilities for disabled people. Small laundry. Motorcaravan services. Shop, takeaway and restaurant (15/5-15/9). Heated swimming pool, paddling pool, slides (15/5-15/9; lifeguard July/Aug). TV room (satellite). Games room. Tennis. Minigolf. Giant chess. Play area. Riding in July/Aug. Fishing. Off site: Supermarket in Dol 3 km. Golf 12 km. Beach 20 km.

Open: 31 March - 22 September.

Directions

Site is by the D576 Dol-de-Bretagne - Pontorson road, just east of Baguer-Pican. It can be reached from the new N176 taking exit for Dol-Est and Baguer-Pican. GPS: N48:32.972 W01:41.050

Charges guide

Per person	€ 4,50 - € 5,75
child (under 13 yrs)	free - € 3,90
pitch incl. electricity	€ 10,00 - € 21,50
dog	€ 1,50

Camping - Caravaning
le Vieux Chêne
BAGUER PICAN
35120 DOL DE BRETAGNE
TÉL. 0033 2 99 48 09 55
FAX 0033 2 99 48 13 37
Website: www.camping-vieuxchene.fr

BRITTANY
- 200 pitches,
- Tennis,
- Aquatic Park,
- Fishing ponds,
- Mini-golf,
- Mini-club,
- Snack-bar, Shop,
- Ponies...

FR35010 Camping le Bois Coudrais

F-35270 Cuguen (Ille-et-Vilaine)

Tel: 02 99 73 27 45. Email: info@vacancebretagne.com

www.alanrogers.com/FR35010

This gem of a campsite, owned and run by a delightful couple from Jersey, is the kind of small, rural site that is becoming a rarity in France. It has 25 medium to large, well kept, grassy pitches, some divided by young shrubs, others by mature trees. They are spread over three small fields, one of which has an area set aside for ball games and is also home to a group of friendly goats and some chickens – a magnet for children. Electrical connections are possible in most areas. In the small bar, Claire is happy to prepare and serve a selection of homemade meals.

Facilities

The toilet block beside the house provides washbasins in cubicles, showers and sinks for dishwashing and laundry, plus facilities for disabled visitors. Bar with meals. Small heated swimming pool. Play area on grass. New sporting activities and children's entertainment. Animal enclosure. Bicycle hire. Games field. Internet access. Off site: Shop in village 500 m. Combourg 5 km. Fishing 5 km. Golf and riding 15 km. Beach 20 km.

Open: 1 May - 30 September.

Directions

From St Malo take the N137 (in the direction of Rennes) to Combourg. Follow signs on D83 for Fougères and Mont St-Michel. Site is 500 m. past Cuguen on the left, well signed.
GPS: N48:27.237 W01:39.080

Charges 2009

Per unit incl. 2 persons and electricity	€ 19,00
extra person	€ 3,00
child (0-14 yrs)	€ 2,50
dog	€ 1,00
No credit cards.	

BOOK THIS SITE
CALL 01580 214000
...we'll arrange everything
The Travel Service

45

The Travel Service
...we'll arrange everything
BOOK THIS SITE
CALL 01580 214000

The Travel Service
...we'll arrange everything
BOOK THIS SITE
CALL 01580 214000

FR35060 Camping la Touesse

171 rue Ville Gehan, F-35800 Saint Lunaire (Ille-et-Vilaine)

Tel: **02 99 46 61 13**. Email: **camping.la.touesse@wanadoo.fr**   www.alanrogers.com/FR35060

This family campsite was purpose built and has been developed since 1987 by Alain Clement who is keen to welcome more British visitors. Set just back from the coast road, 300 metres from a sandy beach, it is in a semi-residential area. It is, nevertheless, an attractive, sheltered site with a range of trees and shrubs. The 142 level, grass pitches in bays (95 for touring units) have electricity and are accessed by circular tarmac roads. The plus factor of this site, besides its proximity to Dinard, is the fine sandy beach which is sheltered and safe for children. The owners speak English.

Facilities

The central toilet block is well maintained, heated in low season with all modern facilities. Part of it may not be open outside July/Aug. Baby bath and toilet for disabled people. Dishwashing sinks. Laundry facilities. Motorcaravan service point. Shop for basics (1/4-20/9). Pleasant bar/restaurant with TV. Video games for children. Sauna. Off site: Buses 100 m. Sandy beach, fishing 300 m. Riding 500 m. Bicycle hire 1 km. Golf 4 km. Many amenities near.

Open: 1 April - 30 September.

Directions

From Dinard take D786 coast road towards St Lunaire; watch for site signs to the left. GPS: N48:37.850 W02:05.051

Charges guide

Per person	€ 4,00 - € 5,10
child (under 7 yrs)	€ 2,40 - € 2,90
pitch incl. electricity	€ 8,20 - € 9,80
dog	€ 1,50

No credit cards.

FR35020 Castel Camping le Domaine des Ormes

Epiniac, F-35120 Dol-de-Bretagne (Ille-et-Vilaine)

Tel: **02 99 73 53 00**. Email: **info@lesormes.com**   www.alanrogers.com/FR35020

This impressive site is in the northern part of Brittany, about 30 km. from the old town of Saint Malo, in the grounds of the Château des Ormes. In an estate of wooded parkland and lakes it has a pleasant atmosphere, busy in high season but peaceful at other times, with a wide range of facilities. The 800 pitches are divided into a series of different sections, each with its own character and offering a choice of terrain – flat or gently sloping, wooded or open. Only 150 pitches, all with electricity, are used for touring units and there is a large variety of other accommodation available.

Facilities

The toilet blocks are of fair standard, including washbasins in cabins and ample facilities for disabled people. Motorcaravan services. Shop, bar, restaurant, pizzeria and takeaway. Games room, bar and disco. Two heated swimming pools and Aqua park. Adventure play area. Golf. Bicycle hire. Fishing. Equestrian centre. Minigolf. Tennis. Sports ground. Paintball. Archery. Cricket club.

Open: 19 May - 9 September, with all services.

Directions

Access road leads off main D795 about 7 km. south of Dol-de-Bretagne, north of Combourg. GPS: N48:29.418 W01:43.672

Charges guide

Per person	€ 4,25 - € 7,25
pitch incl. vehicle	€ 17,75 - € 29,25
electricity (3/6A)	€ 3,50 - € 4,30
water and drainage	€ 1,60 - € 2,00

FR35040 Camping le P'tit Bois

Saint Malo, F-35430 Saint Jouan-des-Guerets (Ille-et-Vilaine)

Tel: **02 99 21 14 30**. Email: **camping.ptitbois@wanadoo.fr**   www.alanrogers.com/FR35040

On the outskirts of Saint Malo, this neat, family oriented site is very popular with British visitors, being ideal for one night stops or for longer stays. Le P'tit Bois provides 274 large level pitches with 114 for touring units. In two main areas, either side of the entrance lane, these are divided into groups by mature hedges and trees, separated by shrubs and flowers and with access from tarmac roads. Nearly all have electrical hook-ups and over half have water taps. There are site-owned mobile homes and chalets but this does mean that the facilities are open over a long season.

Facilities

Two fully equipped toilet blocks, include washbasins in cabins. Baby baths. Laundry facilities. Simple facilities for disabled people. Motorcaravan service point. Small shop. Bar with entertainment in July/Aug. Snack bar with takeaway. TV room. Games rooms. Heated swimming pool, paddling pool and two water slides (from 15/5). Heated indoor pool with Turkish baths and Jacuzzi (from 5/4). Playground. Multisport court. Tennis. Minigolf. Charcoal barbecues not permitted. Off site: Beach, fishing 1.5 km. Bicycle hire or riding 5 km. Golf 15 km.

Open: 5 April - 13 September.

Directions

St Jouan is west off the St Malo - Rennes road (N137) just outside St Malo. Site is signed from the N137 (take second exit for St Jouan on the D4). GPS: N48:36.596 W01:59.199

Charges guide

Per person	€ 5,00 - € 8,00
child (under 7 yrs)	€ 3,00 - € 6,50
pitch and car	€ 8,00 - € 19,00
electricity (10A)	€ 4,00
dog	€ 4,00 - € 6,00

Check real time availability and at-the-gate prices...

www.alanrogers.com

FR35050 Domaine de la Ville Huchet

Route de la Passagère, Quelmer, F-35400 Saint Malo (Ille-et-Vilaine)

Tel: 02 99 81 11 83. Email: info@villehuchet.com www.alanrogers.com/FR35050

Domaine de la Ville Huchet was taken over a few years ago by the owners of Camping Les Ormes (FR35020). It has been transformed into a superb site with modern facilities and lots of character. The pitches are well laid out and of generous size, most with 6A electricity and some with shade. They are set around an old manor house (disused) at the centre of the site. A splendid pool complex with its slides and pirate theme is particularly exciting for children. A range of entertainment for young and old takes place in the spacious bar area and a new crêperie provides a range of food. This is a useful site, positioned on the edge of St Malo with easy access to the ferry terminal, old town and beaches. A bus service to take you into the town is 400 m. away.

Facilities

The sanitary blocks are modern and clean. Facilities for disabled visitors. Shop. Bar, crêperie and snack bar. Aqua park with water slides. Bicycle hire. Play area. Animation programme in peak season (including live bands). Off site: Aquarium 700 m. St Malo (beaches, ferry terminal and old town) 4 km.

Open: 19 April - 13 September.

Directions

From St Malo take D301 heading south. Join D165 signed Quelmer and the site is well signed (2 km). GPS: N48:36.904 W01:59.269

Charges guide

Per person	€ 3,65 - € 5,50
child (2-13 yrs)	€ 2,45 - € 3,30
pitch	€ 9,45 - € 13,15
electricity (6A)	€ 3,85 - € 4,65
dog	€ 1,60

Domaine de la Ville Huchet ★★★★

Holiday resort in Saint-Malo
For your events,
rent a room full of character.
On a 6 hectare estate,
4 km from the beaches.

- Campsite ★★★★
- Aquatic Park
- Mobile-homes O'HARA for rent
- Appartments for rent

Rte de la Passagère. 35400 St Malo
Tel. 33(0)2 99 81 11 83 • Fax 33(0)2 99 81 51 89
E-mail : info@lavillehuchet.com
Internet : www.lavillehuchet.com

FR35070 Camping Longchamp

Boulevard de Saint-Cast, F-35800 Saint Lunaire (Ille-et-Vilaine)

Tel: 02 99 46 33 98. Email: contact@camping-longchamp.com www.alanrogers.com/FR35070

Michel Rault is justifiably proud of his campsite which lies on the 'Emerald Coast', just 100 m. from a magnificent sandy beach. Set in a wooded area and divided into three sections, this site feels like being in a large landscaped garden. Pitches are large and well kept with 240 for touring. Some hedging and shade is provided by Cypress trees and 140 have electricity. The restaurant on site has a cosy atmosphere, an extensive menu and is run by a Michelin recommended chef. Mr Roult's aim is to keep the site simple and peaceful and as a result many families return year after year.

Facilities

Two very clean toilet blocks with washbasins in cabins and open-style and large showers. Covered dishwashing area. Laundry facilities. Restaurant, bar and takeaway. Small shop. Games room and TV. Play area with bouncy castle (Juy/Aug). Minigolf. Tennis. Boules. Some entertainment in high season. Torches useful. Off site: Golf 2 km. Riding 4 km. Bicycle hire 6 km.

Open: 1 May - 10 September.

Directions

Leave St Malo on D301 and follow signs for Dinard. Turn west onto D168. Keep west onto D603 and in about 3 km. turn north on D503 (St Lunaire). Site signed from village. GPS: N48:38.030 W02:07.231

Charges guide

Per person	€ 5,50
child (under 7 yrs)	€ 3,20
pitch with electricity	€ 9,10 - € 10,20
dog	€ 1,50

47

FR35080 Domaine du Logis

Le Logis, F-35190 La Chapelle-aux-Filtzméens (Ille-et-Vilaine)

Tel: **02 99 45 25 45**. Email: **domainedulogis@wanadoo.fr**   www.alanrogers.com/FR35080

This is an attractive rural site, set in the grounds of an old château. The site's facilities are housed in converted barns and farm buildings, which although old, are well maintained and equipped. There are a total of 180 pitches, 88 of which are for touring. The grass pitches are level, of a generous size and divided by mature hedges and trees. All have 10A electricity connections. This site would appeal to most age groups with plenty to offer the active including a new fitness room with a good range of modern equipment or for those who prefer to relax, perhaps a quiet days fishing beside the lake. The site is well placed for excursions to Mont Saint Michel, Dinard and Dinan.

Facilities

Two comfortable toilet blocks with washbasins and showers. Toilet and shower for disabled visitors. Laundry facilities. Shop in reception. Bar with TV (1/4-30/9). Restaurant and takeaway (28/6-31/8). Outdoor swimming pool (from 15/5). Fitness and games rooms. BMX circuit. Bicycle hire. Lake fishing. Unfenced play areas. Children's club (high season). Internet access. Certain breeds of dogs are not accepted. Off site: Boating on the canal. Riding 10 km.

Open: 1 April - 31 October.

Directions

Turn south off N176 onto D795 signed Dol-de-Bretagne. Continue to Combourg and then take D13 to La-Chapelle-aux-Filtzmeens. Continue for 2 km. Site on right. GPS: N48:23.360 W01:50.080

Charges guide

Per unit incl. 2 persons	
and electricity	€ 19,50 - € 32,00
extra person	€ 4,50 - € 5,00
child (3-12 yrs)	free - € 3,50
dog	free - € 2,00

Camping Cheques accepted.

Camping Le Domaine du Logis****

35190 LA CHAPELLE AUX FILTZMEENS (Ille et Vilaine)
Tél.: 02 99 45 25 45 - Fax: 02 99 45 30 40 - E-mail: domainedulogis@wanadoo.fr - www.domainedulogis.com

FR44020 Camping Municipal du Moulin

Route de Nantes, F-44190 Clisson (Loire-Atlantique)

Tel: **02 40 54 44 48**   www.alanrogers.com/FR44020

This good value, small site is conveniently located on one of the main north - south routes on the edge of the interesting old town of Clisson. A typical municipal site, it is useful for short stays. There are 45 good sized, marked and level pitches with electricity and divided by hedges and trees giving a good degree of privacy and some shade. There is also an unmarked area for small tents. A barbecue and camp fire area is to the rear of the site above the river where one can fish or canoe (via a steep path).

Facilities

The fully equipped toilet block, cleaned each afternoon, includes some washbasins in cabins and others in a separate large room, with hot and cold water. Unit for disabled visitors. Dishwashing and laundry facilities. Bread delivered daily. Table tennis, volleyball, and small playground. No double axle or commercial vehicles accepted. Off site: Supermarket with cheap fuel just across the road. Bicycle hire, riding 5 km. Sailing 15 km. Golf 30 km.

Open: Mid April - mid October.

Directions

From N249 Nantes - Cholet road, take exit for Vallet/Clisson and D763 south for 7 km. then fork right towards Clisson town centre. At roundabout after passing Leclerc supermarket on your right take second exit (into site). GPS: N47:05.742 W01:16.965

Charges guide

Per unit incl. 1 person	
and electricity	€ 7,77 - € 8,20
extra person	€ 2,42 - € 2,55
child (0-7 yrs)	€ 1,61 - € 1,70

No credit cards.

Check real time availability and at-the-gate prices...
www.alanrogers.com

FR44040 Castel Camping le Parc Sainte-Brigitte

Mobile homes ▶ page 489

Domaine de Bréhet, Chemin des Routes, F-44420 La Turballe (Loire-Atlantique)

Tel: 02 40 24 88 91. Email: saintebrigitte@wanadoo.fr
www.alanrogers.com/FR44040

Le Parc Sainte-Brigitte is a well established site in the attractive grounds of a manor house, three kilometres from the beaches. It is a spacious site with 150 good pitches, 110 with electricity, water and drainage. Some are arranged in a circular, park-like setting near the entrance, others are in wooded areas under tall trees and the remainder are on more open grass in an unmarked area near the pool. This is a quiet place to stay outside the main season, whilst in high season, it can become very busy. In high season it is mainly used by families with its full share of British visitors. One can walk around many of the areas of the estate not used for camping; there are farm animals to see and a fishing lake is very popular.

Facilities

The main toilet block, supplemented by a second block, is of good quality. They include washbasins in cabins and two bathrooms. Laundry facilities and lines provided. Motorcaravan services. Small shop. Pleasant restaurant/bar with takeaway (both 15/5-15/9). Heated swimming pool with retractable roof and paddling pool. Playground. Bicycle hire. Boules. TV room and traditional 'salle de réunion'. Fishing. Off site: Riding 2 km. Nearest beach 2.5 km. Golf 15 km.

Open: 1 April - 1 October.

Directions

Entrance is off the busy La Turballe-Guérande D99 road, 3 km. east of La Turballe. A one-way system operates - in one lane, out via another. GPS: N47:20.552 W02:28.301

Charges 2009

Per person	€ 6,30
child (under 7 yrs)	€ 5,00
pitch	€ 7,00
incl. water and electricity	€ 13,90
dog	€ 1,60
No credit cards.	

PARC SAINTE-BRIGITTE
★ ★ ★ ★ ★ N.N.
De Luxe Camping Site

HEATED SWIMMING POOL

Close to the fishing village of LaTurballe and neighbouring beaches. 10 km from the well-known resort of La Baule. The charm of the countryside with the pleasures of the seaside. Sanitary facilities as in a first class hotel. Heated and covered swimming pool (approximately 200 m^2 water and 200 m^2 covered terrace around it). The cover can be retracted during warm weather. Children's pool.

campingsaintebrigitte@wanadoo.fr
www.campingsaintebrigitte.com

FR44100 Camping le Patisseau

29 rue du Patisseau, F-44210 Pornic (Loire-Atlantique)

Tel: 02 40 82 10 39. Email: contact@lepatisseau.com
www.alanrogers.com/FR44100

Le Patisseau is situated in the countryside just a short drive from the fishing village of Pornic. It is a relaxed site with a large number of mobile homes and chalets, and popular with young families and teenagers. The 120 touring pitches, all with electrical connections (6A), are divided between the attractive 'forest' area with plenty of shade from mature trees, and the more open 'prairie' area. Some are on a slight slope and access to others might be tricky for larger units. A railway runs along the bottom half of the site with trains several times a day, (but none overnight) and the noise is minimal. The Morice family works very hard to maintain a friendly atmosphere.

Facilities

The modern heated toilet block is very spacious and well fitted; most washbasins are open style, but the controllable showers are all in large cubicles which have washbasins; these are very popular, so it is best to avoid busy times! Also good facilities for disabled visitors and babies. Laundry rooms. Shop (15/5-8/9). Bar, restaurant and takeaway (1/7-31/9). Indoor heated pool with sauna, jacuzzi and spa (all season). Small heated outdoor pools and water slides (15/5-3/9). Play area. Multisport court. Bicycle hire. Off site: Fishing and beach 2.5 km. Riding, golf, sailing and boatlaunching all 5 km.

Open: 4 April - 11 November.

Directions

Pornic is 19 km. south of the St Nazaire bridge. Access to site is at junction of D751 Nantes - Pornic road with the D213 St Nazaire - Noirmoutier 'Route Bleue'. From north take exit for D751 Nantes. From south follow D751 Clion-sur-Mer. At roundabout north of D213 take exit for Le Patisseau and follow signs to site. Avoid Pornic town centre. GPS: N47:07.183 W02:04.397

Charges 2009

Per unit incl. 2 persons and electricity (6A)	€ 25,00 - € 39,00
extra person	€ 3,00 - € 7,00

Check real time availability and at-the-gate prices...

www.alanrogers.com

FR44050 Camping les Ecureuils

24 avenue Gilbert Burlot, F-44760 La Bernerie-en-Retz (Loire-Atlantique)

Tel: 02 40 82 76 95. Email: camping.les-ecureuils@wanadoo.fr   www.alanrogers.com/FR44050

Just 350 metres from both the sea and the centre of the little town of La Bernerie, Les Ecureuils is a family run site. The sandy beach here is great for children; swimming is restricted to high tide, since the sea goes out a long way, but at low tide you can join the locals in collecting shellfish from the rocks. The site has 167 touring pitches, all with electricity (10A) close by and 19 with their own water tap and drain. There are also 80 mobile homes and chalets for rent and a further 70 privately owned. The site prides itself in its pool complex with heated leisure, swimming and paddling pools; water slides and a flume are only open when supervised in July and August. The fishing port of Pornic is worth a visit, as is the Ile de Noirmoutier, just 35 kilometres south.

Facilities

Four toilet blocks are in traditional French style; some have controllable showers and washbasins in cubicles. Facilities for disabled visitors are not all easily accessible. Very basic baby room. All is kept fairly clean but lacking attention to detail. Bar with terrace, also selling bread (15/6-31/8). Snack bar and takeaway (July/Aug). Swimming pools (15/5-15/9). Playground. Off site: Shops, restaurants and bars 350 m. Also beach, fishing, sailing and boat launching. Golf, riding and bicycle hire 6 km.

Open: 1 May - 15 September.

Directions

La Bernerie-en-Retz is 5 km. south of Pornic and 26 km. south of the Saint Nazaire bridge. From the D213/D13 (St Nazaire - Noirmoutier) turn west on D66 to La Bernerie. Site is signed to right by railway station before reaching town.
GPS: N47:05.070 W02:02.200

Charges guide

Per unit incl. 2 persons	€ 14,00 - € 29,00
extra person	€ 4,00 - € 6,50
child (2-10 yrs)	€ 3,00 - € 5,00
electricity (10A)	€ 4,00

CAMPING LES ECUREUILS***

24, Avenue Gilbert Burlot - 44760 La Bernerie-en-Retz
Tel: 0033(0) 240 82 76 95 - Fax: 0033(0) 240 64 79 52
E-mail: camping.les-ecureuils@wanadoo.fr - Internet: www.camping-les-ecureuils.com

FR44160 Camping Armor-Héol

Route de Guérande, F-44420 Piriac-sur-Mer (Loire-Atlantique)

Tel: 02 40 23 57 80. Email: armor.heol@wanadoo.fr   www.alanrogers.com/FR44160

Situated only 700 metres from Piriac town and the beach, and 14 km. from Guérande, this campsite makes an ideal base for a beach holiday or for touring this beautiful corner of southern Brittany. There are 97 good sized level pitches all with 5A electricity and a further 164 are occupied by mobiles and chalets, half privately-owned, the rest available for rent. As the site is attractively laid out with plenty of trees and hedges, these do not feel intrusive. With an impressive leisure complex and programme of activities and entertainment in high season, the site can be very lively, but it is very well run and becomes quiet after 23.00 hrs.

Facilities

Two clean and well maintained toilet blocks include washbasins in cabins, baby rooms, facilities for disabled visitors and family rooms with shower, basin and toilet (free except July/Aug when they are for hire). At busy times facilities may be under pressure. Washing machines and dryers. Bar, takeaway and restaurant (1/6-15/9). Indoor pool with water movement. Outdoor heated pools and water slides (1/6-15/9). Multisports area, tennis, volleyball. Playground. Fitness rooms. Off site: Beach and town, fishing, boat launching, surfing and bicycle hire 700 m. Sailing 1 km. Golf and riding 2 km.

Open: 5 April - 21 September.

Directions

Piriac is 90 km. west of Nantes and 11 km. northwest of Guérande. Bypass Guérande and take D99 then D333 signed Piriac sur Mer. Site on left before Piriac. GPS: N47:22.481 W02:32.131

Charges guide

Per unit incl. 2 persons	€ 16,00 - € 32,00
extra person	€ 4,00 - € 8,00
child (under 4 yrs)	€ 2,50 - € 4,60
animal	€ 3,00 - € 4,50
electricity	€ 3,50

Check real time availability and at-the-gate prices...

www.alanrogers.com

Mobile homes ▶ page 488

B.P. 18 Le Deffay, Sainte Reine-de-Bretagne, F-44160 Pontchâteau (Loire-Atlantique)

Tel: **02 40 88 00 57**. Email: **campingdudeffay@wanadoo.fr**   www.alanrogers.com/FR44090

BOOK THIS SITE
CALL 01580 214000
...we'll arrange everything
The Travel Service

A family managed site, Château du Deffay is a refreshing departure from the usual formula in that it is not over organised or supervised and has no tour operator units. The 142 good sized, fairly level pitches have pleasant views and are either on open grass, on shallow terraces divided by hedges, or informally arranged in a central, slightly sloping wooded area. Most have electricity. The facilities are located within the old courtyard area of the smaller château (that dates from before 1400). With the temptation of free pedaloes and the fairly deep, unfenced lake, parents should ensure that children are supervised. The landscape is natural right down to the molehills, and the site blends well with the rural environment of the estate, lake and farmland which surround it. For these reasons it is enjoyed by many. The larger château (built 1880) and another lake stand away from this area providing pleasant walking. The reception has been built separately to contain the camping area. Alpine type chalets overlook the lake and fit in well with the environment. The site is close to the Brière Regional Park, the Guérande Peninsula, and La Baule with its magnificent beach (20 km).

Facilities

The main toilet block could do with some updating but is well equipped including washbasins in cabins, provision for disabled people and a baby bathroom. Laundry facilities. Maintenance can be variable and hot water can take time to reach temperature in low season. Shop, bar, small restaurant with takeaway (1/5-20/9) and solar heated swimming pool and paddling pool (all season). Play area. TV. Animation in season including miniclub. Torches useful. Off site: Golf and riding 5 km.

Open: 1 May - 18 September.

Directions

Site is signed from D33 Pontchâteau - Herbignac road near Ste Reine. Also signed from the D773 and N165-E60 (exit 13). GPS: N47:26.270 W02:09.350

Charges guide

Per person	€ 3,20 - € 5,10
child (2-12 yrs)	€ 2,15 - € 3,50
pitch	€ 7,60 - € 11,60
incl. electricity (6A)	€ 11,00 - € 15,60
incl. 3 services	€ 12,90 - € 17,70

Camping Cheques accepted.

Le Deffay
Camping Caravaning
✳✳✳✳

Family campsite in the natural surroundings of the Grande Brière only 20 minutes from the beach. Quiet and relaxing camping. All services are open from beginning of May till mid-September. Covered heated swimming pool, tennis, fishing, pedaloes, walks around the property, table-tennis, playgrounds are free of charge.

Camping Cheque

BP 18 - 44160 Pontchateau
Tel: 0033 240 88 00 57 - (winter) 0033 685 21 15 79
Fax: 0033 240 01 66 55
www.camping-le-deffay.com
Email : campingdudeffay@wanadoo.fr

The Travel Service ...we'll arrange everything

BOOK THIS SITE
CALL 01580 214000

FR44070 Camping Parc du Guibel

Mobile homes ▶ page 488

Route de Kerdrien, F-44420 Piriac-sur-Mer (Loire-Atlantique)

Tel: 02 40 23 52 67. Email: camping@parcduguibel.com

www.alanrogers.com/FR44070

This very large site, situated in an extensive wood, describes itself as 'un Hôtel de Plein Air' and prides itself on its spaciousness and its trees. A keen birdwatcher told the owner that he had seen 50 different species of birds. There are 450 pitches of which 307 are for touring scattered among the 14 hectares of woodland, mainly shaded but some in clearings. One section at the top of the site across a minor road is always quiet and peaceful. 110 pitches have electricity (3, 6 or 10A) of which 67 also have water tap and drainage. There are also 134 mobile homes and chalets for rent. A long room houses the bar, snack bar with takeaway and a small restaurant together with an electronic games area. A small shop sells bread and a few basics. A new pool complex of 500 sq.m. should be ready for 2009 including a slide and a paddling pool. A programme of activities and entertainment for children and adults is organised in high season. The sea is just over a kilometre away and nearby are the salt-marshes producing the famous 'Sel de Guérande'.

Facilities

Five sanitary blocks: the newest is smart and well equipped, with controllable showers and washbasins. Two others have been partially refurbished to the same standards. The others are rather old-fashioned, with preset showers and washbasins in cubicles. Facilities for disabled visitors. Baby room. Laundry facilities. Motorcaravan service point. New swimming pool complex (1/5-15/9). Bar, snack bar, takeaway and restaurant (July-Aug only). Off site: Riding 400 m. Fishing 1 km. Beach 1.2 km. Sailing 3.5 km. Golf 18 km.

Open: 1 April - 30 September.

Directions

Piriac-sur-Mer is 90 km. west of Nantes and 18 km. northwest of La Baule. On N165 from Vannes, leave at exit 15 towards La Roche Bernard, turn left to join D774 towards La Baule. 8 km. after Herbignac, turn right on D52 to St Molt and Mesquer towards Piriac. Do not take the coast road but turn left on D52. Site signed on right in 3 km. GPS: N47:23.177 W02:30.604

Charges guide

Per person	€ 3,00 - € 4,95
child (under 7 yrs)	€ 2,00 - € 3,30
pitch incl. electricity	€ 5,85 - € 9,20

camping caravaning ★★★★

Parc du Guibel

New water park in 2009

Rental of mobile homes and chalets, 450 pitches, In an exceptional green area.

route de Kerdrien, 44420 Piriac sur Mer
Tél: 02 40 23 52 67 Fax: 02 40 15 50 24
Email: camping@parcduguibel.com
www.parcduguibel.com

FR44170 Camping les Ajoncs d'Or

Chemin du Rocher, F-44500 La Baule (Loire-Atlantique)

Tel: 02 40 60 33 29. Email: contact@ajoncs.com

www.alanrogers.com/FR44170

This site is situated in pine woods, 1.5 km. on the inland side of La Baule and its beautiful bay. A well maintained, natural woodland setting provides a wide variety of pitch types (just over 200), some level and bordered with hedges and tall trees to provide shade and many others that maintain the natural characteristics of the woodland. Most pitches have electricity and water nearby and are usually of a larger size. The owners who live on site will welcome you.

Facilities

Two good quality sanitary blocks are clean and well maintained providing plenty of facilities including a baby room. Washing machines and dryers. Shop and bar (July/Aug). Snack bar (July/Aug). Good size swimming pool and paddling pool (1/6-5/9). Sports and playground areas. Bicycle hire. Reception with security barrier (closed 22.30-07.30 hrs). Off site: La Baule. Beach 1.5 km. Fishing and riding 1.5 km. Golf 3 km.

Open: 1 April - 30 September.

Directions

From N171 take exit for La Baule les Pins. Follow signs for 'La Baule Centre', then left at roundabout in front of Champion supermarket and follow site signs. GPS: N47:17.370 W02:22.420

Charges guide

Per unit incl. 2 persons	€ 20,00
incl. electricity	€ 23,00
incl. water and drainage	€ 25,00
extra person	€ 6,00

Check real time availability and at-the-gate prices...

www.**alanrogers**.com

FR44150 Camping la Tabardière

F-44770 La Plaine-sur-Mer (Loire-Atlantique)

Tel: 02 40 21 58 83. Email: info@camping-la-tabardiere.com   www.alanrogers.com/FR44150

Owned and managed by the Barre family, this campsite lies next to the family farm. Pleasant, peaceful and immaculate, it will suit those who want to enjoy the local coast and towns but return to an 'oasis' for relaxation. It still, however, provides activities and fun for those with energy remaining. The pitches are mostly terraced and care needs to be taken in manoeuvring caravans into position – although the effort is well worth it. Pitches have access to electricity and water taps are conveniently situated nearby. The site is probably not suitable for wheelchair users. Whilst this is a rural site, its amenities are excellent with covered swimming pool, paddling pool and a water slide, volleyball, tennis, boules and a very challenging 18 hole minigolf to keep you occupied, plus a friendly bar. The beautiful beaches are three kilometres with the fishing harbour town, Pornic, some five kilometres, for cafes, restaurants and the evening strolls. A 'Sites et Paysages' member.

Facilities

Two good, clean toilet blocks are well equipped and include laundry facilities. Motorcaravan service point. Shop, bar, snacks and takeaway (high season). Good sized covered swimming pool, paddling pool and slides (supervised). Playground. Minigolf. Volleyball and basketball. Half size tennis courts. Boules. Fitness programme. Overnight area for motorcaravans (€ 13 per night). Off site: Beach 3 km. Sea fishing 3 km. Golf, riding and bicycle hire all 5 km.

Open: 4 April - 27 September.

Directions

Site is well signed, situated inland off the D13 Pornic - La Plaine-sur-Mer road.
GPS: N47:08.280 W02:09.110

Charges 2009

Per unit incl. 2 persons	€ 15,00 - € 26,70
extra person	€ 3,70 - € 6,40
child (2-9 yrs)	€ 2,75 - € 4,35
dog	€ 3,20
electricity (3/8A)	€ 3,30 - € 4,80

Camping Cheques accepted.

CAMPING LA TABARDIÈRE ★★★★ *Camping Caravaning*

South Loire - North Vendée

Situated in a green environment, with covered heated swimming pool.

3 km from the sea, 4 km from the shops, 6 km from a 18 holes golf terrain in Pornic, 8 km from a thalasso centre.

Open from 4 April till 27 September

44770 la Plaine sur Mer - Tél.: 0033 240 215 883
info@camping-la-tabardiere.com - www.camping-la-tabardiere.com

FR44230 Camping EléoVic

Route de la Pointe St-Gildas, Préfailles, F-44770 Pornic (Loire-Atlantique)

Tel: 02 40 21 61 60. Email: contact@camping-eleovic.com   www.alanrogers.com/FR44230

This is a delightful site overlooking the sea on the attractive Jade Coast west of Pornic. There are 80 touring pitches, some with wonderful views of the sea, and a similar number of mobile homes, many of which are available for rent. The site is well cared for and everything looks neat. All pitches have access to electricity (10A), but you may need a long cable. Much of the ground is sloping, so a really level pitch may not be available. Access for larger units to some pitches may be tricky.

Facilities

Central sanitary block has spacious pre-set showers and washbasins in cabins. Facilities for disabled visitors. Excellent room for dishwashing and laundry. Further facilities are in the pool building and another smaller block should be ready. Good restaurant (July-Aug; not Wednesdays) with small bar and terrace. Fitness room. Playground. Table tennis. Boules. Children's activities and entertainment and sporting events for families (high season). Off site: Sailing and boat launching 800 m. Bicycle hire and golf 7 km. Riding 10 km.

Open: 5 April - 28 October.

Directions

Préfailles is 20 km. south of the St Nazaire bridge and 9 km. west of Pornic. From north on D213 (Route Bleue) turn southwest just south of St Michel-Chef-Chef on D96 to La Plaine-sur-Mer. Follow signs for Préfailles. From Pornic take D13 to La Plaine (do not enter town). Follow signs for Préfailles. Continue on D313 towards La Pointe Saint-Gildas. At 50 km. sign turn left, then left again to site on right. GPS: N47:07.957 W02:13.890

Charges guide

Per unit incl. 2 persons	€ 15,90 - € 31,10
extra person	€ 4,90 - € 8,30
electricity (10A)	€ 4,70

BOOK THIS SITE
CALL 01580 214000
...we'll arrange everything
The Travel Service

53

FR44180 Camping de la Boutinardière

Mobile homes ▶ page 489

Rue de la Plage de la Boutinardière, F-44210 Pornic (Loire-Atlantique)
Tel: **02 40 82 05 68**. Email: **info@laboutinardiere.com**   www.alanrogers.com/FR44180

This is truly a holiday site to suit all the family whatever their ages, just 200 m. from the beach. It has 250 individual good sized pitches, 100-120 sq.m. in size, many bordered by three metre high, well maintained hedges for shade and privacy. All pitches have electricity available. It is a family owned site and English is spoken by the helpful, obliging reception staff. Beside reception is the excellent site shop and across the road is a complex of indoor and outdoor pools, paddling pool and a twin toboggan water slide. On site there are sports and entertainment areas. Facing the water complex, the bar, restaurant and terraces are new and serve excellent food, be it a snack or in the restaurant or perhaps a takeaway. This site is difficult to better in the South Brittany, Loire-Atlantique area. This campsite has it all – 2 km. from the beautiful harbour town of Pornic and 200 metres from the sea, together with the very best of amenities and facilities.

Facilities

Toilet facilities are in three good blocks, one large and centrally situated and two supporting blocks. Washbasins are in cabins. Laundry facilities. Shop. New complex of bar, restaurant, terraces. Three heated swimming pools, one indoor, a paddling pool and water slides (15/5-22/9). Games room. Sports and activity area. Playground. Minigolf. Fitness equipment and sauna. Off site: Sandy cove 200 m. Golf, riding, sea fishing, restaurants, cafés, fishing harbour, boat trips, sailing and windsurfing, all within 5 km.

Open: 5 April - 30 September.

Directions

From north or south on D213, take Nantes D751 exit. At roundabout (with McDonalds) take D13 signed Bemarie-eb-Retz. After 4 km. site is signed to right. Note: do NOT exit from D213 at Pomic Ouest or Centre.
GPS: N47:05.490 W02:03.080

Charges guide

Per unit incl. 2 persons	€ 15,00 - € 34,00
extra person	€ 3,00 - € 7,50
child (under 8 yrs)	€ 2,00 - € 5,50
electricity (6/10A)	€ 4,00 - € 5,50

FR44210 Camping de l'Océan

Mobile homes ▶ page 490

F-44490 Le Croisic (Loire-Atlantique)
Tel: **02 40 23 07 69**. Email: **camping-ocean@wanadoo.fr**   www.alanrogers.com/FR44210

Camping de l'Océan is situated on the Le Croisic peninsula, an attractive part of the Brittany coastline. Out of a total of 400 pitches, just 80 are available for tourers with the remainder being taken by mobile homes either privately owned or for rent. The pitches are level and 80-100 sq.m. in size (they were rather worn when we visited). This site, probably more suitable for families with young teenagers, can be very lively in high season with a wealth of activities and entertainment.

Facilities

Five adequate toilet blocks include facilities for disabled visitors. Washing machines and dryers. Good restaurant and bar. Takeaway. Shop. Motorcaravan service point. Swimming pool complex comprising an indoor pool, outdoor pool and paddling pool. Volleyball. Football. Basketball. Tennis. Off site: Market (most days). Le Croisic for shops, bars and restaurants. Sailing, riding and golf.

Open: 5 April - 30 September.

Directions

From Le Pouliguen, travel west on N171 to Le Croisic. Site is well signed from here and found in about 1.5 km. GPS: N47:17.520 W02:32.090

Charges guide

Per unit incl. 2 persons and electricity (6A)	€ 16,50 - € 36,50
extra person	€ 3,00 - € 7,00
electricity (10A)	€ 1,00 - € 3,00

FR44220 Camping Parc de Léveno

Mobile homes ▶ page 490

Route de Sandun, F-44350 Guérande (Loire-Atlantique)
Tel: **02 40 24 79 30**. Email: **domaine.leveno@wanadoo.fr**   www.alanrogers.com/FR44220

There have been many changes to this extensive site over the past three years and considerable investment has been made to provide some excellent new facilities. The number of mobile homes and chalets has increased considerably, leaving just 47 touring pitches. Pitches are divided by hedges and trees providing good shade and all have electricity (10A). Access is tricky to some and the site is not recommended for larger units. Twin axle caravans and American motorhomes are not accepted.

Facilities

Main refurbished toilet block offers pre-set showers, washbasins in cubicles and facilities for disabled visitors. Laundry facilities. Shop for basics and snacks. Restaurant, bar with TV (July/Aug). Indoor pool. Heated outdoor pool complex with water slides, paddling pool (15/5-15/9). Aquatic centre. Fitness room. Play area. Multisport court. Activities and events (high season). Off site: Hypermarket 1 km. Fishing 2 km. Beach, golf and riding all 5 km.

Open: 4 April - 30 September.

Directions

Site is less than 3 km. from the centre of Guérande. From D774 and from D99/N171 take D99E Guérande by-pass. Turn east for Villejames and Leclerc Hypermarket and continue on D247 to site on right. GPS: N47:19.987 W02:23.478

Charges 2009

Per unit incl. 2 persons, electricity and water	€ 18,00 - € 35,00
extra person	€ 4,00 - € 7,00

3 destinations in Aqua plein' air...

for successful holidays !

Domaine de **Léveno**
Camping - Locations
★★★★

l'Océan
Camping Village ★★★

La Boutinardière
Camping Village
★★★

LE DOMAINE DE LÉVENO	L'OCÉAN	LA BOUTINARDIÈRE
only 5 km from la Baule !	only 150 m from the beach !	only 200 m from the beach !
Lieu dit Léveno	15, route Maison Rouge	23, rue de la plage
44350 GUÉRANDE - France	B.P. 15	de la Boutinardière
tel. : 00 33 2 40 24 79 30	44490 LE CROISIC - France	44210 PORNIC - France
00 33 2 40 24 79 50	tel. : 00 33 2 40 23 07 69	tel. : 00 33 2 40 82 05 68
fax : 00 33 2 40 62 01 23	fax : 00 33 2 40 15 70 63	fax : 00 33 2 40 82 49 01
www.camping-leveno.com	www.camping-ocean.com	www.camping-boutinardiere.com

- -

To recieve our leaflet, please return the voucher to the establishment of your choice   AR-GB-09

Surname : .... Name : ....

Adress : ....

Post code : ....City : .... Country : ....

Phone : .... E-mail : ....

FR44240 Camping le Ranch

Les Hautes Raillères, F-44770 La Plaine-sur-Mer (Loire-Atlantique)

Tel: **02 40 21 52 62**. Email: **info@camping-le-ranch.com**   www.alanrogers.com/FR44240

This is a pleasant, family-run campsite with a friendly atmosphere, close to the beaches of the Jade Coast between Pornic and St Brévin-les-Pins, yet not right on the seashore. The 99 touring pitches all have access to electricity (6A) although on some a long cable may be required; these occupy the central part of the site, with the fringe areas taken up by mobile homes and chalets. 21 are for rent and 74 privately-owned (although 30 of these are also available for rent in high season). The rows of pitches are separated by well-kept hedges, and small trees mark the corners of most plots. In high season there is a very lively atmosphere and it might seem a little crowded on some pitches; at less busy times it is almost certainly a very peaceful site. A pleasant bar and terrace overlook the attractive pool complex with a swimming pool and paddling pool, together with water slides and a flume. Linked to the bar is a large barn with stage and dance floor which at other times is a games room and an indoor volleyball court.

Facilities

The central sanitary block has pre-set showers, facilities for disabled visitors, washbasins in cubicles, a fairly basic baby room, and dishwashing and laundry sinks. Further small toilet block. Pool open 1/5-30/9 (heated 15/6-15/9). Bar has small shop selling bread, basics and camping gaz. Good takeaway (July - Aug). Activities for children and entertainment and sports events for families in high season. Off site: Beach 800 m. Bicycle hire 1.5 km. Boat launching 3 km. Fishing 5 km. Golf, riding and sailing 3 km.

Open: 1 April - 30 September.

Directions

La Plaine-sur-Mer is 16 km. south of the St Nazaire bridge. Site is on D96 5 km. northeast of the town. From D213 (Route Bleue) just south of St Michel-Chef-Chef turn southwest on D96 towards La Plaine. Site on left in about 2 km.
GPS: N47:09.313 W02:09.894

Charges guide

Per unit incl. 2 persons	€ 12,50 - € 23,00
extra person (over 7 yrs)	€ 3,00 - € 5,00
child (under 7 yrs)	€ 2,00 - € 3,30
electricity	€ 3,80

FR44250 Camping Trémondec

48 rue du Château Careil, F-44350 Guérande (Loire-Atlantique)

Tel: **02 40 60 00 07**. Email: **camping.tremondec@wanadoo.fr**   www.alanrogers.com/FR44250

This is a delightful site close to the sophisticated resort of La Baule, the more relaxed beaches of La Turballe, the salt marshes of Guérande and the Natural Reserve of Brière. It is lovingly cared for by the very friendly Schgier family. There are 60 touring pitches on gently sloping ground, divided by hedges and with plenty of trees offering some shade to many; almost all have electricity (6A) nearby. A further 40 pitches are occupied by mobile homes, chalets and family tents either for rent or leased.

Facilities

Two well equipped and clean sanitary blocks with push button showers and some washbasins in cubicles. Facilities for disabled visitors. Dishwashing and laundry facilities. Bar, snack bar/takeaway and restaurant all July/Aug. Good heated swimming pool and paddling pool (1/5-30/9). Small games room. Children's activities and evening events for families in high season. Off site: Supermarkets, restaurants and bars, bicycle hire, sailing and beach all within 2.5 km. Boat launching 4 km. Riding 5 km. Fishing and golf 10 km.

Open: 1 April - 24 September.

Directions

Site is 5 km. southeast of Guérande and 2.5 km. north of La Baule. From east on N171 (St Nazaire - Guérande), turn south at exit for La Baule Centre. Turn right at next roundabout (Château Careil), then turn right signed to château and site. From west on D99E Guérande by-pass, take D92 (La Baule), then left signed to site. GPS: N47:17.856 W02:23.998

Charges guide

Per person	€ 3,40 - € 5,00
pitch incl. electricity	€ 16,50 - € 24,00
pitch without electricity	€ 12,70 - € 20,20

Check real time availability and at-the-gate prices...

www.**alanrogers**.com

57 chemin du Fief, F-44250 Saint Brévin-les-Pins (Loire-Atlantique)

Tel: 02 40 27 23 86. Email: camping@lefief.com

www.alanrogers.com/FR44190

BOOK THIS SITE
CALL 01580 214000
...we'll arrange everything
The Travel Service

If you are a family with young children or lively teenagers, this could be the campsite for you. Le Fief is a well established site only 800 metres from sandy beaches on the southern Brittany coast. It has a magnificent 'aqua park' with outdoor and covered swimming pools, paddling pools, slides, river rapids, fountains, jets and more. The site has 220 pitches for touring units (out of 413). Whilst these all have electricity (5A), they vary in size and many are worn and may be untidy. There are also 143 mobile homes and chalets to rent and 55 privately owned units. This is a lively site in high season with a variety of entertainment and organised activity for all ages. This ranges from a miniclub for 5-12 year olds, to 'Tonic Days' with aquagym, jogging and sports competitions, and to evening events which include karaoke, themed dinners and cabaret. There are plenty of sporting facilities for active youngsters.

Facilities

One excellent new toilet block and three others of a lower standard. Laundry facilities. Shop (15/5-15/9). Bar, restaurant and takeaway (15/4-15/9) with terrace overlooking the pool complex. Outdoor pools, etc. (15/5-15/9). Covered pool (all season). Play area. Tennis. Volleyball. Basketball. Pétanque. Table tennis. Archery. Games room. Internet access. Organised entertainment and activities (July/Aug). Off site: Beach, bicycle hire 800 m. Bus stop 1 km. Riding 1 km. Golf 15 km. Planète Sauvage safari park.

Open: 1 April - 15 October.

Directions

From the St Nazaire bridge take the fourth exit from the D213 signed St Brévin - L'Océan. Continue over first roundabout and bear right at the second to join chemin du Fief. The site is on the right, well signed. GPS: N47:14.188 W02:10.109

Charges guide

Per pitch incl. 2 persons	€ 17,00 - € 37,00
extra person	€ 5,00 - € 9,00
child (0-7 yrs)	€ 2,50 - € 4,50
electricity	€ 5,00 - € 6,00
dog	€ 2,00 - € 5,00

Sunêlia
CAMPING PLUS BRETAGNE
Camping Qualité

le fief

camping & rental accommodations

GROCERIES
BAR - RESTAURANT
TAKE AWAY MEALS
PLAYING AREAS - TENNIS
MULTI SPORTS TERRAIN
COVERED AND HEATED SWIMMING POOL
9 ANIMATORS DURING THE SEASON

WELLNESS CENTRE
sauna, hammam, spa, fitness room, Power Plate®

Full pension - 1/2 pension

Dynamic, refreshing and exotic!

camping le fief

57, chemin du Fief
44250 ST BREVIN LES PINS
Tél.: 0033 2 40 27 23 86
Fax: 0033 2 40 64 46 19

www.lefief.com

SAINT BREVIN LES PINS — CÔTE DE JADE — SOUTH BRITTANY — FRANCE

www.keraomarketing.com © 2007

The Travel Service
...we'll arrange everything
BOOK THIS SITE
CALL 01580 214000

FR44270 Camping le Château du Petit Bois

F-44420 Mesquer (Loire-Atlantique)

Tel: **02 40 42 68 77**. Email: **info@campingdupetitbois.com**   www.alanrogers.com/FR44270

This pleasant campsite is located in the wooded grounds of a small château. The 125 good sized touring pitches, all with electricity (3/6A) have varying degrees of shade and a few are in the open for those who like a sunny plot. Reception is housed in the converted outbuildings of the château, and is welcoming and informative. The Marin family and their staff are friendly and helpful, and the site is very well run. The sea is just over a kilometre away, as is the village of Mesquer and nearby are the salt marshes which produce the famous Sel de Guérande. On site there is an attractive swimming pool complex: a heated main pool and paddling pool, and a separate pool with two good water slides which is only open when the pool is supervised.

Facilities

The main sanitary block has pre-set showers and open style washbasins together with some cubicles with controllable shower and a washbasin. Dishwashing and laundry facilities. Facilities for disabled visitors. Combined bar, snack bar and takeaway (with TV, pool table and 'babyfoot'). Small shop selling bread and basics (July/Aug). Pool complex with heated main pool and paddling pool and pool with water slides (only open when supervised). Programme of activities (all July/Aug). Off site: Fishing, bicycle hire, riding and sailing all nearby. Golf 12 km.

Open: 1 April - 30 October.

Directions

Mesquer is 80 km. northwest of Nantes and 16 km. north of La Baule. From N165 Nantes - Vannes road, leave at exit 15 towards La Roche Bernard, turn left to join D774 towards La Baule. 8 km. after Herbignac, turn right on D52 to St Molt and Mesquer. Site is on D52 just west of village (do not go into village). GPS: N47:23.941 W02:28.279

Charges guide

Per unit incl. 2 persons	€ 15,40 - € 19,20
extra person	€ 4,90 - € 6,10
child (3-7 yrs)	€ 3,40 - € 4,20
electricity (3/6A)	€ 4,30 - € 5,40

Camping & Rental accommodations

the Celtic spirit in Southern Brittany!

LE CHÂTEAU DU PETIT BOIS ★★★

1820, route de Kerlagadec
44420 MESQUER - France
tél. : (+33) (0)2 40 42 68 77
fax : (+33) (0)2 40 42 65 58
www.campingdupetitbois.com

FR44310 Flower Camping les Brillas

Le Bois des Tréans, F-44760 Les Moutiers-en-Retz (Loire-Atlantique)

Tel: **02 40 82 79 78**. Email: **info@campinglesbrillas.com**   www.alanrogers.com/FR44310

You are assured of a warm welcome from M. and Mme. Perret, the owners of this site. The small number of touring pitches are on grass, hedged and small. The larger pitches are being taken up by mobile homes of which there is a much higher ratio compared to touring pitches. This could be a useful base for visiting Pornic and St Nazaire where there are many tourist attractions. The reception, bar and restaurant are housed in the same modern building as the sanitary facilities. Care should be taken on the approach road to the site which is a long narrow lane with no passing places.

Facilities

The toilet block is clean but basic and includes a mix of English and Turkish style toilets and preset showers. Good facilities for disabled visitors. Dishwashing and laundry facilities. Bar and restaurant with limited menu. Shop in bar. Large games area. Small unfenced play area. Basic swimming pool. Bicycle hire. Entertainment (July/Aug). Off site: Fishing and sailing 3 km. Riding 5 km. Golf 12 km.

Open: 1 April - 30 October.

Directions

Site is 1.5 km. from Les Moutiers. Heading northwest from Les Moutiers on D97 turn right onto Route du Bois des Tréans. Site well signed.
GPS: N47:04.30 W02:00.26

Charges guide

Per unit incl. 2 persons and electricity	€ 13,00 - € 22,50
extra person	€ 2,50 - € 5,50
child (under 7 yrs)	free - € 3,00
child (under 18 yrs)	€ 1,50 - € 4,00

www.flowercampings.com

Check real time availability and at-the-gate prices...

www.alanrogers.com

FR44280 Airotel la Roseraie

20 avenue Jean Sohier, route du Golf, F-44500 La Baule (Loire-Atlantique)

Tel: 02 40 60 46 66. Email: camping@laroseraie.com www.alanrogers.com/FR44280

This is a lively site with plenty of potential and some good features. There is a warm welcome from the Burban family and their reception staff in very pleasant and smart surroundings. An excellent pool complex by the entrance is open all season and includes a heated pool with a roof that is opened when the sun shines, a separate flume and a paddling pool. There are 230 level pitches of which 100 are for touring, all with electricity (6 or 10A) and 50 with water and drainage.

Facilities

Two traditional sanitary blocks have controllable showers, some washbasins in cubicles, facilities for disabled visitors, washing machines and dryers. A modern extension to one block has en-suite showers and washbasins and an attractively decorated children's section. Small shop. Bar with snacks and restaurant facility and separate takeaway (all July/Aug). Play area. Games/TV and fitness rooms. Multisport court. Boules. Off site: Riding 1 km. Beach, fishing and golf 2 km. Boat launching 6 km. Fishing 10 km.

Open: 1 April - 30 September.

Directions

Site is beside the N171/D99 Nantes and St Nazaire - Guérande road (Route Bleue). Leave at exit for La Baule Les Pins and Escoublac and go towards La Baule (still N171). At church in Escoublac turn right and site is 500 m. on right, just after bridge over Route Bleue. GPS: N47:17.930 W02:21.936

Charges guide

Per person	€ 4,50 - € 7,50
child (1-5 yrs)	€ 2,50 - € 4,50
pitch	€ 8,00 - € 13,00
electricity (6A)	€ 5,00
Camping Cheques accepted.	

FR44300 Siblu Camping les Pierres Couchées

L'Hermitage, F-44250 Saint Brévin-les-Pins (Loire-Atlantique)

Tel: 02 40 27 85 64 www.alanrogers.com/FR44300

In high season this is a lively and bustling site, just 300 metres from the beach and close to the 'Route Bleue' running south from St Nazaire towards the Vendée. Most of the site is devoted to mobile homes and chalets either privately-owned or for rent. There are 79 touring pitches on the hilly part of the complex, 53 with electricity available. Access to some is not easy. There is a full programme of activities for children, young people and families in high season and good leisure facilities.

Facilities

Several sanitary blocks, but only one serving the touring pitches. It has pre-set showers, washbasins in cubicles and facilities for disabled visitors, although the latter would have great difficulty in getting there as it is on top of a hillock. Washing machines and dryers Bar/restaurant (all season). Shop, bakery and takeaway (July/Aug). Multisport court, tennis courts, boules. Bicycle hire. Play areas. Large covered amphitheatre. Off site: Beach 300 m. Riding 1 km. Fishing and sailing 4 km. Golf 12 km.

Open: 1 April - 8 October.

Directions

St Brévin is 6 km. south of the St Nazaire bridge. The site is south of the town just off the D213 between St Brévin-l'Océan and St Michel-Chef-Chef, on a brief section where the road narrows. GPS: N47:12.282 W02:09.091

Charges guide

Per unit incl. 2 persons and electricity	€ 20,00 - € 30,00
extra person	€ 4,00 - € 6,50
child (3-6 yrs)	€ 2,50 - € 4,00

FR44320 Camping la Pierre Longue

B.P 13, rue Henri Danant, F-44490 Le Croisic (Loire-Atlantique)

Tel: 02 40 23 13 44. Email: lapierrelongue@orange.fr www.alanrogers.com/FR44320

Le Croisic can be found on a peninsula which stretches over 5 km. into the ocean. The friendly owners have a great sense of humour at this delightful site. There are a total of 60 grass touring pitches of ample size which are well tended and divided by small trees and young shrubs. There is a little but not much shade. A comfortable bar and restaurant with a comprehensive menu serving speciality seafood dishes, both open out onto a terrace. This site has a very pleasant ambience.

Facilities

The main modern toilet block is heated with washbasins both open and in cubicles. Large shower area. Facilities for disabled visitors. Dishwashing sinks and laundry facilities. Small shop (June - Sept). Bar, restaurant and takeaway (May - Sept). Outdoor heated swimming pool and paddling pool (May - Sept). Off site: Riding, golf, boat launching within 1.5 km. Medieval town of Guérande. Beaches of La Baule. Salt beds of the Salines.

Open: All year.

Directions

Take D774 from Guerande south to Pouliguen. Follow northwest to Le Croisic. Site is well signed and on left after 1.5 km. GPS: N47:17.32 W02:31.45

Charges guide

Per unit incl. 2 persons and electricity	€ 14,70 - € 25,00
extra person	€ 3,00 - € 6,50
child (3-12 yrs)	€ 1,50 - € 4,50

Check real time availability and at-the-gate prices...

www.alanrogers.com

FR44340 Camping la Falaise

1 boulevard de Belmont, F-44420 La Turballe (Loire-Atlantique)

Tel: **02 40 23 32 53**. Email: **info@camping-de-la-falaise.com**   www.alanrogers.com/FR44340

La Falaise is a simple site enjoying direct access to a wide sandy beach. There are 150 pitches of which 67 are available to tourers with water and electricity. Other pitches are occupied by mobile homes or chalets (some available to rent). The pitches are of a reasonable size but are unshaded and tend to be very sandy. This is a quiet site in low season becoming much livelier in July and August. There are relatively few amenities on site but nearby La Turballe has a good selection of shops and restaurants. There is one main building housing reception and washing and toilet facilities. In high season, a takeaway food service is available. La Turballe is a bustling fishing port and nearby Guérande, on the edge of the Grande Brière natural park, merits a visit with its excellent market.

Facilities

Central toilet block (predominantly Turkish style toilets). Bar, restaurant and takeaway (1/6-15/9). Play area (unfenced). Mobile homes and chalets for rent. Direct access to the beach. Off site: Shops 300 m. Fishing. Boat launching 500 m. Golf 2 km. Riding 10 km. Walking and cycle trails. Shops and restaurants in La Turballe 2 km.

Open: 25 March - 5 November.

Directions

Take the D99 from Guèrande to La Turballe and then continue towards Piriac-sur-Mer. Bypass La Turballe and the site is on this road after a further kilometre. GPS: N47:21.233 W02:31.333

Charges guide

Per unit incl. 2 persons, electricity and water	€ 20,10 - € 30,65
extra person (over 4 yrs)	€ 4,25 - € 4,90

Camping La Falaise

2 entrance to the beach, on 400 m distance from the fisher harbour and marina. The center is at 600 meters distance, you will find a supermarket at 400 meter distance. La Falaise is near various places of interest. The mediaeval city of Guérande, ferries to the islands, the Parc Naturel Régional de Brière and the Côte Sauvage.

1 Boulevard de Belmont - 44420 La Turballe - Tel: 0033 240 23 32 53 - Fax: 0033 240 62 87 07
E-mail: camping-de-lafalaise@orange.fr - www.camping-la-falaise.com

FR44360 Campéole les Paludiers

Rue Nicolas Appert, F-44740 Batz-sur-Mer (Loire-Atlantique)

Tel: **02 40 23 85 84**. Email: **paludiers@campeole.com**   www.alanrogers.com/FR44360

Les Paludiers, part of the Campéole group, is pleasantly situated at Batz-sur-Mer, a typical Breton village between La Baule and the fortified town of Guérande. The site has 300 pitches, with 150 used for touring units on sandy ground, marked and divided by shrubs. There are 70 with 10A electricity. The remainder of the pitches are occupied by mobile homes and canvas bungalows. At the rear of the modern reception building there is a bar and games room. Outside a patio area overlooks a small heated pool and a play area for children. Entertainment is provided for both children and adults in the high season.

Facilities

Three modern toilet bocks each with good facilities for disabled visitors and a baby room. Laundry facilities. Shop with limited but essential stocks. Bar and snacks (1/7-31/8). Swimming and paddling pools (15/5-15/9). Play area. Games room. Barbecues are only permitted in a dedicated area. Off site: Beach 100 m. Fishing 500 m. Golf, bicycle hire and riding 1 km. Town centre 800 m. Salt marshes and coastal walking paths.

Open: 5 April - 23 September.

Directions

From Nantes take the N171 to St Nazaire and then the D213 towards Guérande. At the D774 follow signs to Batz-sur-Mer, continue through village and take exit from the roundabout into rue Nicolas Appert. Site entrance is on the left. GPS: N47:16.733 W02:29.483

Charges guide

Per unit incl. 1-3 persons	€ 13,00 - € 21,30

FR44350 Camping du Chêne

1 route du Lac, Saint Julien de Concelles (Loire-Atlantique)

Tel: 02 40 54 12 00. Email: campingduchene@wanadoo.fr   www.alanrogers.com/FR44350

Situated just east of the Nantes ringroad, Camping du Chêne would make an ideal night halt. However, it would be a pity to push on as a very pleasant few days could be spent here. With the Loire river to the north and the Loire valley wine route to the south, there is no shortage of places to visit. The young owners, Christophe and Muriel Paysan, are keen to attract more British and Dutch visitors and are working hard to make improvements to their site. There are about 100 pitches, 67 for touring and tents, 55 with 10A electricity. The remainder are used for mobile homes of which 25 are for rent. Most of the touring pitches are at the rear of the site, grassy, level, and vary in size and shape. They are divided by shrubs, and a number of taller trees provide shade. Camping du Chêne is part of an immaculate public park, with a lake which some pitches overlook. There are many sports facilities within the park including fishing, sailing, pedalo hire and tennis courts. At busy times there is a bar and snack bar, with outdoor seating overlooking the lake.

Facilities	Directions
Two toilet blocks are unheated with a mix of British and Turkish style toilets, pushbutton showers and some washbasins in cubicles. Bathroom for disabled visitors. Laundry. Motorcaravan service point. Small playground for young children. Two weeks of animation for children in high season. Off site: Swimming pool 1.5 km Bus service to Nantes. Large supermarket within walking distance.	From Nantes ringroad take exit 44 and follow signs for St Julien de Concelles. Ignore town centre sign and continue to roundabout at Champion supermarket. Take third exit and site is 25 m. on the left. GPS: N47:14.966 W01:22.280

Open: 1 April - 31 October (mobile homes all year).

Charges guide

Per person	€ 4,10
child (under 7 yrs)	€ 2,30
pitch incl. car	€ 4,20 - € 5,30
electricity (10A)	€ 3,20

Camping du Chêne

Only 15 minutes from Nantes you find campsite du Chêne on a 2,5 acres green and tranquil terrain. Lovely lake-side location; fishing, sailing, pedaloes and beach-volley.

In the heart of the vineyard and gastronomy of Nantes' area feel free to come and taste typical dishes such as pike with white butter sauce, eels of Loire's area and frog's legs.

Tourist information can be found at the reception.

Camping du Chêne • 1, Route du Lac • 44450 St. Julien de Concelles • France
Tél.: 0033 2 40 54 12 00 • E-mail: campingduchene@wanadoo.fr • www.campingduchene.fr

FR44400 Flower Camping Domaine du Pont Mahé

Pont Mahé, F-44410 Asserac (Loire-Atlantique)

Tel: 02 40 01 74 98. Email: contact@pont-mahe.com   www.alanrogers.com/FR44400

La Grande Brière is a vast area of marshland to the north of the Loire estuary. This is an area rich in flora and fauna, arguably best explored using the traditional punts (chalands). Domaine du Pont Mahé is a seaside site to the north of the Brière. There are 81 pitches, some of which are occupied by mobile homes (available for rent). Pitches are generally well shaded and of a good size. The site's swimming pool is a focal point and is attractively surrounded by a terrace with straw parasols. Bicycle hire is on offer and a number of cycle tracks run close to the site.

Facilities	Directions
Shop. Bar. Snack bar. Takeaway. Swimming pool. Children's pool. Play area. Games room. Bicycle and canoe hire. Activity and entertainment programme. Mobile homes and equipped tents for rent. Off site: Nearest beach 250 m. Grande Brière natural park. Fishing. Cycle tracks. La Baule (18 km).	Leave the N165 at Arzal exit and head south on the D139 (which becomes the D83) as far as Assérac. Head west here on D82 to Pont Mahé and site is well signed. GPS: N47:26.842 W02:27.026

Open: 21 April - 23 October.

Charges 2009

Per unit inc. 2 persons and electricity	€ 13,50 - € 24,50
extra person	€ 3,00 - € 4,00
child (2-7 yrs)	€ 2,00 - € 3,00
dog	€ 3,00

www.flowercampings.com

61

FR56020 Camping de la Plage

Plage de Kervilaine, F-56470 La Trinité-sur-Mer (Morbihan)

Tel: **02 97 55 73 28**. Email: **camping@camping-plage.com**   www.alanrogers.com/FR56020

The Carnac/La Trinité area of Brittany is popular with British holidaymakers. Camping de la Plage is one of two sites, close to each other, owned by members of the same family, and with direct access to the safe sandy beach of Kervilaine Plage. There are 198 grass pitches of which 112 are for touring (58 are used by tour operators). All are hedged and have electricity (6/10A), water and drainage. The site has a pronounced slope and some pitches reflect this. With narrow roads and sharp bends, it is not suitable for large units. The shop, restaurant and bar, 200 m. along the coast opposite Camping de la Baie, are used by local residents and provide excellent value. The restaurant and takeaway have extensive menus. A lively entertainment programme for all ages in high season makes this an attractive site for family holidays.

Facilities

Toilet blocks have washbasins in cubicles and facilities for disabled people and small children. Laundry facilities. Small swimming pool with water slides. Play areas including ball pool. Tennis. TV. Entertainment programme in high season for all ages. Bicycle hire. Beach. Guided tours. Internet access. Communal barbecue areas (gas or electric only on pitches). Off site: Fishing 50 m. Shop with bakery. Bar, restaurant, crêperie, takeaway (all 200 m). Sailing 1.5 km. Riding 3.5 km. Golf 13 km.

Open: 7 May - 20 September.

Directions

From N165 at Auray take D28 (La Trinité-sur-Mer). On through town following signs to Carnac-Plage on D186. Site signed off this road to the south. Take care to take road signed to Kervilaine Plage where it forks. At seafront turn right. Site is 300 m. on right. GPS: N47:34.538 W03:01.734

Charges 2009

Per unit incl. 2 persons and electricity	€ 19,90 - € 39,10
extra person	€ 5,10
child (2-17 yrs)	€ 3,00 - € 4,20
dog	free - € 1,30

www.camping-plage.com

our holiday at La Plage

56470 La Trinité sur Mer
Tel 33 2 97 55 73 28
Fax 33 2 97 55 88 31
email : contact@camping-plage.com

★ ★ ★ ★ CAMPING CARAVANING LA TRINITE SUR MER

FR56030 Camping de la Baie

Plage de Kervilaine, F-56470 La Trinité-sur-Mer (Morbihan)

Tel: **02 97 55 73 42**. Email: **contact@campingdelabaie.com**   www.alanrogers.com/FR56030

This site is one of two owned by members of the same family. It is situated on the coast overlooking the safe, sandy beach of Kervillen Plage, with its little rocky outcrops providing a naturally enclosed swimming area. This is a very friendly site, which is ideal for quiet or family holidays in an area with lots of local interest. There are 170 pitches, of which 60 are used by tour operators. The 91 touring pitches are all of good size, hedged and all have electricity (6/10A) water and drainage. Some shade is provided by mature and maturing trees.

Facilities

Two modern, very clean toilet blocks include well equipped baby rooms and full en-suite facilities for disabled visitors. Laundry facilities. Bar, restaurant and takeaway (open to the public all season). Well stocked shop (all season). Small (12 m) swimming pool with slide. Play areas. Multi-sport pitches. TV room. Indoor games room. Bicycle hire. Internet access. Off site: Beach, fishing and boat ramp 50 m. Tennis and minigolf 200 m (shared with Camping de la Plage). Riding 3 km. Sailing school 1.5 km. Golf 5 km.

Open: 17 May - 14 September.

Directions

From the N165 at Auray take D28 signed La Trinité-sur-Mer. Keep on through the town following signs to Carnac Plage on D186. Site is well signed off this road to the south. Be careful to take the road signed to Kervilaine Plage where it forks. GPS: N47:34.418 W03:01.655

Charges guide

Per person (over 2 yrs)	€ 2,90 - € 7,80
small pitch	€ 7,70 - € 11,95
serviced pitch	€ 11,55 - € 22,60
electricity (6/10A)	€ 2,25 - € 4,50

FR56010 Castel Camping la Grande Métairie

Route des Alignements de Kermario, B.P. 85, F-56342 Carnac (Morbihan)

Tel: **02 97 52 24 01**. Email: **info@lagrandemetairie.com**   www.alanrogers.com/FR56010

La Grande Métairie is a good quality site situated a little back from the sea, close to the impressive rows of the famous 'menhirs' (giant prehistoric standing stones). The site has 575 individual pitches (108 for touring units), surrounded by hedges and trees. All have electricity (some need long leads). The site is well known and popular and has many British visitors with 358 pitches taken by tour operators. It is ideal for families with children of all ages, but probably not suitable for those with walking difficulties. The site has a great deal to offer and is lively and busy over a long season. Musical evenings, barbecues and other organised events including occasional dances are held in an outdoor amphitheatre (pitches near these facilities may be noisy late at night – the bar closes at midnight). Paddocks with ponds are home for ducks, goats and ponies to watch and feed. There are also pony rides around the site. A super swimming pool complex comprises heated indoor and outdoor pools, water slides and toboggans and a jacuzzi. A local market takes place at Carnac on Wednesdays and Sundays.

Facilities

Three large well maintained toilet blocks, with washbasins in cabins. Facilities for babies and people with disabilities. Laundry facilities. Motorcaravan service points. Shops. Bar lounge and terrace. Restaurant. Takeaway. TV and games rooms. Swimming pool complex with bar. Playgrounds and playing field. Tennis. Minigolf. BMX track. Bicycle hire. Fishing. Zip-wire. Paintball. Amphitheatre. Helicopter rides (July/Aug). Organised events and entertainment. American motorhomes accepted up to 27 ft.
Off site: Riding 1 km. Nearest beach 3 km. Golf 12 km.

Open: 1 April - 9 September (all services from 20/5).

Directions

From N165 take Quiberon/Carnac exit onto the D768. After 5 km. turn south onto D119 towards Carnac. At roundabout and after 4 km. turn left (northeast) onto D196 to the site.
GPS: N47:35.837 W03:03.646

Charges guide

Per person	€ 4,00 - € 7,30
child (4-7 yrs)	€ 3,50 - € 5,40
pitch incl. car	€ 8,00 - € 23,90
electricity (6A)	€ 10,00 - € 27,40

Less 20% 22/5-29/6 and after 1/9.

La Grande Métairie
Des Vacances Uniques ★★★★

Route des Alignements de Kermario   **Tél. 33(0)2 97 52 24 01**
B.P. 85 - 56342 Carnac Cedex   **Fax 33(0)2 97 52 83 58**
www.lagrandemetairie.com

Check real time availability and at-the-gate prices...
www.**alanrogers**.com

FR56050 Camping de Kervilor

F-56470 La Trinité-sur-Mer (Morbihan)

Tel: **02 97 55 76 75**. Email: **ebideau@camping-kervilor.com**　　www.alanrogers.com/FR56050

Kervilor may be a good alternative for those who find the beach-side sites in La Trinité too busy and lively. In a village on the outskirts of the town, it has 230 pitches on flat grass and is attractively landscaped with trees (silver birch) and flowers giving a sense of spaciousness. The pitches are in groups divided by hedges, separated by shrubs and trees and all have electricity (6/10A). Around 116 are used for touring units. Used by tour operators (10 pitches). The site has an inviting, well designed pool complex with swimming and paddling pools, slides and fountains. Activities and entertainment are organised in high season. The pleasant port is only 1.5 km. and there are sandy beaches within 2 km.

Facilities

Two modern toilet blocks of a good standard with further facilities in an older block. They include many washbasins in cabins, facilities for disabled people and babies. Small laundry. Small shop and takeaway. Bar with terrace. Pool complex. Play area. Minigolf, pétanque, tennis and volleyball. Bicycle hire. Only charcoal barbecues are permitted. WiFi in bar area. Off site: Town facilities 1.5 km. Sandy beach, fishing or riding 2 km. Golf 12 km.

Open: 1 May - 14 September.

Directions

Site is north of La Trinité-sur-Mer and is signed in the town centre. From Auray take D186 Quiberon road; turn left at site sign at Kergroix on D186 to La Trinité-sur-Mer, and left again at outskirts of town. GPS: N47:36.128 W03:02.203

Charges guide

Per person	€ 5,05
child (under 7 yrs)	€ 3,30
pitch	€ 17,00
electricity (6/10A)	€ 3,50 - € 4,00
dog	€ 2,90

Less 25% outside high season.
7 days for the price of 6 outside July/Aug.

camping **Kervilor**

Near to the port and beaches, Camping de Kervilor will welcome you to its calm, shaded setting - with heated swimming pools, waterslides (including multi-track), spa bath, bar, entertainment tennis court, multi-sport terrain - divertissement room and billards, multi-sport terrain - everything on site. Mobile home rental.

© Photo Luc Vignaud

56470 La Trinité sur Mer - Tel. 0297557675 - Fax. 0297558726
www.camping-kervilor.com - ebideau@camping-kervilor.com

FR56040 Camping de Penboch

9 chemin de Penboch, F-56610 Arradon (Morbihan)

Tel: **02 97 44 71 29**. Email: **camping.penboch@wanadoo.fr**　　www.alanrogers.com/FR56040

Penboch is 200 metres by footpath from the shores of the Golfe du Morbihan with its many islands, and plenty to do including watersports, fishing and boat trips. The site, in a peaceful, rural area, is divided into two – the main part, on open ground, with hedges and young trees, the other across a minor road in woodland with lots of shade. Penboch offers 175 pitches on flat grass, 105 are for touring and they are mostly divided into groups. Electricity (6/10A) is available on all pitches and most also have water and drainage. A 'Sites et Paysages' member.

Facilities

Three toilet blocks, two on the main part (one heated) and one in the annex, include washbasins in cabins. There are new washing facilities including family cabins. Laundry facilities. Motorcaravan service point. Bar with snacks and takeaway. Shop (all 20/5-6/9). Heated pool with slide and paddling pool (1/5-12/9). Indoor pool with relaxation area, jacuzzi and massage tables. Playground. Games room. Caravan storage. American motorhomes accepted in low season. Off site: Beach, fishing 200 m. Windsurfing and sailing 2 km. Bicycle hire 2 km. Golf and riding 6 km.

Open: 4 April - 26 September.

Directions

From N165 at Auray or Vannes, take D101 along northern shores of the Golfe du Morbihan; or leave N165 at D127 signed Ploeren and Arradon. Take turn to Arradon and site is signed. GPS: N47:37.336 W02:48.074

Charges 2009

Per unit incl. 2 persons and electricity	€ 19,40 - € 39,30
extra person	€ 4,00 - € 6,20
child (2-7 yrs)	€ 3,00 - € 4,50
dog	€ 1,50 - € 3,50

BOOK THIS SITE
CALL 01580 214000
...we'll arrange everything
The Travel Service

Check real time availability and at-the-gate prices...
www.alanrogers.com

FR56090 Camping Moulin de Kermaux

F-56340 Carnac (Morbihan)

Tel: 02 97 52 15 90. Email: moulin-de-kermaux@wanadoo.fr   www.alanrogers.com/FR56090

Only 100 metres from the famous Carnac megaliths, Le Moulin de Kermaux is an excellent base from which to see these ancient stones as they portray their ever changing mood, colour and profile. Family run, the site has 150 pitches, all with 6/10A electricity. There are 90 pitches for touring units and 60 mobile homes, mostly separated by hedges and with many mature trees offering welcome shade. The compact nature of the site offers a safe environment for parents and children. Ideal for children of all ages, there is an aquatic complex with a heated pool and a slide with an indoor pool planned for 2009. This is a well run, quiet and comfortable site. Keen walkers and families with young children alike, will enjoy the footpaths in the area. Carnac town provides an assortment of boutiques, crêperies, restaurants and night clubs.

Facilities

The fully equipped toilet block (a few Turkish style) has washbasins in cabins and can be heated. Facilities for disabled visitors. Baby bath. Laundry facilities. Motorcaravan service point. Shop (26/6-31/8). Bar with satellite TV. Takeaway (12/6-31/8) evenings only in low season. Swimming and paddling pools. Sauna and jacuzzi. Adventure playground. Minigolf. Organised activities (July/Aug). Off site: Fishing, bicycle hire and riding 2 km. Beaches 3 km. Bus service 100 m.

Open: 8 April - 15 September.

Directions

From N165 take Quiberon/Carnac exit onto D768. After 5 km. turn south on D119 towards Carnac. At roundabout after 4 km. turn left (northeast) on D196 to site.

Charges guide

Per person	€ 2,70 - € 4,50
child (under 7 yrs)	€ 1,80 - € 3,00
pitch and car	€ 8,70 - € 14,50
electricity (6A)	€ 2,10 - € 3,50
dog	€ 1,20

Less 10-40% outside high season.

Le Moulin de Kermaux* - Route de Kerlescan - 56340 Carnac**
Tél.: +33 (0)297 52 15 90 - Fax: +33 (0)297 52 83 85

moulin-de-kermaux@wanadoo.fr
www.camping-moulinkermaux.com

FR56080 Camping Municipal le Pâtis

3 chemin du Pâtis, F-56130 La Roche Bernard (Morbihan)

Tel: 02 99 90 60 13. Email: camping-info@wanadoo.fr   www.alanrogers.com/FR56080

This is another of those excellent municipal sites one comes across in France. Situated beside the River Vilaine, a five minute walk from the centre of the very attractive old town of La Roche Bernard and beside the port and marina, it provides 69 level grass, part-hedged pitches in bays of four, with 7A electricity and water. 18 special pitches for motorcaravans have been created at the entrance. Next door is a sailing school, boats to hire, fishing, tennis, archery, etc. A restaurant and bar are on the quayside, with others uphill in the town.

Facilities

There are two fully equipped sanitary blocks, one new and very modern, the other fully refurbished. Laundry room behind reception with washing machine and dryer. Small play area. Bicycle hire. Off site: Fishing 500 m. Riding 5 km. Golf 15 km.

Open: April - 30 September.

Directions

Go into town centre and follow signs for the Port around a one-way system and then a sharp turn down hill. GPS: N47:31.090 W02:18.190

Charges guide

Per pitch incl. 2 persons and electricity	€ 13,00
extra person	€ 3,00
child (under 9 yrs)	€ 1,50
animal	€ 1,00

Check real time availability and at-the-gate prices...

www.alanrogers.com

FR56100 Camping de Moulin Neuf

F-56220 Rochefort-en-Terre (Morbihan)

Tel: 02 97 43 37 52

www.alanrogers.com/FR56100

This quiet family site is in wooded countryside, 600 m. from the town. Ian and Norma Hetherington have worked hard to develop Moulin Neuf into a neat, tidy and organised site. There are 72 pitches (60 for tourers, 44 with 10A electricity) of good size (120 sq.m) on neat grass, with two levels. The top level, with a limited number of electrical hook-ups, is flat and pitches are divided by young shrubs. The lower level is partly sloping with mature trees, shade and electricity on all pitches.

Facilities

The modern heated sanitary block is kept very clean and includes large, comfortable showers, cabins with washbasins and British and Turkish style WCs. Provision for disabled people. Baby room. Laundry facilities. Bread delivered each morning. Heated swimming pool (1/6-31/8). Tennis. Football. Two play areas. Off site: Lake 500 m. with watersports. Shop 600 m. Riding and golf. Vannes and the beaches of Golfe du Morbihan.

Open: 15 May - 16 September.

Directions

From Redon take D775 Vannes road west for 25 km. Branch north on D774 signed Rochefort-en-Terre. Follow road past the lake on left, in 800 m. Turn left and follow sign to site. GPS: N47:41.709 W02:20.948

Charges guide

Per unit incl. 2 persons	€ 14,00 - € 16,50
incl. electricity	€ 16,00 - € 19,60
extra person	€ 3,80 - € 4,80

FR56110 Kawan Village le Moustoir

Route du Moustoir, F-56340 Carnac (Morbihan)

Tel: 02 97 52 16 18. Email: info@lemoustoir.com

www.alanrogers.com/FR56110

Camping le Moustoir is a friendly, family run site situated about three kilometres inland from the many beaches of the area and close to the famous 'alignments' of standing stones. Pitches are grassy and separated by shrubs and hedges, with several shaded by tall pine trees. The bar and terrace become the social centre of the site in the evenings. A high season entertainment programme includes a daily 'Kids' Club' attracting children of several nationalities. Several small tour operators use the site.

Facilities

The substantial, traditional style toilet block is well maintained (outside peak season some sections may be closed). Motorcaravan service facilities. Shop, bar, restaurant and takeaway (all season). Heated swimming pool (21 x 8 m), water slides, and paddling pool (from 1/5). Heated indoor swimming pool (all season) added in 2008. Adventure playground. Tennis. Boules. Volleyball, football and basketball. 'Kids' Club'. Barrier deposit € 20. Off site: Watersports at Carnac Plage. Fishing, bicycle hire, riding 2 km. Beach 3 km. Golf 10 km.

Open: 1 April - 30 September.

Directions

From N165, take exit to D768 (Carnac and Quiberon). At second crossroads after 5 km. turn left (D119) towards Carnac. After 3 km. turn left (oblique turning) after a hotel. Site is 500 m. on left. GPS: N47:36.495 W03:03.952

Charges 2009

Per unit incl. 2 persons, car and electricity	€ 22,60 - € 34,60
extra person	€ 4,80
water	€ 4,00

Camping Cheques accepted.

FR56120 Camping des Iles

La Pointe du Bile, B.P. 4, F-56760 Pénestin-sur-Mer (Morbihan)

Tel: 02 99 90 30 24. Email: contact@camping-des-iles.fr

www.alanrogers.com/FR56120

You will receive a warm and friendly welcome at this family run campsite and the owner, Mme. Communal, encourages all her guests to make the most of this beautiful region. Of the 184 pitches, 103 are for touring. Most are flat, hedged and of a reasonable size (larger caravans and American motorhomes are advised to book) and all have electricity. Some pitches have sea views and overlook the beach. There is direct access to cliff-top walks and local beaches.

Facilities

The new large central toilet block is spotlessly clean with washbasins in cabins and showers. Laundry facilities. Facilities for disabled people and baby room. Shop (all season). Bar and restaurant with takeaway (15/5-15/9). Pool complex (1/5-30/9). Bicycle hire. Riding. Activities and entertainment in July/Aug. Across the road in Parc des Iles (mobile home section of site): TV room, multisport pitch, tennis court and motorcaravan service point. Off site: Windsurfing 500 m. Sailing school 3 km. Golf 20 km.

Open: 3 April - 10 October.

Directions

From D34 (La Roche-Bernard), at roundabout just after entering Pénestin take D201 south (Assérac). Take right fork to Pointe du Bile after 2 km. Turn right at crossroads just before beach. Site is on left. GPS: N47:26.735 W02:29.040

Charges 2009

Per unit incl. 2 persons and electricity	€ 19,50 - € 39,50
extra person (over 7 yrs)	€ 2,30 - € 5,00
child (2-7 yrs)	€ 1,30 - € 2,50
pet	€ 1,50 - € 3,00

Check real time availability and at-the-gate prices...

www.**alanrogers**.com

FR56160 Camping la Vallée du Ninian

Le Rocher, F-56800 Taupont (Morbihan)

Tel: **02 97 93 53 01**. Email: **info@camping-ninian.com**   www.alanrogers.com/FR56160

M. and Mme. Joubaud have developed this peaceful family run site in central Brittany from a former farm and they continue to make improvements to ensure that their visitors have an enjoyable holiday. The level site falls into the three areas – the orchard with 100 large, hedged pitches with electricity, the wood with about 13 pitches more suited to tents, and the meadow by the river providing a further 35 pitches delineated by small trees and shrubs, with electricity. The bar has as its centrepiece a working cider press with which M. Joubaud makes his own 'potion magique'.

Facilities

A central building houses unisex toilet facilities including washbasins in cubicles, large cubicle with facilities for disabled visitors and laundry area with washing machines, dryer and ironing board. Shop (July/Aug) selling bread. Small (7 x 12 m) heated swimming pool and children's pool with slide and fountain. Swings, slides and large trampoline. Fishing. Off site: Riding and bicycle hire 4 km. Golf 7 km.

Open: 15 April - 15 September.

Directions

From Ploërmel follow signs to Taupont north on N8. Continue through Taupont and turn left (east) signed Vallée du Ninian. Follow road for 3 km. to site on left. From Josselin follow signs for Hellean. Through village, sharp right after river Ninian bridge. Site is 400 m. on right. GPS: N47:58.159 W02:28.208

Charges 2009

Per person	€ 3,20 - € 4,00
pitch and car	€ 4,80 - € 6,00
electricity (3/6A)	€ 2,00 - € 3,50
Credit cards accepted in July/Aug. only.	

FR56130 Camping Mané Guernehué

52 rue Mané er Groez, F-56870 Baden (Morbihan)

Tel: **02 97 57 02 06**. Email: **mane-guernehue@wanadoo.fr**   www.alanrogers.com/FR56130

Located close to the Morbihan Gulf, Mané Guernehué is a smart, modern site with excellent amenities and a variety of pitches. Some are terraced beneath pine trees, others in a former orchard with delightful views of the surrounding countryside. The 377 pitches are generally large, 200 being occupied by mobile homes and chalets. Most pitches have 10A electricity and a few also have water and drainage. Many are level but a few, particularly in the centre of the site, slope to varying degrees. An impressive new indoor pool complex has been added.

Facilities

Three modern toilet blocks include washbasins in cabins. The maintenance of the blocks does seem to be under some pressure. Facilities for disabled visitors. Laundry facilities. Small shop, bar and takeaway. Heated swimming pool, water slide, jacuzzi and gym. Fishing. Minigolf. Pony trekking. Teenagers' room with games and TV. Play area. Tree top adventure area. Varied entertainment programme in high season. Off site: Beach, golf 3 km.

Open: 1 April - 30 September.

Directions

From Auray or Vannes use the D101 to Baden and watch for signs to site.
GPS: N47:36.907 W02:55.555

Charges guide

Per unit incl. 2 persons	€ 15,00 - € 35,00
extra person	€ 5,00 - € 7,20
child (under 7 yrs)	€ 3,00 - € 5,20
electricity (10A)	€ 4,50
Camping Cheques accepted.	

FR56150 Camping du Haras

Aérodrome Vannes-Meucon, Kersimon, F-56250 Vannes-Meucon-Monterblanc (Morbihan)

Tel: **02 97 44 66 06**. Email: **camping-vannes@wanadoo.fr**   www.alanrogers.com/FR56150

Close to Vannes and the Golfe du Morbihan in southern Brittany, Le Haras is a small, family run, rural site that is open all year. There are 140 pitches at the moment, although there are plans to extend the site. With a variety of settings, both open and wooded, the pitches are well kept and of a good size, all with electricity (4-10A) and most with water and drainage. Whilst M. Danard intends keeping the site quiet and in keeping with its rural setting, he provides plenty of activities for lively youngsters, including some organised games and evening parties.

Facilities

The small modern toilet block (heated in winter) provides a few washbasins in cabins and controllable showers. Facilities for babies and disabled visitors. Laundry facilities. No shop but basics are kept in the bar. Bar. (May - Oct). Takeaway (July/Aug). Swimming pool with waves and slide (1/5-31/10). Play area. Animal park. Trampoline. Minigolf. Bicycle hire. Organised activities (high season). Off site: Riding 400 m. Fishing 3 km. Beach 15 km.

Open: All year.

Directions

From Vannes on N165 take exit signed Pontivy and airport on the D767. Follow signs for airport and Meucon. Turn right on the D778, follow airport and yellow campsite signs. GPS: N47:43.000 W02:43.000

Charges guide

Per person	€ 4,00 - € 5,00
child (0-7 yrs)	€ 2,00 - € 3,00
pitch	€ 2,00 - € 3,00
electricity (4-10A)	€ 3,00 - € 6,00

67

FR56180 Camping le Cénic

F-56760 Pénestin-sur-Mer (Morbihan)

Tel: 02 99 90 33 14. Email: info@lecenic.com

www.alanrogers.com/FR56180

Le Cénic is attractively set amidst trees and flowers, providing activities for all tastes. An attractive covered aquatic complex has water slides, bridges, rivers and a jacuzzi, whilst the outdoor pool comes complete with water slide, 'mushroom' fountain and sunbathing areas. You may fish in the lake or use inflatables, watched by the peacock, the geese and turkeys. There is a hall for table tennis and a range of indoor games. There are 310 pitches, 160 of which are for touring. Of these, 90 have electricity (6A), but long leads will be required. The area has much to offer from the beaches of La Mine d'Or, the harbour at Trébiguier-Pénestin, the Golf du Morbihan with its numerous islands, La Baule with its magnificent beach and the medieval city of Guérande to the unique Brière nature reserve.

Facilities

Good new toilet block includes washbasins in cabins, facilities for disabled visitors, baby room and laundry and dishwashing sinks. Separate laundry. Bar and shop (1/7-31/8). TV and games rooms (1/7-31/8). Indoor (15/4-15/9) and outdoor (1/7-31/8) swimming pools. Play area. Fishing. Off site: Riding 500 m. Bicycle hire 1 km. Sailing 2 km. Pénestin town 2 km. Sandy beaches 2.5 km. Golf 30 km.

Open: 1 May - 30 September.

Directions

From D34 (La Roche-Bernard), at roundabout just after entering Pénestin take D201 south (Assérac). After 100 m. take first turning on left. After 800 m. turn left and campsite is 300 m. on right down a narrow winding lane.
GPS: N47:28.746 W02:27.386

Charges guide

Per person	€ 4,50 - € 6,00
child (under 7 yrs)	€ 2,00 - € 3,00
pitch incl. electricity	€ 9,00 - € 19,00

Covered Aquatic Centre (heated swimming pool, balneotherapy area, children's pool), outdoor pool, water chute, games room, bar, fishing in the lake.
Le Cénic offers a range of accommodation: static caravans, chalets to rent.

www.lecenic.com
56760 Pénestin-sur-Mer

Tél: +33 (0)2 99 90 33 14

info@lecenic.com

Fax: +33 (0)2 99 90 45 05

FR56210 Camping Merlin l'Enchanteur

La Vallée de l'Yvel, 8 rue du Pont, F-56800 Loyat (Morbihan)

Tel: 02 97 93 05 52. Email: qualitypark1@wanadoo.fr

www.alanrogers.com/FR56210

This fairly basic ex-municipal site is located a few hundred metres from the village of Loyat and 5 km. from the large town of Ploermel. The grass touring pitches are level and each pitch is separated by well established trees. Long leads may be required for the electricity hook-ups which are 10A and water points may be some distance from certain pitches. This simple site is open all year and is ideally suited for anglers as there is a fishing lake and river adjacent. A short walk takes you into the village where most basic requirements can be bought. The long distance cycle route 'Voie Vert' is nearby.

Facilities

One small sanitary block has open style washbasins and pre-set showers. No facilities for disabled visitors. Laundry facilities. Covered swimming pool. Play area. Fishing. Bicycle hire. Internet access. Torches useful. Off site: Loyat Village. Ploërmel 5 km. Riding 3 km. Golf 5 km.

Open: All year.

Directions

Site is in a northern direction from Ploërmel on the D766. Take D13 signed Loyat. Site is on left after 1 km. before entering Loyat Village.
GPS: N47:59.055 W02:22.915

Charges guide

Per person	€ 3,50
child (0-13 yrs)	€ 1,50 - € 2,00
pitch	€ 5,00
electricity (10A)	€ 4,50 - € 6,00

Check real time availability and at-the-gate prices...

www.alanrogers.com

FR56200 Camping la Ferme de Lann-Hoëdic

Route du Roaliguen, F-56370 Sarzeau (Morbihan)

Tel: 02 97 48 01 73. Email: contact@camping-lannhoedic.fr   www.alanrogers.com/FR56200

Camping la Ferme is an attractively landscaped site with many flowering shrubs and trees. The 108 touring pitches, all with electricity (10A) are large and mostly level, with maturing trees which are beginning to offer some shade. The 20 pitches with mobile homes are in a separate area. The working farm produces cereal crops and the summer months are an interesting time for children to see the harvest in progress. Mireille and Tim, the owners, go out of their way to make this a welcoming and happy place to stay. Located in the countryside on the Rhuys Peninsula, Golfe du Morbihan, it is an ideal base for cycling, walking and water based activities.

Facilities

Two new, high quality toilet blocks with facilities for people with disabilities, and babies. Washing machines and dryers. Bread delivery. Ice creams and soft drinks available at reception. Takeaway meals and traditional Breton 'soirées' (high season). Bicycle hire. Playground with modern well designed equipment. Pétanque. Off site: Beach, fishing and boating 800 m. Sarzeau 2 km. Riding 2 km. Golf 6 km.

Open: 1 April - 31 October.

Directions

East of Vannes on the N165, join the D780 in the direction of Sarzeau. Exit D780 at the 'Super U'; roundabout south of Sarzeau, following signs for Le Roaliguen. Campsite is signed.
GPS: N47:30.447 W02:45.655

Charges guide

Per person	€ 3,40 - € 4,30
child (under 7 yrs)	€ 1,60 - € 2,10
pitch incl. electricity	€ 8,40 - € 10,60

No credit cards.
Camping Cheques accepted.

Camping ★★★
La Ferme de Lann Hoëdic

SOUTHERN BRITTANY

Only 2 hours south of St Malo, discover the beautiful Gulf of Morbihan from our peaceful and spacious 3 star site. 800 meters from sandy beaches, we offer brand new facilities and a warm welcome waiting just for you.

Open from 01/04 to 31/10

Route du Roaliguen   56370 Sarzeau
Tel : +33 297 48 01 73
Fax : +33 297 41 72 87
contact@camping-lannhoedic.fr

The comfort of a 3-star campsite, the charm of a country setting

FR56220 Camping les Jardins de Kergal

Route de Guidel Plages, F-56520 Guidel (Morbihan)

Tel: 02 97 05 98 18. Email: jardins.kergal@wanadoo.fr   www.alanrogers.com/FR56220

This is a long established campsite that offers a variety of well cared for pitches. Most are shaded by mature trees and unusually many are triangular in shape. Access could be tricky for larger units. The toilet facilities have been refurbished to a very high standard, complete with soft music and potted plants. A comfortable lounge contains a small library, board games and a television. The site's pool complex is impressive with a heated, covered pool, an open pool with slides and a paddling pool. Many sporting facilities are provided, and in high season entertainment and activities are arranged for children.

Facilities

The good toilet block includes facilities for disabled visitors and babies. Washing machine and dryer. Shop. Bar (28/6-30/8). Pizza and rotisserie vans visit (high season). Covered swimming pool (all season). Outdoor pool and slides (15/5-15/9). Multisport court. Bicycle hire. Minigolf. Off site: Beaches 1.5 km. Guidel town for shops and restaurants. Fishing 3 km. Golf 10 km.

Open: 22 March - 2 November.

Directions

From the RN165 west of Lorient take exit for Guidel, then the D306 from Guidel towards the beach (plage). Site is well signed on the left.
GPS: N47:46.480 W03:30.370

Charges guide

Per unit incl. 2 persons and electricity (10A)	€ 8,50 - € 15,90
extra person	€ 4,50 - € 6,90
child (2-10 yrs)	€ 2,90 - € 4,90
dog	€ 3,00 - € 5,00

69

FR56270 Camping les Menhirs

Allée Saint Michel, F-56340 Carnac (Morbihan)

Tel: **02 97 52 94 67**. Email: **contad@lesmenhirs.com**   www.alanrogers.com/FR56270

Although located within the built-up area of the popular resort of Carnac, and only 300 m. from the beach, this campsite feels much more rural. Catering for all ages, this is a friendly site and lively in high season with plenty of activities including evening entertainment and a club for children. There are 350 pitches; 154 touring pitches and the remainder used for mobile homes and chalets, of which the majority are used by tour operators. The touring pitches are in groups and are large, level and hedged. All have electricity (10A), water and drainage, and 14 have hardstanding. The central complex containing the pools and games areas, all overlooked by the bar and its terrace, makes a convivial focal point. The town and seafront can be explored on foot and the Brittany coast and the Gulf of Morbihan are within easy reach by car or bicycle.

Facilities

Three spotless, modern, light toilet blocks with washbasins in cabins, facilities for children, babies and disabled people. A further en-suite unit for disabled people is by the pool complex. Laundry. Shop. Comfortable bar with satellite TV and takeaway (13/5-16/9). Heated indoor and outdoor swimming pools, the latter with slides (all season). Fitness complex with massage, multi-gym, jacuzzi, sauna and solarium. Multisport pitch. Tennis. Boules. Riding (1/7-31/8). Play areas. Children's club and evening entertainment (July/Aug). Off site: Beach 300 m. Bicycle hire 500 m. Golf 800 m. Sailing 1 km. Town centre 1 km. Bars and restaurants within easy walking distance.

Open: 1 May - 26 September.

Directions

From Auray take D786 to Carnac and Quiberon. After 5 km. turn south on D119 towards Carnac at roundabout. 600 m. beyond next roundabout fork left, signed La Trinité-sur-Mer and Plages. Keep straight on at lights. Fork left at first roundabout. Turn left at next roundabout (T-junction) and site is signed at 250 m. on the left.
GPS: N47:34.592 W03:04.134

Charges guide

Per person	€ 3,92 - € 7,83
child (0-6 yrs)	€ 2,92 - € 5,81
pitch with electricity, water and waste water	€ 18,14 - € 32,62

CAMPING LES MENHIRS

Situated 300 m from the sandy beach and close to the centre of Carnac Plage, the Camping des menhirs offers a variety of high standard facilities: heated outdoor swimming pool, heated indoor swimming pool, sauna, jacuzzi, etc...

Bp 167 - Allée St Michel - 56343 Carnac - France
Tel: 0033 (0)2 97 52 94 67 - Fax: 0033 (0)2 97 52 25 38

contact@lesmenhirs.com
www.lesmenhirs.com

FR56240 Yelloh! Village Domaine d'Inly

Route de Couarne, B.P. 24, F-56760 Pénestin-sur-Mer (Morbihan)

Tel: **04 66 73 97 39**. Email: **info@yellohvillage-domaine-inly.com**   www.alanrogers.com/FR56240

This very large site is mainly taken up with mobile homes and chalets, some belonging to the site owner, some private and some belonging to tour operators. Most pitches are arranged in groups of ten to 14 around a central stone circle with a water point in the middle. Of the 500 pitches, 100 are for touring units and all are large (150-200 sq.m) with a 10A electrical connection (Europlug). Most are sloping. There is an attractive lake at the bottom of the site where one can fish or canoe.

Facilities

Two toilet blocks with facilities for disabled visitors and a baby room. Laundry. Shop, comfortable bar, with large screen satellite TV, and attractive restaurant (all 1/5-15/9). Heated swimming pool with slide (15/5-15/9). Play areas. Lake for fishing/canoeing. Riding. Off site: Pénestin town centre 2 km. Supermarket 1 km. Golf 2 km. Sailing and boat ramp 2.5 km. Beach 2 km.

Open: 5 April - 21 September.

Directions

From D34 from La Roche-Bernard, at roundabout just after entering Pénestin take D201 south, signed Assérac. After 100 m. take first turning on left and follow site signs. GPS: N47:28.289 W02:28.036

Charges guide

Per unit incl. 2 persons	€ 17,00 - € 38,00
extra person (over 1 yr)	€ 5,00 - € 6,00

tel: +33 466 739 739   www.yellohvillage.com

Check real time availability and at-the-gate prices...

www.**alanrogers**.com

FR56280 Airotel les Sept Saints

Mobile homes ▶ page 490

B.P. 14, F-56410 Erdeven (Morbihan)

Tel: 02 97 55 52 65. Email: info@septsaints.com

www.alanrogers.com/FR56280

One is attracted to this campsite on arrival, with a well-tended shrubbery and reception to the left of the entrance and a landscaped pool complex on the right. The 200 pitches are divided equally between mobile homes and touring pitches, arranged in three separate groups: 60 normal touring pitches with electricity (10A), mobile homes, and an area under the trees across the play area for tents. Touring pitches are separated by manicured hedges and are level grass. The heated swimming pool complex, with its slides, jacuzzi and padding pool, and overlooked by the bar terrace, provides a focal point. In July and August there are separate children's clubs for younger children and teenagers and a variety of entertainment in the evenings. The site offers a complete holiday within itself as well as access to the Brittany coast.

Facilities

Two modern toilet blocks include en-suite facilities for disabled visitors and attractive baby rooms. Two laundry rooms. Bar, takeaway and shop (10/6-9/9). Heated swimming pool with slides, Jacuzzi, and paddling pool with mushroom and baby slide (15/5-15/9). Excellent play areas. Multisport pitch. Boules. Grass area for ball games. Bicycle hire. Games room. TV room. Gas supplies. Internet. Off site: Fishing 1.5 km. Riding 3 km. Golf 3 km. Beach and sailing 3 km.

Open: 15 May - 15 September.

Directions

From N165 at Auray take exit for D768 to Carnac and Quiberon. At roundabout entering Plouharnel turn west on D781, following signs to Erdeven and L'Orient. Continue through Erdeven, turn left where site is signed after 1.5 km. and site is 150 m. on the right. GPS: N47:39.317 W03:10.307

Charges guide

Per person	€ 4,00 - € 7,00
child (under 7 yrs)	€ 3,00 - € 5,50
pitch	€ 10,00 - € 18,00
electricity	€ 5,50

Camping Les 7 Saints****

Situated near the sea, in a region of rich heritage of the Brittany culture. Our 4-stars camping site offers the comfort of its marked, shaded camping spots and its high quality facilities.... Make the most of the swimming pool and toddlers' pool (both heated from the May 15th to Sept. 15th). And don't forget other facilities: color TV, video games, pool, crazy foot, table tennis, volley ball and toddlers' playground.

Live activities in July and August for the whole family (various games, sports, singers, bands, disco and karaoke).

Other facilities: washing machines, ironing room, bar and terrace, grocer, takeaway food, baby tubs and care room...

We will do our utmost to offer you quality holidays. In the vicinity : beaches 3 km away, sailing, wind-surfing, sail-karts, fishing, scuba diving, water ski-ing, tennis court, 18 hole golf course aero club, horse riding, enjoyable cycling and walking.

56410 Erdeven - Tel 0033 2 97 55 52 65
Fax 0033 2 97 55 22 67 - info@septsaints.com

www.sept-saints.com

FR56300 Camping An Trest

Route de la Plage du Roaliguen, F-56370 Sarzeau (Morbihan)

Tel: 02 97 41 79 60. Email: letreste@campingletreste.com

www.alanrogers.com/FR56300

This is a delightful site offering 198 touring pitches out of a total of 225. The small number of mobile homes are in a separate area. Pitches are of a good size for most but a limited number of larger ones are retained at one end of the site for larger units. The site is attractively laid out with grass pitches and hedged bays for between four and six units. A fair amount of shade is provided by a variety of trees and shrubs. There is no restaurant on site but a mobile takeaway visits six days a week with a different menu each day.

Facilities

The sanitary block is centrally located with mainly British style toilets and a few Turkish. Washbasins are open and in cubicles and showers are pre-set. Two excellent en-suite rooms provide for disabled visitors (key entry). Baby baths. Dishwashing sinks and laundry room with washing machines and dryers. Well stocked shop (July/Aug). Bar. Mobile takeaway. Heated swimming pool with slides and flume. Paddling pool. TV and games room. Off site: Beach 800 m. Supermarket in An Trest 3 km. Markets and shops in Sareau 3 km.

Open: 16 June - 10 September.

Directions

Take N165 from Vannes. Turn on to D780 signed Sarzeau. Turn left at roundabout by large supermarket. Site is 3 km. on left and is well signed. GPS: N47:30.20 W02:46.17

Charges guide

Per person	€ 5,60
child (under 10 yrs)	€ 2,20
pitch	€ 9,85
electricity (10A)	€ 3,30
Less 20% in June and September.	

Check real time availability and at-the-gate prices...
www.alanrogers.com

FR56360 Camping Do Mi Si La Mi

31 rue de la Vierge, Saint Julien-Plage, F-56170 Quiberon (Morbihan)

Tel: 02 97 50 22 52. Email: camping@domisilami.com   www.alanrogers.com/FR56360

Occupying a five hectare site on the Quiberon Peninsula just 100 metres from the sandy beaches, this campsite has plenty to offer. Of the 350 pitches, 194 are for touring and are set amongst high mature hedges giving plenty of shade and privacy; some have sea views. Long leads are required on a few pitches as hook-ups can be shared between three or four pitches. The excellent facilities for children are in a well fenced area and include climbing frames, bouncy castles and multisport courts. Treasure hunts and other activities are organised daily. Staff at the well managed reception gave us excellent customer service and we enjoyed our stay on this site which is ideally situated for exploring this fascinating area.

Facilities

Seven sanitary blocks, with good hot showers. Separate laundry. Shop. Bar. TV room. Bouncy castles. Multisport courts. Children's club. Off site: Bar, restaurant, supermarket 50 m. Beaches 100 m. Bicycle hire 100 m. Town centre 2 km. Golf, riding 3 km.

Open: 1 April - 1 November.

Directions

From the N165 Vannes-Lorient dual carriageway south of Auray, take the exit for Carnac/Ploemel. Continue southwest on D768 through the town of Plouharmel following signs for Quiberon. About 25 km. from the N165 but before reaching the town of Quiberon, the site is signed to the left at St Julien-Plage. GPS: N47:29.984 W03:07.216

Charges guide

Per person	€ 3,00 - € 4,10
child (under 7 yrs)	€ 1,80 - € 2,70
pitch	€ 7,80 - € 12,00
electricity (3/10A)	€ 2,70 - € 4,10

A green oasis at 100m from the beach!

www.domisilami.com

Camping DO MI SI LA MI ★★★
31, rue de la Vierge • St-Julien Plage
56170   QUIBERON - FRANCE
Phone : 0033 2 97 50 22 52
Fax : 0033 2 97 50 26 69
camping@domisilami.com

Quiberon Bay

Open from 01/04/09 till 01/11/09

FR56310 Camping Municipal Beg Er Roch

Route de Lorient, F-56320 Le Faouët (Morbihan)

Tel: 02 97 23 15 11. Email: camping.lefaouet@wanadoo.fr   www.alanrogers.com/FR56310

Like many of today's municipal campsites this one is immaculate and offers excellent value. There are 52 well kept grassy pitches with electricity (3/5A) available but long leads may be needed. There are also a few furnished tents and mobile homes for rent. For those campers who are anglers, a river at the bottom of the site (fenced) provides salmon and trout fishing at a supplement. For the more energetic, the manager can provide details and maps of local walks. For shops and other amenities the town of Le Faouët is only 2 km. away.

Facilities

A single toilet block provides toilets, washbasins and showers. Facilities for campers with disabilities. Washing machine and dryer. Play area. Minigolf. Boules. Fishing. Large games room with TV and bar billiards.

Open: 15 March - 30 September.

Directions

Take the D769 north from Lorient to Le Faouët. Site is well signed from this road. GPS: N48:01.094 W03:28.205

Charges guide

Per person	€ 3,00 - € 3,80
child (2-7 yrs)	€ 1,45 - € 1,70
pitch	€ 4,40 - € 5,50
electricity (5A)	€ 3,00
No credit cards.	

Check real time availability and at-the-gate prices...

www.alanrogers.com

FR56430 Camping Moulin de Cadillac

Route de Berric, F-56190 Noyal-Muzillac (Morbihan)
Tel: 02 97 67 03 47. Email: infos@moulin-cadillac.com　　www.alanrogers.com/FR56430

Le Moulin de Cadillac is a riverside site located 15 minutes by car from the beaches of the Morbihan. Set in the heart of rural Brittany, this attractive site has 192 pitches, 139 of which are for touring. Pitches are generous (100-150 sq.m) although access to some is tight and may not be suitable for larger units. They are well laid out on grass and a profusion of trees and shrubs provides both shade and privacy. Electricity is available to all, but water supply may mean a short walk to one of the three sanitary blocks. A small bar and terrace overlook the swimming pool and a small zoo will keep younger children amused.

Facilities

Three well appointed toilet blocks include facilities for children and disabled visitors. No shop but some basics are kept in reception. Bar (July/Aug). Swimming pool with slides (heated July/Aug) and paddling pool. Games room. TV room. All weather sports pitch. Tennis. Minigolf. Three play areas. Two fishing lakes. Children's zoo. Some entertainment in high season. Mobile homes and chalets for rent. Off site: Muzillac for shopping, restaurants etc. 8 km. Nearest beaches 10 km. Riding and bicycle hire 10 km. Golf 15 km.

Open: 30 May - 30 September.

Directions

From Vannes travel south east on the N165. Exit on D140 in the direction of Berric. After 3 km. at Lauzach, site is well signed on the right. Continue for a further 4 km. GPS: N47:36.786 W02:30.084

Charges guide

Per person	€ 3,50 - € 4,70
child (under 7 yrs)	€ 2,00 - € 2,80
pitch	€ 4,50 - € 7,00
electricity (10A)	€ 3,20

Le Moulin de Cadillac

56190 Noyal-Muzillac - Tel: 0033 297 670 347 - Fax: 0033 297 670 002
www.camping-moulin-cadillac.com - infos@moulin-cadillac.com

FR56440 Camping Moténo

Route du Magou'r, F-56680 Plouhinec (Morbihan)
Tel: 02 97 36 76 63. Email: camping-moteno@wanadoo.fr　　www.alanrogers.com/FR56440

This site is situated on the east side of the river d'Etel just before it enters the sea. The grass pitches are of average size, hedged and shaded by large trees. Of the 256 pitches, 181 are occupied by mobile homes, mostly for rent. The new aqua park complex with covered and open areas is superb and includes slides, flumes and various pools. The beach is easily accessible, just 800 m. as is the little port facing Etel which can be reached by a regular ferry service. Plouhinec, the nearest town, is five kilometres by road where you will find shops and restaurants.

Facilities

Three toilet blocks (only one open when we visited in June) are old and poorly maintained. Washing machines and dryer. Shop and bar (July/Aug). New aqua complex. Multisport court. Gym. Bicycle hire. Play area. Animation (July/Aug). Off site: Beach 800 m. Ferry to Etel for bars and shopping. Nearby towns of Lorient, Auray and the Quiberon peninsular.

Open: 5 April - 13 September.

Directions

From Plouhinec, southeast of Lorient, take the D781 in the direction of Carnac. Site is signed on right in 4 km. Follow signs for Plage. GPS: N47:39.874 W03:13.259

Charges guide

Per pitch incl. 2 persons and electricity	€ 18,20 - € 26,00
extra person (over 7 yrs)	€ 3,60 - € 6,00
child (0-7 yrs)	€ 2,50 - € 4,30
pet	free - € 5,00
Min. stay 7 nights 13/7-17/8.	

Check real time availability and at-the-gate prices...
www.alanrogers.com

FR56460 Flower Camping le Kernest

Bangor, F-56360 Belle Ile-en-Mer (Morbihan)

Tel: **02 97 31 56 26**. Email: **direction.generale@amisep.asso.fr**   www.alanrogers.com/FR56460

Belle Ile is a large island lying around 14 km. off the Quiberon peninsula. Access to the island can be made by ferry from either Quiberon, Vannes or Lorient (reservation is recommended in high season). Le Kernest is a family site and a member of the Flower group. It is located around 800 m. from a sandy beach with direct access by footpath. There are 100 pitches here, some of which are occupied by wooden chalets. Touring pitches are grassy and well shaded, and all have electrical connections. Leisure facilities on site include a tennis court and multisports terrain, as well as a snack bar. Numerous cycle tracks cross the island, including one around the perimeter.

Facilities	Directions
Shop. Snack bar. Takeaway. Tennis. Multisports terrain. Play area. Fishing. TV room. Activity and entertainment programme. Chalets for rent. Off site: Nearest beach 800 m. (direct path). Riding. Fishing. Cycle tracks.	Upon arrival at Le Palais, follow signs to Bangor on D90 and then to Kernest. Site is well signed from here. GPS: N47:18.888 W03:11.347
Open: 1 June - 30 September.	**Charges 2009**

Per unit incl. 2 persons and electricity	€ 13,90 - € 21,90

www.flowercampings.com

FR56470 Flower Camping l'Océan

16 ave de Groix, B.P. 18 Kerhostin, F-56510 St Pierre-de-Quiberon (Morbihan)

Tel: **02 97 30 91 29**. Email: **direction@relaisdelocean.com**   www.alanrogers.com/FR56470

L'Océan is a member of the Flower group and can be found just 100 m. from the nearest beach, halfway down the Quiberon peninsula. The site forms a part of a holiday complex that was established in 1925 and which also includes a hotel. There are 300 pitches which are generally well shaded, although some sunnier pitches are also available. A selection of mobile homes and fully equipped tents are for rent. In peak season, a varied animation programme is on offer, including traditional Celtic folk evenings and magic shows, as well as discos and concerts. The site's bar/restaurant 'Ty Mouss' is the focal point and specializes in pizzas and crêpes, and other light meals.

Facilities	Directions
Shop. Bar/restaurant. Takeaway. Multisports terrain. Tennis. Bicycle hire. Canoe hire. Play area. TV/games room. Activity and entertainment programme. Mobile homes and equipped tents for rent. Off site: Nearest beach 100 m. Riding. Fishing. Cycle tracks. Prehistoric stones at Carnac.	Leave the N165 at the Quiberon exit and head south on the D768. Continue towards St Pierre - Quiberon, passing through Plouharnel. Site is located at Kerhostin and is signed to the right, before St Pierre. GPS: N47:32.060 W03:08.373
Open: April - November.	**Charges guide**

Per unit incl. 2 persons and electricity	€ 16,00 - € 20,00
extra person	€ 3,50 - € 4,50
child (under 7 yrs)	€ 2,50
dog	€ 3,00

www.flowercampings.com

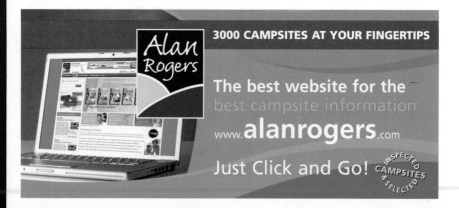

3000 CAMPSITES AT YOUR FINGERTIPS

Alan Rogers

The best website for the best campsite information

www.**alanrogers**.com

Just Click and Go!   INSPECTED & SELECTED CAMPSITES

MAP 2

Normandy

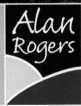

A striking area whose beauty lies not only in the landscape. Famed for its seafood and Celtic tradition, certain areas of Normandy remain untouched and wonderfully old fashioned.

DÉPARTEMENTS: 14 CALVADOS, 27 EURE, 50 MANCHE, 61 ORNE, 76 SEINE MARITIME

MAJOR CITIES: CAEN AND ROUEN

Normandy has a rich landscape full of variety. From the wild craggy granite coastline of the northern Cotentin to the long sandy beaches and chalk cliffs of the south. It also boasts a superb coastline including the Cotentin Peninsula, cliffs of the Côte d'Albâtre and the fine beaches and fashionable resorts of the Côte Fleurie. Plus a wealth of quiet villages and unspoilt countryside for leisurely exploration.

The history of Normandy is closely linked with our own. The famous Bayeux Tapestry chronicles the exploits of the Battle of Hastings and there are many museums, exhibitions, sites and monuments, including the Caen Memorial Museum, which commemorate operations that took place during the D-Day Landings of 1944.

Known as the dairy of France you'll also find plenty of fresh fish, rich cream, butter, and fine cheeses such as Camembert and Pont l'Evêque. The many apple orchards are used in producing cider and the well known Calvados, Normandy's apple brandy.

Places of interest

Bayeux: home to the famous tapestry; 15th-18th-century houses, cathedral, museums.

Caen: feudal castle, Museum of Normandy, Museum for Peace.

Omaha Beach: D-Day beaches, Landing site monuments, American Cemetery.

Deauville: seaside resort, horse racing centre.

Giverny: home of impressionist painter Claude Monet, Monet Museum.

Honfleur: picturesque port city with old town.

Lisieux: pilgrimage site, shrine of Ste Thérèse.

Mont St-Michel: world famous abbey on island.

Rouen: Joan of Arc Museum; Gothic churches, cathedrals, abbey, clock tower.

Cuisine of the region

Andouillette de Vire: small chitterling (tripe) sausage.

Barbue au cidre: brill cooked in cider and Calvados.

Douillons de pommes à la Normande: baked apples in pastry.

Escalope (Vallée d'Auge): veal sautéed and flamed in Calvados and served with cream and apples.

Ficelle Normande: pancake with ham, mushrooms and cheese.

Poulet (Vallée d'Auge): chicken cooked in the same way as Escalope Vallée d'Auge.

Tripes à la Mode de Caen: stewed beef tripe with onions, carrots, leeks, garlic, cider and Calvados.

Normandy

FR14010 Yelloh! Village la Côte de Nacre

Rue du Général Moulton, F-14750 Saint Aubin-sur-Mer (Calvados)
Tel: **04 66 73 97 39**. Email: **info@yellohvillage-cote-de-nacre.com**   www.alanrogers.com/FR14010

La Côte de Nacre is a large, commercial site with many facilities, all of a high standard. This could be an ideal holiday location for families with older children and teenagers. Two thirds of the site is given over to mobile homes and there are five tour operators on the site. The touring pitches are reasonable, both in size and condition. With pleasant, well cared for flowerbeds, there is some hedging to the pitches, but not much, and a few trees, so little shade. There is a 'state of the art' pool complex which includes a covered pool (with lifeguards in attendance).

Facilities	Directions
One open toilet block has showers and washbasins in cubicles. New block (completed in 2007). Laundry room. Bar, restaurant and takeaway. Pool complex with outdoor and indoor pools, slides, etc. Play area. Library. Games room. Children's club. Multisports area. Off site: Town 1 km.	Travel west from Ouistreham on D514 to St Aubin-sur-Mer. Site is well signed, just off the main road in a residential area. GPS: N49:19.566 W00:23.400

Open: 21 March - 14 September.

Charges guide

Per unit incl. 2 persons	€ 17,00 - € 42,00
extra person	€ 5,00 - € 8,00

tel: +33 466 739 739   www.yellohvillage.com ——————

FR14020 Camping Municipal du Bayeux

Boulevard Eindhoven, F-14400 Bayeux (Calvados)
Tel: **02 31 92 08 43**   www.alanrogers.com/FR14020

Only a few kilometres from the coast and the landing beaches this site makes a very useful night stop on the way to or from Cherbourg, whether or not you want to see the tapestry. The 140 pitches are in two areas (many on hardstanding), well marked and generally of good size with electricity. The site is busy over a long season – early arrival is advised as reservations are not taken. There is a full time warden from 15/6-15/9, otherwise reception is open from 08.00-10.00 and 17.00-19.00 hrs. There may be some road noise on one side of the site.

Facilities	Directions
The two good quality toilet blocks have British and Turkish style WCs, washbasins in cabins in main block, and units for disabled people. Motorcaravan service point. Laundry room. Takeaway food and snacks. Two playgrounds. Reading room with TV. Games room. Off site: Large public indoor swimming pool adjoins site with children's pool and jacuzzi. Supermarket nearby (closes 8 pm). Bicycle hire 1 km. Riding 5 km. Beach, golf or fishing 8 km.	Site is on the south side of northern ring road (D613) to town, and just west of the junction with the D516 to autoroute. GPS: N49:17.037 W00:41.857

Open: 1 May - 30 September.

Charges guide

Per person	€ 3,10
child (under 7 yrs)	€ 1,65
pitch and electricity	€ 7,00
No credit cards.	

FR14030 Castel Camping le Château de Martragny

F-14740 Martragny (Calvados)
Tel: **02 31 80 21 40**. Email: **chateau.martragny@wanadoo.fr**   www.alanrogers.com/FR14030

Martragny is an attractive site in a parkland setting adjoining the château. Close to D-Day beaches, it is also convenient for the ports of Caen and Cherbourg, and has the facilities and charm to encourage both long stays and stopovers. The pleasant lawns surrounding and approaching the château take 160 units, with electricity connections for 140. Most pitches are divided by either a small hedge or a few trees. Bed and breakfast (en-suite) accommodation is available in the château all year (reservation essential). Madame de Chassey takes great pride in the site and takes care that peace and quiet is preserved.

Facilities	Directions
Three modernised sanitary blocks include washbasins in cabins, sinks for dishes and clothes and two baby baths. Disabled people are well catered for. Good laundry. Shop and takeaway food bar (21/5-15/9). Bar. Swimming pool (20 x 6 m.) and paddling pool heated in poor weather. Play areas. Tennis. Minigolf. Games and TV room. Fishing. Bicycle and buggy hire. Off site: Riding 1 km. Beach 15 km. Golf 20 km.	Site is off the N13, 8 km. southeast of Bayeux. Take Martragny exit from dual carriageway. GPS: N49:14.595 W00:36.348

Open: 1 May - 12 September.

Charges 2009

Per person	€ 5,50 - € 6,50
child (under 7 yrs)	€ 3,00 - € 3,50
pitch incl. electricity	€ 15,50 - € 17,00
Less 15% outside 1/7-31/8.	
Camping Cheques accepted.	

The Travel Service ...we'll arrange everything
BOOK THIS SITE CALL 01580 214000

Check real time availability and at-the-gate prices...
www.**alanrogers**.com

FR14060 Camping les Hautes Coutures

Route de Ouistreham, F-14970 Bénouville (Calvados)

Tel: **02 31 44 73 08**. Email: **info@campinghautescoutures.com**   www.alanrogers.com/FR14060

Les Hautes Coutures is a pleasant site whose new owner has made considerable improvements to the leisure facilities so that it is now not only an ideal site for overnight stops (being just 4 km. from the Caen-Portsmouth ferry terminal) but also well worth considering for a longer stay. There are 120 good-sized grass touring pitches separated by mature hedges, all with electrical connections (4-10A). An area close to the canal has large, unmarked pitches. There are also around 150 mobile homes, 30 available to rent. The site is beside the Caen ship canal and a short walk along the footpath takes you to Pegasus Bridge and the Pegasus Memorial museum. In the other direction the path (and cycle track) goes to Ouistreham.

Facilities

Two toilet blocks include showers, washbasins in cabins (warm water). Facilities can be under pressure at peak times with variable hot water supply. Laundry facilities. Motorcaravan service point. Small shop, restaurant and takeaway (July/Aug). Bar (May - Sept). Attractive new pool complex with water slides and an outdoor pool linked to another with retractable roof (May - Sept). Small lounge/TV area and games room. Impressive new play area, trampoline and outdoor fitness equipment. Multisport court. Fishing. Minigolf. Boules.
Off site: Pegasus Bridge and Memorial Museum short walk along canal path. Beach, sailing, boat launching, water-skiing and riding all 2-3 km. Golf 4 km.

Open: 1 April - 30 October.

Directions

Bénouville is 10 km. north east of Caen. From northern ring road (N 814) at exit 3, take D515 towards Ouistreham (or follow car ferry signs from other points). After Bénouville (now the D514) take first exit and site entrance is ahead. From ferry take D514 towards Caen; in 4 km. take slip road for Bénouville and at T-junction turn left to site. (Owner awaits arrivals from evening ferry). GPS: N49:15.003 W00:16.396

Charges guide

Per person	€ 8,20
child (under 7 yrs)	€ 5,50
pitch	€ 8,20
electricity (4-10A)	€ 5,00 - € 6,00

Route de Ouistreham 14970 BENOUVILLE
Tel : 02 31 44 73 08   Fax : 02 31 95 30 80
E-mail : info@campinghautescoutures.com   Web site : www.campinghautescoutures.com

FR14070 Camping de la Vallée

88 rue de la Vallée, F-14510 Houlgate (Calvados)

Tel: **02 31 24 40 69**. Email: **camping.lavallee@wanadoo.fr**   www.alanrogers.com/FR14070

Camping de la Vallée is an attractive site with good, well maintained facilities, situated on the rolling hillside above the seaside resort of Houlgate. The site has 373 pitches with 98 for touring units. Large, open and separated by hedges, all the pitches have 4 or 6A electricity and some also have water and drainage. Part of the site is sloping, the rest level, with gravel or tarmac roads. Shade is provided by a variety of well kept trees and shrubs.

Facilities

Three good toilet blocks include washbasins in cabins, mainly British style toilets, facilities for disabled visitors and baby bathrooms. Laundry facilities (no washing lines allowed). Motorcaravan services. Shop (from 1/5). Bar. Snack bar with takeaway in season (from 15/5). Heated swimming pool (1/5-30/9; no shorts). Games room. Playground. Bicycle hire. Volleyball, football, tennis, pétanque. Entertainment in Jul/Aug. Internet access. Only one dog per pitch. Off site: Riding 500 m. Beach, town, fishing 1 km. Golf 2 km.

Open: 1 April - 30 September.

Directions

Houlgate is 30 km. northeast of Caen. From A13 exit for Cabourg follow D400 to Dives-sur-Mer, then D513 (Hougate/Deauville) until the sea front. After 1 km. at lights turn right and follow signs to site. GPS: N49:17.644 W00:04.097

Charges guide

Per unit incl. 2 persons and electricity	€ 21,00 - € 32,00
extra person	€ 5,00 - € 6,00

Credit card minimum € 50.
Camping Cheques accepted.

Check real time availability and at-the-gate prices...

www.alanrogers.com

FR14090 Castel Camping du Brévedent

Le Brévedent, F-14130 Pont-l'Evêque (Calvados)

Tel: 02 31 64 72 88. Email: contact@campinglebrevedent.com

www.alanrogers.com/FR14090

Le Brévedent is a well established, traditional site with 144 pitches (109 for tourists, 31 used by tour operators) set in the grounds of an elegant 18th-century hunting pavilion. Pitches are either around the fishing lake (unfenced), in the lower gardens (level), or in the old orchard (gently sloping). Most have electricity. It is an excellent holiday destination within easy reach of the Channel ports and its peaceful, friendly environment makes it ideal for mature campers or families with younger children.

Facilities

Three toilet blocks include washbasins in cubicles and facilities for disabled visitors. One has been refurbished with spacious en-suite cubicles (shower, washbasin and baby bath). Laundry facilities. Motorcaravan service point. Shop (baker delivers). Restaurant (24/5-19/9). Takeaway (1/5-25/9). Bar (evenings). Clubroom. Internet access. TV and library. Heated swimming and paddling pools (unsupervised) (1/5-25/9). Playground. Minigolf. Games room. Fishing. Rowing. Bicycle hire. Organised excursions. Entertainment and children's club (high season). Dogs are not accepted. Off site: Riding 1 km. Tennis. Golf, boat launching and river swimming 12 km. Beach 25 km.

Open: 28 April - 23 September.

Directions

Pont-l'Evêque is due south of Le Havre. Le Brévedent is 13 km south east from Pont-l'Evêque: take D579 toward Lisieux for 4 km. then D51 towards Moyaux. At Blangy le Château continue ahead on D51 to Le Brévedent. GPS: N49:13.528 E00:18.342

Charges guide

Per person	€ 5,20 - € 6,70
child (1-12 yrs)	€ 2,20 - € 4,50
pitch	€ 7,00 - € 9,00
electricity	€ 2,45 - € 3,20

FR14100 Camping Municipal du Château

3 rue du Val d'Ante, F-14700 Falaise (Calvados)

Tel: 02 31 90 16 55. Email: camping@falaise.fr

www.alanrogers.com/FR14100

The location of this site is really quite spectacular, lying in the shadow of the Château of William the Conqueror, within walking distance of the historic town of Falaise in the 'coeur de Normandie'. The site itself is small, with only 66 pitches (most with electricity) either beside the little river, on a terrace above or on gently sloping ground. With trees and hedges providing some shade as well as open grassed areas, this site has a rather intimate 'up-market' feel about it.

Facilities

Although the sanitary facilities are dated, they are of good quality and kept clean. Free hot water to showers, washbasins in cubicles for the ladies and laundry sinks (all closed overnight). Unit for disabled visitors (shower room and separate WC). Motorcaravan service point. Excellent new play area. New tennis courts and boules pitch. TV room. Fishing. Free WiFi access. Off site: Bicycle hire 300 m. Riding 500 m. Tree-top adventure park 17 km. Kayak club with canoe hire and river descent 19 km.

Open: 1 May - 30 September.

Directions

Falaise is 35 km. south east of Caen on the route to Alençon and Le Mans. Site on western side of town, well signed from ring road. From N158 heading south take first roundabout into Falaise and follow site signs through residential suburb to site. GPS: N48:53.734 W00:12.288

Charges guide

Per person	€ 3,30
pitch	€ 4,00
electricity (5A)	€ 2,50

FR14140 Camping Municipal Pont Farcy

F-14380 Pont-Farcy (Calvados)

Tel: 02 31 68 32 06

www.alanrogers.com/FR14140

This well tended, riverside site is in a tranquil location within easy walking distance of the small village. Just off the A84 motorway it is within easy driving distance of Cherbourg or Caen. A warden lives on site. The 60 numbered pitches are on grass, some separated by small hedges, with electricity (10A) available to all (long leads may be needed). Activities either on site or at the adjacent 'base plein air' include tennis, minigolf, canoe/kayak, pedaloes and cycle hire, walking and fishing.

Facilities

A modern building houses all the facilities, including some washbasins in cubicles and a suite for disabled campers. First floor 'salle' with dining tables for campers. There is a lift from the ground floor. Adventure style playground. Off site: Village garage with a small shop, bakery, butcher, post office. Bar/hotel. Attractions include the Gorges de la Vire and opportunities in the area for riding, climbing and parachuting.

Open: 1 April - 30 September.

Directions

Pont-Farcy is about 25 km. due south of St Lô. From A84, exit 39, take D21 south for 1 km. Site is on left at entrance to village. GPS: N48:56.395 W01:02.120

Charges guide

Per unit incl. 1 or 2 persons	€ 9,00
extra person	€ 2,15
electricity	€ 1,85

No credit cards.

Check real time availability and at-the-gate prices...

www.alanrogers.com

FR14160 Camping Bellevue

Mobile homes ▶ page 491

Route des Dives, F-14640 Villers-sur-Mer (Calvados)

Tel: 02 31 87 05 21. Email: contact@camping-bellevue.com   www.alanrogers.com/FR14160

Bellevue is located just west of Villers-sur-Mer with its sandy beach, and 9.5 km. west of fashionable Deauville. A fairly large site with 249 pitches in total, but including 190 privately owned mobile homes and 20 units for rent, there are only 59 pitches left for tourists. Many of these are on terraces, individual and relatively small with restricted access, so suitable only for smaller units. Double axle caravans will have difficulty and will only be able to access pitches adjacent to the road. There are around half a dozen, further level pitches behind reception mostly used by motorcaravans (unsuitable for American RVs).

Facilities	Directions
Two sanitary units provide unisex facilities, all in individual cubicles, with some wide door cubicles for disabled visitors. Baby changing room. Laundry room with washing machine, dryer and a range of sinks for laundry and dishwashing. Swimming pool complex (15/6-15/9). Bar (1/7-15/9). Takeaway van in July/Aug. Boules court. Video games machines. Pool table. Playground. Organised activities in peak season. Off site: Beach and town 1.5 km. Riding 2 km. Golf 4 km. **Open:** 1 April - 31 October.	Villers-sur-Mer is about 8 km. west of Deauville. The site is 1.5 km. west of Villers on the D513; be ready to turn right into lane (site signed) at the crest of a hill, where the road bends to the right. GPS: N49:18.562 W00:01.178

Charges guide

Per person	€ 6,00
child (0-7 yrs)	€ 3,50
pitch	€ 7,00
electricity	€ 4,00

FR14150 Sunêlia Port'land

Chemin du Castel, F-14520 Port-en-Bessin (Calvados)

Tel: 02 31 51 07 06. Email: campingportland@wanadoo.fr   www.alanrogers.com/FR14150

The Gerardin family will make you most welcome at Port'land, now a mature site lying 700 metres to the east of the little resort of Port en Bessin, one of Normandy's busiest fishing ports. The 300 pitches are large and grassy with 202 available for touring units, including 128 with 15A electricity. There is a separate area for tents without electricity. The camping area has been imaginatively designed into distinct zones, some overlooking small fishing ponds and another radiating out from a central barbecue area. There are ten site-owned mobile homes for rent. A member of the Sunelia group.

Facilities	Directions
The two sanitary blocks are modern and well maintained. Special disabled facilities. Heated swimming pool (covered in low season) and paddling pool. Bar, restaurant, takeaway. Large TV and games room. Multisports pitch. Fishing. Play area. WiFi access. Off site: Beach 4 km. 27-hole Omaha Beach International golf course adjacent. Fishing 600 m. Bicycle hire and riding 10 km. D-Day beaches. Colleville American war Cemetery. Bayeux. **Open:** 29 March - 5 November.	Site is clearly signed off the D514 4 km. west of Port en Bessin. GPS: N49:20.829 W00:46.274

Charges guide

Per unit incl. 2 persons and electricity	€ 25,00 - € 37,00
extra person	€ 4,80 - € 7,30
child (2-10 yrs)	€ 2,80 - € 4,20
dog	€ 3,00

FR14170 Camping la Capricieuse

2 rue Brummel, F-14530 Luc-sur-Mer (Calvados)

Tel: 02 31 97 34 43. Email: info@campinglacapricieuse.com   www.alanrogers.com/FR14170

La Capricieuse is situated on the edge of the delightful small seaside town of Luc-sur-Mer. It is an ideal location for those looking for a superb municipal site just a few minutes drive from the Ouistreham car ferry. This immaculate site has 204 touring pitches of varying sizes, on level grass with hedges and a variety of trees gives some shade. 105 have electricity and 52 also have water and drainage. Although the site does not have its own shop, bar or restaurant, these can be found within walking distance in Luc-sur-Mer.

Facilities	Directions
Three modern toilet blocks with washbasins in cubicles and showers are kept very clean. Fully equipped facilities for disabled visitors. Laundry and dishwashing facilities. Motorcaravan service point. Large TV room. Games room. Adventure playground (unfenced). Tennis. Boules. Off site: Fishing and bicycle hire nearby. Riding 3 km. Golf 30 km. **Open:** 1 April - 30 September.	Take the D514 from Ouistreham car ferry and head west to Luc-sur-Mer. Campsite is well signed from the western end of St Luc. GPS: N49:19.078 W00:21.468

Charges 2009

Per unit incl. 2 persons and electricity	€ 15,90 - € 20,35
extra person	€ 3,60 - € 4,50

BOOK THIS SITE
CALL 01580 214000
...we'll arrange everything
The Travel
Service

Check real time availability and at-the-gate prices...

www.alanrogers.com

FR14180 Camping la Briquerie

Equemauville, F-14600 Honfleur (Calvados)

Tel: **02 31 89 28 32.** Email: **info@campinglabriquerie.com**   www.alanrogers.com/FR14180

La Briquerie is a large, neat municipal site on the outskirts of the attractive and popular harbour town of Honfleur. Very well cared for and efficiently run by a family team, the site has 420 pitches, many of which are let on a seasonal basis. There are also 130 medium to large, hedged touring pitches. All have electricity (5/10A), water and drainage. One of the main attractions here is the close proximity to Honfleur where one can watch the fishing boats from the quay or browse the work of the artists who display their work in the galleries around the town.

Facilities	Directions
Two toilet blocks with washbasins in cubicles and showers. Good facilities for disabled visitors. Laundry room. Large restaurant (July/Aug). Takeaway (1/6-15/9). Bar (1/6-30/9). Small shop (July/Aug). Large pool complex with two flumes (15/5-15/9). Sauna. Jacuzzi. Fitness room. Boules. Minigolf. TV and internet access. Off site: Supermarket adjacent. Riding and bicycle hire 1 km. Beach 2 km. Fishing 5 km. Golf 7 km.	Site is well signed from Honfleur on the D579, beside the Intermarché on the D62. GPS: N49:23.868 E00:12.514

Open: 1 April - 30 September.

Charges guide

Per pitch incl. 2 persons, electricity, water and drainage	€ 20,80 - € 26,80
extra person	€ 5,40 - € 7,40
child (2-7 yrs)	€ 3,00 - € 4,00

FR14190 Camping les Peupliers

Allée des Pins, F-14810 Merville-Franceville (Calvados)

Tel: **02 31 24 05 07.** Email: **asl-mondeville@wanadoo.fr**   www.alanrogers.com/FR14190

Les Peupliers is run by friendly, family managers who keep this site attractive and tidy. It is just 300 metres from a long, wide, sandy beach. The touring pitches, of which there are 85, are on level open ground, all with 10A electricity. Those in the newest part are hedged but, with just a few trees on the edge of the site, there is little shade. The campsite amenities are near the entrance, housed in neat modern buildings. This site is ideally located for visiting Caen, Bayeux and the traditional seaside towns of Deauville and Trouville.

Facilities	Directions
Two excellent heated toilet blocks with washbasins in cabins and showers. Good facilities for disabled visitors and for babies. Laundry room. Small shop, bar with terrace and takeaway (all July/Aug). Heated swimming pool and paddling pool (May-Sept). Play area. Games room. Entertainment and animation in high season. Off site: Fishing, riding and golf all within 1 km. Bicycle hire 2 km.	From Ouistreham take the D514 to Merville-Franceville. Site is well signed off Allée des Pins. From Rouen on A13 (exit 29B), take D400 to Cabourg then the D514 to Merville-Franceville. GPS: N49:16.996 W00:10.232

Open: 1 April - 30 October.

Charges 2009

Per person	€ 6,70
pitch	€ 7,40
electricity (10A)	€ 5,30

FR14220 Camping Loisirs Ariane

100 route de Cabourg, F-14810 Merville-Franceville-Plage (Calvados)

Tel: **02 31 24 52 52.** Email: **info@loisirs-arizne.com**   www.alanrogers.com/FR14220

You will get a warm welcome in English at this spacious, well laid out site, just 300 metres from the beach. It has 144 good-sized pitches, all with 10A electricity, water and waste points close by. Roads and hedges are well maintained with easy access for larger units. The site is well lit and secure with gate controlled entry. There are numerous beaches nearby and possible days out include the D-Day Beaches, Pegasus Bridge, Bayeux and its Tapestry, fashionable Deauville and picturesque Honfleur.

Facilities	Directions
Two bright, recently built sanitary blocks, heated and with tiled walls and floors. Controllable showers. Washbasins in cubicles. Special children's themed shower and toilets. Baby room. Facilities for disabled visitors. Washing machines and dryers. Motorcaravan service point. Shop, bar, snack bar and takeaway. Free use of internet. Bicycle hire. Games room. Children's club and entertainment for adults (July/Aug). Off site: Beach 300 m. Sailing 500 m. Golf and riding 1 km. Boat launching 2 km. Shops, bars and restaurants all close by in Merville.	Merville-Franceville-Plage is just 17 km. northeast of Caen. From A13 motorway exit 29/29b follow D400 north towards Cabourg (5 km); then bear west on D400A towards Cabourg Plage (3 km) and west on D514 to Merville-Franceville. Continue to site on right. From Ouistreham ferry port follow signs for Caen for about 4 km. then turn east and north on D514 to Merville and site on left. GPS: N49:16.974 W00:11.442

Open: 1 April - 30 November.

Charges guide

Per person	€ 4,05 - € 6,10
electricity (10A)	€ 4,00

Check real time availability and at-the-gate prices...

www.**alanrogers**.com

FR14200 Camping la Vallée de Deauville

Avenue de la Vallée, F-14800 Saint Arnoult (Calvados)

Tel: 02 31 88 58 17. Email: contact@camping-deauville.com — www.alanrogers.com/FR14200

Close to the traditional seaside resorts of Deauville and Trouville, this large, modern site is owned and run by a delightful Belgian couple. With a total of 450 pitches, there are many mobile homes, both for rent and privately owned, and 150 used for touring units. These pitches are level, of a reasonable size and mostly hedged, and 60 have 10A electricity connections. A brand new pool complex complete with flumes, lazy river, jacuzzi and fun pool makes an attractive focal point near the entrance and there is a large fishing lake. The bar and restaurant are large and comfortable and there is a very good shop on the site. The wide sandy beaches of this coast are 3 km. With the various new developments at this site, it promises to be a good choice in the Deauville and Caen area.

Facilities

Two new heated toilet blocks with showers and washbasins in cubicles. Good facilities for babies and disabled visitors. Laundry facilities. Small shop, bar and restaurant (high season). Takeaway (all season). New swimming pool complex. Good play area and play room. Entertainment in high season. Off site: Beach 3 km. Golf and riding 2 km. Bicycle hire 3 km.

Open: 1 April - 31 October.

Directions

From the north, take the A29, then the A13 at Pont l'Evêque. Join the N177 (Deauville/Trouville) and after 9 km. take the D27 signed St Arnoult. Site is well signed on edge of village.
GPS: N49:19.430 E00:05.100

Charges guide

Per person	€ 5,40 - € 9,00
child (0-7 yrs)	€ 3,00 - € 5,00
pitch	€ 7,20 - € 12,00
electricity (10A)	€ 2,40 - € 4,00
animal	€ 2,40 - € 4,00

Camping La Vallee de Deauville

Avenue de la Vallée
14800 Deauville-St-Arnoult

Tél: (33) 02 31 88 58 17
Fax: (33) 02 31 88 11 57

Mail: contact@camping-deauville.com
Internet: www.camping-deauville.com

FR27020 Camping du Domaine Catinière

Route de Honfleur, F-27210 Fiquefleur-Equainville (Eure)

Tel: 02 32 57 63 51. Email: info@camping-catiniere.com — www.alanrogers.com/FR27020

A peaceful, friendly site, close to the Normandy coast, in the countryside yet in the middle of a very long village, this site is steadily achieving a modern look. There are 19 rental and 24 privately owned mobile homes, but there should be around 90 pitches for tourists including a large open field for tents and units not needing electricity. Caravan pitches are separated, some with shade, others are more open and all have electricity hook-ups. The site is divided by well fenced streams.

Facilities

Toilet facilities include mostly British style WCs, some washbasins in cubicles, and facilities for disabled visitors and babies (cleaning can be variable). Washing machine and dryer. Reception with shop. Small bar/restaurant with regional dishes and snacks. Heated swimming pool (1/6-15/9). Two playgrounds, trampoline. Boules. Barrier (card deposit). Off site: Large supermarket close to southern end of the bridge. Smaller supermarket in Beuzeville 7 km. Beach 7 km.

Open: 10 April - 27 August.

Directions

From the Pont de Normandie (toll bridge). Take first exit on leaving bridge (exit 3, A29) signed Honfleur. At roundabout turn left under motorway in direction of Le Mans and Alencon on D180. Take second exit on right after about 2.5 km, onto D22 towards Beuzeville. Site is on right after about 1 km.
GPS: N49:24.054 E00:18.365

Charges guide

Per pitch incl. 1 or 2 persons	€ 15,00 - € 21,00
incl. electricity (4A)	€ 19,00 - € 25,00
extra person	€ 4,00 - € 6,00

Credit cards accepted (minimum of € 70).

BOOK THIS SITE
CALL 01580 214000
...we'll arrange everything
Service The Travel

Check real time availability and at-the-gate prices...

www.alanrogers.com

FR27070 Camping de l'Ile des Trois Rois

Mobile homes ▶ page 491

1 rue Gilles Nicolle, F-27700 Andelys (Eure)

Tel: **02 32 54 23 79**. Email: campingtroisrois@aol.com

www.alanrogers.com/FR27070

One hour from Paris and 30 minutes from Rouen, L'Ile des Trois Rois has an attractive setting on the banks of the Seine, with a private fishing lake and is a haven of peace. It is overlooked by the impressive remains of the Château-Gaillard and would be ideal as an overnight stop or for longer. The site has been owned by the Francais Family for the past four years and they live on site. Within walking distance of the town and shops, the site has 100 spacious and partly shady grass pitches, all with electricity (long leads may be required for some). Water taps are rather scarce. There are also five mobile homes for rent and 60 pitches occupied by private mobile homes/seasonal units. Medieval Festival in Les Andelys – last weekend in June. Bread and cakes are available from a vending machine 24 hrs.

Facilities

Four small, unheated toilet blocks have British style toilets (no seats), showers and washbasins all in cubicles, diswashing and laundry sinks. One has facilities for disabled people and another has a laundry facility. Motorcaravan service point. Two heated swimming pools (15/5-15/9). Fishing in the Seine or in the private lake. Fenced play area. Animation. Bar and restaurant, evening entertainment (4/7-30/8). Bicycles and barbecues for hire. Internet access and satellite TV. Off site: Day trips to Paris and Rouen. Cycling and walking trails. Riding 5 km. Golf 9 km.

Open: 15 March - 15 November.

Directions

From the A13 motorway, take exit 17 and join the D316 to Les Andelys. In Les Andelys follow signs to Evreux, and the campsite is located just off the island before passing the bridge over the Seine. GPS: N49:14.155 E01:24.038

Charges guide

Per unit incl. 2 persons	€ 17,00
extra person	€ 5,00
child (under 3 yrs)	free
dog	€ 2,00

L'Ile des Trois Rois

The park Ile des Trois Rois is situated in the most beautiful bend of the Seine nearby Castle Gaillard in Normandy and is a haven of peace. Paris is situated of less than than an hour and Rouen is half an hour driving from the camp site. Facilities: two heated swimming pools, ping pong, camper service, bar and restaurant (high season) and play area

1, Rue Gilles Nicole - F-27700 Les Andelys - France - Tel. 0033 (0) 2 32 54 23 79
Fax 0033 (0) 2 32 51 14 54 - Email campingtroisrois@aol.com - www.camping-troisrois.com

FR27030 Camping Saint-Nicolas

F-27800 Le Bec-Hellouin (Eure)

Tel: **02 32 44 83 55**

www.alanrogers.com/FR27030

This lovely site, operated by the municipal authority and still run by the same resident wardens, is located on a forested hillside above the interesting and attractive small town of Le Bec-Hellouin. The town is quite photogenic, has the usual tourist shops, several bars and restaurants and horse drawn carriage rides. There are 90 marked grassy pitches, 30 used for seasonal units, leaving about 60 for tourists all with 10A hook-ups and some with water taps. There is limited shade from a few trees.

Facilities

A modern heated unit has good showers, British style WCs, open and cubicled washbasins. Extra facilities in the old unit by reception, where you will find the laundry. Reception keeps soft drinks and ices. The baker calls each morning. Playground. Playing field and tennis courts. Off site: Le Bec-Hellouin and its Abbey 1.5 km. Fishing 1.5 km. Riding 2 km. Swimming pool at Brionne 6 km. Golf 7 km.

Open: 1 April - 30 September.

Directions

Le Bec-Hellouin is about 30 km. southwest of Rouen, 24 km. southeast of Pont Audemer, just off the D130 between Pont Authou and Brionne. Turn east onto D39 to Le Bec-Hellouin, pass through edge of town. At far end of one-way section, turn left on minor road. Continue for about 1 km. Take left hand fork, and on for about 500 m. to site on right. GPS: N49:14.086 E00:43.519

Charges guide

Per unit incl. 2 persons and electricity	€ 11,60
extra person	€ 3,20
No credit cards.	

FR50000 Camping l'Etang des Haizes

43 rue Cauticotte, F-50250 Saint Symphorien-le-Valois (Manche)

Tel: **02 33 46 01 16**. Email: **info@campingetangdeshaizes.com**   www.alanrogers.com/FR50000

BOOK THIS SITE
CALL 01580 214000
...we'll arrange everything
The Travel Service

This is an attractive and very friendly site with a swimming pool complex with four-lane slides, jacuzzi and a paddling pool. L'Etang des Haizes has 98 good size pitches, of which 60 are for touring units, on fairly level ground and all with electricity (10A). They are set in a mixture of conifers, orchard and shrubbery, with some very attractive, slightly smaller pitches overlooking the lake and 38 mobile homes inconspicuously sited. The fenced lake has a small beach (swimming is permitted), ducks and pedaloes, and offers good coarse fishing for huge carp (we are told). Believe it or not, a turtle can sometimes be seen on a fine day! Just one kilometre away is La Haye-du-Puits with two supermarkets, good restaurants and a market on Wednesdays. A good sandy beach is within 10 km. and the Normandy landing beaches are 25 km.

Facilities

Two well kept and modern unisex toilet blocks have British style toilets, washbasins in cabins, units for disabled people and two family cabins. Small laundry. Motorcaravan services. Milk, bread and takeaway snacks available (no gas). Snack bar/bar with TV and terrace. Swimming pool complex (all amenities 20/5-10/9). Play areas. Bicycle hire. Pétanque. Organised activities including treasure hunts, archery and food tasting (10/7-25/8). Off site: Beach 10 km.

Open: 1 April - 16 October.

Directions

Site is just north of La Haye-du-Puits on the primary route from Cherbourg to Mont St-Michel, St Malo and Rennes. It is 24 km. south of N13 at Valognes and 29 km. north of Coutances: leave D900 at roundabout at northern end of bypass (towards town). Site signed on right. GPS: N49:17.724 W01:33.296

Charges 2009

Per unit incl. 2 persons	
and electricity	€ 16,00 - € 36,00
person (over 4 yrs)	€ 5,00 - € 6,50
dog	€ 1,00 - € 2,00

Camping Cheques accepted.

Camping Caravaning
★★★★★
L'étang des Haizes
Club Airotel
A very relaxing atmosphere with a fantastic swimming pool the lake is a wonderful attraction and excellent facilities

Camping Cheque

© 02 97 41 68 42
Création 3D

In between Nature Park and a Lovely Coast with sandy beaches

Camping L'étang des Haizes
Tél. : 0033 233 460 116
Fax : 0033 233 472 380
St-Symphorien-le-Valois
F 50250 LA HAYE DU PUITS
in NORMANDY

Http:/www.campingetangdeshaizes.com
Email: info@campingetangdeshaizes.com

Vacances en Normandie

Check real time availability and at-the-gate prices...
www.alanrogers.com

FR50030 Castel Camping le Château de lez Eaux

Mobile homes ▶ page 491

Saint Aubin des Préaux, F-50380 Saint Pair-sur-Mer (Manche)

Tel: **02 33 51 66 09**. Email: **bonjour@lez-eaux.com**   www.alanrogers.com/FR50030

Set in the spacious grounds of a château, Lez Eaux lies in a rural situation just off the main route south, under two hours from Cherbourg. There are 229 pitches of which 113 are for touring, all with electricity (5/10A) and 70 fully serviced. Most of the pitches are of a very good size, partly separated by trees and shrubs on either side, flat or very slightly sloping, grassy ground overlooking Normandy farmland or beside a small lake (with carp and other fish). There is a considerable tour operator presence, but these units by no means dominate, being generally tucked away in their own areas. This is a very pleasant location from which to explore this corner of the Cotentin peninsula, with swimming pools on site and beaches nearby. Saint Pair is 4 km. and Granville 7 km.

Facilities

Three modern clean toilet blocks include hot showers and washbasins in cabins, facilities for children and babies, and for disabled people. Shop, small bar, snacks and takeaway (all from 1/5). Small heated swimming pool and indoor tropical-style fun pool (from 1/5, no T-shirts or Bermuda-style shorts). Play area. Tennis. Games and TV rooms. Bicycle hire. Lake fishing. Torches useful. Only one dog per pitch. Off site: Beach 4 km. Riding 5 km. Golf 7 km.

Open: 1 April - 15 September.

Directions

Lez Eaux is just to the west of the D973 about 17 km. northwest of Avranches and 7 km. southeast of Granville. Site is between the two turnings east to St Aubin des Préaux and well signed. GPS: N48:47.764 W01:31.480

Charges guide

Per unit incl. 2 persons	€ 14,00 - € 30,00
extra person	€ 8,50
child (under 7 yrs)	€ 6,50
electricity (5A)	€ 7,00
all services	€ 10,00

Château de **Lez-Eaux**
★★★★

50380 SAINT PAIR SUR MER
bonjour@lez-eaux.com
Tel. +33 (0)2 33 51 66 09

LES CASTELS
★★★★

www.lez-eaux.com

FR27060 Domaine de Marcilly

Parcs Résidentiels ▶ page 515

Route de Saint-Andre-de-l'Eure, F-27810 Marcilly-sur-Eure (Eure)

Tel: **02 37 48 45 42**. Email: **domainedemarcilly@wanadoo.fr**   www.alanrogers.com/FR27060

Pitches at this campsite are exclusively for chalet accommodation.

FR50010 Camping la Gallouette

F-50550 Saint Vaast-la-Hougue (Manche)

Tel: 02 33 54 20 57. Email: contact@camping-lagallouette.fr

www.alanrogers.com/FR50010

Claudine and Jean Luc Boblin will give you a warm welcome at their seaside campsite which is ideally placed for visiting Barfleur, Ste Mère-Eglise and the Normandy landing beaches. There are 192 level pitches in total, 132 of which are for touring and all have 6A electricity. Some are separated by hedges and there are many colourful flower beds, shrubs and trees but little shade. A light and airy bar faces onto a terrace and swimming pool and there is also a state-of-the-art multisport court.

Facilities

Three modern sanitary blocks, one open and two enclosed, have British style toilets, showers and washbasins (some in cabins). Area for disabled visitors and for babies. Laundry facilities. Small shop. Snack bar. Bar with terrace. Swimming pool. Multisports court. Play area. Pétanque. Fishing. Internet access. Entertainment in high season. Off site: Beach 300 m. Shops and restaurant in St Vaast. Riding 5 km. Golf 12 km.

Open: 1 April - 30 September.

Directions

The D902 runs between Barfleur and Valognes on the eastern side of the Cherbourg peninsula. About half way along at Quettehou take the D1 to St Vaast. Site signed on right on entering town. GPS: N49:35.04 W01:16.07

Charges guide

Per person	€ 4,50 - € 5,80
child (1-10 yrs)	€ 2,80 - € 3,50
pitch with electricity	€ 9,90 - € 14,50
animal	€ 1,60

FR50050 Kawan Village le Cormoran

Ravenoville-Plage, F-50480 Sainte Mère-Eglise (Manche)

Tel: 02 33 41 33 94. Email: lecormoran@wanadoo.fr

www.alanrogers.com/FR50050

This welcoming, family run site, close to Cherbourg (45 km) and Caen (95 km), is situated just across the road from a long sandy beach. It is also close to Utah beach and is ideally located for those wishing to visit the many museums, landing beaches and remembrance gardens of WW2. On flat, quite open ground, the site has 100 good size pitches on level grass, all with 6A electricity. Some extra large pitches are available. The well kept pitches are separated by mature hedges and the site is decorated with flowering shrubs. A covered pool, a sauna and a gym are among improvements for 2009. These facilities, plus a shop, comfortable bar and takeaway are open all season. This modern, clean and fresh looking campsite caters for both families and couples and would be ideal for a holiday in this interesting area of France. The country roads provide opportunities for exploring on foot or by bike. There are many small towns in the area and in early June, you may find historical groups re-enacting battles and the events of 1944-1945.

Facilities

Four toilet blocks, one heated, are of varying styles and ages but all are maintained to a good standard. Laundry. New kitchen facilities. Shop. Bar and terrace. Snacks and takeaway. Outdoor pool (1/6-15/9, unsupervised). New covered pool, sauna and gym (all season). Play areas. Tennis. Boules. Entertainment, TV and games room. Bicycle and shrimp net hire. Riding (July/Aug). Communal barbecues. Off site: Beach 20 m. Sand yachting. Golf (9-holes) 3 km.

Open: 4 April - 27 September.

Directions

From N13 take Ste Mère-Eglise exit and in centre of town take road to Ravenoville (6 km), then Ravenoville-Plage (3 km). Just before beach turn right and site is 500 m. GPS: N49:27.960 W01:14.104

Charges 2009

Per unit incl. 1 or 2 persons and electricity	€ 20,00 - € 32,00
extra person	€ 4,00 - € 7,50
child (3-10 yrs)	€ 2,00 - € 3,00
dog	€ 3,00

Camping Cheques accepted.

Camping Le Cormoran****

2, Rue du Cormoran - 50480 Ravenoville-Plage - France
Tel: 0033 233 41 33 94 - fax: 0033 233 95 16 08
E-mail: lecormoran@wanadoo.fr - www.lecormoran.com

covered heated pool

BOOK THIS SITE
CALL 01580 214000
"we'll arrange everything
The Travel Service

The Travel Service
...we'll arrange everything
CALL 01580 214000
BOOK THIS SITE

FR50060 Kawan Village le Grand Large

F-50340 Les Pieux (Manche)

Tel: **02 33 52 40 75**. Email: **le-grand-large@wanadoo.fr**   www.alanrogers.com/FR50060

Le Grand Large is a well established, quality family site with direct access to a long sandy beach and within a 20 km. drive of Cherbourg. It is a neat and tidy site with 147 touring pitches divided and separated by hedging giving an orderly, well laid out appearance. A separate area has 40 mobile homes for rent. The reception area is at the entrance (with a security barrier) and the forecourt is decorated with flower beds. To the rear of the site and laid out in the sandhills is an excellent play area with swings, slides and climbing frame. Not surprisingly the sandy beach is the big attraction. Roads around the site are tarmac and there are pleasant views across the bay to the tip of the Cherbourg peninsula.

Facilities

Two well maintained toilet blocks. The main one is modern and includes washbasins in cubicles and some family rooms. WCs are mostly to the outside of the building. Provision for disabled people. Baby bathroom. Laundry area. Motorcaravan services. Shop for basics. Bar. Takeaway (4/7-29/8). WiFi. Swimming and paddling pools. Play area. Tennis. Boules. Fishing. TV room. Animation (July/Aug). Off site: Bicycle hire and riding 5 km. Golf 15 km.

Open: 11 April - 20 September.

Directions

From Cherbourg port take N13 south for about 2 km. Branch right on D650 (previously D904) signed Cartaret. Continue for 18 km. to Les Pieux. Take D4 in town and turn left just after 'Super U' supermarket. Follow site signs via D117/517. GPS: N49:29.665 W01:50.544

Charges 2009

Per unit incl. 2 persons	€ 17,00 - € 31,00
extra person	€ 4,00 - € 6,00
child (under 7 yrs)	€ 2,50 - € 3,50
electricity (6A)	€ 4,00
Camping Cheques accepted.	

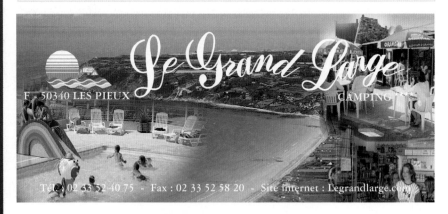

FR50070 Castel Camping Caravaning l'Anse du Brick

Route du Val de Saire, F-50330 Maupertus-sur-Mer (Manche)

Tel: **02 33 54 33 57**. Email: **welcome@anse-du-brick.com**   www.alanrogers.com/FR50070

A friendly, family site, l'Anse du Brick overlooks a picturesque bay on the northern tip of the Cotentin peninsula, eight kilometres east of Cherbourg port. Its pleasing location offers direct access to a small sandy beach and a woodland walk. This is a mature, terraced site with magnificent views from certain pitches. Tarmac roads lead to the 117 touring pitches (all with 10A electricity) which are level, separated and mostly well shaded by many trees, bushes and shrubs.

Facilities

New sanitary facilities are kept spotlessly clean and are well maintained. British style toilets, washbasins mainly in cubicles, push button showers. Provision for disabled visitors. Laundry area. Motorcaravan service point. Shop (1/4-30/9). Restaurant and bar/pizzeria (1/5-10/9). Heated swimming pool (1/5-15/9). Tennis. Play area. Organised entertainment in season. Miniclub (6-12 yrs). Bicycle and kayak hire. Off site: Fishing 100 m. Riding 4 km. Golf 10 km.

Open: 1 April - 30 September.

Directions

From Cherbourg port follow signs for Caen and Rennes. After third roundabout, take slip road to right, under road towards Bretteville-en-Saire (D116). From southeast on N13 at first (Auchan) roundabout, take slip road to right towards Tourlaville (N13 car ferry), ahead at next roundabout, right at third lights on D116 to Bretteville. Continue for 7 km. Site signed. GPS: N49:40.044 W01:29.293

Charges 2009

Per pitch incl. 2 persons and electricity	€ 19,60 - € 38,20
extra person	€ 4,10 - € 7,20

The Travel Service
...we'll arrange everything
CALL 01580 214000
BOOK THIS SITE

Check real time availability and at-the-gate prices...

www.alanrogers.com

FR50080 Kawan Village Haliotis

Chemin des Soupirs, F-50170 Pontorson (Manche)

Tel: 02 33 68 11 59. Email: camping.haliotis@wanadoo.fr   www.alanrogers.com/FR50080

The Duchesne family have achieved a remarkable transformation of this former municipal site. Situated on the edge of the little town of Pontorson and next to the river Couesnon, Camping Haliotis is within walking, cycling and canoeing distance of Mont Saint Michel. The site has 152 pitches, including 118 for touring units. Most pitches have electricity and 34 really large ones also have water and drainage. Private sanitary facilities are now available on some 'luxury' pitches. The large, comfortable reception area has been developed to incorporate a bar and restaurant.

Facilities

Very clean, renovated and well-equipped toilet block. Laundry facilities. Bar where breakfast is served. Bread to order. Heated swimming pool (cleaned daily) with jacuzzi, separate paddling pool. Sauna and solarium. Good fenced play area. Trampoline. Petanque. Archery. Large games room. Tennis court. Bicycle hire. Fishing in the River Couesnon. Japanese garden and animal park. Club for children. Off site: Local services including large supermarket, restaurants and takeaways in Pontorson within walking distance. Riding 3 km. Golf 4 km. Fishing 25 km. Beach 30 km.

Open: 1 April - 5 November.

Directions

Site is 300 m. from the town centre, west of D976, alongside the river, and is well signed from the town. GPS: N48:33.424 W01:30.670

Charges 2009

Per unit incl. 2 persons and electricity	€ 16,50 - € 22,00
with private sanitary facility	€ 18,50 - € 27,00
extra person	€ 4,50 - € 6,00
child (under 12 yrs)	€ 2,00 - € 3,50
dog	€ 0,50

Camping Cheques accepted.

Camping Haliotis ★★★

Located at 5mn from Mont-Saint-Michel along a river

NORMANDIE

Tel : +33(0)2 33 68 11 59   Fax : +33(0)2 33 58 95 36
info@camping-haliotis-mont-saint-michel.com

FR50190 Campéole Saint Grégoire

F-50170 Servon (Manche)

Tel: 02 33 60 26 03. Email: nadine.ferran@atciat.com   www.alanrogers.com/FR50190

This small rural site is simple and well cared for. Modestly sized pitches are in groups of three or four with very little indication of pitch boundaries. Shrubs and well trimmed hedges are planted throughout. Half of the 85 pitches are occupied by chalets and mobile homes. One building houses all of the facilities which are modern, bright and of a high standard. A reasonable car journey will take you to Mont St-Michel, St Malo or Avranches.

Facilities

One modern sanitary block has washbasins in cabins and controllable showers. Baby room. Very good facilities for disabled visitors. Washing machine. Takeaway (July/Aug). Small swimming pool. Boules. Play area (3-8 yrs). Torches required. Off site: Several beaches can be reached by car. Mont St-Michel. St Malo. Avranches.

Open: 1 April - 30 September.

Directions

On the RN175 from Avranches towards St Malo, take exit for Servon on the right. Site is on the right in 200 m. GPS: N48:35.822 W01:24.790

Charges guide

Per unit incl. 2 persons	€ 11,00 - € 15,40
extra person	€ 4,00 - € 6,60
child (2-6 yrs)	free - € 3,70
electricity	€ 4,00

BOOK THIS SITE
CALL 01580 214000
...we'll arrange everything
The Travel Service

Check real time availability and at-the-gate prices...

www.alanrogers.com

BOOK THIS SITE

CALL 01580 214000

...we'll arrange everything

The Travel Service

FR50110 Camping Saint-Michel

35 route du Mont Saint-Michel, F-50220 Courtils (Manche)

Tel: **02 33 70 96 90**. Email: **infos@campingsaintmichel.com**   www.alanrogers.com/FR50110

This delightful site is owned and run by an enthusiastic young couple, the Duchesnes. It is located in a peaceful, rural setting, yet is only 8 km. from the busy tourist attraction of Mont St-Michel. The site has 100 pitches which include 36 for touring units and 25 for mobile homes and chalets to rent. Electricity connections (6A) are available and many trees and shrubs provide shade to the pitches. From the restaurant and its terrace overlooking the pool, the site slopes gently down to a small enclosure of farm animals kept to entertain children and adults alike. Meet Nestor and Napoléon, the donkeys, Linotte the pony and Dédé and Dedette, the Vietnamese potbellied pigs, as well as miniature goats, sheep, chickens and ducks. It is M. and Mme. Duschesne's intention to maintain a quiet and peaceful site, hence there are no discos or organised clubs.

Facilities

The modern, well maintained toilet block has washbasins in cubicles and showers. Separate laundry. Facilities for disabled visitors in the new reception building. All is of an excellent standard. Motorcaravan service point. Shop. Bar (15/3-15/10). Restaurant and takeaway (4/6-13/9). Heated swimming pool (1/5-30/9). Animal farm. Play area. Games room. Bicycle hire. Off site: Fishing 2 km. Riding 3 km. Beach 30 km.

Open: 6 February - 4 November.

Directions

From St Malo take the N137 south and join the N176 east to Pontorson where it becomes the N175. In 20 km. turn northwest on D43 signed Courtils. Site is through village on the left. GPS: N48:37.657 W01:24.960

Charges guide

Per person	€ 4,00 - € 6,00
child (0-7 yrs)	€ 1,80 - € 2,50
pitch incl. car	€ 4,50 - € 6,00
electricity (6A)	€ 3,00
dog	€ 1,00

Camping Saint-Michel***

We invite those seeking respite to our lush floral garden, only 8 km from Mont Saint Michel, for relaxing stays with your family.

Bar, restaurant (15/06 to 15/09), shop, warmed swimming pool (01/05 to 30/09), Animals park with play garden for children, washing and drying machines, fishing (3 km), bay of Mont Saint Michel for walking (3 km)

Open march 15 till october 15

35 • route du Mont-Saint-Michel • 50220 Courtils • France
tel. 02 33 70 96 90 • fax 02 33 70 99 09

FR50200 Yelloh! Village les Vikings

F-50270 Saint Jean de la Riviere (Manche)

Tel: **04 66 73 97 39**. Email: **info@yellohvillage-lesvikings.com**   www.alanrogers.com/FR50200

Les Vikings is located close to the attractive resort of Barneville-Carteret on the western side of the Cherbourg peninsula. The site is just 400 m. from a sandy beach. There are 250 pitches of which around 90 are reserved for touring, the rest being occupied by mobile homes and chalets, some of which are for rent. Pitches are grassy and of a reasonable size. Most of the site's amenities are grouped around the entrance and these include a swimming pool, a restaurant/pizzeria and a bar. During the peak season, various activities are organized including discos and karaoke evenings.

Facilities

Shop. Bar. Restaurant, snack bar and takeaway. Swimming pool. Games room. Play area. Activity and entertainment programme. Mobile homes for rent. Off site: Supermarket. Trips to the Channel Islands and D-day beaches. Mont St-Michel.

Open: 1 April - 4 October.

Directions

From Cherbourg, head southwest on the D650 to Barneville-Carteret. Site is at St Jean de la Rivière, just to the south of the town and clearly signed. GPS: N49:21.846 W01:45.208

Charges 2009

Per unit incl. 2 persons and electricity	€ 15,00 - € 39,00
extra person	€ 5,00 - € 7,00

tel: +33 466 739 739 www.yellohvillage.com ──────

yelloh! VILLAGE

Check real time availability and at-the-gate prices...

www.alanrogers.com

FR50170 Camping le Lac des Charmilles

Route de Vire, F-50160 Torigni-sur-Vire (Manche)

Tel: 02 33 56 91 74. Email: contact@camping-lacdescharmilles.com   www.alanrogers.com/FR50170

The very friendly new owners have recently acquired this former municipal site and have already made some outstanding changes. Situated next to a lake on the outskirts of Torigni-sur-Vire (1 km) and surrounded by farmers' fields the 39 touring pitches are divided by mature hedges giving plenty of privacy. Additions have included an exceptional new bar and restaurant with an attractive wooden terrace, a new sanitary block providing the most modern facilities and a multisport court along with trampolines and bouncy castle. So, although still lacking some facilities, the first-class additions already installed make this a great choice if visiting this area. There are plans to increase the number of pitches and with so much unused land much more may be achieved over the coming months and years.

Facilities

Two sanitary blocks including one new central block with excellent facilities including those for disabled visitors. Bar/restaurant with full menu and takeaway. Outdoor swimming pool (heated 15/6-15/9). TV, table tennis, go-karts, pétanque, multisport court, trampoline, bouncy castle. Motorhome service point. Large units accepted. Off site: Fishing 200 m. Village with shops, bars, banks etc. 1 km. Canoes 5 km. Riding 13 km. Golf 30 km. Beaches of Normandy 45 mins.

Open: Easter - 31 October.

Directions

Exit the A84 Caen - Rennes motorway at junction 40 and head north on the N174 towards St Lô. The campsite is on your right just before you enter the town of Torigni-sur-Vire.
GPS: N49:01.711 W00:58.314

Charges guide

Per pitch incl. 2 persons and electricity	€ 16,20 - € 20,80
extra person	€ 3,90
child (0-6 yrs)	€ 2,90
dog	€ 1,50

Camping Cheques accepted.

Camping le Lac des CHARMILLES TORIGNI-SUR-VIRE — 2 campings ★★★ — Camping DES CHEVALIERS VILLEDIEU-LES-POÊLES

Norman settings, camping-caravaning, holiday homes for rent. Bar, restaurant, take away, sports field, play area, heated swimming pool

Camping le Lac des Charmilles*
Route de Vire - 50160 Torigni sur Vire
Tel: 0033 (0) 233 569 174 - contact@camping-lacdescharmilles.com
www.camping-lacdescharmilles.com

Camping des Chevaliers*
2 Impasse Pré de la Rose - 50800 Villedieu-les-Poêles
Tel: 0033 (0) 233 610 244 - contact@camping-deschevaliers.com
www.camping-deschevaliers.com

FR50180 Camping des Chevaliers

2 impasse Pré de la Rose, F-50800 Villedieu-les-Poêles (Manche)

Tel: 02 33 61 02 44. Email: contact@camping-deschevaliers.com   www.alanrogers.com/FR50180

This pleasant site is situated less than a five minute walk from the attractive and interesting town of Villedieu-les-Poêles with its history of metalwork shops and foundries. This former municipal site is undergoing many modernisations and so far the sanitary facilities have been renovated and a heated (15/6-15/9) outdoor swimming pool added. The 101 touring pitches are separated by low hedges and there are many mature trees giving plenty of shade. There are plenty of electrical hook-ups (4, 8 or 13A). A small river runs alongside the site which is safely fenced with gate access.

Facilities

Two sanitary blocks provide adequate facilities. One main block situated behind reception has all modern facilities, the other centrally located with toilets and sinks only. Bar and restaurant with terrace. Takeaway snacks and pizzas. Multisport court. Purpose-built skateboard park. Playground with trampoline and bouncy castle. Go-karts and bicycle hire. Fishing. Off site: Shops, bars, restaurants in town 500 m.

Open: 11 April - 31 October.

Directions

From the A84 Rennes-Caen motorway, take exit 37 and head east on the D524 to Villedieu-les-Poêles. Follow signs for the Office de Tourisme and continue on, keeping the Office and Post Office on your left. The campsite is 200 m. on your left.
GPS: N48:50.199 W01:13.018

Charges guide

Per unit incl. 2 persons and electricity	€ 19,20 - € 22,80
extra person	€ 3,90

Check real time availability and at-the-gate prices...
www.alanrogers.com

FR50150 Kawan Village la Route Blanche

F-50290 Breville-sur-Mer (Manche)

Tel: 02 33 50 23 31. Email: larouteblanche@camping-breville.com   www.alanrogers.com/FR50150

La Route Blanche has a bright and cheerful atmosphere and Philippe and Corinne, the owners, are working continually to make an excellent site even better. The 140 pitches for touring are generous and numbered on well-cut grass and divided by young conifers. There are many shrubs and flowers and mature trees give shade to some areas. 67 pitches have 6/10A electricity and long leads may be necessary for some. Although the site does not have its own restaurant, there are five to choose from within a short distance and the beaches of Breville-sur-Mer are within a ten minute walk.

Facilities

Well maintained sanitary facilities with British style toilets, washbasins in cabins and showers. Good provision for disabled visitors. Laundry and dishwashing facilities. Bread available all season. Bar and takeaway (July/Aug). New large swimming pool complex with flumes, toboggan and bubble pool. Play area. Multisports court. Entertainment in high season. Off site: Golf (opposite). Fishing 500 m. Riding 1 km.

Open: 1 April - 31 October.

Directions

Take D971 that runs between Granville and Coutance. Then one of the roads west to Breville-sur-Mer. Site is well signed.
GPS: N48:52.176 W01:33.762

Charges guide

Per pitch incl. 2 persons	€ 16,00 - € 24,00
electricity (6/10A)	€ 2,60 - € 3,60
extra person	€ 3,50 - € 4,50
child (2-7 yrs)	€ 1,80 - € 2,20
dog	€ 2,00 - € 2,50
Camping Cheques accepted.	

Camp site La Route Blanche ***

Flowered camp site full with charme and exceptional nature. At 5 km distance from the sea resort of Granville. Located in the bay of the Mount Saint Michel facing the Channel Islands: Jersey and Guernesey.

6, La Route Blanche, 50290 Breville sur Mer
Tel: 0033 (0)2 33 50 23 31
Fax: 0033 (0)2 33 50 26 47
larouteblanche@camping-breville.com
www.camping-breville.com

FR61010 Camping Municipal la Campière

Boulevard du Docteur Dentu, F-61120 Vimoutiers (Orne)

Tel: 02 33 39 18 86. Email: mairie.vimoutiers@wanadoo.fr   www.alanrogers.com/FR61010

This small, well kept site is situated in a valley to the north of the town, which is on both the Normandy Cheese and Cider routes. Indeed the town is famous for its cheese and has a Camembert Museum, five minutes walk away in the town centre. The 40 pitches here are flat and grassy, separated by laurel hedging and laid out amongst attractive and well maintained flower and shrub beds. There is some shade around the perimeter and all pitches have electricity.

Facilities

The single central sanitary block is clean and heated, providing open washbasins, good sized, well designed showers, children's toilets and a bathroom for disabled visitors. Dishwashing and laundry facilities under cover. Off site: No shop but a large supermarket is 300 m. Tennis courts and a park are adjacent. Water sports facilities or riding 2 km.

Open: March - October.

Directions

Site is on northern edge of town, signed from main Lisieux-Argentan road next to large sports complex.
GPS: N48:55.954 E00:11.805

Charges guide

Per person	€ 2,30 - € 2,75
child (under 10 yrs)	€ 1,34 - € 1,60
pitch	€ 1,63 - € 1,95
extra car	€ 1,63 - € 1,95
animal	€ 0,92 - € 1,10
Reductions for 7th and subsequent days.	

FR61040 Camping Municipal du Champ Passais

F-61700 Domfront (Orne)

Tel: 02 33 37 37 66. Email: mairie@domfront.com   www.alanrogers.com/FR61040

Situated on the edge of the fascinating fortified town of Domfront, this small site has 34 individual pitches on a series of level terraces and a separate open grassy area for tents. The nine pitches nearest the entrance are all hardstandings separated by grass and with 10A electricity. Grass pitches on the lower levels, divided by shrubs and hedges, have 5A electricity and most have water and waste water points. The site is cared for by a lady warden who keeps everything immaculate and is justifiably proud of the entries in her visitors' book.

Facilities

Excellent sanitary facilities include British style toilets and some washbasins in cubicles. Facilities for disabled people. Washing machine. Motorcaravan service point outside gate (small charge). No separate chemical disposal point, but a notice tells visitors where to empty toilet cassettes. TV. Boules. Play area. Double axle caravans not accepted under any circumstances; American RVs can be accommodated. Off site: Sports centre adjacent. Supermarket 800 m. Fishing and bicycle hire 1 km. Riding 15 km.

Open: 1 April - 30 September.

Directions

Domfront is on the N176 Alençon - Mont St-Michel road and site is just off this to the south of town; signed to the right up the hill towards town centre - or the left as you leave town heading west. GPS: N48:35.491 W00:39.146

Charges guide

Per unit incl. 2 persons	€ 5,70
extra person	€ 2,65
child (under 10 yrs)	€ 1,35
electricity (10A)	€ 4,00

No credit cards.

FR76010 Camping le Marqueval

1210, rue de la Mer, F-76550 Pourville-sur-Mer (Seine-Maritime)

Tel: 02 35 82 66 46. Email: contact@campinglemarqueval.com   www.alanrogers.com/FR76010

Le Marqueval is a well established family site of 290 pitches, located close to the seaside town of Hautot-sur-Mer, just west of Dieppe. The site has been developed around three small lakes (suitable for fishing). Pitches are grassy and all are separated by hedges and of a good size. All have electrical connections (6A). Leisure amenities include a swimming pool and smaller children's pool. The site's bar also functions as a snack bar and during the high season evening entertainment is occasionally organized here. The site's owners will be happy to recommend places of interest in the area and these include Dieppe, with its old town, and the stylish resort of Le Tréport. This stretch of the Normandy coastline is well known for its towering white cliffs and fine sandy beaches. There are superb coastal walks along the clifftops and quiet lanes, ideal for exploration by cycle. The nearby château at Miromesnil, birthplace of Maupassant, is well worth a visit and has magnificent gardens.

Facilities

Snack bar. Swimming pool. Fishing. Playground. Entertainment and activity programme. Mobile homes for rent. Off site: Nearest beach 1.2 km. Riding 1.5 km. Tennis. Cycle and walking tracks. Dieppe 5 km. St Valery-en-Caux (fishing port).

Open: 17 March - 15 October.

Directions

Head west from Dieppe on the D925 as far as Hautot-sur-Mer. Then turn right onto the D153 towards Pourville. Site is well signed from here. GPS: N49:54.528 E01:02.436

Charges 2009

Per unit incl. 2 persons and electricity	€ 15,00 - € 21,50
extra person	€ 4,00 - € 6,50
child (under 7 yrs)	€ 3,00 - € 3,50
dog	€ 1,00 - € 2,00

CAMPING LE MARQUEVAL**

CAMPING LE MARQUEVAL** - 1210 RUE DE LA MER - 76550 POURVILLE SUR MER
TEL: 0033 235 82 66 46 - FAX: 0033 235 4010 36
CONTACT@CAMPINGLEMARQUEVAL.COM - WWW.CAMPINGLEMARQUEVAL.COM

Check real time availability and at-the-gate prices...

www.alanrogers.com

FR76020 Camping Municipal Le Val Boise

Avenue Du Capitaine Portheous, 76370 Berneval Le Grand (Seine-Maritime)

Tel: 02 35 85 29 18. Email: camping-berneval@wanadoo.fr   www.alanrogers.com/FR76020

This pleasant, well run municipal site is located in a wooded valley running down from the village to the sea. The reception and a group of 14 larger pitches, a few occupied by seasonal caravans, are situated next to the road leading down to the sand and shingle beaches. There are also six attractive wooden chalets for hire. The remaining 16 touring pitches are on wooded terraces. All pitches have 16A electricity but only a few have shade. Ideal for a simple, inexpensive site close to Dieppe.

Facilities

Two well maintained toilet blocks provide free hot showers and some washbasins in cubicles. Facilities for disabled visitors. Laundry facilities. Motorcaravan service point. Activities room. Small play area. Field for kite flying and ball games. Children's activities and tournaments (July/August). Free internet access in reception, plus free WiFi (also on adjacent pitches). Off site: Beach and sea fishing 600 m. Boat launching 3 km. Riding, sailing and bicycle hire 10 km. Golf 12 km. Fishing 15 km.

Open: 1 April - 1 November.

Directions

Berneval is 10 km. east of Dieppe. From A29 take N27 to Dieppe, turn east on ring road to join D925 towards Le Tréport. From ferry: after 2 km. turn east on D925. In about 5 km turn north on D54 to Berneval le Grand and in village follow site signs. GPS: N49:57.722 E01:11.617

Charges guide

Per person	€ 1,60 - € 2,00
pitch	€ 4,55 - € 5,40
electricity (16A)	€ 2,70 - € 3,50

FR76030 Camping Vitamin

865 chemin de Vertus, 76550 St Aubin Surscie (Seine-Maritime)

Tel: 02 35 82 11 11. Email: camping.vitamin@wanadoo.fr   www.alanrogers.com/FR76030

Although the address is St Aubin, this site is actually on the outskirts of Dieppe and is only a couple of kilometres from the seafront and the shops. Those arriving or leaving by ferry could find it useful for a stopover as it is just off the main N27 to Rouen. It has a very French atmosphere, with large numbers of privately owned mobile homes and seasonal caravans. However, the 44 touring pitches (all with 10A electricity) are attractively laid out and there is a sense of spaciousness.

Facilities

Two excellent and well maintained toilet blocks (one unisex) provide free showers and washbasins in cubicles. Facilities for disabled visitors. Baby bath. Washing machines and dryers. Motorcaravan service point. Bar serving snacks (1/6-30/9) and entertainment (July/Aug). Heated swimming pool (15/6-15/9). Adventure playground and field for games. Multisports court. Games barn. Large pétanque pitch. Sports tournaments in high season. Off site: Supermarket 200 m. Centre Commercial 800 m. Golf and riding 1 km. Beach, boat launching, sailing and sea fishing 2 km. Fishing 8 km.

Open: 1 April - 15 October.

Directions

From south on the N27, continue towards Dieppe. After roundabout with D915, take slip road and pass under road following signs for Formule 1 and Hotel B&B. Continue ahead to site. From ferry terminal head southeast to turn west onto ringroad. Follow this, keeping right at large roundabout (Leclerc) and left at next onto N27 (Rouen). At roundabout (Auchan), turn south on N27. Take sliproad and turn right to site. GPS: N49:54.038 E01:04.482

Charges guide

Per unit incl. 2 persons and electricity	€ 16,50
extra person	€ 4,50

FR76040 Camping la Source

Petit Appeville, F-76550 Hautot-sur-Mer (Seine-Maritime)

Tel: 02 35 84 27 04. Email: info@camping-la-source.fr   www.alanrogers.com/FR76040

This friendly, attractive site with a new heated pool is just four kilometres from Dieppe and is useful for those using the Newhaven - Dieppe ferry crossing either as a one night stop-over or for a few days' break before heading on. The 120 pitches are flat and there is some shade. There are good hardstandings for motorcaravans and electricity is available. A fast-flowing small river runs along one border (not protected for young children).

Facilities

A good, clean single toilet block (men left, ladies right) includes washbasins in cubicles and mainly British style WCs. En-suite unit for disabled people but the unmade gravel roads may cause problems. Laundry facilities. Small bar and terrace. Swimming pool. Playing field. TV and games rooms. Fishing. Bicycle hire. Off site: Riding 2 km. Beach 3 km. Golf 4 km.

Open: 15 March - 15 October.

Directions

From Dieppe follow D925 west to Fécamp. At foot of descent at traffic lights in Petit Appeville turn left. From west, turn right (signed D153 St Aubin). Just after railway, turn left under bridge and ahead on narrow road. Site is shortly on left. GPS: N49:53.925 E01:03.398

Charges guide

Per person	€ 4,50 - € 5,00
pitch incl. car	€ 6,30 - € 8,30
electricity (6A)	€ 2,60
Camping Cheques accepted.	

Check real time availability and at-the-gate prices...
www.alanrogers.com

FR76090 Camping Municipal d'Etennemare

Hameau d'Etennemare, F-76460 Saint Valery-en-Caux (Seine-Maritime)

Tel: 02 35 97 15 79   www.alanrogers.com/FR76090

This comfortable, neat municipal site is two kilometres from the harbour and town, 30 km. west of Dieppe. Quietly located, it has 116 pitches of which 49 are available for touring units. The grassy pitches are all on a slight slope, all with electricity (6A), water and drain, but there is very little shade. Reception is open all day in July and August, but in low season is closed 12.00-15.00 hrs daily and all day Wednesday: there is a card-operated security barrier.

Facilities

Two modern, clean and well maintained sanitary buildings are side by side, one containing showers and the other, more recently refitted, has toilets, both open and cubicled washbasins and facilities for disabled people. Both blocks can be heated in winter. Dishwashing and laundry sinks. Washing machines. Small shop (July/Aug). Playground. Table tennis. Off site: Hypermarket 1.5 km. Harbour and beach (pebbles) 2 km.

Open: All year.

Directions

From Dieppe keep to D925 Fécamp road (not through town). At third roundabout turn right on D925E towards hypermarket. From Fécamp turn left on D925E as before. Take first right (site signed) to site on left in 1 km. GPS: N49:51.515 E00:42.279

Charges guide

Per unit incl. 2 persons and electricity	€ 13,40
extra person	€ 2,75
child (under 10 yrs)	€ 1,75

FR76130 Camping de la Forêt

Rue Mainberthe, F-76480 Jumièges (Seine-Maritime)

Tel: 02 35 37 93 43. Email: info@campinglaforet.com   www.alanrogers.com/FR76130

This is a pretty family site with a friendly laid back atmosphere. It is located just 10 km. from the A13 Paris - Caen autoroute. Cars and smaller motorcaravans can approach by ferry across the River Seine (not caravans). The site was formerly a municipal and has recently been taken on by the Joret family. The 111 grassy pitches (84 for tourers) are attractively located in woodland. Many pitches have some shade and all have 10A electrical connections. There is a separate area for tents. The site organises some activities in high season and these include treasure hunts and guided walks. Jumièges is just 600 m. away. The great abbey at Jumièges was founded in 654 by St Philibert, rebuilt by the Normans and consecrated in the presence of William the Conqueror – well worth a visit! A good range of shops, cafes, restaurants etc. can also be found here.

Facilities

Two toilet blocks, both of modern construction and maintained to a good standard with British toilets, some basins in cubicles and pre-set showers. Baby room. Facilities for disabled visitors. Laundry facilities. Motorcaravan service point. Shop. Baker calls daily. Pizzas on Friday and Saturday evenings 18.30 hrs. Small swimming pool and paddling pool (heated 1/6-15/9). Playground. Boules. Games room with TV. Bicycle hire. Chalets and mobile homes to let.

Open: 11 April - 25 October.

Directions

From A29, junction 8, follow Yvetot - Pon de Brotonne. Before bridge, turn left and follow Le Trait and Jumièges. Site clearly signed. GPS: N49:26.092 E00:49.738

Charges guide

Per unit incl. 2 persons	€ 16,00 - € 26,00
extra person	€ 4,00 - € 4,50
child (under 7 yrs)	€ 1,90
electricity	€ 4,00

Reduced charges in low season.
Camping Cheques accepted.

BOOK THIS SITE
CALL 01580 214000
...we'll arrange everything
The Travel Service

CAMPING DE LA FORÊT ★ ★ ★ ★

Rue Mainberte
76480 JUMIÈGES
Tél 02 35 37 93 43
Fax 02 35 37 76 48
www.campinglaforet.com
info@campinglaforet.com

Check real time availability and at-the-gate prices...

www.alanrogers.com

FR76100 Camping Municipal Cany-Barville

Route de Barville, F-76450 Cany-Barville (Seine-Maritime)

Tel: 02 35 97 70 37. Email: camping-canybarville@orange.fr

www.alanrogers.com/FR76100

This good quality site, first opened in 1997 next to the municipal sports stadium, has a floral entrance and tarmac roads. Of the 100 individual hedged pitches 75 are available for tourists. There are around 40 concrete hardstandings (awnings can be a problem) and the remainder are on grass: all are fully serviced with water, drainage and electric hook-ups (10A). Shade from new specimen trees is still very limited. Cany-Barville is a bustling small town with a traditional Normandy market on Monday mornings.

Facilities

The modern, centrally located, sanitary unit can be heated and has British style toilets, controllable showers and washbasins in cubicles. Laundry facilities. Copious hot water. Separate suites for disabled people. Drive-over motorcaravan service point. Boules. Games room. Off site: Bakery, restaurants 600 m. Supermarket 1 km. Sailing and windsurfing centre 2 km. Beach 10 km.

Open: 1 April - 1 October.

Directions

Cany-Barville is 20 km. east of Fécamp on D925 to Dieppe. From traffic lights on east of town turn south on D268 towards Yvetot. Go under railway. Site is 600 m. from town on right, after stadium. GPS: N49:46.990 E00:38.546

Charges guide

Per person	€ 3,05
child (under 14 yrs)	€ 1,30
pitch	€ 2,00 - € 3,05

FR76110 Camping Municipal les Boucaniers

Rue Pierre Mendès France, F-76470 le Tréport (Seine-Maritime)

Tel: 02 35 86 35 47. Email: camping@ville-le-treport.fr

www.alanrogers.com/FR76110

This is a large, good quality, municipal site which has undergone redevelopment. It has an attractive entrance and some floral displays, tarmac roads and site lighting. The 260 pitches are on level grass, some with dividing hedges, and trees to provide a little shade. There are 22 good quality wooden chalets for rent, and some privately owned mobile homes, which leaves around 215 pitches for tourists, all with electric hook-ups (6A; some long leads are needed). A small unit acts as shop, bar and takeaway. The baker calls daily in high season, and every day except Monday in low season.

Facilities

Three well equipped sanitary blocks (one can be heated) provide mainly British style WCs, washbasins in cubicles, pre-set hot showers, with new facilities for small children and disabled persons in one block. Multisport court. Minigolf. Boules. Off site: Tennis, football and gymnasium nearby. Fishing, golf and beach 2 km. Riding 3 km. Markets at Le Tréport (Mon and Sat) and at Eu (Fri).

Open: Easter weekend - 30 September.

Directions

From D925 Abbeville - Dieppe road take D1915 towards Le Tréport centre. At new roundabout take first exit to right and site entrance is 150 m. on the right in rue Pierre Mendès-France. GPS: N50:03.463 E01:23.322

Charges guide

Per person	€ 2,95
child (2-10 yrs)	€ 1,75
pitch	€ 2,85
incl. electricity	€ 6,95

FR76120 Camping Municipal Veulettes-sur-Mer

8 rue de Greenock, F-76450 Veulettes-sur-Mer (Seine-Maritime)

Tel: 02 35 97 53 44

www.alanrogers.com/FR76120

A good value, well kept municipal site in an attractive little coastal town, just 500 m. from the beach and all town services. There are 116 marked pitches on open level grass, 40 of which are seasonal pitches, which leaves 76 pitches for touring units, all with electric hook-ups, water and waste water drainage. Reception keeps soft drinks and ices during July/August. Also on site is an attractive 'salle' (open all day in July/August) with a library and TV, a games area, table tennis, babyfoot and further toilet facilities. There is a traffic free cycle path to the next village 4 km. away.

Facilities

Three good modern sanitary units in traditional style buildings are of varying ages (one can be heated). These provide pre-set hot showers, washbasins in cubicles, and facilities for disabled people in the smallest unit on the far side of the site. Laundry room. Playground. Boules. TV and library. Off site: Public park with tennis courts and large playground, beach (pebble), watersports centre and all shops and services are within 500 m. Golf 200 m. Fishing 1 km. Beach 500 m.

Open: 1 April - 31 October.

Directions

Veulettes-sur-Mer is on the coast about 45 km. west of Dieppe. Site is central in town, lying about 500 m. back from the main promenade (signed). GPS: N49:50.967 E00:35.791

Charges guide

Per person	€ 2,70
child (4-10 yrs)	€ 1,35
pitch	€ 2,35
electricity (10A)	€ 2,70
car	€ 1,10

Check real time availability and at-the-gate prices...

www.alanrogers.com

MAP 3

Northern France, with its lush countryside and market towns, is much more than just a stop off en-route to or from the ports. The peaceful rural unspoilt charms of the region provide a real breath of fresh air.

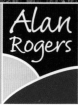

Alan Rogers

NORD/PAS DE CALAIS: 59 NORD, 62 PAS-DE-CALAIS
MAJOR CITY: LILLE

PICARDY: 02 AISNE, 60 OISE, 80 SOMME
MAJOR CITY: AMIENS

This is a region where centuries of invaders have left their mark. At Vimy Ridge near Arras, World War One trenches have been preserved intact, a most poignant sight. Elsewhere almost every village between Arras and Amiens has its memorial. It is also the birthplace of Gothic architecture with six cathedrals, including Laon, Beauvais and Amiens, arguably the grandest in France.

The area however is predominately rural. Inland and south are long vistas of rolling farmland broken by little rivers and well scattered with pockets of forest woodland. The coastline is characterised by sandy beaches, shifting dunes and ports. It is a quiet and sparsely populated area with peaceful villages and churches that provide evidence of the glorious achievements of French Gothic architecture. Boulogne is home to Nausicaa, the world's largest sea-life centre and from Cap Griz-Nez you may be able to see the White Cliffs of Dover. There are also many huge hypermarkets where you may stock up on wine, beer and cheese.

Places of interest

Amiens: Notre Dame cathedral, monument to 1918 Battle of the Somme.

Chantilly: Château of Chantilly with a 17th-century stable with a 'live' Horse museum.

Compiègne: Seven miles east of the town is Clairière de l'Armistice. The railway coach here is a replica of the one in which the 1918 Armistice was signed and in which Hitler received the French surrender in 1942.

Laon: 12th-century cathedral, WW1 trenches, Vauclair Abbey.

Marquenterre: one of Europe's most important bird sanctuaries.

Cuisine of the region

Carbonnade de Boeuf à la Flamande: braised beef with beer, onions and bacon.

Caudière (Chaudière, Caudrée): versions of fish and potato soup.

Ficelles Picardes: ham pancakes with mushroom sauce.

Flamiche aux poireaux: puff pastry tart with cream and leeks.

Hochepot: a thick Flemish soup with virtually everything in it but the kitchen sink.

Soupe courquignoise: soup with white wine, fish, moules, leeks and Gruyère cheese.

Tarte aux Maroilles: a hot creamy tart based on Maroilles cheese.

Waterzooï: a cross between soup and stew, usually of fish or chicken.

BOOK THIS SITE
CALL 01580 214000
...we'll arrange everything
The Travel Service

FR02000 Camping Caravaning du Vivier aux Carpes

10 rue Charles Voyeux, F-02790 Seraucourt-le-Grand (Aisne)

Tel: 03 23 60 50 10. Email: camping.du.vivier@wanadoo.fr   www.alanrogers.com/FR02000

Vivier aux Carpes is a small quiet site, close to the A26, two hours from Calais, so is an ideal overnight stop but is also worthy of a longer stay. The 59 well spaced pitches, are at least 100 sq.m. on flat grass with dividing hedges. The 40 for touring units all have electricity (6A), some also with water points, and there are special pitches for motorcaravans. This is a neat, purpose designed site imaginatively set out with a comfortable feel. The enthusiastic owners and manager speak excellent English and are keen to welcome British visitors.

Facilities

The spacious, clean toilet block has separate, heated facilities for disabled visitors, made available to other campers in the winter. Laundry facilities. Motorcaravan service point (fresh water for large vans is charged). Large TV/games room. Small play area. Bicycle hire. Pétanque. Fishing. Gates close 22.00 hrs, office open 09.00-21.30. Rallies welcome. WiFi. Off site: Village has post office, doctor and supermarket. Riding 500 m. Golf 12 km.

Open: 1 March - 30 October.

Directions

Leave A26 (Calais - Reims) at exit 11. Take D1 left towards Soissons for 4 km. Take D8, on entering Essigny-le-Grand (4 km.) turn sharp right on D72 signed Seraucourt-le-Grand (5 km). Site signed. GPS: N49:46.915 E03:12.850

Charges 2009

Per unit incl. 2 persons and electricity	€ 18,50
extra person	€ 3,70

No credit cards.

FR02030 Caravaning la Croix du Vieux Pont

F-02290 Berny-Riviere (Aisne)

Tel: 03 23 55 50 02. Email: info@la-croix-du-vieux-pont.com   www.alanrogers.com/FR02030

Located on the banks of the River Aisne, La Croix du Vieux Pont is a very smart, modern 34 hectare site offering a high standard of facilities. Many pitches are occupied by mobile homes and tour operator tents, but there are 60 pleasant touring pitches, some on the banks of the Aisne. Maintained to a high standard, the excellent amenities include four heated swimming pools, one indoors with a waterslide and jacuzzi. At the heart of the site is a well stocked fishing lake which is also used for pedaloes and canoes.

Facilities

The six toilet blocks are modern and kept very clean, with washbasins in cabins and free hot showers. Laundry facilities. Facilities for disabled visitors. Large supermarket. Bar, takeaway and good value restaurant (most amenities 1/4-30/9). Swimming pool complex (covered pool 1/4-30/10, outdoor 1/5-30/9). Play area. Fishing. Bicycle hire. Apartments to let. Off site: Riding 100 m. Golf 30 km.

Open: 8 April - 31 October.

Directions

From Compiegne take N31 towards Soissons. At Vic-sur-Aisne turn right, towards Berny-Riviere and site is on right after 400 m. GPS: N49:24.292 E03:07.704

Charges guide

Per unit incl. 2 persons and electricity	€ 21,50 - € 24,00
incl. 4 persons	€ 30,50 - € 33,00

Camping Cheques accepted.

FR59010 Camping Caravaning la Chaumière

529 Langhemast Straete, F-59285 Buysscheure (Nord)

Tel: 03 28 43 03 57. Email: camping.LaChaumiere@wanadoo.fr   www.alanrogers.com/FR59010

This is a very friendly, pleasant site, in the département du Nord with a strong Flanders influence, There is a real welcome here. Set just behind the village of Buysscheure, the site has 29 touring pitches separated by trees and bushes. Each pair shares a light, electricity connections, water points and rubbish container. Access from narrow site roads can be difficult. A small, fenced fishing lake contains some large carp (seen!) A bonus is that Bernadette works for the local vet and can arrange all the documentation for British visitors' pets. English is spoken.

Facilities

Modern unisex toilet facilities are simple and small in number, with two WCs, one shower and one washbasin cabin. Facilities for disabled visitors may also be used (a toilet and separate washbasin/shower room). Dishwashing and laundry facilities. Motorcaravan services. Basic chemical disposal. Bar (daily) and restaurant (weekends only, all day, in season). Dog exercise area. Heated outdoor pools. Play area. Minigolf. Archery. Off site: Local market (Monday) at Bergues. St Omer. Beach 30 km. Lille 60 km.

Open: 1 April - 30 September.

Directions

From Calais take N43 (St Omer) for 25 km. Just beyond Nordausques take D221 left (Watten). In Watten turn left for centre, then right on D26 (Cassel). Soon after Lederzeele site signed to right. On reaching Buysscheure turn left, then right, site signed. Single track road (1 km.) with bend. GPS: N50:48.091 E02:20.354

Charges 2009

Per unit incl. 2 persons and electricity	€ 18,00
extra person	€ 7,00

No credit cards.

Check real time availability and at-the-gate prices...
www.alanrogers.com

FR60020 Aestiva Camping de Sorel

Rue Saint-Claude, F-60490 Orvillers-Sorel (Oise)

Tel: **03 44 85 02 74**. Email: **contact@aestiva.fr**   www.alanrogers.com/FR60020

Aestiva Camping de Sorel is located north of Compiègne, close to the A1 motorway and is ideal as an overnight stop. The site has 80 large grassy pitches, of which 60 are available for touring, all with electrical connections. The original farm buildings have been carefully converted to house the site's amenities including a bar, TV room and the toilet facilities. The site is open for a long season but most amenities are only open from April to September. The site is, however, close to the village of Sorel with its shops and restaurants. There are two mobile homes for rent. Compiègne lies 15 km to the south and its château is well worth a visit and houses a number of interesting museums. There is also an important golf course in the town. Closer to the site, the GR123 long distance footpath runs through Sorel, and offers the opportunity to explore the surrounding countryside on foot.

Facilities

Toilet block with facilities for children and disabled visitors. Motorcaravan service point. Small shop. Bar, snack bar and takeaway (15/4-30/9). TV room. Play area. Boules. Hairdressing service. Bicycle hire. WiFi. Off site: Tennis. Riding 5 km. Fishing 10 km. Golf 15 km. Compiègne 15 km.

Open: 2 February - 14 December.

Directions

Take exit 11 from the A1 motorway (Lille - Paris) and join the northbound N17. Site is signed to the right on reaching village of Sorel after around 8 km. GPS: N49:34.013 E02:42.505

Charges guide

Per unit incl. 2 persons and electricity	€ 29,00
extra person	€ 6,00
child (under 7 yrs)	€ 3,00
Camping Cheques accepted.	

FR60010 Camping Campix

B.P. 37, F-60340 Saint Leu-d'Esserent (Oise)

Tel: **03 44 56 08 48**. Email: **campix@orangel.fr**   www.alanrogers.com/FR60010

This informal site has been unusually developed in a former sandstone quarry on the outskirts of the small town. The quarry walls provide a sheltered, peaceful environment and trees soften the slopes. Not a neat, manicured site, the 160 pitches are in small groups on the different levels with stone and gravel access roads (some fairly steep and muddy in poor weather). Electricity (6A) is available to all the pitches. There are many secluded corners mostly for smaller units and tents and space for children to explore (parents must supervise – some areas, although fenced, could be dangerous). Torches are advised.

Facilities

A large building houses reception and two clean, heated sanitary units - one for tourers, the other (open July/Aug) usually reserved for groups. Two suites for disabled people double as baby rooms. Laundry area. Facilities may be congested at peak times. Motorcaravan services. Daily bread and milk. Pizza and other Italian food delivered in the evenings (July/Aug). Play area. Off site: Fishing 1 or 5 km. Riding and golf 5 km.

Open: 7 March - 30 November.

Directions

St Leu-d'Esserent is 11 km. west of Senlis, 5 km. northwest of Chantilly. From north on A1 autoroute take Senlis exit, from Paris the Chantilly exit. Site north of town off D12 towards Cramoisy, and signed in village. GPS: N49:13.509 E02:25.638

Charges guide

Per person	€ 3,50 - € 5,50
child (under 9 yrs)	€ 2,00 - € 3,50
pitch	€ 4,00 - € 5,50
electricity	€ 2,50 - € 3,50
dog	€ 1,50 - € 2,00
Camping Cheques accepted.	

Check real time availability and at-the-gate prices...
www.alanrogers.com

BOOK THIS SITE
CALL 01580 214000
...we'll arrange everything
The Travel Service

FR62010 Castel Camping Caravaning la Bien-Assise

D231, F-62340 Guines (Pas-de-Calais)

Tel: 03 21 35 20 77. Email: castels@bien-assise.com

www.alanrogers.com/FR62010

A mature and well developed site, the history of La Bien-Assise goes back to the 1500s. There are 198 grass pitches mainly set among mature trees with others on a newer field. Connected by gravel roads and of a good size (up to 300 sq.m), shrubs and bushes divide most of the pitches. Being close to Calais, the Channel Tunnel exit and Boulogne, makes it a good stopping point en-route. At times it can be very busy here (when maintenance can be variable). Used by tour operators (40 pitches).

Facilities

Three well equipped toilet blocks provide many washbasins in cabins, mostly British style WCs and provision for babies, laundry and dishwashing. The main block is in four sections, two unisex. Motorcaravan service point. Shop. Restaurant. Bar/grill and takeaway (evenings from 1/5). TV room. Pool complex (1/5-20/9) with toboggan, covered paddling pool and outdoor pool. Play areas. Minigolf. Tennis. Bicycle hire. Off site: Fishing 8 km. Beach 9 km. Riding 10 km.

Open: 25 April - 20 September.

Directions

From ferry or tunnel follow signs for A16 Boulogne. Take exit 11 (Frethun, Gare TGV) and RD215 (Frethun). At first roundabout take third exit (Guines). Pass under the TGV. In Frethun take RD246 towards Guines and St Tricat and at roundabout take exit for Guines. Pass through St Tricat and Hames Boucres, and in Guines follow site signs turning right towards Marquise for 120 m. GPS: N50:51.979 E01:51.419

Charges guide

Per unit incl. 2 persons and electricity	€ 17,50 - € 28,50
extra person	€ 3,00 - € 5,00

FR62030 Kawan Village Château du Gandspette

133 rue de Gandspette, F-62910 Eperlecques (Pas-de-Calais)

Tel: 03 21 93 43 93. Email: contact@chateau-gandspette.com

www.alanrogers.com/FR62030

This spacious family run site, in the grounds of a 19th-century château, conveniently situated for the Channel ports and tunnel, provides overnight accommodation together with a range of facilities for longer stays. There are 100 touring pitches, all with electric hook-ups, intermingled with 50 French-owned mobile homes and caravans, and a further 18 for hire. Pitches are delineated by trees and hedging. Mature trees form the perimeter of the site, and here there is access to woodland walks.

Facilities

Two sanitary blocks with a mixture of open and cubicled washbasins. Good facilities for disabled people and babies. Laundry facilities. Motorcaravan service point. Bar, grill restaurant and takeaway (all 15/5-15/9). Swimming pools (15/5-30/9). Playground and playing field. Tennis. Pétanque. Children's room. Entertainment in season. Off site: Supermarket 1 km. Fishing 3 km. Riding, golf 5 km. Bicycle hire 9 km. Beach 30 km.

Open: 22 March - 30 September.

Directions

From Calais follow N43 (St Omer) for 25 km. Southeast of Nordausques take D221 (east). Follow site signs for 5-6 km. From St Omer follow N43 to roundabout at junction with D600. Turn right on D600 (Dunkirk). After 5 km. turn left on D221. Site is 1.5 km. on right. GPS: N50:49.137 E02:10.740

Charges guide

Per unit incl. 2 persons and electricity	€ 17,00 - € 27,00
extra person (over 6 yrs)	€ 5,00 - € 6,00
Camping Cheques accepted.	

FR62080 Camping la Paille Haute

145 rue de Sailly, F-62156 Boiry-Notre-Dame (Pas-de-Calais)

Tel: 03 21 48 15 40. Email: la-paillehaute@wanadoo.fr

www.alanrogers.com/FR62080

Quietly situated in a small village overlooking beautiful countryside and easily accessed from the A1 and A26 autoroutes, this site makes an ideal overnight stop. There are 100 pitches here, 65 for touring and all with 6/10A electricity. Some pitches are on open, level grass with lovely views over the countryside, and others are by the site's small fishing lake. You can be sure of a warm welcome here from the friendly owner, who is working hard still developing areas of the site.

Facilities

One modern, basic toilet block, unisex. Extra toilets by pool. One toilet/shower room for disabled visitors. Washing machine and dryer under canopy. Motorcaravan service point. Bar and snacks. Swimming pool (15/6-15/9). Poolside bar and pizza oven. TV in bar. Fishing pond. Playground. Boules. Internet access. Entertainment. Off site: Supermarket 500 m. City of Arras. WW1 Canadian memorial at Vimy Ridge.

Open: 1 April - 31 October.

Directions

From A1 take exit 15 and D939 southeast. Follow signs for Boiry-Notre-Dame. From A26 take exit 8 and D939 northwest following signs for Boiry-Notre-Dame. From village follow camping signs to site. GPS: N50:16.412 E02:56.92

Charges guide

Per unit incl. 2 persons	€ 15,00 - € 18,00
extra person	€ 3,00 - € 3,50
electricity (6A)	€ 3,00

Check real time availability and at-the-gate prices...
www.alanrogers.com

FR62120 Camping l'Eté Indien

Hameau Honvault, F-62930 Wimereux (Pas-de-Calais)

Tel: **03 21 30 23 50**. Email: **ete.indien@wanadoo.fr**   www.alanrogers.com/FR62120

L'Eté Indien is a new site located near the resort of Wimereux, a little to the north of Boulogne. It offers a quiet and tranquil environment in which to enjoy your holiday – apart from some train noise (every 30 minutes, daytime only). Pitches for touring and camping are furthest from the entrance and vary in size. All have electrical connections (10A). In keeping with its Wild West theme, there is a small village of four Indian 'teepees' for rent, as well as more conventional mobile homes and chalets. The swimming pool and children's pool are a fair distance from the touring pitches. Other amenities include a fishing pond and a snack bar, Le Jardin de l'Eté Indien. The site lies at the heart of the Côte d'Opale, which boasts over 130 km. of coastline. Wimereux is an old-fashioned resort with plenty of shops and restaurants, and is renowned as a centre for kite surfing and speed sailing. This is an ideal stop-over for Calais, Dunkerque or Boulogne.

Facilities

Two toilet blocks include facilities for babies and disabled people. Laundry. Small shop. Bar. Snack bar and takeaway. Motorcaravan services. Swimming pool. Children's pool. Play area with trampoline. Boules. Games room. Internet access and WiFi. Bicycle hire. Fishing pond. Off site: Wimereux, Le Touquet, Boulogne and the Nausicaa museum. Cité de l'Europe shopping complex at Calais. Beach 1 km. Riding adjacent. Golf 1.5 km.

Open: All year.

Directions

From the A16 take exit 32 (Wimereux) and follow signs to Wimereux (D96 and D940). After 1.5 km. turn right. Site is well signed from here and is located on the left, close to a riding centre. Approach is rather narrow, with speed ramps and is poorly surfaced. GPS: N50:45.085 E01:36.437

Charges guide

Per unit incl. 2 persons and electricity	€ 15,50 - € 20,00
extra person	€ 3,20 - € 4,00
child (under 13 yrs)	€ 2,00 - € 2,50
dog	€ 1,50 - € 2,00

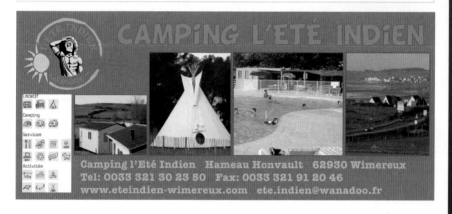

Camping l'Eté Indien   Hameau Honvault   62930 Wimereux
Tel: 0033 321 30 23 50   Fax: 0033 321 91 20 46
www.eteindien-wimereux.com   ete.indien@wanadoo.fr

FR80020 Camping Caravaning le Champ Neuf

Rue du Champ Neuf, F-80120 Saint Quentin en Tourmont (Somme)

Tel: **03 22 25 07 94**. Email: **contact@camping-lechampneuf.com**   www.alanrogers.com/FR80020

Part of a large farm, the campsite was started in 1995 and all the charming family are now involved (although Maman is firmly in charge). There are 157 pitches with 59 for touring, of which 30 are in a new field with the remainder scattered amongst more permanent mobile homes and caravans. All pitches are on level grass with 3/6A electricity. The site is only 75 minutes from Calais, 18 km. off the motorway. This is a quiet site with home cooking and soirées, and with the famous Marquenterre bird reserve next door, bird-watching enthusiasts will appreciate the dawn chorus and migrating birds.

Facilities

Two toilet blocks have British style toilets, washbasins in cubicles, family cubicles and facilities for disabled visitors. Laundry facilities. Motorcaravan service point. Bar, entertainment area and snack bar. Games room. Tennis. Off site: Shops, restaurants, bars in Rue 7 km.

Open: 1 April - 1 November.

Directions

From A16 exit 24, take D32 towards and around Rue. At second roundabout take second exit on D940, then left on D4 for 1.5 km. before turning right on D204 to Le Bout des Crocs. Site is signed to the left. GPS: N50:16.137 E01:36.158

Charges guide

Per unit incl. 2 persons	€ 11,60
extra person	€ 4,10
electricity (3-6A)	€ 3,00 - € 3,60

BOOK THIS SITE
CALL 01580 214000 ...we'll arrange everything
The Travel Service

Check real time availability and at-the-gate prices...

www.**alanrogers**.com

BOOK THIS SITE
CALL 01580 214000
...we'll arrange everything
The Travel **Service**

FR80010 Castel Camping le Château de Drancourt

B.P. 80022, F-80230 Saint Valéry-sur-Somme (Somme)

Tel: 03 22 26 93 45. Email: chateau.drancourt@wanadoo.fr   www.alanrogers.com/FR80010

This is a popular, busy and lively site within easy distance of the Channel ports, between Boulogne and Dieppe. There are 356 pitches in total, of which 220 are occupied by several tour operators; 30 units for rent, and 26 privately owned. The 80 touring pitches are on level grass, of good size, some in shade and others in the open, all with electricity. Fully-serviced pitches are available on reservation. The site is well landscaped and, in spite of the numbers in high season, does not feel overcrowded. It can be dusty around the reception buildings and the château in dry weather. English is spoken and the site is run personally by the energetic owner and his staff. Nearby medieval St Valéry-sur-Somme has a fête each year to celebrate William the Conqueror's embarkation in 1066. The reserve of Le Marquenterre is a must for bird enthusiasts. Pony riding is available in season (stables 15 km).

Facilities

Three toilet blocks include washbasins in cubicles, family bathrooms and facilities for disabled visitors. Laundry facilities. Drainage difficulties can cause occasional problems. Shop, restaurant and takeaway. Several bars. TV rooms, one for children. Games room. Heated pools, one indoor, one outside and paddling pool. Tennis. Golf practice range. Minigolf. Bicycle hire. Fishing. Off site: Beach 14 km.

Open: Easter - 5 November.

Directions

Site is 2.5 km. south of St Valéry and signed from the D940 Berck - Le Tréport road. Turn south on D48 Estreboeuf road. Turn immediately left to Drancourt and site. GPS: N50:09.228 E01:38.156

Charges guide

Per unit incl. 2 persons	€ 12,00 - € 30,00
extra person	€ 5,00 - € 6,70
child (under 5 yrs)	€ 2,00 - € 4,70

Camping le Château de Drancourt

LES CASTELS ★★★★

Camping le Château de Drancourt - BP 80022, 80230 St. Valéry-sur-Somme
Tel.: (33) 3 22 26 93 45 - Fax: (33) 3 22 26 85 87 - E-mail: chateau.drancourt@wanadoo.fr
www.chateau-drancourt.com

FR80210 Camping le Clos Cacheleux

Mobile homes ▶ page 492

Route de Bouillancourt, F-80132 Miannay (Somme)

Tel: 03 22 19 17 47. Email: raphael@camping-lecloscacheleux.fr   www.alanrogers.com/FR80210

Le Clos Cacheleux is a well situated campsite of six hectares bordering woodland in the park of the Château Bouillancourt which dates from the 18th century. First opened in July 2008, it is 11 km. from the Bay of the Somme, regarded as being among the most beautiful bays in France. There are 60 very large, grassy pitches (200 sq.m) and all have electricity hook-ups and water points. The owners aim to make your stay as enjoyable as possible by providing high quality services and activities. Visitors have access to the swimming pool, bar and children's club of the sister site – Le Val de Trie (20 m).

Facilities

The single sanitary block is clean and well maintained. Facilities for disabled visitors. Baby room. Laundry room with washing machine and dryer. Motorcaravan service point. At the sister site: shop, bar with terrace, library and TV room, restaurant and takeaway (26/4-2/9). Play area. Boules. Picnic tables. Freezer for ice packs. Barbecue hire. Bicycle hire. Fishing pond. Caravan storage. Some of the above facilities are on the sister site. Off site: Village 1 km. Hypermarket in Abbéville. Sandy beaches of the Picardy coast 12 km. Golf 7 km. Riding 14 km.

Open: 1 April - 15 October.

Directions

From the A28 at Abbéville take the D925 towards Eu and Le Tréport; do not go towards Moyenville. Turn left in Miannay village on the D86 towards Toeufles. The road to Bouillancourt-sous-Miannay is on the left after 2 km. and site is signed in the village. GPS: N50:05.011 E01:42.806

Charges guide

Per unit incl. 2 persons and electricity	€ 16,70 - € 23,60
extra person	€ 3,10 - € 4,90
child (under 7 yrs)	€ 1,90 - € 2,90
dog	€ 0,80 - € 1,30

Check real time availability and at-the-gate prices...

www.alanrogers.com

FR80060 Camping le Val de Trie

Mobile homes ▶ page 492

Rue des Sources, Bouillancourt-sous-Miannay, F-80870 Moyenneville (Somme)

Tel: 03 22 31 48 88. Email: raphael@camping-levaldetrie.fr   www.alanrogers.com/FR80060

BOOK THIS SITE
CALL 01580 214000
...we'll arrange everything
Service The Travel

Le Val de Trie is a natural countryside site in woodland, near a small village. The 100 numbered, grassy pitches are of a good size, divided by hedges and shrubs with mature trees providing good shade in most areas, and all have electricity (6A) and water. Access roads are gravel (site is possibly not suitable for the largest motorcaravans). It can be very quiet in April, June, September and October. If there is no-one on site, just choose a pitch or call at farm to book in. There are a few Dutch tour operator tents (five). This is maturing into a well managed site with modern facilities and a friendly, relaxed atmosphere. There are good walks around the area and a notice board keeps campers up to date with local market, shopping and activity news. English is spoken. The owners of Le Val de Trie have recently opened a new campsite nearby, Le Clos Cacheleux (FR80210).

Facilities

Two clean sanitary buildings include washbasins in cubicles, units for disabled people, babies and children. Laundry facilities. Motorcaravan services. Shop (from 1/4), bread to order and butcher visits in season. Bar with TV (1/4-15/10), snack bar with takeaway (29/4-10/9). Room above bar for children Off site: Riding 14 km. Golf 10 km. Beach 12 km.

Open: 24 March - 15 October.

Directions

From A28 take exit 2 near Abbeville and D925 to Miannay. Turn left on D86 to Bouillancourt-sous-Miannay: site is signed in village.
GPS: N50:05.038 E01:42.779

Charges guide

Per unit incl. 2 persons	€ 14,60 - € 19,60
incl. electricity	€ 16,70 - € 23,60
extra person	€ 3,10 - € 4,90
child (under 7 yrs)	€ 1,90 - € 2,90
dog	€ 0,80 - € 1,30

Camping Cheques accepted.

Camping le Val de Trie ×××

Online reservation

Cottages to rent

Ideal spot for first or last night or longer stay
Situated at only 1 hour from Calais (A16) 12 km from the coast

Quiet and relaxing   Fishing pond   Swimming pools   Bar
BOUILLANCOURT sous MIANNAY 80870 MOYENNEVILLE
Tel : +33 3 22 31 48 88   Fax : +33 3 22 31 35 33
www.camping-levaldetrie.fr   raphael@camping-levaldetrie.fr

Camping le Clos Cacheleux
Route de Bouillancourt
80132 Miannay
raphael@camping-lecloscacheleux.com
www.camping-lecloscacheleux.com
tel.: +33 3 22 31 48 88
Online reservation

New

Ideal spot for first or last night or longer stay
1 hour from Calais (A16) 12 km from the coast

Check real time availability and at-the-gate prices...
www.alanrogers.com

FR80040 Camping le Royon

1271 route de Quend, F-80120 Fort-Mahon-Plage (Somme)

Tel: **03 22 23 40 30**. Email: **info@campingleroyon.com**   www.alanrogers.com/FR80040

This busy site, some two kilometres from the sea, has 397 pitches of which 116 are used for touring units. Most are near the entrance, some are set amongst the mobile homes. They are of either 95 or 120 sq.m., marked, numbered and divided by hedges and are arranged either side of access roads. Electricity (6A) and water points are available to all. The remaining 281 pitches are used for mobile homes. The site is well lit, fenced and guarded at night (€ 30 deposit for barrier card). Entertainment is organised for adults and children in July/Aug when it will be very full. Nearby there are opportunities for windsurfing, sailing, sand yachting, canoeing, swimming, climbing and shooting. The site is close to the Baie de l'Authie which is an area noted for migrating birds.

Facilities

Four toilet blocks provide unisex facilities with British and Turkish style WCs and washbasins in cubicles. Units for disabled people. Baby baths. Laundry facilities. Shop. Gas supplies. Mobile takeaway calls evenings in July/Aug. Clubroom and bar. Heated, open air and covered pools. Open air children's pool and sun terrace. Play area. Games room with TV. Multicourt. Tennis. Boules. Bicycle hire. Internet access and WiFi. Off site: Fishing, riding, golf and watersports centre within 1 km. Public transport nearby (July/Aug). Train station 15 km.

Open: 7 March - 1 November.

Directions

From A16 exit 24, take D32 around Rue (road becomes D940 for a while) then continues as D32 (Fort-Mahon-Plage). Site is on right after 19 km. GPS: N50:19.937 E01:34.776

Charges guide

Per unit incl. up to 3 persons and electricity	€ 17,00 - € 26,50
extra person (over 1 yr)	€ 7,00
dog	€ 3,00

17€ ✎PRIVILEGE CAMPING TICKET✎ 17€

Present this Privilege Camping Ticket at reception and you will only pay 17 Euros per night for a pitch with electricity up to 3 people

Offer valid for year 2009, except in July and August

SUGGESTED BY AIROTEL CAMPING LE ROYON

Camping Qualité Picardie**** - 1271 Route de Quend - 80120 Fort-Mahon Plage
Tel: (33)3 22 23 40 30 - Fax (33)3 22 23 65 15 - www.campingleroyon.com

FR80090 Kawan Village Caravaning le Val d'Authie

20 route de Vercourt, F-80120 Villers-sur-Authie (Somme)

Tel: **03 22 29 92 47**. Email: **camping@valdauthie.fr**   www.alanrogers.com/FR80090

In a village location, this well organised site is fairly close to several beaches, but also has its own excellent pool complex, small restaurant and bar. The owner has carefully controlled the size of the site, leaving space for a leisure area with an indoor pool complex. There are 170 pitches in total, but with many holiday homes and chalets, there are only 60 for touring units. These are on grass, some are divided by small hedges, with 6/10A electric hook-ups, and ten have full services. A 'Sites et Paysages' member.

Facilities

Good toilet facilities include some shower and washbasin units, washbasins in cubicles, and limited facilities for disabled people and babies. Facilities may be under pressure in high season and cleaning variable. Shop (not October). Bar/restaurant (4/4-12/10; hours vary). Swimming and paddling pools with lifeguards in July/Aug). Playground, club room with TV. Weekend entertainment in season (discos may be noisy until midnight, once weekly). Multicourt, beach volleyball, football, boules and tennis court. Internet room. Fitness room including sauna (charged).

Open: 29 March - 12 October.

Directions

Villers-sur-Authie is about 25 km. NNW of Abbéville. From A16 junction 24 take N1 to Vron, then left on D175 to Villers-sur-Authie. Or use D85 from Rue, or D485 from Nampont St Martin. Site is at southern end of village at road junction. GPS: N50:18.815 E01:41.729

Charges guide

Per unit incl. 2 persons	€ 19,00 - € 25,00
extra person	€ 6,00
child (2-6 yrs)	€ 3,00
electricity (6/10A)	€ 5,00 - € 8,00
Camping Cheques accepted.	

Check real time availability and at-the-gate prices...

✍ www.alanrogers.com

FR80070 Kawan Village la Ferme des Aulnes

Mobile homes ▶ page 492

1 rue du Marais, Fresne-sur-Authie, F-80120 Nampont-Saint Martin (Somme)

Tel: 03 22 29 22 69. Email: contact@fermedesaulnes.com   www.alanrogers.com/FR80070

This peaceful site, with 120 pitches, has been developed on the meadows of a small, 17th-century farm on the edge of Fresne and is lovingly cared for by its enthusiastic owner and his hard-working team. Restored outbuildings house reception and the facilities, around a central courtyard that boasts a fine heated swimming pool. A new development outside, facing the main gate, has 20 large level grass pitches for touring. There is also an area for tents. In the centre, a warden lives above a new facility building. The remaining 22 touring pitches are in the main complex, hedged and fairly level. Activities are organised for children and there are indoor facilities for poor weather. From here you can visit Crécy, Agincourt, St Valéry and Montreuil (where Victor Hugo wrote Les Misérables). The nearby Bay of the Somme has wonderful sandy beaches and many watersports.

Facilities

Both sanitary areas are heated and include washbasins in cubicles with a large cubicle for disabled people. Dishwashing and laundry sinks. Shop. Piano bar and restaurant. Motorcaravan service point. TV room. Swimming pool (16 x 9 m; heated and with cover for cooler weather). Jacuzzi and sauna. Fitness room. Aquagym and balneotherapy. Playground. Boules. Archery. Rooms with play stations and videos. Off site: River fishing 100 m. Golf 1 km. Riding 8 km.

Open: 22 March - 2 November.

Directions

From Calais, take A16 to exit 25 and turn for Arras for 2 km. and then towards Abbeville on N1. At Nampont-St Martin turn west on D485 and site will be found in 2 km. GPS: N50:20.157 E01:42.740

Charges guide

Per person	€ 7,00
child (under 7 yrs)	€ 4,00
pitch	€ 7,00
electricity (6/10A)	€ 6,00 - € 12,00

Camping Cheques accepted.

BOOK THIS SITE
CALL 01580 214000
...we'll arrange everything
The Travel
Service

La Ferme des Aulnes

www.fermedesaulnes.com

Kawan · La Clef Verte · Camping Cheque · Camping Qualité · HOLIDAY CHEQUE

103

FR80120 Camping les Aubépines

Saint Firmin, F-80550 Le Crotoy (Somme)

Tel: **03 22 27 01 34**. Email: **contact@camping-lesaubepines.com**   www.alanrogers.com/FR80120

This peaceful, family-run site is on the edge of the Parc Ornithologique du Marquenterre and is just 1 km. from a beach on the Baie de Somme, a river estuary famous for its resident population of seals. There are 196 pitches, although around 100 are occupied by privately-owned mobile homes with a few available for rent. Consequently there are just 71 touring pitches scattered throughout the site. All on level ground, they are of a reasonable to good size, separated by hedges and trees and with water taps and electricity (3-10A) close by.

Facilities

Two unisex toilet blocks, fairly basic but clean and in good order. British style toilets (seatless), washbasins in cubicles, push button showers and some larger cubicles with shower and basin. Baby bath and toilet. Facilities for disabled visitors are minimal (no grab rails). Laundry room. Shop. Indoor games. Small play area. Bicycle hire. Off site: Riding adjacent. Beaches: 1 km. and 10 km. Fishing 2 km. Bird sanctuary, tennis 3 km. Golf 10 km.

Open: 1 April - 1 November.

Directions

Le Crotoy is on the D940 Berck - Le Tréport road. At roundabout for town, take D4 to St Firmin, turn right at next roundabout. After village sign, turn left to site (signed) on right in about 500 m. GPS: N50:15.004 E01:36.747

Charges guide

Per unit incl. 2 persons and electricity	€ 19,00 - € 29,00
extra person	€ 5,00 - € 5,20

FR80130 Flower Camping les Vertes Feuilles

25 route de la Plage Monchaux, F-80120 Quend Plage les Pins (Somme)

Tel: **03 22 23 55 12**. Email: **contact@lesvertesfeuilles.com**   www.alanrogers.com/FR80130

Situated on the Picardy coast, 3 km. from the beach, this 1.5 hectare site provides 46 touring pitches out of a total of 106. The remainder contain a mix of mobile homes and semi-residential caravans. It is a charming campsite where a pleasant welcome awaits you. The site roads are slightly narrow, so larger units cannot be accommodated. This whole area is bustling in high season with many campsites and holiday villages but this makes for a wonderful French style seaside holiday. Don't forget to visit the nearby Gardens of Valloires and the bird reserve of Le Marquenterre.

Facilities

One large toilet block, old but renovated, has unisex showers, washbasins in cubicles and 3 family rooms. Ramped facilities for disabled visitors. Snack bar in season. Covered heated swimming pool (10/4-30/9). Play areas. Bicycle hire. Off site: Beach 3 km. Golf 2 km. Riding 5 km. Local markets. Aquaclub. Abbey and Gardens of Valloires and the bird reserve of Le Marquenterre.

Open: 1 April - 1 November.

Directions

From A16 Rue exit, take D32 around Rue, when road becomes D940 for a while, then continues again as D32 towards Fort-Mahon-Plage. After left turn for Quend Plage, site on left. GPS: N50:19.170 E01:36.350

Charges 2009

Per unit incl. 2 persons and electricity	€ 16,50 - € 30,40
extra person	€ 4,50 - € 5,50
No credit cards.	

www.flowercampings.com

FR80190 Camping les Galets de la Mollière

Rue Faidherbe, La Mollière, F-80410 Cayeux-sur-Mer (Somme)

Tel: **03 22 26 61 85**. Email: **info@campinglesgaletsdelamolliere.com**   www.alanrogers.com/FR80190

Cayeux-sur-Mer is an attractive, traditional seaside resort close to the Somme estuary and Les Galets de la Mollière is located just to the north of the town. Formerly a municipal site, it has undergone a recent renovation programme. The site extends over six hectares and has 195 pitches, of which 71 are reserved for touring units, all with 10A electrical connections (French style). An attractive swimming pool complex, bar, shop and a games room were added in 2008. A fine sandy beach is adjacent to the site, a short walk across the sand dunes.

Facilities

Toilet blocks housed in small wooden huts include facilities for babies and disabled people. Laundry. Small shop. Bar, snack bar and takeaway. Games room. Play area. Boules. Motorcaravan services (across the road from the site entrance). WiFi (charge). Off site: Nearest beach 300 m. Cayeux sur Mer 3 km. Tennis 3 km. Riding and fishing 1 km. Sailing and windsurfing 1 km. Golf 15 km. Large hypermarket in Abbéville.

Open: 21 March - 5 November.

Directions

From the A16 take exit 24 (Le Crotoy) and join the D32 to Rue, and then the D940 to St Valéry. Bypass St Valéry on the D940 and then join the D3 signed Cayeux sur Mer. After a further 4 km. you will arrive at La Mollière and site is well signed from here. GPS: N50:12.156 E01:31.507

Charges guide

Per unit incl. 3 persons and electricity	€ 17,00 - € 28,50
extra person (over 1 yr)	€ 7,00

Check real time availability and at-the-gate prices...

www.**alanrogers**.com

FR80150 Camping Airotel Le Walric

Route d'Eu, F-80230 Saint Valéry-sur-Somme (Somme)

Tel: **03 22 26 81 97**. Email: **info@campinglewalric.com**   www.alanrogers.com/FR80150

A clean, well-kept and managed site, Le Walric is about 75 minutes from Calais. A former municipal site, it has been completely updated with a new bar and snack bar, a pool complex, two play areas and entertainment in high season. There are 263 well laid out, large and level grass pitches. Of these, 105 with electricity connections are for touring with the remainder used for a mix of new mobile homes and semi-residential caravans. The site's situation on the outskirts of the town make it an ideal holiday location. Medieval Saint Valéry is renowned for its association with William the Conqueror. The cathedral cities of Amiens, St Quentin and Laon are near. The Bay of the Somme is of special interest to bird enthusiasts. Watersports abound in this area. There are two other sites in this group which you may also consider for a stay: Les Galets de la Molliere and Le Bois de Pins.

Facilities

Two toilet blocks include British style WCs, washbasins in cubicles and showers. Facilities for disabled visitors. Laundry room with baby changing. Motorcaravan service point. Bar with snacks and TV. Heated outdoor pool. Off site: Shops, restaurants, bars in St Valéry.

Open: 1 April - 1 November.

Directions

From A16 exit 24, follow D32 across N1. At roundabout take D235 to Morlay; turn left on D940 and continue around St Valéry until second roundabout where take first exit on D3 to site on right. GPS: N50:11.040 E01:37.200

Charges guide

Per unit incl. 3 persons and electricity	€ 17,00 - € 28,50
extra person	€ 7,00
dog	€ 3,00

Le Bois de Pins ★★★ **Le Walric** ★★★★ **Les Galets de la Mollière** ★★★

Privilege Camping Ticket € 18,- per night for a pitch

This offer is not valid for arrivals in July and August

FR80200 Camping le Bois de Pins

Rue Guillaume-le-Conquérant, F-80410 Cayeux-sur-Mer (Somme)

Tel: **03 22 26 71 04**. Email: **info@campingleboisdepins.com**   www.alanrogers.com/FR80200

Cayeux-sur-Mer is a pretty resort to the south of the vast Somme bay. Le Bois de Pins is a quiet family site, close to a fine sandy beach and open for a long season. The site can be found in the small village of Brighton, just outside the resort. There are 163 grassy pitches, all of which have 6/10A electrical connections. Some pitches are occupied by mobile homes and chalets. On site amenities include a small shop and play area for children. Cayeux is a lively resort with a wide variety of watersports available, as well as a good golf course and tennis courts. St Valéry-sur-Somme, a little to the north, has retained its delightful mediaeval character and has a fine Gothic church. There is much else of interest in the area, including the world famous Marquenterre bird reserve, to the north of the bay. The site's friendly owners will be pleased to recommend possible day trips.

Facilities

Shop. Games room. Play area. Tourist information. Mobile homes for rent. Off site: Nearest beach 500 m. Fishing 2 km. Cycle and walking tracks. Cayeux-sur-Mer.

Open: 21 March - 5 November.

Directions

Leave the A16 autoroute at exit 24 and follow signs to St Valéry-sur-Somme on the D32 and D940. Shortly beyond St Valéry, join the D3 towards Cayeux-sur-Mer and, upon arrival at Brighton, the site is well signed. GPS: N50:11.859 E01:31.005

Charges guide

Per unit incl. 3 persons and electricity	€ 17,00 - € 28,50
extra person	€ 7,00

Check real time availability and at-the-gate prices...

www.alanrogers.com

FR80100 Camping Parc des Cygnes

111 avenue des Cygnes, F-80080 Amiens (Somme)

Tel: **03 22 43 29 28**. Email: **camping.amiens@wanadoo.fr**   www.alanrogers.com/FR80100

Formerly Camping de l'Ecluse, this is now a 3.2 hectare site which has been completely levelled and attractively landscaped. Bushes and shrubs divide the site into areas; some 20 mature trees are planned to provide some shade. The 145 pitches are for touring, with plans for a handful of mobile homes for rent. All pitches are grassed with plenty of space on the tarmac roads in front of them for motorcaravans to park in wet conditions. There are 86 pitches with electricity (6-16A), water and drainage and further water points throughout the rest of the site. The site is just a few minutes from the N1, the A16 Paris - Calais motorway and the A29/A26 route to Rouen and the south, so it is useful as a stop-over being about 50 km. from the ports. Amiens itself is an attractive cathedral city where you can eat out on the waterfront of the 'Venice of the North' or take a boat trip around the 'floating gardens' of 'Les Hortillonnages'.

Facilities

Two toilet blocks (one open only when site is busy) with separate toilet facilities but unisex shower and washbasin area. Baby bath. Facilities for disabled people. Dishwashing sinks. Reception building also has toilets, showers and washbasins (heated when necessary). Laundry facilities. Shop (open on request). New bar and takeaway (1/5-15/9; weekends only in low season). Games and TV room. Bicycle hire. Fishing. Off site: Golf and riding 5 km. Beaches 70 km.

Open: 1 April - 15 October.

Directions

From A16, leave at exit 20. Take the Rocade Nord (northern bypass) to exit 40, follow signs for Amiens Longpré. At roundabout take second exit to Parc de Loisirs, then right to site (signs all the way). GPS: N49:55.255 E02:15.530

Charges 2009

Per unit incl. 2 persons and electricity	€ 14,60 - € 20,30
extra person	€ 6,00
child (4-12 yrs)	€ 5,00
dog	€ 2,10

Parc des Cygnes ★★★★
Camping & Caravaning, Cottages

For quality holidays!

PARC DES CYGNES
CAMPING & CARAVANING
★★★★
Le camping au cœur d'Amiens

Camping Qualité

111 Avenue des Cygnes - 80080 AMIENS
Tél.: +33 (0)3 22 43 29 28
Fax: +33 (0)3 22 43 59 42
E-mail: camping.amiens@wanadoo.fr
Web: www.parcdescygnes.com
GPS: 49.920916 / 2.258833

FR80110 Kawan Village le Ridin

Lieu-dit Mayocq, F-80550 Le Crotoy (Somme)

Tel: **03 22 27 03 22**. Email: **contact@campingleridin.com**   www.alanrogers.com/FR80110

Le Ridin is a popular family site in the countryside just 2 km. from Le Crotoy with its beaches and marina, and 6 km. from the famous bird reserve of Le Marquenterre. The site has 162 pitches, including 47 for touring, the remainder occupied by mobile homes and chalets (for rent). There is some shade. The pitches and roads are unsuitable for large units. The site amenities are housed in beautifully converted barns across the road and these include a heated pool, fitness centre, bar/restaurant and bicycles for hire. Reception staff are helpful and will advise on local excursions.

Facilities

Toilet blocks are heated in cool weather and provide good showers and special facilities for children. Restaurant/bar. Small shop. Swimming and paddling pools. Fitness centre. Games room. Play area. TV room. Bicycle hire. Entertainment and activity programme. Off site: Birdwatching 6 km. Golf 10 km.

Open: 21 March - 5 November.

Directions

From A16 (Calais - Abbéville) take exit 24 and follow signs to Le Crotoy. At roundabout on arrival at Le Crotoy turn towards St Férmin, then second road on right. GPS: N50:14.364 E01:37.893

Charges guide

Per unit incl. 2 persons	€ 16,00 - € 24,00
extra person	€ 5,00 - € 5,20
electricity (6-10A)	€ 2,50 - € 5,50

Camping Cheques accepted.

The Travel Service ...we'll arrange everything **CALL 01580 214000** **BOOK THIS SITE**

Check real time availability and at-the-gate prices...

www.**alanrogers**.com

MAP 3

Paris & Ile de France

With its tree lined boulevards, museums, art galleries, the Arc de Triomphe and of course the famous Eiffel Tower, this cosmopolitan city has plenty to offer. Less than 30 miles from the heart of the capital, a fun-packed trip to Disneyland Paris is also within reach.

DÉPARTEMENTS: 75 PARIS, 77 SEINE-ET-MARNE, 78 YVELINES, 91 ESSONE, 92 HAUTS-DE-SEINE, 93 SEINE-ST-DENIS, 94 VAL DE MARNE, 95 VAL D'OISE

MAJOR CITIES: PARIS, VERSAILLES, IVRY, MELUN, NANTERRE, BOBIGNY, CRETEIL AND PONTOISE.

One of the most chic and culturally rewarding cities in the world, Paris has something for everyone. The list of things to do is virtually endless and could easily fill many holidays - window shopping, the Eiffel Tower, Notre Dame, Montmartre, trips on the Seine, pavement cafés and the Moulin Rouge, the list goes on.

As a peaceful retreat, you can relax and enjoy the lush scenery of surrounding hills and secret woodlands of the Ile de France. Square bell towers in gentle valleys, white silos on endless plains of wheat; soft and harmonious landscapes painted and praised by La Fontaine, Corot and all the landscape painters. Paris is surrounded by forests, Fontainebleau, Compiègne, Saint-Germain-en-Laye and majestic châteaux such as Fontainbleau and Vaux-le-Vicomte.

Disneyland Resort Paris provides a great day out for all the family with two fantastic theme parks with over 70 attractions and shows to choose from. On the outskirts of Paris is Parc Astérix. with one of Europe's most impressive roller-coasters.

Places of interest

Fontainebleau: château and national museum, history of Napoléon from 1804-1815.

Malmaison: château and national museum.

Meaux: agricultural centre, Gothic cathedral, chapter house and palace.

Paris: obviously! The list of places is too extensive to include here.

St Germain-en-Laye: château, Gallo-roman and Merovingian archeological museum.

Sèvres: ceramics museum.

Thoiry: château and Parc Zoologique, 450-hectare park with gardens and African reserve containing 800 animals.

Versailles: Royal Castle, Royal Apartments, Hall of Mirrors, Royal Opera and French History Museum.

Cuisine of the region

Although without a specific cuisine of its own, Paris and Ile de France offer a wide selection of dishes from all the regions of France. Paris also has a wide choice of foreign restaurants, such as Vietnamese and North African.

FR75020 Camping du Bois de Boulogne

2 allée du Bord de l'eau, F-75016 Paris (Paris)

Tel: **01 45 24 30 00**. Email: **camping-boulogne@stereau.fr**

www.alanrogers.com/FR75020

A busy site and the nearest to the city, set in a wooded area between the Seine and the Bois de Boulogne. The site is quite extensive but nevertheless becomes very full with many international visitors. There are 510 pitches (including mobile homes and a few chalets) of which 280 are marked, with electricity (10A), water, drainage and TV aerial connections. The site has undergone a huge improvement and development programme including the refurbishment of all toilet blocks. Reservations are made for pitches – if not booked, arrive early in season (mornings).

Facilities

Toilet blocks have British style WCs, washbasins in cubicles and showers with divider and seat (hot water throughout). All these facilities suffer from heavy use in season. Laundry facilities. Five motorcaravan service points. Shop. Bar and restaurant (1/4-15/10). Bar open 07.00-24.00 most times and until 02.00 hrs in peak season. Pizza bar and takeaway. Playground. Information service. Off site: Fishing 1 km. Bicycle hire 2 km.

Open: All year.

Directions

Site is on east side of Seine between the river and the Bois de Boulogne, just north of the Pont de Suresnes. Easiest approach is from Port Maillot. Traffic lights at site entrance. Follow signs closely and use a good map. GPS: N48:52.060 E02:14.050

Charges guide

Per unit incl. 2 persons incl. electricity, water and drainage	€ 20,40 - € 28,30
	€ 24,60 - € 35,70
tent incl. 2 persons	€ 11,00 - € 16,50
extra person	€ 4,50 - € 6,50

FR77020 Camping le Chêne Gris

Mobile homes ▶ page 493

24 place de la Gare de Faremoutiers, F-77515 Pommeuse (Seine-et-Marne)

Tel: **01 64 04 21 80**. Email: **info@lechenegris.com**

www.alanrogers.com/FR77020

This site is being progressively developed by a Dutch holiday company. A principal building houses reception on the ground floor and also an airy restaurant/bar plus a takeaway. Of the 198 pitches, 65 are for touring many of which are on aggregate stone, the rest (higher up the hill on which the site is built) being occupied by over 100 mobile homes and 25 tents belonging to a Dutch tour operator. Terraces look out onto the heated leisure pool complex and an adventure-type play area for over-fives, whilst the play area for under-fives is at the side of the bar with picture windows overlooking it. The site is next to a railway station with trains to Paris (45 minutes). Disneyland is 20 km.

Facilities

One toilet block with push button showers, washbasins in cubicles and a dishwashing and laundry area. At busy times these facilities may be under pressure. A second block is to be added. Facilities for disabled visitors. Bar, restaurant and takeaway. Pool complex (all season). Off site: Shops, bars and restaurants within walking distance. Fishing and riding 2 km.

Open: 25 April - 8 November.

Directions

Pommeuse is 55 km. east of Paris. From A4 at exit 16 take N34 towards Coulommiers. In 10 km. turn south for 2 km. on D25 to Pommeuse; site on right after level-crossing. Also signed from south on D402 Guignes - Coulommiers road, taking D25 to Faremoutiers. GPS: N48:48.514 E02:59.530

Charges guide

Per unit incl. 2 persons and electricity	€ 29,00 - € 35,00
extra person	€ 2,00 - € 3,50
child (3-11 yrs)	€ 2,00 - € 3,00
animal	€ 2,50
Camping Cheques accepted.	

- 15 minutes drive from Disneyland® Resort Paris
- next to the train station at Pommeuse with a direct line to Paris
- rental of luxury mobile homes
- rental of luxury, fully furnished bungalow tents
- pitch reservation with 10 amp electrical hook up
- well shaded campsite
- situated on a gently sloping hillside
- English, Italian, Spanish, French, Dutch and German spoken
- open 25th April 2009 to 8th November 2009

Camping **Le Chêne Gris**
24, Place de la Gare de Faremoutiers
77515 Pommeuse
T: (+33) 1640 42 180 F: (+33) 1642 00 589

- Snack bar
- Restaurant ▪ Bar
- Laguna pool (Children's Pool)
- Covered swimming pool
- Supermarket

Camping **Le Chêne Gris**

www.lechenegris.com

Check real time availability and at-the-gate prices...

 www.**alanrogers**.com

FR77030 Camping International de Jablines

Base de Loisirs, F-77450 Jablines (Seine-et-Marne)

Tel: 01 60 26 09 37. Email: welcome@camping-jablines.com

www.alanrogers.com/FR77030

Jablines is a modern site which, with the accompanying leisure facilities of the adjacent 'Espace Loisirs', provides an interesting, if a little impersonal alternative to other sites in the region. Man-made lakes provide marvellous water activities. The 'Great Lake' as it is called, is said to have the largest beach on the Ile-de-France! The site itself provides 150 pitches, of which 141 are for touring units. Most are of a good size with gravel hardstanding and grass, accessed by tarmac roads and marked by fencing panels and shrubs. All have 10A electricity, 60 with water and drainage also. The whole complex close to the Marne has been developed around old gravel workings. Water activities include dinghy sailing, windsurfing, canoeing, fishing and supervised bathing, plus a large equestrian centre. In season the activities at the leisure complex are supplemented by a bar and restaurant, plus a range of very French style group activities.

Facilities

Two toilet blocks, heated in cool weather, include push button showers, some washbasins in cubicles. Dishwashing and laundry facilities. Motorcaravan service (charged). Shop. Play area. Bar/restaurant adjacent at leisure centre/lake complex with watersports including 'water cable ski', riding activities, tennis and minigolf. Whilst staying on the campsite, admission to the leisure complex is free. Internet point. Ticket sales for Disneyland and Astérix. Off site: Golf 15 km.

Open: 28 March - 25 October.

Directions

From A4 Paris - Rouen turn north on A104. Take exit 8 on D404 Meaux/Base de Loisirs Jablines. From A1 going south, follow signs for Marne-la-Vallée using A104. Take exit 6A Clay-Souilly on N3 (Meaux). After 6 km. turn south on D404 and follow signs. At park entry keep left for campsite. GPS: N48:54.817 E02:44.051

Charges 2009

Per unit incl. 2 persons and 10A electricity	€ 22,00 - € 25,00
serviced pitch	€ 24,00 - € 27,00
extra person	€ 6,00 - € 7,00

Camping Cheques accepted.

Base Régionale de Plein-Air et de Loisirs de Jablines-Annet

Covering more than 450 hectares, a leisure and relaxation area unique in the Ile de France.

L'espace loisirs
Jablines-Annet
www.camping-jablimes.com

Camping ★★★

FR77040 Caravaning des 4 Vents

Rue de Beauregard, F-77610 Crèvecoeur-en-Brie (Seine-et-Marne)

Tel: 01 64 07 41 11. Email: f.george@free.fr

www.alanrogers.com/FR77040

This peaceful, pleasant site has been owned and run by the same family for over 35 years. There are around 200 pitches, with many permanent or seasonal units, however, there are 130 spacious grassy pitches for tourists, well separated by good hedges, all with 6A electricity and a water tap shared between two pitches. The whole site is well landscaped with flowers and trees everywhere. This is a great family site with pool and games facilities at the top end so that campers are not disturbed.

Facilities

Three modern sanitary units (heated in cooler weather) provide British style WCs, washbasins (mainly in cubicles) and push button showers. Facilities for disabled people. Laundry facilities. Motorcaravan service point. In high season a mobile snack bar and pizzeria (16.00-23.00), and a baker (07.30-11.00). Well fenced swimming pool (16 m. diameter; June to Sept). Playground. Games room. Riding (high season). Off site: La Houssaye 1 km.

Open: 1 March - 1 November.

Directions

Crèvecoeur is just off the D231 between A4 exit 13 and Provins. From north, pass obelisk and turn right onto the C3 in 3 km. From south 19 km. after junction with N4, turn left at signs to village. Follow site signs. GPS: N48:45.044 E02:53.775

Charges guide

Per unit incl. 2 persons and electricity	€ 25,00
extra person (over 5 yrs)	€ 5,00

BOOK THIS SITE The Travel Service
CALL 01580 214000
...we'll arrange everything

Check real time availability and at-the-gate prices...

 www.**alanrogers**.com

FR77060 Le Parc de la Colline

Mobile homes ▶ page 493

Route de Lagny, F-77200 Torcy (Seine-et-Marne)

Tel: **01 60 05 42 32**. Email: **camping.parc.de.la.colline@wanadoo.fr**   www.alanrogers.com/FR77060

This is a traditional and fairly basic campsite with just one advantage – its proximity to Paris and to Disneyland. There are shuttle buses to the Metro (RER) station just 3 km. away and also to Disneyland and Parc Astérix. There are two large sports and water parks nearby and weekend fitness sessions on the beach (500 m. from site). The site itself is on the side of a hill with most pitches on level grass terraces. Those at the foot of the hill are separated by mature hedges and bushes. All have electricity (2/6A), but water has to be fetched from the toilet blocks. Access to the terraces is quite steep.

Facilities

Two elderly toilet blocks seem to be reasonably maintained and had just been cleaned when we saw them; an attempt has been made to brighten them up. Mainly Turkish style toilets but a few British with the occasional seat! Controllable showers. Warm and cold water to washbasins (mainly in cubicles). En-suite facility for disabled visitors (stark but fully equipped). Laundry facilities. Small shop for basics. Snack bar (mainly canned drinks and beers) with internet point, TV and some games. Off site: Disneyland 10 mins and central Paris 20 mins (métro), Parc Asterix 30 mins (car). Supermarket and restaurants. Fishing and golf 400 m. Riding 1 km.

Open: All year.

Directions

From Paris and the Péripherique take A4 to the junction with the A104 (Charles de Gaulle - Lille). From A1 Paris - Lille take A104 (Marne la Vallée), leave at exit 10 and head west signed Parc de Loisirs de Torcy to campsite on left in 1 km.
GPS: N48:51.510 E02:39.219

Charges guide

Per person	€ 7,10
child (under 7 yrs)	€ 5,10
pitch incl. electricity	€ 14,50
dog	€ 4,60

FR77070 Kawan Village la Belle Etoile

Quai Joffre, la Rochette, F-77000 Melun (Seine-et-Marne)

Tel: **01 64 39 48 12**. Email: **info@campinglabelleetoile.com**   www.alanrogers.com/FR77070

Alongside the River Seine, this site has an overall mature and neat appearance, although the approach road is somewhat off-putting with several industrial plants. However, you'll discover that La Belle Etoile enjoys a pleasant position with pitches to the fore of the site within view of the barges which continually pass up and down. The 170 touring pitches, with electricity connections (6/10A), are on grass and laid out between the many shrubs and trees. There are ten units for hire. A friendly, family run site with pleasant and helpful English speaking owners, it is ideally situated for visiting Fontainebleau and Paris.

Facilities

The toilet blocks are not new but they are kept very clean and the water is very hot. Laundry room. Baby bath. Facilities for disabled visitors (shower, washbasin and WC). Motorcaravan service point. Small bar, snacks and shop (28/6-30/8). Takeaway (1/5-15/9). Swimming pool (1/5-15/9). Play area. Fishing. Bicycle hire. Tickets for Disney and Vaux le Vicomte are sold by the site. Off site: Fontainebleau and Paris. Golf 15 km.

Open: 28 March - 18 October.

Directions

Travelling north on N6 Fontainebleau - Melun road, on entering La Rochette, pass petrol station on left. Turn immediately right into Ave de la Seine. At end of road turn left at river, site on left in 500 m.
GPS: N48:31.501 E02:40.164

Charges guide

Per person	€ 5,20 - € 6,20
baby (0-2 yrs)	€ 2,20 - € 2,40
child (3-11 yrs)	€ 3,50 - € 4,50
pitch	€ 5,30 - € 6,30
dog	€ 1,50
Camping Cheques accepted.	

Camping La Belle Etoile

* Familycampsite
* Many playfacilities
* Hirefacilities:
 - Tent bungalows with toilet and shower
 - Mobil homes and chalets

GPS: 48,52578/2,66911 (lat / long)
E-mail: info@campinglabelleetoile.com
Internet: www.campinglabelleetoile.com
Tel: ++33(0) 1 64 39 48 12
Fax: ++33(0) 1 64 37 25 55

We accept Camping-Cheque

The Travel Service ...we'll arrange everything BOOK THIS SITE CALL 01580 214000

Check real time availability and at-the-gate prices...

www.**alanrogers**.com

`FR77090` Camping les Etangs Fleuris

Route Couture, F-77131 Touquin (Seine-et-Marne)

Tel: 01 64 04 16 36. Email: contact@etangs-fleuris.com   www.alanrogers.com/FR77090

This is a pleasant, peaceful site which has a very French feel despite the presence of a fair number of mobile homes, since these occupy their own areas round the periphery. The 80 touring pitches are grouped on the level ground around the attractive lakes, all with electricity (10A) and water, separated by hedges and with shade from mature trees. The life of the site centres round a smart bar/function room which doubles as reception and a shop, as well as the lakes and an attractive, irregularly shaped pool. The lakes are home to some sizeable carp as well as being restocked daily with trout (fishing € 5 for half a day). The site is near enough to both Paris (50 km.) and Disneyland (23 km.) to provide a practical alternative to the busier sites nearer the centre.

Facilities

A simple, heated toilet block has push button showers and open washbasins (with dividers and hooks) for men but mainly in cubicles for ladies. No facilities for disabled visitors. Another heated block is only opened when site is very busy. Laundry facilities. Motorcaravan service area. Shop for basics in bar. Heated pool with paddling section (15/4-15/9). Takeaway meals and snacks (15/5-10/9). Internet access and WiFi. Multisports pitch. Minigolf. Trampoline. Off site: Riding 5 km. Golf 15 km. Zoo 5 km.

Open: 15 April - 15 September.

Directions

Touquin is off the D231, 21 km. from exit 13 of A4 motorway and 30 km. northeast of Provins. From D231 follow signs for Touquin, then Etangs Fleuris. Site is 2.5 km. west of village. GPS: N48:43.983 E03:02.819

Charges 2009

Per unit incl. 2 persons	€ 16,00
incl. electricity	€ 18,00
child (2-10 yrs)	€ 3,50 - € 4,00

No credit cards.

CAMPING Les Etangs Fleuris★★★

Only 25 minutes from Disneyland Resort Paris!

CAMPING Les Etangs Fleuris★★★ • Route de la Couture • 77131 Touquin
Tél.: +33 164 04 16 36 • Fax: +33 164 04 12 28
E-mail: contact@etangs-fleuris.com • www.etangs-fleuris.com

GPS location:
48.733054 / 3.046978

`FR77120` Camping le Soleil de Crécy

Route de Serbonne, F-77580 Crécy-la-Chapelle (Seine-et-Marne)

Tel: 01 60 43 57 00. Email: info@campinglesoleil.com   www.alanrogers.com/FR77120

Situated east of Paris in the beautiful Brie region, Le Soleil de Crécy is a site for all the family and is very well positioned for accessing both Disneyland Paris and the city itself. The nearest station is just 100 m. from the site and there is also a good bus service. There are separate areas for those using tents or those with either caravans and motorcaravans, with 4A or 10A electrical connections available for the latter. A number of mobile homes are available for rent. This is a lively site in high season with an entertainment and activity programme, as well as some good amenities including a swimming pool.

Facilities

One toilet block near reception includes facilities for children and disabled visitors. Shop. Restaurant. Snack bar. Takeaway. Swimming pool. Minigolf. Activity and entertainment programme. Bicycle hire. Games room. Mobile homes for rent. Off site: Disneyland Paris 14 km. Vaux le Vicomte 16 km. Val d'Europe shopping complex 14 km. Bus stop at site entrance.

Open: 28 March - 3 November.

Directions

Take exit 16 from the A4 motorway and join the N34 towards Coulommiers. This road passes through Crécy-la-Chapelle. Shortly after passing the church, turn right and the site is signed from here. GPS: N48:51.348 E02:55.532

Charges guide

Per person	€ 6,00
child (3-13 yrs)	€ 3,00
pitch	€ 11,00 - € 18,00
electricity	€ 4,50 - € 8,00

Check real time availability and at-the-gate prices...

www.alanrogers.com

FR77110 Camping Club le Parc de Paris

Rue Adèle Claret, Montjay la Tour, F-77410 Villevaudé (Seine-et-Marne)

Tel: **01 60 26 20 79**. Email: **camping.leparc@club-internet.fr**   www.alanrogers.com/FR77110

This rural, sloping site (open all year) is conveniently situated as an overnight stop or for a visit to Disneyland and is located close to the town of Villevaudé and its shops and services. The 190 largely level, grassy pitches (100 sq.m) all have 4A electricity. There are many mobile homes and chalets for rent on the site. An activity area provides swings and other play equipment. The new owners are redeveloping the site and have modernised the toilet blocks. A new heated outdoor pool with slides should be available for the 2009 season. There are good tarmac and gravel access roads. The site provides a shuttle bus service to the local station and to Disneyland Paris. The man-made lake at nearby Jablines provide marvellous watersports activities including the largest beach in the Ile-de-France region.

Facilities

The four toilet blocks will include washbasins, toilets and showers in cabins. Facilities for babies and disabled persons. Laundry. Motorcaravan service point. Small shop. Bar and snack bar. Takeaway. Outdoor swimming and paddling pools planned. Playground. Games area. Minigolf. TV room. Gas supplies. Bicycle hire, Internet. Shuttle bus service Off site: Golf 10 km. Paris 20 km. Disneyland 20 km. Parc Astérix 40 km.

Open: All year.

Directions

From the north: A1 Paris, join A104 Marne la Vallée and leave at exit 6B onto N3. After Claye Souilly turn right on D404 to Villevaude and follow local camping signs. From the south: A4 Reims, Metz, Nancy, join A104 Lille and take exit 8 to join D404 towards Claye Souilly and Villevaude then follow local camping signs. GPS: N50:19.937 E01:34.776

Charges guide

Per unit incl. 2 persons	
and electricity	€ 29,00 - € 33,00
extra person	€ 7,00 - € 8,00
child (3-6 yrs)	€ 5,50 - € 6,60

open all the year

CAMPING CLUB
LE PARC DE PARIS
★★★

WWW.campingleparc.fr

CAMPING CLUB LE PARC DE PARIS
RUE ADELE CLARET, MONTJAY LA TOUR.
77410 VILLEVAUDE.
TEL: 01-60-26-20-79

Wi Fi

Camping
Caravaning
Accomodation

FR77140 Yelloh! Village Paris/Ile-de-France

Route de Montaiguillon, F-77560 Louan (Seine-et-Marne)

Tel: **04 66 73 97 39**. Email: **info@yellohvillage-paris-iledefrance.com**   www.alanrogers.com/FR77140

Formerly known as La Cerclière, this Yelloh! Village site to the east of Paris lies at the heart of the Montaiguillon forest, around 50 km. from Disneyland Paris and 80 km. from the city itself. This 11 hectare site contains 220 pitches, of which 40 are currently for touring units and 72 for mobile homes and chalets of which 20 are privately owned. Pitches are shaded, although some are rather small and only a few have electricity. The owners plan to include more touring pitches during 2009.

Facilities

Six toilet blocks, but when we visited only three were in use with quite a walk from some pitches. Provision was fairly basic and facilities for disabled visitors, motorcaravans and chemical disposal were very limited. Shop. Bar. Restaurant. Takeaway. Swimming pool complex with slides. Balnéotherapy pool. Tennis. Fishing. Cable runway for over 8 year olds (charged). Pony rides (charged). Activity and entertainment programme. Play area. Internet access and WiFi (charged).

Open: 26 April - 6 September.

Directions

From A4 (Paris - Metz) exit 16 join the N34. Continue on this road as far as La Ferté Gaucher and then turn right to join the southbound D204. At the N4 turn left and then right on D15 to Villiers St Georges. Continue on D60 to Louan Villegruis Fontaine from where the site is signed as Camping la Cerclière. GPS: N48:37.857 E03:29.516

Charges guide

Per unit incl. 2 persons	€ 14,00 - € 35,00

tel: +33 466 739 739 www.yellohvillage.com

Check real time availability and at-the-gate prices...

www.alanrogers.com

FR77130 Camping les Courtilles du Lido

Courtilles du Lido, F-77250 Veneux-les-Sablons (Seine-et-Marne)

Tel: 01 60 70 46 05. Email: lescourtilles-dulido@wanadoo.fr   www.alanrogers.com/FR77130

Les Courtilles du Lido is a well established, family run site located just outside the 14th-century village of Moret-sur-Loing on the edge of the Forêt de Fontainebleau. There are 180 well shaded grassy pitches with 10A electricity, dispersed throughout the five hectare terrain. A good range of amenities includes a pool and an 18-hole minigolf course, as well as a pizzeria and bar. There are 15 mobile homes for rent. Paris lies 55 km. to the north and can be accessed by either the A5 or A6 motorways or by rail from the local station (within walking distance). Some train noise can be heard from the site. The close proximity of Fontainebleau, just 5 km. distant, is, of course, a major attraction and the town merits repeated visits. The château was once the home of the kings of France. Fontainebleau's golf course is the second oldest in France and many other activities are possible in the area, including rock climbing and 300 km. of walking and cycle trails through the forest.

Facilities

A single toilet block provides adequate facilites. No facilities for children and disabled people. Shop. Pizzeria. Bar. Takeaway meals. Swimming pool. Play area. Games room. Motorcaravan services. Minigolf. Short tennis. Boules. Internet access and WiFi. Off site: Moret-sur-Loing (an attractive Gallo-Roman village) 2 km. Fishing 500 m. Canoeing. Riding and golf 15 km. Fontainebleau 5 km. River cruises 5 km. Paris 55 km.

Open: Easter - 22 September.

Directions

Site is close to the point where the Loing joins the Seine. From Fontainebleau take the southbound N6 (towards Sens). Upon arrival at Veneux les Sablons follow signs for Moret-sur-Loing and then St Mammès. Final approach is through a tunnel. Site is well signed. GPS: N48:22.993 E02:48.182

Charges guide

Per person	€ 3,75
child (under 7 yrs)	€ 3,00

Camping Les Courtilles du Lido - Chemin du Passeur - 77250 Veneux les Sablons
Tel: 0033 160 70 46 05 - Fax: 0033 164 70 62 65
E-mail: lescourtilles-dulido@wanadoo.fr - www.les-courtilles-du-lido.fr

FR77150 Flower Camping la Ferté Gaucher

Route de Saint Martin des Champs, F-77320 La Ferté Gaucher (Seine-et-Marne)

Tel: 01 64 20 20 40   www.alanrogers.com/FR77150

La Ferté Gaucher is an attractive town in the valley of the Grand Morin, a tributary of the Marne. The main appeal of this site, however, is probably its proximity to Disneyland Paris and the capital itself. The site is a member of the Flower group and extends over four hectares of parkland. There are 200 grassy pitches of a good size and with electrical connections. The river runs alongside the site and some pitches are adjacent to it. Leisure facilities include fishing and during the peak season, occasional evening entertainment is organized. Municipal tennis courts and a swimming pool can be found 50 m. from the site.

Facilities

Bar. Small restaurant. Takeaway. Fishing. Bicycle hire. Playground. Entertainment and activity programme. Mobile homes for rent. Off site: Tennis. Swimming pool. Cycle and walking tracks. Disneyland Paris 44 km. Paris 74 km.

Open: 1 March - 30 September.

Directions

Head east from Paris on the A4 and leave at exit 16 (Crécy-la-Chapelle). Continue southeast on the D934 through Coulommiers and as far as La Ferté Gaucher. Site is well indicated from here. GPS: N48:46.747 E03:18.644

Charges 2009

Per unit incl. 2 persons and electricity	€ 15,00 - € 26,00
extra person	€ 3,00 - € 4,00
child (2-7 yrs)	€ 2,00 - € 3,00
dog	€ 1,50 - € 2,00

www.flowercampings.com

(113)

The Travel Service
...we'll arrange everything
CALL 01580 214000
BOOK THIS SITE

FR78040 Huttopia Rambouillet

Route du Château d'Eau, F-78120 Rambouillet (Yvelines)

Tel: 01 30 41 07 34. Email: rambouillet@huttopia.com

www.alanrogers.com/FR78040

This pleasant site has recently been taken over by the Huttopia group who will be developing it, starting with an outdoor, heated swimming pool. It is in a peaceful forest location beside a lake, with good tarmac access roads, site lighting and 190 touring pitches of varying size and surfaces. Some of the individual pitches are divided by hedges, others are more open and sunny. All have electricity, 83 also have water and drainage, with a few hardstandings. There are many good cycle and footpaths in the area. Rambouillet itself is an interesting town and Chartres and Versailles are within reach. It is possible to visit Paris by rail; the Mobilis 'transport package' ticket is available from the railway station.

Facilities	Directions
Two heated sanitary buildings include British and Turkish style WCs, washbasins (some in cubicles), dishwashing and laundry sinks, plus basic facilities for baby changing and for disabled persons. Washing machine and dryer. Motorcaravan service point. Café/bar and boutique. Good playground. Swimming pool. Off site: Large supermarket at southern end of the town.	Rambouillet is 52 km. southwest of Paris. Site is southeast of town: from N10 southbound take Rambouillet/Les Eveuses exit, northbound take Rambouillet centre exit, loop round and rejoin N10 southbound, taking next exit. Follow site signs. GPS: N48:37.623 E01:50.727

Open: 4 April - 5 November.

Charges 2009

Per unit incl. 2 persons	€ 22,00 - € 36,40
extra person	€ 5,20 - € 6,80

Camping Cheques accepted.

HUTTOPIA

tel: +33 (0) 4 37 64 22 33 www.huttopia.com

HUTTOPIA

Huttopia Rambouillet

Roulottes, tents and cottages to rent

Natural swimming-pool, Bar restaurant, brand new facilities, children playground...

Route du Château d'eau
78120 Rambouillet
Tel. +33 (0)1 30 41 07 34

In the heart of the famous forest of Rambouillet by the «Etang d'Or» pond...

www.huttopia.com

FR78010 Camping Caravaning International

1 rue Johnson, F-78600 Maisons-Laffitte (Yvelines)

Tel: 01 39 12 21 91. Email: ci.mlaffitte@wanadoo.fr

www.alanrogers.com/FR78010

This site on the banks of the Seine is consistently busy, has multilingual, friendly reception staff and occupies a grassy, tree covered area bordering the river. There are 351 pitches, 57 occupied by mobile homes and 70 used by tour operators, plus two areas dedicated to tents. Most pitches are separated by hedges, are of a good size with some overlooking the Seine (unfenced access), and all 195 touring pitches have electricity hook-ups (6A). The roads leading to the site are a little narrow so large vehicles need to take care. Train noise can be expected.

Facilities	Directions
Three sanitary blocks, two insulated for winter use and one more open (only used in July/August). Facilities are clean with constant supervision necessary, due to volume of visitors. Provision for people with disabilities. Laundry and dishwashing areas. Motorcaravan service point. Self-service shop. Restaurant/bar. Takeaway food and pizzeria. TV room, table tennis, football area. Internet point. SNCF rep each morning 15/6-15/8 for travel advice. Off site: Sports complex adjoining. Riding 500 m. Bicycle hire 5 km.	Best approached from A13 or A15 autoroute. From A13 take exit 7 (Poissy). Follow D153 (Poissy), the D308 (Maisons-Laffitte), then site signs before town centre. From A15 exit 7 take D184 (St Germain), after 11 km. turn left on D308 (Maisons-Laffitte). Follow site signs. From A1 take A86, then at exit 2 (Bezons) take D308 (Maisons-Laffitte). Follow signs to site on left. GPS: N48:56.394 E02:08.740

Open: 1 April - 31 October.

Charges guide

Per unit incl. 2 persons and electricity	€ 24,50 - € 30,00

Check real time availability and at-the-gate prices...

www.alanrogers.com

FR78060 Huttopia Versailles

31 rue Berthelot, F-78000 Versailles (Yvelines)

Tel: 01 39 51 23 61. Email: versailles@huttopia.com

www.alanrogers.com/FR78060

This Huttopia site is rather different. When the French owners visited Canada and experienced 'back to nature' camping, they were so impressed that they decided to introduce the idea to France. This is probably a little like camping as it used to be, but with some big differences. Gone are the formal pitches with neatly trimmed hedges and instead there are 145 places of ample size arranged informally amongst the trees. The terrain is as nature intended with very little grass and much of it steep and rugged (there are plans to introduce some terracing). Long electricity leads are required and be prepared to use blocks and corner steadies on many pitches. Most pitches have good shade. All the site buildings are designed and built to fit into the natural concept. Attractive wooden huts, tents and gypsy style caravans can be rented. This is a different but popular site that will suit campers who, while still wanting their creature comforts, would like to be in more natural surroundings.

Facilities

Three well designed toilet blocks (wood cabin style) provide basic facilities. Special bivouacs set up for cooking and washing up. Restaurant with takeaway food (30/4-27/9 and weekends). Bar. Games room. Simple swimming and paddling pools (May - Sept). Playground. Bicycle hire. Children's club. Off site: Versailles and its château. Fishing 1 km. Golf 3 km. Riding 5 km.

Open: 19 December - 5 November.

Directions

From the front of the château of Versailles take the Avenue de Paris and the site is signed after 2 km. GPS: N48:47.380 E02:09.380

Charges 2009

Per unit with 2 persons	
and electricity	€ 27,30 - € 41,80
extra person	€ 6,20 - € 8,50
child (2-7 yrs)	€ 3,00 - € 4,30
dog	€ 4,00

tel: +33 (0) 4 37 64 22 33 www.huttopia.com

HUTTOPIA Versailles

Roulottes, tents and cottages to rent

Heated swimming-pool, Bar restaurant, Children playground...

31 rue Berthelot 78000 Versailles Tel. +33 (0)1 39 51 23 61

In the heart of the forest
5 minutes from the Palace of Versailles
20 minutes from the Eiffel Tower...

www.huttopia.com

FR78050 Camping le Val de Seine

Base de Loisirs, chemin du Rouillard, F-78480 Verneuil-sur-Seine (Yvelines)

Tel: 01 39 28 16 20. Email: sce-client@valdeseine78.com

www.alanrogers.com/FR78050

This is an excellent little site, completely refurbished to high standards and located in a large leisure and country park on the western outskirts of Paris. Campers have free access to the huge country park (800 m. from site) with its three large lakes, one with a beach for swimming, others for sailing and pedalo hire. The site has 87 pitches in two sections, one each for campers (mainly groups) with its own toilet block, the other for caravans and tents. Here there are 37 level pitches, all but four with electricity (6A), water and drainage. There is some aircraft and train noise.

Facilities

Two modern toilet blocks have controllable showers and some washbasins in cubicles. Facilities for disabled visitors (touring area). Dishwashing provision. Small block for children plus baby room (camping area). Laundry facilities. Motorcaravan service point. Reception sells bread (to order) and basics. Country park with lakes, fishing, sailing, many other sports facilities, a self-service restaurant and brasserie. Tennis courts, 18-hole minigolf. Communal barbecue in camping area. Off site: Riding adjacent. Golf 7 km. Paris 20 mins by train and 30 mins by car.

Open: 15 April - 30 September.

Directions

From A13 take exit 8 (Meulan-les Mureaux). Follow signs for 'Base de Loisirs du Val de Seine'. Go through Les Mureaux and bear right on D154 towards Verneuil. At roundabout turn left (signed 'Base de Loisirs') to site. GPS: N48:59.762 E01:57.548

Charges guide

Per person (4 yrs and over)	€ 3,25 - € 3,75
pitch	€ 4,20 - € 5,30
electricity	€ 4,25

115

MAP 4

Home to the Champagne region, the varied landscapes of Eastern France include dense forests, vineyards and winding rivers. The whole area is dotted with fascinating ancient churches and castles, towns and villages.

Alan Rogers

EASTERN FRANCE IS DEFINED AS:
CHAMPAGNE-ARDENNE: 08 ARDENNES, 51 MARNE, 10 AUBE, 52 HAUTE-MARNE. LORRAINE VOSGES: 54 MEURTHE-ET-MOSELLE, 55 MEUSE, 57 MOSELLE, 88 VOSGES. ALSACE: 67 BAS-RHIN, 68 HAUT-RHIN

Situated on the flatlands of Champagne are the most northerly vineyards in France where special processing turns the light, dry wine into 'le Champagne' and names such as Moët et Chandon and Veuve Clicquot spring to mind. Nowhere else in the world are you allowed to make sparkling wine and call it Champagne. Travelling further east you come across spa towns such as Vittel, the birth place of St Joan of Arc at Domrémy and the beautiful lake and valley around Gérardmer in the Vosges mountains.

Today you can descend from the mountains into the Alsace vineyards and fairy tale wine villages. The 'Route des Vins' follows the vineyards along the Rhine valley from Mulhouse to Colmar and north almost to Strasbourg. Alsace and Lorraine have been frequently fought over and today there are many poignant reminders of the turbulent past, such as at Verdun. There are also many beautiful places to visit, such as the garden-city of Metz and the Art Nouveau capital of Nancy.

Places of interest

Épernay: home of Champagne production.

Gérardmer and La Bresse: the main towns of the Vosges mountains with many opportunities for hiking.

Le Linge: trenches including rusty barbed wire have been left as they were.

Metz and Nancy: the capitals of Lorraine, known for their beautiful cultural heritage.

Reims: 13th-century Gothic cathedral.

Riquewihr: traditional town, fortifications and medieval houses.

Verdun: hill forts such as Fort de Vaux and Fort de Douaumont, large military cemetery at Douaumont.

Cuisine of the region

Bar-le-Duc ('Lorraine caviar'): redcurrant jam de-seeded with a goose quill.

Madeleine de Commercy: small, shell shaped, buttery pastries with orange flavouring.

Quiche Lorraine: made only in the classical manner with cream, eggs and bacon.

Tarte (aux mirabelles): golden plum tart. Also made with other fruits.

Tarte à l'oignon Alsacienne: onion and cream tart.

Credit photo: CRTL.
The Comité Régional du Tourisme de Lorraine's annual Passport brochure suggesting over 150 places to visit (with discounted entrance) is available free of charge from www.tourisme-lorraine.fr

[Ethnology]
STRANGE AQUATIC TRIBES

Playful nature,
Explore the diversity of the vegetation and natural landscapes of Champagne-Ardenne, France's most floral region.

Gourmet delights,
Treat yourself in Champagne-Ardenne to a selection of local produce which will set your taste buds dancing!

Fan of novel adventures,
Champagne-Ardenne frees your traveller's soul. On land, on water and in the air; whether calm or exciting, the adventure can begin!

Lover of eloquent stories,
Attentive observer or gentle rambler, Champagne-Ardenne transports you, beyond the centuries, through the wealth of its heritage.

You'll see, Champagne-Ardenne will be your next conquest!

horizon-bleu.com

Your next conquest

www.tourisme-champagne-ardenne.com

CHAMPAGNE ARDENNE
TOURISME

FR08010 Camping Municipal du Mont Olympe

Rue des Paquis, F-08000 Charleville-Mezieres (Ardennes)

Tel: **03 24 33 23 60**. Email: **camping-charlevillemezieres@wanadoo.fr**   www.alanrogers.com/FR08010

Attractively situated alongside the Meuse River, within easy walking distance across a footbridge to the centre of the pleasant large town, this site was completely rebuilt in 2002. It now offers excellent facilities, with 129 grass pitches, all with electricity (10A), water and waste water connections. There are 66 from 108 to 219 sq.m. in size, 49 up to 106 sq.m. and seven hardstandings for motorcaravans.

Facilities	Directions
Two heated buildings provide first class showers, private cabins, baby rooms and facilities for disabled visitors. Well equipped laundry room. Motorcaravan service point. Shop (July/Aug). Play area. TV and games room. Barbecues allowed at communal area only. Off site: Municipal pool next door. Boat trips on the river. Attractive town centre close by. Bicycle hire 1 km. Golf 20 km.	Site north of Charleville on island of Montcy St Pierre. From north D988/D1 follow river, over bridge, then immediately left. From southeast (A203/N51/N43) take 'centre' exit, head for 'Gare' then follow Avenue Forest north and sharp left after bridge. Site is 150 m. on from old site. GPS: N49:46.741 E04:43.246

Open: 1 April - 15 October.

Charges guide

Per unit incl. 2 persons and electricity	€ 16,00
extra person	€ 3,20
child (2-10 yrs)	€ 1,60 - € 5,80

FR08040 Camping la Samaritaine

Rue des Etangs, F-08240 Buzancy (Ardennes)

Tel: **03 24 30 08 88**. Email: **info@campinglasamaritaine.com**   www.alanrogers.com/FR08040

A delightful new site in the heart of the Ardennes. It is peacefully situated just outside the village beside a stream. There may be some high season noise from a nearby lake where you can swim or fish. Flowers decorate the entrance and bushes and saplings separate the pitches. The 101 numbered touring pitches all have electricity (10A) and are on level grass off hard access roads. They vary in size up to 130 sq.m. 55 have water and drainage, and there are small wooden containers for waste. There are also ten mobile homes and nine chalets for rent.

Facilities	Directions
Sanitary facilities provide private cabins. Baby bath. Facilities for disabled visitors. Laundry facilities. Motorcaravan service point. Bread delivered daily. A few essentials are kept in reception. Snack bar/takeaway (20/6-31/8). Large recreation room with games and tables. Play area. Boules. Accompanied walks and entertainment programme (high season). Off site: Restaurant in village.	Buzancy is about 22 km. east of Vouziers on RD947 towards Stenay and Montmédy. Site is just over 1.5 km. from centre of village down a small road. Well signed. GPS: N49:25.584 E04:56.406

Open: 1 May - 20 September.

Charges 2009

Per unit with 2 persons and electricity	€ 16,50 - € 18,50
extra person	€ 3,00 - € 3,50
child (under 10 yrs)	€ 2,00 - € 2,50
animal	€ 1,50 - € 2,20

FR10010 Camping Municipal de Troyes

7 rue Roger Salengro, F-10150 Pont-Sainte-Marie (Aube)

Tel: **03 25 81 02 64**. Email: **info@troyescamping.net**   www.alanrogers.com/FR10010

This municipal campsite, within the Troyes city boundary and about 2 km. from the centre, has been taken over by two young enthusiastic managers who are turning it into an attractive place to stay. Their plans include adding a covered pool. There are 110 level grassy pitches (six with hardstanding), all for tourers, about equally shaded and open. All have electrical connections (5A, some need long leads), and there are plenty of water taps. Being on one of the main routes from Luxembourg to the southwest of France, and from Calais to the Mediterranean, Troyes makes a good night stop.

Facilities	Directions
Two modern toilet blocks contain British style WCs, washbasins and pre-set showers. Facilities for disabled people. Motorcaravan services. Washing machines and dryer. Shop for basics. Gas supplies. Restaurant, snack bar and takeaway (15/6-15/9). TV room. Games room, free of charge. Playground. Bouncy castle. Minigolf. Boules. Bicycle hire. Off site: Bus to Troyes centre 50 m. Supermarket 100 m. Other shops, restaurants, bars, ATM 300 m. Riding 8 km.	From all routes follow signs for Troyes and Pont Sainte-Marie (just north of the old city centre), then signs for Camping Municipal. Site is on the Chalons road no. 77. GPS: N48:18.666 E04:05.817

Open: 1 April - 15 October.

Charges guide

Per person	€ 4,50
child (2-11 yrs)	€ 3,20
pitch	€ 6,00 - € 7,00
electricity (5A)	€ 2,80
animal	€ 1,00

Check real time availability and at-the-gate prices...

www.alanrogers.com

FR10020 Kawan Resort Lac de la Forêt d'Orient

Rue du Lac, F-10140 Mesnil Saint Père (Aube)

Tel: **03 25 41 27 15**. Email: **info@campinglacdorient.com**   www.alanrogers.com/FR10020

Le Lac d'Orient is a new site which will be opening in 2009. This site will be one of the first Kawan Resorts, a new group of campsites in attractive rural locations and equipped with a good range of leisure amenities. We will be undertaking a full inspection of this site in 2009. The site can be found at the centre of the large Forêt d'Orient natural park and is just 100 m. from a large lake which is ideal for all manner of watersports. Previously, a small municipal site, Le Lac d'Orient has been comprehensively renovated and will offer a new restaurant and bar, as well as indoor and outdoor swimming pools. There are 300 pitches here, some of which will be occupied by mobile homes and chalets. All pitches will have electrical connections and some will also offer water and drainage. There are miles of walking and cycle routes, and further afield, the city of Troyes is worth exploration, with parts dating back to the Roman era.

Facilities	Directions
Restaurant/bar. Takeaway. Shop. Indoor and outdoor swimming pools. Paddling pool. Sauna and spa bath. TV room. Play area. Off site: Troyes centre 20 km. Lac de l'Orient 100 m. Windsurfing and sailing. Canoe and pedalo hire. Fishing. Cycle and walking tracks.	Mesnil Saint Père is close to the intersection of the A5 and A26 motorways. Leave the A26 at exit 23 and join the eastbound D619, signed Lac d'Orient. Turn left on D43 following signs to Mesnil Saint Père and then the site.
Open: 15 May - 30 September.	**Charges 2009**
	To be confirmed; please contact the site. Camping Cheques accepted.

Rue du Lac
10140 Mesnil Saint Père

Tél : 0033 (0)3 85 72 65 96
Fax : 0033 (0)3 85 72 66 07

info@camping-lacdorient.com
www.camping-lacdorient.com

Open from 15/05/2009 to 30/09/2009 (check the dates on the website)

kawan RESORT **LAC D'ORIENT**

Next to the lake with its yacht marina and beach, Camping le Lac d'Orient offers a woodland setting with brand new facilities throughout for 2009.

Check real time availability and at-the-gate prices...

www.**alanrogers**.com

The Travel **Service** ...we'll arrange everything **CALL 01580 214000** **BOOK THIS SITE**

FR51020 Camping Municipal en Champagne

Rue de Plaisance, F-51000 Châlons-en-Champagne (Marne)

Tel: 03 26 68 38 00. Email: camping.mairie.chalons@wanadoo.fr   www.alanrogers.com/FR51020

The location of Châlons, south of Reims and near the A4 and A26 autoroutes, about 200 miles from Calais and Boulogne, makes this an ideal stopover. This site on the southern edge of town is an example of a good municipal site. The wide entrance with its neatly mown grass and flower beds sets the tone for the rest of the site; 96 of the 148 pitches, accessed from tarmac roads, are on a gravel base with the rest on grass. All have electricity (10A). The generously sized gravel pitches are separated by hedges. The newest area of pitches overlooks the small lake.

Facilities

Two toilet blocks (one can be heated) include washbasins in cabins, baby room and hairdressing station. Facilities for disabled visitors. Laundry and dishwashing facilities. Refuse bins. Bread to order. Bar, snack bar and takeaway (20/5-31/9 evenings, lunchtime July/Aug). Gas supplies. Games and TV rooms. Playground. Minigolf, tennis, volleyball, boules, minifootball. Motorcaravan service point. Off site: Bus stop. Fishing.

Open: 1 April - 31 October.

Directions

From north on A4, take La Veuve exit (27) onto N44 which by-passes town. Leave at last exit (St Memmie), follow camping signs. From south on A26, take exit 18 on N77 and towards town. Site well signed 'Camping', (south of town on D60). GPS: N48:56.156 E04:22.994

Charges guide

Per person	€ 4,80
child (under 7 yrs)	€ 1,85
pitch incl. electricity	€ 8,00
vehicle	€ 3,20

FR52030 Kawan Village Lac de la Liez

Mobile homes ▶ page 493

Peigney, F-52200 Langres (Haute-Marne)

Tel: 03 25 90 27 79. Email: campingliez@free.fr   www.alanrogers.com/FR52030

Managed by the enthusiastic Baude family, this newly renovated lakeside site is near the city of Langres. Only 10 minutes from the A5, Camping Lac de la Liez provides an ideal spot for an overnight stop en route to the south of France. There is also a lot on offer for a longer stay. The site provides 131 fully serviced pitches, some with panoramic views of the 250 hectare lake with its sandy beach and small harbour where boats and pedaloes may be hired. Ideal for swimming and watersports; access to the lake is down steps and across quite a fast road (in total 150 m). Amenities on the site include indoor and outdoor swimming pools, a restaurant and bar and a shop. As well as all the activities on the lake, sporting activities on site include a tennis court, archery and bicycle hire. The city pf Langres with its old ramparts and ancient city centre is within easy reach – it was elected one of the 50 most historic cities in France – and it is well worth a visit.

Facilities

Two toilet blocks have all facilities in cabins (only one is open in low season). Facilities for disabled people and babies. Laundry facilities. Motorcaravan services. Shop, bar and restaurant (with takeaway food). Indoor pool complex with spa and sauna. Heated outdoor pool (15/6-15/9). Games room. Playground. Extensive games area. Tennis (free in low season). Off site: Lake with beach. Boat and bicycle hire and cycle tracks around lake. Fishing 100 m. Riding 5 km. Golf 40 km.

Open: 1 April - 1 November.

Directions

From Langres take the N19 towards Vesoul. After 3 km. turn right, straight after the large river bridge, then follow site signs. GPS: N47:52.440 E05:22.628

Charges guide

Per person	€ 5,00 - € 7,00
child (2-12 yrs)	€ 3,00 - € 4,50
pitch	€ 6,00 - € 8,00
electricity	€ 3,50 - € 5,00
dog	€ 3,00

Camping Cheques accepted.

Camping du Lac de la Liez ★★★★

In the heart of the Champagne and Ardennes regions of France, Lac de la Liez is a top quality 4 star site, ideal for the whole family

Open 01st April - 01st November

Peigney, F-52200 Langres • tel 0033 (0)325 90 27 79 • fax 0033 (0)325 90 66 79
e-mail campingliez@free.fr • http://campingliez.free.fr

Check real time availability and at-the-gate prices...

www.**alanrogers**.com

FR52020 Castel Camping la Forge de Sainte-Marie

F-52230 Thonnance-les-Moulins (Haute-Marne)

Tel: 03 25 94 42 00. Email: info@laforgedesaintemarie.com   www.alanrogers.com/FR52020

This most attractive campsite, entered through an arched gateway, was created in 1995 by careful conservation of original forge buildings to create modern facilities in this secluded valley. A picturesque bridge links the upper part with a lower road to the section near the river. Another old building has been converted into gîtes for letting. Grass pitches, 165 for touring units, are of a very generous size on terraces amongst trees or in more open areas. Electricity (6A) and water are available and 120 pitches are fully serviced. There are also 30 mobile homes and chalets, and 22 tour operator units.

Facilities	Directions
Two sanitary blocks (under pressure at peak times). Additional facilities at reception or pool complex. Shop, restaurant and bar with terrace. Pizzeria in high season. Heated indoor pool and one for children (28/4-12/9). Play areas. Bicycle hire. Fishing on payment. Games room. Internet terminal. Organized games for children (high season). Programme for adults including farm visit with barbecue, music, dancing and excursions. Golfing holidays arranged. Off site: Riding 15 km. Golf 45 km. **Open:** 25 April - 11 September.	Site is 12 km. southeast of Joinville between Poissons and Germay on road D427. The site entrance may be a little tight for large units. GPS: N48:24.392 E05:16.270

Charges guide

Per pitch incl. 2 persons	
and electricity	€ 18,70 - € 29,90
extra person	€ 3,60 - € 7,20
child (2-9 yrs)	€ 1,80 - € 3,60
animal	€ 1,50

Camping Cheques accepted.

FR52060 Camping Navarre

9 bld Maréchal de Lattre de Tassigny, F-52200 Langres (Haute-Marne)

Tel: 03 25 87 37 92. Email: campingnavarre@free.fr   www.alanrogers.com/FR52060

Camping Navarre is a small municipal site of 66 pitches, with the advantage of being located within the town of Langres. The pitches here are grassy, well shaded and of a good size, mostly with electrical connections. The site's toilet block has all the usual facilities and has been recently modernised. Although there are few amenities on site, the town centre is just a short walk away and a wide selection of shops, cafés and restaurants is on offer. Langres, with its 3.5 km. of ancient ramparts and imposing towers, is classified as one of the 50 most beautiful towns in France and makes a popular overnight stop. For those choosing to spend longer in the Haute-Marne, the surrounding country stretching across the large Lac de la Liez (resulting from the construction of the Marne - Saône canal) and the Marne valley is well worth exploration. The Liez sailing school offers opportunities for windsurfing and sailing, and canoe and pedalo hire are also available.

Facilities	Directions
Modernised, heated toilet block with facilities for disabled visitors. Play area. Off site: Langres centre. Lac de la Liez 5 km. Fishing (river) 3 km. Cycle and walking tracks. **Open:** 15 March - 31 October.	Langres is close to the intersection of the A5 and A31 motorways. Leave either motorway and head for the town centre. Site is well signed from here. GPS: N47:51.651 E05:19.817

Charges guide

Per unit incl. 2 adults	
and 2 children	€ 12,00 - € 13,40

Camping Navarre

For a one-night stop or a longer stay in the historical city of Langres the campsite Navarre is ready to welcome you with a brand new toilet block

Camping Navarre • 9, Boulevard Marechal de Lattre de Tassigny • 52200 Langres
Tél./fax: 0033 (0)325 87 37 92 • E-mail: campingnavarre@free.fr • www.campingnavarre.fr

FR52050 Yelloh! Village en Champagne

F-52290 Eclaron (Haute-Marne)

Tel: **04 66 73 97 39**. Email: **info@yellohvillage-en-champagne.com**   **www.alanrogers.com/FR52050**

Formerly known as Les Sources du Lac, this Yelloh! Village site has been recommended to us and we plan to undertake a full inspection in 2009. The site is located close to the village of Eclaron and has direct access to the Lac du Der. This is a very large lake with 77 km. of shoreline and is home to over 270 species of birds. Part of the lake is an ornithological reserve but a wide range of water based activities are on offer in other areas. These include including fishing, windsurfing and sailing. There are 55 touring pitches here and around 90 mobile homes and chalets for rent.

Facilities

Shop. Bar. Restaurant. Takeaway. Swimming pool. Paddling pool. Direct access to the lake and beach. Ornithological activities. Activity and entertainment programme. Off site: Walking and cycle trails. Fishing. The 'Champagne route'. Grange aux Abeilles (bee barn) at Giffaumont Champaubert.

Open: 26 April - 6 September.

Directions

Take the southbound N44 from Châlons as far as Vitry-le-François and then join the eastbound N4 as far as St Dizier. From St Dizier ring road take D384 towards Montier-en-Der and at Eclaron-Braucourt follow signs to site. GPS: N48:34.328 E04:50.935

Charges guide

Per unit incl. 2 persons	€ 14,00 - € 29,00
extra person (over 3 yrs)	€ 4,00 - € 5,00

tel: +33 466 739 739   www.yellohvillage.com ————

FR54000 Campéole le Brabois

Avenue Paul Muller, F-54600 Villers-les-Nancy (Meurthe-et-Moselle)

Tel: **03 83 27 18 28**. Email: **nadine.ferran@atciat.com**   **www.alanrogers.com/FR54000**

This former municipal site is within the Nancy city boundary and 5 km. from the centre. Situated within a forest area, there is shade in most parts and, although the site is on a slight slope, the 185 good-sized, numbered and separated pitches are level. Of these, 160 pitches have electrical connections (5/15A) and 30 also have water and drainage. Being on one of the main routes from Luxembourg to the south of France, Le Brabois makes a good night stop.

Facilities

Six sanitary blocks (old and due for refurbishment over the next few years) with a mix of British and Turkish style WCs and some washbasins in cubicles. One can be heated in cool weather. Units for disabled visitors. Laundry facilities. Motorcaravan service point. Shop. Bread to order. Restaurant with bar and small shop (15/6-31/8). Library. Playground. Off site: Restaurants, shops 1 km. Walking and cycling. Regular buses to Nancy.

Open: 1 April - 15 October.

Directions

From autoroute A33 take exit 2b for Brabois and continue for 500 m. to 'Quick' restaurant on left. Turn left, pass racetrack to T-junction, turn right and after 400 m. turn right on to site entrance road. GPS: N48:39.864 E06:08.598

Charges guide

Per unit incl. 2 persons and electricity	€ 15,00 - € 18,20
extra person	€ 4,00 - € 5,50

Credit cards minimum € 15.

FR54010 Camping de Villey-le-Sec

34 rue de la Gare, F-54840 Villey-le-Sec (Meurthe-et-Moselle)

Tel: **03 83 63 64 28**. Email: **info@campingvilleylesec.com**   **www.alanrogers.com/FR54010**

This neat campsite is a popular overnight stop, but the area is worth a longer stay. Villey-le-Sec has its own fortifications, part of the defensive system built along France's frontiers after the 1870 war, and a long cycle track passes near the site. On a bank of the Moselle river, there are 75 level grassy marked touring pitches, with electricity (6A) and plenty of water taps. There are also individual water taps and waste water drainage for eight of these pitches. Another area without electricity accommodates 11 tents. Just outside the site is an overnight stopping place for motorcaravans.

Facilities

Two modern toilet blocks (one heated) contain British style WCs, washbasins in cabins and controllable showers. Facilities for disabled people and babies. Motorcaravan services. Washing machine and dryer. Gas supplies. Shop. Bar/restaurant. Snack bar and takeaway. Games room. Playground. Playing field. Table tennis. Boules. Fishing. Off site: Riding 2 km. Rock climbing 4 km. Golf 15 km.

Open: 1 April - 30 September.

Directions

Villey-le-Sec is 7 km. east of Toul. Leave A31 west of Nancy at exit 15 and after 1 km. at roundabout (Leclerc supermarket) take D909 to Villey-le-Sec. In village follow signs 'Camping, Base de Loisirs' to the right. At bottom of hill turn left to site in 300 m. GPS: N48:39.169 E05:59.491

Charges guide

Per person	€ 3,00
pitch	€ 2,30 - € 3,60
electricity (6-10A)	€ 3,50 - € 4,50

Check real time availability and at-the-gate prices...

www.alanrogers.com

FR55010 Camping les Breuils

Allée des Breuils, F-55100 Verdun (Meuse)

Tel: 03 29 86 15 31. Email: contact@camping-lesbreuils.com   www.alanrogers.com/FR55010

Thousands of soldiers of many nations are buried in the cemeteries around this famous town and the city is justly proud of its determined First World War resistance. Les Breuils is a neat, attractive site beside a small fishing lake and close to the town and Citadel. It provides 166 flat pitches of varying sizes on two levels (144 for touring units), many with shade. Separated by trees or hedges, they are beside the lake and 120 offer electricity connection (6A) – long leads will be necessary for some. The 'Citadelle Souterraine' is well worth a visit and is within walking distance of the site.

Facilities

Two sanitary blocks are a mixture of old and new, including washbasins in cabins for ladies. Laundry facilities. Facilities for disabled visitors and babies. Cleaning variable. Motorcaravan services. Shop (1/5-30/9). Guide books on sale at reception (1/5-31/8). Restaurant (1/6-20/8), bar (evenings 1/5-30/9). Swimming pool (200 sq.m) and children's pool (1/6-31/8). Fenced gravel play area. Multisports complex. Off site: Bicycle hire, town 1 km. Riding 5 km.

Open: 1 April - 30 September.

Directions

The RN3 forms a sort of ring road round the north of the town. Site is signed from this on the west side of the town (500 m. to site).
GPS: N49:09.222 E05:21.938

Charges guide

Per person	€ 4,00 - € 5,50
child (2-10 yrs)	€ 3,00 - € 3,50
pitch	€ 3,00 - € 4,50
electricity (6A)	€ 4,00
dog	€ 1,70

Discounts for low season and longer stays.
Credit cards accepted for minimum of € 15.

FR57050 Camping Municipal de Metz-Plage

Allée de Metz-Plage, F-57000 Metz (Moselle)

Tel: 03 87 68 26 48. Email: campingmetz@mairie-metz.fr   www.alanrogers.com/FR57050

As this site is just a short way from the autoroute exit and within easy walking distance for the city centre, it could make a useful night stop if travelling from Luxembourg to Nancy or for a longer stay if exploring the area. By the Moselle river, the 151 pitches are on fairly level grass and most are under shade from tall trees. 65 pitches are fully serviced and 84 have electricity (10A). Tent pitches have a separate place beside the river.

Facilities

The two sanitary blocks, one newer than the other, are acceptable if not luxurious. Facilities for disabled visitors. Baby room. Laundry and dishwashing facilities. Motorcaravan service point. Shop. Bar, restaurant and takeaway. Hardstanding pitches for over night stops for motorcaravans without electricity. Off site: Indoor pool adjacent. Fishing. Riding 5 km. Golf 8 km.

Open: 5 May - 23 September.

Directions

From autoroute take Metz-Nord - Pontiffray exit (no. 33) and follow site signs.
GPS: N49:07.430 E06:10.135

Charges guide

Per person	€ 2,50
child (4-10 yrs)	€ 1,20
pitch incl. electricity	€ 6,00
incl. water and drainage	€ 7,00
tent and vehicle	€ 2,50

FR57080 Camping la Croix du Bois Sacker

F-57220 Burtoncourt (Moselle)

Tel: 03 87 35 74 08. Email: camping.croixsacker@wanadoo.fr   www.alanrogers.com/FR57080

This very attractive site is quiet and child-friendly and has been run for the last few years by a young and enthusiastic couple who have made many improvements to this former municipal site. For example, the terrace has been enlarged, a small shop added and the facilities for disabled visitors improved. There are 60 pleasant, open pitches, some with shade and all with electricity and water taps. The site is not far from Metz and is well suited for travellers going south to Germany, Switzerland or Italy. Forming part of the site, a lake is good for fishing (carp).

Facilities

The seasonal and touring parts of the site have separate facilities. Showers are on payment (token). Turkish style toilets outnumber British style. Washbasins, some in cabins. Shop. Bar. Sports field and tennis court. Play area. Lake swimming (July/Aug). Fishing. Off site: Woodland walks.

Open: 1 April - 20 October.

Directions

From the A4 take exit 37 (Argancy) and follow signs for Malroy, Chieulles and Vany on RD3 towards Bouzonville. Then take D53 to Burtoncourt and site.
GPS: N49:13.499 E06:23.966

Charges guide

Per unit incl. 2 persons and electricity	€ 15,00
extra person	€ 4,00
child (2-12 yrs)	€ 2,50
dog	€ 1,50

FR67010 Camping l'Oasis

3 rue du Frohret, F-67110 Oberbronn (Bas-Rhin)

Tel: **03 88 09 71 96**. Email: **oasis.oberbronn@laregie.fr**   www.alanrogers.com/FR67010

This is an attractively situated, inexpensive site, amidst the mountains and forests of northern Alsace, not far from the German border. There are good views over the valley to one side and the pretty village with trees sheltering the other. The circular internal road has pitches around the outside (120 for touring units, 30 for seasonal units), and space in the centre where there is a playground. A 'Centre de Vacances' has been added, with a covered swimming pool, sauna and fitness room.

Facilities

The first well appointed toilet block, heated in cool weather, has some washbasins in cabins for ladies, washing machines and dryers, a baby room and facilities for disabled people. The second block is unisex and small. Small shop. General room with table football and air hockey. Swimming pool and children's pool (July/Aug). Indoor pool next to site. Playground. New childrens club. Tennis court. Off site: Riding 700 m. Supermarket 1 km. Fishing 3 km. Fitness circuit in forest. Market selling local produce.

Open: 14 March - 12 November.

Directions

Travel northwest from Haguenau on N62 for 20 km. South of Niederbronn turn left on D28 for Oberbronn-Zinswiller - site is signed from here. From A4 take exit 42 to Sarreguemines, then N62 and D620 towards Haguenau and as above. GPS: N48:55.746 E07:36.244

Charges guide

Per person	€ 3,70
pitch incl. electricity	€ 6,30
car	€ 1,80

No credit cards.

FR67040 Camping la Ferme des Tuileries

F-67860 Rhinau (Bas-Rhin)

Tel: **03 88 74 60 45**. Email: **camping.fermetuileries@neuf.fr**   www.alanrogers.com/FR67040

Close to the German border, this ten hectare, family run site has 150 large open pitches, hardstanding for 15 motorcaravans and room for 50 seasonal caravans. Welcoming reception staff will provide information about the site and the local area. A small lake with two water slides is used for swimming, fishing and boating (divided into two areas) and there is also a small unsupervised swimming pool (hats compulsory). A newly built restaurant and bar are at the lakeside. A ferry crosses the Rhine river into Germany from 7 km. away.

Facilities

Three modern, bright and cheerful blocks with the normal facilities. Two washing machines and two dryers. Controllable showers. Family bathroom at no extra charge. Fully equipped facilities for disabled visitors (no key, no coins). Motorcaravan services. Newly built restaurant and bar. Small lake for swimming, fishing, boating, two water slides. Swimming pool (unguarded) open July/August. Tennis. Petanque. Minigolf. Off site: Supermarket 300 m. Ferry across the Rhine. Good level region for cycling.

Open: 1 April - 30 September.

Directions

Coming from Colmar (A35) take exit 14 (Kogenheim-Benfeld-Erstein) then the N83 to exit for Benfeld-Rhinau, following site signs. From Strasbourg on A35 take exit 7 (Erstein-Fegersheim) then the N83. GPS: N48:19.260 E07:41.880

Charges guide

Per person		€ 3,30
child (under 7 yrs)		€ 1,50
pitch		€ 3,30
electricity (2-6A)	€ 1,40 -	€ 3,20

No credit cards.

FR57090 Parc Résidentiel de la Tensch

Parcs Résidentiels ⏵ page 516

F-57670 Francaltroff (Moselle)

Tel: **03 87 01 79 04**   www.alanrogers.com/FR57090

Pitches at this campsite are exclusively for chalet accommodation.

FR67050 Camping Municipal Wasselonne

Route de Romanswiller, F-67310 Wasselonne (Bas-Rhin)

Tel: 03 88 87 00 08. Email: camping-wasselonne@wanadoo.fr   www.alanrogers.com/FR67050

A good quality municipal site with a resident warden. Facilities include a well stocked small shop, a crêperie in season and the added bonus of free admission to the superb indoor heated swimming pool adjacent to the site. There are 80 tourist pitches and around 20 seasonal units, on grass with a slight slope, all with electricity hook-ups (10A). Four new rental chalets are in a separate fenced area and there are six new private chalets. This could be an excellent base from which to visit Strasbourg.

Facilities

The single, large, and well maintained sanitary unit has unisex facilities with ample sized showers and washbasins in cubicles. Laundry facilities and covered dishwashing sinks. No specific facilities for disabled visitors but the rooms are spacious and should be accessible to many. Excellent drive-over motorcaravan service point. Off site: Heated pool, hotel with restaurant, tennis courts, plus athletics stadium all adjacent. Supermarket 500 m. Fitness trail, riding 1 km.

Open: 15 April - 15 October.

Directions

Wasselonne is 25 km. west of Strasbourg. Site lies southwest of town centre on D224 towards Romanswiller, and is well signed.
GPS: N48:38.264 E07:25.907

Charges guide

Per unit incl. 1 person	€ 7,30 - € 7,70
extra person	€ 3,40 - € 3,60
child (0-10 yrs)	€ 1,80 - € 1,90
electricity	€ 3,00
animal	€ 0,50 - € 0,60

FR68030 Camping de Masevaux

3 rue du Stade, F-68290 Masevaux (Haut-Rhin)

Tel: 03 89 82 42 29. Email: camping-masevaux@tv-com.net   www.alanrogers.com/FR68030

Masevaux is a pleasant little town in the Haut-Rhin département of Alsace, just north of the A36 Belfort - Mulhouse motorway. The neatly mown 120 pitches for tourists are on level grass, of reasonable size, marked by trees and hedges, and all have electricity (3/6A). Most are well shaded with good views of the surrounding hills. The pleasant and helpful Scottish managers, who take pride in the site, would like to welcome more British visitors. A good choice for one night or a longer stay to explore this interesting region, and an ideal destination for serious walkers.

Facilities

A modern, well designed and well equipped sanitary block has most washbasins in private cabins. Baby room. Laundry. Café/bar serving snacks. Baker calls in high season. Ice-creams and soft drinks from reception. TV room, small library. Boules. Play area. Tennis (extra charge). Fishing. Off site: Supermarket, restaurants and indoor pool. Market in Masavaux Wednesdays. Bicycle hire 300 m. Golf 7 km. Riding 10 km.

Open: 15 February - 31 December.

Directions

From D466 in Masevaux follow signs for Belfort and then 'Camping Complexe Sportif'.
GPS: N47:46.677 E06:59.462

Charges guide

Per person	€ 3,60
child (2-12 yrs)	€ 1,50
pitch	€ 3,20
electricity (3/6A)	€ 3,20 - € 3,80
dog	€ 0,50

FR68040 Camping Municipal les Trois Châteaux

10 rue du Bassin, F-68420 Eguisheim (Haut-Rhin)

Tel: 03 89 23 19 39. Email: camping.eguisheim@wanadoo.fr   www.alanrogers.com/FR68040

The village of Eguisheim is on the Alsace 'Rue du Vin' to the west of Colmar. The three châteaux from which the site gets its name are clearly visible on the distant hills. Being close to the village, Les Trois Châteaux is busy and popular. Flowers, shrubs and trees, and well tended grass areas make this a very pleasant place. The 121 pitches, 115 with electricity (6/10A), are either on a slight slope or a terrace, and are marked and numbered, most with good shade. Around 80% of pitches have some gravel hardstandings, most of irregular shape and size.

Facilities

The single sanitary block in the centre of the site has hot showers and warm water only to washbasins. Some washbasins in cubicles and facilities for disabled people. Motorcaravan service point. Playground. Bicycle hire. Off site: Fishing 3 km. Golf, riding 10 km.

Open: 1 April - 8 October.

Directions

Eguisheim is just off the N83 and the site is well signed in the village. GPS: N48:02.553 E07:17.993

Charges 2009

Per unit incl. 2 persons	€ 11,50 - € 13,00
extra person	€ 3,50 - € 4,00
child (0-12 yrs)	€ 0,10 - € 2,50
electricity (6/10A)	€ 3,00 - € 5,00
dog	€ 1,50 - € 2,00

Check real time availability and at-the-gate prices...
www.alanrogers.com

FR68050 Camping Municipal Pierre de Coubertin

23 rue de Landau, F-68150 Ribeauvillé (Haut-Rhin)

Tel: **03 89 73 66 71**. Email: **camping.ribeauville@wanadoo.fr**   www.alanrogers.com/FR68050

The fascinating medieval town of Ribeauvillé on the Alsace Wine Route is within walking distance of this attractive, quietly located site. Popular and well run, it has 226 touring pitches, all with 16A electricity and some separated by shrubs or railings. There are tarmac or gravel access roads. This is a site solely for touring units – there are no mobile homes or seasonal units here. The small shop is open daily for most of the season (hours vary) providing bread, basic supplies and some wines. Only breathable groundsheets are permitted.

Facilities

Large, heated block provides modern facilities with washbasins in cubicles. Baby facilities. Large laundry and dishwashing rooms. A smaller unit at the far end of the site is opened for July/Aug. Very good facilities for disabled campers at both units. Shop (Easter - Oct). Excellent adventure style play area with rubber base. Tennis. Boules. TV room. Off site: Outdoor pool (June-Aug). Bicycle hire 200 m. Fishing 500 m. Golf 12 km.

Open: 15 March - 15 November.

Directions

Ribeauvillé is 13 km. southwest of Sèlestat and site is well signed. Turn north off the D106 at traffic lights by large car park, east of the town centre. GPS: N48:11.697 E07:20.198

Charges 2009

Per person	€ 4,00
child (0-7 yrs)	€ 2,00
pitch	€ 4,00 - € 5,00
electricity (16A)	€ 3,50

FR68060 Camping Intercommunal Riquewihr

Route des Vins, F-68340 Riquewihr (Haut-Rhin)

Tel: **03 89 47 90 08**. Email: **camping.riquewihr@tiscali.fr**   www.alanrogers.com/FR68060

Surrounded by vineyards and minutes from the delightful village of Riquewihr, this is a well run site which has earned its good reputation. Situated in the heart of the Alsace wine region the site covers three hectares with views across the open countryside. A modern, part-timbered building houses reception and close by is a small summer house heavily garlanded with flowers. The 161 spacious individual pitches, many with shade and divided by hedging, have electrical connections (6/10A). Most are on grass but there are also a few with hardstandings. Wine caves are just 200 m. away.

Facilities

Three sanitary blocks, one of a more modern design (not all open in low season). Facilities include private cabins with basins, good nursery room with baby bath, child's WC and changing mat, and excellent facilities for disabled people. Laundry areas. Motorcaravan service point. Campers' room with tables and chairs. Shop for basic necessities, drinks and papers (1/7-31/8). TV room. Playground. Off site: Ball games area and sports field. Fishing 3 km. Swimming pool 4 km. Bicycle hire 5 km.

Open: Easter - 31 December.

Directions

From N83 north of Colmar take D4 westwards (Bennwihr). Turn north on D1bis for 2 km. towards Ribeauvillé. Site signed off roundabout at southern end of Riquewihr bypass. Do not enter village. GPS: N48:09.731 E07:19.014

Charges guide

Per person	€ 3,25 - € 3,60
child (under 7 yrs)	€ 1,55 - € 1,70
pitch incl. electricity	€ 7,10 - € 8,00
dog	€ 1,10 - € 1,20

FR68080 Camping Clair Vacances

Route de Herrlisheim, F-68127 Saint Croix-en-Plaine (Haut-Rhin)

Tel: **03 89 49 27 28**. Email: **clairvacances@wanadoo.fr**   www.alanrogers.com/FR68080

Clair Vacances is a very neat, tidy and pretty site with 130 level pitches of generous size which are numbered and most are separated by trees and shrubs. All have electricity connections (8-13A) and ten are fully serviced with water and drainage. The site has been imaginatively laid out with the pitches reached from hard access roads. This is a quiet family site. The friendly couple who own and run it will be pleased to advise on the attractions of the area. The site is 1 km. from the A35 exit, not far from Colmar in the region of Alsace, a popular and picturesque area.

Facilities

Two excellent, modern toilet blocks include washbasins in cabins, well equipped baby rooms and good facilities for disabled visitors. Laundry facilities. Shop with limited supplies. Swimming and paddling pools (heated) with large sunbathing area (15/6-15/9). Playground. Community room. Archery in high season. Camping Gaz. Dogs are not accepted. No barbecues or football. American motorhomes and twin axle caravans are not accepted. Off site: Colmar with restaurants and shops.

Open: Week before Easter - 15 October.

Directions

Site is signed from exit 27 of the A35 south of Colmar on the Herrlisheim road (D1). GPS: N48:00.957 E07:20.989

Charges guide

Per unit incl. 2 persons and electricity	€ 15,50 - € 25,00
extra person	€ 5,00 - € 7,00
child (0-7 yrs)	€ 0,20 - € 3,00
child (8-12 yrs)	€ 4,00 - € 6,00

FR68100 Village Center Parc de la Fecht

Route de Gunsbach, F-68140 Munster (Haut-Rhin)

Tel: 04 99 57 21 21. Email: contact@village-center.com

www.alanrogers.com/FR68100

This campsite has been recommended by our agent in France and we intend to undertake a full inspection in 2009. Parc de la Fecht is a popular site located close to Colmar and Munster and is attractively sited along the famous Alsace wine route. The site has 260 pitches, some of which are occupied by mobile homes and chalets. Touring pitches are partly shaded and all have electrical connections. The site has direct access to the River Fecht and a good range of leisure facilities including a sports field and play area. Parc de la Fecht is well located for those wishing to explore the region on foot or by mountain bike with many walking and cycle routes close at hand. A member of Village Center group.

Facilities

Heated toilet blocks include facilities for babies and disabled visitors. Small shop. Snack bar. Sports pitch. Play area. Miniclub and entertainment programme (July/Aug). Mobile homes for rent. Off site: Supermarket, shops and restaurants in Munster. Riding 5 km. Swimming pool with water slides. Extensive walking and cycle (mountain bike) opportunities. Many picturesque Alsatian villages.

Open: 12 May - 15 September.

Directions

Site is east of Munster on D417 (Gérardmer - Colmar). From Munster take the D417 towards Turkheim, then head for Colmar on the D10. The site is 2.2 km. from Munster.
GPS: N48:02.595 E07:09.071

Charges guide

Per unit incl. 2 persons	
and electricity	€ 8,00 - € 16,00
extra person	€ 2,00 - € 4,00
child (under 7 yrs)	€ 1,50 - € 3,25

Parc de la Fecht***

Munster > Alsace

- 800 m away from the town centre
- Perfect place for multiples excursions

Village center

BOOK YOUR HOLIDAYS
www.village-center.com
+33 (0)4 99 57 21 21

FR68120 Camping les Lupins

Rue de la Gare, F-68580 Seppois-le-Bas (Haut-Rhin)

Tel: 03 89 25 65 37. Email: leslupins@wanadoo.fr

www.alanrogers.com/FR68120

Only ten kilometres from the Swiss border and within walking distance of a small village (800 m), this is a very attractive site. It has 142 grass touring pitches, which are not separated and 25 chalets to rent. Attractive trees have been planted throughout the site. The main site building houses reception, a small shop, two pool tables and a television and used to be the old local railway station (1910-1970). A very pleasant, small, fenced swimming pool is guarded in July and August, as is a playground for small children. The site is a member of the Village Center group.

Facilities

One good toilet block provides plenty of facilities in a traditional style. A second block is older but with similar facilities. Cabins for disabled visitors. Free hot water. Small shop, bar and terrace. Swimming pool. Play area. Internet access. Off site: Village 800 m. Restaurant across the road. Forest walks.

Open: 7 April - 15 October.

Directions

Leave Belfort - Basel (CH) autoroute at Grandvillars. From Colmar/Strasbourg to Altkirch-Férette and Seppois-le-Bas. Leave A36 at Burnhaupt (exit 14) and take D103 towards Dannemarie, then the D7b to Seppois. From there follow signs to site.
GPS: N47:32.348 E07:10.799

Charges guide

Per unit incl. 2 persons	€ 9,00 - € 18,00
extra person	€ 2,00 - € 3,00

127

FR88020 Camping de Belle-Hutte

1 bis Vouille de Belle-Hutte, Belle-Hutte, F-88250 La Bresse (Vosges)

Tel: **03 29 25 49 75**. Email: **camping-belle-hutte@wanadoo.fr**   www.alanrogers.com/FR88020

Belle-Hutte is a pleasant family run site in the heart of the Vosges mountains on one of the southern routes to the Col de la Schlucht. Attractively situated surrounded by mountains and trees, it occupies an open hill slope (900 m. above sea level) with 125 numbered grass pitches (95 for touring) on six terraces. Pitches of about 120 sq.m. (some are larger) are divided by hedges and all have electrical connections. To reach the site you would have to depart from the usual main through routes but access is easy via good roads.

Facilities

The well built, central sanitary block is of excellent quality. Heated in cool weather, it also has facilities for disabled people and babies. Laundry facilities. Motorcaravan service point. Shop for gifts and basics. Takeaway and bar (hours vary). Rest room with TV. New swimming pool complex (June - Sept; no Bermuda shorts). Playground. Play room. Fishing. Ski storage. Picnic area. Trampoline. Pétanque. Badminton. Internet access. Off site: Ski lift 100 m. Village 400 m. Fishing 4 km. Riding 10 km.

Open: All year.

Directions

Site is about 9 km. from La Bresse on the D34 road towards the Col de la Schlucht.
GPS: N48:02.095 E06:57.758

Charges 2009

Per unit incl. 2 persons	€ 11,00 - € 19,90
extra person	€ 3,70 - € 6,20
child (under 7 yrs)	€ 2,30 - € 3,20
electricity (2-10A)	€ 1,30 - € 10,20

Higher prices are for winter.

FR88030 Camping de Noirrupt

5 chemin de l'Etang, F-88530 Le Tholy (Vosges)

Tel: **03 29 61 81 27**. Email: **info@jpvacances.com**   www.alanrogers.com/FR88030

An attractive, modern, family run site, Camping de Noirrupt has a commanding mountainside position with some magnificent views especially from the upper terraces. This is a very comfortable and high quality site and one that is sure to please. The tarmac site road winds up through the site with pitches being terraced and cars parked in separate small car parks close by. The 70 lawn-like tourist pitches are generally spacious, and the whole site is beautifully landscaped and divided up with many attractive shrubs, flower beds, decking and trees.

Facilities

Two very modern buildings at different levels, plus a small unit behind reception, all immaculate with modern fittings. Washbasins in cubicles, facilities for babies, children and disabled campers. Washing machines and dryer. Shop. Bar, snack bar and takeaway (4/7-20/8). Swimming pool (15 x 10 m. 1/6-15/9). TV room (1/6-15/9). Tennis. Animation in season. No double axle caravans or American RVs. Off site: Riding 300 m. Fishing 2 or 5 km. Golf 30 km. Le Tholy with its supermarket banks and other services 2 km. Gérardmer 10 km.

Open: 15 April - 15 October.

Directions

From Gérardmer take D417 west towards Remiremont. In Le Tholy turn right on D11, continue up hill for 2 km., and site is signed to your left.
GPS: N48:05.334 E06:43.709

Charges guide

Per person	€ 5,50
child (under 7 yrs)	€ 3,20
pitch	€ 8,90
electricity (2/6A)	€ 3,00 - € 5,00

FR88040 Kawan Village Lac de Bouzey   Mobile homes ⊙ page 494

19 rue du Lac, F-88390 Sanchey (Vosges)

Tel: **03 29 82 49 41**. Email: **camping.lac.de.bouzey@wanadoo.fr**   www.alanrogers.com/FR88040

Camping Lac de Bouzey is eight kilometres west of Epinal, overlooking the lake, at the beginning of the Vosges Massif. The 125 individual 100 sq.m. back-to-back grass pitches are arranged on either side of tarmac roads with electricity (6-10A); 100 are fully serviced. They are on a gentle slope, divided by trees and hedging and some overlook the 130 ha. lake with its sandy beaches. Units can be close when site is busy. In high season there is lots going on for all ages, especially teenagers. Open all year, the site is much quieter in low season. English is spoken.

Facilities

Sanitary block includes a baby room and one for disabled people (there is up and down hill walking). In winter a small, heated section in main building with toilet, washbasin and shower is used. Laundry facilities. Motorcaravan service point. Shop. Bar and restaurant. Heated pool (1/5-30/9). Fishing, riding, games room, archery and bicycle hire. Internet. Soundproof room for cinema and discos (high season). Off site: Golf 8 km.

Open: All year.

Directions

Site is 8 km. west of Epinal on D460 and is signed from some parts of Epinal. Follow signs for Lac de Bouzey and Sanchey. GPS: N48:10.015 E06:21.594

Charges guide

Per unit incl. 2 persons	€ 15,00 - € 25,00
extra person	€ 5,00 - € 9,00
electricity (6-10A)	€ 5,00 - € 6,00

Camping Cheques accepted.

The Travel Service ...we'll arrange everything
BOOK THIS SITE CALL 01580 214000

128

FR88050 Domaine de Champé

14 rue des Champs-Navés, F-88540 Bussang (Vosges)

Tel: **03 29 61 61 51**. Email: **info@domaine-de-champe.com**   www.alanrogers.com/FR88050

Bordered by the Moselle river and located just off the town square, this site is open all year making it a good base from which to explore in summer, and ideal for skiing in winter, when you might be tempted to rent one of the 12 chalets. Domaine de Champé is a level site with 110 touring pitches, all with electricity (4-12A), spread over a fairly large area on both sides of a tributary stream, so some are a quite a distance from the facilities. This is an improving site where you will receive a hospitable welcome. Recent additions include a good sized, heated, outdoor pool and a new leisure centre with a sauna, steam room, jacuzzi and massage.

Facilities

Two sanitary units, one behind reception, with a smaller one in a more central position, are adequate rather than luxurious. Facilities for disabled campers. Motorcaravan services. Bar (all year). Restaurant and takeaway (weekends only in low season). Swimming pool (1/5-30/9). Sauna, steam room, jacuzzi and massage. Tennis. Small play area. Fishing. Internet access and WiFi. Off site: Shops and all other services in town. Lake fishing 3.5 km. Riding 4 km. Skiing 3 km.

Open: All year.

Directions

Bussang is about midway between Remiremont and Mulhouse on N66, almost due north of Belfort. Site is signed from town centre.
GPS: N47:53.317 E06:51.429

Charges guide

Per person	€ 4,60 - € 6,00
child (4-10 yrs)	€ 2,40 - € 3,20
pitch	€ 5,20 - € 7,10
electricity (4A)	€ 3,40 - € 4,50

DOMAINE
Champé

Domaine de Champé★★★

14, Rue des Champs Navets
88840 Bussang
Tel.: 0033 (0)3 29 61 61 51
info@domaine-de-champe.com
www.domaine-de-champe.com

FR88080 Yelloh! en Vosges Domaine des Bans

Rue James Wiese, F-88430 Corcieux (Vosges)

Tel: **04 66 73 97 39**. Email: **info@yellohvillage-domaine-des-bans.com**   www.alanrogers.com/FR88080

Domaine des Bans is a large, busy campsite with 630 pitches in a country setting, with plenty of opportunities to be active. There is a very high percentage of static and tour operator units, but room for about 80 touring units. Pitches (with electricity, water and drainage), numbered and separated by hedges, vary in size with some on low terraces. There is good shade. Some are tucked away in quiet areas with others nearer to where activities take place. This is not really a site for short stays, but is a base for exploring the varied and interesting countryside.

Facilities

Three functional toilet blocks. Some washbasins are in cabins. Shop (30/5-30/9). Bar (1/6-15/9). Restaurant (1/5-15/9). Takeaway (30/4-15/9). Swimming pools (outdoor 1/6-15/9, indoor 1/5-15/9). Playground. Tennis. Minigolf. Archery. Bicycle hire. Riding. Lakes for fishing and boating. High season entertainment including discos (soundproof room), theatre performances and live music. 'Goats' Castle' with about two dozen goats. Off site: Restaurant outside site. Others nearby in village.

Open: 26 April - 6 September.

Directions

From D8 St Dié - Gerardmer road, turn west on D60 just north of Gerbepal to Corcieux.
GPS: N48:10.142 E06:52.817

Charges guide

Per unit incl. 2 persons and electricity	€ 14,00 - € 39,00
extra person (over 3 yrs)	€ 5,00 - € 7,00

www.yellohvillage.com tel: +33 466 739 739

Check real time availability and at-the-gate prices...

www.**alanrogers**.com

BOOK THIS SITE
CALL 01580 214000
...we'll arrange everything
The Travel
Service

FR88090 Base de Loisirs du Lac de la Moselotte

Les Amias B.P. 34, F-88290 Saulxures-sur-Moselotte (Vosges)

Tel: 03 29 24 56 56. Email: lac-moselotte@ville-saulxures-mtte.fr   www.alanrogers.com/FR88090

This neat, well run, spacious lakeside site, part of a leisure village complex, has 75 generously sized, grassy and individual hedged pitches. All have electrical hook-ups (10A) and 25 of these are multi-serviced with electricity, water and waste water drainage. The trees currently provide no more than a little shade. The site is fully fenced with security barrier and key for the gates (to site and lakeside). All facilities are modern and well maintained. The adjacent 'Base de Loisirs' has a wide variety of activities on offer, and the area is very good for walking and cycling.

Facilities

The heated toilet block has controllable hot showers, some washbasins in cubicles and good facilities for babies and disabled campers. Laundry facilities. Shop (July/Aug). Bread to order. Bar/snack bar and terrace. Bicycle hire. Play area. Outdoor skittle alley. 30 chalets for rent. Off site: Town an easy walk. The 'Base de Loisirs' with lake (supervised swimming July/Aug), sandy beach, a climbing wall, fishing, archery and hire of pedalos, canoes and kayaks. Golf 15 km.

Open: All year.

Directions

Saulxures-sur-Moselotte is 20 km. east of Remiremont. From Remiremont take D417 east (St Ame), then right (east) on D43 towards La Bresse for 10.5 km. Turn left into Saulxures (site signed), entrance on right after 500 m. by lake. GPS: N47:57.164 E06:45.127

Charges guide

Per person	€ 4,00 - € 5,00
child (4-10 yrs)	€ 2,40 - € 3,00
pitch incl. electricity	€ 9,00 - € 11,00

FR88100 Camping du Barba

45 le village, F-88640 Rehaupal (Vosges)

Tel: 03 29 66 21 17. Email: barba@campingdubarba.com   www.alanrogers.com/FR88100

Located in the refreshing and beautiful Haute-Vosges region, this small, very pleasant campsite is owned and run by a dedicated couple. There is room for 50 units on well tended, unmarked grass where you pitch where you like. This creates a very relaxed, natural environment with hedges and mature trees providing shelter and shade. The site is in the heart of the village with an auberge next door for fine wines and good food, including local specialties. The surrounding hills offer 150 km. of marked walking and bike trails. Gérardmer and the Valley of the Lakes are just 15 minutes away.

Facilities

The single toilet block, built in chalet style, is of a high standard and should be sufficient. Washing machine and dryer. Bread delivered. Auberge next door for meals and takeaway (to order). and small shop. Dogs are not accepted. Off site: Supermarket 5 km. Walking, cycling, skiing and fishing. Riding 6 km.

Open: 1 May - 1 October.

Directions

From Gérardmer follow signs to Rehaupal. Site is very well signed. GPS: N48:07.135 E06:43.878

Charges guide

Per person	€ 3,00
child (under 7 yrs)	€ 2,00
pitch	€ 4,50
electricity (3/6A)	€ 2,80 - € 3,80

FR88110 Camping la Sténiole

1 le Haut Rain, F-88640 Granges-sur-Vologne (Vosges)

Tel: 03 29 51 43 75. Email: steniole@wanadoo.fr   www.alanrogers.com/FR88110

Set in a lovely rural area in the heart of the Vosges massif, this attractive site is run by a dedicated young couple who are constantly improving the site and its facilities. There are 70 pitches, either separated by hedges or beside the water. A small river has been used to form a small lake for fishing and swimming and a series of separate ponds (water quality is checked regularly). An atmosphere of relaxation is encouraged and the whole family can have a good time here. At an altitude of 720 m. there is easy access to 160 km. of paths and tracks for walking and cycling.

Facilities

One toilet block together with further facilities in the main building provide all necessities including 4 private cabins. Washing machines and dryers. Bar. Restaurant (July/Aug). Takeaway (1/6-30/8). Internet access on the terrace. Lake swimming. Fishing. Games room with TV and library. Play area. Tennis. Apartments and mobile homes to rent. Off site: Woods and hills for walking and cycling. Riding 5 km. Bicycle hire 10 km. Golf 30 km.

Open: 1 May - 30 September.

Directions

Take the N420 from Epinal to Gérardmer then the D423 to Granges. There are two sites not far away from each other. GPS: N48:07.302 E06:49.704

Charges guide

Per person	€ 3,00
hild (under 8 yrs)	€ 2,00
pitch	€ 4,00
electricity (4/10A)	€ 3,00 - € 5,00

No credit cards.

BOOK THIS SITE
CALL 01580 214000
...we'll arrange everything
The Travel Service

BOOK THIS SITE
CALL 01580 214000
...we'll arrange everything
The Travel Service

FR88120 Camping Au Clos de la Chaume

21 rue d'Alsace, F-88430 Corcieux (Vosges)

Tel: 03 29 50 76 76. Email: **info@camping-closdelachaume.com** www.alanrogers.com/FR88120

This pleasant site is within walking distance of the town, on level ground with a small stream adjacent. The friendly family owners live on site and do their best to ensure campers have an enjoyable relaxing stay. There are 100 level grassy pitches of varying sizes, with some holiday homes (private and rental) leaving 70 pitches for tourists. All have electricity hook-ups (6/10A) and some are divided by shrubs and trees. Access roads are sandy and large units or American RVs should telephone first to check pitch availability. The site boasts an attractive, well fenced, small swimming pool and an excellent small adventure style playground. The site has some excellent and informative leaflets (available in several languages) which give details of walks and mountain biking routes in the surrounding countryside. Corcieux is in the heart of the 'Ballons des Vosges' and this site would make a good base to explore the area.

Facilities

Two units provide well maintained facilities including a laundry with washing machines and dryers, a dual purpose family/disabled room and dishwashing sinks. Motorcaravan service point. Recycling. Reception keeps basic supplies (July/August). Campingaz stocked. Swimming pool (13 x 7m. June-Sept). Games room with table football and a pool table. Table tennis, boules and volleyball. Off site: Bicycle hire 800 m. Riding 2 km. Fishing 3 and 10 km. Golf 30 km. Corcieux market (Mondays).

Open: 15 April - 20 September.

Directions

Corcieux is about 17 km. southwest of St Dié-des-Vosges. Site is on D60, east of town centre, by the town boundary sign. GPS: N48:10.094 E06:53.401

Charges 2009

Per unit incl. 2 persons and electricity	€ 11,80
extra person	€ 4,50
child (0-7 yrs)	€ 2,80
animal	€ 1,40

FR88130 Kawan Village Vanne de Pierre

Mobile homes ▶ page 494

5 rue du camping, F-88100 Saint Dié-des-Vosges (Vosges)

Tel: 03 29 56 23 56. Email: **vannedepierre@wanadoo.fr** www.alanrogers.com/FR88130

La Vanne de Pierre is a neat and attractive site with 118 pitches, many of which are individual with good well trimmed hedges giving plenty of privacy. There are 13 chalets and mobile homes (for rent) and a few seasonal units, leaving around 101 tourist pitches, all multi-serviced with water, drain and electricity hook-up (6/10A). The reception building has been recently refitted and provides a well stocked small shop plus a restaurant/bar with a takeaway facility (all year but opening hours may vary). A 'Sites et Paysages' member.

Facilities

Main unit is heated with good facilities including washbasins in cubicles. Three family rooms each with WC, basin, and shower and two similar units fully equipped for disabled campers. Dishwashing and laundry rooms. A second, older unit (opened July/Aug). Shop. Bar/restaurant and takeaway. Swimming pool (1/4-30/9, weather permitting). Internet access. Gas supplies. Bicycle hire. Nordic walking is organised. Off site: Golf, tennis, archery and riding all 1 km. Fishing. Supermarkets.

Open: All year.

Directions

St Dié is southeast of Nancy. Site is east of town on north bank of river Meurthe and south of D82 to Nayemont les Fosses. Site is well signed. GPS: N48:17.160 E06:58.199

Charges guide

Per unit incl. 2 persons	€ 15,00 - € 22,00
extra person	€ 4,00 - € 6,00
child (4-10 yrs)	free - € 4,00
electricity	€ 4,00 - € 5,00
Camping Cheques accepted.	

BOOK THIS SITE
CALL 01580 214000
...we'll arrange everything
The Travel Service

Check real time availability and at-the-gate prices...
www.alanrogers.com

FR88150 Camping de Ramberchamp

21 chemin du Tour du Lac, F-88150 Gérardmer (Vosges)

Tel: **03 29 63 03 82**. Email: **boespflug.helene@wanadoo.fr**   www.alanrogers.com/FR88150

A long established, family run site in a beautiful location on the southern side of Lake Gérardmer, de Ramberchamp is very peaceful. It benefits from a bar and restaurant adjacent to reception, which is on one side of the D69, with mostly long stay units on the pitches around it. Most of the 200 touring pitches are on the opposite side of the road by the lakeside, with the larger sanitary building. Pitches here vary in size, larger ones being further from the lake, all with electricity (4A) and quite level. Those by the lakeside are mostly on gravel and are very popular.

Facilities

The main sanitary unit is fairly central and has been refurbished with modern fittings, whilst retaining its old French style and character. Baby room. Unit for disabled campers. Laundry. Motorcaravan service point. A second smaller older unit serves pitches on the other side of the road. Bar/restaurant with takeaway (15/4-15/9). Small play area. Max length of unit 8.5 m. Off site: Fishing, riding and bicycle hire 500 m. Town with shops, banks, buses and railway station 1.5 km.

Open: 15 April - 15 September.

Directions

Site is west of Gérardmer, on D69 on southern side of the lake. Best approached from N417 towards Le Tholy, turning on D69, passing Lido. Site reception on right hand side, site entrance opposite. GPS: N48:03.860 E06:51.222

Charges guide

Per unit incl. 2 persons	€ 16,00
extra person	€ 5,00
electricity (4A)	€ 3,50

No credit cards.

FR88160 Camping les Jonquilles

Route du Lac, F-88400 Xonrupt-Longemer (Vosges)

Tel: **03 29 63 34 01**. Email: **info@camping-jonquilles.com**   www.alanrogers.com/FR88160

Les Jonquilles is a traditional, family run, lakeside site with a friendly reception and some terrific views of the surrounding countryside and lake. The site has an overall slope (blocks advised), with 240 pitches entirely for tourists and no mobile homes, chalets or rental units. All the pitches are marked, many by very small trees and have access to electricity hook-ups (6A), but the site is generally quite open. There are a number of special pitches for motorcaravans by the lakeside, with a full 'aire de service' facility alongside and this area is very popular.

Facilities

Two traditional buildings, modernised at various times, give a good provision and include some Turkish toilets, washbasins in cubicles and spacious showers. Baby bath in ladies. Facilities for disabled campers. Washing machines and dryer. Playground. Pétanque.
Off site: Opposite reception is a food shop, bar, snack bar and crêperie, with takeaway, all operated by the site owner's brother. Bar has internet terminal and satellite TV.

Open: 1 May - 30 September.

Directions

Xonrupt-Longemer is just to the east of Gérardmer. From centre of town take D67a that runs around the southern side of the lake and site is on left opposite a bar/restaurant. GPS: N48:04.057 E06:56.944

Charges 2009

Per unit incl. 2 persons and electricity	€ 12,00 - € 15,50
extra person	€ 2,00 - € 3,00
child (under 7 yrs)	€ 1,30 - € 1,50

FR88170 Camping les Pinasses

215 route de Bruyères, F-88600 La Chapelle-devant-Bruyères (Vosges)

Tel: **03 29 58 51 10**. Email: **pinasses@dial.oleane.com**   www.alanrogers.com/FR88170

Les Pinasses is an orderly, well run family site with a small outdoor swimming pool. Traditional in style, the site is long and narrow with pitches on two levels. The sanitary facilities are good. However the site is fronted by a fairly busy road and a railway track runs immediately behind it, and this is quite close to some pitches. There are around 125 grassy, individual, hedged pitches of varying sizes, all with 4/6A electricity under trees plus 14 units to rent. There are also a number of seasonal units on site. The site organises a little low key animation in July and August.

Facilities

Four blocks of varying styles, upgraded at different times, include a mix of seated and Turkish style toilets, some washbasins in cubicles. Facilities for disabled campers at one block only (ramped entrance). Washing machines, dryers and spin dryer. Small shop (15/4-15/9). Bar and restaurant (July/Aug). Swimming and paddling pools (1/6-15/9). Playground. TV room. Boules. Minigolf. Tennis. Fishing. Some entertainment in high season. American RVs not accepted. Off site: Golf 30 km. Bicycle hire 8 km.

Open: 15 April - 15 September.

Directions

La Chapelle-devant-Bruyères is about 25 km. southwest of St Dié. Site is beside D60 Corcieux to Bruyeres road, 2 km. east of its junction with D423. GPS: N48:11.399 E06:46.538

Charges guide

Per unit incl. 2 persons	€ 17,80
extra person	€ 4,90
child (under 7 yrs)	€ 2,50
electricity (4/6A)	€ 3,50 - € 4,50

Check real time availability and at-the-gate prices...

www.**alanrogers**.com

MAP 5

Vendée & Charente

It's not only the fine beaches that make this holiday region so appealing. Sleepy fishing harbours, historic ports and charming towns all create a great holiday atmosphere.

Alan Rogers

WE HAVE EXERCISED A LITTLE TOURISM LICENSE WITH THIS AREA TAKING ONE DÉPARTEMENT FROM THE OFFICIAL WESTERN LOIRE REGION, 85 VENDÉE, AND ONE FROM THE POITOU-CHARENTES REGION, 17 CHARENTE-MARITIME

With a sunshine record to rival the south of France, the Vendée and Charente regions are among the most popular areas in France. Running alongside the coastal area stretching down from La Rochelle past Rochefort to Royan, it boasts gently shelving sandy beaches, warm shallow waters and fragrant pine forests. Explore the coasts for traditional fishing villages or head inland for fields of sunflowers and unspoilt rural villages.

The Vendée was the centre of the counter-revolutionary movement between 1793 and 1799 and a 'son et lumière' held at Le Puy-du-Fou tells the whole story. Les Sables d'Olonne is its main resort renowned for its excellent sandy beach. The area between the Vendée and Charente, the Marais Poitevin, is one of the most unusual in France – a vast tract of marshland with a thousand or more tree-lined canals and slow moving streams. The port of La Rochelle, with massive medieval towers, buzzes with life and the island of Ré is popular with those seeking beaches and small, quiet ports.

Places of interest

Marais Poitevin: marshes known as the 'Green Venice'.

Angoulême: Hill-top town surrounded by ramparts, cathedral, Renaissance château.

La Rochelle: port, Porte de la Grosse Horloge (clock gate), Museum of the New World.

Le Puy-du-Fou: 15th-16th-century castle, sound and light show involving over 700 participants.

Les Sables d'Olonne: fishing port and seaside resort.

Noirmoutier: linked to the mainland by a 3 mile bridge.

Saint Savin: 17th-century abbey, mural painting.

Cuisine of the region

Fish predominates, both fresh water (eel, trout, pike), sea water (shrimps, mussels, oysters). Light fruity wines from Haut-Poitou, Deux-Sèvres and Charente, and Cognac and Pineau des Charentes – an apéritif of grape juice and Cognac.

Cagouilles: snails from Charentes.

Chaudrée: ragout of fish cooked in white wine, shallots and butter.

Mouclade: mussels cooked in wine, egg and cream, served with Pineau des Charentes.

Soupe de moules à la Rochelaise: soup of various fish, mussels, saffron, garlic, tomatoes, onions and red wine.

Sourdons: cockles from the Charentes.

FR17010 Camping Bois Soleil

Mobile homes ▶ page 494

2 avenue de Suzac, F-17110 Saint Georges-de-Didonne (Charente-Maritime)

Tel: 05 46 05 05 94. Email: camping.bois.soleil@wanadoo.fr   www.alanrogers.com/FR17010

Close to the sea, Bois Soleil is a fairly large site in three parts, with 165 serviced pitches for touring units and a few for tents. All the touring pitches are hedged, and have electricity, with water and drainage between two. The main part, Les Pins, is attractive with trees and shrubs providing shade. Opposite is La Mer with direct access to the beach, some areas with less shade and an area for tents. The third part, La Forêt, is for static holiday homes. It is best to book your preferred area as it can be full mid June - late August. There are a few pitches with lockable gates. The areas are well tended with the named pitches (not numbered) cleared and raked between visitors and with an inclusive charge for electricity and water. This lively site offers something for everyone, whether they like a beach-side spot or a traditional pitch, plenty of activities or the quiet life. The sandy beach here is a wide public one, sheltered from the Atlantic breakers although the sea goes out some way at low tide.

Facilities

Each area has one large sanitary block, and smaller blocks with toilets only. Heated block near reception. Cleaned twice daily, they include washbasins in cubicles, facilities for disabled people and babies. Launderette. Nursery. Supermarket, bakery (July/Aug). Beach shop. Restaurant and bar. Takeaway. Swimming pool (heated 15/6-15/9). Steam room. Tennis. Bicycle hire. Play area. TV room and library. Internet terminal. Charcoal barbecues not permitted. Dogs are not accepted 24/6-2/9. Off site: Fishing, riding 500 m. Golf 20 km.

Open: 4 April - 2 November.

Directions

From Royan centre take coast road (D25) along the seafront of St Georges-de-Didonne towards Meschers. Site is signed at roundabout at end of the main beach. GPS: N45:35.130 W00:59.128

Charges 2009

Per unit incl. 2 persons, 6A electricity	€ 24,00 - € 39,00
tent incl. 2 persons	€ 18,00 - € 35,00
extra person	€ 3,00 - € 8,00
child (3-7 yrs)	free - € 6,00
dog (not 23/6-25/8)	€ 3,50

Less 20% outside July/Aug.
Camping Cheques accepted.

FR17080 Camping le Royan

10 rue des Bleuets, F-17200 Royan (Charente-Maritime)

Tel: 05 46 39 09 06. Email: camping.le.royan@wanadoo.fr   www.alanrogers.com/FR17080

Camping Le Royan is a well established family site located close to the resort of Royan and its beaches. There are 186 good size grassy pitches, of which 80 are for touring. All but 16 have 10A electricity (Euro plugs). Some pitches may suffer from road noise from the nearby Royan bypass. The site has tarmac access roads and well maintained toilet blocks. The swimming pool is particularly attractive with a jacuzzi and a number of slides. A lively entertainment programme and children's club are organised in peak season.

Facilities

Two sanitary buildings with facilities for disabled people. Snack bar and pizzeria. Shop. Swimming pool with waterslides and other features. Paddling pool. Games room. Playground. Bicycle hire. Children's club. Entertainment. Mobile homes and chalets for rent. Gas barbecues allowed. Only small dogs accepted. Off site: Beach 2.5 km. Royan centre 2 km. La Palmyre zoo. Riding and golf 7 km.

Open: 1 April - 15 October.

Directions

Site is close to the Royan bypass to the northwest of the town heading towards La Palmyre. It is well signed. GPS: N45:38.708 W01:02.48

Charges guide

Per pitch including 3 people and electricity	€ 21,50 - € 33,00
extra person	€ 3,50 - € 7,50
child (3-9 yrs)	€ 3,50 - € 6,50

Check real time availability and at-the-gate prices...

www.alanrogers.com

Bois Soleil

Camping ★★★★
Charente-Maritime

Surrounded by pine trees and a sandy beach on the Atlantic Coast, with one direct access to the beach, Bois Soleil proposes to you many attractions like tennis, tabletennis, children playgrounds and entertainment. Shops, take-away and snack-bar with big TV screen.

Spring and Summer

2, avenue de Suzac - 17110 ST GEORGES DE DIDONNE
Tel: 0033 546 05 05 94 - Fax: 0033 546 06 27 43
www.bois-soleil.com / e-mail: camping.bois.soleil@wanadoo.fr

The Travel Service
BOOK THIS SITE
CALL 01580 214000
...we'll arrange everything

FR17040 Siblu Camping Bonne Anse Plage

La Palmyre, F-17570 Les Mathes-La Palmyre (Charente-Maritime)

Tel: 05 46 22 40 90. Email: bonneanseplage@siblu.fr   www.alanrogers.com/FR17040

On the edge of the Forêt de la Coubre, just beyond La Palmyre, Bonne Anse Plage is attractively set amongst pines, just a short stroll from a tidal inlet, and just 600 m from the mouth of the Gironde estuary. This is a spacious, gently undulating site, and is now owned by the Siblu group. There are 850 level, marked pitches, of which around half are for touring units (all with electricity). Most are well shaded, the ones nearer the sea less so and are rather sandier. The reception, restaurant and bar with a spacious outdoor terrace and an impressive pool complex form the social focus. The pool complex also features several giant water slides. A shopping centre which is open all season includes a supermarket, delicatessen and takeaway, bistro, shops for bread and pastries, holiday goods and papers. There is plenty going on in high season with clubs for children of all ages, including Siblu Soccer tournaments throughout the season. Evening entertainment, including children's shows, takes place on the bar's outdoor terrace.

Facilities

Seven well maintained toilet blocks include facilities for disabled visitors and babies. Motorcaravan service point. Shopping centre. Restaurant and bar. Takeaway food. Large pool complex with water slides (including a junior chute). Playground. Video games room. TV. Minigolf. Football. Trampolines. Bicycle hire. Climbing wall. Entertainment and activities in high season. Internet access. Gas barbecues only. Off site: Supervised, safe beaches 500 m. Fishing, riding 1 km. Zoo 1 km. Golf 5 km. Watersports and tennis. Fitness track.

Open: 1 May - 19 September.

Directions

Leave A10 autoroute at Saintes. Head for Royan (N150). In Royan take signs for La Palmyre (D25). At La Palmyre roundabout follow signs for Ronce-les-Bains. Site is 1 km. on left.
GPS: N45:41.886 W01:11.986

Charges guide

Per unit incl. 3 persons and electricity	€ 37,60 - € 44,80
extra person (over 1 yr)	€ 7,60 - € 9,20

A beautiful beach side base in La Palmyre within easy reach of Royan and La Rochelle.

- pool complex with lifeguards, slides and toddler pool
- climbing wall & trampolines
- organised sports & entertainments
- free children's clubs, open all season for 1 - 14s
- 70m sq average pitch size
- friendly bi-lingual staff
- site open 1 May - 19 September

Book a ferry inclusive package on 0871 911 7777
Or direct on parc 0033 546 22 40 90
bonneanseplage@siblu.fr

bonne anse plage ★★★★
La Palmyre, Charente Maritime

siblu
holidays

FR17030 Camping le Bois Roland

82 route Royan - Saujon, F-17600 Médis (Charente-Maritime)

Tel: 05 46 05 47 58. Email: bois.roland@wanadoo.fr   www.alanrogers.com/FR17030

This campsite is in an urban area on a busy N-road but, nevertheless, has some unique features. Over the past 30 years, M. Dupont, the owner, has planted a very large number of tree varieties to mark and separate the pitches and they provide some shade. The site has 88 pitches for touring units, mainly between 80-90 sq.m. All have electricity (some may need long leads) and access to water close at hand. The family run a bar and provide simple takeaway food in July and August and there is a welcoming swimming pool.

Facilities

Two modernised toilet blocks contain a mixture of Turkish and British style toilets (no seats and no paper). Modern showers. Baby changing room. Special facilities for disabled campers. Laundry facilities. Play area for young children. Off site: Buses pass the gate. Supermarket with ATM 2 km. Beach 5 km. Riding 1 km. Fishing 4 km. Bicycle hire 5 km. Golf 10 km.

Open: 23 April - 30 September.

Directions

Site is clearly signed on the west side of the N150, 600 m. north of the village of Medis (the N150 runs between Saujon and Royan).
GPS: N45:38.970 W00:57.470

Charges guide

Per unit incl. 2 persons	€ 14,00 - € 17,50
extra person	€ 4,80
child (0-5 yrs)	€ 2,00 - € 3,50
electricity (5/10A)	€ 4,20 - € 4,90

Check real time availability and at-the-gate prices...

www.alanrogers.com

FR17060 Airotel Oléron

Domaine de Montravail, F-17480 Le Château-d'Oléron (Charente-Maritime)

Tel: **05 46 47 61 82**. Email: **info@camping-airotel-oleron.com**   www.alanrogers.com/FR17060

This family run site on the outskirts of Le Château-d'Oléron with very good facilities, including a superb equestrian centre, a full range of sporting activites and an attractive heated pool complex. This is a mature site with about 270 pitches of a good size, with varying degrees of shade provided by trees and shrubs. It is well laid out with 133 touring pitches and the remainder for mobile homes of which 30 are for rent. Most touring pitches have electricity (10A) and four have their own water and drainage. A full entertainment programme is provided in high season and one can enjoy the exploration of the island with its fine sandy beaches on the Atlantic coast and the miles of flat tracks for walking, cycling or horse riding. The equestrian centre offers courses of up to a week in length for riders ranging from novice to experienced.

Facilities

Two modern toilet blocks with facilities for disabled visitors and babies. Washing machine and dryer. Motorcaravan service point. Shop. Bar, restaurant and takeaway (15/6-15/9). Heated swimming and paddling pools. Equestrian centre. Playground. Multisport court. Tennis. Minigolf. Fishing. Canoe hire. Bicycle hire. TV and games room. Internet access. WiFi. Off site: Supermarket. Local markets. Zoo. Aquarium.

Open: Easter - 30 September.

Directions

Cross the bridge onto the island and continue on D26. At second roundabout turn right, marked Dolus and Le Château. Proceed 500 m. and take first right, marked Campings. Site is 1 km. on the right. GPS: N45:52.933 W01:12.392

Charges guide

Per unit incl. 2 persons	€ 13,50 - € 22,00
extra person	€ 4,00 - € 6,50
electricity (8A)	€ 3,90
dog	€ 2,50

FR17050 Camping l'Orée du Bois

225 route de la Bouverie, la Fouasse, F-17570 Les Mathes (Charente-Maritime)

Tel: **05 46 22 42 43**. Email: **info@camping-oree-du-bois.fr**   www.alanrogers.com/FR17050

L'Orée du Bois has 388 pitches of about 100 sq.m. in a very spacious, pinewood setting. There are 150 for touring units, mainly scattered amongst the permanent chalets and tents. They include 40 large pitches with hardstanding and individual sanitary facilities (in blocks of four with shower, toilet, washbasin and dishwashing sink). Pitches are on flat, fairly sandy ground, separated by trees and hedges and all have electricity (6A). Trees offer some shade. Used by several tour operators.

Facilities

Four main toilet blocks include some washbasins in cabins. Three have a laundry and facilities for disabled people. Shop. Excellent bar, restaurant, crêperie and takeaway service (1/5-13/9). Heated swimming pools (1/5-13/9), water slide and paddling pool (trunks, not shorts). Play areas. Tennis court, boules, football and basketball. Games room and TV lounge. Bicycle hire. Discos. Entertainment in July/Aug. Internet access. Barbecues in special areas only. WiFi. Off site: Riding 300 m. Fishing 4 km. Golf 20 km.

Open: 1 May - 13 September.

Directions

From north follow D14 La Tremblade. At roundabout before Arvert turn on D268 (Les Mathes and La Palmyre). Site on right in Fouasse. From south, at Royan take D25 (La Palmyre). In town turn north to Les Mathes. At first roundabout in Les Mathes follow sign (Fouasse and La Tremblade). Site on left after 2 km. GPS: N45:43.957 W01:10.711

Charges 2009

Per unit incl. 2 persons and electricity	€ 17,00 - € 38,00
incl. private sanitary facility	€ 24,00 - € 46,00
extra person	€ 8,00

Min. stay 7 days in high season. Camping Cheques accepted.

BOOK THIS SITE
CALL 01580 214000
...we'll arrange everything
Service The Travel

FR17070 Camping les Gros Joncs

Mobile homes ▶ page 496

850 route de Ponthezieres, F-17190 Saint Georges-d'Oléron (Charente-Maritime)

Tel: 05 46 76 52 29. Email: camping.gros.joncs@wanadoo.fr   www.alanrogers.com/FR17070

Situated on the west coast of the island of Ile d'Oléron, Les Gros Joncs is owned and run by the Cavel family who strive to keep the site up to date and of high quality. There are 50 or so touring pitches of a good size (some extra large) providing a choice between full sun and varying degrees of shade. All have water and electricity (10A) to hand. Much attention has been given to the needs of visitors with disabilities, including chalets where space and equipment are specially adapted. The restaurant and takeaway are of a standard unusual in a campsite. The shop with its own bakery and patisserie stocks a wide range of foods, drinks and everyday essentials. The site has a heated swimming pool, recently renovated and now including a water slide and with hydrotherapy and beauty treatments available. New indoor pool and fitness room. The Ile d'Oléron has much history to explore and the French are justifiably proud of the oyster and mussel production on the island – probably the best in Europe and well worth a visit (and tasting!)

Facilities

Toilet facilities are of traditional design, kept very clean and very adequate in number. Laundry facilities. Motorcaravan services. Well stocked shop with bakery (1/4-15/9). Bar with TV, restaurant and snack bar with takeaway (all 1/4-15/9). Swimming pool (1/4-15/9) with hydrotherapy and beauty treatments. Bicycle hire. Children's club (1/7-15/9). WiFi internet access. No barbecues. Off site: Beach 200 or 400 m. Bus service from Chéray. Fishing 2 km. Riding 6 km. Golf 8 km.

Open: All year.

Directions

Cross the viaduct onto the Ile d'Oléron. Take D734 (St George d'Oléron). At traffic lights in Chéray turn left. Follow signs for camping and Sable Vignier. Soon signs indicate direction of Les Gros Joncs. GPS: N45:57.214 W01:22.787

Charges guide

Per unit incl. 2 persons	€ 14,70 - € 40,10
incl. 3 persons	€ 17,20 - € 40,10
extra person	€ 5,60 - € 11,20
electricity	€ 3,00

CAMPING LES GROS JONCS

850 Route de Ponthezieres - F-17190 St Georges-d'Oléron - France - Tél.: 05 46 76 52 29
Fax: 05 46 76 67 74 - E-mail: info@les-gros-joncs.fr - www.camping-les-gros-joncs.com

FR17110 Camping Caravaning Monplaisir

26 avenue de la Palmyre, F-17570 Les Mathes-La Palmyre (Charente-Maritime)

Tel: 05 46 22 50 31. Email: campmonplaisir@aol.com   www.alanrogers.com/FR17110

Monplaisir provides a small, quiet haven in an area with some very hectic campsites. It is ideal for couples or families with young children. Quite close to the town, the entrance leads past the owners' home to a well kept, garden-like site. There are 114 level, marked pitches and all but a few have electrical connections (6A); long leads may be required. On 14 there are caravans for rent and a modern building provides flats and studios for rent. Larger units would find this site difficult.

Facilities

The toilet block has some washbasins in cabins and facilities for disabled visitors. Laundry and dishwashing facilities. Ice pack service in reception. Bread delivered daily. TV, games room and library. Heated swimming pool and paddling pool (early May - 30/9). Small play area. Winter caravan storage. Off site: Supermarket short walk. Minigolf adjacent (owned by the site). Fishing 500 m. Riding 1 km. Golf 5 km.

Open: Easter - 1 October.

Directions

Follow D25 to La Palmyre. In town, turn north to Les Mathes. At roundabout turn right to town centre. Site on left. From north on D14 (La Tremblade) turn onto D268 (Les Mathes and La Palmyre) at roundabout just before Arvert. Keep straight on to Les Mathes, road becomes D141 and turn left (north) at roundabout. Site is 600 m. on left. GPS: N45:42.924 W01:09.321

Charges guide

Per unit incl. 2 persons	€ 17,00
extra person	€ 5,00
electricity	€ 3,00

Check real time availability and at-the-gate prices...

www.alanrogers.com

FR17140 Castel Camping Séquoia Parc

La Josephtrie, F-17320 Saint Just-Luzac (Charente-Maritime)

Tel: 05 46 85 55 55. Email: **info@sequoiaparc.com**   www.alanrogers.com/FR17140

This is definitely a site not to be missed. Approached by an avenue of flowers, shrubs and trees, Séquoia Parc is a Castel site set in the grounds of La Josephtrie, a striking château with beautifully restored outbuildings and courtyard area with a bar and restaurant. Most pitches are 140 sq.m. with 6A electricity connections and separated by mature shrubs providing plenty of privacy. The site has 300 mobile homes and chalets, with 126 used by tour operators. This is a popular site and reservation is necessary in high season. Member of Leading Campings Group.

Facilities

Three spotlessly clean luxurious toilet blocks, include units with washbasin and shower and facilities for disabled visitors and children. New large laundry. Motorcaravan service point. Gas supplies. Large new supermarket, Restaurant/bar and takeaway. Swimming pool complex with water slides and large paddling pool. Tennis. Games and TV rooms. Bicycle hire. Pony trekking. Entertainment. Off site: Fishing 5 km. Golf 15 km. Flying trips.

Open: 16 May - 6 September, with all services.

Directions

Site is 5 km. southeast of Marennes. From Rochefort take D733 south for 12 km. Turn west on D123 to Ile d'Oléron. Continue for 12 km. Turn southeast on D728 (Saintes). Site signed, in 1 km. on left. GPS: N45:48.699 W01:03.637

Charges 2009

Per unit incl. 2 persons and electricity	€ 19,00 - € 44,00
extra person	€ 7,00 - € 9,00

FR17170 Domaine des Charmilles

Saint Laurent de la Prée, F-17450 Fouras (Charente-Maritime)

Tel: 08 20 20 23 27. Email: **charmilles17@wanadoo.fr**   www.alanrogers.com/FR17170

Les Charmilles is an impressive quality site which is maintained to a very high standard. Of the 300 large pitches, 55 are for touring. All pitches have electricity (10A) and many also have water and drainage. There is an attractive restaurant and bar and an extensive entertainment programme in high season. A plan is in place for continual improvements to the site. This is one of the very few sites in France to have all its facilities especially adapted for disabled guests, including ten of the chalets and the swimming pools. The owner wishes to ensure that all of his visitors have a great holiday.

Facilities

The modern toilet blocks are conveniently placed. Excellent facilities for babies and disabled people. Laundry facilities. Shop, bar, takeaway and restaurant (all May - Sept). Heated swimming pools (one covered), water slides, paddling pool, aquagym and terrace (all May - Sept). Massage (two days per week). Playground. Multisports court. Bicycle hire. Minibus service to beach in July/Aug. No charcoal barbecues. Off site: Fishing 3 km. Golf 5 km. Sailing 10 km. Riding 15 km.

Open: 7 April - 22 September.

Directions

Leave N137 at exit for Fouras and St Laurent de la Prée, joining D937 towards Fouras. Site is on left in about 800 m. GPS: N45:59.240 W01:03.070

Charges guide

Per pitch incl. 2 persons	€ 15,00 - € 30,00
extra person	€ 6,00
child (under 5 yrs)	€ 4,00
electricity	€ 4,00

FR17210 Sunêlia Interlude

8 route de Gros Jonc, F-17580 Le Bois-Plage-en-Ré (Charente-Maritime)

Tel: 05 46 09 18 22. Email: **infos@interlude.fr**   www.alanrogers.com/FR17210

Camping Interlude enjoys a pleasant location with access to an excellent beach. A popular site even in low season, (may become very crowded with overstretched facilities in high season), it has 387 pitches, 136 of which are for touring units. Pitches are sand based, vary in size from 80-120 sq.m. and are mostly divided by hedges on part undulating, sandy terrain. Many are placed to the left of the site in a pine forest setting, others mingle with the tour operators and new mobile homes.

Facilities

Two modern, clean and well equipped sanitary blocks provide washbasins in cabins and some shower units suitable for families with twin washbasins. Baby room, child size toilets and en-suite facilities for disabled visitors. Laundry and dishwashing facilities. Motorcaravan service point. Newly renovated restaurant/bar and shop. Fresh bread. Swimming pools, one outdoor and one inside. Play area. Boules. Organised events and entertainment. Games/TV room. Tennis. Bicycle hire. Communal barbecues. Multisports area.

Open: 4 April - 27 September.

Directions

After toll bridge to the Ile de Ré follow sign (Le Bois-Plage). Turn left at first roundabout, straight on at next two, then left at fourth roundabout. Site signed. GPS: N46:10.430 W01:22.430

Charges guide

Per pitch incl. 2 persons and electricity	€ 23,00 - € 40,00
incl. water and waste	€ 26,00 - € 42,00
extra person	€ 5,00 - € 10,00
140 sq.m. pitch incl. water and drainage	€ 26,00 - € 44,00

FR17160 Camping le Clos Fleuri

8 impasse du Clos Fleuri, F-17600 Médis (Charente-Maritime)

Tel: **05 46 05 62 17**. Email: **clos-fleuri@wanadoo.fr**   www.alanrogers.com/FR17160

Camping Le Clos Fleuri really does live up to its name. The profusion of different trees and the lawns and flower beds give this small site a very rural atmosphere. There is always a warm welcome from the Devais family who created this pretty site in 1974. The 125 touring pitches are mostly of generous size (a little uneven in places). They vary from being in full sun to well shaded and 110 have electrical connections. The bar/restaurant is a converted barn providing a cool haven on hot days and a very convivial venue for evening gatherings and entertainment. There is occasional noise from light aircraft. The surrounding countryside is very pleasant with crops of sunflowers, wheat and maize, while beaches of all sorts are within easy reach. All in all the Clos Fleuri combines a great deal of charm, beauty and friendliness with a location from which the attractions of the Charente-Maritime may be discovered.

Facilities

Toilet facilities are kept scrupulously clean. One block is segregated male and female, the other is unisex with each unit in its own cubicle. Facility for disabled visitors. Baby baths. Laundry facilities. Small pool and paddling pool. Sauna. Shop (1/7-15/9). Restaurant (1/7-31/8) and bar (1/7-15/9). In high season there are twice weekly 'soirées' and boules and archery competitions. Minigolf. Small football pitch. Security barrier closed at night. Off site: Médis 2 km.

Open: 1 June - 18 September.

Directions

Médis is on the N150 from Saintes, halfway between Saujon and Royan. Drive into village. Site signed to south at various points in Médis and is about 2 km. outside village. GPS: N45:37.782 W00:56.768

Charges guide

Per pitch incl. 2 persons	€ 17,90 - € 25,50
extra person	€ 6,00 - € 7,70
child (2-7 yrs)	€ 4,00 - € 5,20
electricity (5/10A)	€ 3,00 - € 5,60
Less 25% in June and Sept.	

In the land of Sun, Pineau, Cognac, Oysters, Mussels and Melons.

nr.ROYAN

Le Clos Fleuri

www.le-clos-fleuri.com   ☆ ☆ ☆ ☆

Trees, bushes, flowers and birds.....
Beauty and peace. Smart & large
grassy pitches & now chalets !
Bar & restaurant set in
a old stone built barn   Family barbecues are...recommended !

country camping

FR17230 Camping l'Océan

La Passe, la Couarde-sur-Mer, F-17670 Ile de Ré (Charente-Maritime)

Tel: **05 46 29 87 70**. Email: **campingdelocean@wanadoo.fr**   www.alanrogers.com/FR17230

L'Océan lies close to the centre of the Ile de Ré, just 50 m. from a sandy beach. There are 338 pitches here with 161 for touring units, the remainder occupied by mobile homes and chalets. The camping area is well shaded and pitches are of a reasonable size, all with electricity (10A). A pleasant bar/restaurant overlooks the large heated swimming pool which is surrounded by an attractive sunbathing terrace. Bicycle hire is popular here as the island offers over 100 km. of interesting cycle routes. A bus goes to La Rochelle from 300 metres outside the site.

Facilities

The new toilet blocks are modern and well maintained with facilities for disabled visitors. Motorcaravan services. Shop. Bar/restaurant and takeaway. Swimming pool. Riding. Bicycle hire. Tennis. Fishing pond adjacent. Play area. Minigolf (free). Helicopter rides, sub-aqua diving and pony riding (high season). Entertainment in high season. No charcoal barbecues. Internet access. Off site: Beach 50 m. La Couarde 2.5 km. Golf 5 km.

Open: 5 May - 28 September.

Directions

After toll bridge, join D735 which runs along the north side of the island until you pass La Couarde. The site is 2.5 km. beyond village (in direction of Ars-en-Ré). GPS: N46:12.260 W01:28.060

Charges guide

Per unit incl. 1-2 persons	€ 14,95 - € 38,20
extra person	€ 4,35 - € 9,65
electricity	€ 5,20
dog	€ 1,80 - € 4,55
Camping Cheques accepted.	

Check real time availability and at-the-gate prices...

www.**alanrogers**.com

FR17190 Le Logis du Breuil

F-17570 Saint Augustin-sur-Mer (Charente-Maritime)

Tel: 05 46 23 23 45. Email: camping.Logis-du-Breuil@wanadoo.fr   www.alanrogers.com/FR17190

The first impression on arrival at this impressive campsite is space. The camping area is a 200 m. expanse of farm pasture where (on different areas) cattle graze and children play. The camping areas are set among rows of mature and shady trees giving a dappled effect to the tents, caravans and grassy pitches. The 320 pitches (250 with 3/6A electricity) are very large and have direct access to wide, unpaved alleys, which lead on to the few tarmac roads around the site. The amenities are centred around the reception area and pool complex. A 'Sites et Paysages' member. The area around the site is very pleasant agricultural land and the beaches of the Atlantic coast are nearby, as are the oyster and the mussel beds of Marennes and La Tremblade. The Gagnard family started the campsite about 25 years ago and obviously take great pride in what it has now become: a peaceful, friendly and very pleasant site from which to explore a delightful holiday area.

Facilities

Four well maintained toilet blocks are spaced around the camping area. Dishwashing and laundry facilities. Swimming pools. Shop, bar and snacks and takeaway (franchised) are well run. No evening entertainment. Play area. Indoor games area. Bicycle hire. Tennis. Excursions organised. WiFi. Off site: Beach 50 minute walk near St Palais-sur-Mer, another to the 'Cote Sauvage'.

Open: 1 May - 30 September.

Directions

Approaching Royan follow signs to St Palais-sur-Mer. Go straight on past first set of traffic lights and two roundabouts. At second set of lights turn right (St Augustin). Site is 2 km. on left, just before village. GPS: N45:40.463 W01:05.768

Charges 2009

Per unit incl. 2 persons	
and electricity 3A	€ 18,25 - € 24,70
with electricity 6A	€ 18,55 - € 25,00
child (under 7 yrs)	€ 3,40 - € 4,80
dog	€ 1,85 - € 2,35

Quiet and space

Le Logis du Breuil
★ ★ ★
CAMPING   CARAVANING

17570 SAINT-AUGUSTIN-SUR-MER
TEL : (33) 05 46 23 23 45
FAX : (33) 05 46 23 43 33

Chalet and Mobilhomes to rent

www.logis-du-breuil.com
camping.logis-du-breuil@wanadoo.fr

SITES & PAYSAGES DE FRANCE
Camping Qualité

FR17290 Camping les Peupliers

RD735, F-17630 La Flotte-en-Ré (Charente-Maritime)

Tel: 05 46 09 62 35. Email: camping@les-peupliers.com   www.alanrogers.com/FR17290

On the Ile de Ré, you are never far from the sea and the location of this campsite is no exception. It is just 800 metres from the sea with sea views from some of the pitches. English is spoken at reception and the staff go out of their way to make your stay enjoyable. The 21 level touring pitches are in a separate area from 143 chalets for rent, in an area of light woodland. There are few water points. The trees provide some shade, but the very low hedges provide little privacy as the width and length of the pitches varies.

Facilities

Two new but traditionally designed sanitary blocks are clean and well maintained. Both have unisex facilities including showers and vanity type units in cabins. Separate facilities for people with disabilities. Laundry facilities. Shop, restaurant, takeaway and bar with TV (all 8/4-23/9). Outdoor swimming pool (15/5-15/9). Play area. Children's club and entertainment (high season). Fridge hire. Bicycle hire. Off site: Riding 500 m. Beach and sailing 800 m. Fishing 800 m. Golf 20 km.

Open: 5 April - 27 September.

Directions

Over the toll bridge and turn left at second roundabout. Site is well signed. GPS: N46:10.969 W01:18.050

Charges 2009

Per unit incl. 2 persons	
and electricity	€ 21,00 - € 33,00
extra person	€ 5,00 - € 8,00
child (0-5 yrs)	free - € 5,00
dog	€ 5,00
Camping Cheques accepted.	

BOOK THIS SITE The Travel Service
CALL 01580 214000
...we'll arrange everything

141

FR17220 Camping la Brande

Route des Huitres, F-17480 Le Château-d'Oléron (Charente-Maritime)

Tel: **05 46 47 62 37**. Email: **info@camping-labrande.com**   www.alanrogers.com/FR17220

A quality environmentally-friendly site, run and maintained to the highest standard. La Brande offers an ideal holiday environment on the delightful Ile d'Oléron, famed for its oysters. La Brande is situated on the oyster route and close to a sandy beach. Pitches here are generous and mostly separated by hedges and trees, the greater number for touring outfits. All are on level grassy terrain and have electricity hook-ups, some are fully serviced. The many activities during the high season, plus the natural surroundings, make this an ideal choice for families. A feature of this site is the heated indoor pool (28°) open all season. The Barcat family ensures that their visitors not only enjoy quality facilities, but Gerard Barcat offers guided bicycle tours and canoe trips. This way you discover the nature, oyster farming, vineyards and history of Oléron, which is joined to the mainland by a 3 km. bridge.

Facilities

Three heated, clean sanitary blocks have spacious, well equipped showers and washbasins (mainly in cabins). Baby facilities. Excellent facilities for people with disabilities (separate large shower, washbasin and WC). Laundry rooms. Motorcaravan service point. Superb restaurant/takeaway and bar (July/Aug). Shop (July/Aug). Heated indoor swimming pool (all season). Jacuzzi. Sauna. Well equipped playground. Games room. Football field, tennis, minigolf, fishing and archery. Bicycle hire. Canoe hire. Free WiFi. New building for children. Off site: Beach 300 m. Sailing 2 km. Riding 6 km. Golf 7 km.

Open: 15 March - 11 November.

Directions

After crossing bridge to L'Ile d'Oléron turn right towards Le Château-d'Oléron. Continue through village and follow sign for Route des Huitres. Site is on left after 2.5 km. GPS: N45:54.249 W01:12.915

Charges guide

Per unit incl. 2 persons and electricity	€ 19,20 - € 40,00
extra person	€ 5,00 - € 8,00
dog	€ 2,50 - € 8,00

Camping Cheques accepted.

Alain BARCAT and his team welcomes you at La Brande - an open air hotel, camping and caravan site. Situated 1,5 miles outside of Château d'Oléron on la Route de Huîtres nearby the seaside, 28°C heated swimming pool opened from the 15.03 till the 15.11 (free WiFi hotspot)

ROUTE DES HUÎTRES • 17480 LE CHÂTEAU D'OLÉRON
TÉL. +33 (0)5 46 47 62 37 • FAX +33 (0)5 46 47 71 70
info@camping-labrande.com • www.camping-labrande.co.uk

FR17490 Camping les Chirats

Route de la Platère, F-17690 Angoulins-sur-Mer (Charente-Maritime)

Tel: **05 46 56 94 16**. Email: **contact@campingleschirats.fr**   www.alanrogers.com/FR17490

This site is in a good position, being 8 km. south of La Rochelle and with a small sandy beach is just 100 m. from the site. The larger beaches at Aytre and Chatelaillon are three km. away. This is a family run site and a warm and friendly welcome awaits visitors. Of the 240 pitches, 200 are for touring units and the remainder are used for chalets which are for rent. The pitches are mainly open, level and easily accessible with some having views over the sea. Electricity supply is 10A and many have water and drainage. Leisure facilities on this site are excellent.

Facilities

Three modern sanitary blocks all centrally placed with facilities for disabled visitors and babies. Washing machines. Bar, restaurant, snack bar and takeaway. Attractive indoor and outdoor swimming pools. Toboggan. Well equipped 'wellness' centre including sauna, jacuzzi, solarium, spa and gym. Playground. Multisports area. Internet access. Entertainment (July/Aug). Off site: Fishing 100 m. Bicycle hire 500 m. Tennis 1 km. Riding 4 km. Golf 5 km. Aquarium 8 km.

Open: 1 April - 30 September.

Directions

Leave N137 at exit for Angoulins and La Jarne on to the D202. Go through Angoulins turning right on rue de Chay. Carry on to Chemin de la Platere. Site is then well signed. GPS: N46:06.245 W01:07.856

Charges guide

Per unit incl. 2 persons	€ 12,00 - € 18,50
incl. electricity	€ 15,00 - € 21,50
extra person	€ 3,50 - € 4,00
child (under 10 yrs)	€ 2,50 - € 3,00

FR17260 Camping le Cormoran

Route de Radia, Ars-en-Ré, F-17590 Ile de Ré (Charente-Maritime)

Tel: **05 46 29 46 04**. Email: **info@cormoran.com**   www.alanrogers.com/FR17260

Just outside Ars-en-Ré, Le Cormoran offers a quiet rural holiday for families with young children. Pitches vary in size and are a mixture of sand and grass. All have electricity. The restaurant and bar overlook the pool. Basic provisions are stocked in the bar. There are the usual shops in Ars, which is some 800 m. away. Le Cormoran is close to the local oyster beds. The sister site, Camping La Plage, is about 3 km. away and concentrates mainly on its 142 mobile homes. There are 44 pitches for touring units but the facilities for them are a little old fashioned.

Facilities

Unisex toilet facilities are in two blocks with toilets (British and Turkish style), showers and washbasins mainly in cabins. Provision for disabled visitors. Laundry facilities. Motorcaravan service point. Bar, restaurant and takeaway meals. WiFi. Swimming pool (covered in low season). Fitness centre. Tennis. Games room. Play area. Entertainment programme in high season. Bicycle hire. Off site: Nearest beach 500 m. Ars-en-Ré 800 m. Fishing 500 m. Boat launching 1 km. Riding 3 km. Golf 10 km.

Open: 1 April - 30 September.

Directions

Cross the toll bridge from La Rochelle onto the Ile de Ré and continue on D735 to Ars-en-Ré from where site is well signed. GPS: N46:12.673 W01:03.179

Charges guide

Per unit incl. 2 persons	€ 16,80 - € 24,20
extra person	€ 5,50 - € 11,50
child (0-9 yrs)	€ 3,30 - € 11,50
electricity (10A)	€ 5,00
animal	€ 2,70 - € 5,50

Check real time availability and at-the-gate prices...

www.alanrogers.com

FR17280 Camping la Grainetière

Mobile homes ▶ page 496

Route de Saint-Martin, F-17630 La Flotte-en-Ré (Charente-Maritime)

Tel: 05 46 09 68 86. Email: la-grainetiere@free.fr

www.alanrogers.com/FR17280

A truly friendly welcome awaits you from the owners, Isabelle and Eric, at La Grainetière. It is a peaceful campsite set in almost three hectares of pine trees which provide some shade for the 65 touring pitches of various shapes and sizes. There are also 50 well spaced chalets for rent. Some pitches are suitable for units up to seven metres (book in advance). There are no hedges for privacy and the pitches are sandy with some grass. Ample new water points and electricity (10A) hook-ups (Euro plugs) serve the camping area. The site is well lit.

Facilities

The unisex sanitary block is first class, with washbasins in cubicles, showers, British style WCs, facilities for children and people with disabilities. Shop (1/4-30/9). Takeaway (July/Aug). Swimming pool (heated 1/4-30/9). Bicycle hire. Fridge hire. TV room. Charcoal barbecues are not permitted. Off site: Beach and sailing 2 km. Bar and restaurant 2 km. Fishing and boat launching 2 km. Riding 3 km. Golf 10 km.

Open: 1 April - 30 September.

Directions

Follow camping signs from La Flotte, 1 km. from the village. GPS: N46:11.253 W01:20.696

Charges guide

Per unit incl. 2 persons	€ 14,00 - € 24,00
extra person	€ 3,00 - € 7,00
child (0-7 yrs)	€ 2,00 - € 3,00
electricity (10A)	€ 4,00

La Grainetiere

Between St. Martin harbor and la Flotte. All kinds of shops at proximity. Isabelle and Eric welcome you in a wooded park. Friendly family atmosphere.

Route de Saint Martin - 17630 La Flotte - France - Tel: 0033 (0)5 46 09 68 86 - Fax: 0033 (0)5 46 09 53 13
lagrainetiere@free.fr - www.la-grainetiere.com

FR17550 Camping Transhumance

Route de Royan, F-17920 Breuillet (Charente-Maritime)

Tel: 05 46 22 72 15. Email: contact@transhumance.com

www.alanrogers.com/FR17550

The approach to Camping Transhumance looks out over pretty, rolling countryside and leads to a peaceful site with a pleasant social atmosphere. There are 365 pitches here, made up of a mixture of touring, seasonal and mobile homes. They are arranged in avenues with about 20 units in each and divided by hedges. The pitches are mainly on grass, are level and have 10A electricity. Some areas are shaded. Despite the site's rural situation, the beaches of Royan are a just a short drive away and there are many other interesting places to visit nearby, including the oyster beds at Marennes.

Facilities

Two toilet blocks, are unheated but clean and bright. Baby room. Good facilities for disabled visitors (key access). Excellent laundry. Small shop. Bar. Takeaway. Swimming pool. Tennis. Boules. WiFi in reception. Off site: Village of Breuillet 2 km. with shops and bank. La Palmyre Zoo.

Open: 24 May - 6 September.

Directions

From Saujon take the D14 northwest signed to La Tremblade. After about 8 km. turn left on D140 signed Breuiillet. Pass through the village (watch for speed bumps) and site is 2 km. on the left, well signed. GPS: N45:40.703 W01:03.100

Charges guide

Per unit incl. 2 persons	€ 13,00 - € 18,00
extra person	€ 3,50 - € 4,50
child (under 10 yrs)	€ 2,50 - € 3,50
electricity (10A)	€ 4,50

Check real time availability and at-the-gate prices...

www.alanrogers.com

FR17340 **Camping Port-Punay**

Allée Bernard Moreau, les Boucholeurs, F-17340 Châtelaillon-Plage (Charente-Maritime)

Tel: **05 46 56 01 53**. Email: **contact@camping-port-punay.com**   www.alanrogers.com/FR17340

Port-Punay is a friendly, well run site just 200 metres from the beach and 3 km. from the centre of the resort of Châtelaillon-Plage. There are 166 touring pitches laid out on well trimmed grass, with many mature poplars and large shrubs. The site has a well stocked shop, open all season and a small bar and restaurant only open in high season. A heated swimming pool has a separate gated area for paddling. There is a good range of activities available and in high season some entertainment is arranged. This is a family run site (Famille Moreau) and the son of the family speaks excellent English, as does his Dutch wife. Rochefort to the south and La Rochelle to the north are well worth a visit (buses from outside the site), as is the nearby town of Châtelaillon-Plage, which has an all-year covered market and, in summer, a street market every day. Port-Punay has just one large toilet block, centrally positioned on the site, with very good facilities.

Facilities

One large toilet block with good facilities including washbasins in cubicles and large shower cubicles. Facilities for disabled visitors and babies. Washing machines. Shop. Bar, restaurant and takeaway (15/6-15/9). Swimming pool (heated May - Sept). Games area. Play area. Bicycle hire. Internet access. WiFi. Off site: Beach 200 m. Châtelaillon-Plage 3 km. by road, 1.5 km. along the seafront on foot or bike. Buses to Rochefort and La Rochelle from outside site. Riding 2 km. Golf 10 km.

Open: 1 April - 28 September.

Directions

From N137 (La Rochelle - Rochefort) take exit for Châtelaillon-Plage. At the 1st roundabout follow the sign for the town centre. At the 2nd roundabout turn left. Follow signs to the site at the seaside hamlet of Les Boucholeurs. Here drive to the sea wall then turn left through village to site. Take care, as the road has many traffic-calming measures and can be narrow in places. GPS: N46:03.288 W01:05.004

Charges guide

Per unit incl. 2 persons	€ 14,90 - € 22,00
extra person	€ 4,20 - € 5,50
child (0-3 yrs)	€ 3,20 - € 4,20
electricity (10A)	€ 4,00 - € 5,00

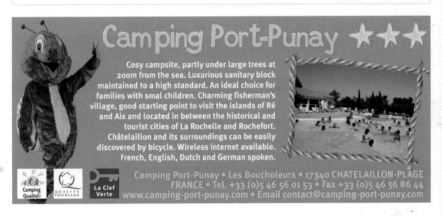

Camping Port-Punay ★★★

Cosy campsite, partly under large trees at 200m from the sea. Luxurious sanitary block maintained to a high standard. An ideal choice for families with smal children. Charming fisherman's village, good starting point to visit the islands of Ré and Aix and located in between the historical and tourist cities of La Rochelle and Rochefort. Châtelaillon and its surroundings can be easily discovered by bicycle. Wireless internet available. French, English, Dutch and German spoken.

Camping Qualité · QUALITÉ TOURISME · La Clef Verte

Camping Port-Punay • Les Boucholeurs • 17340 CHATELAILLON-PLAGE FRANCE • Tel. +33 (0)5 46 56 01 53 • Fax +33 (0)5 46 56 86 44 www.camping-port-punay.com • Email contact@camping-port-punay.com

FR17560 **Campéole le Platin**

125 ave. Gustave Perreau, F-17840 Rivedoux Plage (Charente-Maritime)

Tel: **05 46 09 84 10**. Email: **platin@campeole.com**   www.alanrogers.com/FR17560

Located at the gateway to the Ile de Ré, Le Platin is just a short walk from the pleasant village of Rivedoux Plage where there are several good restaurants and shops. A long, narrow site, the beach is on one side and the main road on the other. It is divided into small avenues with around 20 pitches in each. All have 10A electricity and most are shaded, although the pitches nearest the beach have little shade (but the best views). Of the 200 pitches, 50 are used for canvas bungalows for hire, the rest are seasonal and for touring.

Facilities

The toilet facilities here are a little below standard, although one block has good showers and an en-suite bathroom for disabled visitors. This is only the second year Campéole have been here, and there are plans for improvements. A swimming pool complex is due for completion in June 2009. Small bar. Entertainment in high season. Off site: Bicycle hire 200 m.

Open: 1 April - 30 September.

Directions

After crossing the toll bridge from La Rochelle, continue on the D735 into Rivedoux Plage. Site is well signed on the right. GPS: N46:09.533 W01:16.251

Charges guide

Per unit incl. 2 persons and electricity	€ 16,60 - € 23,90
extra person	€ 4,10 - € 5,90

145

FR17540 Camping la Clé des Champs

1188 route de la Fouasse, F-17570 Les Mathes/La Palmyre (Charente-Maritime)

Tel: 05 46 22 40 53. Email: contact@la-cle-des-champs.net   www.alanrogers.com/FR17540

La Clé des Champs is situated on the edge of the large Forêt de la Coubre and around 1.5 km. from the village of Les Mathes. The sandy beaches of the Gironde estuary are around four kilometres distant. There are 300 pitches, around half occupied by mobile homes and chalets, some of which are available for rent. Pitches are grassy and mostly equipped with electrical connections (6/10A). The swimming pool can be covered in low season and there is a separate paddling pool for children. An entertainment and activity programme is on offer during the 'P'tits Bilous' children's club (4-12 years). Various cycle tracks lead through the forest to the beaches of the Côte Sauvage (bicycle hire is available on site). These stretch for 70 km. and sandy beaches alternate with rocky coves. The nearby zoo at La Palmyre, with over 1,600 animals, is France's second largest. La Palmyre is a stylish resort with many cafes and restaurants, as well as a fine sandy beach.

Facilities	Directions
Bar. Snack bar. Takeaway. Covered swimming pool. Paddling pool. Games room. Play area. Bicycle hire. Activity and entertainment programme. Mobile homes for rent. Off site: Nearest beach 4 km. Les Mathes village 1.5 km. (good range of shops and restaurants). Riding centre nearby. Minigolf 800 m.	From Saujon take the D14 heading north west towards La Tremblade. At Arvert head south on the D141 to Les Mathes. Beyond the village, head right on the Route de la Fouasse and the site is on the right after a further 500 m. GPS: N45:43.259 W01:10.289
Open: 28 March - 31 October.	**Charges 2009**

Per unit incl. 2 persons	
and electricity	€ 14,30 - € 24,00
extra person	€ 3,20 - € 4,50
child (2-7 yrs)	€ 2,50 - € 3,50
dog	€ 2,40 - € 2,60

Covered heated swimming pool · Animation
Mobile homes for rent · Multisports terrain · Minigolf

La Clé des Champs ★★★

1188 route de la Fouasse · 17570 Les Mathes · Tél : 05 46 22 40 53
fax : 05 46 22 56 96 · www.la-cledeschamps.com
E-mail : contact@la-cledeschamps.com or : contact@la-cle-des-champs.net

FR85000 Camping le Petit Rocher

1250 avenue de Docteur Mathevet, F-85560 Longeville-sur-Mer (Vendée)

Tel: 02 51 90 31 57. Email: rocher85@free.fr   www.alanrogers.com/FR85000

A former municipal site, Le Petit Rocher is now under the same management (M. Guignard) as another local campsite, Les Brunelles. With its seaside location set in a pine forest, there is an air of peace and tranquillity. Although the area is undulating, the 150 good size touring pitches are flat and arranged in terraces throughout the wooded area. Electricity hook-ups are available (Euro style plugs) and there are adequate water points. A grassy play area for children is thoughtfully situated in a hollow, but has limited equipment. A fun pool was added in 2008.

Facilities	Directions
Three new, spacious sanitary blocks are clean and well maintained with showers, British style WCs. Facilities for people with disabilities. Washing machine and dryer. Tennis court. New fun pool. Off site: Beach 200 m. Bars, restaurant, and small shops nearby. Riding and bicycle hire 2 km. Boat launching 11 km. Fishing 15 km. Golf 20 km.	From Longeville-sur-Mer follow signs for Le Rocher towards La Tranche-sur-Mer. Turn right at first roundabout, following campsite signs to site on right. GPS: N46:24.226 W01:30.431
Open: 25 April - 12 September.	**Charges 2009**

Per unit with 2 persons	
and electricity	€ 16,00 - € 24,00
extra person	€ 3,00 - € 5,00
No credit cards.	

The Travel Service ...we'll arrange everything
BOOK THIS SITE
CALL 01580 214000

Check real time availability and at-the-gate prices...
www.alanrogers.com

FR85010 Camping le Zagarella

Route de La Tranche, F-85560 Longeville-sur-Mer (Vendée)

Tel: 02 51 33 30 60. Email: contact@campingzagarella.com   www.alanrogers.com/FR85010

This pleasant campsite is set in a wooded, six hectare area, 900 metres walk from the beach (or 1.5 km. by road). As well as 100 chalets to rent, there are 45 small touring pitches (the site is probably unsuitable for units over six metres). On well drained grass and shaded, the pitches are hedged and all have water and 10A electricity (French connections). Access around the site is by tarmac roads. The site has a landscaped pool complex including slides and a covered pool. An area for sports and games including tennis is across the road via an underpass.

Facilities

Two well maintained toilet blocks of traditional design include British style WCs, washbasins in cubicles and free pre-set showers. Separate baby room and facilities for people with disabilities. Washing machines. Shop (25/5-5/9). Bar (20/5-5/9). Restaurant and takeaway (1/5-30/9). Swimming pool (1/6-30/9) and indoor pool (heated 1/4-30/9). Playground. Tennis. Bicycle hire. Gas barbecues permitted (available for rent). Off site: Beach 900 m. Riding 1 km. Golf 30 km.

Open: 1 April - 30 September.

Directions

From Longeville-sur-Mer take road to Tranche-sur-Mer and site is on the left (follow green camping signs). GPS: N46:24.234 W01:29.286

Charges guide

Per unit incl. 2 persons	€ 16,00 - € 28,00
extra person	€ 5,00 - € 6,00
child (0-7 yrs)	€ 3,50 - € 4,00
dog	€ 4,30

CAMPINGS **FranceLoc**

Domaine de Zagarella

Pitches, mobile homes and cha-lets. Indoor pool and heated out-door pool in a natural setting, waterfall, Jacuzzi, waterslide, play area, tennis...
At 900m from the beach

Le Rocher - Route de la Tranche
85560 Longeville Sur Mer
Tél : 33 (0) 251 33 30 60
Fax : 33 (0) 251 33 37 09
www.campings-franceloc.com

Vendée

FR85020 Camping du Jard

123 Mal de Lattre de Tassigny, F-85360 La Tranche-sur-Mer (Vendée)

Tel: 02 51 27 43 79. Email: info@campingdujard.fr   www.alanrogers.com/FR85020

Camping du Jard is a well maintained site between La Rochelle and Les Sables d'Olonne. First impressions are good, with a friendly welcome from M. Marton or his staff. The 242 touring pitches are level and grassy, hedged on two sides by bushes. The smallest are 100 sq.m. (the majority larger) and most are equipped with electricity, half with water and drainage. It is a comparatively new site, but the large variety of trees is beginning to provide a little shade. An impressive pool complex has a toboggan, paddling pool and an indoor pool with jacuzzi. The site is 700 m. from a sandy beach with many shops and restaurants nearby.

Facilities

Three toilet blocks with facilities for babies and disabled people and most washbasins are in cabins. Laundry facilities. Shop (1/6-10/9), restaurant and bar (25/5-10/9). Heated pool with toboggan and paddling pool, plus heated indoor pool with jacuzzi (no Bermuda-style shorts in pools). Sauna, solarium and fitness room. Tennis. Minigolf. Bicycle hire. Play area, games and TV rooms. Internet access. American motorhomes are not accepted. Pets are not accepted.

Open: 26 April - 15 September.

Directions

Site is east of La Tranche-sur-Mer on D46. From D747 (La Roche-sur-Yon - La Tranche) follow signs (La Faute-sur-Mer) along bypass. Take exit for La Grière and then turn east to site. GPS: N46:20.901 W01:23.242

Charges guide

Per unit incl. 2 persons and electricity	€ 22,40 - € 31,00
extra person	€ 4,50 - € 5,50
child (under 5 yrs)	€ 3,00 - € 4,00

BOOK THIS SITE
CALL 01580 214000
...we'll arrange everything
Service The Travel

Check real time availability and at-the-gate prices...
www.alanrogers.com

FR85030 Camping la Loubine

1 route de la Mer, F-85340 Olonne-sur-Mer (Vendée)

Tel: 02 51 33 12 92. Email: camping.la.loubine@wanadoo.fr　　www.alanrogers.com/FR85030

Situated on the edge of a forest, this campsite is just 1.8 kilometres from a sandy beach and five minutes from Les Sables d'Olonne. The 60 grass touring pitches are mostly shaded, all with 6A electricity connections and adequate water points. Only a limited number of pitches is available for large units (over 7 m.) because of difficulties with manoeuvring. It is best to confirm availability and book in advance. The focal point of the site is an excellent bar and entertainment area for karaoke and discos with a patio overlooking the splendid pool complex with its water slides. There are many chalets and mobile homes on the site, both privately owned and to rent.

Facilities

Toilet blocks are clean with British style WCs, washbasins in cubicles and controllable showers. Shop. Bar and restaurant (15/5-15/9). Indoor pool (all season). Outdoor swimming pools (15/5-15/9). Tennis. Fitness room. Minigolf. Play area. Bicycle hire. A new indoor aqua park is planned. Dogs are not allowed in July and August. Off site: Beach 2 km. Fishing and boat launching 6 km. Golf 4 km. Riding 1 km. Boat launching 6.5 km. Restaurant, shop, bar within 1.5 km.

Open: 5 April - September.

Directions

Site is west of Olonne beside the D80 road. Turn towards the coast at roundabout, signed La Forêt d'Olonne and site (75 m). GPS: N46:32.760 W01:48.360

Charges guide

Per pitch incl. 2 persons	€ 15,50 - € 27,00
extra person	€ 3,25 - € 5,00
child (under 6 yrs)	free - € 2,95
electricity (6A)	€ 3,65

Camping La Loubine

Traditional-style facilities set in the grounds of an old farm only 1800 m from the beach; La Loubine is a lively site with one of the best pool complexes in the area. (1 heated indoor pool with 3 waterslides, whirlpool bath and sauna).

Bar - Restaurant - Take Away - Shop - Tennis Court - Crazy Golf - Playground - Fitness Room - Multi Sport Pitch - Bicycle Hire - Entertainment in high season.

1, Route de la Mer - 85340 Olonne Sur mer - France
Tel.: 0033 (0)2 51 33 12 92 - Fax: 0033 (0)2 51 33 12 71

camping.la.loubine@wanadoo.fr
www.la-loubine.fr

FR85040 Castel Camping Caravaning la Garangeoire

Saint Julien-des-Landes, F-85150 la Mothe-Achard (Vendée)

Tel: 02 51 46 65 39. Email: info@garangeoire.com　　www.alanrogers.com/FR85040

La Garangeoire is a stunning campsite, situated some 15 km. inland near the village of St Julien-des-Landes. Set in 200 ha. of parkland surrounding the small château of La Garangeoire of which there is an outstanding view as you approach through the gates. With a spacious, relaxed atmosphere, the main camping areas are on either side of the old road which is edged with mature trees. The 360 pitches, all named after birds, are individually hedged, some with shade. They are well spaced and are especially large (most 150-200 sq.m), most with electricity (8A) and some with water and drainage also.

Facilities

Ample, first class sanitary facilities. All have washbasins in cabins. Facilities for babies and disabled people. Laundry facilities. Motorcaravan service point. Shop, full restaurant and takeaway (2/5-20/9) with bars and terrace (all season). Pool complex with water slides, fountains and a children's pool (all season). Play field with play equipment. Games room. Tennis courts. Bicycle hire. Minigolf. Archery. Riding (July/Aug). Fishing and boating. Off site: Golf 10 km. Beaches 15 km.

Open: 4 April - 26 September.

Directions

Site is signed from St Julien; entrance is to the east off the D21 road, 2.5 km. north of St Julien-des-Landes. GPS: N46:39.936 W01:42.80

Charges 2009

Per unit incl. 2 persons	
and electricity	€ 17,50 - € 36,00
incl. services	€ 19,50 - € 38,50
extra person	€ 4,50 - € 7,80
child (under 10 yrs)	€ 2,50 - € 3,60
dog	€ 3,00 - € 3,50
Camping Cheques accepted.	

The Travel Service ...we'll arrange everything
BOOK THIS SITE CALL 01580 214000

Check real time availability and at-the-gate prices...

www.alanrogers.com

FR85090 Camping l'Abri des Pins

Route de Notre-Dame-de-Monts, F-85160 Saint Jean-de-Monts (Vendée)

Tel: 02 51 58 83 86. Email: contact@abridespins.com

www.alanrogers.com/FR85090

L'Abri des Pins is situated on the outskirts of St Jean-de-Monts and is separated from the sea and long sandy beach by a strip of pinewood. The site has 218 pitches, 78 of which are for touring units with 30 larger than average, with electricity, water and drainage. Electricity is also available for the other pitches which are around 100 sq.m., fully marked out with dividing hedges and shade. Many pitches are occupied by privately owned mobile homes, but there are no tour operators on the site.

Facilities

The two sanitary blocks include washbasins in cabins, laundry and dishwashing sinks. Good small shop (1/7-31/8). Bar/restaurant (eat in and take away). Outdoor, heated swimming pool and water slide, plus small pool for children, with decked sunbathing area (open all season; no Bermuda-style shorts). Daily children's club, football, pétanque, aquarobics. Off site: Supermarket. Restaurants. Beach 700 m. Walking, cycling and fishing 1 km. Riding 2 km. Golf 5 km.

Open: 15 June - 16 September.

Directions

Site is 4 km. from town centre on St Jean-de-Monts - Notre Dame-de Monts/Noirmoutiers road (D38), on left heading north, just after Camping les Amiaux. GPS: N46:48.562 W02:06.540

Charges guide

Per unit incl. 3 persons and electricity	€ 22,50 - € 33,70
extra person	€ 3,60 - € 6,10
Deposit required for armband for access to pool and site (high season only).	

FR85130 Camping Pong

Rue du Stade, F-85220 Landevieille (Vendée)

Tel: 02 51 22 92 63. Email: info@lepong.com

www.alanrogers.com/FR85130

A comfortable family run site, in a rural situation 12 km. southeast of St Gilles-Croix-de-Vie, and five kilometres from the coast at Brétignolles. It has 229 pitches with 187 used for touring units, the remainder for mobile homes and chalets. All have electricity connections (4/6A) and are of a good size. The bar, restaurant, function room, games room, gym and shop have all recently been rebuilt. The original part of the site around the small, lightly fenced fishing lake (there are warning signs) has mature trees, whereas, in the newer areas trees and shrubs are developing well.

Facilities

Four modern, unisex sanitary blocks provide toilets of mixed styles and some washbasins in cabins. Facilities for disabled people, baby room, dishwashing and laundry room. Shop, takeaway, bar and restaurant (15/6-15/9). Swimming pools including heated pool with jacuzzi, toboggan and paddling pool (from 15/5). Gym, TV lounge and games room. Bicycle hire. Fishing. Fenced play area and children's club. Off site: Tennis 200 m. Lac du Jaunay 2.5 km. Beach, golf, riding 5 km.

Open: 1 April - 15 September.

Directions

Site is on the edge of Landevieille and is signed from the D32 (Challans - Les Sables d'Olonne) and D12 (La Mothe Achard-St Gilles Croix-de-Vie). GPS: N46:38.520 W01:47.940

Charges guide

Per unit incl. 2 persons and electricity	€ 15,00 - € 24,00
extra person	€ 3,20 - € 4,90
child (under 5 yrs)	€ 2,50 - € 3,70
water and drainage	€ 1,70

FR85080 Hotellerie de Plein Air la Puerta del Sol

Les Borderies, chemin de Hommeaux, F-85270 Saint Hilaire-de-Riez (Vendée)

Tel: 02 51 49 10 10. Email: info@campinglapuertadelsol.com

www.alanrogers.com/FR85080

La Puerta del Sol is a good quality campsite a short distance away from the busy coast. It is suitable not only for families with teenage children to entertain, but also for those seeking a more peaceful and relaxing holiday. There are 216 pitches, of which 102 are used for touring units. Pitches are level with dividing hedges and many receive shade from the mature trees on the site. Each pitch is fully serviced with water, waste water point and electricity. There is one small French tour operator on site (20 pitches).

Facilities

Three heated toilet blocks have a mix of Turkish and British style WCs, washbasins in cabins and baby baths. Dishwashing and laundry facilities. Facilities for disabled visitors. Shop (1/5-31/8). Bar (1/5-15/9). Self-service restaurant and takeaway (1/5-31/8). Swimming pool, slide and paddling pool (1/5-30/9; no Bermuda-style shorts). Play area. Tennis. Bicycle hire. Games room. American motorhomes accepted with reservation. Off site: Beach, riding, fishing and golf 5 km. St Jean-de-Monts 7 km.

Open: 1 April - 30 September.

Directions

From Le Pissot (7 km. north of St Gilles Croix-de-Vie on D38) take D59 (Le Perrier). Site is 2 km. along this road on the right down a short side road. Site signed. GPS: N46:45.870 W01:57.430

Charges guide

Per unit incl. up to 2 persons and services	€ 19,00 - € 29,00
extra person	€ 5,00 - € 6,50
child (under 7 yrs)	€ 2,50 - € 4,50
animal	€ 4,00

BOOK THIS SITE
CALL 01580 214000
...we'll arrange everything
The Travel Service

BOOK THIS SITE
CALL 01580 214000
...we'll arrange everything
The Travel Service

Check real time availability and at-the-gate prices...

www.alanrogers.com

FR85710 Camping le Bel Air

Mobile homes ▶ page 498

6 chemin de Bel Air, F-85180 Château d'Olonne (Vendée)

Tel: **02 51 22 09 67**

www.alanrogers.com/FR85710

Le Bel Air is a well established site close to the Vendée's largest resort, Les Sables d'Olonne. This is a very well equipped site with a new and impressive pool complex being the focal point. This complex comprises a large covered pool and separate outdoor pool. Both have water slides and the indoor complex also has a sauna, lazy river, spa bath and a fully equipped gym, amongst other features. There are 305 pitches here of which around 70 are available for touring units. The rest are occupied by mobile homes and chalets (available for rent). Pitches are grassy and all have electrical connections. This is a lively site in high season with its own nightclub and entertainment programme. A children's club is available during the daytime. Le Bel Air is just 500 m. from the sea and the nearest sandy beach is 3 km. Les Sables is a stylish resort with a host of enticing seafood restaurants and also now known as the departure point of the Vendée Globe round-the-world solo yacht race.

Facilities

Bar. Snack bar. Takeaway. Shop. TV room. Swimming pool complex. Indoor pool. Multisports terrain. Playground. Mobile homes and chalets for rent. Off site: Nearest beach 2.5 km. Les Sables d'Olonne 2 km. (shops, cafés and restaurants). Motor museum at Talmont-St Hilaire.

Open: 15 March - 15 November.

Directions

Approaching from the north (D160), follow signs to Les Sables d'Olonne and then Talmont-St Hilaire on D949. Site is well signed when you reach Château d'Olonne. GPS: N46:28.325 W01:43.588

Charges 2009

Per unit incl. 2 persons	
and electricity	€ 18,00 - € 29,00
extra person	€ 3,00 - € 4,50
child (under 7 yrs)	€ 2,50 - € 3,50
dog	free - € 3,00

FR85110 Camping l'Océan

Mobile homes ▶ page 496

Rue des Gabelous, F-85470 Brem-sur-Mer (Vendée)

Tel: **02 51 90 59 16**. Email: contact@campingdelocean.fr

www.alanrogers.com/FR85110

Set amongst grapevines and fir trees, Camping L'Océan is situated between the fishing port of St Gilles Croix-de-Ville and Brem-sur-Mer, only 600 metres (15 minutes' walk) from beautiful sandy beaches and the clear Atlantic Ocean. The campsite is family managed (Helen is English) and a very warm welcome awaits at the reception area which is well stocked with local information. The touring pitches are an average of 100 sq.m. in size and have 6A French style electric hook-ups (some require long leads). They are divided by hedges and are centrally located in the campsite with mobile homes to rent on either side. Local excursions arranged on an ad hoc basis. The campsite focus is on family fun and entertainment with organised activities during high season including water aerobics, pétanque, karaoke, discos and wine tasting, plus a club for children three mornings a week.

Facilities

Three old style but very clean unisex toilet blocks have free pre-set showers, British style WCs, and washbasins in cubicles. Separate toilet and shower for people with disabilities. Shop (July/Aug). Bar and restaurant (weekends only May, June, Sept). Swimming pool (heated 15/6-30/8) with slide. Indoor pool (15/4-30/9). Fitness room. Bicycle hire. Playground in two areas (ages 2-6 yrs and 6-12yrs). Organised activities. Children's club. Off site: Brem-sur-Mer 15 minutes walk. Supermarket 5 minute drive. Fishing 1 km. Riding 9 km. Golf 15 km.

Open: 1 April - 15 October.

Directions

Take N160 from La Roche-sur-Yon towards Les Sables d'Olonne. Take exit for La Mothe-Achard and Bretignolles-sur-Mer. Follow D54 to Brem-sur-Mer then D38 Bretignolles-sur-Mer. Site is signed on left before Activity Centre. GPS: N46:36.324 W01:49.908

Charges guide

Per unit incl. 2 persons	€ 13,20 - € 19,00
incl. electricity (6A)	€ 15,80 - € 22,00
extra person	€ 3,50 - € 4,50
child (0-7 yrs)	€ 2,30 - € 2,90

Check real time availability and at-the-gate prices...

www.**alanrogers**.com

Hôtellerie de Plein Air

Bel Air
★★★★

500m from the Atlantic coast

*Covered 1000m² aquatic complex
with Jacuzzi, recreational activities,
fitness room, solarium...*

- Water slide.
- Heated swimming and paddling pools.
- Multi-sports ground.
- Children's club.
- Bar, pizza, snacks.
- Grocery, bakery.
- Activities 7 days a week in high season.
- Rental of mobile homes.
Comfort and High Comfort 6/8 places.
(park less than 3 years old,
half-covered terrace)
- Sales of mobile homes and rental
of annual pitches.

6, Chemin de Bel Air • 85180 CHATEAU D'OLONNE • Tél. 02 51 22 09 67
Fax. 02 51 22 16 47 • Web : www.campingdubelair.com
E-mail : camping.lebelair@wanadoo.fr

Camping l'Océan
★★★

600m from the beach

- Water slide.
- Outdoor pool.
- Heated indoor pool.
- Games and multi-sport areas.
- Children's club.
- Bar, pizza, snacks.
- Activities seven days a week
July and August.
- Rental of mobile homes.
Comfort and High Comfort
6/8 places.
(park less than 3 years old)
- Sales of mobile homes and rental
of annual pitches.

Rue des Gabelous - 85470 BREM SUR MER - Tel : 02.51.90.59.16
Fax : 02 51 90 14 21 • Web : www.campingdelocean.fr
E-mail : contact@campingdelocean.fr

FR85150 Camping la Yole

Mobile homes ▶ page 497

Chemin des Bosses, Orouet, F-85160 Saint Jean-de-Monts (Vendée)

Tel: **02 51 58 67 17.** Email: **contact@la-yole.com**   www.alanrogers.com/FR85150

La Yole is an attractive and well run site, two kilometres from a sandy beach. It offers 356 pitches, the majority of which are occupied by tour operators and mobile homes to rent. There are 150 touring pitches, most with shade and separated by bushes and trees. A newer area at the rear of the site is more open. All the pitches are of at least 100 sq.m. and have electricity (10A), water and drainage. The pool complex includes an outdoor pool, a paddling pool, slide and an indoor heated pool with jacuzzi. Entertainment is organised in high season. This is a clean and tidy site, ideal for families with children and you will receive a helpful and friendly welcome.

Facilities

Two toilet blocks include washbasins in cabins and facilities for disabled people and babies. A third block has a baby room. Laundry facilities. Shop. Bar, restaurant and takeaway (1/5-5/9). Outdoor pool and paddling pool. Indoor heated pool with jacuzzi. Play area. Club room. Tennis. Games room. Entertainment in high season. WiFi. Gas barbecues only. Off site: Beach, bus service, bicycle hire 2 km. Riding 3 km. Fishing, golf and watersports 6 km.

Open: 5 April - 26 September.

Directions

Site is signed off the D38, 6 km. south of St Jean-de-Monts in the village of Orouet. Coming from St Jean-de-Monts turn right at l'Oasis restaurant towards Mouette and follow signs to site.
GPS: N46:45.383 W02:00.466

Charges guide

Per unit incl. 2 persons	
and electricity	€ 16,00 - € 30,00
extra person	€ 3,70 - € 6,50
child (2-9 yrs)	€ 2,15 - € 5,00
baby (0-2 yrs)	free - € 3,50
dog	€ 4,00 - € 5,00

Camping Cheques accepted.

Hot Spot WiFi

Camping La Yole ★★★★

Wake up to the sound of birdsong in a wooded park of 17 acres with four star comfort. Space, security, informal atmosphere:
la yole, tucked away between fields and pine trees, only 2 km from the beach.

– Chemin des Bosses - Orouet - F 85160 Saint Jean de Monts –
– Tel: 0033 251 58 67 17 - Fax: 0033 251 59 05 35 –
– contact@la-yole.com / www.la-yole.com –

Check real time availability and at-the-gate prices...

www.**alanrogers**.com

Route des Goffineaux, F-85520 Jard-sur-Mer (Vendée)
Tel: 02 51 33 42 74. Email: camping-ecureuils@wanadoo.fr
www.alanrogers.com/FR85210

Les Ecureuils is a wooded site in a quieter part of the southern Vendée. It is undoubtedly one of the prettiest sites on this stretch of coast, with an elegant reception area, attractive vegetation and large pitches separated by low hedges with plenty of shade. Of the 261 pitches, some 128 are for touring units, each with water and drainage, as well as easy access to 10A electricity. This site is popular with tour operators (54 pitches). Jard is rated among the most pleasant and least hectic of Vendée towns. The harbour is home to some fishing boats and rather more pleasure craft. There is a public slipway for those bringing their own boats.

Facilities

Two toilet blocks, well equipped and kept very clean, include baby baths, and laundry rooms. Small shop (bread baked on site). Snack bar and takeaway (1/6-15/9). Bar with snacks and ice creams. Good sized L-shaped swimming pool and separate paddling pool (30/5-15/9). Indoor pool and fitness centre (all season). Two play areas for different age groups. Minigolf. Club for children (5-10 yrs, July/Aug). Bicycle hire. Internet access. Only gas barbecues are allowed. Dogs are not accepted. Off site: Beach, fishing 400 m. Marina and town.

Open: 15 April - late September.

Directions

From Les Sables d'Olonne take the N949 towards Talmont-St Hilaire. Keep right in the centre (D21 towards Jard). From la Roche-sur-Yon follow the D474 and the D49 towards Jard-sur-Mer. From the village follow the signs 'Autre campings' or Camping les Ecureuils. Site is on the left.
GPS: N46:24.683 W01:35.382

Charges guide

Per person	€ 5,00 - € 6,90
child (0-9 yrs)	€ 1,50 - € 4,50
pitch incl. electricity, water and drainage	€ 5,00 - € 6,70

LES ECUREUILS

85520 JARD-SUR-MER
Tel. 0033 251 33 42 74
Fax 0033 251 33 91 14

Hôtellerie de Plein Air ★★★★
SUD VENDÉE - FRANCE
WWW.CAMPING-ECUREUILS.COM

Alan Rogers

FREE 2009 brochure
Over 60 French campsites, hand picked for you
Call for your copy today **01580 214000**
FREE CHILD PLACES ON MANY SITES

BOOK THIS SITE
CALL 01580 214000
...we'll arrange everything
The Travel Service

Check real time availability and at-the-gate prices...
www.alanrogers.com

The Travel Service
BOOK THIS SITE
CALL 01580 214000
...we'll arrange everything

FR85220 Camping Acapulco

Avenue des Epines, F-85160 Saint Jean-de-Monts (Vendée)
Tel: **02 51 59 20 64**. Email: **info@sunmarina.com**   www.alanrogers.com/FR85220

Ideal for family beach holidays, this friendly site is situated mid way between St Jean-de-Monts and St Hilaire-de-Riez, and is 600 m. from the beach. It is one of four sites on the Vendée coast owned by the Sunmarina group. Most of the pitches here are taken by mobile homes, leaving about 30 for touring. All are about 100 sq.m. on grass and divided by hedges which give some shade. The central part of the site has an excellent pool complex complete with five slides, a children's pool and a terrace for sunbathing. Adjacent to this is a spacious bar, restaurant and a safe play area.

Facilities

Two sanitary blocks are clean and include washbasins in cabins and showers. Facilities for disabled visitors. Laundry facilities. Motorcaravan service point. Shop with basic supplies. Bar, restaurant and takeaway. Large heated pool complex with five water slides and paddling pool. Play area. Entertainment in high season. Off site: Shopping centre 400 m. Sancy beach 600 m.

Open: 15 May - 15 September.

Directions

Follow the coastal road of St Jean-de-Monts south towards St Hilaire-de-Riez. Just past signs of Commune St Hilaire, turn left at first roundabout. Site is 400 m. on right (signed). GPS: N46:45.822 W02:00.540

Charges guide

Per unit incl. 3 persons and electricity	€ 32,00
extra person	€ 9,00

FR85230 Camping les Ecureuils

100 avenue de la Pège, F-85270 Saint Hilaire-de-Riez (Vendée)
Tel: **02 51 54 33 71**. Email: **info@camping-aux-ecureuils.com**   www.alanrogers.com/FR85230

Of the seaside sites on the Vendée, Les Ecureuils has to be one of the best, run by a friendly and most helpful family. Just 300 m. from a superb beach, the site is ideally situated for exploring from Les Sables d'Olonne to Noirmoutier. Developed on what was originally a farm, there are 230 pitches (55 for touring units). On sandy grass, all have electricity (6A, Euro adaptors avalable), water and drainage. Well kept hedges and mature trees give shade and privacy, although some more open pitches are also available for sun lovers. The site is popular with British tour operators (60%).

Facilities

The two main sanitary blocks are spacious, and include some washbasins in cubicles, and facilities for babies and disabled people. Laundry and dishwashing facilities. Small shop (25/5-6/9). Restaurant. Large, airy bar with screened terrace. Pool complex including pool for small children with its own 'mini aqua park', large heated pool, and water slide with separate splash pool. Indoor pool, paddling pool and jacuzzi. Off site: Beach 300 m. Bicycle hire 200 m. Fishing 4 km. Riding 5 km. Golf 6 km.

Open: 1 May - 15 September.

Directions

Driving south D38 (St Jean-de-Monts - St Gilles), turn right at L'Oasis hotel/restaurant in Orouet (6 km. outside St Jean-de-Monts), signed Les Mouettes. After 1.5 km. at roundabout turn left (St Hilaire-de-Riez). Site is 500 m. on left. GPS: N46:44.167 W02:00.570

Charges guide

Per unit incl. 2 persons and 3 services	€ 26,30 - € 35,40
extra person	€ 5,00 - € 6,15

FR85250 Yelloh! Village le Littoral

Le Porteau, F-85440 Talmont-Saint Hilaire (Vendée)
Tel: **04 66 73 97 39**. Email: **info@yellohvillage-le-littoral.com**   www.alanrogers.com/FR85250

Le Littoral is situated on the southern Vendée coast between the ports and beaches of Les Sables d'Olonne and Bourgenay. It has been fully modernised over recent years by the Boursin family. Although the site's 483 pitches are mainly used for mobile homes and chalets for hire, there are 67 touring pitches which are hedged and of a good size. They are interspersed with the mobile homes and all have water, electricity and drainage. The site has a heated outdoor pool complex together with an indoor heated pool. The restaurant is open daily with frequent themed evenings.

Facilities

New chalets. Three sanitary blocks have both British and Turkish style WCs, showers and washbasins in cubicles. Baby rooms. Facilities for disabled visitors. Laundry facilities. Shop. Bar. Restaurant and takeaway. Indoor pool. Outdoor pool complex with slides (17/5-10/9). Bicycle hire. Tennis. Play area. Activities, entertainment and excursions. Minibus to beach. Off site: Bus. Sea fishing 200 m. Riding 500 m. Golf 1.5 km. Beach 3 km.

Open: 4 April - 13 September.

Directions

From D949 Les Sables - Talmont, take D4 south to Port Bourgenay. Turn onto D129 westward and site is on left in 300 m. GPS: N46:27.098 W01:42.121

Charges guide

Per unit incl. 2 persons	€ 14,00 - € 36,00
extra person	€ 4,00 - € 6,00
child (1-7 yrs)	free - € 6,00

tel: +33 466 739 739 www.yellohvillage.com ━━━━

yelloh! VILLAGE

Check real time availability and at-the-gate prices...

www.**alanrogers**.com

FR85260 Village de la Guyonnière

La Guyonnière, F-85150 Saint Julien-des-Landes (Vendée)

Tel: **02 51 46 62 59**. Email: **info@laguyonniere.com**

www.alanrogers.com/FR85260

La Guyonnière is a spacious, rural site. It is Dutch owned but English is spoken and all visitors are made very welcome. It is a farm type site with eight different fields, each being reasonably level and seven having a toilet block. The 270 mostly large pitches have a mix of sun and shade. Some are open, others are separated by a tree and a few bushes. All have access to electricity connections and 86 are occupied by mobile homes and chalets. Bar and restaurant facilities are housed in the original farm buildings attractively converted. Entertainment is provided in the bar on high season evenings. This is a perfect place for families, with large play areas on sand and grass, and a paddling pond with shower. Being in the country, it is ideal for cyclists and walkers with many signed routes from the site. A pleasant 500 m. walk takes you to the Jaunay Lake where fishing is possible (permits from the village), canoeing (life jackets from reception) and pedaloes to hire. There are no tour operators and, needless to say, no road noise. It is popular for many reasons, the main one being the free and easy atmosphere.

Facilities

Modern toilet blocks. Most cubicles are quite small. Washbasins are in cubicles. Limited provision for babies and disabled visitors. Dishwashing and laundry sinks. Shop. Bar with TV and pool table (both 1/5-15/9). Restaurant (15/6-15/9). Pizzeria with takeaway (1/5-29/9). Small pool and heated pool with jacuzzi and slide. Paddling pool. Play areas, sand pit. Tennis. Bicycle hire. Car wash. WiFi. Off site: Riding 3 km. Golf 8 km. Beaches 10 km.

Open: 25 April - 25 September.

Directions

Site is signed off the D12 road (La Mothe Achard - St Gilles Croix-de-Vie), about 4 km. west of St Julien-des-Landes, down a lane about 1 km. from the main road. GPS: N46:39.152 W01:45.010

Charges 2009

Per unit incl. 2 persons and electricity	€ 18,00 - € 36,90
extra person	€ 4,90 - € 6,00
child (3-9 yrs)	€ 3,30 - € 3,90
animal	€ 3,50

Less 10-20% outside high season.

Camping Vendée ★★★
VILLAGE de lA GUYONNIÈRE

A beautiful, rural campsite with a tranquil atmosphere within 15 minutes' drive of large sandy beaches and 400 m from a large lake. The campsite has many quality amenities and the green spacious pitches, which are up to 225 m², are unique! Children love to see the many animals around the site.

NEW: outdoor pool with contra flow river!

The Vendée is a sunny destination - only a half day's drive from the ferry ports - as it has as many hours of sunshine as the French Rivièra!

Camping Qualité

85150 St Julien des Landes
Tel. 0033 251 46 62 59 Fax 0033 251 46 62 89
Internet: www.laguyonniere.com
E-mail: info@laguyonniere.com

Check real time availability and at-the-gate prices...

www.alanrogers.com

The Travel Service
BOOK THIS SITE
CALL 01580 214000
...we'll arrange everything

FR85270 Chadotel Camping l'Océano d'Or

84 rue Georges Clémenceau, B.P. 12, F-85520 Jard-sur-Mer (Vendée)

Tel: **02 51 33 05 05.** Email: **chadotel@wanadoo.fr**   www.alanrogers.com/FR85270

This site should appeal to families with children of all ages. It is very lively in high season but appears to be well managed, with a full programme of activities (it can therefore be noisy, sometimes late at night). There are 430 flat, grass and sand pitches of which 40% are occupied by tour operators and mobile homes. The 260 for touring units, all with 6A electricity, are quite large (about 100 sq.m). Some are separated by high hedges, others are more open with low bushes between them.

Facilities

Four rather dated, unisex toilet blocks include washbasins all in cabins (cleaning and maintenance is variable). Dishwashing and laundry facilities. Shop (1/6-10/9). Bar and snack bar (1/6-10/9, limited hours outside high season). Swimming pool (heated 20/5-20/9) with slides, waterfalls and children's pool. Play area. Tennis. Pétanque. Minigolf. Electric barbecues are not allowed. Off site: Excellent beach within walking distance. Golf, riding, karting and other activities within 15 km.

Open: 7 April - 23 September.

Directions

Site is on the D21 Talmont-St Hilaire - Longeville sur Mer, just east of the turning to the town centre. GPS: N46:25.264 W01:34.199

Charges guide

Per pitch incl. 2 persons	€ 14,50 - € 24,20
incl. electricity	€ 19,20 - € 28,90
extra person	€ 5,80
child (under 2 yrs)	€ 3,80
animal	€ 3,00

FR85280 Camping les Places Dorées

Route de Notre-Dame-de-Monts, F-85160 Saint Jean-de-Monts (Vendée)

Tel: **02 51 59 02 93.** Email: **contact@placesdorees.com**   www.alanrogers.com/FR85280

Les Places Dorées is owned by the same family as Abri des Pins (FR85090) just across the road. It is a newer site with maturing trees beginning to offer some shade. There are 245 grassy pitches, the quietest being towards the back of the site. Each one is separated, all have 10A electricity and some are also equipped with water and drainage. In low season the site is quiet but it can be noisy in high season with the bar and disco closing late. Recently added are a relaxation area with a heated covered pool, spa facilities (balnéo, hammam and massage), a fitness room and a games room.

Facilities

Three modern toilet blocks include washbasins in cubicles. Facilities for disabled visitors. Laundry facilities. Bread to order. Bar, snack bar and takeaway. Outdoor pool complex with slides, jacuzzi and waterfall (no Bermuda-style shorts). Covered, heated pool, spa facilities, gym. Games room. High season entertainment and children's club at L'Abri des Pins, also activities for adults. Facilities at L'Abri des Pins may be used. Off site: Fishing 500 m. Beach 700 m. Riding 2 km. Golf 5 km.

Open: 1 June - 1 September.

Directions

Site is 4 km. north of St Jean-de-Monts on the D38 St Jean-de-Monts - Notre Dames-de-Monts road on the right hand side, almost opposite L'Abri des Pins. GPS: N46:48.690 W02:06.685

Charges guide

Per pitch incl. 3 persons and electricity	€ 23,00 - € 34,40
extra person	€ 3,70 - € 6,20
No credit cards.	

FR85300 Camping la Grand' Métairie

8 rue de la Vineuse en Plaine, F-85440 Saint Hilaire-la-Forêt (Vendée)

Tel: **02 51 33 32 38.** Email: **info@camping-grandmetairie.com**   www.alanrogers.com/FR85300

Just five kilometres from the super sandy beach at Jard-sur-Mer, La Grand' Métairie offers many of the amenities of its seaside counterparts, but with the important advantage of being on the edge of a delightful, sleepy village otherwise untouched by tourism. It is a busy well run site with a programme of lively entertainment in high season. The site has 180 pitches (50 touring pitches), all with electricity. Some also with water and drainage. The pitches have good shade, are all separated by mature trees and hedges and are reasonable in size.

Facilities

Two modern toilet blocks are very clean and include washbasins mainly in cabins. Units for disabled people. Washing machines and dryers. Fridge hire. Safety deposit boxes. Smart bar/restaurant and takeaway (all 1/5-15/9). Attractive, heated outdoor pool and paddling pool (from 1/5). Indoor pool (all season). Sauna, jacuzzi. Gym. Tennis, minigolf (both free in low season). Visiting hairdressing salon. Internet access. Children's club. Off site: Village shop 100 m. Riding and fishing 5 km. Golf 15 km.

Open: 5 April - 30 September.

Directions

From Les Sables d'Olonne take D949 (La Rochelle) towards Talmont-St Hilaire and Luçon; 7 km. after Talmont turn right on D70 to St Hilaire-la-Forêt. Site is on left before village centre. GPS: N46:26.907 W01:31.580

Charges guide

Per unit incl. 2 persons and electricity	€ 17,00 - € 27,00
extra person	€ 5,00 - € 8,00
Min. stay 7 nights 13/7-17/8.	

Check real time availability and at-the-gate prices...

www.alanrogers.com

FR85350 Camping Caravaning la Ningle

Chemin des Roselières 66, F-85270 Saint Hilaire-de-Riez (Vendée)

Tel: 02 51 54 07 11. Email: campingdelaningle@wanadoo.fr　　www.alanrogers.com/FR85350

At Camping La Ningle you are guaranteed to receive a warm welcome from M. et Mme. Guibert, who have established a very pleasant campsite with a friendly, family atmosphere. There are 155 pitches, 60 available for touring units. All have electricity (6A) and all are fully serviced (electricity, water and drainage). Pitches are spacious with dividing hedges and all have some shade. The nearest beach is a 600 m. walk , but there are also three small heated swimming pools on site.

Facilities

Two clean toilet blocks include some washbasins in cubicles. Toilet/shower room for disabled people and large family shower room. Laundry facilities. Bread (July/Aug). Takeaway three evenings per week. Bar (July/Aug). Main swimming pool, larger children's pool, paddling pool and slide. Fitness suite. Tennis court. Games field. Games room. Fishing lake. Children's activities (July/Aug), and regular pétanque and tennis competitions. WiFi in bar area. Off site: Small supermarket and takeaway 200 m.

Open: 20 May - 10 September.

Directions

Driving south on D38 (St Jean-de-Monts - St Gilles), turn right at L'Oasis hotel/restaurant in Orouet, signed Les Mouettes. After 1.5 km. at roundabout, turn left (St Hilaire-de-Riez). Pass two campsites, then next left, signed La Ningle. GPS: N46:44.686 W02:00.267

Charges guide

Per pitch incl. 2 persons and electricity	€ 17,50 - € 29,80
extra person	€ 3,10 - € 4,60
child (under 7 yrs)	€ 1,65 - € 2,90

FR85360 Camping la Forêt

190 chemin de la Rive, F-85160 Saint Jean-de-Monts (Vendée)

Tel: 02 51 58 84 63. Email: camping-la-foret@wanadoo.fr　　www.alanrogers.com/FR85360

Camping La Forêt is owned by M. and Mme. Jolivet and they work hard to provide a small, quality site. Well run with a friendly, family atmosphere, it provides just 63 pitches with 50 for touring units. Of 100 sq.m. in size, the pitches are surrounded by mature hedges and have water and electricity. Trees provide shade to every pitch. There is one tour operator on site, but their presence is not intrusive. There is a quiet and relaxed atmosphere, ideal for couples or families with young children.

Facilities

The central toilet block includes washbasins in cubicles. Laundry and dishwashing facilities. Baby bath. Facilities for disabled people. Motorcaravan waste tanks can be emptied on request. Basic provisions sold in reception, including fresh bread. Takeaway. Small heated swimming pool (15/5-15/9). Play area. Bicycle hire. Only gas and electric barbecues allowed, communal barbecue in centre of site. Not suitable for American motorhomes. Off site: Beach 400 m. Network of cycle paths through the forest and local marshland.

Open: 15 May - 28 September.

Directions

Follow D38 out of St Jean-de-Monts, towards Notre Dame-de-Monts. After 5.5 km. turn left at sign for site and Plage de Pont d'Yeu. Follow road and site is on left in about 100 m. GPS: N46:48.484 W02:06.830

Charges guide

Per pitch incl. 2 persons	€ 17,00 - € 27,00
extra person	€ 3,50 - € 5,00
child (under 7 yrs)	€ 3,50 - € 3,90
electricity (6A)	€ 3,80

No credit cards.

FR85390 Camping des Batardières

F-85440 Saint Hilaire-la-Forêt (Vendée)

Tel: 02 51 33 33 85　　www.alanrogers.com/FR85390

Camping des Batardières is a haven of tranquility on the edge of an unspoilt village, yet just 5 km. from the sea. It is an attractive, unsophisticated little site, lovingly maintained by its owners for more than 25 years. Many visitors return year after year. There are 75 good-sized pitches (a few up to 130 sq.m) and all are available for touring (there are no mobile homes and no tour operators!) All have easy access to water and electricity (6A, or 2A for tents). There are few facilities on site.

Facilities

The sanitary block is kept very clean and visitors are encouraged to keep it that way (no shoes in the shower cubicles, for instance). Some washbasin and shower combination cubicles. Laundry facilities. Tennis court. Play area and field for games, kite-flying etc. Not suitable for American motorhomes or twin axle caravans. Off site: Village shop and bar 200 m. Jard-sur-Mer 5 km. Bicycle hire 3 km. Fishing 5 km. Golf 16 km.

Open: 27 June - 2 September.

Directions

From Les Sables d'Olonne take D949 (la Rochelle) towards Talmont-St Hilaire and Luçon. 7 km. after Talmont turn right on D70 to St Hilaire-la-Forêt. Site signed to the right approaching village. GPS: N46:26.917 W01:31.719

Charges guide

Per unit incl. 2 persons	€ 20,00
electricity	€ 3,50
extra person	€ 3,00

No credit cards.

Check real time availability and at-the-gate prices...
www.alanrogers.com

FR85480 Camping Caravaning le Chaponnet

Mobile homes ► page 497

Rue du Chaponnet (N16), F-85470 Brem-sur-Mer (Vendée)

Tel: **02 51 90 55 56**. Email: **campingchaponnet@wanadoo.fr**

www.alanrogers.com/FR85480

This well established family run site is within five minutes' walk of Brem village and 1.5 km. from a sandy beach. The 80 touring pitches are level with varying amounts of grass, some with shade from mature trees. Pitches are separated by tall hedges and serviced by tarmac or gravel roads and have frequent water and electricity points (long leads may be required). Tour operators have mobile homes and tents on 70 pitches and there are 55 privately owned mobile homes and chalets. The pool complex also has a jacuzzi, slides and a paddling pool, together with a sauna and fitness centre. It is overlooked by the spacious bar and snack bar. Entertainment is provided for all ages by day and three or four musical evenings a week provide family fun rather than teenage activities.

Facilities

The five sanitary blocks are well maintained with washbasins in cubicles, some showers and basins have controllable water temperature. Facilities for babies and disabled people. Laundry facilities. Bar, snack bar and takeaway (all 1/6-31/8). No shop but bread and croissants available. Indoor (heated) and outdoor pools. Play area with space for ball games. Tennis. Bicycle hire. Indoor games room. Off site: Shops and restaurants. Beach 1.5 km. Fishing 2 km. Golf 12 km. Riding 10 km.

Open: 1 May - 15 September.

Directions

Brem is on the D38 St Gilles - Les Sables d'Olonne road. Site is clearly signed, just off the one-way system in centre of village.
GPS: N46:36.260 W01:49.946

Charges guide

Per unit incl. 3 persons	€ 19,50 - € 30,00
incl. electricity	€ 23,80 - € 33,90
extra person	€ 4,10 - € 5,50
child (under 5 yrs)	€ 2,60 - € 3,70
dog	€ 3,00

CAMPING LE CHAPONNET ★★★★

Camping le Chaponnet ★★★★ • Rue du Chaponnet • F-85470 Brem sur Mer • France
T: [33] 2 51 90 55 56 • F: [33] 2 51 90 91 67 • campingchaponnet@wanadoo.fr
www.le-chaponnet.com

FR85510 Camping le Bois Joli

2 rue de Châteauneuf, F-85710 Bois-de-Céné (Vendée)

Tel: **02 51 68 20 05**. Email: **campingboisjoli@free.fr**

www.alanrogers.com/FR85510

A warm welcome is given by the English speaking Malard family, who make every effort to make your stay enjoyable. On site is a small lake with fishing and a large sports field (with a portacabin style toilet block). The site also has a small swimming pool and paddling pool. The bar has been extended and includes a dancing area. There are 130 pitches of which 90 are for touring units. All pitches have 6A electricity, although not every pitch is serviced with water. A new, separate sanitary block with a laundry and a family room has been added.

Facilities

Three toilet blocks - old, but with modem, bright tiles and very clean. All are unisex with some washbasins in cubicles, some controllable showers, two baby baths, two washing machines, dishwashing and laundry sinks. Bar with evening entertainment. Takeaway (1/7-31/8). Children's activities. Good play area with swings. Table tennis. Tennis court. Volleyball. Pétanque. Bicycle hire. Off site: Supermarket and bus service in village (two minutes' walk). Walking, cycling and canoeing. Riding 5 km. Beach 18 km.

Open: 1 April - 25 September.

Directions

From Challans take D58 direct to Bois de Céné (10 km). Turn left at first road junction and site is immediately on right. GPS: N46:56.029 W01:53.275

Charges guide

Per pitch incl. 2 persons, electricity and car	€ 13,00 - € 17,30
extra person	€ 3,00 - € 4,00
child (1-6 yrs)	€ 1,70 - € 2,60
animal	€ 2,10 - € 3,60

Check real time availability and at-the-gate prices...
www.**alanrogers**.com

FR85720 Camping Indigo Noirmoutier

23 allée des Sableaux, Bois de la Chaize, F-85330 Noirmoutier-en-l'Ile (Vendée)

Tel: **02 51 39 06 24**. Email: **noirmoutier@camping-indigo.com**   www.alanrogers.com/FR85720

Located in woodland and on dunes along a two kilometre stretch of sandy beach just east of the attractive little town of Noirmoutier on the island of the same name, this could be paradise for those who enjoy a simple campsite in a natural setting. On land belonging to the ONF (France's forestry commission), this site is operated by Huttopia whose aim is to adapt to the environment rather than take it over. The 500 touring pitches, all with electricity, are situated among the pine trees and accessed along tracks. Those on the sand dunes have fantastic views across the Bay of Bourgneuf to Pornic and the Jade Coast. Cars are only allowed in these areas on arrival and departure and it is planned eventually to provide more car parking at strategic points so that this rule can apply to the whole site. There are no mobile homes, just ten large, traditional, but well equipped tents for rent. Nearby are salt marshes, an aquarium and a water theme park and there are opportunities to walk, cycle, sail and windsurf.

Facilities	Directions
Five sanitary blocks currently provide basic facilities including pre-set showers and some washbasins in cubicles. The central one is larger and more modern, the others have been refurbished. All have facilities for disabled visitors. Washing machines and dryers. Motorcaravan service point. Playground. Bicycle hire. WiFi (reception, bar, pool). Off site: Riding 4 km. Golf 25 km.	The Ile de Noirmoutier is 70 km. southwest of Nantes. Take D38 road from the mainland, cross bridge to island and continue to Noirmoutier en l'Ile. Go through town past three sets of traffic lights and at roundabout turn right following signs to 'Campings'. GPS: N46:59.815 W02:13.200

Open: 4 April - 4 October.

Charges 2009

Per unit incl. 2 persons and electricity	€ 16,90 - € 28,50
extra person	€ 3,20 - € 4,60

Camping Cheques accepted.

tel: +33 (0) 4 37 64 22 33 www.camping-indigo.com

Camping Indigo
Noirmoutier★★

«Wood & canvas» tents to rent

Direct access to the beach, shady pitches, children
playground, bikes rental, close to the village

23 rue des Sableaux - 85330 Noirmoutier-en-l'île
Tel : (33) 2 51 39 06 24

In the heart of a pine forest,
along a 2 Kilometres coast...

w w w . c a m p i n g - i n d i g o . c o m

FR85420 Camping 'Bel

Rue du Bottereau, F-85360 La Tranche-sur-Mer (Vendée)

Tel: **02 51 30 47 39**. Email: **campbel@wanadoo.fr**   www.alanrogers.com/FR85420

Camping 'Bel's owner, M. Guieau, who has a very dry sense of humour, takes an individual approach. The first priority is the contentment of the children, who receive various small gifts during their stay. A popular site with a large proportion of French clients, despite the large presence of British tour operators (115 pitches). The 85 touring pitches are on level, sandy grass and separated by hedges with mature trees giving good shade. All pitches have electrical connections (6/10A).

Facilities	Directions
Two modern toilet blocks have washbasins in cabins, very good baby units and facilities for disabled visitors. Baker calls daily. Bar. Takeaway. Heated outdoor pool with jacuzzi. Plenty of entertainment for children aged 6-14 yrs (July/Aug). Fitness area. Tennis and badminton. Pets are not accepted. Satellite TV. Internet access. Off site: Beach 150 m. Bicycle hire 100 m. Supermarket 200 m. Fishing and watersports within 150 m. Riding 5 km.	Follow signs from roundabout on La Tranche bypass, near 'Super U' supermarket onto avenue General de Gaulle. Left after 50 m. onto Rue du Bottereau. Site on right after 100 m. GPS: N46:20.916 W01:25.913

Open: 24 May - 6 September, with all services.

Charges guide

Per unit incl. 2 persons and water	€ 22,00
incl. electricity (10A)	€ 26,00
extra person	€ 6,00
child (under 5 yrs)	€ 4,00

BOOK THIS SITE
CALL 01580 214000
...we'll arrange everything
The Travel Service

159

FR85780 Camping Caravaning le Bois Joly

46 route de Notre-Dame-de-Monts, B.P. 207, F-85165 Saint Jean-de-Monts (Vendée)

Tel: **02 51 59 11 63**. Email: **boisjoly@compuserve.com**   www.alanrogers.com/FR85780

This is an attractive, family run holiday site with Indoor and outdoor pool complexes and 385 pitches, most of which are fully serviced. Of these 210 are taken by mobile homes or chalets, leaving around 170 good sized, hedged pitches with 6A electric hook-ups for tourists. Grassy and level, these are served by tarmac roads and four fresh, clean, modern, toilet blocks. A good family holiday location, there are lots of activities and entertainment in July and August. The indoor pool is open all season, the L-shaped outdoor pool complex has a 'menhirs' theme and attractive flower beds. There are four toboggans, a paddling pool and a raised solarium deck On site there are several small playgrounds for younger children, plus a very large and comprehensive adventure playground. The river behind the site offers opportunities for fishing or canoeing.

Facilities

Four modern toilet blocks with controllable showers, washbasins in cubicles. Facilities for babies and disabled persons. Laundry facilities. One block is heated for low season. Bar. Snack bar. Takeaway (July/Aug). Indoor pool (7/4-28/9). Outdoor pools (15/6-15/9). Sauna, solarium and gym. Playgrounds. Multi-sport court. Pétanque. TV room. Games room. Events, entertainment and canoeing on site in July/Aug. River fishing. Drive-over motorcaravan service point. Safety deposit boxes. No charcoal barbecues allowed. No double axle caravans accepted. Off site: Golf 2 km. Riding and tennis 500 m. Bicycle hire 1.5 km. Beach and boat launching 1.5 km. Shops, restaurants and other services all within 2 km.

Open: 2 April - 28 September.

Directions

Site is at the northern end of St Jean-de-Monts, on the eastern side of the D38, about 300 m. north of junction (roundabout) with the D51.
GPS: N46:47.948 W02:04.463

Charges guide

Per unit incl. 2 persons and electricity (6A)	€ 15,00 - € 27,00
extra person	€ 2,00 - € 5,00
child (under 7 yrs)	€ 1,00 - € 2,50

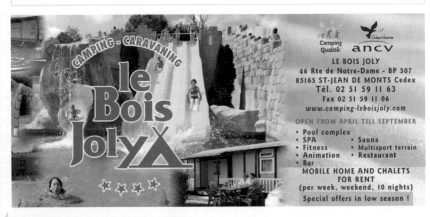

CAMPING - CARAVANING
le Bois Joly

★★★★

Camping Qualité

ancv

LE BOIS JOLY
46 Rte de Notre-Dame - BP 507
85165 ST-JEAN DE MONTS Cedex
Tél. 02 51 59 11 63
Fax 02 51 59 11 06
www.camping-leboisjoly.com

OPEN FROM APRIL TILL SEPTEMBER
• Pool complex
• SPA   • Sauna
• Fitness   • Multisport terrain
• Animation   • Restaurant
• Bar

MOBILE HOME AND CHALETS
FOR RENT
(per week, weekend, 10 nights)
Special offers in low season !

FR85440 Camping les Brunelles

Le Bouil, F-85560 Longeville-sur-Mer (Vendée)

Tel: **02 51 33 50 75**. Email: **camping@les-brunelles.com**   www.alanrogers.com/FR85440

This is a well managed site with good facilities and a varied programme of high season entertainment for all the family. In 2007 Les Brunelles was combined with an adjacent campsite to provide 600 pitches. Many of the new pitches have water, electricity and waste, and are in excess of 100 sq.m. to allow easier access for larger units. On the original Les Brunelles site, the touring pitches are all level on sandy grass and separated by hedges, away from most of the mobile homes.

Facilities

Four old, but well maintained and modernised toilet blocks have British and Turkish style toilets and washbasins, both open style and in cabins. Laundry facilities. Shop. Takeaway and large modern, airy bar. Covered pool with jacuzzi (all season). Outdoor pool with slides and paddling pools (1/5-30/9). Tennis. Bicycle hire. Off site: Golf and riding within 15 km. Good supervised sandy beach 900 m. St Vincent-sur-Jard 2 km.

Open: 4 April - 19 September.

Directions

From D21 (Talmont - Longueville), between St Vincent and Longueville, site signed south from main road towards coast. Turn left in Le Bouil (site signed). Site is 800 m. on left.
GPS: N46:24.798 W01:31.388

Charges 2009

Per unit incl. 2 persons and electricity	€ 21,00 - € 30,00
extra person	€ 5,00 - € 8,00
Camping Cheques accepted.	

The Travel Service
BOOK THIS SITE
CALL 01580 214000
...we'll arrange everything

Check real time availability and at-the-gate prices...
www.alanrogers.com

FR85810 Camping les Dauphins Bleus

16 rue du Rocher, F-85800 Givrand (Vendée)

Tel: 02 51 55 59 34. Email: dauphins-bleus@franceloc.fr
www.alanrogers.com/FR85810

In a rural setting on the edge of the village and only two kilometres from the sea, this large site has 320 pitches, most taken by mobile homes and chalets for rent. There are just 12 level, grassy, touring pitches, generally small and of odd shapes, and suitable only for small units, tents and camper vans. These are scattered around the site between the rental units. The site is served by two large toilet blocks, one centrally located the other at one end of site and nearest to most of the entertainment and sports areas. The site offers an excellent pool complex and many sporting opportunities. Professional animators organise a children's club and evening entertainment in main season. The village of Givrand (walking distance) and nearby St Gilles Croix-de-Vie between them provide supermarkets, shops and services. The region offers a number of markets including St Gilles on Monday, Thursday and Sunday, Croix-de-Vie on Wednesday and Saturday and St Hilaire-de-Reiz Thursdays and Sundays.

Facilities

Two modern toilet blocks with mostly seated toilets, washbasins in cubicles, and compact showers. Facilities for babies. Units for campers with disabilities. Launderette with washing machines and dryers. Shop. Bar with TV (April - Sept) and takeaway (May - Sept). Heated outdoor pool (25 x 19 m, May - Sept). Indoor pool (April - Sept). Gym. Tennis. Pétanque. Multisport court. Playground. Bicycle hire. 'Pluto Club' for children, organised activities and evening entertainment July/Aug. Only gas barbecues permitted. Off site: Beach 2 km. Supermarket, ATM 2 km.

Open: 31 March - 29 September.

Directions

From D38 south of St Gilles Croix-de-Vie, turn east on D42 to Givrand where site is well signed to the left. GPS: N46:40.380 W01:53.697

Charges guide

Per unit incl. 2 persons	€ 11,00 - € 21,00
extra person	€ 5,00 - € 6,00
child (2-7 yrs)	€ 3,50 - € 4,50
electricity (6A)	€ 3,70

CAMPINGS FranceLoc

VENDÉE

LES DAUPHINS BLEUS****

Aquatic Park with heated indoor and outdoor swimming pool and new water slides. Detention and amusement guaranteed!

Givrand • 85800 • 16, rue du Rocher
Tel.: +33 (0)2 51 55 59 34
Email : dauphins-bleus@franceloc.fr
www.camping-franceloc.fr

FR85450 Camping les Roses

Rue des Roses, F-85100 Les Sables-d'Olonne (Vendée)

Tel: 02 51 33 05 05. Email: info@chadotel.com
www.alanrogers.com/FR85450

Les Roses has an urban location, with the town centre and lovely beach just a short walk away. It has an informal air with the 210 pitches arranged interestingly on a knoll. Mature trees give good shade to some areas. There are 107 touring pitches of varying size, many being more suitable for tents than caravans. All pitches have access to electricity (10A) and water (long cables may be needed). In high season caravanners might find site access tricky at times due to overloaded town centre traffic systems. The site has 103 mobile homes and chalets, but no tour operators.

Facilities

Three well maintained toilet blocks have washbasins in cubicles, unit for disabled visitors, baby room and laundry facilities. Simple bar and takeaway (15/5-15/9). Simple shop. Small, heated, outdoor pool with water slide and paddling pool (1/5-30/9). Play area. Volleyball, basketball and pétanque. Bicycle hire. Electric barbecues are not permitted. Off site: Beach 500 m. Golf, riding, karting, watersports, zoo, sea and river fishing within 5 km.

Open: April - 31 October.

Directions

Site is signed from D949 Les Sables to La Rochelle road, north of the 'Géant Casino' roundabout. Turn south at minor junction. GPS: N46:29.500 W01:45.910

Charges guide

Per pitch incl. 2 persons	€ 14,50 - € 24,20
incl. electricity	€ 19,20 - € 28,90
extra person	€ 5,80
child (under 5 yrs)	€ 3,80

Check real time availability and at-the-gate prices...
www.alanrogers.com

FR85850 Flower Camping la Bretonnière

F-85150 Saint Julien-des-Landes (Vendée)

Tel: 02 51 46 62 44. Email: camp.la-bretonniere@wanadoo.fr   www.alanrogers.com/FR85850

An attractive, modern site on a family farm surrounded by beautiful peaceful countryside, this site is sure to please. With 150 pitches in an area of six hectares, there is plenty of space for everyone. There are 132 touring pitches, eight tour operator tents and eight alpine-style chalets, spread around several fields, some quite open, others with some shade from perimeter hedges. The grassy pitches are all of a really generous size with electricity (12/16A). Two swimming pools, one covered, the other outdoor, are surrounded by a pleasant terrace, with the bar and reception close by. Also on site is a lovely large fishing lake (unfenced) with a pleasant walk all around. The bar and takeaway operate in July/August, ices and basic tinned food items are available from reception and there is a really good motorcaravan service point. The village of Saint Julien-des-Landes is 2.5 km. and the larger town of La Mothe-Achard is 7 km.

Facilities

Five modern, clean and well appointed toilet blocks are spread evenly around the site, with baby rooms and facilities for disabled people at two blocks. Motorcaravan service point. Bar, snack bar and takeaway (July/Aug). Covered swimming pool (15.5 x 7 m.) and outdoor pool (11 x 5 m.) open June - Sept. WiFi around bar and reception. Playgrounds. Games/TV room. Tennis. Boules. Fishing lake. Caravan storage. Off site: Village 2.5 km. La Mothe-Achard 7 km. Golf 12 km. Riding 2 km. Boat launching 4 km.

Open: 1 April - 15 October.

Directions

Saint Julien-des-Landes is 18 km. northeast of Les Sables d'Olonne and 5 km. northwest of La Mothe-Achard. From La Mothe-Achard take D12 west towards Bretignolles-sur-Mer, pass through St Julien and after 2 km. take first turn right (site signed). Site is 500 m. GPS: N46:38.679 W01:43.998

Charges 2009

Per unit incl. 2 persons and electricity	€ 11,00 - € 26,00
extra person	€ 3,50 - € 4,50
child (2-7 yrs)	€ 2,50 - € 3,50

www.flowercampings.com

FR85620 Camping le Caravan'ile

B.P. 4, la Guérinière, F-85680 Ile de Noirmoutier (Vendée)

Tel: 02 51 39 50 29. Email: contact@caravanile.com   www.alanrogers.com/FR85620

This well appointed, family run site on the island of Noirmoutier has direct access to the dunes and an extensive sandy beach. It offers heated indoor and outdoor swimming pools with a paddling pool and flume, a sauna, steam room, jacuzzi and mini gym and a variety of entertainment in high season. Most of the 103 level touring pitches are near the beach (shielded by the dune). All have electricity (5A) and are separated by bushes and occasional maturing trees providing a little shade. The site has a very French ambience, with no tour operators, although there are 90 mobile homes for rent and many more privately-owned.

Facilities

Three very clean sanitary blocks, each with showers, some washbasins in cabins and facilities for disabled people (showers are closed overnight). Laundry. Small supermarket at entrance (1/4-15/9). Bar, snack bar and takeaway (1/4-15/9). Indoor pool (all season) and outdoor pools (15/5-15/9; heated July/Aug). Games and sports area. Games room. Off site: Restaurant, bicycle hire and boat launching. Sailing 2 km. Riding 5 km. Golf 20 km.

Open: 1 March - 15 November.

Directions

The Ile de Noirmoutier is 70 km. southwest of Nantes. Take D38 road from the mainland, cross bridge to island and continue to fourth roundabout. Take exit for La Guérinière and immediately turn left to site. GPS: N46:57.980 W02:13.046

Charges guide

Per unit incl. 2 persons	€ 11,80 - € 18,70
incl. 5A electricity	€ 13,80 - € 22,00
extra person	€ 3,00 - € 4,60

The Travel Service ...we'll arrange everything BOOK THIS SITE CALL 01580 214000

FR85860 Camping les Fosses Rouges

8 rue des Fosses Rouges, F-85180 Le Château-d'Olonne (Vendée)

Tel: **02 51 95 17 95**. Email: **info@camping-lesfossesrouges.com**   www.alanrogers.com/FR85860

A family run site, Les Fosses Rouges was created in 1968 on the fields owned by the present owner's grandfather. Since it was built, the site has been surrounded by urban development, but neverthless it is still a good value and well presented, if compact, site. There are 205 well hedged pitches of small to average size, most with some shade and electricity (10A). Some 45 are used for mobile homes, both private and to rent. There are also some seasonal or long stay tourers. There is a good swimming pool and a separate sports and games area. The site offers some low key entertainment in the main season. Nearby are the zoo and seashell museum at Les Sables d'Olonne, the fascinating salt pans and the museum of modern art at the Abbaye Sainte-Croix.

Facilities

Four colourful toilet blocks in traditional style are evenly distributed around the site. Washbasins in cubicles for ladies, push button showers. Facilities for disabled people. Washing machine at two blocks. Bar and takeaway (1/7-31/8). Shop (15/6-30/9). Motorcaravan service point. Swimming pool (heated, open all season and covered when necessary). Playground. Tennis. Minigolf. Giant chess. Open air stage for animation. Internet access (July/Aug). Communal barbecue areas. Off site: ATM at supermarket 1 km. Fishing 1 km. Golf and riding 4 km. Boat launching 5 km.

Open: 4 April - 27 September.

Directions

Site is southeast of Les Sables d'Olonne between the D949 and the sea. From large roundabout by supermarket on D949 turn towards sea on Avenue Dugay Trouin (signed La Pironnière). Continue straight on at mini-roundabout and in 150 m. turn left into rue des Fosses Rouges to site in 500 m. GPS: N46:28.761 W01:44.501

Charges 2009

Per unit incl. 2 persons	€ 12,60 - € 16,00
incl. electricity	€ 16,00 - € 19,50
extra person	€ 2,60 - € 3,60
child (under 7 yrs)	€ 1,30 - € 1,80

Family campsite with clearly defined pitches with an average size of 90 m² for tents, caravans and motor homes, situated 800m from the sea and 2 km from the beach.

At your disposal are sanitary facilities' with free use of hot water, heated covered swimming pool, tennis, mini golf and animation in July and August. Near shopping centre, casino and spa.

Reservations are recommended and necessary in high season.

8 Rue des Fosses Rouges - 85180 Château d'Olonne
Tel : 0033 (0)251 951 795 - Fax : 0033 (0) 251 325 421
E-mail : info@camping-lesfossesrouges.com
Internet : www.camping-lesfossesrouges.com

FR85640 Camping les Chouans

108 avenue de la Faye, F-85270 Saint Hilaire-de-Riez (Vendée)

Tel: **02 51 54 34 90**. Email: **info@sunmarina.com**   www.alanrogers.com/FR85640

This family run campsite is within a short drive of the Vendée beaches. A friendly greeting from Josée and Stephane is a welcome arrival before entering this well organized, smart site. Cleanliness is important here! In high season it is bustling and lively, with numerous activities available. The site mainly caters for privately owned mobile homes and touring pitches are minimal (early booking advised). Some pitches are shaded, and smaller than average but each has electricity. Water points are close by. Late night discos may be noisy in July and August. Tour operators occupy 52 pitches.

Facilities

Two sanitary blocks (one unisex) both have open, vanity style washbasins. Shower room and separate toilet for disabled campers. Baby room. Laundry facilities. Small shop (multi national newspapers available). Bicycle hire. Swimming pool and slides. Good sports area with tennis court, basketball, boules and table tennis. Small fitness gym (charged). Good entertainment programme for all ages. Weekly excursions. Off site: Beach 1.6 km. Small town of St Hilaire-de-Riez approx 3 km. Riding, golf and fishing within 6 km. St Jean-de-Monts and St Gilles Croix-de-Vie nearby, with selection of restaurants and shops.

Open: 15 May - 15 September.

Directions

Travel south on D38 from St Jean-de-Monts and turn right at Oruet towards Les Mouettes. At the coast join D23 southwards and follow this road to first roundabout (2.5 km). Site is signed here and is 2 km. on left. GPS: N46:44.049 W01:58.415

Charges guide

Per unit incl. 3 persons	€ 25,00 - € 32,00
extra person	€ 9,00
child under 5 yrs	€ 6,00

163

FR85870 Camping Baie d'Aunis

10 rue du Pertuis, F-85360 La Tranche-sur-Mer (Vendée)

Tel: **02 51 27 47 36**. Email: **info@camping-baiedaunis.com**   www.alanrogers.com/FR85870

This very popular site has direct access to a sandy beach through a pedestrian gate (with key code) and across a car park. The town centre is also only 500 m. away. Shady and level, there are 150 individual pitches, all with electricity (10A). A good number of pitches are on a gravel base and a few are suitable only for smaller units. There are chalets and mobile homes (19) to rent. On site amenities include a heated swimming pool and a good restaurant and bar. This is a popular seaside resort with 13 km. of good quality sandy beaches.

Facilities

The main centrally located sanitary unit is large, good quality and very well appointed. A smaller simpler unit is at the far end of the site. British style WCs, washbasins in cubicles, provision for babies and disabled campers. Laundry room at each block. Motorcaravan service point. Bar/restaurant and takeaway (1/5 -10/9, w/ends only in low season). Outdoor swimming pool (10 x 20 m; heated May - Sept). Playground. TV room. Dogs and other animals not accepted July/Aug. Off site: La Tranche is a major sail-boarding centre, with teaching facilities in a special lagoon, plus a surf school. Beach, bicycle hire, sea fishing all within 50 m. Town centre 500 m. Golf 38 km. Riding 12 km. Boat launching 100 m.

Open: 28 April - 14 September.

Directions

La Tranche-sur-Mer is 35 km. south of La Roche-sur-Yon. From La Roche-sur-Yon take 0747 to La Tranche. At roundabout (D747 and D1046) carry straight on to next roundabout and turn right towards town centre. At next (new) roundabout continue straight on to site on left (well signed). GPS: N46:20.777 W01:25.918

Charges guide

Per unit incl. 2 persons	€ 7,80 - € 24,70
incl. electricity (10A)	€ 11,80 - € 28,70
extra person	€ 5,00 - € 5,90
child (under 5 yrs)	€ 3,15 - € 3,40

CAMPING BAIE D'AUNIS****

Camping Baie d'Aunis | 10, Rue du Pertuis Breton | 85360 La Tranche sur Mer
Tel: 0033 (0) 251 27 47 36 | Fax: 0033 (0) 251 27 44 54
info@camping-baiedaunis.com | www.camping-baiedaunis.com

FR85680 Camping le Pin Parasol

Lac du Jaunay, F-85220 La Chapelle-Hermier (Vendée)

Tel: **02 51 34 64 72**. Email: **campingpinparasol@free.fr**   www.alanrogers.com/FR85680

Tucked away in the Vendée countryside yet just 15 minutes' drive from the beach, the site enjoys a pleasant rural setting above the Lac du Jaunay, well away from the bustle of the coast. There are 284 good sized touring pitches, all with electricity (6/10A) and 22 with water tap and drainage. The established pitches have some shade, others are in the open with hedges and trees yet to mature. The enthusiastic family owners are very hands-on and the facilities are of a high standard, most notably the pool area with its new indoor pool, jacuzzi, steam room and fitness suite.

Facilities

Four fully equipped toilet blocks include facilities for babies and disabled visitors. Block in new area can be under some pressure at busy times but you can always walk to the next block! Washing machines and dryers. Shop. Restaurant and bar with terrace. Takeaway. (July/Aug). Heated outdoor pool with paddling pool and slides (15/6-15/9). Indoor pool. Play area. Multisport pitch. Boules. Bicycle hire. Entertainment in high season. Fishing. Tennis. Internet boxes for hire giving access via your electric connection. Off site: Golf and riding within 5 km. Beaches and sailing, 12 km.

Open: 28 April - 25 September.

Directions

La Chapelle-Hermier is 26 km. west of La Roche-sur-Yon. Site is to the south of the D42 La Chapelle-Hermier - l'Aiguillon-sur-Vie road, 2 km. east of the junction with the D40 Coëx-La Chaize - Giraud road and is well signed. GPS: N46:39.973 W01:45.317

Charges guide

Per unit incl. 2 persons	€ 11,50 - € 25,50
extra person	€ 4,50 - € 6,00
child (0-10 yrs)	€ 3,00
electricity (6/10A)	€ 3,50 - € 4,00
animal	€ 4,00

The Travel Service ...we'll arrange everything

BOOK THIS SITE
CALL 01580 214000

Check real time availability and at-the-gate prices...

www.**alanrogers**.com

FR85940 Camping Zagarella

Route des Sables, F-85160 Saint Jean-de-Monts (Vendée)

Tel: **02 51 58 19 82**. Email: **zagarella@zagarella.fr**   www.alanrogers.com/FR85940

Camping Zagarella is an ideal site for happy family holidays, with many facilities for children of all ages. A family run site, the management and staff are very friendly and do all they can to ensure everyone has a good time. There are 281 pitches with 77 used for touring units. These vary in size and shape but are mainly level and grassy, and divided by shrubs. Some areas of the site are heavily wooded but there are more open parts for sun lovers. There are two tour operators here which lead to a nice mix of nationalities. The site has both indoor and outdoor heated swimming pools with a water chute and slides, and the play areas provided for younger children are very well equipped. Children's clubs and family entertainment are organised in high season.

Facilities

Two modern, unheated toilet blocks are clean and well maintained. Both contain good facilities for disabled visitors and baby baths. Laundry. Motorcaravan service point. Small shop (1/5-7/9). Bar and takeaway (1/6-8/9). Indoor pool (all season). Outdoor pool (1/5-13/9). Tennis. Multisport court. Bicycle hire. Gym and sauna. Only gas barbecues are permitted. WiFi in bar. Off site: Beach 3 km. Riding 1 km. Golf 3 km.

Open: 4 April - 28 September.

Directions

Travelling south on the D38 St Jean-de-Monts - St Gilles road. About 4 km. south of St Jean keep a sharp look-out for a blue site sign on the right. GPS: N46:46.896 W02:01.086

Charges guide

Per unit incl. up to 3 persons	
and electricity	€ 15,90 - € 37,20
extra person	€ 4,50 - € 5,10
child (under 3 yrs)	€ 3,00 - € 3,60
dog	€ 2,70 - € 3,30

Swimming pool complex with waterchute, waterslides, indoor pool and great children's pool with slides, jacuzzi. Entertainement in english organised by the site'staff and kid's club (6 days/week)

FR85740 Camping Aux Coeurs Vendéens

251 route de Notre-Dame-de-Monts, F-85160 Saint Jean-de-Monts (Vendée)

Tel: **02 51 58 84 91**. Email: **info@coeursvendeens.com**   www.alanrogers.com/FR85740

This is a delightful little site, a real find for those wishing to enjoy the beaches and life-style of this stretch of coastline without the razzmatazz of some of the neighbouring sites. It is family run and everywhere there is attention to detail: flower tubs beside the road as you drive in, whitewashed stones for the pitch numbers, engraved designs on the washbasin mirrors, even plugs for the dishwashing sinks! There are 52 touring pitches, all with electricity available (10A), and a further 65 with mobile homes and chalets, all but five available for rent.

Facilities

Two sanitary blocks are bright and cheerful and kept very clean. Controllable showers, washbasins in cubicles, two pleasant baby rooms. En-suite facilities for disabled visitors (wheelchair users might have minor difficulties accessing this). Internet access. Washing machines and dryer. Small shop with takeaway. Swimming pools (7/5-10/9). TV and games rooms. Playgrounds. Trampoline. Minigolf. Bicycle hire. Off site: Beach, sea fishing and boat launching 700 m. Sailing, riding and golf 3 km. Fresh water fishing 7 km.

Open: 4 April - 19 September.

Directions

Site is on the D38 just over 3 km. north of St Jean-de-Monts, roughly halfway between St Jean-de-Monts and Notre-Dame-de-Monts, on the western side of the road. GPS: N46:48.548 W02:06.610

Charges guide

Per unit incl. 2 persons	
	€ 15,00 - € 26,00
extra person	€ 2,50 - € 4,90
child (under 5 yrs)	free - € 3,30
electricity (10A)	free - € 3,30

165

FR85930 Castel Camping Domaine des Forges

Rue des Forges, F-85440 Avrillé (Vendée)

Tel: 02 51 22 38 85. Email: contact@campingdomainedesforges.com

www.alanrogers.com/FR85930

Le Domaine des Forges has recently been acquired by Cathy and Thierry Pacteau. They already have experience in owning a caravan site, and it is their intention to create a prestige site with the highest quality of services. Arranged in the beautiful grounds of a 16th-century manor house, the pitches are generous in size (170-300 sq.m) and fully serviced including 32A electricity, internet access and cable TV. At present 140 pitches are ready with a further 155 to be developed over the next few years. The owners' aim is to eventually develop a residential site and there are already mobile homes and chalets on site for viewing. A stylish restaurant has been opened and future plans include an indoor pool, gym, bar and games room. An area of hardstanding pitches for motorcaravans is also planned.

Facilities

Two toilet blocks with facilities for disabled visitors and babies. Laundry facilities. Shop (from 2009). Restaurant. Takeaway (1/7-31/8). Outdoor pool (heated 1/7-31/8). Tennis. Minigolf. Fishing lake. Off site: Village 400 m. Les Sables d'Olonne 25 km. Vendée beaches 8 km.

Open: All year.

Directions

Travel south from La Roche-sur-Yon on the D747 for about 21 km. At the D19, turn right for Avrille (about 6 km). At junction with the D949 turn right and first right again into rue des Forges. Site at the end of the road. GPS: N46:28.565 W01:29.672

Charges 2009

Per unit incl. 2 persons and electricity	€ 16,00 - € 26,00
extra person	€ 2,00 - € 6,00
child (2-6 yrs)	free - € 4,00
animal	€ 3,00

Camping Domaine des Forges

Open all year
Very comfortable pitches of 220 m²
Member of 'Les Castels'

• Rue des Forges • F-85440 Avrillé • Tél: 0033 2 51 22 38 85 •
contact@campingdomainedesforges.com • www.campingdomainedesforges.com

Alan Rogers

FREE 2009 brochure
Over 60 French campsites, hand picked for you
Call for your copy today 01580 214000
FREE CHILD PLACES ON MANY SITES

FR85950 Camping le Clos Cottet

Route de la Tranche-sur-Mer, F-85750 Angles (Vendée)

Tel: 02 51 28 90 72. Email: contact@camping-clos-cottet.com

www.alanrogers.com/FR85950

Le Clos Cottet is an attractive family site, based around an old Vendéen farm. There are 196 pitches here, all of which have reasonable shade. Many of them are occupied by mobile homes and chalets. During the high season (July and August) a free shuttle bus service runs to the nearest beach (six kilometres). On site, however, there is a fine swimming pool complex with a large outdoor pool with water slides, as well as a heated indoor pool. This complex also contains a sauna and Turkish bath, and a popular aquagym. This is a lively site in high season with regular discos and karaoke evenings, as well as many sports tournaments and other family activities. Angles is a pretty village with a good range of shops and restaurants. Les Sables d'Olonne lies to the north and is a stylish resort with a long sandy beach and a popular zoo.

Facilities

Shop. Bar. Snack bar. Pool complex with outdoor and covered pools. Water slides. Children's pool. Sauna. Play area. Sports field. Activity and entertainment programme. Mobile homes and chalets for rent. Off site: Angles village centre 1.5 km. Nearest beach 6 km. Les Sables d'Olonne. Cycle and walking tracks.

Open: 4 April - 19 September.

Directions

Leave La Roche-sur-Yon on D747 (towards La Tranche-sur-Mer). Pass Moutiers-les-Mauxfaits and then continue to Angles. Site is well signed from the village. GPS: N46:23.544 W01:24.219

Charges guide

Per unit incl. 2 persons and electricity	€ 16,00 - € 28,00
extra person	€ 4,00 - € 5,00
child (under 4 yrs)	€ 2,50 - € 3,00

Camping Le Clos Cottet ★★★★

.Water slick
.Hamman, Sauna,
.Gym
.Ping Pong
.Mini Golf
.Boule alley
. Fishing Pond
.Picnic area with barbecues
.Mini Farm (Hens, pig, goats, emus...)
Free Bus to the Beach

Many Animations in july and August

COVERED POOL HEATED TO 29°

OPEN FROM APRIL TO SEPTEMBER

Route de la tranche / mer- F.85750 ANGLES
Tel: (0033) 02.51.28.90.72 contact@camping-clos-cottet.com
Internet website: www.camping-closcottet.com

FR85770 RCN Camping la Ferme du Latois

F-85220 Coëx (Vendée)

Tel: 02 51 54 67 30. Email: info@rcn-lafermedulatois.fr

www.alanrogers.com/FR85770

Until recently a simple 'Camping à la ferme', this site is being developed by RCN, the Dutch organisation that now owns it, into an extensive and very well equipped campsite. Naturally a very high proportion of its clientele is Dutch, but the owners are keen to attract more British visitors. Located on the far side of two attractive fishing lakes, the original, very spacious pitches are attractively laid out with plenty of grass, hedges and mature trees. The new ones on the near side of the lakes are equally spacious but here the grass, bushes and trees have yet to start growing.

Facilities

Two modern sanitary blocks built in traditional style have excellent toilets, showers and washbasins in cubicles. Good facilities for visitors with disabilities. Attractively tiled areas for babies and children, with special toilets, basins and showers. Laundry room ('buanderie'). Small shop. Bar counter with terrace. All facilities available all season. Play area. Bicycle hire. Fishing. Off site: Golf and riding 3 km. Beach, sailing, boat launching 12 km.

Open: 14 April - 6 October.

Directions

Coëx is 29 km. west of La Roche-sur-Yon via the D938 to Aizenay, then the D6 St Gilles Croix-de-Vie road. Site is south of the village just off the D40 (La Chaize-Giraud - Brem-sur-Mer) and is clearly signed. GPS: N46:40.622 W01:46.131

Charges guide

Per unit incl. 2 persons, electricity and water	€ 18,00 - € 45,50
incl. 6 persons	€ 39,20 - € 51,00

www.rcn-campings.fr

BOOK THIS SITE
CALL 01580 214000
...we'll arrange everything
The Travel Service

167

FR85840 Campéole la Grande Côte

Route de la Grande Côte, F-85550 La Barre-de-Monts (Vendée)

Tel: 02 51 68 51 89. Email: nadine.ferran@atciat.com

www.alanrogers.com/FR85840

A site that lives up to its name, this one is very large, with 727 pitches. However, 245 are occupied by Bengali tents to rent, 60 by private caravans and 29 by tour operators. There are still 394 numbered touring pitches in rows, all with 10A electricity and spread over undulating sand dunes with sparse grass under pine trees. The site is served by eight fairly modern and fairly well maintained toilet blocks around the site. Some of the terraced pitches at the rear of the site have views of the impressive bridge onto the Ile de Noirmoutier, and there is direct access to a sandy beach via a gate.

Facilities

Eight toilet blocks, all of a similar design, include some washbasins in cubicles, seatless toilets, baby bath, and a good unit for disabled campers. One laundry room. Outdoor swimming pool (15/5-30/9). Shop for bread and basics. Bar and takeaway (1/7- 31/8). Playgrounds, trampoline and bouncy castle. Entertainment and clubs for children (1/7-31/8). Multi-sports court. Boules. Bicycle hire. No charcoal barbecues. Supplement for double axle caravans. Off site: Fishing, sailing 50 m. Golf 15 km. Riding 2 km. Boat launching 25 km. Nearby is Ecomuseum du Oaviaud.

Open: 31 March - 16 September.

Directions

Site is on the mainland at the approach to the Ile de Noirmoutier. From the north via Bourgneuf-en-Retz take D758 to Beauvoir-sur-Mer, then d22 to La Barre-de-Monts. Continue through town ignoring road to Fromentine. At town boundary turn right on D38b (slightly oblique turn), signed Ile de Noirmoutier. In 500 m, straight on at roundabout for about 1 km. then right signed Grand Côte and Fromentine. Take next left for 1 km. to site (entrance on right). GPS: N46:53.137 W02:08.838

Charges guide

Per unit incl. 2 persons	€ 13,00 - € 20,30
extra person	€ 4,50 - € 6,40
electricity (10A)	€ 4,00

FR85890 Camping le Rouge-Gorge

F-85290 Saint Laurent-sur-Sèvre (Vendée)

Tel: 02 51 67 86 39. Email: campinglerougegorge@wanadoo.fr

www.alanrogers.com/FR85890

A family run site, Le Rouge-Gorge is open all year. There are 72 touring pitches, plus some units for rent and privately owned caravans and chalets. The site does accept a small number of workers' units. Slightly sloping and undulating pitches are on grass in a garden-like setting and a small wildlife pond (fenced) is in the centre of the site. It would make a suitable base from which to visit the spectacles of Puy de Fou and the steam railway which runs from Mortagne-sur-Sèvre to Les Herbiers. This is also an excellent stop-over for those heading to and from southern France and Spain, or the ski-resorts.

Facilities

Two toilet blocks, one can be heated, with washbasins in cubicles and facilities for disabled campers and babies. Laundry facilities. Motorcaravan service point. Bread and basic provisions stocked (15/6-15/9). Swimming pool (1/6-30/9). Some low key family entertainment in high season. Boules. Charcoal barbecues are not permitted. TV room. WiFi. Off site: Fishing 500 m. Riding 2 km. Mortagne - Les Herbiers steam railway is close to site.

Open: All year.

Directions

Saint Laurent-sur-Sèvre is about 10 km. due south of Cholet, just south of the N149. Site is on D111 west of town towards la Verrie, entrance at top of hill on right. GPS: N46:57.486 W00:54.205

Charges guide

Per unit incl. 2 persons and electricity	€ 16,20 - € 26,70
extra person	€ 3,70
child (under 10 yrs)	€ 1,95

insure4campers.com — Alan Rogers — BROUGHT TO YOU BY ALAN ROGERS

Personal travel insurance - European vehicle assistance insurance

Whatever form your camping holiday may take, you'll need insurance. Our policies provide exactly the right cover for self-drive campsite-based holidays.

Call us **NOW** for a no-obligation quote

01580 214006

Policies despatched within 24 hours

With over one hundred of France's finest châteaux, this is a region to inspire the imagination. The Loire valley is a charming region of lush countryside, fields of sunflowers, rolling vineyards and of course the great river itself.

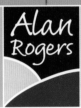

OUR TOURIST REGIONS INCLUDE ALL THE LOIRE VALLEY: 18 CHER, 28 EURE-ET-LOIR, 36 INDRE, 37 INDRE-ET-LOIRE, 41 LOIR-ET-CHER, 45 LOIRET. FROM WESTERN LOIRE: 49 MAINE-ET-LOIRE, 53 MAYENNE, 72 SARTHE. AND FROM POITOU-CHARENTES: 79 DEUX SÈVRES, 86 VIENNE

For centuries the Loire valley was frequented by French royalty and the great river winds its way past some of France's most magnificent châteaux: Amboise, Azay-le-Rideau, Chenonceau, with its famous arches that span the river and appear to 'float' on the water, and the fairytale Ussé with myriad magical turrets are just some of the highlights.

Known as the Garden of France, the Loire's mild climate and fertile landscape of soft green valleys, lush vineyards and fields of flowers makes it a favourite with the visitors. Renowned for its wines, with hundreds to choose from, all are produced from vineyards stretching along the main course of the River Loire. Imposing abbeys, troglodyte caves, tiny Romanesque churches, woodland areas such as the Sologne and sleepy, picturesque villages reward exploration. Cities like Blois and Tours are elegant with fine architecture and museums, and Paris is only one hour by TGV. One of the oldest towns of Loire valley is Saumur. Its old quarter, grouped around the riverbank beneath the imposing château, is particularly pleasant to wander around.

Places of interest

Amboise: château, Leonardo da Vinci museum.

Beauregard: château with Delft tiled floors.

Blois: château with architecture from Middle Ages to Neo-Classical periods.

Chambord: Renaissance château.

Chartres: cathedral with stained glass windows.

Chinon: old town, Joan of Arc museum

Loches: old town, château and its fortifications.

Orléans: Holy Cross cathedral, house of Joan of Arc.

Tours: Renaissance and Neo-Classical mansions, cathedral of St Gatien.

Vendôme: Tour St Martin, La Trinité.

Villandry: famous Renaissance gardens.

Cuisine of the region

Wild duck, pheasant, hare, deer, and quail are classics, and fresh water fish such as salmon, perch and trout are favourites. Specialities include rillettes, andouillettes, tripes, mushrooms and the regional cheeses of Trappiste d'Entrammes and Cremet d'Angers, Petit Sable and Ardoises d'Angers cookies.

Bourdaines: baked apples stuffed with jam.

Tarte a la citrouille: pumpkin tart.

Tarte Tatin: upside-down tart of caramelised apples and pastry.

FR18010 Flower Camping les Etangs

Route de Sancerre, F-18700 Aubigny-sur-Nère (Cher)

Tel: 02 48 58 02 37. Email: camping.aubigny@orange.fr

www.alanrogers.com/FR18010

Les Etangs is a site of 100 pitches, close to the Sancerre vineyards and the lakes of the Sologne. A member of the Flower group, this site extends over two hectares and borders a small lake (suitable for fishing). Pitches are large and grassy (most have electrical connections). There are chalets available for rent. The town of Aubigny-sur-Nère is very close (1 km) and has a close attachment with Scotland, thanks to the 'Auld Alliance'. The town is the only one in France to celebrate French-Scottish friendship on Bastille Day. Bicycle hire is available on site and many tracks are available in the area, running through the surrounding forests.

Facilities

Small shop. Snack bar. Takeaway. Play area. Bicycle hire. Fishing. Activity and entertainment programme. Mobile homes for rent. Off site: Aubigny-sur-Nère 1 km. Walking and cycle tracks. Swimming pool 50 m. (with aqua-gym). Riding 20 km. Sancerre vineyards.

Open: 1 April - 15 October.

Directions

Approaching from the north (Orléans) on the A71 take exit 4 for Salbris and east on D724 and D924 until Aubigny. Take the D923 towards Sancerre and site is 1 km. GPS: N47:29.061 E02:27.422

Charges guide

Per unit incl. 2 persons and electricity	€ 13,70 - € 17,90
extra person	€ 2,30 - € 4,00

FR28100 Flower Camping le Bois Fleuri

Route de Brou, F-28120 Illiers-Combray (Eure-et-Loir)

Tel: 02 37 24 03 04. Email: infos@camping-chartres.com

www.alanrogers.com/FR28100

The elegant city of Chartres is, of course, best known for its sublime cathedral, widely considered to be the finest Gothic cathedral in France, and included on the UNESCO list of World Heritage sites. Le Bois Fleuri is a small, wooded site, 20 km. from Chartres, open for an extended season. There are 89 pitches here as well as a number of mobile homes available for rent. Pitches range from 'Nature' (without electricity) to 'Grand Confort' (large pitches with electricity). Attractive pool and various other amenities, including bicycle hire and a children's playground.

Facilities

The two large toilet blocks (one closed outside July/Aug) are fully tiled, with some washbasins in cabins. Good facilities for disabled people including telephone booths and, although the site is on a slope, it could possibly be acceptable for wheelchair users. Motorcaravan services. Bar. Swimming pool. Fishing. Bicycle hire. Play area. Off site: Fishing. Golf. Chartres 20 km. Illiers Combray 2 km. Riding. Cycle routes.

Open: 1 April - 31 October.

Directions

Leave the A11 (Paris - Le Mans) motorway at the Thivars exit and take the D114 and then the D921 to Illiers Combray. Site is well signed from the town. GPS: N48:17.166 E01:13.645

Charges guide

Per unit incl. 2 persons and electricity	€ 14,50
incl. services	€ 20,00

No credit cards.
Camping Cheques accepted.

FR36110 Camping le Rochat Belle-Isle

17 avenue du Parc des Loisir, F-36000 Châteauroux (Indre)

Tel: 02 54 34 26 56. Email: camping.le-rochat@orange.fr

www.alanrogers.com/FR36110

Set amongst mature trees adjacent to a large lake on one side of the site and a gently-flowing river on two others (not fenced), this attractive municipal site is a peaceful haven tucked away from the large bustling city of Châteauroux. There are 166 numbered level pitches, mainly open but shaded by trees. The site has easy access for larger units. The Belle-Isle lake adjacent to the site offers a bar, restaurant, cycle tracks, fishing and water sports. The modern, well run reception has all the information you need to help you enjoy your stay. English is spoken.

Facilities

Two well equipped sanitary blocks with controllable showers and shower curtain divider. Washbasins in cabins. All very clean. Facilities for disabled visitors (no key required). Laundry. Small play area. Table tennis. Pétanque. Off site: All the attractions of a busy city: shops, bars, restaurants. Swimming pools close by.

Open: 1 May - 30 September.

Directions

The city of Châteauroux is accessed from junctions 12,13 or 14 from the A20 Vierzon to Limoges motorway. Head towards the city centre where Camping Le Rochat Belle-Isle is very well signed. Signs for 'Halls Exposition' also take you to this recreational area, where site is next left after the municipal pool. GPS: N46:49.429 E01:41.690

Charges guide

Per unit incl. 2 persons	€ 13,60
electricity	€ 3,30 - € 4,50

Check real time availability and at-the-gate prices...

www.alanrogers.com

www.flowercampings.com

Visit the glass blow museum !

... get to know this profession and attend a glass blowing demonstration

Open every day from 14 till 19 o'clock except Tuesdays from May till August. The rest of the year open on Wednesday, Friday, Saturday and Sunday from 14 till 18 o'clock. Demonstrations : every first Saturday of the month. Information through +33 238 92 79 06 or please visit www.musee-dordives.fr

Situated in DORDIVES, between Montargis & Fontainebleau. 1,5h from Orléans

FR28140 Huttopia Senonches

Avenue de Badouleau, F-28250 Senonches (Eure-et-Loir)

Tel: 04 37 64 22 35. Email: senonches@huttopia.com   www.alanrogers.com/FR28140

Senonches is the latest addition to the Huttopia group and will be opening for the 2009 season. This site is hidden away in the huge Forêt Dominiale de Senonches and, in keeping with other Huttopia sites, combines a high standard of comfort with a real sense of backwoods camping. There are 150 pitches here, some with electrical connections (6/10A). The pitches are very large ranging from 100 sq.m. to no less than 300 sq.m. There are also 20 Canadian-style log cabins and tents available for rent. There is a good range of on-site amenities including a shop and a bar/restaurant. The swimming pool overlooks a lake and is open from early July until September. The forest can be explored on foot or bike (rental available on site) and beyond the forest, the great city of Chartres is easily visited, with its stunning gothic cathedral, widely considered to be the finest in France.

Facilities

The toilet blocks are modern and are heated in low season, with special facilities for disabled visitors. Shop. Bar. Snack bar. Takeaway. Swimming pool. Fishing. Play area. Bicycle hire. Entertainment and activity programme. Tents and chalets for rent. Off site: Riding 4 km. Senonches (good selection of shops, restaurants and bars). Cycle and walking tracks. Chartres.

Open: 3 July - 5 November.

Directions

Approaching from Chartres, use the ringroad (N154) and then take the D24 in a northwesterly direction. Drive through Digny and continue to Senonches, from where the site is well signed.
GPS: N48:33.341 E01:02.311

Charges guide

Per person	€ 5,10 - € 5,90
child (2-7 yrs)	€ 1,90 - € 2,50
pitch	€ 4,20 - € 10,20
electricity	€ 5,00

tel: +33 (0) 4 37 64 22 33 www.huttopia.com

HUTTOPIA

Huttopia SENONCHES

Tents and cottages to rent

Natural swimming-pool, Bar restaurant, Children playground...

Etang de Badouleau
28250 Senonches
Tél : +33 (0)4 37 64 22 35

In the Perche Regional Park
by the Badouleau pond...

www.huttopia.com

BOOK THIS SITE
CALL 01580 214000
...we'll arrange everything
The Travel Service

FR37010 Camping de la Mignardière

22 avenue des Aubépines, F-37510 Ballan-Miré (Indre-et-Loire)

Tel: 02 47 73 31 00. Email: info@mignardiere.com

www.alanrogers.com/FR37010

Southwest of the city of Tours, this site is within easy reach of several of the Loire châteaux, notably Azay-le-Rideau. There are also many varied sports amenities on the site or very close by. The site has 177 numbered pitches of which 139 are for touring units, all with electricity (6/10A) and 37 with drainage and water. Pitches are of a good size on rather uneven grass with limestone gravel paths (which are rather 'sticky' when wet). The barrier gates (coded access) are closed 22.30 - 07.30 hrs. Reservation is essential for most of July/August.

Facilities

Three toilet blocks include washbasins in private cabins, a unit for disabled people, baby bath and laundry facilities. Motorcaravan service point. Shop. Takeaway. Two large, heated swimming pools (one covered). Paddling pool. Tennis court. Table tennis. Bicycle hire. Off site: Attractive lake 300 m. Family fitness run. Fishing 500 m. Riding 1 km. Golf 3 km. Tours centre 8 km.

Open: 1 April - 25 September.

Directions

From A10 autoroute take exit 24 and D751 towards Chinon. Turn right after 5 km. at Campanile Hotel following signs to site. From Tours take D751 towards Chinon. GPS: N47:21.305 E00:38.045

Charges guide

Per unit incl. 2 persons	€ 14,00 - € 21,00
incl. electricity and water	€ 20,00 - € 29,00
extra person	€ 4,00 - € 5,30
child (2-10 yrs)	€ 2,60 - € 3,20
Camping Cheques accepted.	

FR37050 Kawan Village la Citadelle

Avenue Aristide Briand, F-37600 Loches-en-Touraine (Indre-et-Loire)

Tel: 02 47 59 05 91. Email: camping@lacitadelle.com

www.alanrogers.com/FR37050

A pleasant, well maintained site, La Citadelle's best feature is probably that it is within walking distance of Loches, noted for its perfect architecture and its glorious history, yet at the same time the site has a rural atmosphere. The 86 standard touring pitches are all level, of a good size and with 10A electricity. Numerous trees offer varying degrees of shade. The 30 larger serviced pitches have 16A electricity but little shade. Mobile homes (28 for hire) occupy the other 48 pitches.

Facilities

Three sanitary blocks provide mainly British style WCs, washbasins (mostly in cabins) and controllable showers. Laundry facilities. Motorcaravan service point. Two baby units and provision for disabled visitors (both in need of attention). Heated swimming pool (May - Sept). Play area (adult supervision recommended). Small bar and snack bar (15/6-15/9). Internet access and TV. Off site: Supermarket, station and buses within 1 km. Bicycle hire 50 m. Riding 5 km. Golf and river beach both 10 km.

Open: 19 March - 10 October.

Directions

Loches is 45 km. southeast of Tours. Do not enter town centre. Approach from roundabout by supermarket at southern end of bypass (D943). Site signed towards town centre and is on right in 800 m. GPS: N47:07.382 E01:00.134

Charges guide

Per pitch incl. 2 persons	€ 14,80 - € 31,50
extra person	€ 4,30 - € 6,10
child (0-10 yrs)	free - € 4,60
Camping Cheques accepted.	

FR37070 Camping de l'Ile Auger

Quai Danton, F-37500 Chinon (Indre-et-Loire)

Tel: 02 47 93 08 35. Email: communaute.r.c.sb@wanadoo.fr

www.alanrogers.com/FR37070

This traditional municipal-style site is well placed for exploring the old medieval town of Chinon and lies alongside the River Vienne opposite the impressive castle which was once the home of England's Henry II and includes a museum to Joan of Arc. A five minute walk over the bridge takes you to the town centre. The 277 level pitches are numbered but not separated and trees provide some shade. All have electricity (long leads needed in places). Nearby are châteaux at Azay le Rideau and Villandry and the abbey at Fontevraud.

Facilities

Hot water is provided to showers and basins in two blocks near the entrance and in a small block at the far end of the site. WCs here are mainly British style. Three small blocks around the rest of the site, provide additional WCs (many Turkish style) and basins with cold water. Motorcaravan service point. Laundry facilities. Playground. Boules. Fishing. Canoes. Off site: Town with shops, bars and restaurants 500 m. Bicycle hire and river beach (no swimming) 1 km. Riding 10 km.

Open: 15 March - 15 October.

Directions

From the A85 at exit 9 (Chinon) follow D749 for 10 km. and turn south on D751 for 3 km. Turn east on D751E then north towards town centre. Follow one-way system, cross traffic coming out of town at bridge and continue ahead to campsite on right. GPS: N47:09.827 E00:14.121

Charges guide

Per person	€ 2,00
pitch incl. electricity (4-12A)	€ 6,45 - € 7,85

Check real time availability and at-the-gate prices...

www.alanrogers.com

FR37030 Camping le Moulin Fort

F-37150 Francueil-Chenonceau (Indre-et-Loire)

Tel: 02 47 23 86 22. Email: lemoulinfort@wanadoo.fr   www.alanrogers.com/FR37030

Camping Le Moulin Fort is a tranquil, riverside site that has been redeveloped by British owners, John and Sarah Scarratt. The 137 pitches are enhanced by trees and shrubs offering plenty of shade and 110 pitches have electricity (6A). From the snack bar terrace adjacent to the restored mill building a timber walkway over the mill race leads to the unheated swimming pool and paddling pools. The site is ideal for couples and families with young children, although the river is unfenced. There is occasional noise from trains passing on the opposite bank of the river. All over the campsite, visitors will find little information boards about local nature (birds, fish, trees and shrubs), about the history of the mill and fascinating facts about recycling. The owners are keen to encourage recycling on the site. The picturesque Château of Chenonceau is little more than 1 km. along the Cher riverbank and many of the Loire châteaux are within easy reach, particularly Amboise and its famous Leonardo de Vinci museum.

Facilities

Two toilet blocks with all the usual amenities of a good standard, include washbasins in cubicles, baby baths and facilities for disabled visitors. Motorcaravan service point. Shop, bar (limited hours), restaurant and takeaway (all 21/5-19/9). Swimming pool (21/5-19/9). Excellent play area. Minigolf. Pétanque. Games room and TV. Library. Fishing. Bicycle and canoe hire. In high season regular family entertainment including wine tasting, quiz evenings, activities for children, light-hearted games tournaments and live music events. WiFi in bar area. Off site: Boat launching 2 km. River beach 4 km. Riding 12 km. Golf 20 km. Trains to Tours 1.5 km.

Open: 1 April - 30 September.

Directions

Site is 35 km. east of Tours off the D976 Vierzon road. From A85 at exit 11 take D31 towards Bléré and turn east on D976 (Vierzon) for 7 km. then turn north on D80 (Chenonceau) to site. From north bank of Cher (D140/D40) turn south on D80 to cross river between Chenonceau and Chisseaux. Site on left just after bridge. GPS: N47:19.637 E01:05.338

Charges guide

Per unit incl. 2 persons	€ 9,00 - € 22,00
extra person	€ 3,00 - € 5,00
child (4-12 yrs)	€ 2,00 - € 4,00
electricity (6A)	€ 4,00
dog	€ 2,00 - € 3,00

BOOK THIS SITE
CALL 01580 214000
...we'll arrange everything
The Travel Service

LE MOULIN FORT

CAMPING ✱✱✱
37150 FRANCUEIL-CHENONCEAUX

Téléphone: +33(0) 2 47 23 86 22 - Fax: +33(0) 2 47 23 80 93 - lemoulinfort@wanadoo.fr

We offer you:
- An unbeatable location within walking distance of Chenonceau Castle
- An ideal base for exploring the Loire region of France
- A warm welcome from the English owners
- A perfect place for relaxing by the river or enjoying the wide range of facilities and animation available on site
- A good stopover point within easy reach of the UK ports, well-signposted and easy to find

On-site facilities:
•Shop •Bar •Take-away •Restaurant •Swimming pool •TV room •Animation •Play-area •Themed evenings •Bicycle hire •Canoe hire •Barbecues permitted
Motorcaravan service area • Reservation recommended for high season

BOOK THIS SITE
CALL 01580 214000
...we'll arrange everything

The Travel
Service

FR37060 Kawan Village l'Arada Parc

Mobile homes ▶ page 498

Rue de la Baratière, F-37360 Sonzay (Indre-et-Loire)

Tel: **02 47 24 72 69**. Email: **info@laradaparc.com**   www.alanrogers.com/FR37060

A good, well maintained site in a quiet location, Camping l'Arada Parc is a popular base from which to visit the numerous châteaux in this beautiful part of France. The 77 grass touring pitches all have electricity and 35 have water and drainage. The clearly marked pitches, some slightly sloping, are separated by trees and shrubs some of which are now providing a degree of shade. An attractive, heated pool is on a pleasant terrace beside the restaurant. Entertainment, themed evenings and activities for children are organised in July/August. This is a new site with modern facilities which is developing well.

Facilities

Two modern toilet blocks provide unisex toilets, showers and washbasins in cubicles. Baby room. Facilities for disabled visitors (wheelchair users may find the gravel access difficult). Laundry facilities. Shop, bar, restaurant and takeaway (all season). Outdoor swimming pool (no Bermuda style shorts; 1/5-13/9). Heated, covered pool (all season). Play area. Games area. Boules. TV room. Bicycle hire. Internet access. Off site: Tennis 200 m. Fishing 500 m. Golf 12 km. Riding 14 km.

Open: 28 March - 30 October.

Directions

Sonzay is northwest of Tours. From the new A28 north of Tours take the exit to Neuillé-Pont-Pierre which is on the N138 Le Mans - Tours road. Then take D766 towards Château la Vallière and turn southwest to Sonzay. Follow campsite signs. GPS: N47:31.687 E00:27.180

Charges guide

Per unit incl. 2 persons	€ 13,50 - € 17,50
extra person	€ 3,50 - € 4,50
child (2-10 yrs)	€ 2,75 - € 3,50
electricity (10A)	€ 3,50
animal	€ 1,50

Camping Cheques accepted.

OPEN from 28th March to 30th October

Camping - Caravaning ★★★★

L'Arada Parc

At the heart of the Loire's chateau country and the vineyards of Touraine

Bar, restaurant, activities, tennis, chalets & mobile home renting, indoor & outdoor swimming pool, spa, fitness room, hammam

"Golf at 10mn"

L'ARADA PARC • 37 360 Sonzay
Tél. +33 (0)2 47 24 72 69
Web: www.laradaparc.com
E-mail: info@laradaparc.com

FR37100 Camping la Fritillaire

Rue Basse, F-37420 Savigny-en-Véron (Indre-et-Loire)

Tel: **02 47 58 03 79**. Email: **lafritillaire.veron@ffcc.fr**   www.alanrogers.com/FR37100

A municipal site run by the FFCC (France's Camping and Caravanning Federation), La Fritillaire is a pleasant, no-frills site offering excellent value. There are 94 touring pitches, marked by trees and bushes, on level ground and ringed by tall trees. There are 58 electric connections (10A) so for some of the shadier pitches a hook-up may not be available or you will need a long cable. The central pitches, however, all have electricity and water, and 22 also have drainage.

Facilities

A smart, modern building houses reception and the sanitary facilities which include push-button showers, washbasins in cabins, good provision for disabled visitors and laundry facilities. Motorcaravan service point. Play area. Boules, volleyball and basketball. Off site: Baker's 500 m. Shops, bar and restaurant in village. Fishing 200 m. Golf 3 km. Bicycle hire and boat launching 10 km. Riding 15 km.

Open: 1 April - 30 September.

Directions

Savigny-en-Véron is 20 km. east of Saumur via D947 to Montsoreau, then the D7 road along the south bank of the Loire. Village and campsite are both clearly signed from all approaches. GPS: N47:12.013 E00:08.366

Charges guide

Per unit incl. 2 persons	€ 7,70 - € 10,10
full services	€ 11,50 - € 13,65
extra person	€ 2,10 - € 2,60
child (under 10 yrs)	€ 1,00 - € 1,40
electricity (10A)	€ 3,20

FR37090 Camping du Château de la Rolandière

F-37220 Trogues (Indre-et-Loire)

Tel: **02 47 58 53 71**. Email: **contact@larolandiere.com**   www.alanrogers.com/FR37090

This is a charming site set in the grounds of a château. The owners, Ghislain and Sabine Toulemonde, offer a very warm welcome. There are 50 medium sized, flat or gently sloping pitches, separated by hedges. Most have 6A electricity and water taps nearby and parkland trees give shade. There is a large chalet for hire and the château and adjoining buildings contain rooms to let. The site has a pleasant swimming pool with a sunny terrace and paddling pool, minigolf and an area for ball games, swings and slides. The site is close to both the A10 and the N10, so is convenient for an overnight break. However it certainly merits a longer stay as it is a delightfully peaceful spot from which to visit the châteaux at Chinon, Loches, Villandry or Azay-le-Rideau and the villages of Richelieu and Crissay-sur-Manse. There are interesting excursions to gardens and grottos, and in nearby Azay-le-Rideau, to the wicker craftsmen's workshops. A 'Sites et Paysages' member.

Facilities

The toilet block is older in style but has been refurbished to provide good facilities with modern showers, washbasins and laundry areas around central British style WCs. Provision for disabled visitors. Small shop for basics. Bar with terrace. Snacks and takeaway (July/Aug). Swimming pool (15/5-30/9). Minigolf (no children under 12 yrs). Play area. Fitness room. TV lounge. WiFi. Off site: Fishing 1 km. on River Vienne. River beach and boat launching 4 km. Golf 15 km. Bicycle hire 25 km. Restaurant 4 km. St Maure 7 km.

Open: 15 April - 30 September.

Directions

Trogues is 40 km. south west of Tours on the D760 Loches-Chinon road. Site is east of village, 5 km. west from exit 25 on A10 at St Maure-de-Touraine. Entrance is signed and marked by a model of the château. GPS: N47:06.460 E00:30.631

Charges guide

Per person	€ 4,50 - € 6,00
child (under 10 yrs)	€ 2,50 - € 3,50
pitch	€ 7,00 - € 10,50
electricity	€ 4,00

No credit cards.

FR37150 Camping les Coteaux du Lac

Base de Loisirs, F-37460 Chemillé-sur-Indrois (Indre-et-Loire)

Tel: **02 47 92 77 83**. Email: **lescoteauxdulac@wanadoo.fr**   www.alanrogers.com/FR37150

This former municipal site has been completely refurbished to a high standard and is being operated efficiently by a private company owned by the present enthusiastic manager, Yves Joyaut. There are 49 touring pitches, all with electricity (10A) and individual water tap; four have hard standing for motorcaravans. At present there is little shade apart from that offered by a few mature trees, but new trees and bushes have been planted and flower beds are to be added. In a few years this promises to be a delightful site; meanwhile it is smart and very well tended.

Facilities

Excellent sanitary block with controllable showers, some washbasins in cabins and en-suite facilities for disabled visitors. Dishwashing and laundry facilities. Reception sells a few basic supplies and bread can be ordered. Swimming and paddling pools. Playing field. Play equipment for different ages. Chalets to rent (15) are grouped at far end of site, Off site: Fishing 100 m. Lakeside beach, sailing and other water sports 200 m. Riding 4 km. Golf 15 km.

Open: 5 April - 30 September.

Directions

Chemillé-sur-Indrois is 55 km. southeast of Tours and 14 km. east of Loches, just off the D760 from Loches to Montrésor. Site is to the north of this road and is signed just west of Montrésor.
GPS: N47:09.472 E01:09.592

Charges guide

Per pitch incl. 2 persons	€ 11,50 - € 17,20
extra person	€ 3,50 - € 4,70
electricity	€ 3,70

Check real time availability and at-the-gate prices...

www.**alanrogers**.com

BOOK THIS SITE
CALL 01580 214000
...we'll arrange everything
The Travel Service

The Travel Service

BOOK THIS SITE CALL 01580 214000 ...we'll arrange everything

FR37120 Castel Camping Parc de Fierbois

Sainte Catherine de Fierbois, F-37800 Saint Maure-de-Touraine (Indre-et-Loire)

Tel: 02 47 65 43 35. Email: parc.fierbois@wanadoo.fr   www.alanrogers.com/FR37120

Parc de Fierbois has an impressive entrance and a tree lined driveway and is set among 250 acres of lakes and forest in the heart of the Loire Valley. In all, there are 320 pitches including 100 for touring units, the remainder being used by tour operators and for chalets and mobile homes. There are 80 touring pitches, mostly level and separated by low hedging or small trees, with water, drainage and electricity hook-ups (2-8A). The other pitches are small or medium in size, many unmarked and some sloping and in the shade. This is a lively family holiday site. There is a super pool complex and a sandy beach on the shores of the lake. There is plenty here to occupy and entertain children. English is spoken in reception.

Facilities

Three toilet blocks provide British style WCs, hot showers and washbasins in cubicles. Baby room. Dishwashing and laundry facilities. Motorcaravan service point. Shop. Bar. Restaurant. Takeaway. Water park complex (pools, slides, paddling pool, sunbathing areas). Indoor heated pool. Indoor entertainment and games bar. Tennis. Pétanque. Minigolf. Bicycle hire. Go-karts and electric cars. TV/video room. Gym. Fishing. Pedaloes, canoeing and entertainment programme (July/Aug). Off site: Riding 10 km. Golf 30 km.

Open: 18 May - 11 September.

Directions

Travelling south on N10 from Tours, go through Montbazon and on towards St Maure and Chatellerault. Site signed 16 km. outside Montbazon near Ste Catherine. Turn off main road. Follow site signs. From A10 autoroute use St Maure exit and turn north up N10. GPS: N47:08.899 E00:39.272

Charges 2009

Per unit incl. 2 persons	€ 16,00 - € 42,00
extra person	€ 6,00 - € 8,00
electricity	€ 4,50

Parc de Fierbois
Camping Caravaning ★★★★

Parc de Fierbois Camping Caravaning****
Ste. Catherine de Fierbois - 37800 St. Maure de Touraine
Tel: 0033 (0)247 65 43 35 - Fax: 0033 (0)247 65 53 75
contact@fierbois.com - www.fierbois.com

QUALITÉ TOURISME   LES CASTELS Hôtellerie de Plein Air   Camping Qualité

FR41010 Le Parc du Val de Loire

Route de Fleuray, F-41150 Mesland (Loir-et-Cher)

Tel: 02 54 70 27 18. Email: parcduvaldeloire@wanadoo.fr   www.alanrogers.com/FR41010

Between Blois and Amboise, quietly situated among vineyards away from the main roads and towns, this site is nevertheless centrally placed for visits to the châteaux; Chaumont, Amboise and Blois (21 km.) are the nearest in that order. There are 185 touring pitches of reasonable size, either in light woodland marked by trees or on open meadow with separators. All the pitches have electricity (10A) and 100 of them also have water and drainage. Sports and competitions are organised in July/August with a weekly disco and dance for adults and opportunities for weekly wine tasting.

Facilities

Three original toilet blocks of varying ages are acceptable. Units for disabled visitors, babies and laundry facilities. Motorcaravan services. Shop with bakery (July/Aug). Bar, restaurant, snack service, pizzeria and takeaway (all 15/5-1/9). TV and recreation rooms. Swimming pools, one heated (May-mid Sept), larger one with slide. Tennis. Playgrounds with skate board facilities. Bicycle hire. Minigolf. Barbecue area. Off site: Fishing 2 km. Golf 4 km. Riding 10 km.

Open: 31 March - 29 September.

Directions

From A10 exit 18 (Château-Renault, Amboise) take D31 south to Autrèche (2 km). Turn left on D55 for 3.5 km. In Darne-Marie Les Bois turn left and then right onto D43 to Mesland. Follow site signs. Or, from south, site signed from Onzain. GPS: N47:30.601 E01:06.286

Charges 2009

Per unit incl. 2 persons	€ 14,00 - € 24,00
large pitch (120-170 sq.m)	
with services	€ 22,00 - € 32,00
extra person	€ 4,50 - € 7,00
child (4-14 yrs)	€ 3,50 - € 6,20

Check real time availability and at-the-gate prices...

www.alanrogers.com

FR37130 Village Center Parc des Allais

Domaine du Bois des Allais, F-37220 Trogues (Indre-et-Loire)

Tel: 02 47 58 60 60. Email: contact@parc-des-allais.com   www.alanrogers.com/FR37130

Parc des Allais is a mainly residential site situated in the heart of the Loire Valley. It is convenient for exploring the surrounding countryside and the region's world class châteaux. The site lies within a 16 hectare park and borders an attractive lake. It has a new indoor and outdoor pool complex overlooking the Vienne River. Of the 198 pitches there are only 25 small pitches for touring (10A electricity), separated by hedges and with good shade, all near the entrance.

Facilities

Two basic toilet blocks with facilities for campers with disabilities. Shop, bar, takeaway (31/3-13/10). Restaurant (July/Aug). Swimming pool complex, indoor and outdoor pools, slides, paddling pool (15/4-15/10). Miniclub. Theme evenings. Entertainment (July/Aug). Minigolf. Tennis. Boules. Fishing. Bicycle hire. Boat and go-kart rental (July/Aug). Play area. Fitness facilities. Games room. Internet. Motorcaravan services outside entrance. Off site: Countryside and châteaux of the Loire region. Futuroscope (45 minutes). Tours (less than an hour). Caves. Wine Route. Riding 3 km. Golf 30 km.

Open: 31 March - 15 October.

Directions

South of Tours leave A10 autoroute at exit 25 signed Ste Maure de Touraine. Take D970 west for about 3 km. Turn south on D58 to Pouzay. Turn west on D109 to site. It is between Pouzay and Trogues. GPS: N47:05.954 E00:30.251

Charges guide

Per unit incl. 2 persons	
and electricity	€ 23,00 - € 29,86
extra person	€ 4,00 - € 5,00
child (under 12 yrs)	€ 3,00 - € 4,00

Le Parc des Allais ★★★★

Trogues > The Loire

• A parc closed to the river Vienne
• Covered and heated swimming-pool

Villagecenter

BOOK YOUR HOLIDAYS
www.village-center.com
☎ +33 (0)4 99 57 21 21

FR41020 Castel Camping Château la Grenouillère   Mobile homes ▶ page 499

RN 152, F-41500 Suèvres (Loir-et-Cher)

Tel: 02 54 87 80 37. Email: la.grenouillere@wanadoo.fr   www.alanrogers.com/FR41020

Château de la Grenouillère is a comfortable site with good amenities. It is set in a 28 acre park and the 275 pitches (including 130 for tour operators and mobile homes) are in three distinct areas. The majority are in a wooded area, with about 60 in the old orchard and the remainder in open meadow, although all pitches are separated by hedges. There is one water point for every four pitches and all have electric hook-up (6/10A). Additionally, there are 14 fully serviced pitches with a separate luxury sanitary block in the outbuildings of the château.

Facilities

Three sanitary blocks are modern and well appointed, including some washbasins in cabins. Laundry facilities. Shop (1/6-12/9). Bar. Pizzeria and pizza takeaway. Restaurant and grill takeaway (8/5-12/9). Swimming complex of four pools (one covered) and slide. Tennis. Games room. Internet point. Bicycle and canoe hire (July/Aug). Fishing. Off site: Suèvres 3 km. Riding, and watersports 5 km. Golf 10 km.

Open: 25 April - 12 September.

Directions

Site is between Suèvres and Mer on north side of the N152 and is well signed. GPS: N47:41.134 E01:29.212

Charges 2009

Per unit incl. 2 persons	
and electricity	€ 26,00 - € 39,00
incl. full services	€ 30,00 - € 45,00
extra person	€ 5,00 - € 8,00
child (under 7 yrs)	€ 3,00 - € 6,00
dog	€ 3,00 - € 4,00

The Travel Service ...we'll arrange everything

BOOK THIS SITE
CALL 01580 214000

FR37140 Huttopia Rillé

Lac de Rillé, F-37340 Rillé (Indre-et-Loire)

Tel: **02 47 24 62 97**. Email: **rille@huttopia.com**

www.alanrogers.com/FR37140

This site in a forest by a lake has plenty of potential. It has recently been acquired by the Huttopia group which aims to provide a traffic-free environment. Cars are to be left in a carpark outside the barrier (allowed on site to unload and load). New arrivals must park outside and gain an entry code from reception. There are 146 pitches of which 32 are occupied by rental accommodation and 24 are for motorcaravans in a separate area. The touring pitches are numbered in groups amongst the trees but are not marked; they vary in size and cost.

Facilities

The central toilet block has family rooms (with showers and basins), washbasins in cubicles and facilities for disabled visitors (shower/basin plus separate toilet) but there are no ramps and access for wheelchairs is very difficult. Another smaller block has separate showers, washbasins and slightly better facilities for disabled visitors. Motorcaravan service point. Heated swimming pool with paddling area (May - Sept). Play area. Fishing. Canoes on lake. Communal barbecue areas. Off site: Riding 6 km. Golf 15 km.

Open: 24 April - 5 November.

Directions

Rillé is 40 km. west of Tours. From D766 Angers - Blois road at Château la Vallière take D749 southwest. From N152 Tours - Angers road go northwest at Langeais on D57. In Rillé turn west on D49. Site on right in a short distance. GPS: N47:27.485 E00:13.146

Charges 2009

Per unit incl. 2 persons and electricity	€ 19,20 - € 37,00
extra person	€ 5,20 - € 6,80
child (2-7 yrs)	€ 3,10 - € 4,50
dog	€ 4,00
Camping Cheques accepted.	

tel: +33 (0) 4 37 64 22 33 www.huttopia.com

HUTTOPIA

Huttopia Rillé

Roulottes, tents and cottages to rent

Heated swimming-pool, Bar restaurant, Tennis courts, Beach, Children playground, Hiking, Biking...

In the heart of the forest around Lake Rillé, near the Châteaux of the Loire Valley...

Lac de Rillé - 37340 Rillé
Tel. +33 (0)2 47 24 62 97

www.huttopia.com

FR41030 Leading Camping les Alicourts

Domaine des Alicourts, F-41300 Pierrefitte-sur-Sauldre (Loir-et-Cher)

Tel: **02 54 88 63 34**. Email: info@lesalicourts.com

www.alanrogers.com/FR41030

A secluded holiday village set in the heart of the forest and with many sporting facilities and a super new spa centre, Parc des Alicourts is midway between Orléans and Bourges, to the east of the A71. There are 490 pitches, 150 for touring and the remainder occupied by mobile homes and chalets. All pitches have electricity connections (6A) and good provision for water, and most are 150 sq.m. (min. 100 sq.m). Locations vary from wooded to more open areas, thus giving a choice of amount of shade. All facilities are open all season and the leisure amenities are exceptional. Member of Leading Campings Group.

Facilities

Three modern sanitary blocks include some washbasins in cabins and baby bathrooms. Laundry facilities. Facilities for disabled visitors (shallow step to reach them). Motorcaravan services. Shop. Restaurant. Takeaway in bar with terrace. Pool complex. Spa centre. 7 hectare lake (fishing, bathing, canoes, pedaloes). 9-hole golf course. Play area. Tennis. Roller skating/skateboarding (bring own equipment). Minigolf. Boules. Bicycle hire. Internet access.

Open: 29 April - 12 September.

Directions

From A71, take Lamotte Beuvron exit (no 3) or from N20 Orléans to Vierzon turn left on to D923 towards Aubigny. After 14 km. turn right at camping sign on to D24E. Site signed in about 4 km. GPS: N47:32.639 E02:11.516

Charges 2009

Per unit incl. 2 persons and electricity	€ 19,00 - € 42,00
extra person	€ 6,00 - € 9,00
child (1-7 yrs)	free - € 7,00

Check real time availability and at-the-gate prices...

www.alanrogers.com

3 route de Pontlevoy, F-41120 Candé-sur-Beuvron (Loir-et-Cher)

Tel: **02 54 44 15 20**. Email: **grandetortue@wanadoo.fr**

Mobile homes ▶ page 499

www.alanrogers.com/FR41070

This is a pleasant, shady site that has been developed in the surroundings of an old forest. It provides 169 touring pitches the majority of which are more than 100 sq.m. 150 have 10A electricity and the remainder are fully serviced. The family owners continue to develop the site with a new multisport court already created. During July and August, they organise a programme of trips including wine/cheese tastings, canoeing and horse riding excursions. Used by tour operators. This site is well placed for visiting the châteaux of the Loire or the cities of Orléans and Tours.

Facilities

Three sanitary blocks offer British style WCs, washbasins in cabins and pushbutton showers. Laundry facilities. Shop selling provisions. Terraced bar and restaurant with reasonably priced food and drink (15/4-15/9). Swimming pool and two shallower pools for children (1/5-30/9). Trampolines, a ball crawl with slide and climbing wall, bouncy inflatable. Multisport court. Off site: Walking and cycling. Bicycle hire 1 km. Fishing 500 m. Golf 10 km. Riding 12 km.

Open: 9 April - 30 September.

Directions

Site is just outside Candé-sur-Beuvron on D751, between Amboise and Blois. From Amboise, turn right just before Candé, then left into site. GPS: N47:29.389 E01:15.515

Charges guide

Per unit incl. 2 persons	€ 15,00 - € 26,00
incl. electricity	€ 19,50 - € 30,00
extra person	€ 5,00 - € 7,50
child (3-9 yrs)	€ 3,50 - € 5,50
animal	€ 3,70

Camping Cheques accepted.

LA GRANDE TORTUE

Camping Caravaning International ★★★★

La Grande Tortue

3, route de Pontlevoy
41120 CANDÉ-sur-BEUVRON
Tel: 0033 254 44 15 20 - Fax: 0033 254 44 19 45
Website: www.la-grande-tortue.com

FREE 2009 brochure

Over 60 French campsites, hand picked for you

Call for your copy today **01580 214000**

FREE CHILD PLACES ON MANY SITES

BOOK THIS SITE
CALL 01580 214000
...we'll arrange everything

The Travel Service

Check real time availability and at-the-gate prices...

www.**alanrogers**.com

The Travel Service ...we'll arrange everything BOOK THIS SITE CALL 01580 214000

FR41040 Camping Château des Marais

27 rue de Chambord, F-41500 Muides-sur-Loire (Loir-et-Cher)

Tel: **02 54 87 05 42**. Email: **chateau.des.marais@wanadoo.fr**   www.alanrogers.com/FR41040

The Château des Marais campsite is well situated to visit the chateau at Chambord (its park is impressive) and the other châteaux in the 'Vallée des Rois'. The site, providing 133 large touring pitches, all with electricity (6/10A), water and drainage and with ample shade, is situated in the oak and hornbeam woods of its own small château. An excellent swimming complex offers pools and two flumes. English is spoken and the reception from the enthusiastic owners and the staff is very welcoming. Used by tour operators (90 pitches).

Facilities

Four modern sanitary blocks have good facilities including some large showers and washbasins en-suite. Washing machine. Motorcaravan service point. Shop and takeaway. Bar/restaurant with large terrace. Swimming complex with heated and unheated pools, slide and cover for cooler weather. TV room. Bicycle hire. Fishing pond. Excursions to Paris, an entertainment programme and canoe trips organised in high season. Internet access. Off site: Riding 5 km. Golf 12 km. Muides-sur-Loire (five minutes walk).

Open: 15 May - 15 September.

Directions

From A10 autoroute take exit 16 to Mer, cross the Loire to join D951 and follow signs. Site signed off D103 to southwest of village. 600 m. from junction with D112. GPS: N47°39.948 E01°31.726

Charges guide

Per pitch incl. 2 persons	€ 24,00 - € 32,00
extra person	€ 6,00 - € 8,00
child (under 5 yrs)	free - € 5,00
electricity (6/10A)	€ 5,00 - € 7,00
dog	€ 5,00

Credit cards accepted for amounts over € 80.

FR41100 Camping les Saules

Route de Contres (D102), F-41700 Cheverny (Loir-et-Cher)

Tel: **02 54 79 90 01**. Email: **contact@camping-cheverny.com**   www.alanrogers.com/FR41100

Set in the heart of the châteaux region, has recently been revitalised and re-opened by a local family. The tastefully renovated traditional reception buildings in their lakeside setting give a very pleasant welcome. There are 166 good size, level pitches with 149 available for touring units. All have shade from the many trees on the site, 150 have electrical connections (a few will require leads longer than 25 m.), and there are ample water taps. Cheverny is considered to have the best interior and furnishings of all the châteaux in the Loire region, and many others are within easy reach. A 'Sites et Paysages' member.

Facilities

Two sanitary blocks with toilets, showers, washbasins in cubicles and facilities for disabled visitors. Laundry facilities. Motorcaravan service point. Gas supplies. Shop. Restaurant (July/Aug). Bar. Snack bar and takeaway. Swimming and paddling pools. TV/social room with toys, board games, books. Two play areas. Large grass area for ball games. Minigolf (free). Fishing. Bicycle hire. Internet and WiFi. Off site: Golf 3 km. Riding 3 km.

Open: 1 April - 30 September.

Directions

From Cheverny take D102 south towards Contres. Site is on the right after about 2 km. GPS: N47°30.000 E01°27.668

Charges 2009

Per unit incl. 2 persons, car and electricity	€ 19,50 - € 29,00
extra person	€ 4,50
child (4-10 yrs)	€ 2,00
dog	€ 2,00

CHEVERNY CAMPING LES SAULES ★★★★

In the heart of the Kings Valley, next to the Château of Cheverny and its 18-hole golf course, just near the forest, welcome to the quiet atmosphere of the Camping Les Saules and its green and shady setting of 8 hectares.

Excellent starting point for walking and cycling.

Rental of chalets.

CAMPING LES SAULES F. 41700 CHEVERNY

Tel. : 33 (0) 254 799 001
Fax : 33 (0) 254 792 834

www.camping-cheverny.com - contact@camping-cheverny.com

CHEVERNY
et découvrez Les secrets de Moulinsart

Check real time availability and at-the-gate prices...

www.alanrogers.com

FR45030 Camping Touristique de Gien

Rue des Iris, Poilly-lez-Gien, F-45500 Gien (Loiret)

Tel: 02 38 67 12 50. Email: camping-gien@wanadoo.fr — www.alanrogers.com/FR45030

BOOK THIS SITE
CALL 01580 214000
...we'll arrange everything
The Travel Service

This open, attractive site lies immediately across the river from Gien on the opposite bank of the Loire with views of the château and town. It has a long river frontage, which includes a good expanse of sandy beach. There are 150 well-sized, level, grassed touring pitches. All have electricity (4/10A), 18 have water and drainage (between two). Some are shaded by mature trees. The bar and restaurant, with a large outdoor area, are open to the public and provide a sociable gathering point. Soirées with different themes are held at least weekly in July and August. The town, with its château, is within a kilometre across the bridge. The site makes an excellent base for exploring the eastern end of the Loire valley, and the town of Gien itself is of interest. The festival celebrating the heritage of this part of the Loire at Ascensiontide is well worth a visit.

Facilities

Three toilet blocks (no paper or seats in toilets, some Turkish), one heated, and one new with an en-suite unit for disabled people. Laundry. Bar and restaurant (1/4-30/9), both open to the public. Shop 20 m. outside gates (all year). Swimming pool paddling pools (15/6-15/9). Play area and grassed games area. Minigolf. Bicycle hire. Canoe hire. Fishing. Off site: Town centre less than 1 km. Hypermarket 1 km. Riding 2 km. Golf 25 km.

Open: 1 March - 9 November.

Directions

North of the river, from north (A77 and RN7) take D940 to Gien; from southeast (A77 and RN7) and from west take D952 to Gien. Follow signs to Centre Ville and turn south over bridge. At traffic lights turn west on D951 towards Pouilly-lez-Gien. Site is signed 300 m. on right. If south of the river, from D940 turn west onto D951 and site is 300 m. on right. GPS: N47:40.850 E02:37.090

Charges guide

Per unit incl. 2 persons	€ 13,00 - € 19,00
extra person	€ 6,00
child (under 12 yrs)	€ 4,00
electricity (4/10A)	€ 3,50 - € 5,00

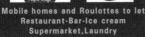

CAMPING TOURISTIQUE DE GIEN
★★★
Rue des iris - 45500 Poilly lez Gien (GIEN)
Tél : 02 38 67 12 50 - Fax : 02 38 67 12 18
Email : camping-gien@wanadoo.fr
www.camping-gien.com
Plenty touristic and cultural sites
Trips, canoes and mountain bikes (to let), fishing
Covered swimming pool, mini golf, maxi trampoline
Entertainment and theme evenings
Mobile homes and Roulottes to let
Restaurant-Bar-Ice cream
Supermarket, Laundry

FR41060 Siblu Camping Domaine de Dugny

La Cabinette (CD45), F-41150 Onzain (Loir-et-Cher)

Tel: 02 54 20 70 66. Email: domainededugny@siblu.fr — www.alanrogers.com/FR41060

This well organised campsite began as an 'à la ferme' back in 1976. Since then it has grown into an eight hectare site surrounded by acres of quiet farmland. Now owned by the Siblu Group, it opens all year round. There are 300 pitches, with mobile homes (privately owned and to rent) leaving 190 tourist pitches. Generously sized, they are partially separated, some with shade and others open. All but 30 have electricity (10A), water and drainage. This is a campsite for active people. Play areas and sports fields includes equipment for youngsters, a trampoline, minigolf, football and basketball.

Facilities

Three sanitary units include some washbasins in cubicles and provision for disabled people. Dishwashing and laundry sinks. Bread, ices, soft drinks and gas are stocked. Restaurant and takeaway. Barbecue evenings. Heated outdoor pool complex (one pool with slides) and paddling pool. Play areas. Minigolf, volleyball, basketball and pétanque. Internet point. Pony and horse riding. Microlight flights. Pedaloes/rowing boats for hire. Children's disco. Campfire evenings.

Open: All year.

Directions

Onzain is southwest of Blois (15 km.), on opposite side of river from Chaumont-sur-Loire. Take N152 (Blois Tours), turn right onto D1 (Onzain). Site signed after railway bridge. Turn right onto D58, then left onto D45. Follow signs. GPS: N47:31.563 E01:11.231

Charges guide

Per person	€ 7,00 - € 14,00
pitch	€ 5,50 - € 9,00
electricity	€ 5,50

Check real time availability and at-the-gate prices...
www.alanrogers.com

FR45040 Camping Hortus

1 route d'Orléans (D60), Sully-sur-Loire, F-45600 Saint Père-sur-Loire (Loiret)

Tel: **02 38 36 35 94**. Email: info@camping-hortus.com   www.alanrogers.com/FR45040

Across the river from Sully-sur-Loire with its imposing château, this site makes a comfortable base for exploring this part of the Loire valley. The present owners acquired it from the local authority in 2005 and their drive and initiative have turned it into an attractive site with many facilities. There are 80 well-sized touring pitches, all with electricity, water and drainage, on level grass and divided into groups of four by hedges. There is also an area for tents between the main pitches and the river. Trees provide a degree of shade. New swimming pools, bar and (open air) restaurant make this an ideal site for a quiet family holiday. A 'Sites et Paysages' member.

Facilities

Two modern toilet blocks, one heated, are well equipped with some washbasins in cabins and separate suite for disabled visitors. Small shop for essentials. Bar and open air restaurant (1/5-30/9). Heated, covered swimming pool (12 x 8 m.) and separate paddling pool (both 1/5-30/9). Fishing. Bicycle hire. Minigolf. Play areas. Off site: Town and Château 1.5 km. Two supermarkets 2 km. Golf 2 km. Riding 4 km.

Open: All year.

Directions

From Orleans take N60 then the D952 towards Gien. Turn south on D948 for Sully-sur-Loire. In St Père-sur-Loire, at roundabout just before river bridge, turn west on D60 signed St Benoit-sur-Loire. Site is 300 m. on left. GPS: N47:46.264 E02:21.728

Charges guide

Per unit incl. 2 persons and electricity	€ 16,50 - € 20,50
extra person	€ 3,70 - € 5,50
child (3-12 yrs)	free - € 3,50
dog	€ 2,00

HORTUS, LE JARDIN DE SULLY

CAMPING *** with 100% pitches for tourism

- **At 135 km of Paris**
- **Covered swimming pool**
- **Rental of mobile homes and tent bungalows**

Open all year long

www.camping-hortus.com

FR45010 Kawan Village les Bois du Bardelet

Route de Bourges, Le Petit Bardelet, F-45500 Gien (Loiret)

Tel: **02 38 67 47 39**. Email: contact@bardelet.com   www.alanrogers.com/FR45010

This attractive, lively family site, in a rural setting, is well situated for exploring the less well known eastern part of the Loire Valley. Two lakes (one for boating, one for fishing) and a pool complex have been attractively landscaped in 12 hectares of former farmland, blending old and new with natural wooded areas and more open field areas with rural views. Bois du Bardelet provides 260 pitches with around 130 for touring units. All are larger than 100 sq.m. and have electrical connections, with some new, luxury pitches of 200 sq.m. with water and waste water. The communal areas are based on attractively converted former farm buildings with a wide range of leisure facilities.

Facilities

Two sanitary blocks (only one open outside 15/6-31/8) include washbasins in cabins. Facilities for disabled visitors and babies. Washing machines. Shop (1/4-30/9). Bar. Snack bar, takeaway, restaurant (all 1/4-14/9) and pizzeria (8/7-21/8). Outside pool (1/5-31/8). Indoor children's pool. Indoor pool, heated (with purchased club card). Aqua-gym, fitness and jacuzzi room. Games area. Archery. Canoeing and fishing. Tennis. Minigolf. Boules. Bicycle hire. Playground. Internet access. Off site: Supermarket 5 km. Riding 7 km. Golf 25 km. Walking and cycling routes.

Open: 1 April - 30 September.

Directions

From Gien take D940 (Bourges). After 5 km. turn right and right again to cross road and follow site signs. From Argent sur Sauldre take D940 (Gien). Site signed to right after 15 km. Entrance is 200 m. past what looks like the first opening to site. GPS: N47:38.491 E02:36.917

Charges 2009

Per unit incl. 2 persons and electricity	€ 19,20 - € 32,00
luxury pitch	€ 33,00 - € 44,00
extra person (over 2 yrs)	€ 4,90 - € 6,50
Camping Cheques accepted.	

The Travel Service ...we'll arrange everything

BOOK THIS SITE CALL 01580 214000

FR49000 Camping du Lac de Maine

Avenue du Lac de Maine, F-49000 Angers (Maine-et-Loire)

Tel: 02 41 73 05 03. Email: camping@lacdemaine.fr   www.alanrogers.com/FR49000

The Lac de Maine campsite is situated in the heart of the Anjou region. Most of the 141 level touring pitches are part grass and part gravel hardstanding, with the remainder all gravel. All have water, drainage and electricity (6/10A). The main entrance has a height restriction of 3.2 m., although there is an alternative gate for higher vehicles. This is a useful site, open for a long season and only five minutes from the centre of Angers. With wide access roads, it is also suitable for American RVs. This site has the advantage of being at the southern end of the Parc de Loisirs du Lac de Maine. The adjacent 100 acre lake has a sandy beach for swimmers, windsurfing, sailing and pedaloes available, while the parkland provides tennis courts and a nature reserve.

Facilities

Two sanitary blocks, one which can be heated and includes some washbasins in cubicles. British style WCs (no seats). Facilities for babies and visitors with disabilities. Dishwashing and laundry facilities. Motorcaravan service point. Reception stocks gas. Restaurant/bar (both 15/6-15/9). Heated L-shaped swimming pool (1/6-15/9). Spa. Volleyball. Pétanque. Bicycle hire. Internet point. Barrier card deposit € 20. Off site: Lake beach 500 m. Fishing 1 km. Riding 3 km. Golf 5 km.

Open: 25 March - 10 October.

Directions

Site is just west of Angers near the N23 (Angers - Nantes road). Turn south at signs for Quartier de Maine and Lac de Maine. Follow signs for Pruniers and Bouchemaine. Site on D111 and signed. GPS: N47:27.277 W00:35.777

Charges guide

Per unit incl. 2 persons	€ 11,85 - € 17,00
extra person	€ 3,00
child (under 13 yrs)	€ 2,00
electricity (10A)	€ 3,40
animal	€ 2,00
Camping Cheques accepted.	

Camping du Lac de Maine
☆☆☆☆

Discover this pretty campsite nestling in the heart of the Anjou wine region, close to the historic town of Angers and a beautiful vast 100 ha lake.

Openingdates: 25/03 to 10/10/2009

Mobile homes and bungalows for rent

Heated Swimming Pool, Paddling pool, SPA, Restaurant, Bar, Takeaway, Bike hire, Internet Facilities (WiFi)...

Avenue du Lac de Maine - F-49000 Angers - Tel: 0033 (0)2.41.73.05.03
Fax: 0033 (0)2.41.73.02.20 - camping@lacdemaine.fr - www.camping-angers.fr

FR49010 Castel Camping l'Etang de la Brèche

5 impasse de la Brèche (RN152), F-49730 Varennes-sur-Loire (Maine-et-Loire)

Tel: 02 41 51 22 92. Email: mail@etang-breche.com   www.alanrogers.com/FR49010

The Saint Cast family have developed L'Etang de la Brèche with care and attention. The site provides 116 large, level touring pitches with shade from trees and bushes. Less shaded areas are used for recreation. There are electrical connections to all pitches (some long cable may be required), with water and drainage on 63 of them. The restaurant, bar and terrace, also open to the public, provides a social base and is popular with British visitors. The pool complex includes one with a removable cover, one outdoor, and one for toddlers. The site is used by tour operators (85 pitches).

Facilities

Three toilet blocks, modernised to good standards, include facilities for babies with two units for people with disabilities. Washing up sinks and laundry. Shop and epicerie. Restaurant, pizzeria and takeaway. Heated pools. Tennis, basketball, minigolf and a field for football. Bicycle hire. General room, games and TV rooms. Internet point. Varied sporting and entertainment programme (10/7-25/8). Pony riding. Child minding is arranged in afternoons. Torch useful. Off site: Golf 7 km.

Open: 30 April - 15 September.

Directions

Site is 100 m. north off the main N152, about 4 km. northeast of Saumur on the north bank of the Loire. GPS: N47:14.839 W00:00.029

Charges 2009

Per unit incl. 2 persons	
and electricity	€ 16,00 - € 36,50
with water and drainage	€ 18,00 - € 39,00
extra person	€ 5,00 - € 8,00
child (4-10 yrs)	€ 3,00 - € 4,00
7th night free in low season.	

Check real time availability and at-the-gate prices...

www.alanrogers.com

BOOK THIS SITE
CALL 01580 214000
...we'll arrange everything
The Travel Service

FR49040 Camping de l'Etang

Mobile homes ▶ page 499

Route de Saint-Mathurin, F-49320 Brissac (Maine-et-Loire)

Tel: **02 41 91 70 61**. Email: **info@campingetang.com**   www.alanrogers.com/FR49040

At Camping de l'Etang many of the 124 level touring pitches have pleasant views across the countryside. Separated and numbered, some have a little shade and all have electricity with water and drainage nearby. 21 are fully serviced. A small bridge crosses the river Aubance which runs through the site (well fenced) and there are two lakes where fisherman can enjoy free fishing. The site has its own vineyard and the wine produced can be purchased on the campsite. The adjacent Parc de Loisirs is a paradise for young children with many activities (entry is free for campers). These include boating, pedaloes, pony rides, miniature train, water slide, bouncy castle and swings. Originally the farm of the Château de Brissac (yet only 24 km. from the lovely town of Angers), this is an attractive campsite retaining much of its rural charm. A 'Sites et Paysages' member.

Facilities

Three well maintained toilet blocks provide all the usual facilities. Laundry facilities. Baby room. Disabled visitors are well catered for. Motorcaravan service point. Small shop and takeaway snacks when bar is closed. Bar/restaurant serves crêpes, salads, etc (evenings 15/6-31/8). Swimming pool (heated and covered) and paddling pool. Fishing. Play area. Bicycle hire. Wide variety of evening entertainment in high season. WiFi. No electric barbecues. Off site: Golf and riding 10 km. Sailing 25 km.

Open: 15 May - 15 September.

Directions

Brissac-Quincé is 17 km. southeast of Angers on D748 towards Poitiers. Do not enter the town but turn north on D55 (site signed) in direction of St Mathurin. GPS: N47:21.560 W00:26.065

Charges guide

Per unit incl. 2 persons	€ 15,00 - € 29,00
extra person	€ 5,00 - € 7,00
child (0-10 yrs)	free - € 4,00
electricity	free - € 3,00
dog	€ 3,00 - € 4,00

On the route of the châteaux of the Loire, 2 campsites welcome you

The same spirit of hospitality

CAMPING DE CHANTEPIE **
S'-Hilaire-S'-Florent - 49400 SAUMUR
Tél. +33 (0)2 41 67 95 34 - Fax +33 (0)2 41 67 95 85
e-mail : info@campingchantepie.com
www.campingchantepie.com

Association de
Chantepie et de l'Etang
N° 2002/DRTEFP/280

CAMPING DE L'ETANG ****
Route de S'-Mathurin
49320 BRISSAC
Tél. +33 (0)2 41 91 70 61 - Fax +33 (0)2 41 91 72 65
e-mail : info@campingetang.com
www.campingetang.com

FR49020 Camping de Chantepie

Saint Hilaire-Saint Florent, F-49400 Saumur (Maine-et-Loire)

Tel: **02 41 67 95 34**. Email: **info@campingchantepie.com**   www.alanrogers.com/FR49020

On arriving at Camping de Chantepie with its colourful, floral entrance, a friendly greeting awaits at reception, set beside a restored farmhouse. The site is owned by a charitable organisation which provides employment for local people with disabilities. Linked by gravel roads (which can be dusty) the 150 grass touring pitches are level and spacious, with some new larger ones (200 sq.m. at extra cost – state preference when booking). All pitches have electricity (6/10A) and are separated by low hedges of flowers and trees which offer some shade. This is a good site for families. The panoramic views over the Loire from the pitches on the terraced perimeter of the meadow are stunning and from here a path leads to the river valley. Leisure activities for all ages are arranged in July/Aug. by the Chantepie Club, including wine tastings, excursions and canoeing. A 'Sites et Paysages' member.

Facilities

The toilet block is clean and facilities are good with washbasins in cubicles, new showers (men and women separately) and facilities for disabled visitors. Laundry facilities. Baby area. Shop, bar, terraced café and takeaway (all 15/6-31/8). Covered and heated pool, outdoor pool and paddling pool. Play area with apparatus. Terraced minigolf. TV. Video games. Pony rides. Bicycle hire. Internet access. WiFi. Off site: Fishing 500 m. Golf, riding 2 km. Sailing 7 km.

Open: 15 May - 15 September.

Directions

St Hilaire-St Florent is 2 km. west of Saumur. Take D751 (Gennes). Right at roundabout in St Hilaire-St Florent and on until Le Poitrineau and campsite sign, then turn left. Continue for 3 km. then turn right into site road. GPS: N47:17.629 W00:08.571

Charges 2009

Per unit incl. 2 persons	€ 15,00 - € 29,00
extra person	€ 5,00 - € 7,00
child (3-10 yrs)	€ 3,00 - € 4,00
electricity	€ 3,00

Check real time availability and at-the-gate prices...
www.alanrogers.com

Rue de Verden, Ile d'Offard, F-49400 Saumur (Maine-et-Loire)

Tel: **02 41 40 30 00**. Email: **iledoffard@cvtloisirs.fr**   www.alanrogers.com/FR49080

This site is situated on an island between the banks of the Loire. The 208 touring pitches are at present on grass at the far end or hardstanding nearer the entrance. Pitches have access to electricity hook-ups (10A). A new heated outdoor swimming pool has been completed together with paddling and spa pools. Within walking distance of the centre of Saumur, this site is useful as an overnight stop en route south or as a short-term base from which to visit the numerous châteaux in the region. Fishing is possible in the Loire (permits are available from Saumur).

Facilities

Three sanitary blocks, one heated in winter, include provision for disabled visitors. Toilet facilities are unisex. Block one has a well equipped laundry. The other blocks are only open in high season. Restaurant and bar (early May - late Sept) with takeaway. Internet access. Play area. Some activities and a children's club, wine tastings, etc. in high season. Off site: Thursday market 500 m. Saturday morning market 2 km. Riding 5 km.

Open: 1 March - 15 November.

Directions

From north and A85 exit 3, take N147 south (Saumur). After 2.5 km. turn left (N147 bears right). Follow old road towards river and town. Cross bridge onto island, then first left and site is ahead. GPS: N47:15.457 W00:03.660

Charges guide

Per unit incl. 2 persons	€ 16,00 - € 25,50
extra person	€ 4,00 - € 5,00
child (5-10 yrs)	€ 2,00 - € 2,50
electricity	€ 3,50

Camping Çheques accepted.

Le Camping Ile d'Offard**

Situated on an island in the Loire River, with an outstanding view over Saumur Castle and within walking distance from the town centre is Campsite Ile d'Offard. With its 258 pitches it is an ideal starting point for discovering the beauty of the Loire valley. Walk in the footsteps of French Kings, visit their famous castles and sample the historical vineyards of Saumur, Champigny, Bourgueil, Chinon, and Anjou.
A new heated swimming complex and restaurant are all ready to give you an unforgettable stay...

CAMPING ILE D'OFFARD
rue de Verden - 49400 SAUMUR
Tél. : 0033 241 403 000
Fax : 0033 241 673 781
www.CVTLOISIRS.com   iledoffard@cvtloisirs.fr

Montsabert, F-49320 Coutures (Maine-et-Loire)

Tel: **04 66 73 97 39**. Email: **info@yellohvillage-parcdemontsabert.com**   www.alanrogers.com/FR49060

This extensive site has recently been taken over by a friendly French couple who already have plans for improvements. It has a rural atmosphere in the shadow of Montsabert château, from where visiting peacocks happily roam in the spacious surroundings. The main features are the heated swimming pool (with cover) and the adjoining refurbished, rustic style restaurant. There are 111 large, well marked touring pitches, divided by hedges and all with water tap, drainage and electricity (10A). Picnic tables are provided. The site is used by several small tour operators (12 pitches). Partially wooded by a variety of trees, this site offers the peace of the countryside.

Facilities

The main toilet block can be heated and has washbasins and bidets in cabins and a baby room. Laundry facilities. A second block serves the pool and another provides more WCs. Shop, bar and takeaway (31/5-31/8). Restaurant(14/6-23/8). Heated pool (no Bermuda style shorts) and paddling pool. Sports hall. Minigolf. Tennis. Play area. Bicycle hire. Entertainment (high season). Archery. Riding. Off site: Canoeing nearby. Fishing 5 km. Golf 8 km.

Open: 12 April - 14 September.

Directions

Coutures is 25 km. southeast of Angers on the D751 to Saumur. From A11 take exit 14 and follow signs for Cholet/Poitiers, then Poitiers on D748. At Brissac-Quincé turn northeast on D55 and in 5 km. turn right to Coutures. Montsabert is north of village. GPS: N47:22.464 W00:20.709

Charges guide

Per pitch incl. 2 persons	€ 16,00 - € 25,00
extra person	€ 4,00 - € 4,75
child (1-13 yrs)	€ 2,50 - € 3,20
electricity (10A)	€ 3,50

www.yellohvillage.com tel: +33 466 739 739

185
Check real time availability and at-the-gate prices...
www.**alanrogers**.com

BOOK THIS SITE
CALL 01580 214000
...we'll arrange everything
The Travel Service

BOOK THIS SITE
CALL 01580 214000
...we'll arrange everything
The Travel Service

BOOK THIS SITE
CALL 01580 214000
...we'll arrange everything
The Travel Service

FR49090 Kawan Village l'Isle Verte

Avenue de la Loire, F-49730 Montsoreau (Maine-et-Loire)

Tel: 02 41 51 76 60. Email: isleverte@cvtloisirs.fr

www.alanrogers.com/FR49090

This friendly, natural site, with pitches overlooking the Loire, is just 100 m. from the centre of Montsoreau, an ideal starting point to visit the western Loire area. Most of the 90 shaded, level and good-sized tourist pitches are separated by low hedges but grass tends to be rather sparse during dry spells. All have electricity (16A). Excellent English is spoken in the reception and bar. Fishermen are particularly well catered for here, there being an area to store equipment and live bait (permits are available in Saumur). Attractions within walking distance of the campsite include the château, Troglodyte (mushroom caves and restaurant), both just 500 m., wine tasting in the cellars nearby, and a Sunday market in the town.

Facilities

A single building provides separate male and female toilets. Washbasins, some in cabins, and showers are unisex. Separate facilities for disabled campers. Baby room. Laundry and dishwashing facilities. Motorcaravan service point. Bar and snack bar (1/5-30/9). Swimming and paddling pools (15/5-30/9). Small play area. Boules. Bicycle hire (June - Aug. or by special request). Fishing. Off site: Golf 6 km. Riding 15 km.

Open: 1 April - 30 September.

Directions

Take D947 from Saumur to Montsoreau and site is clearly signed on left along the road into town. GPS: N47:13.092 E00:03.159

Charges 2009

Per unit incl. 2 persons	€ 14,00 - € 18,00
extra person	€ 3,00 - € 3,50
child (5-10 yrs)	€ 2,00 - € 2,50
electricity	€ 3,00

Camping Cheques accepted.

Le Camping Isle verte***

Residing on the banks of the Loire River, 100 m from centre of Montsoreau, this family campsite with 110 pitches is an excellent destination for discovering the Troglodytes (the champignonnière, wine caves within 500m) and Castles of the Loire.
Isle Verte is situated in natural settings, ideal for relaxing holidays. The site has direct access to the banks of the Loire and offers activities for all tastes and ages : excursions, fishing, walking and cycling.

Avenue de la Loire
49730 MONTSOREAU
Tél. : 0033 241 517 660
Fax : 0033 241 510 883
www.campingisleverte.com
isleverte@cvtloisirs.fr

FR49070 Camping Caravaning la Vallée des Vignes

La Croix Patron, F-49700 Concourson-sur-Layon (Maine-et-Loire)

Tel: 02 41 59 86 35. Email: Campingvdv@wanadoo.fr

www.alanrogers.com/FR49070

The enthusiasm of the English owners here comes across instantly in the warm welcome received by their guests. Bordering the Layon river, the 50 good sized touring pitches are reasonably level and fully serviced (10A electricity, water tap and drain). Five pitches have a hardstanding for cars. Attractions include an enclosed bar and restaurant, a generously sized sun terrace surrounding the pool and high season activities for children and adults. These include wine tasting, a hog roast (or similar), competitions and treasure hunts. An ideal base for visiting the châteaux of the Loire and the many caves and vineyards.

Facilities

The toilet block includes washbasins in cabins, and dishwashing facilities at either end. Baby room. Facilities for disabled visitors. Laundry facilities. Bar (from 15/5 or on request) serving meals, snacks and takeaway (from 15/5). Swimming and paddling pools (from 15/5). Playground, games area and football pitch. Minigolf, volleyball, basketball, table tennis. Internet access. Fishing. Caravan storage. Off site: Zoo and rose gardens at Doué-la-Fontaine. Grand Parc Puy du Fou.

Open: 15 April - 15 October.

Directions

Site signed off D960 Doué - Vihiers road, just west of Concourson-sur-Layon. GPS: N47:10.459 W00:20.838

Charges guide

Per unit incl. 2 persons	€ 16,50 - € 22,00
extra person	€ 4,00 - € 5,00
child (2-12 yrs)	€ 2,50 - € 3,00
electricity (10A)	€ 4,00
dog	€ 3,00

Special offers available.

Check real time availability and at-the-gate prices...

www.alanrogers.com

FR49150 Camping le Thouet

Le Côteaux du Chalet, route Bron, F-49260 Montreuil-Bellay (Maine-et-Loire)

Tel: 02 41 38 74 17. Email: contact@campinglethouet.com   www.alanrogers.com/FR49150

Open all year, this countryside site occupies a grassy, tree-lined area with the River Thouet running along the far side from the reception and terrace. The site covers an area of 20 acres occupied in part by 37 good sized, unmarked pitches, 32 for touring and all with 10A electricity. Reception is part of an old farmhouse, the home of the owners who, in winter, provide a warm bathroom for the use of the campers. The owner is English and his wife is multilingual. Beside the swimming pool is an attractive sun terrace together with a bar and restaurant. There is a large hardstanding area, with electricity and water, ideal for winter visitors. This is a peaceful and quiet campsite with families and couples in separate areas. It is a good base for touring the famous châteaux of the Loire. It is a good site for birdwatching (the RSPB has recorded 90 species of birds). Booking advisable in high season.

Facilities

Two modern toilet block including facilities for campers with disabilities and baby room. Bread and much more available by request. Outdoor pool, no paddling pool (1/5-30/9) surrounded by terrace, bar/restaurant (1/4-15/10). Wine tasting. Bicycle hire. Boules. Fishing. Large play area. Boat launching. Birdwatching. Off site: Golf and canoeing 5 km. Riding 10 km. beautiful village of Montreuil Bellay, shops, restaurants etc. (5 minutes drive).

Open: All year.

Directions

From Saumur take N147 towards Poitiers. About 6 km. after Le Coudray Macouard turn left, signed Montreuil Belley Centre Ville. Immediately turn left again. Site well signed in under 2 km.
GPS: N47:07.891 W00:09.554

Charges guide

Per unit incl. 2 persons and electricity (10A)	€ 20,00
extra person	€ 4,00

Camping Le Thouet
49260 Montreuil Bellay France
Tel: 0033 (0)241 387 417
Mob: 0033 (0)619563275
Fax: 0033 (0)241 509 283
E-mail: campinglethouet@alicepro.fr
www.campinglethouet.com

FR49120 Centre Touristique Lac de Ribou

Allée Léon Mandin, F-49300 Cholet (Maine-et-Loire)

Tel: 02 41 49 74 30. Email: info@lacderibou.com   www.alanrogers.com/FR49120

Situated just 58 km. southeast of Nantes and a similar distance from the River Loire at Angers and Saumur, this could be a useful place to break a journey or to spend a few days relaxing. Camping Lac de Ribou, with the adjacent 'Village Vacances', forms a holiday complex in pleasant parkland next to an extensive lake on the outskirts of the busy market town of Cholet. 162 touring pitches are on undulating land (some are sloping), divided by hedges and with mature trees proving shade on many; most have electricity (10A) and 115 also have individual water tap and drainage.

Facilities

Two sanitary blocks provide preset showers, washbasins in cabins and excellent dishwashing and laundry sinks. Facilities for disabled visitors. Motorcaravan service points. Small shop (July/Aug). Bar and 'snackerie' with takeaway (July/Aug). Large heated swimming pool plus smaller pool with slide and a paddling pool (1/6-30/9). Play area. Very full programme of activities for all ages (July/Aug). Off site: Fishing and small beach (no swimming) 500 m. Sailing 1 km. Supermarket 2 km. Riding 5 km. Golf 7 km.

Open: 1 April - 30 September.

Directions

From Cholet ring road east of town, turn east on D20 towards Maulévrier and Mauléon. At roundabout by Leclerc supermarket, take first exit signed to site which is signed 'Parc de Loisirs de Ribou' all around the town.
GPS: N47:02.182 W00:50.624

Charges guide

Per unit incl. 1 or 2 persons	€ 9,45 - € 17,90
extra person	€ 3,00 - € 4,45
electricity (10A)	€ 3,75 - € 5,20
No credit cards.	

Check real time availability and at-the-gate prices...
www.alanrogers.com

FR49170 Camping de Coulvée

Route de Cholet, F-49120 Chemille (Maine-et-Loire)

Tel: **02 41 30 39 97**. Email: **camping-chemille-49@wanadoo.fr**   www.alanrogers.com/FR49170

An exceptionally well cared for and attractive lakeside site with landscaped entrance and gardens. Each of the 53 pitches has tall mature hedges giving plenty of shade and privacy; 41 pitches have their own water and electricity. The good-sized pitches are mostly level. The snack bar, indoor games room and TV room are located within the modern reception building. A wonderful patio area has views across the lake, play area and lawned gardens. A number of chalets are available to rent. The staff are very helpful and we thoroughly enjoyed this very pleasant rural site.

Facilities

One central modern sanitary block, open style basins, preset showers. Separate facilities for disabled visitors. Laundry facilities. Motorcaravan service point. TV, pool table, electronic games, table football. Very good play area. Pedaloes, canoes (life jackets available from reception). Swimming in lake (lifeguard in afternoons, high season only). Miniclub (afternoons in high season). Fishing. Bicycle hire. Internet access. Off site: Shops, bars, restaurants in town 1 km. (lakeside walk). Riding 2 km.

Open: 30 April - 15 September.

Directions

From A87 Angers - Cholet motorway at junction 25, head south on the N160 for 5 km. to the town of Chemillé. Follow the signs for camping to the south side of the town. GPS: N47:12.151 W00:44.065

Charges guide

Per unit incl. 2 persons	€ 10,00 - € 16,00
extra person	€ 3,50
child (under 7 yrs)	€ 2,00
electricity (10A)	€ 3,50

FR49180 Flower Camping Val de Loire

6 rue Ste Baudruehe, F-49350 Les Roisers Sur Loire (Maine-et-Loire)

Tel: **02 41 51 94 33**. Email: **contact@camping-valdeloire.com**   www.alanrogers.com/FR49180

This former municipal site on the outskirts of a village on the River Loire between Saumur and Angers has 84 touring pitches, all with electricity (5/10A), individual water taps and waste water drainage. A further 28 pitches are used for mobile homes, mostly for hire. Recent additions include a pleasant bar with terrace and a marquee for games and entertainment. There are two new heated swimming pools, one covered, the other surrounded by terraces and with a large paddling pool.

Facilities

The main sanitary block is modern if rather drab, with controllable showers and washbasins in cubicles. Two older blocks and a new 'portacabin' unit provide additional facilities. In the main block there are facilities for disabled visitors and a laundry room. Bar with TV serves snacks and bread to order (July/Aug). Covered pool (1/4-30/9). Outdoor pool (1/5-15/9). Children's activities, outings and entertainment in season. Play area. Games room. Minigolf. Tennis. Bicycle hire. Off site: Fishing 800 m. Riding 2 km. Golf 15 km. Boat launching 1 and 15 km. Shops and restaurant in village 800 m.

Open: 1 April - 30 September.

Directions

Les Rosiers is 17 km northwest of Saumur. From A85 motorway at exit 1 take southbound D144 to Beaufort-en-Vallée, then continue south on D59. Site is signed to right on approach to village. From D952 Saumur-Angers road turn north in village to site on left in 800 m. GPS: N47:21.526 W00:13.562

Charges guide

Per unit incl. 2 persons	€ 14,00 - € 20,00
extra person	€ 4,00 - € 5,00
child (2-10 yrs)	€ 3,00 - € 4,00
electricity	€ 4,00

www.flowercampings.com

FR53020 Camping le Malidor

F-53250 Charchigne (Mayenne)

Tel: **02 43 03 99 88**. Email: **le-malidor@orange.fr**   www.alanrogers.com/FR53020

A warm welcome is given by the English owners of this attractive, small, rural site, open all year. It is surrounded by farmland and it provides a real taste of the French countryside. The three private lakes provide great fishing and only a short walk away the path leads to the village. There are 20 pitches with 15 for touring, all with 10A electricity. They are terraced and divided by mature hedges. The surrounding countryside is well worth exploring and this site is a perfect place from which to do so.

Facilities

One sanitary block provides good facilities but none for campers with disabilities. Bar and restaurant. Play area, paddling pool. Boules. Darts, pool table, hall for groups up to 80. Fishing with three lakes (fishing gear and bait available). Minigolf. Bicycle hire. Walks and painting courses. Off site: Village with bar/restaurant and shop 500 m. Beaches 20 km.

Open: All year.

Directions

From A81 (Rennes - Le Mans) take exit 3 for Laval. Head northeast on N162 to Mayenne. Then take N12 in the same direction towards Alençon for 20 km. Just before Javron turn left on D33 to Cherchigne. Then follow signs to site just before Cherghigné. GPS: N48:25.114 W00:24.085

Charges guide

Per unit incl. 2 persons	€ 15,00
extra person	€ 4,00 - € 7,50

FR72070 Camping du Vieux Moulin

Chemin des Bergivaux, F-72340 La Chartre sur le Loir (Sarthe)

Tel: 02 43 44 41 18. Email: camping@lachartre.com   www.alanrogers.com/FR72070

Le Vieux Moulin is located just 8 km. north of Le Mans and, given its close proximity to the A11 and A28 autoroutes, is a convenient site for an overnight stop. Recommended by a reader, we intend to inspect the site next year. There are 100 grassy and well shaded pitches here, as well as a number of chalets which are available for rent. The site is just five minutes from the village of Neuville sur Sarthe where there is a reasonable array of shops and restaurants. The site borders the River Sarthe and has a good range of amenities including a swimming pool, mini golf course and children's playground. Although open for a short season, Le Vieux Moulin also opens for race days at Le Mans' world famous circuit (special rates apply at these times). The close proximity of Le Mans is, of course, a major attraction and the town merits an extended visit. Its cathedral, motor museum and the nearby abbeys of l'Epau and Solesmes are all of particular interest.

Facilities

Two toilet blocks. Swimming pool. Play area. Minigolf. Off site: Neuville sur Sarthe (attractive mediaeval village) 500 m. Fishing. Riding. Golf 5 km. Le Mans 8 km.

Open: 1 July - 30 August, also for some race events (additional charges apply).

Directions

Site is close to the junction of the A11 and A81 motorways. Leave the A11 at Le Mans Nord exit and head north on the D338, passing St Saturnin. Then turn right to join D197 and follow this road to Neuville sur Sarthe. Site is well signed from here. GPS: N47:43.944 E00:34.257

Charges guide

Per unit incl. 2 persons and electricity	€ 16,00
extra person	€ 4,00

Your peaceful green place in the Loir Valley

www.le-vieux-moulin.fr
camping@lachartre.com
+33 (0)2 43 44 41 18

Camping du Vieux Moulin
72340 LA CHARTRE (France)

★★★
Camping
du Vieux moulin

FR72020 Camping Municipal du Lac

Rue du Lac, F-72120 Saint Calais (Sarthe)

Tel: 02 43 35 04 81   www.alanrogers.com/FR72020

Camping du Lac is a pleasant, traditional municipal site with 75 marked pitches (about 60 for touring), most are separated by hedges and all with electricity (10A), water and drainage. A separate area is for tents. In high season there are themed evening walks, competitions and communal meals (campers take their own food and can join in the dancing). Reception is welcoming, the value is excellent and this would make a good night stop or a base for visiting the Le Mans 24 hour race.

Facilities

Two sanitary blocks are old but kept very clean and provide showers and some washbasins in private cabins. Washing machine. Bread and croissants (to order). Two small play areas. Lake fishing. Two mobile homes for rent. Off site: Swimming pool adjacent (free). Local supermarket just a short walk. Riding 10 km. Bicycle hire 15 km. Golf 40 km.

Open: 1 April - 15 October.

Directions

St Calais is 45 km. east of Le Mans. Well signed from N157, site is beside lake north of the town, near the station. Follow signs for campsite and 'Plan d'eau'. GPS: N47:55.638 E00:44.742

Charges guide

Per person	€ 2,60
child (under 12 yrs)	€ 1,30
pitch	€ 2,30
electricity	€ 2,70

No credit cards.

189

FR72080 Camping Lac des Varennes

F-72340 Marcon (Sarthe)

Tel: **02 43 44 13 72**. Email: **camping.des varennes.marcon@wanadoo.fr**   www.alanrogers.com/FR72080

Lac de Varennes is located at the edge of the massive forest of Bercé in the valley of the Loir and has direct lake access. There are 250 pitches here, all grassy and with electrical connections (6/10A). Many also have lake views. The site has its own sandy beach (with a beach volleyball court) and pedaloes and canoes are available for rent. Other on-site amenities include a bar/restaurant (open in July and August) and a shop. In high season, various activities are organised including a club for children and riding. Mobile homes are available for rent. There are more than 300 km. of footpaths and cycle routes through the Forêt de Bercé and the site owners will be pleased to recommend routes. A little further afield, the vineyards of Côteaux de Loir are of interest and the châteaux of the Loire to the south, will need little introduction.

Facilities

Shop (July/Aug). Bar, restaurant and takeaway (July/Aug). Play area. Games room/TV. Tennis. Archery. Motorcaravan services. Organised entertainment (JulyAug). Direct access to lake. Off site: Walking and cycling in the forest. Châteaux of the Loire. Le Mans.

Open: 27 March - 2 November.

Directions

From Château du Loir, head south on the D938 and cross the Loir. Then head east on the D305 to Marçon, from where the site is well signed. GPS: N47:42.719 E00:29.982

Charges guide

Per unit incl. 2 persons and electricity	€ 12,60 - € 16,50
extra person	€ 3,50 - € 4,70
child (under 13 yrs)	€ 1,70 - € 2,30
dog	€ 1,30 - € 1,80

**Camping
du Lac des Varennes** * * *

Loir Valley

open from 27/01/2009 to 02/11/2009

In the heart of the Loir Valley, in edge of a splendid lake of 50ha, you have found **the ideal place for an unforgatable stay.**

You will be allured by this area with the richest architectural, wine and gastronomical heritage.

72340 Marçon, phone : +33 (0)2 43 44 13 72
camping@lacdesvarennes.com www.lacdesvarennes.com
Le Mans, Tours, direction Chateau du Loir, Marçon,
the site is 800 m west from Marçon by D61

FR72030 Castel Camping le Château de Chanteloup

F-72460 Sillé-le-Philippe (Sarthe)

Tel: **02 43 27 51 07**. Email: **chanteloup.souffront@wanadoo.fr**   www.alanrogers.com/FR72030

An attractive and peaceful site close to Le Mans, Chanteloup is situated in the park of a 19th-century château in the heart of the Sarthe countryside. There are 100 pitches all with 6A electricity although long leads will be required in some places. Some are in the woods, many are around the edges of the lawns and completely open, and a few overlook the lake, so there are differing degrees of shade throughout the site. This lack of regimentation enhances the atmosphere and the spacious feeling in the grounds surrounding the old château.

Facilities

All sanitary facilities are in the château outbuildings and are well maintained and kept very clean. Washbasins are in cabins. Dishwashing and laundry facilities. Small shop, takeaway and restaurant with covered outdoor seating (all 5/7-24/8). Bar (all season). Swimming pool (fenced). Play area (parental supervision essential). Games room, tennis, volleyball, table tennis. Mountain bike hire. Organised activities (high season). WiFi. Off site: Riding 7 km. Golf 10 km. Tennis club in Le Mans.

Open: 30 May - 30 August.

Directions

Sillé-le-Philippe is 18 km. northeast of Le Mans on the D301 to Bonnétable. From autoroute take exit 23, follow signs for Le Mans and Tours, then Le Mans and Savigné l'Evèque. Site is to the east just off main road and signed on southern edge of Sillé. GPS: N48:06.281 E00:20.424

Charges 2009

Per person	€ 6,00 - € 10,30
pitch	€ 9,90 - € 15,50
electricity	€ 3,80

Less 10% outside 24/6-20/8. Charges are higher during the 24 hr race week at Le Mans.

Check real time availability and at-the-gate prices...

www.**alanrogers**.com

FR79050 Kawan Village du Bois Vert

14 rue Boisseau, le Tallud, F-79200 Parthenay (Deux-Sèvres)

Tel: **05 49 64 78 43**. Email: **bois-vert@wanadoo.fr**   www.alanrogers.com/FR79050

This former municipal site is now operated by a campsite group although so far it has changed little. There are 88 pitches of which 74 are for touring, all with electricity (10A) and 30 also with water and drainage. There are 15 mobile homes to rent. Pitches are separated by hedges and there are mature trees providing some shade. The site is on the River Thouet and although there is a secure fence, there is a steep drop to the river bank. Pleasant walkways along both sides and a footbridge close by enable you to walk into the old walled town.

Facilities

Two very traditional sanitary blocks both in need of attention. One has unisex toilets (a few British-style but seatless), showers and washbasins in cubicles. Primitive dishwashing and laundry sinks. The second is slightly better. Facilities for disabled visitors, incl. new mobile homes. Bar with snackbar and takeaway (1/5-30/9). Bread can be ordered. New heated swimming pool. TV. Table tennis and boules. Small play area. Tickets available for Futuroscope and Puy du Fou. Off site: Motorcaravan service point adjacent. Fishing 100 m. Base de Loisirs nearby. Riding and golf 15 km.

Open: 1 April - 30 September.

Directions

Parthenay is 50 km. west of Poitiers (and the A10) via the N149 to Bressuire and Nantes. Site is southwest of the town at Le Tallud on the D949 La Roche sur Yon road. Take ring road and site is on right as you join D949.
GPS: N46:38.486 W00:16.035

Charges guide

Per unit incl. 2 persons and electricity	€ 16,50 - € 19,50
extra person	€ 4,00 - € 5,00
child (2-10 yrs)	€ 2,00

Camping Cheques accepted.

Le Camping du Bois vert****

On the banks of the Thouet River, Camping du Bois Vert will charm you with its tranquillity and serenity.

This 88 pitch site is situated in the heart of Parthenay, a town full of art, culture and history. You will have many things to do and places to see: Visit Le quartier St Jacques, walks in the Poitevin Marsh, discovering the "Moutons Village" or even join one of the many festivals such as "Festival des Jeux"... Camping du Bois Vert sees the completion of its new heated swimming pool in 2007.

14 rue Boisseau - Le Tallud
79200 PARTHENAY

Tél. 0033 549 647 843
Fax : 0033 549 959 668
www.camping-boisvert.com
boisvert@cvtloisirs.fr

FR79020 Camping de Courte Vallée

F-79600 Airvault (Deux-Sèvres)

Tel: **05 49 64 70 65**. Email: **camping@caravanningfrance.com**   www.alanrogers.com/FR79020

This small and beautifully landscaped site is family run. Set in ten acres of parkland close to the Thouet river, it is within walking distance of Airvault (the birthplace of Voltaire). In the heart of rural France and off the main tourist tracks, the site offers tranquility and a warm and friendly atmosphere in surroundings maintained to the highest standards. There are 64 grass pitches, many with electricity, water and drainage which makes the site ideal for a long stay to explore the area. Nearby are Puy du Fou, Fontevraud Abbey, Doué la Fontaine zoo and the châteaux of Saumur and Oiron.

Facilities

A modern unisex block has spacious cubicles for showers and washbasins, and shower and WC cubicles for disabled visitors, all kept to a very high standard of cleanliness. Dishwashing area under cover. Washing machine and dryers. Reception sells 'frites', snacks, a selection of beers and wine and ice cream. Internet access. Swimming pool. Boules. Play area. Caravan storage. Wine tasting events and barbecues. Coffee bar. Off site: Airvault (birthplace of Voltaire) is a 10-15 minute walk. Fishing 300 m. Riding 8 km.

Open: All year.

Directions

From D938 (Parthenay-Thouars) take D725 Airvault. On approaching village turn left over bridge. At T-junction turn sharp left, second exit at roundabout, left at junction to site on left. Note: caravans are not allowed in village. GPS: N46:49.937 W00:08.909

Charges guide

Per person	€ 7,00 - € 8,00
child (under 11 yrs)	€ 3,00 - € 5,00
pitch	€ 10,00 - € 12,00
electricity (8A)	€ 4,00

No credit cards.

BOOK THIS SITE
CALL 01580 214000
...we'll arrange everything
The Travel **Service**

Check real time availability and at-the-gate prices...
www.**alanrogers**.com

The Travel Service ...we'll arrange everything **CALL 01580 214000** **BOOK THIS SITE**

FR79060 Camping Indigo Le Lidon

F-79210 Saint Hilaire-la-Palud (Deux-Sèvres)

Tel: **05 49 35 33 64**. Email: **le-lidon@camping-indigo.com**　　www.alanrogers.com/FR79060

Le Lidon is a member of the Indigo group of campsites. It is located within the Marais Poitevin, an enchanting region of over 400 km. of rivers, canals and fens lying to the west of Niort. This site has 140 grassy pitches scattered across 3 hectares. Larger 'Espace' (120 sq.m) pitches are also available. The site's selection of rented accommodation includes fully equipped, Canadian-style tents, chalets and caravans. The Marais Poitevin is undeniably best explored by canoe or punt and it is possible to rent these on site. During high season, an activity and entertainment programme is organised including a children's club and various family activities. The site bar/restaurant is open in July and August and specializes in local cuisine. The Marais Mouillé makes up around a third of the Marais Poitevin, but it is the best known part, and is otherwise known as La Venise Verte (Green Venice), with miles of conches (channels) and drainage ditches overshadowed by ash and poplars.

Facilities

Shop. Bar. Snack bar. Swimming pool. Play area. Direct access to river. Fishing. Canoe hire. Entertainment and activity programme. Tents, chalets and caravans for rent. Off site: St Hilaire La Palud with a good selection of shops and cafes, as well as an open air cinema. Fishing (river). La Maison des Oiseaux (ornithological centre). Vendee beaches 50 km. Cycle and walking tracks. Riding.

Open: 5 April - 30 September.

Directions

St Hilaire-la-Palud lies midway between Niort and La Rochelle. From the north (Niort) leave A10 at exit 33 and head west on the N248 as far as Epannes. Head north on the D1 to Sansais and then west on the D3 to St Hilaire-la-Palud. Site is well signed to the right after the village. GPS: N46:17.028 W00:44.607

Charges 2009

Per unit incl. 2 persons	€ 19,00 - € 25,40
extra person	€ 5,20 - € 6,00
child (2-7 yrs)	€ 2,00 - € 2,60

tel: +33 (0) 4 37 64 22 33 www.camping-indigo.com

Camping Indigo Le Lidon ★★

In the heart of the Poitou fens, A haven of peace and greenery...

Wood & canvas tents, bungalows and chalets to rent

Heated swimming-pool, Bar restaurant, Nature activities, Boat trips...

Lieu-Dit Lidon - 79210 St-Hilaire-La-Palud
Tel : (33) 5 49 35 33 64

www.camping-indigo.com/le_lidon

FR79030 Puy Rond Camping

Cornet, F-79300 Bressuire (Deux-Sèvres)

Tel: **05 49 72 43 22**. Email: **info@puyrondcamping.com**　　www.alanrogers.com/FR79030

This small site with just 21 pitches is owned and run by Mr and Mrs Robert Smith who have made major changes and improvements. It is particularly well sited for those travelling south on the non-motorway route from the Normandy ferry ports. The flat and level pitches are of a good size and all have 6A electricity. Bressuire, built in the shadow of the walls of an 11th- and 13th-century castle, is the second most important town in the department of Deux Sevres.

Facilities

The small toilet block provides showers, washbasins and WCs, Baby bath. Facilities for disabled visitors. Motorcaravan service point. Swimming pool (unheated). Off site: Bressuire with good range of shops, supermarkets and an interesting market 1 km. Local 'caves' sell a variety of wines. Puy du Fou 35 km.

Open: 1 April - 15 October.

Directions

From northwest keep on N149 towards 'centre ville'. Go down hill, pass car hire outlet and after a few metres turn right on D38. Pass cattle market and turn right, keep on but turn right immediately before STOP sign. Turn left towards the site. GPS: N46:49.780 W00:30.090

Charges guide

Per unit incl. 2 persons	€ 12,00 - € 16,50
extra person	€ 2,50 - € 3,00
electricity	€ 3,50

Check real time availability and at-the-gate prices...

www.**alanrogers**.com

FR79040 Camping de la Venise Verte

178 route des Bords de Sèvre, F-79510 Coulon (Deux-Sèvres)

Tel: 05 49 35 90 36. Email: accueil@camping-laveniseverte.fr

www.alanrogers.com/FR79040

This family run site on the edge of the Sevre Nortaise and the Marais Poitevin is ideal for short or long stays. With canoe and cycle hire on site you have no excuse for not exploring the local area. In the Deux-Sèvres, the 'department of discovery', so named because it has two rivers named Sèvre, the Noirtaise and Nantaise, the Venise Verte provides an excellent site. There are 140 flat pitches here with 100 used for touring units, the remainder occupied by mobile homes. The pitches are of a good size, some with 10A electricity, water and drainage and some shade. A 'Sites et Paysages' member.

Facilities

Modern, heated toilet facilities are of a high standard with free showers. Washing machine and dryer. Motorcaravan services. Restaurant/bar. Takeaway on request. Swimming pool (1/7-31/8). Play area. Bicycle and canoe hire. Boules area. Barbecues are not permitted. Off site: Coulon 1.0 km. and boat trips in the Marais. Ideal for walking, fishing, cycling or canoeing. Fishing 200 m. Golf and riding 15 km.

Open: 1 April - 30 October.

Directions

From Niort take N11 towards La Rochelle. Turn on the D3 towards Sansais and then north on D1 (Coulon). At traffic lights head towards 'centre ville' (Coulon) at mini-roundabout turn slightly right. Follow Sevre Noirtaise for 1.5 km. to site right. GPS: N46:18.888 W00:36.538

Charges 2009

Per unit incl. 2 persons and electricity	€ 18,00 - € 29,00
extra person	€ 4,00 - € 6,00

FR86030 Camping le Relais du Miel

Route d'Antran, F-86100 Châtellerault (Vienne)

Tel: 05 49 02 06 27. Email: camping@lerelaisdumiel.com

www.alanrogers.com/FR86030

With very easy access from the A10 and N10 roads, in the northern outskirts of Châtellerault, this site is in the ten acre grounds of a grand house dating from Napoleonic times. It is surrounded by majestic old trees beside the River Vienne. There is also an orchard and stone gateposts leading onto ground, previously the home farm, that now forms 80 large, flat pitches. Divided by mature trees and bushes providing plenty of shade, all the pitches have electricity (10A) and water, 15 with drainage connections. Twin barns form two sides of a courtyard behind the house, one of which has been converted very stylishly into reception, a high ceilinged function and games room, and a bar and restaurant serving good value meals. Beams taken from the original ceiling now form part of the bar top and act as arm rests. The second barn is being developed into apartments. Mobile homes and apartments to rent.

Facilities

Excellent toilet facilities include washbasins in cabins, facilities for disabled visitors, dishwashing and laundry facilities. Basic essentials and gas. Bar and restaurant. Pizzas (from local pizzeria). Takeaway. Snack bar (open in evenings 1/7-30/8). Swimming and paddling pools (15 x 7 m). Playground. Tennis courts. Bicycle hire. Boules. Games room with electronic games, pool and table tennis. Fishing. Observatory. Internet access. Torch useful. Off site: Supermarket 400 m. Riding 5 km. Golf 11 km. Futuroscope 16 km.

Open: 15 June - 2 September.

Directions

Châtellerault is between Tours and Poitiers. Site is north of town close to A10 autoroute. Take exit 26 (Châtellerault-Nord) and site is signed just off roundabout. From N10 follow signs for motorway (Tours - Péage) and at roundabout take exit for Antran. GPS: N46:50.307 E00:32.071

Charges guide

Per unit incl. 2 persons, electricity	€ 20,00 - € 25,00
extra person over 5 yrs	€ 3,00 - € 4,00
extra tent	€ 3,00 - € 4,00
Less 15% for 1 week, 20% for 2 weeks.	

Enjoy rest and comfort

CAMPING
★★★★
Le Relais du Miel

www.lerelaisdumiel.com
Tel: 0033 (0)549 02 06 27
Easy access : A10 Exit 26
Longitude: 0°32'5"
Latitude: 46°50'17"

BOOK THIS SITE
CALL 01580 214000
...we'll arrange everything
The Travel
Service

FR86010 Castel Camping le Petit Trianon

Saint Ustre, 1 rue du Moulin de St Ustre, F-86220 Ingrandes-sur-Vienne (Vienne)

Tel: **05 49 02 61 47**. Email: **chateau@petit-trianon.fr**   www.alanrogers.com/FR86010

A family owned site for many years, situated between Tours, Poitiers and Futuroscope, the approach to Le Petit Trianon is through a grand, narrow, gateway leading onto a slightly sloping meadow surrounded by trees in front of the château. There is also a large, more open field with a woodland area in between. There are 99 spacious, open but marked pitches which are arranged to leave plenty of free space. There is shade in parts from many attractive trees. All have electricity (10A).

Facilities

The original toilet unit includes washbasins in cabins, some washbasin and shower units, baby baths and laundry facilities. Smaller blocks for newer parts of site and one has facilities for disabled people. Motorcaravan service point. Shop (bread to order). Takeaway. Heated pool and paddling pools. Playground. Badminton, croquet and boules. Minigolf. TV room with games. Bicycle hire. Excursions. Internet access. Caravan storage. Off site: Restaurant 50 m. Fishing 3 km. Riding 15 km.

Open: 20 May - 20 September.

Directions

Ingrandes is signed from N10 north of town (between Dangé and Châtellerault). From autoroute A10 take exit 26 for Châtellerault-Nord, at roundabout follow signs for Tours to Ingrandes where site is signed. GPS: N46:53.248 E00:35.183

Charges 2009

Per person	€ 7,00
child (3-6 yrs)	€ 3,50
pitch incl. electricity (5/10A) and vehicle	€ 12,40 - € 12,80

FR86080 Camping Caravaning les Peupliers

F-86700 Couhé (Vienne)

Tel: **05 49 59 21 16**. Email: **info@lespeupliers.fr**   www.alanrogers.com/FR86080

Family owned and run since 1968, Les Peupliers is located in a valley south of Poitiers. The site is arranged on the banks of a river (unfenced), the 170 pitches on both sides or around a fishing lake. On level grass, most are separated and all have 16A electricity, while 86 are fully serviced. There is a good pool complex that includes water slides and toboggans, a heated main pool, a paddling pool and a lagoon with two slides for younger children, jacuzzi, plus water games. There is some noise from the N10 which runs fairly close to the site.

Facilities

Three toilet blocks of varying ages are in Mediterranean style, with washbasins in cubicles and facilities for babies and disabled people. The newest is in regular use and the other two open as the season progresses. Dishwashing and laundry facilities. TV and fridge rental. Shop. Snack bar, restaurant and bar. Entertainment in peak season. Pool complex. Playgrounds. Fishing lake. Minigolf, table tennis, football, volleyball and boules. Motorcaravan service point. WiFi. Off site: Tennis 800 m. Bicycle hire 1 km. Riding 5 km.

Open: 2 May - 30 September.

Directions

Couhé is 30 km. south of Poitiers on N10. From north, follow signs (Couhé town centre) and campsite (a short distance from slip road on right). From south, take 2nd Couhé exit from N10. Site entrance is opposite end of slip road. GPS: N46:18.706 E00:10.670

Charges 2009

Per person	€ 7,00
pitch with electricity	€ 14,50
with water and drainage	€ 17,50
Credit cards accepted (min € 50).	

FR86090 Flower Camping du Lac de Saint Cyr

F-86130 Saint Cyr (Vienne)

Tel: **05 49 62 57 22**. Email: **contact@parcdesaintcyr.com**   www.alanrogers.com/FR86090

This well organised, five hectare campsite is part of a 300 hectare leisure park, based around a large lake with sailing and associated sports, and an area for swimming (supervised July/Aug). Land-based activities include tennis, two half-courts, fishing, badminton, pétanque, beach volleyball, TV room, and a well equipped fitness suite, all of which are free of charge. The campsite has around 185 tourist pitches, 10 mobile homes and three 'yurts' (canvas and wooden tents) for rent. The marked and generally separated pitches are all fully serviced with electricity (10A), water and drainage.

Facilities

The main toilet block is modern and supplemented for peak season by a second unit, although they do attract some use by day-trippers to the leisure facilities. They include washbasins in cubicles, laundry facilities, and facilities for babies and disabled persons. Shop, restaurant and takeaway (April-Sept). Playground on beach. Bicycle hire. Barrier locked 22.00-07.00 hrs (€ 10 deposit for card). Off site: Riding 200 m. Golf 800 m.

Open: 1 April - 30 September.

Directions

St Cyr is about midway between Châtellerault and Poitiers. Site signed to east of N10 at Beaumont along D82 towards Bonneuil-Matours and is part of the Parc de Loisirs de Saint-Cyr. GPS: N46:43.183 E00:27.611

Charges guide

Per pitch incl. 2 persons and electricity	€ 13,00 - € 29,00
extra person	€ 2,60 - € 5,50

www.flowercampings.com

Check real time availability and at-the-gate prices...
www.alanrogers.com

FR86040 Kawan Village le Futuriste

F-86130 Saint Georges-les-Baillargeaux (Vienne)

Tel: 05 49 52 47 52. Email: camping-le-futuriste@wanadoo.fr

www.alanrogers.com/FR86040

Le Futuriste is a neat, modern site, open all year and close to Futuroscope. With a busy atmosphere, there are early departures and late arrivals. Reception is open 08.00-22.00 hrs. There are 118 individual, flat, grassy pitches divided by young trees and shrubs which are beginning to provide some shelter for this elevated and otherwise rather open site (possibly windy). 82 pitches have electricity (6A) and a further 30 have electricity, water, waste water and sewage connections. All are accessed via neat, level and firmly rolled gravel roads. There are panoramic views over the strikingly modern buildings and night-time bright lights that comprise the popular attraction of Futuroscope. This site is ideal for a short stay to visit the park which is only 1.5 km. away (tickets can be bought at the site) but it is equally good for longer stays to see the region. Details of attractions are available from the enthusiastic young couple who run the site. Note: it is best to see the first evening show at Futuroscope otherwise you will find yourself locked out of the site – the gates are closed at 23.30 hrs.

Facilities

Excellent, clean sanitary facilities in two insulated blocks (can be heated). Those in the newest block are unisex. and include some washbasins in cabins and facilities for disabled people. Laundry facilities. Shop (bread to order), bar/restaurant (all 1/5-30/9). Snack bar and takeaway (1/7-31/8). Two heated outdoor pools, one with slide and paddling pool (15/5-15/9). Games room. TV. Boules. Multisport area. Lake fishing. Youth groups not accepted. Off site: Bicycle hire 500 m. Hypermarket 600 m. Golf 5 km. Riding 10 km.

Open: All year.

Directions

From either A10 autoroute or N10, take Futuroscope exit. Site is east of both roads, off D20 (St Georges-Les-Baillargeaux). Follow signs to St Georges. Site on hill; turn by water tower and site is on left. GPS: N46:39.928 E00:23.668

Charges 2009

Per unit incl. 1-3 persons	
and electricity	€ 18,40 - € 25,00
extra person	€ 2,10 - € 2,90
animal	€ 2,00

Camping Cheques accepted.

Open all year. Panoramic view over the Futuroscope situated at 2 kms. Heated swimming pool, pond, snack, bar, restaurant. Chalets for hire.

FUTURISTE

86130 St-Georges les Baillargeaux
Tel.: 0033 549 52 47 52
Fax: 0033 549 37 23 33
www.camping-le-futuriste.fr

Check real time availability and at-the-gate prices...
www.alanrogers.com

MAP 8

Burgundy is a wonderfully evocative region offering breathtaking châteaux and cathedrals, rolling hills and heady mountain views, vineyards and superlative cuisine, not to mention of course, a wide variety of world renowned wines.

DÉPARTEMENTS: 21 CÔTE D'OR, 58 NIÈVRE, 71 SAÔNE-ET-LOIRE, 89 YONNE

MAJOR CITY: DIJON

In the rich heartland of France, Burgundy was once a powerful independent state and important religious centre. Its golden age is reflected in the area's magnificent art and architecture: the grand palaces and art collections of Dijon, the great pilgrimage church of Vézelay, the Cistercian Abbaye de Fontenay and the evocative abbey remains at Cluny, once the most powerful monastery in Europe.

However, Burgundy is best known for its wine, including some of the world's finest, notably from the great vineyards of the Côte d'Or and Chablis, and also for its sublime cuisine.You'll also notice how driving through the country villages is like reading a wine merchant's list with plenty of opportunities for tasting and choosing your wine.

The area is criss-crossed by navigable waterways and includes the Parc Régional du Morvan; good walking country amidst lush, rolling wooded landscape.

Places of interest

Autun: 12th-century St Lazare cathedral.

Beaune: medieval town; Museum of Burgundy Wine.

Cluny: Europe's largest Benedictine abbey.

Dijon: Palace of the Dukes, Fine Arts Museum, Burgundian Folklore Museum.

Fontenay: Fontenay Abbey and Cloister.

Joigny: medieval town.

Mâcon: Maison des Vins (wine centre).

Paray-le-Monial: Romanesque basilica, pilgrimage centre.

Sens: historic buildings, museum with fine Gallo-Roman collections.

Vézelay: fortified medieval hillside.

Cuisine of the region

Many dishes are wine based, including *Poulet au Meursault* and *Coq au Chambertin*. Dijon is known for its *pain d'épice* (spiced honey cake) and spicy mustard.

Boeuf Bourguignon: braised beef simmered in a red wine-based sauce.

Garbure: heavy soup, a mixture of pork, cabbage, beans and sausages.

Gougère: cheese pastry based on Gruyère.

Jambon persillé: parsley-flavoured ham, served cold in jelly.

Matelote: fresh-water fish soup, usually based on a red wine sauce.

Meurette: red wine-based sauce with small onions, used with fish or poached egg dishes.

FR21000 Sunêlia Lac de Panthier

F-21320 Vandenesse-en-Auxois (Côte d'Or)

Tel: **03 80 49 21 94**. Email: **info@lac-de-panthier.com**   www.alanrogers.com/FR21000

An attractively situated lakeside site in Burgundy countryside, Camping Lac de Panthier is divided into two distinct campsites. The first, smaller section houses the reception, shop, restaurant and other similar facilities. The second, larger area is 200 m. along the lakeside road and is where the site activities take place and the pool can be found. The 207 pitches (157 for touring units) all have electricity connections and are mostly on level grass, although in parts there are shallow terraces. The site's restaurant has panoramic views over the lake which has many watersports facilities. Used by tour operators.

Facilities

Two unisex toilet blocks per site also provide for babies and disabled people. Shop, bar and restaurant. Games and TV rooms. Pool, children's pool and water-slide (15/5-15/9). Indoor pool, sauna and fitness equipment. Fishing. Riding. Bicycle and canoe hire. Watersports. Entertainment and activities organised in high season and clubs for children and teenagers. Off site: Boat excursions from Pouilly-en-Auxois (8 km). Riding and golf 10 km. Dijon, Autun and Beaune. Bus to Dijon and Poilly-en-Auxois 300 m.

Open: 8 April - 15 October.

Directions

From A6 join A38 and exit at junction 24. Take N81 towards Arnay Le Duc (back over A6), turn left on D977 for 5 km. Fork left for Vandenesse-en-Auxois. On through village on D977 for 2.5 km, left again and site is on left. GPS: N47:14.197 E04:37.686

Charges guide

Per pitch incl. 2 persons and electricity	€ 21,10 - € 25,00
extra person	€ 5,10 - € 6,40
child (2-7 yrs)	€ 2,80 - € 3,50
dog	€ 3,00

Camping Cheques accepted.

Sunêlia Zen
Lac de Panthier

www.lac-de-panthier.com - www.restaurant-lac-panthier.com
E-mail: info@lac-de-panthier.com
Tel.: 0033 (0)3 80 49 21 94 - Fax: 0033 (0)3 80 49 25 80

On the shores of a large lake, on the edge of the woods, Pélagie and David Plet warmly welcome you with their team on campsite Le Lac de Panthier. They offer you 200 large, quiet and shady pitches for your tent or caravan.
Mobile homes and chalets for rent.

FR21010 Camping Louis Rigoly

Esplanade Saint-Vorles, F-21400 Châtillon-sur-Seine (Côte d'Or)

Tel: **03 80 91 03 05**. Email: **tourism-chatillon-sur-seine@wanadoo.fr**   www.alanrogers.com/FR21010

This well kept, small, hillside municipal site has 54 touring pitches. Mainly individual and separated, they are on fairly flat grass, all with electricity (4/6A) with mature trees providing shelter. Adjoining the site is the municipal swimming pool complex with both indoor and outdoor pools (free in July and August). There is no shop, but the town is close. The site, which has much transit trade, can become full by evening in season.

Facilities

The main toilet block at the lower end of the site is satisfactory. A smaller heated unit behind reception contains facilities for babies, a washing machine and dryer. Facilities for disabled visitors provided in a separate block. Motorcaravan service point. Snack bar July/Aug. Baker calls every morning (except Tuesday). Play area. Boules. Internet access. Off site: Fishing or bicycle hire 1 km. Riding 4 km.

Open: 1 April - 30 September.

Directions

On northeast outskirts of town; site is signed from centre (steep hills approaching site, narrow roads). GPS: N47:51.592 E04:34.810

Charges 2009

Per person	€ 3,40
child (under 7 yrs)	€ 1,30
pitch	€ 3,20 - € 4,65
vehicle	€ 1,45
motorcycle	€ 1,00

No credit cards.

Check real time availability and at-the-gate prices...
www.**alanrogers**.com

FR21020 Camping Municipal les Cent Vignes

10 rue Auguste Dubois, F-21200 Beaune (Côte d'Or)

Tel: 03 80 22 03 91   www.alanrogers.com/FR21020

Les Cent Vignes is a very well kept site offering 116 individual pitches of good size, separated from each other by neat beech hedges high enough to keep a fair amount of privacy. Over half of the pitches are on grass, ostensibly for tents, the remainder on hardstandings with electricity for caravans. A popular site, within walking distance of the town centre, Les Cent Vignes becomes full mid June to early September but with many short-stay campers there are departures each day and reservations can be made. The Côte de Beaune, situated southeast of the Côte d'Or, produces some of the very best French wines.

Facilities

Two modern, fully equipped and well constructed sanitary blocks, one of which can be heated, should be large enough. Nearly all washbasins are in cabins. Laundry facilities. Shop, restaurant with takeaway (all 1/4-15/10). Playground. Sports area with tennis, basketball, volleyball and boules. TV room. Barbecue area. Off site: Centre of Beaune 1 km. Bicycle hire 1 km. Fishing, golf or windsurfing 4 km.

Open: 15 March - 31 October.

Directions

From autoroute exit 24 follow signs for Beaune centre on D2 road, camping signs to site in about 1 km. Well signed from other routes.
GPS: N47:01.982 E04:50.347

Charges guide

Per person	€ 3,60
child (under 7 yrs)	€ 1,80
pitch	€ 4,35
electricity (10A)	€ 3,65

FR21030 Camping les Premier Pres

Route de Bouilland, F-21420 Savigny-les-Beaune (Côte d'Or)

Tel: 03 80 26 15 06. Email: mairie.savigny-les-beaune@wanadoo.fr   www.alanrogers.com/FR21030

This popular site is ideally located for visiting the Burgundy vineyards, for use as a transit site or for spending time in the town of Beaune. During the high season it is full every evening, so it is best to arrive by 4 pm. The 90 level pitches are marked and numbered, with electric hook-ups and room for an awning. A former municipal site, now privately owned. Whilst the famed wine region alone attracts many visitors, Beaune, its capital, is unrivalled in its richness of art from times gone by. Narrow streets and squares are garlanded with flowers, pavement cafés are crammed with tourists and overlooking the scene is the glistening Hotel Dieu.

Facilities

Well kept sanitary facilities are housed in a modern building behind reception. Additional WCs and water points are conveniently placed towards the middle of the site. Motorcaravan service point. Ice available to purchase. Torch useful. Off site: Sunday market in the village 1 km. Beaune 7 km.

Open: 29 April - 30 September.

Directions

From A6 autoroute take exit 24 signed Beaune and Savigny-les-Beaune onto D2. Turn right towards Savigny-les-Beaune (3 km.) and follow signs to site.
GPS: N47:04.140 E04:48.180

Charges guide

Per person	€ 2,30
pitch	€ 3,20
electricity	€ 3,35
No credit cards.	

FR21040 Camping de l'Etang de Fouché

Rue du 8 Mai 1945, F-21230 Arnay le Duc (Côte d'Or)

Tel: 03 80 90 02 23. Email: info@campingfouche.com   www.alanrogers.com/FR21040

Useful as a stop en route to or from the Mediterranean or indeed for longer stays. This quite large but peaceful, lakeside site with its new bar/restaurant and swimming pool complex, can be very busy during the school holidays, and is probably better visited outside the main season. There are 190 good sized pitches, on fairly level grass and all with 10A electricity (some with water). Many are hedged and offer a choice of shade or more open aspect. In July/August there are regular activities for children and adults. A two kilometre stroll around the lake is very pleasant.

Facilities

Two new toilet blocks and third one (totally refurbished) provide all the necessary modern facilities (male and female are separate). Facilities for disabled visitors. Baby room. Washing machines and dishwashing under cover. Shop, bar, restaurant, takeaway (all 15/5-15/9). TV/games room. New small heated outdoor swimming pool. Boules. Playground. Off site: Town centre 800 m. Lakeside beach with playground, water slides, pedaloes, canoes.

Open: 1 April - 15 October.

Directions

From A6 (exit 24) take D981, 16 km. to the town. Turn left on D906 for about 400 m. and site is signed to left. GPS: N47:08.047 E04:29.904

Charges 2009

Per unit incl. 2 persons and electricity	€ 18,40 - € 22,50
extra person	€ 4,30 - € 5,40
child (2-10 yrs)	€ 2,20 - € 2,90
animal	€ 2,00

198

FR21090 Camping de l'Arquebuse

Route d'Athée, F-21130 Auxonne (Côte d'Or)

Tel: 03 80 31 06 89. Email: camping.arquebuse@wanadoo.fr

www.alanrogers.com/FR21090

This is an all year round site located in the Northern Jura with a riverside setting on the Saône. L'Arquebuse has 100 level, unmarked pitches on grass, of which 30 are occupied by mobile homes and chalets. All have 10A electricity and a variety of trees gove shade to some pitches. Auxonne is close to both the A36 and A39 motorways and this site may prove a useful overnight stop. The site has bar/restaurant, Le Pinocchio, and the adjacent 'base nautique' offers a good range of leisure activities, including canoeing, windsurfing, mountain biking as well as a large swimming pool. Auxonne is an attractive town, fortified by Vauban, and is renowned as the capital of the Saone valley. The town's most famous former occupant is Napoleon and he spent two years at the Auxonne military academy. Not surprisingly there are several monuments celebrating his time here!

Facilities

Basic toilet block, heated in winter, provides mostly Turkish style toilets and open washbasins. Washing machine. Small shop. Restaurant/bar. Takeaway meals. Play area. TV room. WiFi. Chalets for rent. Off site: Swimming pool, windsurfing, canoeing, boat trips and fishing. Motorcaravan services. Fortified town of Auxonne with shops, bars and restaurants 1 km. Dijon 34 km.

Open: All year.

Directions

From the A39 autoroute take exit 5 and the N5 for about 6 km. to Auxonne. Site is signed to the left just before crossing the bridge over the Saône. Site is a few hundred metres. GPS: N47:11.965 E05:23.019

Charges guide

Per person	€ 3,60
child (under 7 yrs)	€ 2,00
pitch	€ 3,50 - € 5,50
electricity (10A)	€ 3,50

Camping l'Arquebuse ***

- 3 star campsite
- Open all year
- Wifi
- Washing machines and dryers
- Restaurant
- At the bank of the Saône
- Pool 10 metres from the campsite

Camping l'Arquebuse - Route d'Athée - 21130 Auxonne - Tel: 0033 (0)380 31 06 89 - Fax: 0033 (0)380 31 12 62
E-mail: camping.arquebuse@wanadoo.fr - www.campingarquebuse.com

FR21060 Camping les Bouleaux

11 rue Jaune, F-21200 Vignoles (Côte d'Or)

Tel: 03 80 22 26 88

www.alanrogers.com/FR21060

Camping Les Bouleaux is an excellent little campsite located at Vignoles, northeast of Beaune. There are just 46 pitches, all with an electrical connection (3-6A, long leads may be required on some pitches). The large flat pitches are attractively laid out and most are separated by hedges and trees giving some shade. Monsieur Rossignal takes great pride in his campsite, keeping the grounds and facilities exceptionally clean and tidy, and by planting bright flowers near the reception. The nearest shops are 3 km.

Facilities

An older unisex building provides Turkish style WCs, while the adjacent modern block houses British style WCs (no paper). Washbasins in cabins or communal; push button controllable showers, excellent facilities for visitors with disabilities. Laundry and dishwashing sinks. No shop, but wine and basic groceries can be bought at reception. Gas exchange. Off site: Beaune 3 km. Bicycle hire, fishing or golf 3 km. Riding 6 km.

Open: All year.

Directions

Leave A6 at junction 24.1 south of Beaune. Turn right at roundabout, straight on at traffic lights (centre lane), then right at next roundabout. Cross autoroute, left (Vignoles). Follow campsite signs. GPS: N47:01.475 E04:53.227

Charges 2009

Per unit incl. 2 persons and electricity	€ 14,40 - € 16,50
extra person	€ 3,65
No credit cards.	

199

Check real time availability and at-the-gate prices...

www.alanrogers.com

BOOK THIS SITE
CALL 01580 214000
...we'll arrange everything
The Travel Service

FR21080 Camping des Sources

Avenue des Sources, F-21590 Santenay (Côte d'Or)

Tel: 03 80 20 66 55. Email: info@campingsantenay.com   www.alanrogers.com/FR21080

Santenay lies in the heart of the Côte de Beaune, a region renowned for its wine and châteaux, and within easy reach of Beaune. After a day's sightseeing or 'dégustation', there is a casino and a spa to visit. It is also alongside a long distance track for cycling, roller skating and walking, from which start a number of shorter circular routes. This relatively new site is next to the village sports and leisure area, with access to the swimming pool and paddling pool (free 1/6-31/8). There are 110 comfortable level grassy touring pitches. All have electrical connections (6A) and a water tap is never far.

Facilities

The modern toilet block contains British style WCs, washbasins and preset showers. Facilities for disabled visitors. Motorcaravan services. Laundry facilities. Gas supplies. Shop. Bar, restaurant, snack bar and takeaway (15/5-15/9). Games room. WiFi. Playground. Playing field. Minigolf. Boules. Skittles. Off site: Tennis courts, skateboarding. Casino 300 m. Spa 400 m. Santenay 1.5 km. Bicycle hire 1.5 km. Riding 2 km. Fishing, boat launching 4 km.

Open: 15 April - 31 October.

Directions

From Beaune take N74 (Autun and Montceau-les-Mines). After 2 km., at roundabout, continue on N74. After 11 km. pass under N6 and in 3 km. turn right into Santenay. Site signed from village. GPS: N46:54.260 E04:41.060

Charges guide

Per unit incl. 2 persons and electricity	€ 16,50 - € 20,00
extra person	€ 3,70
electricity	€ 3,50

Camping Cheques accepted.

FR58010 Camping des Bains

15 avenue Jean Mermoz, F-58360 Saint Honoré-les-Bains (Nièvre)

Tel: 03 86 30 73 44. Email: camping-les-bains@wanadoo.fr   www.alanrogers.com/FR58010

You are assured of a warm welcome at this attractive family run site, in an area of rolling country-side, woods, rivers and country villages, ideal for walking or cycling. The spacious 130 level grassed pitches (all with 6A electricity) are mostly separated by hedges with mature trees offering shade. Next to the camping is the 'thermal spa' where there are opportunities to 'take the waters' for a three day session or a full blown cure of three weeks! Reception has details.

Facilities

Two main sanitary units have mostly British style WCs, washbasins in cabins and showers (one block may be closed in low season). Baby bath. Laundry. Facilities for disabled people. Bar provides food and a takeaway. Swimming pool, slide and paddling pool (15/6-10/10). Play area. Streams for children to fish. Minigolf. Games room. Children's entertainment (July/Aug). TV and DVDs. Internet access. Off site: Excellent restaurant opposite entrance. Bicycle hire or riding 500 m. Fishing 5 km.

Open: 1 April - 25 October.

Directions

From Nevers, travel east on D978; turn right onto D985 (St Honoré-les-Bains). Site is signed on entering town. Care is needed at narrow site entrance. GPS: N46:54.450 E03:49.820

Charges guide

Per unit incl. 2 persons	€ 11,00 - € 16,00
extra person	€ 4,50
electricity (6A)	€ 3,50

Camping Cheques accepted.

FR58030 Castel Camping le Manoir de Bezolle

F-58110 Saint Pereuse-en-Morvan (Nièvre)

Tel: 03 86 84 42 55. Email: stephen.ham@btconnect.com   www.alanrogers.com/FR58030

Manoir de Bezolle, which is under new ownership, is well situated to explore the Morvan Natural Park and the Nivernais area. It has been attractively landscaped to provide a number of different areas, some giving pleasant views over the surrounding countryside. The touring pitches of good size are on level grass with shade, some with terracing and access to electricity (10A). There are three small lakes, stocked with many fish for anglers. This site is good for families, with a range of activities in the area.

Facilities

Two main toilet blocks (opened as needed) provide washbasins in cabins, mostly British style WCs, bath, provision for disabled visitors and a baby bath. A fibreglass unit contains two tiny family WC/basin/shower suites for rent. An older block is by the pools. Laundry. Motorcaravan services. Shop. Bar and restaurant. Pizza and takeaway (all year). Internet point. Two pools (1/5-15/9). Minigolf. Boules. Fishing.

Open: All year.

Directions

Site is between Nevers and Autun (midway between Châtillon-en-Bazois and Château-Chinon), just north of the D978. GPS: N47:03.526 E03:49.030

Charges 2009

Per unit incl. 2 persons and electricity	€ 19,00 - € 25,00
extra person	€ 5,00 - € 6,00
child (0-6 yrs)	free - € 4,00

Check real time availability and at-the-gate prices...
www.alanrogers.com

FR58100 Camping de Nevers

Rue de la Jonction, F-58000 Nevers (Nièvre)

Tel: 06 84 98 69 79. Email: info@campingnevers.com

www.alanrogers.com/FR58100

On the banks of the Loire in Nevers, facing the cathedral and the Palace of the Dukes across the river, this small site has 73 grass pitches. Of these, only two are used for caravan holiday homes and 11 are only suitable for tents The 60 touring pitches all have electricity (6/10A). This site would provide a good base for a short stay to explore the region with its famous Burgundy wines of Sancerre and Pouilly Fumé. The pitches are quite tight and are not suitable for larger units, but the site is ideal for those in motorcaravans or tents because of its proximity to the town.

Facilities

One modern toilet block has unisex toilets and showers. Bright and clean, they may be under pressure in high season. Baby area. Provision for disabled visitors. Laundry. Motorcaravan service point. Very small bar (all season) with snacks in high season. Off site: All the amenities of Nevers, including swimming pool and large stores.

Open: 14 April - 14 October.

Directions

From A6 take exit 6. Follow signs for Nevers. Shortly after town sign, site is on the right. Avoid arriving between 12.00-14.00 (site closed) and there is no waiting place outside. GPS: N46:58.925 E03:09.659

Charges guide

Per unit incl. 2 persons and electricity	€ 16,50 - € 20,30
extra person	€ 2,00 - € 3,00
Camping Cheques accepted.	

FR58050 Airotel Château de Chigy

Chigy, F-58170 Tazilly (Nièvre)

Tel: 03 86 30 10 80. Email: reception@chateaudechigy.com.fr

www.alanrogers.com/FR58050

This very spacious site (20 ha. for pitches and another 50 ha. of fields, lakes and woods) lies just at the southern tip of the Morvan Regional Natural Park. The château houses the reception and apartments for rent. Most of the facilities are nearby, and behind are 54 good sized, shaded pitches, with electricity and water supply near. There is a large woodland area with paths, next to which are 100 or so more pitches, some of up to 150 sq.m. They are open and vary from level, terraced, slightly sloping and some are bumpy. All have electrical connections and there are enough water taps.

Facilities

Two toilet blocks contain British style WCs, washbasins in cubicles, and showers. A 'portacabin' has 4 cubicles, each with toilet, washbasin and shower (can be hired as private in July/August). Facilities for disabled visitors and babies. Laundry facilities. Gas supplies. Shop. Bar, restaurant and takeaway (July/Aug). Two outdoor pools, one with paddling pool (15/5-30/9). Swimming in lake. Covered pool. Games and TV rooms. Playground. Minigolf. Boules. All weather sports terrain. Playing field. Off site: Luzy 4 km. Riding 9 km.

Open: 26 April - 30 September.

Directions

From Luzy (34 km. southwest of Autun via the N81) take the D973 towards Bourbon Lancy. After 4 km. the site is signed to the left. GPS: N46:45.600 E03:56.700

Charges guide

Per person	€ 5,00 - € 6,00
child (6-12 yrs)	€ 4,00 - € 5,00
pitch	€ 6,00 - € 8,00
electricity	€ 4,00
dog	€ 1,50

FR71010 Camping Municipal Mâcon

RN6, F-71000 Mâcon (Saône-et-Loire)

Tel: 03 85 38 16 22

www.alanrogers.com/FR71010

Always useful and well cared for, this site is worth considering as a stopover or for longer stays as it is close to the main route south. The 250 good sized pitches, 190 with 6 A electricity and 60 with fresh and waste water points, are on mown, flat grass, accessed by tarmac roads. Gates closed 10.00-06.30 hrs. but large units note – the security barrier has a 3.8 m. height restriction so watch those top boxes! There is a generally bright and cheerful ambience.

Facilities

Sanitary facilities in three well maintained units, are fully equipped with British and Turkish style WCs, and washbasins in cubicles. A fourth block is modern. Facilities for disabled visitors. Washing machine and dryer. Excellent motorcaravan service point. Shop/tabac. Bar. Takeaway and restaurant (Le Tipi) open midday and evenings. Heated swimming and paddling pools (campers only, 15/5-15/9). Good TV lounge. Playground. Off site: Supermarket nearby. Centre of Mâcon 3 km.

Open: 15 March - 31 October.

Directions

Site is on northern outskirts of Mâcon on main N6, 3 km. from the town centre (just south of A40 autoroute junction). GPS: N46:18.126 E04:49.950

Charges guide

Per unit incl. 2 persons	€ 11,60
with electricity (5A)	€ 14,10
tent pitch incl. 2 persons	€ 9,90
extra person	€ 3,10

BOOK THIS SITE CALL 01580 214000 ...we'll arrange everything The Travel Service

Check real time availability and at-the-gate prices... www.alanrogers.com

BOOK THIS SITE
CALL 01580 214000
...we'll arrange everything
The Travel **Service**

FR71070 Kawan Village Château de l'Epervière

Mobile homes ▶ page 500

F-71240 Gigny-sur-Saône (Saône-et-Loire)

Tel: 03 85 94 16 90. Email: domaine-de-leperviere@wanadoo.fr   www.alanrogers.com/FR71070

This site is peacefully situated in the wooded grounds of the 16th-century Château, near the village of Gigny-sur-Saône, and within walking distance of the river where you can watch the river cruise boats on their way to and from Châlon-sur-Saône. There are 160 pitches in total, of which 45 are occupied by tour operators and five units are for rent. The 110 touring pitches, all with 10A electricity (30 fully serviced) are in two distinct areas. The original part, close to the Château and fishing lake, has semi-hedged pitches on level ground with shade from mature trees. The centre of the second area has a more open aspect. Here there are large hedged pitches and mature trees offering shade around the periphery – birdwatchers will love this area. A partly fenced road across the lake connects the two areas. The main château's restaurant serves regional dishes. Gert-Jan and François, and their team enthusiastically organise many activities for visitors including wine tasting in the cellars of the château. Don't forget, you are in the Maconnais and Châlonnaise wine areas and so close to the A6.

Facilities

Two well equipped toilet blocks include washbasins in cabins, showers, baby rooms facilities for disabled visitors. Washing machine and dryer. Basic shop (1/5-30/9). Second restaurant with basic menu and takeaway (1/4-30/9). Converted barn housing attractive bar, large TV and games room. Unheated outdoor swimming pool (1/5-30/9) partly enclosed by old stone walls. Smaller indoor heated pool, jacuzzi, sauna, paddling pool. Play area. Outdoor paddling pool. Fishing. Bicycle hire. Off site: Riding 15 km. Golf 20 km. Historic towns of Châlon and Tournus, both 20 km. The Monday market of Louhans, to see the famous Bresse chickens 26 km.

Open: 29 March - 30 September.

Directions

From the north, A6 exit Châlon-Sud, or Tournus from the south. Take N6 to Sennecey-le-Grand, turn east on D18 and follow site signs for 6.5 km. GPS: N46:39.100 E04:56.923

Charges guide

Per unit incl. 2 persons and electricity	€ 23,40 - € 32,20
extra person	€ 5,70 - € 7,70
child (under 7 yrs)	€ 3,50 - € 5,30
dog	€ 2,40 - € 3,00
Camping Cheques accepted.	

FR71140 Camping du Pont de Bourgogne

Rue Julien Leneveu, Saint-Marcel, F-71380 Châlon-sur-Saône (Saône-et-Loire)

Tel: 03 85 48 26 86. Email: campingchalon71@wanadoo.fr   www.alanrogers.com/FR71140

This is a well presented site, useful for an overnight stop or for a few days if exploring the local area and you want a simple site without the frills. It does get crowded in the third week of July during the Châlon street theatre festival. There are 93 fairly small pitches with 6/10A electricity, ten with a gravel surface. The new owners of the site plan to replace or improve the facilities in the near future, but when we visited there was a bar/restaurant with an outdoor terrace and serving a good selection of simple, inexpensive meals. Although alongside the Saône river, the site is well fenced. The staff are friendly and helpful.

Facilities

Three toilet blocks, two centrally located amongst the pitches and traditional in style and fittings, the third new and modern, alongside the reception building (including facilities for disabled visitors). Dishwashing facilities but no laundry. No shop but essentials kept in the bar (bread to order). Modern bar/restaurant. Simple play area. Bicycle hire arranged. Off site: Municipal swimming pool 300 m. Golf 1 km. Riding 10 km.

Open: 1 April - 30 September.

Directions

From A6 exit 26 (Châlon-Sud) bear right to roundabout and take N80 (Dole) straight on to roundabout at St Marcel. Turn left (fourth exit) and fork right into Les Chavannes. At central traffic lights turn right and under modern river bridge to site entrance. GPS: N46:46.800 E04:52.377

Charges guide

Per person	€ 4,30 - € 5,20
child (under 7 yrs)	€ 2,10 - € 2,80
pitch	€ 4,30 - € 5,90
electricity	€ 3,20 - € 3,90

Check real time availability and at-the-gate prices...
www.alanrogers.com

3 campsites in the heart of southern burgundy

www.campings-bourgogne.com

Holiday
in château park

Discover Tournus

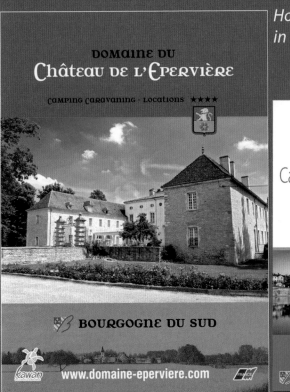

DOMAINE DU
Château de l'Epervière
CAMPING CARAVANING - Locations ★★★★

BOURGOGNE DU SUD

kawan   www.domaine-eperviere.com

Camping de Tournus ★★★

Bourgogne du Sud

www.camping-tournus.com

CAMPING DU Pont de BOURGOGNE

www.camping-chalon.com

Chalon sur Saône - Bourgogne du Sud

Burgundy

Stopover in the city

FR71020 Camping le Village des Meuniers

F-71520 Dompierre-les-Ormes (Saône-et-Loire)

Tel: 03 85 50 36 60. Email: contact@villagedesmeuniers.com   www.alanrogers.com/FR71020

In a tranquil setting with panoramic views, the neat appearance of the reception building sets the tone for the rest of this attractive site. It is an excellent example of current trends in French tourism development. This is a super site, tastefully landscaped, with a high standard of cleanliness in all areas. The main part has 113 terraced, grassy pitches, some with hardstanding, are all fairly level, 86 with electricity and ample water points. Of these, 75 also have waste water outlets. A second section, used only in high season contains 16 standard pitches. All pitches enjoy stunning views.

Facilities	Directions
Sanitary facilities mainly in an unusual, purpose designed hexagonal block, with modern fittings, of high standard. Smaller unit in the lower area of the site, plus further toilets in the main reception building. Motorcaravan service point in car park. Shop. Bar. Café (high season). Takeaway. Swimming pool complex with three heated pools and toboggan run (1/6-31/8). Activities for children (high season). Minigolf. Internet access. Off site: Village 500 m. Fishing 1.5 km. Riding 10 km.	Town is 35 km. west of Mâcon. Follow N79/E62 (Charolles, Paray, Digoin) road and turn south onto D41 to Dompierre-les-Ormes (3 km). Site is clearly signed through village. GPS: N46:21.821 E04:28.476

Charges 2009

Per person	€ 5,10 - € 6,75
child (2-12 yrs)	€ 3,40 - € 4,20
pitch incl. electricity	€ 11,20 - € 14,35
dog	€ 1,50

Open: 1 May - 30 September.

FR71030 Camping Municipal Saint-Vital

Rue des Griottons, F-71250 Cluny (Saône-et-Loire)

Tel: 03 85 59 08 34. Email: cluny-camping@wanadoo.fr   www.alanrogers.com/FR71030

Close to this attractive small town (300 metres walk) with its magnificent abbey (the largest in Christendom) and next to the municipal swimming pool (free for campers), this site has 174 pitches. On gently sloping grass, with some small hedges and shade in parts, electricity is available (long leads may be needed). Some rail noise is noticeable during the day but we are assured that trains do not run 23.30-07.00 hrs. In high season, on Friday evenings, there is a presentation of local produce in the 'salle de réunion'.

Facilities	Directions
Two sanitary buildings provide British and Turkish style WCs, some washbasins in cubicles and controllable showers. Dishwashing and laundry sinks. Washing machine, dryer and ironing board. Off site: Fishing and bicycle hire 100 m. Riding 1 km. Wine routes, châteaux, churches. The excellent traffic free cycle path from Cluny to Givry is highly recommended.	Site is east of town, by the D15 road towards Azé and Blanot. GPS: N46:25.918 E04:40.053

Charges guide

Per unit incl. 2 persons and electricity	€ 13,95
extra person	€ 6,90
child (under 7 yrs)	€ 2,25

Open: 1 May - 30 September.

FR71050 Camping le Moulin de Collonge

F-71390 Saint Boil (Saône-et-Loire)

Tel: 03 85 44 00 32. Email: millofcollonge@wanadoo.fr   www.alanrogers.com/FR71050

This well run, family site offers an 'away from it all' situation surrounded by sloping vineyards and golden wheat fields. It has an instant appeal for those seeking a quiet, relaxing environment. There are 61 level pitches, most with electrical hook-ups although long cables may be required. Flower arrangements are in abundance and, like the shrubs and grounds, are constantly being attended. Beyond the stream that borders the site are a swimming pool, patio and a pizzeria (also open to the public all year). A new lake, 1.8 m. deep, has been created for leisure activities.

Facilities	Directions
Well kept toilet facilities housed in a converted barn. Laundry and dishwashing sinks. Washing machine and dryer. Freezer for campers' use. Bread each morning. Basic shop (1/6-3/9). Pizzeria, snack bar (1/7-31/8). Internet café. Swimming pool covered - some walls can be opened in good weather. Playgrounds. Bouncy castle. Bicycle hire. Table tennis. Fishing. Pony trekking. WiFi (free). Off site: Riding 4 km. Châteaux, wine route, churches. 'Voie Vert', 117 km. track for cycling or walking near the site.	From Châlon-sur-Saône travel 9 km. west on the N80. Turn south on D981 through Buxy (6 km). Continue south for 7 km. to Saint Boil and site is signed at south end of the village. GPS: N46:38.773 E04:41.687

Charges guide

Per person	€ 4,50 - € 5,50
pitch incl. car	€ 5,50 - € 8,00
pitch incl. bicycle	€ 3,50 - € 4,00
electricity	€ 3,50
Camping Cheques accepted.	

Open: 1 April - 30 September.

Check real time availability and at-the-gate prices...

www.alanrogers.com

FR71060 Camping Caravaning Château de Montrouant

F-71800 Gibles (Saône-et-Loire)

Tel: 03 85 84 51 13. Email: campingdemontrouant@wanadoo.fr   www.alanrogers.com/FR71060

A small, pretty site beside a lake in the grounds of an imposing chateau, in a steep valley in the Charolais hills. There is shade from mature trees and the 45 pitches (12 used by Dutch tour operators) are on reasonably flat grassy terraces, separated by hedges. Some pitches overlook the lake and some are next to a field. This site is best for smaller units as the approach roads are narrow. It quickly becomes full mid July - mid August and access becomes difficult with extra traffic. Motorcaravan owners should always check in advance as there may not be a suitable pitch.

Facilities

The sanitary facilities, not too well designed and with variable maintenance, are housed in a part of the château. They include washbasins in cabins. Dishwashing and laundry facilities. Basic supplies available at reception. Small open-air bar/restaurant/takeaway for evening barbecues (only open certain evenings). Swimming pool with secluded sunbathing area. Half-court tennis. Fishing. Torches useful. Off site: The village of Gibles 2 km. Riding 10 km.

Open: 1 June - 4 September.

Directions

Site is to the west of Mâcon and can be reached from A6 (Jn 29) via the N79 to Charolles (50 km). Take D25 southeast for 20 km. to Gibles. The last few kilometers are quite narrow. Just before village, following signs, there is a very sharp turn to the left. Continue with signs. GPS: N46:20.196 E04:22.920

Charges guide

Per person	€ 5,80
pitch incl. electricity	€ 10,30
vehicle	€ 5,30
Camping Cheques accepted.	

FR71080 Camping de l'Etang Neuf

L'Etang Neuf, F-71760 Issy-l'Évêque (Saône-et-Loire)

Tel: 03 85 24 96 05. Email: info@camping-etang-neuf.com   www.alanrogers.com/FR71080

This tranquil campsite overlooking a lake, with views of a forest and the 19th-century Château de Montrifaut, is a real countryside haven for relaxation. Separated by low hedges, the 61 marked, grass pitches have 6A electricity and a small hardstanding area for a car. Young trees offer a little shade. There is a separate area for tents. There is no organised entertainment but a play area, fenced swimming and paddling pools and plenty of space will keep children happily amused.

Facilities

Two very clean sanitary blocks includes washbasins in cabins. Dishwashing and laundry sinks. Washing machine, ironing board and baby room. Separate shower and toilet rooms for disabled people are in the lower block. Motorcaravan services. Bar/restaurant. Bread and croissants to order. Boules pitch. TV and games room. Internet access (WiFi). Off site: Minigolf just outside the site entrance. Riding 500 m. Nearest shop 1 km. in Issy-l'Évêque.

Open: 1 May - 13 September.

Directions

From D973 (Luzy - Bourbon-Lancy) turn left onto D25 (west of Luzy) and continue for about 12 km. Turn right, past D42 in centre of Issy-l'Évêque, signed to campsite. The road narrows slightly, entrance on the right. GPS: N46:42.464 E03:57.611

Charges guide

Per unit incl. 2 persons	€ 16,50 - € 18,00
incl. electricity	€ 16,50 - € 21,00
extra person	€ 3,00 - € 4,50
Camping Cheques accepted.	

FR71120 Camping la Heronnière

Lac de Laives, F-71240 Laives (Saône-et-Loire)

Tel: 03 85 44 98 85. Email: contact@camping-laheronniere.com   www.alanrogers.com/FR71120

Camping la Herronière is a quiet relaxing site on the edge of a leisure lake in pleasant rolling woodland countryside. The 90 touring pitches are good sized, grassy and level. About half have shade, with electrical connections for 88 and there are plenty of water points. The site is within easy reach of Châlon-sur-Saône, Tournus and the Chalonnais vineyards and wine route. Cluny and the former industrial towns of Le Creusot and Montceau-les-Mines are each about 40 km. away.

Facilities

Well equipped modern sanitary block includes facilities for campers with disabilities. Snack bar (June - Aug). Covered area with bread, drinks, ice cream, basic provisions and French breakfast. Heated outdoor pool. Boules. Bicycle hire. Fishing. Marquee with TV, board games. Playground. Off site: Lake swimming, grass area, beach, bar and restaurant 300 m. Exercise circuit, canoeing, windsurfing, pedaloes. Riding 10 km. Golf 15 km. Cluny, Châlon, Le Creusot and Montceau-les-Mines. Shops at Laives 4 km.

Open: 1 May - 15 September.

Directions

Leave N6 (Châlon-sur-Saône - Mâcon) at Sennecy-le-Grand (about 18 km. south of the centre of Châlon), taking D18 west to Laives (4 km). In centre of village, take right fork and continue along D18, 4 km. to the northwest. GPS: N46:40.120 E04:48.480

Charges guide

Per unit incl. 2 persons	€ 16,00 - € 18,20
incl. electricity	€ 20,00 - € 22,50
extra person	€ 4,60
No credit cards.	

BOOK THIS SITE
CALL 01580 214000
...we'll arrange everything
The Travel
Service

205

FR71110 Camping du Lac

Runner up Alan Rogers Awards 2008

Le Fourneau, F-71430 Palinges (Saône-et-Loire)
Tel: **03 85 88 14 49**. Email: **camping.palinges@hotmail.fr**   www.alanrogers.com/FR71110

Camping du Lac is a very special campsite and it is all due to Monsieur Labille, the owner, who thinks of the campsite as his home and every visitor as his guest. The campsite has 50 pitches in total, 16 of which have 10A electricity and 20 are fully serviced. There are six chalets to rent. The site is adjacent to a lake with a beach and safe bathing. Set in the countryside yet within easy reach of many tourist attractions, especially Cluny, the local Château Digoin and Mont St Vincent with distant views of Mont Blanc on a clear day. If you want to visit a specific place, then Monsieur knows exactly where you should go – he never recommends anything that he hasn't personally tried out. Monsieur Labille provides tables and chairs for tent campers and he freezes bottles of water for cyclists to take away (free of charge).

Facilities

The central sanitary block provides all necessary facilities including those for campers with disabilities. Washing machine and fridge. Bread and croissants to order. Boules. Play area. TV room. Sports field, lake beach and swimming adjacent. Bicycle and pedalo hire in July/Aug. Motorcaravan services. Off site: Bar/snack bar outside entrance (weekends only outside 1/7-31/8). Riding 200 m. Palinges is within walking distance, cycle and walking routes, museums, cruises on canals, châteaux, 'museographical' complex.

Open: 1 April - 30 October.

Directions

Palinges is midway between Montceau les Mines and Paray le Monial. From Montceau take N70, then turn left onto D92 to Palinges. Follow campsite signs. Site is also well signed from D985 Toulon-sur-Arroux to Charolles road. GPS: N46:33.674 E04:13.528

Charges guide

Per unit incl. 2 persons and electricity	€ 16,80
extra person	€ 2,20
child (under 12 yrs)	€ 1,10
caravan, 2 axle	€ 34,00

No credit cards.

FR71180 Camping de la Chevrette

Rue de la Chevrette, F-71160 Digoin (Saône-et-Loire)
Tel: **03 85 53 11 49**. Email: **info@lachevrette.com**   www.alanrogers.com/FR71180

This pretty town site has been leased from the municipality for the last few years by an enthusiastic couple. There are 100 neat and tidy pitches which are delineated by hedges (even the pitches for tents) and flowers decorate the site. The level pitches include 75 with electricity (10A) for touring units, 23 for tents and two for caravan holiday homes for rent. At the far end of the site there is direct access to the Loire river and it is this aspect that attracts campers with canoes. The adjacent town swimming pool complex is free for campers. It incorporates a second large pool totally devoted to the sport of water jousting – seven in a boat!

Facilities

Four small toilet blocks, one with cold water only, each provide separate facilities for men and women and some washbasins in cabins. Washing machine and dryer in one block. Facilities for disabled visitors. Small restaurant/snack bar (1/7-31/8). Club room with TV for bad weather. WiFi. Off site: Supermarkets, restaurants and bars in the town. Cycle paths along the canals. Nevers and its cathedral. Riding 3 km. Bicycle hire 15 km.

Open: 1 March - 31 October.

Directions

Digion lies off the N79 and site is well signed from all directions. GPS: N46:28.784 E03:58.053

Charges 2009

Per person	€ 3,10 - € 3,90
child (under 13 yrs)	€ 1,90 - € 2,20
pitch	€ 6,00 - € 6,40
electricity	€ 3,20

Double axle units are charged much more.

Check real time availability and at-the-gate prices...

www.**alanrogers**.com

Burgundy

FR71190 Camping de Tournus

Rue des Canes, F-71700 Tournus (Saône-et-Loire)

Tel: 03 85 51 16 58. Email: info@camping-tournus.com   www.alanrogers.com/FR71190

This very well maintained, pleasant site is just a few minutes from the A6 autoroute, 200 metres from the River Saône and close to the interesting old market town of Tournus. It is ideal for a night halt but deserving of a longer stay. The surrounding area is well worth exploring with its beautiful scenery and many picturesque old towns and villages. The site has 90 fairly level grassy pitches all for touring, 70 having 6A electricity. A few trees give some pitches varying amounts of shade. The new owners have plans for many improvements including some hardstanding pitches.

Facilities

Two clean toilet blocks near the entrance provide all necessary facilities, including for campers with disabilities. Small café (no alcohol) also stocking some daily necessities and bread to order (all season). Small play area. Internet terminal. Bicycle hire. Motorcaravan services planned 2009. Off site: Fishing 200 m. Tournus, Saturday market, shops, bars, cafes, banks etc. short walk/bike ride alongside river. Municipal pool next door.

Open: 1 April - 30 September.

Directions

From the A6 take exit 12 for Tournus and the N6 south for just over 1 km. In Tournus (opposite railway station), turn left signed camping and follow signs to site, about 1 km. GPS: N46:34.459 E04:54.571

Charges guide

Per unit incl. 2 persons	€ 14,30 - € 17,70
extra person	€ 3,90 - € 4,90
electricity (6A)	€ 3,50 - € 4,20

See advertisement on page 203

FR89040 Camping Parc des Joumiers

F-89520 Saint Sauveur en Puisaye (Yonne)

Tel: 03 86 45 66 28. Email: camping-motel-joumiers@wanadoo.fr   www.alanrogers.com/FR89040

This is an attractive, spacious, family run site in the north of Burgundy and east of the Loire. It is set beside a lake and a forest which offers many opportunities for walks and bike rides. There are 100 large, slightly sloping, grass pitches separated by hedges with a variety of trees giving varying amounts of shade. All 74 for touring have 5-16A electricity, water, drain and TV point. There are no organised on-site activities but within 10 km. are many interesting old towns and Château de Saint Fargeau with its pageants and 'son-et-lumière'.

Facilities

Two well appointed toilet blocks with all necessary facilities, including those for children and campers with disabilities. Motorcaravan services. Small swimming and paddling pools (June - mid Sept). Play area with bouncy castle. Bar, restaurant and takeaway overlooking lake (fishing only). WiFi near bar. Fishing. Off site: Large village of St Sauveur 1 km. with small shops, bar, restaurant. Riding 5 km. Bicycle hire 8 km. Château de Saint Fargeau. Chantier de Guédelon, a medieval château under construction. Tourist train. Cyclorail.

Open: 28 March - 5 November.

Directions

Leave A77 at exit 21 and take D965 east for 17 km. to St Fargeau. Turn right on D85 southeast to St Sauveur-en-Puisaye in 11 km. In village turn hard left on D7. In 800 m. turn right (site well signed) to site in 800 m, GPS: N47:37.850 E03:11.643

Charges guide

Per unit incl. 2 persons and electricity	€ 15,60 - € 17,80
extra person	€ 3,70
child (under 7 yrs)	€ 1,80

FR89070 Camping des Platanes

41 route de la Mothe, F-89120 Charny (Yonne)

Tel: 03 86 91 83 60. Email: campingdesplatanes@wanadoo.fr   www.alanrogers.com/FR89070

Peacefully situated in the village of Charny, this is a tranquil, quiet site, yet within easy reach of the A6 autoroute and only one and a half hours from Paris. The important archaeological site of Guédelon castle is nearby, the Chablis wines of the Yonne are ready for discovery and there are delightful walks around two local lakes. There are currently 59 level, grass pitches, all with 16A electricity. With 27 used for touring units, the remainder are used for rented holiday homes and seasonal units. There are plans to enlarge the site and to increase the number of pitches to 82.

Facilities

A modern, purpose-built, heated toilet block provides separate areas for men and women. Washbasins in cabins. Facilities for disabled visitors. Laundry. Motorcaravan service point. Bicycle and barbecue hire. Play area for under fives. Off site: Fishing, riding, walking.

Open: 15 March - 31 October.

Directions

Leave A6 at exit 18 and follow D943 towards Montargis for 14 km. Turn left on D950 and site is on right at start of village. GPS: N47:53.460 E03:05.520

Charges guide

Per unit incl. 2 persons and electricity	€ 14,50 - € 16,00
extra person	€ 3,15 - € 3,50
Camping Cheques accepted.	

Check real time availability and at-the-gate prices...
www.alanrogers.com

MAP 9

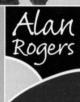

Located to the south of Alsace, the historic province of Franche Comté boasts a varied landscape ranging from flat plains to dense woodlands, rugged dramatic mountains and limestone valleys.

DÉPARTEMENTS: 25 DOUBS, 39 JURA, 70 HAUTE-SAÔNE, 90 TRE. DE BELFORT

MAJOR CITY: BESANÇON

Franche Comté is really made up of two regions. The high valley of the Saône is wide, gently rolling farmland with a certain rustic simplicity, while the Jura mountains are more rugged with dense forests, sheer cliffs, craggy limestone escarpments and torrents of clear, sparkling water gushing through deep gorges. It is for this thrilling scenery that Franche Comté is best known. Nature lovers can climb, bike and hike in the mountains or explore the hills honeycombed with over 4,000 caves. The streams and lakes provide world-class fishing. The spa towns of Salins les Bains and Besançon offer relaxation and a chance to 'take the waters'.

The region has a rich architectural heritage dating from many different periods, including medieval abbeys and châteaux and a poignant chapel in memory of the war. Roman remains, fortresses perched on cliff tops and elegant spa towns can all be explored at leisure. The region's position, bordering Switzerland and close to Germany, is reflected in its culture and also the great diversity of architectural style in the many fine buildings.

Places of interest

Arbois: Pasteur Family Home and Museum, Museum of Wine and Wine Growing.

Belfort: sandstone lion sculpted by Bartholdi; Memorial and Museum of the French Resistance.

Besançon: citadel with good views over the city.

Champlitte: Museum of Folk Art.

Dole: lovely old town, Louis Pasteur's birthplace.

Gray: Baron Martin Museum.

Luxeuil-les-Bains: Tour des Echevins Museum.

Ornans: Gustave Courbet birthplace, museum.

Ronchamp: Chapel of Notre-Dame du Haut de Ronchamp designed by Le Corbusier.

Salins-les-Bains: Salt mines and tunnels.

Sochaux: Peugeot Museum.

Cuisine of the region

Freshwater fish such as trout, grayling, pike and perch are local specialities. The region has a rare wine known as *vin de paille* as well as *vin jaune* (deep yellow and very dry) and *vin du jura*, Jura wine.

Brési: water-thin slices of dried beef; many local hams.

Gougére: hot cheese pastry based on the local *Comté* cheese.

Jésus de Morteau: fat pork sausage smoked over pine and juniper.

Kirsch: cherry flavoured liqueur.

Pontarlier: aniseed liqueur.

Poulet au vin jaune: chicken, cream and morilles cooked in *vin jaune*.

FR25080 Camping les Fuvettes

Mobile homes ▶ page 500

F-25160 Malbuisson (Doubs)

Tel: **03 81 69 31 50**. Email: **les-fuvettes@wanadoo.fr**   www.alanrogers.com/FR25080

High in the Jura and close to the Swiss border, Les Fuvettes is a well established family site with a fine, lakeside setting on Lac Saint Point. The lake is large – over 1000 hectares and a wide range of watersports are possible from the site, including sailing, windsurfing and pedaloes. Most equipment can be hired on site. Pitches here are grassy and of a reasonable size, separated by hedges and small trees. The new swimming pool is impressive with water slides and a separate children's pool. The site's bar/snack bar is housed in an attractive, steep roofed building and offers panoramic views across the lake. Walking and mountain biking are popular pursuits and many trails are available in the surrounding countryside. The Château de Joux is a popular excursion and the nearby Mont d'Or offers fine views towards the Alps. In high season, the site runs an entertainment and excursion programme, including a children's club. Mobile homes and chalets for rent.

Facilities

Three toilet blocks include facilities for babies and disabled people. Shop. Bar and snack bar. Swimming pool with waterslides and jacuzzi. Paddling pool. Play area. Minigolf. Archery. Bicycle hire. Sports pitch. Fishing (permit needed). Boat and pedalo hire. Games room. TV room. Children's club in peak season. Entertainment and excursion programme (July and August). Mobile homes and chalets for rent. Off site: Sailing school. Tennis. Many cycling and walking trails. Many restaurants, cafes and shops in nearby Malbuisson (walking distance).

Open: 1 April - 30 September.

Directions

From Besançon, head south on the N57 and join the D437 beyond Pontarlier signed Lac St Point and Mouthe. This road runs along the easten shores of the lake and passes through Malbuisson. Site is at the end of the village on the right.
GPS: N46:47.518 E06:17.600

Charges 2009

Per unit incl. 2 persons	
and electricity	€ 17,60 - € 26,10
extra person	€ 3,50 - € 5,20
child (under 7 yrs)	€ 1,80 - € 2,90
dog	free - € 1,50

CAMPING
LES FUVETTES

F-25160 Malbuisson
France

Tél.: 03 81 69 31 50
Fax: 03 81 69 70 46

les-fuvettes@wanadoo.fr

FR25000 Castel Camping le Val de Bonnal

Bonnal, F-25680 Rougemont (Doubs)

Tel: **03 81 86 90 87**. Email: **val-de-bonnal@wanadoo.fr**   www.alanrogers.com/FR25000

This is an impressive, generally peaceful, well managed site in a large country estate, harmoniously designed in keeping with the surrounding countryside, well away from main roads and other intrusions. The site itself is very busy, with a wide range of activities and amenities. The 350 good sized, landscaped pitches (190 for touring) with electricity (5A) are separated by a mixture of trees and bushes. A newer area has pitches of 200-250 sq.m. but are less secluded. The main attraction must be the variety of watersports on the three large lakes and nearby river.

Facilities

Four clean toilet blocks include washbasins in cabins, suites for disabled visitors and facilities for children and babies. Laundry facilities. Riverside restaurant, snack bar/takeaway, bar and terrace, shop (all 20/5-8/9). Swimming pool complex with water slides. Well equipped play areas. Sport facilities. Boules. Bicycle hire. Watersports. Fishing on the river and lake. Fitness suite. Internet access. Off site: Rougemont 3.5 km. Golf 6 km. Day trips to Switzerland.

Open: 4 May - 4 September.

Directions

From Vesoul take D9 towards Villersexel. After about 20 km. turn right in Esprels signed Val de Bonnal. Continue for 3.5 km. to site on left. From autoroute A36, exit Baume-les-Dames; go north on D50, then D486 to Rougemont and follow site signs.
GPS: N47:30.211 E06:21.116

Charges guide

Per pitch incl. 2 persons	
and electricity	€ 35,00
extra person	€ 9,00

Check real time availability and at-the-gate prices...

www.alanrogers.com

The Travel Service — **BOOK THIS SITE** **CALL 01580 214000** ...we'll arrange everything

FR25030 Camping du Bois de Reveuge

F-25680 Huanne-Montmartin (Doubs)

Tel: **03 81 84 38 60**. Email: **info@campingduboisdereveuge.com**   www.alanrogers.com/FR25030

Bois de Reveuge has 340 pitches including 150 mobile homes located in woodland to one side of the site. The terraced pitches have good views across the surrounding countryside and lead down to two lakes which may be used for fishing and canoeing. 190 pitches available for tourers have water and electricity and some are extra large (150-180 sq.m). Tall trees have been left standing at the top of the hill but there is little shade in the touring areas. There is a good solar heated swimming pool which can be covered in cool weather and another pool with four water slides and paddling pool.

Facilities

Four modern sanitary blocks with all necessary facilities (only two open in low season). Facilities for disabled visitors, children and babies. Laundry facilities. Kiosk for basics, restaurant/pizzeria (1/5-15/9). Swimming pools. Play areas. Miniclub (high season). Video screen, music and other entertainment. Bowling alley. Shooting range. Pony club. BMX track. Aqua-gym. Groups may request activities such as orienteering. Package deal includes use of canoes, archery, fishing, bicycle hire and pedaloes.

Open: 23 April - 17 September.

Directions

Site is well signed from the D50. From A36 autoroute south of the site, take exit for Baume-les-Dames and head north on D50 towards Villersexel for about 7 km. to camp signs. GPS: N47:26.472 E06:20.352

Charges 2009

Per unit incl. 2 persons and electricity	€ 19,00 - € 37,00
extra person	€ 4,00 - € 7,00
child (2-5 yrs)	€ 2,00 - € 5,00

FR25050 Camping Municipal de Saint Point-Lac

8 rue du Port, F-25160 Saint Point-Lac (Doubs)

Tel: **03 81 69 61 64**. Email: **camping-saintpointlac@wanadoo.fr**   www.alanrogers.com/FR25050

A good example of a municipal campsite in which the village takes a pride, this site is on the banks of a small lake with views to the distant hills. The 84 level, numbered pitches are on grass and 60 have electricity (16A). It is worth making a detour from the Pontarlier - Vallorbe road or for a longer stay. The village shop and restaurant are an easy 200 m. walk from the site entrance. Units over seven metres are not accepted.

Facilities

Well maintained, older style central sanitary block (partly refurbished) has British style WCs and free hot water. Suite for disabled visitors. Dishwashing and laundry facilities. Hot snacks and takeaway in high season (July/Aug). Fishing. Off site: Lakeside walk. Motorcaravan services opposite. Beach and swimming area. Pedalo hire. Bicycle hire 5 km.

Open: 1 May - 30 September.

Directions

From north, take D437 south of Pontarlier and keep on west side of the lake to the second village (Saint Point-Lac); from south exit N57 at Les Hopitaux-Neufs and turn west to lake. GPS: N46:48.709 E06:18.186

Charges guide

Per pitch incl. 2 persons and electricity	€ 12,80 - € 14,50
extra person	€ 2,00 - € 2,50

FR39010 Kawan Village la Plage Blanche

3 rue de la Plage, F-39380 Ounans (Jura)

Tel: **03 84 37 69 63**. Email: **reservation@la-plage-blanche.com**   www.alanrogers.com/FR39010

Situated in open countryside, along the banks of the River Loue, this site has 220 marked pitches on level ground, most of which are for touring units. All have 6A electricity connections. Many of the pitches are of a good size, although those actually along the river bank are smaller. Trees provide both fully shaded and semi-shaded pitches. Approximately a kilometre of riverside provides points of access, some with a small beach area. At low water levels this provides an ideal setting for children to swim and play safely in the gently flowing, shallow water. Inflatables are popular and there is a canoe/kayak base.

Facilities

Modern, well kept sanitary facilities in three unusual blocks. Launderette. Motorcaravan service area. No shop but bread to order. Bar/restaurant with terrace (1/5-30/9). Pizzeria and takeaway (all season). TV room. Library. Swimming and paddling pools (15/5-15/10). Play area. River fishing and fishing lake. Canoeing. Entertainment and activities (1/7-30/8). Internet access. Off site: Shop 1.5 km. Supermarket 6 km. Riding 10 km. Golf 13 km. Paragliding and hang gliding.

Open: 1 April - 15 October.

Directions

Ounans is 20 km. southeast of Dole. From autoroute A36, exit Dole, then D405 to Parcey, N5 to Mont-Sous-Vaudrey (8 km) then D472 towards Pontarlier. In Ounans site is signed. GPS: N47:00.177 E05:39.823

Charges guide

Per person	€ 5,50
child (1-7 yrs)	€ 3,50
pitch with electricity	€ 11,00
Camping Cheques accepted.	

Check real time availability and at-the-gate prices...

www.alanrogers.com

1 rue des Vernois, F-39130 Marigny (Jura)

Tel: **03 84 25 70 03**. Email: **contact@lapergola.com**   www.alanrogers.com/FR39040

Close to the Swiss border and overlooking the sparkling waters of Lac de Chalain, La Pergola is a neat, tidy, terraced site set amongst the rolling hills of the Jura. It is very well appointed, with 350 pitches, 127 for touring, mainly on gravel and separated by small bushes, all with electricity, water and drainage. Arranged on numerous terraces, connected by steep steps, some have shade and the higher ones have good views over the lake. The bar/restaurant terrace is beautiful and leads to a landscaped waterfall area next to the three swimming pools and entertainment area. English is spoken. It is awaiting discovery as it is not on the main tourist routes. A tall fence protects the site from the public footpath that separates the site from the lakeside but there are frequent access gates. The entrance is very attractive and the work that Mme. Gicquaire puts into the preparation of the flowerbeds is very evident. The terrace features grape vines for welcome shade and a colourful array of spectacular flowers.

Facilities

Latest sanitary block serving the lower pitches is well appointed. Slightly older blocks serve the other terraces. Facilities for disabled visitors on lower terraces. Shop (1/6-15/9). Bar. Self service restaurant. Pizzeria/takeaway. Pool complex, two pools heated. Good play areas and children's club. Archery. Boules. Pedaloes, canoes and small boats for hire. Organised programme in high season, evening entertainment with disco twice weekly. Internet access. Off site: Hang-gliding 2 km. Riding 3 km.

Open: 15 May - 15 September.

Directions

Site is 2.5 km. north of Doucier on D27 next to Lake Chalain. It is signed from Marigny. GPS: N46:40.621 E05:46.851

Charges 2009

Per unit incl. 2 persons and electricity	€ 21,00 - € 36,00
extra person	€ 5,50 - € 7,00
child (3-7 yrs)	free - € 5,50

Various special offers available.
Camping Cheques accepted.

Camping La Pergola ★★★★

Restaurant, Entertainment, Heated outdoor swimming pools, Mobilhomes to rent

A spectacular view of the magnificent Chalain Lake

What a perfect spot for lovers of nature, wide-open space and water sports

La Pergola : lac de Chalain - 39130 Marigny
Tel. : 03 84 25 70 03 - Fax : 03 84 25 75 96
E-mail : contact@lapergola.com - www.lapergola.com

B.P. 52, F-39130 Clairvaux-les-Lacs (Jura)

Tel: **04 66 73 97 39**. Email: **info@yellohvillage-fayolan.com**   www.alanrogers.com/FR39050

This modern site, backed by wooded hills, is situated on the shores of Le Petit Lac about a mile from the town of Clairvaux-les-Lacs amid the lakes and forests of the Jura. The neat, tidy site is in two parts, with pitches from 80-100 sq.m. either on terraces overlooking the lake or on the flatter area near the shore. There are electrical connections (6A) and 200 pitches fully serviced. The upper part has little shade until the young trees grow but there is some on the lower section.

Facilities

Four modern well equipped toilet units. Baby room. Laundry facilities. Shop. Restaurant. Bar. Snack bar/pizzeria and takeaway. Two good pools (heated from mid May) and a smaller one for children (trunks, not shorts). Fitness centre with covered pool, sauna, steam bath, massage. Entertainment area. Playground. Organised activities. Fishing. Internet access. Off site: Bicycle hire 800 m.

Open: 30 April - 6 September.

Directions

Clairvaux-les-Lacs is on the N78 between Lons-le-Saunier and Morez. In Clairvaux follow signs for 'Lacs Campings' and Fayolan. GPS: N46:33.866 E05:45.367

Charges guide

Per unit incl. 2 persons and electricity	€ 17,00 - € 36,00
extra person	€ 5,00 - € 6,50

www.yellohvillage.com tel: +33 466 739 739

BOOK THIS SITE
CALL 01580 214000
...we'll arrange everything
The Travel Service

211

FR39080 Kawan Village Domaine de l'Epinette

15 rue de l'Epinette, F-39130 Chatillon (Jura)

Tel: **03 84 25 71 44**. Email: **info@domaine-epinette.com**   www.alanrogers.com/FR39080

This site is set in charming wooded countryside on land sloping down to the river Ain, which is shallow and slow moving. There are 150 grassy pitches, 126 are available for touring units, some slightly sloping. These are arranged on terraces and separated by hedges and young bushes and trees, about half being shaded. Nearly all have electricity hook-ups, although some long leads are needed. There is an attractive swimming pool (heated 1/7-31/8), paddling pool and surrounds. An activity club for children takes place in July/August. Guided canoe trips on the river start and finish at the campsite. This quiet site has the same owners as FR39040, but is more recently established and less than half the size. Four hard standing pitches.

Facilities

Two modern toilet blocks. Unit for disabled visitors. Baby bath. Dishwashing and laundry sinks. Washing machine and dryer. Small shop for basics. Snack bar and takeaway (evenings). New reception, bar, TV room and shop. Playground. Table tennis under marquee. Boules. Direct access to river for swimming and canoeing. Off site: Riding 6 km. Golf 25 km. Shops, etc. in Doucier 6 km.

Open: 9 June - 15 September.

Directions

From Lons-le-Saunier take D471 eastwards towards Champagnole. After about 8 km. fork right onto D39 towards Doucier. After about 11 km. at Chatillon turn right onto D151 south towards Blye. Site is less than 2 km. on the left. GPS: N46:39.532 E05:43.787

Charges 2009

Per unit incl. 2 persons	
and electricity	€ 16,50 - € 27,00
extra person	€ 3,50 - € 4,50
child (2-7 yrs)	free - € 3,00
animal	€ 2,00

Camping Cheques accepted.

Camping Domaine de L'Épinette ★★★

Domaine de l'Épinette
15, rue de l'Épinette - 39130 Châtillon
Tel. : 03 84 25 71 44
E-mail : info@domaine-epinette.com
www.domaine-epinette.com

FR39060 Camping la Marjorie

640 boulevard de l'Europe, F-39000 Lons-le-Saunier (Jura)

Tel: **03 84 24 26 94**. Email: **info@camping-marjorie.com**   www.alanrogers.com/FR39060

La Marjorie is a spacious site set on the outskirts of the spa town of Lons-le-Saunier. Bordering one area of the site are open fields and woodlands. It is a former municipal site with 200 level pitches, 185 for tourists. Mainly on hardstanding they are separated by well trimmed hedges interspersed with tall trees which gives privacy plus a little shade at some part of the day. There are 130 pitches with electricity (6/10A) and 37 are fully serviced. There is a cycle path from the site into town (2.5 km) and a mountain bike track behind the site.

Facilities

Three well maintained toilet blocks, two modern and heated, Baby baths, facilities for disabled people. Small shop (15/6-31/8). Small bar with takeaway meals (all 15/6-31/8). TV room, table tennis, small play area, boules pitch, volleyball and football field. Archery, canoeing and riding. Motorcaravan service point (charge). Off site: Swimming pool 200 m. Bus stop 400 m. Restaurants 500 m. Bicycle hire 1.5 km. Fishing 3 km. Riding 5 km. Golf 6 km. Caves and waterfalls 17 km.

Open: 1 April - 15 October.

Directions

Site is off N83 Lons-le-Saunier - Besancon road. From south site signed from first roundabout on the outskirts of Lons. Approaching from Bescancon on N83, follow signs for Club Nautique on outskirts of Lons. Take care entering site. GPS: N46:41.053 E05:34.096

Charges guide

Per unit incl. 2 persons	€ 12,60 - € 15,40
incl. electricity (6A)	€ 14,40 - € 17,90
tent pitch incl. 2 persons	€ 10,00 - € 17,90

Check real time availability and at-the-gate prices...

www.alanrogers.com

FR39100 Camping Trélachaume

Lac de Vouglans, F-39260 Maisod (Jura)

Tel: **03 84 42 03 26**. Email: **info@trelachaume.fr** www.alanrogers.com/FR39100

This spacious campsite is situated in an attractive part of the Jura. The site has 180 pitches of varying sizes, many quite large. There are 153 for touring units and of these, 133 have electricity (6/16A, long leads may be needed). Young trees have been planted to create more shaded areas. There is no restaurant on the site, but a good bar with snacks and a takeaway operates 20 metres from the site entrance (1/6-31/8). In high season events and activities are organised, many of them in the municipal 'salle des fêtes' on the edge of the site.

Facilities	Directions
Three modern toilet blocks contain British style WCs, washbasins and pre-set showers. En-suite facilities for disabled people. Baby room. Washing machine, spin dryer and ironing board. Shop for basics (1/6-31/8). Gas supplies. Paddling pool (20/6-31/8). Playground. Boules. Off site: Bathing, boating, canoeing, sailing and fishing 1 km. Bus stop 2 km. Riding 3 km.	From the south, at the north end of the A404 motorway, continue north towards Orgelet and Lons-le-Saunier on the D31, D436, D27, and D470. Just before Charchilla go left on D301 to Maisod and follow site signs. GPS: N46:28.830 E05:41.540

Open: 18 April - 6 September.

Charges guide

Per unit incl. 2 persons	€ 12,00 - € 14,10
extra person (over 4 yrs)	€ 3,50
electricity	€ 2,70

FR39090 Camping les Bords de Loue

Chemin du Val d'Amour, F-39100 Parcey (Jura)

Tel: **03 84 71 03 82**. Email: **contact@jura-camping.com** www.alanrogers.com/FR39090

This spacious campsite, beside the river Loue, enables canoeing, boating and fishing to be enjoyed direct from the site. It is also at the western end of the Val d'Amour, where the attractive countryside and villages make for pleasant walking and cycling. The site has 284 grass pitches, 216 are for touring. Some are undulating and/or slightly sloping, and only a few have shade. All have electricity (6A), some long leads. Some pitches at the western end of the site are some distance from the nearest water tap. In July/August there are organised events and activities, including pony rides.

Facilities	Directions
Three modern toilet blocks with all the necessary facilities, including for disabled people. Motorcaravan services. Washing machines and dryers. Gas supplies. Bar (all season). Snack bar and takeaway (July/Aug). Satellite TV. Swimming pool and paddling pool (1/5-1/9). Playground. Tennis (free outside July/Aug). Archery. Boules. Off site: Parcey 1 km. with shops, bar, ATM. Golf 1.5 km. Riding 4 km. Bicycle hire 7 km.	Parcey is 8 km. south of Dole. From north, leave A39 exit 6 (Dole). Go southwest for 1 km. on N75/N5 (Beaune and Châlon-sur-Saône). At roundabout, turn left (southeast) (N5) to Parcey. Site is well signed. GPS: N47:01.011 E05:28.913

Open: 15 April - 10 September.

Charges guide

Per person	€ 4,30
child (0-7 yrs)	€ 2,00
pitch incl. electricity (6A)	€ 7,30

FR39110 Camping le Moulin

Patornay, F-39130 Clairvaux-les-Lacs (Jura)

Tel: **03 84 48 31 21**. Email: **contact@camping-moulin.com** www.alanrogers.com/FR39110

Patornay is a pleasant village, just by the river Ain where it starts to widen on its way to the Lac de Vouglans. This well equipped five hectare campsite lies right on the river bank, with direct access for boating, canoeing and fishing. Of the 160 touring pitches, 120 are between well trimmed hedges and trees, with electricity (6A), and water taps very near. The other 40 are in a more natural area, where there is no electricity and water taps are a bit further apart. In July/August the site arranges activities and events for both children and adults.

Facilities	Directions
Two modern heated toilet blocks. Facilities for disabled people. Baby room. Motorcaravan services. Washing machines and dryers. Basic shop. Bar, snack bar, takeaway and terrace (29/5-31/8). Satellite TV. Internet. Games room. Swimming pool with slides and flume, paddling pool (29/5-31/8). Playground. Sports field. Boules. Off site: Pont-de-Poitte (200 m) with supermarket, shops, restaurants, bars, takeaway, ATM, bus stop. Bicycle hire 1 km. Riding 4 km. Sailing 10 km. Golf 17 km.	From Lons-le-Saunier, take the N78 in a southeasterly direction to Pont-de-Poitte. After about 17 km. in village, cross bridge over River Ain, towards Clairvaux-les-Lacs. After 100 m., turn left at site sign and immediately fork left. GPS: N46:35.360 E05:42.200

Open: 25 April - 13 September.

Charges guide

Per unit incl. 2 persons, car and electricity	€ 17,00 - € 28,00
extra person	€ 5,00

BOOK THIS SITE
CALL 01580 214000
...we'll arrange everything
The Travel Service

BOOK THIS SITE
CALL 01580 214000
...we'll arrange everything
The Travel Service

213

The Travel Service
BOOK THIS SITE
CALL 01580 214000
...we'll arrange everything

FR39120 Camping Beauregard

F-39130 Mesnois (Jura)

Tel: **03 84 48 32 51**. Email: reception@juracampingbeauregard.com   www.alanrogers.com/FR39120

A hillside site on the edge of a small village with views of the rolling countryside, Beauregard has 192 pitches. A fenced oval swimming pool and a circular children's pool provide the main attraction on sunny days. Mobile homes and tents for rent leave around 155 for touring units, all with 6A electricity (long leads may be necessary). The tarmac roads are narrow in places, and many pitches are compact and could be more level. Larger outfits may have difficulty fitting everything on the pitch and with levelling. Newer pitches on the lower level could be more suitable (but no shade).

Facilities

Three toilet blocks fairly evenly distributed around the site make a good provision, although the newest one on the lower section is only opened in peak season. Generally modern facilities, some Turkish toilets. The WCs at the block nearest the pool suffer from overuse by unsupervised children. Baby room and facilities for disabled campers. Outdoor pool (15/6-31/8). Play areas. Off site: Restaurant bar and takeway (1/4-30/9) adjacent to site. Fishing 500 m. Riding 5 km. Boat launching 2 km. Other shops and services in Pont-de-Poitte 2 km.

Open: 1 April - 30 September.

Directions

From Lons-le-Saunier (easily accessed from A39) take N78 southeast towards Clairvaux-les-Lacs. After about 17 km. in Thuron (before Pont-de-Poitte) turn left on D151 to Mesnois. Site is 1 km. on left by road junction. GPS: N46:35.980 E05:41.293

Charges guide

Per unit incl. 2 persons	€ 17,20 - € 21,50
extra person	€ 3,28 - € 4,10
child (2-8 yrs)	€ 2,24 - € 2,80
electricity	€ 3,00

Less 20% in low season.

FR90000 Camping l'Etang des Forges

11 rue Béthouart, F-90000 Belfort (Tre.-de-Belfort)

Tel: **03 84 22 54 92**. Email: contact@camping-belfort.com   www.alanrogers.com/FR90000

Belfort (known as the City of the Lion) is a historic fortified town with much history. Although 178 pitches are marked out, this very spacious site only uses 90 of them, and you should always be able to find room here. The pitches are all on level, mostly open ground divided by bushes. A few trees around one end give a little shade to some pitches and there are electricity hook-ups (6A) to all and a good supply of water taps. The reception building also contains a small shop and café.

Facilities

A single modern sanitary building (heated in cool weather) provides washbasins in cubicles, a suite for disabled people, dishwashing and laundry sinks, a washing machine and dryer. Motorcaravan services. Outdoor swimming pool (10/6-9/9). Volleyball. Table tennis. Small playground. TV Room. Shop and café (1/7-31/8). Internet terminal. Off site: Large supermarket is on edge of town on the Mulhouse road.

Open: 7 April - 30 September.

Directions

Site is northeast of town centre towards Offemont, adjacent to the lake and sports facilities (well signed). GPS: N47:39.200 E06:51.866

Charges guide

Per person	€ 3,50 - € 3,80
child (4-9 yrs)	€ 2,50 - € 3,10
pitch	€ 7,50 - € 8,50
electricity	€ 3,00

Camping Cheques accepted.

FR70020 Camping International du Lac

Avenue des Rives du Lac, F-70000 Vesoul-Vaivre (Haute-Saône)

Tel: **03 84 76 22 86**. Email: camping_dulac@yahoo.fr   www.alanrogers.com/FR70020

This is one of the better examples of a town site and is part of a leisure park around a large lake. The campsite does not have direct access to the lake as it is separated by a security fence, but access is possible at the site entrance. There are 160 good sized, level, grass pitches, all with electricity (10A). Access is from hard roads and pitches are separated by shrubs and bushes. There is a large area in the centre of the site with a play area. A five kilometre path has been created around the lake for jogging, walking and cycling.

Facilities

Three good quality toilet blocks, one heated, are well spaced around the site and provide a mix of British and Turkish style WCs, washbasins and showers. Baby room. Two superb suites for disabled visitors. Laundry facilities. Motorcaravan service point. Baker calls daily (July/Aug); bread ordered from reception at other times. Animation (July/Aug). Bicycle hire. TV and games room. Boules. Internet access. Fishing. Off site: Bar and restaurant adjacent. Lake beach 100 m. Sailing 2 km. Riding 4 km.

Open: 1 March - 31 October.

Directions

On road D457 to west of Vesoul on route to Besançon, well signed around the town. GPS: N47:37.812 E06:07.700

Charges guide

Per person	€ 3,55
child (under 7 yrs)	€ 1,65
pitch	€ 3,40
incl. electricity	€ 5,40
vehicle	€ 2,60

Check real time availability and at-the-gate prices...

www.alanrogers.com

MAP 9

Deep valleys dividing mountain slopes, covered in lush alpine pastures and evergreen woods – this is the Savoy Alps bordering Switzerland. Further south you'll come across the Dauphiné Alps which, although they can appear harsh and forbidding, offer spectacular scenery.

Savoy & Dauphiny Alps

DÉPARTEMENTS: 38 ISÈRE, 73 SAVOIE, 74 HAUTE-SAVOIE

MAJOR CITY: GRENOBLE

Lying between the Rhône Valley and the Alpine borders with Switzerland and Italy are the old provinces of Savoie and Dauphiné. This is an area of enormous granite outcrops, deeply riven by spectacular glacier hewn and river etched valleys. One of the world's leading winter playgrounds there is also a range of outdoor activities in the summer. Despite development, great care has been taken to blend the old with the new and many traditional villages still retain their charm and historical interest. For many, it is an opportunity to escape the crowds and enjoy some clean air, unusual wildlife, stunning views, hidden lakes and sometimes isolated villages in spectacular mountain settings.

From Chambéry, north to the shores of Lac Léman (Lake Geneva) are many towns and villages that, since Roman times, have attracted visitors to take the waters. Aix-les-Bains, Evian and Annecy were three major lakeside spa resorts of the Victorian period; while Chamonix and Grenoble attracted the19th-century travellers who pioneered modern skiing and 'alpinism'. To the north is the region of Chartreuse famous for its monastery and liqueur!

Places of interest

Aix-les-Bains: spa resort on the Lac du Bourget, boat excursions to the Royal Abbey of Hautecombe.

Albertville: 1992 Winter Olympics, museum, now has an active nightlife!

Annecy: canal-filled lakeside town, 12th-century château, old quarter.

Bourg-St-Maurice: centre of Savoie café society.

Chambéry: old quarter, Dukes of Savoie château, Savoie museum.

Chamonix: site of first Winter Olympics in 1924, world capital of mountain climbing.

Evian-les-Bains: spa and casino on Lake Geneva.

Grenoble: University city, Fort de la Bastille.

Cuisine of the region

Plat gratiné applies to a wide variety of dishes; in the Alps this means cooked in breadcrumbs.

Farcement (Farçon Savoyard): potatoes baked with cream, eggs, bacon, dried pears and prunes.

Féra: a freshwater lake fish.

Fondue: hot melted cheese and white wine.

Gratin Dauphinois: potato dish with cream, cheese and garlic.

Gratin Savoyard: another potato dish with cheese and butter.

Lavaret: a freshwater lake fish, like salmon.

Longeole: a country sausage.

Lotte: a burbot, not unlike an eel.

Tartiflette: potato, bacon, onions and Reblochon cheese.

215

The Travel Service BOOK THIS SITE CALL 01580 214000 ...we'll arrange everything

FR38030 Camping la Cascade

Route de l'Alpe d'Huez, F-38520 Bourg-d'Oisans (Isère)

Tel: **04 76 80 02 42**. Email: **lacascade@wanadoo.fr**   www.alanrogers.com/FR38030

La Cascade has a long season and it is within sight and sound of the waterfall from which it takes its name. It is only 2 km. from Bourg-d'Oisans which lies in the Romanche valley 725 m. above sea level surrounded by high mountains. The area is a sun trap and gets very hot in summer. The site has 133 individual grassy pitches, 106 for touring units on mainly flat ground and of varying size. Although most are quite adequate, larger units are best near the entrance as the pitches and roads do become narrow. All have 16A electricity.

Facilities

Two heated sanitary blocks are of good quality with mainly British style toilets, washbasins in cabins and showers. Laundry facilities. Bar and snack bar (25/6-30/8). Good sized, heated and sheltered swimming pool and paddling pool (1/6-30/9) surrounded by large, enclosed sunbathing area. TV in bar. Off site: Supermarket or fishing 500 m. Bicycle hire or riding 1 km. Bourg-d'Oisans 1 km. with bars, restaurants, shops and banks. Ski resorts of Alpe d'Huez 13 km. and Les Deux Alpes 25 km.

Open: 20 December - 30 September.

Directions

From Grenoble take N91 to Bourg-d'Oisans, cross river bridge, after 730 m. turn left on to D211, signed Alpe d'Huez. Site is on right in 600 m. GPS: N45:03.832 E06:02.362

Charges guide

Per unit incl. 2 persons and electricity	€ 21,80 - € 29,30
extra person (over 5 yrs)	€ 4,80 - € 6,50
animal	free

FR38010 Kawan Village le Coin Tranquille

F-38490 Les Abrets (Isère)

Tel: **04 76 32 13 48**. Email: **contact@coin-tranquille.com**   www.alanrogers.com/FR38010

Les Abrets is well placed for visits to the Savoie regions and the Alps. It is an attractive, well maintained site of 192 grass pitches (178 for tourers), all with electricity. They are separated by neat hedges and trees to make a lovely environment doubly enhanced by the rural aspect and mountain views. This is a popular, family run site with friendly staff that makes a wonderful base for exploring the area. Set in the Dauphiny countryside north of Grenoble, Le Coin Tranquille is truly a 'quiet corner', especially outside school holiday times, although still popular with families in high season.

Facilities

The central well appointed sanitary block is well kept, heated in low season. Facilities for children and disabled people. Two smaller blocks provide facilities in high season. Busy shop. Excellent restaurant. Swimming pool and paddling pool (15/5-30/9; no Bermuda-style shorts) with sunbathing areas. Play area. TV and games in bar. Quiet reading room. Weekly entertainment for children and adults (July/Aug) including live music (not discos). Bicycle hire (limited). Off site: Riding 6 km. Fishing 8 km. Golf 25 km. Les Abrets with shops 2 km.

Open: 1 April - 31 October.

Directions

Les Abrets is 70 km. southeast of Lyon at junction of N6 and N75. From roundabout in town take N6 towards Chambéry, turning left in just under 2 km. (signed Restaurant and Camping). Follow signs along country lane for just over 1 km. and entrance is on right. GPS: N45:32.482 E05:36.489

Charges 2009

Per unit incl. 2 persons and electricity	€ 16,30 - € 32,00
extra person	€ 4,00 - € 7,50

Camping Cheques accepted.

FR38020 Camping Ser Sirant

Lac de Laffrey, Petichet, F-38119 Saint Théoffrey (Isère)

Tel: **04 76 83 91 97**. Email: **campingsersirant@wanadoo.fr**   www.alanrogers.com/FR38020

This small lakeside site, a few kilometres from La Route Napoléon, has 87 touring pitches (6A reverse polarity) and 6 chalets, set on a level, partly terraced, grassed area. There is a pleasant lakeside terrace just outside the bar and reception, whilst about 70 metres up the lakeside there is a sailing school for you to improve (or start) your sailboarding skills. On site there are kayaks for hire and fishing on the lake. This is a picturesque site with the minimum of extras which will appeal especially to water lovers.

Facilities

A single toilet block is at one end of the site. Equipped to basic standards it could be under pressure at peak times. Half the WCs are Turkish style. No facilities for children. Launderette. Small bar with shop for basic supplies. Takeaway at weekends in July/Aug. Kayak hire. Fishing. Chalets to rent. Off site: Shops and restaurants within 1 km. Riding and bicycle hire 5 km.

Open: 1 May - 30 September.

Directions

Petichet is on the Route Napoléon between Grenoble and La Mure. Site is well signed and easy to find by the lake. GPS: N45:00.490 E05:47.560

Charges guide

Per unit incl. 2 persons and electricity	€ 19,50 - € 22,00
extra person	€ 3,50 - € 4,90

No credit cards.

Check real time availability and at-the-gate prices... www.alanrogers.com

FR38060 Domaine les Trois Lacs du Soleil

La Plaine, F-38460 Trept (Isère)

Tel: 04 74 92 92 06. Email: info@les3lacsdusoleil.com   www.alanrogers.com/FR38060

Les Trois Lacs is situated on the edge of three lakes in flat, open country in the north of Dauphine. The camping area is on one side of the largest lake with tall trees on one edge and views of distant mountains. The 200 good sized pitches, with 180 for tourists, are well spaced and separated by trees and hedges. All have 6A electricity. There is plenty of activity on offer for the whole family including fishing in one lake, swimming in the other two and, for the more energetic, roller blading. There is plenty of space around the lake for children to play. The land around the lakes has been well landscaped with grassy banks and a variety of shrubs and trees. This is a good base from which to enjoy either the countryside, the historic places of the region or the programme of leisure activities provided by the site (in July/Aug).

Facilities

Two fully equipped toilet blocks are in the centre of the camping area. Toilets for children. Baby room. Laundry facilities. Small shop (July/Aug). Bar/restaurant. Snack bars. Outdoor pool (all June-Sept). Lakeside beach and water slide. Discos and entertainment in high season. TV and sports hall. Roller blade hire. Walking. Fishing. Gas barbecues only. Off site: Riding 500 m. Trept 2 km. Mountain bike hire 10 km.

Open: 1 May - 13 September.

Directions

From A43 take exit 7 on to D522 north. Turn left after 7 km. on to D65 then after 5 km. turn right on to D517. Site is 2 km. east of Trept. Signs in village. GPS: N45:41.219 E05:21.115

Charges guide

Per unit incl. 2 persons	
and electricity	€ 18,50 - € 31,00
extra person	€ 3,00 - € 7,00
child (0-10 yrs)	free - € 3,50
animal	€ 1,50

CAMPING VILLAGE
DOMAINE
LES 3 LACS DU SOLEIL
Cat.1 ★ ★ ★ ★

A holiday park of 26 acres with 3 lakes, a 'nature' swimming pool of 5000 m², swimming pool, paddling pool, shady pitches of 100 m², tennis, mini golf, sporting facilities, fishing. Cottages, chalets and bungalow tents for rent

Opening dates: 01/05/2009 - 13/09/2009

Camping Village les 3 Lacs du Soleil****
38460 Trept | Tél.: 0033 4 74 92 92 06
info@les3lacsdusoleil.com | www.les3lacsdusoleil.com

FR38040 Camping à la Rencontre du Soleil

Route de l'Alpe d'Huez, F-38520 Bourg-d'Oisans (Isère)

Tel: 04 76 79 12 22. Email: rencontre.soleil@wanadoo.fr   www.alanrogers.com/FR38040

The Isère is an attractive and popular region with exceptional scenery. Bourg-d'Oisans lies in the Romanche valley 725 m. above sea level surrounded by high mountains. This compact site, pleasant, friendly and family run, nestles between two impressive mountain ranges, at the base of France's largest National Park, Le Parc des Ecrins. It is a real sun trap and gets very hot in summer. It is only two kilometres from Bourg-d'Oisans and has 73 level, hedged pitches, most of average size, with mature trees offering good shade (43 for touring). Electricity is available (2-10A). Rock pegs are advised. A 'Sites et Paysages' member.

Facilities

Heated toilet block provides all the usual amenities, but no facilities for disabled people. Washing machine and dryer. Motorcaravan services. Bread to order. Restaurant and takeaway (all season). Room with TV, children's play room. Small, sheltered swimming pool (all season). Play area. Children's club. Activities in high season include walking, mountain biking. Off site: Supermarket 1 km. Fishing 5 km. Bicycle hire, riding 2 km. Canoeing, rafting, riding, hiking, climbing. Cable car at Alpe d'Huez.

Open: 1 May - 30 September.

Directions

Leave Bourg-d'Oisans on N91 towards Briançon. Shortly on a sharp right hand bend, turn left on D211 signed Alpe d'Huez. Site is on left just beyond Camping la Piscine. Entrance is on a sharp bend - take care. GPS: N45:03.940 E06:02.381

Charges 2009

Per unit incl. 2 persons	
and electricity	€ 19,00 - € 30,80
extra person	€ 5,10 - € 6,60

Camping Cheques accepted.

B O O K   T H I S   S I T E
CALL 01580 214000
...we'll arrange everything
The Travel Service

217

BOOK THIS SITE
CALL 01580 214000
...we'll arrange everything

The Travel
Service

FR38070 Camping l'Oursière

F-38250 Villard-de-Lans (Isère)

Tel: **04 76 95 14 77**. Email: **info@camping-oursiere.fr**   www.alanrogers.com/FR38070

This friendly, family run site is ideally situated within easy walking distance of the attractive resort of Villard de Lans which provides a very wide range of activities. It is ideal for those who prefer a peaceful site in a more natural setting. The good sized grass and stone pitches are slightly uneven but have magnificent views over the surrounding mountains. There are 186 marked pitches, 146 for touring, most have electricity (6/10A). A variety of trees offers some shade. Rock pegs essential. Because the town of Villard-de-Lans offers so much entertainment, little is organised on site. There are good shops, bars and restaurants (all July/August only), a bank, swimming pool complex, ice skating rink (last two open most of the year) and a gambling casino. There are many marked walks and bike rides (on and off road) around the town, several starting from the site. This is an excellent value for money base for those seeking a relaxing or active holiday, both summer and winter.

Facilities

Clean, heated toilet blocks with all necessary facilities including those for disabled campers, ski store and drying room. Motorcaravan services. Single building houses reception, bar (July/Aug), cosy lounge with open fireplace, TV room, games rooms. Snack bar (July/Aug). Internet access. Play area. Boules. Volleyball. Trout fishing. Off site: Bus to Autrans and Grenoble. Free bus to ski resorts (winter). Supermarket 1 km. Bicycle hire 1 km. Riding 2 km. Golf 5 km.

Open: All year excl. 28 September - 4 December.

Directions

Northwest of Grenoble, leave Autoroute A48 exit 13 or 3A. Follow N532 to Sassenage, at roundabout take D531. Entering Villard-de-Lans (25 km), fork left signed Villard Centre, site is shortly on left. Only route for caravans and motorcaravans. GPS: N45:04.655 E05:33.37

Charges 2009

Per unit incl. 2 persons and electricity	€ 18,00 - € 24,00
extra person	€ 4,10 - € 4,85
child (2-12 yrs)	€ 3,60 - € 4,25
dog	€ 0,90

Camping Caravaneige L'Oursière

Situated in the heart of the Vercors Regional Park, we offer you all ingredients for a relaxing or active holiday

Camping Caravaneige L'Oursière
38250 Villard de Lans - France
www.camping-oursiere.fr
info@camping-oursiere.fr
Tel. +33 (0)4 76 95 14 77
Fax +33 (0)4 76 95 58 11

open from 05-12-2008 till 27-09-2009

FR38050 Camping Caravaning le Temps Libre

F-38150 Bougé-Chambalud (Isère)

Tel: **04 74 84 04 09**. Email: **camping.temps-libre@libertysurf.fr**   www.alanrogers.com/FR38050

You will receive a warm welcome at this spacious, family run site which is close to the A7 motorway, between Lyon and Valence. There are 199 pitches, with 90 available for tourers. Mobile homes and seasonal pitches are in a separate area. The medium to large, partly sloping, grassy pitches are mostly separated by hedges and trees giving privacy and some shade. All have 9A electricity and water close by. Most are in cul-de-sacs, in groups of 8, and a few have tricky access. There is a large hardstanding area with electricity for motorcaravans and overnight stays. A 'Sites et Paysages' member.

Facilities

Three toilet blocks, two for tourers, providing all the necessary facilities. Motorcaravan service point. Good shop (1/5-31/8), bar/restaurant and takeaway (all 1/7-31/8). Large pool complex (15/5-30/9, no Bermuda style shorts). Two playgrounds. Club/TV room. Boules. Tennis. Fishing. Minigolf. Organised activities and pony cart rides (July and Aug). Internet access. Off site: Disco 3 km. Canoeing. Shops. Supermarket. Lafuma factory shop at Anneyron 8 km. Golf and riding 10 km.

Open: 1 April - 30 September.

Directions

From A7 motorway take exit 12 (Chanas) or from N7 take D510 east towards Grenoble for about 7 km. to Bougé-Chambalud. Turn right in village. Site is a few hundred metres (signed). GPS: N45:19.426 E04:54.155

Charges guide

Per unit incl. 2 persons	€ 14,50 - € 20,50
extra person	€ 4,50 - € 7,00
electricity (9A)	€ 4,50
Camping Cheques accepted.	

Check real time availability and at-the-gate prices...

www.alanrogers.com

FR38080 Kawan Village Au Joyeux Réveil

Le Château, F-38880 Autrans (Isère)

Tel: 04 76 95 33 44. Email: camping-au-joyeux-reveil@wanadoo.fr   www.alanrogers.com/FR38080

The small town of Autrans is set on a plateau, 1,050 m. high, in the Vercors region. The well organised site is run by a very friendly family (English is spoken). It is on the outskirts of the town, set below a ski jump and short lift. There are 108 pitches with 78 for touring, electricity 2-10A. They are mainly on grass, in a sunny location with fantastic views over the surrounding wooded mountains with small trees giving little shade. There is a new swimming pool area with a separate paddling pool and two other pools with river and slide. Here the days can be very hot and sunny and the nights quite chilly. It is ideally situated for any of the activities that this wonderful area has to offer – from walking, mountain biking and potholing in summer to downhill and cross-country skiing in winter, it is all there for you in magnificent scenery. The D531 and the D106 look a little daunting on the map and do involve a stiff climb but they are good roads and have no difficult bends.

Facilities

The new toilet block is very well appointed, with under-floor heating and all the expected facilities. Another new building houses a bar with terrace, snack bar/takeaway (July and August). New pool area with two pools, toboggan for children, sunbathing area and a separate paddling pool. Small play area. TV room. Internet point. Off site: Autrans with a few shops 500 m. Villard de Lans, supermarket, shops, restaurants, bars, ice rink and many other activities 16 km. Short ski lift is near the site and a shuttle bus runs (in winter) to the longer runs (5 km). Fishing, bicycle hire and riding 300 m. Bus to Villard de Lans and Grenoble.

Open: 1 December - 31 March, 1 May - 30 September.

Directions

From A48, northwest of Grenoble use exit 13 (going south) or 3A (going north). Follow N532 to Sassenage, turn west at roundabout on D531 to Lans en Vercors. At a roundabout turn right on D106 signed Autrans. On entering Autrans turn right at roundabout (site signed) and very shortly right again. This is the only route recommended for caravans and motorcaravans. GPS: N45:10.515 E05:32.870

Charges guide

Per unit incl. 1 or 2 persons	€ 18,50 - € 30,00
extra person	€ 5,00
electricity (2-6A)	€ 2,00 - € 8,00

Winter prices - apply to site.
Camping Cheques accepted.

CAMPING AU JOYEUX REVEIL

We take pride in providing our guests with the very best service, including sharing our love of the Vercors, one of France's most beautiful regions. Our campsite is open in both summer and winter and offers a quiet, friendly environment perfect as a base for discovering all that nature has to offer in the Vercors.

The campsite has a very nice heated pool complex, including a covered pool, modern sanitary facilities with under-floor heating in winter and the pitches with clear views of the mountains.

Located right at the heart of the Vercors natural park (history, tradition and nature) in a beautiful, restful setting, our site is located just across from the Olympic ski jump from the 1968 Games and is just 300m from the town of Autrans (1050m) which offers a full range of shops and activities.

Christine and Franck Blanc

Camping Au Joyeux Réveil • 38880 Autrans • Tel: 0033.4.76.95.33.44 • www.camping-au-joyeux-reveil.fr

FR38090 Camping Caravaning Belle Roche

F-38930 Lalley (Isère)

Tel: 04 76 34 75 33. Email: gildapatt@aol.com   www.alanrogers.com/FR38090

Belle Roche is a good, spacious, family run site. The level site is only a few years old, so is rather open at present with very little shade, but it is nonetheless neat and well maintained throughout. There are 57 large, slightly uneven and slightly sloping pitches, many part grass with a gravel hardstanding, partially delineated by shrubs and young trees. Rock pegs are necessary. All have 10A electricity (long leads may be necessary) and there are ample water points.

Facilities

Two modern, well equipped and clean toilet blocks. Facilities for disabled visitors. Laundry and dishwashing. Motorcaravan services. Bar/TV room, terrace serving simple meals (all season). Bread. Swimming pool (mid May - Sept) with large sunbathing area and sunbeds. Very large play area. Off site: Village shop 400 m. Many marked cycling, walking and climbs to suit all capabilities. Bicycle hire 8 km. Riding 15 km.

Open: 4 April - 27 September.

Directions

Follow N75 south from Grenoble (about 65 km.) turn left onto D66, signed Lalley, Mens and campsite, and then follow camping signs through the village. The campsite is on the right just beyond the village. GPS: N44:45.295 E05:40.736

Charges 2009

Per unit incl. 2 persons	€ 16,10 - € 19,00
extra person	€ 3,60

Camping Cheques accepted.

Check real time availability and at-the-gate prices...

www.alanrogers.com

BOOK THIS SITE
CALL 01580 214000
...we'll arrange everything

The Travel
Service

FR38100 Camping Belledonne

Rochetaillée, F-38520 Bourg-d'Oisans (Isère)

Tel: 04 76 80 07 18. Email: belledon@club-internet.fr www.alanrogers.com/FR38100

This extremely neat and spacious site, takes its name from the nearby Belledonne mountain range. The 180 well drained, level, generous, grassy pitches, 148 for touring have electricity (3/6A). There is some road noise for a few pitches. Beech hedges and abundant mature trees provide ample privacy and shade. A bar/restaurant with terrace is next to an attractive pool complex with sunbathing space, surrounded by well tended gardens and grass spaces. In July and August the site becomes quite lively with a daily programme of organised activities. A 'Sites et Paysages' member.

Facilities

Two well appointed sanitary blocks with baby room and facilities for disabled visitors. Shop. Bar/restaurant and takeaway (all open all season). TV/games room. Swimming and paddling pools. Tennis. Good play area, large meadow with fitness course. Bicycle hire (July/Aug). Off site: Allemont, shops 2 km. Bourg-d'Oisans, shops, bars, restaurants 8 km. Hiking, mountain biking, white water rafting, canoeing, bungee jumping, paragliding and much more. Cable car (high season).

Open: 15 May - 13 September.

Directions

Site is 8 km. west of Bourg-d'Oisans. From Grenoble take N85 to Vizille and then N91 towards Bourg-d'Oisans. In Rochetaillée branch left (site signed) onto D526, signed Allemont. Site is 250 m. on right. GPS: N45:06.854 E06:00.459

Charges 2009

Per pitch incl. 2 persons, car and electricity	€ 19,70 - € 29,10
extra person	€ 3,20 - € 6,30

Camping Cheques accepted.

FR38130 Camping Belvédère de l'Obiou

Les Egats, F-38350 Saint Laurent-en-Beaumont (Isère)

Tel: 04 76 30 40 80. Email: info@camping-obiou.com www.alanrogers.com/FR38130

This very good, small Alpine site with just 45 pitches is in the centre of the Ecrins National Park. It is therefore ideal for walkers and cyclists looking to take advantage of the well marked trails. It has most things a good site should have, with its restaurant (high season), heated pool and sitting room with TV and library. The welcoming owners will even supply you with breakfast. The views from the terraced pitches are spectacular and there is a wealth of activities in the area.

Facilities

Two modern toilet blocks, one part of the main building, the other 'Portacabin' style, are immaculate and can be heated. High standard facilities for disabled visitors. Excellent laundry. Motorcaravan services. Restaurant (May - Sept) with Savoyard menu, high quality takeaway and breakfast. Small shop with ice cream. Swimming pool (June - Sept). Bicycle hire. Good play area. Off site: Fishing 3 km. Walking. Cycling. Mountain activities.

Open: 15 April - 30 September.

Directions

From Grenoble take exit 8 onto the RN85. After 9 km. left onto D529 (La Motte d'Aveillans) and back onto the RN85 at La Mure. 7 km. south of La Mure site signed on the left. GPS: N44:52.564 E05:50.270

Charges 2009

Per unit incl. 2 persons	€ 13,00 - € 18,00
extra person	€ 3,00 - € 5,00
electricity (4-10A)	€ 3,00 - € 5,50

Camping Cheques accepted.

FR38110 Camping le Champ du Moulin

Bourg d'Arud, F-38520 Venosc (Isère)

Tel: 04 76 80 07 38. Email: info@champ-du-moulin.com www.alanrogers.com/FR38110

Le Champ du Moulin lies on the floor of the narrow Vénéon valley. It has generous stone and grass pitches that are part-shaded by large trees with electricity (up to 10A). Rock pegs are essential. When the mountain snows melts in late May/early June, the river beside the site changes from its winter trickle to an impressive torrent. Parents with small children need to be especially vigilant. On the edge of the Ecrins National Park with stunning mountain scenery and miles of marked cycling and walking trails, it is an ideal site for active outdoor families. A 'Sites et Paysages' member.

Facilities

Heated, well equipped toilet block. Drying racks for clothes. Baby room. Facilities for disabled people. Motorcaravan services. Chalet restaurant/bar with home cooking. Small shop sharing reception with bread. Play area. TV room. Internet access. Fishing. Off site: Municipal heated outdoor pools and flume next door open in summer, playground, tennis, tree-top adventure park. Rafting, canoeing, paragliding, bungee jumping, hill walking and summer mountain biking available nearby. Discounted ski passes. Golf 3 km. (summer only).

Open: 15 December - 30 April, 1 June - 15 September.

Directions

From Grenoble, pass through Bourg-d'Oisans on the RD1091, signed Briancon. After 3 km. turn right on D530 signed Venosc. In 8 km. pass the telecabin on left. Site on right in 400 m. GPS: N44:59.069 E06:07.198

Charges 2009

Per unit incl. 1 or 2 persons	€ 13,60 - € 19,40
extra person	€ 4,00 - € 4,90
child (3-7 yrs)	€ 2,40 - € 3,00
electricity (3/6/10A)	€ 4,20 - € 8,30

Check real time availability and at-the-gate prices...
www.alanrogers.com

FR38120 Kawan Village le Bontemps

5 impasse du Bontemps, F-38150 Vernioz (Isère)

Tel: 04 74 57 83 52. Email: **info@campinglebontemps.com**   www.alanrogers.com/FR38120

Acquired in April 2008 by Kawan Villages, this spacious, attractive and well cared for site is enhanced by a variety of trees planted by the original owner nearly 30 years ago. The 175 large, level and grassy pitches are arranged in groups, partly separated by neat hedges, all with water and electricity. There are 15 pitches which are used for mobile homes and chalets and a group at the back is used by weekenders. The shop, bar/restaurant and leisure facilities are conveniently placed near the entrance and there is a large sports area and activity hall to one side. This is an excellent site for both short and long stays.

Facilities

Two toilet blocks. Motorcaravan service points. Shop, bar (all season). Restaurant and takeaway (15/4-15/9). Swimming pool (all season). Several play areas. Minigolf. Tennis. Badminton. Electronic games. Fitness equipment. Extensive list of activities for all the family (high season). Small fishing lake. Volleyball. Table-tennis. Off site: Small river for fishing. Vernioz 2 km. Bicycle hire 20 km. Vienne 20 km. Golf 20 km. Pilat Regional Park 15 km.

Open: 28 March - 31 October.

Directions

Exit A7 south of Lyons at junction 9. Continue south for about 7 km. on N7. Just north of Auberives turn left on D37. Follow campsite signs for 7 km. Entrance is on right 4 km. beyond Vernioz. GPS: N45:25.698 E04:55.694

Charges 2009

Per unit incl. 2 persons and electricity	€ 21,50 - € 28,00
extra person	€ 5,00 - € 6,00
child (under 7 yrs)	€ 2,50 - € 3,00
dog	€ 2,00

Camping Cheques accepted.

Kawan Village Le Bontemps

Just 10 minutes off the N7 and short distance from A7, spacious, private pitches set in parkland.
On A7, from the North take exit 9 and from the South exit 12. Perfect for visiting Roman Vienne & the Pilat Regional Park.

Open from 28/03/2009 to 31/10/2009

5 impasse du Bontemps
38150 Vernioz / Saint Alban de Varèze
Tél : 0033 (0)4 74 57 83 52
Fax : 0033 (0)4 74 57 83 70
info@camping-lebontemps.com
www.camping-lebontemps.com

Check real time availability and at-the-gate prices...
www.**alanrogers**.com

The Travel Service ...we'll arrange everything
BOOK THIS SITE
CALL 01580 214000

FR38140 Camping le Colporteur

Le Mas du Plan, F-38521 Bourg-d'Oisans (Isère)

Tel: **04 76 79 11 44**. Email: **info@camping-colporteur.com**   www.alanrogers.com/FR38140

The site is within a few minutes level walk of the attractive market town making this an ideal spot for motorcaravanners. The owners have recently put in much effort to improve this site. There are 150 level grassy pitches, 130 for touring, mostly separated by hedging and a variety of mature trees that offer some shade. All pitches have 15A electricity and rock pegs are advised. Although there is no pool on the site, campers are given free entry to the adjacent municipal pool. In July and August the attractive bar/restaurant is the focal point for evening activities. At over 700 metres above sea level, Bourg-d'Oisans is in the largest national park in France. It is surrounded by high mountains making it a real suntrap and can be very hot in summer. The area is revered by serious cyclists as several mountain roads close by are regularly used by the Tour de France. This is an ideal base for exploring this scenic region with its abundance of wild flowers, old villages and rushing waterfalls; by car, on foot or by bike.

Facilities

Large well equipped, modern, airy toilet block has all the necessary facilities including washbasins in cabins, a baby room and an en-suite room for disabled campers. Games room. Boules. Table tennis. Volleyball. Small play area. Organised family activities (July/Aug). Off site: Shops, bars, restaurants in town and supermarket 500 m. Cycling, mountain biking, hiking, rafting, canoeing, climbing, riding, hang-gliding, Parc des Ecrins, cable cars (July/August) and many mountain passes. Bus services.

Open: 1 May - 30 September.

Directions

Site is in Bourg-d'Oisans. From Grenoble follow the N91 into town and shortly after the road bears left in the town centre and just beyond a petrol station, turn right (site signed). Follow signs to site, a few hundred metres. GPS: N45:03.156 E06:02.130

Charges guide

Per unit incl. 2 persons	
and electricity	€ 20,50 - € 26,00
extra person	€ 5,80
child (5-10 yrs)	€ 3,50

Camping le Colporteur

5 minutes walk from the town. Grassy touring pitches. Complete tranquility. Views of Alpe d'Huez.

info@camping-colporteur.com - www.camping-colporteur.com

FR38160 Camping de Martinière

Route du Col de Porte, F-38380 Saint Pierre-de-Chartreuse (Isère)

Tel: **04 76 88 60 36**. Email: **camping-de-martiniere@orange.fr**   www.alanrogers.com/FR38160

Chamechaude, the 2,082 m. Eiger-like peak, presides benevolently over the 86 touring pitches at this beautiful, high alpine site open from May to September for the summer season. The 86 large touring pitches, with electricity available (2-10A), have some shade and are slightly sloping. The site has a heated pool in the open air so that not a moment of the views is lost. This well run, family owned enterprise, is a peaceful centre for walking, climbing, cycling or just soaking up the air and ambience. It is in the centre of the Chartreuse National Forest. A 'Sites et Paysages' member.

Facilities

Two heated toilet blocks, one at each end of the site provide excellent, clean facilities. Facilities for babies but not for disabled visitors. Laundry facilities. Shop (1/6-15/9). Bar (1/6-15/9) with snacks (1/7-1/9). Heated swimming and paddling pools (1/6-5/9). Play area. Indoor sitting area for poor weather. Extensive paperback library (NL. IT, Fr, UK). Off site: Restaurant 50 m. from site entrance. Bicycle hire 3 km. Skiing 6 km. Walking, cycling and mountain activities.

Open: 1 May - 13 September.

Directions

From St Laurent du Pont (north from Voiron or south from Chambery), take D512 (St Pierre-de-Chartreuse). Site is well signed in the village (the road south from St Pierre d'Entremont is not recommended for towing). GPS: N45:19.330 E05:47.498

Charges 2009

Per unit incl. 2 persons	
and electricity	€ 16,50 - € 25,70
extra person	€ 4,80 - € 5,50
Camping Cheques accepted.	

Check real time availability and at-the-gate prices...
www.**alanrogers**.com

FR38180 Castel Camping le Château de Rochetaillée

Chemin de Bouthean, Rochetaillée, F-38520 Bourg-d'Oisans (Isère)

Tel: **04 76 11 04 40**. Email: **jcp@camping-le-chateau.com**　　　www.alanrogers.com/FR38180

Set in the grounds of the small château, with spectacular views, this site has recently been upgraded to provide high quality amenities. The grounds are shared with chalets and tents to rent, with these in a separate area. There are 94 touring pitches, all with 6/10A electricity hook-ups on level areas (some large) separated by hedges and trees. The site has an excellent heated swimming pool, a fitness room, sauna, bar/restaurant and takeaway food together with a small shop with bread and basic groceries. The site is in the centre of an area ideal for walkers, cyclists and climbers.

Facilities

Three very good toilet blocks are colourful and very clean. Shower room with facilities for babies. Excellent, spacious facilities for disabled visitors. Small launderette. Shop, bar, snacks, takeaway and separate restaurant (all 1/6-7/9). Swimming pool. Sauna, fitness room and jacuzzi. Climbing wall. Daily activities for children (July/Aug). Guided mountain walks and other activities. Fishing. Safe hire. Barbecue area. Internet and WiFi. Off site: Many mountain activities. Riding and bicycle hire 4 km.

Open: 13 May - 14 September.

Directions

Site is signed from the N91, just north of Rochetaillée. GPS: N45:06.918 E06:00.329

Charges 2009

Per unit incl. 2 persons	€ 17,00 - € 27,00
extra person	€ 5,00 - € 6,80
child (0-10 yrs)	€ 3,30 - € 4,30
electricity (6/10A)	€ 4,00 - € 4,50

FR38190 Camping le Champ Long

Le Champ Long, F-38350 La Salle-en-Beaumont (Isère)

Tel: **04 76 30 41 81**　　　www.alanrogers.com/FR38190

Set at the entrance to the Ecran National Park and overlooked by the great Obiou massif, this site has been carved from a hilly forest. It provides 97 pitches (8/10A electricity) arranged in glades between mature trees. The setting is such that it is hard to see the other units around you, yet the mountain views through the trees are wonderful. The site is terraced and hilly and adequate power for towing is needed for the winding access tracks. Very large outfits are best near the entrance as the distant pitches could be difficult to get to. There are some steep paths to the sanitary blocks.

Facilities

Two sanitary blocks, one at reception, the other high on the steep terraces provide British and Turkish style WCs, washbasins in cabins and unexceptional showers. Facilities for children and babies. Laundry facilities. Motorcaravan service point. Milk, bread and a few essentials kept (May-Sept). Bar. Good restaurant and takeaway (May-Sept). Heated outdoor swimming pool (1/5-31/8). Play area and games room. Barbecues to rent. Caravan storage. Off site: Riding and bicycle hire 6 km.

Open: 1 April - 15 October.

Directions

From the RN85 turn off at sign for La Roche which is close to La Salle-en-Beaumont. Site is signed. GPS: N44:51.332 E05:50.702

Charges guide

Per unit incl. 2 persons	€ 13,00 - € 15,00
extra person	€ 3,50 - € 3,80
child (0-7 yrs)	€ 2,50 - € 2,80

FR73020 Camping Caravaneige le Versoyen

Route des Arcs, F-73700 Bourg-Saint-Maurice (Savoie)

Tel: **04 79 07 03 45**. Email: **leversoyen@wanadoo.fr**　　　www.alanrogers.com/FR73020

Bourg-St-Maurice is on a small, level plain at an altitude of 830 m. on the River Isère, surrounded by mountains. Le Versoyen attracts visitors all year round (except for a short time when they close). The site's 205 unseparated, flat pitches (180 for touring) are marked by numbers on the tarmac roads and all have electrical connections (4/6/10A). Most are on grass but some are on tarmac hardstanding making them ideal for use by motorcaravans or in winter. Trees give shade in some parts, although most pitches have almost none. Duckboards are provided for snow and wet weather.

Facilities

Two acceptable toilet blocks can be heated, although the provision may be hard pressed in high season. British and Turkish style WCs. Laundry. Motorcaravan service facilities. Outdoor and covered pools (July/Aug). Heated restroom with TV. Small bar with takeaway in summer. Free shuttle in high season to funicular railway. Off site: Fishing or bicycle hire 200 m. Tennis and swimming pool 500 m. Riding 1 km. Golf 15 km. Cross-country ski track.

Open: All year (excl. 7/11-14/12 and 2/5-25/5).

Directions

Site is 1.5 km. east of Bourg-St-Maurice on CD119 Les Arcs road. GPS: N45:37.324 E06:47.010

Charges guide

Per unit incl. 2 persons and electricity	€ 16,10 - € 21,00
extra person	€ 4,00 - € 4,60
child (4-13 yrs)	€ 2,50 - € 4,40
dog	€ 0,50

Check real time availability and at-the-gate prices...
www.alanrogers.com

BOOK THIS SITE
The Travel Service
CALL 01580 214000
...we'll arrange everything

FR73040 Camping Municipal le Savoy

Avenue du Parc, F-73190 Challes-les-Eaux (Savoie)

Tel: 04 79 72 97 31. Email: camping73challes-les-eaux@wanadoo.fr   www.alanrogers.com/FR73040

This attractive municipal site is surrounded by mountains and only a few hundred metres from the centre of Challes-les-Eaux. There are 99 level pitches, mostly for touring. Some are separated by beech hedges and mature trees offer some shade. There are 12 pitches for motorcaravans, 44 part hardstanding super pitches with 10A electricity and 19 with 6A electricity. Rock pegs are advised. This site is a very good base for touring this scenic region and makes an ideal stop over for those on route to the Fréjus Tunnel and Italy.

Facilities

Two well equipped toilet blocks with all the necessary facilities. Facilities for disabled visitors. Bar with simple snacks (July/Aug). Good sized playground. Boules, table tennis and table football. Off site: Small park with lake for swimming, tennis and volleyball courts adjacent. Challes-les-Eaux, with shops, banks, bars, restaurants, small supermarket, casino and minigolf, a few hundred metres. Interesting old town of Chambéry 6 km. Fréjus Tunnel 96 km. and Bardonecchia (Italy) 110 km.

Open: 1 May - 30 September.

Directions

Challes is 7 km. southeast of Chambéry. From south on autoroute A41, join N6 north at exit 21. Head towards Challes-les-Eaux. From north on A43/A41 head south towards A41 (Grenoble/Albertville) and join N6 at exit 18. Site is on the N6 at northern edge of town. Turn east at traffic lights, site signed. GPS: N45:33.094 E05:59.036

Charges guide

Per unit incl. 2 persons, car and electricity	€ 13,05
extra person	€ 1,35 - € 3,20

FR73030 Camping les Lanchettes

Mobile homes ▶ page 500

F-73210 Peisey-Nancroix (Savoie)

Tel: 04 79 07 93 07. Email: lanchettes@free.fr   www.alanrogers.com/FR73030

A natural, terraced site, it has 90 good size, reasonably level and well drained, grassy/stony pitches, with 80 used for touring units, 70 having electricity (3-10A). Because it is very cold in winter and quite cold on some spring and autumn evenings (warm bedding necessary) there are no outside taps. For those who love walking and biking and wonderful scenery, this is the site for you. In winter it is ideal for the serious skier being close to the resort of Les Arcs. Underpowered units not advised.

Facilities

Well appointed heated toilet block. Motorcaravan services. Restaurant, takeaway (July/Aug. and winter). Playground. Club/TV room. Large tent/marquee used in bad weather. In winter a small bus (free) runs to all the hotels, bars, ski tows. Off site: Walks in National Park. Riding next to site. Peisey-Nancroix, restaurants, bars and shops 3 km. Les Arcs winter sports centre 6 km. Outdoor swimming pool and bicycle hire 6 km. Golf and indoor pool 8 km.

Open: 15 December - 15 October.

Directions

From Albertville take N90 towards Bourg-St-Maurice, through Aime. In 9 km. turn right on D87, signed Peisey-Nancroix. Follow a winding hilly road (with hairpin bends) for 10 km. Pass through Peisey-Nancroix; site on right about 1 km. beyond Nancroix. GPS: N45:31.882 E06:46.536

Charges guide

Per unit incl. 2 persons	€ 11,80 - € 13,50
extra person	€ 4,05 - € 4,50
electricity (3-10A)	€ 3,00 - € 8,00

Camping Cheques accepted.

FR73050 Camping les Trois Lacs

Les Chaudannes (D916a), F-73330 Belmont Tramonet (Savoie)

Tel: 04 76 37 04 03. Email: info@les3lacs.com   www.alanrogers.com/FR73050

If you would enjoy a site surrounded by lakes with views of the distant mountains, then this is ideal for you. The site takes 100 touring units on large, well spaced pitches separated by hedges in a park with mature trees. This rural site has excellent facilities for fishing and boating and there is a hall with lots of entertainment ranging from pool to electronic games. Well away from the pitches, this hall also hosts music and discos in the evenings in high season.

Facilities

Three sanitary blocks are supplemented by small units with WCs around the site. Well equipped showers. Special new block for children. Excellent facilities for visitors with disabilities. Laundry facilities. Shop, bar and restaurant (full menu in high season) and takeaway (all 1/6-1/9). Small swimming pool (1/5-1/9; unheated). TV and sports hall. Entertainment in high season. Chalets and rooms to rent. Access to all three lakes 15 km.

Open: 1 May - 20 September.

Directions

From the A43 take exit 11 (St Genix-sur-Guiers) onto D916. Site is 2 km. GPS: N45:33.560 E05:40.490

Charges guide

Per unit incl. 1 or 2 persons	€ 14,00 - € 28,00
extra person	€ 3,50 - € 6,50
child (1-6 yrs)	€ 2,50 - € 5,00
electricity (6/10A)	€ 4,00 - € 5,00

No credit cards.

Check real time availability and at-the-gate prices...
www.alanrogers.com

FR73060 Camping Caravaneige l'Eden

F-73210 Landry (Savoie)

Tel: 04 79 07 61 81. Email: info@camping-eden.net   www.alanrogers.com/FR73060

L'Eden is open almost all year round (it is closed for three weeks in May). Beside the Iser river and set in beautiful woodland glades, it is perfect for winter skiing and summer walking and cycling. The site is set in a valley with the Alpine peaks as a backdrop. The 132 good, spacious pitches all have 10A electrical hook-ups and individual water supplies (available when no frost is likely). The pristine, modern sanitary blocks are heated in colder weather and include a large drying room. There is a pool for summer lounging, a bar and a welcoming communal area with bar, TV and internet access.

Facilities	Directions
Two heated toilet blocks include drying rooms, good facilities for disabled visitors and for babies. Small launderette. Communal area with bar, TV and internet. Snack bar and takeaway (July/Aug). Swimming pool (13.5 x 5 m; June - Sept). Games room. Play area. Fishing. Ski passes for sale on-site. Off site: Shops and restaurants in village. Many leisure pursuits including rafting, paragliding, cycle and cross country ski tracks. Riding 10 km. Golf 15 km.	From the RN90 take D87 towards Landry. Site is on left after 250 m. and is well signed from the RN90. GPS: N45:34.591 E06:44.074

Charges guide

Per unit incl. 2 persons	€ 10,70 - € 21,40
extra person	€ 2,90 - € 5,70
child (0-7 yrs)	€ 2,30 - € 4,50
electricity (10A)	€ 2,00 - € 6,00

Open: All year excl. 1-23 May.

FR73080 Flower Camping Lacs de Chevelu

F-73170 Saint Jean-de-Chevelu (Savoie)

Tel: 04 79 36 72 21. Email: camping-des-lacs@wanadoo.fr   www.alanrogers.com/FR73080

This is a small, family orientated campsite which is run by a friendly family and surrounded by delightful scenery, not far from Lac du Bourget. Beside the site is a small lake which is fed by springs and has a sandy beach ideal for swimming and playing around in small boats. The site has 120 average to large size, grass pitches with 110 for touring. There are 50 with 10A electricity (long leads advised). They are numbered and marked by very small trees with a few having some shade. This site ideal for families who are happy to make their own entertainment.

Facilities	Directions
Excellent newly refurbished toilet block with all necessary facilities including those for babies and campers with disabilities. Motorcaravan services. Shop. Bar (1/6-30/8). Takeaway snacks (1/6-30/8). Fishing. Lake bathing (lifeguard in high season). Walks and bike rides. Games area. Boules. TV room. Play area. Some entertainment in high season. Off site: Riding, bicycle hire, canoeing, hang gliding 5 km. Boat ramp 7 km. Golf 10 km. Yenne with shops, bars and restaurants 5 km. Chambéry 13 km.	Leave A43 at exit 13 (Chambery) and take N504 north towards Belley. After the 'Tunnel du Chat', in Saint Jean-de-Chevelu, turn right (site signed). Site is just over 1 km. GPS: N45:41.627 E05:49.495

Charges guide

Per unit incl. 2 persons	€ 12,50 - € 17,90
with electricity (10A)	€ 13,90 - € 20,90
extra person	€ 2,60 - € 3,90
child (2-7 yrs)	€ 2,10 - € 2,90

Open: 1 May - 28 September.

FR73090 Flower Camping du Lac de Carouge

Base de Loisirs, F-73250 Saint Pierre-d'Albigny (Savoie)

Tel: 04 79 28 58 16. Email: campinglacdecarouge@orange.fr   www.alanrogers.com/FR73090

Camping Lac de Carouge is a well maintained and pleasant campsite next to a very clean, gently shelving, spring fed lake. This is ideal for swimming and playing around in small boats. There are many marked walks and cycle tracks in this beautiful regional park. The site provides 80 large, level, grass pitches with 67 for touring (electricity 6/10A), separated by hedges giving privacy and some shade. There are good views of the mountains but not of the lake. Access to the site is easy from the A41, A43 and A430 autoroutes, ideal for a short stay but you may be tempted to stay longer.

Facilities	Directions
Two new (2007) toilet blocks with excellent facilities, including a superb family room and suite for campers with disabilities. Large tent for bar and children's room (July/Aug). Volleyball, table tennis, boules. Off site: Lake bathing, play area, shaded picnic and play area, pedaloes 200 m. Bar/restaurant 200 m. and 500 m. Bike rides and walks around lake. Supermarket 1 km. St-Pierre d'Albigny some shops restaurants 2 km. Albertville with large range of shops, bars, restaurants 26 km.	St-Pierre d'Albigny is just north of the N90/N6, midway between Albertville and Chambery. Site is well signed on the outskirts of the village. GPS: N45:33.398 E06:09.970

Charges 2009

Per unit incl. 2 persons and electricity	€ 15,50 - € 19,50
extra person	€ 3,00 - € 4,00
child (2-7 yrs)	€ 2,00 - € 3,00

Open: 25 April - 15 September.

Check real time availability and at-the-gate prices...
www.alanrogers.com

www.flowercampings.com

FR73120 Camping le Sougey

Lac Rive Ouest, F-73610 Saint Alban-de-Montbel (Savoie)

Tel: **04 79 36 01 44**. Email: info@camping-sougey.com   www.alanrogers.com/FR73120

In scenic surroundings, this site is only 200 m. from Lake Aiguebelette, the third largest natural lake in France. The 165 pitches (140 for touring units) all have 6/10A electricity and are set amongst many mature trees and well-manicured hedges, giving a tropical feel and plenty of shade and privacy. Most pitches are flat, but some are on a steep hillside and therefore sloping. There are adequate water points around the site and there are 30 serviced pitches are available. This is a very peaceful quality site with good views of the surrounding countryside and mountains. The owner, Philippe Kremer, is very friendly and speaks excellent English. The restaurant and shop are in a converted barn just outside the main entrance and the patio has terrific views across the lake. A traditional wood oven is used for pancakes and pizzas or there is a good choice of speciality Savoyard dishes. The lake offers many types of water sports, but to keep the purity of the water, motorboats are not allowed. The beach is free for campsite users, and lifeguards are present in July and August (dogs are not permitted). Walks with llamas and paragliding are organised from reception.

Facilities

Two identical sanitary blocks provide excellent facilities, washbasins in cabins, controllable showers, baby bath, 2 shower units with en-suite washbasin. Good facilities for disabled visitors. Separate laundry. Freezer. Shop (1/7-31/8). Bar and restaurant (open to public, just outside main gate). Well maintained play area. Miniclub. TV room. Chalets to rent. Off site: Fishing, boating, swimming, rafting at lake 200 m. Bicycle hire 3 km. Walks with llamas and paragliding.

Open: 1 May - 16 September.

Directions

From A43 Chambéry - Lyon motorway, take exit 12 and D921 south towards Lac d'Aiguebelette. Follow signs to Plage du Sougey. Site is on the left just before the Plage. GPS: N45:33.349 E05:47.449

Charges guide

Per unit incl. 2 persons	€ 12,70 - € 16,70
incl. electricity (6A)	€ 15,80 - € 19,80
with full services	€ 17,30 - € 24,10
extra person (over 5 yrs)	€ 3,60
dog	€ 1,70

CAMPING LE SOUGEY★★★★

Campsite du Sougey is nestled in the heart of a site naturally rich in exceptional panoramas, located at a height of 380 meters at the foot of the 'Massif de l'Epine'. You are looking for quality services and service, for a complete and diversified atmosphere of tourism then do not hesitate: **you found your place for holidays!**

Lac Rive Ouest - 73610 Saint Alban de Montbel
Tel : 0033 479 36 01 44 - Fax : 0033 479 44 19 01
E-mail : info@camping-sougey.com - Internet : www.camping-sougey.com

FR73100 Camping le Reclus

F-73700 Séez (Savoie)

Tel: **04 79 41 01 05**. Email: contact@campinglerecus.com   www.alanrogers.com/FR73100

This small mountain campsite, set in the hills above Bourg St Maurice, is enthusiastically run by the Bonato sisters who have great plans to offer the unexpected. The 108 pitches, some gently sloping, are set amongst mature pine trees giving plenty of shade; 90 have electrical connections. The site borders a fast-flowing mountain stream, which is well fenced. The site is undergoing redevelopment, with many new facilities being introduced. A new TV room was just about to open on our visit. The village of Séez is a few minutes' walk away. This site is not recommended for larger units.

Facilities

Two sanitary blocks, the central one more modern, have small shower cubicles with preset hot water; and open style basins. Laundry room with washer/dryer and indoor drying area. Restaurant and takeaway (June - Sept). Small play area. Bread, drinks and ice cream for sale. Bicycle hire. Off site: Shops and bars in the village of Séez. Access to the ski resort of Les Arcs via the funicular railway in Bourg St Maurice 2 km. Riding 1 km. Swimming pools 2 km.

Open: All year excl. November.

Directions

From A43 Lyon - Chambéry - Grenoble motorway take A430 to Albertville and RN90 to Moutiers and Bourg St Maurice. Drive through town, at third roundabout follow signs for Tignes and Val d'Isère. Site is 2 km.up the hill on the right on entering village of Séez. GPS: N45:37.555 E06:47.623

Charges guide

Per unit incl. 2 persons	€ 11,20 - € 12,40
extra person	€ 3,60 - € 4,00
electricity (4-10A)	€ 4,00 - € 4,70

Check real time availability and at-the-gate prices...

www.alanrogers.com

FR73130 Camping International l'Ile aux Cygnes

501 bvd Ernest Couturier, F-73370 Le Bourget-du-Lac (Savoie)

Tel: 04 79 25 01 76. Email: camping@bourgetdulac.com   www.alanrogers.com/FR73130

This is a large municipal site in a fantastic location with wonderful views on the shores of Lake Bourget, the largest natural lake in France. The surrounding mountains create a scenic backdrop. The 235 pitches are level and a few have dividing hedges. Mature trees give some shade, but the site is mostly open. Many pitches border the lake or rivers which run along two sides of the site. Caution must be taken as there are some unfenced stretches. All pitches have easy access to electricity (10A) and there are adequate water points around the site. The lake offers many watersports.

Facilities

Four sanitary blocks with some basins in cubicles, preset showers, baby room, children's washbasins, en-suite facilities for visitors with disabilities. Washing machines and dryer. Motorcaravan service point. Well stocked shop. Bar, restaurant with terrace, takeaway and pizzas. Play area. TV room. Internet access. Fishing, swimming, canoes. Bicycle hire. Off site: Minigolf, archery, tennis, boat launching, sailing all within 500 m.

Open: 1 April - 30 September.

Directions

From motorway junction of A43 Lyon - Chambéry with A41 Annecy - Grenoble (junction 14 at Chambéry), head north on N201/N504 for 8 km. to Lac-du-Bourget. Then follow signs for 'Plage Municipal' and yacht club. Site is 300 m. after the yacht club. GPS: N45:39.318 E05:51.678

Charges guide

Per person	€ 2,78 - € 4,08
pitch	€ 4,89 - € 5,67
electricity (10A)	€ 3,57

FR74010 Camping les Deux Glaciers

80 route des Tissières, les Bossons, F-74400 Chamonix (Haute-Savoie)

Tel: 04 50 53 15 84. Email: glaciers@clubinternet.fr   www.alanrogers.com/FR74010

A pleasant and well kept, naturally laid out, small mountain site for summer and winter use. Les Deux Glaciers lies at the foot of two glaciers and is close to the well known ski resort of Chamonix. The site has 135 terraced pitches, 100 for touring, with electricity (2-10A). Rock pegs are advised. It is pleasantly laid out with trees and floral displays. There are magnificent views of Mont Blanc Range and the Aiguille-de-Midi. There is significant road noise. Reservations are not taken in summer. Not ideal for large outfits and those with walking difficulties.

Facilities

Two small, heated, sanitary blocks, have dated facilities. Facilities for disabled visitors. Washing machine and drying room. Restaurant/takeaway (all year). Mobile traders call. Room (for winter use only). Table tennis. Small play area. WiFi. Off site: Shop 500 m. Fishing 600 m. Bicycle hire or riding 3 km. Golf 4 km. Chamonix, swimming, hang-gliding, cable cars, ski lifts, funicular railway all within 3 km. Walks and bike rides. Bus to Chamonix and other villages all season. Fantastic skiing in winter.

Open: All year (except 15 November - 15 December).

Directions

From Geneva (N205) take second exit for Les Bossons; site shortly on right. From Chamonix turn right at sign for Les Bossons, left at T-junction and pass under the main road; site shortly on right. GPS: N45:54.123 E06:50.233

Charges guide

Per unit incl. 2 persons	€ 14,30
extra person	€ 5,10
electricity (2-10A; higher in winter)	€ 2,30 - € 7,00

FR74030 Camping Belvédère

8 route du Semnoz, F-74000 Annecy (Haute-Savoie)

Tel: 04 50 45 48 30. Email: camping@ville-annecy.fr   www.alanrogers.com/FR74030

This municipal site is the nearest campsite to Annecy which can be reached in 15 minutes by a quiet, but steep footpath. There are 120 good sized pitches, 106 of which are for touring and 80 have electricity (10A). Many have part hardstanding and are fully serviced and some grass pitches are reserved for tents (rock pegs essential). Space may be limited if the site is busy. A variety of trees provide some shade. This site is ideally placed for visiting Annecy but is not suitable for large units.

Facilities

Three modern toilet blocks, one heated in cold weather, with washroom for visitors with disabilities. Laundry facilities. Small shop, bar and takeaway (June-Aug). Games/wet weather room. Playground. Bicycle hire. Communal area for barbecues. Sporting activities arranged. Off site: Boat launching 600 m. Lakeside beach 800 m. Swimming pool 800 m. Bicycle hire 1 km. Other activities on and around Lake Annecy. Boat trips. Lakeside cycle track. Hang-gliding and canyoning.

Open: 4 April - 10 October.

Directions

Leave A41, Annecy Sud, take N508 to Annecy. After some traffic lights descend a hill looking for 'H' and 'Silence' signs. Turn right up hill, signed Le Semnoz. Fork right, then turn left, signed Camping, site shortly on right. GPS: N45:53.454 E06:07.890

Charges guide

Per unit incl. 2 persons	€ 14,20 - € 18,50
tent/car incl. 2 persons	€ 10,20 - € 13,90
extra person	€ 4,10 - € 4,90
electricity (10A)	€ 2,60

227

BOOK THIS SITE
CALL 01580 214000
...we'll arrange everything

The Travel
Service

FR74040 Camp de la Ravoire

Bout-du-Lac, route de la Ravoire, F-74210 Doussard (Haute-Savoie)

Tel: **04 50 44 37 80**. Email: **info@camping-la-ravoire.fr**   www.alanrogers.com/FR74040

La Ravoire is a high quality site, 800 m. from Lake Annecy, noted for its neat and tidy appearance and the quietness of its location in this popular tourist region. The 112 level pitches are on well mown grass with some shade and separated by small shrubs and some hedging. The 90 pitches for touring (21 with water and drain) have electricity (5-15A). Those looking for a campsite in this attractive region without the 'animation' programmes, will find this a peaceful base.

Facilities

Very good toilet block, facilities for disabled people, laundry room, washing machines, dryers and irons. Bar, snack bar, takeaway. Shop. Outdoor pool, water slide and paddling pool. All open all season. Good play area. Sports areas. Off site: Fishing, boat launching, bicycle hire 1 km. Riding 6 km. Golf 8 km. Good restaurants on the lakeside, shops in Doussard and Annecy. Cycle track (20 km) almost to Annecy passes close by. Canyoning and hang gliding close. Boat trips.

Open: 15 May - 7 September.

Directions

Site signed from N508 Annecy - Albertville road. About 13 km. south of Annecy, at traffic lights in Brédannaz, turn right (site signed) and then immediately left. Site on left in about 1 km. GPS: N45:48.147 E06:12.579

Charges guide

Per unit incl. 2 persons, water and electricity (5A)	€ 30,00 - € 33,50
extra person	€ 6,50
Camping Cheques accepted.	

FR74060 Kawan Village la Colombière

Saint Julien-en-Genevois, F-74160 Neydens (Haute-Savoie)

Tel: **04 50 35 13 14**. Email: **la.colombiere@wanadoo.fr**   www.alanrogers.com/FR74060

La Colombière, a family owned site, is on the edge of the small village of Neydens, a few minutes from the A40 autoroute and only a short drive from Geneva. It is an attractive site with only 104 pitches (82 for touring with electricity 5-15A), all reasonably level and separated by fruit trees, flowering shrubs and hedges. Neydens makes a good base for visiting Geneva and the region around the lake. It is a very pleasant, friendly site where you may drop in for a night stop – and stay for several days! English is spoken. A 'Sites et Paysages' member.

Facilities

Good sanitary blocks (one heated) include facilities for disabled people. Motorcaravan services. Fridge hire. Gas supplies. Good bar/restaurant (all season) and terrace overlooking the pool (1/5-15/9). New heated, indoor pool, spa pool and jacuzzi (21/3-11/11). Games room. Organised visits and activities. Bicycle hire. Archery. Boules. Playground. Internet (WiFi). Off site: Fishing, riding 1 km. Golf 7 km. Lake beach and windsurfing 12 km. Switzerland 3 km. St Julien-en-Genevois 5 km. Geneva.

Open: 20 March - 11 November
(all year for motorcaravans and suitable caravans).

Directions

From A40 south of Geneva take exit 13 and then N201 towards Annecy. After 2 km. turn left into village of Neydens and follow campsite signs to site in just over 1 km. GPS: N46:07.214 E06:06.331

Charges guide

Per unit incl. 2 persons	€ 16,00 - € 25,50
extra person	€ 3,70 - € 5,70
child (2-12 yrs)	€ 3,50 - € 4,50
electricity (5/6A)	€ 4,70
dog	€ 2,00
Camping Cheques accepted.	

FR74090 Camping le Plan du Fernuy

Route des Confins, F-74220 La Clusaz (Haute-Savoie)

Tel: **04 50 02 44 75**. Email: **info@plandufernuy.com**   www.alanrogers.com/FR74090

This neat and open site has separate summer and winter seasons. It has 80 average sized, stony, grassy, pitches, 58 for tourists with electricity and 22 fully serviced. There are good mountain views but little shade, rock pegs essential. The site's crowning glory is an excellent indoor heated pool with window views to the mountains. This is a good site for skiing in winter (with access to a ski-tow from the campsite). In summer it is a good base for walking and cycling and other sporting opportunities.

Facilities

Very good heated sanitary provision. Baby room. Facilities for disabled visitors. Washing machine and dryer. Drying room for ski clothing and boots. Motorcaravan services. Small shop and bar, snacks, takeaway. Games, TV room. Heated indoor pool and paddling pool. Skiing from site and ski excursions organised. Off site: Shops and restaurants in village 2 km. Riding 800 m. Golf, bicycle hire and fishing 1.5 km.

Open: 4 June - 4 September, 18 December - 24 April.

Directions

From Annecy take D909 to La Clusaz and at roundabout turn towards Les Confins. Site is on right after 2 km. (well signed). It is best to avoid using D909 from Flumat particularly with caravans or motorhomes. GPS: N45:54.567 E06:27.114

Charges guide

Per pitch incl. 2 persons	€ 20,00 - € 24,00
incl. electricity (4-13A)	€ 23,50 - € 32,00
extra person	€ 5,50 - € 6,50
Winter prices are higher.	

Check real time availability and at-the-gate prices...

www.**alanrogers**.com

FR74070 Camping Caravaning l'Escale

F-74450 Le Grand-Bornand (Haute-Savoie)

Tel: **04 50 02 20 69**. Email: **contact@campinglescale.com**   www.alanrogers.com/FR74070

You are assured a good welcome in English from the Baur family at this beautifully maintained and picturesque site, situated at the foot of the Aravis mountain range. There are 149 pitches with 122 for touring. Of average size, part grass, part gravel they are separated by trees and shrubs that give a little shade. All pitches have electricity (2-10A) and 86 are fully serviced. Rock pegs are essential. A 200 year old building houses a bar/restaurant decorated in traditional style and offering regional dishes in a delightful, warm ambience. The village is 200 m. has all the facilities of a resort with activities for summer or winter holidays. An excellent choice for an outdoor holiday, in summer a variety of well signed footpaths and cycle tracks provide forest or mountain excursions. In winter the area provides superb facilities for downhill and cross-country skiing. This very popular campsite, set beside the picture postcard ski resort of Le Grand-Bornand, has wonderful views and is surrounded by fields of flowers in summer.

Facilities

Good toilet blocks (heated in winter) have all the necessary facilities. Drying room for skis, clothing and boots. Superb pool complex with interconnected indoor (all season) and outdoor pools and paddling pools (10/6-31/8), jacuzzi and water jets. Cosy bar/restaurant and takeaway. Play area. Tennis. WiFi. Activities for adults and children. Discounts on organised walks and visits to Chamonix-Mont Blanc. Off site: Village (5 minutes walk), shops, bars, restaurants, archery, paragliding, golf, minigolf. 150 km. of signed walks. Bicycle hire 200 m. Riding and golf 3 km. Free bus for cable car (500 m) for skiing and snowboarding.

Open: 5 December - 19 April, 20 May - 27 September.

Directions

From Annecy follow D16 and D909 towards La Clusaz. At St Jean-de-Sixt, turn left at roundabout D4 signed Grand Bornand. Just before village fork right signed Vallée de Bouchet and camping. Site entrance is on right at roundabout in 1.2 km. GPS: N45:56.412 E06:25.692

Charges guide

Per unit incl. 2 persons	€ 16,00 - € 22,50
incl. services	€ 18,00 - € 27,50
extra person	€ 4,90 - € 5,70
electricity (2-10A)	€ 3,80 - € 6,90

Camping Caravaneige L'Escale

74450 Le Grand Bornand - France - Tel: +33 (0)4 50 02 20 69 - Fax: +33 (0)4 50 02 36 04
Email: contact@campinglescale.com - www.rentlescale.com

FR74100 Village Camping Europa

1444 route Albertville, F-74410 Saint Jorioz (Haute-Savoie)

Tel: **04 50 68 51 01**. Email: **info@camping-europa.com**   www.alanrogers.com/FR74100

You will receive a friendly welcome at this quality, family run site. The flowers, shrubs and trees are lovely and everything is kept neat and tidy. There are 210 medium to large size pitches (110 for touring) on level stony grass. Rock pegs are advised. All pitches have electricity (6A) close by and 18 have water and drainage. The static units are separated from the touring section by high hedges. There may be some noise from the main road. A good base from which to tour the Lake Annecy area.

Facilities

Two very good toilet blocks, recently modernised to a high standard, include some large cubicles with both showers and washbasins. Motorcaravan service point. Good bar and restaurant (1/6-31/8). Swimming pool complex. Bicycle hire. Internet access. Miniclub. Musical evenings. Off site: Fishing 300 m. Boat launching 500 m. Lakeside beach 2 km. Riding 3 km. Golf 8 km. Lakeside bike ride (40 km). St Joriz. Canyoning and hang-gliding.

Open: 30 April - 20 September.

Directions

From Annecy take N508 signed Albertville. Site is well signed on the right on leaving Saint-Jorioz. GPS: N45:49.480 E06:10.550

Charges guide

Per unit incl. 2 persons and electricity	€ 14,50 - € 29,10
serviced pitch	€ 22,70 - € 37,30
extra person	€ 4,20 - € 6,20

Check real time availability and at-the-gate prices...
www.alanrogers.com

FR74110 Camping le Taillefer

1530 route de Chaparon, F-74210 Doussard (Haute-Savoie)

Tel: **04 50 44 30 30**. Email: **info@campingletaillefer.com**   www.alanrogers.com/FR74110

This excellent, small site is family run and friendly with stunning views over the lakeside mountains. It is only 1.5 km. from Lake Annecy, yet it offers a quiet, very relaxing and beautiful environment all at a very good price. This site is terraced and abounds with flowers, shrubs and small trees. It only has 32 average sized, grassy, reasonably level and sunny pitches, 28 with electricity (6A). In high season the site is quiet as there are no organised events, although there are plenty on and around the lake close by. Explore the countryside and picturesque villages by taking to the back roads.

Facilities

Modern toilet block with facilities for disabled visitors. Small shop selling bread, drinks and ices etc. Small bar in high season. Playground. Small club/TV room. Bicycle hire. Torches needed (no site lighting). Off site: Doussard, shops, bank. Lake Annecy with beaches (2 km), restaurants, snack bars, fishing and many watersports. Cycle track 800 m. Minigolf, boat launching, small nature reserve. Canyoning, hang-gliding. Boat trips. Fishing 1.5 km. Golf 8 km. Riding 10 km. Cycle ride of 20 km.

Open: 1 May - 30 September.

Directions

From Annecy take N508 signed Albertville. At traffic lights in Brédannaz turn right and left. Site on left in 1.5 km. Do not turn in by reception (this is a dead end) - wait in road until directions are received. GPS: N45:48.141 E06:12.339

Charges guide

Per unit incl. 2 persons	€ 13,00 - € 15,00
extra person	€ 3,00 - € 3,50
electricity (6A)	€ 3,40

FR74130 Camping de la Plage

304 rue de la Garenne, F-74500 Amphion-les-Bains (Haute-Savoie)

Tel: **04 50 70 00 46**. Email: **info@camping-dela-plage.com**   www.alanrogers.com/FR74130

This very good, family run site is small, quiet and friendly. It has a very long season and is only a few hundred metres from Lake Geneva and the village of Amphion making it an excellent centre to relax and explore this wonderful region. The 53 fully serviced pitches (electricity 2-6A), only a few used by mobile homes, are level, medium sized and separated by trees. There is an adjacent large aqua park plus an excellent spacious playground. The site does not accept large unit or double axle caravans.

Facilities

Excellent toilet facilities, heated off season. Washing machine, dryer, iron. Small bar and takeaway (high season). Very small heated swimming pool, covered in cool weather. Sauna. Small playground for young children. Boules. TV room. Exercise room with play area. Wifi. Off site: Excellent aqua park with beach adjacent. Lake Geneva, beaches, restaurants, snack bars, fishing, water sports. Ferry service around lake to Geneva and Lausanne. Small shops, restaurants, supermarket within walking distance. Hypermarket 1 km. Golf 3 km.

Open: All year excl. 2 November - 24 December.

Directions

Site is between Thonon-les-Bains and Evian-les-Bains. Turn north off the N5 at Amphion-les-Bains (at roundabout with statue and fountains) and follow site signs - site is a few hundred metres on the right. GPS: N46:23.728 E06:32.079

Charges guide

Per unit incl. 2 persons	€ 16,50 - € 22,00
extra person	€ 6,10 - € 6,50
child (under 8 yrs)	€ 3,00 - € 3,20
electricity (2-6A)	€ 2,00 - € 4,20

FR74150 Camping de la Mer de Glace

200 chemin de la Bagna, les Praz, F-74400 Chamonix (Haute-Savoie)

Tel: **04 50 53 44 03**. Email: **info@chamonix-camping.com**   www.alanrogers.com/FR74150

This attractive site is convenient for Chamonix but is in a tranquil setting away from its hustle and bustle. The buildings are of typical regional timber construction, decorated with traditional painted flower designs. Set in a large level clearing, with a view of the Mont Blanc range, it has been kept as natural as possible without a pool, restaurant, bar or disco and is well suited to those looking for quiet and relaxation. The area is rich in trails for walking and mountain biking and many pass nearby. There are 150 pitches of varying sizes, most with shade and 75 have electricity connections (3-10A).

Facilities

Three sanitary blocks with facilities for disabled visitors. Washing machine, dryer. Motorcaravan services. Bread. Pizza van twice weekly in July/Aug. Meeting room, snack room. Small playground for young children. Free internet and WiFi access. Off site: Fishing and golf 500 m. Bicycle hire 1 km. Riding 5 km. Shops, etc. 700 m. in Les Praz or 1.5 km. in Chamonix. Indoor and outdoor swimming pools in Chamonix 1.5 km. Free bus/train pass in locality.

Open: 25 April - 4 October.

Directions

From Chamonix take N506 northeast towards Les Praz. After 1 km. site signed to right. NOTE: the first two signs direct you under a 2.4 m. high bridge. Continue to a small roundabout at entrance to Les Praz, turn right and follow signs. GPS: N45:56.283 E06:53.560

Charges 2009

Per person	€ 5,90 - € 6,70
pitch	€ 5,60 - € 7,50
electricity (3A)	€ 2,80

Check real time availability and at-the-gate prices...

www.**alanrogers**.com

FR74140 Camping les Dômes de Miage

197 route des Contamines, F-74170 Saint Gervais-les-Bains (Haute-Savoie)

Tel: **04 50 93 45 96**. Email: **info@camping-mont-blanc.com**   www.alanrogers.com/FR74140

Saint Gervais is a pretty spa town in the picturesque Val-Monjoie valley and this site is two kilometres from its centre. It is 22 km. west of Chamonix and centrally located for discovering this marvellous mountain region. Nestled among the mountains, this sheltered, well equipped site provides 150 flat grassy pitches. Of a good size, about half have shade and there are 100 with electricity points (3/10A). The remainder on terraced ground are used for tents. Third generation hosts, Stéphane and Sophie, will welcome you to the site and their passion for this area at the foot of Mont Blanc is infectious. A number of Savoyard style chalets to let are planned for the future. This is a good site for large motorcaravans. There is no on-site entertainment programme, but a wealth of information about the area and activities available nearby is provided at reception where they will help you plan your itinerary. The region is good for walking and there is a bus service into Saint Gervais, from where there is a frequent shuttle bus to its spa and a tramway to the Mont Blanc range. There is also good public transport between the town and Chamonix.

Facilities

Two sanitary blocks, one heated, with a suite for disabled visitors and baby room. Washing machines, dryer. Motorcaravan services. Small basic shop. Bar/restaurant. TV room, library, ironing board. Excellent playground. Playing field. Off site: Fishing 100 m. Bicycle hire 1 km. Riding 7 km. Shops, etc. and outdoor swimming pool in St Gervais.

Open: 1 May - 21 September.

Directions

From St Gervais take D902 towards Les Contamines and site is on left after 2 km.
GPS: N45:52.423 E06:43.205

Charges guide

Per unit incl. 1 or 2 persons	€ 16,50 - € 20,50
extra person	€ 3,00 - € 4,00
child (2-10 yrs)	€ 2,50 - € 3,50
electricity (3/6A)	€ 2,90 - € 3,90
dog	€ 2,00

Camping Cheques accepted.

A NEW WAY TO DISCOVER THE MOUNTAINS...

A campsite in the middle of untouched nature, in a quiet location at the foot of Mont-Blanc, in the center of many hiking paths. A wide choice of activities and services, sports centre with swiming pool, tennis, etc... 800 yards away.
Aiguille du Midi, Mer de glace & Chamonix 15 miles, St-Gervais 1,2 miles, Megève 7 miles.

CAMPING

Les Dômes de Miage
★ ★ ★

197, route des Contamines - F-74170 Saint-Gervais-les-bains
Tél. + 33 (0)4 50 93 45 96
e-mail : info@camping-mont-blanc.com
WWW.CAMPING-MONT-BLANC.COM

La Clef Verte

Camping Qualité

Check real time availability and at-the-gate prices...
www.**alanrogers**.com

FR74210 Village Center des Iles de Passy

245 chemin de la Cavettaz, F-74190 Passy (Haute-Savoie)

Tel: **04 99 57 21 21**. Email: **contact@village-center.com**   www.alanrogers.com/FR74210

This Alpine site is approached by a lakeside road with mountains to the left and with unrivalled views of Mont Blanc straight ahead. Set in an area with oak trees giving shade, there are 260 very good touring pitches which are all large and divided by 1.2 m. high, well trimmed beech hedges. A small, high season takeaway is located beside the play area allowing relaxed child supervision. An electric railway may cause some noise. This is an ideal site for Alpine lovers, a perfect base for walking and cycling, while the municipal water sports area in which the site is set offers a whole range of water based activities.

Facilities

Two toilet blocks, screened by attractive hedges, are not modern but are acceptable and include hot showers and a WC/shower for disabled visitors. Laundry facilities. Basic takeaway in high season. Chalets to rent. Off site: Site is in the centre of a large municipal water sports complex. Fishing 500 m. Riding 10 km. Golf 20 km. Excellent centre for walking and cycling. Passy has shopping, restaurants and bars, 2 km.

Open: 22 May - 26 September.

Directions

Site is west of Passy. From the A40 take exit 21 (Chamonix) and drive through Passy to site (well signed). GPS: N45:55.434 E06:39.024

Charges guide

Per person	€ 4,00 - € 5,00
pitch	€ 13,00 - € 18,00

AltaVia Link

Les Iles**

Passy > Savoie

- **150 m away from the lake of Passy**
- **Near the Mont Blanc**

Villagecenter

BOOK YOUR HOLIDAYS
www.village-center.com
+33 (0)4 99 57 21 21

FR74160 Camping l'Ile des Barrats

185 chemin de l'Ile des Barrats, F-74400 Chamonix (Haute-Savoie)

Tel: **04 50 53 51 44**. Email: **campingiledesbarrats74@orange.fr**   www.alanrogers.com/FR74160

l'Ile de Barrats is a delightful neat, tidy, small and tranquil site. It is within easy walking distance of the beautiful town of Chamonix, although there are bus and train services close by if needed. There are 53 slightly sloping, grassy pitches all for touring mostly separated by small hedges and a variety of trees offering some shade. All have electricity (5/10A) and 32 have water and drainage. This is an ideal site for those wishing to roam the mountain trails and for those seeking a peaceful and relaxing holiday in a most superb setting. No twin axle caravans.

Facilities

A modern, clean toilet block offers all necessary facilities, including those for disabled visitors. Covered picnic area with table and benches, ideal for those with small tents. Motorcaravan services. Store room for mountaineers. Mobile shop in July/Aug. No organised activities. Off site: Baker 500 m. Chamonix 800 m. level walk (high class summer and winter resort with colourful Saturday market). Hang gliding, funicular railway, cable cars and chair lifts nearby.

Open: 15 May - 1 October.

Directions

On entering Chamonix from Geneva, turn left at first roundabout after turn off for the Mont Blanc Tunnel (follow signs for Hospital). Shortly, at next roundabout, turn left and site is on right opposite hospital. GPS: N45:54.855 E06:51.689

Charges guide

Per person	€ 6,40
child (0-7 yrs)	€ 4,90
pitch incl. car	€ 7,90
electricity (5/10A)	€ 3,30 - € 4,30
dog	€ 1,00

No credit cards.

Check real time availability and at-the-gate prices...
www.**alanrogers**.com

FR74180 Camping International le Lac Bleu

Route de la Plage, F-74210 Doussard (Haute-Savoie)

Tel: 04 50 44 30 18. Email: lac-bleu@nwc.fr   www.alanrogers.com/FR74180

This lakeside site has its own beach and jetty and a short walk brings you to the lake ferry. The site has breathtaking views, a swimming pool and 220 pitches divided by privet and beech hedges. This site is perfect for walking, cycling or sailing and in low season provides a tranquil base for those just wishing to relax. In high season it will be busy and popular. The proximity of the public lakeside area which is often used as a festival venue could be either a source of noise or an exciting place to be depending on your point of view. When we visited the music stopped at 23.00. A nearby cycle track on a disused railway to Annecy gives a level 16 km. ride with mountains on the left and the lake to the right. In high season there is a children's club for the under eights. The bar has a thriving takeaway (roast whole chickens and pizza) and an 'al fresco' eating area.

Facilities

Three toilet blocks are of a high standard with free showers. Good provision for babies and disabled visitors. Bar (15/5-15/9) and integral small shop. Takeaway. Swimming pool (15/5-15/9). Bicycle hire. Boat launching (sailing lessons and boat hire nearby). Multisports pitch. Private beach. Off site: Small supermarket 100 m. Hypermarket 4 km. Village close with bars and restaurants. Fishing 100 m. Riding and golf 7 km.

Open: 1 April - 25 September.

Directions

Site is 16 km. south of Annecy on Route d'Albertville, well signed.
GPS: N45:79.042 E06:21.778

Charges guide

Per unit incl. 2 persons	€ 16,00 - € 28,00
extra person	€ 4,00 - € 5,90
child	free - € 5,90
electricity (8A)	€ 3,80

Route de la Plage - 74210 Doussard
Tel: 0033 450 44 30 18
Fax: 0033 450 44 84 35
lac-blue@nwc.fr
www.camping-lac-blue.com

Welcome to Camping Le Lac Bleu!
The whole team here will ensure that you have a great holiday on the shores of Lake Annecy on a wonderful site at the heart of the French Alps. You'll be sure to enjoy the fine beach and swimming pool, and, of course, a stunning natural setting which is the ideal place for outstanding holidays! This really is a great spot too for all watersports - waterskiing, windsurfing, sailing, pedaloes and much more.

FR74200 Camping l'Idéal

715 route de Chaparon, F-74210 Lathuile (Haute-Savoie)

Tel: 04 50 44 32 97. Email: camping-ideal@wanadoo.fr   www.alanrogers.com/FR74200

For panoramic views of mountains and the lake, this family run site is excellent. Trim and neat, the site is well cared for and the welcome is warm. The 300 pitches are generally large and well drained, some with small hedges but mostly open and with 6A electricity. These pitches share the site with chalets which are located at the top of the site well away from the tourers. L'Idéal is far enough from the lake to avoid the noise and crowds but close enough to take advantage of the facilities there. From the site you can cycle downhill to the Annecy cycle route.

Facilities

Three very well designed toilet blocks include excellent facilities for babies and disabled visitors. A further new block is planned. Laundry facilities. Shop (June - Sept). Bar. Restaurant, snack bar and takeaway (June - mid August). Two swimming pools. Tennis. Paragliding lessons. Bicycle hire. Play area. Children's club. Activities and excursions in high season. Off site: Lake 900 m. Golf and riding 5 km.

Open: 8 May - 5 September.

Directions

Lathuile is 18 km. southeast of Annecy and site is well signed in the village.
GPS: N45:47.708 E06:12.338

Charges guide

Per unit incl. 2 persons and electricity	€ 18,70 - € 25,20
extra person	€ 3,50 - € 5,00
child (2-7 yrs)	€ 2,50 - € 4,20
dog	€ 2,50

Check real time availability and at-the-gate prices...
www.alanrogers.com

The Travel Service

BOOK THIS SITE

CALL 01580 214000

...we'll arrange everything

FR74220 Camping Saint Disdille

117 ave de Saint Disdille, F-74200 Thonon-les-Bains (Haute-Savoie)

Tel: **04 50 71 14 11**. Email: **camping@disdille.com**   www.alanrogers.com/FR74220

Saint Disdille is situated close to the beautiful Lake Geneva and the famous spa town of Thonon-les-Bains, which can be reached on a bus that passes the site. There are 600 large, level pitches on stone and rough grass (rock pegs are essential). Large trees give some shade. The 300 pitches reserved for touring (200 with 6-10A electricity) are scattered amongst mobile homes and permanent weekender caravans and can be some distance from the facilities. The site is ideally situated for the large range of watersports in the area and Switzerland is easily accessible by car, bus, train or boat. This site will be lively in the high season due to the large number of long stay units and the on-site and adjacent discos finish after midnight. Although there are no problems with large units on the site, access is not easy due to the urban location. For 2009 a new bypass around Thonon will make access easier.

Facilities

Five adequate toilet blocks, 4 recently refurbished inside. Shop. Bar with TV, restaurant with takeaways (all season). Diving and rafting clubs. Play area with bouncy castle. Multisport court. Boules. Games room with pool table. WiFi (free) and internet point (fee). Twin axle vans are not accepted. Off site: Small lakeside public beach and disco 300 m. Fishing 500 m. Large open air pool 1 km. Boat ramp, windsurfing, bicycle hire 2 km. Many other water sports in the area. Golf 5 km. Thonon-les-Bains 2 km.

Open: 1 April - 30 September.

Directions

From Annemasse take N5 to Thonon-les-Bains. In Thonon follow signs for Evian to Intermarché supermarket. At next roundabout follow signs to campsite and Parc de la Chataigneraie. GPS: N46:23.859 E06:30.201

Charges guide

Per unit incl. 2 persons	€ 14,00 - € 17,00
extra person	€ 4,00
child (3-10 yrs)	€ 2,50
electricity (6/10A)	€ 3,00 - € 4,00

CAMPING SAINT DISDILLE***

Lac Leman

Very shady
Pitches of 100 m²

www.disdille.com

Mobile homes for rent

Beach with supervision on 200m
Free diving and pedalos
Close by river 'La Dranse'

Rafting-Kayak Bar-Restaurant-Shop-Baker-Newspapers-Playground-Table tennis tournaments-Jeu de Boules Tennis-Multisports terrain

117, Avenue de Saint Disdille - 74200 Thonon
Tel: 0033 450 71 14 11 - Fax: 0033 450 71 93 67

FR74170 Camping Moulin Dollay

206 rue du Moulin Dollay, F-74570 Groisy (Haute-Savoie)

Tel: **04 50 68 00 31**. Email: **moulin.dollay@orange.fr**   www.alanrogers.com/FR74170

This spacious site is a gem with only 30 pitches, all for touring. The friendly and enthusiastic owner has worked hard to develop this site to a high quality over the last few years. The large to very large, level, grass pitches are partially separated by hedging and a variety of trees provide some shade. All pitches have 6A electricity and 15 also have sole use of a tap and a drain. Rock pegs are recommended. As there are only a few activities organised for youngsters on site it is perhaps better suited to independent couples and young families.

Facilities

Spacious, well appointed, heated toilet block, including facilities for disabled visitors and a baby room. Washing machine, dryer. Motorcaravan services. Bar, TV corner. Large open play and sports area. River fishing. Off site: Shops, restaurants, bank and supermarkets at Groisy 1 km. Interesting little town of Thorens-Glières with its 11th century château 5 km. Riding 4 km. Golf 6 km.

Open: 1 May - 30 September.

Directions

Site about 12 km. north of Annecy. Heading north on N203 Annecy - Bonneville road, turn left on D2d at Groisy le Plot. Cross river and go under road bridge and immediately turn right and then left, following site signs. GPS: N46:00.146 E06:11.450

Charges 2009

Per unit incl. 2 persons and electricity	€ 17,00 - € 20,00
extra person	€ 5,00
child (under 7 yrs)	€ 2,00
dog	€ 1,00
No credit cards.	

234

Check real time availability and at-the-gate prices...

www.**alanrogers**.com

FR74230 Camping Caravaneige le Giffre

La Glière, F-74340 Samoëns (Haute-Savoie)

Tel: 04 50 34 41 92. Email: camping.samoens@wanadoo.fr   www.alanrogers.com/FR74230

Surrounded by magnificent mountains in this lesser known Alpine area, yet accessible to major ski resorts, Le Giffre could be the perfect spot for those seeking an active, yet relaxing holiday. There are 300 firm, level pitches on stony grass (rock pegs advised) with 270 for touring units. Most have electricity (6/10A) but long leads may be needed. They are spaced out amongst mature trees which give varying amounts of shade and some overlook the attractive lake and leisure park. The small winter/summer resort of Samoëns is only a 15 minutes level stroll away. Mr Dominach loves gardening and the site is bedecked with flowers. Make sure you do not miss the small vegetable and herb garden at the entrance. There is little in the way of on site entertainment but there are many activities available in Samo'ns and the surrounding area.

Facilities	Directions
Three adequate toilet blocks, heated in winter with facilities for campers with disabilities. Games room. Play area. Boules. Fishing. Off site: Leisure park next to site - pool (entry free summer), ice skating (entry free winter), tennis (summer), archery, adventure park. Paragliding. Rafting, many walks and bike rides (summer) and ski runs (winter). Snack bar and baker (high season) 100 m. Samoëns with a good range of shops, bars, restaurants 1 km. Grand Massif Express cable car 150 m. Bicycle hire 200 m. Riding 2 km.	Leave A40 autoroute at Cluses (exit 18 or 19). Go north on D902 towards Taninges. Just before Taninges turn east on D4 to Samoëns. After crossing river, at roundabout, turn left and site is immediately on the left. Park outside the entrance. GPS: N46:04.681 E06:43.117

Open: All year.

Charges guide

Per unit incl. 2 persons	€ 11,00 - € 16,00
extra person	€ 3,50
child (4-12 yrs)	€ 2,50
electricity (5A)	€ 3,00 - € 4,50

Camping Caravaneige Le Giffre***

Open all year, located on the edge of the Giffre and the 'Lacs aux Dames', 700m from the town and its shops and at the heart of the leisure park, our campsite has 312 level grass pitches on a well shaded site of 6.9h.

In winter, departures for cross-country skiing from the campsite and ski lifts 150m away. Access within 8 min to 265 km of downhill slopes.

Camping Caravaneige Le Giffre • La Glière• F-74340 Samoens
www.camping-samoens.com

FR74240 Camping le Chamaloup

Contamine Sarzin, F-74270 Frangy (Haute-Savoie)

Tel: 04 50 77 88 28. Email: camping@chamaloup.com   www.alanrogers.com/FR74240

Le Chamaloup is a neat and tidy site run by a very friendly family. It is situated midway between the lakes of Annecy, Geneva and de Bourget and only 10 minutes from the A40 autoroute making it an ideal centre for exploring this beautiful region. There are only 60 level, grass pitches which are separated by small fences. Mature trees give varying amounts of shade. The 43 pitches for touring (with 10A electricity) are well separated from authentic wooden chalets for rent. The emphasis here on quiet family holidays with occasional soirées in the high season. Although access is easy for large units, twin axle caravans are not accepted.

Facilities	Directions
Two modern toilet blocks with all necessary facilities including those for campers with disabilities. Small shop, bar, restaurant, takeaway (July/Aug). Heated swimming and paddling pools (1/6-15/9). Games/TV room. Some organised family activities (July/Aug). Internet access (WiFi). Off site: Riding 4 km. Golf, bicycle hire, lake beach, windsurfing, boat ramp 15 km. Frangy with small range of shops, bars, restaurants 4 km. Annecy 23 km. Geneva 34 km.	Leave A40 autoroute at exit 11, signed Frangy. Take N508 14 km. southeast, and after bypassing Frangy, site is on the left in 4 km. GPS: N46:00.637 E05:58.573

Open: 1 June - 15 September.

Charges guide

Per unit incl. 2 persons	€ 16,00 - € 18,00
extra person	€ 4,50 - € 5,50
child (1-12 yrs)	€ 3,50
electricity (10A)	€ 4,00

Check real time availability and at-the-gate prices...

www.alanrogers.com

MAP 10

Endless shimmering beaches, huge sand dunes, watersports aplenty, fragrant pine forests, the fine wines of Bordeaux, and the chic city of Biarritz: it's easy to see the allure of the Atlantic Coast.

Alan Rogers

THE COASTAL DÉPARTEMENTS OF THE OFFICIAL REGION OF AQUITAINE, STRETCHING FROM BORDEAUX IN THE NORTH TO THE PYRÉNÉES AND THE SPANISH BORDER ARE INCLUDED IN OUR 'TOURIST' REGION: 33 GIRONDE, 40 LANDES, 64 PYRÉNÉES ATLANTIQUES

The Atlantic Coast stretches north from Biarritz to Arcachon. The most notable features are the uninterrupted line of vast sandy beaches, over 100 miles long, and the endless pine woods in the hinterland - this is Europe's largest man-made forest. There are also many lakes to see, ideal for watersports activities.

The département of the Gironde covers the area from the Bassin d'Arcachon, famed for its oysters and Europe's highest sand dune, to the Gironde estuary and Bordeaux. The vineyards of Bordeaux are world famous and especially well known for their Médoc, Sauternes, and St Emilion wines.

The Pays Basque area in the southwest corner is much influenced by Spain. The most famous Basque towns are Biarritz, Bayonne and the picturesque old port of St-Jean-de-Luz. Further inland and nearer the Pyrénées is the attractive town of St-Jean-Pied-de-Port on the pilgrims' route to northern Spain and Santiago de Compostela, close to the forest of Iraty with its lakes and ski runs.

Places of interest

Bayonne: old streets and fortifications; Basque Museum.

Bordeaux: 14,000 piece Bohemian glass chandelier in foyer of the Grand Theatre, 29 acre Esplanade des Quinconces.

Pau: famous motor racing circuit on (closed) public highway; stadium for the Basque game of *pelota*.

St Emilion: visit the castle ramparts or drink premier cru St Emilion at pavement cafés.

St Jean-de-Luz: seaside resort and fishing village.

St Jean-Pied-de-Port: ancient city with citadel, bright Basque houses in steep streets.

Cuisine of the region

Seafood is popular, local specialities include carp stuffed with foie gras and mullet in red wine.

Chorizos: spicy sausages.

Chou farci: stuffed cabbage, sometimes *aux marrons* (with chestnuts).

Foie Gras: specially prepared livers of geese and ducks, seasoned and stuffed with truffles.

Gâteau Basque: shallow custard pastry with fillings.

Jambon de Bayonne: raw ham, cured in salt and sliced paper thin.

Lamproie: eel-like fish with leeks, onions and red Bordeaux wine.

3 quality labels

2nd camping provider in France

1 wide range of destinations

© Dylan Ellis/Corbis

Villagecenter

Escape with Village Center !

Village Center invites you in the heart of the nicest areas in France (Provence, Périgord...). Our large range of recent holiday homes and our labelled services are waiting for you. No matter if you choose tent, camping car or holiday homes we offer you a large choice of enjoyable places (sunny, shady...), various activities and multiple facilities (swimming-pool, mini-club, restaurant...).

Village Center, the best choice for your holiday !

Altavia Link

Villagecenter

BOOK YOUR HOLIDAYS
www.village-center.com
+33 (0)4 99 57 21 21

FR33020 Camping Caravaning Fontaine-Vieille

4 boulevard du Colonel Wurtz, F-33510 Andernos-les-Bains (Gironde)

Tel: 05 56 82 01 67. Email: contact@fontaine-vieille.com   www.alanrogers.com/FR33020

Fontaine-Vieille is a large, traditional site that has been operating for over 50 years. The site stretches along the eastern edge of the Bassin d'Arcachon under light woodland in the residential area of the small town of Andernos. Popular with the French, it has nearly 700 individual pitches, of which 520 are touring pitches (about 400 with electricity). On flat, grassy or sandy ground, they are marked by stones in the ground or young trees. Some pitches have excellent views of the Bassin, but a premium is charged for these.

Facilities

Seven adequate sanitary blocks with facilities for people with disabilities and children. Shop (1/6-15/9). Bar, terrace, takeaway and restaurant (15/5-15/9). Swimming pool complex. Tennis. TV room. Play areas. Minigolf. Boats, sailboards. Sports organised (high season). Internet access. Communal barbecue areas (only gas may be used on pitches). Off site: Grocery shop and bakery 1 km. Town centre 2.5 km. Golf 3 km. Riding 5 km.

Open: 1 April - 30 September.

Directions

From A63 exit 22, take A660 towards Arcachon. Turn off A660 at exit 2 towards Facture then take RD3 north along the Bassin. Site signed to left entering Andernos. GPS: N44:43.562 W01:04.846

Charges guide

Per unit incl. 2 persons	€ 13,30 - € 20,40
incl. electricity (5A)	€ 17,10 - € 27,10
extra person	€ 3,50 - € 6,00
child (2-6 yrs)	free - € 2,60
Camping Cheques accepted.	

FR33030 Camping Club Arcachon

5 allée Galarie, B.P. 46, F-33312 Arcachon (Gironde)

Tel: 05 56 83 24 15. Email: info@camping-arcachon.com   www.alanrogers.com/FR33030

The Camping Club of Arcachon enjoys a situation well back from the hustle and bustle, where nights are quiet and facilities are of a high standard. Caravans, motorcaravans and tents all have their own area. The latter have pitches of varying sizes on neatly formed terraces. There are 250 pitches, with 150 for touring, electricity (6/10A). The site enjoys good security with day and night time 'guardians'. The site restaurant is well thought of, and in season the outdoor pool with its water slide is open all day. The Arcachon basin is an ideal base for those seeking an 'out and about' holiday.

Facilities

Three sanitary blocks with the usual facilities. Motorcaravan services. Washing machine, dryers. Fridge hire. Shop (15/6-15/9). Bar, restaurant, snack bar, takeaway (April - Oct). Swimming pool (1/6-30/9). Bicycle hire. Play area. Games room. Children's club (15/6-15/9). Entertainment for all age groups (15/6-15/9). Barbecues are only permitted in communal areas. Off site: Beach 1.8 km. Arcachon 2-3 km. Riding 1 km. Golf 2 km.

Open: All year (excl. 12 November - 12 December).

Directions

Approaching Arcachon on bypass (from Bordeaux) take exit for 'Hopital Jean Hameau'. Cross over bypass following signs for hospital, then signs for Abatilles. At next roundabout follow signs for 'Camping'. Take care as the route travels through suburban housing. GPS: N44:39.078 W01:10.445

Charges guide

Per person	€ 4,00 - € 7,00
pitch incl. electricity	€ 6,00 - € 19,00

FR33040 Camping la Pinèda

Route de Cazaux, F-33260 Cazaux la Teste-de-Buch (Gironde)

Tel: 05 56 22 23 24. Email: info@campinglapinede.net   www.alanrogers.com/FR33040

La Pinèda is a popular, family site with an attractive forest setting, close to the Dune de Pyla and the lively resort of Arcachon. The site boasts a very impressive swimming pool complex which includes a large children's pirate ship, a covered pool and water slides. There are 200 pitches here, around 130 of which are occupied by mobile homes. Pitches are mostly well shaded and with electrical connections (6A). The site is just three kilometres from the very large Lac de Cazaux where there are many watersport activities. It also has direct access to a canal with mooring opportunities.

Facilities

Two modern sanitary blocks are generally clean and well maintained providing facilities mostly in private cabins. Facilities for disabled visitors (access is fairly steep). Laundry rooms. Shop (1/7-31/8). Restaurant, bar and takeaway (1/7-31/8). Pool complex (1/6-30/9) abd covered pool (all season). Games room. Playground. Bicycle hire. Fishing. Canoe hire. Barbecues are not permitted except on communal area. Off site: Riding 1 km. Lac de Cazaux (fishing and watersports) 3 km. Nearest beach 7 km.

Open: 5 April - 27 September.

Directions

From Arcachon head south towards Cazaux on the D112. Site is located north of the village and is well signed to the left. GPS: N44:33.300 W01:09.040

Charges guide

Per unit incl. 2 persons	€ 16,00 - € 26,00
extra person	€ 4,60 - € 7,00
child (2-7 yrs)	€ 2,60 - € 4,50
electricity	€ 4,70

Check real time availability and at-the-gate prices...

www.alanrogers.com

FR33050 Camping les Ourmes

Avenue du Lac, F-33990 Hourtin (Gironde)

Tel: 05 56 09 12 76. Email: lesourmes@free.fr

www.alanrogers.com/FR33050

Located only 500 metres from the largest fresh water lake in France, only ten minutes' drive from the beach and with its own pool, this is essentially a holiday site. Of the 270 pitches, 240 are for tourers, marked but in most cases not actually separated, and arranged amongst tall pines and other trees which give good shade. All have electricity connections. The site's amenities are arranged around a pleasant entrance courtyard with an evening entertainment programme in season. This site has a busy, cosmopolitan feel, with visitors of many different nationalities.

Facilities	Directions
Three refurbished toilet blocks. Washing machine, dryer. Small shop (1/7-31/8). Bar/restaurant with outdoor tables, takeaway snacks and reasonably priced meals (1/7-31/8). Medium sized swimming pool, paddling pool (1/5-15/9). Large leisure area, play area, volleyball, basketball, table tennis. TV, games rooms. Boules. Off site: Watersports and fishing possible on the lake, with bicycle hire, tennis and riding within 500 m.	Follow Houroin Port (Ave du Lac) from the town centre and site is signed on left. GPS: N45:10.926 W01:04.566

Open: 1 April - 30 September.

Charges guide

Per unit incl. 2 persons	€ 12,00 - € 20,00
incl. electricity	€ 15,00 - € 23,00
extra person (over 2 yrs)	€ 2,00 - € 4,00
dog	€ 2,00

FR33080 Camping le Domaine de la Barbanne

Route de Montagne, F-33330 Saint Emilion (Gironde)

Tel: 05 57 24 75 80. Email: barbanne@wanadoo.fr

www.alanrogers.com/FR33080

La Barbanne is a pleasant, friendly, family owned site in the heart of the Bordeaux wine region, only two and a half kilometres from the famous town of St Emilion. With 174 pitches, most for touring, the owners have created a carefully maintained, well equipped site. The large, level and grassy pitches have dividing hedges and electricity (long leads necessary). The original parts of the site bordering the lake have mature trees, good shade and pleasant surroundings, whilst in the newer area the trees have yet to provide full shade and it can be hot in summer. Twelve pitches for motorcaravans are on tarmac surrounded by grass.

Facilities	Directions
Two modern, fully equipped toilet blocks include facilities for campers with disabilities. Motorcaravan services. Well stocked shop. Bar, terrace, takeaway, restaurant (1/6-20/9). Two swimming pools, one heated with water slide (15/4-22/9). Enclosed play area with seats for parents. Children's club (from 1/7). Tennis. Boules. Minigolf. Bicycle hire. Evening entertainment (from 1/7). Off site: St Emilion and shops 2.5 km. Riding 8 km.	Site is 2.5 km. north of St Emilion. Caravans and motorhomes are forbidden through the village of St Emilion and they must approach the site from Libourne on D243 or from Castillon leave D936 and take D130/D243. GPS: N44:54.997 W00:08.513

Open: 1 April - 22 September.

Charges guide

Per unit incl. 1 or 2 persons	€ 20,00 - € 30,00
extra person	€ 5,00 - € 8,00

Camping Cheques accepted.

FR33090 Flower Camping le Pressoir

Petit Palais et Cornemps, F-33570 Lussac (Gironde)

Tel: 05 57 69 73 25. Email: contact@campinglepressoir.com

www.alanrogers.com/FR33090

Buried in the famous wine producing countryside of the Lussac, Pomerol and St Emilion areas north of Bordeaux, Le Pressoir is surrounded by fields of vines. The 100 large pitches are arranged on either side of a gravel road leading up a slight hill. Most are shaded by attractive trees, but almost all are sloping. They are over 100 sq.m. and equipped with electricity. The old barn has been converted into a stylish bar and a really charming, separate restaurant. A quiet, family site, Le Pressoir provides a comfortable base for a holiday in this area famous for good food and wine.

Facilities	Directions
Fully equipped toilet block with facilities for visitors with disabilities, and washing machine. Bar and pleasant restaurant (all season). Heated swimming pool (15/5-15/9, no Bermuda shorts). Playground with timber equipment. Petanque. Mountain bike hire. Free WiFi. Mobile homes to rent (5). Off site: Tennis nearby. Fishing 3 km. Riding and bicycle hire 9 km.	From N89 Bordeaux - Périgueux at Saint Médard de Guizières turn south towards Lussac (D21). From Castillon-la-Bataille on D936 Libourne-Bergerac road, south of site, take D17 north towards St Médard then D21 through Petit Palais. Site signed. GPS: N44:59.824 W00:03.801

Open: All year.

Charges guide

Per person	€ 5,60 - € 7,50
pitch	€ 13,00 - € 15,00
incl. 6A electricity	€ 13,00 - € 26,00

BOOK THIS SITE
CALL 01580 214000
...we'll arrange everything
The Travel
Service

239

BOOK THIS SITE
CALL 01580 214000
...we'll arrange everything

The Travel
Service

FR33110 Airotel Camping de la Côte d'Argent

Mobile homes ▶ page 501

F-33990 Hourtin-Plage (Gironde)

Tel: **05 56 09 10 25**. Email: **info@camping-cote-dargent.com**   www.alanrogers.com/FR33110

Côte d'Argent is a large, well equipped site for leisurely family holidays. It makes an ideal base for walkers and cyclists with over 100 km. of cycle lanes in the area. Hourtin-Plage is a pleasant invigorating resort on the Atlantic coast and a popular location for watersports enthusiasts, The site's top attraction is its pool complex where wooden bridges connect the pools and islands and there are sunbathing and play areas plus an indoor heated pool. The site has 550 touring pitches, not clearly defined, arranged under trees with some on soft sand. Entertainment takes place at the bar near the entrance (until 00.30). Spread over 20 hectares of undulating sand-based terrain and in the midst of a pine forest. There are 48 hardstandings for motorcaravans outside the site, providing a cheap stop-over, but with no access to site facilities. The site is well organised and ideal for children.

Facilities

Very clean sanitary blocks include provision for visitors with disabilities. Washing machines. Motorcaravan service points. Large supermarket, restaurant, takeaway, pizzeria bar. Four outdoor pools with slides and flumes. Indoor pool. Massage (institut de beauté). Tennis. Play areas. Miniclub, organised entertainment in season. Bicycle hire. Internet. ATM. Charcoal barbecues are not permitted. Hotel (12 rooms). Off site: Path to the beach 300 m. Fishing and riding. Golf 30 km.

Open: 16 May - 13 September.

Directions

Turn off D101 Hourtin-Soulac road 3 km. north of Hourtin. Then join D101E signed Hourtin-Plage. Site is 300 m. from the beach.
GPS: N45:13.381 W01:09.868

Charges guide

Per unit incl. 2 persons and electricity	€ 25,00 - € 44,00
extra person	€ 3,00 - € 7,00
child (2-10 yrs)	€ 2,50 - € 6,00

Camping Cheques accepted.

FR33120 Camping la Cigale

Route de Lège, F-33740 Arès (Gironde)

Tel: **05 56 60 22 59**. Email: **campinglacigaleares@wanadoo.fr**   www.alanrogers.com/FR33120

La Cigale is an attractive little site with charm and ambience where the owners extend a very warm welcome. Small and beautifully maintained, it is set amid pine trees and M. Pallet's floral displays. The 95 level, grassy pitches, most with electricity and of 100 sq.m. in size, are divided by hedges and flower borders. The majority have shade from the pine trees. There are two small swimming pools in a pleasant setting and under the ample shade of a large plane tree, where drinks, meals and snacks are served on the bar terrace.

Facilities

The well equipped toilet block includes a family room with two showers and facilities for disabled visitors. Washing machine and dryer. Motorcaravan services. Simple shop. Bar, terrace, meals, snacks. Pizza takeaway (all 17/6-10/9). Two small swimming pools (15/5-12/9). Small play area. Entertainment in July/Aug. Free donkey cart rides every Sunday. Off site: Site is convenient for a choice of beaches. Village 800 m. Fishing or riding 1 km.

Open: 5 May - 30 September.

Directions

Leave Bordeaux ring road at exit 10 (D213) or exit 11 (D106) and continue direct to Arès. Turn into Arès following road to church square. Turn right following signs for Lège/Cap Ferret. Site is 800 m. on left.
GPS: N44:46.366 W01:08.537

Charges guide

Per unit incl. 1 or 2 persons	€ 27,00 - € 47,00
extra person	€ 6,00
electricity (4/6A)	€ 5,50

FR33150 Camping Municipal les Gabarreys

Route de la Rivière, F-33250 Pauillac (Gironde)

Tel: **05 56 59 10 03**. Email: **camping.les.gabarreys@wanadoo.fr**   www.alanrogers.com/FR33150

An attractive, small site with well tended flower beds, Les Gabarreys is surrounded by vineyards of the Médoc region. An excellent site, it has 59 pitches, most with hardstanding for caravans or motorcaravans (so pegging out awnings could be a problem), some grass pitches for tents and six mobile homes, all with electric hook-ups (5/10A, some may require long leads).

Facilities

Two immaculate toilet blocks provide open and cubicle washbasins and excellent facilities for disabled visitors. Motorcaravan services. General room with satellite TV, fridge-freezer and a small library. New play area. Minigolf (free) and volleyball. New spa and sauna.

Open: 3 April - 9 October.

Directions

From Bordeaux take D1 to St Laurent, then D206 to Pauillac. At roundabout turn right to Pauillac Guais, then straight on at next roundabout and turn right before Maison du Tourisme.
GPS: N45:11.098 W00:45.524

Charges guide

Per unit incl. 2 persons	€ 12,30 - € 13,50
electricity (5/10A)	€ 3,80 - € 5,20

Check real time availability and at-the-gate prices...
www.alanrogers.com

Airotel Camping Caravaning
Côte d'Argent

★★★

POOL COMPLEX OF 3500 M² WITH WATERSLIDES, JACUZZI AND COVERED HEATED SWIMMING POOL

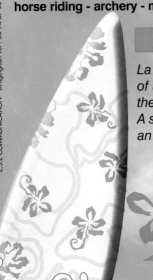

Special low season offers (not in July and August)
14 = 11 and 7 = 6
campsite or accommodations

wifi - hotel - shops - restaurant - bar - provisions - animation (sports) - tennis - horse riding - archery - mini club - games room - sailing (4 km) - surfing (300 m)

E.S.E COMMUNICATION - Draguignan Tél : 04 94 67 06 00

Hourtin Plage - Aquitaine - Atlantique Sud

La Côte d'Argent is a beautiful sloping park of 20 ha in the heart of a pine tree forest. At 300 m of a long winding sandy beach at the Atlantic Ocean.
A site in the lee of dunes and the forest, this holiday village enjoys an ideal climate for enjoying relaxing nature holidays.

Sun, Life and fun

Airotel Camping Caravaning de la Côte d'Argent
33990 Hourtin Plage
Tél : 00033 (0)5.56.09.10.25
Fax : 0033 (0)5.56.09.24.96
www.camping-cote-dargent.com   -   www.cca33.com -
www.campingcoteouest.com

FR33140 Camping le Grand Pré

Route de Casteljaloux, F-33430 Bazas (Gironde)

Tel: **05 56 65 13 17**. Email: **legrandpre@wanadoo.fr**

www.alanrogers.com/FR33140

In a rural position, where the owners stated philosophy of tranquillity is realised. There are only 30 grass pitches, separated by flowering shrubs and bushes. There are plans to expand and four pitches are occupied by mobile homes. All have electricity (6-16A), water and drainage. Reception facilities and a bar are in a very tastefully converted old barn, where you may have breakfast or collect bread. There is a traffic free footpath from the site to the town, which we can recommend. A new cycle path runs from Bazas to the Atlantic coast (on 80 km. of old railway track).

Facilities

The high quality toilet block may not be adequate for demand, but we are told more units will be built. Laundry facilities. Baby room. Facilities for disabled persons. Motorcaravan services. Swimming pool and paddling pool. Sunbathing area. Playground. Boules. B&B nearby at the Château. By prior arrangement touring motorcaravans may park overnight (with electricity) when site is closed. Off site: Shops, bars and restaurants in Bazas, 1.5 km.

Open: 1 April - 30 September.

Directions

Bazas is around 55 km. southeast of Bordeaux, and 15 km. south of Langon. From Bazas centre take the D655 east towards Casteljaloux, and the site entrance is about 1 km. on your right (well signed). GPS: N44:25.856 W00:12.141

Charges guide

Per unit incl. 1 or 2 persons	€ 7,90 - € 18,90
electricity (6-16A)	€ 3,20 - € 4,75
extra person over 10 yrs	€ 2,40 - € 3,50

FR33170 Camping les Acacias

44 route de Saint Vivien, F-33590 Vensac (Gironde)

Tel: **05 56 09 58 81**. Email: **contact@les-acacias-du-medoc.fr**

www.alanrogers.com/FR33170

Les Acacias is a medium sized, family run site in a lovely, rural location on the edge of the pretty little village of Vensac. This attractive site has been owned by the Gomes family for 16 years, and they offer a very warm welcome in the chalet-style reception. The mixed woodland setting, with lots of flowering shrubs, makes a welcome change from the ubiquitous pines on the coast. There are 175 pitches (141 for touring) and electrical connections were being refurbished when we visited.

Facilities

Maintenance and cleaning of the attractive toilet block is of a high standard. Facilities for disabled visitors. Mother and baby room with good facilities. Washing machines and dryers. Small shop (1/7-30/8). Bar, café and takeaway (1/7-30/8). Swimming and paddling pools (unheated, 1/6-24/9). Minigolf (free). Play area. Mobile homes to rent. Off site: Bicycle hire in St Vivien 3 km. Fishing and riding 5 km. Nearest beach 12 km. Bus service to Lesparre and Le Verdon outside site.

Open: 1 April - 24 September.

Directions

From Bordeaux ringroad take exit 8 towards St Medard, then a quick right-left onto D1 towards Castelnau-de-Medoc. Continue on D1 as it becomes the N215, past Lesparre-Medoc. After a further 15 km. ignore first left turn to Vensac (despite campings sign), take second and site is on left in 200 m. From the north, take ferry from Royan to Le Verdon then N215 south and turn off to Vensac (about 20 km). GPS: N45:24.532 W01:01.964

Charges guide

Per unit incl. 2 persons and electricity	€ 11,00 - € 20,00
extra person	€ 3,20

FR33210 Sunêlia la Pointe du Medoc

Route de la Pointe de Grave, F-33123 Le Verdon-sur-Mer (Gironde)

Tel: **05 56 73 39 99**. Email: **info@camping-lapointedumedoc.com**

www.alanrogers.com/FR33210

This site has 260 pitches, with around half for touring (6A electricity and many fully serviced). It is situated roughly equi-distant between the sandy Atlantic beach (accessed by a pleasant walk through the forest opposite) and that of the Gironde estuary, both around one kilometre away. Pitches are generally large. Some are in full sun but those towards the rear of the site offer much more shade. A large converted office provides a library with internet access and a billiard table.

Facilities

Swimming pool, small waterfalls, paddling pool. Massage room. Minigolf. Multisport terrain. Bicycle hire. Communal barbecues. Organised entertainment and children's club (ages 4-11) all season. Small farm and children's garden. Activities for teenagers in July/Aug. Off site: Sea fishing 1 km. Riding 5 km.

Open: 26 April - 12 September.

Directions

Site is on the RN215 just south of Le Verdon and can be accessed either from the south (Bordeaux or the Blaye ferry), or from the north using the regular Royan - Pointe de Grave car ferry. GPS: N45:32.724 W01:04.770

Charges guide

Per unit incl. 1 or 2 persons	€ 13,00 - € 20,00
incl. electricity	€ 16,00 - € 24,00
incl. water and drainage	€ 18,00 - € 26,00
extra person (over 1 yr)	€ 3,00 - € 6,00

FR33130 Yelloh! Village les Grands Pins

Mobile homes ▶ page 501

Plage Nord, F-33680 Lacanau-Océan (Gironde)

Tel: **04 66 73 97 39**. Email: **info@yellohvillage-les-grands-pins.com**

www.alanrogers.com/FR33130

This Atlantic coast holiday site with direct access to a fine sandy beach, is on undulating terrain amongst tall pine trees. A large site with 600 pitches, there are 430 of varying sizes for touring units. One half of the site is a traffic free zone (except for arrival or departure day, caravans are placed on the pitch, with separate areas outside for parking). There is a good number of tent pitches, those in the centre of the site having some of the best views. This popular site has an excellent range of facilities available for the whole season. Especially useful for tent campers are safety deposit and fridge boxes which are available for rent. Mobile homes (2 persons) are for hire. The large sandy beach is a 350 m. stroll from the gate at the back of the site.

Facilities

Four well equipped toilet blocks, one heated, including baby room and facilities for disabled people. Launderette. Motorcaravan services. Supermarket. Bar, restaurant, snack bar, takeaway. Heated swimming pool (lifeguard in July/Aug) with sunbathing surround. Jacuzzi. Free fitness activities. Games room. Fitness suite. Tennis. Two playgrounds. Adventure playground. Bicycle hire. Organised activities. WiFi in the bar (on payment). Only gas barbecues are permitted. Off site: Fishing, golf, riding and bicycle hire 5 km.

Open: 26 April - 20 September.

Directions

From Bordeaux take N125/D6 west to Lacanau-Océan. At second roundabout, take second exit: Plage Nord, follow signs to 'campings'. Les Grand Pins signed to right at the far end of road. GPS: N45:00.664 W01:11.602

Charges guide

Per unit incl. 2 persons	
and electricity	€ 14,00 - € 43,00
extra person	€ 5,00 - € 9,00
child (2-12 yrs)	free - € 5,00
dog	€ 4,00

Half-board arrangements available.

www.yellohvillage.com tel: +33 466 739 739

Les Grands Pins
camping village ★★★★

Directly at the beach in the heart of an extensive pine forest, this is an ideal choice for family holidays, where you can relax in the open air. Discover Lacanau, the popular surfing spot, play golf, go cycling on one of the nice cycle tracks or choose a canoe trip on the lakes. For a full day excursion, visit a château in the famous Medoc Wine area, make a boat trip on the Bassin d'Arcachon or go shopping in the majestic town of Bordeaux.

NEW in 2009: 'La Baïne' aquatic area with external river and lagoon, children's paddling pool, heated indoor leisure pool and fitness area, sauna, hammam

• **Pitch for 1 night from €15,-*** • **1 night in a cottage for €29,-***

*between May 9th to May 20th 2009

Book your flight to Bordeaux-Mérignac Airport (45km)!

Yelloh! Village Les Grands Pins
33680 Lacanau Ocean
Tel: 0033 556 032 077
E-mail: reception@lesgrandspins.com

For information, special offers and online secure booking visit:
www.lesgrandspins.com

yelloh! VILLAGE

Check real time availability and at-the-gate prices...

www.alanrogers.com

FR33220 Sunêlia le Petit Nice

Route de Biscarosse, F-33115 Pyla-sur-Mer (Gironde)

Tel: **05 56 22 74 03**. Email: **info@petitnice.com**

www.alanrogers.com/FR33220

Le Petit Nice is a traditional seaside site, just south of the great Dune du Pyla (Europe's largest sand dune, and a genuinely remarkable sight). It is a friendly, if relatively unsophisticated, site with direct (steep) access to an excellent sandy beach. The 225 pitches are for the most part terraced, descending towards the sea. Many are quite small, with larger pitches generally occupied by mobile homes. For this reason it is likely to appeal more to campers and those with smaller motorcaravans and caravans. Most pitches are shaded by pine trees but those closest to the sea are unshaded.

Facilities

Two refurbished toilet blocks include washbasins in cubicles, baby rooms and facilities for disabled visitors. New, very smart bar/restaurant. Well stocked shop. Games room. Attractive swimming pool with small slide, children's pool and jacuzzi. Good fenced play area. Tennis. Boules.

Open: 1 April - 30 September.

Directions

The site is on the D218 (Arcachon - Biscarosse) south of the Dune du Pyla and is the fifth site you pass after the Dune. GPS: N44:34.339 W01:13.255

Charges guide

Per pitch incl. 2 persons	€ 14,00 - € 28,00
incl. electricity (6A)	€ 17,00 - € 32,00
extra person	€ 4,00 - € 7,00

Camping Cheques accepted.

FR33230 Camping International le Truc Vert

Route du Truc-Vert, F-33950 Lège-Cap-Ferret (Gironde)

Tel: **05 56 60 89 55**. Email: **truc-vert@tiscali.fr**

www.alanrogers.com/FR33230

Relaxing amidst the tall pines of this ten hectare hillside site is pleasant, but if you are looking for more activity there are many cycle ways and walks to enjoy in the lovely local countryside. The site provides over 480 pitches (280 with 6A electricity) with trees giving shade. Some pitches are level but for many you will need levelling blocks. Some site roads are a little steep so care is needed and also while travelling on the local main roads through the woods (keep to speed limits) as the occasional wild boar ventures out onto the roads. The entrance area is decked with flowers and a blaze of colour when in bloom and very welcoming.

Facilities

Seven toilet blocks (not all open all season) spread well around the site offer satisfactory facilities with showers and washbasins in cubicles, facilities for disabled people (although some may find the roads on site a little steep). Motorcaravan service area. Laundry facilities. Bar/brasserie (1/5-30/9). Restaurant (1/6-30/9). Shop. Play area. TV/games room. Some evening entertainment in season. Internet access. Charcoal barbecues are not permiited. Off site: Riding 500 m. Fishing and beach 300 m.

Open: 1 May - 30 September.

Directions

From Bordeaux take D106 towards Lège-Cap Ferret. Continue on D106 through town and in Les Jacquets, just before village sign for Le Petit Piquey, turn right. Follow through residential area and woods for about 4 km. Site is on left. GPS: N44:42.930 W01:14.573

Charges guide

Per unit incl. 2 persons	€ 112,90 - € 19,00
extra person	€ 3,00 - € 4,20
electricity (6A)	€ 3,10

FR33240 Camping Airotel de l'Océan

F-33680 Lacanau-Océan (Gironde)

Tel: **05 56 03 24 45**. Email: **airotel.lacanau@wanadoo.fr**

www.alanrogers.com/FR33240

Its location on the Atlantic coast, 600 m. from a lovely sandy beach makes this site extremely popular. Set in ten hectares of wooded sand dunes, the site offers the total holiday experience with 550 pitches set amongst pine trees with areas for peace and quiet and areas for those who want to be on top of it all. Some pitches are quite spacious, some level and others requiring blocks. At the time of our visit everywhere was very dry and there was very little grass. There is a large swimming pool complex, a bar and soundproofed disco.

Facilities

Six toilet blocks provide spacious facilities including a room for disabled visitors in each block (although the site is quite hilly), baby rooms, washing machines. Motorcaravan services. Supermarket. Bar, restaurant, takeaway. Large leisure pool complex. Various sports facilities. Fitness gym. TV, games rooms. Internet access. Bicycle hire. Barbecue area. Off site: Beach 600 m. Shops 1 km. Many cycle routes through the woods.

Open: 9 April - 25 September.

Directions

From Bordeaux take D106 then onto D3 to Royan and through the wooded areas of the Atlantic coast. At Lacanau join D6 to Lacanau-Océan. At roundabout before village turn right and site is 800 m. on the right. GPS: N45:00.511 W01:11.544

Charges guide

Per unit incl. 2 persons	€ 15,50 - € 37,00
incl. electricity	€ 15,50 - € 37,00
extra person	€ 3,50 - € 8,00

FR33280 Village Center la Forêt

Route de Biscarrosse, F-33115 Pyla-sur-Mer (Gironde)
Tel: 05 56 22 73 28. Email: camping.foret@wanadoo.fr   www.alanrogers.com/FR33280

Camping de la Forêt is one of a number of sites in this area that is dominated by the massive Dune du Pyla. The dune has to be negotiated in order to get to the beach (either over it or around, which is about 3 km), and the virtual wall of bright sand is all you have by way of a view to the east. This is a very well kept site with good facilities, easy access for all types of unit, and plenty of attractions for adults and children. Set on a gentle slope, mixed pine and oak trees give shade on most pitches. There are 24 pitches on hardstanding for motorcaravans, and all of the remaining touring pitches (on well-kept grass) have good access to water and electricity. A large area nearest to the dune has unserviced pitches for tents. Modern mobile-homes for hire have their own area. The pool is perhaps a little basic, being a simple rectangular affair with no loungers, and no separate paddling area for the little ones. However the other facilities are very good, with a large bar and terrace with takeaway food available, and a separate more up-market restaurant. For more active campers there are quite good sports facilities on site, and nearby a network of cycle paths, GR walks, horse riding and (for the really brave) para-gliding. Dances and games evenings are on offer in high season.

Facilities

Six unisex toilet blocks (not all open in low season) have good facilities. No special facilities for babies. Facilities for disabled visitors (key from reception). Washing machines and dryers. Motorcaravan service area. Well stocked shop. Bar, takeaway and restaurant (1/5-30/9). Swimming and paddling pools. Tennis (free except in July/Aug). Minigolf. Boules. Bicycle hire. Large play area. Children's club in July/Aug. Off site: Golf, riding and sailing all within 5 km.

Open: 7 April - 5 November.

Directions

From A63 (north or south) take A660 towards Arcachon. At La Teste turn off towards Dune du Pyla and at Dune car park roundabout take left turn towards Biscarrosse. Site is about 2 km. on the right. GPS: N44:35.706 W01:11.796

Charges guide

Per unit incl. 2 persons	€ 14,00 - € 29,00
incl. electricity	€ 19,00 - € 33,00
extra person	€ 5,00 - € 8,00
child (under 7 yrs)	€ 2,50 - € 4,50

Altavia Link

La Forêt***

Pyla-sur-Mer > Atlantic coast

- Situated at the bottom of the Dune of Pilat
- Stairs to easy reach the top of the great Dune of Pilat

Villagecenter

BOOK YOUR HOLIDAYS
www.village-center.com
+33 (0)4 99 57 21 21

QUALITÉ TOURISME

Camping Qualité

FR33260 Camping le Braou

Route de Bordeaux, F-33980 Audenge (Gironde)
Tel: 05 56 26 90 03. Email: info@camping-audenge.com   www.alanrogers.com/FR33260

The present owners, M. and Mme. Gharbi, were the wardens of this simple, former municipal site and now lease it from the town. They have funded several developments since they took over in 2003. The site is flat with easy access, and the large pitches are in avenues, separated by newly-planted small shrubs. There is little natural shade. The new electric hook-ups (on 116 of the 148 pitches) are 10A. Outside high season this is a pleasant, reasonably priced place to stay while exploring the Bassin d'Arcachon with its bird reserve, oyster-beds, walks and cycle tracks.

Facilities

The two toilet blocks have been refurbished and are very adequate. Washbasins are in cubicles. Shop for basics. Bar and snack bar (July/Aug). Swimming pool (1/6-31/8). Play area. Internet access. Motorcaravan service point and overnight pitches outside site. Mobile homes to rent. Off site: Town facilities 800 m. Beach and fishing 15 km. Riding 2 km. Golf 5 km.

Open: 1 April - 30 September.

Directions

From A63 take exit 22 onto A660 towards Arcachon. From A660 take exit 2 towards Facture, then D3 through Biganos to Audenge. Site is signed 'Camping Municipal' at lights in town. GPS: N44:40.950 W01:00.870

Charges guide

Per person	€ 3,00 - € 5,00
pitch incl. electricity	€ 14,00 - € 21,00

BOOK THIS SITE
CALL 01580 214000
...we'll arrange everything
The Travel Service

FR33290 Camping le Tedey

Par le Moutchic, route de Longarisse, F-33680 Lacanau-Lac (Gironde)

Tel: **05 56 03 00 15**. Email: **camping@le-tedey.com**   www.alanrogers.com/FR33290

With direct access to a large lake and beach, this site enjoys a beautiful tranquil position set in an area of 14 hectares amidst mature pine trees. There are 700 pitches of which 630 are for touring units with 36 mobile homes and chalets available for rent. The pitches are generally level and grassy although the site is on a slope. Dappled sunlight is available through the trees. Electricity is available to all pitches and 223 also have water and waste water drainage. The bar is close to the lake with a large indoor and outdoor seating area. The owners and staff are friendly and helpful and English is spoken. There is an open air cinema on Saturdays and Wednesdays as well as other entertainment in July and August. A children's club is also organised. The takeaway sells a variety of food and the shop next door is well stocked. This is an attractive well maintained site where you get a feeling of space and calm. There are many places of interest nearby and a short drive from Bordeaux.

Facilities

Four modern sanitary blocks with facilities for disabled visitors and babies. Laundry facilities. Bar with terrace. Creperie. Takeaway. Bicycle hire. Boating on the lake. Petanque. Playground. Gas barbecues only on pitches. Dogs accepted but not in July or August. Internet access. Off site: Surfing. Riding. Golf. Cycling.

Open: 28 April - 19 September.

Directions

From Lacanau take the D6 to Lacanau-Océan. Take Route de Longarisse and camping is well signed. GPS: N44:59.172 W01:08.046

Charges guide

Per unit incl. 1 or 2 persons	€ 16,00 - € 20,00
incl. water and drainage	€ 19,80 - € 24,00
extra person	€ 3,00 - € 5,00
child (2-10 yrs)	€ 2,50 - € 3,00

ROUTE DE LONGARISSE
33680 LACANAU
TEL: 0033(0) 5 56 03 00 15
FAX: 0033(0) 5 56 03 01 90

Le Tedey — CAMPING CARAVANING ★★★

L A C A N A U - C O T E A T L A N T I Q U E

E-MAIL: CAMPING@LE-TEDEY.COM - INTERNET: WWW.LE-TEDEY.COM

FR33340 Camping Club de Soulac

Boulevard de l'Amélie, F-33780 Soulac-sur-Mer (Gironde)

Tel: **05 56 09 82 87**. Email: **sables@lelilhan.com**   www.alanrogers.com/FR33340

This site is also known as Les Sables d'Argent and forms a group (Camping Club de Soulac) with its sister site Le Lilhan. Set amongst pine trees and undulating sand dunes, this seaside holiday site has direct access to the beach and some pitches have fine views of the sea. There are 152 individual, hedged pitches on sandy grass with some terracing (some do slope). Many are under tall pines with some very large fir cones, but a few are in the open right on the shore. There are 72 pitches for touring units, the remainder being used for a mix of rented and private mobile homes and chalets. Five pitches are fully serviced and 70 have 10A electricity.

Facilities

Two toilet blocks, both recently refitted, provide washbasins (some in cubicles), facilities for babies and disabled campers. Washing machine and dryer. Small shop for bread and basic provisions. Bar with satellite TV, games machines, internet access and WiFi. Restaurant, crêperie, pizzeria and takeaway (everything open 1/4-30/9). Children's club and entertainment (July/Aug). New beachside games area. Good adventure playground and communal barbecue area. Sea fishing, surfing and other watersports. Bicycle hire. Only gas and electric barbecues on pitches. American RVs not accepted. Off site: Riding. Boat launching. Over 100 km. of cycleways in the area.

Open: 1 April - 30 September.

Directions

Soulac-sur-Mer is on the Atlantic coast just south of the tip of the Gironde peninsula. Les Sables d'Argent is on the long straight boulevard which runs parallel to the sea, south of town centre towards Amélie-sur-Mer (also signed from D101 along with numerous other sites (signs are small and easy to miss). GPS: N45:29.981 W01:08.409

Charges guide

Per unit incl. 2 persons	€ 15,95 - € 19,95
extra person	€ 3,00 - € 4,50
child (2-10 yrs)	€ 2,70 - € 3,50
electricity (10A)	€ 4,00 - € 4,20
Camping Cheques accepted.	

Check real time availability and at-the-gate prices...

www.**alanrogers**.com

FR33310 Yelloh! Village Panorama du Pyla

Grande Dune du Pyla, route de Biscarrosse, F-33260 Pyla-sur-Mer (Gironde)

Tel: 04 66 73 97 39. Email: **info@yellohvillage-panorama.com**   www.alanrogers.com/FR33310

Many campsites set amongst pine trees have a rather untidy look, but Panorama is different. Here the entrance is inviting with well tended flower beds and a pleasant, airy reception. There is a steep climb up to the first of the touring pitches, passing the swimming pool and play area. Some pitches are suitable for caravans and motorcaravans and others suitable for tents. The touring pitches are on terraces amongst the tall pines and most have electricity (3-10A). The sea views from almost all pitches are stunning. Access to the toilet blocks may involve a steep climb (the site is probably not suitable for people with disabilities). All potentially noisy activities – pool, play areas, shop, discos, concerts, bar and takeaway – are grouped on the entrance side of the dune, away from the pitches. A track leads down to the beach with a staircase and right next door is Europe's largest dune, the Dune du Pyla, a favourite with parascenders. The area is a maze of off road cycle tracks. There are many activities and entertainments organised in high season, even classical concerts.

Facilities

Seven toilet blocks are clean and well maintained with baby rooms and facilities for disabled people. Fridge hire. Laundry facilities. Motorcaravan services. Restaurant with view of the ocean. Three heated pools and jacuzzi. Adjacent play area. Tennis. Minigolf. Paragliding. Sub-aqua diving. Entertainment in high season. Internet access. Off site: Riding and golf 10 km.

Open: 18 April - 29 September.

Directions

From N250, just before La Teste, take D259 signed Biscarrosse and Dune du Pyla. At roundabout turn left (south) on D218 coast road signed and Dune di Pyla. Site is 4 km. GPS: N44:34.359 W01:13.232

Charges guide

Per unit incl. 2 persons and electricity	€ 17,00 - € 40,00
extra person	€ 4,00 - € 7,00
child (under 12 yrs)	€ 3,00 - € 4,00

 ──────── www.yellohvillage.com tel: +33 466 739 739

Between the dunes and the ocean, a glimpse of what's in store

★★★
camping village
panorama du pyla
A R C A C H O N - F R A N C E

The PANORAMA is the only campsite in the region which is right by the sea and protected against the noise of motor traffic. The parking lot is patrolled by security guards at night. There is a panoramic view of the ocean, with a private staircase down to the beach. Customers have free use of the heated pool, minigolf, sauna, children's club, classical music auditorium. Tennis is free in the low season. You can find almost anything you need in the shops on the campsite. The entertainments hall and discotheque are some distance away from the camping area. There is a take-off zone for paragliding and hanggliding. The great PYLA dune can be reached directly from the campsite. Chalets and trailer homes over looking the sea, for rent.

Reductions in low season. www.camping-panorama.com

TEL: +33 (0) 556 221 044 FAX: +33 (0) 556 221 012 E-MAIL: mail@camping-panorama.com   yelloh!

FR33350 Camping Chez Gendron

2 Jandeon, F-33820 Saint Palais (Gironde)

Tel: 05 57 32 96 47. Email: **info@chezgendron.com**   www.alanrogers.com/FR33350

This useful all year site is Dutch-owned and in traditional style. In a rural setting, there are views over the Gironde estuary from the bar terrace above the small (unheated) swimming pool. The site is arranged in a number of paddocks and is part terraced, part sloping. There are 50 pitches, all on grass with electricity hook-ups (6/10A), well spaced and quite shady. Some are a fair distance from the facilities. It can be quite a steep walk up from the lowest pitches. Access to some pitches may be difficult for large or tall units especially in inclement weather.

Facilities

One small traditional toilet block, with modern fittings and underfloor heating. Facilities for babies and a suite for disabled visitors. Washing machine. These facilities could be stretched in peak season. Bar/restaurant and takeaway with terrace (1/5-30/9). Outdoor pool (1/5-30/9). Playground. Trampoline. Boules. Bicycle hire. Games room with WiFi and internet terminal. Low key animation in season. No charcoal barbecues in summer. Off site: Fishing 8 km. Boat launching 8 km. Golf 15 km.

Open: All year.

Directions

Saint-Palais is on the D255, just west of the N137 and about 6 km. south of Mirambeau and A10 exit 37. Site lies southwest of village on minor road off the D255 and is well signed. GPS: N45:18.861 W00:36.183

Charges guide

Per person	€ 3,50
child (under 4 yrs)	free
pitch	€ 10,50
Discounts in low season.	

247

FR33360 Camping de la Bastide

2 les Tuilleries, Pineuilh, F-33220 Sainte Foy-la-Grande (Gironde)

Tel: **05 57 46 13 84**. Email: **contact@camping-bastide.com** www.alanrogers.com/FR33360

A pleasant location on the bank of the River Dordogne, this small site is about a kilometre from the town centre. Neatly presented, there are only 38 pitches, of which just 26 are available for tourists (12 mobile homes for rent). All are on grass with 10A electricity. The site roads are narrow and the pitches not large (so unsuitable for large RVs and double axle caravans) with kerbs and some low tree branches to negotiate. Some pitches are drive through style and some also have some low ranch style fence dividers. An oval swimming pool has a decking surround.

Facilities

Central refurbished toilet block is traditional in style with modern fittings. Good facility for disabled campers. Washing machine and dryer. WiFi zone around reception and pool area. Games room with TV. Playground. Boules. Fishing in the adjacent river. No charcoal barbecues allowed. Off site: Bicycle hire 1 km. Golf 5 km. Riding 5 km.

Open: 1 April - 31 October.

Directions

Sainte-Foy-la-Grande is about 20 km. west of Bergerac. Site is 1 km. east of the town centre on D130, on south bank of the river Dordogne (well signed). GPS: N44:50.648 E00:13.488

Charges guide

Per unit incl. 1 person	€ 8,50 - € 11,00
incl. 2 persons and electricity (6A)	€ 14,50 - € 19,00
extra person	€ 2,00 - € 3,00
child	free - € 2,50

FR33380 Camping Pasteur

1 rue du Pilote, F-33740 Arès (Gironde)

Tel: **05 56 60 33 33**. Email: **pasteur.vacances@wanadoo.fr** www.alanrogers.com/FR33380

Arès is a pleasant resort on the northern fringe of the Bassin d'Arcachon, around 45 minutes west of Bordeaux. Camping Pasteur is a small site with an extended season offering just 50 pitches, of which around 30 are occupied by mobile homes and chalets. The touring pitches are well shaded and equipped with electrical connections (6A). The site is 300 m. from the village centre and 200 m. from the nearest beach. Amenities include a small swimming pool and snack bar (high season). This is a good area for cycling with a number of trails running close to the site and bicycles may be hired from the site.

Facilities

A single toilet block near the site entrance is in traditional style and kept very clean. Washbasins are in roomy cabins. Facilities for disabled visitors. Washing machine and dryer. Basic provisions kept in reception. Small bar and snack bar with takeaway (1/6-1/9). Small swimming pool (1/6-1/9). Play area. TV hire. Bicycle hire. Mobile homes and chalets for rent. Off site: Nearest beach 200 m. Village centre 300 m. Fishing 2 km. Golf 8 km. Riding 10 km.

Open: 1 March - 15 October.

Directions

From Bordeaux western ring road take the westbound D213 and then the D106 to Arès. Site is well signed in the village. GPS: N44:45.714 W01:08.221

Charges guide

Per pitch incl. 2 persons	€ 13,00 - € 23,50
extra person	€ 3,00 - € 5,00
electricity	€ 4,00

FR33390 Camping la Prairie

93 avenue du Médoc, F-33950 Lège-Cap-Ferret (Gironde)

Tel: **05 56 60 09 75**. Email: **camping.la.prairie@wanadoo.fr** www.alanrogers.com/FR33390

La Prairie is located to the north of the Bassin d'Arcachon. This is a pleasant, grassy site with 118 pitches, of which 101 are available for touring units. The pool can be found at the site entrance and is very inviting with a large sunbathing terrace and separate paddling pool for children. Pitches are large and level and all have electrical connections (10A). Shade is limited. The village of Lège is one kilometre to the south and there is a good selection of shops and restaurants here. On-site amenities include a small bar and snack bar, although these only operate in July and August.

Facilities

Two good quality toilet blocks with pre-set showers and washbasins in cubicles. Facilities for visitors with disabilities. Washing machines. Bar and snack bar (1/7-31/8). Swimming and paddling pools (1/6-30/9). Playground. Sports field. Entertainment and children's club in peak season. Mobile homes to rent. Off site: Beach 7 km. Bicycle hire 2 km. Golf 10 km. Riding 15 km. Sailing 5 km.

Open: 20 March - 27 September.

Directions

The site is 1 km. north of Lège on the D3 (Avenue du Médoc). GPS: N44:48.179 W01:08.014

Charges guide

Per unit incl. 2 persons	€ 9,80 - € 14,40
extra person	€ 2,40 - € 3,10
child (2-10 yrs)	€ 2,00 - € 2,50
electricity (10A)	€ 3,10

Check real time availability and at-the-gate prices...

www.alanrogers.com

FR33400 Camping Club Les Lacs

126 route des Lacs, F-33780 Soulac-Sur-Mer (Gironde)

Tel: 05 56 09 76 63. Email: **info@camping-les-lacs.com**   www.alanrogers.com/FR33400

Given its proximity to the Gironde ferry terminal at Le Verdon, many campers head south through Soulac. It is, however, a smart resort with a fine sandy beach. Camping Club Les Lacs is one of the best sites here and has 228 pitches on offer, of which 114 are available to touring units. All pitches have electrical connnections (5A). Site amenities are impressive with a large, modern complex at the entrance housing a large bar, restaurant, shop and stage for evening entertainment (high season). There is a large outdoor pool and covered pool adjacent. Member 'Sites et Paysages'.

Facilities	Directions
Good quality, modern toilet blocks.with showers and washbasins in cubicles. Facilities for visitors with disabilities. Washing machines and dryers. Shop. Bar, restaurant and takeaway (1/6-15/9). Swimming and paddling pools (1/6-15/9). Indoor pool all season. Water slide. Minigolf. Games room. Playground. Entertainment and children's club in peak season. Off site: Nearest beach 2.5 km. Bicycle hire 2 km. Riding 12 km. Fishing 4 km.	Site is 1 km. south of Soulac on the D101 (Routes des Lacs) and is well signed. GPS: N45:29.013 W01:07.171

Open: 5 April - 8 November.

Charges guide

Per unit incl. 2 persons	€ 16,00 - € 26,00
extra person	€ 4,00 - € 5,00
child (3-10 yrs)	€ 2,00 - € 4,00
electricity (5A)	€ 5,00

FR33420 Flower Camping la Canadienne

Route de Lège, 82 rue Gen. de Gaulle, F-33740 Arès (Gironde)

Tel: 05 56 60 24 91. Email: **info@lacanadienne.com**   www.alanrogers.com/FR33420

Arès is a pleasant little resort town on the northern edge of the Arcachon basin. La Canadienne is a member of the Flower group and is a well established family site with 105 pitches, many of which are now occupied by mobile homes and fully equipped tents (available for rent). There are two grades of touring pitch: 'Nature' (without electricity) and 'Comfort' with 15A electricity. The pitches are shaded and of a good size. The site has direct access to 150 km. of cycle tracks around the bay.

Facilities	Directions
Shop. Bar. Snack bar. Takeaway. Swimming pool. Play area. Bicycle hire. TV room. Activity and entertainment programme. Mobile homes and equipped tents for rent. Children's club in high season and activities including nature discovery and art workshops. Off site: Village centre 1 km. Fishing. Dune de Pyla. Cycle tracks.	Leave the Bordeaux ring road at exit 10 (D213) and drive to Arès. Continue tothe village centre and then follow signs for Lège and Cap Ferret. Site is on this road after a further 1 km. GPS: N44:46.675 W01:08.568

Open: 1 February - 29 November.

Charges 2009

Per unit incl. 2 persons and electricity	€ 17,90 - € 31,90
extra person	€ 4,00 - € 6,00
child (2-7 yrs)	€ 3,00 - € 4,00

www.flowercampings.com

FR33410 Camping Bordeaux Lac

Chemin de Bretous, F-33000 Bordeaux Lac (Gironde)

Tel: 05 57 87 70 60   www.alanrogers.com/FR33410

Bordeaux is undeniably one of France's major cities, but, until now has not had a campsite of quality. Bordeaux Lac is a large commercial area to the north of the city, centred around a massive lake and exhibition centre. This site is under construction at the time of writing and we will undertake a full inspection in 2009. 190 touring pitches are planned and will be arranged around a 14 hectare park. The pitches will all be 'grand confort' (i.e with electricity, water and drainage). A further 106 pitches will be occupied by mobile homes and chalets (available for rent). Leisure amenities will include a swimming pool and a restaurant.

Facilities	Directions
Restaurant. Swimming pool. Play area. Mobile homes and chalets for rent. Off site: Golf (Bordeaux Lac complex). Fishing. Large shopping centre. Cycle and walking tracks. Bordeaux centre 5 km.	Approaching from the north use the A630 (Bordeaux ring road) and leave at exit 4 (Bordeaux Lac) and follow signs to the site. GPS: N44:53.883 W00:34.917

Open: 10 May - September.

Charges 2009

Not yet available; contact the site.

FR40020 Camping les Chênes

Bois de Boulogne, F-40100 Dax (Landes)

Tel: 05 58 90 05 53. Email: camping-chenes@wanadoo.fr   www.alanrogers.com/FR40020

Les Chênes is a well established site, popular with the French themselves and situated on the edge of town amongst parkland (also near the river) and close to the spa for the thermal treatments. The 176 touring pitches are of two types, some large and traditional with hedges, 109 with electricity, water and drainage, and others more informal, set amongst tall pines with electricity if required. This is a reliable, well run site, with a little of something for everyone, but probably most popular for adults taking the 'treatments'. Dax is not a place that springs at once to mind as a holiday town but, as well as being a spa, it promotes a comprehensive programme of events and shows during the summer season.

Facilities

Two toilet blocks, one new and modern with heating, washbasins in cubicles, facilities for people with disabilities, babies and young children. The older block has been refurbished. Laundry facilities. Shop also providing takeaway food (4/4-31/10). Swimming and paddling pools (2/5-19/9). Play area. Field for ball games. Boules. Bicycle hire. Miniclub for children (July/Aug). Occasional special evenings for adults. Charcoal barbecues are not permitted. Off site: Restaurant opposite. Riding, fishing and golf all within 100 m. Beaches 28 km.

Open: 21 March - 7 November.

Directions

Site is west of town on south side of river, signed after main river bridge and at many junctions in town - Bois de Boulogne (1.5 km). In very wet weather the access road to the site (but not the site itself) may be flooded.
GPS: N43:42.721 W01:04.385

Charges guide

Per pitch incl. 2 persons and electricity (5A)	€ 13,90 - € 16,70
incl. water and drainage	€ 16,60 - € 19,40
extra person	€ 6,00
child (2-10 yrs)	€ 4,00
animal	€ 1,50

Camping Les Chênes ★★★★

Hôtel de plein air
du Bois de Boulogne
4 0 1 0 0   D A X
Tel. 0033 558 90 05 53
Fax 0033 558 90 42 43

FR40030 Les Pins du Soleil

Route des Minieres, quartier la Pince, F-40990 Saint Paul-lès-Dax (Landes)

Tel: 05 58 91 37 91. Email: info@pinsoleil.com   www.alanrogers.com/FR40030

This site will appeal to families, particularly those with younger children, or those who prefer to be some way back from the coast within easy reach of shops, cultural activities, etc. and well placed for touring the area. The new young owners are keen to make improvements to what is already a very pleasant site with 145 good sized pitches. There are 62 pitches for touring units all of which have electricity and drainage. The site benefits from being developed in light woodland so there is a fair amount of shade from the many small trees.

Facilities

Sanitary facilities include washbasins, hot showers and provision for disabled visitors. Laundry. Motorcaravn services. Small supermarket (1/6-31/10). Bar. Takeaway. Attractive, medium sized swimming pool with café, new paddling pool and jacuzzi (all 2/6-15/9). Playground and children's miniclub in high season. Covered entertain-metns area. Bicycle hire. Off site: Bus to the thermal baths 1 km. Fishing 1 km. Riding 3 km.

Open: 1 April - 31 October.

Directions

From west on N124, avoid bypass, follow signs for Dax and St Paul. Almost immediately turn right at roundabout onto D459 and follow signs. Site shortly on left. It is well signed from town centre, north of river. GPS: N43:43.224 W01:05.64

Charges guide

Per pitch incl. 2 persons	€ 8,00 - € 18,00
incl. electricity, water and drainage	€ 15,00 - € 24,00
extra person	€ 6,00
Camping Cheques accepted.	

FR40040 Camping Village la Paillotte

66, route des Campings, F-40140 Azur (Landes)

Tel: **05 58 48 12 12**. Email: **info@paillotte.com**   www.alanrogers.com/FR40040

La Paillotte, in the Landes area of southwest France, is a site with a character of its own. It lies beside the Soustons Lake only 1.5 km. from Azur village, with its own sandy beach. This is suitable for young children because the lake is shallow and slopes gradually. All 310 pitches at La Paillotte are mostly shady with shrubs and trees. The 132 pitches for touring vary in price according to size, position and whether they are serviced. La Paillotte is an unusual site with its own atmosphere which appeals to many regular clients. The campsite buildings (reception, shop, restaurant, even sanitary blocks) are all Tahitian in style. Circular in shape and constructed from local woods with the typical straw roof (and a layer of waterproof material underneath), some are now being replaced but still in character. For boating the site has a small private harbour where you can keep your own non-powered boat (of shallow draught).

Facilities

Well equipped toilet blocks. Washing machines and dryers. Motorcaravan services. Shop (1/6-1/9). Good restaurant with terrace overlooking lake, bar, takeaway (all 22/4-24/9). Swimming pool complex (22/4-24/9). Sports, games and organised activities. Miniclub. TV room, library. Fishing. Bicycle hire. Sailing, rowing boats and pedaloes for hire. Torches useful. Dogs are not accepted. Off site: Riding 5 km. Golf 10 km. Atlantic beaches 10 km.

Open: 24 April - 20 September.

Directions

Coming from the north along N10, turn west on D150 at Magescq. From south go via Soustons. In Azur turn left before church (site signed). GPS: N43:47.229 W01:18.570

Charges guide

Per unit incl. 2 persons and 10A electricity	€ 15,50 - € 38,00
incl. electricity and water	€ 17,50 - € 40,00
pitch by the lake with electricity	€ 20,00 - € 46,00
extra person (over 4 yrs)	€ 3,00 - € 7,50

CAMPINGS FranceLoc

Domaine de La Paillotte

At the banks of lake Soustons : Cottages and bungalows in Polynesian style. Heated swimming pool. Animation for all tastes and ages.

Domaine de la Paillotte
40140 Azur
*Tél. 0033(0)5 58 48 12 12
Fax. 0033(0)5 58 48 10 73*
www.campings-franceloc.fr

Landes

FR40050 Sunêlia le Col-Vert

Lac de Leon, F-40560 Vielle-Saint-Girons (Landes)

Tel: **0890 710 001**. Email: **contact@colvert.com**   www.alanrogers.com/FR40050

There are some 800 pitches in total, the 380 for touring being flat and covered by light pinewood, most with good shade and many along the lake side. They range from around 100 to 130 sq.m, partly separated and some 120 have water and electricity points and others have their own sanitary unit. Activities are organised in season: children's games, tournaments, etc. by day and dancing or shows in the evenings. Used by tour operators (80 pitches). The site has a supervised beach in July and August, sail-boarding courses in high season and there are some boats and boards for hire.

Facilities

Four toilet blocks, one heated. Washing machines, dryer, dishwasher, facilities for disabled people. Motorcaravan services. Shops (4/4-6/9). Bar/restaurant, takeaway. Two pools (all season, supervised), one covered and heated. New play area. TV room. Games room. Sports areas, boules, tennis. Fitness centre and sauna. Jogging tracks. Safety deposit boxes. Riding, bicycle hire, minigolf. Fishing. Riding. Sailing school (15/6-15/9). Communal barbecues. Off site: Walking and cycle ways in the forest. Atlantic beaches 5 km. Golf 10 km.

Open: 4 April - 20 September.

Directions

Site is off D652 Mimizan-Léon road, 4 km. south of crossroads with D42 at St-Girons. Road to lake and site is signed at Vielle. GPS: N43:54.190 W01:18.631

Charges guide

Per unit incl. 2 persons	€ 11,00 - € 47,90
extra person	€ 2,00 - € 6,40
child (3-13 yrs)	€ 1,50 - € 5,40
electricity (3/6/10A)	€ 4,10 - € 5,50
dog	€ 1,00 - € 4,30

The Travel Service
...we'll arrange everything

BOOK THIS SITE
CALL 01580 214000

FR40060 Camping Club International Eurosol

Route de la Plage, F-40560 Vielle-Saint-Girons (Landes)

Tel: **05 58 47 90 14**. Email: **contact@camping-eurosol.com**   www.alanrogers.com/FR40060

This attractive and well maintained site is set on undulating ground amongst mature pine trees giving good shade. The 356 pitches for touring are numbered and 209 have electricity with 120 fully serviced. A family site with multilingual entertainers, many games and tournaments are organised and a beach volleyball competition is held each evening in front of the bar. A third covered pool has recently been added to the smart, landscaped pool complex. A sandy beach 700 metres from the site has supervised bathing in high season.

Facilities

Four main toilet blocks and two smaller blocks are comfortable and clean with facilities for babies and disabled visitors. Motorcaravan services. Fridge rental. Well stocked shop and bar. Restaurant, takeaway (from 1/6). Stage for live shows arranged in July/Aug. Outdoor swimming pool complex. Tennis. Multisport court. Bicycle hire. Internet and WiFi. Charcoal barbecues are not permitted. Off site: Riding school opposite. Fishing 700 m.

Open: 9 May - 12 September.

Directions

Turn off D652 at St Girons on D42 towards St Girons-Plage. Site is on left before coming to beach (4.5 km). GPS: N43:57.100 W01:21.087

Charges 2009

Per unit incl.1 or 2 persons and electricity	€ 18,00 - € 33,50
extra person (over 4 yrs)	€ 5,00
dog	€ 2,50

EUROSOL ★★★★ Camping Club International

Route de la Plage • F-40560 Saint Girons Plage • Tel: 0033 558 479 014 • Fax: 0033 558 477 674
contact@camping-eurosol.com • www.camping-eurosol.com

FR40070 Yelloh! Village Lous Seurrots

Contis Plage, F-40170 Saint Julien-en-Born (Landes)

Tel: **04 66 73 97 39**. Email: **info@yellohvillage-lous-seurrots.com**   www.alanrogers.com/FR40070

Lous Seurrots is only a short 300 m. walk from the beach and parts of the site have views across the estuary. There are 610 pitches, mainly in pine woods on sandy undulating ground. They are numbered but only roughly marked out, most have good shade and over 80% have electrical hook-ups (adaptors required). The site's pool complex (two heated) is in a superb setting of palm trees and flower beds and the paved sunbathing areas have wonderful views out to the estuary and the sea. For all its size, Lous Seurrots is a family site with the emphasis on peace and tranquillity (no discos).

Facilities

Six well kept, modern toilet blocks, baby rooms and facilities for people with disabilities. Washing machines. Motorcaravan services. Large shop (15/5-15/9). Bar, restaurant (15/5-15/9). Takeaway (1/7-27/9). Swimming pool complex (2/4-30/9) and a Jacuzzi with keep fit classes (July/Aug). Tennis. Archery. Minigolf. Canoeing. Bicycle hire. Fishing. Miniclub. Evening entertainment twice weekly in high season in open-air auditorium. Only gas barbecues are permitted. Internet. Off site: Riding 3 km.

Open: 5 April - 27 September.

Directions

Turn off D652 on D41 (15 km. south of Mimizan) to Contis-Plage and site is on left as you reach it. GPS: N44:05.347 W01:18.990

Charges guide

Per unit incl. 2 persons and electricity	€ 17,00 - € 36,00
extra person	€ 4,00 - € 6,00
child (3-7 yrs)	free - € 4,00
animal	€ 3,00

tel: +33 466 739 739 www.yellohvillage.com   ━━━━━━━ **yelloh!** VILLAGE

Check real time availability and at-the-gate prices...
www.**alanrogers**.com

FR40080 Airotel Club Marina-Landes

Rue Marina, F-40200 Mimizan (Landes)

Tel: 05 58 09 12 66. Email: contact@clubmarina.com   www.alanrogers.com/FR40080

Well maintained and clean, with helpful staff, Club Marina-Landes would be a very good choice for a family holiday. Activities include discos, play groups for children, specially trained staff to entertain teenagers and concerts for more mature campers. There are numerous sports opportunities and a superb beach nearby. A nightly curfew ensures that all have a good night's sleep. The site has 444 touring pitches (298 with 10A electricity) and 128 mobile homes and chalets for rent. The pitches are on firm grass, most with hedges and they are large (mostly 100 sq.m. or larger). If ever a campsite could be said to have two separate identities, then Club Marina-Landes is surely the one. In early and late season it is quiet, with the pace of life in low gear – come July and until 1 September, all the facilities are open and there is fun for all the family with the chance that family members will only meet together at meal times.

Facilities

Five toilet blocks (opened as required), well maintained with showers and many washbasins in cabins. Facilities for babies, children and disabled visitors. Laundry facilities. Motorcaravan services. Fridge hire. Shop (freshly baked bread). Bar and restaurant. Snack bar, pizzas and takeaway (1/5-11/9). Covered pool. Outdoor pool. Minigolf. Tennis. Bicycle hire. Play area. Internet access. Entertainment and activities (high season). Gas or electric barbecues only. Off site: Beach and fishing 500 m. Bus service 1 km. Riding 1 km. Golf 7 km. Mimizan 8 km.

Open: 30 April - 14 September.

Directions

Heading west from Mimizan centre, take D626 passing Abbey Museum. Staright on at lights (crossing D87/D67). Next lights turn left. After 2 km. at T-junction turn left. Follow signs to site. GPS: N44:12.234 W01:17.472

Charges guide

Per unit incl. 3 persons	€ 14,00 - € 38,00
incl. electricity	€ 17,00 - € 42,00
child	€ 3,00 - € 8,00
dog	€ 2,00 - € 4,00

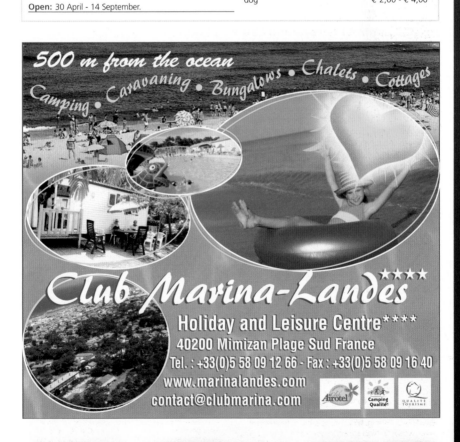

Check real time availability and at-the-gate prices...
www.alanrogers.com

The Travel Service

BOOK THIS SITE

CALL 01580 214000 ...we'll arrange everything

FR40100 Camping du Domaine de la Rive

Mobile homes ▶ page 501

Route de Bordeaux, F-40600 Biscarrosse (Landes)

Tel: 05 58 78 12 33. Email: info@camping-de-la-rive.fr

www.alanrogers.com/FR40100

Surrounded by pine woods, La Rive has a superb beach-side location on Lac de Sanguinet. It provides mostly level, numbered and clearly defined pitches of 100 sq.m. all with electricity connections (6A). The swimming pool complex is wonderful with pools linked by water channels and bridges. There is also a jacuzzi, paddling pool and two large swimming pools all surrounded by sunbathing areas and decorated with palm trees. An indoor pool is heated and open all season. There may be some aircraft noise from a nearby army base. This is a friendly site with a good mix of nationalities. The latest addition is a super children's aquapark with various games. The beach is excellent, shelving gently to provide safe bathing. There are windsurfers and small craft can be launched from the site's slipway.

Facilities

Five good clean toilet blocks have washbasins in cabins and mainly British style toilets. Facilities for disabled visitors. Baby baths. Motorcaravan service point. Shop with gas. Restaurant. Bar serving snacks and takeaway. Swimming pool complex (supervised July/Aug). Games room. Play area. Tennis. Bicycle hire. Boules. Archery. Fishing. Waterskiing. Watersports equipment hire. Tournaments (June-Aug). Skateboard park. Trampolines. Miniclub. No charcoal barbecues on pitches. Off site: Golf 8 km.

Open: 1 April - 30 September.

Directions

Take D652 from Sanguinet to Biscarrosse and site is signed on the right in about 6 km. Turn right and follow tarmac road for 2 km.
GPS: N44:27.607 W01:07.808

Charges guide

Per pitch incl. 2 persons	
and electricity	€ 20,00 - € 42,00
incl. water and drainage	€ 23,00 - € 45,00
extra person	€ 3,40 - € 7,50
child (3-7 yrs)	€ 2,30 - € 6,00
dog	€ 2,10 - € 5,00

Camping Cheques accepted.

FR40140 Camping Caravaning Lou P'tit Poun

Mobile homes ▶ page 502

110 avenue du Quartier Neuf, F-40390 St Martin-de-Seignanx (Landes)

Tel: 05 59 56 55 79. Email: contact@louptitpoun.com

www.alanrogers.com/FR40140

The manicured grounds surrounding Lou P'tit Poun give it a well kept appearance, a theme carried out throughout this very pleasing site which celebrates its 20th anniversary in 2009. It is only after arriving at the car park that you feel confident it is not a private estate. Beyond this point an abundance of shrubs and trees are revealed. Behind a central sloping flower bed lies the open plan reception area. The avenues around the site are wide and the 168 pitches (142 for touring) are spacious. All have 10A electricity, many also have water and drainage and some are separated by low hedges. A 'Sites et Paysages' member. The jovial owners not only make their guests welcome, but extend their enthusiasm to organising weekly entertainment for young and old during high season.

Facilities

Two unisex sanitary blocks, maintained to a high standard and kept clean, include washbasins in cabins, a baby bath and provision for disabled people. Laundry facilities with washing machine and dryer. Motorcaravan service point. Small shop (1/7-31/8). Café/restaurant (1/7-31/8). Swimming pool (1/6-15/9) Play area. Games room, TV. Half court tennis. Off site: Bayonne 6 km. Fishing and riding 7 km. Golf 10 km. Sandy beaches 10 minutes drive.

Open: 2 June - 12 September.

Directions

Leave A63 at exit 6 and join D817 in the direction of Pau. Site is signed at Leclerc supermarket. Continue for 3.5 km. and site is clearly signed on right.
GPS: N43:31.451 W01:24.730

Charges guide

Per pitch incl. 2 persons	
and electricity	€ 21,50 - € 32,50
extra person	€ 6,00 - € 7,00
child (under 7 yrs)	€ 4,00 - € 5,00

Lou P'tit Poun ★★★

At 10 km from the ocean, a friendly welcome awaits you at this quality campsite between Les Landes and the Basque country.

Rental of bungalows and mobil-homes

CAMPING LOU P'TIT POUN
40390 ST MARTIN DE SEIGNANX
Tél : 05 59 56 55 79   Fax : 05 59 56 53 71
E-mail : contact@louptitpoun.com
LANDES - AQUITAINE - FRANCE

Check real time availability and at-the-gate prices...

www.alanrogers.com

★ ★ ★

Club Airotel

Domaine de La Rive

a Paradise for Children

www.larive.fr

Pool complex and a covered heated swimming pool

Route de Bordeaux
40600 Biscarosse
Tél : 00 33 5 58 78 12 33
Fax : 00 33 5 58 78 12 92
info@camping-de-la-rive.fr

La Clef Verte

Chalets and mobile homes for rent. At the banks of a lake, in the heart of the landaise forest

E.S.E COMMUNICATION · Draguignan- Tél : 04.94.67.06.00

FR40160 Village Center les Vignes

Route de la Plage du Cap de L'Homy, F-40170 Lit-et-Mixe (Landes)

Tel: **04 99 57 21 21**. Email: **contact@les-vignes.com**   www.alanrogers.com/FR40160

Les Vignes is a large holiday site close to the Atlantic coast with 450 pitches, of which 262 are occupied by a mix of mobile homes, bungalows and tents, most of which are for rent. The 188 tourist pitches are relatively level on a sandy base, all serviced with electricity (10A) and water, some with waste water drains. The site's amenities, including a supermarket, restaurant and bar, are located at the entrance to the site. The rather stylish swimming pool complex includes a six lane water slide. A wide range of activities is provided and during July and August a great variety of entertainment options for both adults and children, some of which take place in the new entertainment 'Big Top'.

Facilities

Four sanitary units with washing machines, dryers, facilities for babies and disabled people. Large supermarket (15/6-10/9). Restaurant, bar (15/6-10/9). Takeaway (July/Aug). Swimming pool complex (1/6-15/9). Tennis. Table tennis. Golf driving range. Minigolf. Volleyball, basketball. Pétanque. Kids club and playground. Bicycle hire. Internet access. Barrier closed 23.00-07.00 hrs. Off site: Golf course, canoeing, kayaking, surfing, riding. Many cycle tracks.

Open: 1 June - 15 September.

Directions

Lit-et-Mixe is on the D652 20 km. south of Mimizan. Turn west on D88 1 km. south of town towards Cap de l'Homy for 1.5 km. where site entrance is on left. GPS: N44:01.375 W01:16.787

Charges guide

Per pitch incl. 2 persons, electricity and water	€ 16,00 - € 37,00
extra person (over 5 yrs)	€ 5,00
child (under 5 yrs)	free

Les Vignes★★★★

Lit-et-Mixe > Atlantic coast

• Wild aspect and natural surroundings of the Gascony Landes area
• Close to the beaches of the Atlantic ocean

Villagecenter

BOOK YOUR HOLIDAYS
www.village-center.com
+33 (0)4 99 57 21 21

FR40110 Le Village Tropical Sen-Yan

Le Village Tropical, F-40170 Mézos (Landes)

Tel: **05 58 42 60 05**. Email: **reception@sen-yan.com**   www.alanrogers.com/FR40110

This exotic family site is about 12 km. from the Atlantic coast in the Landes forest area, just outside the village. There are 140 touring pitches set around a similar number of mobile homes. Pitches are marked with hedges and have electricity (6A). The reception, bar and pool area is almost tropical with the luxuriant greenery of its banana trees, palm trees, tropical flowers and its straw sunshades. The covered, heated pool, new water slide, gym with sauna and jacuzzi all add to the attractiveness. A new covered animation area provides entertainment and discos during high season.

Facilities

Three well maintained and clean toilet blocks with good quality fittings have showers, washbasins in cabins and British style WCs. The newest block is especially suitable for low season visitors with a special section for babies, plus excellent facilities for disabled people. Shop (from 15/6). Bar, restaurant and snacks (1/7-31/8). Outdoor swimming pools (1/7-15/9). Heated indoor pool (1/6-15/9). Archery. Practice golf. Bicycle hire. No charcoal barbecues. Off site: Fishing 500 m. Riding 6 km. Beach 12 km.

Open: 1 June - 15 September.

Directions

From N10 take exit 14 (Onesse-Laharie), then D38 Bias/Mimizan road. After 13 km. turn south to Mézos from where site is signed. GPS: N44:04.337 W01:09.380

Charges guide

Per unit incl. 2 persons	€ 20,00 - € 30,00
incl. 6A electricity	€ 24,00 - € 34,00
extra person	€ 5,00 - € 6,00
child (under 7 yrs)	free - € 5,00

Check real time availability and at-the-gate prices...

www.**alanrogers**.com

FR40180 Camping le Vieux Port

Plage Sud, F-40660 Messanges (Landes)

Tel: 01 72 03 91 60. Email: contact@levieuxport.com

Mobile homes ▶ page 502

www.alanrogers.com/FR40180

BOOK THIS SITE
...we'll arrange everything
CALL 01580 214000
The Travel Service

A well established destination appealing particularly to families with teenage children, this lively site has 1,406 pitches of mixed size, most with electricity (6A) and some fully serviced. The camping area is well shaded by pines and pitches are generally of a good size, attractively grouped around the toilet blocks. There are many tour operators here and well over a third of the site is taken up with mobile homes and another 400 pitches are used for tents. The heated pool complex is exceptional boasting five outdoor pools and three large water slides. There is also a heated indoor pool. An enormous 7000 sq.m. Aquatic Parc is planned for 2009 and all the sanitary facilities are to be renovated. The area to the north of Bayonne is heavily forested and a number of very large campsites are attractively located close to the superb Atlantic beaches. Le Vieux Port is probably the largest and certainly one of the most impressive of these. At the back of the site a path leads across the dunes to a good beach (500 m). A little train also trundles to the beach on a fairly regular basis in high season (small charge). All in all, this is a lively site with a great deal to offer an active family.

Facilities

Nine well appointed, recently renovated toilet blocks with facilities for disabled people. Motorcaravan services. Good supermarket and various smaller shops in high season. Several restaurants, takeaway and three bars (all open all season). Large pool complex (no Bermuda shorts) including new covered pool and Polynesian themed bar. Tennis. Multisport pitch. Minigolf. Bicycle hire. Riding centre. Organised activities in high season including frequent discos and karaoke evenings. Only communal barbecues are allowed. Off site: Fishing 1 km. Golf 8 km.

Open: 1 April - 30 September.

Directions

Leave RN10 at Magescq exit heading for Soustons. Pass through Soustons following signs for Vieux-Boucau. Bypass this town and site is clearly signed to the left at second roundabout.
GPS: N43:47.867 W01:24.067

Charges 2009

Per unit incl. 2 persons	€ 13,00 - € 44,00
extra person	€ 4,00 - € 8,00
child (under 13 yrs)	€ 3,00 - € 5,50
electricity (6/8A)	€ 4,50 - € 8,00
animal	€ 2,50 - € 5,00

Camping Cheques accepted.

LE VIEUX PORT direct access to the beach

South Atlantic Coast - MESSANGES - LANDES - FRANCE

New water park planned in 2009. 1400 sq meters of water

Tél. 0 825 70 40 40 (0,15€/mn)   Tél. +33 176 76 70 00

www.levieuxport.com

Le Vieux Port ★★★★

Club Airotel

Check real time availability and at-the-gate prices...
www.alanrogers.com

FR40190 Le Saint-Martin Airotel Camping

Mobile homes ▶ page 502

Avenue de l'Océan, F-40660 Moliets-Plage (Landes)

Tel: 05 58 48 52 30. Email: contact@camping-saint-martin.fr

www.alanrogers.com/FR40190

A family site aimed mainly at couples and young families, Airotel St-Martin is a welcome change to most of the sites in this area in that it has only a small number of chalets (85) compared to the number of touring pitches (575). First impressions are of a neat, tidy, well cared for site and the direct access to the beach is an added bonus. The pitches are mainly typically French in style with low hedges separating them plus some shade. Electricity hook ups are 10-15A and a number of pitches also have water and drainage. Entertainment in high season is low key (with the emphasis on quiet nights) – daytime competitions and a miniclub, plus the occasional evening entertainment, well away from the pitches and with no discos or karaoke. With pleasant chalets and mobile homes to rent, and an 18-hole golf course 700 m. away (special rates negotiated), this would be an ideal destination for a golfing weekend or longer stay.

Facilities

Seven toilet blocks of a high standard and very well maintained, have washbasins in cabins, large showers, baby rooms and facilities for visitors with disabilities. Motorcaravan service point. Washing machines and dryers. Fridge rental. Supermarket. Bars, restaurants and takeaways. Indoor pool (22/3-1/11), jacuzzi and sauna (charged July/Aug). Outdoor pool area with jacuzzi and paddling pool (15/6-15/9). Multisport pitch. Play area. Internet access. Electric barbecues only. Off site: Bicycle hire 500 m. Golf and tennis 700 m. Riding 8 km.

Open: 19 March - 11 November.

Directions

From the N10 take D142 to Lèon, then D652 to Moliets-et-Mar. Follow signs to Moliets-Plage, site is well signed. GPS: N43:51.145 W01:23.239

Charges guide

Per unit incl. 1 or 2 adults,	
1 child	€ 17,50 - € 39,00
incl. electricity	€ 21,00 - € 43,20
service pitch	€ 24,00 - € 48,50
extra person	€ 6,00
dog	€ 3,50

Prices are for reserved pitches.

★ ★ ★ ★

Le Saint Martin

Airotel Camping
Caravaning

Avenue de l'Océan
40660 Moliets-Plage

Tél : (33) 05.58.48.52.30
Fax : (33) 05.58.48.50.73

www.camping-saint-martin.fr
contact @camping-saint-martin.fr

FR40200 Yelloh! Village le Sylvamar

Avenue de l'Océan, F-40530 Labenne-Océan (Landes)

Tel: 04 66 73 97 39. Email: info@yellohvillage-sylvamar.com

www.alanrogers.com/FR40200

Less than a kilometre from a long sandy beach, this campsite has a good mix of tidy, well maintained chalets, mobile homes and touring pitches. The 562 pitches (216 for touring) are level, numbered and mostly separated by low hedges. Most have electricity (10A), many also have water and drainage and there is welcoming shade. The swimming pool complex is superbly set in a sunny location. The pools are of various sizes (one is heated) with a large one for paddling. With four toboggans and a fast flowing channel for sailing down in the inflatable rubber rings provided, this is great fun for children.

Facilities

Four modern toilet blocks have washbasins in cabins, and facilities for babies and disabled visitors. Washing machines. Fridge hire. Shop. Bar/restaurant and takeaway. Play area. Cinema and video room. TV room. Miniclub (July/Aug). Fitness centre. Tennis. Entertainment programme. Bicycle hire. No charcoal barbecues. Off site: Beach 900 m. Fishing, riding 1 km. Golf 7 km.

Open: 26 April - 17 September.

Directions

Labenne is on the N10. In Labenne, head west on D126 signed Labenne-Océan and site is on right in 4 km. GPS: N43:35.742 W01:27.383

Charges guide

Per unit incl. 2 persons	
and electricity	€ 17,00 - € 38,00
extra person (over 7 yrs)	€ 3,00 - € 7,00

tel: +33 466 739 739 www.yellohvillage.com

Check real time availability and at-the-gate prices...

www.**alanrogers**.com

FR40220 Camping les Acacias

Route d'Azur, quartier Delest, F-40660 Messanges (Landes)

Tel: 05 58 48 01 78. Email: lesacacias@lesacacias.com

www.alanrogers.com/FR40220

Close to the Atlantic beaches of Les Landes, this small family run site is quiet and peaceful. There are 79 large, generally flat touring pitches separated by trees and shrubs, with chalets and mobile homes arranged unobtrusively on two sides of the site. There are also some seasonal caravans. All the touring pitches have electricity (5/10A), 8 have water, which is also available at the toilet block. Pitches are easily accessed by tarmac internal roads. M. and Mme. Dourthe are constantly improving the site and the facilities and services show the care taken in design.

Facilities	Directions
One modern, clean and well designed toilet block with facilities for disabled people. Laundry facilities. Fridge hire. Motorcaravan services. Shop (15/6-15/9). Takeaway (high season). Games room. Small play area. Football. Boules. Bicycle hire. Off site: Bus 1 km. Beach 2 km. Fishing 3 km. Riding 1.5 km. Golf 4 km. Supermarket 2 km.	Site is signed off the D652, turning inland (east) 2 km. north of Vieux-Boucau; 3 km. south of Messanges. GPS: N43:47.902 W01:22.530

Open: 25 March - 25 October.

Charges guide

Per unit incl. 1 or 2 persons	€ 9,40 - € 14,00
extra person	€ 2,80 - € 3,60
electricity	€ 2,90 - € 4,20

FR40240 Camping Mayotte Vacances

368 chemin des Roseaux, F-40600 Biscarrosse (Landes)

Tel: 05 58 78 00 00. Email: mayotte@yellohvillage.com

www.alanrogers.com/FR40240

This appealing site is set amongst pine trees on the edge of Lac de Biscarrosse. Drive down a tree and flower lined avenue and proceed toward the lake to shady, good sized pitches which blend well with the many tidy mobile homes that share the area. Divided by hedges, all the pitches have electricity (10A) and water taps. There may be some aircraft noise at times from a nearby army base. The pool complex is impressive, with various pools, slides, chutes, jacuzzi and sauna, all surrounded by paved sunbathing areas. The excellent lakeside beach provides safe bathing with plenty of watersports.

Facilities	Directions
Four good quality, clean toilet blocks (one open early season). Good facilities for visitors with disabilities. Baby/toddler bathroom. Motorcaravan services. Laundry. Supermarket. Boutique. Rental shop (July/Aug). Restaurant. Swimming pools (one heated; supervised July/Aug. and weekends). Play area. Further children's area (extra cost) with trampolines, inflatables and a small train. Bicycle hire. Fishing. Watersports. Organised activities and entertainment and clubs for toddlers and teenagers (all July/Aug). Charcoal barbecues not permitted. Internet access. Off site: Golf 4 km. Riding 100 m. Beach 10 km. Town 2 km. with restaurants, shops and bars.	From the north on D652 turn right on D333 (Chemin de Goubern). Pass through Goubern and Mayotte Village. Take next right (signed to site) into Chemin des Roseaux. GPS: N44:26.097 W01:09.303

Open: 30 April - 24 September.

Charges guide

Per unit incl. 2 persons	€ 17,00 - € 39,00
extra person	€ 3,50 - € 7,50
child (3-7 yrs)	free - € 3,50
dog	€ 3,00 - € 5,00

FR40280 Airotel Lou Puntaou

Au bord du Lac, F-40550 Léon (Landes)

Tel: 05 58 48 74 20. Email: reception@loupuntaou.com

www.alanrogers.com/FR40280

Set between Lac de Léon and the nature reserve park of Huchet, this site offers plenty for young families. The level pitches are mainly grass, hedged and have electricity (15A). Trees offer reasonable shade. In July and August only, there may be some noise from the lake car park and activities. The lake is 200 metres away with watersports, fishing, restaurants and bars, plus plenty of cycle rides. In July and August a full range of activities is organised on the site with sports and clubs for children and activities and evening entertainment for adults. A number of tour operators use the site.

Facilities	Directions
Three traditional style toilet blocks include facilities for disabled visitors and children. Laundry facilities. Motorcaravan service point. Simple shop at site entrance. Bar, restaurant and takeaway. TV and games rooms. Tennis. ATM. Internet. Only electric barbecues are permitted (communal area available). Off site: Village 500 m. with shops, restaurants and bars. Lake 200 m. Beach 7 km. Riding 10 km. Golf 7 km.	From N10 take exit 12 towards Castets. Take D142 to Léon and at island take first exit 'Centre Ville'. At T- junction turn left on D652. After 300 m. turn left at sign for site and lake. After 500 m. site is on left. GPS: N43:53.081 W1:18.898

Open: 1 April - 30 September.

Charges guide

Per person	€ 3,00 - € 6,00
child (2-13 yrs)	free - € 4,00
pitch incl. electricity	€ 9,00 - € 27,00

Check real time availability and at-the-gate prices...

www.alanrogers.com

FR40250 Camping les Grands Pins

Mobile homes ▶ page 503

1039 avenue de Losa, F-40460 Sanguinet (Landes)

Tel: **05 58 78 61 74**. Email: **info@campinglesgrandspins.com**   www.alanrogers.com/FR40250

Approached by a road alongside the lake, this site is set amongst tall pine trees. The gravel pitches are of average size, mostly level and shaded. Hedges divide those available for tourers and these are set amongst the many mobile homes. Large units may find manoeuvring difficult. There may be some aircraft noise at times from a nearby army base. A central pool complex includes a covered heated indoor pool, an outdoor pool, water slide and flume. In early and late season this is a very quiet site with very few facilities open. However, there are plenty of walks, cycle rides and the lake to enjoy. The poolside bar, restaurant and shops are only open in July/August. In July and August the site becomes busy, offering watersports, minigolf, a children's club, boat trips and organised activities. Fishing is also available. The charming small village of Sanguinet is 2 km. away with shops, bars, restaurants and an archaeological museum.

Facilities

Four toilet blocks include washbasins in cabins, showers and British style toilets. Baby bath and provision for disabled visitors. Laundry facilities. Motorcaravan service point. Shop, bar, restaurant and takeaway (1/7-31/8). Indoor pool (all seson). Outdoor pool complex (1/7-31/8). Play area. Games room and TV in bar. Tennis. Bicycle hire (July/Aug). Children's club. Pets not accepted in July/Aug. Barbecues not allowed (dedicated area). Off site: Beach 30 m. Fishing 2 km. Golf and riding 15 km.

Open: 1 April - 31 October.

Directions

Enter Sanguinet from the north on the D46. At one way system turn right. Do not continue on one way system but go straight ahead toward lake (signed) on Rue de Lac. Site is 2 km. on left.
GPS: N44:29.038 W01:05.383

Charges guide

Per person incl. 2 persons and electricity	€ 16,00 - € 37,00
extra person	€ 4,50 - € 6,50
child (3-7 yrs)	€ 4,00 - € 5,00

FR40270 Village Center Eurolac

Promenade de l'Etang, F-40200 Aureilhan (Landes)

Tel: **05 58 09 02 87**. Email: **eurolac@camping-parcsaintjames.com**   www.alanrogers.com/FR40270

This well shaded and wooded site is located on the banks of Lac de l'Aureillan (with a road in between), just 8 km. from the Atlantic beaches. The natural surroundings of the lake shore provide many bicycle and walking tracks, together with a sandy beach. Consisting mainly of pitches for mobile homes (most privately owned), there are only 11 small pitches available for tourers, each with electricity. They are really only suitable for small units and tents as negotiating the sometimes low lying branches and trees along the roadways may prove difficult. Facilities for sport and activities are excellent, with a heated swimming pool, two tennis courts, volleyball pitches, bicycle hire and more.

Facilities

Four traditional toilet blocks provide washbasins in cabins, showers and British style toilets. Ramped facilities for disabled visitors. (key provided). Laundry. Heated swimming pool (May - Sept) Games room. Minigolf. Bicycle hire. Fishing (licence from Mimizan). Sandy play area. Miniclub (4-12 yrs) and evening entertainment (July/Aug). Barbecues not permitted (communal area provided). Off site: Fishing 20 m. (permit). Boat launching. Riding 1 km. Golf 5 km. Sea and beach 8 km.

Open: 8 April - 30 September.

Directions

Heading east from the centre of Mimizan take the D626. After 2 km. take next left signed Aureilhan. Continue to 'stop' sign and turn left. Go through the village to the lake and turn right to site on the right.
GPS: N44:13.347 W01:12.207

Charges guide

Per unit incl. 1 person and electricity (6A)	€ 8,50 - € 22,00
extra person	€ 1,50 - € 4,50
child (4-10 yrs)	€ 1,50 - € 2,50

Altavia Link

Eurolac★★★★

Aureilhan > Atlantic coast

- Close to the lake of Aureilhan
- A lot of entertainment

Villagecenter

BOOK YOUR HOLIDAYS
www.village-center.com
☎ +33 (0)4 99 57 21 21

Les Grands Pins

CAMPING CARAVANING ★★★★
Sanguinet

www.campinglesgrandspins.com

Lac de Biscarosse

Lake, Pool complex;
many activities under the landaise sun

Chalets and mobile homes for rent

Avenue de Losa (route du lac) 40460 SANGUINET
Tél : 00 33 5 58 78 61 74 - Fax : 00 33 5 58 78 69 15
info@campinglesgrandspins.com

LANDES

ESE COMMUNICATION : 04 94 67 06 00

FR40300 Village Center Aurilandes

1001 promenade de l'Étang, F-40200 Aureilhan (Landes)

Tel: **04 99 57 21 21**. Email: **contact@village-center.com**   www.alanrogers.com/FR40300

In the heart of the Landes forest and five minutes from the popular resort of Mimizan, Aurilandes offers 440 pitches spread over 8 hectares. They are mostly shaded and some have pleasant views over the Etang d'Aureilhan. A new pool complex incorporates a sauna, spa, solarium and gym. The site is part of the Village Center group and provides a good range of facilities and amenities including a club for children in high season. Cité du Bois at nearby Mimizan and the huge Dune du Pyla to the north are popular for excursions. Mobile homes are available for rent.

Facilities

Snack bar. Shop. Swimming pool, paddling pool, solarium and fitness area (sauna, spa, gym). TV room. Play area and miniclub. Facilities for disabled visitors. Entertainment in peak season. Off site: Fishing. Golf. Parachuting. Riding. Watersports. Hiking trails. Fitness trail. Cycle routes.

Open: 13 May - 16 September.

Directions

Aureilhan is on the D626 (Labouheyre - Mimizan road). Site is well signed from this road. GPS: N44:13.378 W01:11.667

Charges guide

Per unit incl. 2 persons and electricity	€ 14,00 - € 29,00
extra person	€ 2,00 - € 5,00

Altavia Link

Aurilandes★★

Aureilhan > Atlantic coast

- Close to the lake of Aureilhan
- Fitness area and sauna

Villagecenter

BOOK YOUR HOLIDAYS
www.village-center.com
+33 (0)4 99 57 21 21

The Travel Service ...we'll arrange everything
BOOK THIS SITE CALL 01580 214000

FR40290 Yelloh! Village Punta Lago

Avenue du Lac, F-40550 Léon (Landes)

Tel: **04 66 73 97 39**. Email: **info@yellohvillage-punta-lago.com**   www.alanrogers.com/FR40290

Five hundred metres from the charming village of Léon, this site offers above average size, level, grass pitches (some sandy). Most have electricity, water and drainage and they are separated by hedges. Shade is welcome from the tall oak trees. Whilst the pitches would be considered typical for the region, the buildings are a mix of old and new, the old being the sanitary block, in good order, clean and with all the usual facilities including a lovely new children's bathroom and facilities for disabled visitors. The new encompasses an indoor heated pool, a recreation room serving as a gym and a TV room.

Facilities

The single toilet block is old, but kept clean and well maintained. Facilities for children and disabled visitors. Laundry facilities. Large shop. Restaurant and takeaway. Bar. Heated indoor and outdoor pools. Bicycle hire. Play area. Fridge hire. Entertainment and activities (July/Aug). Barbecues are not permitted. Off site: Lake 300 m. with sailing, windsurfing, kayak, swimming and fishing. Léon 500 m. with market at every day (June/Sept). Beach 7 km. Golf 8 km. Riding 5 km.

Open: 18 April - 27 September.

Directions

From N10 take exit 12 towards Castets. Take D142 to Léon and at island take first exit to 'Centre Ville'. At T-junction turn left on D652 and after 300 m. turn left at sign for site and lake. After 500 m. site is on the left. GPS: N43:53.050 W01:18.780

Charges guide

Per unit incl. 2 persons and electricity	€ 17,00 - € 38,00
extra person (over 3 yrs)	free - € 5,50

tel: +33 466 739 739 www.yellohvillage.com

yelloh! VILLAGE

Check real time availability and at-the-gate prices...

 www.alanrogers.com

FR40340 Village Camping Océliances

Avenue des Tucs, F-40510 Seignosse (Landes)

Tel: 05 58 43 30 30. Email: oceliances@wanadoo.fr

www.alanrogers.com/FR40340

This is a very large campsite situated 600 m. from the beach and 600 m. from Seignosse golf course. It has been totally modernised to a very high standard with a new reception area, outdoor pool complex with extensive decking, bar, restaurant and takeaway. You can be assured of a warm welcome here. There are 542 sandy/grass pitches with tall pine trees giving some shade, 320 for touring with 121 having electricity (6A). This site will appeal to a large variety of visitors, in low season, quiet but with plenty to do in the area, and in high season, a site for families with children.

Facilities	Directions
Six refurbished toilet blocks include facilities for babies and campers with disabilities. Large laundry. Fridge hire. Large shop. Bar and restaurant (all 1/7-31/8). Pool complex (1/6-30/9). Games room. Floodlit sports court. Surf school. Play area. Children's clubs. Bicycle hire. Internet. Off site: Beach and golf 600 m. Sailing 3 km. Fishing and riding 10 km. **Open:** 26 April - 28 September.	From Seignosse Bourg take D86 west, passing golf course. Go straight on at roundabout, D86 and Ave des Tucs, to site on left. GPS: N43:41.634 W01:25.825

Charges guide

Per unit incl. 2 persons and electricity	€ 16,10 - € 28,50
incl. water and drainage	€ 18,10 - € 31,00
extra person	€ 4,00 - € 6,30

FR40350 Camping l'Arbre d'Or

75 route du Lac, F-40160 Parentis-en-Born (Landes)

Tel: 05 58 78 41 56. Email: contact@arbre-dor.com

www.alanrogers.com/FR40350

L'Arbre d'Or is a friendly, family site on the outskirts of Parentis-en-Born. There are 200 pitches here, all well shaded by tall pine trees and most offering electrical connections. Around 90 pitches are occupied by mobile homes and chalets. L'Arbre d'Or lies 400 m. from the large Lac de Parentis where many watersports are available. The nearest coastal beach is at Biscarosse Plage, 19 km. distant. The site boasts two swimming pools, one of which is covered in inclement weather, as well as a restaurant and an activity programme. Bicycle hire is available and there are hundreds of kilometres of cycle trails through the surrounding forest.

Facilities	Directions
Two well located toilet blocks are a good provision and are kept clean. Pre-set showers. Facilities for disabled visitors. Bar, restaurant and takeaway (15/5-15/9). Two heated swimming pools. Play area. Bicycle hire. Entertainment and activities in peak season. Games room. Mobile homes and chalets for rent. Off site: Shop 800 m. Golf and riding 9 km. Lac de Parentis 400 m. **Open:** 1 April - 31 October.	From Bordeaux head south on the A63 and then the N10 as far as Liposthey. Then head west on the D43 to Parentis en Born. The site is well signed from here on the Route du Lac. GPS: N44:20.773 W01:05.574

Charges guide

Per unit incl. 2 persons	€ 13,00 - € 17,70
incl. electricity	€ 16,00 - € 19,80
extra person	€ 4,00 - € 4,30

FR64020 Camping Barétous-Pyrénées

Quartier Ripaude, F-64570 Aramits (Pyrénées-Atlantiques)

Tel: 05 59 34 12 21. Email: atso64@hotmail.com

www.alanrogers.com/FR64020

Located on the edge of the Pyrénées, this quiet site is well away from the tourist bustle, particularly in early or late season. It has a rural location, yet is close to the town. This is a wonderful location for exploring the region and offers a peaceful haven for those wishing to stay in quiet surroundings. The shady, grass pitches are attractive and of a good size with hedges. They offer both water and electricity (10A). The welcoming reception (English spoken) sells local produce and organic food. The heated swimming and paddling pool area is overlooked by a small sun terrace with a café/bar.

Facilities	Directions
Two sanitary blocks, one old, one modern, offer clean facilities with unisex toilets and showers. Facilities for disabled visitors. Café/bar with hot and cold meals (July/Aug). Heated swimming and paddling pools (May - Sept). Communal room with TV, games, library and drinks. Small shop selling organic food. Boules. Small play area with sandpit. Off site: Town with supermarket and ATM 250 m. Fishing 50 m. Riding 3 km. Snow skiing 25 km. **Open:** 1 Feburary - 15 October.	From Oloron Sainte Marie, head southwest on D919 to Aramits. Through village bear right on D918. Cross river and immediately turn right at campsite sign. GPS: N43:07.284 W00:43.939

Charges guide

Per unit incl. 2 persons	€ 13,00 - € 19,00
extra person	€ 3,50 - € 5,00
electricity	€ 3,50

No credit cards.
Camping Cheques accepted.

FR64030 Camping Ametza

Boulevard de l'Empereur, B.P. 19, F-64700 Hendaye (Pyrénées-Atlantiques)

Tel: **05 59 20 07 05**. Email: **ametza@meuf.fr**   www.alanrogers.com/FR64030

With a beautiful long sandy beach and the town of Hendaye only 900 metres away (a 20 minute walk) this well cared for, family run campsite, offers plenty for everyone. Attractively laid out, the grass pitches are flat and shady, most having electricity (6A). We found the railway line running nearby was not intrusive. There is a pleasant bar and restaurant together with an excellent pool area (comfortable and with good quality sunbeds and umbrellas). The beach at Hendaye is popular for surfing, particularly for beginners. Having shallow water, it offers safe bathing.

Facilities

Two clean and bright sanitary blocks have good facilities with a laundry and en-suite facility for disabled people. Excellent bathroom for babies and children. Fridge hire. Shop (w/ends only in early season). Bar and restaurant. Swimming pool (from May). TV room. Small playground. Entertainment and activities (July/Aug). Electric barbecues are not permitted. Internet access. Shuttle bus to beach (July/Aug). Off site: Beach and town 900 m. Bicycle hire 1 km. Boat launching 2 km. Fishing 5 km. Golf and riding 10 km.

Open: 8 April - 31 October.

Directions

From the A63 exit 2 (St-Jean-de-Luz Sud) take D913 signed Hendaye. At roundabout turn left on coast road D912. In 6 km. turn left on D358 (San Sebastian) Cross railway bridge and site is on left. GPS: N43:22.379 W01:45.351

Charges guide

Per unit incl. 2 persons	€ 16,80 - € 21,50
extra person	€ 4,20 - € 4,90
child (2-10 yrs)	€ 2,10 - € 3,50
electricity	€ 3,90

FR64040 Camping des Gaves

Quanitien Pon, F-64440 Laruns (Pyrénées-Atlantiques)

Tel: **05 59 05 32 37**. Email: **campingdesgaves@wanadoo.fr**   www.alanrogers.com/FR64040

Set in a secluded valley, Camping Des Gaves is a clean, small and well managed site, open all year, with very friendly owners and staff. It is set high in Pyrennean walking country on one of the routes to Spain and is only 30 km. from the Spanish border. There are 99 pitches including 50 level grassed touring pitches of which 38 are fully serviced, numbered and separated (the remainder are used for seasonal units). Mature trees provide plenty of shade.

Facilities

The very clean toilet block can be heated in cool weather and has modern fittings. Washbasins for ladies in curtained cubicles and one shower in ladies' suitable for showering children. Laundry room. No shop but baker calls daily (July/Aug). Small bar with large screen TV, pool and video games (July/Aug). Larger bar with table tennis. Small play area. Boules. Volleyball. Fishing. Card operated barrier (€ 20 deposit). Off site: Bicycle hire 800 m. Shops, restaurant and bars 1 km.

Open: All year.

Directions

Take N134 from Pau towards Olorons and branch left on D934 at Gan. Follow to Laruns and just after town, turn left following signs to site. GPS: N42:58.929 W00:25.057

Charges guide

Per unit with 2 persons and electricity	€ 13,90 - € 24,10
extra person	€ 3,20 - € 4,10
child (4-10 yrs)	€ 2,10 - € 2,90

FR64050 Camping Itsas Mendi

Acotz, F-64500 Saint Jean-de-Luz (Pyrénées-Atlantiques)

Tel: **05 59 26 56 50**. Email: **itsas@wanadoo.fr**   www.alanrogers.com/FR64050

This large campsite is ideal for families. Set close to the beach (400 metres), it boasts two swimming areas. Both fenced, one is overlooked by a terrace and has a jacuzzi and the other is made for children with a paddling pool, whirlpool and water slides. During July and August entertainment, activities and excursions are organised. Together with surfing, scuba and children's clubs, rafting and mountain bike trails, there is something for all. All pitches are of medium size, shaded with electricity (10A). May be difficult for large vehicles to manoeuvre and have full choice of pitches.

Facilities

Five sanitary blocks (not all open early season) are clean and one has facilities for disabled visitors. Laundry facilities. Motorcaravan service point. Fridge hire. Bar and restaurant (1/6-15/9). Tennis. Football field. TV room. Entertainment, activities and excursion in July and August. Internet access. Off site: Large supermarket 1 km. Bus (50 m.) runs every hour to St Jean-de-Luz. Fishing 1 km. Golf, riding and bicycle hire 4 km.

Open: 1 April - 30 September.

Directions

From the A63 take exit 3, then the N10 toward Bayonne. Turn second left signed 'Acotz Campings Plages'. At T-junction turn right and site is on left. GPS: N43:24.822 W01:37.007

Charges guide

Per unit incl. 2 persons	€ 16,20 - € 32,50
extra person	€ 3,70 - € 6,00
child (2-10 yrs)	€ 2,20 - € 3,70
Camping Cheques accepted.	

Check real time availability and at-the-gate prices...
www.alanrogers.com

FR64060 Camping le Pavillon Royal

Avenue du Prince de Galles, F-64210 Bidart (Pyrénées-Atlantiques)

Tel: 05 59 23 00 54. Email: info@pavillon-royal.com

www.alanrogers.com/FR64060

Le Pavillon Royal has an excellent situation on raised ground overlooking the sea, with good views along the coast to the south and to the north coast of Spain beyond. There is a large heated swimming pool and sunbathing area in the centre of the site. The camping area is divided up into 303 marked, level pitches, many of a good size. About 50 are reserved for tents and are only accessible on foot. The remainder are connected by asphalt roads. All have electricity and most are fully serviced. Much of the campsite is in full sun, although the area for tents is shaded. Beneath the site – and only a very short walk down – stretches a wide sandy beach where the Atlantic rollers provide ideal conditions for surfing. A central, marked-out section of the beach is supervised by lifeguards (from mid June). There is also a section with rocks and pools. Reservation for this site in high season is advisable.

Facilities

Good quality toilet blocks with baby baths and unit for disabled people. Washing facilities are closed at night except for two single night units. Washing machines, dryers. Motorcaravan services. Shop (including gas). Restaurant and takeaway (from 1/6). Bar (all season). Heated swimming and paddling pools. Playground. General room, TV room, games room, films. Fishing. Surf school. Dogs are not accepted. Off site: Golf 0.5 km. Bicycle hire 2 km. Riding 3 km. Sailing 5 km.

Open: 15 May - 30 September.

Directions

From A63 exit 4, take the N10 south towards Bidart. At roundabout after the 'Intermarché' supermarket turn right (signed for Biarritz). After 600 m. turn left at site sign. GPS: N43:27.275 W01:34.562

Charges guide

Per unit incl. 2 persons, electricity and water	€ 27,00 - € 45,00
tent pitch incl. 1 or 2 persons	€ 20,00 - € 33,00
extra person (over 4 yrs)	€ 6,50 - € 9,00

Le Pavillon Royal
camping caravaning **** NN

64210 BIDART
Tél: 05.59.23.00.54
Website: www.pavillon-royal.com
E-mail: info@pavillon-royal.com

- Right by a sandy beach with direct access
- On the outskirts of Biarritz
- Very peaceful situation
- Sanitary installations of really exceptional quality

FR64070 Castel Camping le Ruisseau des Pyrénées

Route d'Arbonne, F-64210 Bidart (Pyrénées-Atlantiques)

Tel: 05 59 41 94 50. Email: francoise.dumont3@wanadoo.fr

www.alanrogers.com/FR64070

This busy site, with a large play area filled with equipment is ideal for young families. It is about 2 km. from Bidart and 2.5 km. from a sandy beach. There are two swimming pools with slides on the main site and across the road, an indoor heated pool and new spa complex (charged July/Aug) with outdoor fitness equipment. Pitches on the main campsite are individual, marked and of a good size, either on flat terraces or around the lake. The terrain is wooded so the great majority of them have some shade. Electrical connections are available throughout. The site has a number of steep slopes to negotiate.

Facilities

Two main blocks and some extra smaller units. Washing machines. Motorcaravan service point. Shop. Large self-service restaurant with takeaway and bar with terraces, and TV. Outdoor swimming pools, indoor pool and spa complex (all season). Sauna. Large play area. Two tennis courts (free outside July/Aug). Fitness track. TV and games rooms. Minigolf. Bicycle hire. Fishing. Internet access. Off site: Riding and golf 2 km.

Open: 23 May - 19 September.

Directions

Site is east of Bidart on a minor road towards Arbonne. From A63 autoroute take Biarritz exit (4), turn towards St Jean-de-Luz and Bidart on N10. After Intermarche turn left at roundabout and follow signs to site. GPS: N43:26.207 W01:34.068

Charges guide

Per unit incl. 2 persons	€ 15,00 - € 32,00
extra person	€ 5,00 - € 6,50
child (under 7 yrs)	€ 2,50 - € 4,00
electricity	€ 3,00 - € 5,00

BOOK THIS SITE
CALL 01580 214000
...we'll arrange everything
The Travel Service

Check real time availability and at-the-gate prices...
www.alanrogers.com

FR64080 Camping les Tamaris Plage

Quartier Acotz, F-64500 Saint Jean-de-Luz (Pyrénées-Atlantiques)

Tel: **05 59 26 55 90**. Email: **tamaris1@wanadoo.fr**   www.alanrogers.com/FR64080

This is a popular, small and pleasant site which is well kept. It is situated outside the town and just across the road from a sandy beach. The 35 touring pitches, all with 7/10A electricity, are of good size and separated by hedges, on slightly sloping ground with some shade. The site becomes full for July and August with families on long stays, so reservation then is essential. Mobile homes for rent occupy a further 40 pitches. A leisure centre and club provides a heated pool and various other free facilities for adults and children. A gym, Turkish bath, massage and other relaxing amenities are also available at an extra charge. There is no shop, but bread is available daily across the road. Opposite the site, a popular surf school offers instruction to new and experienced surfers.

Facilities

The single toilet block of good quality and unusual design should be an ample provision. Facilities for disabled people. Washing machine. Wellness health club with free facilities: swimming pool, TV and play room and club for children (4-11 yrs) and on payment: gym, Turkish bath and other health facilities, sunbathing area, jacuzzi, adult TV lounge. Off site: Beach, fishing, surfing 30 m. Bicycle hire or club 4 km. Riding 7 km.

Open: 1 April - 5 November.

Directions

Proceed south on N10 and 1.5 km. after Guethary take first road on right (before access to the motorway and Carrefour centre commercial) and follow site signs. GPS: N43:25.077 W01:37.429

Charges guide

Per unit incl. 2 persons and electricity (5A)	€ 15,00 - € 28,00
tent pitch incl. 2 persons	€ 12,00 - € 21,00
extra person (over 2 yrs)	€ 4,00 - € 6,00
dog	€ 5,00

TAMARIS PLAGE**** CAMPSITE HOLIDAY VILLAGE

ACOTZ 64500 ST. JEAN DE LUZ | TEL. 00 33 5 59 26 55 90 | FAX 0033 5 59 47 70 15
WWW.TAMARIS-PLAGE.COM | GPS: 43.413499. - 1.607297

FR64100 Camping Etche Zahar

Allée de Mesplès, F-64240 Urt (Pyrénées-Atlantiques)

Tel: **05 59 56 27 36**. Email: **info@etche-zahar.fr**   www.alanrogers.com/FR64100

Although this attractive site is small, the hardcore roads give access to remarkably large grass pitches separated by small hedges. The larger pitches have little shade but at the far end an area of trees offers smaller shaded pitches for tents.There are also nine immaculate mobile homes and nine chalets. Electricty (10A) is available for 14 pitches. The site is 'Tourisme & Handicap' approved and offers two chalet and facilities specifically for disabled visitors. The English speaking owner is justly proud and offers a warm welcome to her eco-friendly site. Quietly positioned, it is ideal for those who wish to enjoy relaxed rural pursuits.

Facilities

The single sanitary block was very clean when we visited. Laundry facilities. Meals (July/Aug).Swimming pool (June - Oct). Small Library. Motorcaravan grey water point (hose required). Some play equipment. Bicycle hire. Internet facilities. WiFi. Pets not accepted 1-20 Aug. Off site: Town with supermarket, shops, restaurants and bars 10 minute walk. Fishing 1 km. Boat launching 1 km. Sailing 10 km. Golf 20 km. Beach 22 km.

Open: 20 March - 3 November.

Directions

From Bayonne go east on D1 and join the A64. Take exit 4 turning right on D936. Turn left on D123 to Urt. Follow 'Toute Directions' to D257. Turn right at fire station to site on the left.
GPS: N43:29.494 W01:17.792

Charges guide

Per person	€ 3,70
child (0-10 yrs)	€ 2,50
pitch	€ 8,40 - € 11,00
electricity (10A)	€ 3,20

F-64122 Urrugne (Pyrénées-Atlantiques)
Tel: **05 59 54 31 21**. Email: **info@col-ibardin.com**

Mobile homes ▶ page 503

www.alanrogers.com/FR64110

This family owned site at the foot of the Basque Pyrénées is highly recommended and deserves praise. It is well run with emphasis on personal attention, the friendly family and their staff ensuring that all are made welcome and is attractively set in the middle of an oak wood with a mountain stream cascading through it. Behind the forecourt, with its brightly coloured shrubs and modern reception area, various roadways lead to the 191 pitches. These are individual, spacious and enjoy the benefit of the shade (if preferred a more open aspect can be found). There are electricity hook-ups (4/10A) and adequate water points. A very attractive chalet 'village' has recently been added. From this site you can enjoy the mountain scenery, be on the beach in 7-10 km. or cross the border into Spain in about 14 km.

Facilities

Two toilet blocks, one rebuilt to a high specification, are kept very clean. WC for disabled people. Dishwashing and laundry facilities. Motorcaravan service point. Shop for basics and bread orders (15/6-15/9). Restaurant, takeaway service and bar (15/6-15/9). Heated swimming pool and paddling pool. Playground and club (adult supervision). Tennis. Boules. Video games. Bicycle hire. Multisport area. Not suitable for American motorhomes. Off site: Supermarket and shopping centre 5 km. Fishing and golf 7 km. Riding 20 km.

Open: 1 April - 30 September.

Directions

Leave A63 at St Jean-de-Luz sud, exit no. 2 and join RN10 in direction of Urrugne. Turn left at roundabout (Col d'Ibardin) on D4. Site on right after 5 km. Do not turn off to the Col itself, carry on towards Ascain. GPS: N43:20.035 W01:41.077

Charges guide

Per unit incl. 2 persons	
and electricity	€ 16,50 - € 34,00
extra person	€ 3,00 - € 6,00
child (2-7 yrs)	€ 2,00 - € 3,50
pet	€ 2,50

BOOK THIS SITE
CALL 01580 214000
...we'll arrange everything
Service The Travel

Camping Caravaning
Du Col D'Ibardin

Open 01 April – 30 September
Swimming pool ● Tennis ● Bar ● Children's Pool and Club
Launderette ● Hot Water ● Snacks ● Playground ● Bicycle Hire
● Little farm with animals for children
● Mobil-homes to rent

Tel: (0033) (0)559.54.31.21
Fax: (0033) (0)559.54.62.28
Site: www.col-ibardin.com
E-mail: info@col-ibardin.com

64122 URRUGNE
PAYS BASQUE

Alan Rogers

FREE 2009 **brochure**
Over 60 French campsites, hand picked for you

Call for your copy today **01580 214000**

FREE CHILD PLACES ON MANY SITES

Check real time availability and at-the-gate prices...
 www.**alanrogers**.com

FR64120 Camping Beau Rivage

Allée des Maronniers, F-64190 Navarrenx (Pyrénées-Atlantiques)

Tel: **05 59 66 10 00**. Email: **beaucamping@free.fr**   www.alanrogers.com/FR64120

Cross the picturesque river and follow the old town walls to discover this well cared for family owned campsite (English). The site is tiered and the large, well maintained grass pitches are surrounded by mature hedges offering a peaceful and relaxed setting. Currently torches may be needed. The attention to well cared for detail is carried into the two sanitary blocks. Recent projects include a heated swimming pool, low key entertainment area (wine tasting, barbecues, etc), additional chalets, hardstandings and a baby room, adding to an already impressive campsite.

Facilities

Two very clean sanitary blocks with good separate facilities for ladies and men include provision for disabled visitors. Laundry facilities in top block. Playground for small children (rubber matting). Play field. Off site: Shop at end of road. Town is five minutes walk for further shops, bars, restaurants, ATM and bicycle hire. Fishing 200 m. Riding 15 km.

Open: 15 March - 15 October.

Directions

From the north take D936 to Navarrenx. Turn left at first roundabout on D115 into Navarrenx. Turn left at T-junction, go over bridge and follow walls of town all the way around. At next island turn right on D947 and site is signed from here.
GPS: N43:19.200 W00:45.660

Charges guide

Per unit incl. 2 persons	€ 12,00 - € 17,00
incl. electricity	€ 15,50 - € 20,50
extra person	€ 3,50 - € 4,50

FR64140 Sunêlia Berrua

Rue Berrua, F-64210 Bidart (Pyrénées-Atlantiques)

Tel: **05 59 54 96 66**. Email: **contact@berrua.com**   www.alanrogers.com/FR64140

Berrua is in a useful situation on the Basque coast, 10 km. from the Pyrenees, 20 km. from Spain and a five minute drive from Biarritz. Just 1 km. from the sea, it an ideal location for visiting the beaches in southwest France. A neat and tidy site, it has 270 level pitches (120 for touring units) set amongst trees. Most have electricity (6A) and some are fully serviced. The focal point of the site is an excellent swimming pool complex with several pools, slides and paddling pools which is surrounded by sunbeds. A member of the Sunêlia group.

Facilities

Toilet facilities are good (unisex) consisting of two blocks with washbasins in cabins, baby rooms, facilities for disabled visitors, washing machines and dishwashing sinks (cold water only). Motorcaravan services. Shop (July/Aug). Bar/restaurant and takeaway (15/4-15/9). New pool complex. Games room. Play area (3-10 yrs only). Bicycle hire. Archery. Boules. Off site: Fishing 1 km. Golf and riding 3 km. Beach 1 km.

Open: 6 April - 5 October.

Directions

From A63 exit 4, take N10 south towards Bidart. At roundabout after the 'Intermarché' supermarket, turn left. Bear right then take next right (site signed).
GPS: N43:26.293 W01:34.942

Charges guide

Per unit incl. 2 persons	€ 16,10 - € 30,20
extra person	€ 3,20 - € 6,15
electricity (6A)	€ 2,90 - € 4,90
Camping Cheques accepted.	

FR64150 Yelloh! Village Ilbarritz

Avenue de Biarritz, F-64210 Bidart (Pyrénées-Atlantiques)

Tel: **04 66 73 97 39**. Email: **info@yellohvillage-ilbarritz.com**   www.alanrogers.com/FR64150

This is a very pleasant, reasonably priced site which will appeal greatly to couples and young families. Set on a fairly gentle hillside, the top level has reception and bar. Slightly lower are the paddling and swimming pools in a sunny location with sunbeds. Next comes the well stocked shop, tennis courts and the rest of the pitches. Some pitches are behind reception and others, lower down, some slightly sloping, are under trees and separated by hydrangea hedges. Some have electricity (10A, long leads required). The site is not suitable for American motorhomes.

Facilities

The two toilet blocks have some washbasins and showers together. Washing machines, dryers, ironing boards and facilities for disabled people. Motorcaravan services. Shop and bar. Restaurant (1/6-10/9) and takeaway (1/7-31/8). Pool. Tennis (charged in July/Aug). Play area. Bicycle hire. Off site: Lake 600 m. Golf 1 km. Riding 1 km.

Open: 8 May - 20 September.

Directions

Heading south on the A63 towards Spain, take exit J4 onto the N10 towards Bidart. At the roundabout straight after Intermarche turn right towards Biarritz. The site is 1 km. GPS: N43:27.185 W01:34.425

Charges guide

Per unit incl. 2 persons	€ 15,90 - € 24,50
Camping Cheques accepted.	

tel: +33 466 739 739 www.yellohvillage.com

Check real time availability and at-the-gate prices...

 www.alanrogers.com

FR64230 Camping Municipal de Mosqueros

F-64270 Salies-de-Béarn (Pyrénées-Atlantiques)

Tel: 05 59 38 12 94   www.alanrogers.com/FR64230

In scenic surroundings convenient for the A64, this three-star municipal site is worthy of its grading and is attractively located in a parkland situation one kilometre from the pretty little town of Salies-de-Béarn. It has an immaculate appearance, welcoming wardens and very clean facilities. Tarmac roads lead from the entrance barrier (locked at night), past reception to spacious, numbered pitches. Most have electricity (10A), some have water taps and drainage and all are separated by tall shrubs and hedges giving privacy. Salies-de-Béarn, with its old houses overhanging the river and its thermal baths, is minutes away. Large units should take care when negotiating narrow roadways and trees.

Facilities

The two fully equipped toilet blocks are maintained to a high standard. Dishwashing and laundry area with sinks, washing machine, dryer and iron. TV and recreation room. Off site: Swimming pool (special rates for campers) and tennis court adjacent. Golf and riding 2 km. Fishing 7 km.

Open: 15 March - 31 October.

Directions

Site is well signed in the town and is on the D17 Bayonne road, west of the town. GPS: N43:28.850 W00:56.282

Charges guide

Per person	€ 2,60
pitch	€ 2,70 - € 5,30
electricity	€ 2,55

FR64160 Camping Merko-Lacarra

820 Route des Plage, F-64500 Saint Jean-de-Luz (Pyrénées-Atlantiques)

Tel: 05 59 26 56 76. Email: contact@merkolacarra.com   www.alanrogers.com/FR64160

Positioned 50 metres from the beach, scattered with pretty Tamaris trees and enjoying views of the surrrounding coutryside, this beautifully cared for campsite offers everything for a relaxing stay. The proud owners maintain the campsite to a high standard. The site is sloping but the 89 touring pitches are predominately level and are all of grass. All have electricity (16A via French connectors; adaptors not available). There is little shade. Tidy mobile homes are on the boundaries of the site. There may be some railway noise but we did not find this intrusive.

Facilities

The single toilet block is well kept and clean. Facilities for disabled visitors. Baby room. Laundry facilities. Motorcaravan service point (charged). New mobile home and washblock. Small shop and snack bar (15/6-15/9). Excellent play area. Electric barbecues are not permitted. WiFi. Off site: Limited public transport July/Aug. Beach and fishing (sea) 50 m. Golf 5 km. Bicycle hire 5 km. Riding 12 km. Mountains (8 km) for walking and cycling.

Open: 28 March - 17 October.

Directions

From the A63 take exit 3, then the N10 toward Bayonne. Turn second left signed 'Acotz Campings Plages'. At T-junction turn right and follow signs for site. However this right turn leads to a low bridge - height restriction 3.5 m. To avoid the bridge, turn left at T-junction and continue along road until reaching the site on the right. GPS: N43:25.116 W01:37.389

Charges guide

Per pitch incl. 2 persons and electricity	€ 18,50 - € 31,00
extra person	€ 4,20 - € 6,00

FR64240 Camping Uhaitza le Saison

Route de Libarrenx, F-64130 Mauleon-Licharre (Pyrénées-Atlantiques)

Tel: 05 59 28 18 79. Email: camping.uhaitza@.fr   www.alanrogers.com/FR64240

Like its sister sites in the Campings de Charme group, this campsite is small and attractive with 50 good sized grass, shady pitches. There are 43 for touring, all with electricity (4-10A) and 37 with water and a drain. The clear waters of the river cascade directly behind the site and offer fishing and swimming from the man-made rock formations. This quiet location offers peace and relaxation but also for the adventurous, mountain walks are only 30 minutes drive away. The medieval town of Mauleon is within a 1.5 km. level walk. American RVs and twin axle caravans are not accepted.

Facilities

One traditional style sanitary block (plus one small unit opened in high season) is clean and comfortable. Facilities for babies and campers with disabilities. Motorcaravan services. Laundry. Gas. Small play area. Bread to order. Small bar, snacks (1/6-30/9). Off site: Town 1.5 km. with banks, shops, restaurants and bicycle hire. Riding 4 km.

Open: 1 March - 15 November.

Directions

From north, take D23 to Mauleon Licharre. In town, follow bypass. At large roundabout take second exit, D611. At T-junction turn right. Campsite is on right in 0.8 km. and is well signed from the town. GPS: N43:12.476 W00:53.800

Charges guide

Per unit incl. 2 persons	€ 12,80 - € 17,00
extra person	€ 3,40 - € 4,50
electricity (4/10A)	€ 2,60 - € 4,80

BOOK THIS SITE
CALL 01580 214000
...we'll arrange everything
The Travel Service

269

FR64250 Camping Atlantica

Quartier Acotz, F-64500 Saint Jean-de-Luz (Pyrénées-Atlantiques)
Tel: **05 59 47 72 44**. Email: **info@campingatlantica.com**   www.alanrogers.com/FR64250

This is a friendly, family run site with 200 shady and well kept grass pitches set amongst many shrubs, flowers and hedges. There are 99 pitches for touring, 69 have 6A electricity and 41 have water and drainage. The excellent swimming pool area is attractively landscaped with plenty of sunbeds. With a bar, restaurant and takeaway open June to September, the beach 500 m. and the cosmopolitan town of St Jean-de-Luz only 3 km. away, this site is suitable for families and couples of all ages. If excessively wet, motor caravans are advised to call ahead to check availability. The three bright and very clean sanitary blocks are well maintained with large showers and piped music. A comprehensive fitness room includes a sauna and during July and August a trained attendant is available for advice.

Facilities

Three immaculate toilet blocks include facilities for babies and campers with disabilities. Excellent laundry. Swimming pool and fitness room (April-Sept). Bar, restaurant, shop, takeaway (all 15/6-15/9). Games Room. Multisport court. Motorcaravan services. Modern, fenced children's play area. Family entertainment (July/Aug). Off site: Bus to major town 400 m. Large supermarket 1 km. Golf 4 km.

Open: 1 April - 30 September.

Directions

Leave A63, exit 3, taking N10 toward Bayonne. Take the second left turn signed 'Acotz Campings Plages'. At T-junction turn right and follow signs. Campsite is on the right. GPS: N43:24.919 W01:37.013

Charges guide

Per unit incl. 2 persons	
and electricity	€ 17,50 - € 31,50
extra person	€ 3,20 - € 6,15
child (under 7 yrs)	€ 2,20 - € 3,70
dog	free - € 2,50

CAMPING ATLANTICA***

Quartier Acotz - 64500 Saint-Jean-de-Luz
Tel: 0033 559 47 72 44 - Fax: 0033 559 54 72 27
info@campingatlantica.com - www.campingatlantica.com

On 500 m distance from the beach in a green and floral environment for a quiet and pleasant stay in a pleasant family ambiance. Water park, relaxing area with spa and sauna, mini golf, sports terrain. All facilities present for pleasant stay. Mobile homes for rent. Dogs not allowed in accommodation.
Campsite open from 1st April till 30th September.

FR64280 Camping Ur-Onea

Rue de la Chapelle, F-64210 Bidart (Pyrénées-Atlantiques)
Tel: **05 59 26 53 61**. Email: **uronea@wanadoo.fr**   www.alanrogers.com/FR64280

Situated on the outskirts of Bidart and 600 m. away from a fine sandy beach, this large, attractively terraced site has 280 grass pitches with little shade, 142 are for touring with electricity (10A) and ten have water and drainage. There are some hardstandings for motorcaravans. A separate area is reserved for washing surf boards, barbecues and there is even a shower for washing dogs. With local transport available all year (600 m.) this campsite is ideal for exploring the surrounding areas. During the summer months, aquarobics, dancing and discos are arranged together with organised sports events and children's clubs.

Facilities

Three well maintained and clean sanitary blocks are of good size with large showers (all also have washbasins) and wall mounted hairdryers. Facilities for babies and disabled visitors. Laundry. Shop (all season). Bar, restaurant and takeaway (13/6-5/9). Swimming pool (May-Sept). Two excellent play areas for younger children. Organised activities in high season. Internet. Off site: Beach 600 m. Bars, restaurants and shops 600 m. Golf 700 m. Riding 2 km.

Open: 4 April - 20 September.

Directions

Take N10 north from St-Jean-de-Luz. Continue through Guethary and site sign is on the right. Turn right and site is on the left in 800 m. GPS: N43:26.028 W01:35.433

Charges guide

Per unit incl. 2 persons	
and electricity (10A)	€ 17,00 - € 29,50
with water and drainage	€ 19,50 - € 32,50
extra person	€ 3,50 - € 5,50
child (under 10 yrs)	€ 2,50 - € 4,50
dog	€ 2,00

Check real time availability and at-the-gate prices...
www.alanrogers.com

MAP 11

The Dordogne is an historical region of great beauty, full of pretty golden-stoned villages and ancient castles. Home to delicacies such as foie gras, truffles and walnuts, plus Roquefort cheese and Cognac, it is one of the gastronomic centres of France.

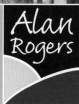

TO FORM 'THE DORDOGNE' WE HAVE USED DÉPARTEMENTS FROM THESE OFFICIAL REGIONS: FROM AQUITAINE: 24 DORDOGNE AND 47 LOT-ET-GARONNE, FROM MIDI-PYRÉNÉES: 12 AVEYRON, 46 LOT, FROM POITOU-CHARENTES: 16 CHARENTE

The Dordogne's history goes back many thousands of years when man lived in the caves of Périgord and left cave paintings at sites such as Les Eyzies and Lascaux. Aquitaine was ruled by the English for 300 years following the marriage of Eleanor of Aquitaine to Henry Plantagenet, who became King of England in 1154.

The villages and castles of the area bear evidence of the resulting conflict between the French and English, and today add charm and character to the countryside. Monpazier is the best example of the 'bastides' (fortified towns) and is set in a diverse region of mountains, vineyards, and fertile river valleys. The rolling grasslands and dense forests include the beautiful valleys of the Dordogne and Vézère.

South of the cultivated fields and cliff-side villages beside the river Lot lie the higher, stony lands of the Quercy Causse and the rocky gorges of the Rivers Aveyron and Tarn. Centred around Millau, there are tortuous gorges and valleys, spectacular rivers, underground caves and grottes, and thickly forested mountains.

Places of interest

Agen: rich agricultural area, famous for its prunes.

Angoulême: Hill-top town surrounded by ramparts, cathedral, Renaissance château.

Cognac: the most celebrated *eau de vie* in the world, cellars, Valois Castle.

Cordes: medieval walled hilltop village.

Monflanquin: well preserved fortified village.

Rocamadour: cliffside medieval pilgrimage site.

Saint Cirq-La Popie: medieval village perched on a cliff.

Sarlat: Saturday market.

Cuisine of the region

Local specialities include the fish dishes: carp stuffed with foie gras, mullet in red wine and *besugo* (sea bream), plus *cagouilles* (snails from Charentes).

Cassoulet: a hearty stew of duck, sausages and beans.

Cèpes: fine, delicate mushrooms; sometimes dried.

Chou farci: stuffed cabbage, sometimes aux marrons (with chestnuts).

Confit de Canard (d'oie): preserved duck meat.

Foie Gras: specially prepared livers of geese and ducks, seasoned and stuffed with truffles.

Magret de canard: duck breast fillets.

Mouclade: mussels cooked in wine, egg yolks and cream, served with Pineau des Charentes.

The Travel Service ...we'll arrange everything **CALL 01580 214000** **BOOK THIS SITE**

FR12000 Flower Camping Caravaning de Peyrelade

Route des Gorges du Tarn, F-12640 Rivière-sur-Tarn (Aveyron)

Tel: **05 65 62 62 54**. Email: **campingpeyrelade@orange.fr**   www.alanrogers.com/FR12000

The 145 touring pitches (100-150 sq.m) are terraced, level and shady with 6A electricity hook-ups (long leads may be required for the riverside pitches). There are also 43 mobile homes. The site is ideally placed for visiting the Tarn, Jonte and Dourbie gorges, and centres for rafting and canoeing are a short drive up the river. Other nearby attractions include the Caves of Aven Armand, the Chaos de Montpellier, Roquefort (of cheese fame) and the pleasant town of Millau. Many of the roads along and between the Gorges are breathtaking for passengers, but worrying for drivers who may not like looking down! Situated at the foot of the Tarn gorges on the banks of the river, this attractive site is dominated by the ruins of the Château de Peyrelade. Bathing from the pebble beach is safe and the water is clean.

Facilities

Two well equipped toilet blocks. Young children are catered for, also people with disabilities. Washing machines, dryer. Bar, restaurant, pizzeria, takeaway (all from 1/6). Paddling pool, attractive heated swimming pool (proper swimming trunks, no shorts). Good playground. Games room. Miniclub. Fishing. Off site: Bicycle hire 100 m. Riding 3 km. Nearby leisure centre can be booked at reception at reduced charges. Millau, hypermarket, shops, night markets.

Open: 15 May - 15 September.

Directions

Take autoroute A75 to exit 44-1 Aguessac then onto D907 (follow Gorges du Tarn signs). Site is 2 km. past Rivière sur Tarn, on the right - the access road is quite steep. GPS: N44:11.428 E03:09.383

Charges 2009

Per unit incl. 2 persons and electricity	€ 19,00 - € 34,00
extra person	€ 3,50 - € 6,00
child (under 7 yrs)	€ 2,00 - € 4,00
dog	€ 2,00

www.flowercampings.com

Camping de Peyrelade ★★★★

Route des Gorges du Tarn - 12640 Rivière-Sur-Tarn
Tél. 00 33 (0)5 65 62 62 54 - Fax. 00 33 (0)5 65 62 65 61
campingpeyrelade@orange.fr - www.campingpeyrelade.com

le camping c'est humain.

www.flowercampings.com

The Travel Service ...we'll arrange everything **CALL 01580 214000** **BOOK THIS SITE**

FR12010 RCN Val de Cantobre

F-12230 Nant-d'Aveyron (Aveyron)

Tel: **05 65 58 43 00**. Email: **info@rcn-valdecantobre.fr**   www.alanrogers.com/FR12010

Imaginatively and tastefully developed by the Dupond family over the past 30 years, this very pleasant terraced site is now owned by the RCN group. Most of the 200 touring pitches (all with electricity and water) are peaceful, generous in size and blessed with views of the valley. The terrace design provides some peace and privacy, especially on the upper levels. Rock pegs are advised. An activity programme is supervised by qualified instructors in July and August and a new pleasure pool has been added. The magnificent carved features in the bar create a delightful ambience, complemented by a recently built terrace.

Facilities

The fully equipped toilet block is well appointed. Fridge hire. Small shop including many regional specialities. Attractive bar, restaurant, pizzeria, takeaway (some fairly steep up and down walking from furthest pitches to some facilities). Swimming pools. Minigolf. Play area. Activity programme. All weather sports pitch. Torch useful. Off site: Fishing 4 km. Riding 15 km. Bicycle hire 25 km.

Open: 11 April - 10 October.

Directions

Site is 4 km. north of Nant, on D991 road to Millau. From Millau direction take D991 signed Gorge du Dourbie. Site is on left, just past turn to Cantobre. GPS: N44:02.664 E03:18.710

Charges 2009

Per unit incl. 2 persons, electricity and water	€ 17,50 - € 47,25
dog	€ 5,00 - € 3,00
Camping Cheques accepted.	

www.rcn-campings.fr

Check real time availability and at-the-gate prices...

www.**alanrogers**.com

FR12040 Village Center les Tours

F-12460 Saint Amans-des-Cots (Aveyron)

Tel: **05 65 44 88 10**. Email: **contact@village-center.com**　　　www.alanrogers.com/FR12040

This impressive campsite is set in beautiful countryside close to the Truyère Gorges, Upper Lot valley and the Aubrac Plateau. Efficiently run, it is situated on the shores of the Lac de la Selves. There are 275 average sized pitches with 6A electricity, some bordering the lake, the rest terraced and hedged with views of the lake. About 100 pitches also have water points. The site has a spacious feel, enhanced by the thoughtfully planned terraced layout and it is well kept and very clean. There is some up and down walking to the facilities, especially from the upper terraces. Used by tour operators (70 pitches).

Facilities

Four very well equipped toilet blocks. Attractive central complex housing the amenities. Shop (with gas). Restaurant, bar. Takeaway (high season). Swimming pools (June-Aug). Play area. Tennis. Varied programme of daytime and evening activities, with miniclub, archery and tree climbing (all supervised). Lake activities include fishing, canoeing, pedaloes, windsurfing, water skiing and provision for launching small boats. Internet terminal. Off site: Riding and golf 6 km.

Open: 20 May - 9 September.

Directions

Take D34 from Entraygues-sur-Truyère to St Amans-des-Cots (14 km). In St Amans take D97 to Colombez and then D599 to Lac de la Selves (site signed, 5 km. from St Amans).
GPS: N44:40.001 E02:40.801

Charges guide

Per unit incl. 2 persons	€ 16,00 - € 38,00
with services	€ 18,00 - € 40,00
extra person	€ 4,00 - € 8,00

Camping Cheques accepted.

Altavia Link

Les Tours ★★★★

Saint-Amans-des-Cots > Aveyron

- **Pitches with direct acces to the lake**
- **Tree climbing**

Camping Qualité

Villagecenter

🌿 BOOK YOUR HOLIDAYS
www.village-center.com
📞 +33 (0)4 99 57 21 21

FR12020 Camping Caravaning les Rivages

Avenue de l'Aigoual, route de Nant, F-12100 Millau (Aveyron)

Tel: **05 65 61 01 07**. Email: **campinglesrivages@wanadoo.fr**　　　www.alanrogers.com/FR12020

Les Rivages is a large, well established site on the outskirts of the town. It is well situated, being close to the high limestone Causses and the dramatic gorges of the Tarn and Dourbie. Smaller pitches, used for small units, abut a pleasant riverside space suitable for sunbathing, fishing or picnics. Most of the 314 pitches are large, and well shaded. A newer part of the site has less shade but larger pitches. All pitches have electricity (6A), and 282 have water and drainage. The site offers a very wide range of sporting activities close to 30 in all (see facilities).

Facilities

Four well kept modern toilet blocks have all necessary facilities. Special block for children. Small shop (1/6-15/9). Terrace, restaurant and bar overlooking swimming pool, children's pool (from 10/5). Play area. Entertainment, largely for children, child-minding, miniclub. Impressive sports centre with tennis (indoor and outdoor), squash and badminton. Boules. River activities, walking, bird watching, fishing. Off site: Rafting and canoeing arranged. Bicycle hire 1 km. Riding 10 km. Hypermarket in Millau.

Open: 1 April - 15 October.

Directions

From Millau, cross the Tarn bridge and take D991 road east towards Nant. Site is about 400 m. from the roundabout on the right, on the banks of the Dourbie river. GPS: N44:06.052 E03:05.769

Charges guide

Per pitch incl. 2 persons and electricity	€ 18,60 - € 26,60
incl. water and drainage	€ 20,60 - € 28,60
extra person (over 3 yrs)	€ 3,30 - € 4,80
pet	€ 1,50 - € 3,50

BOOK THIS SITE
CALL 01580 214000
...we'll arrange everything
The Travel Service

273

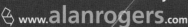

The Travel Service
...we'll arrange everything
BOOK THIS SITE CALL 01580 214000

FR12050 Flower Camping les Terrasses du Lac

Route du Vibal, F-12290 Pont-de-Salars (Aveyron)

Tel: 05 65 46 88 18. Email: campinglesterrasses@orange.fr   www.alanrogers.com/FR12050

A terraced site, it provides 180 good sized, level pitches, 112 for touring, with or without shade, all with electricity. Some pitches have good views over the lake which has direct access from the site at two places – one for pedestrians and swimmers, the other for cars and trailers for launching small boats. This site is well placed for excursions into the Gorges du Tarn, Caves du Roquefort and nearby historic towns and villages. Although there are good facilities for disabled visitors, the terracing on the site may prove difficult. At an altitude of some 700 m. on the plateau of Le Lévézou, this outlying site enjoys attractive views over Lac de Pont-de-Salars. The site seems largely undiscovered by the British, perhaps as it is only open for a short season.

Facilities

Four toilet blocks with adequate facilities. Fridge hire. Shop. Bar/restaurant with a lively French ambience serving full meals (high season) snacks (other times), takeaway (all 1/7-31/8). Heated swimming pool, children's pool (1/6-30/9). Solarium. Playground. Pétanque. Billiards. Games, TV rooms. Activities high season. Barbecue area. Off site: Tennis 3 km. Riding 5 km. Golf 20 km.

Open: 1 April - 30 September.

Directions

Using D911 Millau - Rodez road, turn north at Pont-de-Salars towards lake on D523. Follow site signs. Ignore first site and continue, following lake until Les Terraces (about 5 km). GPS: N44:18.316 E02:44.030

Charges 2009

Per pitch incl. 2 persons	
and electricity	€ 14,90 - € 26,50
with water and waste water	€ 15,90 - € 28,50
extra person	€ 4,00 - € 5,50
child (2-7 yrs)	€ 3,00 - € 4,00
dog	€ 1,75

www.flowercampings.com

In overhanging of the lake, discover an exceptional place for your relaxation and your escape. Chalets and Mobile homes to rent. A 200 m² heated swimming pool. Free activities

LES TERRASSES
DU LAC ★★★★

Route de Vibal 12 290 PONT DE SALARS
Tel : 0033 565 46 88 18
Fax : 0033 565 46 85 38
www.campinglesterrasses.com
campinglesterrasses@wanadoo.fr

FR12060 Camping Beau Rivage

Lac de Pareloup, route de Vernhes, F-12410 Salles-Curan (Aveyron)

Tel: 05 65 46 33 32. Email: camping-beau-rivage@wanadoo.fr   www.alanrogers.com/FR12060

This family run, immaculate site has a wonderful position alongside the beautiful Lac de Paraloup. There are 80 level, grassy pitches (60 for touring) attractively arranged on terraces, separated by neat hedges and a variety of small trees offering little shade. All have electricity (10A). A range of watersports is available on the lake (mostly July and August) and many activities are organised both in high season. On arrival at the site, park outside and go to reception. The site entrance is narrow and quite steep and tractor assistance is available. Once on site access to pitches is easy.

Facilities

Two well equipped and clean toilets blocks provide all the necessary facilities, including those for visitors with disabilities. Washing machines. Small shop, bar, snacks, terrace and takeaway (all July/Aug). Heated swimming pool (10/6-20/9). Games rooms. TV room. Pool table. Play area. Fishing, boating, lake bathing. Off site: Salles-Curan with shops, bars, restaurants 4 km. Boat ramp 200 m. Watercraft for hire (July/Aug). Bicycle hire 2 km. Tennis 3 km. Riding 12 km. Golf 35 km. Canoeing, rafting, paragliding, caving, windsurfing.

Open: 1 May - 30 September.

Directions

From D911 Rodez - Millau road turn south on D993 signed Salles-Curan. In 7 km, just after bridge over the lake, turn right on D243 (site signed). Entrance is on right in just over 1 km. Park outside gate. GPS: N44:12.550 E02:46.376

Charges guide

Per unit incl. 2 persons	
and electricity	€ 15,50 - € 29,50
extra person	€ 4,00 - € 6,50
child (2-7 yrs)	€ 2,00 - € 4,50
animal	€ 2,00 - € 4,00

FR12070 Flower Camping la Grange de Monteillac

F-12310 Sévérac-l'Eglise (Aveyron)

Tel: 05 65 70 21 00. Email: info@la-grange-de-monteillac.com   www.alanrogers.com/FR12070

La Grange de Monteillac is a modern, well equipped site in the beautiful, well preserved small village of Sévérac-l'Église. A spacious site, it provides 105 individual pitches, 70 for touring, on gently sloping grass, separated by flowering shrubs and mostly young trees offering little shade. All pitches have electricity (6A, long leads may be required), and 24 have water and waste water connections. There are 35 chalets, mobile homes and tents for rent in separate areas. The friendly owner will advise about the interesting activities in the region. An evening stroll around this delightful village is a must.

Facilities

Modern toilet block with facilities for babies and disabled people. Washing machine, dryer. Shop (1/7-31/8). Poolside restaurant/snack bar serving pizzas, grills etc, takeaway (1/7-31/8). Music in the bar (July/Aug). Two swimming pools (1/6-15/9). Well equipped playground. Bicycle hire. Archery. Boules. Organised activities. Children's club. Off site: Fishing 1 km. Shops in village 3 km. Riding 9 km. Golf 25 km. Many marked walks and bicycle rides, canoeing, rafting, canyoning, climbing and hang gliding.

Open: 1 May - 15 September.

Directions

Site is on the edge of Sévérac-l'Église village, just off N88 Rodez - Sévérac Le Château road. From A75 use exit 42. At Sévérac-l'Église turn south onto D28, site is signed. Site entrance is very shortly on left. GPS: N44:21.911 E02:51.086

Charges 2009

Per unit incl. 2 persons and electricity	€ 15,50 - € 26,30
extra person	€ 3,00 - € 6,00
child (2-7 yrs)	€ 2,00 - € 3,80

www.flowercampings.com

FR12080 Kawan Village les Genêts

Lac de Pareloup, F-12410 Salles-Curan (Aveyron)

Tel: 05 65 46 35 34. Email: contact@camping-les-genets.fr   www.alanrogers.com/FR12080

The 163 pitches include 80 grassy, mostly individual pitches for touring units. These are in two areas, one on each side of the entrance lane, and are divided by hedges, shrubs and trees. Most have electricity (6A) and many also have water and waste water drainage. This family run site slopes gently down to the shores of Lac de Pareloup and offers both family holiday and watersports facilities. A full animation and activities programme is organised in high season, and there is much to see and do in this very attractive corner of Aveyron.

Facilities

Two sanitary units with suite for disabled people. The older unit has been refurbished. Baby room. Laundry. Well stocked shop. Bar, restaurant, snacks (main season). Swimming pool, spa pool (from 1/6; unsupervised). Playground. Minigolf. Boules. Bicycle hire. Pedaloes, windsurfers, kayaks. Fishing licences available. WiFi in bar.

Open: 31 May - 11 September.

Directions

From Salles-Curan take D577 for about 4 km. and turn right into a narrow lane immediately after a sharp right hand bend. Site is signed at junction. GPS: N44:10.670 E02:46.650

Charges guide

Per unit incl. 1 or 2 persons and 6A electricity	€ 13,00 - € 39,00
extra person	€ 4,00 - € 7,00
Camping Cheques accepted.	

FR12160 Kawan Village les Peupliers

Route des Gorges du Tarn, F-12640 Rivière-sur-Tarn (Aveyron)

Tel: 05 65 59 85 17. Email: lespeupliers12640@orange.fr   www.alanrogers.com/FR12160

Les Peupliers is a friendly, family site on the banks of the Tarn river. Most of the good-sized pitches have shade, all have electricity, water and a waste water point and are divided by low hedges. It is possible to swim in the river and there is a landing place for canoes. The site has its own canoes (to rent). In a lovely, sunny situation on the site is a swimming pool with a paddling pool, sun beds and a new slide, all protected by a beautifully clipped hedge and with a super view to the surrounding hills and the Château du Peyrelade perched above the village.

Facilities

Large, light and airy toilet facilities, baby facilities with baths, showers and WCs, facilities for disabled visitors. Washing machines. Shop (1/6-30/9). Bar, TV. Internet. Snack bar, takeaway (1/5-30/9). Swimming pool (from 1/5). Games, competitions July/Aug. Fishing. Play area. Weekly dances July/Aug. Canoe hire. Off site: Village with shops and restaurant 300 m. Riding 500 m. Bicycle hire 2 km. Golf 25 km. Rock climbing, canyoning, cycling and walking.

Open: 25 April - 30 September.

Directions

Heading south on the A75 autoroute take exit 44-1 signed Aguessac/Gorges du Tarn. In Aguessac turn left and follow signs to Riviere-sur-Tarn (5 km). Site is clearly signed down a short road to the right. GPS: N44:11.146 E03:07.841

Charges 2009

Per unit incl. 2 persons and electricity	€ 20,00 - € 28,00
extra person	€ 5,00 - € 7,00
Camping Cheques accepted.	

BOOK THIS SITE
CALL 01580 214000
...we'll arrange everything
The Travel Service

Check real time availability and at-the-gate prices...
www.alanrogers.com

The Travel Service
BOOK THIS SITE
CALL 01580 214000
...we'll arrange everything

FR12150 Kawan Village Marmotel

F-12130 Saint Geniez-d'Olt (Aveyron)

Tel: 05 65 70 46 51. Email: info@marmotel.com   www.alanrogers.com/FR12150

The road into Marmotel passes various industrial buildings and is a little off-putting – persevere, as they are soon left behind. The campsite itself is a mixture of old and new. The old part provides many pitches with lots of shade and separated by hedges. The new area is sunny until the trees grow. These pitches each have a private sanitary unit, with shower, WC, washbasin and dishwashing. New and very well designed, they are reasonably priced for such luxury. All the pitches have electricity (10A). A lovely restaurant has a wide terrace with views of the hills and overlooking the heated swimming and paddling pools. These have fountains, a toboggan and sun beds either on grass or the tiled surrounds. The Lot river runs alongside the site where you can fish or canoe.

Facilities

Good sanitary facilities include baby baths and facilities for disabled visitors. Washing machines. Bar/restaurant, takeaway. Swimming pools. Small play area. Multisports area. Entertainment July/Aug. including disco below bar, cinema, karaoke, dances, miniclub for 4-12 yr olds. Bicycle hire. Fishing. Canoeing. Off site: Large supermarket 500 m. Riding 10 km. Bicycle tours and canoe trips on the Lot and rafting on the Tarn are organised.

Open: 10 May - 14 September.

Directions

Heading south on autoroute 75 (free) take exit 41 and follow signs for St Geniez d'Olt. Site is at western end of village. Site is signed onto D19 to Prades d'Aubrac, then 500 m. on left. GPS: N44:28.040 E02:58.390

Charges 2009

Per unit incl. 1 or 2 persons and electricity	€ 17,80 - € 27,00
with private sanitary facilities	€ 21,40 - € 32,00
extra person	€ 2,10 - € 6,10
child (under 5 yrs)	free - € 3,20
dog	€ 1,50

Camping Cheques accepted.

Marmotel
★ ★ ★ ★ Camping-Village

"VERY COMFORTABLE, VERY NATURAL"
5 ha in the Lot Valley, by the riverside. 180 pitches, 42 of which have individual toilet. Chalets and Mobile homes for hire. 350 sqm swimming pools, waterslides, multi sports area, animations, kids club, bar, restaurant.
Open 10/05 – 14/09 2008
w w w . m a r m o t e l . c o m

The Travel Service
BOOK THIS SITE
CALL 01580 214000
...we'll arrange everything

FR12210 Flower Camping la Source

Presqu'île de Laussac, F-12600 Therondels (Aveyron)

Tel: 05 65 66 27 10. Email: info@camping-la-source.com   www.alanrogers.com/FR12210

This extremely spacious, steeply terraced site borders the long and narrow Lac de Sarrans with its steep wooded sides. The site is run by a very friendly family and is better suited for the younger family wanting to 'get away from it all'. All the facilities are first class, although the layout of the site means that pitches may be some distance and a steep climb away. The owners prefer to provide tractor assistance for caravans. There are 110 medium to large, slightly sloping, grassy pitches with 64 for touring, all with 6/10A electricity, water and drainage.

Facilities

Two large, well appointed and clean toilet blocks with all the necessary facilities including those for babies and campers with disabilities. Shop (28/6-29/8). Bar with TV (17/5-7/9). Restaurant and takeaway (28/6-29/8). Swimming pool with toboggan and paddling pool (17/5-7/9, heated 17/5-7/9). Play area. TV room. Activities in high season for all the family. Lake fishing. Off site: Boat ramp 500 m. Golf 6 km. Riding and bicycle hire 15 km.

Open: 17 May - 7 September.

Directions

Leave the A75 at exit 28 or 29 (St Flour). Go through town and take D921 (Rodez). After 12 km. turn right on D990 (Pierrefort) and 3 km. after village turn left on D34 (Laussac). Follow narrow twisting lanes down to site (about 9 km). GPS: N44:51.223 E02:46.263

Charges guide

Per unit incl. 2 persons	€ 15,50 - € 25,90
extra person	€ 3,00 - € 4,70
electricity (6/10A)	€ 2,00

Camping Cheques accepted.

www.flowercampings.com

Check real time availability and at-the-gate prices...
www.alanrogers.com

FR12170 Castel Camping le Caussanel

Lac de Pareloup, F-12290 Canet-de-Salars (Aveyron)

Tel: **05 65 46 85 19**. Email: **info@lecaussanel.com**   www.alanrogers.com/FR12170

The site has 235 large, fairly level, grassy pitches, 135 for touring. Most have 6-10A electricity but very long leads may be necessary, and 33 are fully serviced. The pitches are defined by a tree or boulder in each corner and offer little privacy but many have wonderful views over the lake. Most pitches have little shade, a few having good shade. The site has swimming pools with toboggan and slides and a large paddling pool for children with small slides. The adjacent lake offers a large area, one kilometre long, for swimming and all the usual watersports. This large, extremely spacious site on the banks of Lac de Pareloup is greatly improved. It is ideal, in low season, for those seeking a tranquil holiday in a beautiful region of France or in high season, for those seeking an active holiday. One tour operator takes 20 pitches.

Facilities

Modern toilet blocks have all the necessary facilities. Motorcaravan services. Shop. Bar. Restaurant, takeaway (7/6-6/9). Swimming pool complex from June. Large play area. Boules. Tennis. Football. TV room, clubhouse. Organised activities (July/Aug). Fishing. Bicycle hire (July/Aug). Motor boat launching. Water sports (July/Aug). Swimming in lake. Internet access. Off site: Paths around lake (24 km). Other marked walks and cycle rides. Shops, banks, restaurants 8 km. Riding 10 km. Golf 30 km. Canoeing, rafting, paragliding caving, windsurfing.

Open: 16 April - 12 September.

Directions

From D911 Rodez - Millau road, just east of Pont de Salars, turn south on D993 signed Salles-Curan. In 6 km. at crossroads turn right on D538 signed Le Caussanel. Very shortly turn left and continue to site. GPS: N44:12.877 E02:45.995

Charges guide

Per unit incl. 2 persons	€ 13,20 - € 26,90
extra person	€ 3,50 - € 6,90
child (2-7 yrs)	€ 2,60 - € 4,80
incl. electricity	€ 16,30 - € 31,10
incl. water and drainage	€ 18,70 - € 34,70
Camping Cheques accepted.	

Le Caussanel

Take the advantage of the fresh air in an unspoilt region with a wealth of natural treasures. Wide open spaces, great expanses of water and greenery... You are in the heart of Aveyron on the shores of Lac de Pareloup.

aquatic park, water slide, pentagliss, watergames (16-05 to 05-09), miniature farm and multisports area

CHALETS & MOBILE HOMES FOR RENT

Services open from 06-06 to 05-09
(shop, bar, pizzeria-grill, entertainment...)

Openingdates:
16-05 to 12-09 2009

Lac de Pareloup - 12290 Canet de Salars - Tél.: 05 65 46 85 19 - Fax: 05 65 46 89 85
Email: info@lecaussanel.com - www.lecaussanel.com

FR12240 Camping Saint-Pal

Route du Gorges du Tarn, F-12720 Mostuéjouls (Aveyron)

Tel: **05 65 62 64 46**. Email: **saintpal@wanadoo.fr**   www.alanrogers.com/FR12240

Saint-Pal is ideally situated on the approach road to the Gorges du Tarn, so access to the site is easy. This small, very neat site is run by a very friendly family and is aimed at those who prefer peace and quiet and less in the way of organised activity. Beside the Tarn river, the site is arranged in the open valley and is fairly flat. There are 74 large, level, grassy pitches, with 64 for touring. Separated by hedging, most are shaded by mature trees and 6A electricity is available. Some pitches are alongside the attractive river.

Facilities

One very clean, modern toilet block with good facilities includes a room for babies and campers with disabilities. Motorcaravan service point. Small shop (1/6-15/9). Bar/restaurant and takeaway (1/7-31/8). Small swimming pool (all season). Play area, TV/games room. River bathing, boating and fishing. Organised walks and low key entertainment in July and August. Off site: Bicycle hire 500 m. Riding 5 km. Le Rozier 1 km. Millau 20 km.

Open: 19 May - 15 September.

Directions

Leave A75 at exit 44, north of Millau. Take N9 south for 14 km. to Aquessac. Turn left on D907 and site is on right in 14 km. just before village of Le Rosier. GPS: N44:11.751 E03:11.983

Charges guide

Per unit incl. 2 persons and electricity	€ 14,60 - € 23,20
extra person	€ 3,30 - € 4,80
child (under 5 yrs)	€ 23,00 - € 3,50

Check real time availability and at-the-gate prices...
www.alanrogers.com

BOOK THIS SITE
CALL 01580 214000
...we'll arrange everything
The Travel Service

The Travel
Service ...we'll arrange everything

BOOK THIS SITE
CALL 01580 214000

FR12260 Camping du Val de Saures

Village de Gîtes le Bastie, F-12140 Entraygues-sur-Truyère (Aveyron)

Tel: 05 65 44 56 92. Email: info@camping-valdesaures.com   www.alanrogers.com/FR12260

Camping Le Val de Saures is a well presented, value for money site only five minutes across a river bridge from the interesting old town of Entraygues. Situated at the confluence of the rivers Lot and Truyère, it is a good base for relaxing and exploring this beautiful area of Aveyron. There are 110 good sized level grassy pitches (6A electricity) separated by small shrubs and trees with varying amount of shade. Many overlook the river Lot. Although the site has no shop, bar or restaurant these are all available in the town. In the area there are many wonderful medieval villages, with their narrow streets and Tudor houses with the famous grey Lauze tiles. Canoeing or rafting are possible and there are marked paths to explore on foot, on horseback or by bike.

Facilities

Three very clean and well appointed toilet blocks with all the necessary facilities including facilities for campers with disabilities. Motorcaravan service point. TV/games room. WiFi. Playground. River fishing but no bathing. Off site: Fortified town of Entraygues (400 m. by footbridge) with a good range of shops, banks, bars and restaurants. Swimming pool (free), tennis courts and large playground close by. Watersports excursion 400 m. Riding 10 km.

Open: 1 May - 24 September.

Directions

Entraygues sur Truyère is 42 km. southeast of Aurillac on the D920. At southern end of Entraygues on the D920 turn right (site signed), over river bridge onto the D904 and immediately right again. Just past the tennis courts fork right and follow lane down to site. GPS: N44:38.546 E02:33.849

Charges guide

Per unit incl. 2 persons	€ 9,00 - € 16,00
extra person	€ 2,50 - € 4,00
child (2-13 yrs)	free - € 3,00
electricity	€ 3,00

Camping **le Val de Saures** ★ ★ ★

126 pitches • 11 chalets • at the riverside of the Lot • family campsite • 'municipal' swimming pool • games room with free WiFi • animation for children and adults • all shops on 300 meters distance • chalets for rent

Village de Gîtes du Bastié • 12140 Entraygues sur Truyère • Tel : 0033 565 44 56 92 • Fax : 0033 565 44 27 21
www.camping-valdesaures.com • info@camping-valdesaures.com

FR12250 Flower Camping du Lac de Bonnefon

L'Etang de Bonnefon, F-12800 Naucelle (Aveyron)

Tel: 05 65 69 33 20   www.alanrogers.com/FR12250

This small family run site, popular with French campers, lies in a picturesque region waiting to be discovered, with rolling hills, deep river valleys, lakes and many old fortified villages. This site is more suitable for those seeking a quieter holiday with less in the way of entertainment. There are 112 good sized, grassy, slightly sloping pitches with 74 for touring (50 with 10A electricity). Some are separated by laurel hedging with others more open and maturing trees give a little shade. The new enthusiastic and friendly owners have recently extended the site and refurbished the facilities to a high standard.

Facilities

Two toilet blocks include some washbasins in cabins and good facilities for disabled visitors. No shop but bread to order. Bar with TV (all season). Snack bar (July/Aug, other times on demand). Swimming and paddling pools (1/6-30/9). Playground. Archery. Good lake fishing but no bathing. Activities for all the family in July/Aug. Off site: Riding 500 m. Small village of Naucelle with a few shops and large heated pool complex 1 km.

Open: 1 April - 31 October.

Directions

Site is just off the N88 about halfway between Rodez and Albi. From Naucelle Gare take D997 towards Naucelle. In just over 1 km. turn left on D58 and follow signs to site in just under 1 km. GPS: N44:11.283 E02:20.896

Charges guide

Per unit incl. 2 persons and electricity	€ 13,50 - € 22,00
extra person	€ 4,00 - € 5,00
child (2-10 yrs)	€ 2,00 - € 3,00
Camping Cheques accepted.	

www.flowercampings.com

FR12290 Flower Camping le Port de Lacombe

F-12300 Flagnac (Aveyron)
Tel: 05 65 64 10 08   www.alanrogers.com/FR12290

The new managers, Patrick and Marie-Claude Comtat, have plans to improve this leased municipal site. It is well kept and is situated on the banks of the Lot river, a location ideal for walking, cycling, fishing and canoeing. The 91 grass touring pitches are level and range in size from 100-130 sq.m. A large natural swimming pool is fed by the river and provides a separate paddling area and a large slide. Using the D42, one can wind through the valley and climb to over 2,000 feet to the Plateau de la Viadene. The scenery is panoramic and picturesque.

Facilities

Two separate sanitary blocks, each with the usual facilities including provision for disabled visitors. Washing machine. Bar (all season) with restaurant and takeaway (both 15/6-15/9). TV in function room. Play area. Swimming pool fed from the river and paddling pool (1/7-31/8). Bicycle hire. Fishing in river. Entertainment (July/Aug).

Open: 1 April - 30 September.

Directions

Driving south from Brive-la-Gaillarde, take N140 to Decazeville, turning north on D963 to Flagnac. Site is well signed on the left. From Rodez take N140 to Decazeville, then as above.
GPS: N44:36.340 E02:14.110

Charges guide

Per unit incl. 2 persons	€ 8,00 - € 22,00
incl. electricity (6A)	€ 11,00 - € 20,00
extra person	€ 2,00 - € 4,00

FR12350 Camping Côté Sud

Avenue de l'Aigoual, F-12100 Millau (Aveyron)
Tel: 05 65 61 18 83. Email: camping-cotesud@orange.fr   www.alanrogers.com/FR12350

Le Côté Sud is a family run site just 500 m. from the lively market town of Millau which lies in the valley below the imposing Millau suspension bridge. The owners speak German, Dutch and English so all will get a great welcome here. There are 160 good sized, slightly sloping grassy pitches with varying degrees of shade and good views over the wooded hills. There are 140 pitches for tourers, 6/10A electricity – long leads needed. The site has a heated swimming pool, sauna and snack bar/bar, pleasant for unwinding after a busy day touring making it ideal for long or short stays.

Facilities

Modern well equipped, clean toilet blocks with all necessary facilities including those for campers with disabilities. Snack bar/bar (July/Aug). Swimming pool, sauna (June - Sept). Small TV room. Play area. Activity and entertainment programme, mainly off site. River fishing and bathing. Off site: Millau centre 500 m. Bicycle hire 300 m. Riding 2 km. Walking and cycling in the Grands Causses park. Roquefort cheese cellars. Caves (Aven Armand and Dargilan).

Open: 1 April - 30 September.

Directions

Leave A75 autoroute at exit 45 before crossing viaduct and follow signs to Millau. On entering Millau turn left at roundabout, signed Zone Commerciale and follow signs for 'Campings'. Turn left at roundabout, cross river and shortly turn right to campsite. GPS: N44:06.144 E03:05.460

Charges guide

Per unit incl. 2 persons and electricity	€ 10,00 - € 24,00
extra person	€ 3,00 - € 4,50

FR12360 Camping la Plaine

F-12300 Saint Parthem (Aveyron)
Tel: 05 65 64 05 24. Email: infos@camping-laplaine.fr   www.alanrogers.com/FR12360

Strung out along the bank of the Lot river, this small, spacious, delightful site is family run. The enthusiastic and very friendly Dutch owners are making many improvements here including the addition of a new swimming pool in 2008. There are 65 grassy, fairly level pitches with 61 for touring (6A electricity, long leads advised). The pitches are separated by maturing trees and some hedging with views over the river and the wooded gorge. Some pitches have little shade. Swimming and canoeing are possible from the small pebbly beach. The site makes a good base for exploring this interesting and beautiful region by car, bike or on foot.

Facilities

Old style but very clean central block and small satellite block with all necessary facilities. Facilities for visitors with disabilities. Washing machine, ironing board. Small bar/restaurant with takeaway (all season). Bread to order. Swimming pool with patio. River fishing and bathing from pebble beach. Tennis. Boules. Off site: Small village, small shop, 500 m. Riding 8 km. Canoeing 15 km. Medieval towns and villages, e.g. Conques 14 km.

Open: 5 April - 14 September.

Directions

Site is northeast of Decazeville. Leave Decazeville on the D963 signed Aurillac. After 6 km. cross river and turn east onto D42 to St Parthem (6 km). Site is well signed. GPS: N44:37.752 E02:19.235

Charges guide

Per unit incl. 2 persons	€ 12,50
extra person	€ 3,50
electricity (6A)	€ 3,00
No credit cards.	

www.flowercampings.com

Check real time availability and at-the-gate prices...
www.alanrogers.com

FR12390 Camping Le Millau Plage

Rte de Millau Plage, F-12100 Millau (Aveyron)

Tel: 05 65 60 10 97. Email: **info@campingmillauplage.com**   www.alanrogers.com/FR12390

This slightly old site is situated on the banks of the Tarn river one and a half kilometres outside Millau. This is an historical town in its own right and a very popular place for hang-gliding and watersports, as well as for people wishing to get a view of the Millau suspension bridge further down the valley. Plenty of trees provide ample shade and the site could be a little dark on cloudy or dull days. The river will attract older children who will love to climb the trees and jump or dive into the water, but as the site is open onto the river younger children would need supervision. Everyone will enjoy the large pool that is next to the restaurant and bar area.

Facilities

Four toilet blocks along the middle of the site provide easy access from most pitches. The blocks are old and due some modernisation. Motorcaravan services. Small shop (9/7-15/8). Bar with TV and snack type restaurant. Large irregular shaped pool filled with river water. Limited children's club in high season along with video and non-professional entertainment for adults in the evening in high season. Off site: Historic town of Millau. Hang-gliding, fishing and canoeing and walking in the impressive Massive Central.

Open: 29 March - 30 September.

Directions

Millau is best accessed from the A75 motorway. From either north or south take the N9, following it round the town until roundabout signed for Millau Plage. Cross the river and take third exit at next roundabout. Site is on left 1.5 km. after the final roundabout and after passing two other sites. GPS: N44:06.931 E03:05.215

Charges guide

Per unit incl. 2 persons and electricity	€ 15,50 - € 26,00
extra person	€ 3,00 - € 5,00
child (2-4 yrs)	€ 2,00 - € 3,50
dog	€ 2,00 - € 4,00

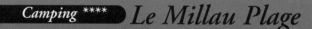

Camping **** Le Millau Plage

Route de Millau Plage • F-12100 Millau • Tél.: 0033 (0)5 65 60 10 97
Mail: info@campingmillauplage.com • www.campingmillauplage.com

FR12380 Camping Belle Rive

Rue du Terral, F-12500 Saint Come d'Olt (Aveyron)

Tel: 05 65 44 05 85. Email: **bellerive12@voila.fr**   www.alanrogers.com/FR12380

Small and simple, this family run campsite, beside the River Lot, is on the edge of a delightful medieval village. The region has many historic towns and villages with chateaux and ancient churches and is close to the Pilgrim route. The local produce, for example Roquefort cheese, is well worth sampling. The site is good for those seeking a tranquil spot with little in the way of on site activities. There are 71 good sized grassy pitches delineated by a variety of tall trees giving good shade on most pitches (6A electricity). Access to the site is not suitable for large outfits due to the many small twisting roads.

Facilities

Adequate but very clean old style central block with combined shower and washbasin cubicles. Washing machine. Facilities for disabled campers. Play area. Some family activities (high season). River bathing and fishing. Off site: Village, small shops, bank, bar/restaurants 400 m. Espalion with larger shops and market 4 km. Swimming pool 4 km. Riding 12 km. Canoeing. Ancient villages, chateaux, churches. Many walking and cycling routes.

Open: 1 May - 30 September.

Directions

Leave A75 at exit 42, signed Sévérac le Château. Take N88 west, then D28 to Espalion. Cross river on D987 to St Côme d'Olt (4 km). On entering village bear left, following signs to site. Do not drive through the village. GPS: N44:30.826 E02:49.108

Charges guide

Per unit incl. 2 persons and electricity	€ 12,21
extra person	€ 2,98
child (under 7 yrs)	€ 1,49
No credit cards.	

Check real time availability and at-the-gate prices...

www.**alanrogers**.com

FR16020 Castel Camping les Gorges du Chambon

Eymouthiers, F-16220 Montbron (Charente)

Tel: 05 45 70 71 70. Email: gorges.chambon@wanadoo.fr   www.alanrogers.com/FR16020

This is a wonderful Castels site with 28 hectares of protected natural environment to be enjoyed in the rolling Périgord Vert countryside. The 90 pitches are extremely generous in size (150 sq.m), mostly level and enjoy a mixture of sunshine and shade. There are 85 with water and 10A electricity, the remaining five are fully serviced. The spaciousness is immense, with fine walks through the woodlands and around the grounds. Flora, fauna and wildlife are as nature intended. Here you can feel at peace and enjoy precious moments of quiet. There has been much work done with the ecology association. The songs of the birds can be heard against the backdrop of water flowing gently down a small river on one side of the campsite. Guided walks are a feature. Les Gorges du Chambon is arranged around a restored Charentaise farmhouse and its outbuildings. A converted barn provides space for the restaurant and bar and the food is excellent, at a reasonable price. There is a pleasant pool together with a paddling pool. There is also a sand beach area along the river and canoes can be hired. The site owners are friendly and helpful and want you to enjoy your stay.

Facilities

Traditional style blocks include facilities for disabled people. Washing machine, dryer. Basic shop. Bar, restaurant (all season). Takeaway (all season). Swimming pool, children's pool. Play area. Games room, TV and library with English books. Tennis. Archery. Minigolf. Bicycle and canoe hire. Organised activities July/Aug, children's club, youth disco, teenagers' corner. Internet access. Dogs are not accepted. Off site: Private fishing (free) 6 km, with licence 200 m. Golf 6 km. Riding 6 km.

Open: 19 April - 20 September
(rented accommodation 1 May - 31 October).

Directions

From N141 Angoulême - Limoges road at Rochefoucauld take D6 to Montbron village. Follow D6 in direction of Piegut-Pluviers and site is signed to the north on D163 on entering La Tricherie.
GPS: N45:39.588 E00:33.460

Charges guide

Per person	€ 4,00 - € 7,10
child (1-7 yrs)	€ 1,60 - € 3,55
pitch and car	€ 8,30 - € 11,00
electricity (6A)	€ 3,50

Camping Cheques accepted.

GORGES DU CHAMBON ★★★★

Jacques Petit invites you to relax in a setting of outstanding natural beauty - real rural France, with the opportunity to fish, hire a bike to explore the lanes, observe unspoilt nature, swim in an outdoor pool, relax in the bar with a drink and a bar snack, dine in their restaurant, enjoy a takeaway meal. For a real family holiday !

Gite & Chalets, Mobile home to let.

Mail: gorges.chambon@wanadoo.fr
Web: gorgesduchambon.fr
Tel: (33) 545 70 71 70 - Fax: (33) 545 70 80 02

FR16040 Camping Devezeau

F-16230 Saint Angeau (Charente)

Tel: 05 45 39 21 29. Email: bookings@campingdevezeau.com   www.alanrogers.com/FR16040

Camping Devezeau is open all year and provides a pleasant stopping place on the way to and from the south. It is also within easy reach of Cognac. The site has British owners who are working hard to upgrade what is already an attractive site. There are just 39 pitches (29 for touring units) mainly on grass and separated by small shrubs, although there are four hardstandings for motorcaravans. Most have electricity. Set in the gently rolling Charente countryside, a short drive from the N10.

Facilities

The toilet block in a converted barn provides single sex facilities. Facilities for people with disabilities. Laundry sinks and a washing machine. Gas supplies. New snack bar. Swimming pool (12 x 12 m; 1/5-30/9). Play area. Off site: Shop and bar in village 1.5 km. Fishing 2 km.

Open: All year.

Directions

From north, N10 exit for Mansle. Turn left (east) at lights onto D6 for St Angeau (9 km). At St Angeau turn right on the D15 signed Tourriers. Take first left, after 300 m, site signed, site is then 300 m.
GPS: N45:50.356 E00:16.318

Charges guide

Per unit incl. 2 persons	€ 13,00 - € 18,00
electricity	€ 2,00

No credit cards.

Check real time availability and at-the-gate prices...
www.alanrogers.com

FR16050 Camping de Cognac

Boulevard de Châtenay, route de Sainte-Sévère, F-16100 Cognac (Charente)

Tel: **05 45 32 13 32**. Email: **info@campingdecognac.com**   www.alanrogers.com/FR16050

Situated close to the historic town of Cognac, this municipal site is set in a rural area next to the Charente river. It has 168 pitches, 160 for touring caravans and 8 mobile homes which are all available for rent. All have 6A electricity and a water tap but no drain. The pitches are separated by shrubs and hedging, with tarmac or gravel roads all around. This area is naturally very suitable for those who enjoy brandy, with all the famous Cognac houses offering tours for visitors.

Facilities

Two well equipped, fairly modern toilet blocks (access by steps) include children's toilets and washing machines. Separate ground level facilities for disabled visitors. Motorcaravan services. Small swimming pool on site (municipal pool nearby). Shop. Snack bar and takeaway. Fishing. Play area on grass. Minigolf. Double axle caravans not accepted. Off site: Bicycle hire 2 km. Riverside walks. Restaurants, bars and shops in the town (2.3 km). Golf 5 km. Riding 6 km.

Open: 26 April - 30 September.

Directions

Site is to the north of the town beside the river on the D24 to St Sévère. GPS: N45:42.544 W00:18.759

Charges guide

Per unit incl. 2 persons and electricity	€ 13,00 - € 20,00
extra person	€ 4,00 - € 5,50
child (2-12 yrs)	€ 3,50 - € 4,00
animal	€ 1,50

Less for stays over 7 days.

FR16060 Camping Marco de Bignac

Lieu-dit Les Sablons, F-16170 Bignac (Charente)

Tel: **05 45 21 78 41**. Email: **info@marcodebignac.com**   www.alanrogers.com/FR16060

The small village of Bignac is set in peaceful countryside not too far from the N10 road, north of Angoulême. This mature, British owned site is arranged alongside an attractive lake on a level, grassy meadow. The 87 large touring pitches are marked by a trees so there is shade, 80 have electricity (3/6A). There is a hedged swimming pool and plenty of grassy space for ball games. This site is popular with British visitors and is a peaceful, relaxing location for couples or young families. There is no noisy entertainment and all the activities are free of charge.

Facilities

Two traditional style toilet blocks have functional facilities. Washing machine. Bar all year with food high season and weekends. Small shop. Swimming pool (June-September, unsupervised). Football, badminton, tennis, pedaloes, minigolf, boules, fishing, all free. Library. Play area. Pets' corner. Organised activities in high season. A torch may be useful. Off site: Local markets. Riding 5 km. Golf 25 km.

Open: All year.

Directions

From N10 south of Poitiers, 14 km. north of Angoulême, take D11 west to Vars and Basse. Turn right onto D117 to Bignac. Site is signed at several junctions and in village (Camping Bignac). GPS: N45:47.857 E00:03.770

Charges guide

Per pitch incl. 2 persons	€ 15,00 - € 21,00
extra person	€ 3,00 - € 5,00
electricity (3/6A)	€ 2,00 - € 3,00

FR24010 Kawan Village Château le Verdoyer

Champs Romain, F-24470 Saint Pardoux (Dordogne)

Tel: **05 53 56 94 64**. Email: **chateau@verdoyer.fr**   www.alanrogers.com/FR24010

The 26 hectare estate has three lakes, two for fishing and one with a sandy beach and safe swimming area. There are 135 good sized touring pitches, level, terraced and hedged. With a choice of wooded area or open field, all have electricity (5/10A) and most share a water supply between four pitches. There is a swimming pool complex and in high season activities are organised for children (5-13 yrs) but there is no disco. This site is well adapted for those with disabilities, with two fully adapted chalets, wheelchair access to all facilities and even a lift into the pool.

Facilities

Well appointed toilet blocks include facilities for people with disabilities, and baby baths. Serviced launderette. Motorcaravan services. Fridge rental. Shop with gas. Bar, snacks, takeaway and restaurant, both open all season. Bistro (July/Aug). Two pools the smaller covered in low season, slide, paddling pool. Play areas. Tennis. Minigolf. Bicycle hire. Small library. Off site: Riding 5 km.

Open: 26 April - 6 October.

Directions

Site is 2 km. from the Limoges (N21) - Chalus (D6bis-D85) - Nontron road, 20 km. south of Chalus and is well signed from main road. Site on D96 about 4 km. north of village of Champs Romain. GPS: N45:33.083 E00:47.683

Charges guide

Per unit incl. 2 persons and electricity	€ 18,00 - € 29,00
full services	€ 18,00 - € 33,50
extra person	€ 5,00 - € 6,50

Camping Cheques accepted.

The Travel Service ...we'll arrange everything
BOOK THIS SITE CALL 01580 214000

Check real time availability and at-the-gate prices...

www.**alanrogers**.com

FR24020 Camping Caravaning les Granges

Mobile homes ▶ page 503

F-24250 Groléjac-en-Périgord (Dordogne)

Tel: 05 53 28 11 15. Email: contact@lesgranges-fr.com

www.alanrogers.com/FR24020

Situated only 500 metres from the village of Groléjac, Les Granges is a lively and well maintained campsite set on sloping ground in woodland. There are 188 pitches, of which 100 are available for touring units. The pitches are marked and numbered on level terraces, and most receive good shade from mature trees and shrubs. All pitches have electricity (6A) and water either on the pitch or close by. The site has a good sized swimming pool and a large shallow pool for children. A bridge connects these to a fun pool with water slides. Around 88 pitches are used by tour operators. Regular entertainment is organised in high season, along with a children's club every weekday morning.

Facilities

The toilet blocks are of a very high standard with good facilities for disabled visitors. Bar/restaurant and snack bar also providing takeaway food (15/5-15/9). No shop, but bread and milk can be ordered. Play area. Minigolf. Climbing wall. Canoe and bicycle hire. Off site: Shops in the nearby village of Groléjac and hypermarkets of Sarlat or Gourdon are not far away. Golf and riding 6 km.

Open: 25 April - 13 September.

Directions

In centre of village of Groléjac on main D704 road. Site signed through a gravel parking area on west side of road. Drive through this area and follow road around to T-junction. Turn right, under railway bridge, and immediately left (site signed). Site is just along this road on left. GPS: N44:48.955 E01:17.451

Charges guide

Per unit incl. 2 persons and electricity	€ 15,25 - € 27,60
extra person (over 5 yrs)	€ 6,50 - € 7,30
dog	free - € 3,00

CAMPING LES GRANGES 4 ★★★★

24250 GROLEJAC
Tél :+ 33.(0)5.53.28.11.15. - Fax : + 33. (0)5.53.28.57.13.
www.lesgranges-fr.com
Email : contact@lesgranges-fr.com

In pure Perigord-style buildings, les Granges welcomes you in lush vegetation and offers all the modern confort of a 4 star campsite. You will find spacious terraced emplacements 100 m², bordered by hedges in bloom and more. 3 pools including 1 heated, 2 water chutes. At 500m The Dordogne with canoê hire and cycle paths, mountain bike hire, washing machine, dryer, iron, fridge...

All the services are open from 03/05: restaurant, take away, pizza, bar.
From 01/07 till 29/08 : Animations, Childrens Club
Hire mobil homes and chalets available from 27/04 till 13/09.

Acces A20 from Paris to Toulouse, exit at Souillac. D704 between Sarlat 10 km and Gourdon 12 km.

FR24030 Camping les Périères

Rue Jean Gabin, F-24203 Sarlat-la-Canéda (Dordogne)

Tel: 05 53 59 05 84. Email: les-perieres@wanadoo.fr

www.alanrogers.com/FR24030

Les Périères is a good quality small site set on an attractive hillside within walking distance of the beautiful medieval town of Sarlat. The 100 pitches are arranged on wide terraces around the semi-circle of a fairly steep valley, overlooking a central leisure area that includes indoor and outdoor swimming pools and two tennis courts. The pitches are of a very good size, all equipped with electricity (6A), individual water and drainage points and many have dappled shade from the numerous walnut trees on the site (the walnuts can be bought in the campsite shop).

Facilities

Good toilet blocks with facilities for disabled visitors, baby bathroom, washing machines and dryers. Motorcaravan services. Small shop. Pleasant bar. Small snack bar/takeaway (July/August). Outdoor swimming pool (no shorts), paddling pool, indoor spa pool and sauna (all season). Tennis, football, fitness track. Stone cottages to rent. No electric barbecues allowed. Off site: Bicycle hire 1 km. Fishing 5 km. Riding and golf 7 km.

Open: Easter - 30 September.

Directions

Site is on the east side of Sarlat, on the D47 to Ste Nathalene (negotiating Sarlat town centre is best done outside peak hours).
GPS: N44:53.622 E01:13.648

Charges guide

Per unit incl. 2 persons	€ 19,70 - € 26,90
incl. electricity	€ 23,50 - € 30,90
extra person	€ 6,30
child (under 7 yrs)	€ 4,30
Credit cards accepted with 2% fee.	

Check real time availability and at-the-gate prices...
www.alanrogers.com

FR24050 Camping les Hauts de Ratebout

Saint Foy de Belvès, F-24170 Belvès (Dordogne)

Tel: **05 53 29 02 10**. Email: **camping@hauts-ratebout.fr**   www.alanrogers.com/FR24050

Situated southwest of Sarlat, there are some stunning views of the surrounding countryside from many of the 200 pitches at this pretty hilltop campsite. The terraced pitches vary in size (80-130 sq.m), some flat and some sloping. All have electricity (6A) and water. Housed in an older building, the restaurant/bar has plenty of atmosphere and is interestingly furnished. The swimming pool complex includes a 200 sq.m. unheated pool with slide, a shallow 100 sq.m. pool which is covered and heated as necessary, a fun pool with another slide and a small paddling pool. The site is used by tour operators (57 pitches). The walled town of Belvès is worth a visit.

Facilities

Four high standard toilet blocks offer the usual amenities including private washbasins and facilities for people with disabilities. Washing machines and dryers. Small shop (with gas) and takeaway service. Restaurant/bar and second bar and terrace. Swimming pool complex (proper trunks). Adventure playground on gravel. General room with pool and football tables and TV. Tennis. Organised activities in season. Nightly videos and sporting events. Off site: Fishing and bicycle hire 6 km. Riding 7 km. Golf 8 km.

Open: 13 May - 10 September.

Directions

From Belvès, take D710 southwards for 2 km. then turn east on D54. After 2 km. turn left, and after a further 500 m. left again (following campsite signs all the way). Site is 1.5 km. along on the right. GPS: N44:44.505 E01:02.708

Charges guide

Per unit incl. 2 persons, water and electricity	€ 20,00 - € 32,00
incl. drainage	€ 20,00 - € 33,00
extra person	€ 5,00 - € 7,00
child (3-7 yrs)	€ 3,00 - € 5,50

Camping Cheques accepted.

DORDOGNE

FranceLoc

Les hauts de ratebout****

Indoor heated swimming pool, outdoor pool of 300m² with water slide. Mobil homes and cottages in Périgourdines style.

Sainte Foy de Belvès
24170 • Tel.: +33 (0)5 53 29 02 10
Email : ratebout@franceloc.fr
www.camping-franceloc.fr

FR24040 Castel Camping le Moulin du Roch

Route des Eyzies-Le Roch (D47), F-24200 Sarlat-la-Canéda (Dordogne)

Tel: **05 53 59 20 27**. Email: **moulin.du.roch@wanadoo.fr**   www.alanrogers.com/FR24040

The site has 195 pitches, of which 124 are for touring units. They are mostly flat (some slope slightly) and grassy and all have electricity (6A). Pitches on the upper levels have plenty of shade, whilst those on the lower level near the amenities and the fishing lake are more open. Entertainment and activities are organised from June to September, with something for everyone from craft workshops and sports tournaments to canoeing and caving for the more adventurous. An excellent multi-lingual children's club runs in July and August. Walking and mountain biking lead from the site through surrounding woodland.

Facilities

Modern, well maintained, clean toilet blocks. Washing machines, dryers. Good shop, Bar with WiFi and terrace, Takeaway, Superb restaurant, Attractive swimming pool, paddling pool, sun terrace, (all open all season) Fishing lake. Tennis. Boules. Playground. Discos twice weekly in high season. Pets are not accepted. Off site: Supermarkets, banks, etc. at Sarlat 10 km. Bicycle hire and riding 10 km. Golf 15 km.

Open: 7 May - 25 September.

Directions

Site is 10 km. west of Sarlat la Canéda, on south side of D47 Sarlat - Les Eyzies road. GPS: N44:54.516 E01:06.883

Charges 2009

Per pitch incl. 2 persons and electricity	€ 19,00 - € 33,00
incl. full services	€ 23,00 - € 37,00
extra person	€ 5,00 - € 9,50
child (3-7 yrs)	free - € 4,50

Camping Cheques accepted.

Check real time availability and at-the-gate prices...

www.alanrogers.com

FR24090 Domaine de Soleil Plage

Mobile homes ▶ page 504

Caudon par Montfort, Vitrac, F-24200 Sarlat-la-Canéda (Dordogne)

Tel: 05 53 28 33 33. Email: info@soleilplage.fr

www.alanrogers.com/FR24090

This site is in one of the most attractive sections of the Dordogne valley, with a riverside location. The site has 199 pitches, in three sections, with 104 for touring units. The smallest section surrounds the main reception and other facilities. There are 40 mobile homes, 20 chalets and 17 bungalow tents. The site offers river bathing from a sizeable pebble or sand bank. All pitches are bounded by hedges and are of adequate size. Most pitches have some shade and have electricity and many have water and drainage. If you like a holiday with lots going on, you will like this one. Various activities are organised during high season including walks and sports tournaments, and daily canoe hire is available from the site. Once a week in July and August there is a 'soirée' (charged for) usually involving a barbecue or paella, with band and lots of free wine – worth catching! The site is busy and reservation is advisable. Used by a UK tour operators (35 pitches). English is spoken. The site is quite expensive in high season and you also pay more for a riverside pitch, but these have fine river views.

Facilities

Toilet facilities are in three modern unisex blocks. You will need to borrow a plug for the baby bath (€ 5 deposit). Washing machines and dryer. Motorcaravan service point. Well stocked shop. Pleasant bar with TV. Attractive, newly refurbished restaurant with terrace. Very impressive main pool, paddling pool, spa pool and two water slides. Tennis. Minigolf. Playground. Fishing. Canoe and kayak hire. Bicycle hire. Currency exchange. Small library. Off site: Golf 1 km. Riding 5 km.

Open: 1 April - 30 September.

Directions

Site is 6 km. south of Sarlat. From A20 take exit 55 (Souillac) towards Sarlat. Follow the D703 to Carsac and on to Montfort. At Montfort castle turn left for 2 km. down to the river.
GPS: N44:49.500 E01:15.233

Charges guide

Per person	€ 4,50 - € 7,00
child (2-9 yrs)	€ 2,50 - € 4,50
pitch incl. electricity	€ 9,00 - € 15,50
incl. full services	€ 12,00 - € 23,00

Camping Cheques accepted.

Take advantage of our prices in low season to enjoy our heated pool & the beautiful scenery from your chalet or your pitch along the river

Right on the Dordogne riverside
(Sand beach, swimming, fishing, canoeing) An exceptional site, 6 km from Sarlat mediaeval town. In the heart of Périgord beautiful landscapes & castles

Many quality facilities for couples, families or groups: Mini-mart (fresh bread & croissants), restaurant périgourdin, pizzeria, take-away, bar, meeting room. Numerous activities: heated pool complex, tennis, mini-golf, multi-sport pitch, hiking, cycling, golf (1 km), riding (5 km), numerous visits (caves, castles, vines, farms...)

English fluently spoken

Domaine de Soleil Plage****
Caudon par Montfort, VITRAC, 24200 SARLAT
Tel: +33 5 53 28 33 33 - Fax: +33 5 53 28 30 24
www.soleilplage.fr - GPS: 44° 49' 30N - 1° 15' 14E

Awards
Alan Rogers Welcome Award
ANWB Camping of the Year

Check real time availability and at-the-gate prices...
www.alanrogers.com

BOOK THIS SITE · The Travel Service · CALL 01580 214000 · ...we'll arrange everything

FR24060 Camping le Paradis

Saint Léon-sur-Vézère, F-24290 Montignac (Dordogne)

Tel: 05 53 50 72 64. Email: le-paradis@perigord.com   www.alanrogers.com/FR24060

Le Paradis is a well maintained riverside site, halfway between Les Eyzies and Montignac. Well situated for exploring places of interest in the Dordogne region, the site is very well kept and laid out with mature shrubs and bushes of different types. It has 200 individual pitches of good size on flat grass, divided by trees and shrubs (148 for touring units). All have electricity, water and drainage, and there are some special pitches for motorcaravans. At the far end of the site, steps down to the Vézère river give access for canoe launching and swimming. The site welcomes a good quota of Dutch and British visitors, many through a tour operator. Organised games, competitions and evening events are aimed at maintaining a true French flavour. English is spoken. This is a site of real quality, which we thoroughly recommend.

Facilities

High quality, well equipped, heated toilet blocks (unisex), baby baths and toilets,. Well stocked shop (with gas). Good restaurant, takeaway. Good pool complex heated in low season, paddling pool. Play area. Tennis. BMX track. Multisport court. Canoe hire. Fishing. Bicycle hire. Quad bike and horse riding excursions. Off site: Riding 3 km. Various trips organised to surrounding area.

Open: 31 May - 30 September.

Directions

Site is 12 km. north of Les Eyzies and 3 km. south of St Léon-sur-Vézère, on the east side of the D706. GPS: N45:00.124 E01:04.266

Charges guide

Per unit incl. 2 persons	€ 17,50 - € 26,00
extra person	€ 5,20 - € 7,20
child (3-12 yrs)	€ 4,20 - € 6,20
electricity (10A)	€ 3,50

10% discount for pensioners in low season.
Camping Cheques accepted.

Camping Le Paradis

Camping Le Paradis - 24290 St. Leon sur Vézère
tel.: 05 53 50 72 64 - fax: 05 53 50 75 90 - le-paradis@perigord.com - www.le-paradis.com

FR24100 Camping le Moulinal

F-24540 Biron (Dordogne)

Tel: 05 53 40 84 60. Email: lemoulinal@perigord.com   www.alanrogers.com/FR24100

A rural, lakeside site in woodland, Le Moulinal offers activities for everyone of all ages. Of the 280 grassy pitches, only around 62 are available for touring units and these are spread amongst the site's own mobile homes, chalets and a small number of British tour operator tents. All pitches are flat, grassy and have 6A electricity, but vary considerably in size (75-100 sq.m). The five-acre lake has a sandy beach and is suitable for boating (canoe hire available), swimming and fishing. Ambitious, well organised animation is run throughout the season including craft activities and a children's club.

Facilities

Toilet facilities, built to harmonise with the surroundings, include facilities for disabled people and babies. Washing machines, dryers. Motorcaravan services. Excellent restaurant. Bar. Snack bar/takeaway. Large, heated swimming pool with jacuzzi and paddling pool. Rustic play area. Multisport court. Boules. Tennis. Archery. Roller skating. Mountain bike hire. All facilities are open all season. Off site: Riding and climbing 5 km. Potholing 10 km. Bastide towns of Monpazier, Villeréal and Monflanquin 15 km.

Open: 1 April - 16 September.

Directions

Site is 53 km. southeast of Bergerac. From D104 Villeréal - Monpazier road take the D53/D150 south. Just before Lacapelle Biron turn right onto D255 towards Dévillac, (site signed). Site is 1.5 km. on the left. GPS: N44:35.988 E00:52.249

Charges guide

Per pitch incl. 2 persons and electricity	€ 20,00 - € 43,00

Camping Cheques accepted.

Check real time availability and at-the-gate prices...

www.alanrogers.com

FR24080 Village Center le Moulin de David

Gaugeac, F-24540 Monpazier (Dordogne)

Tel: 08 25 00 20 30. Email: contact@village-center.com   www.alanrogers.com/FR24080

Set in a 14 hectare wooded valley, it has 160 pitches split into two sections, 102 are available for touring units – 33 below the central reception complex in a shaded situation, and 69 above on partly terraced ground with varying degrees of shade. All pitches have electricity (3/6/10A). Spacing is good and there is no crowding. The site has been attractively planted with a pleasing variety of shrubs and trees and combined with the small stream that runs through the centre of the site they create a beautiful and tranquil setting. Purchased in 2006 by Village Centre Group, this pleasant and attractive site is one for those who enjoy peace, away from the hustle and bustle of the main Dordogne attractions, yet sufficiently close for them to be accessible. There is a delightful wooded walk via a long distance footpath (GR36) to Château Biron, about 2-3 km. distance.

Facilities

Three good toilet blocks, including facilities for visitors with disabilities, and babies. New mobile home. Laundry room. Good shop. Bar/restaurant with shaded patio, takeaway. Swimming pool and paddling pool, freshwater pool with waterslide. Play area. Boules. Half-court tennis. Trampoline. Library. Bicycle hire. Events, games and canoe trips. Off site: Small supermarket and ATM in Monpazier 2.5 km.

Open: 17 May - 13 September.

Directions

From Monpazier take the D2 Villeréal road. Take third turning left (after about 2 km), signed to Moulin de David and Gaugeac Mairie. Site is about 500 m. along this road on the left. GPS: N44:39.569 E00:52.739

Charges guide

Per person (over 5 yrs)	€ 5,00
pitch incl. water and drainage	€ 16,00 - € 32,00

Le Moulin de David ★★★★

Monpazier Gaugeac > Dordogne

- A verdant camp site close to nature
- An artificial lake fed by natural spring

Villagecenter

BOOK YOUR HOLIDAYS
www.village-center.com
+33 (0)4 99 57 21 21

QUALITE TOURISME   Camping Qualité   La Clef Verte

FR24120 Camping la Plage

F-24230 Saint Seurin-de-Prats (Dordogne)

Tel: 05 53 58 61 07. Email: info@camping-in-france.net   www.alanrogers.com/FR24120

This is a beautiful site where the natural environment blends in perfect harmony with nature. It is more like a park than a campsite with a differing array of trees and shrubs. Camping la Plage nestles gently beside the River Dordogne where there is a feeling of spaciousness, tranquillity and calm. The owners are friendly and helpful and are keen to ensure you enjoy your holiday. The 85 pitches are generous in size with some being open and some shaded, and 15A electricity is provided. They are separated by shrubs and hedges. Access for motorcaravans and large units does not cause a problem.

Facilities

Two traditional style sanitary blocks. No facilities for visitors with disabilities. Bar (all year) and restaurant (April-Oct). Takeaway. TV. Swimming pool. Pétanque. Play area. Private access to the river. Fishing. Communal barbecues only. Off site: Golf 12 km. Riding 6 km.

Open: 15 May - 15 September (gites longer).

Directions

Take the D936 from Bergerac to Bordeaux. Bypass St Foy Le Grande and a few kilometres further on is a roundabout with St Seurin de Prats on the left. Take that road and site is on the right, well signed. GPS: N44:49.323 E00:04.501

Charges guide

Per unit incl. 2 persons	€ 15,00 - € 18,50
extra person	€ 4,00 - € 6,00
child (under 7 yrs)	€ 3,00 - € 4,00
electricity (15A)	€ 4,00

287

FR24110 Village Center Caravaning Aqua Viva

Route Sarlac-Souillac, Carsac-Aillac, F-24200 Sarlat-la-Canéda (Dordogne)

Tel: 05 53 31 46 00. Email: contact@village-center.com   www.alanrogers.com/FR24110

This shaded woodland site is ideally situated for visits to Rocamadour and Padirac, as well as exploring the Dordogne region, including the medieval town of Sarlat, only 7 km. away. The site is divided into two sections, separated by a small access road. Pitches are flat, mainly on grass, divided by shrubs and they vary from average to large size. Many have shade from the numerous trees. All have electricity (6/10A). A wide range of organised activities, children's clubs and entertainments run throughout the season, making this site popular with families, especially those with pre-teen and younger teenage children. One small tour operator uses the site, but it attracts a good mixture of nationalities, resulting in a very international ambience. English is spoken.

Facilities

Each part of the site has a modern toilet block, with facilities for disabled people and babies. Bar, restaurant/takeaway with terrace. Good shop. Heated swimming pool, children's pool. Small fishing lake. Minigolf. Half tennis. Good play park for under 7s. Floodlit boules pitch and multisport court. Bicycle hire. Off site: Aerial woodland assault course 500 m. Riding and golf 5 km.

Open: 24 April - 16 September.

Directions

Site is 7 km. from Sarlat south of the D704A road from Sarlat to Souillac. From Souillac, the access road to the site is just around a left hand bend, not easy to see. GPS: N44:52.046 E01:16.765

Charges guide

Per person	€ 5,00
child (0-7 yrs)	€ 4,00
pitch incl. electricity (6/10A)	€ 16,00 - € 30,00
animal	€ 3,00

Altavia Link

Aqua Viva ★★★★
Carsac-Aillac > Dordogne

- Very natural camp site
- Pitches surrounding an artificial lake

Villagecenter
BOOK YOUR HOLIDAYS
www.village-center.com
+33 (0)4 99 57 21 21

QUALITÉ TOURISME   Camping Qualité

FR24170 Camping le Port de Limeuil

F-24480 Allès-sur-Dordogne (Dordogne)

Tel: 05 53 63 29 76. Email: didierbonvallet@aol.com   www.alanrogers.com/FR24170

At the confluence of Dordogne and Vézère rivers, opposite the picturesque village of Limieul, this delightful family site exudes a peaceful and relaxed ambience. There are 65 marked touring pitches on grass, some spacious and all with electricity (5A). The buildings are in traditional Périgourdine style and surrounded by flowers and shrubs. A sports area on a large open grassy space between the river bank and the main camping area adds to the feeling of space and provides an additional recreation and picnic area (there are additional unmarked pitches for tents and camper vans along the bank here).

Facilities

Two clean, modern toilet blocks provide excellent facilities. Bar/restaurant with snacks and takeaway (all 20/5-5/9). Small shop. Swimming pool with jacuzzi, paddling pool and children's slide (1/5-30/9). Badminton, football and boules. Mountain bike hire. Canoe hire, launched from the site's own pebble beach. WiFi in bar area. Off site: The pretty medieval village of Limeuil 200 m. Riding 1 km. Golf 10 km.

Open: 1 May - 30 September.

Directions

Site is 7 km. south of Le Bugue. From D51/D31E Le Buisson to Le Bugue road turn west towards Limieul. Just before bridge into Limieul, turn left (site signed), across another bridge. Site shortly on the right. GPS: N44:52.878 E00:53.444

Charges 2009

Per pitch incl. 2 persons	€ 14,00 - € 25,40
extra person	€ 4,50 - € 6,50
child (under 10 yrs)	€ 2,50 - € 3,50
electricity (5A)	€ 2,50 - € 3,50
dog	€ 1,40 - € 2,00

FR24130 Camping les Grottes de Roffy

Mobile homes ▶ page 504

Sainte Nathalène, F-24200 Sarlat-la-Canéda (Dordogne)

Tel: 05 53 59 15 61. Email: roffy@perigord.com

www.alanrogers.com/FR24130

BOOK THIS SITE

CALL 01580 214000

...we'll arrange everything

The Travel Service

About five kilometres east of Sarlat, Les Grottes de Roffy is a pleasantly laid out, family site. There are 162 clearly marked pitches, some very large, set on very well kept grass terraces. They have easy access and good views across an attractive valley. Some have plentiful shade, although others are more open, and all have electricity (6A). The reception, bar, restaurant and shop are located within converted farm buildings surrounding a semi-courtyard. The site shop is well stocked with a variety of goods and a tempting epicerie (home made on site) with plenty of ideas for the barbecue and to takeaway. In season there is something for all the family, with evening entertainment (including Jazz and Latin evenings) and daily activities for children. A variety of activities and excursions for all ages includes quad biking, pottery, massage and yoga. Conveniently located for Sarlat and all other Dordogne attractions, this is a good site for families. Used by tour operators.

Facilities

Two toilet blocks with modern facilities are more than adequate. Well stocked shop. Bar and 'gastronomique' restaurant with imaginative and sensibly priced menu. Takeaway (all amenities from 6/5). Good swimming pool complex comprising two deep pools (one heated), a fountain, paddling pool and heated jacuzzi. Tennis. Games room. Play area. Entertainment and activities for all ages. Off site: Fishing 2 km. Bicycle hire 7 km. Riding 10 km. Golf 15 km.

Open: 26 April - 21 September.

Directions

Take D47 east from Sarlat to Ste Nathalène. Just before Ste Nathalène the site is signed on the right hand side of the road. Turn here, and the site is about 800 m. along the lane.
GPS: N44:54.242 E01:16.926

Charges guide

Per person	€ 5,50 - € 7,20
child (2-7 yrs)	€ 4,00 - € 5,50
pitch	€ 7,10 - € 10,30
incl. electricity	€ 9,80 - € 13,10
with full services	€ 11,80 - € 15,10

les Grottes de **Roffy** camping caravaning
★ ★ ★ ★
Sainte-Nathalèle • 24200 Sarlat • France
E-mail roffy@perigord.com   Tél. +33 (0)5 53 59 15 61 • Fax +33 (0)5 53 31 09 11

FR24180 Camping Caravaning Saint-Avit Loisirs

Le Bugue, F-24260 Saint Avit-de-Vialard (Dordogne)

Tel: 05 53 02 64 00. Email: contact@saint-avit-loisirs.com

www.alanrogers.com/FR24180

Although Saint Avit Loisirs is set in the middle of rolling countryside, far from the hustle and bustle of the main tourist areas of the Dordogne the facilities are first class, providing virtually everything you could possibly want without the need to leave the site. This makes it ideal for families with children of all ages. The site is in two sections. One part is dedicated to chalets and mobile homes, whilst the main section of the site contains 199 flat and mainly grassy, good sized pitches, 99 for touring, with electricity (6A), arranged in cul-de-sacs off a main access road.

Facilities

Three modern unisex toilet blocks provide high quality facilities, but could become overstretched (particularly laundry and dishwashing sinks) in high season. Shop, bar, restaurant, cafeteria. Outdoor swimming pool, children's pool, water slide, 'crazy river', heated indoor pool with jacuzzi, fitness room. Soundproofed disco. Minigolf. Boules. BMX track. Tennis. Play area. Canoe trips and other sporting activities. Good walks. Off site: Sarlat and Périgeux for markets and hypermarkets.

Open: 1 April - 27 September.

Directions

Site is 6 km. north of Le Bugue. From D710 Le Bugue - Périgueux road, turn west on narrow and bumpy C201 towards St Avit-de-Vialard. Follow road through St Avit, bearing right and site is 1.5 km.
GPS: N44:57.082 E00:50.825

Charges guide

Per person	€ 4,00 - € 9,70
pitch	€ 6,20 - € 14,00
incl. electricity	€ 10,10 - € 19,30
incl. water and drainage	€ 12,90 - € 22,90

Check real time availability and at-the-gate prices...
www.alanrogers.com

FR24140 Camping Bel Ombrage

F-24250 Saint Cybranet (Dordogne)

Tel: 05 53 28 34 14. Email: belombrage@wanadoo.fr

www.alanrogers.com/FR24140

Bel Ombrage is a quiet, well maintained site located in a pretty location by the little River Céou, with a pebble beach that is safe and clean for bathing. The site has a good pool complex, but otherwise there are few on site facilities. The 180 well shaded, good sized and flat grass pitches are marked by trees and bushes and all with electricity. The quiet and tranquil setting makes the site particularly popular with couples. Bel Ombrage is very close to Domme and Castelnaud and would make an ideal and inexpensive base for visiting the southern Dordogne area. It is a short walk to the village of St Cybranet, with bar, restaurant and a small well stocked supermarket, and a short drive takes you to the beautifully restored village of Daglan.

Facilities

Two modern toilet blocks are kept spotlessly clean, with facilities for disabled visitors and babies. Laundry facilities. Bread van. Large swimming pool with sun terrace, children's pool. Paddling pool. Play area. Games room. Fishing. Excursions can be booked at reception. Off site: Pizzeria next door. Tennis and canoeing close. Riding and bicycle hire 3 km. Golf 6 km. More shops at Cénac.

Open: 1 June - 5 September.

Directions

Site is about 14 km. south of Sarlat, on the east side of the D57 Castelnaud-la-Chapelle - St Cybranet road, about 1 km. north of the junction with the D50. GPS: N44:47.442 E01:09.740

Charges 2009

Per person	€ 5,30
child (under 7 yrs)	€ 3,30
pitch	€ 7,00
electricity (10A)	€ 3,80

No credit cards.

Bel Ombrage camping-caravaning

24250 St. Cybranet • Tel: 0033 (0)553 28 34 14 • Fax: 0033 (0)553 59 64 64
E-mail: belombrage@wanadoo.fr • www.belombrage.com

FR24220 Camping Domaine des Chênes Verts

Route de Sarlat, F-24370 Calviac-en-Périgord (Dordogne)

Tel: 05 53 59 21 07. Email: chenes-verts@wanadoo.fr

www.alanrogers.com/FR24220

This peaceful countryside family campsite is set in a beautiful area of the Dordogne valley, and is complemented by the renovated Périgourdine farm buildings which house the amenities at the centre of the site. The spacious grounds which contain many trees provide 143 pitches on either side of the main buildings, of which 63 are for touring units. Most of the good sized, grassy pitches are shaded, and all are separated by hedging. There is electricity (6A) to all pitches, and water points nearby. The majority of pitches are large and level but some are gently sloping.

Facilities

Two fully equipped unisex toilet blocks include washbasins in cabins, dishwashing and laundry areas. Washing machine. Small shop (fresh bread daily), bar, snack bar and takeaway. Motorcaravan service point. Fridge hire. Gas supplies. Medium sized swimming pool with large sunbathing area (15/6-15/9), covered, heated pool (1/4-20/9) and paddling pool. Play area. Multisport court. Animation for children. TV and games room. Charcoal barbecues provided. Off site: Forest walks and cycle tracks lead from the site.

Open: 1 May - 28 September.

Directions

From D704 Sarlat - Gourdon road turn east on D704A towards Souillac and Calviac (this turning is about 3.5 km. from Sarlat). Site is about 5 km. along this road on the left. GPS: N44:51.794 E01:17.824

Charges guide

Per person	€ 3,75 - € 4,70
child (under 7 yrs)	€ 2,15 - € 2,70
pitch incl. electricity	€ 11,70 - € 13,90
dog	€ 1,75 - € 2,20

FR24150 **Camping les Deux Vallées**

La Gare, F-24220 Vézac (Dordogne)

Tel: 05 53 29 53 55. Email: les2v@perigord.com

www.alanrogers.com/FR24150

This site is enviably situated almost under the shadow of Beynac castle in the heart of the Dordogne. There are 96 flat marked touring pitches, most of a good size, some large, and with electricity (6/10A). There is plenty of shade and the general feel is of unspoilt but well managed woodland. There is a small fishing lake on site and it is only a short distance to the Dordogne river for bathing or canoeing. The site is being steadily upgraded by its Dutch owners who provide a warm and friendly welcome. English is spoken. This site would be ideal for those wanting a quiet and relatively inexpensive base from which to visit the Dordogne region, particularly in low season, as the site has the advantage of being open all year.

Facilities	Directions
The modern unisex, clean toilet blocks (one heated) have facilities for disabled visitors and babies. Shop, bar/restaurant with takeaway (24/4-30/10). Good sized pool complex (24/4-30/9). Minigolf. Boules. Play area. Games room. Fishing. Entertainment including quiz nights and barbecues (July/Aug). Off site: Bicycle hire 0.2 km. Riding 2 km. Golf 8 km. Lake beach 450 m.	Leave A20 at exit 55 and follow D804 to Sarlat. From Sarlat continue onto the D57 towards Beynac-et-Cazenac and directly after village sign for Vézac take first right turn to site. GPS: N44:50.136 E01:09.524

Open: All year.

Charges guide

Per person	€ 3,20 - € 5,20
child (0-18 yrs)	€ 0,20 - € 5,20
pitch	€ 4,00 - € 6,75
electricity (6A)	€ 3,50
animal	€ 1,00 - € 1,50

Dutch/French owned, idyllic in nature 8 kms from Sarlat.
450 m from Dordogne riverside and château Beynac.
Canoeing and walking trails.
Comfortable Chalets and Mobil homes and Caravan storage.

Caroline & Derrick
www.les-2-vallees.com
GPS: 44.8356/1.15873 (lat.long)

Open all year

FR24230 **Camping le Moulin de Paulhiac**

F-24520 Daglan (Dordogne)

Tel: 05 53 28 20 88. Email: Francis.Armagnac@wanadoo.fr

www.alanrogers.com/FR24230

You will be guaranteed a friendly welcome from the Armagnac family, who are justifiably proud of their well-kept and attractive site, built in the grounds surrounding an old mill. The 150 shady pitches (98 for touring) are separated by hedges and shrubs, all fully serviced. Many pitches are next to a stream that runs through the site and joins the River Ceou along the far edge. A tent field slopes gently down to the river, which is quite shallow and used for bathing. This site will appeal especially to families with younger children. Used by a tour operator (44 pitches).

Facilities	Directions
Two clean toilet blocks provide modern facilities, including those for visitors with disabilities. Good shop, restaurant, takeaway. Main pool, heated and covered by a sliding roof in low season, children's pool, a further small pool and two slides. Boules. Bicycle hire. Canoe trips organised on the Dordogne. Organised evening activities. Children's club in high season.	Site is about 17 km. south of Sarlat, and is on the east side of the D57, about 5 km. north of the village of Daglan. GPS: N44:46.057 E01:10.581

Open: 15 May - 15 September.

Charges guide

Per person	€ 6,75
child (2-10 yrs)	€ 4,95
pitch incl. electricity	€ 20,50 - € 24,00
dog	€ 1,80
Special offers in low season.	

291

FR24160 Camping le Grand Dague

Mobile homes ▶ page 504

Route du Grand Dague, Atur, F-24750 Périgueux (Dordogne)

Tel: 05 53 04 21 01. Email: info@legranddague.fr

www.alanrogers.com/FR24160

Le Grand Dague is close to Périgueux, in a rural and tranquil setting. Built on a hillside, the site is clean, attractive and very spacious and 68 of the 93 pitches are for touring units. The pitches are only slightly sloping and are divided by tall, mature hedging (electricity 6A). There is a large field suitable for large motorhomes. Those with disabilities might find the roads quite steep. Several large, open grassy areas provide space for youngsters to play. A good range of equipment in the play area helps make this an ideal site for young families.

Facilities

Excellent, part heated sanitary facilities include a baby room and facilities for people with disabilities. Small shop (15/6-15/9). Bar, attractive restaurant with appetising menu and takeaway (both from June). Swimming pool, water slide and paddling pool (from early May). Pétanque. Minigolf. Play area. Fishing. Off site: Paintball outside gate. Riding 5 km. Bicycle hire 8 km. Golf 10 km.

Open: 28 April - 15 September.

Directions

From the Bordeaux - Brive inner ring road in Périgueux take D2 south, signed Atur. Campsite signed. Turn east at roundabout just before entering Atur. Site is in 3 km. GPS: N45:08.880 E00:46.657

Charges guide

Per unit incl. 2 persons and electricity	€ 17,50 - € 27,00
extra person	€ 4,50 - € 6,75
child (0-7 yrs)	€ 3,00 - € 4,50
animal	€ 2,00

LE GRAND DAGUE ★ ★ ★ ★

A campsite set in one of the most beautiful and green parts of the Dordogne region, with a magnificent view over the surrounding countryside. The site is easily accessed and is ideal for all manner of sports, jogging and excellent bicycle rides. The campsite is centrally situated in a perfect spot for exploring the entire Dordogne region. The spacious pitches have water and electricity plus we have brand new luxury mobile homes waiting for you or you may prefer to choose for a fully equipped, spacious bungalow tent. The campsite has a large swimming pool and a shallow children's pool, a restaurant with many local specialities and a well-stocked grocery shop. Open from 31 May to 30 September 2009.

Address: 24750 Atur/Périgueux   Tel. 0033(0)553 042 101, Fax. 0033(0)553 042 201
Website: www.legranddague.fr

FR24250 Camping les Tourterelles

F-24390 Tourtoirac (Dordogne)

Tel: 05 53 51 11 17. Email: les-tourterelles@tiscali.fr

www.alanrogers.com/FR24250

This is a well maintained, Dutch owned site with its own equestrian centre that will appeal to lovers of the countryside, in an area that is ideal for walking or horse riding, yet is within easy reach of Périgueux and the better known sights of the Dordogne. There are 125 pitches in total, but the site has some chalets, bungalows and mobile homes which leaves around 88 grassy pitches for tourists. These are on several different levels most with good shade from mature trees and all have electricity hook-ups (6A). In low season the site can organise tours to local walnut farms, dairies etc. Rallies are welcome and themed programmes can be arranged.

Facilities

Three good, fully equipped toilet blocks include facilities for disabled visitors and a baby unit. Laundry. Bread to order. Bar/restaurant serving good value meals, with takeaway. Freezer pack service. Swimming pool (20 x 10 m.) and paddling pool. Riding. Tennis. Badminton. Children's club and comprehensive activity and entertainment programme in main season. Off site: Shop at Tourtoirac 1 km. Supermarket at Hautefort 6 km. Fishing 1 km. Bicycle hire 6 km.

Open: 16 April - 30 September.

Directions

Site is 46 km. northeast of Périgueux. From Périgueux, take D5 east to Tourtoirac. Turn north onto D67 on entering village (site signed) and shortly fork left on D73 towards Coulaures; site is on left in 1 km. GPS: N45:16.833 E01:02.913

Charges guide

Per pitch incl. 2 persons, car and electricity	€ 15,00 - € 25,00
extra person	€ 3,00 - € 4,20
child (under 13 yrs)	free - € 3,50
animal	free - € 4,00

Low season discounts for over 55s.
No credit cards.

BOOK THIS SITE
CALL 01580 214000
...we'll arrange everything
The Travel Service

292
Check real time availability and at-the-gate prices...
www.alanrogers.com

FR24300 Flower Camping la Rivière Fleurie

Saint Aulaye de Breuilh, F-24230 Saint Antoine-de-Breuilh (Dordogne)

Tel: 05 53 24 82 80. Email: info@la-riviere-fleurie.com   www.alanrogers.com/FR24300

This quiet and pleasant campsite is close to the vineyards of Pomerol and St Emilion, and not far from the extensive shopping of St Foy la Grande and Bergerac. The 60 pitches are all spacious, divided by shrubs and maturing trees are beginning to provide shade. All pitches have electricity (4/10A) There are no tour operators, but 14 pitches are used for site owned mobile home, and there are also studio apartments to let throughout the year. The site has a tranquil and peaceful ambience, suitable for anyone looking for a quiet and relaxing holiday.

Facilities

Sanitary facilities are plentiful and modern (no toilet paper). Bar and terrace restaurant serving a range of basic meals. Swimming pool (100 sq.m) and toddlers' pool. Football, volleyball, table football and TV room. Weekly 'soirées' where the owners host an evening of French food and entertainment. Canoe trips arranged. Off site: Municipal tennis court adjacent (free to campers). Fishing 100 m. Riding 4 km. Bicycle hire 8 km.

Open: 1 April - 30 September.

Directions

Site is in St Aulaye, about 3 km. south of D936 Bordeaux - Bergerac road. 6 km. east of Lamothe-Montravel turn south on local roads and follow signs to site 150 m. from river.
GPS: N44:49.743 E00:07.343

Charges guide

Per unit incl. 2 persons	€ 14,50 - € 18,00
extra person	€ 4,50 - € 5,50
child (under 7 yrs)	€ 2,80 - € 3,50
electricity	€ 3,10 - € 4,50

FR24290 Camping le Moulin du Bleufond

Avenue Aristide Briand, F-24290 Montignac (Dordogne)

Tel: 05 53 51 83 95. Email: le.moulin.du.bleufond@wanadoo.fr   www.alanrogers.com/FR24290

Built on flat ground around a 17th century mill, this former municipal site has its own pool and is nearby town sporting facilities. The 83 pitches (66 for touring units) are marked and divided by mature hedges, all have electricity and most have some shade. Pitches vary considerably in size. The small town of Montignac is only five minutes' walk, with shops, restaurants and bars. The site is separated from the river by a reasonably quiet road; there is a sizeable bank for fishing. This is an ideal base from which to visit a fascinating and beautiful part of the Périgord.

Facilities

Modern, clean, heated sanitary facilities are well cared for. Bread and a few essentials available at reception. Bar, snack bar, terrace restaurant (all season). Heated swimming pool, paddling pool. Sauna. Games room with table games and giant TV. Canoe trips and bicycle hire. Musical evenings weekly in high season. WiFi. Off site: Shops, supermarkets, bars and a range of restaurants in the town only 5 minutes' walk away.

Open: 1 April - 15 October.

Directions

Site is just south of Montignac, on D65 to Sergeac. Just after crossing stone bridge on one way system in centre of town turn sharp right (allow for a wide sweep!) The site is 750 m. on left.
GPS: N45:03.444 E01:09.888

Charges guide

Per person	€ 3,98 - € 5,30
pitch	€ 4,72 - € 6,30
electricity (10A)	€ 3,20

FR24310 Camping Caravaning la Bouquerie

F-24590 Saint Geniès-en-Périgord (Dordogne)

Tel: 05 53 28 98 22. Email: labouquerie@wanadoo.fr   www.alanrogers.com/FR24310

La Bouquerie is a well maintained site, situated within easy reach of the main road network in the Dordogne, but without any associated traffic noise. The main complex is based around some beautifully restored Périgordin buildings. It includes a shop and a bar and restaurant overlooking the pool complex, with a large outdoor terrace for fine weather. The excellent restaurant menu is varied and reasonably priced. Of the 180 pitches, 91 are used for touring units and these are of varying size (80-120 sq.m), flat and grassy, some with shade, and all with electrical connections (10A).

Facilities

Three well maintained toilet blocks with facilities for disabled visitors and baby rooms. Washing machines and covered drying lines. Small shop (15/5-15/9), takeaway food. Bar, restaurant (both 15/5-15/9). Paddling pool, large shallow pool (heated), large deep pool, sunbathing areas with loungers. Carp fishing in lake on site. Bicycle hire. Riding. Off site: Shops and restaurants, etc. in the nearby village of St Geniès.

Open: 19 April - 19 September.

Directions

Site is signed on east side D704 Sarlat - Montignac, about 500 m. north of junction with D64 St Geniès road. Turn off D704 at campsite sign and take first left turn signed La Bouquerie - site is straight ahead.
GPS: N44:59.919 E01:14.729

Charges guide

Per pitch incl. 2 persons and electricity	€ 19,00 - € 25,50
extra person	€ 4,60 - € 6,50

BOOK THIS SITE
CALL 01580 214000
...we'll arrange everything
The Travel
Service
www.flowercampings.com

Check real time availability and at-the-gate prices...
www.alanrogers.com

FR24320 Camping les Peneyrals

Mobile homes ▶ page 505

Le Poujol, F-24590 Saint Crépin-Carlucet (Dordogne)

Tel: 05 53 28 85 71. Email: camping.peneyrals@wanadoo.fr

www.alanrogers.com/FR24320

Within easy reach of all the attractions of the Périgord region, M. and Mme. Havel have created an attractive and friendly family campsite at Les Peneyrals. There are 199 pitches, 80 of which are for touring. The pitches at the bottom of the hill tend to be quieter as they are further from the main facilities, but are all level and grassy (some on terraces), with electricity (5/10A), and most have some shade. An attractive bar and restaurant with terrace overlook the excellent pool complex and at the bottom of the site is a small fishing lake. The site is set on a wooded hillside, with flowers in abundance (thanks to the dedication of Mme. Havel's mother). Activities are organised over a long season, including archery, various sports tournaments, aquagym, discos and a children's club. It is used fairly unobtrusively by a UK tour operator (70 pitches).

Facilities

Two modern, unisex toilet blocks provide good quality facilities, including provision for babies and disabled visitors. Motorcaravan services. Good value shop, excellent restaurant and takeaway. Pool complex with two large pools (one heated), paddling pool and four slides with splash pool. Indoor heated pool. Bicycle hire. Minigolf. Tennis (charged). Badminton. Play area. Games room, TV room and small library. Off site: Supermarkets, banks, etc. in Sarlat 11 km.

Open: 10 May - 13 September.

Directions

Site is 11 km. north of Sarlat. From D704 Sarlat - Montignac road turn east on D60 towards Salignac-Eyvigues. After 4 km. turn south on D56 towards St Crépin-Carlucet. Site is about 500 m. along this road on the right. GPS: N44:57.465 E01:16.374

Charges guide

Per person	€ 4,60 - € 7,60
child (under 7 yrs)	free - € 5,40
pitch	€ 6,70 - € 10,70
electricity (5/10A)	€ 2,00 - € 3,70

10 Km from Sarlat
In the heart of the Périgord!

2 heated swimming pools and heated paddling-pool

Heated sanitary installations (low season)

CHALETS AND MOBIL HOMES FOR HIRE

All facitilies operational from 10th May to 13th September

CAMPING LES PENEYRALS
24590 ST CREPIN-CARLUCET
Tél : 0033.55 32 88 571
Fax : 0033.55 32 88 099

35% Discount in May, June and September

Internet : www.peneyrals.com

FR24330 Camping de l'Etang Bleu

F-24340 Vieux-Mareuil (Dordogne)

Tel: 05 53 60 92 70. Email: marc@letangbleu.com

www.alanrogers.com/FR24330

There are 169 pitches, 151 for touring, with the remainder taken up by site owned mobile homes for rent. The pitches are a good size, flat and grassy, with mature hedging and trees providing privacy and plenty of shade. All pitches have water and 90 have electricity (10/16A). At the bottom of the site is a fishing lake stocked with carp (permit required) and various woodland walks start from the campsite grounds. The bright and cheerful 'bistro bar' provides good value food and drinks, and becomes a focal point for evening socialising on site.

Facilities

Modern well maintained toilet block provides facilities for babies and disabled people. Laundry. Small playground, paddling pool. Swimming pool, sun terrace. Bar with terrace (all season), restaurant (1/6-30/9), poolside bar. Takeaway (1/6-30/9). Small shop. Boules, volleyball, badminton. Canoe and bicycle hire. Entertainments, sporting activities, excursions in high season. Off site: Restaurant 'Auberge de L'Etang Bleu' adjacent to campsite, small supermarket, post office etc. in Mareuil 7 km.

Open: Easter/1 April - 18 October.

Directions

Site is between Angoulême and Périgueux. Leave D939 in Vieux Mareuil, take D93, and follow narrow road. Just after leaving village site signed on right, just past Auberge de L'Etang Bleu. Turn right, follow signs to site. GPS: N45:26.768 E00:30.515

Charges guide

Per person	€ 3,75 - € 5,50
child (2-7 yrs)	€ 1,25 - € 2,00
pitch and car	€ 7,75 - € 9,25
incl. electricity	€ 9,75 - € 13,50
pet	€ 3,00

The Travel Service ...we'll arrange everything
BOOK THIS SITE
CALL 01580 214000

Check real time availability and at-the-gate prices...

www.alanrogers.com

FR24360 Camping le Mondou

F-24370 Saint Julien-de-Lampon (Dordogne)

Tel: 05 53 29 70 37. Email: lemondou@camping-dordogne.info

www.alanrogers.com/FR24360

This quiet and peaceful site mid-way between Sarlat and Souillac is ideally situated for exploring the Dordogne and Lot departments. It is set amongst countryside at the edge of the small village of St Julien and only two kilometres from the Dordogne river. The 62 grassy pitches are of medium to large size, divided by shrubs and with some shade from a wide variety of trees. All have electricity (6A). The friendly and helpful owners, John and Lia, organise regular evening entertainment during high season and they work hard to ensure that everyone enjoys their stay at Le Mondou.

Facilities

Two sanitary blocks provide basic facilities, including facilities for disabled visitors, baby baths, washing machine, ironing board and iron. Terrace bar and snack bar with reasonably priced menu. Restaurant (1/5-1/10). Large swimming pool with sun terrace and children's paddling pool (1/5-30/9). Rustic style play area and large playing field. WiFi. Boules pitch, volleyball/badminton net. Bicycle hire. Off site: Bar, restaurant and small shop in St Julien-de-Lampon about 1 km. away. Fishing 2 km.

Open: 1 April - 15 October.

Directions

Site about 12 km. southwest of Souillac. From D807, at Rouffillac, turn south across the river Dordogne (D61 signed St Julien-de-Lampon). Entering village turn left (D50, signed to Mareuil). Site in 500 m. beyond village. GPS: N44:51.783 E01:22.433

Charges guide

Per person	€ 4,75
pitch	€ 2,00 - € 4,50
electricity (6/10A)	€ 2,75 - € 3,50

No credit cards.

FR24350 RCN le Moulin de la Pique

F-24170 Belvès (Dordogne)

Tel: 05 53 29 01 15. Email: info@rcn-lemoulindelapique.fr

www.alanrogers.com/FR24350

This high quality campsite set in the heart of the Dordogne has fine views looking up to the fortified town of Belves. It is a splendid rural estate where there is plenty of space and a good mixture of trees and shrubs. Set in the grounds of a former mill, the superb traditional buildings date back to the 18th-century. There are 200 level pitches with 154 for touring units, all with 6A electricity, a water point and drainage. The remainder are used for mobile homes to rent. The site is ideally suited for families with young and teenage children as there is so much to do, both on site and in the surrounding area.

Facilities

Three modern sanitary blocks include facilities for people with disabilities. Launderette. Shop. Bar. Restaurant. Snack bar and takeaway. Swimming pools (2 heated). Recreational lake. Playgrounds. Library. Fossil field. Sports field. Tennis. Minigolf. Boules. Satelite TV. Games room. Bicycle hire. Internet facilities. WiFi. Off site: Bars, restaurants and shops in the village of Belvès 2 km. Canoeing 2 km. Riding 5 km. Golf 7 km.

Open: 12 April - 11 October.

Directions

Site is 35 km. southwest of Sarlat on the D710, about 7 km. south of Siorac-en-Périgord. GPS: N44:45.737 E01:00.847

Charges guide

Per pitch incl. 2 persons, electricity and water	€ 18,00 - € 45,50
extra person (over 6 yrs)	€ 5,50

www.rcn-campings.fr

FR24370 Camping le Pech Charmant

F-24620 Les Eyzies-de-Tayac (Dordogne)

Tel: 05 53 35 97 08. Email: info@lepech.com

www.alanrogers.com/FR24370

As the name suggests, this is a charming site set on the top of a hill in the heart of the Périgord Noir, yet just two kilometres from Les Eyzies. The site is on two levels and the lower, quieter level has a superb spacious feeling with touring caravans and tents being positioned around its perimeter, leaving the centre clear. There are 80 level pitches, of which ten are used for mobile homes and two new chalets. The pitches have dappled shade and 10A electricity. Donkey renting is popular with donkeys being used to help out with walks lasting from half a day to three days and more.

Facilities

Modern sanitary block with facilities for disabled visitors. Bar. Restaurant/snack bar. Takeaway. TV, internet access and WiFi in the bar. Swimming and paddling pools. Boules. Play area. Private access to the river. Fishing. Sports field. Only gas barbecues are permitted. American type motorhomes are not accepted. Off site: Bicycle hire 2 km. Riding 3 km. Golf 13 km.

Open: 15 April - 1 October.

Directions

From Les Eyzies head south on the D706 towards Le Bugue. Turn left immediately after the Renault garage and follow road for about 2 km. Site is signed along this road. GPS: N44:55.442 E01:01.789

Charges guide

Per person	€ 3,00 - € 5,50
pitch	€ 6,00 - € 9,00
electricity (10A)	€ 3,00

BOOK THIS SITE
CALL 01580 214000
"...we'll arrange everything"
The Travel Service

Check real time availability and at-the-gate prices...
www.alanrogers.com

FR24380 Camping BleuSoleil

Domaine Touvent, F-24580 Rouffignac-Saint-Cernin (Dordogne)

Tel: 05 53 05 48 30. Email: infos@camping-bleusoleil.com   www.alanrogers.com/FR24380

Camping BleuSoleil is delightfully and quietly located in the countryside and has magnificent views from all areas of the site. It comprises 70 acres and, at present, has 110 pitches, 95 for touring and 15 used for wooden chalets. Electricity is avaliable on every pitch. Set in an open, woody, and hilly area, some of the pitches have partial shade from well sited trees and hedges. There is some terracing. You will receive a warm welcome at BleuSoleil and a comfortable stay. The village of Rouffignac-St Cernin-de-Reilhac, is one kilometre away and is within walking distance.

Facilities

Three modern unisex sanitary blocks are clean, well maintained and adequate for the number of pitches. En-suite toilet for disabled visitors. Baby room with bath. Enclosed laundry area with two washing machines and dryer. Shop, small bar with TV, and restaurant (high season) Large 200 sq.m. swimming pool and paddling pool. New multisports area. Boules. Small play area and a pen with donkeys and goats. Off site: Village facilities 1 km. Fishing 2 km. Riding 4 km.

Open: 3 April - 30 September.

Directions

From Périgueux take N89 east for 17 km. to Thenon, then D31 south signed Balou. Continue from Balou for 3 km. to the outskirts of Rouffignac-St Cernin-de-Reilhac and look for site sign on the left. Turn off main road to site (less than 1 km).
GPS: N45:03.298 E00:59.214

Charges guide

Per person	€ 3,20 - € 4,60
pitch	€ 5,20 - € 6,90
electricity (10A)	€ 3,90

FR24410 Camping Caravaning le Bois du Coderc

Route des Gaunies, F-24420 Antonne-et-Trigonant (Dordogne)

Tel: 05 53 05 99 83. Email: coderc-camping@wanadoo.fr   www.alanrogers.com/FR24410

Located in the scenic Périgord region, ten kilometres from Périgueux, Les Bois du Coderc, under new ownership, has been completely renovated. It is a calm, picturesque, part wooded, riverside site, ideally situated for visiting many interesting places. The touring pitches (there are no individual markedout pitches) and a mobile home are spaced out over a field and woodland, with electricity hook-ups (10A) and water points. This campsite has a calm, relaxing atmosphere. However, it is well placed near the historical town of Périgueux which is rich in history and full of charm and character.

Facilities

One male and female sanitary block with pre-set showers (no charge) clean and well maintained (only one toilet and a shower are open in winter). Baby changing area. Dishwashing area. Laundry facilities. Small shop. Snacks and takeaway. Bar/games room. Small play area. The river Isle runs through the campsite and is suitable for paddling. WiFi. Heated (15/5-15/9) outdoor swimming pool.

Open: 10 January - 20 December.

Directions

Heading north on the N21 Limoges - Périgueux road, 2.5 km. north of Antonne et Trigonant turn right at Routier Restaurant (near km. marker 49). Continue along this road following signs. Travelling south from Limoges direction turn is on left 3 km. south of Sarliac sur L'Isle. GPS: N45:13.166 E00:51.816

Charges 2009

Per person	€ 3,00 - € 3,50
pitch with electricity	€ 8,20 - € 10,00

FR24440 Camping les Acacias

Bourg de la Canéda, F-24200 Sarlat-la-Canéda (Dordogne)

Tel: 05 53 31 08 50. Email: camping-acacias@wanadoo.fr   www.alanrogers.com/FR24440

Only 2.5 km. from the historic medieval town centre of Sarlat, and yet surrounded by peaceful countryside, this campsite is well suited to those seeking a relaxing and peaceful site within easy reach of the major attractions of the Dordogne. The 122 grassy pitches are mostly flat, divided by hedges or trees, with plenty of shade, and all have electricity (6A). The small but welcoming bar and terrace are the focal point for daily events and entertainment during high season, with activities for all ages. A bus service 50 m. from the campsite entrance runs six times daily into Sarlat centre.

Facilities

Two toilet blocks provide clean and comfortable showers, washbasins in cabins, British style toilets, facilities for disabled people, baby bath and children's shower, toilet and washbasin. Laundry facilities. Shop with bread to order. Bar serving snacks and takeaway food (15/5-30/9). Swimming pool and paddling pool (1/5-20/9). Multisport area. Play area. Bicycle hire. Canoe excursions arranged. Off site: Supermarket, bar/restaurant, pizza takeaway all 1.5 km. Golf 2 km. River fishing and riding 3 km.

Open: 1 April - 30 September.

Directions

From Sarlat follow signs for Souillac and Cahors. Pass under impressive stone railway viaduct and take second right signed La Canéda. Follow until small sports field and stadium on the left and bear right into village of La Canéda. Site is signed 500 m. on the right. GPS: N44:51.293 E01:14.260

Charges 2009

Per unit incl. 2 persons	€ 11,00 - € 16,00
extra person	€ 3,50 - € 5,00
electricity	€ 3,00

Check real time availability and at-the-gate prices...

www.alanrogers.com

FR24420 Camping les Valades

D703, F-24220 Coux-et-Bigaroque (Dordogne)

Tel: 05 53 29 14 27. Email: camping.valades@wanadoo.fr www.alanrogers.com/FR24420

Sometimes we come across small but beautifully kept campsites which seem to have been a well kept secret and Les Valades certainly fits the bill. Set on a hillside overlooking countryside between the Dordogne and Vezère rivers each of the 49 touring pitches is surrounded by variety of flowers, shrubs and trees. Pitches are flat and grassy, mostly on terraces, all with electricity (10A) and most with individual water and drainage as well. At the bottom of the hill, away from the main area, is the swimming pool, a good sized lake for carp fishing, swimming or canoeing (free canoes). From the moment you arrive you can see that the owners, M. and Mme. Berger, take enormous pride in the appearance of their campsite, with an abundance of well tended flowers and shrubs everywhere you look. There are also a few well shaded woodland camping pitches.

Facilities

The clean modern toilet block includes facilties for disabled people. Washing machine. Main reception building houses bar, snack bar (both July/Aug), enlarged terrace overlooking valley. Swimming pool, sun terrace, paddling pool (all season). New play area near the lake and pool. Off site: Small shop, bar, restaurant in Coux-et-Bigaroque 5 km. Supermarket at Le Bugue 10 km. Riding and bicycle hire 5 km. Golf 6 km.

Open: 1 April - 15 October.

Directions

Site is signed down a turning on west side of D703 Le Bugue - Siorac-en-Périgord road, about 3.5 km. north of village of Coux-et-Bigaroque. Turn off D703 and site is 1.5 km. along on right. GPS: N44:51.633 E00:57.831

Charges 2009

Per unit incl. 2 persons and electricity	€ 23,50
extra person	€ 5,60
child (0-6 yrs)	€ 3,90
dog	€ 2,90

No credit cards.

24220 Coux et Bigaroque
FRANCE

www.lesvalades.com

FR24460 Flower Camping le Temps de Vivre

F-24590 Salignac-Eyvigues (Dordogne)

Tel: 05 53 28 93 21. Email: contact@temps-de-vivre.com www.alanrogers.com/FR24460

Le Temps de Vivre is situated in the centre of the Périgord Noir, in the countryside and lies about 250 m. above sea level. The area of the campsite covers about four and a half acres in total, with one and a half acres in use at present. It is a small, friendly, family run site with 50 pitches, 30 of which are for touring and 20 for mobile homes. The pitches are wide and terraces separate some of them. All have electricity connections available (10A) and you will find a variety of trees and bushes often as a natural separation. This is a delightful and peaceful rural site.

Facilities

One modern unisex sanitary block, very clean, well maintained, serviced, and adequate for the number of pitches. En-suite toilet for disabled visitors. Baby room with bath. Covered laundry area. Small shop all season in the reception area. Small bar, restaurant and takeaway (July/Aug). Two swimming pools (one for children). Boules. Play area. Off site: Shops and restaurants, etc. within walking distance in the nearby village of Salignac-Eyvigues.

Open: 1 April - 1 November.

Directions

From Brive-La-Gaillarde heading south on the A20 continue for 30 km. to exit 55 signed Souillac. Take D62/D15 northwest for 12 km. until Salignac-Eyvigues. As you drive through the town centre look for blue sign for site. Follow the sign of the main road for about 2 km. GPS: N44:57.804 E01:19.698

Charges guide

Per unit incl. 1 person	€ 11,00 - € 18,50
extra person	€ 2,50 - € 4,50
child (2-7 yrs)	€ 2,00 - € 3,00

www.flowercampings.com

BOOK THIS SITE
CALL 01580 214000
...we'll arrange everything
The Travel Service

297

FR24480 Camping les Tailladis

Marcillac Saint-Quentin, F-24200 Sarlat (Dordogne)

Tel: 05 53 59 10 95. Email: tailladis@wanadoo.fr

www.alanrogers.com/FR24480

Les Tailladis is a well situated, mature campsite of some 17 hectares of woodland, owned by the same Dutch and French family for over 42 years. It is about 12 km. from Sarlat, Eyzies and Montignac-Lascauax, and 35 km. from Souillac. Four hectares of the total provides medium to large pitches which are grassy, terraced and partially shaded, with electricity (6A), and water points close by. There is also a small stream and pond. The access road and campsite roads/tracks are narrow and winding, which may cause difficulties for some larger units. The hosts are welcoming and you will be greeted with a drink and warm, friendly service.

Facilities

One heated sanitary block is well sited for all pitches. En-suite toilet for disabled visitors. Baby bath and changing area. Laundry room. Motorcaravan service point. Large shop (fresh bread and milk can be ordered). Restaurant, bar. Library. Swimming pool and paddling pool. Play area with trampoline. Activities organised during high season. Internet access (charged for). Off site: Riding 3 km. Bicycle hire 12 km. Golf 25 km. Boat launching 25 km.

Open: All year.

Directions

From Sarlat-la-Canéda, take D704 heading north. After 10 km. look for signs on the left for Marcillac St Quentin. Take this road heading northwest, and site is less than 3 km. after Marcillac St Quentin on the left hand side. Access and site roads are narrow for large units. GPS: N44:58.470 E01:11.299

Charges guide

Per person	€ 3,21 - € 5,35
child (3-8 yrs)	€ 2,28 - € 3,80
pitch with electricity	€ 7,77 - € 10,55

FR24470 Flower Camping les Nauves

Le Bos Rouge, F-24170 Belvès (Dordogne)

Tel: 05 53 29 12 64. Email: campinglesnauves@hotmail.com

www.alanrogers.com/FR24470

Les Nauves is a pretty and well maintained site, four kilometres from the beautiful medieval village of Belvès in the Périgord Noir region of the Dordogne. The site consists of 100 pitches, 60 for touring and 40 dedicated to mobile homes, chalets and bungalow tents. There are some pitches that are separated and shaded by mature trees, while others are open with good views of the surrounding countryside. The ground on most of the pitches is soft, sandy soil and may cause some difficulty for large vehicles in wet weather. The owners are very dedicated to providing a quality site.

Facilities

New Chalet. The single sanitary block is clean and well maintained. Facilities for disabled visitors. Baby room (with adult shower). Laundry area with one washing machine. Good shop. Bar/restaurant with patio, and takeaway on request. Swimming pool and paddling pool. Good play area. Boules. Library (French and Dutch books). Games room. Riding. Off site: Fishing 2 km. Golf 10 km. Bicycle hire 4 km.

Open: 29 April - 23 September.

Directions

From Belvès take D53 southwest towards Monpazier. Site is 4 km. from Belvès on the left hand side. Follow signs and site is 800 m. off the main road. GPS: N44:45.130 E00:58.890

Charges guide

Per person	€ 2,50 - € 4,50
child (0-7 yrs)	€ 2,00 - € 3,00
pitch	€ 10,50 - € 16,70
electricity (6A)	€ 3,20

FR24510 Camping les Trois Caupain

Le Port, F-24260 Le Bugue (Dordogne)

Tel: 05 53 07 24 60. Email: info@camping-bugue.com

www.alanrogers.com/FR24510

A superb, mature, ex-municipal site, Les Trois Caupain is less than one kilometre from Le Bugue, which has a range of supermarkets and tourist attractions. The site carefully blends mobile homes and camping pitches and fruiting plum trees abound on the site. The well marked pitches are neat, level and mostly shaded, with water and electricity hook ups close by. The current owners, the three Caupain family members, will do all they can to make your stay a pleasant one. The campsite is less than fifty metres away from the river. Popular with tourists, Le Bugue is a delightful town.

Facilities

Two clean and well maintained sanitary blocks include toilet and shower for disabled people. Excellent laundry room. Baby room with bath. Motorcaravan service point. Small shop selling local produce. Bar with TV. Restaurant with terrace (high season). Heated swimming pool and paddling pool. Play area. Boules. Animation and entertainment in high season. Fishing. Off site: Riding 3 km. Golf 8 km. Supermarkets in Le Bugue.

Open: 1 April - 30 October.

Directions

From Le Bugue, take D703 heading southeast and site is less than 1 km. from the town centre, well signed. Turn right off the main road and site is less than 800 m. along this road on the left. GPS: N44:54.559 E00:55.886

Charges 2009

Per unit incl. 2 persons	€ 12,40 - € 16,50
extra person	€ 3,50 - € 4,75
child (2-12 yrs)	€ 1,90 - € 3,20

BOOK THIS SITE

The Travel Service

CALL 01580 214000

...we'll arrange everything

www.flowercampings.com

FR24530 Camping Port Vieux

1 rue de la Paix, F-24700 Montpon-Ménestérol (Dordogne)

Tel: 05 53 80 22 16. Email: daniel.taillez455@orange.fr   www.alanrogers.com/FR24530

Port Vieux was originally a municipal site established over 25 years ago, but for the last two years, it has been managed by the Terre Océane group. There are 120 pitches, of which 115 are used for touring pitches, most with partial shade and separated by well established hedges. Three mobile homes and two bungalow tents are available to rent. The beautiful river Isle runs through the site, which is within walking distance of the town of Montpon Ménestérol. Also within walking distance there is a tree lined recreational park with a man-made river beach for swimming and paddling.

Facilities

Two sanitary blocks are clean, well maintained and adequate for the number of pitches. En-suite toilet for disabled visitors. Laundry area with washing machine. Bread ordering service, ice cream and cold drinks vending machine. Bar open in the evening with TV (acc. to demand). Small play area. Boules. Fishing. Canoe hire. Off site: Lake beach and large play area, boat hire and bicycle hire 500 m. Good supermarkets less than 1 km. Riding 10 km. Golf 20 km.

Open: 1 April - 30 September.

Directions

From N89 (Périgueux - Bordeaux) exit 12, head north to Montpon Ménestérol on the D708. Look for signs to site, which is just over the river bridge. Entrance to site is on a sharp steep bend to the right. GPS: N45:00.706 E00:09.397

Charges guide

Per unit incl. 2 persons	€ 5,00 - € 9,00
extra person	€ 2,10 - € 3,00
child (under 12 yrs)	€ 1,70 - € 2,50
electricity	€ 3,00

FR24560 Domaine le Cro Magnon

Le Raisse, Allas-les-Mines, F-24220 Saint Cyprien (Dordogne)

Tel: 05 53 29 13 70. Email: contact@domaine-cro-magnon.com   www.alanrogers.com/FR24560

Le Cro Magnon is pleasantly situated in the heart of the Dordogne valley in the Périgord Noir. The 160 spacious, mostly shady pitches are divided in two different types: tent pitches without electricity and serviced pitches (6A electricity hook up, water and waste water drain). The site also offers various accommodation for rent. The swimming complex includes two pools (one outdoor, one indoor), one heated, water slides, a jacuzzi and a sauna. Near the entrance of the site are a snack bar, pizzeria, bar, a well stocked shop and the reception. From a viewpoint on the site there are incredible views over the Dordogne valley.

Facilities

Two toilet blocks provide the usual facilities including facilities for disabled visitors. Washing machines. Motorcaravan services. Shop. Bar with TV. Snack bar and takeaway. Swimming pools with slides, jacuzzi and sauna. Multisport court. Boules. Play area. Off site: Canoeing, walking and cycling. Fishing.

Open: 11 May - 30 September.

Directions

From the A20 (Limoges - Brive) take exit 55 for Souillac and Sarlat. In Sarlat take D57 to Vézac, then D703 to St Cyprien. In St Cyprien follow D703, then D50 (left) to Berbiguières and follow signs for site. GPS: N44:50.165 E01:03.754

Charges guide

Per person (over 4 yrs)	€ 3,40 - € 7,00
pitch	€ 5,00 - € 10,40
incl. services	€ 8,10 - € 17,10

FR24570 Camping la Palombière

Sainte Nathalène, F-24200 Sarlat (Dordogne)

Tel: 05 53 59 42 34. Email: la.palombiere@wanadoo.fr   www.alanrogers.com/FR24570

This site is set in a gorgeous, rural part of France amongst the beauty of the Périgord countryside with its rolling green hills and ancient buildings. The restored and preserved buildings at La Palombière add to the pleasure of this delightful site. It is evident that much investment has gone into making this holiday destination a place to remember. There are 177 pitches of which 88 are for touring caravans and tents. All have electricity (10A) and some are fully serviced. Most are level and shaded from the sun, with some terracing because of the different levels. There are 89 mobile homes with 45 to rent.

Facilities

Two modern sanitary blocks include facilities for babies and disabled people. Laundry facilities. Shop. Bar. Restaurant. Snack bar and takeaway. Heated swimming pool complex with slide and toboggan. Gymnasium. Playgrounds. Library. Sports field. Tennis. Minigolf. Boules. Satellite TV. Games room. Bicycle hire. Internet facilities. WiFi. Off site: Riding 3 km. Canoeing 3 km. Golf 10 km.

Open: 26 April - 14 September.

Directions

Take the D47 east from Sarlat to Ste Nathalène. Site is signed from village and is reached by taking a left turn just beyond it. GPS: N44:54.482 E01:17.527

Charges guide

Per person	€ 4,80 - € 7,30
simple pitch	€ 7,00 - € 10,40
incl. services	€ 11,50 - € 15,10
incl. electricity	€ 9,70 - € 13,40

Check real time availability and at-the-gate prices... www.alanrogers.com

BOOK THIS SITE CALL 01580 214000 ...we'll arrange everything The Travel Service

FR24660 Camping Brin d'Amour

Saint Cirq, F-24260 le Bugue (Dordogne)

Tel: **05 53 07 23 73**. Email: campingbrindamour@orange.fr | www.alanrogers.com/FR24660

This really is one of the most beautiful sites in the Dordogne. Situated in the Périgord Noir with wonderful views across the undulating hills and the Vezere valley. Here there is a feeling of tranquility, spaciousness and calm. The owners offer a welcome and outstanding customer service. Of the 80 pitches, 60 are for touring units and the remaining 20 are for chalets and mobile homes which are all available to rent. All are level, easily accessible and mostly shaded. There is also a pond at the far end of the site. This is a small site where you can relax in a family atmosphere. The main building is of fine traditional Perigordine quality and houses a very attractive restaurant and bar. This is an ideal place from which you can explore the countryside by foot or by bicycle, take an excursion, visit the caves or canoe down the river. With a romantic history, the site's name translates as 'a piece of love'. Definitely a site not to be missed.

Facilities

Modern sanitary block with facilities for disabled visitors and babies. Washing machine. Shop (15/5-20/10). Bar (1/4-15/9). Restaurant and takeaway (1/6-15/9). Swimming and paddling pools (1/4-30/9, heated from 1/5). Tennis. Fishing. Pétanque. Play area. Children's club July and August. Bicycle hire. Electric and charcoal barbecues only. Fridge hire. WiFi. Charcoal barbecues are not permitted. Max. 1 dog per pitch. Off site: Riding 2 km. Canoeing 5 km. Sailing, golf 10 km. Prehistoric Park. Caves.

Open: 1 April - 30 October.

Directions

Take D710 from Perigueux to Le Bugue and 500 m. after Le Bugue entry sign turn sharp left on D32e to St Cirq. Site is signed from here. GPS: N44:56.41 E00:57.36

Charges guide

Per unit incl. 2 persons	€ 12,00 - € 18,00
extra person	€ 3,50 - € 5,00
child (1-10 yrs)	€ 2,50 - € 4,00
electricity	€ 3,00
dog (max. 1)	€ 2,00

Camping Brin d'Amour***

Camping Brin d'Amour*** - 24260 Saint Cirq/Le Bugue
Tél/Fax: 0033 553 07 23 73

campingbrindamour@orange.fr
www.brindamourcamping.com

FR24640 Camping de Nontron

Saint Martial de Valette, F-24300 Nontron (Dordogne)

Tel: **05 53 56 02 04**. Email: camping-de-nontron@orange.fr | www.alanrogers.com/FR24640

Open for almost all the year, this site is ideally situated in the Périgord Vert either as a first stop on route South, or for a much longer stay. This is a neat and well presented site against a background of tall trees. There are 70 pitches of which 60 are for touring units, two are for mobile homes and eight are studios which are all available to rent. All are level with easy access and separated by hedges. A new sports complex has been opened next to the site which includes a swimming pool, toboggan, jacuzzi, sauna, solarium and tennis court and the site sells discounted entry tickets.

Facilities

Well equipped sanitary block with facilities for disabled visitors and babies. Laundry with washing machines and ironing boards. Motorcaravan service point. Shop (1/7-31/8). Takeaway (July/Aug). TV and games room. Boules. Play area. Gas and electric barbecues only on pitches, special areas for charcoal. Off site: New sports complex next to site. Riding, karting 10 km. Bicycle hire 20 km. Golf.

Open: 1 January - 15 December.

Directions

From Angoulême take D939 to Périgueux. Branch left to Nontron on D4, then carry onto D75. After Nontron take D675 towards Brantôme and campsite is 200 m. on the left after entering St Martial de Valette. GPS: N45:30.839 E00:39.475

Charges guide

Per person	€ 3,00
child (under 10 yrs)	€ 1,50
pitch	€ 3,00
electricity (6A)	€ 3,50 - € 4,50

FR24670 Camping les Terrasses du Périgord

Pech-d'Orance, F-24200 Sarlat-la-Canéda (Dordogne)

Tel: 05 53 59 02 25. Email: terrasses-du-perigord@wanadoo.fr

Set on a hill top on the edge of Sarlat, this site has panoramic views acros
105 pitches, of which 90 are for touring units, with the remaining 15 bein
homes for rent. The site is sloping on different levels but the pitches are ge
marked and separated by trees. Electricity is 6, 10 or 16A. For those with la
phone in advance for pitch availability, as not all are suitable. A warm and
by the French owners. An old, fully restored farmhouse fitted out as a bar a
tasting together with a bistro. A well stocked shop is next to the games ro
evening entertainment. This includes Périgordine dancing and shows. The swimming pool and
children's pool have only recently been added and a large playground has a cable slide. There are
many places to visit in the surrounding area. Sarlat is 2 km. away.

Facilities

One modern sanitary block divided into two provides all facilities including those for disabled visitors and babies. Washing machine and dryer. Motorcaravan services. Shop. Bar with snack bar and takeaway. Wine tastings. Swimming pool and toddler's pool. Play area with cable slide. Minigolf. Bicycle hire. Gas and electric barbecues only. Evening entertainment. Off site: Caves. Châteaux. Fishing 2 km. Canoeing 2 km. Riding 8 km.

Open: 27 April - 8 September.

Directions

From Sarlat, take D47 to Proissans. Continue on D56 to Proissans and site is 500 m. on the left. In Sarlat, follow the signs for hospital as it is nearby. GPS: N44:54.372 E01:14.201

Charges guide

Per person	€ 3,80 - € 4,90
child (under 7 yrs)	€ 2,20 - € 2,90
pitch	€ 4,90 - € 6,50
electricity	€ 2,90 - € 4,10

No credit cards.

Camping Les Terrasses du Périgord*

2 km from the medieval city of Sarlat.

Arranged in a former wine field of 6ha bordered with a truffle field on the top of a hill, the panorama is exeptional. Very quiet, the seperated and flowering pitches are shaded, grassy and level with electricity and fountain. Wine tasting in wine cellar.

3229 Les Terrasses du Périgord - 24200 SARLAT - France - Tel: (33) 05 53 59 02 25
Fax: (33) 05 53 59 16 48 - terrasses-du-perigord@wanadoo.fr - www.terrasses-du-perigord.com

FR24690 Yelloh! Village Lascaux Vacances

F-24290 Saint Amand de Coly (Dordogne)

Tel: 04 66 73 97 39. Email: info@yellohvillage-lascaux-vacances.com   www.alanrogers.com/FR24690

St Amand de Coly can be found at the heart of the Périgord Noir, just five minutes from the world-renowned caves at Lascaux. The site, formerly known as Les Malénies, is a recent member of the Yelloh! Village group and an extensive programme of renovation and development has been carried out since its current owners took over in 2003. There are 44 pitches here, some of which are occupied by mobile homes and chalets (available for rent). The new swimming pool complex is impressive and incorporates a spa bath and sauna. Other on-site amenities include a supermarket and restaurant.

Facilities

Shop. Bar. Restaurant. Takeaway food. Swimming pools with sauna and spa bath. Play area. Bicycle hire. Riding. Activity and entertainment programme. Mobile homes and chalets for rent. Off site: Fishing. Walking and cycle tracks. Lascaux caves 2 km. Sarlat 20 km.

Open: 5 April - 30 September.

Directions

Leave the A89 (Bordeaux - Clermont Ferrand) at exit 17 (Peyrignac) and head south on D6089 as far as Le Lardin - St Lazare. Join southbound D62 to Coly and then follow signs to Saint Amand de Coly. Site is signed from here. GPS: N45:03.296 E01:14.794

Charges 2009

Per unit incl. 2 persons and electricity	€ 15,00 - € 29,00
extra person	€ 5,00 - € 6,00

www.yellohvillage.com tel: +33 466 739 739

Check real time availability and at-the-gate prices...

www.alanrogers.com

FR24720 Ca

Le Coux et B

Tel: 05 53

mping Le Clou

igaroque (Dordogne)

31 63 32. Email: info@camping-le-clou.com

www.alanrogers.com/FR24720

mping Le Clou is located in the hills between the Dordogne and Vézère rivers. A wide variety of shrubs and trees give the site a parkland appearance. Two farm buildings, typical of the Périgord, are at the heart of the site. One overlooks the swimming pool and the hills beyond. The site extends over nine acres and has 94 pitches with sizes varying from 80 to 150 sq.m. In high season an animation team organises various sports activities for all ages. In low season the owners provide more relaxing activities, such as wine tasting, boules and film screenings. During this time, guests have the opportunity to join the site owners at their table for dinner (table d'hôte). There are many walking and cycle tracks in the area, some leading directly from the site. Both the Dordogne and the Vézère are, of course, popular for swimming or fishing and the opportunity to make a unforgettable canoe trip.

Facilities

Modern toilet blocks with special family rooms. Bar. Restaurant. Swimming pool with water slide and paddling pool. Minigolf. Boules. Play area. Multisport terrain. Trampolines. Off site: Sarlat and Domme. Aquapark. Riding centre. 18 holes golf. Caves. Tennis. Mountain bike hire.

Open: 19 April - 5 October.

Directions

Site is between Le Bugue and Le Coux et Bigaroque on the D703 and is well signed.
GPS: N44:51.751 E00:58.916

Charges guide

Per unit incl. 2 persons and electricity	€ 16,75 - € 24,00

Camping le Clou ★★★
Camping, caravanning, mobilehomes, chalets and tents

Participant CampingCard and ACSI

Dutch owners ~ English spoken ~ Restaurant and Table d'hôte
www.camping-le-clou.com ~ info@camping-le-clou.com
Tél.: +33 553 31 63 32

FR24700 Camping le Tiradou

F-24220 Saint Vincent de Cosse (Dordogne)

Tel: 05 53 30 30 73. Email: contact@camping-le-tiradou.com

www.alanrogers.com/FR24700

Situated in the Périgord Noir, some 12 km. southwest of Sarlat, this is a really well presented small campsite where the owners have worked hard to make sure that the site is maintained to the highest standards possible. Eliane and Eric are friendly and helpful and are keen to ensure that you enjoy your holiday. There are 60 pitches of which 40 are for touring units, the remaining 20 for mobile homes to rent. Trees provide a mixture of sunshine and shade and all the pitches are level and have electricity (6A). There is one serviced pitch with its own water point and drain. Facilities at this site really are commendable.

Facilities

Two modern sanitary blocks include facilities for babies and disabled persons. Washing machine. Small shop. Bar. Snack bar. Takeaway. Swimming and paddling pools. Jacuzzi. Playground. Bicycle hire. Internet access. WIFI. Library. Trampoline. Pétanque. Family games. Organised acticities (July/Aug). Off site: Fishing and canoeing 1 km. Riding 7 km. Golf 12 km.

Open: 5 April - 25 October.

Directions

From Sarlat take the D703 to St Cyprien. Site is 1 km. after Beynac on the right hand side and it is well signed. GPS: N44:50.257 E01:06.780

Charges guide

Per unit incl. 2 persons and electricity	€ 14,80 - € 19,10
extra person	€ 3,40 - € 4,70
child (3-7 yrs)	€ 2,20 - € 2,90
dog	€ 1,80

FR24710 Camping le Pont de Mazerat

F-24620 Tamniès (Dordogne)

Tel: 05 53 29 14 95. Email: le.pont.de.mazerat@wanadoo.fr

www.alanrogers.com/FR24710

This site is very nicely presented with good attention to detail throughout. It is situated ten minutes north of Sarlat in the hills of the Périgord Noir in a very rural position with plenty of greenery all around. The beautiful lake at Tamnies is 300 m. away and provides fishing, boating, a beach and good walks. There are 83 pitches, 53 for touring units and the remaining 30 for mobile homes for rent. The level pitches are of a good size with no access problems for larger units and roads around the site are tarmac. Electricity supplied is 6/10A. Trees provide good levels of shade.

Facilities

Single, central toilet block with facilities for visitors with disabilities. Motorcaravan service point. Small shop.Bar and restaurant/snack bar. Swimming and paddling pools. Playground. Minigolf. Multisport field. Pétanque. Television. WIFI. Gas and charcoal BBQs permitted. Organised entertainment in high season. Children's club. Off site: Fishing and boating 300 m. Riding and bicycle hire 1 km. Golf 20 km.

Open: Easter (April) - 30 September.

Directions

Leave Sarlat on theD704, direction Montignac. Shortly after passing a hamlet, Les Presses, follow signs for Etang de Tamnies to the left. Site is well signed from this point. GPS: N44:57.895 E01:09.905

Charges guide

Per unit incl. 2 persons	
and electricity	€ 13,84 - € 20,15
extra person	€ 3,35 - € 5,00
child (2-7 yrs)	€ 2,15 - € 3,55

FR46030 Flower Camping les Pins

F-46350 Payrac-en-Quercy (Lot)

Tel: 05 65 37 96 32. Email: info@les-pins-camping.com

www.alanrogers.com/FR46030

Set amongst four hectares of beautiful pine forest, Camping Les Pins is well situated for exploring the historical and natural splendours of the Dordogne region, as well as being a convenient overnight stop when heading north or south. There are 125 clearly marked, level pitches (100 sq.m), of which 55 are for touring units. The pitches are well marked and separated by small shrubs or hedges. Many have shade from the abundant pine trees and all have 10A electricity connections. There is a bar and a good value restaurant with a terrace overlooking the pool area.

Facilities

Three toilet blocks (heated April and May), well maintained and including washbasins in cabins and good baby bath facilites. Laundry facilities (with plenty of drying lines). Motorcaravan service point. Shop with basics (1/6-14/9). Bar with TV. Restaurant and takeaway. Heated swimming pool (1/5-14/9), three slides and smaller paddling pool. Tennis. Small library. Some entertainment in season. Off site: Fishing 7 km. Riding 10 km.

Open: 12 April - 13 September.

Directions

Site entrance is 16 km. from Souillac on western side of the N20 just south of the village of Payrac-en-Quercy. GPS: N44:47.495 E01:28.306

Charges 2009

Per unit incl. 2 persons	
and electricity	€ 17,50 - € 28,00
extra person	€ 4,00 - € 6,60
child (under 7 yrs)	€ 1,50 - € 4,50

FR46050 Camping le Rêve

F-46300 Le Vigan (Lot)

Tel: 05 65 41 25 20. Email: info@campinglereve.com

www.alanrogers.com/FR46050

Le Rêve is a peaceful site situated in the heart of rolling countryside where the Perigord runs into Quercy. You are assured of a warm reception from the Van Iersels, a Dutch couple who have been providing a friendly and hospitable welcome to their clients for the past 19 years. The 56 flat and grassy touring pitches are all of good size, with access to electricity (6A) and divided by shrubs and trees. A few of the pitches are situated at the edge of the forest and provide plenty of shade.

Facilities

The toilet block includes an enclosed area for cooler weather. Washbasins in cabins, special cubicles for disabled people and a baby room. New laundry facilities. Small shop for basics (bread, milk etc.), pleasant bar, restaurant and takeaway (all open all season). Heated swimming pool (all season) and large paddling pool with 'mushroom' fountain. Play area. Boules. Internet access and WiFi. Off site: Fishing 5 km. Riding 8 km. Golf 20 km.

Open: 25 April - 21 September.

Directions

From D820 Souillac - Cahors road turn west onto D673 3 km. south of Payrac. After 2 km. site signed down lane on west side of road. Turn here, follow signs, site in 2.5 km. GPS: N44:46.382 E01:26.458

Charges guide

Per person	€ 4,75
child (under 7 yrs)	€ 2,70
pitch	€ 6,75
electricity (6A)	€ 2,70

Credit cards accepted July and August only.

BOOK THIS SITE
CALL 01580 214000
"...we'll arrange everything
Service The Travel

www.flowercampings.com

BOOK THIS SITE CALL 01580 214000 ...we'll arrange everything The Travel Service

FR46040 Camping Moulin de Laborde

F-46700 Montcabrier (Lot)

Tel: 05 65 24 62 06. Email: moulindelaborde@wanadoo.fr   www.alanrogers.com/FR46040

Based around a converted 17th-century watermill, Moulin de Laborde has been created by the Van Bommel family to provide a tranquil and uncommercialised campsite for the whole family to enjoy. Bordered by woods, hills and a small river, there are 90 flat and grassy pitches, all of at least 100 sq.m. with electricity (6A). Pretty shrubs and trees divide the pitches and provide a moderate amount of shade. A gate leads walkers onto a 'Grand Randonée' footpath which passes through Montcabrier.

Facilities

Well designed, clean toilet block, unit for people with disabilities. Washing machine, dryer. Basic shop. Small bar, restaurant, takeaway. Swimming pool, sunbathing area, paddling pool (all season). Play area. Small lake, free rafts and rowing boats. Fishing. Volleyball. Badminton. Boules. Covered recreation area. Mountain bike hire. Rock climbing. Archery. Dogs are not accepted. WiFi (free). Off site: Riding 5 km. Golf 8 km. Canoeing on the Lot. The Château of Bonaguil 6 km. Fumel 12 km.

Open: 4 April - 26 September.

Directions

Site is on the north side of the D673 Fumel - Gourdon road about 1 km. northeast of the turn to village of Montcabrier. GPS: N44:32.919 E01:04.937

Charges guide

Per person	€ 6,20
child (under 7 yrs)	€ 3,30
pitch	€ 8,40
electricity (6A)	€ 2,60

Less 20% outside July/August. No credit cards.

FR46150 Camping la Truffière

F-46330 Saint Cirq-Lapopie (Lot)

Tel: 05 65 30 20 22. Email: contact@camping-truffiere.com   www.alanrogers.com/FR46150

Set in 4 hectares of mature oak woodland, only two and a half kilometres from the cliff top village of St Cirq-Lapopie, La Truffière is well suited to those seeking a peaceful countryside holiday amongst the stunning natural scenery of the 'Parc naturel régional des Causses de Quercy'. The 90 terraced touring pitches are of varying sizes and on a mixture of grass and gravel (larger units should reserve pitches in advance). All pitches have electricity (6A) and most have shade from the abundant trees.

Facilities

Two well appointed, clean, modern toilet blocks (one heated) include facilities for disabled visitors. Motorcaravan services. Fridge hire. Small shop (open all season). Bar/restaurant (1/6-31/8), terrace overlooking pool and playing field. Snack bar (1/6-31/8). Swimming pool, paddling pool, sun terrace (1/5-15/5). Playing field. Adventure style play area. Trampolines. Boules. English spoken. Off site: Small shop in village. Supermarkets in Cahors 25 km. Riding 3 km. Fishing (in the River Lot) 3 km. Mountain bike trails (bikes can be hired on site).

Open: 1 April - 30 September.

Directions

From D911 Cahors - Rodez road, turn north on D42 at Concots (signed St Cirq-Lapopie). Site about 5 km. on right. Approaching from north on D42 via St Cirq-Lapopie not recommended due to extremely tight left turn in village. GPS: N44:26.913 E01:40.473

Charges guide

Per person	€ 5,10
pitch	€ 5,50
electricity	€ 3,50

Camping Cheques accepted.

FR46070 Camping de la Plage

F-46330 Saint Cirq-Lapopie (Lot)

Tel: 05 65 30 29 51. Email: camping-laplage@wanadoo.fr   www.alanrogers.com/FR46070

The site is situated next to the River Lot and is a good base for those who want an active holiday, with many sporting activities available either on site or in the immediate area. It does attract organised groups of young people and can be quite lively at times. The site is a rental base for canoeing and kayaking (lifejackets and all equipment included in hire charge). The campsite has 120 pitches including 109 for touring pitches, all with electricity, a few fully serviced and some hardstandings. Most are on a very slight slope and have good shade from mature trees and bushes.

Facilities

Two practical sanitary blocks are clean and well maintained. Facilites for disabled people. Two washing machines and dryer. Motorcaravan service point (charge). Bar (April - Oct). Restaurant (1/5-30/9). Takeaway (1/6-30/9). Internet terminal. WiFi. Play area. Large children's room for animation. Canoeing, kayaking and swimming from beach at the rear of the site (lifeguard July/Aug). Fishing. Off site: Rock climbing, caving and canyoning all near by. Bicycle hire 5 km. Riding 9 km.

Open: All year.

Directions

From Cahors take D653 east to Vers, then take D662 for 17 km. to Tour de Faure. Cross river on narrow bridge and site entrance is on right by bar/restaurant. Do not approach via Saint Cirq-Lapopie. GPS: N44:28.156 E01:40.881

Charges guide

Per person	€ 5,00
child (under 7 yrs)	€ 3,00
pitch	€ 5,00 - € 7,00
electricity (6/10A)	€ 4,00 - € 5,00

Check real time availability and at-the-gate prices...
www.alanrogers.com

FR46010 Castel Camping le Domaine de la Paille Basse

F-46200 Souillac-sur-Dordogne (Lot)

Tel: 05 65 37 85 48. Email: paille.basse@wanadoo.fr

www.alanrogers.com/FR46010

Set in a rural location some 8 km. from Souillac, this family owned site is easily accessible from the N20 and well placed to take advantage of excursions into the Dordogne. It is part of a large domain of 80 hectares, all available to campers for walks and recreation. The site is quite high up and there are excellent views over the surrounding countryside. The 262 pitches are in two main areas – one is level in cleared woodland with good shade, and the other on grass without shade. Numbered and marked, the pitches are a minimum 100 sq.m. and often considerably more. All have electricity (3/6A) with about 80 fully serviced. The site is well placed to take advantage of excursions into the Dordogne. A wide range of activities and entertainment are organised in high season. The site can get very busy in high season and is popular with three tour operators. If you like a livelier type of site, you will enjoy La Paille Basse.

Facilities

Three main toilet blocks all have modern equipment and are kept very clean. Laundry. Small shop with a large selection of wine. Restaurant, bar (open until 02.00 in high season), terrace, pizza takeaway. Crêperie. main swimming pool, a smaller one, paddling pool (unheated), water slides. Sun terrace. Sound-proofed disco (three times weekly in season). TV (with satellite). Cinema below the pool area. Tennis. Play area. Library. Off site: Golf 4 km.

Open: 15 May - 15 September.

Directions

From Souillac take D15 and then D62 roads leading northwest towards Salignac-Eyvignes and after 6 km. turn right at site sign and follow steep and narrow approach road for 2 km. GPS: N44:56.836 E01:26.354

Charges guide

Per person	€ 5,40 - € 7,00
child (under 7 yrs)	€ 3,80 - € 5,00
pitch	€ 7,80 - € 10,80
incl. water and drainage	€ 9,80 - € 13,00
dog	€ 4,00

Camping Cheques accepted.

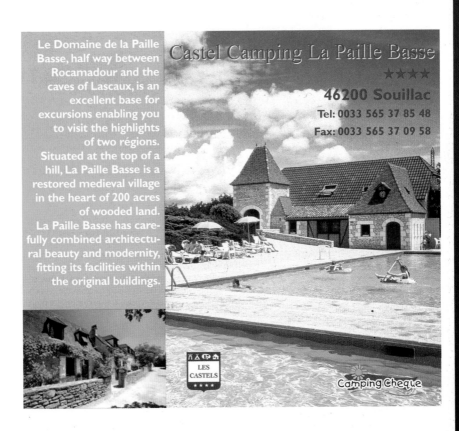

Le Domaine de la Paille Basse, half way between Rocamadour and the caves of Lascaux, is an excellent base for excursions enabling you to visit the highlights of two régions. Situated at the top of a hill, La Paille Basse is a restored medieval village in the heart of 200 acres of wooded land. La Paille Basse has carefully combined architectural beauty and modernity, fitting its facilities within the original buildings.

Castel Camping La Paille Basse

★★★★

46200 Souillac

Tel: 0033 565 37 85 48

Fax: 0033 565 37 09 58

LES CASTELS ★★★★

Camping Cheque

Check real time availability and at-the-gate prices...

www.alanrogers.com

FR46170 Campéole les Reflets du Quercy

Mas de Bastide, F-46150 Crayssac (Lot)

Tel: **05 65 30 00 27**. Email: **nadine.ferran@atciat.com**   www.alanrogers.com/FR46170

Set in the west of the Lot department, about 16 km. from the large town of Cahors, this site is owned by the Campéole group and is classed as a holiday village. Located on a hill with good views of the surrounding countryside, the pitches are hilly and terraced. Most are partially shaded with Quercy oak trees and some are set apart by small Crayssac stone walls. Almost half of the touring pitches are located on good, level hardstanding. At the rear of the site is a large area of independently owned mobile homes and residents here also have access to the campsite facilities. The site has a good 25 m. swimming pool overlooked by the terrace of the bar and snack bar. The site is managed by a very friendly French couple and a welcoming Campéole team.

Facilities

Three clean and well maintained sanitary blocks (not all open outside high season). Facilities for visitors with disabilities. Baby room with bath. Laundry facilities. Motorcaravan service point. Shop (July/Aug). Bar and snacks (July/Aug). Swimming and paddling pools (July/Aug). TV and games room. Boules. Tennis court. Play area with large bouncy castle. Animation in high season. Off site: Fishing and riding 7 km. Bicycle hire 15 km. Good shops 16 km.

Open: 5 April - 28 September.

Directions

From Cahors on the RN20, follow D911 northwest towards Puy-l'Évêque, Mercuès and Prayssac. Several kilometres after Labarthe, take D23, on the left near Crayssac. Site is well signed from Crayssac. GPS: N44:30.414 E01:19.446

Charges guide

Per unit incl. 2 persons	€ 13,00 - € 18,90
extra person	€ 4,00 - € 6,10
child (2-5 yrs)	free - € 3,90
electricity (10A)	€ 3,90

Camping Les Reflets du Quercy

Mas de Bastide - 46510 Crayssac (Lot) - France
Tél.: +33 (0)5 65 30 00 27 - Fax: +33 (0)5 65 30 01 43
www.camping-lot.info

Campéole
CAMPSITES AND RENTED ACCOMMODATION

FR46180 Camping le Ventoulou

Ventoulou, F-46500 Thégra (Lot)

Tel: **05 65 33 67 01**. Email: **contact@leventoulou.com**   www.alanrogers.com/FR46180

Le Ventoulou is a small, well kept and peaceful site on the Périgord 'walnut' route, at the heart of the Quercy Causses natural park. The site is based around an ancient farmhouse located between the quaint villages of Padirac and Thégra. Of just over half a hectare, the site is compact, yet because of careful spacing of pitches does not seem crowded. You will receive a warm welcome from the French owners. The Padirac Aqua Park is just three kilometres away. There is a weekly soirée during the high season.

Facilities

One very well equipped sanitary block is clean and well maintained. Good facilities for disabled visitors. Baby room with bath. Laundry facilities. Shop. Bar with TV. Restaurant and takeaway. Swimming pool and paddling pool. Bicycle hire. Boules. Play area with two trampolines. Games room and library. Off site: Riding 2 km. Fishing 10 km. Golf 15 km.

Open: 4 April - 28 September.

Directions

From A20 south exit 54 follow the N140 southeast to Gramat. Take the D807 northeast to Lavergne, then the D11 to Thégra and look for signs to the site which is less than 2 km. GPS: N44:49.600 E01:46.500

Charges guide

Per unit incl. 2 persons	€ 11,50 - € 19,50
extra person	€ 3,50 - € 6,00
child (under 7 yrs)	€ 1,90 - € 4,50
electricity (10A)	€ 4,20 - € 4,20

The Travel Service ...we'll arrange everything CALL 01580 214000 BOOK THIS SITE

Check real time availability and at-the-gate prices...

www.**alanrogers**.com

FR46140 Club de Vacances Duravel

Port de Vire, F-46700 Duravel (Lot)

Tel: 05 65 24 65 06. Email: clubduravel@wanadoo.fr

www.alanrogers.com/FR46140

This quality site is beautifully situated on the banks of the Lot River, only 35 km. from the historic town of Cahors. The site has 300 clearly defined, large pitches all with electricity. Some of these are fully serviced with water and drainage, and private sanitary facilities. The reception, bar, restaurant, snack bar and the shop are all located beside the river and from the terrace you can enjoy lovely views over the water. The pool complex offers two large pools (one is heated) with water slides and a children's pool. Duravel is a holiday destination which would suit all ages. Bridge and pétanque contests are organised in low season. During high season an animation team provides plenty of activities to suit all tastes and ages, including 'anything can happen' evenings when you will be surprised with a special theme night. The region also offers many possibilities for exploring, canoeing on the river, visiting wine cellars or strolling around local markets.

Facilities

Two clean toilet blocks include facilities for disabled people. Baby rooms. Laundry facilities. Serviced pitch facility provides a toilet, shower and sink (with hot water; cleaning charge € 13,50 per stay). Well stocked shop. Restaurant. Bar. Pizzeria and takeaway. Two tennis courts. Multisport area. Play area. Fishing. Boat launching. WiFi.

Open: 25 April - end September.

Directions

From Paris A10 towards Orleans and A71 towards Vierzon. Follow A20 and take exit 57 to Villeneuve sur Lot. Take the D811 to Cahors, Puy l'Evêque and the D58 to Duravel. Site is well signed.
GPS: N44:29.782 E01:04.906

Charges guide

Per person	€ 4,30 - € 6,35
pitch	€ 6,85 - € 10,00
incl. individual sanitary facilitiy	€ 14,75 - € 18,00
electricity	€ 3,50

active relax comfort charm

You will find it at Club de Vacances Duravel!

Club de Vacances
Duravel ★★★★

CampingCard ACSI · ACSI

- ANWB Euro-Top campsite
- Large demarcated, shaded pitches, if necessary with private sanitary facilities
- Swimming pools, 2 heated
- Rental bungalows, mobile homes and tents
- Various recreation- and animation program
- Shop, restaurant, snack bar and pizzeria are available from 25th of April
- Appealing discounts in May, June and September
- Special arrangements like bridge, hiking tours, cycling and golf
- For more information and internet booking: **www.clubdevacances.eu**

Club de Vacances Duravel
46700 Duravel - France
Tel. 00 31 (0) 74 266 64 99
Fax 00 31 (0) 74 266 82 05
info@clubdevacances.eu
www.clubdevacances.eu

Alan Rogers

FREE 2009 brochure
Over 60 French campsites, hand picked for you
Call for your copy today **01580 214000**
FREE CHILD PLACES ON MANY SITES

Check real time availability and at-the-gate prices...

www.**alanrogers**.com

FR46190 Kawan Village Domaine de la Faurie

F-46240 Séniergues (Lot)

Tel: 05 65 21 14 36. Email: contact@camping-lafaurie.com   www.alanrogers.com/FR46190

A stunning array of tended shrubs and thoughtful flower plantings is spread throughout this very pretty site which is located on a hilltop with wide open views of the surrounding hills and valleys. Although hidden away, it is an excellent base for exploring the Lot and Dordogne regions. The site is separated into two distinct areas, an open, lightly shaded front section and a much more densely shaded area with tall pine trees all around the pitches. The pitches are large and most are at least 100 sq.m. The friendly French owners consider the three hectacre site their personal garden.

Facilities

The single sanitary block is clean and well maintained. Facilities for disabled visitors. Washing machine. Motorcaravan service point. Excellent gift shop selling regional and local produce (bread available). Bar, restaurant and takeaway. Swimming pool and paddling pool. TV and games rooms. Boules. Bicycle hire. Play area. Small library. Weekly soirées in high season. Max. 1 dog per pitch. Off site: Fishing 3 km. Golf 8 km. Riding 15 km.

Open: 7 April - 30 September.

Directions

From the A20 exit on N56 and turn right towards St Germain du Bel Air. Continue for 5 km. and the site is on the right. GPS: N44:41.518 E01:32.077

Charges guide

Per person	€ 6,50
child (1-7 yrs)	€ 4,50
pitch	€ 9,00
electricity (6A)	€ 3,50
Camping Cheques accepted.	

FR46220 Camping les 3 Sources

Peyratel, F-46190 Calviac-Sousceyrac (Lot)

Tel: 05 65 33 03 01. Email: info@les-trois-sources.com   www.alanrogers.com/FR46220

This rural site is beautifully situated in the hilly surroundings of the Lot region, only 20 km. from the Dordogne river. The site offers 120 well maintained pitches in an attractive, wooded area. There are also 16 chalets and 20 mobile homes for rent. The pitches are numbered and have 6/10A electricity connections and water points within easy reach. Following a fire in 2005 when the site's facilities burned down, and at the time of our visit, the reception and snack bar were housed in chalets on what was the terrace of the restaurant. A new restaurant, shop and reception are promised.

Facilities

Two toilet blocks provide good facilities including washbasins in cabins. Facilities for babies and disabled visitors. Laundry facilities including ironing. Snack bar (to be replaced by new bar and restaurant). Swimming and paddling pools. Games room. Trim trail on island in the lake. Fishing. Play area. Activities and entertainment including children's club. Off site: Riding 15 km. Lake beach 17 km.

Open: 29 April - 17 September.

Directions

From A20 (Chateauroux, Limoges, Brive) follow D8/D20 towards Vayrac and Bretenoux. Do not go through Martel. Follow signs for St Cère and Sousceyrac (D673) and turn left to Calviac after 6 km. (towards Lamativie). After 2 km. site is on right hand side. GPS: N44:56.369 E02:03.073

Charges guide

Per unit incl. 2 persons and electricity	€ 6,35 - € 10,35
extra person	€ 2,15 - € 4,50
dog	€ 2,95 - € 3,45

FR46230 Camping des Arcades

Moulin de Saint Martial, F-46800 Saint Pantaléon (Lot)

Tel: 05 65 22 92 27. Email: info@des-arcades.com   www.alanrogers.com/FR46230

Recently taken over by an enthusiastic, young Dutch couple, Camping des Arcades is situated in the hilly surroundings of the Lot Valley. There are 80 level, grass pitches with 6A electricity hook ups. The heated swimming pool is small but provides plenty of fun during hot summer days. Those who enjoy fishing can enjoy lazy afternoons on the banks of the site's lake (the lake is unfenced). The site's facilities such as the reception, the bar and the restaurant are housed in a 13th-century watermill. Entertainment and excursions are organised all season. The D653 road runs beside the site, which may cause some nuisance.

Facilities

Two toilet blocks provide good facilities with facilities for disabled visitors in one block. Laundry facilities. Shop for basics in high season (bread available all season). Bar, restaurant and takeaway. Swimming pool. Fishing. Activities and entertainment. Off site: Canoeing, walking, cycling and riding nearby.

Open: 28 April - 30 September.

Directions

From the A20 take the N20 to Cahors. Continue until roundabout (Atrium wine), then take D653 towards Agen and Montcuq. Site is on left after 10 km. GPS: N44:22.071 E01:18.380

Charges guide

Per person	€ 5,00
pitch	€ 7,00 - € 10,00
electricity	€ 3,00

Check real time availability and at-the-gate prices...

www.alanrogers.com

FR46310 Camping les Granges

F-46110 Vayrac (Lot)

Tel: 05 65 32 46 58. Email: info@les-granges.com   www.alanrogers.com/FR46310

Situated just over three kilometres outside Vayrac in a very rural position, this site nestles quietly beside the river in a tranquil and peaceful area. Pitches along the river frontage are popular and this should be remembered when reserving a space if that area is preferred. There is direct access to the river at one end of the site which can be useful for setting off in a canoe and enjoying the pleasures of the Dordogne river. There are 150 pitches with 116 of average size for touring units and the remaining 34 for mobile homes, the latter all available for rent. The pitches are level, mostly shaded and have 10A electricity. Entertainment is organised in high season. The owners are friendly and helpful and are keen to ensure you enjoy your holiday whilst on their family orientated site. This part of France offers many places of interest to visit with many fine châteaux and historic sites. Restaurants abound and offer a gastronomic experience with great local cuisine. Off site activities are numerous and the staff at the tourist office in Vayrac are very helpful. In this area, the natural environment is protected and you can explore the beautiful countryside on foot or on a bicycle.

Facilities	Directions
Two modern sanitary blocks include facilities for visitors with disabilities. Washing machine and ironing board. Snack bar and takeaway Swimming pool and fun pool for small children. Play area. Organised entertainment (12/7-16/8). Fishing. Off site: Bicycle hire 1 km. Golf and riding 10 km.	From Brive, take the D20 towards Figeac. In Vayrac turn right just before the church at sign for 'Campings' and 'Stade'. Site is signed from here. GPS: N44:56.077 E01:40.789

Open: 1 May - 20 September.

Charges guide

Per person	€ 4,90
child (2-10 yrs)	€ 2,70
pitch	€ 5,50
electricity (10A)	€ 4,00
dog (max. 1)	€ 1,60

Vallée de la Dordogne

3-stars campsite at the Dordogne river side, mobile homes for rent, 150 shady pitches, 5 acres, swimming pool, play ground, snack, shop, bar, close to Rocamadour

Camping les Granges***
4611 Vayrac
Tél. +33 (0)565 32 46 58
info@les-granges.com
www.les-granges.com

FR46240 Camping Quercy Vacances

Mas de la Combe, F-46090 Sainte Pierre-Lafeuille (Lot)

Tel: 05 65 36 87 15. Email: quercy-vacances@wanadoo.fr   www.alanrogers.com/FR46240

This clean and well run site is owned by a young, English speaking, French couple who are determined to improve the facilities and ambiance. It is only 4.5 km. from the A20 and is an ideal stopover site for holidaymakers travelling to and from Spain. However, it is better than just a stopover site and is worth staying a few extra days. It has 70 large unmarked touring pitches most of which have 6/10A hook-ups. The site facilities include a rustic bar and restaurant.

Facilities	Directions
Clean, modern toilet block, recently refurbished. Facilities for campers with disabilities are located in a separate building adjacent to the camping area. Small basic shop. Bar and takeaway. Restaurant serving specials like couscous and paella once per week. Large round swimming pool (20/6-15/9), unsuitable for young children, minimum depth 1.2 m. Live music, dancing (July/Aug). Small play area. Off site: Riding 5 km. Bicycle hire, fishing 10 km.	Leave A20 exit 57 (Cahors). Shortly turn left on N20 and then turn right on small un-named road (site signed) before reaching St Pierre Lafeuille (about 4.5 km. from the A20). Site on right in about 600 m. GPS: N44:31.889 E01:27.585

Open: 1 April - 31 October.

Charges guide

Per person	€ 3,80 - € 5,00
child (3-9 yrs)	€ 3,00 - € 4,00
pitch	€ 5,00 - € 8,80
electricity (6/10A)	€ 3,30 - € 5,50

309

FR46320 Camping les Rives du Célé

Domaine du Surgié, F-46100 Figeac (Lot)

Tel: 05 61 64 88 54. Email: contact@marc-montmija.com   www.alanrogers.com/FR46320

Very conveniently placed, two kilometres from the town centre of Figeac, this site has a rural location. It is a campsite where activities on site and in the surrounding areas are numerous and it would therefore suit an active family including teenagers. Navigation around the park is easy for larger units due to good design. There are 163 pitches, 103 for touring units, the remaining 60 for mobile homes and gites, all of which are for rent. The pitches are level, with a mixture of shade and sun and all have 10A electricity. The site is split into different areas with the aquatic centre next to the camping area.

Facilities

Three fully equipped, modern sanitary blocks include facilities for babies and disabled people. Laundry. Shop, bar, restaurant and takeaway (all from 30/4). Swimming pool complex. Sports competitions and party nights with themed dining. Children's clubs. Canoeing. Fishing. Minigolf. Boules. Bicycle hire. Off site: Riding 2 km.

Open: 30 April - 30 September.

Directions

From Cahors, take the D653 to Figeac from where the site is well signed. GPS: N44:36.593 E02:03.009

Charges guide

Per unit incl. 2 persons and electricity	€ 12,00 - € 39,00
extra person	€ 3,50 - € 6,00
child (3-12 yrs)	€ 2,00 - € 3,00
dog	€ 1,50 - € 2,50

FR46330 Village Club l'Evasion

Martignac, F-46700 Puy-L'Evèque (Lot)

Tel: 05 65 30 80 09. Email: evasion@wanadoo.fr   www.alanrogers.com/FR46330

Situated on a sunny hilltop, this good quality site has fine views over the Lot countryside and deserves to be visited. It is a small site with 65 pitches of average size and 35 chalets and mobile homes, all available to rent. The majority of the pitches are on level, gravel hardstandings with a few on grass. They enjoy dappled shade through tall oak trees and 5A electricity hook-ups, with a water point between two pitches. Large motorhomes are accepted although booking is necessary to ensure a large enough space is available. Access is good. This site has a most agreeable restaurant and bar with a varied and reasonably priced menu.

Facilities

Traditional sanitary block centrally placed includes facilities for disabled people. Washing machine, dryer, ironing board. Shop (all year). Bar, restaurant and takeaway (July/Aug). Large swimming pool.Games room. Organised entertainment. Internet access and WIFI. Only communal charcoal barbecues are permitted. Off site: Fishing 2 km. Riding 5 km. Bicycle hire 6 km. Golf 25 km. Sporting trips arranged.

Open: 1 April - 30 September (chalets all year).

Directions

From Cahors take the D911 and D656. 1 km after Puy-L'Eveque turn right onto D28 and site is signed. 3 km from Puy-L'Eveque up a hill. GPS: N44:31.670 E01:07.508

Charges guide

Per unit incl. 2 persons and electricity	€ 16,20 - € 23,20
extra person	€ 6,50 - € 10,00
child (under 10 yrs)	€ 5,00 - € 8,70

FR47050 Camping Moulin de Campech

F-47160 Villefranche-de-Queyran (Lot-et-Garonne)

Tel: 05 53 88 72 43. Email: campech@wanadoo.fr   www.alanrogers.com/FR47050

This well shaded, pretty site is run by Sue and George Thomas along with Sue's parents, Dot and Bob Dunn. At the entrance to the site, a trout lake with graceful weeping willows feeds under the restored mill house which is home to the owners as well as housing the bar and restaurant. Children will need supervision around the lake and at the pool which is on an elevated area above the mill house. The 60 large-sized pitches are mostly divided by hedges, with electricity (6A, long leads may be necessary in places, but can be borrowed free of charge).

Facilities

The single, rather ordinary toilet block has modern fittings. Washing machine and tumble dryer. Bar, restaurant. Terraced swimming pool. Open grassy games area. Board games and English library. Boules. Barbecue, gourmet nights in high season. Fishing (discounted rate for campers, no permit required). Torch useful. Off site: Watersports, bicycle hire, golf or riding 10 km. Markets every day in villages and towns around the region. Numerous wine caves and armagnac products.

Open: 1 April - 19 October.

Directions

Take A10 south to Bordeaux. Join A62 for Toulouse and take exit 6 for Damazan. Follow D8 to Mont de Marsan, at Cap du Bosc turn right onto D11 for Casteljaloux. Site is signed, 5 km. on right. GPS: N44:16.307 E00:11.456

Charges guide

Per person	€ 3,95 - € 5,75
child (under 7 yrs)	€ 2,90 - € 4,00
pitch with electricity	€ 11,60 - € 14,60
dog	€ 2,40

Check real time availability and at-the-gate prices...

www.alanrogers.com

F-47500 Sauveterre-la-Lemance (Lot-et-Garonne)

Tel: 05 53 40 67 26. Email: moulinduperie@wanadoo.fr

www.alanrogers.com/FR47010

BOOK THIS SITE
CALL 01580 214000
...we'll arrange everything
The Travel Service

Set in a quiet area and surrounded by woodlands this peaceful little site is well away from much of the tourist bustle. It has 125 reasonably sized, grassy pitches, all with 6A electricity, divided by mixed trees and bushes with most having good shade. All are extremely well kept, as indeed is the entire site. The attractive front courtyard is complemented by an equally pleasant terrace at the rear. Two small, clean swimming pools overlook a shallow, spring water lake, ideal for inflatable boats and paddling and bordering the lake, a large grass field is popular for games. The picturesque old mill buildings, adorned with flowers and creepers, now house the bar and restaurant. The food is to be recommended here, as is the owner's extensive knowledge of wine that he is pleased to share with visitors. A quiet, friendly site with regular visitors – reservation is advised for July/Aug. Bergerac Airport is an hour away so it may suit those choosing a mobile home or bungalow tent and wanting to travel light.

Facilities

Two clean, modern and well maintained toilet blocks include facilities for disabled visitors. Motorcaravan services. Fridge, barbecue, chemical toilet hire (book in advance). Basic shop. Bar/reception, restaurant and takeaway. Two small swimming pools (no Bermuda-style shorts). Boules. Outdoor chess. Playground. trampoline. Small indoor play area. Bicycle hire. Organised activities in high season; including canoeing, riding, wine tasting visits, sightseeing trips, barbecues, gastronomic meals. Winter caravan storage. Off site: Fishing 1 km. Small supermarket in village and larger stores in Fumel.

Open: 15 May - 18 September.

Directions

From D710, Fumel - Périgueux, turn southeast into Sauveterre-le-Lemance. Turn left (northeast) at far end on C201 signed Château Sauveterre and Loubejec (site also signed). Site is 3 km. on right. GPS: N44:35.410 E01:02.857

Charges guide

Per unit incl. 2 persons	€ 13,05 - € 21,85
incl. electricity	€ 16,95 - € 25,75
extra person	€ 4,20 - € 6,50
child (under 7 yrs)	€ 1,80 - € 3,45
animal	€ 2,15 - € 4,10

Camping Cheques accepted.

MOULIN DU PÉRIÉ ★★★★

Camping - Caravaning

CAMPING - CARAVANING **Open from 15/05/2009 to 18/09/2009**

All services open during the opening:
• restaurant, bar, basic shop with fresh bread, take away food & house made pizzas, swimming pools, jumping castles.

During the high season:
• sports, children's activities, music, circus

Comfortable accommodations for hire are available at the site: chalets, mobile homes and large bungalow tents.

Special Inclusive Holidays
Two weeks holiday discovering the natural and scenic Perigord / Dordogne area. Interesting & Complete Programmes Local wine and food tasting in June and September

For more information and free brochure :
Henri or Anne-Marie BAUDOT
tel: 0033 553 40 67 26
fax: 0033 553 40 62 46
Moulin du Périé
47500 Sauveterre la Lémance France
www.camping-moulin-perie.com
MOULINDUPERIE@wanadoo.fr
DIRECT BOOKING ON LINE

HOLIDAY CHEQUE

kawan

DORDOGNE - PERIGORD

Check real time availability and at-the-gate prices...
www.alanrogers.com

FR47030 Camping le Château de Fonrives

Rives, F-47210 Villeréal (Lot-et-Garonne)

Tel: 05 53 36 63 38. Email: chateau.de.fonrives@wanadoo.fr   www.alanrogers.com/FR47030

Le Château de Fonrives is situated in Lot-et-Garonne. The site is set in pretty part-farmed, part-wooded countryside. It is a mixture of hazelnut woodland with lake and château (mostly 16th-century). An attractive avenue leads to the barns adjacent to the château which have been converted. There are 200 pitches, 96 of which are for touring units, with electricity. Pitches near the woodland receive moderate shade, but elsewhere there is light shade from hedges and young trees. Former barns have been converted to provide a restaurant with covered terrace and bar with an open terrace overlooking the outdoor pool.

Facilities

One sanitary block. Shop. Restaurant, snacks and takeaway. Bar with disco area and terrace. Covered swimming pool (April - Oct), outdoor pool, water slides, paddling pool. Small play area. Small field for volleyball and football. Library. Minigolf, tennis, bicycle hire (all charged). Activities organised for children and adults in season, including excursions and walks. Caravan storage. Off site: Riding 8 km.

Open: 4 May - 14 September.

Directions

Site is about 2 km. northwest of Villeréal, on west side of the D14/D207 Bergerac - Villaréal road. GPS: N44:39.434 E00:43.708

Charges guide

Per unit incl. 2 persons	€ 16,00 - € 24,50
extra person	€ 4,00 - € 4,30
child (under 6 yrs)	€ 2,00 - € 2,30
electricity (6A)	€ 2,50 - € 4,50

CAMPING le Château de Fonrives ****
47210 RIVES (périgord-Dordogne)
Tél.: 0033 553.366.338 Fax: 0033 553.360.998
www.campingchateaufonrives.com
Contact@campingchateaufonrives.com

FonriveS

Mobil-home/ Chalet rental
touring pitch rental

Special offer
Out of july /auguts
Pitch for 2 pers.
With electricity
15€ per night

Indoor heated swimming pool-jacuzzi

FR47090 Flower Camping du Lac de Lislebonne

Le Bétous, F-47170 Mézin-Réaup-Lisse (Lot-et-Garonne)

Tel: 05 53 65 65 28. Email: domainedelislebonne@free.fr   www.alanrogers.com/FR47090

Lac de Lislebonne can be found on the eastern edge of the vast Landes forest, in the Lot et Garonne département. This small site has just 40 pitches, some of which are occupied by attractive wooden chalets (available for rent). There are 22 touring pitches. These are of a good size and all have electricity (10A). The site lake is a pleasant spot to cool off and has a sandy beach. Various activities are organised in and around the lake, including water polo, canoeing and beach volleyball. Bicycle hire is available on site and there are over 250 km. of marked cycle tracks in the area

Facilities

Shop. Bar. Snack bar. Takeaway. Lake swimming. Play area. Bicycle and canoe hire. Fishing. TV room. Activity and entertainment programme. Chalets for rent. Off site: Riding. Golf. Tennis. Château du Moulin 10 km. Cycle tracks.

Open: 25 April - 25 September.

Directions

Leave the A62 autoroute at exit for Agen and head southwest on the D656 to Nérac and then Mézin. Join the 149 towards Réaup-Lisse and follow signs to Base de Loisirs. GPS: N44:04.401 E00:12.584

Charges 2009

Per unit incl. 2 persons and electricity	€ 12,90 - € 18,50

www.flowercampings.com

Check real time availability and at-the-gate prices...

www.alanrogers.com

FR47110 Le Cabri Holiday Village

Route de Savignac, F-47120 Duras (Lot-et-Garonne)

Tel: 05 53 83 81 03. Email: holidays@lecabri.eu.com

www.alanrogers.com/FR47110

This is a good quality site set in 14 acres of beautiful countryside, on the border of the Dordogne and the Lot-et-Garonne, between the two rivers of the same name. The views are superb. Le Cabri Holiday Village is an English owned and run, small holiday complex. The new owners, Peter and Eileen Marston who are keen caravanners themselves, have developed 24 new spacious pitches (generally 150 sq.m), all with electricity (4/16A) and water. The open, level pitches are all on hardstandings surrounded by grass and separated by shrubs. Access for large motorhomes causes no problems whatsoever as they were considered when the site was planned. Open all year round, the site has excellent facilities including a swimming pool, a fishing pond and other leisure facilities. Wildlife watching is another pastime with red deer and wild boar populating the area. Le Cabri also benefits from its own high quality restaurant which specialises in local cuisine. Open all year, it draws clientele from the local area as well as those staying on the site. Although situated in a very rural and peaceful area, the historic village of Duras is only a ten minute walk, with its good selection of shops, restaurants, bars and the famous fortified château standing guard at the head of the village square.

Facilities

A recently refurbished sanitary block is centrally located, heated in low season and includes three new private cabins. Separate cabin for disabled visitors. Washing machines, dryers and ironing board. Shop (all year). Restaurant (15/3-20/1) with occasional entertainment year round. Internet access. Swimming pool. Large play area. Boules. Well stocked fishing pond. Off site: Riding 1 km. Golf (international course) 10 km. Tennis 1 km. Watersports 7 km. Canoeing 8 km.

Open: All year.

Directions

In Duras, look for the D203 and follow signs for site. It is less than 1 km. away. GPS: N44:40.978 E00:11.169

Charges guide

Per person	€ 4,00 - € 5,00
child (under 11 yrs)	€ 2,00 - € 3,00
pitch	€ 5,00 - € 7,00
electricity (4/10A)	€ 3,00 - € 5,00
Special offer (not July/Aug): stay 6 nights, pay for only 5.	

Le Cabri Holiday Village
Route de Savignac - 47120 Duras
Tel-fax: 0033 (0) 553 838 103
Mobile: 0033 (0) 685 449 711
E-mail: holidays@lecabri.eu.com - www.lecabri.eu.com

FR47120 Camping la Vallée de Gardeleau

F-47410 Sérignac-Péboudou (Lot-et-Garonne)

Tel: 05 53 36 96 96. Email: valleegardeleau@Wanadoo.fr

www.alanrogers.com/FR47120

Camping La Vallée is a delightful, small, family run site established over 12 years ago. It is well hidden and private, some 9 km. from civilization and deep in the countryside of Lot-et-Garonne, very close to the border of the Dordogne and 150 km. from the Atlantic coast. It has a total of 33 pitches, 26 for touring, seven mobile homes, and 4 bungalow tents. The medium sized pitches are well laid out, all with hedges and some shade, some with views.

Facilities

Two sanitary blocks are well sited and clean. Facilities for disabled visitors. Baby room. Washing machine. Shop with daily deliveries of fresh bread. Bar with snack bar and TV. Restaurant (high season). Swimming pool. Small play area. Communal stone barbecue. Animation for children (high season). Off site: Fishing and riding 2 km. Bicycle hire 9 km. Golf 20 km. Atlantic coast 150 km.

Open: 1 April - 31 October.

Directions

From Castillones on the N21 find the D254 to Sérignac-Péboudou and follow this. Some 10 km. along this road, look for signs to site which is on the left hand side. GPS: N44:36.918 E00:32.364

Charges guide

Per person	€ 2,55 - € 3,95
child (under 7 yrs)	€ 1,55 - € 2,40
pitch with electricity	€ 7,05 - € 12,15

Check real time availability and at-the-gate prices...

www.alanrogers.com

FR47100 Camping Municipal le Robinson

Le Robinson (RN113), F-47400 Tonneins (Lot-et-Garonne)

Tel: 05 53 79 02 28

www.alanrogers.com/FR47100

Close to the River Garonne, this small site has a rather formal charm with neat flower beds, well mown lawns and an extremely well cared for appearance. With a small reception, the Gardien based on site and a security barrier, it only has 32 pitches plus a meadow for additional camping. All with electricity (15A), the pitches are of a reasonable size, separated by small trees which provide a little shade. There is some road and rail noise at times. This is a good stopping off point or base from which to explore the local area.

Facilities

Sanitary facilities are roomy but of fairly old design, they are adequate rather than luxurious. Washing machine. No proper chemical disposal point. Ice and cold drinks available. Under cover area with fridge, freezer, tables and chairs. Small play area, sandpit, table tennis. Torch useful. Off site: Tonneins town centre 1.5 km, with full range of supermarkets, bars and restaurants.

Open: 1 June - 30 September.

Directions

Take either exit 5 from autoroute to Marmande then the N113 south or exit 6 to Aiguillon (avoid town) and follow N113 north. Site on west side of N113 just south of Tonneins.
GPS: N44:22.896 E00:19.092

Charges guide

Per pitch incl. 2 persons	€ 8,00
extra person	€ 3,00
electricity	€ 3,50
No credit cards.	

FR47130 Camping des Bastides

Terre Rouge, F-47150 Salles (Lot-et-Garonne)

Tel: 05 53 40 83 09. Email: info@campingdesbastides.com

www.alanrogers.com/FR47130

Attractive and well maintained, this six and a half hectares is hilly and terraced with good views from the top of the site. Although the terrain is hilly, most of the 90 medium sized touring pitches are fairly level and moderately shaded. The friendly Dutch owners of 11 years are warm and welcoming. Tight turns with narrow gravel paths and overhanging trees may cause some difficulties for larger units. Reception keeps information on a variety of local walking and cycling routes. Weekly trips are arranged to one of the wine growing châteaux in the region.

Facilities

Two modern, clean and well maintained sanitary blocks can be heated. Facilities for disabled visitors. Excellent children's facilities with baby bath and child-size facilities. Private en-suite facilities for hire. Shop. Bar/reception and snack restaurant (including takeaway). Swimming pool with slides, and two paddling pools. Boules. Play area. WiFi access. Animation (high season). Weekly excursions and weekly barbecues. Off site: Fumel 8 km. Fishing 1 km. Riding and bicycle hire 10 km. Golf 25 km.

Open: 1 May - 15 September.

Directions

From Fumel, take D710 north towards Cuzorn. Before reaching Cuzorn, turn northwest on D162 and site is 6 km. on the right hand side (well signed). GPS: N44:33.150 E00:52.890

Charges guide

Per unit incl. 2 persons and electricity (6A)	€ 15,00 - € 25,00
extra person	€ 4,00 - € 5,50
child (2-12 yrs)	€ 2,25 - € 2,75

FR47150 Domaine de Guillalmes

Condat, F-47500 Fumel (Lot-et-Garonne)

Tel: 05 53 71 01 99. Email: info@guillalmes.com

www.alanrogers.com/FR47150

Domaine de Guillalmes is a very attractive site on the banks of the River Lot and close to the village of Fumel. It was until recently exclusively for 18 chalets but the British owners have now added a 10 pitch touring caravan area all with 4/16A electricity and water. These pitches are on hardstandings divided by small hedges and small trees giving some shade. They are spacious and ideal for very large outfits and American motorhomes. All the facilities are available to tourers including the magnificent pool and bar terrace. The site is an ideal stopover but you may decide to stay longer.

Facilities

Shower and toilet available to tourers, other facilities including those for disabled campers in the restaurant area (08.00-22.00). The owners are building two additional showers. Washing machine and dryer. Bar, terrace and takeaway. Restaurant. Bread to order. Swimming pool (June - Oct) with jacuzzi. Tennis. Boules. Free use of bikes and canoes. Soirées. Children's activities. Off site: Fummel, Rocamadour and Cahors.

Open: All year.

Directions

Site is between Fumel and Soturac. From Fumel, take D911 signed Cahors, then follow signs to Domaine de Guillalmes. Turn right 150 m. before Soturac (site signed). GPS: N44:28.983 E01:00.562

Charges guide

Per unit incl. 2 persons	€ 18,00 - € 22,00
extra person	€ 3,50 - € 5,50
child (under 7 yrs)	€ 2,50 - € 4,50
electricity (4/6A)	€ 5,00 - € 6,00

MAP 12

These two quiet and deeply rural provinces are right in the centre of France and are surrounded by the tourist regions of the Loire Valley and the Dordogne. Unknown to many, it is often 'forgotten territory' but by some it's considered close to paradise.

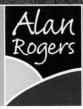

Alan Rogers

Limousin & Auvergne

WE HAVE COMBINED TWO OFFICIAL REGIONS: LIMOUSIN WITH DÉPARTEMENTS 19 CORRÈZE, 23 CREUSE, 87 HAUTE-VIENNE; AND AUVERGNE, 03 ALLIER, 15 CANTAL 43 HAUTE-LOIRE, 63 PUY-DE-DÔME. ALSO INCLUDED IS 48 LOZÈRE, PART OF THE OFFICAL REGION OF LANGUEDOC-ROUSSILLON

This is the home of Limoges porcelain and Aubusson tapestry, of exceptional Romanesque and Gothic churches and fairytale Renaissance châteaux. Limousin is an unspoilt, thinly populated region on the western side of the Massif Central. With hills and gorges and lush green meadows, numerous ancient village churches dot the landscape as well as more imposing abbey churches and fortresses. The many lakes and rivers of the Limousin provide endless possibilities for canoeing, sailing, wind-surfing and other watersports. To the south, fortified cities cling to mountain sides, home to many religious events and legends.

The Auvergne, set in the heart of the Massif Central, was formed by a series of volcanic eruptions and is a dramatic region of awe-inspiring non-active volcanoes, lakes, sparkling rivers, green valleys and forests. There are also numerous underground streams that have carved out extensive and fantastic cave systems, for which the region is famous. It is a wonderful destination for nature lovers, those who enjoy active outdoor pursuits or for people who want to relax at spa resorts.

Places of interest

Aubusson: long tradition of tapestry making, Hotel de Ville tapestry collections.

Clermont-Ferrand: old city centre, 11th- and 12th-century Notre Dame du Port Basilica, 13th-century cathedral; known as *ville noire* for its houses built in local black volcanic rock.

Limoges: porcelain, enamel and faience work, château, church of St Michel-de-Lions, cathedral of St Etienne.

Vichy: spa, natural spring park.

Cuisine of the region

Limousin is known for a thick soup called *bréjaude* and its beef, which is extremely tender and full of flavour. Local specialties in the Auvergne include ham and andouille sausages, stuffed cabbage, and bacon with lentil and *cèpes* (mushrooms). Le Puy is famed for its lentils and *Vereine du Velay* – yellow and green liqueurs made from over 30 mountain plants.

Aligot: purée of potatoes with Tomme de Cantal cheese, cream, garlic and butter.

Friand Sanflorin: pork meat and herbs in pastry.

Jambon d'Auvergne: a tasty mountain ham.

Perdrix à l'Auvergnate: partridge stewed in white wine.

Potée Auvergnate: a stew of vegetables, cabbage, pork and sausage.

315

FR03030 Camping Beau Rivage

Rue Claude Decloître, les Berges de l'Allier, F-03700 Bellerive-sur-Allier (Allier)

Tel: **04 70 32 26 85**. Email: **camping-beaurivage@wanadoo.fr**　　www.alanrogers.com/FR03030

This well maintained, compact, urban site beside the River Allier is on the outskirts of the famous spa town of Vichy. It has recently been completely refurbished by the enthusiastic new owners (good English and Dutch spoken). Some of the 80 medium sized, reasonably level pitches have delightful views across the river to the beautiful Parc Napoléon beyond. They are separated by flowering shrubs and hedging, and mature trees offer some shade; 10A electricity is available on all pitches and 12 are fully serviced. Almost 50% of the pitches are occupied by mobile homes and chalets to rent.

Facilities	Directions
Very clean, modern airy sanitary facilities in individual cubicles in pleasantly decorated buildings. Fully equipped, they include mostly British type toilets and a baby room. Laundry facilities. Motorcaravan service point. Small bar with snacks (March - Oct). River fishing. Play area. Bicycles and pedaloes. Minigolf. Archery. Internet including WiFi. Off site: Riding, canoeing and tennis nearby. Very close to the site are several bars and restaurants. Hypermarket complex within 1 km. Vichy 2 km.	Well signed in Bellerive on the west bank of the River Allier. Leave A71 at exit 12 (Vichy). After about 15 km. turn right at large roundabout with fountains and follow signs, Berges des Allier, Campings and Beaurivage. GPS: N46:05.817 E03:26.407

Open: 22 March - 30 October.

Charges guide

Per person	€ 3,80 - € 4,90
child (0-7 yrs)	€ 2,90 - € 3,80
pitch incl. electricity (10A)	€ 6,80 - € 9,00
Camping Cheques accepted.	

FR03050 Camping Caravaning la Petite Valette

Sazeret, F-03390 Montmarault (Allier)

Tel: **04 70 07 64 57**. Email: **la.petite.valette@wanadoo.fr**　　www.alanrogers.com/FR03050

Originally a working farm, La Petite Valette has been transformed by its hard working Dutch and German owners into a very attractive and peaceful, secluded campsite. There are 55 level grassy pitches of good size, many with rural views, each with an electricity point (6A). They are separated by flowering bushes and trees giving some shade and privacy and many have pleasant, rural views. A small lake in one of the lower fields is stocked with fish for anglers. The countryside is ideal for cycling and there are many interesting old villages nearby.

Facilities	Directions
Good clean toilet facilities in outbuildings. Unit for people with disabilities, families and babies. Laundry. Bread. Meals, snacks (to order). Takeaway. Small swimming and paddling pools. Sunbathing areas. Play area with seating. Mountain bike hire. Organised activities in July/Aug. Off site: Tennis, riding and sailing in the area. Small town of Montmarault 6 km. for shops.	Leave A71 exit 11. First roundabout take D46 signed St Pourcain. Shortly at roundabout take D945 signed Deux-Chaises and La Valette. After 3 km. take third left, site sign, follow narrow lanes to site (just under 2 km). GPS: N46:32.568 E02:59.581

Open: 1 April - 30 October.

Charges guide

Per person	€ 3,95 - € 4,95
pitch incl. electricity	€ 9,20 - € 10,90
For one night stay 1/7-31/8, plus 10%.	

FR03080 Camping les Acacias

Rue Claude Decloître, F-03700 Bellerive-sur-Allier (Allier)

Tel: **04 70 32 36 22**. Email: **camping-acacias03@orange.fr**　　www.alanrogers.com/FR03080

Les Acacias is a compact, urban site on the west bank of the Allier river. It is opposite the historic spa town of Vichy which has many attractions including spas, theatre, a racecourse, ample sporting opportunities and numerous shops bars and restaurants. There are 85 level, grass/gravel pitches in the four star section of this site. Separated by hedges and shaded by mature trees, there are 57 for touring (10A electricity) and some fully serviced. Access is easy for large units, although some busy roads must be negotiated. It is a good short stay site for visiting Vichy and the region around.

Facilities	Directions
Adequate toilet blocks but with no facilities for campers with disabilities; otherwise all necessary facilities. Motorcaravan services. Small shop (10/5-30/9). Bar and takeaway (20/6-15/9). Swimming pool with sunbathing area and slides. Boules. Play area. Games/TV rooms. Organised family activities in July/Aug. Canoes and pedaloes to rent. WiFi. Off site: Shops and hypermarket 500 m. River beach, boat hire and golf 1 km. Bicycle hire, large swimming pool 2 km. Riding 5 km. Vichy 2 km.	From the A71 take exit 12 (Vichy) and head east on A719 then N209 to Bellerive-sur-Allier. Turn right at roundabout with fountains, follow signs to Berges des Allier, Campings and then Acacias. Site is 3 km. GPS: N46:06.986 E03:25.543

Open: 1 April - 15 October.

Charges guide

Per person	€ 3,80 - € 4,90
child (under 7 yrs)	€ 2,30 - € 3,50
pitch	€ 3,80 - € 5,80
electricity (10A)	€ 3,00

Check real time availability and at-the-gate prices...

www.alanrogers.com

FR03010 Camping de la Filature

Ile de Nieres, F-03450 Ebreuil (Allier)

Tel: 04 70 90 72 01. Email: camping.filature@libertysurf.fr   www.alanrogers.com/FR03010

Near the spa town of Vichy and beside a fine fly fishing river, this traditional touring and camping site makes a good base to explore the Auvergne including the nearby river gorges, châteaux, mountains and lakes. There are 80 spacious, grassy pitches, most with shade from mature trees and many directly by the river. The river is clean, shallow and pleasant to play in with a deeper swimming area 500 m. away. Most pitches have electricity (3/6A). You will receive a warm welcome from the English owners, who provide good value and very popular takeaway food. The quiet country roads are ideal for walking and cycling, especially mountain biking, and for touring by car.

Facilities

Very clean sanitary facilities are in individual cubicles. Fully equipped, they include mostly British type toilets, a bathroom and a room for disabled visitors. Laundry facilities. Small shop for essentials (1/5-30/9). Baker calls. Bar (1/6-30/9). Excellent takeaway (1/6-30/9). Barbecues and pizza nights organised in high season. River bathing and fishing. Play area. Bicycle hire. Minigolf. Off site: Riding, canoeing and tennis nearby. Ébreuil with shops and restaurants 1 km.

Open: 31 March - 1 October.

Directions

Site is well signed from exit 12 of A71 autoroute to Clermont Ferrand in the direction of Ebreuil. It is about 6 km. from the A71 and 1 km. west of Ebreuil beside the river on the D915 towards the Chouvigny gorges. GPS: N46:06.526 E03:04.403

Charges guide

Per unit incl. 2 persons	€ 17,00
extra person	€ 5,00
child (under 16 yrs)	€ 3,00
electricity (3/6A)	€ 3,50
Discounts in low season.	

Don't wait to die to go to heaven, visit the: ★★★★

CAMPING DE LA FILATURE DE LA SIOULE

03450 EBREUIL, FRANCE - 0033 (0)4 70 90 72 01

camping.filature@aliceadsl.fr

• Clean facilities with really hot water • Bar and takeaway (real home cooking) • Orchard setting by lovely clean trout river with swimming areas • Spacious pitches with shade • Free wifi link • Play areas • Economic and luxury mobile homes to rent • Canoeing, riding, fabulous walking and cycling • Ideal centre to visit Auvergne • 10 minutes from exit 12 Autoroute A71-A75 (free) to Millau and Montpellier • 30 days for 2 persons, including electricity, € 360,- except 14 July to 15 August.

www.campingfilature.com

FR03120 Flower Camping la Roseraie

Route de Randan, F-03700 Brugheas (Allier)

Tel: 04 70 32 43 33. Email: camping.laroseraie@wanadoo.fr   www.alanrogers.com/FR03120

La Roseraie is a member of the Flower group of campsites and can be found in the volcanic region of the Auvergne with fine mountain views all around. The site is on the edge of the pretty village of Brugheas, parts of which date back to the Roman era. The attractive spa town of Vichy with its parks stretching along the banks of the Allier is very close and easily visited by bicycle. There are 80 pitches here, some of which are occupied by mobile homes and chalets. The pitches, grassy and mostly shaded, are large (minimum 100 sq.m), some very large (250 sq.m), and the majority have electrical connections.

Facilities

Shop. Bar. Restaurant/snack bar and takeaway. Swimming pool. Games room. Play area. Archery. Bicycle hire. Minigolf. Activity and entertainment programme. Mobile homes for rent. Off site: Vichy 7 km. Cycle and walking tracks. Puy de Dome. Le Pal theme park.

Open: 1 April - 30 October.

Directions

From Vichy, cross the Allier and head south west on the D1093 and then the D117 as far as Brugheas. Site is clearly signed. GPS: N46:04.777 E03:22.928

Charges guide

Per unit incl. 2 persons and electricity	€ 17,80
extra person	€ 4,00 - € 6,00
child (under 7 yrs)	€ 3,00

www.flowercampings.com

Check real time availability and at-the-gate prices...

www.alanrogers.com

FR03170 Camping Municipal Dompierre-sur-Besbre

F-03290 Dompierre-sur-Besbre (Allier)

Tel: **04 70 34 55 57**   www.alanrogers.com/FR03170

This immaculate, attractive and excellent value for money site has 68 level, partly shaded and individually hedged, grassy pitches, all with easy access. There are a few long stay units, leaving about 65 for tourers, all with electricity (10A) and most being fully serviced. It is located next to the municipal sports fields and is ideal for motorcaravans being within easy walking distance of the town centre and supermarket (700 m). The warden is very proud of his efficiently run site and its award-winning floral displays. Twin axle caravans are not accepted.

Facilities

Modernised, heated toilet blocks, very clean with all necessary facilities including provision for disabled visitors. Some washbasins in curtained cubicles for ladies. Washing machine. Excellent motorcaravan services. Charcoal barbecues are not permitted. Off site: The small town has shops, restaurants and a Saturday market. Vallée de la Besbre has a wealth of activities, several rivers and small lakes nearby for fishing. Cycle tracks, footpaths, equestrian centres. Le Pal theme park and zoo 8 km.

Open: 15 May - 15 September.

Directions

Dompierre is 35 km. east of Moulins. Leave N79 at eastern end of Dompierre bypass, turn southwest on N2079 towards town. Entrance to sports complex and campsite is on left beyond D55 before the river bridge and town centre. GPS: N46:31.052 E03:41.24

Charges guide

Per person	€ 2,20
child (5-12 yrs)	€ 1,30
pitch	€ 1,80 - € 2,10
electricity	€ 2,10

FR15030 Camping Caravaning le Val Saint-Jean

F-15200 Mauriac (Cantal)

Tel: **04 71 67 31 13**. Email: contact@revea-vacances.com   www.alanrogers.com/FR15030

Le Val Saint-Jean is set beside a lake in the heart of the département of Cantal. The campsite has 100 generously sized, slightly sloping, touring pitches (with 10A electricity), many with good views. It is organised for maximum privacy and you are never far from a sanitary block. Most of the activities are situated by the lake where you can use all the facilities of the leisure club (high season) including cycling, canoeing, kayaking and pedaloes. This less well known region is well worth exploring and the local gastronomy can be experienced in the village of Mauriac with its attractive architecture typical of the area. Salers, one of the most beautiful French towns is 20 km.

Facilities

The two toilet blocks are well equipped with hot water throughout, providing some washbasins in cabins, dishwashing sinks and a laundry room. Facilities for people with disabilities. Limited shop. Bar, snack bar and restaurant (all May - Sept). Play area and playing field. Activities organised for children in July/Aug. Off site: Sandy beach. Lake fishing and swimming. Swimming pool (1-6/15-9). Golf. Guided walks. Mauriac village 1.6 km. Riding 3 km.

Open: 25 April - 27 September.

Directions

Mauriac is around 120 km. southwest of Clermont-Ferrand. Leave A89 autoroute at junction 23 (Ussel West), take D979 (Bort-les-Orgues) for 5 km. Turn right onto D982 (Mauriac) for 40 km. Follow site signs in town. GPS: N45:13.120 E02:18.953

Charges 2009

Per unit incl. 2 persons and electricity	€ 17,10 - € 23,10
extra person	€ 4,40 - € 5,40
child (2-7 yrs)	free - € 3,30
dog	€ 1,50

Holidays in chalets and mobile homes Pitches and natural settings

REVEA
Vacances Couleurs Nature

Brochures, information and reservation
+33 (0)473 938 044
www.revea-vacances.fr
23, rue Jean Claret
63000 Clermont-Ferrand

Check real time availability and at-the-gate prices...

www.**alanrogers**.com

FR19090 **Camping le Vaurette**

Monceaux-sur-Dordogne, F-19400 Argentat (Corrèze)

Tel: 05 55 28 09 67. Email: **info@vaurette.com**   www.alanrogers.com/FR19090

You are assured of a warm welcome at this immaculate site, beautifully situated beside the shallow river Dordogne and just a few kilometres from Argentat. There are 120 large, gently sloping grass pitches, 118 for touring. Separated by a large variety of beautiful trees and shrubs offering varying amounts of shade, all have 6A electricity and many have good views over the river Dordogne as the pitches nearest the river are slightly terraced. The owners run an active campsite for all the family whilst maintaining an air of tranquility (no radios). Excellent English is spoken. The ancient barn at the far end of the site houses the bar and a large TV room (large screen) and the terrace overlooks the good sized and attractive, heated swimming and paddling pools (all season).

Facilities

Two very clean traditional toilet blocks offer all the expected facilities, including facilities for people with disabilities. Further facilities are near the bar and heated pool. Motorcaravan service point. Shop and takeaway (July/Aug). Football. Gym. Badminton. Boules. Tennis. Fishing. River bathing. Accompanied canoe trips, walks and mountain bike rides. Organised activities for all the family (July and Aug) but no late night discos etc. WiFi. Off site: Argentat with shops and watersports centre 9 km. Riding 15 km.

Open: 1 May - 21 September.

Directions

A20 or A89 - Tulle exit - then N120 to Argentat, onto D12 towards Beaulieu. Site is on the left. GPS: N45:02.739 E01:53.058

Charges 2009

Per unit incl. 2 persons	€ 15,50 - € 23,50
extra person (over 2 yrs)	€ 3,30 - € 5,00
electricity (6A)	€ 3,30
dog	€ 2,00 - € 3,50

Camping ★★★★ **Le Vaurette**
Vallée de la Dordogne
19400 Argentat
Tél. +33 5 55 28 09 67   Fax +33 5 55 28 81 14   www.vaurette.com

FR19060 **Camping Domaine le Mialaret**

Route d'Egletons, F-19160 Neuvic (Corrèze)

Tel: 05 55 46 02 50. Email: **info@lemialaret.com**   www.alanrogers.com/FR19060

Mialaret is 4 km. from the village of Neuvic and only 6 km. from the Gorges of the Dordogne. It is set in the grounds of a 19th century château, now a hotel and restaurant with a good reputation. Most pitches are set in a gently sloping parkland situation where 80 trees and many bushes have been planted. Some pitches are level and separated by small bushes, most have some shade and 10A electricity. Entertainment and activities are organised in high season including Djembe drum workshops, a circus school, fishing lessons and evening concerts. In low season there are cooking courses with the chefs of the hotel.

Facilities

Refurbished sanitary blocks give an adequate provision, one heated, facilities for disabled people, washing machines. Motorcaravan services. Shop with bread. Bar, snacks, takeaway. Dinner and bar. Swimming pool with shallow area. Play areas. Tennis. Fishing. Off site: Village with shops and lake 4 km. Golf 4 km. Canoeing, cycling and riding trips organised.

Open: 1 April - 31 October.

Directions

From Clermont-Ferrand or Brives on the A89, take exit 23 for and follow signs for Neuvic (20 km). In Neuvic follow signs for La Mialaret (take first right after Ecomarché). Site is 4 km. GPS: N45:22.945 E02:13.746

Charges guide

Per person	€ 5,00 - € 7,50
child (2-8 yrs)	free - € 5,00
pitch incl. electricity	€ 8,50 - € 12,50
dog	free

Camping Cheques accepted.

Check real time availability and at-the-gate prices...

www.alanrogers.com

CALL 01580 214000
...we'll arrange everything

Service

FR19100 Sunêlia Au Soleil d'Oc

Monceaux-sur-Dordogne, F-19400 Argentat (Corrèze)

Tel: **05 55 28 84 84**. Email: **info@dordogne-soleil.com**   www.alanrogers.com/FR19100

You will be assured of a very warm welcome, throughout the long season, at this attractive family run site set amongst a variety of tall trees on the banks of the river Dordogne. The 120 large, level, grass pitches, 80 for tourists, all with 6A electricity, are mostly separated by neatly trimmed shrubs and hedges. They are set out on two levels; the lower level nearer the river, with fewer static pitches, being some distance from the toilet facilities and sports area. This site should appeal to lovers of watersports and other activities, particularly in July and August when there are many to choose from for all the family. The shop, bar, restaurant and swimming pools are near the entrance and just across the little road is the large sports area. This region is famous for its prehistoric caves, castles and ancient villages and their markets.

Facilities

Two unisex toilet blocks offer all the facilities one would expect. Baby facilities. Shop. Bar. Restaurant and takeaway (1/6-30/9). Outdoor pool (1/5-15/10). New indoor pool planned. Motorcaravan service point. Bathing in the river Dordogne. Canoe hire and organised trips. Volleyball, football, pool table and electronic games. Archery. Minigolf. Fishing. Bicycle hire. Guided walks and bike rides. Entertainment programme (July/Aug). WiFi. Off site: River Dordogne. Argentat 4 km. Riding 15 km.

Open: 1 April - 1 November.

Directions

Leave Argentat on D12 heading southwest (Beaulieu). In 3.5 km. (village of Laygue) turn left across a single track bridge spanning the river Dordogne. Immediately turn left and site is a few hundred metres on left.
GPS: N45:04.514 E01:55.025

Charges guide

Per unit incl. 2 persons	€ 14,50 - € 20,70
extra person	€ 3,80 - € 5,80
child (2-13 yrs)	free - € 3,90
dog	free - € 3,00
Camping Cheques accepted.	

Sunêlia Au Soleil d'Oc****

Sun, Nature, Patrimony, Activities.

Our ingredients for a lovely holiday at the borders of the Dordogne River.

Open from 1st of April - 1st of November

Monceaux sur Dordogne - 19400 Argentat - tél. +33 (0) 555 28 84 84
info@dordogne-soleil.com - www.dordogne-soleil.com - www.campingsoleildoc.com
Camping Cheque
Camping Qualité

FR19070 Camping Château de Gibanel

Saint Martial Entraygues, F-19400 Argentat (Corrèze)

Tel: **05 55 28 10 11**. Email: **contact@camping-gibanel.com**   www.alanrogers.com/FR19070

This slightly terraced campsite is located in a beautiful estate, dominated by the 16th-century château, on the banks of a very clean lake in this lesser known part of the Dordogne valley. The very friendly family ensures that everything is of a very high standard. Nearly all of the 250 grassy pitches are used for touring units. All have electricity (6A) and are separated by a variety of mature trees giving varying amounts of shade. Many of the trees have low branches making access to most pitches rather difficult for large motorcaravans. Some pitches have an ideal position alongside the lake.

Facilities

Four modern, spacious and very clean toilet blocks include many large cubicles with a shower and washbasin. Good provision for disabled visitors. Washing machine and dryer. Good shop for basics. Bar, snack and takeaway (July/Aug). Swimming and paddling pools. Range of family activities in July/Aug, including dance evenings, folklore events, watersports, walking and cycling. Bicycle hire (July/Aug). TV room. Boules. Off site: Argentat 5 km.

Open: 29 May - 5 September.

Directions

Site is 5 km. northeast of Argentat. Take D18, signed Eggletons, and after 4 km. alongside the lake, fork right at site sign. Follow lane down to site.
GPS: N45:06.650 E01:57.536

Charges 2009

Per unit incl. 2 persons and electricity	€ 22,20
extra person	€ 5,00
child (2-7 yrs)	€ 2,70
dog	€ 1,50

Check real time availability and at-the-gate prices...

www.alanrogers.com

FR19140 Campéole le Coiroux

Centre Touristique du Coiroux, F-19190 Aubazine (Corrèze)

Tel: 05 55 27 21 96. Email: nadine.ferran@atciat.com   www.alanrogers.com/FR19140

Le Coiroux, part of the Campeole group, is set in a picturesque location in the heart of a forest on the edge of a large leisure park and lake. There are 174 large pitches, 62 for touring all with 10A electricity. They are flat and grassy with small dividing hedges and trees giving shade. The large number of mobile homes and chalets on site are separate from the camping area and not intrusive. There is everything one needs for a family holiday at this site which caters for adults and children of all ages. There is an excellent 27-hole golf complex 800 m. away and lake fishing within 300 m. Activities in the area for youngsters include a tree walking adventure course and paintball. Rocamadour and many other tourist destinations are within 1 hours drive.

Facilities

One large modern very well equipped sanitary block with all necessary facilities including those for campers with disabilities and baby room. Washing machines and tumble dryers. Motorcaravan service point. Large heated swimming pool (17/5-28/9). Poolside bar and snack bar and large shop selling groceries, fruit and vegetables (14/6-14/9). Boules. Tennis. Organised activities for children, teenagers and adults throughout the day (July/Aug). Off site: Leisure park (reduced fees charged).

Open: 28 March - 27 September.

Directions

Leave A20 exit 50 Brive centre, take N28 towards Tulle. At the village of Gare d'Aubazine turn right to Aubazine. Continue for 6 km. through village, take road to Chastang and follow signs to Parc Touristique du Coiroux about 4 km.
GPS: N45:11.180 E01:42.465

Charges guide

Per unit incl. 2 persons	€ 13,00 - € 19,80
extra person	€ 4,00 - € 6,40
child (2-5 yrs)	€ 3,40 - € 4,10
electricity	€ 4,00

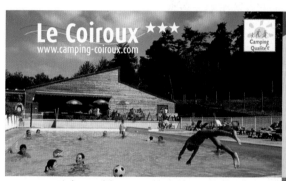

Le Coiroux ★★★
www.camping-coiroux.com

Camping Qualité

Pitches, Mobil Home and bungalows rental

Campéole
CAMPINGS ET LOCATIONS

Quiet, Spacey and Cheerful
Nearby the Dordogne Valley and
the Périgord Noir
Forests, lakes, rivers
nature everywhere !
Picturesque villages
English spoken
Open from 28/03 au 27/09/2009

Heated swimmingpool from 01/05 to 27/09/2009

FR19080 Camping le Vianon

F-19160 Palisse (Corrèze)

Tel: 05 55 95 87 22. Email: camping.vianon@wanadoo.fr   www.alanrogers.com/FR19080

You will receive a very warm welcome from the Dutch owners of this spacious and peaceful site and they speak excellent English. The site is tucked away in the lesser known, very beautiful Corrèze region yet it is only a few kilometres from the river Dordogne. This region is reputed to have the purest air in France. The grassy, slightly sloping pitches are of a good size in a natural woodland setting with tall trees offering shade and all have 16A electricity. The bar, restaurant and terrace overlook the swimming pool and sunbathing area and are open all season.

Facilities

Modern toilet blocks with all the necessary facilities. Unit for disabled visitors. Bar. Restaurant, takeaway. Shop. Boules. Spacious play area. Bicycle hire. Lake fishing. Off site: Small town Neuvic with shops, restaurants 9 km. Large lake with water sports, swimming. Canoeing in the Dordogne (30 minutes). Riding and golf course at Neuvic. Marked walks and cycle rides.

Open: All year (telephone first Oct - Apr).

Directions

Leave A89 southwest of Ussel and take N89 towards Egletons. In about 7 km. just before Combressol, turn left on D47 signed Palisse and Camping le Vianon. Site entrance is on the left in 7 km.
GPS: N45:25.607 E02:12.350

Charges 2009

Per unit incl. 2 persons and electricity	€ 20,00 - € 29,35
extra person (over 2 yrs)	€ 4,00 - € 5,50
dog	€ 1,50 - € 2,00
Special rates for long stays.	

321

The Travel Service ...we'll arrange everything
BOOK THIS SITE CALL 01580 214000

FR19130 Flower Camping des Iles

Boulevard Rodolphe de Turenne, F-19120 Beaulieu-sur-Dordogne (Corrèze)
Tel: 05 55 91 02 65. Email: info@campingdesiles.fr   www.alanrogers.com/FR19130

This is a very pleasant and well equipped site in a beautiful location on a small island in the river Dordogne. Camping des Iles is a very attractive family run site only five minutes walk away from the centre of the medieval town of Beaulieu-sur-Dordogne with its ancient streets, old churches, many shops and restaurants. This five hectare site has 120 shady, grass pitches, 90 of which are available for touring all with 10A electricity.

Facilities

Three modern, clean toilet blocks. Baby room. Facilities for campers with disabilities. Laundry room. Motorcaravan service point. Heated pool (June- September), poolside bar, snacks. Boules. Canoe hire. Fishing. Children's entertainment (3-12 yrs). Evening soirees. No shop or bread on site because of its close proximity to the town. Off site: Pizzeria and takeaway 200 m. Tennis 600 m. Bicycle hire 8 km. Golf or riding 18 km.

Open: 7 April - 15 October.

Directions

The site is in the centre of the Beaulieu-sur-Dordogne on the D940. From Tulle turn right or from Montal turn left. Approach site with care through the narrow streets. Enter site through narrow archway. GPS: N44:58.782 E01:50.409

Charges guide

Per unit incl. 2 persons	€ 11,90 - € 19,90
with electricity	€ 14,90 - € 23,50
extra person	€ 3,90 - € 6,50

FR43030 Kawan Village de Vaubarlet

Vaubarlet, F-43600 Sainte Sigolène (Haute-Loire)
Tel: 04 71 66 64 95. Email: camping@vaubarlet.com   www.alanrogers.com/FR43030

This peacefully located, spacious riverside family site has 131 marked, level, grassy, open pitches, with those around the perimeter having shade, all having electricity (6A). With 102 pitches for tourists, the remainder are occupied by site owned tents or mobile homes. Those who really like to get away from it all can use a small 'wild camping' area on the opposite side of the river with its own very basic facilities. This area is reached either by footbridge or a separate road access. The main site is separated from the river (unfenced) by a large field used for sports activities.

Facilities

Good, clean toilet blocks, baby room, washing machine, dryer. Two family bathrooms are also suitable for people with disabilities. WiFi. Small shop, bread. Takeaway, bar (all season). Attractive swimming pool, children's pool. Bicycle hire. Boules. Large games area. Playground. Activities in season include camp fire, music evenings, children's canoe lessons. Trout fishing. Birdwatching. Off site: Shops in Ste-Sigolène 6 km. Riding 15 km. Walks and cycle tracks from site.

Open: 1 May - 30 September.

Directions

Site is 6 km. southwest of Ste Sigolène on the D43 signed Grazac. Keep left by river bridge, site signed. Site shortly on right. GPS: N45:12.936 E04:12.766

Charges 2009

Per unit incl. 2 persons	€ 19,00
extra person	€ 4,00
child (2-7 yrs)	€ 3,00
electricity	€ 3,00
Camping Cheques accepted.	

FR48000 Camping Caravaning le Champ d'Ayres

Route de la Brèze, F-48150 Meyrueis (Lozère)
Tel: 04 66 45 60 51. Email: campinglechampdayres@wanadoo.fr   www.alanrogers.com/FR48000

This is a traditional family run site, set in the heart of the Cevennes Champ d'Ayres. Neat, tidy and well kept, it is run with young families in mind (teenagers might be bored). The site is slightly sloping with 85 grass pitches, 64 for touring, the majority hedged with well trimmed bushes and most with some shade. All have electricity (6/10A) but some may require long leads. The area is surrounded by mountains and gorges and some of the roads are not for the faint-hearted or those with large and under-powered units. Being very centrally located, there are many attractions in the area.

Facilities

The excellent toilet block is kept very clean and has all the necessary facilities. Baby room. Facilities for visitors with disabilities. Laundry facilities. Shop, small bar and takeaway (all 1/5-15/9). New heated swimming and paddling pool (16/5-15/9). Play area. Games room. Boules. Bicycle hire. Activities arranged (July/Aug). WiFi. Off site: The small, pretty town of Meyrueis (500 m) has many shops and restaurants. Fishing 100 m. Riding 1 km.

Open: 11 April - 19 September.

Directions

From N9 at Aquessac (5 km. north of Millau) take D907 (Gorge du Tarn). At Rozier turn right on D996 (Meyrueis and Gorges de la Jonte). In Meyrueis follow signs for Château d'Ayres and site signs. Site is 500 m. east of town. GPS: N44:10.860 E03:26.135

Charges 2009

Per unit incl. 2 persons	€ 10,00 - € 21,00
extra person	€ 3,00 - € 4,50
electricity	€ 3,00

Check real time availability and at-the-gate prices...
www.alanrogers.com

www.flowercampings.com

Route de la Châtre, B.P. 12, F-23600 Boussac-Bourg (Creuse)

Tel: 05 55 65 02 21. Email: info.camping-de.poinsouze@orange.fr

Mobile homes ▶ page 505

www.alanrogers.com/FR23010

BOOK THIS SITE
CALL 01580 214000
...we'll arrange everything
Service The Travel

Le Château de Poinsouze is a well established site with pitches arranged on the open, gently sloping, grassy park to one side of the Château's main drive – a beautiful plane tree avenue. It is a well designed, high quality site. The 145 touring pitches, some with lake frontage, all have electricity (6-25A), water, drain and 66 have sewerage connections. The site has a friendly family atmosphere, there are organised activities in main season including dances, children's games and crafts, family triathlons and there are marked walks around the park and woods. All facilities are open all season. This is a top class site with a formula which should ensure a stress-free, enjoyable family holiday. Boussac (2.5 km) has a market every Thursday morning. The massive 12/15th century fortress, Château de Boussac, is open daily all year. The Château (not open to the public) lies across the lake from the site. Exceptionally well restored outbuildings on the opposite side of the drive house a new restaurant serving superb cuisine, other facilities and the pool area.

Facilities

High quality, sanitary unit, washing machines, dryer, ironing, suites for disabled people. Motorcaravan services. Well stocked shop. Takeaway. Bar, internet, two satellite TVs, library. Restaurant with new mini-bar for low season. Heated swimming pool, slide, children's pool. Fenced playground. Pétanque. Bicycle hire. Free fishing in the lake, boats and lifejackets can be hired. Sports facilities. Dogs are only allowed for one overnight stay between 5/7-16/8.

Open: 8 May - 13 September.

Directions

Site entrance is 2.5 km. north of Boussac on D917 (towards La Châtre). GPS: N46:22.356 E02:12.157

Charges 2009

Per unit incl. 2 persons incl. electricity (6A) water,	€ 13,00 - € 22,00
waste water	€ 16,00 - € 25,00
extra person	€ 3,00 - € 6,00
child (2-7 yrs)	€ 2,00 - € 5,00
dog	€ 3,00

Camping Cheques accepted.

Centre of France

Château de Poinsouze

★★★★

Family Campsite. Calm & Nature. Exceptional fully enclosed sanitary facilities.
Heated swimming pool. Animation 4-12 years, Chalets & mobil-homes for hire. Gites all year long.
Route de la Châtre 23600 Boussac-Bourg - Tel: 0033 555 65 02 21 - Fax: 0033 555 65 86 49
info.camping-de.poinsouze@orange.fr / www.camping-de-poinsouze.com

Check real time availability and at-the-gate prices...
www.**alanrogers**.com

BOOK THIS SITE
CALL 01580 214000
...we'll arrange everything
The Travel Service

FR48020 Kawan Village de Capelan

F-48150 Meyrueis (Lozère)

Tel: **04 66 45 60 50**. Email: **camping.le.capelan@wanadoo.fr**

www.alanrogers.com/FR48020

The Lozère is one of France's least populated regions but offers some truly spectacular, rugged scenery, wonderful flora and fauna and old towns and villages. Le Capelan has 119 grassy pitches in total, 79 are for touring and are strung out alongside the river, most with some shade and all with electrical connections (6/10A). Around 40 pitches are used for mobile homes. There is direct river access from the site and trout fishing is popular. Although there are special facilities, the site is not ideal for visitors with disabilities. English is spoken.

Facilities

Well maintained toilet blocks, facilities for visitors with disabilities (but not ideal). Three bathrooms for rent. Small shop. Bar (both from 1/6). Takeaway (from 1/7). Swimming, paddling pools, sunbathing terrace (from 1/6), access via 60 steps. Multisports terrain. Satellite TV. Play area. Leisure activities including supervised rock climbing. Fishing. Internet. Communal barbecue area, only gas and electric barbecues. Off site: Town centre with shops 1 km. Bicycle hire 1 km. Riding 3 km. Canoeing. Cévennes national park. Caves. Vulture visitor centre.

Open: 1 May - 15 September.

Directions

From Clermont Ferrand on the A75 take exit 44-1 Aguessac-le Rozier towards Meyrueis. The site is 1 km. west of Meyruels on the D996, the road to La Jonte. It is well signed from the centre of the town. GPS: N44:11.150 E03:25.193

Charges 2009

Per unit incl. 2 persons	€ 13,50 - € 21,00
incl. electricity	€ 16,50 - € 24,00
extra person	€ 3,00 - € 4,70
child (under 7 yrs)	€ 2,00 - € 3,20
Camping Cheques accepted.	

FR48030 Camping Beldoire

F-48210 Les Vignes (Lozère)

Tel: **04 66 48 82 79**. Email: **camping-beldoire@wanadoo.fr**

www.alanrogers.com/FR48030

Situated in the wonderful Gorges du Tarn area, Beldoire is arranged in two sections on either side of the road. There are 142 average sized, stony pitches (with 127 for touring), all with 6A electricity and most having shade. Rock pegs are essential. The flatter section next to the river (101 pitches) takes all units. All the amenities are in the steeply terraced, upper section on the other side of the busy road, The 41 pitches are only available in July/August and only take tents. The tortuous, narrow, hilly roads makes access difficult for large and underpowered units.

Facilities

Four basic toilet blocks, two in each section, have the necessary facilities. The steepness of the roads means that this site is not suitable for those with walking difficulties. Small shop. Bar/restaurant and takeaway (15/6-30/8). Small swimming pool (10/6-14/9). Games room. Play area. Fishing and bathing in river. Off site: Riding and bicycle hire 10 km. Rafting, canoeing, canyoning, climbing.

Open: 14 April - 14 September.

Directions

Leave A75 at exit 44 and go south on N9 to Aquessac (14 km). Turn left on D907, signed Gorges du Tarn and site entrance is just past les Vignes (25 km). GPS: N44:17.224 E03:14.044

Charges guide

Per unit incl. 2 persons	€ 10,30 - € 14,30
extra person	€ 3,20 - € 3,80
electricity	€ 3,00

FR48040 Camping la Cascade

Salvinsac, F-48150 Meyrueis (Lozère)

Tel: **04 66 45 45 45**. Email: **contact@camping-la-cascade.com**

www.alanrogers.com/FR48040

A delightful small site run by a friendly family, La Cascade is located in the Lozère, one of France's least populated regions. There is some truly spectacular, rugged scenery, wonderful flora and fauna and old towns and villages. This site has only 50 good sized, grassy pitches, separated by trees giving varying amounts of shade. There are 37 for touring and 24 with 10A electricity. It is not recommended for large outfits due to the narrow access road. This is an ideal site for unwinding and exploring this wonderful region on foot, on bike or by car.

Facilities

Two small heated toilet blocks with good facilities including baby bath. Washing machine. Bread to order, cold drinks and local specialities. Family room. Play area. Trout fishing. Communal barbecue. Bicycle hire. Guided walks. Off site: Meyrueis, shops, bars, restaurant, banks 3 km. Riding 3 km. Canoeing. Cévennes National Park. Caves. Vulture visitor centre.

Open: 15 April - 30 September.

Directions

From Clermont Ferrand on the A75 take exit 44-1, Aguessac-le Rozier, towards Meyrueis. Pass through Meyrueis on to the D996 (signed Florac). In 3 km. turn right down narrow road to site. GPS: N44:11.800 E03:27.383

Charges 2009

Per unit incl. 2 persons	€ 11,20 - € 15,40
extra person	€ 2,90 - € 3,90
electricity (6A)	€ 2,10 - € 3,00

Check real time availability and at-the-gate prices...

www.alanrogers.com

FR48060 Camping les Terrasses du Lac de Naussac

Lac de Naussac, F-48300 Langogne (Lozère)

Tel: **04 66 69 29 62**. Email: **info@naussac.com**

www.alanrogers.com/FR48060

With friendly, family owners, this very spacious campsite and hotel complex is on the side of a steep hill at nearly 1,000 m. altitude (nights can be cold). There are 180 good size, grassy, sloping pitches, often with part hardstanding (165 for touring). All have 6/10A electricity and many have panoramic views over the lake and surrounding hills. There are small trees on site offering a little shade. The lake offers a wide range of water based activities, notably sailing and fishing. The Lac de Naussac is the largest in the Lozère and this site has direct access to the lake.

Facilities

Three modern and well maintained, newly refurbished toilet blocks. Motorcaravan service point. Small shop (1/5-30/9). Restaurant/takeaway in hotel. Small swimming pool (1/6-30/9). Lively 'animation' programme in peak season including children's club but no discos. Play area. Communal barbecue area. Gas and electric barbecues only. Internet point and WiFi. Off site: Disco 300 m. Watersorts. Cycle ride around lake of 30 km. Langogne 2 km. Golf 3 km. Riding and bicycle hire 3 km.

Open: 15 April - 30 September.

Directions

Leave N88 (Le Puy - Mende) just southwest of Langogne. Turn north on D26 towards Lac de Naussac and follow signs to site (2.5 km). Park beside lake and just before hotel. Reception inside hotel. GPS: N44:44.083 E03:50.116

Charges guide

Per pitch incl. 2 persons	€ 12,50 - € 13,50
extra person	€ 3,50
electricity	€ 2,50

Camping Cheques accepted.

FR48080 Camping Couderc

Route de Millau, F-48210 Saint Enimie (Lozère)

Tel: **04 66 48 50 53**. Email: **campingcouderc@wanadoo.fr**

www.alanrogers.com/FR48080

A spacious rural site, Couderc is strung out along 1 km. of the clear shallow River Tarn, although access to the river is not easy. The Gorges du Tarn and the high plateaux are well worth exploring. Come in May and June to see the wonderful flowers and butterflies with vultures soaring overhead. There are 130 good sized, level grassy/stony pitches here, separated by vines and mature trees. With 123 for touring units, most have welcome shade and 10A electricity (long leads may be needed). Rock pegs are advised. Although the local roads are winding and narrow, access on the site is good.

Facilities

Several toilet blocks with adequate facilities including those for children. Facilities for visitors with disabilities (but the terrain makes it not ideal for those with walking difficulties). Bar/TV room. Breakfast (all season). Basic shop, bread to order. Swimming and paddling pools (a steep climb from pitches). Play area. Canoe hire and trips run from site. Boules. River fishing. Electric barbecues only - communal barbecues provided. Off site: Ste Enimie 1.5 km. with shops, restaurants, bars, bank. Grottes, canyoning, rock climbing, caving. Gorges of Tarn.

Open: 1 April - 30 September.

Directions

Leave A75 at exit 40 for La Canourgue. Take the D998 to Ste Enimie (28 km) following signs for Millau, Gorges du Tarn. Take the D907 to site on left in 1.5 km. Approach from south not recommended for large outfits. GPS: N44:21.20 E03:24.08

Charges guide

Per unit incl. 2 persons	€ 11,00 - € 17,00
extra person	€ 3,00 - € 4,00
child (under 7 yrs)	€ 1,30 - € 1,60
electricity	€ 3,00

FR63000 Les Chalets du Hameau du Lac

Parcs Résidentiels ▶ page 517

Lieu dit le Pré Bad, le Lac Chambon, F-63790 Chambon-sur-Lac (Puy-de-Dôme)

Tel: **06 12 03 91 56**. E-mail: **auvergne-chalets-location@orange.fr**

www.alanrogers.nl/FR63000

The pitches at this campsite are used exclusively for mobile home and chalet accommodation.

Check real time availability and at-the-gate prices...

www.alanrogers.com

FR63030 Camping Caravaning de l'Europe

Route de Jassat, F-63790 Murol (Puy-de-Dôme)

Tel: **04 73 39 76 66**. Email: **europe.camping@wanadoo.fr**   www.alanrogers.com/FR63030

L'Europe is, in high season, a lively site, dominated by its mobile homes, on the edge of the little town of Murol. The site is 800 m. from the Lac de Chambon which boasts a sandy beach and range of water sports. There are 219 level grassy pitches, 59 for touring, all with electricity and of good size with reasonable shade. With a busy activities programme including evening entertainment. The bar and restaurant overlook the pool complex and is the site's focal point and entertainment centre. The site organises a number of popular excursions.

Facilities

Sanitary facilities include washbasins in cabins and showers and provision for disabled visitors. Laundry facilities. Bar, restaurant and takeaway (6/7-30/8). Swimming pool with toboggan and paddling pool. Tennis. Archery. Boules. Football. Aquagym. Water polo. Play area and large sports area. Internet access and WiFi. Off site: Fishing and bicycle hire 300 m. Riding 5 km. Golf 20 km. Murol 1.5 km. Lac Chambon 2 km.

Open: 30 May - 30 August.

Directions

Site is about 40 km. southwest of Clermont Ferrand. Leave A75 autoroute at exit 6 (St Nectaire). Take D978 to Murol (34 km). At far end of village turn left onto D5. In 300 m. turn right onto D618 (Jassat). Site on left in 300 m. GPS: N45:34.097 E2:56.401

Charges guide

Per unit incl. 2 persons and electricity	€ 14,45 - € 27,60
extra person (over 5 yrs)	€ 2,40 - € 5,45

FR63040 Château Camping la Grange Fort

Les Pradeaux, F-63500 Issoire (Puy-de-Dôme)

Tel: **04 73 71 02 43**. Email: **chateau@lagrangefort.com**   www.alanrogers.com/FR63040

This site has good, modern facilities, yet is oozing with character. It is very popular with the Dutch. The new reception is well stocked with tourist information and an internet access point. The cosy bar still has the old stable stalls and hay racks. The 120 pitches (90 for touring units) are of average size, mostly on grass but with some crushed stone hardstandings, and they are connected by rather narrow roads with limited play space for children. Some of the smaller pitches are in sunny fields around the castle, others in bays with hedges and trees. All have 6A electricity.

Facilities

Refurbished sanitary blocks have facilities for disabled visitors and a 'hydra shower'. Laundry room. Bread. Restaurant and takeaway (1/5-15/9). Bar (15/6-15/9). Indoor pool with sauna, massage (15/4-15/10). Outdoor pools (15/6-1/10). New swimming pool (24.5 x 14.5 m) with jacuzzi. Play area. Internet. WiFi. Tennis, minigolf, football, boules. Organised activities in season. Torches useful. Off site: Fishing 250 m. Riding 8 km.

Open: 10 April - 15 October.

Directions

From A75 autoroute take exit 13 onto D996 east towards Parentignat. At first roundabout take first exit on D999 new road (St Remy, La Vernet). At next roundabout take first exit (D34) and follow campsite signs. GPS: N45:30.525 E03:17.093

Charges guide

Per unit incl. 2 persons	€ 17,40 - € 24,50
extra person	€ 4,75 - € 6,10
electricity	€ 3,25

FR63050 Sunêlia la Ribeyre

Jassat, F-63790 Murol (Puy-de-Dôme)

Tel: **04 73 88 64 29**. Email: **laribeyre@free.fr**   www.alanrogers.com/FR63050

The friendly Pommier family have put much personal care into the construction of this site. There are 400 level, grassy pitches, of which 310 are for tourers and 200 of these have electricity (6/10A). Electricity, water and drainage is available for 51 pitches. A superb large indoor/outdoor water park includes slides, toboggan and lazy river and a small man-made lake at one end provides facilities for water sports. It is a great base for touring being only 1 km. from Murol, dominated by its ancient Château, 6 km. from St Nectaire and about 20 km. from Le Mont Dore.

Facilities

Six excellent, very clean modern toilet blocks with facilities for disabled persons. Washing machines, dryers. Snack bar in peak season (1/6-31/8). Large indoor/outdoor water park (heated). TV. Games room. Tennis. Fishing. Lake swimming and canoeing. Many organised activities in high season. Off site: Riding 300 m. Shops and restaurants and a large Wednesday market (high season) in Murol 1.5 km. Bicycle hire 1 km. Fishing and watersports at Lac Chambon 3 km.

Open: 1 May - 15 September.

Directions

From A75 Autoroute, exit 6 signed St Nectaire. Continue to Murol, D978 then D996, several sites signed in town. Turn left up hill, D5, shortly turn right opposite car park, D618, site signed. Site is second on left. GPS: N45:33.770 E02:56.377

Charges 2009

Per unit incl. 2 persons and electricity	€ 23,95 - € 31,30
with services	€ 27,25 - € 36,10
extra person	€ 5,40 - € 6,90

FR63070 Camping le Pré Bas

Lac Chambon, F-63790 Murol (Puy-de-Dôme)

Tel: 04 73 88 63 04. Email: prebas@campingauvergne.com   www.alanrogers.com/FR63070

Le Pré Bas is especially suitable for families and those seeking the watersports opportunities that the lake provides. Level, grassy pitches are divided up by mature hedging and trees and, with 106 mobile homes for rent, around 74 pitches are available for tourists, all with electricity (6A). A gate leads to the lakeside where, in high season, there is windsurfing, pedaloes, canoes and fishing, and 50 m. away is a beach with supervised bathing and a snack bar. The site has a pool complex with heated swimming pools (one covered), a large slide and a paddling pool. A 'Family Center' comprising a 300 sq.m. covered area with sauna, jacuzzi and Turkish bath, was added in 2008. The site is in the heart of the Parc des Volcans d'Auvergne, beside the beautiful Lac Chambon with its clear, clean water, The cable car ride up to the Puy de Sancy, the highest peak in the area, provides superb views offering an excellent opportunity for trekking and mountain bike rides. Superb scenery abounds; wooded mountains rising to over 6,000 feet, flower filled valleys and deep blue lakes.

Facilities

Refurbished toilet building with facilities for guests with disabilities plus four smaller units. Washing machines, dryers, ironing, baby room. Motorcaravan services. Snack bar (10/6-10/9 and some weekends in low season). Three pools of different depths (20/5-10/9, lifeguard in July/Aug). Watersports, fishing in lake. Games room, table tennis, table football, pool, TV, library. Adventure style playground, football, basketball. Organised activities. WiFi. Off site: Lakeside bars, restaurants, shops. Murol 4 km. St Nectaire famous for cheese. Puy-de-Dôme, hang gliding, Vulcania Exhibition.

Open: 1 May - 30 September.

Directions

Leave A75 autoroute at exit 6 and take D978 signed St Nectaire and Murol, then D996. Site is located on left, 3 km. west of Murol towards Mont Dore, at the far end of Lac Chambon.
GPS: N45:34.513 E02:54.854

Charges guide

Per pitch incl. 2 persons	
and electricity	€ 17,90 - € 26,60
extra person	€ 4,10 - € 5,80
child (0-10 yrs)	€ 2,70 - € 5,80
dog	free - € 2,00

Camping ★★★★ du Pré Bas

New for 2008: opening of a ludic and wellness area for moments of pleasure with the whole family!

This area of more than 300 sqm, called 'Family Center', is entirely covered. It includes spa, hammam, sauna, rest area and massage -on demand - for the adults and a play area for children. This one is made of 4 levels (pool with balls, slides, trampoline and a mini-football pitches) for the greatest joy of children from 3 to 12. Mobile homes for rent. Situated at the Lac Chambon

Lac Chambon - 63790 Murol - www.leprebas.com - prebas@campingauvergne.com

FR63060 Camping le Clos Auroy

Rue de la Narse, F-63670 Orcet (Puy-de-Dôme)

Tel: 04 73 84 26 97. Email: info@campingclub.info   www.alanrogers.com/FR63060

You are assured a friendly welcome at Le Clos Auroy. It is a very well maintained and popular site, 300 m. from Orcet, a typical Auvergne village just south of Clermont Ferrand. Being close (3 km) to the A75, and open all year, it makes an excellent stopping off point on the journey north and south but you may be tempted to stay longer. The 90 good size pitches are on level grass, separated by very high, neatly trimmed conifer hedges, offering lots of privacy but not much shade. All have electricity (5/10A) and 25 are fully serviced.

Facilities

High quality, very clean toilet blocks. Washing machine, dryer. Motorcaravan services. Small shop, takeaway (1/7-15/9). Heated pool, jacuzzi, large pool for children (15/5-30/9), terrace near bar (15/5-30/9). Playground. Coffee mornings. Tennis. Children's activities.
Off site: Large playground nearby and riverside walk just outside gate. Village 300 m. Fishing and canoeing 500 m. Parc des Volcans with fantastic scenery.

Open: All year.

Directions

From A75 take exit 4 or 5 towards Orcet and follow campsite signs. It is just before the village.
GPS: N45:42.030 E03:10.154

Charges guide

Per unit incl. 2 persons	
extra person	€ 14,50
child (1-7 yrs)	€ 4,50
electricity (5/10A)	€ 3,05
	€ 3,25 - € 4,75

Less for longer stays in low season. No credit cards.

Check real time availability and at-the-gate prices...

www.alanrogers.com

The Travel Service

BOOK THIS SITE

CALL 01580 214000

...we'll arrange everything

FR63080 Camping le Moulin de Serre

Vallée de la Burande (D73), F-63690 Singles (Puy-de-Dôme)

Tel: **04 73 21 16 06**. Email: **moulin-de-serre@wanadoo.fr**   www.alanrogers.com/FR63080

Off the beaten track, this spacious and well maintained site is set in a wooded valley beside a river where one can pan for gold. It offers a good base for those seeking quiet relaxation in this lesser known area of the Auvergne. The 90 large pitches (55 for touring) are separated by a variety of trees and hedges giving good shade. Some pitches have hardstanding and all have electricity (3-10A), long leads may be necessary. Access around the site is easy but the narrow lanes leading to it are twisting which might prove difficult for larger units.

Facilities

Well appointed. Clean toilet blocks, one heated having excellent facilities for disabled people and babies. New communal barbecue. Heated swimming pool, terrace (8/6-28/9). Takeaway (July/August), bar/restaurant (July/Aug). Bread ((19/5-16/9). Washing machine, dryer. Motorcaravan services. Large play area. Tennis. Canoe hire in high season. Organised activities (July/Aug). Off site: Lake for fishing 2 km. Château de Val 20 km. Spa town of La Bourboule 25 km. Barrage de Bort les Orgues offers watersports. Many marked walks and cycle tracks. Riding.

Open: 14 June - 17 September.

Directions

Site is about 25 km. southwest of La Bourboule. Turn west off the D922 just south of Tauves at site sign. Follow site signs along the D29 and then the D73 for about 10 km. GPS: N45:32.590 E02:32.565

Charges guide

Per unit incl. 2 persons	
and electricity	€ 13,50 - € 22,55
extra person	€ 2,30 - € 4,20
child (under 10 yrs)	€ 1,60 - € 2,90
dog	€ 1,00 - € 1,80

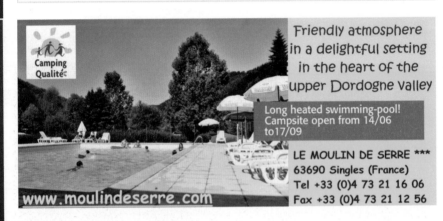

Camping Qualité

Friendly atmosphere in a delightful setting in the heart of the upper Dordogne valley

Long heated swimming-pool! Campsite open from 14/06 to17/09

LE MOULIN DE SERRE ★★★
63690 Singles (France)
Tel +33 (0)4 73 21 16 06
Fax +33 (0)4 73 21 12 56

www.moulindeserre.com

FR63090 Camping les Domes

Les Quatre Routes de Nébouzat, F-63210 Nébouzat (Puy-de-Dôme)

Tel: **04 73 87 14 06**. Email: **camping.les-domes@wanadoo.fr**   www.alanrogers.com/FR63090

A popular site, it is ideally situated for exploring the beautiful region around the Puy-de-Dôme. The site has 65 small to medium sized pitches, most for touring, 50 with 10/15A electricity, separated by trees and hedges. Some pitches have a level, paved area ideal for caravans and motorcaravans. Rock pegs are advised. The attractive reception area comprising the office, a small shop for essentials (high season only) and a meeting room has lots of local information and interesting artefacts. An added small attraction is a heated, covered swimming pool, which can be opened in good weather.

Facilities

Well appointed, clean toilet block, no special facilities for disabled visitors. Basic shop (baker calls). Breakfast, snacks. Boules, pool table, table football, table tennis, giant chess, drafts. Small play area. TV and games room. Off site: Fishing 100 m. Restaurant 200 m. Nebouzat 1.3 km. (shops etc). Riding 6 km. Hang gliding and parascending 8 km. (Puy de Dôme). New Vulcania exhibition 15 minutes drive. Watersports 9 km. Golf 10 km. Clermond Ferrand with its interesting old town and hypermarkets (18 km). Many walks and cycle routes.

Open: 1 May - 30 September.

Directions

Site is 18 km. southwest of Clermont Ferrand and is well signed from the roundabout at the junction of the D2089 and the D941A. It is a few hundred metres from the roundabout along the D216 towards Orcival. GPS: N45:43.537 E02:53.403

Charges guide

Per unit incl. 2 persons	€ 10,00
extra person	€ 6,50
child (under 5 yrs)	€ 4,00
electricity (10A)	€ 5,00
No credit cards.	

Check real time availability and at-the-gate prices...

www.**alanrogers**.com

FR63120 Camping Indigo Royat

Route de Gravenoire, F-63130 Royat (Puy-de-Dôme)

Tel: 04 73 35 97 05. Email: royat@camping-indigo.com
www.alanrogers.com/FR63120

This is a spacious and attractive site sitting high on a hillside on the outskirts of Clermont Ferrand, but close to the beautiful Auvergne countryside. It has nearly 200 terraced pitches on part hardstanding. There are 142 available for touring units, all with 6/10A electricity (long leads may be needed). The pitches are informally arranged in groups, with each group widely separated by attractive trees and shrubs. The bar and terrace overlooks the irregularly shaped swimming pool, paddling pool, sunbathing area, tennis courts and play areas. Although very peaceful off season, the site could be busy and lively in July and August. This site would be ideal for those who would like a taste of both the town and the countryside.

Facilities

Five well appointed toilet blocks, some heated. They have all the usual amenities but it could be a long walk from some pitches. Small shop. Bar, takeaway. Attractive swimming, paddling pools, sunbathing area. Tennis. Boules. Bicycle hire. Two lay areas. Organised entertainment in high season. Internet. Off site: Royat 20 minutes walk but bus every 30 minutes in the mornings. Clermont Ferrand, Puy-de-Dôme, Parc des Volcans, Vulcania.

Open: 4 April - 18 October.

Directions

From A75 exit 2 (Clermont Ferrand) follow signs for Bordeaux (D799). At third roundabout exit left signed Bordeaux. Shortly take exit right then turn right, signed Ceyrat. Leaving Ceyrat, at traffic lights take D941C signed Royat and Puy-de-Dôme. At top of hill turn left (D5) site signed. Entrance 800 m. GPS: N45:45.526 E03:03.308

Charges 2009

| Per unit incl. 2 persons and electricity | € 18,90 - € 27,70 |
| extra person | € 4,50 - € 5,30 |

Camping Cheques accepted.

tel: +33 (0) 4 37 64 22 33   www.camping-indigo.com

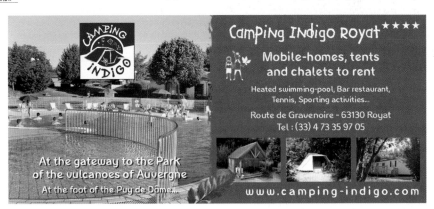

Camping Indigo Royat ★★★★

Mobile-homes, tents and chalets to rent

Heated swimming-pool, Bar restaurant, Tennis, Sporting activities...

Route de Gravenoire - 63130 Royat
Tel : (33) 4 73 35 97 05

www.camping-indigo.com

At the gateway to the Park of the vulcanoes of Auvergne
At the foot of the Puy de Dôme...

FR63130 Camping le Repos du Baladin

Groire, F-63790 Murol (Puy-de-Dôme)

Tel: 04 73 88 61 93. Email: reposbaladin@free.fr
www.alanrogers.com/FR63130

Recommended by a reader, this is a lovely small and friendly campsite that offers an alternative to the larger sites in this area. The owners are aiming for a quiet, relaxing site, attracting nature lovers who want to spend time walking, cycling or touring in this beautiful region rather than creating a holiday park with everything on site. Attractively and well laid out, there are 62 good sized pitches, 49 for touring (5A electricity), and many with good privacy. They are separated by neat conifer hedges with mature trees offer varying amounts of shade. Murol with its ancient castle is 1.5 km.

Facilities

One excellent, very clean and central toilet block provides all the necessary facilities. TV/games room in same block. Small shop (15/6-15/9). Bar with TV (1/6-15/9). Restaurant with snacks and takeaway (1/6-15/9). Heated swimming pool and sunbathing area (1/6-15/9). Large play area. Boules. Off site: Murol 1.5 km. Fishing, bicycle hire and boat launching at Lac Chambon, 2 km.

Open: 1 May - 15 September.

Directions

Site is 40 km. southwest of Clermont Ferrand. Leave A75 at exit 6 (St Nectaire) and take D978 beyond St Nectaire to Murol (34 km). At far end of the village turn left up hill on D5. In 800 m. turn right on D146, signed Groire and site. Entrance on right in 900 m. GPS: N45:34.437 E02:59.449

Charges guide

Per unit incl. 2 persons	€ 12,20 - € 16,90
extra person	€ 3,20 - € 3,90
electricity (5A)	€ 4,00

Check real time availability and at-the-gate prices...

www.alanrogers.com

FR63140 Camping les Loges

F-63340 Nonette (Puy-de-Dôme)

Tel: **04 73 71 65 82**. Email: **les.loges.nonette@wanadoo.fr**   www.alanrogers.com/FR63140

A pleasant, spacious, rural site bordering the River Allier and close to the A75 Autoroute. There are 126 good sized, level, grassy pitches offering plenty of shade, 100 for touring and all with 6A electricity. This site would suit those seeking a quieter holiday without too many organised activities. The river is good for bathing and canoeing and there are many walks and bike rides in the area. It is also well placed to explore the beautiful Auvergne countryside, the extinct volcanoes and the many attractive old towns and villages.

Facilities

Modern toilet blocks contain all the usual facilities. Small shop (July/Aug). Bar, restaurant, takeaway (mid June-mid September). TV room. Heated swimming pool with toboggan, paddling pool (June-Sept). Sauna, spa room (July/Aug). Volleyball. Table tennis. Play areas, play room. River fishing, bathing. Sunday evening dances in high season. Canoe trips. Off site: Walking and cycling routes. Riding 5 km. Small village of Nonette 3 km. Saint Germain 5 km. Issoire 13 km.

Open: Easter - 13 October.

Directions

From A75 exit 17 (south of Issoire), turn left (D214) signed Le Breuil. Bypass Le Breuil, turn left (D123) signed Nonette. Cross river, turn left then immediately very sharp left just after roundabout - take care (site signed). Entrance is 1 km. GPS: N45:28.386 E03:16.334

Charges guide

Per unit incl. 2 persons	€ 12,00 - € 16,20
extra person	€ 3,60 - € 4,60
electricity (6A)	€ 3,50

FR63160 Camping Bel-Air

F-63230 Saint Ours (Puy-de-Dôme)

Tel: **04 73 88 72 14**. Email: **camping.belair@free.fr**   www.alanrogers.com/FR63160

This is an attractive, family run site. In traditional style, but with modern facilities, it has a rural location lying within the Parc des Volcans. There are 60 level grass pitches, 25 with 6/10A electricity, including three with hardstanding for larger motorcaravans and three chalets. The pitches are spaced around a wooded clearing, most with varying degrees of shade. This site is ideal for those seeking a peaceful holiday in a wonderful area yearning for exploration – there are no organised activities here. Its position only 6 km. from the A89 autoroute makes it ideal for both short and long stays. Double axle caravans are not accepted.

Facilities

Modern well equipped toilet block with baby room and facilities for disabled visitors. Washing machine and dryer. Motorcaravan service point. Small shop (bread to order). Minigolf and boules. Gas and electric barbecues only (communal barbecue provided). Play area. WiFi in reception. Off site: Pontgibaud 3 km.

Open: 1 May - 30 September.

Directions

Leave A89 west of Clermont Ferrand at exit 26. Take D941 bypassing Pontgibaud. At roundabout turn left, D943 St Ours. Site shortly on left. GPS: N45:50.662 E02:52.604

Charges 2009

Per person	€ 4,60
pitch incl. electricity (6/10A)	€ 7,80 - € 8,50
No credit cards.	

FR63180 Camping la Vallée Verte

Route des Granges, F-63710 Saint Nectaire (Puy-de-Dôme)

Tel: **04 73 88 52 68**. Email: **lavalleeverte@libertysurf.fr**   www.alanrogers.com/FR63180

Vallée Verte is a very well tended, peaceful, good value campsite. Set in the heart of the beautiful Parc des Volcans d'Auvergne, it is only a short walk from the small spa town of Saint Nectaire and close to Lac Chambon with its sandy beach and some water sports. There are many other interesting towns and villages waiting to be explored. The site has 90 level grass pitches (5/8A electricity) with 74 for touring units. Separated by wooden rails or a variety of hedging, a mixture of trees gives shade to some of the pitches. Twin axle caravans are not accepted.

Facilities

Excellent new toilet block with all necessary facilities including a superb room for families and campers with disabilities. Motorcaravan services. Shop, bar and restaurant with takeaway (all season). Play areas. Boules. Organised meals and walks in high season. Off site: St Nectaire with shops, bars, restaurants. Casino. Caves. Lac Chambon with beach, windsurfing, bicycle hire, bars and restaurants 6 km.

Open: 15 April - 15 September.

Directions

Leave autoroute A75 at exit 6 south of Clermont Ferrand. Take D978 then D996 to St Nectaire. On entering St Nectaire turn left, D642 (site signed). Entrance is a few hundred metres. GPS: N45:34.519 E02:59.972

Charges guide

Per unit incl. 2 persons	€ 9,50 - € 13,50
extra person	€ 3,00 - € 4,60
electricity (5/8A)	€ 3,00 - € 3,50

Check real time availability and at-the-gate prices...

www.alanrogers.com

FR63210 Camping de la Haute Sioule

Route du Camping, F-63210 St Bonnet/Orcival (Puy-de-Dôme)

Tel: 04 73 65 83 32. Email: info@chalets-auvergne.info

www.alanrogers.com/FR63210

This simple, small site is family run in a quiet, rural location in the heart of the beautiful Parc des Volcans. With good views over the surrounding hills, it is close to the Puy-de-Dôme and several winter and summer resorts. Developed from a farm with sheep and geese roaming freely until mid June, the site has 70 sloping, slightly uneven, grassy pitches with about 45 for touring (4-13A electricity, long leads needed). Access is not easy for motorhomes and large outfits. It would be a good base for touring the region but may be noisy in the high season due to the seasonal caravans.

Facilities

Central basic toilet block with mainly Turkish toilets. No facilities for campers with disabilities. Washing machine and dryer. Bar with TV, restaurant and snacks (all season). Play area for younger children. Minigolf. Boules. WiFi. Off site: St Bonnet 200 m. Orcival 4 km. with larger range shops etc. Puy-de-Dôme and other extinct volcanoes. Volcania exhibition. Winter ski resorts 20 km. Lakes. Fishing 5 km. Riding 7 km.

Open: 15 March - 1 November.

Directions

A75 just south of Clermont Ferrand at exit 2, signed Bordeaux and La Bourboule. Continue on D2089 until Les Quatre Routes. Turn left at roundabout, D216. Bear left to site entrance in just over 500 m. GPS: N45:42.504 E02:51.652

Charges guide

Per unit incl. 2 persons	€ 12,00
extra person	€ 3,90
electricity (4-13A)	€ 2,70 - € 5,90

FR63220 Camping les Chelles

F-63880 Olliergues (Puy-de-Dôme)

Tel: 04 73 95 54 34. Email: info@camping-les-chelles.com

www.alanrogers.com/FR63220

A very rural, rustic site, les Chelles is run by enthusiastic Dutch owners. It is situated in the Parc Naturel Livradois, 25 km. south of Thiers, and is ideal for nature lovers and those seeking a quiet retreat. There are many marked walks and challenging cycle routes close by. There are 60 pitches with 50 slightly sloping grassy pitches for touring, some with views over the surrounding wooded hills (15A electricity, long leads advised). The pitches are naturally laid out on woodland terraces but not ideal for those with walking difficulties or for large or underpowered units due to the hilly terrain.

Facilities

Centrally placed basic toilet block. Washing machine and dryer. Motorcaravan service point (charge). Bar/restaurant (all season) with TV. Bread to order. Small swimming and paddling pools near small play area. Tennis. Boules. Bicycle hire (high season). Small fishing lake. Some activities for younger children, bike rides (high season). WiFi (charge). Off site: Olliergues 5 km. Thiers 25 km. Many challenging cycle rides and walks.

Open: 1 April - 30 October.

Directions

Olliergues is on D906 25 km. south of Thiers. On entering Olliergues bear left up hill, D37. Shortly turn sharp left on D87. In 1.5 km. at church turn right and shortly left to site. Well signed from Olliergues. GPS: N45:41.392 E03:38.002

Charges 2009

Per unit incl. 2 persons and electricity	€ 14,80
extra person	€ 3,00
No credit cards.	

FR63230 Camping le Pré des Laveuses

Rue des Laveuses, F-63800 Cournon-d'Auvergne (Puy-de-Dôme)

Tel: 04 73 84 81 30. Email: camping@cournon-auvergne.fr

www.alanrogers.com/FR63230

A well equipped municipal site, le Pré des Laveuses is adjacent to a boating and fishing lake and its beach, alongside the River Allier, close to Cournon d'Auvergne and the A75 autoroute. This site will be busy in the high season due to its public bar/restaurant, new heated swimming pool complex, nearby activities and its proximity to Clermont Ferrand. There are 150 large, grassy, mostly level pitches with 120 for touring (all with 10A electricity, long leads advised). They are separated by neat hedges with mature trees giving some shade and many have pleasant views over the surrounding hills and the town, although hedging obscures views of the lake.

Facilities

Two modern toilet blocks with all necessary facilities, including those for campers with disabilities, possibly stretched when site busy. Washing machine and dryer. Public bar/restaurant with TV (June/Sept). New heated swimming pool complex. Children's room (TV). Play area. Boules. WiFi (free). Many high season sporting and family activities, children's club. Off site: Lake, bathing, boating and fishing (adjacent). Cournon 2 km. Clermont Ferrand 12 km. Bicycle hire 2.5 km. Riding 10 km.

Open: 1 April - 31 October.

Directions

Site is 12 km. southeast of Clermont Ferrand. Leave autoroute A75 at exit 1, taking D212 to Cournon d'Auvergne. Site is well signed to east of town, beside River Allier. Follow Zone de Loisirs. GPS: N45:44.411 E03:13.360

Charges guide

Per unit incl. 2 persons	€ 14,50 - € 16,60
extra person	€ 4,20 - € 4,70
child (under 7 yrs)	€ 2,10 - € 2,60
electricity (10A)	€ 2,00 - € 3,10

Check real time availability and at-the-gate prices...
www.alanrogers.com

FR87020 Castel Camping le Château de Leychoisier

Domaine de Leychoisier, 1 route de Leychoisier, F-87270 Bonnac-la-Côte (Haute-Vienne)

Tel: **05 55 39 93 43**. Email: **contact@leychoisier.com**   www.alanrogers.com/FR87020

You will receive a warm welcome at this beautiful, family run 15th-century château site. It offers peace and quiet in superb surroundings. It is ideally situated for short or long stays being only 2 km. from the A20/N20 and 10 km. north of Limoges. The large, slightly sloping and grassy pitches are in a parkland setting with many magnificent mature trees offering a fair amount of shade. Of the 90 pitches, 85 are for touring, 80 have 10A electricity and many have a tap, although long leads and hoses may be necessary. Explore the grounds and walk down to the four hectare lake. The lake provides free fishing, boating, canoeing and a marked off area for swimming.

Facilities

The toilet block is very clean, but perhaps cramped at busy times. Some washbasins in cabins with good provision for disabled visitors. Washing machine. Basic food provisions. Restaurant (from 10/5). Bar, TV room and snack bar. Small swimming pool with sunbathing area (proper trunks, no shorts). Lake. Play area. Tennis and boules courts (in need of repair when we visited). Torch useful. Off site: Shop 2 km. Supermarket 5 km. Riding 7 km. Golf 20 km.

Open: 15 April - 20 September.

Directions

From A20, north of Limoges, take exit 27 (west) signed Bonnac-La-Côte. In village turn left and follow signs to site. GPS: N45:55.958 E01:17.404

Charges 2009

Per person	€ 6,00 - € 7,50
child (under 7 yrs)	€ 4,00 - € 5,00
pitch	€ 9,00
electricity	€ 5,00
dog	€ 1,00

No credit cards.

Château de Leychoisier
Camping & caravaning ★★★★

1 Route de Leychoisier
F-87270 Bonnac-la-Côte
Tél./fax: +33 (0)55 53 99 343
E-mail: contact@leychoisier.com
www.leychoisier.com

FR87040 Domaine Cévéo de Pierrefitte

Parcs Résidentiels ▶ page 518

Lac de Vassivière, F-87120 Beaumont du Lac (Haute-Vienne)

Tel: **05 55 69 15 88**. Email: **resa@ceveo.com**   www.alanrogers.com/FR87040

Pitches at this campsite are exclusively for chalet accommodation.

Check real time availability and at-the-gate prices...
www.alanrogers.com

MAP 13

With such a rich and varied landscape, the Rhône Valley offers a spectacular region of craggy gorges and scented hills, ideal for life at a leisurely pace – easy to do when there are so many stunning views to take in.

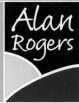

DÉPARTEMENTS: 01 AIN, 07 ARDÈCHE, 26 DRÔME, 42 LOIRE, 69 RHÔNE

MAJOR CITY: LYON

The region's 2,000 year history as a cultural crossroads has blessed the area with a rich blend of customs, architecture and sights of interest. The city of Lyon was developed by the Romans as a trading centre, and was once the capital. It is now the second largest city of France. The Place de la Terreur in the centre of the city is where the guillotine was placed during the French revolution – until it wore out through over-use. Not far from Lyon lies the Dombes, the land of a thousand lakes, and the medieval village of Pérouges and Roman ruins of Vienne.

The Rhône valley holds areas of great interest and natural beauty. From the sun-baked Drôme, with its ever-changing landscapes and the isolated mountains of the Vercors to the deep gorges and high plateaux of the Ardèche, studded with prehistoric caves and lush valleys filled with orchards; and encompassing the vineyards of the Beaujolais and the Rhône Valley. For the energetic there are cycling, horse riding and even white water rafting opportunities, while for the more leisurely inclined, the remote areas are a haven for bird watching and walking.

Places of interest

Beaujolais: vineyards and golden-stone villages.

Bourg-en-Bresse: church of Notre-Dame, craft shops, museum of Ain.

Dombes: lakes, ornithological park.

Lyon: Gallo-Roman artifacts, Renaissance quarter, historical Fabric Museum, silk museum.

Pérouges: medieval village, Galette de Pérouges.

St Etienne: museum of Modern Art.

Vallon-Pont d'Arc: base from which to visit Gorges de l'Ardèche; canoe and rafting centre.

Vienne: Gothic style cathedral, 6th-century church St Pierre.

Cuisine of the region

The poultry, cheese, freshwater fish and mushrooms are superb. Local wines include Beaujolais, Côte Rotie, St Julien, Condrieu, Tain-Hermitage, Chiroubles and Julienas.

Bresse (Poulet, Poularde, Volaille de): the best French poultry, fed on corn and when killed bathed in milk; flesh is white and delicate.

Gras-double: ox tripe, served with onions.

Poulet au vinaigre: chicken, shallots, tomatoes, white wine, wine vinegar and a cream sauce.

Poulet demi-deuil (half-mourning): called this because of thin slices of truffle placed under the chicken breast.

Rosette: a large pork sausage.

Sabodet: Lyonnais sausage of pig's head, pork and beef, served hot.

FR01040 Camping Lac du Lit du Roi

La Tuillière, F-01300 Massignieu-de-Rives (Ain)

Tel: **04 79 42 12 03**. Email: **acamp@wanadoo.fr**   www.alanrogers.com/FR01040

This attractive and well cared for, family run site is ideal for those seeking an active holiday in a peaceful setting. This superb, picturesque area offers wonderful opportunities for exploration by foot, bicycle, car and boat. Take time to sample the wines and other local produce on offer. Of the 120 pitches (electricity 10A), 90 are available for touring, all being close to the lake and many having wonderful views over the lake and the wooded hills beyond. The slightly sloping, grassy pitches are set on low terraces and are partly separated by hedging and a variety of trees give some shade. It has a commanding position beside a beautiful lake which forms part of the River Rhône waterway giving direct access to the much larger Lac du Bourget. In July and August a few social events are organised, suitable for all the family, but this site is best suited for those not requiring a programme of organised activities.

Facilities

Two modern toilet blocks offer all necessary facilities with provision for disabled visitors. Washing machines. Motorcaravan services. Bar, snack bar, terrace. Bread. Small heated swimming pool. Tennis. Play area beside lake. Grassy beach, pedaloes, canoes, surf bikes for hire. Bicycle hire. Lake fishing. Winter caravan storage. Off site: Shops at Belley 8 km. Lac du Bourget (watersports, boat hire). Nature reserve. Cycle tracks and walks (maps available). Marina, boat ramp nearby. Golf 8 km. Riding 15 km.

Open: 14 April - 30 September.

Directions

Site is about 8 km. east of Belley. Turn east off N504 at roundabout (Champion supermarket) on D992 signed Culoz and Seyssel. After 4 km. turn right over bridge, D37 signed Massignieu. Follow signs to campsite (2 km).
GPS: N45:46.122 E05:46.92

Charges guide

Per unit incl. 2 persons	
and electricity	€ 17,00 - € 23,00
extra person	€ 5,00 - € 6,50
child (0-7 yrs)	€ 3,00 - € 5,00
Camping Cheques accepted.	

AU BORD DU LAC ET AUX PORTES DES SAVOIES
★★★★
CAMPING DU *Lac du Lit du Roi*
EMPLACEMENTS OMBRAGÉS
LOCATIONS MOBILES-HOMES, PISCINE...
01300 Massignieu-de-rives - Tél : 33(0)4 79 42 12 03 - Fax : 33(0)4 79 42 19 94
Email : info@camping-savoie.com - www.camping-savoie.com - www.via-camp.com

FR01060 Flower Camping Ile de la Comtesse

Route des Abrets, F-01300 Murs-et-Gélignieux (Ain)

Tel: **04 79 87 23 33**. Email: **camping.comtesse@wanadoo.fr**   www.alanrogers.com/FR01060

A very pleasant, family run, lakeside site, there are 100 medium to large, level grassy pitches here. With 69 for touring, many are separated by low hedges and tall poplar trees offer some shade. All have 6A electricity (but very long leads may be necessary) and most have views over the lake and craggy hills beyond. High season activities are aimed mainly at younger children and the family. Fishing, sailing, canoeing and bathing are possible on the lake that borders the site. There is plenty of space around the lake for leisure activities, including marked walks and cycle trails.

Facilities

Traditionally styled, modern and well appointed toilet block with all the necessary facilities. Facilities for disabled visitors. Motorcaravan service point. Small bar/restaurant with takeaway and small shop. Large marquee used for TV and organised activities. Swimming and paddling pools. Daily programme of activities for young children and the family in high season. Bicycle hire. WiFi. Off site: Restaurant adjacent. Aost with shops, etc. 5 km. Walaibi Theme Park 10 km. Riding 10 km. Golf 20 km.

Open: 30 April - 14 September.

Directions

From the A43 (Lyon - Chambery) autoroute, take exit 10 and go north on D592 for about 10 km. After crossing the lake turn right on the D992 and site is shortly on the right. GPS: N45:38.407 E05:38.948

Charges 2009

Per unit incl. 2 persons	
and electricity	€ 14,90 - € 30,50
extra person	€ 4,90 - € 7,50
child (2-7 yrs)	€ 2,90 - € 5,40
dog	€ 3,00 - € 3,90

BOOK THIS SITE
The Travel Service
CALL 01580 214000
...we'll arrange everything

www.flowercampings.com

Check real time availability and at-the-gate prices...
www.**alanrogers**.com

FR01090 Camping la Pierre Thorion

Base de Loisirs, les Luizants, F-01290 Cormoranche-sur-Saône (Ain)

Tel: **03 85 23 97 10**. Email: **contact@lac-cormoranche.com**   www.alanrogers.com/FR01090

Situated in a region famous for its wines, gastronomy and picturesque old villages, this site is part of the 42 hectare landscaped recreation park that surrounds a tree lined lake. The 117 generous pitches are level, grassed and enclosed by hedges, all with electricity and drainage. A small dam divides the lake into two areas, one for swimming, the other, larger part for fishing (also permitted at night) and boating. To the far side of the park is a TGV railway track. During the day the trains are fairly frequent, but there are no night services and the daytime noise is a moderate rumble. The reception office has a good selection of tourist information on a region lined with the wine routes of Beaujolais, Macon and Bourgogne. In addition, this is the region of Bresse chickens and fresh water fish and in the surrounding picturesque towns and villages there are many good restaurants, the most famous being that of Geoges Blanc in Vonnas.

Facilities

Modern sanitary building provides free pre-set showers and (a little small), washbasins in cabins. Facilities for disabled people. Laundry room with washing machine. Motorcaravan service point. Small shop (order bread for following morning). Bar and restaurant with takeaway, overlooking lake. Lake swimming with a separate area for small children. Off site: Macon, Bourg-en-Bresse and the village of Perouges.

Open: 1 April - 30 September.

Directions

Site is 5 km. south-southwest of Macon on the eastern site of the Saône. It is well signed from all directions 'Base de Loisirs'. If approaching from the west via Creches, there is a 2.6 m. height restriction. GPS: N46:15.100 E4:49.566

Charges guide

Per person	€ 4,10 - € 5,00
child (2-12 yrs)	€ 1,60 - € 2,50
pitch incl. electricity	€ 5,80 - € 8,50

CAMPING LA PIERRE THORION

01290 Cormoranche-sur-Saône · Tel.: 0033 (0)3 85 23 97 10
contact@lac-cormoranche.com · www.lac-cormoranche.com

FR01030 Camping les Ripettes

Chavannes-sur-Reyssouze, F-01190 Pont-de-Vaux (Ain)

Tel: **03 85 30 66 58**. Email: **info@camping-les-ripettes.com**   www.alanrogers.com/FR01030

A friendly welcome is assured from the owners of this spacious site situated in quiet, flat countryside near the pleasant small town of Pont-de-Vaux. The 2.5 hectare (six acre) site has 54 large (100 sq.m. to 400 sq.m) level grassy pitches, 51 of which are available to tourists. Nearly all are separated by hedges and about half are shaded by the many trees on the site. All but two have electrical connections (10A), and there are ample water points. The site is a useful stop on the way to or from the south of France, and also serves as a centre to explore the interesting surrounding area.

Facilities

Two well appointed, small sanitary blocks contain a suite for disabled visitors. Washing machine and dryer. Limited range of food stocked and wine, ice cream, meat for barbecues at reception. Two swimming pools. Small play area, sandpit. Areas for ball games. Board games, books. Bicycle hire. WiFi. Communal Sunday barbecues are popular. Off site: Restaurant 1 km. Riding 2 km. Shops, etc., in Pont-de-Vaux 4 km. Fishing 4 km. Golf 15 km.

Open: 1 April - 30 September.

Directions

Site is 18 km. northeast of Macon. Leave N6 at Fleurville (14 km. south of Tournus). Go east on D933A to Pont-de-Vaux (5 km) where site is signed. Take D2 east towards St Trivier-de-Courtes. After 3 km. turn left after water tower, left again at next junction (100 m). Site is 300 m. GPS: N46:26.620 E04:58.841

Charges 2009

Per unit with 2 persons and electricity	€ 15,60 - € 19,00
extra person	€ 3,15 - € 3,50
child (under 10 yrs)	€ 2,25 - € 2,50

BOOK THIS SITE The Travel Service
CALL 01580 214000 ...we'll arrange everything

Check real time availability and at-the-gate prices...

www.alanrogers.com

FR01050 Camping des Gorges de l'Oignin

Rue du Lac, F-01580 Matafelon-Granges (Ain)

Tel: **04 74 76 80 97**. Email: **camping.lesgorgesdeloignin@wanadoo.fr** www.alanrogers.com/FR01050

This family run, terraced site (English spoken) offers lovely views across the lake to the hills beyond. There are 132 good sized pitches, 70 for touring, separated by young trees and flowering shrubs and with a choice of grass or hardstanding. About half have their own water point and all have 10A electricity. Twin axle caravans are not accepted. The reception, bar/restaurant and pool complex are at the top of the site with a steep road down to the terraces and the rest of the campsite. At the bottom of the site is a large grassy area next to the lake for sunbathing and activities.

Facilities

Two modern, well equipped and clean toilet blocks with all the usual facilities excepting facilities for disabled people. Bar/restaurant, takeaway and TV room (July/Aug). Swimming pool, paddling pool and new 'lazy river' (1/6-30/9). Playground and sports area. Swimming, fishing and boating on the lake (no motorboats). Off site: Golf 2 km. Riding 2 km. Matafelon 800 m. Thoirette 6 km. Oyonnax with range of shops, market, bar/restaurants 10 km.

Open: 1 April - 30 September.

Directions

Matafelon is 40 km. east of Bourg-en-Bresse. Leave autoroute A404 at Oyonnax, exit 11 and head west on D13 to Matafelon (10 km). On entering village and opposite the Mairie turn left, signed camping, and descend to site (800 m). GPS: N46:15.321 E5:33.430

Charges guide

Per unit incl. 2 persons	
and electricity	€ 15,20 - € 23,00
extra person	€ 3,40 - € 4,80
child (3-10 yrs)	€ 2,20 - € 3,60
dog	€ 1,00 - € 2,00

FR01120 Camping la Nizière

F-01320 Saint Nizier-le-Désert (Ain)

Tel: **04 74 30 35 16**. Email: **laniziere@cc-chalamont.com** www.alanrogers.com/FR01120

La Nizière is a small site belonging to the département of the Ain. There are 70 pitches and 8 chalets which are available for rent. The site is midway between Lyon and Bourg-en-Bresse, between the Ain and the Saône in the Dombes, a region of farmland, forests and hundreds of lakes. Pitches are all equipped with electrical connections and some also have water and drainage. A well stocked lake ensures that this is a popular site for anglers. However, there are over 40 km. of walking and cycle tracks around the site, which extends over 25 hectares. There is also a small snack bar and a picnic area. The nearby town of Chalamont is typical of the area, surrounded by 50 small lakes and with a pretty centre and plenty of shops, cafés and restaurants. Bourg-en-Bresse is a much larger town, 20 km. distant and the capital of the former province of Bresse. Now, it is an interesting place to visit with a fine cathedral in the suburb of Brou.

Facilities

Snack bar. Fishing (two lakes). Play area. Games room. Activity and entertainment programme. Chalets for rent. Off site: Riding. Cycle and walking tracks. Bourg-en-Bresse 20 km. Lyon 40 km.

Open: 15 April - 15 October.

Directions

Approaching from the north, leave the A40 at first Bourg-en-Bresse exit (number 5). Head for the town and use the ringroad (D117) and then the D1083 to St Paul de Varax. Follow signs to St Nizier-le-Désert on the D70b and site is well signed from the village. GPS: N46:03.272 E05:09.590

Charges guide

Per unit incl. 2 persons	€ 10,80

Enjoy a stay in harmony with nature right in the Dombes area close by a bird park in Villars les Dombes. The campsite La Nizière with its 3 stars ensures you green nature, peace and family atmosphere. Fishing, hiking and mountain biking are waiting for you to discover the wonderful landscapes of the region! Our region is very famous for its gastronomy and offers you typical dishes of the region. Our project for 2009 is to create an ecological swimming pool!

La Nizière* - 01320 Saint Nizier le Désert**
Tel: 0033 (0)4 74 30 35 16 - laniziere@orange.fr
www.cc-chalamont.com/Base_loisir/index.php

FR07020 Camping Caravaning l'Ardéchois

Le Chambon, Gluiras, F-07190 Saint Sauveur-de-Montagut (Ardèche)

Tel: 04 75 66 61 87. Email: ardechois.camping@wanadoo.fr   www.alanrogers.com/FR07020

This attractive site is quite a way off the beaten track and the approach road is winding and narrow in places. However, it is worth the effort, to find it in such a spectacular setting. This site has 106 pitches (83 for touring with 10A electricity) laid out on steep terraces and many separated by trees and plants. Some are alongside the small, fast-flowing stream, while the rest (60%) are on higher, sloping ground nearer the restaurant/bar and pool. The main site access roads are tarmac but are quite steep and larger units may find access to some terraces difficult.

Facilities	Directions
Two very good sanitary blocks include facilities for families and people with disabilities. Laundry facilities. Motorcaravan services. Shop. Cosy restaurant. Swimming and paddling pools (heated), adjacent bar, snack bar, terrace. TV. Bicycle hire, archery, fishing. Comprehensive entertainment programme. Only gas/electric barbecues. Off site: Canyoning, climbing, river walking and canoeing trips organised. **Open:** 27 April - 30 September.	From Valence take N86 south for 12 km. At La Voulte-sur-Rhône turn right onto D120 to St Sauveur-de-Montagut (site well signed), in centre turn left onto D102 towards Mézilhac for 8 km. to site. GPS: N44:49.705 E4:31.399

Charges guide

Per unit incl. 2 persons	€ 28,30 - € 47,50
extra person	€ 5,50 - € 8,50
Camping Cheques accepted.	

FR07030 Yelloh! Village Soleil Vivarais

Soleil Vivarais, F-07120 Sampzon (Ardèche)

Tel: 04 66 73 97 39. Email: info@yellohvillage-soleil-vivarais.com   www.alanrogers.com/FR07030

A large, lively, high quality site bordering the River Ardèche, complete with beach, Soleil Vivarais offers much to visitors, particularly families with children. Of the 350 pitches, 110 generously sized, shady and level pitches are for tourers, all with 10A electricity. Rock pegs are advised. During the day the proximity of the swimming pools to the terraces of the bar and restaurant make it a pleasantly social area. In the evening the purpose built stage, with professional lighting and sound system, provides an ideal platform for the regular family entertainment programmes.

Facilities	Directions
Modern, clean, well equipped toilet blocks, facilities for people with disabilities. Washing machines, dryers. Motorcaravan services. Small supermarket. Bar/restaurant, takeaways and pizzas. Heated pool. Fishing. Boules. Archery. Bicycle hire. River bathing. Extensive animation programme June - Aug. Off site: Riding 800 m. **Open:** 5 April - 14 September.	On D579, 2 km. south of Ruoms, turn left at roundabout, signed Vallon-Pont-d'Arc. Shortly turn right over river bridge, site on right. GPS: N44:25.774 E04:21.317

Charges 2009

Per unit incl. 2 persons and electricity	€ 15,00 - € 43,00
extra person	€ 5,00 - € 7,00

www.yellohvillage.com   tel: +33 466 739 739

FR07070 Kawan Village les Ranchisses

Route de Rocher, F-07110 Largentière (Ardèche)

Tel: 04 75 88 31 97. Email: reception@lesranchisses.fr   www.alanrogers.com/FR07070

This is a very well equipped, modern campsite in a lesser known area of the Ardèche. There are 165 good-sized, level, grassy pitches, 88 for tourists with electricity (10A) including 44 which are fully serviced. There are two distinct areas, one which is well shaded and the lower part with less shade. There is traffic noise in some areas. A small river pool provides opportunities for bathing, fishing or canoeing (free life jackets) with one part of the bathing area quite safe for youngsters. Well run and with the emphasis on personal attention, this is a highly recommended site.

Facilities	Directions
Comprehensive toilet buildings include facilities for babies and disabled visitors. Laundry facilities. Motorcaravan services. Shop. Bar. Restaurant (regional specialities), takeaway/pizzeria and terrace. Two large pools, paddling pool (heated). New indoor pool complex. Adventure style playground. Organised amusements for children (from 1/6). Skate park. Tennis. Minigolf. Boules. Canoeing. Internet access. Off site: Largentière 1.5 km. Riding 8 km. Bicycle hire 10 km. **Open:** 12 April - 30 October.	Largentière is southwest of Aubenas best approached using D104. Just beyond Uzer, 16 km. From Aubenas, turn northwest on D5. After 5 km. at far end of Largentière, fork left downhill signed Rocher and Valgorge. Site on left in about 1.8 km. GPS: N44:33.601 E04:17.081

Charges 2009

Per unit incl. 2 persons	€ 18,00 - € 43,00
extra person (over 1 yr)	€ 4,50 - € 8,50
Camping Cheques accepted.	

337

FR07050 Sunêlia le Ranc Davaine

Saint Alban-Auriolles, F-07120 Ruoms (Ardèche)

Tel: **04 75 39 60 55**. Email: **camping.ranc.davaine@wanadoo.fr**   www.alanrogers.com/FR07050

Le Ranc Davaine is a large, busy, family oriented site with direct access to the River Chassezac. There are 435 pitches with 87 for touring, all with electricity (10/16A) for which very long leads are required (some may cross roads). Most pitches are scattered between static caravan and tour operator pitches on fairly flat, stony ground under a variety of trees, some of which are quite low giving much needed shade. Rock pegs are advised. The site can get very busy for much of the season. A lively programme of entertainment is aimed at young children and teenagers with enclosed disco four nights a week until 03.00. Sunbathing areas surround the pool complex, overlooked by the restaurant terrace, providing very pleasant surroundings, especially attractive with evening floodlighting. The site is popular with tour operators (113 pitches) and there are 170 mobile homes.

Facilities

Fully equipped, very clean and modern toilet blocks include facilities for disabled visitors. Washing machines, dryers. Large shop. Internet. Bar/restaurant, pizzeria, takeaway. Swimming pool, covered pool (heated), two small square pools, slide (all facilities, all season; no shorts allowed). Large play area. Tennis. Minigolf. Fishing. Extensive activity and entertainment programme (July/Aug). Discos. Fitness hall (charged). Off site: Canoe hire nearby for excursions down the River Ardèche. Canyoning. Bicycle and quadbike hire 2 km. Riding 5 km.

Open: 4 April - 13 September.

Directions

From Ruoms go south on the D111. Just before Grospierres turn right onto D246, cross the river bridge (2.5 m. width restriction) and then left on D208 towards Chandolas and site. GPS: N44:24.848 E04:16.374

Charges guide

Per unit incl. 2 persons	€ 20,60 - € 36,00
incl. electricity	€ 25,75 - € 40,20
extra person	€ 6,40 - € 9,60
child (2-13 yrs)	€ 3,75 - € 9,60

Le Ranc Davaine★★★★   **Aluna Vacances**★★★★

Saint Alban Auriolles - 07120 Ruoms
www.camping-ranc-davaine.fr
camping.ranc.davaine@wanadoo.fr

Route de Lagorce - 07120 Ruoms
www.alunavacances.fr
alunavacances@wanadoo.fr

FR07630 Aluna Vacances

Route de Lagorce, F-07120 Ruoms (Ardèche)

Tel: **04 75 93 93 15**. Email: **alunavacances@wanadoo.fr**   www.alanrogers.com/FR07630

Aluna is a large holiday park close to the market town of Ruoms in the southern Ardèche, famous for its Gorges and the large range of watersports and other tourist activities. This will be a very lively site in July and August with a wide range of activities organised for all age groups, all day and into the night. There are 200 pitches mainly occupied by mobile homes and tour operators with only 40 slightly uneven and sloping pitches for touring (electricity 6A, rock pegs advised). All the main activities take place in a single area, including a magnificent aqua park.

Facilities

Facilities: Well appointed and very clean modern toilet blocks with all necessary facilities including those for campers with disabilities. Motorcaravan services. Shop, bar, restaurant, takeaway (26/4-14/9). Superb aqua park complex (all season, heated March and April). Fitness room (all season). Large play area. Miniclubs (over 5 years). Tennis. Multisport court. Boules. Underground disco (until 02.00), outdoor stage (both July/Aug). Extensive activity programme (July/Aug). Only electric barbecues on site. Off site: Bicycle hire 2 km. River bathing 2 km. Horse riding 5 km.

Open: Late March - 16 September.

Directions

Site is in the southern Ardèche south of Aubenas. Leave Aubenas on D104 signed Alès. Shortly turn left on D579 signed Vallon-Pont-d'Arc. Bypass Vogüé, cross river and keep right. At Ruoms turn left at roundabout on D559 signed Lagorce. In about 1 km. turn right to site on right. GPS: N44:26.644 E04:22.022

Charges guide

Per unit incl. 2 persons and electricity	€ 36,70 - € 41,00
extra person (over 2 yrs)	€ 8,70 - € 9,80
dog	€ 4,10

Check real time availability and at-the-gate prices...

www.alanrogers.com

FR07090 Camping le Domaine des Plantas

F-07360 Les Ollières-sur-Eyrieux (Ardèche)

Tel: 04 75 66 21 53. Email: plantas.ardeche@wanadoo.fr   www.alanrogers.com/FR07090

Under new ownership, this is a good quality site in a spectacular setting on the steep banks of the Eyrieux river. Old, original buildings house the reception, restaurant and bar. The terrace provides a stunning viewpoint. The 169 pitches (100 for touring) are steeply terraced and shaded with electricity (10A, long leads may be needed). Much up and down walking is required making this site unsuitable for those with walking difficulties There is a sandy beach beside the quite fast-flowing, but fairly shallow river (used for bathing). The 3 km. approach road is a twisting, single track and may present a problem to those with larger outfits. Domaine des Plantas offers an attractive alternative to those in the more popular southern parts of the Ardèche. The Eyrieux valley is less well known, but arguably just as attractive as those further south and a good deal less crowded, particularly in the main season.

Facilities

Two excellent well equipped toilet blocks (one heated). There are some facilities which will certainly please the very young. Washing machine. Motorcaravan services. Small shop, bar, restaurant, disco. Heated, covered and outdoor swimming pools, paddling pool and toboggans. Adventure play area. High season children's activities, discos for 14-18 year olds held in cellar (strictly no alcohol). Many activities and excursions. Only gas and electric barbecues. Off site: Riding 15 km. Mountain biking, canoeing, canyoning, riding and walking. A wonderful area for touring.

Open: 21 April - 5 October.

Directions

Leave A7 exit 15 (Valence Sud). Turn right to Valence centre, follow signs to Montélimar via N7 for 7 km. Turn right towards Charmes sur Rhône to Beauchastel. Take D120 to Ollières-sur-Eyrieux. Cross river, turn left and follow site signs (3 km) along narrow track. GPS: N44:48.520 E04:38.125

Charges guide

Per unit incl. 2 persons and electricity	€ 19,00 - € 31,00
extra person over 4 yrs	€ 4,00 - € 7,50
child (2-4 yrs)	€ 2,00 - € 3,00

Camping Cheques accepted.

CAMPINGS FranceLoc

ARDÈCHE

Domaine des Plantas ★★★★

Two heated swimming pools, of which one is covered. Water slides. You will stay in a green environment, bounded by a river.

Les Ollières sur Eyrieux
07360 • Tel.: +33 (0)4 75 66 21 53
Email : plantas.ardèche@wanadoo.fr
www.camping-franceloc.fr

FR07080 RCN la Bastide en Ardèche

Route d'Alès (RD111), Sampzon, F-07120 Ruoms (Ardèche)

Tel: 04 75 39 64 72. Email: info@rcn-labastideenardeche.fr   www.alanrogers.com/FR07080

You can be assured of a good welcome at this recently upgraded site. There are 300 good sized, level, grassy pitches marked out by trees which give plenty of shade. All have electricity 3/5A, and 86 are fully serviced. On driving down to your pitch, it seems that there are many mobile homes, actually there are only 46 with 25 small chalets plus another 16 pitches used by a tour operator. Canoe trips are arranged down the Gorge d'Ardèche and in mid June each year a large section of the river bank next to the site is cleared of boulders and sand put down. Security patrols ensure quiet nights.

Facilities

Two well equipped toilet blocks, one new and one refurbished, with baby room and facilities for disabled people. Shop. Attractive restaurant, pizzeria and bar. Heated swimming pool and sunbathing area. Play area. Tennis. Fishing. Organised activities. Recreation room in cellar. Only gas barbecues are permitted. Off site: Riding, bicycle hire 3 km. Watersports on River Ardèche. Ruoms 4 km. Vallon-Pont-d'Arc 7 km. Medieval villages of Balazuc, Labaume and Largentière.

Open: 15 March - 15 October.

Directions

Going south from Ruoms on the D579, after 2.5 km. at roundabout, turn right on D111 signed Alès. After 1 km. cross river bridge and site is 200 m. on the left. GPS: N44:25.375 E04:19.297

Charges guide

Per unit incl. 2 persons, electricity and water	€ 18,00 - € 45,50

Many discounts offered in low season.

www.rcn-campings.fr

BOOK THIS SITE
CALL 01580 214000
...we'll arrange everything
The Travel Service

339

FR07100 Camping la Garenne

Chemin de la Garenne, F-07800 Saint Laurent-du-Pape (Ardèche)

Tel: **04 75 62 24 62**. Email: **info@lagarenne.org**   www.alanrogers.com/FR07100

This spacious, family orientated site has a long season and is within easy reach of the A7/N7 south of Valence. It is only a short stroll from the village which has a range of small shops. Guests are predominantly Dutch but all are made welcome and English is widely spoken. The 120 hard pitches (rock pegs advised), some terraced and some sloping, have varying degrees of shade. Some are separated by hedges and all have electricity, but only 4A (some need long leads). Visitors' pursuits have been carefully considered resulting in a variety of family activities from mid May to mid September. People with diverse interests are therefore attracted throughout the season for example, bridge evenings are organised during May, June and September. There is a lively activity and entertainment programme in peak season.

Facilities

Excellent and very clean, modern toilet blocks provide all necessary facilities including those for children and disabled visitors. Small shop for basics. Bar, restaurant and takeaway (all 15/5-15/9). Swimming pool and sunbathing terrace (20/5-30/9). Paddling pool. Boules. Games room. Barbecues are not permitted. Off site: Village. Fishing 1 km. Riding 2 km. Bicycle hire 3 km. Walking, biking, canoeing, canyoning and exploring the Ardèche region.

Open: 1 March - 1 November.

Directions

Leave the N86 at Beauchastel, 20 km. south of Valence and follow the D21 to Saint Laurent du Pape. In the village, turn right just before the post office and the site is at the end of this road, beyond the tennis court. GPS: N44:49.574 E04:45.732

Charges guide

| Per unit incl. 2 persons and electricity | € 18,50 - € 30,50 |
| extra person | € 5,50 |

Reductions in low season for over 55s.

Camping **La Garenne*****

- Ardèche -

... Where Alps, Provence and Massif Central meet ...

• between Valence and Montélimar
• at entrance of beautiful Eyrieux Valley
• at five minutes walk from the village centre
• mobile homes for rent

Family camp site (120 pitches) under Dutch ownership with large swimming pool, toddlers pool, bar/restaurant, shop and recreation room.

low season: bridge - jeu de boules - walking
high season: extensive recreation program

07800 St. Laurent-du-Pape • Ardèche
www.lagarenne.org

FR07130 Camping les Coudoulets

Pradons, F-07120 Ruoms (Ardèche)

Tel: **04 75 93 94 95**. Email: **camping@coudoulets.com**   www.alanrogers.com/FR07130

For those who prefer a more intimate, peaceful campsite beside the river Ardèche, only a short distance away from the main centre, then this very well cared for site, run by a very friendly family, could be for you. There are 125 good sized, grassy and well shaded pitches, separated by trees and shrubs. There are 109 for touring, all with 10A electricity. Organised family activities take place in July/August such as barbecues and musical evenings (no discos). There is an area for bathing in the river and it is an ideal spot for canoeists. The family own a small vineyard and their wine is on sale in the bar; we fully recommend it.

Facilities

Good, clean, recently refurbished block has all the necessary facilities including excellent facilities for disabled people. Motorcaravan services. Bar, TV, terrace (May - Sept) bread, ices, drinks. Snacks (July/Aug). Butcher calls in high season. Small heated swimming pool, paddling pool. Superb new aquatic play area and pool for children (May - Sept). Fishing. WiFi. Off site: Shop 300 m. Ruoms with range of shops 4 km.

Open: 1 May - 10 September.

Directions

Leave Montélimar westwards on N102 towards Aubenas. After passing Villeneuve-de-Berg turn left on D103 towards Vogüé for 5 km. Turn left on D579 towards Ruoms, site on right on entering Pradons (10 km). GPS: N44:28.598 E04:21.514

Charges 2009

Per unit incl. 2 persons	€ 14,00 - € 25,00
extra person	€ 4,50 - € 6,00
child (under 7 yrs)	€ 3,80 - € 4,80
electricity (6A)	€ 4,00

BOOK THIS SITE
The Travel Service ...we'll arrange everything
CALL 01580 214000

Check real time availability and at-the-gate prices...
www.alanrogers.com

FR07110 Domaine le Pommier

RN102, F-07170 Villeneuve-de-Berg (Ardèche)

Tel: **04 75 94 82 81**. Email: **info@campinglepommier.com**   www.alanrogers.com/FR07110

Domaine Le Pommier is an extremely spacious Dutch owned site of ten hectares in 32 hectares of wooded grounds. The site is steeply terraced (a tractor is available for assistance) and has wonderful views over the Ardèche mountains and beyond. There are 400 pitches with 275 for tourists. They are grassy/stony, of good size and well spaced. Separated by young trees and hedges, some have little or no shade. All have access to electricity and water is close by. The site is not recommended for large units. Recent developments include a mini-farm, including llamas, goats and ponies, and an unusual pancake restaurant. This serves an excellent range of pancakes of various flavours. The site has first class facilities, including the most up-to-date toilet blocks, a very good bar/restaurant and one of the best swimming and paddling pool complexes we have seen, ideal for all the family.

Facilities

Four excellent toilet blocks, one with under-floor heating, provide all the necessary facilities. Comprehensive shop. Bar/restaurant. Swimming pool complex with slides, paddling pools, etc. Everything opens from the end of April. Boules. Minigolf. Activities including games in the woods, archery, water polo and tug-of-war. Bridge and water colour classes. Tennis. Soundproof disco. Very extensive programme of events on and off site. Low season excursions. Off site: Villeneuve-de-Berg 1.5 km. River Ardèche 12 km. Potholing, rock climbing, canoeing, canyoning, mountain biking, walking or riding.

Open: 25 April - 30 September.

Directions

Site is west of Montélimar on the N102. The entrance is adjacent to the roundabout at the eastern end of the Villeneuve-de-Berg bypass. GPS: N44:34.350 E04:30.669

Charges guide

Per unit incl. 2 persons	€ 15,50 - € 29,50
extra person over 4 yrs	€ 4,00 - € 6,50
electricity	€ 4,00
dog	free - € 4,00

Max. 6 persons per pitch.
Special offers for longer stays in low season.

Camping - Domaine ★★★★

Le Pómmier

- Pleasant family campsite on a 30 ha domain
- 275 spacious, shady and sunny pitches.
- Hire of chalets and mobile homes.
- À la carte restaurant, pizzeria, pancake restaurant / children's farm, snack / take away. All restaurants offer beautiful views from the terrace.
- Bar with terrace, discotheque, supermarket whith own bakery.
- Waterpark, slides, paddling pool, children's shallow pool, whirlpool.
- River, mini golf 18 holes, internet corner, WIFI.
- Play area, multi sports area, aero-parcour, bicycle hire, table tennis
- Extensive entertainment programme with children's club, day and evening programmes.
- Special senior activity programme in low season, organised boules matches, bridge drives, water colour painting classes.

SPECIAL OFFERS IN LOW SEASON !

Ardèche

New in 2009 : pool with pirateship and slides

Camping Domaine "Le Pommier" ★★★★
07170 VILLENEUVE DE BERG, France
Tel. 00 33 4 75 94 82 81 (English spoken) - FAX : 00 33 4 75 94 83 90
www.campinglepommier.com - e-mail : info@campinglepommier.com

Check real time availability and at-the-gate prices...

www.alanrogers.com

FR07150 Camping Domaine de Gil

Mobile homes ▶ page 506

Route de Vals-les-Bains, Ucel, F-07200 Aubenas (Ardèche)

Tel: **04 75 94 63 63**. Email: **info@domaine-de-gil.com**

www.alanrogers.com/FR07150

Under new ownership, this very attractive and well organised, smaller site in a less busy part of the Ardèche should appeal to couples and families with younger children. The 80, good sized, level pitches, 43 for touring, are surrounded by a variety of trees offering plenty of shade. All have 10A electricity. The focal point of the site is formed by the beautiful swimming pool, paddling pool and large sunbathing area, with the bar, restaurant and well appointed children's play areas all adjacent. A spacious sports area and shady picnic/play area are alongside the river Ardèche an ideal spot to cool off on a hot day.

Facilities

Modern well appointed toilet block, washing machine and iron. Motorcaravan services. Basic shop. Bar/restaurant, takeaway (from June). Heated swimming pool, paddling pool. Two play areas. Boules, minigolf, football and tennis. Canoeing, boating and fishing. Organised activities in high season. Only gas and electric barbecues. Off site: Shops at Vals-les-Bain 1.5 km. Interesting old town of Aubenas with larger range of shops, restaurants, bars 3 km. Organised canoe trips, canyoning on river Ardèche. Bicycle hire, riding 4 km.

Open: 14 April - 23 September.

Directions

Site north of Aubenas. From southeast (N102), after tunnel, turn right, roundabout (signed Ucel), cross river into Pont d'Ucel (3.5 tonne limit). Bear right and at roundabout, last exit (signed Ucel). Shortly turn left (signed Ucel D218), then right (Ucel D578B). Site is 2 km. GPS: N44:38.558 E04:22.775

Charges guide

Per unit incl. 2 persons	€ 14,00 - € 29,00
extra person	€ 3,50 - € 5,75
child (under 10 yrs)	free - € 4,25
electricity	€ 4,00
animal	€ 2,00 - € 3,00

Domaine de gil ★★★★
CAMPING-CARAVANING
On the banks of the river Ardèche
Heated Swimmingpool
Rent of Mobilhomes
07200 Ucel-Aubenas - Ardèche
Tel. +33 4 75 94 63 63 (english spoken)
www.domaine-de-gil.com
e-mail: info@domaine-de-gil.com

FR07140 Camping les Lavandes

Le Village, F-07170 Darbres (Ardèche)

Tel: **04 75 94 20 65**. Email: **sarl.leslavandes@online.fr**

www.alanrogers.com/FR07140

Situated to the northeast of Aubenas, in a quieter part of this region, Les Lavandes is surrounded by magnificent countryside, vineyards and orchards. The enthusiastic French owners, who speak good English, run a site that appeals to all nationalities. The 70 pitches (58 for touring) are arranged on low terraces separated by a variety of trees and shrubs that give welcome shade in summer. Electricity 6/10A is available to all. Visit at the end of May to see the campsite trees laden with luscious cherries. Organised activities include wine tasting, shows, musical evenings and children's games.

Facilities

Comprehensive and well maintained facilities, baby room and excellent facilities for disabled people. Washing machine. Small shop (1/7-31/8). Bar, terrace (1/6-31/8). Restaurant (15/6-31/8). Takeaway (15/4-31/8). Swimming pool, paddling pool, sunbathing areas, all with super views. Two small play areas for younger children. Games room. Outdoor chess. Electric barbecues are not permitted. Off site: Fishing 1 km. Riding 3 km. Tennis 5 km. Bicycle hire 15 km. Canoeing, walking, cycling, riding, carting nearby. Climbing (Courpatas, Chabanne, Saint Michel de Boulogne, Lavilledieu). Wonderful area for birds (Golden Orioles and Bonellis eagle).

Open: 15 April - 30 September.

Directions

Site is best approached from the south. From Montélimar take N102 towards Aubenas. After Villeneuve, in Lavilledieu, turn right at traffic lights on D224 to Darbres (10 km). In Darbres turn sharp left by post office (care needed) and follow site signs. GPS: N44:38.873 E04:30.203

Charges guide

Per unit incl. 2 persons	€ 12,50 - € 18,50
extra person	€ 2,80 - € 3,50
child (under 8 yrs)	€ 1,50 - € 2,60
electricity	€ 3,50
dog	€ 1,50 - € 2,50

The Travel Service

BOOK THIS SITE CALL 01580 214000 ...we'll arrange everything

Check real time availability and at-the-gate prices...

www.**alanrogers**.com

FR07120 Camping Nature Parc l'Ardéchois

Route touristique des Gorges, F-07150 Vallon-Pont-d'Arc (Ardèche)

Tel: **04 75 88 06 63**. Email: **ardecamp@bigfoot.com**   www.alanrogers.com/FR07120

This very high quality, family run site is within walking distance of Vallon-Pont-d'Arc. It borders the River Ardèche and canoe trips are run, professionally, direct from the site. This campsite is ideal for families with younger children seeking an active holiday. The facilities are comprehensive and of an extremely high standard, particularly the central toilet block. Of the 244 pitches, there are 225 for tourers, separated by trees and individual shrubs. All have electrical connections (6/10A) and 125 have full services. Forming a focal point is the bar and restaurant (good menus), with a terrace and stage overlooking the attractive heated pool. There is also a large paddling pool and sunbathing terrace. For children, there is a well thought out play area plus plenty of other space for youngsters to play, both on the site and along the river. Activities are organised throughout the season; these are family based no discos. Patrols at night ensure a good night's sleep. Access to the site is easy and suitable for large outfits. Member of Leading Campings Group.

Facilities

Two well equipped toilet blocks, one superb with everything working automatically. Facilities are of the highest standard, very clean and include good facilities for babies, those with disabilities, washing up and laundry. Four private bathrooms to hire. Washing machines. Well stocked shop. Swimming pool and paddling pool (no Bermuda shorts). Tennis. Very good play area. Internet access. Organised activities, canoe trips. Only gas barbecues are permitted. Communal barbecue area. Off site: Canoeing, rafting, walking, riding, mountain biking, golf, rock climbing, bowling, wine tasting and dining. Vallon-Pont-d'Arc 800 m. Explore the real Ardèche on the minor roads and visit Labaume, Bazakuc and Largentière (market Tuesday).

Open: 1 April - 30 September.

Directions

From Vallon-Pont-d'Arc (western end of the Ardèche Gorge) at a roundabout go east on the D290. Site entrance is shortly on the right. GPS: N44:23.873 E04:23.929

Charges guide

Per pitch incl. 2 persons and electricity   € 42,00

Camping Nature Park ★★★★
L'Ardéchois
VALLON PONT D'ARC - ARDÈCHE - SÜD
Along the Ardèche river

GPS : N 44° 23' 87"
E 04° 23' 93"

Open : 01.04 - 30.09

Pont d'Arc : 3 km
Village : 1 km

Leading Camping

• Heated waterpark
• Heated sanitary
+ family bathrooms
• Mobilhome rentals
• Comfortable sites
• Bar, Restaurant, Supermarket
• Canoe Nature Paradise
• Animations for children
• Tennis
• Midget golf
• LudoPark (Multisports)
• English spoken
• Off-season discounts

Camping Nature Park l'Ardéchois
Route des Gorges de l'Ardèche / F-07150 Vallon pont d'Arc
Tel. 33 (0)4 75 88 06 63 - Fax 33 (0)4 75 37 14 97
ardecamp@bigfoot.com   www.ardechois-camping.com

ADAC Super-Platz

DCC Europa Preis '99

2006

2006 ANWB

The Travel Service
...we'll arrange everything
CALL 01580 214000
BOOK THIS SITE

FR07170 **Ludocamping**

F-07170 Lussas (Ardèche)

Tel: **04 75 94 21 22**. Email: **info@ludocamping.com**

www.alanrogers.com/FR07170

This is a quiet family campsite offering a really wide range of activities. From mid July - early August, only families with children under 14 yrs are accepted which allows the activities to be focused on this age group. The 160 grassy pitches, all for touring, 5-10A electricity, are in two areas. The upper area has large super pitches with wonderful views but little shade. The lower area, closer to the small river, has pitches set naturally amongst the trees and they have good shade. There is an attractive swimming pool (heated all season), good sized paddling pool and large sunbathing area.

Facilities

Clean, good quality toilet blocks offer all necessary facilities. Bar (all season), takeaway (from 1/5), terrace overlooking the valley. Play area. Recreational area next to river. Fishing. Bicycle hire. Club for over 6/7 yr olds offering a very wide range of activities. Off season club for older children. Seniors excursions in campsite coach. Only gas and electric barbecues. Off site: Lussas (few shops, restaurant, bar) 600 m. Riding 6 km. Gliding, hang-gliding, canoeing, speed boating.

Open: 1 April - 15 October.

Directions

From Montélimar take N102 west towards Aubenas, pass around Villeneuve, at traffic lights in Lavilledieu turn right onto D224 towards Lussas. Site entrance is on right just before village (about 4 km. from N102). GPS: N44:36.297 E04:28.276

Charges guide

Per unit incl. 2 persons	€ 11,00 - € 25,00
extra person	€ 2,00 - € 6,00
electricity (6A)	€ 3,00

Special long stay, low season offers. No credit cards.

FR07180 **Kawan Village Ardèche**

Boulevard de Paste, F-07000 Privas (Ardèche)

Tel: **04 75 64 05 80**. Email: **jcray@wanadoo.fr**

www.alanrogers.com/FR07180

This spacious, family run site is on the southern outskirts of Privas and would be a good base for exploring the lesser known parts of the Ardèche. Bus and coach trips are available to explore these areas. The site has 166 large, grass, reasonably level pitches, of which 153 are for tourers. A wide variety of trees provide reasonable shade and electricity (6/10A) should now be available on most pitches. Two tour operators use the site. Recent additions include new heated pools. There is a play area for children and a miniclub, but (deliberately) no provision for teenagers.

Facilities

Two toilet blocks, only one open in low season. Facilities for disabled people. Motorcaravan service point. Bar and restaurant (1/5-30/9). Boules. Play area. Miniclub. Entertainment (high season). Only gas barbecues are permitted. Tents (4) for rent. Off site: Swimming pool and tennis courts adjacent. Supermarket 100 m. Bicycle hire 2 km. Riding 5 km.

Open: 1 April - 30 September.

Directions

At traffic lights in the centre of town take D2, signed Montélimar. Descend the winding road for 1 km. then at roundabout turn right and then shortly left, signed Espace Ouvèze. The entrance is straight on. GPS: N44:43.569 E04:35.898

Charges guide

Per unit incl. 2 persons	€ 14,50 - € 19,00
electricity (6A)	€ 3,50

Camping Cheques accepted.

FR07240 **Domaine des Chênes**

Chassagnes Haut, F-07140 Les Vans (Ardèche)

Tel: **04 75 37 34 35**. Email: **reception@domaine-des-chenes.fr**

www.alanrogers.com/FR07240

The campsite is run by a friendly family in the southwest Ardèche, only 2 km. from the village of Les Vans. There are 122 pitches with only 28 small to medium sized pitches for touring. Electricity 10A is available. The pitches are laid out on steep terraces with some having good shade and others having good views over the surrounding hillside. There is a magnificent pool complex ideal for young children. A bar and restaurant with a takeaway is open all season. The site is not suitable for large outfits due to a narrow approach road and steep site roads with tight bends.

Facilities

Two very well appointed toilet blocks with all the necessary facilities including those for children and campers with disabilities. Washing machine. Motorcaravan services. Shop (Jul/Aug). Bar/restaurant with takeaway. Small bar and games room by pool. Excellent pool complex, fitness room and sauna (May - Sept). Some organised activities in high season. Only gas barbecues are permitted. Off site: Fishing 500 m. Bicycle hire 1 km. Riding 2 km. Village of Les Vans 2 km.

Open: 1 April - 30 September.

Directions

Leave Alès northeast on the D904,signed Aubenas. Continue through St Ambroix, and after a further 13 km. just beyond St Paul-le-Jeune, turn left on D901. After about 6 km. turn right on D295, site signed. Descend to sharp right hand turn and shortly to site. GPS: N44:24.567 E04:10.050

Charges guide

Per unit incl. 2 persons and electricity (10A)	€ 14,00 - € 25,00
extra person	€ 2,50 - € 4,40

Check real time availability and at-the-gate prices...

 www.**alanrogers**.com

FR07190 Camping le Chambourlas

F-07360 Les Ollières-sur-Eyrieux (Ardèche)

Tel: **04 75 66 24 31**. Email: **info@chambourlas.com**   www.alanrogers.com/FR07190

Tucked away in a beautiful setting, in the hills above Privas, this is a small, neat and tidy family owned site (Dutch and English spoken). The 78 grassy, sloping pitches (72 for touring, electricity 10A) are set on low terraces, separated by an interesting variety of trees with excellent views over the wooded hills. The attractive reception, restaurant and shop are in one building close to all the facilities. Although there are special facilities, this is not an ideal site for those with walking difficulties. It is not ideal for very large units due to the steep and narrow local roads. There is a wide range of family orientated activities, especially in July and August, but these do not extend late into the night.

Facilities

One modern very clean toilet block with all the necessary facilities including those for disabled visitors. Bar, restaurant and takeaway (all 15/5-28/8). Small shop (mid May - Oct). Swimming pool, paddling pool and sunbathing area (1/5-30/9). Play area. Boules. Good range of activities, some in low season, no discos. River fishing. Only gas barbecues. Off site: Many walks and bike rides. Bicycle hire 6 km. Excursions. Village of les Ollières-sur-Eyrieux 6 km. Riding 15 km. Privas 19 km. Cévennes Regional Mountain Park.

Open: 1 May - 1 October.

Directions

At traffic lights in Privas take D2 north, signed Le Cheylard. Follow road over two river bridges. Site entrance is on right (about 11 km. after traffic lights). Take care - this is a fairly tortuous climb. GPS: N44:46.870 E04:37.016

Charges guide

Per unit incl. 2 persons and electricity	€ 15,00 - € 29,00
extra person	€ 4,90 - € 5,90
child (2-12 yrs)	€ 4,60 - € 5,60
dog	free - € 2,50
Camping Cheques accepted.	

07360 **Les Ollières sur Eyrieux**   **Between Privas and Les Ollières**
0033 475 66 24 31
www.chambourlas.com

FR07250 Yelloh! Village la Plaine

F-07120 Ruoms (Ardèche)

Tel: **04 66 73 97 39**. Email: **info@yellohvillage-la-plaine.com**   www.alanrogers.com/FR07250

One of the 'all singing, all dancing' type of campsite, La Plaine is quiet in low season, but in high season with all-day and evening activities for both teenagers and adults, and a miniclub each day, there is no reason to feel bored! There are 212 pitches of moderate size (75 used for their air conditioned mobile homes), of which 160 have electricity. They are protected from the sun and marked by many trees. A stage and sound equipment are in use most nights and might cause some noise problems. This is a young family site for people with lots of energy, perhaps not for a quiet holiday in high season!

Facilities

Three sanitary blocks, clean and modern provide all facilities under cover. Good facilities for disabled visitors. Excellent laundry room. Fridge hire. Shop, restaurant, bar and takeaway. Heated pool complex. Gym. Play area. Fitness room. Entertainment programme. Miniclub (5-12 yrs). Fishing. River beach. New multisport area. Bicycle hire. Off site: Town 3 km. Riding 2 km.

Open: 5 April - 14 September.

Directions

Exit Ruoms south on the D579 and at junction 2 km, south, take D111 signed St Ambroix. Site is on the left. GPS: N44:25.624 E04:20.137

Charges guide

Per unit incl. 2 persons and electricity (6A)	€ 14,00 - € 35,00
extra person	€ 5,00 - € 7,00
child (under 3 yrs)	free
pet	€ 4,00 - € 5,00

www.yellohvillage.com   tel: +33 466 739 739

(345)

FR07290 La Domaine d'Imbours

F-07220 Larnas (Ardèche)

Tel: **04 75 54 39 50**. Email: **info@domaine-imbours.com**   www.alanrogers.com/FR07290

This large site is part of a holiday complex with many mobile homes (99), chalets (41), hotel and 200 camping pitches. These are on scrub grass, not marked, with some shade from mature trees and 6A electricity (long leads may be helpful). For those looking for more or less everything organised for them in high season, this complex may suit. Out of season it is different, with not much happening. The complex is dominated by the hotel which is about 1 km. from the camping area along a descending site road. Around the hotel is a large and well designed pool complex. In high season there are evening shows and dancing, again at the hotel. Here too one can play tennis on one of four courts. To use the laundry one needs to transport washing to the hotel complex, where there are machines. There are quad bikes for hire which seem to be driven round the camping area with some speed As the complex is rather remote, there is a well stocked, small supermarket. For those who visit towing a caravan, please do use the recommended route – other roads are not suitable.

Facilities

Good sanitary blocks with well designed showers and hot and cold water for washing (in cubicles). Facilities for children and disabled visitors. Laundry. Small but well stocked supermarket (the site is quite remote). ATM. Bar and restaurant. Takeaway (1/6-31/8). Swimming pool complex (outdoor pools heated 1/430/9, indoor pool all season). Play area on sand. Tennis. Bicycle and quad bike hire. Archery. Riding. Activity clubs for all ages and entertainment (high season). Barbecues are not permitted.

Open: 24 March - 6 October.

Directions

From the N86 Bagnols - Aubanas road, exit onto the D4 at Bourg St Andeo to Remeze (a good road). Turn right at entrance to village on the D362 towards Larnas and site is on the right in Imbours. Do not attempt other routes with a caravan. GPS: N44:26.209 E04:34.652

Charges guide

Per person	€ 4,20 - € 7,00
child (0-7 yrs)	€ 2,30 - € 4,20
pitch (low season)	€ 4,20
pitch incl. 3 persons (high season)	€ 26,00 - € 29,00

CAMPINGS FranceLoc

Domaine d'Imbours

Le Domaine d'Imbours offers a large choice of facilities: pool complex with heated indoor pool, outdoor pools, paddling pools and many activities.

Le Domaine d'Imbours
07220 Larnas
Tél. 0033(0)4 75 54 39 50
Fax. 0033(0)4 75 54 39 20
www.campings-franceloc.com

FR07340 Domaine du Cros d'Auzon

Saint Maurice-d'Ardèche, F-07200 Vogüé-Gare (Ardèche)

Tel: **04 75 37 75 86**. Email: **camping.auzon@wanadoo.fr**   www.alanrogers.com/FR07340

This site can be described with the word 'immaculate'. The 55 pitches on well cut grass, are all of a very generous size and all have water, drainage and electricity. On the banks of the Ardèche, the site is part of a holiday complex which includes a hotel and conference centre, separated by a 300 m. driveway. Out of season it is very quiet, but in July and August a newly built bar, takeaway and restaurant together with an 'animations' building, become the focal point of the evenings. There are 55 mobile homes for hire (some tour operators).

Facilities

Two excellent, modern toilet blocks of an unusual design are kept very clean. Well equipped laundry room. Fridge hire. Bar, takeaway, restaurant and shop (July/Aug). At the hotel: swimming pool (1/5-15/9), minigolf and tennis. Play area of generous size. Bicycle hire. Internet access. Charcoal barbecues are not permitted. Off site: Village 500 m. Golf. Riding 10 km.

Open: 1 April - 15 September.

Directions

The D579 between Ruoms and Aubenas passes through the village of Vogüé. At the only roundabout take road to the southwest. Site is signed from the roundabout (about 800 m). GPS: N44:32.050 E04:24.414

Charges guide

Per unit incl. 2 persons and electricity	€ 17,50 - € 27,50
extra person	€ 4,00 - € 6,70

Check real time availability and at-the-gate prices...

www.alanrogers.com

FR07310 Camping la Roubine

Route de Ruoms, F-07150 Vallon-Pont-d'Arc (Ardèche)

Tel: 04 75 88 04 56. Email: roubine.ardeche@wanadoo.fr

www.alanrogers.com/FR07310

This site on the bank of the Ardèche has been in the same family ownership for some 30 years. During this time there has been constant upgrading and it must now be considered one of the best sites in the area. There are 114 touring pitches, all with electricity (10A) and quite spacious. Well tended grass, trimmed hedging and mature trees and smart tarmac roads create a calm and well kept atmosphere. The proprietors, M. Moulin and Mme. Van Eck like to welcome their guests and are available to help during the day – they are rightly proud of their well run campsite. Much attention is given to cleanliness – the toilet blocks are cleaned three times a day. A variety of sporting facilities are available on the site. The pool complex is heated when necessary throughout the season. There is a bar and restaurant of most modern design which, together with a mini-market, are open throughout the season. The site also caters for their young visitors with children's club in high season complete with an adventure playground and even an amphitheatre. There is an internet room.

Facilities

Several small sanitary blocks include washbasins in cubicles. The main toilet block has showers, washbasins in vanity units, a baby bathroom and facilities for visitors with disabilities. Laundry. Swimming pools, paddling pool and seperate childrens pool. Tennis. Boules. Fishing. Barbecues only permitted on communal sites. River beach. Off site: Bicycle hire and riding 1 km. Footpath to town 700 m. Supermarket in town.

Open: 20 April - 15 September.

Directions

From Vallon take the D579 towards Ruoms. Site is well signed on left 400 m. from town. From west (Ruoms) site signed on right near Vallon town sign. If missed proceed to roundabout at entrance to Vallon, go around and return some 400 m. (as above). GPS: N44:24.328 E04:22.750

Charges guide

Per unit incl. 2 persons	€ 19,00 - € 33,00
extra person	€ 3,40 - € 7,00
child (0-13 yrs)	free - € 7,00
electricity	€ 4,20

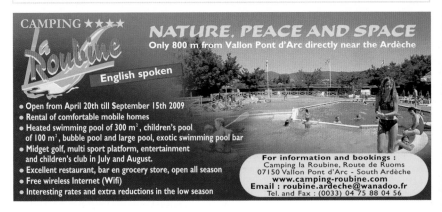

CAMPING ★★★★ la Roubine

NATURE, PEACE AND SPACE

Only 800 m from Vallon Pont d'Arc directly near the Ardèche

English spoken

- Open from April 20th till September 15th 2009
- Rental of comfortable mobile homes
- Heated swimming pool of 300 m², children's pool of 100 m², bubble pool and large pool, exotic swimming pool bar
- Midget golf, multi sport platform, entertainment and children's club in July and August.
- Excellent restaurant, bar en grocery store, open all season
- Free wireless Internet (Wifi)
- Interesting rates and extra reductions in the low season

For information and bookings :
Camping la Roubine, Route de Ruoms
07150 Vallon Pont d'Arc - South Ardèche
www.camping-roubine.com
Email : roubine.ardeche@wanadoo.fr
Tel. and Fax : (0033) 04 75 88 04 56

FR07360 Camping le Petit Bois

87 rue du Petit Bois, F-07120 Ruoms (Ardèche)

Tel: 04 75 39 60 72. Email: vacances@campinglepetitbois.fr

www.alanrogers.com/FR07360

Situated only 800 m from the ancient town centre of Ruoms, and yet within an area of trees and rocky outcrops, this site offers a centre for those wishing to explore this part of the Ardèche valley. The 118 pitches are of irregular shape and size and are a mix of stone and grass (76 are used for mobile homes). There is some shade. The site is now 30 years old and is needing some restoration, which is now underway. Some standpipes have coils of tubing attached. Perhaps these should not be used for domestic water purposes. A 'Sites et Paysages' member.

Facilities

Three toilet blocks (only one open in low season) were in need of some maintenance when we visited. Cleaning appeared somewhat erratic. Motorcaravan service point. Bar (all season). Restaurant and takeaway (1/7-31/8). New heated swimming pool (1/4-30/6) and solarium. Playground. Games and TV rooms in season. Fishing. Entertainment organised in high season. Off site: Town with shops, etc. 300 m. Riding and bicycle hire 1 km.

Open: 1 April - 30 September.

Directions

Approaching Ruoms on the D579 from Vallon-Pont-d'Arc go straight on at first (Super U) and second roundabouts. At third roundabout turn left (southwest) signed Largentier (site is signed). GPS: N44:27.638 E04:20.240

Charges guide

Per unit incl. 2 persons	€ 15,00 - € 28,00
with electricity (10A)	€ 19,00 - € 28,00
extra person	€ 4,80 - € 5,80
child (1-7 yrs)	€ 2,80 - € 3,80

347

flower
camping

FR07400 Flower Camping le Riviera

F-07120 Sampzon (Ardèche)

Tel: **04 75 39 67 57**. Email: **leriviera@wanadoo.fr**   www.alanrogers.com/FR07400

This large, well organised, family run site is situated beside the River Ardèche not far from Vallon-Pont-d'Arc. There are 180 pitches in total with 144 of average size on grass and stone for touring (rock pegs are advised). Separated by hedges and trees, pitches have varying degrees of shade and 10A electricity connections are available. In July and August daily and evening activities are organised for all the family. The site's facilities are of a high standard and disabled visitors are well provided for. Access to some of the pitches is not ideal in some parts and may prove to be difficult for larger units.

Facilities

Two toilet blocks, one new and excellent, providing cubicles with washbasins, showers, baby room and excellent facilities for disabled visitors. Washing machines and dryer. Swimming and paddling pools and terrace (all season, heated). Bar, restaurant with covered terrace (6/8-8/9 and weekends). Shop (July/Aug). Bicycle and canoe hire (July/Aug). Fishing. Stony river beach. Disco or karaoke every evening until midnight. Off site: Shop close to entrance. Riding 1 km. Bicycle hire 3 km.

Open: 1 April - 30 September.

Directions

On D579 2 km. south of Ruoms, turn left at roundabout signed Vallon-Pont-d'Arc. Shortly turn right over river bridge. Site on left.
GPS: N44:25.770 E04:21.370

Charges guide

Per unit incl. 2 persons and electricity (10A)	€ 16,00 - € 38,00
extra person	€ 4,50 - € 8,40
child (under 7 yrs)	free - € 7,40

FR07420 Camping du Pont

Route de Chauzon, F-07120 Pradons (Ardèche)

Tel: **04 75 93 93 98**. Email: **campingdupont07@wanadoo.fr**   www.alanrogers.com/FR07420

This is a lovely small campsite, run by a friendly outgoing family who have recently moved here. Beside the Ardèche river, the site has a small sandy beach and a deep river pool for swimming. There are 65 average sized, grassy pitches with 52 for touring (6/10A electricity), all separated by hedges and trees giving good shade. The welcoming bar, takeaway, small shop and pool are open all season. Family activities are organised in July and August. The site is ideal for those seeking a less commercialised site close to the Ardèche Gorges.

Facilities

The good toilet block provides separate facilities for men and ladies, an excellent room for children and facilities for disabled visitors. Small shop. Bar, snacks and takeaway. Heated swimming and paddling pools (1/4-30/9). Games/TV room. Play areas. Small sandy river beach, deep pool for swimming. Fishing. Canoe trips. Organised walks from site. Charcoal barbecues are not allowed. Off site: Supermarket 200 m. Bicycle hire 3 km. Riding 4 km. Vallon-Pont-d'Arc 12 km.

Open: Easter - 30 September.

Directions

Leave Montélimar westwards on N102 towards Aubenas. Passing Villeneuve-de-Berg, turn left on D103 towards Vogüé for 5 km. Turn left on D579 towards Ruoms. In Pradons turn right D308, signed Chauzon. Site shortly on left before river bridge. GPS: N44:24.430 E04:21.200

Charges guide

Per unit incl. 2 persons	€ 13,80 - € 21,50
extra person	€ 3,50 - € 5,00
electricity	€ 3,80

FR07440 Camping Mas de Champel

Quartier Champel, F-07360 Les Ollières-sur-Eyrieux (Ardèche)

Tel: **04 75 66 23 23**. Email: **masdechampel@wanadoo.fr**   www.alanrogers.com/FR07440

This is a simple campsite with easy access and within walking distance of a small village. It has a lively entertainment programme plus many organised activities in the high season. There are 95 unmarked, level grassy pitches, 51 for touring (electricity 6A, may need long leads) with almost no shade. A small sandy beach alongside the Eyrieux river offers lots of space for children to play in the shallow water. The bar and restaurant offer arrange of meals including breakfast and entertainment is provided in the area adjacent.

Facilities

Two small old, adequate toilet blocks with all necessary facilities. Bar, restaurant/takeaway. Swimming pool, heated paddling pool and sunbathing area. Games/TV room. Small, simple play area. Fishing. Bicycle hire. Motorcaravan services. Only gas barbecues permitted. Many organised family activities in July/Aug. Off site: Ollières-sur-Eyrieux, small shops, bar, restaurant 500 m. Riding 7 km.

Open: 20 April - 22 September.

Directions

Leave N86 south of Valence at Beauchastel. Turn west, D120, to Ollières sur Eyrieux (about 20 km). Site is on right at entrance to village and is signed. GPS: N44:48.356 E04:36.916

Charges guide

Per unit incl. 2 persons and electricity	€ 17,90 - € 28,80
extra person	€ 3,90 - € 6,90
child (2-7 yrs)	free - € 4,90

www.flowercampings.com

Check real time availability and at-the-gate prices...

www.alanrogers.com

FR07610 Camping les Charmilles

D 258, les Clapas, F-07170 Darbres (Ardèche)

Tel: **04 75 88 56 27**. Email: **info@campinglescharmilles.fr**   www.alanrogers.com/FR07610

A delightful and well maintained, rural site, les Charmilles is run by a very friendly Dutch family. It is situated in the Auzon Valley of the Ardèche, high up on the hills overlooking Aubenas and far beyond. The air here is cooler and fresher than in the valley below. There are 100 grassy/stony pitches of varying size laid out on low terraces, many with panoramic views. There are 75 for touring units with a variety of trees giving some shade. Electricity (5/10A) is available (long leads may be necessary) and rock pegs are advised. Many family activities are arranged in July and August with some also during low season. A spacious bar and its terrace overlook the pool, with wonderful views over the valley and mountains beyond; just the place to relax and watch the colourful sunsets and the twinkling lights in Aubenas far below. This is a good family base for those who enjoy the outdoor life; walking, cycling, watersports and nature. Some of the most beautiful villages in France are close by and well worth a visit and the local narrow lanes are just waiting to be explored.

Facilities

Excellent toilet block (new 2007), very clean with all necessary facilities including those for young children and campers with disabilities. Shop (May - Sept). Bar with TV and restaurant (overlooking pool) with takeaway (May - Sept). Swimming pool and large, separated paddling pool, sunbathing terrace. Many family activities, including miniclub, walks, excursions (high season) with some in the low season. Boules. WiFi. Charcoal barbecues are not permitted. Off site: Gorges Ardèche. Medieval market towns and villages. Aubenas 15 km.

Open: Easter - 30 September.

Directions

Site is east of Aubenas in the Ardèche. Leave Aubenas on the N102 signed Montélimar. At Lavilledieu turn onto D224 signed Darbres. After 10 km. in Darbres fork right on D258 signed Mirabel. Site is on left in about 2 km.
GPS: N44:38.011 E04:30.507

Charges guide

Per unit incl. 2 persons and electricity	€ 19,00 - € 39,50
extra person (over 3 yrs)	€ 3,50 - € 5,00
dog	€ 2,00

LES CHARMILLES CAMPING***

Panoramic view   In the south of France

English spoken   Ardèche   Beautiful scenery

Child friendly

CC

New sanitary facilities!
Mobile homes for rent!
Reduction in the low season!

CAMPING LES CHARMILLES***

Phone: 0033 (0)4 75 88 56 27 • www.campinglescharmilles.fr • info@campinglescharmilles.fr

FR07570 Domaine de la Plage

Neyrac-les-Bains, F-07380 Aubenas (Ardèche)

Tel: **04 75 36 40 59**. Email: **contact@lecampingdelaplage.com**   www.alanrogers.com/FR07570

A great deal of care and attention to detail has gone into developing this compact site and its superb facilities. However, of its 45 pitches, only eight are for camping. The site is beautifully landscaped with flora and fauna and the facilities are sympathetically incorporated into a former textile factory. It has a very attractive solar heated pool and sunbathing terrace, with bar and snack service. The river can be directly accessed from the site and the owners have constructed a delightful bridge walkway crossing a waterfall and into a small picnic area. A 'Sites et Paysages' member.

Facilities

Modern sanitary facilities include superb facilities for disabled visitors although access around the site is quite steep. Laundry room. Fridge hire. Microwave and oven facilities. Gas. Bar. Snack service. Shop. Solar heated swimming pool and poolside bar. Large games room, library and TV room. Pétanque. Play area. Entertainment and children's animation programmes. Fishing. Canoeing excursions with site pickup. Off site: Thermal baths 700 m. Bicycle hire 2 km. Tennis 3 km. Golf 8 km.

Open: 30 March - 26 October.

Directions

From A7 exit 17 take N7 (Montelimar) for 20 km. Turn west on N102 to Aubenas. Continue on N102 for 30 km. towards Neyrac-les-Bains. Cross river at Pont-de-Labeaume and site is 2 km. on left just before entering village.
GPS: N44:40.398 E04:15.564

Charges guide

Per unit incl. 2 persons	€ 14,00 - € 22,00
extra person	€ 4,00 - € 5,00
electricity (4-10A)	€ 3,00 - € 4,00

349

FR26030 Le Grand Lierne

B.P. 8, F-26120 Chabeuil (Drôme)

Tel: **04 75 59 83 14**. Email: **contact@grandlierne.com**   www.alanrogers.com/FR26030

In addition to its obvious attraction as an overnight stop, fairly convenient for the A7 autoroute, this site provides a pleasant base to explore this little known area between the Ardèche and the Vercors mountains and the Côtes du Rhône wine area. It has 198 marked, stony pitches, 90 for touring units (6/10A electricity), separated by hedges and oak trees which offer varying amounts of shade. A more open area exists for those who prefer less shade and a view of the mountains, but this area contains many mobile homes. The site has an attractive pool complex with several pools. They are surrounded by terraces with loungers for sunbathing and one small pool is covered in poor weather. There are very good sporting facilities with many organised activities making this a lively site in July and August. English and Dutch are spoken. The site is used by tour operators (30%).

Facilities

Two old sanitary blocks with modern facilities including those for disabled people. Washing machines, dryers. Motorcaravan services. Shop/restaurant, terrace (1/7-31/8). Bar/takeaway (1/5-8/9). Fridge rental. Three pools 1/5-30/9, one very small, covered and heated. Paddling pool, water slide, toboggans and lazy river. Playgrounds. Minigolf. Archery. Library. Extensive entertainment programme. WiFi. Only gas and electric barbecues are permitted. Dogs are not accepted 8/7-18/8. Off site: Golf 3 km. Bicycle hire 4.5 km. Fishing 5 km. Riding 7 km. Chabeuil 5 km. Valence 11 km.

Open: 28 April - 30 September, with all services.

Directions

Site signed from Chabeuil about 11 km. east of Valence. Best approached from south side of Valence via Valence ring road. D68 to Chabeuil. Site is off D125 to Charpey, 5 km. from Chabeuil, well signed. GPS: N44:54.951 E05:03.907

Charges guide

Per unit incl. 2 persons	€ 16,90 - € 30,20
extra person	€ 7,90 - € 8,50
child (2-7 yrs)	€ 4,80 - € 6,20
electricity (6/10A)	€ 4,30 - € 5,70

Camping Cheques accepted.

DRÔME

CAMPINGS FranceLoc

grand Lierne

Aquatic Park of 200 m² with water slide. Discover our natural campsite at the foot of the Vercors with mobile homes and chalets.

New in 2008: new indoor swimming pool.

Chabeuil • BP 8 • F • 26120
Tel.: +33 (0)4 75 59 83 14
Email : grand-lierne@franceloc.fr
www.camping-franceloc.fr

FR07600 Camping le Castelet

113 route du Grand Pont, F-07300 St Jean-de-Muzols (Ardèche)

Tel: **04 75 08 09 48**. Email: **courrier@camping-lecastelet.com**   www.alanrogers.com/FR07600

This is a gem of a site run by a very friendly French family. Developed over a period of 30 years, it is situated in the valley of the River Rhône surrounded by wooded hills and terraces of vines. Everything here is neat and tidy and maintained to a high standard. There are 60 grassy, fairly level pitches separated by low fences, flowering shrubs and hedges and small trees give limited shade. All the 53 pitches used for touring units have good access and 6A electricity but long leads are advised. The site is ideal for couples and families with pre-teenage children.

Facilities

Two excellent, modern toilet blocks are fully equipped. Facilities for young children and campers with disabilities. Washing machine. Small bar. TV room next to reception. Bread to order (all season). Swimming and paddling pools with sunbathing terrace (15/5-10/9). Very good play area adjacent to bar. Large playing field with shaded area for picnics. Small river for paddling. Organised excursions and activities for children (high season). WiFi and internet point. Only gas barbecues permitted. Off site: River beach (500 m). Bicycle hire 4 km. Riding 10 km.

Open: 1 April - 15 September.

Directions

Leave A7 at exit 13 westwards to Tournon-sur-Rhône. Cross the River Rhône and turn right on N86 signed St Jean-de-Muzols. After 1.5 km. turn left at roundabout on D532 signed Lamastre. After 3 km. turn right across river, then immediately turn sharp right to site entrance. GPS: N45:04.072 E04:47.110

Charges guide

Per unit incl. 2 persons	€ 13,50 - € 15,00
extra person	€ 4,00
electricity (5A)	€ 3,30

No credit cards.

Check real time availability and at-the-gate prices...

www.**alanrogers**.com

FR26100 Camping le Sagittaire

Pont de Mirabel, F-26110 Vinsobres (Drôme)

Tel: 04 75 27 00 00. Email: camping.sagittaire@wanadoo.fr   www.alanrogers.com/FR26100

Le Sagittaire is beautifully situated in this picturesque region with its Côtes du Rhône vineyards, lavender fields and medieval hilltop villages. It is only 2.5 km. from Vinsobres and 6 km. from Nyons, well known for its olives and its Provençal market. There are 270 level grassy pitches with 124 for touring, all with electricity (6/10A). Most are separated by hedges and there are mature trees offering some shade. The hub of the site is a water park with indoor and outdoor pools, slides and toboggans. A one hectare lake surrounded by a sandy beach is ideal for children. Leisure activities for all ages are organised in July and August, with sports during the day and barbecues, discos, karaoke and live shows in the evening, making this a lively site. This is a good base for a family holiday in a wonderful region which can be explored on foot, bike or by car.

Facilities

Three excellent modern toilet blocks. Facilities for campers with disabilities and families. Motorcaravan services. Shop. Bar with TVs. Restaurant. Takeaway. Games room (1/4-30/9). Outdoor swimming pool, toboggan, slides, lazy river, cascades (1/5-30/8). Heated covered pool, paddling pool, jacuzzi (1/4-30/9). Small lake with sandy beach, picnic area. Excellent range of sporting facilities. Play areas. Fitness room. Extensive programme of family activities in July/Aug. Fishing. Bicycle hire. Minigolf. Charcoal barbecues not allowed. Cycling is forbidden. Off site: Riding. Mediterranean beaches 1.5 hours away.

Open: All year.

Directions

Leave A7 at exit 19 (Bollène) and follow signs for Nyons (D94). Site is well signed on right just beyond Vinsobres (about 30 km).
GPS: N44:19.664 E05:04.743

Charges guide

Per unit incl. 2 persons	€ 17,50 - € 31,00
extra person	€ 3,60 - € 7,50
child (under 7 yrs)	€ 2,10 - € 4,50
electricity (3/6A)	€ 3,70 - € 4,80

Long stay off season discounts.

Domaine du Sagittaire

3 hectares of relaxation with a 7600 m² waterpark parc and lake, tennis, Californian mini golf, volleyball. New in 2007 200 m² swimming pool.

Vinsobres 26110 Nyons
Tél. 0033(0)4 75 27 00 00
Fax. 0033(0)4 75 27 00 39
www.campings-franceloc.com

Drôme

FR07620 Camping le Chamadou

Mas de Chaussy, F-07120 Balazuc (Ardèche)

Tel: 0820 366 197. Email: infos@camping-le-chamadou.com   www.alanrogers.com/FR07620

La Chamadou is a delightful, well maintained and peaceful site run by an enthusiastic and friendly family. It is situated in the southern Ardèche, close to the medieval, perched village of Balazuc, not far from the river Ardèche. There are 86 slightly sloping grassy/stony pitches with 69 for touring (electricity 10A). They are separated by hedges and flowering shrubs with a variety of trees giving some shade. There are several small very clean toilet blocks with excellent facilities. A cosy restaurant and terrace have panoramic views. The approach road is narrow for large outfits.

Facilities

Several small, well appointed and very clean toilet blocks have all the necessary facilities including those for campers with disabilities. Bar/TV (all season). Tiny shop with necessities. Restaurant and takeaway (July/Aug and some special occasions). Swimming pool, paddling pool, toboggan (all season). Good play area. Games room. Lake fishing. Canoe trips and bike hire organised. Only electric and gas barbecues allowed. Off site: Small village of Vogüé 3 km. Small shop 2 km. River bathing 2 km. Riding and bicycle hire 4 km.

Open: 1 April - 31 October.

Directions

Site in is in southern Ardèche south of Aubenas. Leave Aubenas on the D104, signed Alès. Shortly turn left on D579 signed Vallon-Pont-d'Arc. Bypass Vogüé, cross river and keep right. In 4.5 km. turn left at site sign along narrow lane to site in 2 km.
GPS: N44:30.467 E04:24.208

Charges guide

Per unit incl. 2 persons	€ 17,00 - € 22,50
extra person	€ 4,30 - € 5,10
child (1-7 yrs)	€ 3,40 - € 3,70
electricity (10A)	€ 4,00 - € 4,20

351

FR26110 Kawan Village Les Quatre Saisons

Route de Roche-sur-Grâne, F-26400 Grâne (Drôme)

Tel: **04 75 62 64 17**. Email: **camping4saisons@wanadoo.fr**   www.alanrogers.com/FR26110

This small, terraced site, open all year, nestles in the hillsides of the lower Drôme valley close to the Vercors Mountains. With its 80 pitches (73 for touring units), it provides mainly accommodation for overnight but it is worth a longer stay. The pitches are level and stony, of variable size, cut out of the hillside and reached by a one-way system on tarmac roads. All pitches have electricity (6/10A), some with water and drain. The modern main building houses reception on the top floor, with other facilities below, and provides commanding views across the valley towards Crest and the Vercors.

Facilities

Good sanitary facilities, heated in low season, include, baby room, en-suite facilities for disabled visitors (but site is very sloping and not suitable for wheelchairs). Washing machine. Bar (15/4-15/10). TV room. Small swimming pool (15/4-15/9). Play area. Bicycle hire. Off site: Village nearby with shops catering for most needs. Fishing 1 km. Riding 3 km. Crest.

Open: All year.

Directions

From A7 exit 17, or the N7 at Loriol, take the D104 towards Crest. After 8 km. in Grâne take D113 south. Site is on left about 600 m. beyond the village. GPS: N44:43.661 E04:55.592

Charges guide

Per unit incl. 2 persons	€ 13,00 - € 16,00
extra person	€ 3,00 - € 5,00
child (under 13 yrs)	€ 2,00 - € 4,00
electricity	€ 4,00
dog	€ 3,00

Camping Cheques accepted.

Les 4 Saisons Camping et Caravanning★★★★

Only 10 minutes from exit 16 of the A7 highway. Ideal for a stop-over or a longer stay in a quiet and relaxing environment with lovely well situated pitches with a nice view on the Vercors. The campsite is perfectly located for cyclists and walkers. Lovers of antiquity will love the magnificent high situated villages.

Route de Roche sur Grâne - 26400 Grane
Tél. 0031 (0)4 75 62 64 17 - Fax 0031 (0)4 75 62 69 06
E-mail contact@camping-4-saisons.com

www.camping-4-saisons.com

FR07640 Flower Camping Saint-Amand

F-07110 Laurac (Ardèche)

Tel: **Sitetel**. Email: **st-amand@wanadoo.fr**   www.alanrogers.com/FR07640

Saint Amand is a member of the Flower group and can be found around 15 km. west of Vallon Pont d'Arc, close to the appropriately named village of Bellevue. There are 116 pitches, most with electrical connections and good shade. A number of pitches are occupied by mobile homes and fully equipped tents (available for rent). From the site's pool, there are some fine views across the surrounding scrubland and vineyards. Other amenities include a small restaurant, specialising in home-made pizzas and a new playing area for children. The closest shops are in the village of Laurac (2.5 km. away).

Facilities

Small shop. Pizzeria and snack bar. Takeaway. Swimming pool. Children's pool. Play area. Activity and entertainment programme. Mobile homes for rent. Off site: Laurac 2.5 km. Vallon Pont d'Arc 15 km. Cycle and walking tracks.

Open: 1 April - 19 September.

Directions

Approaching from the north (Privas), head southwest on the D104 to Aubenas and then continue to Bellevue. Site is clearly signed from here. GPS: N44:29.978 E04:18.371

Charges 2009

Per unit incl. 2 persons and electricity	€ 13,90 - € 21,50
extra person	€ 2,30 - € 3,50
child (2-6 yrs)	free - € 3,00
dog	€ 1,50

www.flowercampings.com

FR26140 Flower Camping la Châtaigneraie

Route de Mantaille, F-26140 Anneyron (Drôme)

Tel: 04 75 31 43 33. Email: contact@chataigneraie.com

www.alanrogers.com/FR26140

Small and neat, La Châtaigneraie is a family run, terraced site (English spoken) tucked away in the countryside and will suit those seeking a quieter, relaxing family orientated site. It is not ideal for those with walking difficulties. There are 71 medium sized, slightly sloping, grassy pitches, 30 for touring away from the static units. They are separated by a variety of hedges and young trees provide varying degrees of shade and all have 6/10A electricity. The Drôme is a beautiful area to explore with many old towns and villages with their markets and museums. Enjoy the local produce and the wines of the Rhône valley.

Facilities

The single toilet block at the top of the site is a good, modern building kept very clean. Bar and small shop. Good restaurant/takeaway with full menu at weekends and high season, otherwise a 'menu de jour'. Swimming and paddling pools (15/5-15/9). Short tennis. Two small play areas, TV and games room. Bicycle hire. Farmer's market twice a week. Entertainment for children and adults (July/Aug). WiFi internet access near bar. Only electric barbecues can be allowed. Off site: Marked walks and cycle tracks in the hills around. Fishing and golf 3 km. Riding 8 km.

Open: 1 April - 30 September.

Directions

Leave A7 south of Lyons at exit 12 and go south on the N7 for 7 km. Turn left on D1 to Anneyron. In the village turn right on D161 signed Mantaille and in 3 km. turn right on D301, signed Albon. Site is shortly on the right, well signed.
GPS: N45:15.282 E04:54.239

Charges guide

Per unit incl. 2 persons	
and electricity	€ 14,90 - € 23,50
extra person	€ 4,00 - € 5,00
child (3-14 yrs)	€ 2,00 - € 3,80
dog	€ 2,00 - € 2,20

Camping La Châtaigneraie ★★★

Route de Mantaille - 26140 Anneyron
Tél. 00 33 (0)4 75 31 43 33 - Fax. 00 33 (0)4 75 03 84 67
contact@chataigneraie.com - www.chataigneraie.com

flower campings

le camping c'est humain.

www.flowercampings.com

FR26010 Domaine du Lac de Champos

Mobile homes ▶ page 506

F-26260 Saint-Donat-sur-l'Herbasse (Drôme)

Tel: 04 75 45 17 81. Email: contact@lacdechampos.com

www.alanrogers.com/FR26010

Lac de Champos is a spacious park surrounding a 9 hectare lake. There are large grassy areas for recreation with fishing, bathing and boating (no motors) on the lake all open to both the public and to campers. The public area of the park is at one end near entrance and the campsite at the other. There are 98 pitches close to the lake with 75 for touring units, some stony and some grassy. Most have some shade and 6/10A electricity (long leads advised). A separate sunny, level, tarmac area adjacent to a grassy public picnic area and overlooking the lake is available for motorcaravans.

Facilities

Two toilet blocks, one rather old provide all necessary facilities including those for campers with disabilities. Motorcaravan services. Bar and midday snacks (July/Aug). Games room with TV near entrance. Wifi at reception. Fishing, boating (no motors) on lake, canoes and pedaloes for hire (July/Aug and weekends). Separate lake swimming area (supervised high season) with beach, paddling pool and large toboggan. Tennis. Organised activities in high season. Charcoal barbecues are not permitted; electric barbecues for hire. Off site: St Donat 3 km riverside walk. Riding 1 km. Bicycle hire 10 km.

Open: 26 April - 14 September.

Directions

Leave A7 autoroute at exit 13 and take D532 signed Romans-sur-Isère. After about 5 km. at Curson turn north on D67. Continue through St Donat (site well signed) to site on right in 3 km.
GPS: N45:07.911 E05:00.256

Charges guide

Per unit incl. 2 persons	
and electricity	€ 11,50 - € 16,50
extra person	€ 2,50 - € 3,60
child (3-12 yrs)	€ 2,00 - € 3,00
dog	€ 1,00

www.flowercampings.com

353

Check real time availability and at-the-gate prices...

www.alanrogers.com

BOOK THIS SITE
CALL 01580 214000
...we'll arrange everything
The Travel Service

The Travel

Service

BOOK THIS SITE

CALL 01580 214000

...we'll arrange everything

FR26150 Flower Camping Lac Bleu

Quarter la Touche, F-26410 Chatillon-en-Diois (Drôme)

Tel: 04 75 21 85 30. Email: info@lacbleu-diois.com

www.alanrogers.com/FR26150

This spacious and peaceful site is run by a very friendly family who have made many improvements to the site with many more in the pipeline. It lies in a beautiful valley surrounded by mountains, south of the Vercors National Park. The 90 pitches (78 for touring) are large, level, with rough grass, slightly bumpy and separated by a variety of trees offering some shade (rock pegs advised). All have electricity (6-10A). At the centre of the site is a lake of 2.5 hectares with warm clean water fed by springs making it ideal for swimming and fishing. A good bar, restaurant and terrace overlook the lake and there is plenty of space for children to play. An evening stroll around the lake is recommended. The site is near the very small River Bez and not far from the interesting and ancient small town of Die, the home of the famous Clairette de Die. It is a very good site for exploring this picturesque part of France, yet to completely unwind and enjoy the views, the beautiful sunset over the mountains and the very clean air.

Facilities

Two clean toilet blocks one new, the other refurbished for 2007. Baby room and facilities for disabled campers. Motorcaravan service point. Small shop. Bar/restaurant. Takeaway. Games room. Play area bordering the lake. Large sports/play area. Bicycle hire. Footpaths around lake. Lake bathing and fishing. Pedaloes. Internet point. Only gas and electric barbecues allowed. Off site: Medieval villages (Châtillon 2 km). Canoeing, canyoning, grottos.

Open: 1 April - 30 September.

Directions

Head southeast from Die on the D93, signed Gap. After about 5 km. turn left on D539 signed Châtillon-en-Diois. After 4.5 km. bear right onto D140, site signed. Follow signs to site, shortly on left. GPS: N44:40.947 E05:26.799

Charges guide

Per unit incl. 2 persons	€ 9,90 - € 23,00

www.flowercampings.com

Camping Le Lac Bleu ★★★

Quartier La Touche - 26410 Châtillon-en-Diois
Tél. 00 33 (0)4 75 21 85 30 - Fax. 00 33 (0)4 75 21 82 05
info@lacbleu-diois.com - www.lacbleu-diois.com

le camping c'est humain.

www.flowercampings.com

FR26040 Kawan Village le Couspeau

F-26460 Le Poët-Célard (Drôme)

Tel: 04 75 53 30 14. Email: info@couspeau.com

www.alanrogers.com/FR26040

As one approaches this site, a magnificent landscape of mountains and valleys unfolds. The site has 127 pitches with 83 for touring (6A electricity). Access to the older section of the site is reasonably easy and mature trees here provide some shade. The 30 fully serviced pitches on the lower section are large and separated by small hedges with little shade. Access is via a steep road but tractor assistance is available. Rock pegs are advised. The most direct approach to the site is via a steep road with hairpin bends to negotiate, so care is required (not advised for underpowered or large units).

Facilities

Three sanitary blocks. Washing machines, dryer. Facilities for disabled campers (the site is not ideal with steep roads and steps). Shop (15/4-14/9). Bar (20/6-14/9). Restaurant and takeaway (25/6-25/8). Swimming pool (1/6-30/8) and small, heated, covered paddling pool (14/4-14/9). Play area, organised activities. Tennis. Bicycle hire. Rafting, canoe trips (on River Drôme), riding, paragliding. Off site: Riding, fishing 5 km. Ideal area for the serious cyclist, mountain biker and hiker. Medieval towns and villages, markets and châteaux. Crest, Poët-Laval. Vercors mountains.

Open: 15 April - 14 September.

Directions

From A7, exit 16, take D104 towards Crest. At traffic lights on Crest bypass, turn right, D538 towards Bourdeaux. Before Bourdeaux turn right over bridge, D328B, signed Le Po't Célard. Climb for 1.5 km. to T-junction, turn right. D328. Before Le Poët-Célard turn left, D328A to site. GPS: N44:35.744 E05:06.680

Charges guide

Per unit incl. 2 persons	€ 14,00 - € 30,00
extra person	€ 5,00
electricity (6A)	€ 3,00

Camping Cheques accepted.

FR26210 Camping les Bois du Chatelas

Mobile homes ▶ page 506

Route de Dieulefit, F-26460 Bourdeaux (Drôme)

Tel: **04 75 00 60 80**. Email: **contact@chatelas.com**

www.alanrogers.com/FR26210

Located at the heart of the the Drôme Provencale, Les Bois du Chatelas is a smart, family run site which has undergone many recent improvements. The site is just 1 km. from the delightful village of Bourdeaux which offers a good range of shops, cafés, etc. There are 120 pitches here of which 69 are occupied by mobile homes. Although situated on a hillside, the pitches are level and of a good size. They all offer electricity, water and drainage. Les Bois du Chatelas is a particularly good choice for those seeking an active holiday. Member 'Sites et Paysages'. The long distance GR9 footpath passes through the site and there are very many walking and cycle routes close at hand. A popular aquagym is organised in the large outdoor pool in peak season. In the high season, a lively entertainment programme is organized as well as a number of cycling and walking excursions.

Facilities

Two heated toilet blocks (on upper and lower levels) with facilities for babies and disabled people (note: the site is hilly and may be unsuitable). Shop. Bar. Restaurant/pizzeria. Indoor swimming pool. Outdoor pool with water slide, waterfall and jacuzzi. Sports pitch. Archery. Play area. Bicycle hire. Entertainment and excursion programme (July/Aug). Mobile homes for rent. Off site: Rafting and canoe trips. Riding 5 km. Fishing 1 km. Very extensive walking and cycle (mountain bike) opportunities. Vercors mountain range.

Open: 7 April - 30 September.

Directions

From the north, leave A7 at exit 16 and join the eastbound D104 to Crest. Upon reaching Crest take D538 south to Bourdeaux and continue towards Dieulefit. Site is on the left 1 km. beyond Bourdeaux and is well signed. GPS: N44:34.737 E05:07.674

Charges guide

Per unit incl. 2 persons	€ 14,00 - € 24,00
extra person	€ 4,20 - € 5,00
child (1-7 yrs)	€ 2,70 - € 2,90
electricity (10A)	€ 4,30 - € 4,50

Camping Les Bois du Chatelas

Route de Dieulefit - F-26460 Bourdeaux - Tl.: (33) 4 75 00 60 80 - Fax (33) 4 75 00 60 81
E-mail: contact@chatelas.com - www.chatelas.com

FR26130 Kawan Village l'Hirondelle

Bois de Saint Ferreol, F-26410 Menglon (Drôme)

Tel: **04 75 21 82 08**. Email: **contact@campinghirondelle.com**

www.alanrogers.com/FR26130

This natural, spacious and peaceful site is run by a very friendly family and you are assured a good welcome. It lies in a beautiful valley, south of the Vercors mountains and the Vercors National Park, beside the River Bez, a tributary of the River Drôme which is also close by. In natural openings in woodland, the 100 large to very large pitches all have electricity (3/6A) and are stony and slightly bumpy (rock pegs advised). There are 58 for touring units. The large pitches are separated from others by a wide variety of trees with the 1.5 km. of river bank on one side.

Facilities

Two large toilet blocks offer all the necessary facilities. Very good bar/restaurant with good menus and takeaway (all season). Small range of supplies, including bread, on sale from the bar. Excellent pool complex with small slide, paddling pool and jacuzzi (1/5-13/9). Ample room to play and paddle in the river. Playground. Club/TV room. Internet access. Fishing. Football, boules, volleyball, archery. Multisport court. Bicycle hire. Organised events for young children and adults. Occasional evening events. Off site: Riding 5 km.

Open: 28 April - 17 September.

Directions

From Die follow D93 southwards and after 5 km, at Pont de Quart, turn left on D539 signed Châtillon. After about 4 km. turn right on D140, signed Menglon. Site entrance is shortly on the right just after crossing a small river. GPS: N44:40.885 E05:26.846

Charges 2009

Per pitch incl. 2 persons	€ 16,40 - € 25,70
extra person	€ 4,85 - € 7,20
child (2-10 yrs)	€ 3,30 - € 6,00
electricity (3/6A)	€ 3,15 - € 4,20

Camping Cheques accepted.

Check real time availability and at-the-gate prices...

www.alanrogers.com

BOOK THIS SITE
CALL 01580 214000
...we'll arrange everything
The Travel Service

FR26260 Camping les Acacias

F-26340 Vercheny (Drôme)

Tel: **04 75 21 72 51**. Email: **info@campinglesacacias.com**   www.alanrogers.com/FR26260

Located midway between Crest and Die, Camping les Acacias is a comfortable riverside site. There are 90 pitches here with 6 or 10A electrical connections supplied to most. The pitches are of a good size and generally well shaded. They are separated by trees and hedges and some are available along the riverside. The site slopes down to the banks of the Drôme river and some up and down walking will probably be required. A small canoe base has been established here and canoe excursions to the Gorges de Saillans are justifiably popular. Given the proximity of the D93 and railway line, there may be some background road and rail noise. Walking and mountain biking are popular pursuits and many trails are available in the surrounding countryside. Nearby mountains such as Archiane and Les Trois Becs are popular excursions. In high season, the site runs an entertainment and excursion programme, including a club for children. The site's bar and snack bar is housed below reception and has a small terrace.

Facilities

Three toilet blocks with facilities for babies and disabled visitors. Bar and snack bar. Small shop. Play areas. Canoe hire. Fishing (permit needed). TV room. Entertainment and children's club (peak season). Excursion programme (July/Aug). Mobile homes and chalets for rent. Off site: Many cycling and walking trails. Restaurants, cafés and shops in nearby Saillans and Vercheny.

Open: 1 April - 30 September.

Directions

Head east from Crest on the D93. Site is located on the right, midway between Saillans and Vercheny. GPS: N44:41.782 E05:14.484

Charges guide

Per pitch incl. 2 persons	€ 12,00 - € 14,50
extra person	€ 3,20 - € 3,90
child (under 4 yrs)	free
electricity (6A)	€ 3,10

Situated between the Vercors and Provence, nestled at the foot of the mountain 'Les Trois Becs' at the riverside of the Drôme with crystal blue water. Les Acacias is the right place to be for relaxing and activities. Flat and wooded terrain amidst nature. We offer canoes for rent for a discovery tour through the Drôme.

26340 Vercheny - France
Tél. 04 75 21 72 51 - Fax 04 75 21 73 98
E-mail info@campinglesacacias.com

www.campinglesacacias.com

FR26160 Domaine la Garenne

RD53, F-26330 Saint Avit (Drôme)

Tel: **04 75 68 62 26**. Email: **garenne.drome@wanadoo.fr**   www.alanrogers.com/FR26160

This very spacious, partly terraced rural site lies in pleasant countryside to the east of the Rhône valley. Most of the very large pitches are spread out naturally under pine trees but a grassy lower area is more open and young trees give little shade at present. Although all the pitches have electricity (3/6A) very long leads are necessary. Of the 100 pitches, 25 are taken up by long stay units. The facilities are old but very clean and could entail a long walk. The small pool and its sunbathing area are next to the reception but there are few other amenities. Torches and rock pegs essential.

Facilities

Four small basic toilet blocks with washbasins in cabins. Some facilities for disabled people but the rough paths and terracing make this site unsuitable for those with walking difficulties. Washing machine. Motorcaravan services. Baker calls July/Aug. Small bar (July/Aug). Kitchen area with tables under cover. Small swimming pool. Large sports area. Play area. Communal barbecue (not allowed on the pitches). Some family activities (July/Aug). WiFi at reception. Off site: Fishing 1 km. Riding 2 km. Golf 15 km. Village shops at Châteauneuf 3 km. Many marked walks and cycle routes.

Open: 1 May - 15 September.

Directions

Leave the N7 16 km. north of Tournon. Turn east on D51, signed Châteauneuf. After about 15 km. at Mureils, turn right on D363, signed St Avit. After 2 km. turn left on D53 (site signed) and site entrance is shortly on the right. GPS: N45:12.123 E04:57.431

Charges guide

Per unit incl. 2 persons	€ 15,00
Low season discounts.	

Check real time availability and at-the-gate prices...

www.**alanrogers**.com

FR26270 Camping Champ la Chèvre

F-26220 Lus-la-Croix-Haute (Drôme)

Tel: 04 92 58 50 14. Email: info@campingchamplachevre.com   www.alanrogers.com/FR26270

This is a pleasant, unpretentious site with some really magnificent views across towards the western Alps. Formerly a farm (hence its name!) and now under new management, Champ la Chèvre is undergoing a steady process of refurbishment and is attractively located just 200 m. from the village and 500 m. from the N75. There are 100 pitches, for the most part sunny and quite spacious, and many with fine mountain views. Some pitches are sloping and most pitches have 6A electrical connections. Although there is no swimming pool on site, the large municipal pool adjacent is free for all campers. This is a good base for exploring the mountains and the owners have many ideas for excursions in the area, including downhill mountain biking, swimming in local rivers and hundreds of kilometres of walking trails. The nearby village of Lus La Croix Haute is pretty and has a good range of shops and a small railway station.

Facilities

Centrally located toilet block with facilities for disabled visitors. Motorcaravan services. Play area. Minigolf. Mobile homes and chalets for rent. Off site: Heated swimming pool adjacent (free to campers). Village of Lus La Croix Haute 200 m. Railway station 300 m. Tennis. Many walking and cycle trails.

Open: 26 April - 28 September.

Directions

From the north, head south from Grenoble initially on the A480 and then the A51 towards Sisteron. Then join the southbound N75 for around 35 km. to Lus La Croix Haute. Drive through the village and site is well signed. GPS: N44:39.864 E05:42.445

Charges 2009

Per unit incl. 2 persons	€ 13,80 - € 16,40
extra person	€ 4,00 - € 4,90
child (under 10 yrs)	€ 3,00 - € 3,90
electricity (6A)	€ 4,05

Camping** Champ la Chèvre

Mobile Homes, chalets and cabins for rent
Bar, restaurant, take-away and pizza during high season
New sanitary facilities, table tennis, soccer, volleyball, jeu de boules and evening entertainment

Please make reservations for high season

D505 - 26620 Lus La Croix Haute - Tel.: 0033 (0)4 92 58 50 14
E-mail: info@campingchamplachevre.com - www.campingchamplachevre.com

Summerseason from 26/4 to 28/9
Winterseason from 28/9 to 26/4

FR26200 Camping Domaine de l'Ecluse

Bénivay, F-26170 Buis les Baronnies (Drôme)

Tel: 04 75 28 07 32. Email: camp.ecluse@wanadoo.fr   www.alanrogers.com/FR26200

Tucked away in the beautiful Drôme Provençale region, this quiet, rural site is situated high in the hills northeast of the Roman city of Vaison-la-Romaine. There are 75 level, stony pitches of average size, with 53 for touring (6A electricity, long leads necessary). They are separated by hedges and mature poplar trees giving varying amounts of shade. Rock pegs are advised. The attractive pool has a toboggan and terrace. This site would make an ideal base for those who love serious hill-walking and biking. Visitors in June will be amazed by the variety of wild flowers and butterflies.

Facilities

Two toilet blocks with all the necessary modern facilities include rooms for babies and campers with disabilities. Small shop (May - Sept). Bar and restaurant (July/Aug). Takeaway (1/5-9/8). Swimming pool (April - Sept). Games field. Simple progamme of events and some excursions (July/Aug). Gas barbecues only. Internet link via a cable. Off site: Restaurant nearby. Bicycle hire, fishing and riding 8 km. Lake bathing 8 km. Historic villages of Buis-les-Boronies 8 km. Mollans 8 km. Vaison la Romaine 14 km. Nyons with excellent market and large range of shops 20 km. Mont Ventoux.

Open: 5 April - 15 November.

Directions

Site is northeast of Vaison la Romaine. Only recommended access is via Buis le Baronnies. Just south of the village turn northwest on the D147 for 7 km. over the pass to Propiac. Turn right on D347 and climb to site in 2 km. At entry pull hard over to the right to take sharp left hand bend down slope. GPS: N44:17.397 E05:11.502

Charges guide

Per person	€ 3,50 - € 4,00
child (0-7 yrs)	€ 1,50 - € 2,00
pitch	€ 5,50 - € 7,00
electricity (6A)	€ 3,20

357

FR26290 Camping Château de Galaure

Mobile homes ▶ page 507

F-26330 Châteauneuf-de-Galaure (Drôme)

Tel: **04 75 68 65 22**

www.alanrogers.com/FR26290

Châteauneuf-de-Galaure is tucked away at the heart of the Drôme département, between Lyon and Valence. This is a spacious site, extending over 11 hectares, with 200 large, grassy pitches (mostly with 10A electrical connections). The river Galaure runs close by and there are three swimming pools on site, including one for children and a large water slide. Châteauneuf is a typically sleepy Provençal village with a couple of good restaurants and surrounded by some very fine countryside. This is excellent walking country and the site's owners will be delighted to recommend routes. Châteauneuf has a fine Franciscan abbey which is currently being restored. A little further afield, Hauterives, is home to the Palais Idéal du Facteur Cheval. This is surely one of Europe's most unexpected tourist sights, an amazing palace built by a postman over a period of 33 years.

Facilities

Two swimming pools with water slides. Children's pool. Play area. Tourist information. Off site: River (fishing) 250 m. Cycle and walking tracks in the surrounding hills. Palais Idéal 8 km.

Open: All year.

Directions

From Lyon head south on the A7 leaving at exit 12 (Chanas) and head east on the D519 as far as Bougé-Chambalud. Head south on the D53 as far as Chateauneuf de Galaure, from where site is clearly signed. GPS: N45:13.413 E04:57.118

Charges guide

Per unit incl. 2 persons and electricity	€ 30,00

camping Château de Galaure

A charming campsite situated in a quiet area. It features spacious pitches and is 100km south of Lyon. An ideal choice for families with children with good sanitary facilities, three pools with water slides and a shallow pool for smaller children. In addition, there is a large covered play area and a sports field. Enjoy the beauty of the Drôme area with its lovely climate and friendly atmosphere. The village shops and terraces can be found just a short walk from the campsite.

F 26330 Chateauneuf-de-Galaure
Tel. +33 (0)4 75 68 65 22, Fax +33 (0)4 75 68 60 60   Internet: www.galaure.com

FR26280 Camping la Vallée Bleue

La Plaine du Pont, F-26510 Sahune (Drôme)

Tel: **04 75 27 44 42**. Email: **welcome@lavalleebleue.com**

www.alanrogers.com/FR26280

La Vallée Bleue is an immaculate, small site run by a very friendly family, set in the beautiful Drôme Provençale famous for its vineyards, olive trees and lavender fields. There are only 55 mainly level stony, grassy pitches with 52 for touring. All have electricity connections (6A), water and drain. The site is carefully landscaped with a very wide variety of fruit trees and flowering shrubs giving varying amounts of shade to the spacious pitches. This site should appeal to those seeking a peaceful and relaxing holiday, happy to organise their own entertainment. This site is vey popular and advanced booking is advised.

Facilities

Superb modern toilet block with all necessary facilities including for disabled campers. Washing machine. Small bar with TV. Restaurant with terrace overlooking garden and attractive pool and sunbathing area (all open all season). Swimming pool. Access to shallow River Eygues with stony beach, ideal for children. WiFi. Off site: Sahune with shop 400 m. Nyons 15 km. with famous market, olive museum and wide range of shops. Good area for walking, cycling, flora, fauna and birdwatching.

Open: 1 April - 30 September.

Directions

Site is about 15 km. northwest of Nyons on the D94. It is well signed on the right just before Sahune. GPS: N44:24.753 E05:15.700

Charges guide

Per unit incl. 2 persons	€ 11,50 - € 18,00
extra person	€ 3,50 - € 5,00
child (under 8 yrs)	€ 2,50 - € 4,00
electricity (6A)	€ 3,00

No credit cards.

FR26300 Camping Indigo la Ferme de Clareau

Route de Die (RD 61), F-26470 La Motte Chalancon (Drôme)

Tel: 04 75 27 26 03. Email: fermedeclareau@camping-indigo.com

www.alanrogers.com/FR26300

La Ferme de Clareau is a recent addition to the Indigo group of campsites. It is located at the heart of La Drôme Provençale, close to the pretty village of La Motte Chalancon. There are 50 spacious pitches here, mostly with electrical connections. There are also no fewer than three toilet blocks, dispersed around the site. La Ferme de Clareau is situated within a large natural park and one side stretches along the River Oule (suitable for swimming and fishing). A new swimming pool was opened in 2008. The old farm buildings have been sensitively restored and now house the site's bar and shop (specializing in local produce including Pre Chorier naturally leavened bread). La Motte Chalancon is a delight to explore with its unique covered streets (calades). There are innumerable walking and cycling opportunities in the area and the campsite organizes family hikes, as well as various sports tournaments and a club for children. Further afield, the Vercors and Ardèche ranges are both within easy reach.

Facilities

Shop. Bar. Snack bar (farmhouse breakfasts available). Swimming pool. Direct access to river. Bicycle hire. Play area. Entertainment and activity programme. Fully equipped tents for rent. Off site: La Motte Chalancon 1 km. Fishing (river). Maison des Vautours wildlife centre. Cycle and walking tracks.

Open: 18 April - 19 October.

Directions

La Motte Chalancon lies midway between Nyons and Gap. Approaching from the west (Nyons) use the D94 as far as Rémuzat. Then take the northbound D61 to La Motte Chalancon. Site is a short distance beyond the village. GPS: N44:28.813 E05:23.675

Charges guide

Per unit inc. 2 persons and electricity	€ 13,60 - € 16,60
extra person	€ 3,10 - € 4,00
child (2-7 yrs)	€ 1,70 - € 2,30

 tel: +33 (0) 4 37 64 22 33 www.camping-indigo.com

Camping Indigo
La Ferme de Clareau
Wood & canvas tents to rent
Swimming-pool,
Nature activities, Hiking...
Route de Die - 26470 La Motte Chalancon
Tel : (33) 4 75 27 26 03
In the heart of the Drome Provençale Region,
at the edge of a river...
www.camping-indigo.com

FR69020 Camping Municipal la Grappe Fleurie

La Lie, F-69820 Fleurie (Rhône)

Tel: 04 74 69 80 07. Email: camping@fleurie.org

www.alanrogers.com/FR69020

With easy access from both the A6 autoroute and the N6, this site is ideally situated for night stops or indeed for longer stays to explore the vineyards and historic attractions of the Beaujolais region. Virtually surrounded by vineyards, but within walking distance (less than 1 km) of the pretty village of Fleurie, this is an immaculate small site, with 85 grass touring pitches. All are fairly level with the benefit of individual access to water, drainage and electrical connections (10A). Baker calls 07.30 hrs - 08.30 hrs. Wine tasting is arranged twice weekly in high season. Restaurant and shopping facilities are available in the village.

Facilities

Sanitary facilities in two blocks have British and Turkish style toilets and very satisfactory shower and washing facilities (showers closed 22.00-07.00 hrs). Facilities for disabled visitors. Washing machine and dryer. Outdoor swimming pool (15 x 7 m). Small playground. Only gas or electric barbecues are allowed. Off site: Fishing 10 km. Fleurie 600 m.

Open: Late March - end October.

Directions

From N6 at Le Maison Blanche/Romanech-Thorins, take D32 to village of Fleurie from where site is signed. GPS: N46:11.258 E04:41.955

Charges guide

Per unit incl. 2 persons and electricity	€ 13,50 - € 16,00
extra person	€ 4,70 - € 5,70
child (5-10 yrs)	€ 3,20 - € 3,70

BOOK THIS SITE The Travel Service
CALL 01580 214000
...we'll arrange everything

359
Check real time availability and at-the-gate prices...
www.alanrogers.com

The Travel Service ...we'll arrange everything

BOOK THIS SITE

CALL 01580 214000

FR69010 Camping Indigo Lyon

Porte de Lyon, F-69570 Dardilly (Rhône)

Tel: **04 78 35 64 55**. Email: **lyon@camping-indigo.com**   www.alanrogers.com/FR69010

Camping International is a modern overnight site just off the A6 autoroute. Kept busy with overnight trade, reception and the café (in the main season) open until quite late. There are 180 separate numbered plots. Many have electricity (10A), water and waste water drainage. Those for caravans are mostly on hardstandings on a slight slope, with another small grassy part, while those for tents are on a flatter area of grass. A very large commercial centre has been developed just outside the site, with eight hotels, restaurants, a supermarket, petrol station, etc. There is some road noise. Lyon is a very attractive city, especially noted for the excellence of its food, and well worth a visit. A bus stop for the centre (8 km.) is nearby (timetables in reception).

Facilities

Three heated sanitary blocks have free hot water (solar heated) and washbasins in cabins. Dishwashing and laundry sinks. Baby changing facilities and washing machines. Motorcaravan service point. Swimming and paddling pools (1/6-15/9, supervised and free). Playground. TV room. Games room. Reading room (books and local information). Boules. Picnic and barbecue area.

Open: All year.

Directions

Travelling south, do not take A46 motorway around Lyon, continue on A6, take exit Limonest, Dardilly, Porte de Lyon. About 8 km. north of Lyon tunnel; turn left for Porte de Lyon (well signed).
GPS: N45:49.221 E04:45.624

Charges 2009

Per unit inc 2 persons and electricity	€ 20,40 - € 25,20
extra person	€ 4,10 - € 4,40
child (2-7 yrs)	€ 2,70 - € 3,00

Camping Cheques accepted.

tel: +33 (0) 4 37 64 22 33 www.camping-indigo.com

Camping Indigo International de Lyon★★★★

Mobile-homes,
Wood & canvas tents to rent

Swimming-pool, Children playground,
Bar, Shopping centre nearby

Open all year round

Porte de Lyon - 69570 Dardilly - tel : (33) 4 78 35 64 55

Only a few minutes from the centre of Lyon, part of the Unesco World Heritage list

www.camping-indigo.com

FR69030 Camping les Portes du Beaujolais

Avenue Jean Vacher, F-69480 Anse (Rhône)

Tel: **04 74 67 12 87**. Email: **campingbeaujolais@wanadoo.fr**   www.alanrogers.com/FR69030

Being just off the main motorway south to the Mediterranean, this campsite would make a good overnight stop. Also the good public transport from Anse means that it could be used as a base for visiting Lyon. However, despite some noise from the motorway and the main line railway, there is much more to it than that. The well run site has good facilities and modern buildings of traditional design and materials. Its 150 formal pitches are shady, level, numbered and marked, with neatly trimmed grass and hedges, and electrical connections (6A). There are 20 fully serviced pitches.

Facilities

New reception area, chalets and mobile homes. Modern toilet blocks, facilities for disabled people. Baby room. Motorcaravan services. Washing machines. Shop (all season). Gas supplies. Bar, restaurant, takeaway (1/6-15/9). Games room. Internet. Swimming pool, paddling pool (1/5-30/9). Playground. Playing field. Tennis. Minigolf. Boules. Free loan of barbecues. Off site: Anse 1 km. Narrow gauge railway at exit. Fishing 200 m. Boat launching 500 m. Bicycle hire 1 km. Riding 1.5 km. Sailing 1.5 km. Golf 2 km.

Open: 1 March - 31 October.

Directions

Anse is on N6, 6 km. south of Villefranche-sur-Saône, 21 km. north of Lyon. Site signed from northern and southern ends of village. There are height limits on all approaches (3 or 3.2 m.).
GPS: N45:56.418 E04:43.596

Charges guide

Per unit incl. 2 persons and electricity	€ 17,20 - € 24,00
extra person	€ 4,00 - € 4,80
child (2-7 yrs)	€ 3,40 - € 3,60

Camping Cheques accepted.

Check real time availability and at-the-gate prices...

www.**alanrogers**.com

MAP 14

Provence

This is a corner of France that evokes dreamy images of lazy afternoons amongst sleepy village squares, sunny vineyards and beautiful lavender fields basking under the dazzling blue of the sky.

Alan Rogers

ONLY THE DÉPARTEMENTS FROM THE MOUNTAINOUS REGION OF PROVENCE HAVE BEEN INCLUDED IN THIS SECTION: 04 ALPES-DE-HAUTE-PROVENCE, 05 HAUTES-ALPES, 84 VAUCLUSE

Provence is a region of magical light, bleached landscapes, olive groves, herb-scented garrigue, vineyards and Roman and medieval antiquities. The river valleys provide natural routes through the mountain barrier. Roman monuments can be seen at Orange, and Vaison-la-Romaine, where a 2,000 year old bridge is still in use. Avignon was the site of the papal court and the Palais des Papes at Avignon is a spectacular construction.

The Hautes-Alpes will reward with stunning vistas, peace and quiet. Briançon is the highest town in Europe and many of the high passes are not for the faint-hearted. The Vaucluse, where in the late spring the southern slopes of the Montagne du Luberon are a mass of colour with wild flowers. The extinct volcanic cone of Mont Ventoux provides dramatic views. The scents, the colours and an amazing intensity of light have encouraged artists and writers to settle amidst the sleepy villages, with narrow streets and ancient dwellings topped with sun-baked terracotta tiles, where the air is fragrant with the perfume of wild herbs and lavender.

Places of interest

Avignon: ramparts, old city, Papal Palace, old palace, Calvet museum.

Mont Ventoux: near Carpentras, one of the best known stages of the classic Tour de France annual cycle race.

Orange: Roman city, gateway to the Midi, Colline St Europe.

St Vaison la Romaine: Roman city, the French Pompei.

Cuisine of the region

Influenced by the Savoie area to the north and the Côte d'Azur to the south, with emphasis on herbs and garlic, and fish. The wine region is mainly known for its dry, fruity rosé wines: Bandol, Bellet, Palette, Cassis. Red wines include Côtes du Rhône and Châteauneuf-du-Pape.

Aigo Bouido: garlic and sage soup with bread (or eggs and cheese).

Farcement (Farçon Savoyard): potatoes baked with cream, eggs, bacon, dried pears and prunes.

Pissaladière: Provencal bread dough with onions, anchovies, olives.

Ratatouille: aubergines, courgettes, onions, garlic, red peppers and tomatoes in olive oil.

Tartiflette: potato, bacon, onions and Reblochon cheese.

FR04010 Sunêlia Hippocampe

Route de Napoléon, F-04290 Volonne (Alpes-de-Haute-Provence)

Tel: **04 92 33 50 00**. Email: **camping@l-hippocampe.com**

Mobile homes ▶ page 507

www.alanrogers.com/FR04010

Hippocampe is a friendly family run, 'all action' lakeside site, organised with families in mind and situated in a beautiful area of France. The perfumes of thyme, lavender and wild herbs are everywhere and the higher hills of Haute Provence are not too far away. There are 447 level, numbered pitches (221 for touring units), medium to very large (130 sq.m) in size. All have electricity (10A) and 243 have water and drainage, most are separated by bushes and cherry trees. Some of the best pitches border the lake. The site's restaurant, bar, takeaway and shop have all been completely renewed. Games, aerobics, competitions, entertainment and shows, plus a daily club for younger family members are organised in July/August. A soundproof underground disco is set well away from the pitches and is very popular with teenage customers. Staff tour the site at night ensuring a good night's sleep. The site is, however, much quieter in low season and, with its good discounts, is the time for those who do not want or need entertaining. The Gorges du Verdon is a sight not to be missed and rafting, paragliding or canoe trips can be booked from the site's own tourist information office. Being on the lower slopes of the hills of Haute-Provence, the surrounding area is good for both walking and mountain biking. All in all, this is a very good site for an active or restful holiday and is suitable for outfits of all sizes. English is spoken.

Facilities

Toilet blocks vary from old to modern, all with good clean facilities that include washbasins in cabins. Washing machines. Motorcaravan service point. Bread available (from 26/4). Shop, bar, restaurant and pizzeria (26/4-7/9). Large, pool complex (from 5/4, heated in early and late seasons). Tennis. Fishing. Canoeing. Boules. Several sports facilities (some with free instruction). Charcoal barbecues are not permitted. Off site: Village of Volonne 600 m. Bicycle hire 2 km. Riding 12 km. Various sporting opportunities.

Open: 22 March - 30 September.

Directions

Approaching from the north turn off N85 across river bridge to Volonne, then right to site. From the south right on D4, 1 km. before Château Arnoux. GPS: N44:06.366 E06:00.933

Charges guide

Per unit incl. 2 persons	€ 13,00 - € 27,00
incl. electricity	€ 16,00 - € 32,00
incl. water/drainage	€ 16,00 - € 39,00
extra person (over 4 yrs)	€ 3,00 - € 6,50

Special low season offers.
Camping Cheques accepted.

In the heart of the ALPS OF HAUTE PROVENCE, near VERDON and LUBERON, 12 km south of Sisteron. Relaxing holiday amidst olive and cherry orchards with a wide selection of activities.

heated pools open from April 5th

Camping L'Hippocampe ★★★★

L'Hippocampe - Route Napoléon - 04290 VOLONNE
Tel: 00 33 492 33 50 00 - Fax: 00 33 492 33 50 49
http://www.l-hippocampe.com - e-mail: camping@l-hippocampe.com

Sunêlia

Reservation required

Camping Cheque

Check real time availability and at-the-gate prices...
www.alanrogers.com

FR04020 Castel Camping le Domaine du Verdon

Mobile homes ▶ page 507

Domaine du Verdon, F-04120 Castellane (Alpes-de-Haute-Provence)

Tel: **04 92 83 61 29**. Email: **contact@camp-du-verdon.com**   www.alanrogers.com/FR04020

Close to the 'Route des Alpes' and the Gorges du Verdon. Two heated swimming pools and numerous on-site activities during high season help to keep non-canoeists here. Du Verdon is a large level site, part meadow, part wooded, with 500 partly shaded, rather stony pitches (390 for tourists). Numbered and separated by bushes, they vary in size, have 6A electricity, and 125 also have water and waste water. They are mostly separate from the mobile homes (60) and pitches used by tour operators (110). Some overlook the unfenced river Verdon, so watch the children. This is a very popular holiday area, the gorge, canoeing and rafting being the main attractions, ideal for active families. One can walk to Castellane without using the main road. Dances and discos in July and August suit all age groups – the latest finishing time is around 23.00 hrs. (after that time patrols make sure that the site is quiet). The site is popular and very busy in July and August.

Facilities

Refurbished toilet blocks include facilities for disabled visitors. Washing machines. Motorcaravan services. Restaurant, terrace, log fire for cooler evenings. New supermarket. Pizzeria/crêperie. Takeaway. Heated swimming pools, paddling pool with 'mushroom' fountain (all open all season). Organised entertainments (July and August). Play areas. Minigolf. Archery. Organised walks. Bicycle hire. Riding. Small fishing lake. ATM. Room for games and TV. Internet access and WiFi. Off site: Castellane and the Verdon Gorge 1 km. Riding 2 km. Boat launching 4.5 km. Golf 20 km. Watersports.

Open: 15 May - 15 September.

Directions

From Castellane take D952 westwards towards Gorges du Verdon and Moustiers. Site is 1 km. on left. GPS: N43:50.353 E6:29.638

Charges 2009

Per unit incl. 2 or 3 persons	€ 20,00 - € 33,00
incl. 6A electricity	€ 25,00 - € 41,00
extra person (over 3 yrs)	€ 8,00 - € 13,00
dog	€ 3,00

Camping Cheques accepted.

Domaine du VERDON
Camping Caravanning
★ ★ ★ ★

Close to the famous Gorges du Verdon on only 1,2 kilometres distance from the typical Provence village of Castellane you will love this lovely harmonius estate with many flowers and trees. Direct access to the river Verdon.

Animation in July and August - 500 pitches
14 acres - 220 mobile homes

Castel Camping Caravanning Domaine du Verdon
04120 Castellane - Tel.: +33 492 836 129 - Fax: +33 492 836 937
E-mail: contact@camp-du-verdon.com - www.camp-du-verdon.com

LES ★★★★
CASTELS
Hôtellerie de Plein Air

Check real time availability and at-the-gate prices...
www.alanrogers.com

The Travel Service

BOOK THIS SITE
CALL 01580 214000
...we'll arrange everything

FR04040 RCN les Collines de Castellane

Route de Grasse, F-04120 Castellane (Alpes-de-Haute-Provence)
Tel: **04 92 83 68 96**. Email: **info@rcn-lescollinesdecastellane.fr**   www.alanrogers.com/FR04040

RCN, a Dutch company, runs a chain of good campsites in the Netherlands. They now operate six sites in France, all with Dutch managers who speak good French and English. Les Collines de Castellane is pleasantly situated in the mountainous landscape of the Alpes-de-Haute-Provence. There are 160 touring pitches spread over a series of flat terraces under umbrella pines with electric tricycles provided for transport up and down the quite steep pathways. At the top of the site, near the entrance, is a combined reception and small restaurant area. The adjoining swimming pool is quite large and offers a water slide and a paddling pool for small children.

Facilities

Tiled, modern toilet facilities include individual cabins and facilities for disabled visitors and babies. Washing machines, dryers and ironing area. Shop. Library. Small restaurant (including takeaway) with terrace. Heated swimming pool with slides and paddling pool. Tennis court. Boules. Three play areas. Organised activities (May - Sept). Off site: Golf 10 km.

Open: 22 April - 22 September.

Directions

Take the N85 (Route Napoleon) from Digné-les-Bains towards Castellane and Grasse. Site is 6 km. south of Castellane, on the right hand side of the road. GPS: N43:48.979 E06:34.378

Charges guide

Per unit incl. 2 persons, electricity and water	€ 18,00 - € 45,50
incl. up to 6 persons	€ 23,40 - € 46,00

www.rcn-campings.fr

FR04060 Camping Caravaning le Haut-Verdon

RD908, F-04370 Villars-Colmars (Alpes-de-Haute-Provence)
Tel: **04 92 83 40 09**. Email: **campinglehautverdon@wanadoo.fr**   www.alanrogers.com/FR04060

For those seeking a quiet, family site set in most spectacular scenery, Camping Le Haut-Verdon is ideal. It is on the banks of the Verdon, an excellent trout river, which flows through the spectacular gorge. Surrounded by the majestic peaks of the Alpes-de-Haute-Provence, it is on the doorstep of the Mercantour National Park. Set amongst the pines, the 109 pitches are mostly on the large size but are rather stony. With 73 for touring units, all have electricity (6/10A) but some require long leads. There is a small village nearby and the town of St André is 23 km.

Facilities

Refurbished, heated toilet block. Washing machines. Freezer for ice packs. Room for tenters for inclement weather. Motorcaravan services. Small shop. Bar/restaurant, takeaway. Heated swimming, paddling pools (from 1/6). Small play area. Giant chess. Boules. Skittle alley. Tennis. TV room. Organised games and competitions. Fishing. Barbecue areas (portable ones banned). Off site: Riding 1 km. Bicycle hire 3 km.

Open: 5 May - 16 September.

Directions

Follow D955 north from St André les Alpes towards Colmar. After 11 km. road number changes to D908. Site on right at southern edge of Villars-Colmars. Caravans not advised to use the D908 from Annot or Col d'Allos from Barcelonnette. GPS: N44:11.489 E06:35.814

Charges guide

Per unit incl. 2 persons	€ 13,00 - € 25,00
extra person	€ 3,00 - € 5,00
electricity (6/10A)	€ 3,00 - € 4,00

FR04080 Yelloh! Village l'Etoile des Neiges

F-04140 Montclar (Alpes-de-Haute-Provence)
Tel: **04 66 73 97 39**. Email: **info@yellohvillage-etoile-des-neiges.com**   www.alanrogers.com/FR04080

This attractive, family run site near the mountain village and ski resort of St Jean Montclar is open most of the year. Being at an altitude of 1,300 m. the nights can get quite cold in summer. The 130 shady terraced pitches, with 70 for touring, are separated by small shrubs and alpine trees. All pitches are close to electricity and water points. An attractive bar and restaurant overlooks the two swimming pools, with the shallow pool having a water slide ideal for children. The site has no shop but local shops are only a few minutes walk away. A 'Sites et Paysages' member.

Facilities

Central toilet block (heated in winter) and facilities for disabled visitors. Two washing machines. Motorcaravan services. Bar/restaurant. Swimming pool (all amenities open 15/5-9/9). Tennis. Boules. Two play areas. Rafting, walking (July/Aug). Off site: Shops in village a few minutes walk. Bicycle hire and riding in village. Fishing 1.5 km. Watersports and beach at Lac Serre Ponçon 7 km.

Open: All year excl. 26/3-29/4 and 16/9-19/12.

Directions

Site is 35 km. south of Gap via D900B. Beyond Serre Ponçon, turn right, D900 signed Selonnet, St Jean Montclar. Entering St Jean Montclar turn left, pass shops, fork right to site. Approach roads are steep and icy in winter. GPS: N44:23.620 E06:20.640

Charges guide

Per unit incl. 2 persons	€ 17,00 - € 31,00
Camping Cheques accepted.	

yelloh! VILLAGE

tel: +33 466 739 739 www.yellohvillage.com

Check real time availability and at-the-gate prices...
www.alanrogers.com

FR04030 Camping le Moulin de Ventre

Niozelles, F-04300 Forcalquier (Alpes-de-Haute-Provence)

Tel: 04 92 78 63 31. Email: moulindeventre@aol.com   www.alanrogers.com/FR04030

This is a friendly, family run site in the heart of Haute-Provence, near Forcalquier, a bustling small French market town. Attractively located beside a small lake and 28 acres of wooded, hilly land, which is available for walking. Herbs of Provence can be found growing wild and flowers, birds and butterflies abound – a nature lovers' delight. The 124 level, grassy pitches for tourists are separated by a variety of trees and small shrubs, 114 of them having electricity (6A; long leads may be necessary). Some pitches are particularly attractive, bordering a small stream. The site is well situated to visit Mont Ventoux, the Luberon National Park, the Gorges du Verdon and a wide range of ancient hill villages with their markets and museums etc. English is spoken. A 'Sites et Paysages' member.

Facilities

Refurbished toilet block. Facilities for disabled people. Baby bath. Washing, drying machines. Fridge hire. Bread. Bar/restaurant, takeaway (all season), themed evenings (high season). Pizzeria. Swimming pools (15/5-15/9). New playground. Bouncy castle. Fishing, boules. Some activities organised in high season. No discos. Only electric or gas barbecues. Internet access. Off site: Shops, local market, doctor, tennis 2 km. Supermarket, chemist, riding, bicycle hire 5 km. Golf 20 km. Walking, cycling.

Open: 5 April - 30 September.

Directions

From A51 motorway take exit 19 (Brillanne). Turn right on N96 then turn left on N100 westwards (signed Forcalquier) for about 3 km. Site is signed on left, just after a bridge 3 km. southeast of Niozelles. GPS: N43:56.100 E05:52.520

Charges guide

Per unit incl. 2 persons and electricity	€ 17,20 - € 26,70
extra person (over 4 yrs)	€ 3,50 - € 5,50
child (2-4 yrs)	€ 2,00 - € 3,00
dog	€ 1,50 - € 3,00

No credit cards.

BOOK THIS SITE
CALL 01580 214000
...we'll arrange everything
The Travel Service

Haute-Provence
Camping
Moulin de Ventre
04300 Niozelles
Tel: 0033 492 78 63 31
Fax: 0033 492 79 86 92
www.moulin-de-ventre.com
Situated between Verdon and Luberon

Alan Rogers

FREE 2009 brochure
Over 60 French campsites, hand picked for you
Call for your copy today 01580 214000
FREE CHILD PLACES ON MANY SITES

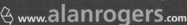

Check real time availability and at-the-gate prices...
www.alanrogers.com

FR04100 Kawan Village International

Route Napoléon, F-04120 Castellane (Alpes-de-Haute-Provence)

Tel: **04 92 83 66 67**. Email: **info@camping-international.fr**   www.alanrogers.com/FR04100

Camping International has very friendly, English speaking owners and is a reasonably priced, less commercialised site situated in some of the most dramatic scenery in France with good views. The 274 pitches, 130 good sized ones for touring, are clearly marked, separated by trees and small hedges, and all have electricity and water. The bar/restaurant overlooks the swimming pool with its sunbathing area set in a sunny location, and all have fantastic views. In high season English speaking young people entertain children (3-8 years) and teenagers. Access is good for larger units.

Facilities	Directions
Small toilet blocks are of an older design. One newer block has modern facilities, including those for visitors with disabilities. Washing machines and dryer. Motorcaravan services. Fridge hire. Shop. Restaurant and takeaway (May - Sept). Swimming pool (1/5-30/9). Children's animation, occasional evening entertainment (July/Aug). Internet access. Free WiFi. Off site: Riding `800 m. Castellane 1.5 km). Boat launching 5 km.	Site is 1 km. north of Castellane on the N85 'Route Napoléon'. GPS: N43:51.539 E06:29.902
Open: 31 March - 1 October.	

Charges 2009

Per unit incl. 2 persons and electricity	€ 18,00 - € 23,50
extra person	€ 3,00 - € 4,50
dog	€ 2,00

Camping Cheques accepted.

FR04110 Yelloh! Village Verdon Parc

Domaine de la Paludette, F-04800 Gréoux-les-Bains (Alpes-de-Haute-Provence)

Tel: **04 66 73 97 39**. Email: **info@yellohvillage-verdon-parc.com**   www.alanrogers.com/FR04110

Friendly and family run, this very spacious site borders the River Ardèche and is close to the attractive spa town of Gréoux les Bains. The 280 medium to very large, stony or gravel pitches (150 for tourists) are in two sections. The main part of the site has large pitches laid out in rows separated by poplar trees. Along the river bank the larger, more natural pitches are scattered amongst the trees and are of irregular shape and size. These have pleasant views across the river to the town beyond. Electrical connections (10A) and water taps are reasonably close to most pitches.

Facilities	Directions
Several toilet blocks (one heated in low season) are clean and to a high standard, with all the necessary facilities including those for disabled visitors. Laundry room. Motorcaravan service point. Small shop. Bar and courtyard terrace. Restaurant and takeaway (April - Sept). TV. Internet point. Large play area. Miniclub (high season). Organised sports. Evening entertainment. Dogs are not accepted in high season. Gas and electric barbeques only. Off site: Gréoux les Bains 1 km. Bicycle hire 1 km.	Leave A51 at Manosque and take D907 southeast towards Gréoux les Bains. Turn right on D4, then left on D82 to Gréoux les Bains. Follow main road downhill through town to roundabout with fountain. Take second right, signed D8 St Pierre and descend for 1 km. Cross river and turn left. Site shortly on the left. GPS: N43:45.612 E5:52.950
Open: 21 March - 29 October.	

Charges guide

Per unit incl. 2 persons	€ 13,00 - € 28,00

tel: +33 466 739 739 www.yellohvillage.com ────────── **yelloh!** VILLAGE

FR04140 Camping les Prairies

Haute-Greyere, F-04140 Seyne-les-Alpes (Alpes-de-Haute-Provence)

Tel: **04 92 35 10 21**. Email: **info@campinglesprairies.com**   www.alanrogers.com/FR04140

Les Prairies lies in a beautiful part of the French Alps, at the foot of the Grand Puy (1,800 m), at the entrance to the once fortified town of Seyne. This quiet site is run by a brother and sister team who grew up on a campsite on the French Riviera. With lovely views of the mountains and the river running beside the site, there are 91 good grass pitches (with 10A electricity) and 17 mobile homes. There is a pleasant pool and a bar forming part of the reception area.

Facilities	Directions
The two toilet blocks near the pool are immaculate and regularly kept that way. Pre-set showers are quite small. Facilities for disabled visitors and babies. Laundry room. Bar and snack bar (15/6-20/8). Heated swimming pool (1/6-15/9). Pétanque. Occasional entertainment in high season. Fishing. Off site: Riding adjacent. Bicycle hire 5 km.	From Gap take D900B and turn right at T-junction where it joins the D900. Cross Col de St Jean and go through Seyne to small airfield on the left. Turn right, following signs to site (do not take an earlier sign as road is very narrow). Coming from Digne, turn left at the airfield. GPS: N44:20.539 E6:21.538
Open: 15 April - 13 September.	

Charges guide

Per unit incl. 2 persons	€ 13,00 - € 22,00
extra person	€ 5,00
electricity (10A)	€ 3,50

Check real time availability and at-the-gate prices...

www.alanrogers.com

FR04120 Camping Indigo Forcalquier

Route de Sigonce, F-04300 Forcalquier (Alpes-de-Haute-Provence)

Tel: **04 92 75 27 94**. Email: **forcalquier@camping-indigo.com**   www.alanrogers.com/FR04120

Although Camping Indigo is an urban site, there are extensive views over the surrounding country-side where there are some excellent walks. The pitches are on grass and are of good size, all with electricity, 6 fully serviced. The site is secure, with an electronic barrier (card deposit required) and there is no entry between 22.30 and 07.00. Local guides lead tours of the historic town and areas. This is an excellent base for visiting Forcalquier, a 15th-century fortified hill town and the Monday market (the best in HauteProvence). Since this site has acquired new owners, an extensive programme of modernisation has been put into effect.

Facilities

Two refurbished toilet blocks with washbasins in cubicles and excellent facilities for disabled visitors. They are cleaned twice daily. Bar. Snack bar and takeaway (15/6-1/9). Play area. Heated swimming and paddling pools. Off site: All shops, banks etc. in town centre 200 m.

Open: 4 April - 18 October.

Directions

From town centre, follow signs for Digne, Sisteron for 400 m, turning sharp left onto Sigonce road after Esso petrol station, then first right and site is 200 m. on the right. Well signed from town.
GPS: N43:57.660 E05:47.226

Charges 2009

Per unit with 2 persons and electricity	€ 18,40 - € 27,40
extra person	€ 4,80 - € 5,80
child (2-7 yrs)	€ 3,10 - € 3,90
dog	€ 3,00 - € 4,00

tel: +33 (0) 4 37 64 22 33   www.camping-indigo.com

FR04150 Camping Rose de Provence

F-04500 Riez-la-Romaine (Alpes-de-Haute-Provence)

Tel: **04 92 77 75 45**. Email: **info@rose-de-provence.com**   www.alanrogers.com/FR04150

This site in the heart of the Verdon Regional Nature Park, originally a municipal site, is a good example of what can be achieved by dedication and imagination. On the lowest reaches of a hill, 81 attractive, small pitches are delineated by shrubs and small trees offering good shade, 54 with 6A electricity. The two toilet blocks are tiled and decorated in imaginative style. Riez is a charming Provençal village with markets, all the usual facilities and shops; including bike hire, allowing one to explore this ancient and historical area. No large outfits and twin axle caravans.

Facilities

Two attractive, well appointed toilet blocks including facilities for campers with disabilities. Small play area. Table football, table tennis. Gas and electric barbecues only. Off site: Village shops, bicycle hire 500 m. Riding 3 km. Lake beach, fishing, sailing 10 km.

Open: 1 April - 6 October.

Directions

Riez is situated between Gréoux and Moustiers on the D952. Sie is 500 m. southeast of Riez. Follow signs for site and municpal tennis oourts.
GPS: N43:48.783 E06:05.955

Charges guide

Per unit incl. 2 persons	€ 11,70 - € 13,80
extra person	€ 2,90 - € 3,70
child (under 7 yrs)	€ 2,10 - € 2,50
electricity (6A)	€ 3,00
Credit cards accepted for reservations only.	

367

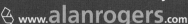

FR04160 Camping les Relarguiers

Route de Colmar, F-04370 Beauvezer (Alpes-de-Haute-Provence)

Tel: 04 92 83 47 73. Email: contact@relarguiers.com

www.alanrogers.com/FR04160

With a very long season, Les Relarguiers is situated at an attitude of 1,150 m. beside the river in the valley of the Haut Verdon. It is ideal for summer and winter holidays, although the nights may be chilly. The new enthusiastic owners are undertaking a complete renovation of this site and the bar/restaurant is already complete. This mountainous area is a haven for nature lovers, hikers and mountain bikers. There are 172 good sized, level, stony, grass pitches shaded by mature trees with 75 for touring all with 10A electricity though long leads may be needed.

Facilities

Two toilet blocks with facilities for campers with disabilities (plans for renovation). Shop. Bar, restaurant and takeaway. Heated pool (15/6-15/9). Boules. Play area. Organised activities in high season. Wifi. Only gas and electric barbecues are permitted. Off site: Bicycle hire 1 km. Riding 5 km. Skiing 15 km. Picturesque mountain villages and scenery.

Open: All year excl. 1 November - 14 December.

Directions

Follow D955 north from St André les Alpes towards Beauvezer. After 11 km. the road number changes to D908. Site on right in village. This is the only recommended route to the site for caravans. GPS: N44:08.816 E06:35.472

Charges guide

Per unit incl. 2 persons	€ 11,50 - € 36,00
extra person	€ 3,00 - € 4,00
child (3-10 yrs)	€ 1,50 - € 3,00
electricity (10A)	€ 3,50

FR04170 Camping les Matherons

F-04700 Puimichel (Alpes-de-Haute-Provence)

Tel: 04 92 79 60 10. Email: lesmatherons@wanadoo.fr

www.alanrogers.com/FR04170

Small, but perfectly formed, Les Matherons is attractively laid out amongst a variety of trees and wild flower meadows. Surrounded by olive trees and herb gardens it Is secluded, but not remote, and offers a calming experience of gentle living. It is owned and run by a Dutch couple and offers just 25 large, terraced, grassy and well separated pitches, within a natural setting of 52 hectares. Many pitches have good views and all have 3A electricity (rock pegs advised). Campers with caravans and tents are asked to keep their vehicles in a car park. Tractor assistance is available.

Facilities

Modern well appointed toilet block with facilities for campers with disabilities. Daily free coffee hour. Snacks. Twice weekly meals (all season). Boules. Giant chess. Sand pit. Play area. Organised walks. Children's activities (high season). Rafting organised from site. Only gas barbecues permitted. Off site: Fishing 2 km. Bicycle hire 9 km. Riding 13 km. Village of Puimichel 2.5 km. Oraison with lake swimming 10 km.

Open: 20 April - 1 October.

Directions

From A51 junction 19 take road through Oraison past square and church and then take second left, D12 signed Castellet, towards Puimichel. Site is well signed 2 km.before Puimichel. GPS: N43:57.625 E6:00.451

Charges guide

Per person	€ 4,00
child (under 9 ys)	€ 3,00
pitch	€ 7,50
electricity (3A)	€ 2,50
No credit cards.	

FR04200 Village Center Côteau de la Marine

F-04500 Montagnac-Montpezat (Alpes-de-Haute-Provence)

Tel: 04 92 77 53 33. Email: contact@village-center.com   www.alanrogers.com/FR04200

Located to the west of the Lac de Sainte Croix and the Gorges de Verdon, Côteau de la Marine is a well equipped site with a fine setting. The site is a member of the Village Center group and has direct access to the river Verdon and its own small harbour. There are 116 touring pitches (60-120 sq.m), mostly with electrical connections (10A). There is plenty of activity in high season, with a club for children and various competitions and tournaments. There is a large swimming pool and a separate children's pool. Other on-site amenities include a sports field, bar and restaurant. The adjacent watersports centre has canoe and electric boat hire. The Gorges de Verdon are, of course, an essential day trip but there is much of picture postcard Provence in the area, including the lavender fields of the Valensole plateau and the valley of the Durance. A number of cycle and walking tracks run very close to the site and it is possible to hire bikes in the sleepy village of Montagnac-Montpezat, where nothing much happens other than the occasional truffle hunt!

Facilities

Shop. Restaurant/snack bar and takeaway. Bar. Swimming and paddling pools. Play area. Activity and entertainment programme. Direct river access. Mobile homes for rent. Off site: Montagnac-Montpezat 5 km. Bicycle and walking tracks. Gorges de Verdon. Lac de Sainte Croix (watersports).

Open: 30 March - 30 September.

Directions

Approaching from the north (Gap), leave the A51 at exit 19 (La Brillane) and follow signs to Oraison. From here, head south on D4 and then D15 to Valensole. Then head southeast on D6 to Riez and then follow signs to Montagnac-Montpezat. Site is clearly signed from here. GPS: N43:44.861 E06:05.907

Charges 2009

Per unit incl. 2 persons and electricity	€ 18,00 - € 31,00

Altavia Link

Coteau de la Marine ****

Montagnac-Montpezat > Provence

- Direct acces to the Verdon gorges area
- Water sports centre next to the camp site

Villagecenter

BOOK YOUR HOLIDAYS
www.village-center.com
+33 (0)4 99 57 21 21

QUALITÉ TOURISME   Camping Qualité

FR05100 Camping la Vieille Ferme

La Clapière, F-05200 Embrun (Hautes-Alpes)

Tel: 04 92 43 04 08. Email: info@campingembrun.com   www.alanrogers.com/FR05100

This is a quiet, urban site in the Hautes-Alpes region. Surrounded by imposing mountains and with a rural ambience, the 100 large, spacious pitches are all for touring. There is good shade and all the pitches have water, 6A electricity, drainage and sewage disposal. The Dutch owners have created a unique mix of activities. In high season one can explore the grandeur of the area and enjoy activities on site including musical evenings, jazz groups and community barbecues. The pretty Roman historical town of Embrun with its 12th-century cathedral is well worth a visit and the modern bustling town of Gap is only 20 km. away.

Facilities

Modern, spotless, well equipped toilet block with family rooms and facilities for campers with disabilities. Bar, restaurant. Takeaway (1/6-30/8). Play area. Family activities (July/Aug). Off site: Embrun, range of shops and facilities. Bicycle hire 300 m. Lakeside sports complex 400 m. Golf 1 km. Riding 1.5 km. Boat ramp 2 km. Gap 10 km. Good transport links in town. Rafting, canoeing. Mountain bike rides, hiking.

Open: 1 May - 1 October.

Directions

Site is clearly signed at the western end of Embrun on the N94. It is about 200 m. south of the main road. GPS: N44:33.244 E06:29.186

Charges guide

Per unit incl. 2 persons	€ 14,00 - € 23,00
extra person	€ 6,00
child (1-12 yrs)	€ 4,00
electricity (6/10A)	€ 3,00 - € 5,00
No credit cards.	

Check real time availability and at-the-gate prices...

www.alanrogers.com

FR05000 Camping des Princes d'Orange

F-05700 Orpierre (Hautes-Alpes)

Tel: 04 92 66 22 53. Email: campingorpierre@wanadoo.fr   www.alanrogers.com/FR05000

This attractive, terraced site, set on a hillside above the village has been thoughtfully developed. The genuine, friendly welcome means many families return year upon year, bringing in turn new generations. Divided into five terraces, each with its own toilet block, all its 100 generously sized pitches (96 for tourists) enjoy good shade from trees and wicker canopies and have electricity connections (4/6/10A). In high season one terrace is reserved as a one-star camping area for young people. Orpierre also has an enchanting maze of medieval streets and houses, almost like a trip back through the centuries. zWhether you choose to drive, climb, walk or cycle there is plenty of wonderful scenery to discover in the immediate vicinity, whilst not far away, some exhilarating hang-gliding and parascending can be enjoyed. For those seeking to 'get away from it all' in an area of outstanding natural beauty, there can be few more tranquil sites. There can be no doubt that you will be made most welcome and will enjoy the quiet splendours the region has to offer. Renowned as a serious rock climbing venue.

Facilities

Six well equipped toilet blocks. Baby bath. Laundry facilities. Bread. Bar, takeaway (1/4-25/10). Heated swimming pool, paddling pool (15/6-15/9). Play area with small trampoline with safety net. Boules. Games room. Fridge hire. Only gas barbecues are permitted. Off site: Orpierre with a few shops and bicycle hire 500 m. Fishing 7 km. Nearest shopping centre Laragne 12 km. Riding 19 km. Hang gliding, parascending. Gorges de Guil.

Open: 1 April - 25 October.

Directions

Turn off N75 road at Eyguians onto D30 - site is signed on left at crossroads in centre Orpierre village. GPS: N44:18.675 E05:41.801

Charges guide

Per unit incl. 2 persons	€ 20,00
incl. 3 persons	€ 21,50
extra person	€ 4,10
child (under 7 yrs)	€ 3,10
electricity	€ 3,10

Less 25% in low season. No credit cards.

Camping des Princes d'Orange

05700 Orpierre
Tel: 0033 492 662 253
Fax: 0033 492 663 108
campingorpierre@wanadoo.fr
www.camping-orpierre.com

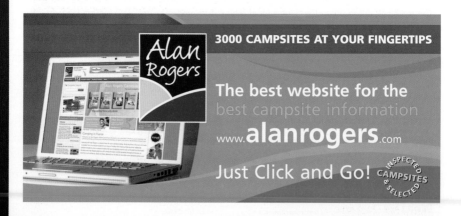

Alan Rogers

3000 CAMPSITES AT YOUR FINGERTIPS

The best website for the best campsite information

www.alanrogers.com

Just Click and Go!

INSPECTED CAMPSITES & SELECTED

FR05070 Camping les Cariamas

Fontmolines, F-05380 Châteauroux-les-Alpes (Hautes-Alpes)

Tel: 04 92 43 22 63. Email: p.tim@free.fr   www.alanrogers.com/FR05070

Set 1,000 metres up in the stunning scenery of the Alps, Les Cariamas is at the gateway to Ecrin National Park and within easy reach of the Serre-Ponçon lake and the Rabioux-Durance river. The 150 pitches, which all have electrical connections, are pleasantly shaded and many offer beautiful views of the surrounding countryside. There are some mobile homes and chalets to rent. Amenities on the site include an outdoor heated swimming pool.

Facilities

Sanitary facilities include washbasins in cabins and hot showers. No failities for disabled visitors. Laundry. Small shop and takeaway (from 1/5). Communal barbecue area. Swimming pool (1/5-30/9). Play area. Mountain bike hire. Fishing. Off site: Riding 15 km. Canoeing, climbing, hiking, mountain biking and rafting. Tennis.

Open: 1 April - 31 October.

Directions

From Gap follow signs to Embrun Briançon. Take turning for Châteauroux-les- Alpes at first roundabout after Embrun. Shortly (800 m.) before the village turn right and follow signs to site. GPS: N44:36.870 E06:31.190

Charges 2009

Per person	€ 4,75
child (under 6 yrs)	€ 2,10
pitch	€ 5,50
electricity	€ 3,50

Camping, hôtel de plein air Les Cariamas

Les Cariamas
Fontmolines
05380 Châteauroux-les-Alpes

t. 00 33 (0)4 92 43 22 63
f. 00 33 (0)6 30 11 30 57
e. p.tim@free.fr
http://les.cariamas.free.fr

FR84040 Domaine le Jantou

535 Chemin des Coudeliéres, F-84250 Le Thor (Vaucluse)

Tel: 04 90 33 90 07. Email: accueil@lejantou.com   www.alanrogers.com/FR84040

Le Jantou has been expanded over the years from an 18th-century farm and farmhouse. It is bordered by a small river said to be good for trout fishing. The 160 level, small to medium sized, fairly stony pitches (rock pegs advised) are in small groups separated by tall hedges and mature trees giving heavy shade to many. All have electricity (3-10A). About half of them are used for touring with most of them in a separate section. There is a large pool, children's pool and paddling pool surrounded by paved and grass sunbathing areas.

Facilities

Two central toilet blocks partially refurbished with all the necessary facilities, include washbasins in cabins, a baby room and facilities for disabled visitors (key access). Washing machine and dryer. Motorcaravan service point. Small bar/restaurant with takeaway (July/Aug). Small shop with basic provisions. Swimming pools. Play area. Large sports area. Fishing. Bicycle hire. Small games room. TV and internet access. Barbecues are not allowed (four communal barbecue areas). Barrier key € 15 deposit. Off site: Riding 5 km. Supermarket 1 km. Canoeing. Thor, shops, bars, restaurants, bank 2 km. Isle sur la Sorgue (antiques and Provencal markets) 5 km.

Open: 1 April - 31 October.

Directions

Site is just west of Le Thor. Leave A7 autoroute at Avignon north (exit 23) onto D942 signed Carpentras. Shortly turn south on D6 and in 8 km. turn east on N100, signed Le Thor. Just before bridge turn left on D1 and shortly left again to site entrance. GPS: N43:55.764 E04:58.989

Charges guide

Per unit incl. 2 persons	€ 19,00 - € 22,00
extra person	€ 4,60 - € 6,50
child (2-12 yrs)	€ 2,50 - € 4,00
electricity	€ 3,00 - € 4,70
animal	€ 4,30

BOOK THIS SITE
CALL 01580 214000
...we'll arrange everything
The Travel Service

Check real time availability and at-the-gate prices...

www.alanrogers.com

FR84070 Camping Club International Carpe Diem

Route de Saint-Marcellin, B.P. 68, F-84110 Vaison-la-Romaine (Vaucluse)

Tel: **04 90 36 02 02**. Email: **contact@camping-carpe-diem.com**   www.alanrogers.com/FR84070

Carpe Diem is a new site, attractively themed with Greek statues and an amphitheatre surround to its main pool. This is a good site for active families seeking all day entertainment and the situation is quite impressive with magnificent views over one of the most beautiful parts of France, yet only 800 m. from the fascinating town of Vaison-la-Romaine. There are 232 pitches with 119 small to medium sized, grass touring pitches all with electricity and many with some degree of shade. A new terraced area has mobile homes, chalets and unshaded touring pitches. The main pool is impressive with its tiered seating, plants, etc. It is used as a theatre for evening entertainment. A simple square pool with grass surrounds is near the play area. Organised activities off the site include canoeing, riding, climbing, walking and mountain biking.

Facilities

Central toilet block with fountain and super children's facilities. Washing machine. Motorcaravan services. Reception, small shop (25/3-1/11). Bar (3/6-2/9), pizzeria (14/4-30/9). TV. Swimming pools including slides and flumes, one new, covered and heated (all season). Play area. Minigolf, archery, volleyball, football, basketball. Mountain bike hire. Miniclub. Extensive entertainment programme. Barbecues for hire. Off site: Fishing 1 km. Riding 2 km. Golf 20 km. Organised canoeing, riding, climbing, walking, mountain biking. Vaison-la-Romaine (800 m), magnificent Roman ruins, shops, restaurants, market.

Open: 25 March - 1 November.

Directions

Leave Vaison-la-Romaine on D938 heading south towards Carpentras. 1 km. beyond the 'Super U' roundabout turn left on D151, signed St Marcellin. Site entrance is on the left immediately after the junction. GPS: N44:14.064 E05:05.381

Charges guide

Per pitch incl. 2 persons	€ 16,00 - € 29,00
extra person	€ 4,60 - € 7,00
child (under 10 yrs)	€ 2,50 - € 4,20
electricity (6/10A)	€ 3,70 - € 4,70
Camping Cheques accepted.	

VAUCLUSE

CAMPINGS FranceLoc

Le carpe Diem***

Indoor heated swimming pool, water slides, outdoor swimming pool, mobile homes and chalets… In an impressive Roman environment!

Vaison La Romaine
BP 68 • 84110 • Tel.: +33 (0)4 90 36 02 02
Email : contact@camping-carpe-diem.com
www.camping-franceloc.fr

FR84050 Camping Caravaning la Sorguette

Route d'Apt, F-84800 L'Isle-sur-la Sorgue (Vaucluse)

Tel: **04 90 38 05 71**. Email: **sorguette@wanadoo.fr**   www.alanrogers.com/FR84050

This popular, well organised site is well placed, 1.5 km. from Isle sur la Sorgue. Arranged in groups of four, the 164 medium sized level pitches (124 for touring) all have electricity (4-10A). Each group is separated by tall hedges and most have a little shade during the day. In high season a few competitions are organised (boules or volleyball), plus some children's entertainment, but this is quite low key. Running alongside the site, the river Sorgue is only six kilometres from its source in the mountains. It is still very clear and used for canoeing, swimming or fishing.

Facilities

Well maintained toilet blocks, washing machines. Units for disabled people. Baby room. Motorcaravan services. Fridge hire. Shop, bar, snacks (1/7-25/8). Entertainment in July/Aug. Play area, volleyball, half-court tennis, basketball. Canoe, bicycle hire. Internet. Indian tipis, yurts; Mongolian circular tents and Inuit style tents with kitchens. WiFi. Off site: Indoor/outdoor swimming pools (preferential rates) 2 km. Fishing and riding 5 km. Walking and cycling circuits. Canoeing on River Sorgue.

Open: 15 March - 15 October.

Directions

Site is 1.5 km. east of L'Isle sur la Sorgue on the N100 towards Apt. It is well signed from the town. GPS: N43:54.893 E05:04.655

Charges 2009

Per unit incl. 2 persons	€ 11,40 - € 14,40
extra person	€ 5,70 - € 7,20
child (1-11 yrs)	€ 2,90 - € 3,60
electricity (4/10A)	€ 3,80 - € 4,40

The Travel Service   BOOK THIS SITE CALL 01580 214000 ...we'll arrange everything

Check real time availability and at-the-gate prices...

www.alanrogers.com

FR84130 Camping les Chênes Blancs

Route de Gargas, F-84490 Saint Saturnin-les-Apt (Vaucluse)

Tel: **04 90 74 09 20**. Email: **robert@les-chenes-blancs.com**   www.alanrogers.com/FR84130

Les Chênes Blancs lies in the Pays d'Apt, between the mountains of the Luberon and the Vaucluse. This region has a wealth of history and natural beauty including the medieval hill top villages of Gordes and Roussillon and the yellow ochre mines. It has something for everyone, for those seeking to unwind as well as for the young and old who prefer a more active break. There are 192 irregular shaped shady pitches of varying size scattered amongst the trees. Some of the 172 touring pitches can accommodate large outfits and all have 6A electricity.

Facilities

Two clean toilet blocks, the newer one centrally located with older one on the perimeter of the site. Facilities for campers with disabilities. Motorcaravan services. Small shop, bar (15/3-31/10). Restaurant, takeaway, outside terrace (1/5-30/9). Unheated swimming pool, 2 paddling pools (1/5-30/9). Playground. Boules. Table tennis. Multisport court. Electric barbecues only (1200W). Off site: Rock climbing at Buoux and the Dentelles de Montmirail. Canoeing and kayaking on the Sorgue and Durance. The Fontaine de Vaucluse. Fishing 5 km. Riding, bicycle hire 10 km. Hiking trails at all levels, for all ages. Provençal markets. Isle sur la Sorgue, famous for its antiques.

Open: 15 March - 31 October.

Directions

Exit A7, junction 24 Avignon Sud, take D22 and then N100 towards Apt. Through le Chêne to the end of the town, turn left, D4 for 3 km, then turn right, follow signs to site (3 km).
GPS: N43:55.267 E05:20.150

Charges 2009

Per unit incl. car, 2 persons	
and electricity	€ 17,60 - € 22,90
extra person (over 7 yrs)	€ 3,90 - € 5,60
extra person (0-7 yrs)	€ 2,70 - € 3,90
dog	€ 1,60 - € 2,60

Camping Cheques accepted.

Camping Les Chênes Blancs***
Route de Gargas - 84490 St. Saturnin Les Apt
Tel: 0033 490 74 09 20 - Fax: 0033 490 74 26 98
E-mail: robert@les-chenes-blancs.com - Internet: www.les-chenes-blancs.com

FR84090 Camping du Pont d'Avignon

10 chemin de la Barthelasse, Ile de la Barthelasse, F-84000 Avignon (Vaucluse)

Tel: **04 90 80 63 50**. Email: **info@camping-avignon.com**   www.alanrogers.com/FR84090

This is a city site, yet it is in a quiet location and only a short walk or free ferry ride from the town. There are 300 level pitches, some on grass and some with hardstanding. 118 with electricity (10A). All have some shade but those with electricity are well shaded. A good play area, tennis courts and volleyball pitch are in the centre of the site separating the tent pitches on one side and the electric pitches on the other. Many pitches are separated by hedges. The restaurant, bar and terrace overlook the attractive pool.

Facilities

Well maintained and clean toilet blocks, facilities for disabled visitors. Washing machines, dryer. Motorcaravan services. Well stocked shop (4/4-3/10). Bar/restaurant, takeaway (4/4-20/9). Swimming pool, paddling pool (2/5-20/9). Play area with new climbing frame. Tennis (free). Volleyball. Bicycle hire (July/Aug). Internet. Off site: Avignon with famous bridge and Pope's Palace. Ferry to town centre.

Open: 16 March - 1 November.

Directions

Site is on an island in River Rhône. Well signed from roads into Avignon, ring road has complex junctions. Accessed from Pont Daladier towards Villeneuve les Avignon. Just after crossing first section of river fork right, site signed, site about 1 km.
GPS: N43:57.092 E04:48.116

Charges 2009

Per unit incl. 2 persons	
and electricity	€ 16,82 - € 26,72
extra person	€ 3,41 - € 4,86

Camping Cheques accepted.

Check real time availability and at-the-gate prices...
www.alanrogers.com

FR84140 Camping Beauregard

Route d'Uchaux, F-84550 Mornas (Vaucluse)

Tel: **04 90 37 02 08**. Email: **beauregard@wanadoo.fr**   www.alanrogers.com/FR84140

Just a kilometre off the D7 and near an A7 exit, this site may appeal to those needing a night stop when travelling to or from the Mediterranean coast. Although there are many mobile homes, there are 89 pitches available for tourists. The pitches are under large pine trees and are rather sandy. Firm pegging might be difficult. They are of various shapes and sizes, mainly about 90 sq.m. Efforts are being made to upgrade what was an old fashioned campsite. There is a new and attractive pool complex including a covered pool (heated from April) – the pools are used by some local people. Entertainment is organised for high season evenings. A good sized shop sells the essentials.

Facilities

Two toilet blocks, one of which is heated when necessary, with washbasins in cabins. Facilities for disabled visitors (access by key). Laundry facilities. Shop (April - Oct). Bar, restaurant and takeaway (April - Sept). Swimming pools, one covered. Tennis. Play area. Boules. Quad bike hire. Fitness trail. Entertainment (high season). Barbecues are not permitted. Off site: Fishing and riding 5 km. Golf 12 km.

Open: 25 March - 4 November.

Directions

From the A7 take exit for Bollene, then the N7 towards Orange. At north end of Mornas village, turn left on D74 signed Uchaux. Site is on left after 1.7 km. GPS: N44:12.924 E04:44.718

Charges guide

Per unit incl. 2 persons	€ 21,00 - € 24,00
extra person	€ 4,60 - € 7,00
child (under 7 yrs)	€ 2,50 - € 4,20
electricity	€ 4,70

CAMPINGS FranceLoc

Domaine de Beauregard

Pitches, mobile homes and chalets, heated swimming pool, indoor pool. Waterslides, paddling pool. Many activities in high season.

Route d'Uchaux 84550 Mornas
Tél. 0033(0)4 90 37 02 08
Fax. 0033(0)4 90 37 07 23
www.campings-franceloc.com

Provence

FR84100 Camping le Soleil de Provence

Route de Nyons, F-84110 Saint Romain-en-Viennois (Vaucluse)

Tel: **04 90 46 46 00**. Email: **info@camping-soleil-de-provence.fr**   www.alanrogers.com/FR84100

The site has been developed to a high standard. The 162 average sized pitches, 150 for touring are separated by hedges and a variety of young trees offering only a little shade (10A electricity). The excellent pool, surrounded by a sunbathing terrace, and overlooked by the bar, is an unusual shape with an island in the centre. Although there is no paddling pool one end of the pool is very shallow. There is some organised entertainment in July and August but the emphasis is on a quiet and peaceful environment and is an ideal site for relaxing and unwinding.

Facilities

Modern well appointed, heated toilet blocks, facilities for disabled visitors, baby room. Washing machine, dryer. Motorcaravan services. Small shop for bread, open on demand. Bar, snack bar, all season. New aqua park with waterslides and paddling pool. Small play area. Boules. Off site: Tennis 1 km. Vaison-la-Romaine 4 km. Rafting, hiking, cycling, mountain biking 4 km. (Mont Ventoux is a real challenge). Bicycle hire 5 km. Fishing 15 km. Medieval villages, market towns. vineyards, wine tasting.

Open: 15 March - 31 October.

Directions

Site is 4 km. north of Vaison-la-Romaine on the D938 road to Nyons. Turn right, signed St Romain-en-Viennois (site signed) and take first left to site. GPS: N44:16.141 E05:06.358

Charges guide

Per person	€ 3,50 - € 5,50
child (0-7 yrs)	€ 2,50 - € 3,00
pitch	€ 3,00 - € 5,00
car	€ 3,00 - € 4,00
electricity (10A)	€ 3,50
No credit cards.	

Check real time availability and at-the-gate prices...

www.alanrogers.com

FR84150 Camping Flory

Route d'Entraigues, F-84270 Vedène (Vaucluse)

Tel: **04 90 31 00 51**. Email: **campingflory@wanadoo.fr**   www.alanrogers.com/FR84150

Camping Flory is a traditional, country site in the heart of Provence and only ten minutes drive from the historic Papal town of Avignon. The area dedicated to camping is somewhat sloping, with shade provided by mature pine trees. There are 100 touring pitches, all with electricity (10A). Mobile homes occupy a separate area. Vedène lies in a low area not far from the confluence of the Rhône and Durance rivers, but the site is on a hillside and the danger of flooding is minimal with excellent precautions in place. A warm welcome is offered by owners, Ernest and Jeannine Guindos.

Facilities

Three toilet blocks, two of the buildings are old but have been refurbished to a good standard, with some washbasins in cabins and pre-set showers. Very basic facilities for disabled visitors. Motorcaravan services. Small restaurant (1/7-30/8) and takeaway. Shop for basic supplies. Swimming pool (no shorts). Play area. Boules. Some organised activities in high season. Off site: Golf 2 km. Riding 3 km. Bicycle hire and fishing 10 km.

Open: 15 March - 30 September.

Directions

From A7 Autoroute du Soleil, take exit 23 (Avignon Nord) and follow D942 towards Carpentras for 3 km.then turn right at the second sign for Vedène. GPS: N43:59.260 E04:54.470

Charges guide

Per unit incl. 2 persons and electricity	€ 18,00 - € 23,00
extra person	€ 4,50 - € 5,50
child (under 7 yrs)	€ 2,50 - € 3,40

FR84160 Camping Bagatelle

Ile de la Barthelasse, F-84000 Avignon (Vaucluse)

Tel: **04 90 86 30 39**. Email: **camping.bagatelle@wanadoo.fr**   www.alanrogers.com/FR84160

Open all year, Camping Bagatelle is a combination of a city campsite, backpacker's hostel and restaurant. It may be a bit noisy because of its location at the edge of the town – the city sights are just across the bridge. From the restaurant and terrace there are good views across the river of the historical Papal Palaces and the city walls of Avignon. There are 227 shaded gravel pitches, all for touring, with 6-10A electricity and are suitable for larger outfits. The site is hard to find and one must be very careful not to take wrong turns.

Facilities

Two toilet blocks, one of which is being slowly renovated, situated near the touring pitches and heated in low season. The second block is near the hostel. Private bathroom (key at reception). Heated baby room. Good shop. Two restaurants and a bar with counter meals (all year). Playground. Motorcaravan services. Occasional organised activities. Off site: Ferry across river to city.

Open: All year.

Directions

Autoroute A9, exit 22 take N580 to Avignon Centre. Follow signs 'Barthelasse', then 'Camping Bagatelle'. Alternatively, from A7, exit 23 then D942 to 'Avignon Centre'. Follow signs 'Barthelasse', when across river follow 'Camping Bagatelle'. GPS: N43:56.550 E04:48.367

Charges guide

Per unit incl. 2 persons and electricity	€ 16,22 - € 21,22
extra person	€ 3,06 - € 3,46

FR84180 Flower Camping Lou Comtadou

881 ave Pierre de Coubertin, F-84200 Carpentras (Vaucluse)

Tel: **04 90 67 03 16**. Email: **info@loucomtadou.com**   www.alanrogers.com/FR84180

Lou Comtadou can be found 20 km. from Avignon at the foot of the Mont Ventoux. This is an area which is often considered to be the gateway to Provence. It is also a region of fine cuisine, lavender fields and wonderful sunlight, which has always attracted artists to this corner of the region. Lou Comtadou is open for a long season and has 100 pitches, some of which are occupied by mobile homes and fully equipped tents available for rent. Pitches are grassy and generally well shaded. All are equipped with electricity (6A).

Facilities

Bar. Snack bar. Takeaway. Shop. TV room. Motorcaravan services. Playground. Mobile homes and equipped tents for rent. Off site: Tennis. Swimming pool. Shops, cafés and restaurants in Carpentras. Avignon 20 km. Mont Ventoux.

Open: 1 March - 31 October.

Directions

Approaching from the north, leave the A7 at exit 22 (Orange Sud) and follow signs to Carpentras on D907 and D950. Upon arrival in Carpentras follow signs to St Didier and then Complexe Sportif. The site forms part of this complex. GPS: N44:02.627 E05:03.218

Charges 2009

Per unit incl. 2 persons and electricity	€ 17,50 - € 24,50
extra person	€ 5,50 - € 6,90

Check real time availability and at-the-gate prices...

www.**alanrogers**.com

MAP 15

Rolling fields of yellow sunflowers, the Armagnac vineyards and crumbling, ancient stone buildings amidst the sleepy villages make this colourful region popular with those who enjoy good food, good wine and a taste of the good life.

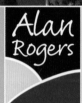

Alan Rogers

DÉPARTEMENTS: 09 ARIÈGE, 31 HAUTE-GARONNE, 32 GERS, 65 HAUTES-PYRÉNÉES, 81 TARN, 82 TARN-ET GARONNE. WE HAVE LEFT OUT THE DÉPARTEMENTS OF AVEYRON (12) AND LOT (46), WHICH ARE IN OUR DORDOGNE/AVEYRON REGION

Still a relatively unknown region, the Midi-Pyrénées is the largest region of France, extending from the Dordogne in the north to the Spanish border. It is blessed by radiant sunshine and a fascinating range of scenery. High chalk plateaux, majestic peaks, tiny hidden valleys and small fortified sleepy villages, which seem to have changed little since the Middle Ages, contrast with the high-tech, industrial and vibrant university city of Toulouse.

Lourdes is one of the most visited pilgrimage sites in the world. Toulouse-Lautrec, the artist, was born at Albi, the capital of the département of Tarn. Much of the town is built of pink brick which seems to glow when seen from a distance. In the east, the little town of Foix, with its maze of steep, winding streets, is a convenient centre from which to explore the prehistoric caves at Niaux and the Aladdin's Cave of duty-free gift shops in the independent state of Andorra. The Canal du Midi that links Bordeaux to the Mediterranean was commissioned by Louis XIV in 1666 and is still in working order.

Places of interest

Albi: birthplace and Museum of Toulouse-Lautrec, imposing Ste Cécile cathedral with 15th century fresco of 'The Last Judgement'.

Auch: capital of ancient Gascony, boasts a fine statue of d'Artágnan.

Collonges-la-Rouge: picturesque village of Medieval and Renaissance style mansions and manors.

Conques: 11th-century Ste Foy Romanesque church.

Cordes: medieval walled hilltop village.

Foix: 11th/12th-century towers on rocky peak above town; 14th century cathedral.

Lourdes: famous pilgrimage site where Ste Bernadette is said to have spoken to the Virgin Mary in a grotto and known for the miracles said to have been performed there.

Cuisine of the region

Food is rich and strongly seasoned, making generous use of garlic and goose fat, and there are some excellent regional wines. Seafood such as oysters, salt-water fish, or piballes from the Adour river are popular.

Cassoulet: stew of duck, sausages and beans.

Confit de Canard (d'oie): preserved duck meat.

Grattons (Graisserons): a mélange of small pieces of rendered down duck, goose and pork fat.

Magret de canard: duck breast fillets

Poule au pot: chicken simmered with vegetables.

Ouillat (Ouliat): Pyrénées soup: onions, tomatoes, goose fat and garlic.

Tourtière Landaise: a sweet of Agen prunes, apples and Armagnac.

FR09060 Kawan Village le Pré Lombard

F-09400 Tarascon-sur-Ariege (Ariège)

Tel: 05 61 05 61 94. Email: leprelombard@wanadoo.fr

www.alanrogers.com/FR09060

This busy, good value site is located beside the attractive river Ariège near the town. There are 180 level, grassy, pitches with shade provided by a variety of trees (electricity 10A). At the rear of the site are 69 site-owned chalets and mobile homes. A gate in the fence provides access to the river bank for fishing. Open for a long season, it is an excellent choice for early or late breaks, or as a stop-over en-route to the winter sun destinations in Spain. This region of Ariège is in the foothills of the Pyrénées and 85 km. from Andorra. Didier Mioni, the manager follows the town motto S'y passos, y demoros – 'if you wish to come here, you will stay here' in his aim to ensure your satisfaction on his site. At Tarascon itself you can visit the Parc Pyrénéen de l'Art Préhistorique to view prehistoric rock paintings, or the really adventurous can take to the air for paragliding or hang gliding.

Facilities

Five toilet blocks of varying age, facilities for people with disabilities. Laundry. Motorcaravan services. Bar and takeaway. Shop. Restaurant, entertainment, dancing (1/5-30/9). Heated swimming pool (1/5-30/9). Playgrounds for toddlers and older children. Video games machines. Boules. Multisport court. Fishing. Internet and WiFi on payment. Satellite TV. Entertainment (high season), nightclub, children's club, sports tournaments. Activity programmes for small groups. Off site: Supermarket 300 m. Town 600 m. Archery, kayaking and fishing nearby. Riding 5 km. Golf 30 km. Skiing 20 km.

Open: 22 March - 11 November.

Directions

Site is 600 m. south of town, adjacent to the river. From north, turn off main N20 into the town, site well signed. From south (Andorra) site signed at roundabout on town approach.
GPS: N42:50.391 E01:36.720

Charges guide

Per unit incl. 2 persons and 10A electricity	€ 15,00 - € 29,50
extra person	€ 4,00 - € 8,50
child (2-7 yrs)	free - € 6,50
dog	free - € 2,00

Camping Cheques accepted.

FR09020 Camping l'Arize

Mobile homes ▶ page 508

Lieu-dit Bourtol, F-09240 La Bastide-de-Sérou (Ariège)

Tel: 05 61 65 81 51. Email: camparize@aol.com

www.alanrogers.com/FR09020

The site sits in a delightful, tranquil valley among the foothills of the Pyrénées and is just east of the interesting village of La Bastide-de-Sérou beside the River Arize (good trout fishing). The river is fenced for the safety of children on the site, but may be accessed just outside the gate. The 70 large pitches are neatly laid out on level grass within the spacious site. All have 3/6A electricity and are separated into bays by hedges and young trees. An extension to the site gives 24 large, fully serviced pitches and a small toilet block.

Facilities

Toilet block includes facilities for babies and disabled visitors. Laundry room. Motorcaravan services. Small swimming pool and sunbathing area. Entertainment in high season. Weekly barbecues and welcome drinks on Sundays. Fishing, riding and bicycle hire. WiFi. Off site: Several restaurants and shops within a few minutes' drive. The nearest restaurant is located at the national stud for the famous Merens horses just 200 m. away and will deliver takeaway meals to your pitch. Golf 5 km.

Open: 7 March - 12 November.

Directions

Site is southeast of the village La Bastide-de-Sérou. Take the D15 towards Nescus and site is on right after about 1 km. GPS: N43:00.109 E01:26.723

Charges guide

Per pitch incl. 2 persons and electricity	€ 16,40 - € 31,60
extra person	€ 4,00 - € 5,40
child (0-7 yrs)	€ 3,00 - € 3,60
dog	€ 1,00 - € 1,80

Discounts for longer stays in mid and low season.

BOOK THIS SITE
CALL 01580 214000
...we'll arrange everything
The Travel Service

Check real time availability and at-the-gate prices...
www.alanrogers.com

FR09050 Camping Municipal la Prade

F-09110 Sorgeat (Ariège)

Tel: **05 61 64 36 34**. Email: **sorgeat.mainie@wanadoo.fr**   www.alanrogers.com/FR09050

Superbly situated high on the mountainside overlooking a valley, this site has magnificent views, with a river 300 m. and a lake two kilometres away. A small site, it provides just 40 pitches on terraces, some of which are occupied by long stay units, (electricity 5-10A). Well supervised, with the warden present at varying times, the site is kept very clean. A small stream tinkles through the edge of the site and the attractive hills towering above it reverberate with the sound of goat bells. A separate area has permanent brick barbecues for use by campers. A most reasonably priced campsite.

Facilities

The original, rather small sanitary block has only two showers and two WCs in each half. However, a second block has now been added and standards are very high. Facilities for disabled visiotrs are also very good with special washbasin and a very large shower suite. Washing machine. Small play area. Off site: Shop and café in village. Fishing 500 m. Riding and bicycle hire 5 km.

Open: All year.

Directions

From Ax-les-Thermes take D613 towards Quillan for 4 km. Turn onto D52 and continue for 1 km. Follow site signs. Bear left at first junction up through Sorgeat village to site. Mountain roads may be difficult for large units. GPS: N42:43.974 E01:51.234

Charges guide

Per person	€ 3,00
child (0-10 yrs)	€ 1,50
pitch incl. electricity	€ 4,50 - € 7,30

No credit cards.

FR09100 Parc d'Audinac les Bains

Montjoie-Audinac, F-09200 Saint Girons (Ariège)

Tel: **05 61 66 44 50**. Email: **accueil@audinac.com**   www.alanrogers.com/FR09100

Remnants of an old thermal springs can be found on the site at Parc d'Audinac les Bains, a tranquil haven with wonderful views of the surrounding mountains. Owned by a charming French couple, Olivia and Jérôme Barbry, you are guaranteed a friendly welcome on this site which has 90 touring pitches and 25 chalets for rent. The terraced touring pitches are mostly level, although some do have a slight slope. They are on well drained grass and each has 10A electricity supplied (the older part of the site via French sockets). Water supplies are conveniently located for all of the pitches, as are the modern sanitary facilities.

Facilities

New chalets. Two small bright and modern toilet blocks (one unisex) with hot and cold water to showers and washbasins. British and Turkish style WC's. Washing machines. Motorcaravan service point. Good sized outdoor swimming pool and paddling pool. Small shop for drinks and ice creams (July/Aug) in the old thermal spring building by the pool. Children's club (July/Aug). Tennis. Boules. Sports area. Off site: St Girons 3 km.

Open: 1 May - 30 September.

Directions

From St Girons take D117 towards Foix. Turn left on D627 signed St Croix and Merigon. Site is on the right just after Audinac-les-Bains.
GPS: N43:00.444 E01:10.956

Charges guide

Per unit incl. 2 persons	€ 11,50 - € 16,00
extra person	€ 4,00 - € 6,00
child (0-6 yrs)	€ 3,00 - € 5,00
electricity (10A)	€ 3,50

FR09120 Camping Ascou la Forge

F-09110 Ascou (Ariège)

Tel: **05 61 64 60 03**. Email: **mountain.sports@wanadoo.fr**   www.alanrogers.com/FR09120

The Dutch owners of Ascou La Forge will give you a warm, friendly welcome at their oasis in the mountains of the Pyrénées, close to the borders of Andorra and Spain. The site is 3,500 feet above sea level but is easily accessible for motorhomes and caravans. Lying alongside the Lauze river, there are 50 pitches. In low season 44 mainly level, grass touring pitches with electricity are available, but this number reduces to 20 in July and August to allow more room for the large influx of campers with tents. There are also two chalets available to rent.

Facilities

Modern, bright, sanitary block is fully equipped including facilities for disabled visitors which double as a family shower room with a baby bath. Shop. Bar with large screen for major sports events and films about the local flora/fauna. Play area. Maps and walking routes are available from reception. Free WiFi. Off site: Restaurant next door to site (all year). Ax-les-Thermes 7 km.

Open: All year.

Directions

From Ax-Les-Thermes take D613 signed Quérigat, Quillan and Ascou-Pailhéres. After 3.6 km. turn right on D25 to site on right after 3.4 km.
GPS: N42:43.466 E01:53.564

Charges guide

Per unit incl. 2 persons and electricity	€ 16,00 - € 19,00
extra person	€ 3,50 - € 4,25

Check real time availability and at-the-gate prices...
www.alanrogers.com

Winner Alan Rogers Awards 2008

FR32010 Kawan Village le Camp de Florence

Mobile homes ▶ page 508

Route Astaffort, F-32480 La Romieu (Gers)

Tel: **05 62 28 15 58**. Email: **info@lecampdeflorence.com**

www.alanrogers.com/FR32010

Camp de Florence is an attractive site on the edge of an historic village in pleasantly undulating Gers countryside. The 183 large, part terraced pitches (95 for tourers) all have electricity, 14 with hardstanding and 25 fully serviced. They are arranged around a large field (full of sunflowers when we visited) with rural views, giving a feeling of spaciousness. The 13th-century village of La Romieu is on the Santiago de Compostela pilgrim route. The Pyrénées are a two hour drive, the Atlantic coast a similar distance. The site has been developed by the friendly Mynsbergen family who are Dutch (although Susan is English). They have sympathetically converted the old farmhouse buildings to provide facilities for the site. The collegiate church, visible from the site, is well worth a visit (the views are magnificent from the top of the tower), as is the local arboretum, the biggest collection of trees in the Midi-Pyrénées.

Facilities

Three toilet blocks provide all the necessary facilities. Washing machines and dryers. Motorcaravan services. Restaurant (1/5-30/9, also open to the public). Takeaway. Bread. Swimming pool area with water slide. Jacuzzi, protected children's pool (open to public in afternoons). Adventure playground, games and pets areas. Bouncy castle, trampoline. Outdoor fitness machines. Games room. Tennis. Pétanque. Bicycle hire. Video shows, discos, picnics, musical evenings. Excursions. Internet and WiFi. Off site: Shop 500 m. in village. Fishing 5 km. Riding 10 km. Walking tours, excursions and wine tasting.

Open: 1 April - 10 October.

Directions

Site signed from D931 Agen - Condom road. Small units turn left at Ligardes (signed), follow D36 for 1 km, turn right turn La Romieu (signed). Otherwise continue until outskirts of Condom and take D41 left to La Romieu, through village to site. GPS: N43:58.975 E00:30.091

Charges guide

Per unit incl. 2 persons and electricity	€ 16,00 - € 30,90
extra person	€ 3,50 - € 6,90
dog (max. 2)	€ 1,50 - € 2,10

Camping Cheques accepted.

Le Camp de Florence - 32480 La Romieu

Sun * Comfort * Nature * Water

The Gers - A region waiting to be discovered, an unspoilt landscape of rolling hills, sunflowers and historic fortified villages and castles. Peace, tranquillity, the home of Armagnac, Fois Gras and Magret de Canard. A 4* site with spacious pitches, panoramic views and luxury mobile homes for hire.

Tel: 0033 562 28 15 58 - Fax: 0033 562 28 20 04
E-mail: info@lecampdeflorence.com - www.lecampdeflorence.com

FR31000 Camping le Moulin

F-31220 Martres-Tolosane (Haute-Garonne)

Tel: **05 61 98 86 40**. Email: **info@campinglemoulin.com**

www.alanrogers.com/FR31000

Set in a 12 hectare estate of woods and fields, Camping Le Moulin is a family run campsite in the foothills of the Pyrénées, close to the interesting medieval village of Martres-Tolosane and situated on the site of an old mill on the bank of the River Garonne. There are 99 pitches (60 for tourers) all with electrical connections. Most pitches are level and grassy, of a good size and with shade from mature trees. A number of very large (150-200 sq.m) 'super' pitches are also available.

Facilities

Large modern sanitary block with separate ladies and gents WCs. Communal area with showers and washbasins in cubicles. Separate heated area for visitors with disabilities. Baby bath. Laundry facilities. Motorcaravan services. Outdoor bar with WiFi. Snack bar and takeaway (July/August). Daily baker's van (except Monday). Heated swimming pool (July/Aug). Tennis. Canoeing. Archery. BMX track. Playground. Games room. Entertainment programme and children's club (high season). Off site: Martres-Tolosane 1.5 km.

Open: 22 March - 30 September.

Directions

From the A64 motorway (Toulouse-Tarbes) take exit 21 (Boussens) or exit 22 (Martres-Tolosane) and follow signs to Martres-Tolosane. Site is well signed from village. GPS: N43:11.429 E01:01.073

Charges guide

Per person	€ 4,20 - € 6,00
child (2-7 yrs)	€ 2,10 - € 3,00
pitch incl. electricity	€ 8,40 - € 18,00

Less 20% outside July/Aug.

BOOK THIS SITE CALL 01580 214000 ...we'll arrange everything The Travel Service

BOOK THIS SITE CALL 01580 214000 ...we'll arrange everything The Travel Service

THE TRAVEL SERVICE
BOOK THIS SITE
CALL 01580 214000
...we'll arrange everything

FR32020 Camping du Lac

F-32230 Marciac (Gers)

Tel: 05 62 08 21 19. Email: camping.marciac@wanadoo.fr

www.alanrogers.com/FR32020

Set in the rolling countryside of the beautiful Gers region, Camping du Lac is on the edge of the ancient fortified town of Marciac. Rob and Louise Robinson, the English owners since 2002, offer a friendly welcome and a quiet, relaxing stay. The well shaded site has 95 pitches, including 15 used for mobile homes and chalets to rent. There are 60 touring pitches with electricity connections (6/10A, Europlug) on the lower, reasonably level area of the site, including five with hardstanding for motorcaravans. On an informal, slightly sloping terraced area giving a 'back to nature' feeling are 20 pitches without electricity, mainly used for tents.

Facilities

The centrally situated sanitary block uses solar energy to help to heat water. Washbasins in cubicles. Facilities for disabled visitors (two separate bathrooms with shower, WC and washbasin). Washing machine. Motorcaravan service point. Shop. Bar. Takeaway. Bread delivered daily (order at reception). Swimming pool (15/4-30/9). Small library and reading room. Play area. Internet access. Off site: Shops, restaurant and bars 1 km. Marciac 1 km. Fishing, watersports, sailing and riding 300 m. Golf 7 km.

Open: 16 March - 30 October.

Directions

From Auch take the D943 west towards Bassoues and Marciac. Just before Marciac turn left opposite the floating restaurant on the lake (site is signed). Site is 200 m. on the left.
GPS: N43:31.510 E00:09.860

Charges guide

Per unit incl. 2 persons and electricity (6A)	€ 12,50 - € 21,00
extra person	€ 2,50 - € 5,00
child (4-16 yrs)	€ 1,50 - € 3,50

FR32050 Camping Domaine les Angeles

Les Angeles, F-32410 Cézan (Gers)

Tel: Sitetel. Email: lesangeles@gmail.com

www.alanrogers.com/FR32050

Les Angeles is a small site based around an old Gascon farmhouse. Its young Dutch owners, Clara and Guido, took over the site in Spring 2008 and have ambitious development plans. There are 40 pitches, all of a good size and all with electrical connections (6/10A). A number of chalets and mobile homes are available for rent. The site enjoys a very quiet, rural location and guarantees that there will be no discos! Instead, the emphasis is on relaxation and tranquility, and the owners are happy to offer advice on the many walking and cycling opportunities in the area.

Facilities

Shop. Bar. 'Table d'hôte' meals. Takeaway. Library. Games room/lounge. TV for major sports events. Swimming pool. Bicycle hire. Fishing. Play area. Mobile homes and chalets for rent. Off site: Fleurance (shops and restaurants) 12 km. Golf (3 courses nearby). Cycle and walking tracks.

Open: 1 May - 30 September.

Directions

Head south from Fleurance on the D103 as far as Préchac. Head west here towards Cézan and the site is signed before you reach the village.
GPS: N43:47.617 E00:31.167

Charges guide

Per unit incl. 2 persons	€ 11,00 - € 15,50
extra person	€ 4,00 - € 5,50
electricity (6A)	€ 3,00

FR32060 Yelloh! Village le Lac des Trois Vallées

F-32700 Lectoure (Gers)

Tel: 04 66 73 97 39. Email: info@yellohvillage-lac-des-3-vallees.com

www.alanrogers.com/FR32060

This is a large 140 hectare site with many facilities. It is a large holiday complex and good for families with young children or teenagers. The large lake provides the opportunity for canoeing, swimming, diving and there are four water slides. There is a large safe paddling area and a separate fishing lake. The impressive heated pool complex complete with gymnasium and jacuzzi also has paved areas for sunbathing and a large paddling pool. Of the 500 pitches, over 200 are well situated for touring on shaded or open ground, all with electricity (10A). Used by tour operators (100 pitches).

Facilities

Eight modern sanitary blocks each with baby bathing facilities. Provision for disabled visitors. Laundry facilities. Motorcaravan services. Shop. Restaurants and bars. Lakeside snack bar and kiosk. Heated swimming pool complex. Lake complex. BMX/skateboard area. Fishing. Tennis. Minigolf. Video games room. Disco. Cinema. Children's club. Off site: Golf 10 km. Riding 20 km.

Open: 24 May - 7 September with all facilities.

Directions

Take N21 south from Lectoure for 2 km. Site is well signed and is a further 2 km. after turning left off the N21. GPS: N43:54.750 E00:38.911

Charges guide

Per unit incl. 2 persons incl. electricity and water	€ 17,00 - € 42,00
	€ 18,00 - € 43,00
extra person	€ 5,00 - € 8,00

tel: +33 466 739 739 www.yellohvillage.com

yelloh! VILLAGE

Check real time availability and at-the-gate prices...

www.alanrogers.com

FR32110 Camping du Lac de l'Uby

Barbothan-les-Thermes, F-32150 Gaubazon (Gers)

Tel: 05 62 09 53 91. Email: balia-vacances@wanadoo.fr

www.alanrogers.com/FR32110

Camping du Lac de l'Uby is a large, mature site set alongside a lake and close to the thermal spa town of Barbotan-Les-Thermes in the Gers Gascogne region. The site is well shaded by mature trees in most areas and has 280 pitches with 240 available for tourers, the remainder taken up with mobile homes and chalets to rent. The mixture of large and average sized pitches are on level grass and gravel, all having 5/10A electricity (French sockets). Children are well catered for with a good play area and organised activities in July and August, including a circus school two days each week. Evening entertainment is organised in high season. The municipal leisure centre (which is open from June to September) with a large outdoor pool, a lakeside beach and a large play area, is only 500 m. from the site (campers are given free entry). The local tennis club is also just outside the site and four all weather courts are available to hire.

Facilities

Five well distributed sanitary blocks include facilities for disabled visitors and a separate baby bathroom. Separate laundry room. Motorcaravan service point. Shop, restaurant and bar, (1/6-30/9). Play area and covered entertainment area. Fishing. Bicycle hire. Off site: Leisure centre with pool, beach, and large play area 500 m. All weather tennis courts 400 m. Thermal spa facilities 1 km. Golf 20 km. Minigolf 50 m. Lakeside path.

Open: 15 March - 30 November.

Directions

From Condom take D931 to Eauze then head west on N524 to Cazaubon. From Cazaubon continue on the N524 towards Barbotan-Les-Thermes, site is signed on right after 2 km.
GPS: N43:56.401 W00:02.679

Charges guide

Per person	€ 3,50 - € 5,50
child (3-12 yrs)	€ 2,00 - € 4,00
pitch	€ 6,50 - € 13,00
electricity (6A)	€ 2,50 - € 5,50
No credit cards.	

Camping caravaning du Lac de l'UBY

Rediscover your true nature !

Lac de l'Uby welcomes you to its world of tradition and well-being.

Exceptionnal location on the banks of a splendid 80ha lake. Sunny or shady pitches to choose from rental of confortable and spacious mobil homes and gîtes. Kids garden, snack bar, Internet and Wifi spot, Service point for motor homes.

Lac de l'Uby offers a friendly family atmosphere with entertainment and a range of services, sporting and cultural activities.

Free acces to leisure area with sandy beach, swimming pool (high season). Fishing and water sports.

Your relaxing corner in the heart of Gascony!

Open from 15 march to 30 november

Tel: +33 562 095 391
www.camping-uby.com
32150 Barbotan les Thermes

Check real time availability and at-the-gate prices...

www.alanrogers.com

Winner Alan Rogers Awards 2008

FR32080 Kawan Village le Talouch

F-32810 Roquelaure (Gers)

Tel: 05 62 65 52 43. Email: info@camping-talouch.com

www.alanrogers.com/FR32080

Although enjoying a quiet and rural location, this neat and tidy site is only a short drive from the town of Auch with its famous legendary son, d'Artagnan. The entrance is fronted by a parking area with reception to the right and the bar and restaurant facing. Beyond this point lies the top half of the touring area with generous pitches of at least 120 sq.m. located between mature trees and divided by hedges, some with chalets. There are 100 pitches for touring, with electricity (6A). The rear half of the site has unshaded pitches in a more open aspect.

Facilities

Two toilet blocks with open style washbasins and controllable showers. Baby unit. One toilet for disabled visitors. Coin operated washing machine and laundry sinks. Small shop (1/4-30/9). Bar, restaurant and takeaway. Two excellent swimming pools, one heated and covered. Sauna and spa. Bicycle hire. GPS hire with pre-programmed walking routes and special activities for children. Play areas. Tennis and hard surface sports area. Organised entertainment in high season. Small library. Internet and WiFi in reception. Off site: Walking routes. Fishing and riding within 8 km.

Open: 1 April - 30 September.

Directions

Situated some 11 km. north of Auch on the D149, and 64 km. east of Toulouse the site is well signed. From the north approach via the A62 motorway, leaving at Layrac and heading towards Auch on the N21.
GPS: N43:42.890 E00:33.780

Charges guide

Per unit incl. 2 persons and electricity	€ 17,20 - € 31,50
extra person	€ 4,50 - € 7,20
child (under 7 yrs)	€ 3,85 - € 5,90
Camping Cheques accepted.	

FR32090 Camping le Pardaillan

27 rue Pardaillan, F-32330 Gondrin (Gers)

Tel: 05 62 29 16 69. Email: camplepardaillan@wanadoo.fr

www.alanrogers.com/FR32090

In the heart of the Armagnac region of the Gers between Condom and Eauze make a stop at the village of Gondrin and stay at the attractive, family run campsite of Le Pardaillan. Neatly manicured and well laid out, the site has 115 pitches arranged on four separate terraced areas; 51 of these are for tourers, the remainder used for chalets (to rent all year). Level and grassy, the touring pitches are small to average in size, separated by tidy hedges and partially shaded by mature trees. Each has 6/10A electricity and 30 also have water and waste water points.

Facilities

Three toilet blocks include WCs, hot showers and washbasins in cubicles. Facilities for disabled visitors. Heated family shower room. Washing machines, dryers, and ironing board. Bar, restaurant and takeaway (mid June - mid Sept). WiFi internet access. Play area. Children's club and excursions (July/Aug). Fishing lake. Off site: Leisure centre 200 m. Shops, restaurant and bars 500 m. Golf 6 km. Riding 15 km.

Open: Easter - mid October.

Directions

From the A62 exit at Agen and take the D931 west towards Eauze. Site is in village of Gondrin (between Condom and Eauze) and is signed.
GPS: N43:52.990 E00:14.310

Charges guide

Per unit incl. 2 persons and electricity (6A)	€ 12,00 - € 23,50
extra person (over 4 yrs)	€ 3,00 - € 5,50
10A electricity	€ 2,00 - € 2,00

FR32100 Camping les Lacs de Courtés

F-32240 Estang (Gers)

Tel: 05 62 09 61 98. Email: contact@lacs-de-courtes.com

www.alanrogers.com/FR32100

This small site has been owned and managed by a friendly French couple for the last 24 years. It is situated on a hillside overlooking a lake and has 114 pitches neatly arranged on terraces. There are 50 level touring pitches each with adjacent 6A electricity supply (French sockets), the remaining pitches being used for 64 mobile homes and chalets of which 29 are to rent. The touring pitches are mainly grassed and are well separated by hedges and mature trees which provide shade. Some are situated alongside a private lake that is used for fishing and canoeing.

Facilities

Centrally situated toilet block with showers, WCs ans washbasins. Separate facilities for disabled visitors at entrance to site. Laundry room. Motorcaravan services. Bar and small restaurant (1/7-31/8) with covered entertainment area. Two outdoor pools. Jacuzzi. Play area. Lake for fishing and canoeing. Off site: Estang 200 m. Riding 12 km. Golf 18 km. Barbotan-Les-Thermes 11 km.

Open: Easter - 30 September.

Directions

From Condom take D931 to Eauze then N524 west to Cazaubon. After 4 km. take D30 to Estang. Site is on left as you enter the village of Estang.
GPS: N43:52.060 W00:06.100

Charges guide

Per unit incl. 2 persons	€ 7,80 - € 13,00
extra person	€ 3,00 - € 5,00
electricity (6A)	€ 3,00

BOOK THIS SITE
CALL 01580 214000
...we'll arrange everything
The Travel Service

Check real time availability and at-the-gate prices...
www.alanrogers.com

FR32130 Camping Lac du Thoux Saint-Cricq

F-32430 Thoux-Saint-Cricq (Gers)

Tel: 05 62 65 71 29. Email: lacdethoux@cacg.fr

www.alanrogers.com/FR32130

Camping Lac de Thoux-Saint Cricq in the Gers Gascogne region is a mature site set alongside a 70 hectare lake with lots of watersports on offer. The site is well shaded by mature trees in most parts and provides 130 pitches with 125 available for tourers and the remainder taken up with mobile homes and chalets for rent. Several pitches are take up by 'permanent' residents and these are rather untidy looking. The mixture of large, average sized and small pitches are level or slightly sloping grass and gravel and most have 10A electricity available.

Facilities

Two sanitary blocks (only one open outside July/Aug) with showers, WCs and washbasins. Separate facilities for disabled visitors. Baby room. Laundry facilities. Motorcaravan service point. Shop (1/7-31/8). Bar, restaurant and takeaway (1/5-30/10). Swimming pool (1/6-30/9). Play area. Off site: Lake leisure area adjacent. Restaurant 200 m. Golf 10 km. Riding 20 km.

Open: 1 April - 15 October.

Directions

From Auch head east on N124 to Toulouse. At L'Isle-Jourdain take the D654 north towards Cologne. Site is on right after 11 km. and is signed.
GPS: N43:41.132 E01:00.145

Charges guide

Per unit incl. 2 persons	€ 14,00 - € 16,00
extra person	€ 5,00 - € 6,00
electricity (10A)	€ 4,00

FR65020 Sunêlia les Trois Vallées

Avenue des Pyrénées, F-65400 Argelès-Gazost (Hautes-Pyrénées)

Tel: 05 62 90 35 47. Email: 3-vallees@wanadoo.fr

www.alanrogers.com/FR65020

This is a large, ever-expanding site on the road from Lourdes into the Pyrénées mountains. It has an unprepossessing entrance and pitches near the road suffer from noise, but at the back, open fields allow views of surrounding mountains on all sides. Amenities include an indoor pool, two jacuzzis and an enormous play area that seems to have everything! The site has 483 flat, grassy pitches of reasonable size, 200 are for tourers, all with 3 or 6A electricity, some fully serviced. The site is popular with young people and could be quite lively at times.

Facilities

The toilet blocks are a little dated, facilities for disabled people. Cleaning can be variable and facilities could be under pressure at peak times. Bread. Bar/disco. Café, takeaway. Pool complex (from 15/5), paddling pool, spa bath, large jacuzzi and two slides. Good playground. Entertainment in high season. Off site: Supermarket across the road. Bicycle hire 50 m. Fishing 500 m. Riding 3 km. Nearby is 'La Voie Verte', a 17 km. traffic-free cycle path from Lourdes south to Soulom.

Open: 3 April - 5 November.

Directions

Argelès-Gazost is 13 km. south of Lourdes. From A64 take exit for Lourdes and follow D821 towards Argelès-Gazost, then onto 'La Voie Rapide' and turn right at the first roundabout, after 300 m. right at the new roundabout and you are at the site.
GPS: N43:00.733 W00:05.833

Charges 2009

Per pitch incl. 2 persons and electricity	€ 13,00 - € 33,00
extra person	€ 5,00 - € 9,50

FR65030 Airotel Pyrénées

46 avenue du Barège, F-65120 Esquieze-Sere (Hautes-Pyrénées)

Tel: 05 62 92 89 18. Email: airotel.pyrenees@wanadoo.fr

www.alanrogers.com/FR65030

It is located on the main road into the mountains, south from Argelès-Gazost and surrounded by the high peaks (some pitches will have daytime road noise). There are 163 level pitches, with 85 for touring units, all with electricity and 90 fully serviced. They are on terraced ground and separated by bushes. Lighting runs through the site and across some pitches. The layout of the pitches with the mobile homes can give a rather crowded feel. In high season a programme of activities is arranged, from walking and mountain bike trips to rafting. There are tour operator pitches.

Facilities

Fairly modern, well appointed, toilet blocks (one heated), facilities for disabled people also doubling as a baby room. Bottled water is advised for drinking and cooking. Motorcaravan services. Small shop (1/7-31/8), bread (15/5-15/9). Outdoor pool (15/6-15/9). Indoor pool, balneotherapy pool, sauna, fitness room (1/12-30/9). Water slides. Practice climbing wall, half-court tennis and boules. Small playground. Off site: Bicycle hire and fishing 1 km. Skiing 10 km.

Open: All year, excl. 1 October - 30 November.

Directions

Take N21 (Voie rapide) south from Lourdes past Argelès-Gazost towards Luz-St-Sauveur. The site is on left at Esquièze-Sere, just before Luz-St-Sauveur. Site is on left immediately after Camping International.
GPS: N42:52.749 W00:00.610

Charges guide

Per unit incl. 2 persons	€ 15,50 - € 26,00
extra person	€ 5,00 - € 6,00
child (2-7 yrs)	€ 3,50
electricity (3-10A)	€ 3,50 - € 6,50
dog	€ 1,50

BOOK THIS SITE
CALL 01580 214000
...we'll arrange everything
The Travel Service

Check real time availability and at-the-gate prices...
www.alanrogers.com

The Travel Service · BOOK THIS SITE · CALL 01580 214000 · ...we'll arrange everything

FR65040 Camping International

F-65120 Luz-Saint-Sauveur (Hautes-Pyrénées)

Tel: **05 62 92 82 02**. Email: **reception@international-camping.fr**   www.alanrogers.com/FR65040

Located in the foothills of the Pyrénées, Camping International is an attractive, family run site with 180 pitches, most are on the fairly level lower section. There are 146 grassy pitches for tourists all with electricity (2/6A), many divided by hedges and some with a little shade. Around 40 pitches (more for tents) are on terraces on the mountainside at back of the site, all accessed by tarmac roads and with stunning views. However some fairly steep up and down walking will be necessary. Most of the amenities are grouped around the reception area along the front of the site.

Facilities

Well equipped toilet blocks (one heated), facilities for babies and campers with disabilites. Shop. Snack bar, takeaway. Heated swimming pool and jacuzzi, all open (1/6-30/9). Bar (20/6-10/9). Half-court tennis. Table tennis. Boules. Minigolf. Volleyball. Badminton. Playground. Organised activities, main season. WiFi. Off site: Luz-St-Sauveur Jazz Festival in July, Internet (free). Paragliding near Barèges, cable car to the Pic du Midi observatory. Climbing, rafting, walking, winter skiing. Fishing 500 m. Bicycle hire 1 km. Riding 7 km. Golf 30 km.

Open: 1 June - 30 September.

Directions

From Lourdes take new N21 (Voie rapide) south, pass Argelès-Gazost continuing towards Luz-St-Sauveur on D921. Site is on left at Esquièze-Sere (just before Luz), proceed carefully, site entrance is well signed but congested at peak times. GPS: N42:52.961 W00:00.806

Charges guide

Per unit incl. 2 persons and electricity	€ 14,60 - € 25,50
extra person	€ 3,00 - € 5,00

Camping Cheques accepted.

FR65060 Castel Camping Pyrénées Natura

Route du Lac, F-65400 Estaing (Hautes-Pyrénées)

Tel: **05 62 97 45 44**. Email: **info@camping-pyrenees-natura.com**   www.alanrogers.com/FR65060

Pyrénées Natura, at an altitude of 1,000 m, on the edge of the National Park is the perfect site for nature lovers. The 60 pitches (46 for touring), all with electricity, are in a large, level, open and sunny field. Around 75 varieties of trees and shrubs have been planted – but they do not spoil the fantastic views. The reception and bar are in a traditional stone building with an open staircase. A small shop in the old water mill stocks a variety of produce and is unmanned and open all day – pay at reception.

Facilities

First class toilet blocks include facilities for disabled visitors and babies. Washing machine and airers (no lines allowed). Motorcaravan services. Small shop, takeaway (15/5-15/9). Small bar (15/5-15/9). Lounge, library, TV (mainly used for videos of the National Park). Sauna, solarium (free between 12.00-17.00). Music room. Play area for the very young. Small 'beach' beside river. Boules. Giant chess. Weekly evening meal in May, June and Sept. Internet. Off site: Village with two restaurants.

Open: 1 May - 20 September.

Directions

From Lourdes take N21 towards Argelès-Gazost, then exit 2, N2021/D21, into Argelès. Approaching town turn onto D918 towards Aucun. After 8 km, turn left on D13 to Bun, cross the river, then right on D103 to site (5.5 km). Narrow road, few passing places. GPS: N42:56.451 W00:10.631

Charges guide

Per unit incl. 2 persons and electricity (3A)	€ 15,50 - € 24,50
extra person	€ 5,25

FR65080 Kawan Village du Lavedan

Lau-Balagnas, F-65400 Argelès-Gazost (Hautes-Pyrénées)

Tel: **05 62 97 18 84**. Email: **contact@lavedan.com**   www.alanrogers.com/FR65080

Camping du Lavedan is an old established and very French site set in the Argelès-Gazost valley south of the Lourdes. It is beside the main road so there is some daytime road noise. The 105 touring pitches are set very close together on grass with some shade and all have electricity (2-10A). The area is fine for walking, biking, rafting and of course, in winter, skiing. There is a pool which can be covered in inclement weather and a twice weekly event is organised in July/Aug, weekly in June.

Facilities

Acceptable toilet block. Baby room. Facilities for disabled visitors. Washing machines and dryer in separate block heated in winter. Restaurant with takeaway and terrace (1/5-15/9). Bar, TV (all year). No shop, bread delivery (1/5-15/9). Swimming pool (with cover), paddling pool. Excellent play area. Internet (July/Aug). Boules, table tennis. Off site: Fishing or bicycle hire 1 km. Supermarket or rafting 2 km. Riding 5 km. Golf 15 km.

Open: All year.

Directions

From Lourdes take the N21 (Voie rapide) south, exit 3 (Argelès-Gazost). Take N2021, D921 or D21 towards Luz-St-Sauveur for 2 km. to Lau-Balagnas. Site on right, southern edge of town. GPS: N42:59.293 W00:05.340

Charges guide

Per unit incl. 2 persons	€ 15,00 - € 23,00
electricity (10A max)	€ 1,00
extra person	€ 4,50 - € 6,50

Camping Cheques accepted.

Check real time availability and at-the-gate prices...
www.alanrogers.com

FR65090 Camping Soleil du Pibeste

16 avenue du Lavedan, F-65400 Agos-Vidalos (Hautes-Pyrénées)

Tel: 05 62 97 53 23. Email: info@campingpibeste.com

www.alanrogers.com/FR65090

Soleil du Pibeste is a quiet, rural site with well tended grass and flower beds. It has 67 pitches for touring, all having electricity (3-15A) with some shade. The Dusserm family welcomes all arrivals with a drink and they are determined to ensure that you have a good stay. There is no shop but the supermarket is only five kilometres and ordered bread is delivered to your door daily. The swimming pool is on a terrace above the pitches, with sun beds, a paddling pool and waterfall and has the most magnificent view of the mountains.

Facilities

Two heated toilet blocks. Baby room. Facilities for disabled visitors (key). Cleaning can be variable. Washing machine, dryer. Motorcaravan services. Bar, snacks, piano, internet. Room for playing cards or reading. Swimming, paddling pools. Small play area. Boules. Archery. Bicycle hire. Tai Chi and other relaxation classes. Off site: Fishing 800 m. Golf 10 km. Rafting 2 km. Skiing 2 km.

Open: 1 May - 30 September.

Directions

Agos Vidalos is on the N21, 5 km. south of Lourdes. Leave express-way at second exit, signed Agos Vidalos and continue to site, a short distance on the right. GPS: N43:02.134 W00:04.256

Charges guide

Per unit incl. 2 persons and 3A electricity	€ 12,00 - € 24,00
extra person	€ 3,00 - € 5,00

FR65100 Camping le Moulin du Monge

Avenue Jean Moulin, F-65100 Lourdes (Hautes-Pyrénées)

Tel: 05 62 94 28 15. Email: camping.moulin.monge@wanadoo.fr

www.alanrogers.com/FR65100

A well organised, family run site with a friendly welcome, Moulin du Monge has a convenient location for visiting Lourdes, only 3 km. away. There will be some traffic noise from the nearby N21 and railway line. This attractive garden-like site has 57 grassy pitches in several different areas and on different levels. Some are in a level orchard area and are closest to the main road. A few pitches are on a little woodland knoll behind reception, with the remainder on a higher level at the back of the site. All have electricity hook-ups (2-6A).

Facilities

The heated toilet blocks have all necessary facilities, including washing machine and dryer. Facilities for campers with disabilities. Baby room. Motorcaravan services. Well stocked shop (15/6-20/9). Heated swimming pool, sliding cover (1/5-20/9), paddling pool. Games/TV room. Barbecue, terrace. Sauna. Boules. Playground, trampolines. Off site: Good transport links to the city centre with its famous grotto and all shops and services. Fishing 3 km. Golf 4 km. Bicycle hire 500 m.

Open: 1 April - 10 October.

Directions

Site is just off the N21 on northern outskirts of Lourdes. From north, on N21 (2 km. south of Adé) be prepared to take slip lane in centre of road. Turn left into Ave. Jean Moulin. Site shortly on left. GPS: N43:06.931 W00:01.895

Charges guide

Per unit incl. 2 persons	€ 14,40
incl. electricity (2-6A)	€ 16,40 - € 18,40
extra person	€ 4,80
child (0-7 yrs)	€ 3,00

FR65110 Camping Cabaliros

Pont de Secours, F-65110 Cauterets (Hautes-Pyrénées)

Tel: 05 62 92 55 36. Email: info@camping-cabaliros.com

www.alanrogers.com/FR65110

After driving up a steady incline through a sheer sided, tree lined valley, the terrain opens up just before you reach the town of Cauterets. Here you will find the delightful Camping Cabaliros where you will receive a warm and friendly welcome. With wonderful views, the site is owned by Jean and Chantal Boyrie and has been in the family since it was opened in 1959. There are four chalets for rent, 36 pitches without electricity (mainly for tents) and 60 pitches with 6A electricity (French sockets) for tourers. All of the touring pitches are on well manicured grass and those around the perimeter of the site are reasonably level with some shade provided by mature trees.

Facilities

Sanitary block near to site entrance with WCs, hot showers and washbasins in cubicles. Washing machine and dryer. Motorcaravan service point. Large library (mainly French) and excellent meeting room with televi-sion. Play area for over 7s. Fishing. Off site: Restaurant (July/Aug) 50 m. Supermarket 1 km. Shops, restaurants and bars 2 km. Riding 10 km.

Open: 1 June - 30 September.

Directions

From Lourdes head south on the N21 to Argelès-Gazost then take D921 followed by the D920 to Cauterets. Site is on right 1 km. after 'SHOPI' supermarket just before Cauterets. GPS: N42:54.100 W00:06.250

Charges 2009

Per unit incl. 2 persons and electricity (6A)	€ 15,60 - € 17,30
extra person	€ 4,30 - € 4,80

BOOK THIS SITE
CALL 01580 214000
...we'll arrange everything
The Travel Service

Check real time availability and at-the-gate prices...
www.alanrogers.com

FR65130 Camping Pyrenevasion

Route de Luz-Ardiden, Sazos, F-65120 Luz-Saint-Sauveur (Hautes-Pyrénées)

Tel: **05 62 92 91 54**. Email: **camping-pyrenevasion@wanadoo.fr** www.alanrogers.com/FR65130

In the heart of the Pyrénées, Camping Pyrenevasion is at a height of 830 m. on a picturesque hillside with panoramic views of the mountains and the town of Luz-St-Sauveur in the valley below. This family run site, where you will receive a warm and friendly welcome, has 60 well laid out, tidy touring pitches. On level, grassy terraces on the hillside which are partially shaded by young trees, each pitch has electricity (French sockets) adjacent and all are reasonably close to the modern heated sanitary block. There are 12 modern, comfortable chalets for rent (all year).

Facilities

Heated sanitary block with showers, WCs, washbasins (cubicles and open area). Facilities for disabled visitors. Baby bath. Washing machine and dryer. Motorcaravan services. Bread can be ordered at reception for next morning delivery. Bar (all year). Takeaway (1/6-1/10). Heated swimming and paddling pools (15/5-1/10). Small play area (up to 6 yrs). Sports area. Off site: Shops, restaurant and bar 2 km. Fishing 200 m. Riding 10 km. Golf 30 km. Skiing 10 km.

Open: All year.

Directions

From Lourdes take N21 south to Pierrefit-Nestalas then the D921 to Luz-St-Sauveur. Follow signs from Luz-St-Sauveur to Luz-Ardiden (D12). Site is on right as you enter the village of Sazos.
GPS: N42:52.970 W00:01.345

Charges guide

Per unit incl. 2 persons	€ 10,00 - € 16,00
extra person	€ 5,00
child (2-6 yrs)	€ 3,00
electricity (3-10A)	€ 3,50 - € 11,50

FR65140 Flower Camping Pène Blanche

F-65510 Loudenvielle (Hautes-Pyrénées)

Tel: **05 62 99 68 85**. Email: **info@peneblanche.com** www.alanrogers.com/FR65140

La Pène Blanche is spacious and well kept, in an idyllic location standing high over Lake Loudenvielle and surrounded by high mountains. There are 120 small, pitches which are not separated, 80 are for touring (40 with 5/10A electricity). The area is ideal for walking, hiking or biking in the mountains. An outdoor pool is just 200 m. away and nearby is the Balnea centre with its spa waters. The resorts of Val Louron and Peyragudes are within easy reach for skiing. For the very brave there is paragliding and hang-gliding or you can relax in the park to watch them gracefully coming in to land.

Facilities

Two toilet blocks, one traditional, one modern and heated including facilities for the campers with disabilities. Indoor dishwashing and laundry room with washing machine, dryer and ironing board. Children's play area. Off site: Restaurant, snack bar, bar and local shops all within 100 m. Cinema 200 m. Motorcaravan services 300 m. Within walking distance are the Balnea Centre with its spa water baths and adjacent swimming pool with waterslide. Tennis. Minigolf. Hiking. Mountain Biking. Paragliding. Hang gliding. Skiing.

Open: All year except November.

Directions

A64 Tarbes to Toulouse, exit junction 16, on D929 follow signs to Arreau, then D618 to D25 signed Loudenvielle.
GPS: N42:47.719 E00:24.517

Charges guide

Per unit incl. 2 persons	€ 11,50 - € 16,90
with electricity (5/10A)	€ 15,30 - € 21,90
extra person	€ 3,80 - € 5,10
child (0-7 yrs)	free - € 3,90

www.flowercampings.com

FR65180 Village Cévéo de Luz

Quartier Maoubèze, F-65120 Luz Saint Sauveur (Hautes-Pyrénées)

Parcs Résidentiels page 517

Tel: **05 62 92 84 72**. Email: **luz@ceveo.com** www.alanrogers.com/FR65180

The pitches at this campsite are used exclusively for mobile home and chalet accommodation.

Check real time availability and at-the-gate prices...

www.**alanrogers**.com

FR65160 Camping le Monlôo

Chemin du Monlou (RD8), F-65200 Bagnères-de-Bigorre (Hautes-Pyrénées)

Tel: **05 62 95 19 65**. Email: **campingmonloo@yahoo.com**   www.alanrogers.com/FR65160

A relatively small site of 120 pitches, Le Monlôo is set in a wide valley in the Pyrénées. The immediate surroundings of farmland, with crops growing and cows at pasture, give way to some magnificent views of the mountains towering away from the front of the site, whilst the back is right at the foot of some smaller foothills. This area is a paradise for walkers and cyclists and just traveling a short distance opens up new horizons with some large waterfalls not far away. The friendly family take their job seriously and will even show you the available pitches from the comfort of their electric car.

Facilities	Directions
Ample toilet facilities are provided in three blocks. Facilities for disabled visitors. Washing machines. Motorcaravan services. Bread to order. Open air heated pool with slide. Simple play area. Gas or electric barbecues are permitted. Off site: Spa town of Bagnères-de-Bigorre 2 km.	From the A64 take exit 14 signed Bagnères-de-Bigorre. Enter town and take D8 road to the right for Ordizan. Site is just a few hundred metres along this road, well signed. GPS: N43:04.908 E00:09.083

Open: All year.

Charges guide

Per unit incl. 2 persons	€ 11,00 - € 16,50
extra person	€ 3,50 - € 4,00
electricity (2-6A)	€ 2,00 - € 5,50

FR65170 Aire Naturelle de Camping l'Arrayade

Arrayade, F-65100 Ger (Hautes-Pyrénées)

Tel: **05 59 56 10 60**   www.alanrogers.com/FR65170

This unique little campsite, situated quite high up in the Pyrénées with some amazing views down the valley, could well be perfect for anyone seeking a relaxing, informal and friendly atmosphere. On a very small site of just 15 pitches, Mme. Pique is a gracious host who will do her utmost to ensure your stay is as pleasant as possible. She has prepared plenty of information on the local area, the best walks to go on and the cycle pathway that takes you into Lourdes centre in just 3 km. You can taste the freshness of the air up here and outdoor lovers will feel really at one with nature.

Facilities	Directions
One very modern toilet block situated in the reception area. Provision is adequate. All fittings are very new and the arrangement makes this area feel almost like a private bathroom. Washing machine and dryer. Small bar where breakfast and evening meals are served. Peaceful lounge. Sauna, jacuzzi and small gym. Internet access.	From Lourdes head south on the D921 signed Lugagnan. After 3 km. bear right on D13 for Ger. As you approach a few houses on your left the site entrance is on the right, set back a little in a lay-by. GPS: N43:03.463 W00:02.491

Open: 15 May - 15 September.

Charges guide

Per unit incl. 2 persons	€ 10,00
electricity	€ 2,50 - € 5,00

FR81070 Camping Rieu Montagné

Lac du Laouzas, F-81320 Nages (Tarn)

Tel: **05 63 37 24 71**   www.alanrogers.com/FR81070

Rieu Montagné is a delightful site in the heart of the Haut Languedoc Regional park and at the corner of the départements of the Tarn, Aveyron and Hérault. There are 127 touring pitches, mostly on broad terraces with reasonable shade, all with electrical connections (6/10A) and 56 fully serviced. A heated swimming pool overlooks the lake and is used for occasional aquagym. In high season there is a varied entertainment programme, and a number of guided walks. Most leisure facilities are available at the lakeside complex.

Facilities	Directions
The two toilet blocks, comprehensively refitted in 2005, provide mostly British style toilets, washbasins in cubicles and facilities for disabled people and babies. Laundry. Shop with basic provisions (July/Aug). Bar and snack bar with takeaway. Swimming pool (14/6-14/9). Entertainment programme (high season). Chalets, tents and mobile homes to let (53). Off site: Lakeside leisure complex.	Nages about 80 km. southeast of Albi. From Albi, D999 east towards St Affrique. 11 km. after Albon right, D607, to Lacaune. At T-junction left, D622, for 6.5 km. Right, D62, 2 km. South of town left over bridge, D162. First left uphill to site. GPS: N43:38.877 E02:46.888

Open: 12 June - 13 September.

Charges guide

Per unit with 2 persons and electricity	€ 17,80 - € 18,00
extra person	€ 4,80 - € 5,50
child (2-7 yrs)	€ 3,00 - € 3,50

BOOK THIS SITE
CALL 01580 214000
...we'll arrange everything
The Travel Service

387

FR81090 Camping le Manoir de Boutaric

Route de Lacabarède, F-81260 Anglès (Tarn)

Tel: 05 63 70 96 06. Email: manoir.boutaric@accesinter.com

www.alanrogers.com/FR81090

Le Manoir de Boutaric is a 19th-century château hidden deep in the Haut Languedoc countryside. The château lies in a attractive park and offers 110 touring pitches as well as a number of mobile homes and chalets. Pitches are spacious, well shaded and all have electrical connections (5A), as well as a water and drainage point. Leisure facilities include a swimming pool and paddling pool and the site also has an attractive restaurant. In high season, entertainment includes discos and film screenings in the château cellars. The village of Anglès-du-Tarn is just 100 m. from the site and has a good range of shops.

Facilities

Restaurant and bar. Takeaway. Swimming pool, paddling pool. Mountain bike hire. Entertainment in high season. Children's club (high season). Mobile homes and chalets for rent. Off site: Off site: Fishing, lake with private beach 6 km. Tennis, riding, golf nearby.

Open: 15 April - 30 October.

Directions

From Toulouse, take the westbound N126 to Castres and then the D622 to Brassac. From Brassac head southeast on the D68 to Angles. Site is well signed from the village. GPS: N43:33.668 E02:33.628

Charges guide

Per unit incl. 2 persons and electricity	€ 13,00 - € 26,00
extra person	€ 3,10 - € 5,50
child (0-5 yrs)	€ 1,60 - € 4,50

FR81100 Camping de la Rigole

Route de Barrage, F-81540 Les Cammazes (Tarn)

Tel: 05 63 73 28 99. Email: campings.occitanie@orange.fr

www.alanrogers.com/FR81100

A pleasant, traditional site with 64 pitches in a countryside location, La Rigole is partly wooded, and gives a friendly reception. A slightly sloping site, most of the 40 touring pitches are on small terraces and many have quite deep shade. All have electricity (4-13A). There is a small bar and a snack bar. One evening each week in main season a regional meal is organised. Small children are well catered for with play areas for tiny tots and under sevens, and a delightful children's farm with animals. The site is totally unsuitable for American RVs.

Facilities

Fairly modern toilet block. Baby room. Facilities for disabled campers (althought the slopes might be difficult). Washing machines, dryer. Small shop. Bar. Takeaway. Swimming pool. All open 15/4-15/10. Table tennis. Badminton. Volleyball. Boules. Small animal farm. Off site: Lac des Cammazes with its dam 400 m. Lac de St Ferréol 5 km., with large sandy beach. Fishing 0.4 km. Riding 1.5 km.

Open: 15 April - 15 September.

Directions

Les Cammazes is 25 km. northeast of Castelnaudary, 10 km. southeast of Revel. From Revel take D629 to Cammazes, continue on D629 through village, after 1 km. turn left towards Barrage (site signed), site entrance 200 m. on right. GPS: N43:24.472 E02:05.196

Charges 2009

Per unit incl. 2 persons and electricity	€ 15,85 - € 19,80

FR81130 Camping l'Amitié

Vallée du Tarn, F-81340 Trébas (Tarn)

Tel: 05 63 55 84 07. Email: amitie@trebas.net

www.alanrogers.com/FR81130

A winding road with wonderful views of the surrounding countryside leads down to the small unspoilt village of Trébas in the Vallée du Tarn, and there on the banks of the Tarn river lies the small friendly site of Camping L'Amitié. There are 60 level, well drained and manicured grass pitches, 49 of which are available for tourers. A few wooden chalets are also available to rent. All with electricity (French sockets), the pitches are on terraces which slope gently towards the riverbank and most have partial shading although some are in the open area close to the river.

Facilities

The toilet block is near the site entrance with Turkish and British style toilets, hot showers and washbasins in cubicles (cold water only). No shop. Bar/restaurant (1/5-15/9). Swimming pool (1/6-31/8). Play area. Some activities and entertainment in high season. Off site: Site is in small village with mini-supermarket, pharmacy, baker and butcher. Bar/restaurant 250 m. (July/Aug. only).

Open: 1 April - 15 September.

Directions

From Albi take D999 east (signed Millau). At Alban take D53 north to St Andre and Trébas. Cross river at Villeneuve sur Tarn to Trébas, the site is in the village and signed. GPS: N43:56.521 E02:28.902

Charges guide

Per unit incl. 2 persons	€ 8,30 - € 11,80
extra person	€ 2,80 - € 3,90
child (2-7 yrs)	€ 1,80 - € 2,60

Check real time availability and at-the-gate prices...
www.alanrogers.com

FR82040 **Flower Camping les Gorges de l'Aveyron**

Marsac bas, F-82140 Saint Antonin-Noble-Val (Tarn-et-Garonne)

Tel: **05 63 30 69 76**. Email: **info@camping-gorges-aveyron.com**   **www.alanrogers.com/FR82040**

This is a friendly, family site which is undergoing a process of renovation by its new owners, Stephane and Johanna Batlo. The site has an attractive wooded location, sloping down to the River Aveyron and facing the Roc d'Anglars. Reception and the two toilet blocks are housed in traditional, converted farm buildings. There are 80 pitches of which 65 are for touring units and these all have electrical connections (3-10A). The pitches are grassy and well shaded and may become very soft in times of poor weather. Some pitches are available close to the river but we would suggest that these are unsuitable for younger children as the river is unfenced. The owners have ambitious plans for the future and are planning to add a swimming pool and third toilet block. This is a very quiet site in low season and some amenities, notably the snack bar and shop are only available in the peak season. The nearby town of St Antonin-Noble-Val dates back to the eighth century and is just 1.5 km. from the site. The town is well worth a visit and has a good range of shops and restaurants.

Facilities

Two toilet blocks with washing machines and dryers. Small shop (June - Oct). Bar, snack bar and takeaway (April - Oct). Direct access to river. Fishing. Canoeing. Play area. Entertainment and activities in high season. Mobile homes for rent. Off site: St Antonin-Noble-Val with a wide choice of shops, restaurants and bars 1.5 km. Cordes-sur-Ciel 35 km. Bicycle hire 1.5 km. Riding 2 km. Many walking paths and cycle trails.

Open: 1 February - 30 November.

Directions

From the north, take exit 59 from the A20 autoroute joining the D926 and follow signs to St Antonin. Site can be found on the D115, 1.5 km. east of the town. GPS: N44:09.114 E01:46.290

Charges guide

Per pitch incl. 2 persons	
and electricity	€ 9,40 - € 16,30
extra person	€ 2,90 - € 5,00
child (under 7 yrs)	€ 1,60 - € 2,50

Les Gorges de l'Aveyron***
The soothing beauty of the extensive nature

New for 2008! Swimming pool

82140 St. Antonin Noble Val - Tel: 0033 (0)563 306 976 - Fax: 0033 (0)563 306 761
E-mail: info@camping-gorges-aveyron.com · www.camping-gorges-aveyron.com

FR82010 **Camping les Trois Cantons**

F-82140 Saint Antonin-Noble-Val (Tarn-et-Garonne)

Tel: **05 63 31 98 57**. Email: **info@3cantons.fr**   **www.alanrogers.com/FR82010**

Les Trois Cantons is a well established and very friendly family run with 100 pitches (85 for tourers) set among mature trees that give dappled shade. The pitches are of average size, reasonably level and all have electricity connections. The swimming pool is covered and heated in early and late season, with activities organised there in July and August. There are also walks, archery and boules, clay modelling plus wine tastings and a weekly dance. When the trees are bare early in the season, there could be a little road noise when the wind is in a certain direction.

Facilities

The two sanitary blocks include British and Turkish style WCs, showers, washbasins (some in cubicles) and facilities for disabled visitors, which have recently been refurbished. Laundry and dishwashing facilities. Very limited shop (bread daily). Bar serving snacks and takeaways. Swimming pool (heated from 15/5-30/9) and paddling pool. Games/TV room. Play area. Small farm area. Tennis. Volleyball. Boules. English spoken. Off site: Riding 1 km. Fishing 7 km. Many pretty medieval villages to visit.

Open: 15 April - 30 September.

Directions

From A20 or N20 at Caussade, take D926 signed Caylus and Septfonds. Site is signed to right 5 km. after Septfonds. Do not take the D5 towards St Antonin-Noble-Val as it involves 5 km. of narrow road. GPS: N44:11.580 E01:41.780

Charges guide

Per pitch incl. 2 persons	€ 14,50 - € 21,00
extra person	€ 4,55 - € 6,40
child (2-9 yrs)	€ 2,70 - € 4,20
electricity (2-10A)	€ 2,70 - € 6,80
Camping Cheques accepted.	

BOOK THIS SITE   CALL 01580 214000 ...we'll arrange everything   The Travel Service

389

www.flowercampings.com

Languedoc and Roussillon form part of the Massif Central. With its huge sandy beaches the mountainous Languedoc region is renowned for its long sunshine records, and the pretty coastal villages of Roussillon are at their most beautiful at sunset erupting in a riot of colour.

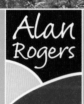

Alan Rogers

THIS SECTION COVERS THE SOUTH WEST COASTAL REGION OF THE MEDITERRANEAN, DÉPARTEMENTS: 11 AUDE, 30 GARD, 34 HÉRAULT, 66 PYRÉNÉES-ORIENTALES.

Once an independent duchy, the ancient land of Languedoc combines two distinct regions: the vineyards of the Corbières and Minervois and the coastal plain stretching from the Rhône to the Spanish border. Much of the region is rugged and unspoilt, offering opportunities for walking and climbing.

There is ample evidence of the dramatic past. Ruins of the former Cathar castles can be seen throughout the region. The walled city of Carcassonne with its towers, dungeons, moats and drawbridges is one of the most impressive examples of medieval France.

Today, Languedoc and Roussillon are wine and agricultural regions. Languedoc, with considerable success, is now a producer of much of the nation's better value wines. But above all, vast hot sandy beaches and long hours of sunshine make this a paradise for beach enthusiasts. La Grande Motte, Cap d'Agde and Canet, are all being promoted as an alternative to the more famous Mediterranean stretches of the Côte d'Azur.

Places of interest

Aigues-Mortes: medieval city.

Béziers: wine capital of the region, St Nazaire cathedral, Canal du Midi.

Carcassonne: largest medieval walled city in Europe.

Limoux: medieval town, Notre Dame de Marseilla Basilica, St Martin church.

Montpellier: universities, Roman sites; Gothic cathedral.

Nîmes: Roman remains, Pont du Gard.

Perpignan: Kings Palace; Catalan characteristics, old fortress.

Pézenas: Molière's home.

Villeneuve-lés-Avignon: Royal City and residence of popes in 14th century.

Cuisine of the region

Cooking is Provençal, characterised by garlic and olive oil with sausages and smoked hams. Fish is popular along the coast. Wines include Corbières, Minervois, Banyuls and Muscat.

Aïgo Bouido: garlic soup.

Boles de picoulat: small balls of chopped-up beef and pork, garlic and eggs.

Bouillinade: a type of *bouillabaisse* with potatoes, oil, garlic and onions.

Boutifare: a sausage-shaped pudding of bacon and herbs.

Cargolade: snails, stewed in wine.

Ouillade: heavy soup of *boutifare* leeks, carrots, and potatoes..

Touron: a pastry of almonds, pistachio nuts and fruit.

FR11030 Camping la Pinède

Rue des Rousillons, F-11200 Lézignan-Corbières (Aude)

Tel: **04 68 27 05 08**. Email: **reception@orange.fr**   www.alanrogers.com/FR11030

Within walking distance of the town and only 35 km. from Narbonne Plage, La Pinède is set on terraces on a hillside, with good internal access on made-up roads. The 90 individual, level pitches vary in size and are divided up mainly by various trees and shrubs with 6A electricity (17 mobile homes). The guardian organises weekly local wine tasting and local walks to show visitors what is growing in the garden and how plants can be used as natural remedies. Outside the gates are a municipal swimming pool (July/Aug), a disco, a restaurant and tennis courts.

Facilities

Three fully equipped sanitary blocks. Not all blocks are opened outside high season. Washing machine. Motorcaravan service point. Gas. Pleasant bar providing decently priced hot food (July/Aug). Fresh vegetables can be sampled from the garden (small charge). Communal barbecue (private barbecues are not permitted). Torches necessary. Caravan storage. Off site: Bicycle hire 1 km. Riding 3 km. Fishing 4 km.

Open: 1 March - 30 October.

Directions

Access is directly off the main N113 on west side of Lézignan-Corbières. From A61 (to avoid low bridge) exit at Carcassonne or Narbonne onto N113 and follow to site. GPS: N43:12.276 E02:45.156

Charges guide

Per person	€ 3,30 - € 4,50
child (under 10 yrs)	€ 2,10 - € 3,40
pitch	€ 6,00 - € 7,70
animal	€ 1,50

FR11240 LVL les Ayguades

Avenue de la Jonque, F-11430 Gruissan (Aude)

Tel: **04 68 49 81 59**. Email: **loisirs-vacances-languedoc@wanadoo.fr**   www.alanrogers.com/FR11240

Sites with direct access to the sea are popular, particularly those with a long season. Les Ayguades is situated between Gruissan Plage and Narbonne Plage and is overlooked by the Montagne de la Clape. The site is owned by an association which has recently updated the facilities and is committed to preserving the environment running the site with this in mind. There are 290 sandy pitches of various sizes, all with 10A electricity. The pitches are hedged and there is some shade. The site also has 70 chalets and mobile homes to rent, plus 15 privately owned. An upstairs restaurant has panoramic views of the sea.

Facilities

Three fully equipped toilet blocks, two with facilities for disabled people. Launderette. Motorcaravan service point. Shop, bar and takeaway (28/6-31/8). Restaurant (15/4-10/11). Play area and skate park. WiFi. Children's club, Evening entertainment in high season. Beach. Off site: Bicycle hire and riding 1 km.

Open: 15 March - 15 November.

Directions

From the A9 at exit 37 (Narbonne Est), follow the D32 then the D332 towards Gruissan, then Les Ayguades until you come to site signs. GPS: N43:07.962 E03:08.334

Charges guide

Per unit incl. 2 persons	€ 12,90 - € 19,70
incl. electricity	€ 16,50 - € 25,40
extra person	€ 4,10 - € 5,70
child (2-10 yrs)	€ 1,55 - € 2,40
pet	€ 2,10 - € 2,40

FR11020 Cottage Village Aux Hamacs

Parcs Résidentiels ▶ page 520

Route des Cabanes, F-11560 Fleury (Aude)

Tel: **04 68 33 22 22**. Email: **info@cottagevillage.fr**   www.alanrogers.com/FR11020

Pitches at this campsite are exclusively for mobile home and chalet accommodation.

Check real time availability and at-the-gate prices...
www.alanrogers.com

FR11040 Camping le Martinet Rouge Birdie

F-11390 Brousses-et-Villaret (Aude)

Tel: **04 68 26 51 98**. Email: **campinglemartinetrouge@orange.fr**   www.alanrogers.com/FR11040

Le Martinet Rouge provides a peaceful retreat in the Aude countryside to the north of Carcassonne. It is a small site where the owners have been working hard to improve the facilities. The most striking features of the site are the massive granite boulders (outcrops of smooth rock from the last ice age). The site offers 63 pitches for touring units, all with electricity (3/10A), in two contrasting areas – one is well secluded with irregularly shaped, fairly level, large pitches amongst a variety of trees and shrubs, while the other is on a landscaped gentle hill with mature trees.

Facilities

Four sanitary blocks of various ages, including facilities for disabled visitors, baby bathroom. Laundry facilities. Swimming pool and water slide (15/6-15/9). Small shop (no others locally). Bar, terrace, TV (1/7-15/9). Snack bar (1/7-31/8). Barbecue area. Fitness room. Croquet. Half court tennis. Multisport court. Small play area. Internet access. Off site: Tennis, riding and fishing quite close.

Open: March - November.

Directions

Site is best approached via D118, Carcassonne - Mazamet road. Turn onto D103 15 km. north of Carcassonne to Brousses-et-Villaret. Western outskirts of village turn south to site (signed) in 50 m. GPS: N43:20.350 E02:15.127

Charges guide

Per unit incl. 2 persons	€ 12,50 - € 18,00
extra person	€ 4,50 - € 5,50
No credit cards.	

FR11050 Camping Rives des Corbières

Avenue du Languedoc, F-11370 Port Leucate (Aude)

Tel: **04 68 40 90 31**. Email: **rivescamping@wanadoo.fr**   www.alanrogers.com/FR11050

Port Leucate is part of the major Languedoc development which took place during the sixties and seventies and it is now a thriving resort. The campsite is situated on the old coast road into Port Leucate between the Etang de Salas and the beach, 800 m. from the centre of the town and port and only 150 m. from the beach. A mixture of tall poplars and pine trees provide reasonable shade for the 305 pitches. On good-sized sandy plots, all have 6A electricity connections. About 90 are used for mobile homes. With no tour operators this is a good value site, essentially French.

Facilities

Four toilet blocks opened as required. Two have mainly Turkish toilets. Facilities for disabled people. Laundry room. Small supermarket, bar and takeaway (July/Aug). Swimming pools. Play area. Daytime games and tournaments and in the evening, live music, karaoke and dancing. Off site: Beach 150 m. (lifeguards July/Aug). Port 800 m. Watersports, tennis, riding and water park. African wildlife reserve at Sigean Fort at Salses.

Open: 1 April - 30 September.

Directions

From the A9 exit 40 follow signs for Port Leucate on D627 (passing Leucate village) for 14 km. Exit the D627 into Port Leucate village. Go right at roundabout into Ave du Languedoc and site is on right after 800 m. GPS: N42:50.009 E03:02.004

Charges guide

Per unit incl. 2 persons and electricity	€ 17,00 - € 21,00
extra person	€ 3,70 - € 4,70

FR11060 Yelloh! Village Domaine d'Arnauteille

F-11250 Montclar (Aude)

Tel: **04 66 73 97 39**. Email: **info@yellohvillage-domaine-arnauteille.com**   www.alanrogers.com/FR11060

Enjoying some beautiful and varied views, this site is ideal exploring the little known Aude Département and for visiting the walled city of Carcassonne. The site is set in farmland on hilly ground with the original pitches on gently sloping, lightly wooded land. Newer ones are on open ground, of good size, with water, drainage and electricity (5/10A), semi-terraced and partly hedged. Of the 198 pitches, 140 are for touring. The facilities are quite spread out with the pool complex set in a basin surrounded by fine views. Access could be difficult for large, twin axle vans.

Facilities

Toilet blocks, one with a Roman theme. Laundry, facilities for disabled people and a baby bath. Motorcaravan services. Small shop (15/5-30/9). Restaurant in converted stable block, takeaway (15/5-30/9). Swimming pool (25 m), paddling pool, river with water massage and sunbathing terrace. Boules. Play area. Riding (1/7-31/8). Off site: Fishing 3 km. Bicycle hire 8 km. Golf 10 km.

Open: 20 March - 3 October.

Directions

D118 from Carcassonne, pass Rouffiac d'Aude. Before the end of dual carriageway, turn right to Montclar up narrow road (passing places) for 2.5 km. Site signed very sharp left up hill before village. GPS: N43:07.636 E02:15.571

Charges guide

Per pitch incl. 2 persons	€ 14,00 - € 29,00
Camping Cheques accepted.	

tel: +33 466 739 739   www.yellohvillage.com ———— **yelloh!** VILLAGE

Check real time availability and at-the-gate prices...

www.**alanrogers**.com

FR11070 Kawan Village les Mimosas

Mobile homes ▶ page 509

Chaussée de Mandirac, F-11100 Narbonne (Aude)

Tel: **04 68 49 03 72**. Email: info@lesmimosas.com

www.alanrogers.com/FR11070

Six kilometres inland from the beaches of Narbonne and Gruissan, this site benefits from a less hectic situation than others by the sea. The site is lively with plenty to amuse and entertain the younger generation whilst offering facilities for the whole family. A free club card is available in July/Aug. to use the children's club, gym, sauna, tennis, minigolf, billiards etc. There are 250 pitches, 150 for touring, many in a circular layout of very good size, most with electricity (6A). There are a few 'grand confort', with reasonable shade, mostly from two metre high hedges. There are also a number of mobile homes and chalets to rent. This could be a very useful site offering many possibilities to meet a variety of needs, on-site entertainment (including an evening on Cathar history), and easy access to popular beaches. Nearby Gruissan is a fascinating village with its wooden houses on stilts, beaches, ruined castle, port and salt beds. Narbonne has Roman remains and inland Cathar castles are to be found perched on rugged hill tops.

Facilities

Sanitary buildings refurbished to a high standard. Washing machines. Shop and 'Auberge' restaurant (open all season). Takeaway. Bar. Small lounge, amusements (July and Aug). Landscaped heated pool with slides and islands (open 1 May), plus the original pool and children's pool (high season). New play area. Minigolf. Mountain bike hire. Tennis. Sauna, gym. Children's activities, sports, entertainment (high season). Bicycle hire. Multisports ground. Off site: Riding. Windsurfing/sailing school 300 m. Gruissan's beach 10 minutes. Lagoon, boating fishing via footpath (200 m).

Open: 21 March - 1 November.

Directions

From A9 exit 38 (Narbonne Sud) take last exit on roundabout, back over the autoroute (site signed from here). Follow signs La Nautique and then Mandirac and site (6 km. from autoroute). Also signed from Narbonne centre.
GPS: N43:08.197 E03:01.537

Charges guide

Per unit incl. 1 or 2 persons	€ 14,00 - € 23,30
incl. electricity	€ 17,50 - € 30,00
incl. water and waste water	€ 21,70 - € 34,00
extra person	€ 4,10 - € 6,50

Camping Cheques accepted.

Village-camping Les Mimosas

Discover the secret of successful holidays.

Nestling in the heart of lush greenery in the regional nature park, between the beaches of Gruissan and the Bages lagoon, Les Mimosas ensures pleasant holiday experience.
The 2000 m² water complex with 3 swimming pools, 4 waterslides, Jacuzzi, sauna, mini-golf, fitness centre, children games, restaurant, bar, grocery shop and the proposed animation in July and August offer long hours of fun and relaxation for all ages. Without forgetting the large choice of rentals and half shaded places.

A pitch for 3 weeks or longer*
For 2 persons with electricity
Longer period of stay

12,70 €/day
from 01/05 till 27/06 and from the 01/09 till 30/09/09

and **11,70 €/day**
from 24/03 till 30/04 and from 01/10 till 31/10/09

*non combinable offer

Un Air de Vacances, RCS Toulouse 2002 B 329

Les Mimosas VILLAGE-CAMPING
NARBONNE ★★★ MÉDITERRANÉE

INFORMATIONS-RESERVATION
Chaussée de Mandirac
11100 Narbonne - France
Tel. +33 (0)4 68 49 03 72
www.lesmimosas.com

BOOK THIS SITE

CALL 01580 214000

...we'll arrange everything

The Travel Service

FR11080 Camping la Nautique

Mobile homes ▶ page 509

La Nautique, F-11100 Narbonne (Aude)

Tel: 04 68 90 48 19. Email: info@campinglanautique.com

www.alanrogers.com/FR11080

Owned and run by a very welcoming Dutch family, this well established site has pitches each with individual sanitary units. It is an extremely spacious site situated on the Etang de Bages, where flat water combined with strong winds make it one of the best windsurfing areas in France. La Nautique has 390 huge, level pitches, 270 for touring, all with 10A electricity and water. Six or seven overnight pitches with electricity are in a separate area. The flowering shrubs and trees give a pleasant feel. Each pitch is separated by hedges making some quite private and providing shade. Entertainment is organised for adults and children from Easter to September (increasing in high season), plus a sports club for supervised surfing, sailing, rafting, walking and canoeing (some activities are charged for). The unspoilt surrounding countryside is excellent for walking or cycling and locally there is horse riding and fishing. English is spoken in reception by the very welcoming Schutjes family. This site caters for families with children including teenagers and is fenced off from the water for safety. Windsurfers can have a key for the gate (with deposit) that leads to launching points on the lake.

Facilities

Each pitch has its own fully equipped sanitary unit. Special facilities for disabled visitors. Laundry. Shop. Bar and restaurant, terrace, TV. Takeaway. All 1/5-30/9. Snack bar 1/7-31/8. Swimming pools, water slide, paddling pool. Play area. Tennis. Minigolf. Miniclub (high season). Games room. Internet. Only electric barbecues are permitted. Off site: Large sandy beaches at Gruissan (12 km) and Narbonne Plage (20 km). Narbonne 4 km.

Open: 15 February - 15 November.

Directions

From A9 take exit 38 (Narbonne Sud). Go round roundabout to last exit and follow signs for La Nautique and site, then further site signs to site on right in 2.5 km. GPS: N43:08.500 E03:00.140

Charges guide

Per person	€ 5,00 - € 7,50
child (1-7 yrs)	€ 3,00 - € 5,50
pitch incl. electricity, water and sanitary unit	€ 9,50 - € 22,00

Enjoy a luxury holiday!

Private sanitary facilities

LA NAUTIQUE
★ ★ ★ ★
CAMPING - CARAVANING NARBONNE

(+33) 04 68 90 48 19
www.campinglanautique.com

FR11110 Camping Val d'Aleth

F-11580 Alet-les-Bains (Aude)

Tel: 04 68 69 90 40. Email: camping@valdaleth.com

www.alanrogers.com/FR11110

In the gateway to the upper Aude valley, open all year round, this popular small site is run by Christopher and Christine Cranmer who offer a warm welcome. The mellow medieval walls of Alet-les-Bains form one boundary of the site, while on the other and popular with anglers, is the River Aude (fenced for safety). Beyond this is the D118 and a railway which produces noise at times. The 37 mainly small, numbered pitches, around half of which are on hardstandings, all have electricity hook-ups (4-10A) and are separated by hedges and mature trees which give shade.

Facilities

New bright toilet blocks, fully equipped and heated in winter. Facilities for disabled visitors. Washing machine and dryer. New reception with small shop, drinks, wine, beer, use of freezer. Small play area. Mountain bike hire. Internet. Off site: White water sports. The area is very popular with walkers and mountain-bikers. Bus and train services to Carcassonne and Quillan. Some shops and restaurants in town, full range at Limoux (10 km. north). Second weekend in June 'Fete de l'eau' in village (water festival with jazz, food and wine).

Open: All year.

Directions

From Carcassonne take D118 south for 32 km. Ignore first sign to Alet (to avoid narrow stone bridge) and after crossing the river, turn into town. Site is 800 m. on the left (signed). GPS: N42:59.682 E02:15.333

Charges guide

Per unit incl. 2 persons and electricity	€ 17,00 - € 19,00
extra person	€ 3,60
child (under 10 yrs)	€ 2,20
dog	€ 1,40

FR11250 Camping Côte Vermeille

Chemin des Vignes, F-11210 Port-La-Nouvelle (Aude)

Tel: **04 68 48 05 80**. Email: info@camping-cote-vermeille.com   www.alanrogers.com/FR11250

Port la Nouvelle is a traditional seaside resort with a long sandy beach, a large marina and a busy commercial port. Côte Vermeille is a member of the France Loc group and can be found close to the resort and 150 m. from the beach (with direct access). There are 300 pitches, of which around 200 are used for for touring units. These are of a reasonable size and generally well shaded. Most have electrical connections. A large new pool complex was added in 2008 and this features three pools as well as several large water slides and a paddling pool. There is plenty of activity here during the high season with a children's club (5-12 years) and daily aquagym and aerobics sessions. Although the beach and the campsite's pools are likely to be the main appeal here, there is much to see in the area. This includes the often filmed city of Carcassonne and the African safari park at Sigean. The Spanish border is around an hour's drive to the south. Port la Nouvelle is a lively resort with a good selection of restaurants and shops, as well as plenty of nightlife.

Facilities

Shop. Bar and snack bar. Takeaway. Swimming pool complex with paddling pool and water slides. Play area. Activity and entertainment programme. Mobile homes for rent. Off site: Beach 150 m. Port la Nouvelle 2 km. African safari park at Sigean 9 km. Narbonne 20 km.

Open: 15 June - 15 September.

Directions

Approaching from the north, leave the A9 at exit 39 and head east on the D6139 to Sigean and then Port la Nouvelle. Site is clearly signed. GPS: N42:59.880 E03:02.957

Charges guide

Per unit incl. 2 persons and electricity   € 21,50

CAMPINGS FranceLoc

COTE VERMEILLE **

Languedoc

Côte Vermeille is situated in the Languedoc Roussillon et Port-La-Nouvelle with his 13 km long fine, golden sandy beaches. In a warm family friendly environment you will be able to participate a great number of free activities. The fishing port and marina with their activities will guarantee Port-La-Nouvelle an authentic character.

Côte Vermeille
11210 Port la Nouvelle • Languedoc Roussillon
Tel.: +33 (0)4 68 48 05 80 • Email : infos@camping-cote-vermeille.com
www.campings-franceloc.fr

FR11210 Camping le Moulin de Sainte Anne

Chemin De Sainte-Anne, F-11600 Villegly-en-Minervois (Aude)

Tel: **04 68 72 20 80**. Email: campingstanne@wanadoo.fr   www.alanrogers.com/FR11210

Just a few years ago Le Moulin Sainte Anne was a vineyard but, with much hard work by Antoine and Magali Laclive and the backing of the Mairie, there is now a flourishing campsite on the edge of the town. There are 45 level grass pitches of a good size and hedged. All have water and electricity and are terraced where necessary and landscaped with growing trees and shrubs. The facilities are modern, well kept and in keeping with the area. They include a heated pool and a very attractive entertainment area. There is close co-operation with the village and villagers are welcome to the evening entertainment. A 'Sites et Paysages' member.

Facilities

A modern toilet block is very well equipped. Shared facilities for disabled visitors and babies. Washing machine. Motorcaravan service point. Bar, snack bar with takeaway (15/6-25/8). Heated swimming and paddling pools (1/5-30/9). Games room. Play area. Communal barbecue (no barbecues on pitches). Chalets to rent (15). Off site: Multisport pitch, tennis (free), fishing (licence from garage). Shops. Bus stop by bridge. Carcassonne 12 km. Golf 18 km. Bicycle hire 12 km.

Open: 1 March - 15 November.

Directions

Driving north from Carcassonne on D118 turn on D620 signed Villalier and Villegly for 7 km. Site is at entrance to village. Turn right over bridge just before the cemetery. GPS: N43:16.985 E02:26.491

Charges guide

Per person	€ 3,00 - € 4,40
child (under 13 yrs)	€ 1,90 - € 3,20
pitch incl. electricity	€ 6,20 - € 7,80
dog	€ 1,50 - € 2,00

FR11230 Yelloh! Village le Bout du Monde

Ferme de Rhodes, Verdun en Lauragais, F-11400 Castelnaudary (Aude)

Tel: **04 66 73 97 39**. Email: **info@yellohvillage-leboutdumonde.com**   www.alanrogers.com/FR11230

Le Bout du Monde can be found at the heart of the Montagne Noire, on the edge of the Haut Languedoc regional park. This small site is a member of the Yelloh! Village group and has 53 touring pitches with a further 27 pitches occupied by mobile homes. This is a very remote rural setting (hence the site's name!) with large, grassy pitches, a fishing lake and a stream rushing through the site. There is also a children's farm and riding stable. Farm produce is available for purchase.

Facilities

Shop. Restaurant (specialising in local cuisine). Takeaway meals. Swimming pool. Fishing lake. Archery. Sports field. Children's farm. Bicycle hire. Riding. Entertainment and activity programme. Mobile homes for rent.
Off site: Multisports pitch. GR7 long distance footpath. Haut Languedoc Regional Park. Sailing. Canoeing. 'Accrobranche' aerial assault course.

Open: 20 June - 14 September.

Directions

From the A61 take exit to Castenaudary. Here, take the D103 towards Saissac. Pass through St Papoul, turn left to join D803 to Verdun-en-Lauragais. Join northbound D903 and site is well signed. GPS: N43:22.603 E02:04.478

Charges guide

Per unit incl. 2 persons   € 17,00 - € 27,00

tel: +33 466 739 739 www.yellohvillage.com

FR30000 Kawan Village Domaine de Gaujac

Boisset-et-Gaujac, F-30140 Anduze (Gard)

Tel: **04 66 61 67 57**. Email: **gravieres@club-internet.fr**   www.alanrogers.com/FR30000

The 293 level, well shaded pitches include 175 for touring with electricity (4-10A) with 22 fully serviced. Access to some areas can be difficult for larger units due to narrow winding access roads, trees and hedges. Larger units should ask for lower numbered pitches (1-148) where access is a little easier. In high season this region is dry and hot, thus grass quickly wears off many pitches leaving just a sandy base. There are 12 special hardstanding pitches for motorcaravans near the entrance. The site has a new covered animation area and courtyard terrace.

Facilities

Heated toilet blocks include facilities for visitors with disabilities. Washing machines and dryer. Motorcaravan services. Good shop (2/6-27/8). Newsagent. Takeaway and crêperie (15/4-15/9). Bar, restaurant (15/4-15/9). New heated swimming, paddling pool (all season with lifeguard 5/7-15/8) and jacuzzi. Playground, sports field. Tennis. Minigolf. Only gas and electric barbecues.
Off site: Fishing 100 m. Bicycle hire 5 km. Riding, golf 8 km. River beach 70 km.

Open: 1 April - 30 September.

Directions

From Alès take N110 towards Montpellier. At St Christol-les-Alès fork right on D910 towards Anduze and in Bagard, at roundabout, turn left on D246 to Boisset et Gaujac. Follow signs to site in 5 km. GPS: N44:02.148 E04:01.455

Charges guide

Per unit incl. 2 persons	€ 15,00 - € 25,00
extra person	€ 4,50 - € 5,70
electricity (4-10A)	€ 3,00 - € 5,00

Camping Cheques accepted.

FR30020 Yelloh! Village la Petite Camargue

B.P. 21, F-30220 Aigues-Mortes (Gard)

Tel: **04 66 73 97 39**. Email: **info@yellohvillage-petite-camargue.com**   www.alanrogers.com/FR30020

This is a large, impressive site (553 pitches) with a huge swimming pool complex and other amenities to match, conveniently situated beside one of the main routes across the famous Camargue. The busy road is an advantage for access but could perhaps be a drawback in terms of traffic, although when we stayed overnight in season it was virtually silent. It offers a variety of good sized pitches, regularly laid out and with varying amounts of shade. There are 70 touring pitches (with 6/10A electricity) interspersed amongst more than 300 mobile homes and 145 tour operator pitches.

Facilities

Three toilet blocks provide modern facilities. Laundry facilities. Motorcaravan service point. Range of shops, bar/restaurant with pizzeria and takeaway. Hairdresser and beauty centre. Pool complex with jacuzzi. Play area and children's club. Ridings. Tennis. Bicycle hire. Quad bikes. Disco. Diving school. Off site: Fishing 3 km. Beach 3.5 km. with free bus service July/Aug. Golf 8 km.

Open: 26 April - 19 September, with all services.

Directions

From A9, exit 26 (Gallargues), towards Le Grau-du-Roi, site 18 km. Continue past Aigues-Mortes on D62, site is 2 km. on the right, just before large roundabout for La Grand-Motte and Le Grau-du-Roi junction. GPS: N43:33.766 E04:09.583

Charges guide

Per unit incl. 1 or 2 persons   € 17,00 - € 43,00

tel: +33 466 739 739 www.yellohvillage.com

Check real time availability and at-the-gate prices...
www.alanrogers.com

FR30060 Camping Domaine des Fumades

Les Fumades, F-30500 Allègre (Gard)

Tel: **04 66 24 80 78**. Email: **domaine.des.fumades@wanadoo.fr**   www.alanrogers.com/FR30060

Domaine des Fumades is a pleasant, busy site with a friendly atmosphere near the thermal springs at Allègre. The entrance as a whole has a very tropical feel with its banana plants and palm trees. The 230 pitches, 80 for touring, are large and level, all with 4A electricity. A variety of trees add privacy and welcome shade. Three pleasantly landscaped swimming pools have ample sunbathing space, bridges and new jacuzzis. This is a good area for walking, cycling, riding, climbing and fishing. Used by tour operators (80 pitches). Reception at the site is a joy to behold. Set in an attractive courtyard, within the farmhouse, it has a central fountain and masses of tubs and baskets of colourful flowers.

Facilities

Well appointed sanitary blocks with facilities for people with disabilities are well maintained but cleaning is variable. Laundry. Shop. Bar, restaurant, snack bar, takeaway. Barbecue areas. Swimming pools and sunbathing space. Large, well equipped and fenced playground. Games room. Tennis, volleyball and boules. Well planned animation and entertainment programme, designed to appeal to families. No barbecues. Off site: Riding 2 km.

Open: 14 May - 2 September.

Directions

From Alès take D16 through Salindres, continue towards Allègre, until signs for Fumades (and thermal springs) on the right. GPS: N44:11.123 E04:13.751

Charges guide

Per unit incl. 2 persons	
and electricity	€ 16,00 - € 30,00
extra person	€ 3,00 - € 7,00
child (under 7 yrs)	€ 2,50 - € 4,00
pet	€ 4,30

Domaine des Fumades

A beautiful oasis situated between the Ardeche and the Mediterranée. Chalets, mobile homes and pitches. Mini club during the season, swimming pools, Jacuzzis, heated indoor swimming pool.

Domaine des Fumades
30500 ALLEGRE
Tél : 33 (0) 466 24 80 78
Fax : 33 (0) 466 24 82 42
www.campings-franceloc.com

Gard

FR30030 Camping Abri de Camargue

320 route du Phare de l'Espiguette, Port Camargue, F-30240 Le Grau-du-Roi (Gard)

Tel: **04 66 51 54 83**. Email: **contact@abridecamargue.fr**   www.alanrogers.com/FR30030

This pleasant site has an attractive pool area overlooked by the bar with its outdoor tables on a pleasant sheltered terrace. The larger outdoor pool has surrounds for sunbathing and the smaller indoor one is heated. With 277 level pitches, there are 51 for touring units, mainly of 100 sq.m. (there are also smaller ones). Electricity and water are available on most, and the pitches are well maintained and shaded, with trees and flowering shrubs, quite luxuriant in parts. Recent additions include an air-conditioned cinema room and a club for children in high season.

Facilities

Well appointed toilet blocks and facilities for visitors with disabilities. Motorcaravan services. Shop. Bar, TV, restaurant, takeaway. Heated indoor pool, outdoor pool and paddling pool. Cinema. Entertainment programme. High quality play area. Children's club. Pétanque. New music room for young people in high season. Off site: Tennis 800 m. Riding, bicycle hire 1 km. Fishing 2 km. Golf 5 km. Nearest beach Port Camargue 900 m. L'Espiguette 4 km. (free bus passes the gate – July/Aug). Boat, surfboard hire nearby.

Open: 1 April - 30 September.

Directions

Site is 45 km. southwest of Nimes. From A9 autoroute, exit 26, Gallargues to Le Grau-du-Roi. From bypass follow signs Port Camargue and Campings. Then follow Rive gauche signs towards Phare l'Espiguette. Site is on right opposite Toboggan Park. GPS: N43:31.350 E04:08.947

Charges 2009

Per unit incl. 1 or 2 persons	
and electricity	€ 27,00 - € 56,00
incl. 3-5 persons	€ 32,00 - € 61,00
pet	€ 7,00
Campsite access card deposit of € 15.	

Check real time availability and at-the-gate prices...
www.alanrogers.com

FR30080 Kawan Village le Mas de Reilhe

F-30260 Crespian (Gard)

Tel: **04 66 77 82 12.** Email: **info@camping-mas-de-reilhe.fr**   www.alanrogers.com/FR30080

This is a comfortable family site nestling in a valley with 95 pitches (76 for touring), most have electricity (6/10A), some also have water and waste water and some of the upper ones may require long leads. The large lower pitches are separated by tall poplar trees and hedges, close to the main facilities but may experience some road noise. The large terraced pitches on the hillside are scattered under mature pine trees, some with good views, more suited to tents and trailer tents but with their own modern sanitary facilities. The heated pool is in a sunny position overlooked by the attractive bar/restaurant. There are no shops in the village, the nearest being at the medieval city of Sommières 10 km. away (and well worth a visit). From here you can explore the Cevennes gorges, enjoy the Mediterranean beaches or visit the Petite Camargue or Nîmes with its Roman remains. The entertainment in July and August is for children with just the occasional competition for adults.

Facilities

Good toilet facilities with washbasins in cabins and pre-set showers. Dishwashing and laundry sinks. Washing machine. Reception with limited shop (bread can be ordered). Bar (6/4-23/9), takeaway and restaurant (1/6-15/9). Small play area on grass. Pentaque. Heated swimming pool (all season). Internet access (WiFi on each pitch on payment). Motorcaravan services. Off site: Tennis 500 m. Fishing 3 km. Riding 5 km. Bicycle hire 10 km. Golf 25 km. The sea and the gorges are about 30 km. and Nîmes 25 km.

Open: 4 April - 20 September.

Directions

From the A9 take exit Nîmes -ouest signed Alès, then onto the D999 towards Le Vigan. The site is on the N110 just north of the junction with the D999 at the southern end of the village of Crespian. GPS: N43:52.759 E04:05.783

Charges guide

Per unit incl. 2 persons	€ 14,00 - € 20,00
extra person	€ 3,50 - € 5,50
child (2-6 yrs)	€ 2,00 - € 3,50
electricity (6/10A)	€ 3,30 - € 4,30
Camping Cheques accepted.	

LE MAS DE REILHE ★★★★

Camping Caravaning

"Situated between the Cevennes Mountains and the Mediterranean sea, a small charming & shaded camp site in the sun". Mobil-homes, chalets and bungalows A. Trigano to rent.

- Heated swimming-pool 140 m²(4/4 - 20/9)
- Restaurant, pizzeria & takeaway (1/6 - 13/9)
- Animations for children (July - August)
- New heated sanitary blocks

Tél : 0033 466 77 82 12 - Fax : 0033 466 80 26 50
E-mail : info@camping-mas-de-reilhe.fr
Website : www.camping-mas-de-reilhe.fr

FR30040 Flower Camping Mas de Mourgues

Gallician, F-30600 Vauvert (Gard)

Tel: **04 66 73 30 88.** Email: **info@masdemourgues.com**   www.alanrogers.com/FR30040

This is an English-owned campsite on the edge of the Petite Camargue region, popular with those who choose not to use the autoroutes. It can be hot here, the Mistral can blow and you may have some road noise, but having said all that, the previous owners and the present owners, the Foster family, have created quite a rural idyll. There are 80 pitches with 70 for touring and 62 with 10A electricity. Originally a vineyard on stony ground, some of the vines are now used to mark the pitches, although many other varieties of trees and shrubs have been planted.

Facilities

Two small toilet blocks provide for all needs. Facilities for disabled visitors. Washing machine. Motorcaravan service point. Chips and panini to takeaway. Reception keeps essentials and bottled water. Bread to order (evening before). Communal barbecue but gas or electric ones are allowed. Apartments, mobile homes and tents to rent. Off site: Fishing 2 km. (licence not required). Riding 8 km. Golf 20 km. Bicycle hire and boat launching 25 km. Beach 27 km.

Open: 1 April - 30 September.

Directions

Leave A9 autoroute at exit 26 (Gallargues) and follow signs for Vauvert. At Vauvert take N572 towards Arles and St Gilles. Site is on left after 4 km. at crossroads for Gallician. GPS: N43:39.450 E04:17.660

Charges guide

Per unit incl. 2 persons	€ 13,00 - € 16,00

BOOK THIS SITE
CALL 01580 214000
...we'll arrange everything

The Travel Service

www.flowercampings.com

Check real time availability and at-the-gate prices...

www.alanrogers.com

FR30140 Camping la Soubeyranne

Route de Beaucaire, F-30210 Remoulins (Gard)

Tel: **04 66 37 03 21**. Email: **soubeyranne@franceloc.fr**   www.alanrogers.com/FR30140

Owned by the group FranceLoc, this site is well positioned for visiting the Pont du Gard, Nîmes and Uzès, famed for their Roman connections. It is approached by a short tree-lined avenue which leads to reception. The 217 pitches offer extremely generous amounts of shade and keeping the six hectares watered involves over five kilometres of hosepipe. The touring pitches, of which there are 126, are large, level, numbered and separated, and all have 6A electricity connections. An animation programme (July/Aug) is aimed mainly at young children (teenagers may find the site rather quiet). Whilst quiet in some respects, train noise both by day and night can be an irritant.

Facilities

Two well appointed, unisex toilet blocks are basic but clean and give more than adequate facilities and include washbasins in cubicles. Motorcaravan service point. Fridges for hire. Small shop selling basics. Restaurant, bar and takeaway (all 31/3-6/9) – menu not extensive but adequate and moderately priced. Heated swimming pool complex (31/3-6/9) with 20 x 10 m. pool and smaller toddlers' pool (unsupervised), and partly shaded. Play area including trampoline. Infatable castle. Minigolf. Boules. Tennis. Bicycle hire. Off site: Fishing 1 km. Remoulins 1.5 km.

Open: 31 March - 6 October.

Directions

From Uzès take D981 to Remoulins, turn right at lights over river bridge, left at roundabout, then left (signed D986 Beaucaire). Site is 1.5 km. further on left. GPS: N43:55.320 E04:33.470

Charges guide

Per unit incl. 2 persons	€ 14,80 - € 24,00
electricity	€ 4,00
extra person	€ 4,60 - € 7,00
child (under 7 yrs)	€ 2,50 - € 4,20
animal	€ 4,15 - € 4,30

Camping Cheques accepted.

Domaine de La Soubeyranne

Shady pitches, mobile homes, heated indoor pool, waterslides, paddling pool, volleyball, table tennis, boules, mountain biking, entertainment.

Route de Beaucaire
30210 Remoulins
Tél. 0033(0)4 66 37 03 21
Fax. 0033(0)4 66 37 14 65
www.campings-franceloc.com

Gard

FR30070 Castel Camping le Château de Boisson

Boisson, F-30500 Allègre-les-Fumades (Gard)

Tel: **04 66 24 82 21**. Email: **reception@chateaudeboisson.com**   www.alanrogers.com/FR30070

Château de Boisson is a quiet family site within easy reach of the Cévennes, Ardèche or Provence. Reception at the entrance is new, light and cool, built from the stone in the local style. The site is hilly so the pitches are on two levels, many of which slope slightly and all have 5A electricity. Five have personal bathrooms. Rock pegs are essential. Trees provide some shade. The large attractive swimming pool with a slide and paddling pool is at the castle in a sunny location and there is also an indoor pool (all season) of excellent quality.

Facilities

Refurbished, clean and well maintained toilet blocks. Washing machines, baby room, facilities for visitors with disabilities. Small shop. Good restaurant, bar, snacks (all season). Play area. Indoor (all season) and outdoor pools (1/5-29/9). Bridge tournaments in low season. Painting classes. Tennis. Boules. Internet. WiFi. Animation in July and Aug for 4-12 yr olds, outdoor competitions for adults. Appartments to rent in the castle. Barbecues are not permitted. Dogs are not accepted.

Open: Easter - 29 September.

Directions

From Alès take D16 northeast towards Salindres and Auzon. After Auzon turn right across river, immediately left, signed Barjac and site. Shortly turn right, site signed. Only route for trailers and motorcaravans. Do not drive through the village of Boissons. GPS: N44:12.551 E04:15.400

Charges guide

Per unit incl. 2 persons and electricity	€ 19,00 - € 33,00
incl. water and drainage	€ 22,00 - € 37,00
incl. private sanitary unit	€ 25,00 - € 40,00
dog (not allowed 7/7-18/8)	€ 3,20

Check real time availability and at-the-gate prices...
www.alanrogers.com

FR30160 Camping Caravaning le Boucanet

B.P. 206, F-30240 Le Grau-du-Roi (Gard)

Tel: **04 66 51 41 48**. Email: **contact@campingboucanet.fr**   www.alanrogers.com/FR30160

On the beach between La Grande Motte and Le Grau-du-Roi. Many trees have been planted and are growing but as yet most are not tall enough to give much shade. As to be expected, the 458 pitches are sandy but level. The 317 for touring are separated by small bushes, most with electricity (6A). Plenty of flowers decorate the site and the pleasant restaurant (open lunchtimes and evenings) overlooks the large pool (heated at beginning and end of season). An excellent shopping arcade provides groceries, fruit, newspapers, a butcher and cooked meats, rotisserie and pizzas. In July and August organised activities include games, competitions, gymnastics, water polo and jogging for adults. There is access to the river for fishing and horse riding on the white horses of the Camargue is to be found within a few kilometres.

Facilities

The toilet blocks include facilities for disabled people. Baby rooms. Laundry facilities. Fridge hire. Motorcaravan services. Range of shops. Restaurant (1/5). Takeaway (June to end Aug). Bar, snacks. Large swimming pool, paddling pool. Play area on sand. Miniclub in July/Aug. Tennis. Bicycle hire. Dogs are not accepted. Off site: Riding 500 m. Golf 1.5 km. Shops, restaurants and bars within 3 km.

Open: 7 April - 7 October.

Directions

Site is between La Grande Motte and Le Grau-du-Roi on the D255 coastal road, on the seaward side of the road. GPS: N43:33.258 E04:06.424

Charges guide

Per unit incl. 2 persons	€ 17,00 - € 34,00
electricity	€ 3,50 - € 3,70
pitch on first row of beach, plus	€ 5,00 - € 6,00
extra person	€ 6,00 - € 8,70
child (under 7 yrs)	€ 4,50 - € 7,70

Camping Cheques accepted.

CAMPINGS FranceLoc

Domaine du Boucanet

Pitches, mobile homes, heated swimming pool (1 indoor pool), many sports and leisure activities during the season on this family site ideal for relaxation!

B.P. 206
30240 Le Grau du Roi
Tél. 0033(0)4 66 51 41 48
Fax. 0033(0)4 66 51 41 87
www.campings-franceloc.com

Méditerranée

FR30120 Campéole Ile des Papes

Barrage de Villeneuve, F-30400 Villeneuve-lez-Avignon (Gard)

Tel: **04 90 15 15 90**. Email: **ile.papes@wanadoo.fr**   www.alanrogers.com/FR30120

Quite a new site, Camping Ile des Papes is large, open and very well equipped. Avignon and its Palace and museums are 8 km. away. The site has an extensive swimming pool area and a fishing lake with beautiful mature gardens. The railway is quite near but noise is not too intrusive. The 450 pitches are of a good size on level grass and all have electricity, 150 taken by mobile homes or chalets. Games and competitions for all ages are organised in high season.

Facilities

Toilet blocks of very good quality include baby rooms. Washing machines. Motorcaravan services. Well stocked shop (limited hours in low seasons). Bar and restaurant. Two large swimming pools and one for children. Play area. Lake for fishing. Archery, tennis, minigolf and basketball (all free). Bicycle hire. Off site: Riding 3 km.

Open: 25 March - 20 October.

Directions

From Avignon take N100 Nîmes road towards Bagnoles-sur-Cèze, after crossing Rhône turn right. Turn left along river bank, follow signs for Roquemaure (D980). After 6 km. turn right on D228, signed Barrage de Villeneuve, site is 1 km. GPS: N43:58.596 E04:47.664

Charges guide

Per unit incl. 2 persons	€ 16,00 - € 23,00
extra person	€ 4,50 - € 6,30
child (2-5 yrs)	free - € 3,70
electricity (6A)	€ 3,90

Various special offers.

FR30180 Camping Mas de la Cam

Route de Saint-André de Valborgne, F-30270 Saint Jean-du-Gard (Gard)

Tel: 04 66 85 12 02. Email: camping@masdelacam.fr   www.alanrogers.com/FR30180

Camping Mas de la Cam is rather unusual in that all the pitches are used for touring. It is a very pleasant and spacious site with well trimmed grass and hedges and a profusion of flowers and shrubs. Lying alongside the small Gardon river, the banks have been left free of pitches giving neat grass for sunbathing and some trees for shade, whilst children can amuse themselves in the water (no good for canoes). Slightly sloping, the 200 medium to large pitches are on level terraces, some with varying amounts of shade, electricity (6A). There is no evening entertainment. Nearby one can walk in the footsteps of Robert Louis Stevenson (Travels with a Donkey), ride on a steam train, explore the deep underground caverns, visit a giant bamboo forest and explore the region by foot, on bike or by car. Entrance is via a narrow unfenced bridge, but wide enough for large outfits. Nine gîtes for rent in beautiful old farmhouse. A quiet, family site; you are assured of a good welcome here (English is spoken).

Facilities

High quality toilet blocks also provide a baby bath and facilities for disabled visitors. Washing machines. Bar/restaurant, terrace. Small shop. Attractive large swimming (heated) and paddling pools. Huge play and sports areas, multisport court for football, volleyball and basketball. Club, used in low season for bridge, in high season as games room. Fishing. Off site: St Jean-du-Gard (3 km.) with shops, market. Bus twice a day. Riding 5 km. Bicycle hire 15 km.

Open: 28 April - 20 September.

Directions

Site is 3 km. northwest of St Jean-du-Gard in direction of St André de Valborgne on D907, site signed, fork left, descend across a narrow unfenced bridge to site. Site entrance not accessible from north. GPS: N44:06.741 E03:51.246

Charges guide

Per unit incl. 2 persons	€ 14,00 - € 23,00
incl. electricity	€ 17,00 - € 27,00
extra person	€ 3,30 - € 5,70
child (under 7 yrs)	free - € 3,80

camping mas de la cam ★★★
F-30270 St Jean du Gard
Cévennes
www.masdelacam.fr

FR30150 Camping les Sources

Route de Mialet, F-30270 Saint Jean-du-Gard (Gard)

Tel: 04 66 85 38 03. Email: camping-des-sources@wanadoo.fr   www.alanrogers.com/FR30150

This is a lovely, small, family run site situated in the foothills of the beautiful Cévennes. There are 92 average to good sized, slightly sloping pitches on small terraces with 80 used for touring units, all with electricity (6/10A). They are separated by a variety of flowering shrubs and trees offering good shade. Near the entrance is the attractive reception, bar, restaurant and terrace overlooking the swimming pools and play area. In May, June and September a pottery and stone polishing workshop can be arranged locally. The emphasis here is on a quiet family holiday with little organised activity.

Facilities

Two well appointed, modern toilet blocks with washbasins in cabins and special facilities for babies and disabled visitors. Washing machine. Motorcaravan service point. Bar/restaurant with takeaway and small shop. Good swimming and paddling pools (from late May). Games/TV room. Play area. Barbecues are not permitted. Occasional children's activities and family evening meals. Off site: St Jean-du-Gard 1.5 km. Bus service to Nîmes and Alès a few times daily. Fishing and bathing 1.5 km. Riding 12 km. Bicycle hire 14 km. Golf 20 km.

Open: 1 April - 30 September.

Directions

From Alès take D907 through Anduze to St Jean-du-Gard. Take the ring road (autre directions) towards Florac. Turn right at traffic lights on D983, then right onto D50. Very shortly, on sharp right bend, fork right (site signed) and descend to site. Take care not to overshoot the entrance, as access is impossible from the north. GPS: N44:06.843 E03:53.523

Charges guide

Per unit incl. 2 persons	€ 13,00 - € 19,00
incl. electricity	€ 14,50 - € 22,00
extra person	€ 3,20 - € 4,50

Check real time availability and at-the-gate prices...

www.alanrogers.com

FR30190 Camping International des Gorges du Gardon

Chemin de la Barque Vieille, F-30210 Vers-Pont-du-Gard (Gard)

Tel: 04 66 22 81 81. Email: camping.international@wanadoo.fr   www.alanrogers.com/FR30190

Probably the main attraction in the Gardon area of France is the Pont du Gard, an amazing Roman aqueduct built around 50AD. It provides 200 level, mostly good-sized pitches, 180 for touring. Many are on stony terraces in a woodland setting offering good shade while others are more open, all with electricity (10-15A). Rock pegs are essential. There is direct access to the river where swimming is permitted, although in summer the water level may be a little low. Attractive, heated swimming and paddling pools (unsupervised) provide an alternative. The owners, Joseph and Sylvie Gonzales speak a little English, and visitors will receive a warm and friendly welcome. Joseph previously owned a restaurant and we highly recommend his site restaurant. Tourist information is in the reception and Sylvie will share her local knowledge if you need any additional help. There are other attractions worthy of a visit, such as the medieval village of Castillon-du-Gard perched on a rocky peak with narrow cobbled streets, and Collias at the bottom of the gorge from where you can hire canoes.

Facilities

Two toilet blocks provide facilities for visitors with disabilities. Baby room. Washing machine, dishwashing and laundry sinks. Bar and good restaurant (table service and takeaway). Heated swimming, paddling pools (unsupervised). Play areas. Games room and TV. Organised family entertainment during July/Aug. Canoeing arranged. Off site: Many old towns and villages with colourful markets (Uzès Saturday 10 km). Historic cities of Nîmes and Avignon. Good area for walking and cycling.

Open: 15 March - 31 October.

Directions

Exit A9 at Remoulins, then take D981 towards Uzès. About 4 km. after Remoulins, just after the junction for the Pont du Gard, turn left, site signed and follow signs to site (a few hundred metres). GPS: N43:57.446 E04:30.902

Charges guide

Per unit incl. 2 persons	€ 12,50 - € 18,50
extra person	€ 4,00 - € 6,50
child (under 7 yrs)	€ 2,70 - € 4,00
electricity	€ 3,20

FranceLoc CAMPINGS

gorges du gardon

Provence

This campsite at the riverbank of the Gardon with a somewhat rural charm offers you a beach and shady marked pitches. An oasis of peace, shade in the vicinity of a river. An excellent holiday destination for tourists and families.

Gorges du Gardon
30210 Vers Pont-du-Gard • Provence
Tel.: +33 (0)4 66 22 81 81 • Email : camping.international@wanadoo.fr
www.campings-franceloc.fr

FR30290 Castel Camping Domaine de Massereau

Les Hauteurs de Sommieres, route d'Aubais, F-30250 Sommieres (Gard)

Tel: 04 66 53 11 20. Email: info@massereau.fr   www.alanrogers.com/FR30290

A member of the Castels group, de Massereau was opened in August 2006 and is set within a 50 hectare vineyard dating back to 1804. There are now 120 pitches, with 75 available for touring units. Pitch sizes range from 150-250 sq.m. but the positioning of trees on some of the pitches severely limits the useable space. There is an attractive pool complex and a wide range of leisure facilities for all ages. The restaurant offers a reasonable range of good value cuisine and there is a well stocked shop including the vineyard's wines. Good English is spoken.

Facilities

The modern toilet block incorporates excellent facilities for children and disabled visitors. Laundry area. Motorcaravan service point. Well stocked shop and newspapers. Restaurant. Bar. Pizzeria and outdoor grill. Takeaway. Heated swimming pool with slide. New sauna, steam bath and jacuzzi. Play area. Trampoline. Minigolf. Bicycle hire. Fitness trail. Pétanque. Short tennis. TV room. Barbecue hire. Cooker and fridge hire. Gas. WiFi. Charcoal barbecues are not allowed. Off site: Fishing 3 km. Riding 3 km. Golf 30 km. Sailing 30 km.

Open: 27 March - 15 November.

Directions

From the south on A9 take exit 27 and D12 towards Sommieres. Site is 5 km. on right. From the north, there is a width and weight restriction in Sommieres. To avoid this remain on the N110 and then take the N2110 into Sommieres, crossing the river and turn right onto the D12. Site is on left in 1 km. GPS: N43:46.614 E04:05.574

Charges guide

Per unit incl. 2 persons	€ 15,00 - € 31,00
extra person	€ 3,00 - € 9,00
electricity (16A)	€ 4,00 - € 6,20

Check real time availability and at-the-gate prices...

www.alanrogers.com

FR30200 Camping Cévennes-Provence

Corbés-Thoiras, F-30140 Anduze (Gard)

Tel: **04 66 61 73 10**. Email: castelrose@wanadoo.fr   www.alanrogers.com/FR30200

Whenever a new guest arrives at this spectacular and family owned site, one of the seven members of the family takes time to drive the visitors around to enable them to choose what best suits them. From a place on river bank, to the highest pitch some 330 feet higher, the emphasis is on calmness and tranquillity. There are 250 pitches on the various levels, 200 with electricity (3-15A). The river is very popular for swimming and in a separate section for enjoying the rough and tumble of a small 'rapids'. There are no activities arranged on site but the family will spend time with any visitor who wishes to explore off site, perhaps negotiating a discount on their behalf. There is a special area, away from the main site, where teenagers can safely 'let off steam'. This is easily accomplished in the 30 hectares of this natural and unusual site. The site lighting is turned off at 22.30, to encourage people to retire quietly. Young children can enjoy one of the best and most comprehensive play areas we have seen. The family's ethos is perhaps summed up in the way that shrub beds in the minigolf area are sown with culinary herbs, which guests are encouraged to cut and use, at no cost.

Facilities

The 10 toilet blocks are excellent with modern equipment and are kept exceptionally clean and a new sanitary facility is planned for 2009. Good facilities for visitors with disabilities. Large and well stocked shop. Restaurant, takeaway and bar (26/4-15/9). Comprehensive play area. Minigolf. River bathing and fishing. Internet and WiFi. Off site: Bicycle hire 3 km. Riding 4 km. Golf 10 km. Adventure and discovery park on opposite bank of river offering many sports facilities.

Open: 20 March - 1 November.

Directions

From Anduze on the D907 take D284 alongside the river. Site is signed on right about 3 km. from the town. Take care on the approach – there is a narrow lane for 100 m, then a narrow bridge to cross, but visibility is good. GPS: N44:04.666 E03:57.883

Charges 2009

Per unit incl. 2 persons,	
vehicle and electricity	€ 16,20 - € 25,30
extra person	€ 3,30 - € 5,90
child (2-12 yrs)	€ 2,30 - € 4,90

Camping-Caravaning "CEVENNES-PROVENCE"

Open from 20/03 to 01/11

At your service for 50 years...

Calm, shaded
Places with open view
Fishing, pedestrian path
Swimming in river:
direct access and private beach

Corbès - Thoiras F30140 Anduze Gard ☎: 00 334 66 61 73 10 www.camping-cevennes-provence.fr

FR30360 Camping Castel Rose

610 chemin de Recoulin, F-30140 Anduze (Gard)

Tel: **04 66 61 80 15**. Email: castelrose@wanadoo.fr   www.alanrogers.com/FR30360

Spacious and wooded, Le Castel Rose campsite stretches for more than a kilometre along the banks of one of France's most beautiful rivers, the Gardon d'Anduze. The site's long, private river beach is protected from the currents of the river by an artificial breakwater. The site is set away from the busy main road and at night all you will hear is the sound of the water. The pretty town of Anduze is just a 15 minute walk from the site where you can admire and buy its world famous pottery.

Facilities

Five toilet blocks with open style washbasins, private cabins and spacious shower cubicles. Baby bath and children's toilets. Washing machines and dryers. Bar and restaurant with terrace. Games room. Children's club (July/Aug). Fishing, swimming, and canoeing in the river. Play area. Boules. Multisports area. Off site: Anduze with small shops, cafés, crafts. Nearby supermarkets. Steam train. Bamboo forest of La Bambouseraie. Riding 2 km.

Open: 8 April - 16 September.

Directions

From Alès take the N110 (D6110) towards Sommières, then the D910a to Anduze. From the village follow signs for St Jean du Gard and then site. There is a viaduct over this road and shortly after a sign on the right: 'Chemin de Recoulin'. Here turn sharp right. GPS: N44:03.833 E03:58.617

Charges guide

Per unit incl. 2 persons	€ 10,80 - € 13,20
extra person	€ 2,80 - € 3,60
electricity (6A)	€ 2,95
No credit cards.	

403

Check real time availability and at-the-gate prices...

www.alanrogers.com

BOOK THIS SITE
CALL 01580 214000
...we'll arrange everything
The Travel Service

The Travel Service

BOOK THIS SITE
CALL 01580 214000
...we'll arrange everything

FR30230 Camping le Val de l'Arre

Route du Pont de la Croix, F-30120 Le Vigan (Gard)

Tel: 04 67 81 02 77. Email: valdelarre@wanadoo.fr   www.alanrogers.com/FR30230

Camping Val de l'Arre is situated along the Arre river, a tributary of the Herault river, and in the centre of the Cevennes National Park. The site is well managed by M. & Mme. Triaire and his Dutch wife, who between them speak English, Dutch and Spanish, as well as French. There are 180 pitches, 156 for touring of which most have electricity (10A). On well drained grass, there is shade from deciduous trees. There is a pleasant swimming pool with an outdoor bar. A pebble beach at the river bank provides opportunities for play and fishing enthusiasts will certainly also appreciate the river. There are numerous possibilities for outdoor activities such as white water rafting, canoeing or mountain biking. Qualified guides may take you on mountain expeditions on foot or by bicycle. The nearby Les Grottes des Demoiselles, are some of France's foremost caves. There is also the chance to taste the great wines of the Herault region.

Facilities

Three toilet blocks are well spaced around the site. Washbasins, both open style and in cabins, and controllable showers. Facilities for babies and disabled visitors. Washing machines. Shop, open air bar with snacks and restaurant (all 1/6-31/8). Swimming and paddling pools (1/6-31/8). Boules. Play area. Guided walks organised. Off site: Bicycle hire 2.5 km. Riding 8 km. Golf 25 km.

Open: 1 April - 30 September.

Directions

Coming from A75 (Millau - Beziers) leave at exit 48 and follow D7 and D999 to Le Vigan. From Montpellier take D986 to Ganges, then D999 to Le Vigan. Site is signed in the town. GPS: N43:59.524 E03:38.244

Charges guide

Per unit incl. 2 persons	€ 12,50 - € 16,00
extra person	€ 3,50 - € 5,00
child (2-7 yrs)	€ 2,50 - € 3,00
electricity	€ 3,50

Le Val de l'Arre ★★★

Cosy and shady family campsite in the south of the Cevennes region, situated at the Arre riverside. Many walking paths are close at hand for a day trip or excursion. We offer a swimming pool, modern sanitary facilities, a playground, WIFI, shop and a snack bar/restaurant with terrace. Mobile homes for rent. All ready to give you a relaxing and comfortable holiday.

Le Val de l'Arre - Route Du Pont de la Croix - Roudoulouse - 30120 Le Vigan
Tel: 0033 467 810 277 - Fax: 0033 467 817 123
E-mail: valdelarre@wanadoo.fr - www.valdelarre.com

FR30370 Camping Domaine de l'Abeiller

F-30500 Saint Victor-de-Malcap (Gard)

Tel: 04 66 24 15 27. Email: campinglabeiller@wanadoo.fr   www.alanrogers.com/FR30370

Domaine de l'Abeiller is a well equipped family site at the edge of the Cevénnes National Park. There are 216 pitches with 132 for touring, some rather stony with oak trees giving dappled shade. Others are more grassy, with less shade. Most have electricity (6A). There are some mobile homes and chalets for rent. The pool complex is impressive with several pools, a paddling pool, jacuzzi and a water slide for young children. Canoeing and swimming are possible in the nearby river and canoe trips are organised on both the Ceze and Ardèche rivers. A few activities and competitions are organised in high season.

Facilities

Two well appointed, modern toilet blocks and several smaller blocks with all necessary facilities including those for campers with disabilities and children. Large shower cubicles with washbasins. Small shop. Bar, restaurant and takeaway (all 7/6-30/8). Swimming pool complex (1/5-30/9). Excellent play area. TV room. WiFi. A little entertainment and activities in high season. Mobile homes and chalets for rent. Off site: Small supermarket in St Victor. St Ambroix 3 km. Tennis 400 m. River for fishing and bathing 800 m. Bicycle hire 3 km. Riding 12 km.

Open: 1 May - 30 September.

Directions

Laeve Alès northeast on the D904, signed Aubinas. After about 20 km, in the cenre of St Ambroix, turn right on the D51, signed St Victor-de-Malcap. Bypass the village on the D51 and shortly turn left into site. GPS: N44:14.498 E04:13.645

Charges guide

Per unit incl. 2 persons	€ 13,50 - € 27,00
extra person	€ 3,00 - € 6,00
child (under 7 yrs)	€ 2,25 - € 4,50
electricity	€ 4,00

Check real time availability and at-the-gate prices...

www.alanrogers.com

FR30380 Yelloh! Village les Secrets de Camargue

Route de l'Espiguette, F-30240 Le Grau-du-Roi (Gard)

Tel: **04 66 73 97 39**. Email: info@yellohvillage-secrets-de-camargue.com   www.alanrogers.com/FR30380

Les Secrets de Camargue is a recent addition to the Yelloh! Village group, best described as 'stylish and elegant'. It has the unusual feature that it is reserved for over 18s and for families with children under three years old. In total there are 177 pitches with 25 for touring units on level sandy grass (all with 6A electricity, water and waste water). The majority of pitches are for mobile homes and chalets with the unusual feature of thatched roofs. The heart of the site is the Lodge Club which faces the pool and the surrounding sand dunes.

Facilities	Directions
Fully equipped sanitary block includes facilities for visitors with disabilities. Small shop. Restaurant. Bar. Takeaway. Swimming pool. Aquagym. Activities and entertainment. Mobile homes and chalets for rent. Off site: Nearest beach 1.5 km. Riding 1 km. Fishing 2 km. Golf 3 km.	Leave the A9 at exit for Gallargues and head for Aigues Mortes on the D979. Continue to Le Grau-du-Roi and then follow signs to Port Camargue on the D62, continuing to join the D255. Site is well signed from this point. GPS: N43:29.242 E04:08.521
Open: 19 April - 5 October.	**Charges guide**
	Per unit incl. 2 persons € 17,00 - € 43,00

www.yellohvillage.com tel: +33 466 739 739

FR30390 Yelloh! Village les Petits Camarguais

F-30240 Le Grau-du-Roi (Gard)

Tel: **04 66 73 97 39**. Email: info@yellohvillage-petits-camarguais.com   www.alanrogers.com/FR30390

Les Petits Camarguais is sister site to FR30020 and FR30380 and is also a member of the Yelloh! Village group. There are some 220 pitches here, all for mobile homes or chalets, with a good range of facilities including an impressive pool complex with slides, whirlpools and a balneotherapy spa. The facilities are all of of a high quality and there are lots of organised activities for children during the day, and entertainment for adults during the evenings. In high season there is a free shuttle to the nearest beach (1.8 km), L'Espiguette, reputedly the largest French Mediterranean beach.

Facilities	Directions
Mobile homes and chalets for rent. Shop. Bar. Restaurant. Takeaway food. Swimming pool complex with slides, paddling pools and a balneotherapy spa. Activity and entertainment programme. Off site: Beach 1.8 km. (free shuttle in peak season). Riding. Sea fishing. Golf. Casino.	Leave the A9 at the Gallargues exit and head for Aigues Mortes on the D979. Continue to Le Grau du Roi and then follow signs to Port Camargue on the D62, continuing to join the D255b. The site is well signed from this point. GPS: N43:30.508 E04:08.732
Open: 5 April - 19 September.	**Charges 2009**
	Contact the site for charges.

www.yellohvillage.com tel: +33 466 739 739

FR34030 Camping International le Napoléon

Avenue de la Méditérranée, F-34450 Vias-Plage (Hérault)

Tel: **04 67 01 07 80**. Email: reception@camping-napoleon.fr   www.alanrogers.com/FR34030

Le Napoléon is a smaller, family run site in the village of Vias-Plage bordering the Mediterranean. Vias-Plage is hectic to say the least in season, but once through the security barrier and entrance to Le Napoléon, the contrast is marked – tranquility, yet still only a few yards from the beach and other attractions. It has a Californian style pool, amphitheatre for entertainment and other new facilities, but thoughtful planning and design ensure that the camping area is quiet. With good shade from many tall trees, the 239 mainly small, hedged pitches (134 for touring) most have electricity.

Facilities	Directions
Sanitary blocks are of a reasonable standard. Baby bath. Facilities for disabled visitors. Laundry. Motorcaravan services. Fridge hire. Supermarket. Bar. Restaurant/pizzeria. Heated swimming pool with lively piped music. Fitness room with new equipment. Sauna, sun room. Bicycle hire. Tennis, archery, boules. TV. Rooms for young campers. Children's club. Amphitheatre, wide range of free entertainment until midnight. Disco outside site (Easter - Sept). Off site: Shops, restaurants, and laundry adjacent. Fishing 100 m. Riding 800 m. Golf 6 km.	From autoroute take exit for Vias. From town, take D137 towards Vias-Plage. Site is on the right near the beach; watch carefully for turning between restaurant and shops. GPS: N43:17.508 E03:24.991

Charges guide

Per unit incl. 2 persons and electricity	€ 19,00 - € 39,00
extra person (over 4 yrs)	€ 6,00 - € 7,00
dog	€ 3,50 - € 4,00

Show this guide for special rate
(€ 15 for 2 persons) outside July/Aug (2009).

Open: 4 April - 30 September.

405

FR34020 Camping le Garden

44 place des Tamaris, F-34280 La Grande Motte (Hérault)

Tel: **04 67 56 50 09**. Email: **campinglegarden@orange.fr**

www.alanrogers.com/FR34020

Le Garden is a mature site, situated 300 m. back from a fine sandy beach and with all the choice of sports, entertainment and other facilities of the popular holiday resort of La Grand Motte. With space for 86 caravans and 118 mobile homes, the 100 sq.m. pitches are hedged with good shade on sandy/grass base. All have electricity (10A), water and waste water drains. The fine sandy beach and port are only 300 m. away, with a shopping complex, bar and restaurant next to site.

Facilities

Three well situated toilet blocks, smartly refurbished in Mediterranean colours, include washbasins in cabins and baby bath. Laundry facilities. Unit for disabled visitors. Shop to one side of the site with groceries, cigarettes, newspapers, boutique, etc, restaurant, bar and takeaway service (from 15/5). Swimming pool and paddling pool (from 15/5). Children's play area. Off site: Tennis courts, riding club, casino and a nightclub nearby.

Open: 1 April - 15 October.

Directions

Entering La Grande Motte from D62 dual-carriageway, keep right following signs for 'campings' and petite Motte. Turn right at traffic lights by the Office de Tourism and right again by the Bar Le Garden and site almost immediately on right. GPS: N43:33.793 E04:04.367

Charges guide

Per unit incl. 1-3 persons	€ 27,50
incl. electricity, water and drainage	€ 37,50
extra person	€ 9,00

Bracelet required for pool € 10.

CAMPING ★ ★ ★ ★
LE GARDEN
LA GRANDE MOTTE
www.legarden.fr

FR34090 Camping Caravaning Domaine de la Yole

B.P. 23, F-34350 Valras-Plage (Hérault)

Tel: **04 67 37 33 87**. Email: **info@campinglayole.com**

www.alanrogers.com/FR34090

A busy happy holiday village with over 1,100 pitches could seem a little daunting. There are 590 pitches for touring. Most pitches are of a good size, all are level, hedged and have electricity, water and waste water points and, very importantly for this area, they all have shade. The extensive pool area is attractive with lots of sunbathing areas and the impressive activities are located in a central area. The beach, a long stretch of beautiful sand, is 500 m. and here is trampolining, paragliding and jet-skis. This is a busy site with something for all the family.

Facilities

Well maintained toilet blocks include baby rooms. Facilities for families and/or disabled visitors. Washing machines, dryers. Motorcaravan service points. Fridge hire. Shops. Good restaurant, terrace, amphitheatre for daily entertainment (in season). Two large pools, paddling pool (all season). Full and half size tennis courts. Multisports court. Play areas. Children's club. Boules. Internet. Off site: Fishing or riding 2 km. Beach 500 m, path from site.

Open: 25 April - 19 September.

Directions

From A9 autoroute take Béziers Ouest exit for Valras-Plage (13-14 km) and follow Casino signs. Site is on left, just after sign for Vendres-Plage. GPS: N43:14.242 E03:15.695

Charges guide

Per unit incl. 2 persons	€ 18,00 - € 37,35
extra person	€ 5,70 - € 6,30
child (7-16 yrs)	free - € 3,75
child (under 7 yrs)	free - € 1,90
dog	free - € 3,50

FR34110 Yelloh! Village le Club Farret

Mobile homes ▶ page 510

F-34450 Vias-Plage (Hérault)

Tel: **04 66 73 97 39**. Email: **info@yellohvillage-club-farret.com**

www.alanrogers.com/FR34110

Well maintained and with welcoming, helpful staff, everywhere is neat and tidy. It is a large, busy site but the atmosphere is very relaxed. There are 756 good size, level, grassy pitches, with 370 for touring with 6A electricity. And there is some shade from many trees. The large heated pool has lots of sunbathing room. The safe beach is alongside the site so some pitches have sea views. There is a wide range of entertainments and the activities include an extensive art programme. The campsite restaurant is high above the pool with views of the sea, everything is open all season. This superb site of excellent quality has been developed by the Giner family with love and care over the last 40 years. There is no advance booking for the touring pitches – they say that they rarely turn anyone away and will give details of availability. If you wish you can try your hand at catamaran sailing or windsurfing – free of charge for one hour. Activities include pottery, silk painting, mosaics and water colours. The mobile home areas are very smart, and have been attractively landscaped, with African or Balinese themes. A new area for mobile homes is 'vehicle free'. Tour operators occupy 15% of the mobile home pitches in the older areas.

Facilities

Very clean toilet blocks, children's toilets, baby rooms, facilities for disabled visitors. Washing machines. Dog shower. Well stocked supermarket. Hairdresser. Bars with pizzas, snacks, takeaway. Restaurant. Heated swimming pool complex. Excellent play area. Miniclub (5-10 yrs). Teenagers' club (11-15 yrs). Tennis. Archery. Programme of games. Multisports court. Bicycle hire. Off site: Riding 1 km. Golf 10 km. Sailing and windsurfing on beach.

Open: 2 April - 26 September.

Directions

Site is south of Vias at Vias-Plage. From the N112 (Béziers - Agde) take D137 signed Vias-Plage. Site is signed on the left. GPS: N43:17.462 E03:25.147

Charges guide

Per unit incl. 1 or 2 persons	€ 14,00 - € 44,00
extra person	€ 6,00 - € 8,00
extra tent	€ 3,00
pet	€ 3,00

www.yellohvillage.com tel: +33 466 739 739

L'Esprit de Famille

At Club Farret, the family spirit is allowed free rein. The high quality pitches and accommodations set among tenderly cared-for flowery gardens ensure that you will have a pleasant stay in a comfortable home-from-home.

From April to September, everyone can choose their own leisure activities and take full advantage of the pleasures of the pool that is heated in cooler weather, and of course of the beach that is only a stone's throw away. **Request our brochure as soon as possible by e-mail, telephone or letter!**

OPEN FROM 2ND APRIL TO 26TH SEPTEMBER 2009

Le Club Farret - 34450 VIAS PLAGE
Tel. : +33 (0)4 67 21 64 45 - Fax : +33 (0)4 67 21 70 49
E-mail : farret@wanadoo.fr - www.farret.com

Check real time availability and at-the-gate prices...
www.alanrogers.com

FR34070 Yelloh! Village le Sérignan Plage

Mobile homes ▶ page 509

Le Sérignan Plage, F-34410 Sérignan (Hérault)

Tel: 04 66 73 97 39. Email: info@yellohvillage-serignan-plage.com   www.alanrogers.com/FR34070

With direct access onto a superb 600 m. sandy beach (including a naturist section) and with three swimming pools and another planned for next year, this is a must for a Mediterranean holiday. It is a friendly, family orientated site with perhaps the most comprehensive range of amenities we have come across. The enthusiastic owners, Jean-Guy and Catherine continually surprise us with their unique style and new developments. A collection of spa pools (balnéo) built in Romanesque style with colourful terracing and columns, overlooked by a very smart restaurant 'Le Villa' is the 'piece de resistance'. The balnéo spa is shared with the adjoining naturist site (under the same ownership). Having recently acquired an adjacent site, there are now over 1,000 pitches with 400 available for touring units and this is now a pretty large campsite. The touring pitches vary in size and in terms of shade and are mainly on sandy soil, all with electricity. There are over 300 mobile homes and chalets to let, plus some 400 privately owned units. The heart of the site developed in the local Catalonian style is some distance from reception and is a busy and informal area with shops, another good restaurant, the Au Pas d'Oc, an indoor pool and a super roof-top bar. A range of entertainment is provided for adults and children in the evenings.

Facilities

Several modern blocks of individual design with good facilities including showers with washbasin and WC. Facilities for disabled people. Baby bathroom. Launderette. Motorcaravan services. Supermarket, bakery and newsagent (all season). Other shops (1/6-15/9). ATM. Restaurants, bar and takeaway. Hairdresser. Balneo spa. Gym. Heated indoor pool. Outdoor pools (24/4-21/9). Children's clubs. Evening entertainment. Sporting activities. Bicycle hire. Bus to Sérignan village July/Aug. Beach (lifeguards 1/6-15/9). Off site: Riding 2 km. Golf 10 km. Sailing and windsurfing school on beach.

Open: 23 April - 27 September.

Directions

From A9 exit 35 (Béziers Est) follow signs for Sérignan, D64 (9 km). Before Sérignan, turn left, Sérignan Plage (4 km). At small sign (blue) turn right. At T-junction turn left over small road bridge and after left hand bend. Site is 100 m.
GPS: N43:15.838 E03:19.260

Charges guide

Per unit incl. 1 or 2 persons and 6A electricity	€ 14,00 - € 44,00
extra person	€ 5,00 - € 8,00
pet	€ 3,00 - € 4,00

Low season offers.

tel: +33 466 739 739 www.yellohvillage.com ────────

yelloh! VILLAGE

FR34130 Kawan Village le Neptune

46 boulevard du St Christ, F-34300 Agde (Hérault)

Tel: 04 67 94 23 94. Email: info@campingleneptune.com   www.alanrogers.com/FR34130

Camping Neptune is a rare find in this area. This small, family run site with only 165 pitches makes a delightful change. The pitches are mostly separated by flowering bushes, with some shade, most with 6/10A electricity. The Fray family are welcoming and, even though in a busy area, this site is an oasis of calm, suited to couples and young families. Alongside the D32 there may be a little daytime road noise. The swimming pool is in a sunny position overlooked by the bar. The only entertainment is in high season and is a twice weekly miniclub for children.

Facilities

Two toilet blocks provide roomy pre-set showers, washbasins in cabins, three cold showers for hot weather. Laundry facilities. Small shop and bar (both 15/5-30/9). Heated swimming pool heated, bracelets required. Field for sports. Boat mooring facility on the River Hérault across the road. Only one dog allowed. No barbecues. Off site: Beach 1.5 km. Golf and riding 1.5 km.

Open: 1 April - 30 September.

Directions

From A9 exit 34 follow signs for (Agde, Bessau, Vias), then Cap d'Agde. Exit for Grau d'Agde. At roundabout (with statue) follow signs for Grau d'Agde, and again at second roundabout (left). Keep straight on to fifth roundabout where left and under bridge. Site is 600 m. on left.
GPS: N43:17.882 E03:27.377

Charges guide

Per unit incl. 2 persons	€ 16,80 - € 24,20
incl. electricity	€ 18,90 - € 28,90
extra person	€ 4,70 - € 5,60
child (under 7 yrs)	€ 2,35 - € 2,80

Camping Cheques accepted.

Check real time availability and at-the-gate prices...

www.alanrogers.com

Le Sérignan Plage

The magic of the Mediterranean

Imagine – hot sunshine, blue sea, vineyards, olive and eucalyptus trees, alongside a sandy beach – what a setting for a campsite – not just any campsite either !

With three pool areas, one with four toboggans surrounded by sun bathing areas, an indoor pool for baby swimmers plus a magnificent landscaped, Romanesque spa-complex with half Olympic size pool and a superb range of hydro-massage baths to let you unwind and re-charge after the stresses of work.

And that's not all – two attractive restaurants, including the atmospheric "Villa" in its romantic Roman setting beside the spa, three bars, a mini-club and entertainment for all ages, all add up to a fantastic opportunity to enjoy a genuinely unique holiday experience.

Le Sérignan-Plage - F-34410 SERIGNAN
Tel: 00 33 467 32 35 33 - Fax: 00 33 467 32 26 36
info@leserignanplage.com - www.leserignanplage.com

CAMPING VILLAGES
yelloh! VILLAGE

FR34150 Yelloh! Village les Méditerranées

262 avenue des campings, F-34340 Marseillan-Plage (Hérault)

Tel: **04 66 73 97 39**. Email: **info@yellohvillage-mediterranees.com**   www.alanrogers.com/FR34150

Marseillan Plage is a small, busy resort east of Cap d'Adge and it enjoys a super position immediately beside a long gently shelving sandy beach. It is a good quality site set under tall trees with neat hedges separating the 520 pitches (370 for tourers), on sandy soil all having water and electricity (6A). Many newer pitches and the hardstanding pitches have little shade. Amenities and facilities are generally of excellent quality and include a strikingly attractive bar area overlooking the beach with a raised stage for entertainment. This is a well run, family owned site with lots to offer.

Facilities	Directions
Impressive toilet blocks. Facilities for disabled visitors. Motorcaravan services. Shop. Bar, restaurant. Swimming pool complex, slides, Jacuzzi, paddling pools (all season). Play area. Fitness centre. Multisport court. Watersports. Weekly films, games, competitions, dances. WiFi. Miniclub. Bicycle hire. Off site: Shops at Charlemagne across the road. Riding, bicycle hire 500 m. Golf 5 km.	From A9 autoroute exit 34, follow N312 to Agde then take N112 towards Sete. Watch for signs to Marseillan Plage from where site is well signed. GPS: N43:18.522 E03:32.501

Open: 25 April - 27 September.

Charges guide

Per unit incl. 2 persons, water	€ 14,00 - € 44,00
extra person (over 1 yr)	€ 6,00 - € 8,00

tel: +33 466 739 739 www.yellohvillage.com

FR34180 Camping la Borio de Roque

Route de la Salvetat, F-34220 Saint Pons-de-Thomières (Hérault)

Tel: **04 67 97 10 97**. Email: **info@borioderoque.com**   www.alanrogers.com/FR34180

La Borio de Roque is a peaceful site in a very rural location hidden in a wooded valley four kilometres from St Pons. It lies at the end of a one and a half kilometre rough track but it is well worth the effort and it is set around a lovely restored farmhouse with the outbuildings made into four very attractive gites. The 25 large, individually shaped, terraced pitches have 10A electricity and some shade. Some are private to which the owners will escort you. When the site was developed, many different varieties of trees were planted which has created a very attractive environment.

Facilities	Directions
Toilet block, baby bath. Use of large freezer. Bread all season. Local wine, coffee and tea. Swimming pool (from 1/6). Small fishing lake. Small grassy play area. Barbecue areas. Not suitable for American motorhomes. Off site: Bicycle hire 5 km. Golf and riding 20 km. Beach 50 km.	St Pons-de-Thomières is on the N112 northwest of Béziers. Site is 4.5 km. north of the town on the D907 signed Salvetat, on the right on a bend, then 1.5 km. on a rough track (signed). GPS: N43:30.656 E02:44.789

Open: 15 May - 15 September.

Charges guide

Per person	€ 3,50 - € 4,50
pitch incl. electricity	€ 12,75 - € 14,25
No credit cards.	

FR34190 Kawan Village les Champs Blancs

Route de Rochelongue, F-34300 Agde (Hérault)

Tel: **04 67 94 23 42**. Email: **champs.blancs@wanadoo.fr**   www.alanrogers.com/FR34190

Les Champs Blancs is set in high trees, two kilometres from both Agde and the sea in a shady environment. The 169 level, sandy, touring pitches are bordered with bushes and plenty of trees, all with 10A electricity and 60 have private sanitary cabins. Mobile homes occupy separate areas. The pool area has been augmented by a super irregular pool, with toboggans, cascade, jacuzzi, bridges and palms but retaining the original pool and paddling pool. There are tennis courts and other leisure facilities. Games, shows and competitions are arranged in July and August. The area nearest the road is bordered by trees to deaden possible road noise.

Facilities	Directions
Refurbished toilet blocks, unit for disabled visitors, 60 en-suite private cabins containing WC, shower and washbasin. Washing machines and dryers. Motorcaravan services. Well stocked shop (high season, bread only in low season). Bar (from 1/6). Restaurant (20/6-15/9). Swimming complex (from 8/4 depending on weather). Good play area. Minigolf. Tennis. Multisport court. Off site: Riding 1 km. Golf 1.5 km. Beach 2 km.	From A9 exit 34, follow N312 for Agde, joins N112 Béziers - Sète road. Cross bridge over river, take first turn signed Rochelongue, turn right, next left, then next left (signed Agde). Site on left. GPS: N43:17.821 E03:28.528

Open: 8 April - 30 September.

Charges guide

Per pitch incl. 2 persons	€ 20,00 - € 41,00
incl. individual sanitary facilities	€ 23,00 - € 48,00
extra person	€ 10,00
Camping Cheques accepted.	

Check real time availability and at-the-gate prices...

www.**alanrogers**.com

FR34220 Camping la Creole

74 avenue des Campings, F-34340 Marseillan-Plage (Hérault)

Tel: **04 67 21 92 69**. Email: **campinglacreole@wanadoo.fr**   www.alanrogers.com/FR34220

This is a surprisingly tranquil, well cared for small campsite in the middle of this bustling resort that will appeal to those seeking a rather less frenetic ambience typical of many sites in this area. Essentially a family orientated site, it offers around 110 good-sized, level grass pitches, all with 6A electricity and mostly with shade from trees and shrubs. It also benefits from direct access to an extensive sandy beach and the fact that there is no swimming pool or bar actually contributes to the tranquillity. It may even be seen as an advantage for families with younger children. The beach will be the main attraction here no doubt, and the town's extensive range of bars, restaurants and shops are all within a couple of minutes walk.

Facilities	Directions
Toilet facilities are housed in a traditional building, modernised inside to provide perfectly adequate, if not particularly luxurious facilities including some washbasins in private cabins, a baby room and dog shower. Small play area. In high season beach games, dances, sangria evenings etc, are organised, all aimed particularly towards families. Barbecue area. Bicycle hire. Off site: Local market day Tuesday. Riding 1 km.	From A9 exit 34 take N312 towards Agde, then N112 towards Sète keeping a look-out for signs to Marseillan Plage off this road. Site is well signed in Marseillan Plage. GPS: N43:18.765 E03:32.779

Open: 2 April - 10 October.

Charges guide

Per unit incl. 2 persons	€ 13,50 - € 25,80
extra person	€ 2,50 - € 4,80
electricity	€ 2,80
dog	€ 2,00 - € 3,00

CAMPING ★★★
LA CREOLE

Direct access to the beach
Located in the Heart of Marseillan-Plage
Mobile home to rent
Low prices in low season
Open from 2/04 to 10/10

74 avenue des campings
34340 Marseillan-Plage
Tel : +33 (0)4 67 21 92 69
Fax : +33 (0)4 67 26 58 16

campinglacreole@wanadoo.fr
www.campinglacreole.com

FR34210 Camping les Berges du Canal

Promenade les Vernets, F-34420 Villeneuve-les-Béziers (Hérault)

Tel: **04 67 39 36 09**. Email: **contact@lesbergesducanal.com**   www.alanrogers.com/FR34210

There are surprisingly few campsites which provide an opportunity to enjoy the rather special ambience for which the Canal du Midi is renowned, so we were really pleased to discover this delightful campsite right alongside the canal at Villeneuve-les-Béziers. The campsite has 75 level pitches on sandy grass of average size, mostly with 10A electricity, in a peaceful and shady situation, separated from the canal by an access road. There is a pleasant pool complex, one of the two pools being fitted with a Jacuzzi-style facility, but there are no slides or toboggans thereby ensuring that it is relatively peaceful.

Facilities	Directions
A fully equipped toilet block has mainly British style WCs and some Turkish style, and some washbasins in cabins. Facilities for disabled visitors (with key) and children. Beauty therapist visits weekly. Laundry facilities. Motorcaravan service point. Two swimming pools. Bar/snack bar (serving breakfast too). Small restaurant attached to site. Evening entertainment during high season. Off site: Attractive old village centre of Villeneuve-les-Béziers. Beach at Portiragnes Plage. Riding 5 km. Canal du Midi.	From A9 exit 35, follow signs for Agde, at first roundabout take N112 (Béziers). First left onto D37 signed Villenueve-les-Béziers and Valras Plage. Pass traffic lights, left at roundabout and follow site signs (take care at junction beside bridge). GPS: N43:18.990 E03:17.080

Open: 15 April - 15 September.

Charges guide

Per unit incl. 2 persons	€ 14,00 - € 19,00
incl. electricity	€ 16,00 - € 23,00
extra person	€ 2,50 - € 4,50
animal	€ 3,00

411

FR34370 Camping Blue Bayou

Vendres Plage Ouest, F-34350 Valras-Plage (Hérault)

Tel: **04 67 37 41 97**. Email: **bluebayou@infonie.fr**

www.alanrogers.com/FR34370

A pleasant site, Blue Bayou is situated at the far end of Vendres Plage near Le Grau Vendres (the port of Vendres). It is therefore in a much quieter location than many other sites, away from the more hectic, built-up areas of Vendres and Valras Plage The beach is 300 m. across sand dunes and there are open views from the site creating a feeling of spaciousness. There are 256 pitches, all with 10A electricity, with 74 privately owned mobile homes and 92 to let, including some chalets. The touring pitches are large, some with their own sanitary arrangements. Light shade is provided by a mixture of trees. The restaurant and bar area is very attractive, overlooking two swimming pools, one with a toboggan, joined by a bridge where lifeguards station themselves. The site is under new ownership with all the family involved and you are made to feel very welcome. The site would make a very good choice for couples and families, perhaps best visited outside the height of the season when it becomes very busy.

Facilities

Individual toilet units for about half the touring pitches. Two separate blocks are fully equipped (may come under pressure at peak times). Baby bath. Facilities for disabled visitors. Laundry. Bar, restaurant and takeaway (open on demand in early season). Swimming pool (heated all season). Multisport court. Play area. Bicycle hire.
Off site: Fishing, boat launching and riding 1 km. Golf 25 km.

Open: 22 March - 13 September.

Directions

From A9 exit 36 (Béziers Ouest) follow directions for Valras Plage and Vendres Plage over four roundabouts. At fifth roundabout (Port Conchylicole) follow sign for Vendres Plage Ouest and site is 500 m. on the left. The entrance is quite tight. GPS: N43:13.380 E03:14.370

Charges guide

Per unit incl. 2 persons	€ 19,00 - € 37,00
incl. private sanitary facility	€ 23,00 - € 45,00
extra person	€ 5,00 - € 9,00

Blue Bayou ★★★★

300 meters from one of the most beautiful Mediterranean find-sand beaches, Blue Bayou welcomes you with its heated swimming pool area and with its various hosting arrangements in comfortable Mobile Homes, Chalets or its Camping area for tents and caravans.
We offer 40 pitches with private sanitary

Tennis, beach ball, biking, swimming for sportive holidays!
Entertainment, shows or thematic dinners for unforgettable holidays!

Open: 22/3/2008 - 13/09/2008

Vendres Plage Ouest - F-34350 Valras-Plage - France
Tel: 0033 (0)4 67 37 41 97 - Fax: 0033 (0)4 67 37 53 00

bluebayou@infonie.fr
www.bluebayou.fr

FR34260 Kawan Village Beau Rivage

F-34140 Mèze (Hérault)

Tel: **04 67 43 81 48**. Email: **reception@camping-beaurivage.fr**

www.alanrogers.com/FR34260

Beau Rivage is situated on the inland shore of the 4.5 km. by 19.5 km. Etang du Thau. This inland salt lake, lying parallel to the Mediterranean and separated by a very narrow strip of land, is well known for its oyster beds. It also popular for fishing, diving and watersports. The campsite on the edge of the town is within easy walking distance in the direction of Sète. The site has 150 level, sandy-grass pitches all with 6A electricity, plus 35 with mobile homes. The main features of the site are a pleasant pool and paddling pool with a bar and snack restaurant for the high season.

Facilities

One fully equipped small toilet block is open all season and a larger block for the main season. Baby bath. Facilities for disabled people. Washing machine. Motorcaravan service point. Bar providing snacks and simple takeaway food (July/Aug). Heated swimming and paddling pools (all season). Play area. Activities in July and August. Communal barbecues. Off site: Restaurant 300 m. Supermarket 200 m. Beach 500 m. All facilities of the town within easy walking distance. Tennis and bicycle hire 1 km.

Open: 5 April - 20 September.

Directions

From A9 autoroute take exit 33 for Sète. Follow RN113 for Poussan, Bouzigues and Mèze. Continue for 5 km. to outskirts of Mèze and site is on left just after a petrol station. The entrance is between the petrol station and a pottery (not too easy to see). GPS: N43:25.831 E03:36.623

Charges guide

Per unit incl. 2 persons	€ 18,00 - € 35,00
extra person	€ 4,00 - € 7,00

Camping Cheques accepted.

Check real time availability and at-the-gate prices...

www.**alanrogers**.com

FR34400 Camping les Sablons

F-34420 Portiragnes-Plage (Hérault)

Tel: **04 67 90 90 55**. Email: contact@les-sablons.com

www.alanrogers.com/FR34400

Les Sablons is an impressive and popular site with lots going on. Most of the facilities are arranged around the entrance with shops, a restaurant, bar and a large pool complex with no less than five slides, three heated pools and large stage for entertainment. There is also direct access to the white sandy beach at the back of the site close to a small lake. There is good shade on the majority of the site, although some of the newer touring pitches have less shade but are nearer the gate to the beach. On level sandy grass, all have 6A electricity. Of around 800 pitches, around half are taken by a range of mobile homes and chalets (many for hire, some by British tour operators). A wide range of sporting activities, and evening entertainment is arranged with much for children to do. In fact, this is a real holiday venue aiming to keep all the family happy.

Facilities

Well equipped, modernised toilet blocks include large showers some with washbasins. Baby baths and facilities for disabled visitors. Supermarket, bakery and newsagent. Restaurant, bar and takeaway. Pool complex. Entertainment and activity programme with sports, music and cultural activities. Beach club. Tennis. Archery. Play areas. Electronic games. Bicycle hire. ATM. Internet access. Off site: Riding 200 m.

Open: 1 April - 30 September.

Directions

From A9 exit 35 (Béziers Est) follow signs for Vias and Agde (N112). After large roundabout pass exit to Cers then take exit for Portiragnes (D37). Follow for about 5 km. and pass over Canal du Midi towards Portiragnes Plage. Site is on left after roundabout. GPS: N43:16.800 E03:21.800

Charges guide

Per unit incl. 2 persons	€ 16,00 - € 45,00
extra person (max. 6)	€ 6,00 - € 8,00
child (0-4 yrs)	free - € 4,00
dog	€ 2,00 - € 4,00

DIRECT ACCESS TO THE SANDY BEACH

OPEN FROM 01/04 UNTIL 30/09

ALL FACILITIES ON PLACE...
Restaurant, supermarket, fresh bakery...

LES SABLONS
VILLAGE CLUB
CAMPING ★★★★
www.les-sablons.com

WEEK-ENDS' SPECIAL PRICES

26°C

Aquaticamp
www.aquaticamp.com

FRANCE

Check real time availability and at-the-gate prices...

www.alanrogers.com

FR34410 Camping le Méditerranée Plage

Côte Ouest, F-34450 Vias (Hérault)

Tel: **04 67 90 99 07**. Email: contact@mediterranee-plage.com   www.alanrogers.com/FR34410

Set beside the beach in a quiet part of the coast, this site is somewhat different from the majority of beach sites. It has a most impressive entertainment complex situated to one side of the site with very comfortable outdoor seating facing a large stage for entertainment and a very smart bar and restaurant. The colourful furnishings and modern design reflect its Mediterranean setting. The site is very well cared for, with 410 pitches (some 185 used for touring units). Either grassy with a degree of shade or, as you get nearer the beach, more sandy with less shade, all have 6A electricity. The site's other claim to being different is its circus workshop weeks for children (6-12 years) designed to introduce them to the magical world of circus and culminating in a performance for parents each Friday. A new half-board 'country week' includes a dancing course. The pool area, shops including a bakery and snack bar are near the entrance which is busy during the day. The site and the white sandy beach are very popular with Dutch and German visitors.

Facilities

Two large toilet blocks are modern, one very impressive with a special smart nursery unit. Two small ones are more traditional. Facilities for disabled visitors. Laundry. Motorcaravan service point. Smart restaurant (facing stage for animation) and bar. Supermarket. Snack bar. Hairdressers. TV room. Play area. Games room. Tennis. Archery. Windsurfing. Activity programme, children's entertainment, circus school, evening shows and dancing. Internet access. Off site: Riding 2 km.

Open: 4 April - 20 September.

Directions

From A9 exit 35 (Béziers Est) follow directions for Agde and Sète on N112. After 4.2 km. turn for Portiragnes. Pass village and continue for 2.5 km. over Canal du Midi then turn left and follow site signs. GPS: N43:16.949 E03:22.260

Charges guide

Per unit incl. 2 persons	
and electricity	€ 16,50 - € 36,40
extra person	€ 3,00 - € 6,20
child (2-10 yrs)	€ 2,00 - € 4,60

OPEN FROM 4 APRIL TO 20 SEPTEMBER 2009

★ ★ ★ Le Méditerranée CAMPING VILLAGE plage

UNIQUE! CIRCUS WORK SHOPS FOR 6/12 YEARS OLD From 6 April to 1 May From 29 June to 3 July From 24 August to 4 September

A radiant village by the Mediterranean Sea. A place in touch with nature, where you can enjoy the pleasures of a true holiday: a warm and friendly atmosphere, entertaining activities and the wellbeing and comfort of a quality campsite. Le Méditerranée plage, my second homeland Direct access to the beach.

Tel: 00 33 467 90 99 07 - Fax: 00 33 467 90 99 17 - 34450 Vias Plage contact@mediterranee-plage.com **www.mediterranee-plage.com**

FR34290 Yelloh! Village Mer et Soleil

Route de Rochelongue, F-34300 Cap d'Agde (Hérault)

Tel: **04 66 73 97 39**. Email: info@yellohvillage-mer-et-soleil.com   www.alanrogers.com/FR34290

Close to Cap d'Agde, this is a popular, well equipped site with many facilities. The pool area is particularly attractive with large palm trees, a whirlpool, slides and a gym. An upstairs restaurant overlooks this area and the entertainment stage next to it. There are 500 pitches, around half taken by mobile homes and chalets (some to let, some privately owned). The touring pitches are hedged and have good shade, all with 6A electricity. A path from the back of the site leads to a 1 km. long path leading to the white sandy beach at Rochelongue.

Facilities

One large toilet block plus three smaller ones are fully equipped. Attractive units for children with small toilets, etc. Units for disabled visitors. Motorcaravan service point. Washing machine. Shop. Bar and restaurant. Swimming pools. Gym. Tennis. Archery. Sporting activities and evening entertainment. Off site: Beach 1 km. Riding 1 km. Sports complex opposite site.

Open: 5 April - 11 October.

Directions

From A9 exit 34, follow N312 for Agde. It joins the N112 Béziers - Sète.road. Cross bridge over Hérault river and turn right for Rochelongue. Turn left at next roundabout and site is a little further on the right. GPS: N43:17.171 E03:28.680

Charges guide

Per unit incl. 2 persons	€ 17,00 - € 41,00

tel: +33 466 739 739   www.yellohvillage.com   yelloh! VILLAGE

BOOK THIS SITE

CALL 01580 214000
...we'll arrange everything

The Travel Service

FR34430 Siblu Camping les Sables du Midi

B.P. 29, F-34350 Valras-Plage (Hérault)

Tel: **04 67 39 59 06**. Email: **campingoccitanie@wanadoo.fr**

www.alanrogers.com/FR34430

Les Sables du Midi (formerly known as L'Occitanie) is a good value site, particularly for low season visits, and is within walking distance of Valras Plage. The site is virtually a straight road from the autoroute exit (12 km). On arrival, don't be put off by the entrance (it could be more inspiring). You can find a more open pitch in the higher part of the site which is lightly wooded with some views of the surrounding countryside, or choose the lower area with plenty of shade which French visitors seem to do. A right of way divides the site into two parts. The bar, restaurant and pool make a nice social area in the higher part.There are 400 pitches with 30 privately owned mobile homes and 58 for hire. All pitches have 6A electricity and are of reasonable size on level rough grass. The town is a 20 minute walk and the beach 1 km. It is therefore a relatively peaceful location and seems to attract a mix of visitors.

Facilities

Five toilet blocks are fully equipped and opened as required. En-suite unit with ramped access for disabled visitors. Baby bath. Washing machine. Motorcaravan service point. Bar, restaurant and takeaway. Swimming and paddling pools. Play area. Minigolf. Daytime activities for children and sports for adults in high season and some evening entertainment.

Open: 25 April - 12 September.

Directions

From A9 exit 35 (Béziers Est) follow signs for Valras Plage (12 km). Continue straight on at roundabout beside McDonalds and Hyper U and again at next one towards Valras. Then turn immediately left into site. GPS: N43:15.433 E03:17.083

Charges guide

Per unit incl. 2 persons and electricity	€ 17,00 - € 29,00
extra person	€ 2,00 - € 5,00
child (0-7 yrs)	free - € 3,00

Les Sables du Midi, the perfect base for a family-friendly Mediteranean beach holiday.

- pool complex with lifeguards & slides
- organised sports & entertainments
- free children's clubs, open all season for 1 - 14s
- 80m sq average pitch size
- friendly bi-lingual staff
- site open 25 April - 12 September

Book a ferry inclusive package on
0871 911 7777
Or direct on parc **0033 467 32 33 86**
sablesdumidi@siblu.fr

les sables du midi ★★★

Valras Plage, Languedoc

siblu holidays

FR34390 Yelloh! Village Aloha

F-34410 Sérignan-Plage (Hérault)

Tel: **04 66 73 97 39**. Email: **info@yellohvillage-aloha.com**

www.alanrogers.com/FR34390

A well run, orderly site beside the beach at Sérignan Plage, Aloha offers a wide range of good quality facilities all open when the site is open. There are 472 pitches with over 170 mobile homes for hire in attractively landscaped settings. The 295 pitches for touring units are of good size, regularly laid out on level, sandy grass. Easily accessed from tarmac roads, all have 10A electricity. Half are on one side of the small beach road with the swimming pools and other facilities, the other half are somewhat quieter with more grass but less shade across the road.

Facilities

Seven toilet blocks, including three large ones, offer all modern facilities and are well equipped for children. Laundry. Motorcaravan service point. Supermarket. Bakery, newsagent, bazaar, hairdresser. Bar, restaurant, snack bar, pizzeria, takeaway. Large heated pool and fun pools. Playground. Tennis. Multisports facility. Beach and sailing club. Bicycle hire. Evening entertainment. Off site: Riding 800 m. Boat launching 8 km. Golf 20 km.

Open: 25 April - 13 September.

Directions

From A9 exit 35 (Béziers Est) follow signs for Sérignan then Sérignan Plage (D64, about 10 km). Once at Sérignan-Plage continue straight. Follow the sign for Aloha to right after the pink building. GPS: N43:16.400 E03:20.900

Charges 2009

Per unit incl. 2 persons and electricity	€ 15,00 - € 45,00
extra person	€ 5,00 - € 6,00

Long-stay early season discounts.

yelloh! VILLAGE

www.yellohvillage.com tel: +33 466 739 739

Check real time availability and at-the-gate prices...

www.**alanrogers**.com

FR34460 Camping Club International de l'Hérault

Route de la Tamarissière, F-34300 Agde (Hérault)

Tel: 04 67 94 01 01. Email: infos@interdelherault.com   www.alanrogers.com/FR34460

This comfortable site beside the Hérault river is opposite the town of Agde with its famous black cathedral. The site was taken over by the Caron family last year. With one of their sons, Ludovic who manages the site, they have built a super new pool complex and generally upgraded the facilities, whilst the other son, a trained chef, manages the modern restaurant. The 417 level grassy hedged pitches are of reasonable size with 180 available for touring units. All have 6/10A electricity. This is a well run, family orientated site in a quiet situation, albeit with a little road and rail noise possible in high season. The family's enthusiasm for their new project and their wish to make this a truly international site with a wide range of facilities and entertainment should be a recipe for success. It enjoys a quiet situation close to Agde city and to the beach at Tamarissière with its pedestrian ferry connection to the fishing port and village of Grau d'Agde. A free shuttle bus service to the beach is offered in July and August.

Facilities

Two sanitary blocks are of older design but are fully equipped. Access for disabled people. Baby bath. Laundry. Gas. Shop. Bar, restaurant and takeaway (all season). Super pool complex with cascade and bridge separating the paddling pool (heated 1/5-31/8). Separate water slide. Tennis. Games room. TV in bar. Playground. Sporting activities. Entertainment for adults and children. Chalets and mobile homes to let or buy. Off site: Fishing outside site in river. Beach 2.5 km. Riding and boat launching 2 km. Golf 4 km.

Open: 1 May - 31 August.

Directions

From the A9 use exit 34 and follow N112 towards Sète and Agde. Exit at junction for Tamarissiere and Agde centre. Follow signs for Agde centre and site, first left and site on right 500 m.
GPS: N43:18.234 E03:27.768

Charges guide

Per unit incl. 2 persons and electricity	€ 17,00 - € 35,00
extra person	€ 4,00 - € 7,00
child (4-10 yrs)	€ 3,00 - € 4,00

Pitches for tents and caravans, chalets of Mobil homes for rent
Near the beach. Free shuttle service in July and August.
Animation for young and old
Swimming pool with water slide
For more information
www.interdelherault.com of 33 4 67 94 01 01
Camping Club International de l'Hérault
Route de la Tamarissière • 34300 AGDE

AGDE - CAP D'AGDE – MEDITERRANEE

FR34440 Camping les Tamaris

140 avenue d'Ingril, F-34110 Frontignan-Plage (Hérault)

Tel: 04 67 43 44 77. Email: les-tamaris@wanadoo.fr   www.alanrogers.com/FR34440

This is a super site, unusually situated on a strip of land that separates the sea from the étang or inland lake, and therefore Fontignan Ville from Fontignan Plage. The design of the site is unusual which adds to its attractiveness. The pitches are laid out in hexagons divided by tall hedging and colourful shrubs. In total, there are 250 pitches with 100 taken by mobile homes which are let by the site. All have 10A electricity and are on level sandy grass. Direct access to the sandy beach is possible.

Facilities

Three modern toilet blocks with en-suite showers and washbasins. Excellent facilities for children. Unit for disabled visitors. Motorcaravan service point. Shop. Bar, restaurant and takeaway (all season). Swimming pool (from 1/5). Hairdresser. Gym. Play area. Miniclub. Archery. Bicycle hire. Internet access. Entertainment for all ages. Off site: Riding 150 m. Sailing 1 km. Boat launching 2.5 km. Golf 15 km.

Open: 1 April - 22 September.

Directions

From the north on the A9 take exit 32 and follow N112 towards Sète and Frontignan. After 16 km. ignore sign for Frontignan town and continue to Frontignan Plage following site signs. From the south use exit 33 and follow N300 to roundabout by Sète (11 km). Turn left on N112 and take second exit for Frontignan Plage. GPS: N43:26.982 E03:48.362

Charges guide

| Per unit incl. 2 persons | € 24,00 - € 38,00 |
| extra person | € 4,00 - € 8,00 |

Camping Cheques accepted.

Check real time availability and at-the-gate prices...
www.alanrogers.com

FR34480 Village Center l'Europe

Vic la Gardiole (CD114), F-34110 Frontignan (Hérault)

Tel: 04 67 78 11 50. Email: hmarques@village-center.com

www.alanrogers.com/FR34480

Situated between Montpellier and Sète and surrounded by vineyards which produce Muscat wine, L'Europe could make an interesting holiday venue, particularly for those without their own unit. Of its 306 pitches, the site has just 26 for touring units (with 10A electricity). The remainder feature a range of chalets and mobile homes to rent. All the pitches are level and of reasonable size with good shade from flowering hedges. The site boasts one of the best equipped children's play areas we have seen and indeed the focus is on families. There could be some noise from the nearby railway. The site has a wide range of facilities around the central area and provides entertainment from June onwards. The Montagne de la Gardiole is behind the site and the Mediterranean is nearby. Vic la Gardiole is a traditional fishing village and only 700 m. from the site. The unspoilt Aresquiers beach is a further 3.5 km along the road running beside the 'etangs' (sea water lakes) for which this coast is well known. The Canal du Rhône at Sète is a navigable channel running between them amongst the oyster beds. Sète is a must, a miniature Venice and well known for its water jousting games.

Facilities

Two fully equipped toilet blocks. Laundry. Shop. Bar, restaurant and takeaway (June-Sept; hours may vary). Two swimming pools, one with toboggan and paddling pool (June-Sept). Large play area. Internet access. Shuttle bus to beach (July/Aug). Miniclub. Sports activities. Evening entertainment. Part of the Village-Centre group who ensure excellent sports and entertainment teams at all their sites. Off site: Fishing 200 m. Riding 3 km. Boat launching 5 km.

Open: Late May - early September.

Directions

From the A9 take exit 32 for St Jean-de-Védas, then N112 (Séte). After Mireval, follow signs for Vic la Gardiole taking second left on CD114. This is a small road. Site is 800 m. on the right (park on the left). GPS: N43:29.504 E03:46.759

Charges guide

Per unit incl. 2 persons and electricity	€ 16,00 - € 32,00
extra person (over 5 yrs)	€ 6,00
child (0-5 yrs)	€ 3,00

L'Europe ★★★★

Vic La Gardiole > Mediterranean sea

• Near to the beaches of Aresquiers
• Children's play area and waterslides

Villagecenter

BOOK YOUR HOLIDAYS
www.village-center.com
+33 (0)4 99 57 21 21

FR34470 Camping le Fou du Roi

Chemin des Codoniers, F-34130 Lansargues (Hérault)

Tel: 08 74 56 00 27. Email: campinglefouduroi@free.fr

www.alanrogers.com/FR34470

Beside the mellow stone village of Lansargues on the edge of the Camargue, Le Fou du Roi was taken over by the Brunel family two years ago. They have done much to update it with a new reception/bar area complete with an attractive Tahitian style construction which can be left open or closed depending on the weather. Altogether this a lovely little site. There are 82 pitches with 30 for touring units with 10A electricity, arranged in light shade amongst the vineyards. A small pool and play area for children make it a very comfortable site with a nice long season.

Facilities

Two toilet blocks, the first modern and fully equipped, the second not open when we visited. Facilities for visitors with disabilities. Washing machine and dryer. Motorcaravan service point. Small shop (July/Aug). Bar, simple snacks and takeaway (fully open July/Aug). Swimming pool (1/5-15/9). Play area. Only gas barbecues are permitted (communal area provided). Off site: Fishing and riding 3 km. Golf 4 km. Tennis in village. Village within easy walking distance with restaurants and shops.

Open: 30 March - 14 October.

Directions

From A9 exit 27 follow signs for Lunel and from there pick up D24 going south. Lansargues is 7 km. Do not take 'village centre' sign but continue past and pick up site sign just past village on right. GPS: N43:39.109 E04:03.981

Charges guide

Per unit incl. 2 persons	€ 13,50 - € 18,60
extra person	€ 3,00 - € 6,00
child (under 7 yrs)	free - € 3,00
electricity	€ 4,00

Check real time availability and at-the-gate prices...

www.alanrogers.com

FR34490 Flower Camping de Fondespierre

277 route de Fontmarie, F-34160 Castries (Hérault)

Tel: 04 67 91 20 03. Email: pcomtat@free.fr

www.alanrogers.com/FR34490

Interesting sites can be hard to find in this area, particularly so close to Montpellier. Camping du Fondespierre does offer something a little different to the big, run of the mill holiday sites around here. Its situation in a quiet location a few miles northeast of Montpellier provides a relaxing spot to enjoy the natural surroundings of the uneven terrain of the 'garrigue', but with plenty of shade from the wild olive trees and the gnarled evergreen oaks. There are only 103 pitches on stony ground, of which 80 are used for touring units, all with 10A electricity. The site is open all year round.

Facilities

The modern toilet block is fully equipped and can be heated in winter. Washing machine and dryer. Motorcaravan service point. Bar. Some emergency supplies in bar. Two swimming pools one with reverse current. Play area. Football field. Internet. Bicycle hire. Off site: Village 1 km. with shops, restaurants and bars. Riding 3 km. Golf 5 km. Lake for leisure activities and fishing 10 km. Beaches 25 km.

Open: All year.

Directions

From the A9 take exit 28 (Vendargues) towards Castries via the RN110. Pass through village following signs 'Domaine de Fondespierre'. Turn left 800 m. after the village, then second left and right at 'cross' to site. GPS: N43:41.604 E03:59.772

Charges guide

Per unit incl. 2 persons	€ 15,00 - € 22,00
incl. electricity (10A)	€ 19,50 - € 26,50
extra person	€ 4,50

www.flowercampings.com

FR34510 Camping Club du Soleil

60 avenue d'Ingrill, F-34110 Frontignan-Plage (Hérault)

Tel: 04 67 43 02 02. Email: campingdusoleil@wanadoo.fr

www.alanrogers.com/FR34510

Camping Club du Soleil is a pretty and relaxed seaside site just 80 m. from the beach. An attractive little heated pool was added in 2007 and the site boasts a good bar and restaurant, also open to the public. This busy little site offering some entertainment and excursions in peak season, is interesting situated on the strip of land between the sea and the Etang d'Ingril. There are 95 level pitches in total, half of which are used by mobile homes, some available to rent. All pitches are generally well shaded and of a reasonable size, separated by flowering shubs and trees with 6A electricity.

Facilities

Modern fully equipped toilet block. En-suite facilities for visitors with disabilities. Washing machine. Restaurant/snack bar. Bar. Takeaway meals. Heated swimming pool. Play area. Entertainment, activities and excursions in high season. Bicycle hire. Mobile homes and chalets for rent. WiFi in reception area. Off site: Beach 80 m. Supermarket 50 m. Other shops 100 m. Marina and boat launching 1.5 km. Sailing 2 km.

Open: 4 April - 28 September.

Directions

From the A9 autoroute take exit 32 (St Jean-de-Védas) and join the N112 towards Sète. After 13 km. at a roundabout take the third exit following signs for Plage les Aresquiers (D114). Site is a further 4 km. GPS: N43:26.692 E03:47.935

Charges guide

Per pitch incl. 2 persons	€ 15,00 - € 30,00
extra person	€ 4,00 - € 5,50
electricity	€ 2,00

FR34520 Camping les Salisses

Route de la Mer, F-34450 Vias-Plage (Hérault)

Tel: 04 67 21 64 07. Email: info@salisses.com

www.alanrogers.com/FR34520

A traditional style French campsite, Les Salisses is well run and managed with an impressive range of swimming pools and other facilities. The 400 plus level pitches of average size are separated by flowering shrubs and trees that provide shade – all rather pretty. There are just over 100 places for touring units with 8A electricity, the rest being taken by mobile homes, some to let. Vias Plage is a busy, somewhat hectic resort and Les Salisses has its own section of beach with a bar. However, the site's own pools are also very welcoming, the indoor one reserved for naturists in the high season.

Facilities

Four fully equipped toilet blocks. Facilities for disabled visitors. Laundry. Shop. Bar and restaurant. Takeaway pizzeria (1/7-31/8). One indoor pool heated for low season used for naturists in high season, Two other pool complexes, one large pool for real swimming plus a long slide and a smashing complex for all the family with cascades and islands. Play area. Sports field (rugby posts). Multisport court. Tennis. Minigolf. Bicycle hire. Watersports at beach (800 m). Wide range of entertainment and activities. Off site: Riding 1 km Golf 5 km.

Open: 5 April - 13 September.

Directions

From the A9 take exit 34, then the N312 towards Vias and Agde. Join the N112 to avoid Vias town to pick up sign for Vias Plage. Site is first on the right. GPS: N43:17.794 E03:24.984

Charges guide

Per unit incl. 2 persons and electricity	€ 24,00 - € 36,00
extra person	€ 6,50 - € 8,50
pet	€ 4,50 - € 5,50

Check real time availability and at-the-gate prices...

www.alanrogers.com

FR34530 Camping l'Air Marin

F-34450 Vias Plage (Hérault)

Tel: **04 67 21 64 90**. Email: **info@camping-air-marin.fr**   www.alanrogers.com/FR34530

A shaded haven, L'Air Marin is set back beside the Canal du Midi, away from the busy hectic centre of Vias Plage. This site exudes its own identity with distinctive sculptures and artwork all around, including decoratively tiled water points. The facilities are to one side and form the core of the site, attractively arranged overlooking the pool complex. Flowering shrubs separate the 150 pitches for chalets and mobile homes to let, while the 150 level grass places for touring units are more open among tall trees. All have 6A electricity. The site opens quite early in the season compared with some in the area, with all facilities also said to be open all season.

Facilities

Two fully equipped toilet blocks provide a baby bath and a unit for disabled people. Laundry facilities. Shop. Restaurant, bar and takeaway café. Pool complex with covered heated pool, larger outdoor one and paddling pool. Gym. Play area. Tennis (30/6-30/8). Multisport court. Playing field. Activities and entertainment organised in high season. Communal barbecues. Off site: Fishing (permission needed). Beach 800 m. Minigolf, riding, bicycle hire 300 m. Karting 500 m. Golf 10 km.

Open: 15 April - 15 September.

Directions

From the A9 autoroute exit 34, follow N312 towards Agde for about 9 km. Pick up the N112 direction Beziers and take next left for Vias Plage. At tourist centre follow signs for Campings Est alongside the Canal du Midi to pick up site signs.
GPS: N43:18.081 E03:25.382

Charges guide

Per unit incl. 2 persons and electricity	€ 35,00
extra person	€ 7,00

No credit cards.

FR34550 Camping Municipal les Vailhés

BP 62, F-34702 Lodève (Hérault)

Tel: **04 67 44 25 98**   www.alanrogers.com/FR34550

Les Vailhés is a popular municipal site with a wonderful situation on the shores of the Lac du Salagou which is a haven for watersports. The views across the lake are good, and the red rocks are most unusual. In total there are 200 pitches, most with electricity; some are for mobile homes on ground sloping towards the lakeside beach. The majority are hedged and there is a fair amount of shade from various types of trees. The site is fenced off from the lake but the gates are open each day.

Facilities

Two toilet blocks, fully equipped if a little Spartan include washing machines. Play area with small climbing wall. Lake amenities (lifeguards July/Aug) and beach café (July/Aug). Windsurfing, sailing, canoes, and pedalos. Archery. Off site: Ancient town of Lodève 6 km. Beaches of the Mediterranean one hours drive.

Open: 1 April - 30 September.

Directions

From the A75 take exit 54 or 55, and follow directions to Lac du Salagou. Then follow site signs to left. GPS: N43:40.216 E03:21.343

Charges guide

Per person	€ 3,11
child (under 7 yrs)	€ 1,84
pitch incl. electricity	€ 5,94 - € 6,76

FREE CHILDPLACES ON MANY SITES

2009

FREE 2009 brochure
Over 60 French campsites, hand picked for you

Let the Alan Rogers Travel Service take care of your campsite holiday in 2009. Great service, fantastic prices - total convenience.

Call for your copy today
01580 214000

Alan Rogers

The Travel Service ...we'll arrange everything CALL 01580 214000 BOOK THIS SITE

FR34560 Camping le Paradis

Route de Valras, F-34410 Sérignan (Hérault)

Tel: 04 67 32 24 03. Email: paradiscamping34@aol.com

www.alanrogers.com/FR34560

Family owned and run, Le Paradis is a little haven of tranquillity set some three kilometres back from the sea. With only 129 average sized, grassy pitches, of which 22 are taken by mobile homes to rent, it is comfortable and peaceful. Even the pool is hidden behind fencing so it does not intrude. A mix of trees and shrubs give shade and all the pitches are level with 6A electricity. There is a pleasant shaded area to one corner of the pool near the bar. Entertainment is arranged on simple lines – music evenings two nights a week in July and August with darts or tennis tournaments for children.

Facilities

Fully equipped central toilet facilities. Provision for disabled visitors and a baby bath. Washing machine and drier. Small shop for essentials. Bar/restaurant (meals need to be pre-booked). Takeaway. Reasonably sized pool. Play area. Gas and electric barbecues only. Dogs are not accepted. Off site: Supermarket 200 m. Beach 2.5 km. Fishing and boat launching 2 km. Bicycle hire 1 km. Riding 3 km. Golf 15 km.

Open: 1 April - 30 September.

Directions

From A9 exit 35 (Béziers ouest), follow signs for Valras Plage. At second roundabout beside McDonalds and Hyper U take left turn to site on right, clearly signed. GPS: N43:16.156 E03:17.236

Charges guide

Per unit incl. 2 persons	€ 10,00 - € 17,00
incl. electricity	€ 13,00 - € 28,00
extra person	€ 3,00 - € 4,50
child (under 7 yrs)	€ 2,00 - € 3,00

FR66020 Kawan Village Caravaning Ma Prairie

Route de Saint-Nazaire, F-66140 Canet-en-Roussillon (Pyrénées-Orientales)

Tel: 04 68 73 26 17. Email: ma.prairie@wanadoo.fr

www.alanrogers.com/FR66020

Ma Prairie is an excellent site and its place in this guide goes back over 30 years. Then it was simply a field surrounded by vineyards. The trees planted then have now matured, more have been planted, along with colourful shrubs providing a comfortable, park-like setting with some 260 pitches, all with electricity and 35 with water and drainage. It is a peaceful haven some 3 km. back from the sea but within walking distance of Canet village itself. The Gil family still provide a warm welcome and reception boasts an impressive international collection of hats, helmets and uniform caps.

Facilities

Fully equipped toilet blocks, baby bath. Washing machines and dryers. No shop but bread can be ordered. Covered snack bar and takeaway. Air-conditioned bar and restaurant. Large adult pool, splendid children's pool. Play area. Tennis. Bicycle hire. TV. Amusement machines. Dancing three times weekly, busy daily activity programme in season. Caravan storage. Off site: Supermarket 400 m. Riding 600 m. Golf 6 km. Canet Village within walking distance with all amenities. Bus/tram services to the busy modern resort of Canet Plage.

Open: 5 May - 25 September.

Directions

Leave autoroute A9 at Perpignan North towards Barcarès. Site access is from the D11 Perpignan road (exit 5), close to the junction with D617 in Canet-Village. Go under bridge, right at roundabout the left to site. GPS: N42:42.081 E02:59.981

Charges guide

Per unit incl. 2 persons	€ 17,00 - € 30,00
extra person	€ 4,00 - € 7,00
child (4-9 yrs)	€ 3,00 - € 6,00
electricity (10A)	€ 4,00 - € 5,00
Camping Cheques accepted.	

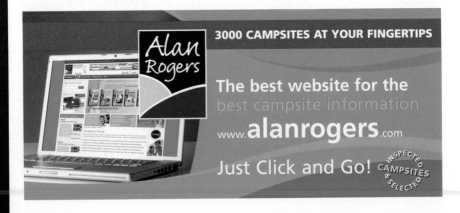

3000 CAMPSITES AT YOUR FINGERTIPS

Alan Rogers

The best website for the best campsite information

www.alanrogers.com

Just Click and Go!

INSPECTED CAMPSITES & SELECTED

Check real time availability and at-the-gate prices...

www.alanrogers.com

FR66070 Yelloh! Village le Brasilia

Mobile homes ▶ page 510

B.P. 204, F-66141 Canet-en-Roussillon (Pyrénées-Orientales)

Tel: **04 66 73 97 39**. Email: info@yellohvillage-brasilia.com

www.alanrogers.com/FR66070

An impressive family site beside the beach and well managed, Le Brasilia is pretty, neat and well kept with an amazingly wide range of facilities. There are 475 neatly hedged touring pitches all with electricity and many with water and drainage, varying in size from 80 to 120 sq.m. Some of the longer pitches are suitable for two families together. With a range of shade from pines and flowering shrubs, less on pitches near the beach, there are neat access roads (sometimes narrow for large units). There are also over 100 pitches with mobile homes or chalets to rent. The sandy beach here is busy, with a beach club (you can hire windsurfing boards) and a naturist section is on the beach to the west of the site. There is a large California type pool, with sunbathing areas bounded by an attractive mosaic wall and bar. The village area of the site provides bars, a busy restaurant, entertainment (including a night club) and a range of shops. In fact you do not need to stir from the site which is almost a resort in itself also providing a cash dispenser, exchange facilities, telephone, post office, gas supplies and even weather forecasts. It does have a nice, lively atmosphere but is orderly and well run – very good for a site with beach access. Although it is a large site it does not seem so. They seem to have thought of everything, including an escort to your pitch and advice on the best way to site your unit. A 'Yelloh Village' member. Member of Leading Campings Group.

Facilities

Ten modern sanitary blocks are very well equipped and maintained, with British style WCs (some Turkish) and washbasins in cabins. Good facilities for children and for disabled people. Laundry room. Hairdresser. Bars and restaurant. Swimming pool (heated). Play areas. Tennis. Sporting activities. Internet café. Entertainment. Bicycle hire. Fishing. Off site: Riding 5 km. Golf 12 km.

Open: 26 April - 27 September.

Directions

From A9 exit 41 (Perpignan Centre/Rivesaltes) follow signs for Le Barcarès/Canet on D83 for 10 km, then for Canet (D81). At first Canet roundabout, turn fully back on yourself (direction Sainte-Marie) and watch for Brasilia sign almost immediately on right. GPS: N42:42.280 E03:02.090

Charges guide

Per unit incl. 2 persons and electricity (6A)	€ 17,00 - € 44,00

www.yellohvillage.com   tel: +33 466 739 739

Your peninsula, your secret

Le Brasilia has chosen as its home base a beautiful, peaceful beach located at the end of Canet-en-Roussillon. It is there, between the river and the port, in the hollow of a deep pine forest with its Mediterranean scents, that Le Brasilia will reveal to you all the little secrets of well-being and the good life. Our village is a garden of nature where you can get away from it all, and draw so much closer to your dream holidays.

Rental of cottages and bungalows, pool heated out of season, cardio-fitness training room, tennis, multi-sports pitches, entertainment, shops, disco, bar restaurant, cabaret, children's clubs, and so much more. All our shops and services are open throughout the whole time that the site is open.

Camping-Village Le Brasilia
BP 204 - 66141 Canet-en-Roussillon Cedex - FRANCE
tél. 04 68 80 23 82 - fax 04 68 73 32 97
e-mail : camping-le-brasilia@wanadoo.fr - www.brasilia.fr

Leading Campings

Check real time availability and at-the-gate prices...
www.alanrogers.com

FR66030 Camping Cala Gogo

Avenue Armand Lanoux, les Capellans, F-66750 Saint Cyprien-Plage (Pyrénées-Orientales)

Tel: **04 68 21 07 12**. Email: **camping.calagogo@wanadoo.fr**   www.alanrogers.com/FR66030

This is an excellent, well organised site and it is agreeably situated by a superb sandy beach with a beach bar and boat launching. There are 654 pitches in total with 450 average sized, level, pitches for touring, electrical connections (6A) everywhere and some shade. The site has a most impressive pool complex carefully laid out with palm trees in ample sunbathing areas. The large bar complex becomes very busy in season and dancing or entertainment is arranged on some evenings on a large stage recently built alongside the bar. A feature of the site is the provision of special beach buggies for visitors with disabilities. The site is now part of the 'Les Pieds dans l'Eau' group (having direct access to water, either sea, river or lake). A large Aquapark, reputed to be amongst the best in southern France, is nearby. Used by tour operators (148 pitches). There are 57 chalets and mobile homes to rent.

Facilities

Fully equipped toilet blocks are of a high standard. Good supermarket and small shopping mall. Sophisticated restaurant with excellent cuisine. Self-service restaurant with simple menu. Takeaway. Bar. Small beach bar (high season). Fridge hire. Disco. TV. Three swimming pools plus one for children, water-jets, jacuzzi, waterfall. Play area. Tennis. Fishing. Diving club. Internet access and WiFi. Events, sports and entertainment organised in season. Torches useful. Off site: Bicycle hire 1 km. Golf, riding and boat launching 3 km. Boat excursions and courses in skin-diving, windsurfing or sailing nearby.

Open: 12 May - 22 September.

Directions

Using D81 (southward) avoid St Cyprien-Plage and continue towards Argelès. Turn right at roundabout signed Le Port and Aquapark and pick up site signs. Site is just past the Aquapark.
GPS: N42:35.963 E03:02.257

Charges 2009

Per unit incl. 2 persons and electricity	€ 23,25 - € 33,20

FR66040 Camping le Soleil

Route du Littoral, F-66702 Argelès-sur-Mer (Pyrénées-Orientales)

Tel: **04 68 81 14 48**. Email: **camping.lesoleil@wanadoo.fr**   www.alanrogers.com/FR66040

Le Soleil is an attractive site with direct access to the sandy beach. It is a busy, popular, family owned site which over the years has developed into a small village. It has over 800 pitches of ample size, of which around 550 are used for touring units, on sandy/grassy ground and with a mixture of trees and shrubs providing plenty of shade, all with electricity (6A). Access for caravans may need care on the narrow access roads. The site has a wide range of amenities, including an impressive pool complex with activities and entertainment for all the family. All facilities are open when the site is open. Spain and the Pyrénées are near enough for excursions. There are over 200 pitches used by tour operators and 70 occupied by mobile homes. English is spoken and there is a comprehensive reservation system (advised for most of July/Aug). Le Soleil also works with the group 'Les Pieds dans l'Eau' (sites with direct access to water such as the sea, river or lake).

Facilities

Seven toilet blocks of the type with external access to individual units. Some family cabins with washbasins, showers. Washing machines. Supermarket, general shop, press, tabac. Restaurant. Takeaway. Bar with disco (July/Aug), beach bar. California type swimming pool complex and entertainment area. Adventure playground. TV room. Internet. WiFi. Tennis. Diving and riding in high season (charge). Dogs are not accepted. Off site: Fishing and mooring boats on the adjacent river. Golf 5 km.

Open: 16 May - 19 September.

Directions

Site is at north end of the beach, about 1 km. from Argelès-Plage village. GPS: N42:34.531 E03:02.539

Charges 2009

Per person (over 5 yrs)	€ 9,30
pitch	€ 13,90
electricity (6A)	€ 3,70

Less 30% in May, June and August.

Check real time availability and at-the-gate prices...
www.**alanrogers**.com

2 Campsites DIRECT ON THE BEACH !

- 30 % in may, june and september on the pitchprices.

Cala-Gogo

Avenue Armand Lanoux
F-66750 SAINT CYPRIEN
Tél. +33 4 68 95 90 11
Fax +33 4 68 95 92 82
www.campmed.com
e-mail : calagogo@campmed.com

le Soleil ★★★★

Route du Littoral
F-66702 Argelès sur Mer
☎ +33 4 68 95 94 62 • Fax +33 4 68 95 92 81
www.campmed.com
e-mail : lesoleil@campmed.com

FR66110 Camping le Dauphin

Route de Taxo-d'Avall, F-66704 Argelès-sur-Mer (Pyrénées-Orientales)

Tel: **04 68 81 17 54**. Email: **info@campingledauphin.com**   www.alanrogers.com/FR66110

Near Taxo in the quieter, northern part of Argelès (a somewhat frenzied resort in season), this family owned site on flat, grassy parkland with plenty of tall trees enjoys good views of the Pyrénées from the terrace area surrounding its excellent complex of swimming pools. There are 346 level, grassy well shaded pitches, all with 10A electricity and some with individual sanitary units. Located some 1.5 km. from the town and beach, there is a regular connecting 'road train' service to and fro throughout the day and evening until midnight. There are 168 pitches taken by mobile homes and chalets either privately owned or for rent. Tour operators use 76 of the pitches.

Facilities

A central sanitary block completly renovated provides all essential facilities including washbasins en-suite. One third of the pitches have their own fully equipped individual sanitary unit. Shops, bar/restaurant, pizzeria with takeaway (all 16/5-5/9). Two large swimming pools and padding pool. Two play areas. Tennis. Multisport courts. Minigolf. Games room. Full entertainment programme in high season. Torches useful in some areas. Off site: Riding 1 km. Fishing 2 km.

Open: 16 May - 5 September.

Directions

Site is on north side of Argelès. From autoroute take exit Perpignan-Nord for Argelès and follow directions for Plage-Nord and Taxo-d'Avall (similarly from the N114). GPS: N42:34.337 E03:01.300

Charges guide

Per unit incl. 2 persons and electricity	€ 16,00 - € 26,70
individual sanitary unit	€ 4,00 - € 10,00
water and drainage	€ 3,00 - € 4,20
extra person	€ 4,00 - € 6,50
electricity	€ 2,00 - € 4,20

LE DAUPHIN

CAMPING LE DAUPHIN ★★★★

route de Taxo à la Mer - BP 57
66704 ARGELES SUR MER cédex
☎ +33 4.68.81.17.54 - FAX : +33 4.68.95.82.60
www.campingledauphin.com
Bar - Restaurant
Supermarket - Takeaway
Game room - Entertainment
Mini-club - Multisport court
Tennis - Playground ...
Mobile home rental - Pitches with private bathrooms
3 separate swimming pools to suit the whole family !!! - Free brochure on request

FR66050 Kawan Village le Haras

Domaine Saint Galdric, F-66690 Palau-del-Vidre (Pyrénées-Orientales)

Tel: **04 68 22 14 50**. Email: **haras8@wanadoo.fr**   www.alanrogers.com/FR66050

A distinctly 'French' style site, Le Haras is midway between the coast (about 8 km.) and the Pyrénées, in quiet countryside away from the bustle of the coastal resorts. Le Haras has 75 pitches with electricity, 18 fully serviced, arranged informally in bays of four, in the grounds of an old hunting lodge. A mixture of trees, shrubs and flowers provides colour and shade. Some access roads are narrow. There is an attractive pool complex with a bar and a courtyard area beside the restaurant and large function room. Rail noise is possible, although this is offset by large trees.

Facilities

Fully equipped toilet blocks, Renovation of smaller block near the pool planned. Covered dishwashing and laundry sinks. Washing machines. Fridge hire. Bar. Restaurant, open to the public (all year). Takeaway. Swimming, paddling pools (1/5-15/9). Play area. No charcoal barbecues. Internet access. Off site: Three bakers in the village, two butchers and a general stores. Beaches 10 minutes drive. Fishing 500 m. Riding 2 km. Bicycle hire 6 km. Golf 7 km.

Open: 20 March - 20 October.

Directions

From A9, exit 43 (Le Boulou) follow D618 towards Argelès for 13 km. On bypassing St André, turn left, Palau-del-Vidre (D11). Bear right through village, on D11 towards Elne. Site on right at end of village, before railway bridge. GPS: N42:34.583 E02:57.866

Charges guide

Per pitch incl. two persons	€ 14,00 - € 24,50
extra person	€ 3,50 - € 5,20
child (under 7 yrs)	free - € 3,60
electricity (5A)	€ 4,00
dog	€ 3,00 - € 3,50

Camping Cheques accepted.

Check real time availability and at-the-gate prices...
www.alanrogers.com

FR66090 Camping Mar Estang

Route de Saint-Cyprien, F-66140 Canet-en-Roussillon (Pyrénées-Orientales)

Tel: **04 68 80 35 53**. Email: **marestang@wanadoo.fr**   www.alanrogers.com/FR66090

Le Mar Estang is a large, 'all singing, all dancing' site with something for everyone. Situated on the edge of Canet, between the Etang (part of the Réserve Naturelle de Canet/St Nazaire) and the sea, there is access to the beach from the site by a tunnel under the road. If you don't fancy the beach, there are four swimming pools to choose from, complete with fun pool, water slides and a heated covered pool. There are 600 pitches, some 200 used for mobile homes or Bengali tents, with 5A electricity, some degree of shade and on sandy ground.

Facilities	Directions
Nine well equipped sanitary blocks are well placed around the site. Facilities for babies. Laundry. Motorcaravan service point. Shop, bars, restaurant and takeaway all open when site is open. Swimming pools, Jacuzzi and solarium. Fitness club. Entertainment. Disco. Communal barbecue. Sailing club. Tennis. Bicycle hire. Play areas. Direct access to beach. Off site: Riding. Canet 500 m. with tourist train in high season. Perpignan 10 km.	Take exit 41 from A9 autoroute and follow signs for Canet. On outskirts of town follow signs for St Cyprien/Plage Sud. Site is very clearly signed on southern edge of Canet Plage. GPS: N42:40.542 E03:01.881

Charges 2009

Per unit incl. 2 persons	€ 21,00 - € 40,00
extra person	€ 7,00 - € 12,00

Open: 29 April - 23 September.

FR66150 Castel Camping les Criques de Porteils

RD114, route de Collioure, F-66701 Argelès-sur-Mer (Pyrénées-Orientales)

Tel: **04 68 81 12 73**. Email: **criquesdeporteils@wanadoo.fr**   www.alanrogers.com/FR66150

This is an amazing site situated on the cliff top with views across the sea to Argelès, set against a backdrop of mountains and close to Collioure, the artist's paradise. What more could you ask? Under new ownership, the facilities are being renovated and some of the pitches being redesigned for easier access. There are around 250 of varying sizes and shapes due to the nature of the terrain, level in places up and down in others. Most have sea views and 5A electricity available. There are three small coves of grey sand accessed by steep steps (gated).

Facilities	Directions
Two renovated toilet blocks, fully equipped with super children's room, all small equipment and colourful. Laundry room with internet point. Motorcaravan service point. Shop. Bar. Restaurant with takeaway. Swimming pool. Play area. Sports field. Off site: Collioure 5 mins.	Exit A9 at Perpignan Sud or Le Boulou. Head for Argelès to pick up signs for 'Collioure par la Corniche'. Watch for signs coming into a bend going down a hill by hotel. GPS: N42:32.000 E03:04.001

Charges 2009

Per unit incl. 2 persons and electricity	€ 24,00 - € 39,00
extra person	€ 6,00 - € 9,00

Open: 1 April - 9 September.

FR66130 Hotel de Plein Air l'Eau Vive

Chemin de Saint-Saturnin, F-66820 Vernet-les-Bains (Pyrénées-Orientales)

Tel: **04 68 05 54 14**. Email: **info@leauvive.com**   www.alanrogers.com/FR66130

Enjoying dramatic views of the Pic du Canigou (3,000 m.), this small site is one and a half kilometres from the centre of Vernet-les-Bains in the Pyrénées. It is approached via a twisting road through a residential area. The 70 tourist pitches, with electricity (4/10A) and 45 fully serviced, are on a slight slope, part hedged and some terraced, with a separate tent field. Most pitches have some shade. Although there is no swimming pool, the site has a very attractive, natural pool with water pumped from the nearby stream, with a small beach. There is a central floating safety line across the pool but parents should keep an eye on children around the pool as there is no supervision or safety fence.

Facilities	Directions
First class toilet facilities and provision for disabled people. Washing machine. Bread, main season. Bar/reception, pool table, library. Snack bar, takeaway (15/5-15/9). A 'meal of the day' can be ordered. Play area. Natural pool for children. Sports field. Bicycle hire. Off site: Fishing 200 m. Swimming pool, thermal centre in village 1 km. Organised rafting, canoeing, hydrospeed trips.	Following N116 towards Andorra. At Ville Franche, turn south, D116, for Vernet-les-Bains. After 5 km, keep right avoiding town. Turn right over bridge towards Sahorre. Immediately turn right (ave de Saturnin) for 1 km. GPS: N42:33.304 E02:22.667

Charges guide

Per unit incl. 2 persons	€ 12,50 - € 21,50
incl. electricity	€ 15,00 - € 25,00
extra person (over 4 yrs)	€ 1,50 - € 2,50
Discounts for weekly stays.	
Credit cards accepted 1/6-31/8 only.	

Open: 16 December - 25 October.

BOOK THIS SITE
CALL 01580 214000
...we'll arrange everything
The Travel Service

BOOK THIS SITE
CALL 01580 214000
...we'll arrange everything
The Travel Service

425

FR66160 Camping la Palmeraie

Boulevard de la Plage, F-66440 Torreilles-Plage (Pyrénées-Orientales)

Tel: **04 68 28 20 64**. Email: **info@camping-la-palmeraie.com**   www.alanrogers.com/FR66160

La Palmeraie is a very attractive, top quality campsite situated some 600 metres from the beach at Torreilles-Plage. Arguably the prettiest campsite in the area, there is an abundance of foliage, including a variety of trees and flowering shrubs which provide ample shade – unusual in a situation on the littoral and so close to the sea. The site is a credit to the owners. The 110 touring pitches (out of a total of 240 in all) are generally on the large side. All the facilities, including an attractive pool and surrounding terrace area, are of a good quality and lend an air of elegance to this excellent site.

Facilities

Three well equipped, modern sanitary blocks are traditional in style with modern fittings. Facilities for disabled visitors and children. Laundry facilities. Fridge hire. Shop. Bar, restaurant and takeaway. Swimming and paddling pools. Play area. Games room. Multisport court. Safety depost. Internet access. Evening entertainment and organised sports activities in July/Aug. Children's club (6-12 yrs). Off site: Beach 600 m. Riding 500 m. Sailing, beach club, minigolf and other activities in the local area.

Open: 27 May - 30 September.

Directions

From A9 take exit 41 and follow signs for Canet via D81 and D83. Once on D83 look for signs for Torreilles Plage. Site is on right hand side as you approach from the roundabout on the D83. GPS: N42:45.942 E03:01.644

Charges guide

Per unit incl. 2 persons	€ 15,70 - € 24,50
extra person	€ 5,00 - € 7,50
child (3-7 yrs)	€ 4,00 - € 5,50
electricity (5/10A)	€ 3,50 - € 6,60

FR66170 Village Camping Spa Marisol

Boulevard de la Plage, F-66440 Torreilles (Pyrénées-Orientales)

Tel: **04 68 28 04 07**. Email: **marisol@camping-marisol.com**   www.alanrogers.com/FR66170

Good quality sites with direct access to the beach are hard to find and Marisol is a useful option. It is a fairly large site with 377 pitches with a significant number of mobile homes, but with 170 for touring. These are sandy grass pitches of good size with some shade. All have electricity (10A). There is a beauty centre where you can enjoy a sauna, Turkish or spa bath. This is essentially a 'holiday' site with all the popular facilities and an extensive entertainment programme, fitness courses and children's club throughout the main season. The owners have renovated the pool area and continue with other improvements.

Facilities

Fully equipped toilet blocks, baby bath. Washing machine. Small supermarket. Bar. TV. Restaurant. Takeaway. Heated swimming pool, water slide, children's pool. Beauty centre (including special packages). Fitness room. Play area. Tennis. Archery. Side gate with access to path across dunes to sandy beach. Watersports activities. Off site: Sea fishing, watersports on beach. Riding 500 m. Bicycle hire 2 km. Golf 10 km.

Open: 5 April - 30 September.

Directions

From A9 take exit 41 (Perpignan-Nord) towards Le Barcarès for 9 km. Then south on D81 towards Canet for 3 km. before turning to Torreilles Plage. Site is signed. GPS: N42:47.059 E03:01.974

Charges guide

Per unit incl. 2 persons and electricity (10A)	€ 15,00 - € 47,50
extra person	€ 5,00 - € 8,90

FR66190 Sunêlia les Tropiques

Boulevard de la Méditerranée, F-66440 Torreilles-Plage (Pyrénées-Orientales)

Tel: **04 68 28 05 09**. Email: **contact@camping-les-tropiques.com**   www.alanrogers.com/FR66190

Les Tropiques makes a pleasant holiday destination, only 400 metres from a sandy beach and also boasting two pools. It will provide families with children of all ages with an ideal seaside holiday. There are 450 pitches with 200 given over to mobile homes and chalets. Pleasant pine and palm trees with other Mediterranean vegetation give shade and provide an attractive environment. Activities are provided for all including a large range of sports, activities, caberets and shows.

Facilities

Modern, fully equipped sanitary facilities, provision for disabled visitors. Launderette. Shop (1/5-15/9). Bar (1/5-15/9). Restaurant, takeaway, pizzeria (all 1/6-15/9). Heated pool (all season), another pool (15/5-30/9) and water slides. Paddling pool. Tennis (floodlit). Multisport area. Pétanque. Archery (1/7-31/8). Play area. Disco (every evening), miniclub for 6-12 ys in July/Aug. Bicycle hire (15/6-15/9). WiFi. Off site: Minigolf 300 m. Windsurf board hire, sea fishing 400 m. Riding 400 m. Golf 15 km.

Open: 5 April - 4 October.

Directions

From A9 exit Perpignan Nord, follow D83 towards Le Barcarès for 9 km. Take D81 south towards Canet for 3 km. turn left at roundabout for Torreilles-Plage. Site is the last but one on left. GPS: N42:46.050 E03:01.783

Charges guide

Per unit incl. 2 persons and electricity	€ 17,00 - € 35,50
extra person	€ 3,70 - € 8,20

BOOK THIS SITE CALL 01580 214000 ...we'll arrange everything

The Travel Service

Check real time availability and at-the-gate prices...

www.alanrogers.com

FR66230 Camping Caravaning le Romarin

Route de Sorède, chemin des Vignes, F-66702 Argelès-sur-Mer (Pyrénées-Orientales)

Tel: **04 68 81 02 63**. Email: **contact@camping-romarin.com**   www.alanrogers.com/FR66230

In an area dominated by 'all-singing, all-dancing' holiday sites, this charming little gem of a site is tucked away some 2 km. behind the busy resort of Argelès. Essentially a site for families with younger children, or for adults seeking peace and quiet, it provides 94 good sized touring pitches, with electricity (6-10A) set among pine, eucalyptus, oak and mimosa trees. There are also 25 mobile homes for rent and a further ten which are privately owned. Ideal for exploring this area, especially the Albères range of Pyrénéen mountains and the ancient city of Perpignan.

Facilities

Good, large toilet block provides a mix of British and Turkish WCs, showers, washbasins in cabins, washing machine. Snack bar (20/6-8/9). Swimming pool (10/6-30/9). Play area. Some traditional (local) family entertainment in high season. Internet access. Dogs only accepted in low season and on touring pitches only. Off site: Riding and bicycle hire 2 km. Beach and fishing 4 km. Golf 8 km. Within reach of shops, supermarket (2 km), all the attractions of Argelès, both village and plage.

Open: 15 May - 30 September.

Directions

From A9 exit 42 (Perpignan Sud), N114 towards Argelès for 25 km, exit 11a. At roundabout, take direction for St André, for 300 m. then make an acute left turn (site signed), up a rather poor road. After 2 km, turn right on the D2, take third right and follow lane to site. It is possible to follow D2 (direction Soredè) from Argelès village. GPS: N42:32.399 E02:59.709

Charges 2009

Per unit incl. 2 persons and electricity	€ 13,00 - € 31,50
extra person	€ 2,00 - € 4,50
child (2-5 yrs)	free - € 2,50
dog	free - € 2,00

CAMPING LE ROMARIN

Great pleasure in a small camping site, in the middle of olive groves, between the sea and the mountain, you will enjoy your stay in natural surroundings. Welcome to the Romarin

Route de Sorède - Chemin des Vignes - F-66702 Argelès-sur-Mer - France
Tél.: 04 68 81 02 063 - Fax: 04 68 81 57 43
Email: contact@camping-romarin.com - www.camping-romarin.com

FR66240 Chadotel Camping le Trivoly

Route des Plages, F-66440 Torreilles-Plage (Pyrénées-Orientales)

Tel: **04 68 28 20 28**. Email: **info@chadotel.com**   www.alanrogers.com/FR66240

The popularity of Torreilles derives mainly from its huge sandy beach and for some off-site nightlife, shopping, etc. but for smarter resorts one really needs to visit Le Barcares or Canet a few kilometres distance in either direction. Le Trivoly (a member of the French Chadotel Group) is about 800 m. gentle stroll from the beach, in a fairly tranquil setting. In total there are 273 pitches, of which 60 are used for touring. These are of a good size, well shaded and hedged with electricity (6A). The remainder are either used by tour operators or for mobile homes. It perhaps offers a rather more peaceful situation than do the other sites here.

Facilities

Four toilet blocks, although not new, provide modern facilities, including washbasins in (rather small) cabins, and were all clean and well cared for when we visited. Small shop (June - mid Sept). Snack-restaurant and takeaway (June-mid Sept). Reasonably sized pool with water slide and paddling pool. Terraced restaurant. Play area. Tennis. Minigolf. Bicycle hire. Entertainment programme in high season. Off site: Centre Commercial 500 m.

Open: 1 April - 24 September.

Directions

From A9 exit 42 (Perpignan-Nord) towards Le Barcarès for 9 km, then turn south on D81 towards Canet. After 3 km. turn left at roundabout, signed Torreilles Plage. Site is on left, in about 500 m. GPS: N42:45.934 E03:01.626

Charges guide

Per unit incl. 2 persons	€ 14,50 - € 24,70
incl. electricity	€ 19,70 - € 29,90
extra person	€ 5,80
child (2-13 yrs)	€ 3,80

427

The Travel Service
...we'll arrange everything
CALL 01580 214000
BOOK THIS SITE

FR66250 Huttopia Font-Romeu

Route de Mont-Louis, F-66120 Font-Romeu (Pyrénées-Orientales)

Tel: 04 68 30 09 32. Email: font-romeu@huttopia.com

www.alanrogers.com/FR66250

This is a large, open site of some seven hectares, nestling on the side of the mountain at the entrance to Font-Romeu. This part of the Pyrénées offer some staggering views and the famous Mont Louis is close by. An ideal base for climbing, hiking or cycling, it would also provide a good stop over for a night or so whilst traveling between Spain and France or to or from Andorra into France. The terraced pitches are easily accessed, with those dedicated to caravans and motorcaravans at the top of the site, whilst tents go on the lower slopes. Trees provide shade to many of the pitches from the sun which can be quite hot at this altitude. Facilities on site are limited to very good toilet blocks and a very large games room and assembly hall which is used by those in tents when it rains.

Facilities

Two toilet blocks, one behind reception, the other in the centre of the tent pitches. Traditional in style, they are bright and clean with modern fittings. Toilet for children and excellent facilities for visitors with disabilities. Washing machines and dryers at each block. large games hall. Only gas barbecues are permitted. Off site: Opportunities for walking and climbing are close by as are golf, riding, fishing, cycling and tennis. The small town of Font-Romeu is very near with all the usual shops and banking facilities.

Open: 24 May - 27 September, 5 December - 12 April.

Directions

Font-Romeu is on the D118, some 12 km. after it branches off the N116 heading west, just after Mont Louis. This is an interesting road with magnificent views and well worth the climb. Site is just before the town, on the left and accessed off the car park. GPS: N42:30.907 E02:03.110

Charges 2009

Per unit with 2 persons and electricity	€ 18,80 - € 34,20
extra person	€ 5,00 - € 6,20
child (2-7 yrs)	€ 3,00 - € 4,20
Camping Cheques accepted.	

tel: +33 (0) 4 37 64 22 33 www.huttopia.com

HUTTOPIA

HUTTOPIA

Huttopia FONT-ROMEU

Tents and cottages to rent

In the heart of the Catalan Pyrenees
on the gorgeous plateau of the Cerdagne...

Heated swimming-pool, Bar restaurant, Brand new facilities, Children playground...

Route de Mont Louis
66120 Font-Romeu - France
Tel. +33 (0)4 68 30 09 32

www.huttopia.com

FR66260 Camping la Massane

25 avenue Molière, F-66702 Argelès-sur-Mer (Pyrénées-Orientales)

Tel: 04 68 81 06 85. Email: camping.massane@infonie.fr

www.alanrogers.com/FR66260

Set a little bit back from the seafront, La Massane is one of the traditional older sites with good views of the Canigou and a pool open for a longer season. With 184 pitches and only 26 taken by mobile homes, it could make a good, quiet and relaxing choice. In July and August it will be a little more hectic (as is the whole resort) with a bar and some family entertainment. Other amenities are within walking distance. Pitches are divided, level and semi-grassed with a mixture of shade from tall trees or shrubs. Electricity (6/10A) is available.

Facilities

Two toilet blocks, one large and modernized with a baby room and facilities for visitors with disabilities. A smaller, traditional block is used early in the season. Laundry room. Swimming pool (heated 15/4-30/9) with paddling pool. Shop, bar, takeaway and entertainment July/Aug only. Play area. Charcoal barbecues not permitted. WiFi free. New adult exercise/games area. Off site: Village of Argelès. Beach 1 km. Bicycle hire 1 km. Spain, Collioure and the Pyrénées within driving distance.

Open: 15 March - 15 October.

Directions

From the A9 take exit 42 (Perpignan Sud) and follow N114 for Argelès to exit 10.for Pujols. At first roundabout take 'Centre Plage'. Pass school on left and site is almost immediately on left. GPS: N42:33.043 E03:01.876

Charges 2009

Per unit incl. 2 persons and electricity	€ 11,50 - € 30,50
extra person	€ 2,50 - € 5,50

Check real time availability and at-the-gate prices...

www.alanrogers.com

FR66290 Camping Club le Floride et l'Embouchure

Route de Saint-Laurent, F-66423 Le Barcarès (Pyrénées-Orientales)

Tel: 04 68 86 11 75. Email: campingfloride@aol.com   www.alanrogers.com/FR66290

Essentially a family run enterprise, Le Floride et l'Embouchure is really two sites in one – l'Embouchure, smaller with direct access to the beach and Le Floride on the opposite side of the fairly busy road into Le Barcarès village. Apart from having some very unusual accommodation to rent ('Bungahomes') and a few pitches with a private sanitary unit, the sites are fairly unremarkable, albeit within a very friendly family-centred environment, popular with Dutch visitors. In total there are 632 pitches, all with 10A electricity. The site is relatively inexpensive, especially outside the July and August peak period. It offers a comfortable, if unpretentious, holiday opportunity with reasonably sized pitches (300 for touring units) and ample shade. In the case of L'Embouchure, there is direct access to a popular beach, but Le Floride has the pool complex complete with toboggan.

Facilities

Four fully equipped toilet blocks on Le Floride and two on L'Embouchure where 50 pitches near the beach have individual facilities. Shop, bar, restaurant and takeaway (all 15/6-5/9). Three swimming pools (one heated outside July/Aug). Play area. Entertainment programme (July/Aug). Charcoal barbecues are not permitted. Off site: Fishing 1 km. Riding 1.5 km. Bicycle hire 3 km. Beach 100 m.

Open: 1 April - 30 September.

Directions

From A9 take exit 41 (Perpignan Nord) and follow signs for Canet and Le Barcarès via D83. At J9 follow D81 (Canet) then next left into Le Barcarès Village. Site is 1 km. on the left and right sides of the road. GPS: N42:46.713 E03:01.806

Charges guide

Per unit incl. 2 persons and electricity	€ 12,50 - € 34,00
incl. individual sanitary facility	€ 16,00 - € 42,00
extra person	€ 2,60 - € 6,20
child (1-4 yrs)	free - € 3,60

FR66490 Flower Camping la Garenne

RD916, F-66170 Néfiach (Pyrénées-Orientales)

Tel: 04 68 57 15 76.   www.alanrogers.com/FR66490

Situated just off the N116 which runs through the foothills of the Pyrénées from Perpignan to Andorra, this site is ideally situated for hiking, climbing, cycling and canoeing. The pitches are all level with very easy access and have a degree of privacy to them, and all are close to the swimming pool and children's play area. A few mobile homes are on the site and some of these are attractively designed to look like chalets found high up in the mountains. Great views of the surrounding hills and mountains are enjoyable from all areas of the site whilst at the back there are vineyards with black grapes in abundance.

Facilities

Single toilet block in the centre of the site provides modern facilities. Baby area and facilities for disabled visitors. Washing machine. Cozy bar area and snack type restaurant with covered area for singing and dancing. Weekly Paella evening. Swimming pool with sunbathing terrace and small pool for young children. Play area. Outdoor fitness machines for adults. Off site: Hiking, climbing, cycling and canoeing all nearby. Attractive town of Ile sur Tet 3 km.

Open: All year.

Directions

From the N116 (Perpignan - Andorra), take exit for Nefiach and head up the old road to Ile sur Tet and the site is on the right. GPS: N42:41.440 E02:39.471

Charges guide

Per unit incl. 2 persons and electricity	€ 17,50 - € 23,50
extra person	€ 4,00 - € 6,00
child (2-7 yrs)	€ 3,00 - € 4,00

Check real time availability and at-the-gate prices...

www.alanrogers.com

FR66300 Yelloh! Village le Pré Catalan

Route de Saint-Laurent, F-66420 Le Barcarès (Pyrénées-Orientales)

Tel: **04 66 73 97 39**. Email: **info@yellohvillage-pre-catalan.com**   www.alanrogers.com/FR66300

The green foliage from the mixed trees and the flowering shrubs makes the site very attractive and an avenue of palms is particularly spectacular. There has been a camping site on the spot since 1960 but the present owners, the Galidie family, took over in 1982 and the site is now run by their son Francois and his English wife Jenny. With 250 pitches in total, there are 158 taken by mobile homes and chalets, half to let and half privately owned. These are mixed amongst the touring pitches which are on level, sandy ground, clearly divided by hedging and with 10A electricity. The newer part has been planted in the same way as the original areas. It has less shade but enjoys views across to the mountains. The facilities are opened all season but hours are adapted according to the number of visitors on site. An upstairs bar has a long terrace which overlooks the pool area. A footpath of just less than 1 km. leads to the sandy beach. All in all, this a pleasant and comfortable place to stay.

Facilities

Good modern facilities include small showers for children. Laundry. Small shop. Bar, restaurant and takeaway (all season). Heated swimming pool and paddling pool. Excellent play area. Tennis. Archery. Internet access. Library. Miniclub and evening entertainment (July/Aug). Gas barbecues only. Off site: Beach 900 m. River fishing 1 km. Riding 1.5 km. Boat launching 3 km. Nearby La Réserve Africaine de Sigean and Le Château de Salses.

Open: 30 April - 20 September.

Directions

From A9 exit 41 (Perpignan Nord), follow signs for Le Barcarès and Canet (D83). At junction 9 take D81 (Canet), then first left to Le Barcarès (D90). Site is on left after 500 m. next to Le California. Follow narrow lane to site entrance. GPS: N42:46.864 E03:01.369

Charges 2009

Per unit incl. 2 persons	€ 15,00 - € 37,00

tel: +33 466 739 739 www.yellohvillage.com

66420 Le Barcarès - Tel : 0033 468 86 12 60
Internet : www.precatalan.com - Email : info@precatalan.com

New swimming pool complex, 1 heated pool of 200 m² and 1 pool of 300 m² with paddling pool. Bar, snack, restaurant, shop and animation for all ages. All our services are available from the opening date. Beach at 900 meter distance on foot. French/English owned.

FR66620 Camping le Texas

Taxo d'Avall, F-66700 Argelès-Sur-Mer (Pyrénées-Orientales)

Tel: **04 68 81 00 17**. Email: **contact@camping-letexas.fr**   www.alanrogers.com/FR66620

Le Texas is situated on the outskirts of Argelès and has been in the hands of the same family for over 35 years. It is now run by Evelyn, the daughter, who has her own baby and speaks English. With only 144 level, sandy pitches, 50 of which have mobile homes to rent, another 50 being privately owned, it has a comfortable, relaxed atmosphere with shade from tall trees. In high season the 'Little Train' will take you to the beach, although there is a pleasant pool on the site. A popular little bar/shop selling local wines and traditional gifts is only 50 m. down the road.

Facilities

Two fully equipped sanitary blocks were being upgraded when we visited. Facilities for disabled visitors. Bread and essentials available high season along with simple takeaway. Outdoor heated pool (24/5-13/9). Multisports court. Play area. Off site: Bar 50 m. Supermarket within 2 km. Riding 2 km. Fishing 2 or 7 km. Bicycle hire 4 km. Boat launching 8 km.

Open: 7 June - 6 September.

Directions

From the N114 which runs around the back of Argelès take exit 10. Follow signs for Taxo d'Avall and Plages Nord. Almost immediately turn left then right by wine cave and site is ahead. Watch out for small road running across the entrance. GPS: N42:34.205 E03:00.167

Charges guide

Per unit incl. 2 persons	€ 13,00 - € 17,80
extra person	€ 4,00 - € 5,80
child (under 5 yrs)	€ 3,00
electricity (3/5A)	€ 3,00 - € 4,30

FR66310 Camping le Rotja

F-66820 Fuilla (Pyrénées-Orientales)

Tel: **04 68 96 52 75**. Email: **campinglerotja.ellenetwim@wanadoo.fr**   **www.alanrogers.com/FR66310**

La Rotja is a pretty, Dutch-owned site, set up a little valley above the fortified old town of Villefranche-de-Conflent and watched over by the impressive, snow-capped Pic d'Canigou. The older part of the site is semi-wooded with wonderful silver birches, whilst the newer part further up the hill is more open and terraced. There is room for 100 fairly level pitches of which 80 have electricity and one can chose a shaded place or not. A small pool at the top of the site is very welcome in high season. Trips are organized into the mountains, along with barbecue evenings. A small bar doubles as reception and a rustic outside area allows 'al fresco' enjoyment of the daily menu. The site has a wonderful situation and whilst having all 'mod cons', the naturalness of the area has been retained. The spa town of Vernet-le-Bains in the next valley is worth visiting, as is the celebrated Fort Libéria, or walk around the walls of Villefranche-de-Conflent or even enjoy a jaunt on the Petit Train Jaune to enjoy the magnificent scenery.

Facilities

Two toilet blocks, both fully equipped. The older one beside the bar area can be heated, a larger, more modern one is in the new area. Facilities for disabled visitors and babies. Bar, outside restaurant (15/5-30/9). Swimming and paddling pools (1/5-30/9). Gas barbecues only. Bicycle hire. Off site: Tennis 100 m. Fishing 300 m. Riding 7 km. Beach 55 km. Rafting, canyoning, hydro-speed and 'parc-aventure' possible with trained guides. Walking, VTT.

Open: 1 April - 31 October.

Directions

Follow the N116 from Perpignan (route to Andorra). After about 50 km. bypass Prades and continue to Villefranche-de-Conflent. Follow around and past it to take left turn signed Fuilla and Sahorre. After 2 km. turn right at village to site.
GPS: N42:33.745 E02:21.565

Charges guide

per unit incl. 2 persons	€ 13,25 - € 18,25
incl. electricity	€ 15,50 - € 20,50
extra person	€ 2,75 - € 3,75
child (0-7 yrs)	€ 1,75 - € 2,75

CAMPING LE ROTJA

Away from the traffic noise awaits camp site Le Rotja you in the nice Apple Valley

34, Avenue de la Rotja - 66820 Fuilla
Tél.: 0033 (0) 4 68 96 52 75
Email: camping@camping-lerotja.com
www.camping-lerotja.com

Activities:
• Historical sight seeing
• Hiking
• Mountain biking
• Fishing
• Horse riding
• Rafting
• Canyoning

FR66630 L'Oasis Camping Club

Route de Saint-Laurent, F-66420 Le Barcarès (Pyrénées-Orientales)

Tel: **04 68 86 12 43**   www.alanrogers.com/FR66630

L'Oasis has quite a park-like feel with mixed deciduous trees and grass of sorts. The 496 pitches are well spaced with 249 for touring units and some 49 used by tour operators. The remainder feature mobile homes or chalets to rent. All have 10A electricity and are most are fairly level on sandy soil and grass, with varying degrees of shade. A smart new bar and restaurant area with a stage for entertainment was just being finished adjacent to the pool area when we visited. A sandy beach is within walking distance (about 1 km.) but the site also has a comfortably sized pool complex.

Facilities

Two modern toilet blocks are fully equipped and include facilities for babies and disabled people. Laundry room. Bar, restaurant, takeaway and shop (open by early July). Heated outdoor pool (14/06-13/09). Tennis. Play area. Off site: Fishing 1 km. Riding 1 km. Minigolf 1 km. Boat launching and wind surfing 3 km.

Open: 14 June - 13 September.

Directions

From A9 autoroute exit 41, follow the D83 towards Barcarès for about 9 km. At exit 9 take D81 towards Canet. Take first left turn signed Le Barcarès village and site is on left after 500 m. past Camping California. GPS: N42:46.585 E03:01.496

Charges guide

Per unit incl. 2 persons and electricity	€ 12,50 - € 29,00
extra person	€ 3,50 - € 6,50

FR66560 Camping la Sirène

Route de Taxo à la Mer, F-66702 Argelès-sur-Mer (Pyrénées-Orientales)

Tel: 04 68 81 04 61. Email: contact@camping-lasirene.fr   www.alanrogers.com/FR66560

From the moment you step into the hotel-like reception area you realise that this large site offers the holiday maker everything they could want in a well managed and convenient location close to Argelès-sur-Mer and the beaches. The 740 mobile homes and chalets vary in standard but all are less than five years old, very clean, comfortable and located on neat tidy pitches. There are also some touring pitches. In the summer there are 170 staff on duty to ensure your stay is as enjoyable as they can make it. All the shops and amenities are near reception making the accommodation areas quite peaceful and relaxing. There are many things to do and summer visitors have the option of using the free bus service to the beach where the site has its own club where you can even go windsurfing at no charge.

Facilities

Restaurant, bar and takeaway. Large shop (all season). Large aqua park, paddling pools, slides, jacuzzi. Games room. Multisports field, tennis, archery, minigolf, football. Theatre, evening entertainment, discos, show time spectacular. Off site: Resort of Argelès sur Mer and its beaches 2 km, as is karting, 10-pin bowling, amusement park and the sites private beach club Emeraude. Interesting old town of Collioure close by.

Open: 7 April - 28 September.

Directions

Leave A9 motorway, junction 42, take D114, towards Argelès. Leave D114, junction 10 and follow signs for Plage Nord. Site signed after first roundabout. Site on right 2 km. after last roundabout. GPS: N42:34.256 E03:01.744

Charges 2009

Per unit incl. 1-3 persons	
and electricity	€ 26,00 - € 43,00
extra person	€ 6,00 - € 9,00
child (under 5 yrs)	€ 4,00 - € 6,00
dog	free

FR66570 Camping l'Hippocampe

Route de Taxo à la Mer, F-66702 Argelès-sur-Mer (Pyrénées-Orientales)

Tel: 04 68 81 04 61. Email: contact@camping-lasirene.fr   www.alanrogers.com/FR66570

A sister site to La Sirène just opposite, this site has some touring pitches along with 170 mobile home and chalet pitches and is aimed at families with young children and adults looking for a quieter site. The mobile homes and chalets are all modern, well maintained and have space around them to provide privacy. The pool on site is dedicated to the smaller children and is a great place for them to gain confidence in the water whilst still being able to play. Entertainment, shops, bars and the full range of activities offered by La Sirène, just across the road. Visitors here also have free access to the beach club Emeraude which offers free transport to Plage Nord where the club is situated complete with bar and snacks.

Facilities

Pool and laundry. Shop, small bar (all season). All other facilities are at La Sirène just across the road. Off site: Beach, Argelès sur Mer within 2 km. Karting, 10-bowling, amusement park and riding within 1 km.

Open: 6 April - 28 September.

Directions

Leave A9 junction 42. Take D114, Argelès road. Leave D114 junction 10, follow signs for Plage Nord. Site signed after the first roundabout, on left 2 km. after last roundabout. GPS: N42:34.230 E03:01.839

Charges 2009

Per unit incl. 1-3 persons	
and electricity	€ 26,00 - € 43,00
extra person	€ 6,00 - € 9,00
child (under 5 yrs)	€ 4,00 - € 6,00
dog	free

FR66590 Camping le Bois du Valmarie

Parcs Résidentiels ▶ page 518

F-66702 Argelès-sur-Mer (Pyrénées-Orientales)

Tel: 04 68 81 04 61. Email: contact@camping-lasirene.fr   www.alanrogers.com/FR66590

Pitches here are exclusively for mobile home and chalet accommodation.

Check real time availability and at-the-gate prices...

www.alanrogers.com

CAMPINGS
CLUBS ★★★★
ARGELÈS/MER
MÉDITERRANÉE

LA SIRÈNE • LE BOIS DE VALMARIE • L'HIPPOCAMPE

Quick and easy, **your reservation in just one click on:**

route de Taxo
66702 Argelès-sur-Mer
Tél. : +33 (0)4 68 81 04 61
Fax : +33 (0)4 68 81 69 74
e-mail : contact@camping-lasirene.fr

www.camping-lasirene.fr

FR66480 Camping Club las Bousigues

Avenue des Corbières, F-66423 Le Barcarès (Pyrénées-Orientales)

Tel: **04 68 86 16 19**. Email: **info@camping-barcares.com**

www.alanrogers.com/FR66480

Under new ownership, Las Bousigues enjoys a quiet situation set well back from Le Barcarès amongst the vineyards. A mature site with lots of greenery, it provides a mix of mobile homes or chalets to rent and pitches for touring, some of which have individual sanitary blocks. The area in front of the pool, bar and restaurant with its plane trees is like a village square. Indeed, the site has a distinctly French ambience unlike some of the 'all singing, all dancing' sites nearer the beach. With around 200 pitches, most with 10A electricity, the site is of a comfortable size and would suit families with younger children. Le Barcarès is a popular holiday destination with long sandy beaches. It is not far from the Spanish border and the Pyrénées should the beach pall and you wish to explore the area.

Facilities

Two fully equipped toilet blocks, one with access for disabled people. Small shower and toilet for children. Individual en-suite units on some pitches. Dog shower. Laundry. Shop. Bar, restaurant and takeaway (holiday weekends and main season). Swimming pool (heated in low season) with small toboggan. Good sized play area beside communal barbecue. Internet access.

Open: 31 March - 30 September.

Directions

From the A9 take exit 40 signed Leucate. Follow D627 towards Port Leucate, then D83 towards Le Barcarès. Take exit 10 for Le Barcarès village. At first roundabout follow campsite sign to right. Site short distance on left. GPS: N42:47.150 E03:01.156

Charges guide

Per unit incl. 2 persons	€ 9,00 - € 25,00
incl. electricity (10A)	€ 11,00 - € 34,00
extra person	€ 4,60 - € 7,00
child (under 10 yrs)	free - € 4,50

Roussillon

CAMPINGS FranceLoc

BOUSiGUES SaIanque ***

Only on 900 meters distance from the beach! You will find a shady campsite with marked pitches and a swimming pool, surrounded by meadows with horses which are happy to greet you. Enjoy the relaxing and hospitable atmosphere.

Bousigues Salanque
66420 Le Barcarès• Roussillon
Tel.: +33 (0)4 68 86 16 19 • Email : lasbousigues@wanadoo.fr
www.campings-franceloc.fr

FR66640 Camping le Soleil Bleu

Route de Saint Laurent, Mas de la Tourre, F-66423 Le Barcarès (Pyrénées-Orientales)

Tel: **04 68 86 15 50**. Email: **info@lesoleilbleu.com**

www.alanrogers.com/FR66640

Formerly Paris Camping and situated close to a wide sandy beach (600 m), Le Soleil Bleu concentrates mainly on chalets and mobile homes. Of the 176 pitches only 16 are available for touring units. Pleasantly shaded with trees and flowering shrubs, the site has a fairly large pool overlooked by the bar area. In high season it is quite lively with a range of entertainment and activities for children. Le Barcarès Plage has grown in recent years and has a range of restaurants and a yacht marina. There are many opportunities for watersports including windsurfing, jet ski, kite surfing and water skiing.

Facilities

Traditional toilet block with modern facilities. Unit for disabled visitors. Laundry room. Shop, bar, restaurant and takeaway (open all season but fewer hours in low season). Two heated outdoor swimming pools (lifeguards July/Aug). Good play area with climbing wall and ropes. Range of activities and entertainment in high season. Internet access. Off site: Beach 600 m. Fishing 200 m. Watersports 2 km. Riding 2 km. Boat launching 3 km.

Open: 5 April - 1 November.

Directions

From A9 exit 41 (Perpigan Nord) follow the D83 towards Le Barcarès. At exit 9 take the D81 towards Canet. Take next left (Le Barcarès village) for 500 m. and site on right as road bends to left. GPS: N42:46.608 E03:01.710

Charges guide

Per unit incl. 2 persons and electricity	€ 21,00 - € 43,00
extra person	€ 4,00
dog	€ 3,00

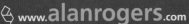
Check real time availability and at-the-gate prices...
www.alanrogers.com

MAP 15 & 16

Bathed in sunshine
from early spring to
late autumn, surrounded
by stunning scenery,
cosmopolitan towns and
superb sandy beaches, no
wonder this is one of France's
most sought-after destinations.

THIS SECTION COVERS THE EASTERN COASTAL
REGION OF THE MEDITERRANEAN. WE INCLUDE
TWO DÉPARTEMENTS FROM THE OFFICIAL REGION
OF PROVENCE AND THE REGION OF CÔTE D'AZUR:
13 BOUCHES-DU-RHÔNE, 83 VAR, 06 ALPES-MARITIME

The glittering Côte d'Azur, perhaps better
known as the French Riviera, is a beautiful
stretch of coast studded with sophisticated
towns such as the famous Monte Carlo,
Nice, and Cannes, not forgetting the other
famous and arguably the most glamorous
resort of St Tropez. With its vast expanses
of golden sandy beaches and long lazy
hours of sunshine, this is a paradise for
sun worshippers and beach enthusiasts.
It's a spectacular coast of rugged coves,
sweeping beaches and warm seas.

The quaint harbours and fishing villages
have become chic destinations, now full
of pleasure yachts, harbour-side cafés and
crowded summertime beaches. Further
up in the hills are quieter tiny medieval
villages with winding streets and
white-walled houses with terracotta roofs,
which have attracted artists for many years.
In St Paul-de-Vence visitors browse through
shops and galleries set on narrow winding
cobblestone streets and inland Grasse is the
perfume capital of the world, surrounded
by the Provencal lavender fields and shady
olive groves which pervade the air with
a magical scent at certain times of the year.

Places of interest

Aix-en-Provence: old town with 17th-18th
century character, Paul Cézanne and
Tapestry museums.

Cannes: popular for conventions and
festivals, Cannes Film Festival, la Croisette,
old city.

Monte Carlo: main city of Monaco,
casinos, gardens, Napoleon Museum.
Motorsport circuit.

Cuisine of the region

Aigo Bouido: garlic and sage soup.

Bouillabaisse: fish soup.

Rouille: an orange coloured sauce with
peppers, garlic and saffron.

Bourride: a creamy fish soup.

Pissaladière: Provençal bread dough with
onions, anchovies and olives.

Pistou (Soupe au): vegetable soup bound
with *pommade*.

Pommade: a thick paste of garlic, basil,
cheese and olive oil.

Ratatouille: aubergines, courgettes, onions,
garlic, red peppers and tomatoes in olive oil.

Salade Niçoise: tomatoes, beans, potatoes,
black olives, anchovy, lettuce, olive oil and
tuna fish.

FR06010 Camping Domaine Sainte Madeleine

Route de Moulinet, F-06380 Sospel (Alpes-Maritimes)

Tel: **04 93 04 10 48**. Email: **camp@camping-sainte-madeleine.com**   www.alanrogers.com/FR06010

Domaine Sainte Madeleine is an attractive, peaceful site, with swimming pool, in spectacular mountain scenery. It is about 20 km. inland from Menton, and very near the Italian border. The approach to this site involves a 17 km. climb with hairpin bends and then a choice of going through the pass or an 800 m. long tunnel (3.5 m. high, 3 m. wide). Situated on a terraced hillside with mountain views towards Italy, manoeuvring within the site presents no problem as the pitches are on level, well drained grass. The lower ones have shade but those higher up on the hill have none. Electricity is available to 60 of the 66 pitches.

Facilities

Good quality toilet block with hot showers (token required). Hot water (often only warm) for dishwashing and laundry sinks drawn from single tap. Washing machines. Motorcaravan services. Gas supplies. Bread can be ordered. Swimming pool (140 sq.m. and heated in spring and autumn). Off site: Sospel is 4 km. with many restaurants, bars, cafés and shops. Tennis, riding and a centre for mountain biking. Fishing 1 km.

Open: 31 March - 30 September.

Directions

From A8 take Menton exit towards Sospel from where you turn onto the D2566 (route de Moulinet). Site is 4 km. north of Sospel on the left. GPS: N43:53.821 E07:25.011

Charges guide

Per unit incl. 2 persons	€ 19,00
extra person	€ 4,20
electricity (10A)	€ 2,90

Less 15% outside July/Aug. No credit cards.

FR06030 Camping Caravaning Domaine de la Bergerie

1330 chemin de la Sine, F-06140 Vence (Alpes-Maritimes)

Tel: **04 93 58 09 36**. Email: **info@camping-domainedelabergerie.com**   www.alanrogers.com/FR06030

La Bergerie is a quiet, family owned site, situated in the hills 3 km. from Vence and 10 km. from the sea at Cagnes-sur-Mer. This extensive, natural, lightly wooded site is in a secluded position about 300 m. above sea level. Most of the pitches are shaded and all are of a good size. There are 450 pitches, 224 with electricity (2/5A), water and drainage. Because of the nature of this site, some pitches are a little distance from the toilet blocks. There are no organised activities and definitely no groups allowed. It is a large site but because it is so extensive it does not give that impression.

Facilities

Refurbished toilet blocks, excellent provision for disabled people (pitches near the block are reserved for disabled people). Good shop. Small bar/restaurant, takeaway (all 1/5-30/9). Large swimming pool, paddling pool, spacious sunbathing area (1/5-30/9). Playground. Bicycle hire. Tennis. 12 shaded boules pitches (lit at night) with competitions in season. No barbecues. Off site: Riding and fishing 10 km. Golf 18 km.

Open: 25 March - 15 October.

Directions

From A8 exit 47 take Cagnes-sur-Mer road towards Vence. Site west of Vence – follow 'toutes directions' around town, join D2210 Grasse road. In 2 km. at roundabout, turn left, follow site signs, 1.5 km. Site on right. GPS: N43:42.421 E07:05.258

Charges guide

Per unit incl. 2 persons	€ 18,50 - € 31,50
extra person	€ 5,00

Camping Cheques accepted.

FR06050 Castel Camping la Vieille Ferme

296 boulevard des Groules, F-06270 Villeneuve-Loubet-Plage (Alpes-Maritimes)

Tel: **04 93 33 41 44**. Email: **info@vieilleferme.com**   www.alanrogers.com/FR06050

In a popular resort area and open all year, La Vieille Ferme is a family owned site with good facilities. It has 113 level gravel-based touring pitches, 95 fully serviced and the majority separated by hedges. Some are only small, simple pitches for little tents. There is also a fully serviced pitch on tarmac for motorhomes. There are special winter rates for long stays with quite a few long stay units on site. The entrance to the site is very colourful with well tended flower beds. English is spoken at reception and the whole place has a very friendly feel to it.

Facilities

Modern, heated, well kept toilet blocks, children's toilets, baby room, facilities for disabled people. Motorcaravan services. Washing machines, dryer. Shop (Easter - Sept). Refrigerator hire. Swimming pool, children's pool, heated and covered for winter use (closed mid Nov-mid Dec). Jacuzzi. Internet. Boules. Games, competitions organised in July/Aug. Off site: Bus from outside site. Beach 1 km. Fishing 1 km. Golf and bicycle hire 2 km. Riding 6 km.

Open: All year.

Directions

From west, A8, exit 44 Antibes, D35, 3.5 km. Left towards Nice, N7. After 3.5 km. turn left for site between Marine Land and Parc de Vaugrenier. Site is 150 m. on right. Avoid N98 Route du Bord de Mer. GPS: N43:37.211 E07:07.555

Charges guide

Per unit incl. 2 persons	€ 13,50 - € 31,00
extra person	€ 3,90 - € 5,00
electricity (2-10A)	€ 2,50 - € 6,00

Check real time availability and at-the-gate prices...

www.**alanrogers**.com

FR06080 Camping Caravaning les Cigales

Mobile homes ▶ page 510

505 avenue de la Mer, F-06210 Mandelieu-la-Napoule (Alpes-Maritimes)

Tel: **04 93 49 23 53**. Email: **campingcigales@wanadoo.fr**   www.alanrogers.com/FR06080

It is hard to imagine that such a quiet, peaceful site could be in the middle of such a busy town and so near Cannes. The entrance (easily missed) has large electronic gates that ensure that the site is very secure. There are only 115 pitches (40 mobile homes) so this is quite a small, personal site. There are three pitch sizes, from small ones for tents to pitches for larger units and all have electricity (6A), some fully serviced. All are level with much needed shade in summer, although the sun will get through in winter when it is needed. The site is alongside the Canal de Siagne and for a fee, small boats can be launched at La Napoule, then moored outside the campsite's side gate. Les Cigales is open all year so it is useful for the Monte Carlo Rally, the Cannes Film Festival and the Mimosa Festival, all held out of the main season. English is spoken.

Facilities

Well appointed, clean, heated toilet blocks. Facilities for babies and disabled visitors. Washing machine. Motorcaravan services. Restaurant and takeaway (May - Oct). Heated swimming pool and large sunbathing area (April - Oct). Small play area. Two games machines. Canal fishing. Off site: Beach 800 m. The town is an easy walk. Two golf courses within 1 km. Railway station 1 km. for trains to Cannes, Nice, Antibes, Monte Carlo. Hypermarket 2 km. Bus stop 10 minutes.

Open: All year.

Directions

From A8, exit 40, bear right. Remain in right hand lane, continue right signed Plages-Ports, Creche-Campings. Casino supermarket on right. Continue under motorway to T-junction. Turn left, site is 60 m. on left opposite Chinese restaurant.
GPS: N43:32.348 E06:56.564

Charges 2009

Per unit incl. 2 persons	
and electricity	€ 37,00 - € 49,50
extra person	€ 7,00
child	€ 3,50

FR06090 Camping Caravaning les Gorges du Loup

965 chemin des Vergers, F-06620 Le Bar-sur-Loup (Alpes-Maritimes)

Tel: **04 93 42 45 06**. Email: **info@lesgorgesduloup.com**   www.alanrogers.com/FR06090

Les Gorges du Loup is situated on a steep hillside above Grasse. The one kilometre lane which leads to the site is narrow with passing places. The 70 pitches are on level terraces, all with electricity and many have stupendous views. Some pitches are only suitable for tents and the site roads are quite steep. A quiet family site, there is no organised entertainment. Grasse (nine kilometres) is surrounded by fields of lavender, mimosa and jasmine and has been famous for the manufacture of perfume since the 16th-century. The very friendly and enthusiastic owners provide 4 x 4 assistance.

Facilities

Clean toilet blocks with washbasins and hot showers, dishwashing and laundry sinks have only a single hot tap. Washing machine and iron. Reception, small shop, bread. Small bar/restaurant with terrace, takeaway (all 3/6-8/9). Swimming pool, small slide, diving board, but no pool for small children. Boules. Skittles. TV room, board games, library. Children's climbing frame, slide. No charcoal barbecues. Chalets, mobile homes for hire. Off site: Bar-de-Loup with its few shops, restaurants is 500 m. walk.

Open: 1 April - 30 September.

Directions

From Grasse, D2085 Nice road. D3 briefly to Châteauneuf Pré du Lac. D2210 to Pont-de-Loup, Vence. Site signed on right. Pass village of Bar-sur-Loup on left, after sharp right turn, follow narrow access road 750 m. (passing places).
GPS: N43:42.148 E06:59.726

Charges guide

Per unit incl. 2 persons	
and electricity	€ 17,40 - € 28,70
extra person	€ 4,50
No credit cards.	

Check real time availability and at-the-gate prices...
www.**alanrogers**.com

FR06190 Parc Saint-James le Sourire

Route de Grasse, F-06270 Villeneuve-Loubet (Alpes-Maritimes)

Tel: **04 93 20 96 11**. Email: **info@camping-parcsaintjames.com** www.alanrogers.com/FR06190

This campsite has been recommended by our agent in France and we intend to undertake a full inspection next year. Le Sourire is a member of the Parc Saint James group. There are 411 pitches here and many are occupied by mobile homes and chalets. There are however 241 touring pitches dispersed throughout the wooded terrain. The site is close to the impressive La Vanade sports complex which has a massive range of activities including no fewer than 55 tennis courts, a riding centre and a nine-hole golf course. There is a good range of activities on site too, including a large swimming pool with a regular programme of aqua gym, water polo and other activities. Le Sourire is a good base for exploring the area and lies close to the Provencal village of Villeneuve Loubet, midway between Cannes and Nice. The nearest beach is just 4 km. Children are well catered for here with an active children's club and a good play area. There is a lively activity programme including excursions and entertainment is arranged regularly during the peak season.

Facilities

Laundry. Supermarket. Swimming pool and separate children's pool. Bar and restaurant. Takeaway. Play area. TV room. Gym. Games room. Sports competitions. Children's club. Evening entertainment. Disco. Mobile homes and chalets to rent. Off site: Cannes and Nice. Nearest beaches 4 km. Marineland water park. Leisure park at La Vanade.

Open: 15 May - 15 September.

Directions

Take the Villeneuve Loubet exit from the A8 autoroute and follow signs to Grasse joining the D2085. The site can be found on the left, 2 km. from Villeneuve Loubet.
GPS: N43:39.618 E07:06.257

Charges guide

Per unit incl. 2 persons and electricity	€ 17,00 - € 28,00
extra person	€ 2,50 - € 4,50
child (under 10 yrs)	€ 1,50 - € 4,00

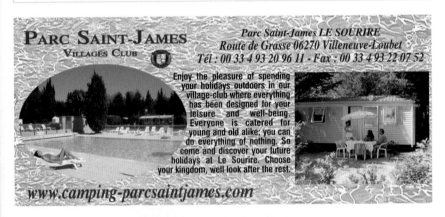

PARC SAINT-JAMES
VILLAGES CLUB

Parc Saint-James LE SOURIRE
Route de Grasse 06270 Villeneuve-Loubet
Tél : 00 33 4 93 20 96 11 - Fax : 00 33 4 93 22 07 52

Enjoy the pleasure of spending your holidays outdoors in our village-club where everything has been designed for your leisure and well-being. Everyone is catered for young and old alike; you can do everything of nothing. So come and discover your future holidays at Le Sourire. Choose your kingdom, well look after the rest.

www.camping-parcsaintjames.com

FR06100 Camping les Pinèdes

Route du Pont de Pierre, F-06480 La Colle-sur-Loup (Alpes-Maritimes)

Tel: **04 93 32 98 94**. Email: **camplespinedes06@aol.com** www.alanrogers.com/FR06100

Les Pinèdes is seven kilometres inland from the busy coast, at the centre of all the attractions of the Côte d'Azur, yet far enough away to be a peaceful retreat at the end of a busy day. It is terraced on a wooded hillside where olives and vines used to grow, All the level pitches have electricity (3-10A), most also with water and they are separated by low bushes. There are plans for 12 new pitches at the top of the site and also a small children's pool. The restaurant at the site entrance has an excellent reputation. In May the evenings are alive with fireflies. A 'Sites et Paysages' member.

Facilities

Two excellent new toilet blocks. One block has facilities for disabled visitors. Baby room. Shop. Bakery. Bar, restaurant, takeaway. Swimming pool. Play area. Field for volleyball, basketball, football, archery, boules. Entertainment for young and old, July/Aug. Weekly walks in the hills June - September (light breakfast carried by the donkeys). Off site: River fishing 50 m. Village 1 km. (tennis, riding, leisure park, keep fit course, antiques quarter). St Paul de Vence is 15 minutes away.

Open: 15 March - 30 September.

Directions

From A8 take D2 towards Vence. At Colle sur Loup roundabout take D6 signed Grasse, site on right in 3 km. at large sign after the restaurant entrance.
GPS: N43:40.902 E7:05.001

Charges guide

Per unit incl. 2 persons	€ 14,00 - € 21,00
caravan or motorcaravan	€ 16,00 - € 24,00
extra person	€ 4,00 - € 5,20
electricity (3-10A)	€ 3,50 - € 4,80
dog	€ 2,00 - € 2,90

Check real time availability and at-the-gate prices...

www.**alanrogers**.com

FR06120 Camping Green Park

159 Vallon des Vaux, F-06800 Cagnes-sur-Mer (Alpes-Maritimes)

Tel: **04 93 07 09 96**. Email: **info@greenpark.fr**   www.alanrogers.com/FR06120

Green Park has many facilities of a high standard and the family owners are justifiably proud. Situated just over 4 km. from the beaches at Cagnes-sur-Mer, Green Park is at the centre of the Côte d'Azur. The newer part of the site keeps all the family occupied with activities for children, teenagers and adults, while on the other side of the road is a quieter, traditional site, with limited facilities. There are 78 touring pitches mainly on grass, with electricity and 24 are fully serviced. The site has two swimming pools, one on each side of the quiet road.

Facilities

All the toilets are modern and mostly British, with facilities for children and disabled visitors (the disabled facilities are superb). Showers and washbasins are modern and kept very clean. Dishwashing and laundry sinks and three washing machines. Bar, restaurant and takeaway (28/4-24/9). Two swimming pools (all season, one heated 5/5-24/9). Internet point. Games room. Electronic barrier (€ 5 card deposit) and a gate keeper on duty all night. Off site: Beach 4 km. Golf and riding 9 km.

Open: 31 March - 15 October.

Directions

From Aix, A8, exit 47 onto N7 towards Nice. Straight on at traffic lights, by racecourse, for 2 km. Turn left towards Val Fleuri, Av. du Val Fleuri. Over roundabouts to Chemin Vallon des Vaux, site on right 2 km. Avoid the town centre. GPS: N43:41.355 E07:09.409

Charges guide

Per unit incl. 2 persons	€ 13,00 - € 44,00
extra person	€ 4,60 - € 6,00
child (7-17 yrs)	€ 3,90 - € 4,50
electricity	€ 5,50 - € 6,50

FR13010 Camping Municipal les Romarins

Route de Saint-Remy, F-13520 Maussane (Bouches du Rhône)

Tel: **04 90 54 33 60**. Email: **camping_municipal_maussane@wanadoo.fr**   www.alanrogers.com/FR13010

A well kept, neat municipal site, Les Romarins has been in the guide for several years and remains popular with our readers. Tarmac access roads lead to 145 good sized grassy pitches separated by hedges and bushes, all with electrical connections (6A). The municipal swimming pool (with discounts) is near and shops and restaurants are in the pleasant little town. Les Baux and St Remy-de-Provence are tourist attractions not to be missed, especially St Remy's Roman ruins. Les Romarins is popular and becomes very busy from 1 July - late August.

Facilities

Three toilet blocks, two refurbished, showers (on payment). An older block opens for July and August. Facilities for disabled visitors. Baby room. Laundry facilities. Motorcaravan services. Municipal swimming pool (50 m. from site) free to campers 15/6-31/8. Play area. Free tennis. Reading room. Internet access. Off site: Bicycle hire or golf 1 km. Fishing or riding 3 km.

Open: 15 March - 15 October.

Directions

Site is within the little town of Maussane on the eastern edge. GPS: N43:43.277 E04:48.580

Charges guide

Per unit incl. 1 or 2 adults	€ 16,50 - € 18,15
extra person	€ 3,80 - € 4,20
electricity	€ 3,30
Less 10-20% for longer stays.	

FR13030 Camping le Nostradamus

Route d'Eyguières, F-13300 Salon-de-Provence (Bouches du Rhône)

Tel: **04 90 56 08 36**. Email: **gilles.nostra@wanadoo.fr**   www.alanrogers.com/FR13030

Only some five kilometres from Salon-de-Provence, near the village of Eyguières, this is a very pleasant campsite with grassy shaded pitches thanks to the many trees which have been preserved here as a result of the imaginative irrigation scheme developed by the owners in the 18th century. The campsite edging the canal was opened 42 years ago as a farm site but has now been developed to offer 83 hedged pitches including 10 used for mobile homes. There are 20 with full services, the rest having electricity (4/6/10A). This is a family site but having said that, the canal is unfenced.

Facilities

One large block with showers and toilets upstairs, and one small toilet block both provide all modern facilities including an en-suite unit for babies and children and another for disabled visitors (key). Washing machine (key). Motorcaravan service point. Shop (basic essentials) and bar (1/3-31/10). Takeaway/restaurant (limited in early season). Swimming and paddling pools (15/5-30/9). Play area outside entrance. Fishing. Off site: Riding 5 km.

Open: 1 March - end October.

Directions

From A7 exit 26 (Senas) follow N538 south for 5 km. Then D175 west and pick up the D17 going south to Salon. Site is at junction of the D17 and CD72 with the entrance off the CD72. From A54 exit 13 go north towards Eyguières and take first right on CD72 (site signed). GPS: N43:40.380 E05:03.500

Charges guide

Per unit incl. 2 persons	€ 12,90 - € 17,10
electricity	€ 2,95 - € 5,95
Camping Cheques accepted.	

439

FR13040 Camping Monplaisir

Chemin de Monplaisir, F-13210 Saint Rémy-de-Provence (Bouches du Rhône)

Tel: **04 90 92 22 70**. Email: **reception@camping-monplaisir.fr**   www.alanrogers.com/FR13040

Only a kilometre from the centre of St Rémy, in the foothills of the Alpilles mountains, this is one of the most pleasant and well run sites we have come across. Everything about the site is of a high standard and quality. The good impression created by the reception and shop continues through the rest of the site. In all there are 130 level grass pitches with nine taken by smart mobile homes, with 6A electricity everywhere. Flowering shrubs and greenery abounds, roads are tarmac and all is neat and tidy. There are five toilet blocks strategically placed for all areas, two heated and one larger, but all unisex. The recreation area with a swimming pool (18 x 10 m), jacuzzi and paddling pool is overlooked by the bar. Open in July and August, it provides light meals and snacks and some entertainment. St Rémy is a very popular town and the site was full when we visited in mid June.

Facilities

Five good quality toilet blocks all have some washbasins in cabins. Family rooms and en-suite facilities for disabled people in two. Washing machines. Two motorcaravan service points. Shop with essentials (good cheese and cold meat counter), also takeaway pizzas. Bar with snacks (July/Aug). Swimming pool. New play area. Boules. Charcoal barbecues are not permitted. Off site: St Rémy 1 km. Les Baux 5 km. Bicycle hire 1 km. Fishing 2 km. Riding 5 km. Golf 10 km.

Open: 1 March - 3 November.

Directions

From St Rémy town centre follow signs for Arles and Nîmes. At roundabout on western side of town take D5 signed Maillane and immediately left by a supermarket. Site is signed and is on the left a little further on. GPS: N43:47.817 E04:49.423

Charges guide

Per unit incl. 2 persons	€ 14,00 - € 19,50
extra person	€ 4,50 - € 6,50
child (2-7 yrs)	€ 2,50 - € 4,50
electricity (6A)	€ 3,50
dog	€ 1,80

CAMPING MONPLAISIR

- Overflowing swimming and paddling pool
- Snack bar in high season, Laundry

- 130 pitches, 2.8 ha of comfort, quietness and garden area
- Boules, children's games, table tennis, grocery

- Chalets & mobile homes to let

CHEMIN MONPLAISIR - F-13210 ST. RÉMY DE PROVENCE - FRANCE
TEL : +33 (0)4 90 92 22 70 - FAX : +33 (0)4 90 92 18 57
www.camping-monplaisir.fr
reception@camping-monplaisir.fr

FR13050 Camping Mas de Nicolas

Avenue Plaisance du Touch, F-13210 Saint Rémy-de-Provence (Bouches du Rhône)

Tel: **04 90 92 27 05**. Email: **camping-masdenicolas@nerim.fr**   www.alanrogers.com/FR13050

The site has a very spacious feel to it, due mainly to the central area of gently sloping grass, dotted with shrubs, that is kept clear of pitches and used for leisure and sunbathing. The 140 pitches are separated by hedges, 120 with electricity, water and drainage, and access roads are wide. Some pitches are an irregular shape and some are sloping, but many have views and they are mostly organised into groups of two and four. There is an attractive pool area with new 'balneotherapie et remise en form', or as we would call it a spa and gym.

Facilities

Good, modern toilet blocks including baby bathroom. Plans to refurbish one block. Dishwashing and laundry sinks, washing machines. Small bar (May-Sept), occasional Paella evenings. Swimming pool (15/5-15/9). Sauna, steam room, spa bath, gym. Play area. Internet access. Off site: Adjacent municipal gym, tennis, volleyball courts. Bicycle hire, riding 1 km. Fishing 2 km. Golf 15 km. St Rémy has a wide selection of restaurants, Wednesday market.

Open: 1 March - 31 October.

Directions

St Rémy de Provence is located where the D571 from Avignon connects with the D99 Tarascon - Cavaillon road. Site is signed from the village centre on the north side. Leave autoroute A7 at Cavaillon or Avignon-Sud. GPS: N43:47.773 E04:50.327

Charges guide

Per unit incl. 2 persons and electricity	€ 17,30 - € 22,50
extra person	€ 4,50 - € 6,30
child (under 10 yrs)	€ 2,20 - € 3,70
animal	€ 1,50 - € 1,70

FR13070 Village Center des Iscles

B.P. 47, F-13640 La Roque d'Anthéron (Bouches du Rhône)

Tel: 04 99 57 21 21. Email: contact@village-center.com
www.alanrogers.com/FR13070

Domaine des Iscles is probably the best of the three sites in this area. There are over 400 pitches, including 160 mobile homes for rent. The remaining pitches for touring units are well laid out with shared electricity and water points. There is shade for some. An attractive feature is a lake with a pebble beach, used for swimming and with a high slide into the water. Fishing is also permitted here in the low seasons. There are 150 km. of footpaths around La Roque d'Anthéron and the Luberon hills are only 10 km. with good opportunities for excursions in this very pleasant landscape. In July and August there an international piano festival is held at the nearby town of Silvacane. Another cultural centre is Aix en Provence which is only 30 km. away. Those interested in fishing will be delighted to choose between the Durance river 100 m. away or the Canal de Marseilles which borders the site.

Facilities

Three basic toilet blocks (only one open in low season) have only two British WCs, the remainder are Turkish style. Small shower cubicles. Facilities for disabled visitors but none for babies. One washing machine at each block. Shop and bar (June-Sept). Restaurant and snack bar (July/Aug). Circular swimming pool. Lake for swimming with slide. Some entertainment and activities for children (July/Aug). Bicycle hire. Fishing (low season). Off site: Fishing nearby. Riding 3 km.

Open: 30 April - 17 September.

Directions

From the A7 (Avignon - Marseille) take exit 26 (Senas) and N7 towards Pertuis. Turn left at Pont Royal on D561 towards Peyrolles. Pass town of La Roque d'Antheron and site is signed where the access road passes under the Canal de Marseille. GPS: N43:43.781 E05:19.097

Charges guide

Per unit incl. 1 or 2 persons and electricity	€ 13,50 - € 28,00
extra person	€ 3,00 - € 4,50
child (4-10 yrs)	€ 1,90 - € 3,00

Altavia Link

Les Iscles★★★

La Roque d'Anthéron > Provence

• 2 km away from La Roque d'Anthéron
• An artificial lake

Villagecenter

BOOK YOUR HOLIDAYS
www.village-center.com
+33 (0)4 99 57 21 21

QUALITÉ TOURISME   Camping Qualité   La Clef Verte

FR13060 Camping les Micocouliers

445 route de Cassoulen, F-13690 Graveson-en-Provence (Bouches du Rhône)

Tel: 04 90 95 81 49. Email: micocou@free.fr
www.alanrogers.com/FR13060

M. et Mme. Riehl started work on Les Micocouliers in 1997 and they have developed a comfortable site. On the outskirts of the town it only some 10 km. from St Rémy and Avignon. A purpose built, terracotta 'house' in a raised position provides all the facilities. The 65 pitches radiate out from here with the pool and entrance to one side. The pitches are on level grass, separated by small bushes, and shade is developing. Electricity connections are possible (4-13A). There are also a few mobile homes. The popular swimming pool is a welcome addition.

Facilities

Unisex facilities in one unit provide toilets and facilities for disabled visitors (by key), another showers and washbasins in cabins and another dishwashing and laundry facilities. Reception and limited shop (July/Aug) are in another. Swimming pool (12 x 8 m; 5/5-15/9). Paddling pool (1/7-31/8). Play area. Off site: Fishing 5 km. Bicycle hire 1 km. Riding next door. Golf 5 km. Beach 60 km. at Ste Marie de la Mer.

Open: 15 March - 15 October.

Directions

Site is southeast of Graveson. From the N570 at new roundabout take D5 towards St Rémy and Maillane and site is 500 m. on the left. GPS: N43:50.638 E04:46.879

Charges guide

Per unit incl. 2 persons	€ 14,00 - € 18,10
extra person	€ 4,70 - € 6,00
child (2-12 yrs)	€ 3,70 - € 4,70
electricity	€ 3,70 - € 6,60
Camping Cheques accepted.	

Check real time availability and at-the-gate prices...

www.alanrogers.com

FR13120 Airotel Parc de Chantecler

41 avenue du Val Saint André, F-13100 Aix-en-Provence (Bouches du Rhône)

Tel: 04 42 26 12 98. Email: info@campingchantecler.com   www.alanrogers.com/FR13120

Cézanne is amongst Aix's most famous former residents, but many just see the town as a stop on the journey south. This good, quiet campsite might change that image; on the southeast edge of the town, close to the motorway it is only minutes by the good bus service from the city centre. The site provides 240 pitches (160 for tourers) in mature woodland with good facilities. Under the new leadership of Serge Carcolse, the site is destined to change for the good whilst retaining the best that already exists. Cézanne's studio is amongst the numerous places to visit in Aix.

Facilities

Four sanitary blocks provide ample WCs, washbasins and hot showers around the site. Facilities for campers.with disabilities Motorcaravan service point. Bar and restaurant (1/7-30/8). Swimming pool (1/5-15/9). Tennis. Boules. Internet access and WiFi. Mobile homes to rent. Barbecues are not permitted. Off site: Bus service 200 m. Aix-en-Provence 2 km. Riding 2 km. Golf 5 km.

Open: All year.

Directions

Leave the A8 at exit 31 (Aix-Sud) and at roundabout turn right. At second set of lights turn left and within 300 m. at roundabout turn right to the site in 200 m. GPS: N43:30.989 E05:28.512

Charges guide

Per person	€ 5,40 - € 5,80
child (under 7 yrs)	€ 3,40 - € 3,60
pitch	€ 6,10 - € 7,00
electricity (5A)	€ 3,40 - € 3,70

Camping Chantecler★★★★

Situated in a green quiet oasis and offering you all the sweetness of life, on only 5 minutes from Aix en Provence.
We warmly welcome you on this green 8 acres park, the favorite surroundings of Cézanne on only 30 minutes form Marseille and Cassis, and on only 45 minutes form Baux de Provence and Avignon.

Val St. André - 13100 Aix en Provence - Tel.: 0033 (0)4 42 26 12 98
info@campingchantecler.com - www.campingchantecler.com

FR13130 Camping le Canet Plage

F-13250 Saint Chamas-en-Provence (Bouches du Rhône)

Tel: 04 90 50 96 89. Email: canet-plage@wanadoo.fr   www.alanrogers.com/FR13130

Recently acquired by dynamic new owners, Le Canet Plage is a family site with 185 pitches (all with electrical connections). Many improvements are scheduled for completion for the 2009 season with a significant investment also made in new mobile homes. The site can be found 15 km. south of Salon de Provence and five kilometres from the Gallo-Roman town of St Chamas, on the banks of the Etang de Berre. Pitches are of a good size with a number of very large (120 sq.m) pitches available. There is direct access to the lake and many watersports are available, including windsurfing, sailing and waterskiing.

Facilities

Restaurant/bar. Takeaway meals. Small shop. Swimming pool. Play area. Games room. Direct access to lake. Mobile homes and chalets for rent. Off site: Nearest sandy beach 3 km. Windsurfing. Sailing. Fishing. Footpath around lake. Golf 8 km. Mediterranean coast 40 km.

Open: All year.

Directions

From the A7 autoroute take Salon-de-Provence Centre exit and pick up signs for Lançon-Provence (D113). Carry on the D113 until La Fare-les-Oliviers and turn right onto the D10 towards St Chamas. The site is well signposted on this road, just before St Chamas. GPS: N43:31.674 E05:05.607

Charges guide

Per person	€ 3,60
child (under 7 yrs)	€ 2,00
pitch	€ 3,50
electricity	€ 3,50

Check real time availability and at-the-gate prices...
www.alanrogers.com

`FR13140` Flower Camping Marius

Plage de la Saulce, La Couronne, F-13500 Martigues (Bouches du Rhône)
Tel: 04 42 80 70 29. Email: contact@camping-marius.com   www.alanrogers.com/FR13140

Martigues is a large town west of Marseille. The old centre is charming with Provencal houses lining the Canal de Caronte and earning the town the epithet, Venice of Provence. Camping Marius can be found to the south of the town and extends over two acres with 119 pitches (of which around 46 are occupied by mobile homes and other rented accommodation). Pitches are of a good size and well shaded. The nearest beach is just a 200 m. stroll away, and there are no roads to cross. On-site amenities include a snack bar and takeaway food service. Cycles and canoes are available for hire.

www.flowercampings.com

Facilities
Snack bar. Takeaway. Play area. Bicycle hire. Canoe hire. Activity and entertainment programme. Direct access to beach 200 m. Mobile homes for rent. Off site: Nearest village is La Couronne (good range of shops and restaurants and railway station). Fishing village of Carro (3 km.) with daily fish market.

Open: 29 March - 10 November.

Directions
Approach Martigues (west side of Etang de Berre) on the D5 and cross the Canal de Caronte, continuing south on the D5 and then the D49 to La Couronne. Site is clearly signed from here.
GPS: N43:20.106 E05:04.056

Charges 2009
Per unit incl. 2 persons	
and electricity	€ 18,40 - € 25,40
extra person	€ 3,80 - € 6,20
child (2-7 yrs)	€ 1,90 - € 3,10
dog	free

`FR83010` Camping Caravaning les Pins Parasols

3360 rue des Combattants d'Afrique du Nord, F-83600 Fréjus (Var)
Tel: 04 94 40 88 43. Email: lespinsparasols@wanadoo.fr   www.alanrogers.com/FR83010

Not everyone likes very big sites and Les Pins Parasols with its 189 pitches is of a comfortable size which is quite easy to walk around. It is family owned and run. Although on very slightly undulating ground, virtually all the pitches (all have electricity) are levelled or terraced and separated by hedges or bushes with pine trees for shade. There are 48 pitches equipped with their own fully enclosed, sanitary unit, with WC, washbasin, hot shower and dishwashing sink. These pitches naturally cost more but may well be of interest to those seeking a little bit of extra comfort.

Facilities
Average quality toilet blocks (one heated) providing facilities for disabled people. Small shop with reasonable stocks, restaurant, takeaway (both 15/4-30/9). General room, TV. Swimming pool, attractive rock backdrop, separate long slide with landing pool, small paddling pool (heated). Half-court tennis. Off site: Bicycle hire or riding 2 km. Fishing 6 km. Golf 10 km. Bus from the gate into Fréjus 5 km. Beach 6 km.

Open: 5 April - 27 September.

Directions
From A8 take exit 38 for Fréjus Est. Turn right immediately on leaving pay booths on a small road which leads across to D4, then right again and under 1 km. to site. GPS: N43:27.774 E06:43.542

Charges guide
Per unit incl. 2 persons	
and electricity	€ 18,00 - € 27,30
pitch with sanitary unit	€ 22,70 - € 34,00
extra person	€ 4,50 - € 6,35
child (under 7 yrs)	€ 3,00 - € 3,85
dog	€ 1,85 - € 2,80

LES PINS PARASOLS CAMPING CARAVANNING ★★★★

3360 Rue des Combattants d'Afrique du Nord
ROUTE DE BAGNOLS - F-83600 FRÉJUS
Tel.: 0033 494.40.88.43

SWIMMING POOL
Supermarket - Snackbar - Individual washing cabins and hot water in all sanitary facilities - Separated pitches (80-100m²) all with electricity. Pitches with individual sanitary facilities (shower, washbasin, sink with hot water, WC) - Children's playground and solarium - Caravan pitches - Water points - Mini-tennis **SUN AND SHADE** near the beaches

Fax : 0033 494.40.81.99
Email : lespinsparasols@wanadoo.fr
Internet : www.lespinsparasols.com

443

FR83020 Castel Camping Caravaning Esterel

Avenue des Golf, Agay, F-83530 Saint Raphaël (Var)

Tel: 04 94 82 03 28. Email: contact@esterel-caravaning.fr   www.alanrogers.com/FR83020

Esterel is a quality caravan site east of St Raphaël, set among the hills at the back of Agay. The site is three and a half kilometres from the sandy beach at Agay where parking is perhaps a little easier than at most places on this coast. It has 230 pitches for tourers, for caravans but not tents, all have electricity and water tap, 18 special ones have their own en-suite washroom adjoining. Pitches are on shallow terraces, attractively landscaped with good shade and a variety of flowers, giving a feeling of spaciousness. Some 'maxi-pitches' from 110 to 160 sq.m. are available with 10A electricity. Developed by the Laroche family for over 30 years, the site has an attractive, quiet situation with good views of the Esterel mountains. Wild boar occasionally come to the perimeter fence to be fed by visitors. This is a very good site, well run and organised in a deservedly popular area. A pleasant courtyard area contains the shop and bar, with a terrace overlooking the attractively landscaped (floodlit at night) pool complex. A member of 'Les Castels' group.

Facilities

Excellent refurbished, heated toilet blocks. Individual toilet units on 18 pitches. Facilities for disabled people. Laundry room. Motorcaravan services. Shop. Gift shop. Takeaway. Bar/restaurant. Five circular swimming pools (two heated), one for adults, one for children, three arranged as a waterfall (1/4-30/9). Disco. Archery. Minigolf. Tennis. Pony rides. Pétanque. Squash. Playground. Nursery. Bicycle hire. Internet access. Organised events in season. No barbecues. Off site: Golf nearby. Trekking by foot, bicycle or by pony in L'Esterel forest park. Fishing, beach 3 km.

Open: 1 April - 6 October.

Directions

From A8, exit Fréjus, follow signs for Valescure, then for Agay, site on left. The road from Agay is the easiest to follow but it is possible to approach from St Raphaël via Valescure.
GPS: N43:27.253 E06:49.945

Charges guide

Per unit incl. 2 persons,	
standard pitch	€ 23,00 - € 38,00
'maxi' pitch	€ 28,00 - € 47,00
deluxe pitch	€ 32,00 - € 51,00
extra person	€ 8,50
child (1-7 yrs)	€ 6,50

FR83040 Camping Club la Bastiane

1056 chemin de Suvières, F-83480 Puget-sur-Argens (Var)

Tel: 04 94 55 55 94. Email: info@labastiane.com   www.alanrogers.com/FR83040

With a shady woodland setting, La Bastiane is a well established site with good amenities, well located for exploring the Côte d'Azur and with easy access to nearby beaches. There are 180 pitches here of which 100 are reserved for touring. They are generally of a good size and are all supplied with electrical connections (6A). The terrain is somewhat undulating but most of the pitches are on level terraces. There is a good swimming pool and a range of amenities including a shop, bar and restaurant. The site becomes lively in peak season with a range of activities including sports tournaments, discos, a children's club and excursions to nearby places of interest such as Monaco and the Gorges de Verdon.

Facilities

Four toilet blocks, three of modern construction, one refurbished. Facilities for disabled visitors. Washing machines, dryers. Shop and Bar (11/4-17/10). Takeaway (11/4-25/9). Restaurant (6/6-12/9). Heated swimming pool (11/4-17/10). Tennis. Multisport terrain. Children's club. Play area. Games/TV room. Bicycle hire. Evening entertainment in peak season. Excursion programme. Only electric barbecues. One dog only. Mobile homes and chalets for rent. Off site: Beach 7 km. Lake beach 8 km. Riding 500 m. Fishing 3 km. Golf 9 km.

Open: 26 March - 17 October.

Directions

Leave A8 at exit 37 (Puget), take right turn at first roundabout (signed Roquebrune), join N7. Turn right, first traffic lights (200 m), then left at T-junction. Site signed from here, on the right 2.5 km. from the motorway. GPS: N43:28.180 E06:40.707

Charges 2009

Per unit incl. 2 persons and electricity	€ 19,00 - € 38,50

Mediterranean East

The Travel Service ...we'll arrange everything

BOOK THIS SITE

CALL 01580 214000

Check real time availability and at-the-gate prices...

 www.alanrogers.com

Esterel CARAVANING

★★★★

Avenue des Golfs - 83530 Saint-Raphaël - France
Tel : +33 4.94.82.03.28 - Fax : +33 4.94.82.87.37

EASTER Special : 28/03 - 25/04/2009,
from 160 € per week in Mini luxe mobile home 2/4 persons
from 18 € per night for 2 pers. in standard pitch for caravan/camper van.

w w w . e s t e r e l - c a r a v a n i n g . f r

On the Côte d'Azur, between Cannes and Saint-Tropez.

In the heart of the Esterel mountains,
3 km away from the sandy beaches of Agay.

New

Indoor heated
swimming pool
for children.

"Jungle Paradise"

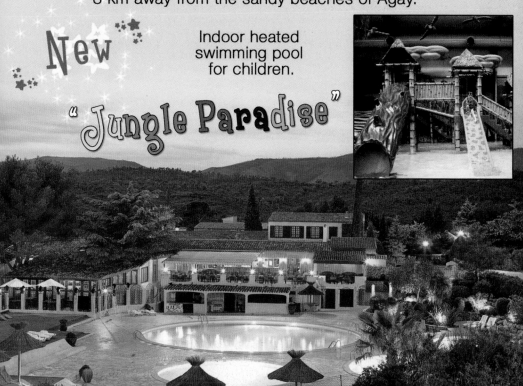

The Travel Service

BOOK THIS SITE
CALL 01580 214000
...we'll arrange everything

FR83080 Au Paradis des Campeurs

La Gaillarde-Plage, F-83380 Les Issambres (Var)

Tel: 04 94 96 93 55

www.alanrogers.com/FR83080

Family owned and run, this popular site has 180 pitches, all with 6A electricity and 132 with water and drainage. The original pitches vary in size and shape but all are satisfactory and most have some shade. The newer pitches are all large and have rather less shade although trees and bushes are maturing nicely. There is no entertainment which gives peaceful nights. The gates are surveyed by TV (especially the beach gate) and a security man patrols all day. With direct access to a sandy beach (via an underpass) and being so well maintained, the site has become deservedly popular so it is essential to book for June, July and August.

Facilities	Directions
Excellent, refurbished, well maintained toilet blocks. Facilities for babies and children with shower at suitable height. En-suite for disabled visitors. Washing machines and dryer. Motorcaravan services. Shop, restaurant and takeaway service (all season). TV room. Internet and WiFi. Excellent play areas with top quality safety bases, catering for the under and over 5s. Boules. Car wash area. Off site: Bicycle hire 2.5 km. Riding 3 km. Golf 6 km.	Site is signed from N98 coast road at La Gaillarde, 2 km. south of St Aygulf. GPS: N43:21.956 E06:42.738

Open: 28 March - 16 October.

Charges guide

Per unit incl. 2 persons	€ 14,00 - € 23,00
incl. water and drainage	€ 16,00 - € 27,00
extra person	€ 6,00
child (under 5 yrs)	€ 3,00
electricity (6A)	€ 4,00

FR83090 RCN Domaine de la Noguière

Route de Fréjus, F-83490 Le Muy (Var)

Tel: 04 94 45 13 78. Email: info@rcn-domainedelanoguiere.fr   www.alanrogers.com/FR83090

A Dutch company, RCN runs a chain of good campsites in the Netherlands. They now operate six sites in France, all with Dutch managers who speak good French and English. Domaine de la Noguière is located amongst beautiful Provençal scenery with lavender fields, mimosa trees and reddish brown rocks. The Mediterranean beaches at the famous resorts of Fréjus and St Raphaël are only 16 km. There are 200 pitches with 6A electricity, arranged on small terraces on the slightly sloping ground. At the entrance to the site there is a reception, a shop and a restaurant serving regional specialities.

Facilities	Directions
Toilets are fully tiled with individual cabins and access for disabled visitors. Washing machines, dryers and ironing area. Bar/restaurant with terrace. Small meeting room with library, snooker table, table football and large TV. Swimming pool with large slides. Tennis. Boules.	From the A8, take exit 37 toward Roquebrune sur Argens and Puget sur Argens (this is the second exit towards Roquebrune, drive past exit 36). At roundabout, take first right turn toward Roquebrune and Le Muy (N7). Continue on this road for 8 km. to site on the right. GPS: N43:28.099 E06:35.521

Open: 21 March - 31 October.

Charges 2009

Per unit incl. 2 persons, electricity and water	€ 21,00 - € 47,50
incl. up to 6 persons	€ 23,50 - € 63,00
Camping Cheques accepted.	

www.rcn-campings.fr

FR83100 Camping de la Plage

RD559, F-83310 Grimaud (Var)

Tel: 04 94 56 31 15. Email: campingplagegrimaud@wanadoo.fr   www.alanrogers.com/FR83100

A site on the beach is always in great demand, and Camping de la Plage is no exception, consequently it becomes very crowded. With 450 pitches, the site is divided into two parts by the N98 although a dangerous crossing is avoided by an underpass. The pitches in the area away from the beach will be the more peaceful and have more shade as they are in light woodland. They are mostly of a good size. In the area over the road there is more grass. There is some traffic noise on the pitches close to the busy road. All pitches have electricity (2-10A) but long leads may be required.

Facilities	Directions
Three toilet blocks of varying quality but well equipped and clean. Baby bath. Facilities for disabled visitors. Motorcaravan services. Large supermarket (all season). Bar, restaurant, takeaway (from May). Tennis. Small play area. Bicycle hire. Fridge rental. Charcoal barbecues are not permitted. Off site: Golf and riding 3 km. Boat hire.	Site is on N98 main coast road about 6 km. southwest of Ste Maxime. This road is very busy in main season. GPS: N43:16.913 E06:35.159

Open: One week before Easter - 6 October.

Charges guide

Per unit incl. 2 persons	€ 23,00 - € 28,00
extra person	€ 6,00 - € 7,10
electricity (2-10A)	€ 4,00 - € 8,50

Check real time availability and at-the-gate prices...
www.alanrogers.com

FR83030 Camping Caravaning Leï Suves

Mobile homes ▶ page 511

Quartier du Blavet, F-83520 Roquebrune-sur-Argens (Var)

Tel: **04 94 45 43 95**. Email: **camping.lei.suves@wanadoo.fr**

www.alanrogers.com/FR83030

This quiet, pretty site is a few kilometres inland from the coast, two kilometres north of the N7. Close to the unusual Roquebrune rock, it is within easy reach of St Tropez, Ste Maxime, St Raphaël and Cannes. The site entrance is appealing – wide and spacious, with a large bank of well tended flowers. Mainly on a gently sloping hillside, the 310 pitches are terraced with shade provided by the many cork trees which give the site its name. All pitches have electricity and access to water. A pleasant pool area is beside the bar/restaurant and entertainment area. It is possible to walk in the surrounding woods as long as there is no fire alert. Many of the pitches are used for mobile homes.

Facilities

Modern, well kept toilet blocks include washing machines, facilities for disabled visitors. Shop. Good sized swimming pool, paddling pool. Bar, terrace, snack bar, takeaway (all 1/4-30/9). Outdoor stage near the bar for evening entertainment, high season. Excellent play area. Table tennis, tennis, sports area. Internet terminal. Only gas barbecues. Off site: Bus stop at site entrance. Riding 1 km. Fishing 3 km. Bicycle hire 5 km. Golf 7 km. Beach at St Aygulf 15 km.

Open: 1 April - 15 October.

Directions

Leave autoroute at Le Muy and take N7 towards St Rapha'l. Turn left at roundabout onto D7 heading north signed La Boverie (site also signed). Site on right in 2 km. GPS: N43:28.677 E06:38.324

Charges guide

Per unit incl. 2 persons	€ 19,00 - € 34,50
incl. 3 persons	€ 21,00 - € 37,00
extra person	€ 4,50 - € 7,50
electricity	€ 4,50

Leï Suves is beautifully located at the Cote d'Azur close to Saint-Tropez Sainte Maxime, Saint-Raphaël and Cannes.

www.camping-lei-suves.com

Camping Caravaning ★★★★
Leï Suves
Quartier du Blavet
83520
Roquebrune sur Argens
Tél : (0033) 4 94 45 43 95
Fax : (0033) 4 94 81 63 13

Roquebrune sur Argens Provence

Check real time availability and at-the-gate prices...
www.**alanrogers**.com

FR83060 Camping Resort la Baume – la Palmeraie

Mobile homes ▶ page 511

Route de Bagnols, F-83618 Fréjus (Var)

Tel: **04 94 19 88 88**. Email: reception@labaume-lapalmeraie.com

www.alanrogers.com/FR83060

La Baume is large, busy site about five and a half kilometres from the long sandy beach of Fréjus-Plage, although with its fine and varied selection of swimming pools many people do not bother to make the trip. The pools with their palm trees are remarkable for their size and variety (water slides, etc.) – the very large 'feature' pool a highlight. Recent additions are an aquatic play area and two indoor pools with a slide and a spa area. The site has nearly 250 adequately sized, fully serviced pitches, with some separators and most have shade. Although tents are accepted, the site concentrates mainly on caravanning. It becomes full in season. Adjoining La Baume is its sister site La Palmeraie, providing self-catering accommodation, its own landscaped pool and offering some entertainment to supplement that at La Baume. There are 500 large pitches with mains sewerage for mobile homes. La Baume's convenient location has its 'downside' as there is some traffic noise on a few pitches from the nearby autoroute – somewhat obtrusive at first but we soon failed to notice it. It is a popular site with tour operators.

Facilities

Seven refurbished toilet blocks. Supermarket, several shops. Two bars, terrace overlooking pools, TV. Restaurant, takeaway. Six swimming pools (heated all season, two covered, plus steam room and jacuzzi). Fitness centre. Tennis. Archery (July/Aug). Skateboard park. Organised events, daytime and evening entertainment, some English. Amphitheatre. Discos all season. Children's club (all season). Off site: Bus to Fréjus passes gate. Riding 2 km. Fishing 3 km. Golf 5 km. Beach 5 km.

Open: 4 April - 26 September, with full services.

Directions

From west, A8, exit Fréjus, take N7 southwest (Fréjus). After 4 km, turn left on D4 and site is 3 km. From east, A8, exit 38 Fréjus and follow signs for Cais. Site is signed. GPS: N43:27.599 E06:43.229

Charges 2009

Per unit incl. 2 persons, electricity, water and drainage	€ 19,00 - € 43,00
extra person	€ 5,00 - € 12,00
child (under 7 yrs)	free - € 7,00
dog	€ 4,00 - € 5,00

Min. stay for motorhomes 2 nights.
Large units should book.

FR83110 Camping de la Baie

Boulevard Pasteur, B.P. 12, F-83240 Cavalaire-sur-Mer (Var)

Tel: **04 94 64 08 15**. Email: campbaie@club-internet.com

www.alanrogers.com/FR83110

This busy site is only a short walk from the main street of the popular holiday resort of Cavalaire with it's harbour, restaurants and shops. A long, sandy beach runs right round the bay and there are plenty of watersport activities nearby. The site is only 400 metres from the beach, very well positioned for a family holiday. The 253 individual touring pitches are on slightly sloping, sandy ground with terracing and good access roads, and all have electricity hook-ups (10A). Trees give plenty of shade. The remaining 190 pitches are used for mobile homes and chalets. English is spoken.

Facilities

Four main modern toilet blocks include washbasins in cabins, and four smaller units have open washbasins behind. Toilets are mainly British style, with some Turkish. Launderette. Small shop. Restaurant. Bar. Takeaway. Entertainment with dance evenings. Kidney-shaped pool with sunbathing terrace (Easter - end Nov), small paddling pool and new jacuzzi. Playground. Table tennis. TV room. Exchange facilities. Off site: Bicycle hire 200 m. Beach 400 m. Golf 10 km. Riding 12 km.

Open: 15 March - 15 November.

Directions

Take D559 to Cavalaire-sur-Mer (not Cavalière, some 4 km. away). Site is signed by yellow signs from the main street, some 400 m. north of the harbour. GPS: N43:10.176 E06:31.816

Charges guide

Per unit incl. 1-3 persons	€ 22,00 - € 41,80
extra person	€ 6,00 - € 10,70
child (under 10 yrs)	€ 3,00 - € 5,90
electricity	€ 4,90
animal	€ 2,50 - € 4,20

Check real time availability and at-the-gate prices...

www.**alanrogers**.com

La Baume   La Palmeraie

Camping Resort ★★★★   *Résidence de Tourisme* ★★

www.labaume-lapalmeraie.com

Heated sanitary blocks, marked-out pitches, 6 swimming pools including 2 covered and heated, 6 water-slides and jacuzzis.
5 kilometers from the sandy beaches of Fréjus and Saint Raphaël.

Fréjus Côte d'Azur

from April to September :

On going entertainment

Cabaret - Show

Disco

Children's club

E.S.E COMMUNICATION - Draguignan Tél : 04 94 67 06 00

Le Sud Grandeur Nature

Rental for
Bastidons
2 or 3 rooms
Mobil-homes
4/6 persons
Appartment
6 of 10 persons

Rue des Combattants d'Afrique du Nord   83618 FREJUS Cedex
Tel: +33(0)4 94 19 88 88   -   Fax:+33(0)4 94 19 83 50
E-mail : reception@labaume-lapalmeraie.com

FR83050 Camping Résidence du Campeur

Mobile homes ▶ page 511

B.P. 12, D7, F-83371 Saint Aygulf (Var)

Tel: **04 94 81 01 59**. Email: **info@residence-campeur.com**   www.alanrogers.com/FR83050

This excellent site near the Côte d'Azur will take you away from all the bustle of the Mediterranean coast. Spread out over ten hectares, there are separate areas for mobile homes and touring caravans and tents, with pitches arranged along avenues. The touring pitches average 100 sq.m. in size and all have electricity connections and private sanitary facilities (although washbasins double as dishwashing sinks). The bar/restaurant is surrounded by a shady terrace, whilst friendly staff provide an excellent service. A pleasant pool complex is available for those who wish to stay on site instead of going swimming in the nearby lake or from the Mediterranean beaches.

Facilities	Directions
Private toilet blocks are cleaned at regular intervals and include a washbasin, shower and WC. Laundry area with washing machines. Well stocked supermarket. Bar and restaurant. Takeaway. New swimming pool complex with four toboggans (all season). Two tennis courts. Minigolf. Boules. Fishing. Bicycle hire. Play area. Games/TV room. Only gas or electric barbecues are permitted. Off site: Beach and St Aygulf 2.5 km. Riding 1.5 km. Golf 2 km. Water skiing nearby.	Leave A8 at Le Muy exit (no. 36) on N555 towards Draguignan then onto the N7 towards Fréjus. Turn right on D7 signed St Aygulf and site is on the right about 2.5 km. before the town. GPS: N43:21.935 E06:42.742

Open: 28 March - 30 September.

Charges guide

Per unit incl. 3 persons and electricity (10A)	€ 28,05 - € 48,10
extra person	€ 8,30
child (under 7 yrs)	€ 5,65

La Résidence du Campeur
Camping Club ★★★★
Provence - Côte d'Azur
Open from 28 March till 30 Septembe

2,5 km away from the fine sandy beaches, discover the charm of this shady campsite where one can enjoy well being and comfort: small supermarket, bar, restaurant, open air cinema. Disco, playing room, mini golf, multi sports terrain, petanque, archery. Animations and Club Mickey in July and August.

B.P 12   Les grands châteaux de Villepey 83371 Saint-Aygulf cedex
Tél : +33(0)4.94.81.01.59   Fax : +33(0)4.94.81.01.64
www.residence-campeur.com   Email : info@residence-campeur.com

FR83120 Camp du Domaine

B.P. 207 La Favière, F-83230 Bormes-les-Mimosas (Var)

Tel: **04 94 71 03 12**. Email: **mail@campdudomaine.com**   www.alanrogers.com/FR83120

Camp du Domaine, three kilometres south of Le Lavandou, is a large, attractive beach-side site with 1,200 pitches set in 45 hectares of pine woods, although surprisingly it does not give the impression of being so big. Most pitches are reasonably level and 800 have 10A electricity. The most popular pitches are at the beach, but the ones furthest away are, on the whole, larger and have more shade amongst the trees, although many of them are more suitable for tents. The beach is the attraction however and everyone tries to get close. American motorhomes are not accepted.

Facilities	Directions
Ten modern, well used but clean toilet blocks. Mostly Turkish WCs. Facilities for disabled visitors (but steep steps). Children and baby room. Washing machines. Fridges to hire. Well stocked supermarket, bars, pizzeria (all open all season). Excellent play area. Boats, pedaloes for hire. Wide range of watersports. Games, competitions July/Aug. Children's club. Tennis. Multisport courts. Barbecues are strictly forbidden. Dogs are not accepted 3/7-31/8. Off site: Bicycle hire 500 m. Riding or golf 15 km.	Just outside and to west of Le Lavandou, at roundabout, turn off D559 towards the sea on road signed Favière. After 2 km. turn left at site signs. GPS: N43:07.080 E06:21.076

Charges guide

Per unit incl. 2 persons	€ 18,00 - € 29,00
incl. electricity and water	€ 26,00 - € 35,50
extra person	€ 5,40 - € 7,50
child (under 7 yrs)	€ 1,00 - € 3,80

Open: 15 March - 31 October.

Check real time availability and at-the-gate prices...
www.alanrogers.com

FR83170 Camping Domaine de la Bergerie

Vallée du Fournel, route du Col-du-Bougnon, F-83520 Roquebrune-sur-Argens (Var)

Tel: **04 98 11 45 45**. Email: **info@domainelabergerie.com**   www.alanrogers.com/FR83170

This excellent site near the Côte d'Azur will take you away from all the bustle of the Mediterranean to total relaxation amongst the cork, oak, pine and mimosa in its woodland setting. The 60 hectare site is quite spread out with semi-landscaped areas for mobile homes and, grassy avenues of 200 separated pitches for touring caravans and tents. All pitches average over 80 sq.m. and have electricity, with those in one area also having water and drainage. The restaurant/bar, a converted farm building, is surrounded by shady patios, whilst inside it oozes character with high beams and archways leading to intimate corners. Activities are organised daily and, in the evening, shows, cabarets, discos, cinema, karaoke and dancing at the amphitheatre prove popular (possibly until midnight). A superb new pool complex supplements the original pool adding more outdoor pools with slides and a river feature, an indoor pool and a fitness centre with jacuzzi, sauna, Turkish bath, massage, reflexology and gym.

Facilities

Four toilet blocks (all refurbished in 2007) are kept clean and include washbasins in cubicles, facilities for people with disabilities, and babies. Supermarket. Bar/restaurant. Takeaway. Pool complex (5/4-30/9) with indoor pool and fitness centre (body building, sauna, gym, etc). Tennis courts. Archery. Roller skating. Minigolf. English speaking childrens club. Mini-farm for children. Fishing. Only gas barbecues are permitted. Off site: Riding or golf 2 km. Bicycle hire 7 km. Beach, St Aygulf or Ste Maxime 7 km. Water skiing and rock climbing nearby.

Open: 25 April - 30 September
(mobile homes 15 February - 15 November).

Directions

Leave A8 at Le Muy exit on N7 towards Fréjus. Proceed for 9 km. then right onto D7 signed St Aygulf. Continue for 8 km. and then right at roundabout on D8; site is on the right. GPS: N43:24.547 E06:40.481

Charges guide

Per unit incl. 2 persons and electricity (6A)	€ 18,50 - € 40,00
incl. water and drainage	€ 24,00 - € 45,00
extra person	€ 5,00 - € 9,00
child (under 7 yrs)	€ 3,60 - € 6,50
dog	free - € 5,00

Between Frejus en St. Tropez, in a natural wooded area of 60 ha., at only 10 min drive from the coast...

DOMAINE DE LA BERGERIE ★★★★

○ Aquatic park with slides and Jacuzzi
○ Steam bath ○ Fitness center ○ 5 tennis
○ Shows ○ Animations ○ Kid's club

COTTAGES FOR RENT 15/02 to 15/11

Low season : Special price for two weeks or longer !

Camping : 25/04 to 30/09
Inside Pool : 04/04 to 30/10

DOMAINE DE LA BERGERIE
Rte du Col du Bougnon
83520 Roquebrune sur Argens
℡ 04 98 11 45 45 • Fax 04 98 11 45 46
www.domainelabergerie.com

451

FR83070 Caravaning l'Etoile d'Argens

F-83370 Saint Aygulf (Var)

Tel: **04 94 81 01 41**. Email: **info@etoiledargens.com**   www.alanrogers.com/FR83070

First impressions of l'Etoile d'Argens are of space, cleanliness and calm. This is a site run with families in mind and many of the activities are free, making for a good value holiday. There are 493 level, fully serviced, grass pitches (265 for touring units, with 10A electricity), separated by hedges, with five sizes, ranging from 50 sq.m. (for small tents) to 250 sq.m. mainly with good shade. The pool and bar area is attractively landscaped with olive and palm trees on beautifully kept grass. Two heated pools (one for adults, one for children) – both very much with families in mind. Reception staff are very friendly and English is spoken. The exceptionally large pitches could easily take two caravans and cars or one family could have a very spacious plot with a garden like atmosphere. The river runs alongside the site with a free boat service to the beach (15/6-15/9). This is a good family site for the summer but also good in low season for a quiet stay in a superb location with excellent pitches. Tour operators take 85 pitches and there are 175 mobile homes but for a large site it is unusually calm and peaceful even in July.

Facilities

Over 20, well kept, small toilet blocks. Supermarket and gas supplies. Bar, restaurant, pizzeria, takeaway. Two swimming pools (heated 1/4-20/6), paddling pool, Jacuzzi, solarium. Floodlit tennis with coaching. Minigolf. Aerobics. Archery (July/Aug). Football and swimming lessons. Boules. Good play area. Children's entertainment (July/Aug). Activity programme with games, dances and escorted walking trips to the surrounding hills within 3 km. Off site: Golf and riding 2 km. Beach 3.5 km.

Open: 1 April - 30 September, with all services.

Directions

From A8 exit 36, take N7, Le Muy, Fréjus. After 8 km. at roundabout take D7 signed Roquebrune, St Aygulf. In 9.5 km. (after roundabout) turn left signed Fréjus. Site signed. Ignore width and height limit signs as site is before limit (500 m). GPS: N43:24.947 E06:42.326

Charges guide

Per tent pitch incl. 2 persons and electricity	€ 20,00 - € 46,00
'comfort pitch' incl. 3 persons	€ 32,00 - € 58,00
'luxury pitch' incl. 4 persons	€ 38,00 - € 68,00
extra person	€ 5,00 - € 8,50
child (under 7 yrs)	€ 4,00 - € 6,50

FR83140 Camping les Lacs du Verdon

Domaine de Roquelande, F-83630 Régusse (Var)

Tel: **04 94 70 17 95**. Email: **info@lacs-verdon.com**   www.alanrogers.com/FR83140

In beautiful countryside and within easy reach of the Grand Canyon du Verdon and its nearby lakes, this site is only 90 minutes from Cannes. This bustling and possible noisy campsite is suitable for active families and teenagers. The 30 acre wooded park is divided in two by a minor road. The 480 very stony, but level pitches (rock pegs advised) are marked and separated by stones and trees. 130 pitches are for tourists, many an irregular shape, but all are of average size with 10A electricity (long leads may be necessary).

Facilities

Modernised toilet blocks have mainly have British style WCs and some washbasins in cubicles. Laundry and dishwashing facilities. Motorcaravan service point. Shop. Bar. Restaurant and pizzeria. Excellent swimming pool/paddling pool complex. Artificial grass tennis courts. Boules. Bicycle hire. Playground. TV and teenage games room. Entertainment programme. Discos, dances and theme nights. Only electric barbecues are permitted. Off site: Régusse 2.5 km. Aups 7 km. Riding 10 km. Fishing, beach, sailing and windsurfing at Saint Croix 15 km.

Open: 29 April - 23 September.

Directions

Leave A8 motorway at St Maximin and take D560 northeast (Barjols). At Barjols turn left on D71 (Montmeyan), turn right on D30 (Régusse) and follow site signs. GPS: N43:39.612 E06:09.064

Charges guide

Per pitch incl. 1 or 2 persons	€ 18,00 - € 27,00
extra person	€ 5,00 - € 7,50
child (3-7 yrs)	€ 4,00 - € 6,00
electricity (10A)	€ 4,00
dog	€ 3,00

L'Étoile d'Argens

✧✧✧✧

2009

Camping-Caravaning

www.etoiledargens.com

E-mail : info@etoiledargens.com

83370 Saint Aygulf - Tel : +33 4 94 81 01 41

The Travel Service
BOOK THIS SITE
CALL 01580 214000
...we'll arrange everything

www.flowercampings.com

FR83130 ✿ **Flower Camping le Beau Vezé**

Route de la Moutonne, F-83320 Carqueiranne (Var)

Tel: **04 94 57 65 30**. Email: **info@camping-beauveze.com**   **www.alanrogers.com/FR83130**

Le Beau Vezé is a quiet site, some way inland from the busy resort of Hyères. The owner tries to keep it as a family site with its quiet position, although the superb beaches and hectic coastal areas are within easy reach. On a steep hillside it has terraced pitches and a plateau with more pitches on the top. The 150 pitches are well shaded but unfortunately some will be rather difficult to manoeuvre onto due to over-hanging trees and could be difficult for motorcaravans. There is some road noise on the lower pitches.

Facilities	Directions
Reasonable standard sanitary blocks, two heated, although maintenance may be variable. Some showers with washbasin. Baby room. Washing machines. Bar/restaurant, takeaway. Bread. Medium sized pool, paddling pool. Play area. Minigolf, boules and tennis. Bicycle hire. Jet-ski hire. Walking tours, visits to vineyard. Evening entertainment in restaurant. Off site: Golf 2 km. Fishing 3 km. Riding 5 km. The lovely old town of Hyères is only 8 km.	From A57 take exit for Toulon Est and follow D559 between Carqueiranne and Le Pradet. Take D76 northwards signed La Moutonne and site is signed on right of D76. GPS: N43:06.848 E06:03.384

Open: 15 May - 15 September.

Charges guide

Per unit incl. 2 persons	€ 21,50 - € 27,00
extra person	€ 5,50 - € 6,30
electricity (6A)	€ 4,00
No credit cards.	

FR83210 **Yelloh! Village les Tournels**

Route de Camarat, F-83350 Ramatuelle (Var)

Tel: **04 66 73 97 39**. Email: **info@yellohvillage-les-tournels.com**   **www.alanrogers.com/FR83210**

Les Tournels is a large site set on a hillside and pitches have panoramic views of the Gulf of St Tropez and Pampelonne beach. The hillside is covered in parasol pines and old olive trees. The pitches are reasonably level, shady, variable size, most with electricity (long leads). The pool, play area, shop and bar maybe some distance away. Recent additions include a superb spa centre with gym, sauna and jacuzzi, with an excellent pool alongside, all for over 18s, and a new restaurant with a large terrace.

Facilities	Directions
Well equipped toilet blocks, some heated, baby baths, children's WCs, facilities for disabled visitors. Laundry facilities. Fridge hire. Bar and restaurant (1/4-15/10). Takeaway. Bar and disco. Large heated swimming pool 1/4-20/10. Fitness centre and pool. Good play area. Miniclub. Gas barbecues permitted. Off site: Shopping centre 500 m, shuttle bus. Golf 6 km. Beach 1.5 km.	From A8 exit 36 take D25 to Ste Maxime, then D98 towards St Tropez. On outskirts of St Tropez, take D93 to Ramatuelle. Site is signed on left in 9 km. GPS: N43:12.315 E06:39.043

Open: 13 March - 7 January.

Charges guide

Per unit incl. 2 persons, extra person	€ 17,00 - € 40,00 € 6,00 - € 8,00

tel: +33 466 739 739   www.yellohvillage.com ────── **yelloh!** VILLAGE

FR83230 **Yelloh! Village Domaine du Colombier**

Route de Bagnols-en-Forêt, 1052 rue des Combattants d'AFN, F-83600 Fréjus (Var)

Tel: **04 66 73 97 39**. Email: **info@domaine-du-colombier.com**   **www.alanrogers.com/FR83230**

Domaine du Colombier is located between Cannes and St Tropez, alongside a main road 2 km. from the centre of Fréjus and 4 km. from the sandy beaches of Fréjus Saint Raphaël. There are 70 touring pitches, ranging in size from 80-150 sq.m. and all with 16A electricity. An attractive pool complex water slides and Jacuzzis and is surrounded by sunloungers, a fitness area and a grill restaurant. Plenty of activities and excursions are arranged all season and the site caters principally for families.

Facilities	Directions
Three well maintained, fully equipped toilet blocks (two heated and with baby rooms). Facilities for visitors with disabilities. Laundry. Well stocked shop. Bar/restaurant, takeaway. Soundproofed nightclub. Large heated swimming pool with paddling pool, slides and jacuzzis (all season). Fitness facilities. Three play areas and four sports areas. Picnic area with communal barbecue. Internet access and WiFi. Fridge, safe and barbecue hire. Off site: Bus stop 50 m.	From A8 exit 37, follow signs for Fréjus, turning left at second lights (D4) and site is 1 km. on the right. From A8 exit 38 east (Nice) straight on at three roundabouts, then right at fourth and fifth. Site is 300 m. on right. From west (Aix) turn right at first roundabout, after 1 km. turn left and site is 1 km. on the left. GPS: N43:26.750 E06:43.636

Open: 31 March - 15 October.

Charges guide

Per unit incl. up to 3 persons	€ 26,00 - € 30,00
Camping Cheques accepted.	

tel: +33 466 739 739   www.yellohvillage.com ────── **yelloh!** VILLAGE

Check real time availability and at-the-gate prices...
www.**alanrogers**.com

FR83190 Camping la Presqu'île de Giens

Mobile homes ▶ page 512

153 route de la Madraque-Giens, F-83400 Hyères (Var)

Tel: **04 94 58 22 86**. Email: **info@camping-giens.com**

www.alanrogers.com/FR83190

La Presqu'île de Giens a good family campsite at the southern end of the Giens peninsula. The site is well maintained and extends over 17 acres of undulating terrain. Of the site's 460 pitches, 170 are reserved for touring. These are generally of a good size and well shaded – there is a separate area of smaller pitches reserved for tents. Electrical connections (16A) are available on all pitches. In high season this becomes a lively site with a well run children's club (small charge) and an evening entertainment programme including discos, singers and dancers. Although there is no swimming pool, the site lies between two sandy beaches, and in July and August a free shuttle bus runs to the nearest, 800 metres away. Excursions are organised to the adjacent islands of Porquerolles, Port Cros and Le Levant. There is a beautiful walking trail set out all around the peninsula.

Facilities

Five toilet blocks, three very good new ones (heated in low season), and two refurbished with a higher proportion of Turkish style toilets. All was clean and well maintained. Facilities for disabled visitors. Washing machines and dryers. Shop. Bar, restaurant and takeaway (to 30/9). Play area. Children's club. Sports tournaments. Evening entertainment. Sports pitch. Diving classes. Excursion programme. Only electric barbecues are permitted. Off site: Beach 800 m. Fishing 1 km. Bicycle hire 1 km. Riding 5 km. Golf 20 km. 'Golden islands' excursions.

Open: 28 March - 4 October.

Directions

From the west, leave A57 at Hyères and continue to Hyères on the A570. At Hyères follow signs to Giens - Les Iles (D97). At end of this road, after 11 km. turn right towards Madraque. Site is on the left. GPS: N43:02.458 E06:08.583

Charges guide

Per unit incl. 2 persons	€ 13,50 - € 20,90
extra person	€ 4,10 - € 6,60
child (0-5 yrs)	free
electricity	€ 4,90 - € 5,70
pet	€ 2,80

Camping Cheques accepted.

camping caravaning

CAMPING

Camping
La Presqu'île de Giens★★★
Côte d'Azur

An exceptional location on Giens Peninsula, right in the heart of the Mediterranean, between two beautiful sandy beaches. A top-quality, well-shaded campsite, featuring a bar, restaurant, supermarket, boulangerie, play area, children club, etc...

High quality and varied leisure and entertainment during summer season, including cinema, sea kayak, scuba diving, gym, walks, and a choice of shows and evening events.

MOBILE HOME AND CHALET RENTAL from 231€ per week
Free brochures available on request.

Special offer from 28/03 - 27/06 and 29/08 - 04/10 :
For 2 weeks rental, 3rd week free.

New features. Apartment hotel on sea front, set facing the islands off the coast of Hyères. Top-comfort air-conditioned apartements to rent (3-7 guests).

153, route de la Madrague - Giens - 83400 HYÈRES
Tél. 00 33 494 58 22 86 - Fax. 00 33 494 58 11 63
www.camping-giens.com - E.mail : info@camping-giens.com

FR83240 Camping Caravaning Moulin des Iscles

Quartier la Valette, F-83520 Roquebrune-sur-Argens (Var)

Tel: 04 94 45 70 74. Email: moulin.iscles@wanadoo.fr   www.alanrogers.com/FR83240

Moulin des Iscles is a small, pretty site beside the river Argens with access to the river in places for fishing, canoeing and some sought after pitches overlooking the river. The 90 grassy, level pitches have water and electricity (6A). A nice mixture of deciduous trees provides natural shade and colour and the old mill house is near the entrance, which has the security barrier closed at night. This is a quiet site with little on site entertainment, but with a nice restaurant. Handicapped visitors are made very welcome. It is a real campsite not a 'camping village'.

Facilities

Fully equipped toilet block, plus small block near entrance, ramped access for disabled visitors. Some Turkish style toilets. Washbasins have cold water. Baby bath and changing facilities. Washing machine. Restaurant, home cooked dish-of-the-day. Well stocked shop. Library with some English books. TV, pool table, table tennis. Play area, minigolf, boules all outside the barrier. Internet terminal. Canoeing possible. Off site: Bicycle hire 1 km. (cycle way to St Aygulf). Riding and golf 4 km. Beach 9 km.

Open: 1 April - 30 September.

Directions

From A8, exit Le Muy, follow N7 towards Fréjus for 13 km. Cross over A8 and turn right at roundabout through Roquebrune sur Argens towards St Aygulf for 1 km. Site signed on left. Follow private unmade road for 500 m. GPS: N43:26.708 E06:39.470

Charges guide

Per unit incl. 2 or 3 persons	€ 20,00
extra person	€ 3,30

Prices are lower out of high season.
Camping Cheques accepted.

FR83250 Kawan Village Douce Quiétude

3435 boulevard Jacques Baudino, F-83700 Saint Raphaël (Var)

Tel: 04 94 44 30 00. Email: sunelia@douce-quietude.com   www.alanrogers.com/FR83250

Douce Quiétude is five kilometres from the beaches at Saint Raphaël and Agay but is quietly situated at the foot of the Estérel massif. There are 400 pitches, only 70 of these are for touring set in pleasant pine woodland or shaded, green areas. The pitches are of a comfortable size, separated by bushes and trees with electricity (6A), water, drainage and telephone/TV points provided. This mature site offers a wide range of services and facilities complete with a pool complex. It can be busy in the main season yet is relaxed and spacious.

Facilities

Fully equipped modern toilet blocks, facilities for babies and disabled visitors. Launderette. Bar, restaurant, takeaway, pizzeria (3/4-3/9). Shop. Three swimming pools (two heated), water slide, Jacuzzi. Play area. Children's club, activities for teenagers (all July/Aug). Sports area. Games room. Tennis. Minigolf. Archery. Fitness centre, sauna. Evening entertainment, shows, karaoke, discos (July/Aug). Mountain bike hire. Only gas barbecues. Off site: Bus route 1 km. Golf and riding 2 km. Windsurf hire and sea fishing 5 km.

Open: 3 April - 2 October.

Directions

From A8 exit 38 (Fréjus/St Rapha'l) take D100, signed Valescure then Agay. Follow site signs (round the back of Fréjus/St Rapha'l). Access via N98 coast road turning north at Agay on D100. Pass Esterel Camping, then site signed. GPS: N43:26.836 E06:48.360

Charges guide

Per unit incl. 2 persons and electricity	€ 18,00 - € 47,50
extra person	€ 5,00 - € 9,00

Camping Cheques accepted.

FR83290 Camping de Saint Aygulf Plage

270 avenue Salvarelli, F-83370 Saint Aygulf-Plage (Var)

Tel: 04 94 17 62 49. Email: info@camping-cote-azur.com   www.alanrogers.com/FR83290

This is a large, well run and self-sufficient campsite with a range of good facilities and direct access to the beach. The pitches here are well marked, flat and arranged in long rows, many with good shade from the pine trees. There are 1,100 in total, with 700 for touring units and the remainder used for mobile homes and chalets. Electricity is available on 500 touring pitches. Although there is no pool on the site, the direct access to the beach makes this is a fine family holidaying campsite.

Facilities

Four large toilet blocks provide good, clean facilities. No facilities for disabled visitors. Laundry facilities. Supermarket. Bakery. Two restaurants. Bar with patio and stage for discos and entertainmanet. Pizzeria and takeaways. Multi-sports court. Play areas. Boules. First aid. Caravan storage. Beach. Only gas and electric barbecues are permitted. Off site: Bicycle hire 100 m. Riding 1 km. Golf 6 km.

Open: 1 May - 19 September.

Directions

From A8 take exits for Puget or Fréjus and RN7 to Fréjus town. Follow signs to sea front and join RN98 towards St Tropez. Saint Aygulf is 2 km towards St Tropez. Site signed and is behind Hotel Van der Valk. GPS: N43:23.574 E06:43.608

Charges guide

Per unit incl. 2 persons	€ 11,50 - € 40,00
incl. electricity	€ 14,50 - € 50,00
extra person	€ 3,00 - € 8,00

Check real time availability and at-the-gate prices...
www.alanrogers.com

FR83200 Kawan Village les Pêcheurs

F-83520 Roquebrune-sur-Argens (Var)

Tel: 04 94 45 71 25. Email: info@camping-les-pecheurs.com

Mobile homes ▶ page 512

www.alanrogers.com/FR83200

BOOK THIS SITE The Travel
CALL 01580 214000 Service
...we'll arrange everything

Les Pêcheurs will appeal to families who appreciate natural surroundings together with many activities, cultural and sporting. Interspersed with mobile homes, the 150 good sized touring pitches (electricity 6/10A) are separated by trees or flowering bushes. The Provencal style buildings are delightful, especially the bar, restaurant and games room, with its terrace down to the river and the site's own canoe station (locked gate). Across the road is a lake used exclusively for water skiing with a sandy beach, a restaurant and minigolf. This popular Riviera site has some new spa facilities including steam pool and sauna. Developed over three generations by the Simoncini family, this peaceful, friendly site is set in more than four hectares of mature, well shaded countryside at the foot of the Roquebrune Rock. Activities include climbing the 'Rock' with a guide. We became more and more intrigued with stories about the Rock and the Holy Hole, the Three Crosses and the Hermit all call for further exploration which reception staff are happy to arrange, likewise trips to Monte Carlo, Ventimigua (Italy) and the Gorges du Verdon, etc. The medieval village of Roquebrune is within walking distance.

Facilities

Modern, refurbished, well designed toilet blocks, baby baths, facilities for disabled visitors. Washing machines. Shop. Bar and restaurant (all open all season). Heated outdoor swimming pool (all season), separate paddling pool (lifeguard in high season), ice cream bar. Games room. Spa facilities. Playing field. Fishing. Canoeing. Waterskiing. Rafting and diving schools. Activities for children and adults (high season), visits to local wine caves. Only gas or electric barbecues. WiFi in reception, bar/restaurant and pool area. Off site: Bicycle hire 1 km. Riding 5 km. Golf 5 km. (reduced fees).

Open: 1 April - 30 September.

Directions

From A8 take Le Muy exit, follow N7 towards Fréjus for 13 km. bypassing Le Muy. After crossing A8, turn right at roundabout towards Roquebrune-sur-Argens. Site is on left after 1 km. just before bridge over river. GPS: N43:27.047 E06:38.010

Charges 2009

Per unit incl. 2 persons and electricity	€ 23,00 - € 41,70
incl. 3 persons	€ 25,50 - € 44,50
extra person	€ 4,00 - € 7,50
child (5-10 yrs)	€ 3,20 - € 6,00
dog (max. 1)	€ 3,10

Camping Cheques accepted.

UN JARDIN EN PROVENCE

10 km away from the beaches of Fréjus St Raphaël, calm and shady. Wellness : spa, spa aqua trainer, sauna, Restaurant, canoeing, Mini tennis Mini golf, Family atmosphere, Rental of mobile homes, Cycle tracks to the beach, Wifi.

Camping ★★★★ Caravaning Les Pêcheurs
83520 Roquebrune sur Argens
Tél : 00 33 (0)4 94 45 71 25   Fax : 00 33 (0)4 94 81 65 13
www.camping-les-pecheurs.com

457

FR83300 Camping Clos Sainte-Thérèse

Route de Bandol, F-83270 Saint Cyr-sur-Mer (Var)

Tel: **04 94 32 12 21**. Email: **camping@clos-therese.com**   www.alanrogers.com/FR83300

This is a very attractive, family run campsite set in hilly terrain four kilometres from the beaches of Saint Cyr. The terraced pitches are level, some with sea views, the friendly owners offering a tractor service if required. There is a good shade from pines, olives, almonds and evergreen oaks. There are 86 pitches for touring units, all with electricity and 30 for chalets or mobile homes. Five pitches are fully serviced. The landscaped pool is pretty and well kept, with a small slide, jacuzzi and a separate paddling pool. This is a friendly, small site, ideal for couples of families with younger children.

Facilities	Directions
Clean, well maintained toilet facilities. Fridge hire. Shop. Bar, restaurant (15/6-15/9). Swimming pools (one heated) and paddling pool. Games room. TV room and library. Boules. Play area. Activities in high season. Off site: Golf course (9 and 18 holes, driving range) 500 m. Tennis opposite site. Bicycle hire 2 km. Beach 4 km. Fishing 4 km. Riding 8 km. **Open:** 1 April - 30 September.	From A50 take D559 to Saint Cyr. Continue towards Bandol and site is 3 km. on the left. GPS: N43:09.587 E05:43.772

Charges guide	
Per unit incl. 2 persons	€ 15,00 - € 22,50
extra person	€ 3,60 - € 5,40
child (3-7 yrs)	€ 2,20 - € 3,30
electricity (6/10A)	€ 4,00 - € 5,20
Camping Cheques accepted.	

FR83310 Camping l'Argentière

Chemin de l'Argentière (D48), F-83310 Cogolin (Var)

Tel: **04 94 54 63 63**. Email: **campinglargentiere@wanadoo.fr**   www.alanrogers.com/FR83310

This little jewel of a site is in a pleasant setting and the intervening wooded area seems to give it sufficient screening to make the campsite itself quite peaceful. It is only five kilometres from the beach at Gogolin or St Tropez, so its position is handy for one of the showplaces of the Riviera, but away from the hustle and bustle of the beach resorts. There are 150 good sized touring pitches (out of 238 with the others used for mobile homes to rent). All have electricity although long leads may be necessary. The site is very well maintained.

Facilities	Directions
Two of three toilet blocks are near the touring pitches and are well kept and clean. Washbasins have warm water (some in cabins). Washing machines (near site entrance). Water has to be taken from the sanitary block. Fridge hire. Shop (1/6-30/9). Bar (1/6-30/9). Restaurant and takeaway (15/6-31/8). Large swimming pool (1/6-30/9). Play equipment. Bicycle hire. Barbecues are only permitted on a communal area. Off site: Shops close. Riding 2 km. Fishing 4 km. Golf 6 km. Beach 5 km. **Open:** 1 April - 30 September.	From the A8 take exit 36 (Le Muy), then, D25 to Ste Maxime and the coast road N98 towards St Tropez. After Grimaud keep following signs for Cogolin. When near that village follow D48 towards St Maur-en-Collobrière, then signs to site in the suburb of L'Argentière. GPS: N43:15.365 E06:30.744

Charges guide	
Per unit incl. 2 persons	€ 14,00 - € 28,00
extra person	€ 3,00 - € 4,00
electricity (3-10A)	€ 2,00 - € 6,00

FR83320 Campasun Parc Mogador

167 chemin de Beaucours, F-83110 Sanary-sur-Mer (Var)

Tel: **04 94 74 53 16**. Email: **mogador@campasun.com** / **campasun@free.fr**   www.alanrogers.com/FR83320

This site in the Mediterranean countryside is very much geared for family holidays with children. Some 20 minutes on foot from the beach, the site has a very large and well kept pool area and a stage for entertainment. Somewhat smaller than other sites of this type, there are 180 good sized pitches (160 for touring units). The ground is mainly level, if rather stony and sandy. Variable shade is available and all pitches have 10A electricity. There are plans to enlarge some of the smaller, 80 sq.m. pitches. The attractive pool, is surrounded by ample paved sunbathing areas.

Facilities	Directions
Two large, super de-luxe toilet blocks, one including washbasins and showers in cabins. The high-tech toilets are automatically cleaned after every use. Laundry. Motorcaravan services. Restaurant with varied and full menu (1/4-5/11), also snacks, pizzas and takeaway. Swimming and paddling pools, solarium. Boules. TV room. Miniclub. Evening entertainment in season. Dogs are not accepted. Off site: Beach 800 m. Golf 6 km. Fishing 800 m. **Open:** 15 March - 5 November.	Take Bandol exit 12 from A50 and head for Six Fours on the N 559. Arriving at Sanary-sur-Mer turn left towards Beaucours and site is on left after 100 m. GPS: N43:08.928 E05:46.392

Charges guide	
Per unit incl. 2 persons and electricity (10A)	€ 18,00 - € 36,00
with individual sanitary facility	€ 22,00 - € 42,00
extra person	€ 5,00 - € 7,00
Camping Cheques accepted.	

Check real time availability and at-the-gate prices...
www.alanrogers.com

FR83220 Kawan Village Cros de Mouton

Mobile homes ▶ page 512

B.P. 116, F-83240 Cavalaire-sur-Mer (Var)

Tel: **04 94 64 10 87**. Email: **campingcrosdemouton@wanadoo.fr**

www.alanrogers.com/FR83220

Cros de Mouton is a reasonably priced campsite in a popular area. High on a steep hillside, about two kilometres from Cavalaire and its popular beaches, the site is a calm oasis away from the coast. There are stunning views of the bay but, due to the nature of the terrain, some of the site roads are very steep – the higher pitches with the best views are especially so. There are 199 large, terraced pitches (electricity 10A) under cork trees with 73 suitable only for tents with parking close by, and 80 for touring caravans. English is spoken by the welcoming and helpful owners. The terrace of the restaurant and the pool area share the wonderful view of Cavalaire and the bay. Olivier and Andre are happy to take your caravan up with their 4x4 Jeep if you are worried.

Facilities

Clean, well maintained toilet blocks have all the usual facilities including those for disabled customers (although site is perhaps a little steep in places for wheelchairs). Washing machine. Shop. Bar/restaurant with reasonably priced meals and takeaway. Swimming and paddling pools with many sunbeds on the terrace and small bar for snacks and cold drinks. Small play area. Games room. Off site: Beach 1.5 km. Bicycle hire 1.5 km. Riding 3 km. Golf 15 km.

Open: 15 March - 9 November.

Directions

Take the D559 to Cavalaire-sur-Mer (not Cavalière 4 km. away). Site is about 1.5 km. north of the town, very well signed from the centre. GPS: N43:10.933 E06:30.966

Charges 2009

Per person	€ 6,30 - € 7,90
child (under 7 yrs)	€ 4,10 - € 4,50
pitch	€ 6,30 - € 7,90
electricity (10A)	€ 4,10 - € 4,50
dog	free - € 2,00

Camping Cheques accepted.

Le Cros de Mouton
Cavalaire - Côte d'Azur

Under the Mediterranean sun, 1.6 km from the beach and the town centre, appreciate the peace, comfort, quietness and the welcome of a family camping site in the heart of a shady forest. Heated swimming pool. Bungalows and mobile-homes for hire.

BP 116 – 83240 Cavalaire
Tel: 0033 494 64 10 87
Fax: 0033 494 64 63 12
campingcrosdemouton@wanadoo.fr
www.crosdemouton.com

The Travel Service
BOOK THIS SITE
CALL 01580 214000
...we'll arrange everything

FR83340 Camping Bonporteau

Mobile homes ▶ page 513

B.P. 18 (RD559), F-83240 Cavalaire-sur-Mer (Var)

Tel: 04 94 64 03 24. Email: contact@bonporteau.fr

www.alanrogers.com/FR83340

This terraced site is situated northeast of and above the pleasant and popular holiday resort of Cavalaire where there is a harbour, restaurants and shops. A long, sandy beach runs right round the bay and there are plenty of watersport activities nearby. The site is only 200 metres from the beach, very well positioned for a family holiday, and only a short walk from a very good hypermarket. The 170 individual touring pitches are on sloping, sandy ground with terracing and good access roads, and all have electricity hook-ups (10A). The remaining 70 pitches are used for mobile homes and chalets. There is a special entrance gate to bring larger units in and the site has a strong 4x4 available for towing heavy units. Trees have grown well to give plenty of shade and there is a very attractive swimming pool. English is spoken by the young and enthusiastic management team.

Facilities

Three main toilet blocks are modern and include washbasins in cabins, Toilets are mainly British style. Launderette. Small shop. Small but attractive, restaurant (1/4-30/9). Bar. Takeaway. Entertainment with dance evenings. Swimming pool with terrace (15/3-30/9) and small paddling pool. Playground. Table tennis. TV and games room. Off site: Beach 200 m. Bicycle hire 800 m. Riding 2 km. Golf 20 km.

Open: 15 March - 15 October.

Directions

Take D559 to Cavalaire-sur-Mer (not Cavalière, some 4 km. away). Site is signed by yellow signs from the main road before entering the town.
GPS: N43:10.009 E06:31.172

Charges guide

Per unit incl. 1-3 persons	€ 25,00 - € 57,15
extra person	€ 5,00 - € 9,00
child	€ 2,50 - € 4,50
dog	€ 2,70 - € 4,50

From 28/6-22/8 weekly bookings only.

BP 18, RD 559
83240 Cavalaire s/mer
Tél. (33) 04 94 64 03 24
Fax (33) 04 94 64 18 62
contact@bonporteau.fr

Camping - Caravaning
Bonporteau
★★★★
www.bonporteau.fr

FR83370 Camping le Fréjus

Route de Bagnols, F-83600 Fréjus (Var)

Tel: 04 94 19 94 60. Email: contact@lefrejus.com

www.alanrogers.com/FR83370

Set on a hillside away from busy Fréjus, this attractively terraced site was developed over 35 years from a farm into a modern, pleasant campsite where there is a warm and genuine welcome. Divided into slightly sloping terraces, its 190 rather small pitches enjoy good shade from trees and have access to 6A electricity. In high season one terrace is reserved as a simple camping area for young people (reservation not required). Whether you choose to drive, walk or cycle, there is plenty of wonderful scenery to discover in the immediate vicinity, whilst not far away beautiful beaches can be enjoyed.

Facilities

Three clean and well positioned toilet blocks have mostly British style WCs and washbasins in cubicles. Baby bath. Laundry facilities. Well stocked shop in high season, bread available from bar at other times. Bar (1/5-31/8) with reasonably priced takeaway service. Heated swimming pool (15 x 10 m) and paddling pool (1/5-31/8). Simple play area. Tennis. Sports court. Boules. Fridge hire. Barbecues are not permitted. Off site: A few shops and a restaurant 500 m. Nearest shopping centre Fréjus 6 km. Bicycle hire 3 km. Fishing 6 km. Riding 2 km. Beach and water based activities 6 km.

Open: All year excl. 16 December - 15 January.

Directions

From the A8 (Aix-en-Provence - Nice) take exit 38 onto D4 towards Fréjus. Site lies along this road on the right. GPS: N43:27.877 E06:43.451

Charges guide

Per unit incl. 2 persons and electricity (6A)	€ 16,00 - € 30,50
extra person	€ 4,60 - € 6,60
child (2-8 yrs)	€ 2,50 - € 3,10

Check real time availability and at-the-gate prices...

www.alanrogers.com

FR83360 La Pierre Verte Camping Village

Route de Bagnols-en-Forêt, F-83600 Fréjus (Var)

Tel: **04 94 40 88 30**. Email: info@campinglapierreverte.com   www.alanrogers.com/FR83360

This attractive, terraced site, set on a hillside under umbrella pines, has been gradually and thoughtfully developed. The genuine, friendly welcome means many families return year upon year, bringing in turn new generations. The site is divided into terraces, each with its own toilet block. All the generously sized pitches (200 for touring units) enjoy good shade from trees and have electricity (6A). For those seeking to 'get away from it all' in an area of outstanding natural beauty, there can be few more tranquil sites, but the many beaches, watersports and excursions the Gulf of St Tropez has to offer can also be enjoyed. For those staying on site, there are two large, heated swimming pools with large sunbathing areas and exciting water slides. Not far away, some exhilarating hanggliding and parascending can be enjoyed.

Facilities

Five toilet blocks with mostly British style WCs and washbasins in cubicles are extremely clean and accessible from all levels. Baby bath. Laundry facilities. Bread available each morning. Bar with reasonably priced takeaway service. Heated swimming pools (25 x 15 m. and 15 x 15m.) and paddling pool. Play area Boules. Games room. Fridge hire. Entertainment and activities in high season. Barbecues are not permitted. Off site: A few shops 2 km. Nearest shopping centre Fréjus 8 km. Riding 1 km. Bicycle hire 5 km. Fishing 8 km. Golf 12 km.

Open: 4 April - 28 September.

Directions

From the A8 (Aix-en-Provence - Nice) take exit 38 onto D4 towards Bagnols-en-Forêt. Site lies along this road past a military camp. GPS: N43:29.033 E06:43.235

Charges guide

Per unit incl. 2 persons and electricity	€ 23,00 - € 38,00
extra person	€ 6,00 - € 8,00
child (2-6 yrs)	€ 4,00 - € 5,00
dog	€ 3,00 - € 4,00

La Pierre Verte Camping Village ★★★★
www.campinglapierreverte.com
E-mail : info@campinglapierreverte.com
8 km from the sandy beaches of Fréjus
Rte de Bagnols en Forêt
83600 FREJUS
FRANCE
Tél : 00 33 4 94 40 88 30
Fax : 00 33 4 94 40 75 41

FR83380 Camping des Prairies de la Mer

Quartier Saint-Pons (RN98), les Mûres, F-83310 Grimaud (Var)

Tel: **04 94 79 09 09**. Email: prairies@riviera-villages.com   www.alanrogers.com/FR83380

This busy site is in the pleasant and popular holiday resort of Port Grimaud where there is a luxurious harbour, restaurants and shops. A long, sandy beach runs right round the bay. The site is right on the beach and is very well equipped for a family holiday. In fact, it is a complete holiday resort, even including its own amusement park for children. There are 500 individual touring pitches on flat, sandy ground, all with electricity. A further 900 pitches are used for mobile homes and chalets. Trees have grown well to give plenty of shade and but there is no swimming pool.

Facilities

Nine modern toilet blocks with three near the touring pitches include washbasins in cabins. Toilets are all British style, Launderette. Large shopping complex. Bar. Attractive, Italian style restaurant (all season). Good takeaway. Entertainment programme with live music evenings. Play area. Sports ground. TV room. Bicycle hire. Sailing and diving schools. Miniclub. ATM. Excursions. Beach. Off site: Golf 3 km. Riding 2 km.

Open: 1 April - 8 October.

Directions

From the A8 (Aix-en-Provence - Cannes) exit 36 (Le Muy) take the D25 to St Maxime, then the coast road N98 towards St Tropez. Site is 6 km. on the left. GPS: N43:16.628 E06:34.910

Charges guide

Per unit incl. 2 persons	€ 18,00 - € 42,00
extra person	€ 3,00 - € 7,00
child (5-13 yrs)	€ 2,00 - € 4,00
electricity	free - € 5,00

461

The Travel Service ...we'll arrange everything

BOOK THIS SITE CALL 01580 214000

FR83440 Domaine de la Malissone

F-83740 La Cadière d'Azur (Var)

Tel: **04 94 90 10 60**. Email: **info@domainemalissonne.com**   www.alanrogers.com/FR83440

This pleasant site is part of the FranceLoc group and is a park for caravan holiday homes with over 200 mobile homes. There are just four pitches without electricity for touring campers and these are really only for tents. Although the site is close to the A50 we heard little noise and site does provide a good base for touring the western Var and Bouche du Rhône departments. Surrounded by vineyards, this sloping site is very well maintained. It is a quiet and restful environment, yet is only minutes from the coast at Les Lecques. Jean Marc, the son of the former owners, manages the site to perfection.

Facilities

Two good sanitary blocks. Launderette. Bar. Restaurant and shop. Three swimming pools. Fitness area. Play area. Gym. Volleyball. Boules. Archery. Minigolf. Animation in high season. TV room and electronic games room. WiFi. Dogs are not accepted 1/7-30/8. Off site: Massif de la Sainte Baume.

Open: 1 March - 13 November.

Directions

Site is on the D66 about 2 km. west of Cadière. Leave the A50 at exit 11 and go towards the town. Then follow signs to the site which itself is close to a motorway bridge. GPS: N43:12.142 E05:44.294

Charges guide

Per unit incl. 2 persons	€ 20,50 - € 27,50
extra person	€ 6,10
child (under 7 yrs)	€ 4,50

CAMPINGS FranceLoc

VAR

La malissone ****

At 4km distance of the sea, this estate consist of a aquatic park with a heated swimming pool, water slides, a lagoon with cascade and a large choice of accommodation.

La Cadière d'Azur
83740 • Tel.: +33 (0)4 94 90 10 60
Email : domainemalissonne@wanadoo.fr
www.camping-franceloc.fr

FR83400 Club Holiday Marina

Le Ginestrel (RN98), F-83310 Grimaud (Var)

Tel: **04 94 56 08 43**. Email: **info@holiday-marina.com**   www.alanrogers.com/FR83400

Owned and operated by an English family this site is an established favourite with British families. It is located in the busy holiday area of the Gulf of St Tropez. The site has a large and well kept pool area and its own adjacent moorings for small yachts. Smaller than many sites in this area, there are 230 good sized pitches of which 49 for touring units. Each of these has its own spacious bathroom with a good shower, washbasin and WC and a shared outdoor sink. On level, rather sandy ground, with variable shade, all have 20A electricity. Cars are parked separately to reduce noise.

Facilities

Private toilet blocks include washbasin, shower and WC, heated in low seasons. Dishwashing sinks. Laundry. Two restaurants with varied and full menu (15/6-31/8). Snacks and takeaway. Separate building houses a bar and games room. TV room. Swimming and paddling pools. Miniclub for children and evening entertainment in season. Fishing in adjacent canal. Off site: Beach 850 m. Golf 4 km.

Open: 1 April - 31 October.

Directions

From the A8 (Aix-en-Provence - Cannes) take exit 36 (Le Muy) and D25 to St Maxime. Follow N98 coast road towards St Tropez and site is 10 km. after very busy roundabout at Grimaud. GPS: N43:16.368 E06:31.290

Charges guide

Per unit incl. 2 persons and electricity	€ 19,00 - € 49,00
family rate (2 adults, up to 3 childen)	€ 29,00 - € 59,00
extra person	€ 5,00 - € 19,00

Check real time availability and at-the-gate prices...

www.alanrogers.com

FR83490 Camping les Lauriers Roses

Route de Roquebrune (D7), F-83370 Saint Aygulf (Var)

Tel: 04 94 81 24 46. Email: camp.leslauriersroses@wanadoo.fr

www.alanrogers.com/FR83490

Les Lauriers Roses is an attractive, small site, steeply terraced over two hectares. It is owned by a friendly Dutch family who will personally site caravans on some of the more challenging areas of the site. There are 95 pitches (85 for touring units) of a good size, the majority set out on individual terraces. The site has a large outdoor swimming pool with an adjoining bar and restaurant area offering a good selection of meals. Units over 7.5 metres and twin axle caravans are not accepted. A family orientated site, a wide choice of both day and evening entertainment is organised in high season. Good English is spoken. Situated a few minutes from sandy beaches, the site has panoramic views over the bay of Fréjus and St-Raphaël and the Esterel mountains. The local town of Saint Aygulf is a lively resort town offering good shops, restaurants and attractions. Many visitors to this site return year after year – always a good indicator of a good quality campsite.

Facilities

Two sanitary blocks, one modernised for 2007, the other due for 2008. Laundry and dishwashing areas. Bread to order. Bar and restaurant (19/4-29/9). Takeaway (19/4-29/9). Large heated outdoor swimming pool and paddling pool. Pétanque. Multisports court. Play area. Entertainment (July/Aug). Internet access. Only gas barbecues are permitted. Caravan storage area. Off site: Supermarket 200 m. Fishing 1 km. Boat hire 200 m. Riding 2 km. Beach 3 km. Golf 2 km.

Open: 18 April - 26 September.

Directions

From A8 take exit 37 towards Puget-sur-Argens. Turn onto N7 (Fréjus). At first roundabout after Fréjus town sign, turn right (first exit) to Saint Aygulf at junction after roundabout. Pass under bridge (4.5 m.) and turn right on D8. At T-junction, turn left on D7. Site is 2 km. GPS: N43:24.416 E06:42.548

Charges 2009

Per unit incl. 2 persons and electricity	€ 33,00
extra person	€ 7,50

No credit cards.
Discounts up to 40% outside high season.

LES LAURIERS ROSES ★★★★

Small family campsite with a wonderful view on the Mediterranean Sea and the Esterel from the terraces.

Shady pitches
Bar / Restaurant
Heated swimming pool / paddling pool
Sports and games activities in high season
Dutch owned
www.info-lauriersroses.com
or tel. 0031 (0)55 3559997

FR83410 Camping Club le Ruou

Les Esparrus, 309, RD560, F-83690 Villecroze-les-Grottes (Var)

Tel: 04 94 70 67 70. Email: info@leruou.com

www.alanrogers.com/FR83410

This is a family oriented site in the Provencal countryside, very much geared for family holidays with children. Some 45 minutes by car from the coast at Fréjus, the site has a large and well kept pool area and a mobile stage for entertainment. Smaller than some other sites of this type, there are 110 good sized pitches (52 for touring units). On mainly terraced, rather stony, ground with good shade, all have 6/10A electricity. Some of the pitches for caravans are along a steep path but a 4x4 is available to assist. The attractive pool complex with slides is surrounded by a sunbathing area and some shade.

Facilities

One new super de-luxe toilet block includes washbasins in cabins. Facilities for babies and disabled visitors. Laundry facilities. Snacks and takeaway (15/6-31/8). The main building houses a bar and entertainment room with TV. Area for shows, cabarets, etc. with mobile stage. Two swimming pools. Tennis. Boules. Play area. Miniclub for children and evening entertainment in season. Charcoal barbecues are not permitted. Off site: Beach 35 km. Fishing, riding and bicycle hire 5 km. Golf 17 km.

Open: 1 April - 30 October.

Directions

Villecroze-les-Grottes is northwest of Fréjus. From the A8 (Toulon - Mandelieu-la-Napoule) take exit 13 onto the N7 towards Le Muy. At Les Arcs turn left on D555 (Draguignan), then onto D557 to Villecroze. Site is on the left side of this road. GPS: N43:33.333 E06:18.000

Charges guide

Per unit incl. 2 persons	€ 15,00 - € 28,80
extra person	€ 3,30 - € 5,50
electricity (6/10A)	€ 2,20 - € 5,30

Camping Cheques accepted.

BOOK THIS SITE
CALL 01580 214000
...we'll arrange everything
The Travel Service

Check real time availability and at-the-gate prices...

www.alanrogers.com

FR83620 Camping Parc Saint James-Gassin

Route de Bourrian, F-83580 Gassin (Var)

Tel: 04 94 55 20 20. Email: gassin@camping-parcsaintjames.com   www.alanrogers.com/FR83620

A member of the Parc Saint James group, this attractive campsite, formerly known as Parc Montana, is very well positioned close to St Tropez. The majority of the pitches are occupied by individually owned mobile homes and chalets but there are also 50 touring pitches on the lower part of the site. The 30 hectare estate clings to the hillside with fragrant woodland providing good shade to the mainly terraced pitches. There is a good range of activities here, many concentrated around the large swimming pool complex. In high season, the activity and entertainment programme is popular and includes soirées on the site's attractive bar terrace.

Facilities

Five toilet blocks provide adequate facilities although rather dated. Facility for disabled visitors in one block. Laundry. Small supermarket. Swimming pools and separate children's pool. Bar and restaurant. Takeaway. Play area. Tennis. Multisports area. Games room. Children's club. Evening entertainment. Disco. Mobile homes and chalets for rent. Off site: St Tropez, Port Grimaud and Cogolin. Nearest beaches 5 km. Riding. Fishing. Walking trails.

Open: 6 January - 24 November.

Directions

From A8 autoroute take Le Muy exit and follow signs to St Tropez and La Croix-Valmer. Pass Sainte Maxime and continue on the N98. At large roundabout take signs to Gassin. Cross first roundabout and turn left at next traffic lights. Site is also signed as Parc Montana in places. GPS: N43:14.421 E06:34.407

Charges guide

Per unit incl. 2 persons and electricity	€ 18,00 - € 35,00
extra person	€ 2,50 - € 5,00
child (under 10 yrs)	€ 1,50 - € 4,00

FR83610 Parc Saint-James Oasis

Route de la Bouverie, F-83480 Puget-sur-Argens (Var)

Tel: 04 98 11 85 60. Email: oasis@camping-parcsaintjames.com   www.alanrogers.com/FR83610

This campsite has been recommended by our agent in France and we intend to undertake a full inspection next year. Oasis Village is a member of the Parc Saint James group and the 450 pitches here are all occupied by mobile homes and chalets. The site extends over 42 hectares of pine and oak woods with an attractive Provençal village at the centre, housing various shops and the restaurant. The swimming pool is impressive and understandably popular. Activities and sports are available free of charge and during the high season, water polo is organised. At the end of the day, the restaurant is a pleasant place to enjoy a meal and the site's regular entertainment programme.

Facilities

Laundry. Supermarket. Large swimming pool complex with children's pool. Bar and restaurant. Takeaway. Play area. TV room. Gym. Tennis. Sports competitions. Children's club. Evening entertainment. Disco. Off site: Frejus and St Raphael. Aquatica water park. Riding 4 km. Golf 5 km. Nearest beaches 8 km.

Open: 31 March - 22 September.

Directions

Take the Puget sur Argens exit from the A8 and join the N7 in the direction of Le Muy. After 2.5 km. turn right into the Route de la Bouverie. The site can be found after a further 1.5 km. on the right. GPS: N43:28.138 E06:39.599

Charges 2009

Pitches at this site are used exclusively for mobile homes and chalets. Contact the site for information and charges.

FR83510 Camping la Pinède

Chemin des Mannes, F-83240 Cavalaire-sur-Mer (Var)

Tel: 04 94 64 11 14   www.alanrogers.com/FR83510

La Pinede is an attractive small site, the appeal being in its proximity to the local town, superb beaches and excellent off site facilities making it ideal for motorcaravanners. Laurent is proud of his site and this is reflected in the number of campers who return year after year to this delightful stretch of the Cote d'Azur. Everything you could want is within a 500 m. walk. There are 140 pitches of mixed size, screened with trees and beautiful flowering hedges. This is a good value site for the area.

Facilities

Recently modernised sanitary block. Laundry and dishwashing areas. Bread service. Gas supplies. Fridge hire. Play area. Pétanque. Charcoal barbecues are not allowed. Excellent English is spoken. Off site: Supermarket 400 m. Boat hire and launching 500 m. Beach 300 m. Riding 2 km. Tennis 4 km. Golf 14 km.

Open: 15 March - 15 October.

Directions

On the N98 from Hyères, take D559 towards Le Lavandou. Follow D559 for 20 km. At Cavalaire-sur-Mer, turn left at roundabout into Chemin des Mannes. Site is 50 m. GPS: N43:10.322 E06:31.477

Charges guide

Per unit incl. 2 persons	€ 15,00 - € 21,00
electricity (5A)	€ 3,00

Check real time availability and at-the-gate prices...

www.alanrogers.com

PARC SAINT-JAMES
VILLAGES CLUB

Parc Saint-James
GASSIN

2 campsites Riviera-Côte d'Azur

Route de Bourrian
83580 Gassin
Tél : 00 33 4 94 55 20 20
Fax : 00 33 4 94 56 34 77

Enjoy the pleasure of spending your holidays outdoors in our village-clubs where everything has been designed for your leisure and well-being. Everyone is catered for young and old alike; you can do everything of nothing. So come and discover your future holidays at Gassin or Oasis. Choose your kingdom, well look after the rest.

OASIS Village

Route de Bouverie
83480 Puget sur Argens
Tél : 00 33 4 98 11 85 60
Fax : 00 33 4 98 11 85 79

23, 27 rue Victor Pauchet 92420 Vaucresson
Tél : 00 33 1 47 95 53 63/62
Fax : 00 33 1 47 95 53 68
www.camping-parcsaintjames.com
E-mail : info@camping-parcsaintjames.com

MAP 16

The island of Corsica is both dramatic and beautiful. The scenery is spectacular with bays of white sand lapped by the clear blue waters of the Mediterranean. At certain times of the year the entire island is ablaze with exotic flowers, aided by Corsica's excellent sunshine record.

Alan Rogers

DÉPARTEMENTS: 2A CORSE-SUD; 2B HAUTE-CORSE

MAJOR CITIES: AJACCIO AND BASTIA

Corsica is regarded by some as the jewel of the Mediterranean islands and is made up of two départements: Haute Corse (upper Corsica) and Corse du Sud (southern Corsica). The island has endured a bloody history, having being much disputed the Greeks, Romans and Lombards. Five hundred years of Italian rule has influenced the look of the island with Italian-style hilltop hamlets and villages developed alongside mountain springs. Many of the villages feature rustic, unadorned churches and also a few Romanesque examples too.

The variety of scenery is spectacular. Across much of the island one can discover dramatic gorges, glacial lakes, gushing mountain torrents and magnificent pine and chestnut forests. You'll also experience the celebrated perfume of the Corsican maquis: a tangled undergrowth of fragrant herbs, flowers and bushes that fills the warm spring and summer air. The highest mountains lie to the west, while the gentler ranges, weathered to strange and often bizarre shapes, lie to the south and a continuous barrier forms the island's backbone.

Places of interest

Ajaccio: a dazzling white city full of Napoleonic memorabilia.

Bastia: historic citadel towering over the headland. The old town has preserved its streets in the form of steps connected by vaulted passages, converging on the Vieux port (the old port). The new port is the real commercial port of the island.

Cuisine of the region

Brocchui: sheeps' milk cheese is used much in cooking in both its soft form (savoury or sweet) or more mature and ripened.

Capone: local eels, cut up and grilled on a spit over a charcoal fire.

Dziminu: fish soup, like bouillabaise but much hotter. Made with peppers and pimentos.

Figatelli: a sausage made of dried and spiced pork with liver. Favourite between-meal snack.

Pibronata: a highly spiced local sauce.

Prizzutu: a peppered smoked ham; resembles the Italian prosciutto, but with chestnut flavour added.

FR20010 Camping Arinella Bianca

Route de la Mer, F-20240 Ghisonaccia (Haute-Corse)

Tel: 04 95 56 04 78. Email: arinella@arinellabianca.com

www.alanrogers.com/FR20010

Arinella is a lively, family oriented site on Corsica's east coast. The 415 level, grassy, good size, irregular shape pitches (198 for touring units) have a variety of trees and shrubs providing ample shade and 6A electricity (long leads needed). Some pitches overlook the attractive lakes which have fountains and are lit at night. The site has direct acess to a huge long beach of soft sand. The brilliantly designed resort style pools and paddling pool, overlooked by an attractive large restaurant, terraced bar and entertainment area, form the hub of Arinella Bianca. When we visited the area was buzzing with activity at night and appeared to delight everyone by incorporating excellent family entertainment. The extremely active children's club with an information point, boutique and supermarket complete the area. A huge range of sport and leisure facilities is also available. Evening entertainment starts at 21.00. Unfortunately a local disco can continue until the early hours. This site is a tribute to its owner's design and development skills as it appears to be in entirely natural glades where, in fact, these have been created from former marshland with a fresh water lake.

Facilities

Four open plan sanitary blocks provide showers, (some with dressing area), washbasins in cabins, mainly British style WCs. Laundry. Motorcaravan services. Shop, bar, terrace, restaurant, amphitheatre, snack bar (all 10/5-15/9). Swimming pool (from 1/5). Windsurfing. Canoeing. Fishing. Tennis. Riding. Bicycle hire. Miniclub. Play area. Disco. Good entertainment programme in the main season. Communal barbecue area. WiFi. Off site: Sailing 300 m. Boat launching 2 km.

Open: mid April - 30 September.

Directions

Site is 4 km. east of Ghisonaccia. From N198 in Ghisonaccia look for sign 'La Plage, Li Mare'. Turn east on D144 at roundabout just south of town. Continue for 3.5 km. to further roundabout where site is signed to right. Site is 500 m. Watch for speed bumps on approach road and on site. GPS: N41:59.904 E09:26.520

Charges 2009

Per unit incl. 2 persons	€ 22,00 - € 38,00
extra person	€ 8,00 - € 10,50
electricity (6A)	€ 5,50
Camping Cheques accepted.	

ARINELLA *Bianca*

Camping Caravaning

20240 Ghisonaccia

Tel: 0033 495 56 04 78 - Fax: 0033 495 56 12 54

www.arinellabianca.com

Camping Cheque

FR20000 Camping U-Farniente de Pertamina Village

RN198, F-20169 Bonifacio (Corse-du-Sud)

Tel: 04 95 73 05 47. Email: pertamina@wanadoo.fr

www.alanrogers.com/FR20000

Whether or not you are using the ferry to Sardinia, Bonifacio deserves a visit and this is a convenient site for a night stop or longer stay. The 120 pitches, many in delightful settings, have electricity (3A), are partially terraced and are hedged with trees and bushes, providing shade. They are fairly flat and vary in size, many over 100 sq.m. A central feature of the site is the large attractive pool, surrounded by terraces. The bar, restaurant, pizzeria/grill and creperie are on terraces above the pool and patios.

Facilities

Two toilet blocks include washbasins in semi-private cubicles, British and Turkish style WCs, washing machines plus drying and ironing facilities. Motorcaravan service point at entrance (public). Shop. Takeaway. Bar, restaurant, pizzeria/grill serving set meals and á la carte menu at reasonable prices (shorter opening hours in May, June and Oct). Swimming pool. Tennis. Play area. TV room. Excellent gym. Off site: Bonifacio 4 km.

Open: Easter - 15 October.

Directions

Site is on the RN198 road, 4 km. north of Bonifacio to the east. Well signed as Pertamina Village. GPS: N41:25.074 E09:10.794

Charges guide

Per unit incl. 2 persons and electricity	€ 19,50 - € 30,00
extra person	€ 6,50 - € 9,50
Camping Cheques accepted.	

467

FR20030 Camping Merendella

Moriani-Plage, F-20230 San-Nicolao (Haute-Corse)

Tel: 04 95 38 53 47. Email: merendel@club-internet.fr

www.alanrogers.com/FR20030

This attractive family run site has the advantage of direct access to a pleasant, long sandy beach. It is peacefully situated on level grass with many well tended trees and shrubs providing shade and colour. Level green sites such as this are unusual in Corsica and are ideal for families or those with mobility problems. There are 196 pitches, all with electricity (2/5A, long leads required) and a minimum of 100 sq.m. There is a dedicated night parking area if you arrive late. An excellent bar, restaurant/pizzeria is close to the site entrance (takeaway pizzas are available).

Facilities	Directions
Modern blocks, two individual cabin units near the beach. Washbasins in private cubicles. British and Turkish style WCs. Facilities for disabled campers. Laundry facilities. Motorcaravan services. Shop. Bar/restaurant, pizzeria. TV room. Games room. Late arrival area. Diving centre. Play area. Torches essential. No pets. Off site: Restaurant outside gate. Watersports 200 m. Town 800 m. Bicycle hire 800 m. Tennis and riding 2 km.	Site is to seaward side of the RN198, 800 m. south of Moriani Plage. GPS: N42:21.882 E9:31.791

Directions

Site is to seaward side of the RN198, 800 m. south of Moriani Plage. GPS: N42:21.882 E9:31.791

Charges guide

Per person	€ 6,35 - € 7,50
caravan and car	€ 6,15 - € 6,95
motorcaravan	€ 5,95 - € 7,10
electricity (2/5A)	€ 3,30 - € 4,30

Open: 15 May - 30 September.

FR20060 Camping la Vetta

Route de Bastia, la Trinité, F-20137 Porto-Vecchio (Corse-du-Sud)

Tel: 04 95 70 09 86. Email: info@campinglavetta.com

www.alanrogers.com/FR20060

This is a site not to be missed in Corsica, the English/French owners Nick and Marieline Long having created a very friendly and peaceful country park setting for their campsite to the north of La Trinité village. The 8.5 hectares of well maintained campsite are part sloping, part terraced with an informal pitch allocation system. It seems to stretch endlessly. The abundance of tree varieties including many cork oaks give shade to 111 pitches which all have 10A electricity. The site has a brilliant new lagoon-style pool, all landscaped and serviced by its own snack bar and crêperie.

Facilities	Directions
Spotless, traditional style toilet facilities have plenty of hot water. Laundry facilities. Shop (July/Aug), gas supplies. Excellent restaurant, patio, bar (July/Aug). Swimming pool, paddling pool and water play area (all season). Snooker table. Play area. TV. Entertainment in high season. Off site: Beach 1.5 km. Supermarket 2 km. Fishing, watersports and boat launching 1.5 km. Riding 4 km. Bicycle hire 5 km. Golf 7 km. Public transport 800 m.	Site is in La Trinité village, off the RN198 (east side), north of Porto-Vecchio. GPS: N41:37.896 E09:17.574

Directions

Site is in La Trinité village, off the RN198 (east side), north of Porto-Vecchio. GPS: N41:37.896 E09:17.574

Charges guide

Per person	€ 6,00 - € 7,50
child (under 7 yrs)	€ 3,00 - € 4,00
pitch	€ 4,50 - € 7,00
electricity	€ 3,00

Open: 1 June - 1 October.

FR20070 Camping Caravaning Santa Lucia

Lieu-dit Mulindinu, F-20144 Sainte Lucie-de-Porto-Vecchio (Corse-du-Sud)

Tel: 04 95 71 45 28. Email: information@campingsantalucia.com

www.alanrogers.com/FR20070

Camping Santa Lucia is a very small, friendly, family run site in a delightful southern Corsican setting, where little English is spoken. Behind the little reception hut is an unsophisticated restaurant and bar which have terraces overlooking the pool. It is very pleasant in the evenings when ornamental lamps light up the area. There are 160 pitches, 60 with 6A electrical connections and 18 serviced pitches. Some of the pitches are in enclosed bays created from huge boulders, making them very private. This site is only minutes by car from Porto Vecchio and with very reasonable prices, will suit many.

Facilities	Directions
Two clean and pleasant toilet blocks include British style toilets, some washbasins in cubicles, dishwashing and laundry sinks, and a washing machine. Facilities for disabled visitors. Bread to order. Bar (15/6-15/9). Restaurant and takeaway (1/7-31/8). Swimming and paddling pools. Play area and high season miniclub for children. Minigolf. Communal barbecues. Satellite TV. WiFi. Off site: Beach, fishing and watersports 5 km. Golf 20 km. Supermarket opposite site entrance.	Site is at south end of Sainte-Lucie-de-Porto-Vecchio village, off N198 and well signed. GPS: N41:41.796 E09:20.604

Directions

Site is at south end of Sainte-Lucie-de-Porto-Vecchio village, off N198 and well signed. GPS: N41:41.796 E09:20.604

Charges guide

Per person	€ 5,00 - € 7,00
child (2-10 yrs)	free - € 3,30
pitch	€ 3,20 - € 4,75
incl. electricity	€ 5,00 - € 7,50

Open: 15 May - 10 October.

Check real time availability and at-the-gate prices...

www.alanrogers.com

FR20110 Camping Restonica

Faubourg Saint Antoine, F-20250 Corte (Haute-Corse)

Tel: **04 95 46 11 59**. Email: **vero.camp@worldonline.fr**   www.alanrogers.com/FR20110

Tucked away alongside the pretty Restonica river and near the Pont Neuf leading into the stunning mountainside old city of Corte, Camping Restonica is ideally placed for tourists wanting to visit Corte or travel on the popular inland mountain railway (the station is only a few hundred metres from the site). This is a small, simple site catering for those who want to enjoy the many delights of Corte. The entrance is steep but manageable for all but very large units, there are flat pitches for campers and caravans in the middle of the site, and many beautiful terraced pitches for tents dotted along the river bank under shady trees.

Facilities

Single, central toilet block is unisex and somewhat dated, although very clean. Toilet for disabled visitors but site not really suitable. Washing machine. Bread to order. Bar and snack bar. River fishing. Off site: Sightseeing. Famous train journeys across Corsica. Museum. Only university in Corsica (politically significant).

Open: 15 April - 30 September.

Directions

Site is south of Corte town and the rivers Tavignano and Restonica. Approaching the town, turn left at first roundabout onto Ave du 9 Septembre. Site is 300 m. on the right. It is signed from the roundabout and at the top of the steep, narrow access road. GPS: N42:18.090 E09:09.120

Charges guide

Per person	€ 6,50
pitch	€ 5,00 - € 7,50
No credit cards.	

FR20140 Camping Dolce-Vita

Route de Bastia, F-20260 Calvi (Haute-Corse)

Tel: **04 95 65 05 99**   www.alanrogers.com/FR20140

Tucked under mature trees, this family site has direct access to the river and across a little bridge to a soft sand beach with fabulous views of Calvi. It is rustic, as are all sites on the west coast, but is a cut above most. Small boats may be moored by the river bridge (caution with children) and the sea is 30 m. away. A pleasant little traditional restaurant and bar are in the centre of the site. There are 200 informal touring pitches, under shade and with 10A electricity (long leads needed in some areas).

Facilities

Three sanitary blocks are dated but well looked after and kept clean. Solar powered for hot water and British style toilets. Push button hot showers. Basic baby area. Shop. Bar and restaurant with TV and pleasant patio. Pizzeria. (May-Sept). Play area. Tennis. Communal barbecue area. Torches are required. Mooring for small boats. Fishing. Off site: Beach 30 m. Riding 1 km. Boat launching 3 km. Town 3 km.

Open: 1 May - 30 September.

Directions

Site is north of Bastia on RN197. On approach to the town from the north it is well signed, 3 km. from town down a minor road towards l'Ile Rousse and the beach. GPS: N42:33.390 E08:47.322

Charges guide

Per person	€ 8,60
pitch incl. car	€ 6,00 - € 7,50
electricity (10A)	€ 4,00
No credit cards.	

FR20150 Camping d'Olzo

L.D. Strutta, F-20217 Saint Florent (Haute-Corse)

Tel: **04 95 37 03 34**. Email: **info@campingolzo.com**   www.alanrogers.com/FR20150

The friendly Barenghi family who own this site are delightful. They are pleased to welcome you to their compact site and Dutch, Italian and English are spoken. The site is flat and very peaceful with a wide variety of trees, including gums and olives, which offer shade to most of the informal pitches. There is ample room to manoeuvre for large units. All 60 pitches have electricity (10A) and are not far from the central sanitary block or the facilities which are grouped near reception. The site is a short walk from the beach. A swimming pool was added in 2008.

Facilities

Single central block has unisex toilets (Turkish and British style) and single sex hot showers. Everything is kept very clean and smart. Washing machines. Motorcaravan service point. Facilities for disabled campers. Small shop (July/Aug), bread to order. Restaurant/pizzeria and bar. Swimming pool planned. Internet access. Play area. Communal barbecue area. Off site: Town of St Florent. Bus from gate. Riding 500 m. Bicycle hire 2 km. Boat launching 2 km. Sailing 2 km. Fishing 500 m.

Open: 1 April - 30 September.

Directions

From Bastia take the D81 west to St Florent. After some 30 minutes the site is well signed as you enter the village on the right. GPS: N42:41.616 E09:19.590

Charges guide

Per person	€ 5,80 - € 6,50
child (under 10 yrs)	€ 3,00 - € 3,50
pitch	€ 2,50 - € 7,50

Check real time availability and at-the-gate prices...

www.alanrogers.com

FR20160 Camping Paradella

Route de la Forêt de Bonifato, Suare, F-20214 Calenzana (Haute-Corse)

Tel: 04 95 65 00 97. Email: info@camping-paradella.com   www.alanrogers.com/FR20160

This site is owned by Antoine Hatt, once a winemaker, but now keen that you enjoy this out of town site with its natural surroundings. The facilities here are of a high standard and it has a new, fresh look, unlike many of the traditional sites on this coast. It is a back to nature site with 130 touring pitches, all with access to 3A electricity. Access is good, even for large units and the pitches are neat, shaded and level. One central tarmac road serves the pitches and the sanitary block is centrally placed. The site is very peaceful, other than a little road noise on one side.

Facilities	Directions
One central, modern sanitary block is very clean with British style toilets and hot showers. Hot water for sinks and laundry. Astro-turf ramps to facilities for disabled campers. Washing machines. Separate small kitchen for groups. Good motorcaravan service point. Shop. Bar and snack bar/restaurant.(June - Sept). Pizzeria (June - Sept). Swimming pool with pleasant patio (May - Sept). Satellite TV. Open sports area. Off site: Riding 1 km. Beach, sailing, boat launching, fishing 7 km. Bicycle hire 9 km.	Site is off the RN197 north of Calvi. Take the GR20 towards Suare and the 'Forêt de Bonifacio'. Site is well signed 7 km. along this road. GPS: N42:30.132 E08:47.520

Charges guide

Per person	€ 5,70 - € 6,60
child (under 7 yrs)	€ 3,00 - € 3,50
pitch incl. car	€ 4,70 - € 6,00
electricity (3A)	€ 3,30

Open: 15 April - 30 September.

FR20170 Camping Paduella

Route de Bastia, F-20260 Calvi (Haute-Corse)

Tel: 04 95 65 06 16   www.alanrogers.com/FR20170

Camping Paduella is a beautifully maintained, simple site which has been run by the friendly Peretti family for 40 years. As it is a popular site, it is best to book ahead for high season. There is a wide choice of pleasant pitches, some shaded under pines, others grassed and hedged with less shade. All are well maintained on level terraces with good access. The lovely white sand beach is 300 m. away and the picturesque town of Calvi is a delightful 30 minute walk. There is a fairly busy road and light railway to cross to get to the beach but most of the walk is through the shaded beach parkland.

Facilities	Directions
Two centrally located spotless modern sanitary blocks (British style WCs). Well equipped showers. Laundry with washing machines, ironing board. Small shop with basic supplies and fresh bread. Pizzeria and bar. Internet access. Play area. Sports ground. Fridge hire can be arranged. Off site: Supermarket and ATM 200 m. Adventure activities 200 m. Riding and bicycle hire 700 m. Boat launching and marina 1 km. Scuba diving, rowing and sailing nearby.	From the north, site is just before the town of Calvi. It is directly off the RN197 on the left and is well signed. GPS: N42:33.126 E08:45.846

Charges guide

Per person	€ 6,00 - € 7,30
child	€ 3,00 - € 3,65
pitch	€ 9,60 - € 10,60
No credit cards.	

Open: 1 May - 15 October.

FR20180 Camping la Pinède

Route de la Pinède, F-20260 Calvi (Haute-Corse)

Tel: 04 95 65 17 80. Email: info@camping-calvi.com   www.alanrogers.com/FR20180

Camping La Pinède is a well ordered, family site of 185 touring pitches, all with 4-16A electricity. The pitches are marked and level (although the pine roots are a nuisance in places). There is access for large units in some areas. Water points are spread around the site and everything is kept tidy and clean. Under the mature pines it can be quite dark but there are plenty of alternatives in the light. The site is divided into areas of accommodation – pitches for tour operators, mobile homes and tourers. Unusually all facilities are in separate buildings.

Facilities	Directions
Three well maintained and well placed concrete sanitary buildings offer hot showers and facilities for campers with disabilities. Washing machines. Clean and fresh, these blocks are better than most on the west coast. Motorcaravan service point. Shop (June - Sept). Bar. Restaurant (May - Sept). Swimming pool (no lifeguard). Internet access. Play area. Tennis. Off site: Beach 200 m. Fishing 200 m. Riding 500 m. Bicycle hire 2 km..	Site is north of Calvi off the RN197, just south of the D251 road to the airport. Look for signs off the roundabout here and take care along a narrow road with leaning fir trees. GPS: N42:33.192 E08:46.116

Charges guide

Per person	€ 6,50 - € 8,50
child (under 7 yrs)	€ 3,50 - € 4,50

Open: 1 April - 31 October.

Check real time availability and at-the-gate prices...

www.alanrogers.com

FR20220 Camping les Oliviers

F-20150 Porto (Corse-du-Sud)

Tel: **04 95 26 14 49**. Email: **lesoliviersporto@wanadoo.fr**   www.alanrogers.com/FR20220

This attractive and modern, resort style campsite is by the Bay of Porto, set alongside a charming river suitable for fishing and swimming. The surrounding area is listed as a World heritage site. It is located on the difficult to access and remote west coast of Corsica and reservations are essential. The site is is on very steep slopes and has 190 mainly small and terraced touring pitches, with 64 having electricity (10A). The quality of the pitches reflect the rugged terrain, large units will find the few motorhome pitches very challenging to access.

Facilities	Directions
Toilet facilities are unisex and in four blocks spread throughout the site. Some washbasins in cubicles, British style WCs. Four washing machines. No facilities for visitors with disabilities and unsuitable for those with mobility problems. Fridge hire. Bread supplies. Restaurant, pizzeria and bar (1/5-mid Sept). Swimming pool, gym, sauna, massage and Turkish bath. Play area. Internet access. Fishing. Torches useful. Corsican trek agency. Off site: Supermarket 50 m. Corsican Trek organises active sports. Bicycle hire 200 m. Golf and fishing 1.5 km.	When approaching Porto from the North the road crosses a bridge over the river. Les Oliviers is on the left, well signed. GPS: N42:15.714 E08:42.618

Charges 2009

Per person	€ 6,80 - € 9,10
child (under 7 yrs)	€ 3,50 - € 4,80
caravan incl. electricity	€ 11,50 - € 14,00
motorcaravan incl. electricity	€ 9,00 - € 10,50

Open: 28 March - 7 November.

FR20230 Camping le Sagone

Route de Vico, F-20118 Sagone (Corse-du-Sud)

Tel: **04 95 28 04 15**. Email: **sagone.camping@wanadoo.fr**   www.alanrogers.com/FR20230

Situated outside the bustling seaside resort of Sagone, surrounded by protective hills, this campsite which used to be a fruit farm is in an ideal location for exploring Corsica's wild and rocky west coast or its mountainous interior. The large site borders a pleasant river and has 300 marked, shaded pitches, 250 with electricity (6A). There are 105 bungalows offered for rent, which are generally separated. The restaurant/bar and games room overlook the pool and they are the focal point of this well managed site. Animation takes place in the central area by the pool during the high season.

Facilities	Directions
Clean, fully equipped toilet blocks with washbasins in cubicles. Facilities for disabled people. Baby baths. Washing machines, dryers. Motorcaravan services. Large supermarket (all year). Restaurant, pizzeria, bar, games room. Swimming pool (June - Sept). Half court tennis. Play area. Sub-aqua experience in pool. Communal barbecues. Satellite TV. Internet. Car wash. New putting and golf practise area. Off site: Riding 500 m. Diving, windsurfing, mountain biking, fishing, bicycle hire.	From Ajaccio take the RD81 in direction of Cergése and Calvilby (by coast road). In Sagone take RD70 in direction of Vico, Sagone can be found on left after 1.5 km. next to supermarket. GPS: N42:07.824 E08:42.330

Charges guide

Per unit incl. 2 persons	€ 14,50 - € 23,00
extra person	€ 4,50 - € 7,70
electricity	€ 3,00
Camping Cheques accepted.	

Open: 1 May - 30 September.

FR20240 Camping Rondinara

Suartone, F-20169 Bonifacio (Corse-du-Sud)

Tel: **04 95 70 43 15**. Email: **reception@rondinara.fr**   www.alanrogers.com/FR20240

The views from every pitch in this site are stunning, either coastal or the rolling hills and cliffs inland. The 'great outdoors' describes this campsite which is away from the any tourist over-development and is at one with nature. The natural and informal pitches sit on the hillside above a superb bay with sheltered water, fine silver sand and safe swimming. Most pitches have shade but most tree foliage is relatively low as yet. Large boulders make natural divisions and some pitches need long leads for the 6A electricity. The beach is a 400 m. walk down a rough track through the maquis.

Facilities	Directions
Three excellent, modern toilet blocks are very clean and offer hot water throughout, hot showers and single sex British style toilets. Motorcaravan service point. Shop. Pizza restaurant. Bar. Swimming pool. Play area. Games room. Electronic games. Animation and family activities. Torches essential here. Off site: Beach, boat launching and fishing 400 m. Golf, riding and sailing 15 km.	Site is mid-way between Bonifacio and Porto Vecchio off the RN 198. Take the D158 to Baie de la Rondinara for 7 km. (site is well signed). The road is rough and narrow but large units will have no trouble negotiating it. GPS: N41:28.394 E09:15.790

Charges guide

Per person	€ 5,50 - € 6,90
pitch	€ 5,50 - € 10,20

Open: 15 May - 30 September.

Check real time availability and at-the-gate prices...
www.alanrogers.com

The best website for the
best campsite information
www.**alanrogers**.com

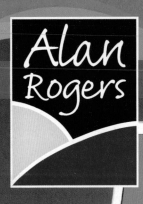

3000 CAMPSITES AT YOUR FINGERTIPS

- Search for the best campsite for *your* holiday
- Full, detailed reviews of the best campsites
- Independent and impartial - for your peace of mind
- Book direct or with the convenience of our Travel Service
- Pitches and mobile homes

Just Click and Go!

INSPECTED CAMPSITES & SELECTED

Naturist campsites

Today there are many more people that enjoy naturist campsites than one would at first think. Some are dedicated naturists who practice their way of life wherever they may and who in the UK may well belong to clubs of like-minded people. For others, especially those who have enjoyed sunbathing on one of the many designated naturist areas on European beaches and feel comfortable with it, the logical next step is to try a holiday in a naturist village or campsite.

This growing number of 'holiday naturists' clearly enjoy the relaxed atmosphere prevailing on naturist sites. If they are not members of British Naturism they can pick up a naturist card on the first site they visit. The rules are simple: respect for the environment and for other visitors. You are encouraged to strip off but, in reality, it is up to you, except in and around the swimming pool where there is always a 'no clothes' rule. Clothes do tend to label people and without them there is a relaxed informality and sense of equality often missing in today's 'designer society'.

We feature some 24 naturist campsites in this guide and have been impressed by the friendly welcome and cultural aspects of their entertainment and range of activities – classical music beside the pool, walking trails to discover local wildlife or book-binding classes, for example. Most campsites make an effort to provide good entertainment and to make your holiday memorable; on the naturist sites in particular this is usually achieved quite elegantly without the frenzy that sometimes pervades more commercially-minded sites.

FR85140 Camping Naturiste le Colombier

Le Colombier, F-85210 St Martin-Lars en Ste Hermine (Vendée)

Tel: 02 51 27 83 84. Email: lecolombier.nat@wanadoo.fr

www.alanrogers.com/FR85140

A countryside site for naturists near La Roche sur Yon, just right for those seeking a peaceful holiday. It provides around 160 pitches in seven very natural fields on different levels linked by informal tracks. There are level, terraced areas for caravans and a feeling of spaciousness with pitches around the edges of fields, unmarked and with electricity (6/10A, some may require long leads). The bar/restaurant is in a converted barn. The site's 125 acres provide many walks throughout the attractive, wooded valley and around the lake.

Facilities

Fully equipped toilet blocks are good, providing some showers in cubicles. Dishwashing sinks. Motorcaravan service point. Grocer/baker calls daily. Bar/restaurant with à la carte and full menu (order before 1 pm), home baked bread and pizzas. Heated swimming pool. Fishing. Playground. Pony and trap rides and one day a week children can make their own bread. Plans for a sauna and aquagym. Off site: Shop 1 km.

Open: 1 April - 30 October.

Directions

From N148, La Roche-sur-Yon - Niort road, at St Hermine, turn onto D8 eastward for 4 km. Turn left on D10 to St Martin-Lars. Site is signed. GPS: N46:35.877 W00:58.162

Charges guide

Per pitch incl. 2 persons and electricity	€ 18,50 - € 21,50
child (3-9 yrs)	€ 3,40 - € 3,50
child (10-16 yrs)	€ 4,70 - € 4,80

FR58060 Domaine Naturiste de la Gagère

F-58170 Luzy (Nièvre)

Tel: 03 86 30 48 11. Email: info@la-gagere.com

www.alanrogers.com/FR58060

At this spacious, attractive, well equipped campsite, you will receive a really good welcome from the enthusiastic founders of Naturocamp. There are 120 good sized level grassy pitches, some shaded, some open, of which 100 are available for tourers. Many are arranged around three sides of rectangles between hedges. There is electricity to 84 pitches, 6 of which are fully serviced, but some will need leads of up to 40 m. In high season there are organised activities and entertainment.

Facilities

Three modern unisex toilet blocks, one heated, contain British style WCs, washbasins and pre-set showers. En-suite facilities for disabled people. Baby changing. Motorcaravan services. Laundry facilities. Shop (31/5-15/9). Bar. Restaurant with snack bar and takeaway (1/5-15/9). Satellite TV. Two heated swimming pools (one all season, the other 15/5-15/9). Sauna and health suite. Playgrounds. Volleyball. Boules. Bicycle hire. Only gas barbecues permitted (available for hire). Off site: Fishing 5 km. Luzy 10 km. Riding 10 km.

Open: 1 April - 1 October.

Directions

Luzy is 34 km. southwest of Autun, on the N81. Travel northeast from Luzy towards Autun. After 6 km. site is signed to the right, then reached by 3 km. of winding (often narrow) road. GPS: N46:49.010 E04:03.260

Charges guide

Per person	€ 6,25
pitch	€ 13,00
electricity	€ 2,50 - € 4,00

Less 10-30% outside July/Aug.
Admin fee for stays of 3 nights or less (€ 5).

FR33160 Espace Naturiste Euronat

F-33590 Grayan et l'Hopital (Gironde)

Tel: 05 56 09 33 33. Email: info@euronat.fr

www.alanrogers.com/FR33160

Euronat is really a large naturist town with extensive facilities, direct access to one and a half kilometres of sandy beach and a thalassotherapy centre. The caravan and camping sites are in two areas separate from the chalets and mobile homes. A variety of good sized, fairly flat and sandy pitches, includes some suitable for large motorhomes. All pitches have 10A electricity and some also have water and drainage. The 'town centre' is superb with supermarkets, an organic supermarket, butcher, fish shop, bakery, restaurants including fish, brasserie, pizzeria/crêperie, and a takeaway.

Facilities

Sanitary blocks are well maintained with some heated (not all open in low season). Facilities for people with disabilities. Launderette. Motorcaravan services. Shops, restaurants. Swimming pool, flumes, children's pool. Swimming lessons. Activities and workshops, archery, pony club, riding, tennis, petanque. Children's activities and day care. TMulti-purpose hall for dances, film nights, music evenings,. Supervised beach. No barbecues (communal areas provided). Torch may be useful.

Open: 23 March - 3 November.

Directions

From Bordeaux ring road take exit 7, then D1215 to Lesparre and Vensac, then follow (large) signed route. GPS: N45:24.976 W01:07.907

Charges guide

Per unit incl. 2 persons	€ 16,00 - € 30,60
incl. electricity (10A)	€ 19,50 - € 38,00
incl. services	€ 23,00 - € 43,50
extra person	€ 4,00 - € 7,00

Camping Cheques accepted.

Check real time availability and at-the-gate prices...

www.alanrogers.com

FR24190 Centre Naturiste le Couderc

Le Couderc, F-24440 Naussannes (Dordogne)

Tel: 05 53 22 40 40. Email: info@lecouderc.com

www.alanrogers.com/FR24190

This is one of the most beautiful camping sites in the Dordogne. Set in 28 hectares of open country-side, there is a feeling of spaciousness, calm and tranquility. The family go the extra mile to ensure visitors enjoy their visit. There are 188 pitches of which 170 are for touring units and the remainder being chalets which are available for rent. One is adapted for disabled visitors. The site is on different levels with undulating slopes but the generous pitches are level and easily accessible. Generally open but mature trees all around offer some shade. There is a very attractive restaurant and bar housed in a fine old Perigordine style building. A dining terrace outside adds to the ambiance on a summer evening. The swimming pool is solar heated as is the pool for toddlers. A jacuzzi and sauna are in the same area. Children will enjoy a well equipped play area in plenty of space together with a children's club in July and August. Music evenings and sporting competitions are also laid on.

Facilities

Five very clean modern toilet blocks with facilities for children and visitors with disabilities. Washing machines. Dryer. Superb restaurant and bar. Takeaway. Terrace. Shop. Heated swimming pools. Jacuzzi. Sauna. Bicycle Hire. Two ponds, one for fishing the other with cable slide. Children's club with sculpture and circus lessons. Play area. Some entertainment. Walking tracks. Caravan storage. Off site: Caves. Châteaux. Market towns. Walking. Riding 10 km. Golf 20 km.

Open: 1 April - 1 October.

Directions

From Bergerac take N21. Turn left on D25 to Issigeac. Continue towards Naussannes for 8 km. Turn left at signpost indicating Naussannes 2 km. Le Couderc is 350 m. on the right.
GPS: N44:45.361 E00:42.127

Charges guide

Per person	€ 4,10 - € 6,80
child (under 12 yrs)	€ 2,70 - € 4,50
pitch	€ 8,10 - € 13,50
electricity	€ 4,50
dog	€ 2,70 - € 4,50

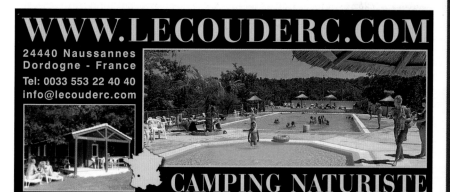

FR46300 Camping Naturiste le Clos Barrat

Mauroux, F-46700 Sérignac (Lot)

Tel: 05 65 31 97 93. Email: contact@leclosbarrat.com

www.alanrogers.com/FR46300

This site is southwest of Cahors in ten hectares of forest and pasture amongst the rich countryside of the Lot/Quercy area. This is a family run naturist site where you will receive a warm and friendly welcome which is extended throughout your stay. It offers spaciousness and tranquillity with 90 generous pitches (over 120 sq.m), all with 6/10A electricity. There are also six mobile homes, chalets or apartments to rent. The site is on a gentle rolling slope and this is reflected in some of the pitches although most are mainly level, and access for larger units is not a problem.

Facilities

Three traditional style sanitary blocks with two offering facilities for disabled visitors. Bar and restaurant. Small shop. Swimming pool and paddling pool. Play area. Trampoline. Tennis. Archery. Organised activities. Library. Barbecues are not permitted. Mobile homes, chalets and apartments for rent. Off site: Many cycle and walking trails. Fishing 6 km. Riding 6 km. Golf 20 km.

Open: 29 April - 31 December.

Directions

From Cahors take the D653 to Villesque. Join the D656 towards Tournon d'Argenais and at St Matre follow signs to Serignac on the D4. Site is signed from there. GPS: N44:25.848 E01:04.110

Charges guide

Per person	€ 5,00 - € 6,50
child (3-18 yrs)	€ 1,00 - € 2,00
pitch	€ 4,80 - € 6,50
incl. electricity	€ 7,70 - € 9,50
pet	€ 1,60

Check real time availability and at-the-gate prices...
www.alanrogers.com

FR33370 Centre Helio-Marin de Montalivet

46 avenue de l'Europe, F-33930 Montalivet (Gironde)

Tel: **05 56 73 73 73**. Email: **infos@chm-montalivet.com**   www.alanrogers.com/FR33370

This is a large naturist village with everything that you would need without leaving the site during your holiday. It has direct access to the sea with its own beautiful golden sandy beaches with coastguard surveillance in high season. Watersports are numerous with lessons if you require. The main emphasis here is to keep the family entertained. There are a total of 2,800 pitches, of which 1,700 are for touring. Pitches are level, on grass or sand, and mature trees provide shade in some areas. Circus school, dancing classes and skate boarding are just some of the activities organised here. Both the swimming pools are different, from tropical to traditional. Four slides and a toboggan are available to use in the aquatic park. There are a number of restaurants and bars to choose from. Alternatively you can choose a takeaway from a number of places available. Mobile homes and chalets are available for rent.

Facilities

Numerous sanitary blocks with facilities for disabled visitors and children. Shops, restaurants and bars. Launderette. Motorcaravan service point. Children's clubs. Evening entertainment. Two swimming pool complexes with slides and toboggan. Playgrounds. Sports grounds. TV rooms and cinema. Large library. Wellness centre offering numerous treatments and massage as well as saunas and jacuzzis. Off site: Golf. Riding. Cycling. Sailing and fishing.

Open: All year.

Directions

From Royan, take the ferry to Verdon-Sur-Mer and continue on N215 for 34 km. Turn right on D102 to Montalivet. Nearing the sea turn left for Hourtins and site is 1 km. on the right.
GPS: N45:21.809 W01:08.745

Charges guide

Per unit incl. 2 persons	
and electricity	€ 16,30 - € 31,50
extra person	€ 3,30 - € 7,50
dog	€ 6,50 - € 7,00

FR30400 Camping Naturiste la Genèse

Route de la Genèse, F-30430 Méjannes-le-Clap (Gard)

Tel: **04 66 24 51 82**. Email: **info@lagenese.com**   www.alanrogers.com/FR30400

La Genèse is a well equipped naturist site close on the banks of the River Cèze on the northern edge of the Cévennes national park. This is a large site with 483 well shaded pitches. These are divided into 'sauvage' (without electricity) and 'prairie' (with electricity 6A). A number of chalets and mobile homes are also available for rent. A wide variety of activities are on offer here, including art and craft workshops, bridge evenings and a cinema. Sports amenities include a large swimming pool with a daily aquagym session in high season, separate children's pool, tennis and archery.

Facilities

Shop. Bar. Restaurant. Swimming pool and children's pool. Sauna. Archery. Games room. Art and craft workshops. Cinema. Canoe hire. Play area. Activity and entertainment programme. Direct access to river. Mobile homes and chalets for rent. Off site: Cycle and walking tracks in the Cévennes national park. Méjannes-le-Clap (shops and restaurants). Orange 50 km.

Open: 29 March - 30 September.

Directions

Approaching from the west (Pont St Esprit) use the D901 to Barjac and then the D979 to Rochegude. Shortly beyond Rochegude, join the D176 to Méjannes le Clap and follow signs to the site.
GPS: N44:16.064 E04:22.208

Charges guide

Per unit incl. 2 persons	
and electricity	€ 19,00 - € 26,00
extra person	€ 4,00 - € 6,00

FR33300 Domaine Naturiste la Jenny

F-33680 Le Porge (Gironde)   Parcs Résidentiels ⊙ pagina 516

Tel: **05 56 26 56 90**. Email: **info@lajenny.fr**   www.alanrogers.com/FR33300

Pitches at this campsite are exclusively for chalet accommodation.

Check real time availability and at-the-gate prices...

www.**alanrogers**.com

live the natural way, live nude...

Domaine Naturiste

46, AV DE L'EUROPE - 33930 MONTALIVET - FRANCE
Tél : 00 33(0)5 56 73 73 73 Fax : 00 33(0)5 56 09 32 15
www.chm-montalivet.com - Email : infos@chm-montalivet.com

www.lagenese.com

La Genèse
Domaine Naturiste

A real sense of nature for the family...

Route de la Genèse - 30430 Mejannes-le-Clap- FRANCE
Tél : 00 33(0)4 66 24 51 82 Fax : 00 33(0)4 66 24 50 38 - Email : info@lagenese.com

The Travel Service ...we'll arrange everything BOOK THIS SITE CALL 01580 214000

FR40120 Domaine Naturiste Arnaoutchot

F-40560 Vielle-Saint-Girons (Landes)

Tel: 05 58 49 11 11. Email: contact@arna.com

www.alanrogers.com/FR40120

'Arna' is a large naturist site with extensive facilities and direct access to the beach. Even with 500 pitches, its layout in the form of a number of sections, each with its own character, make it quite relaxing and very natural. These sections amongst the trees and bushes of the Landes provide a variety of reasonably sized pitches, most with electricity (3/6A), although the hilly terrain means that only a limited number are flat enough for motorcaravans. The centrally located amenities are extensive and of excellent quality. There are several new mobile homes. American motorhomes are not accepted.

Facilities

Heated sanitary facilities include the usual naturist site type of blocks with communal hot showers and also a number of tiny blocks. Motorcaravan services. Supermarket, other shops. Bar/restaurant, pizzeria and tapita (fish) bar. Pizza. Heated indoor pool with solarium, whirlpool and slide. Outdoor and new paddling pool. Spa, sauna, steam, whirlpool, massages. Cinema. Library. Internet point. Bicycle hire. Fishing. Torches useful. Gas and electric barbecues. Off site: Riding or golf 5 km.

Open: 4 April - 27 September.

Directions

Site is signed off the D652 road at Vielle-Saint-Girons. Follow D328 for 3-4 km. GPS: N43:54.450 W01:21.667

Charges guide

Per unit incl. 1 person	€ 9,90 - € 35,90
extra person (over 3 yrs)	€ 2,00 - € 7,40
electricity (3/6A)	€ 5,40

Camping Cheques accepted.

FR23030 Creuse Nature Naturisme

Route de Bétête (D15), F-23600 Boussac (Creuse)

Tel: 05 55 65 18 01. Email: creuse.nature@wanadoo.fr

www.alanrogers.com/FR23030

This is a very spacious and well maintained naturist site set in the beautiful Limousin region in the centre of France. The 100 large grassy pitches, some slightly sloping, are laid out in an open wooded parkland setting. The 80 touring pitches are mainly positioned around the perimeter of the site or the small fishing lake. A central feature is the pool, bar and restaurant complex. Various activities are organised for all the family and there are many footpaths to enjoy around the borders of the site.

Facilities

Four modern, very clean toilet blocks with the usual facilities (open plan, so little privacy). Facilities for visitors with disabilities. Dishwashing and laundry facilities. Small shop (baker calls). Indoor (heated) and outdoor pools. Paddling pool. Sauna. Bar (all season). Restaurant (July/Aug). Archery (high season). Boules. Bicycle hire. Lake fishing. Internet access. Gas barbecues only on pitches. Off site: Small market town of Boussac 5 km.

Open: 15 April - 31 October.

Directions

Boussac lies 35 km. west of Montluçon, midway between the A20 and A71 autoroutes. In Boussac, site is well signed. Take D15 west for about 3 km. Site is on right. GPS: N46:21.060 E02:10.660

Charges guide

Per person	€ 3,50 - € 6,50
child (under 3 yrs)	free - € 2,00
child (3-11 yrs)	€ 2,50 - € 4,00
pitch with electricity	€ 13,50 - € 15,50

FR47140 Camping Naturiste Domaine Laborde

Paulhiac, F-47150 Monflanquin (Lot-et-Garonne)

Tel: 05 53 36 08 16. Email: fontaine.du.roc@wanadoo.fr

www.alanrogers.com/FR47140

Ideally situated on the border of Lot-et-Garonne and Dordogne, Domain Laborde is a naturist site of outstanding quality, with sweeping views from many of the higher pitches. This hilly and terraced site has 120 well maintained touring pitches, many shaded, some partially shaded and all surrounded by woodland. Electricity is available, although some need long leads. There are also 25 chalets for rent. The site has something for everyone and even in low season it is very popular. If you are new to naturist sites, then this is a must. The ambience is good and you will make new friends.

Facilities

New washblock as well as three sanitary blocks are well sited and clean. Washing machines and dryer. Shop with daily deliveries of fresh bread and milk. Bar with TV. Snack bar serving pizzas. Restaurant. Large swimming pool, whirlpool, children's pool and indoor heated pool. Two play areas. Boules. Giant chess board. Communal stone barbecue. Animation for children (high season). Various excursions and other activities for adults and children are organised. Off site: Riding 2 km. Golf 30 km.

Open: 1 April - 1 October.

Directions

From Monflanquin take D272 towards Monpazier. About 10 km. along the road look for the signs to site. It is very well signed at regular intervals and will read 'Laborde FFN'. GPS: N44:36.750 E00:50.232

Charges guide

Per person	€ 4,50 - € 5,50
child (under 6 yrs)	€ 3,50 - € 4,00
pitch	€ 9,00 - € 12,00
electricity (6A)	€ 3,50 - € 4,50

Check real time availability and at-the-gate prices... www.alanrogers.com

FR84020 Domaine Naturiste de Bélézy

Mobile homes ▶ page 508

F-84410 Bédoin (Vaucluse)

Tel: **04 90 65 60 18**. Email: info@belezy.com

www.alanrogers.com/FR84020

At the foot of Mont Ventoux, surrounded by beautiful scenery, Bélézy is an excellent naturist site with many amenities and activities and the ambience is relaxed and comfortable. The 238 marked pitches are set amongst many varieties of trees and shrubs. Electricity points (12A) are plentiful but long leads are necessary. So far as naturism is concerned, the emphasis is on personal choice, the only stipulation being the requirement for complete nudity in the pools and pool area. An area of natural parkland with an orchard, fishpond and woodland (complete with red squirrels), has a good range of sports facilities.

Facilities

Sanitary blocks differ – newer ones are excellent, with showers and washbasins in cubicles, others have hot showers in the open air, screened by stone dividers. One block has a superb children's section. Shop (22/3-21/9). Excellent restaurant and takeaway. Two swimming pools. Sauna. Tennis. Adventure play area. Activities in low season. Archery. Guided walks. Children's club. Hydrotherapy centre (1/4-30/9). Barbecues are prohibited. Pets are not accepted. Off site: Bédoin 1.5 km.

Open: 23 March - 2 October.

Directions

From A7 autoroute or RN7 at Orange, take D950 southeast to Carpentras, then northeast via D974 to Bédoin. Site is signed in Bédoin, being about 1.5 km. northeast of the village. GPS: N44:08.011 E05:11.247

Charges guide

Per unit incl. 2 persons and electricity	€ 27,00 - € 43,00
extra person	€ 5,00 - € 8,50
child (3-8 yrs)	€ 5,80 - € 9,10

Various offers and reductions outside high season. Camping Cheques accepted.

FR09090 Naturiste Camping Millfleurs

Le Tuilier Gudas, F-09120 Varilhes (Ariège)

Tel: **05 61 60 77 56**. Email: ag.kos@wanadoo.fr

www.alanrogers.com/FR09090

Millfleurs is a quiet site in a secluded location for naturists. It is peaceful with some 70 acres of woods and meadows providing guided naturist walks in total privacy. The site has 40 large, flat, mostly terraced pitches (26 with 4/6/8A electricity), long leads if pitching off the terraces. There are also very secluded pitches in wooded areas with shade, or you can pitch a tent in the meadows if you prefer. There are few of the normal camping leisure facilities here and the site is definitely aimed at the more mature naturist camper.

Facilities

An excellent toilet block with facilities for disabled campers. Bread available to order in high season. Guests dine together in the 'salle de reunion' within the farmhouse two nights a week or just meet friends for a drink. Refrigerator with drinks. Pétanque. Guide book for walks and cycle rides. Torches essential. Pick ups from airports and stations arranged. Off site: The coast is approximately 1.5 hours.

Open: 15 April - 30 September.

Directions

From Varilhes, 8 km. south of Pamiers on D624 (parallel to N20). Take D13 for Dalou and Gudas cross railway and N20. The site is 2 km. past Gudas, on right. GPS: N42:59.566 E01:40.731

Charges guide

Per person (all ages)	€ 4,60 - € 5,40
pitch	€ 4,60 - € 5,40
dog	€ 1,80
electricity	€ 2,60

No credit cards.

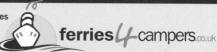

Need a **low cost ferry?**

It couldn't be simpler - just click, choose a ferry and book...

■ Special deals for caravans and motorhomes
■ View routes and compare prices
■ Fully searchable by route and operator

ferries4campers.co.uk

FR65010 Domaine Naturiste l'Eglantière

Ariès-Espénan, F-65230 Castelnau-Magnoac (Hautes-Pyrénées)

Tel: 05 62 39 88 00. Email: info@leglantiere.com

www.alanrogers.com/FR65010

Alongside a small, fast flowing river, in woods it comprises 12 hectares for camping and caravanning, with a further 32 for walking and relaxing. The river is suitable for swimming and canoeing, with fishing nearby. The 83 traditional, varying size, grassy, level pitches have 10A electricity (long leads). The older secluded ones are separated by a variety of tall trees and bushes, the newer ones more open. There is a tenting area across the river. The site has a medium sized swimming pool with sunbathing areas and a children's pool, overlooked by the clubhouse and terrace.

Facilities

Two toilet blocks in typically naturist style, providing under cover, open plan, facilities. Small block has individual cubicles. Shop (July/Aug). Clubhouse, bar (all season), small restaurant (June-Sept), pizzeria, takeaway (July-Aug), internet. Soundproofed activities/disco area, play room for younger children. Swimming pool (all season). Play area, children's entertainment in season. River activities. Canoe, mountain bike hire. No barbecues. Torches useful. Off site: Restaurants in the nearby village.

Open: Easter - October.

Directions

From Auch take D929 south towards Lannemezan. After Castelnau-Magnoac continue past aerodrome and turn onto the D9 towards Monleon-Magnoac. Take the first left towards Ariès-Espénan and follow site signs. GPS: N43:15.829 E00:31.252

Charges guide

Per pitch incl. 2 persons	€ 9,50 - € 32,90
extra person	free - € 5,90
electricity (10A)	€ 4,90
Camping Cheques accepted.	

FR11090 Camping Naturiste le Clapotis

Lieu dit Pech-Redon, F-11480 Lapalme (Aude)

Tel: 04 68 48 15 40. Email: info@leclapotis.com

www.alanrogers.com/FR11090

Le Clapotis is a small and tranquil naturist site, situated between Narbonne and Perpignan in a secluded pine wood beside the Etang de Lapalme (a large sea lagoon). There is direct access to the lagoon which is popular for windsurfing. The site comprises 173 touring pitches, all with electricity (4A) and are of a good size on stony or sandy ground. Pitches in the older part have excellent shade from the pine trees and in the newer area, shade will be provided as the hedges grow. There is a relaxed feeling of harmony and freedom about this site.

Facilities

Two large and one small sanitary block, a little basic but fully equipped. Showers are both open and in cabins. Facilities for babies and disabled campers. Washing machines. Well stocked shop (end May - mid Sept). Bar and restaurant (from 15/6) and takeaway (from midday). Swimming pool (15/6-15/9). Pétanque. Windsurfing. Fishing. Torches useful. Off site: Sandy beach 4 km. Riding 4 km. Bicycle hire 9 km. Golf 10 km.

Open: 15 March - 31 October.

Directions

Exit the N9 junction 40 in direction of Port Leucate. At roundabout take N9 north for 3 km. to next roundabout. Turn right (Port-la-Nouvelle). Site sign in 500 m. Follow narrow, poorly made up road for 2 km to site. GPS: N42:57.480 E02:59.752

Charges guide

Per pitch incl. 2 persons and electricity	€ 22,00 - € 26,00
extra person	€ 4,00 - € 5,00

FR11190 Domaine Naturiste la Grande Cosse

Saint Pierre la Mer, F-11560 Fleury (Aude)

Tel: 04 68 33 61 87. Email: contact@grandecosse.com

www.alanrogers.com/FR11190

Any slight difficulty in finding this secluded naturist site is compensated for immediately you arrive. The abundance of flowers, shrubs and the generally peaceful ambience makes this a delightful place for a relaxing naturist holiday, and the extensive facilities mean you only need to leave the site for sightseeing rather than for necessities. In total there are a total of 480 pitches, of which about 150 are for mobile homes, and the mainly large touring pitches, all with 8A electrical connections, are informally and very attractively arranged in a variety of different areas. Naturism here is pretty relaxed – the only area where clothing is not permitted is in the swimming pools.

Facilities

Five sanitary blocks are opened progressively throughout the season. Fully equipped modern facilities, including a choice of private or communal showers, and some washbasins in cabins. Laundry facilities. Motorcaravan service point. Gas. Well stocked shop. (8/4-30/9). Bar (15/5-30/9). Restaurant (1/6-30/9). Takeaway (30/6-30/9). Swimming pools (5/5-30/9). Play area. Tennis. Internet. Communal barbecues. Off site: Boat launching 5 km.

Open: 28 March - 4 October.

Directions

From the A9 take exit 36 to Vendres. Pass through town, continue to Lespignan, then Fleury. At roundabout turn left signed Cabanes de Fleury. Follow for 4 km. to site sign to left. After 2 km. site signed to right. GPS: N43:12.349 E03:12.659

Charges 2009

Per unit incl. 2 persons and electricitry	€ 20,50 - € 36,50
extra person	€ 5,20 - € 6,90

FR34080 Camping le Sérignan Plage Nature

L'Orpellière, F-34410 Sérignan (Hérault)

Tel: **04 67 32 09 61**. Email: **info@leserignannature.com**

www.alanrogers.com/FR34080

Sérignam Plage Nature benefits from the same 600 m. of white, sandy beach as its sister site next door. Being a naturist site, it actually abuts the naturist section of the beach with direct access to it. It also has the use of the Sérignan Plage balnéo pool in the mornings. The site has 400 good sized pitches on level sandy grass of which 120 are used for touring (6A electricity). There is plenty of shade except on the pitches beside the beach. Many mobile homes and chalets are available to rent. A friendly bar and shop serve the site although visitors may use the facilities at Le Sérignan Plage.

Facilities

Two toilet blocks of differing designs (one refurbished to a very modern design) offer modern facilities with some washbasins in cabins. All clean and well maintained. Washing machines. Supermarket, fresh fruit and vegetables, newsagent/souvenir shop and ice cream kiosk. Small bar/café. Evening entertainment. Play area, miniclub and disco for children. Facilities and pools at Sérignan Plage. Off site: Riding 1.5 km.

Open: 23 April - 27 September.

Directions

From A9 exit 35 (Béziers Est) towards Sérignan, D64 (9 km). Before Sérignan, take road to Sérignan Plage. At small sign (blue) turn right for 500 m. At T-junction turn left over bridge, site is 75 m. after left hand bend. GPS: N43:15.470 E03:19.130

Charges guide

Per unit incl. 1 or 2 persons and electricity	€ 16,00 - € 42,00
extra person	€ 6,00 - € 8,00
Camping Cheques accepted.	

FR30100 Camping Naturiste de la Sablière

Domaine de la Sablière, Saint Privat-de-Champclos, F-30430 Barjac (Gard)

Tel: **04 66 24 51 16**. Email: **contact@villagesabliere.com**

www.alanrogers.com/FR30100

Spectacularly situated in the Cèze Gorges, this naturist site with a surprising 497 pitches, 240 for touring, tucked away within its wild terrain offers a wide variety of facilities, all within a peaceful, wooded and dramatic setting. The pitches themselves are mainly on flat stony terraces, attractively situated among a variety of trees and shrubs (some with a low overhang). Many are of a good size and have electricity (6/10A), very long leads may be needed. Nudity is obligatory only around the pool complex. You must expect some fairly steep walking between the pitches and facilities.

Facilities

Six good unisex sanitary blocks have excellent free hot showers in typical open plan, naturist style, washbasins (cold water) and facilities for people with disabilities. Laundry. Good supermarket. Bar (1/4-22/9). Excellent covered restaurant and takeaway (1/4-22/9). Small café. Swimming pool complex. Fitness room. TV room and disco. Tennis. Minigolf. Fitness trail. Archery. Activity and entertainment programme. Barbecues are not permitted. Off site: Bicycle hire 8 km. Riding 10 km. Golf 12 km.

Open: 1 April - 1 October.

Directions

From Barjac take D901 east for 3 km. Turn right at site sign just before St Privat-de-Champclos and follow site signs along winding country lane to site entrance in 4 km. GPS: N44:16.021 E04:21.125

Charges guide

Per pitch incl. 2 persons	€ 19,00 - € 37,00
extra person	€ 5,00 - € 7,00
Camping Cheques accepted.	

FR34050 Camping Naturiste le Mas de Lignières

Cesseras-en-Minervois, F-34210 Olonzac (Hérault)

Tel: **04 68 91 24 86**. Email: **lemas1@tiscali.fr**

www.alanrogers.com/FR34050

A naturist site hidden in the hills of the Minervois, only three kilometres from the medieval town of Minerve. There are marvellous views to the Pyrénées, the Corbières and the coast at Narbonne. The owners Jeanne and Gilles, offer a warm welcome and promote an enjoyable family atmosphere. The site has 50 large pitches (electricity 6/10A), and 25 super pitches. Mainly on level grass, separated by mature hedges giving considerable privacy. Some smaller pitches are available for tents, with cars parked elsewhere. There is natural shade and a variety of flora and fauna including types of orchid.

Facilities

Clean toilet block has open wash basins and showers, facilities for visitors with disabilities. Washing machine. Simple shop. Bread (15/6-15/9). Bar (15/7-15/8). Swimming pool, sliding cover for use when cold. Paddling pool. Room for general use with TV, library, separate provision for young people. Playground. Tennis, volleyball, boules. Torch useful. Only gas barbecues. Off site: Sailing, riding and canoeing nearby. Canal du Midi.

Open: 1 May - 2 October.

Directions

From A61 take exit for Lézignan-Corbières, D611 to Homps, then D910 to Olonzac. Through village following signs to Minerve (D10). Continue. 4 km. Turn left to Cesseras (D168). At Cesseras follow signs Fauzan for 4 km. (site signed) on right, narrow, winding road. GPS: N43:20.455 E02:42.389

Charges guide

Per unit incl. 2 persons,	€ 22,00 - € 25,00
extra person	€ 4,00

BOOK THIS SITE
CALL 01580 214000
...we'll arrange everything
The Travel Service

FR34540 Domaine de Lambeyran

Hameau de Lambeyran, F-34700 Lodève (Hérault)

Tel: 04 67 44 13 99. Email: lambeyran@wanadoo.fr

www.alanrogers.com/FR34540

A wooded valley covering 340 hectares allows Domaine de Lambeyran a place in the Guinness Book of Records for having the largest area available for naturists in the world. It is a wonderful natural area with amazing views across to Lodève. Naturists can enjoy the marked trails around the valley or the welcome pool whilst choosing from 160 huge (200 sq.m) pitches. Where necessary the pitches have been levelled with local stone which has also been used to create short stairways in the terrain. Electricity (3/6A) is available on 110 pitches.

Facilities

Two large tiled toilet blocks and a smaller one are fully equipped and give good coverage for the various areas. Washing machine. Small shop. Bar and simple restaurant (in the evenings from 7/7). Swimming pool with sunbathing terrace. Mountain biking. Dancing, films and organised trips such as canoeing down the Orb Gorges. Communal barbecue area. Dogs are only allowed in one area. Off site: Tennis and riding 4 km. Watersports and beaches at Lac du Salagou 16 km.

Open: 1 May - 20 September.

Directions

From A75 take exit for Lodève and follow signs for town centre. Cross town following signs for Lunas (D35) picking up site signs. Ignore right turn for les Plans and take next right and follow up hill for 3 km. to site. The road is good but is single file in parts. GPS: N43:44.169 E03:15.992

Charges guide

Per person	€ 4,20 - € 6,20
pitch	€ 7,60 - € 12,80
electricity (3/6A)	€ 4,20
No credit cards.	

FR06070 Domaine Naturiste Club Origan

F-06260 Puget-Theniers (Alpes-Maritimes)

Tel: 04 93 05 06 00. Email: origan@wanadoo.fr

www.alanrogers.com/FR06070

Origan is a naturist site set in the mountains behind Nice, at a height of 500 m. The access road is single track and winding with a few passing places, so arrival is not recommended until late afternoon. The site's terrain is fairly wild and the roads stony and it is not suitable for caravans longer than six metres due to the steep slopes, although the site will assist with a 4 x 4 vehicle if requested. The 100 touring pitches, in three areas, are of irregular size and shape with good views. Electricity connection (6A) is possible on most pitches (by long cable). Member 'France 4 Naturisme'.

Facilities

Sanitary facilities, are clean and of a standard and type associated with most good naturist sites. Laundry facilities. Shop (1/6-30/8). Bar/restaurant. Takeaway. Heated pools. Jacuzzi and sauna. Disco. Tennis. Fishing. Bicycle hire. Organised activities for all (high season). Only gas or electric barbecues are permitted. Torches advised. Off site: Puget-Theniers offers bars, cafés, shops, etc.

Open: 15 April - 30 September.

Directions

Heading west on the N202, just past the town of Puget-Theniers, turn right at campsite sign at level crossing; site is 1 km. GPS: N43:57.458 E6:51.653

Charges guide

Per unit incl. 2 persons	€ 29,50 - € 36,50
extra person	€ 4,00 - € 8,00
Camping Cheques accepted.	

FR20050 Village Naturiste la Chiappa

Mobile homes ▶ page 513

F-20137 Porto-Vecchio (Corse-du-Sud)

Tel: 04 95 70 00 31. Email: chiappa@wanadoo.fr

www.alanrogers.com/FR20050

This is a large naturist campsite on the Chiappa peninsula with 220 pitches for tourers and tents, plus 250 bungalows. A few touring pitches have sea views and are taken first in high season. The pitches are informally marked and have a variety of shapes and sizes, some with difficult slopes and access, especially for large units. (75-125 sq.m). Cars are parked separately. Very long electricity leads are necessary here for most pitches (10A) electricity. The beaches are between long rocky outcrops and it is generally safe to swim, or alternatively enjoy the swimming pool by the main beach.

Facilities

The sanitary facilities were tired and in need of refurbishment when we visited. Washing machines. Motorcaravan service point. Well stocked shop. Two bars and restaurants with snacks. Swimming pool. Play area for children. Riding. Tennis. Minigolf. Fishing. Diving, windsurfing and sailing schools. Keep fit, sauna (extra cost). Bistro. Internet. Torches essential. Off site: Excursions. Car rental.

Open: 9 May - 10 October.

Directions

From Bastia, N198 heading south, take Porto-Vecchio bypass (signed Bonofaccio). At southern end, take first left signed Pont de La Chiappa, unclassified road. After 8 km. site signed. Turn left and follow rough track for 2 km. to site. GPS: N41:35.632 E09:21.428

Charges guide

Per person	€ 8,00 - € 10,00
pitch incl. electricity	€ 11,00 - € 14,00

Check real time availability and at-the-gate prices...

www.alanrogers.com

FR20080 Camping Bagheera Naturisme

Route 198, F-20230 Bravone (Haute-Corse)

Tel: **04 95 38 80 30**. Email: **bagheera@bagheera.fr**   www.alanrogers.com/FR20080

An extremely long private road leads you to this naturist site which is alongside a three kilometre fine sand beach and has been run by the same family for 30 years. There are 190 pitches which are separated from the numerous bungalows. Well shaded under huge eucalyptus trees, all have 10A electricity (long leads may be necessary). Some beach-side pitches have sea views but most others are further back from the sea. All pitches are on sandy grass and are kept clean and neat. Large units will have no problems with access here. The restaurant and beach bar have superb panoramic views of the sea.

Facilities

Four sanitary blocks (one new in 2008) offer hot water throughout. Washing machines. Excellent restaurant (Corsican menu, children's menu). Bar. Comprehensive beach snack bar and bar. Pizzeria. Shop. All amenities 1/6-30/10. Swimming pool. New play area. Gym. Massage. Sauna. Pedaloes. Pétanque. Sub-aqua diving. Beach umbrella rental. Refrigerated lockers for hire. Tennis. Bicycle hire. Fishing. Entertainment programme all season. TV. Internet. Off site: Riding. Boat launching 15 km. Town 11 km.

Open: 1 April - 30 October (bungalows all year).

Directions

Site is between Bastia and Aleria near Bravone, 7 km. north of Aleria on the N198. It is well signed off the N198. Follow site road 4 km. east to beach. GPS: N42:13.164 E09:33.246

Charges guide

Per unit incl. 2 persons	€ 16,00 - € 22,40
extra person	€ 3,60 - € 5,80
child (3-15 yrs)	€ 1,60 - € 3,25

FR20040 Riva Bella Nature Resort & Spa

Mobile homes ▶ page 513

B.P. 21, F-20270 Alèria (Haute-Corse)

Tel: **04 95 38 81 10**. Email: **riva-bella@wanadoo.fr**   www.alanrogers.com/FR20040

This is a relaxed, informal, spacious site alongside an extremely long and beautiful beach. Riva Bella is naturist from 15 May to 20 September only. It offers a variety of pitches, situated in beautiful countryside and seaside. The site is divided into several areas with 200 pitches and bungalows, some alongside the sandy beach with little shade, others in a wooded glade with ample shade. The huge fish-laden lakes are a fine feature of this site. Although electricity is available in most parts, a long cable may be needed. The ground is fairly flat with terracing for tents.

Facilities

High standard toilet facilities. Provision for disabled people, children and babies. Laundry. Large shop (15/5-15/10). Fridge hire. Restaurant with lake views (all season) with reasonable prices. Excellent beach/snack bar. Bar. Watersports, sailing school, fishing, sub-aqua. Balneotherapy centre. Sauna. Aerobics. Giant draughts. Archery. Fishing. Riding. Mountain bike hire. Half-court tennis. Walk with llamas. Internet. WiFi. Professional evening entertainment programme.

Open: 30 March - 2 November.

Directions

Site is 12 km. north of Aleria on N198 (Bastia) road. Watch for large signs and unmade road to site and follow for 4 km. GPS: N42:09.691 E09:33.161

Charges 2009

Per unit incl. 2 persons	
and electricity	€ 15,00 - € 38,00
extra person	€ 5,00 - € 9,00
child (3-8 yrs)	€ 2,00 - € 6,00
dog	€ 3,00

Special offers and half-board arrangements available. Camping Cheques accepted.

Are you missing out?

You are ...

... if you're not a member of British Naturism

The UK's national body is more active than ever – come and find out about Nudefest, the BN Alton Towers weekend and other big events, Special Interest Groups, discounted holidays, e-zine, Members' Forum, lively and informative quarterly magazine on naturism in the UK and around the world, and our campaigning activity for naturists everywhere.

Get more out of naturism by joining our community for less than £3 a month and help us to do the work that is needed to ensure a great future for naturism in the UK.

www.british-naturism.org.uk

CCBN, 30-32 Wycliffe Road, Northampton, NN1 5JF. Telephone: 01604 620361

BOOK THIS SITE The Travel **Service** CALL 01580 214000 ...we'll arrange everything

Check real time availability and at-the-gate prices...
www.**alanrogers**.com

Accommodation

Over recent years many of the campsites featured in this guide have added large numbers of high quality mobile homes and chalets. Many site owners believe that some former caravanners and motorcaravanners have been enticed by the extra comfort they can now provide, and that maybe this is the ideal solution to combine the freedom of camping with all the comforts of home.

Quality is consistently high and, although the exact size and inventory may vary from site to site, if you choose any of the sites detailed here, you can be sure that you're staying in some of the best quality and best value mobile homes available.

Home comforts are provided and typically these include a fridge with freezer compartment, gas hob, proper shower – often a microwave and radio/cassette hi-fi too but do check for details. All mobile homes and chalets come fully equipped with a good range of kitchen utensils, pots and pans, crockery, cutlery and outdoor furniture. Some even have an attractive wooden sundeck or paved terrace – a perfect spot for outdoors eating or relaxing with a book and watching the world go by.

Regardless of model, colourful soft furnishings are the norm and a generally breezy décor helps to provide a real holiday feel.

Although some sites may have a large number of different accommodation types, we have restricted our choice to one or two of the most popular accommodation units (either mobile homes or chalets) for each of the sites listed.

The mobile homes here will be of modern design, and recent innovations, for example, often include pitched roofs which substantially improve their appearance.

Design will invariably include clever use of space and fittings/furniture to provide for comfortable holidays – usually light and airy, with big windows and patio-style doors, fully equipped kitchen areas, a shower room with shower, washbasin and WC, cleverly designed bedrooms and a comfortable lounge/dining area (often incorporating a sofa bed).

In general, modern campsite chalets incorporate all the best features of mobile homes in a more traditional structure, sometimes with the advantage of an upper mezzanine floor for an additional bedroom.

Our selected campsites offer a massive range of different types of mobile home and chalet, and it would be impractical to inspect every single accommodation unit. Our selection criteria, therefore, primarily takes account of the quality standards of the campsite itself.

However, there are a couple of important ground rules:

- FEATURED MOBILE HOMES MUST BE NO MORE THAN 5 YEARS OLD

- CHALETS NO MORE THAN 10 YEARS OLD

- ALL LISTED ACCOMMODATION MUST, OF COURSE, FULLY CONFORM WITH ALL APPLICABLE LOCAL, NATIONAL AND EUROPEAN SAFETY LEGISLATION.

For each campsite we given details of the type, or types, of accommodation available to rent, but these details are necessarily quite brief. Sometimes internal layouts can differ quite substantially, particularly with regard to sleeping arrangements, where these include the flexible provision for 'extra persons' on sofa beds located in the living area. These arrangements may vary from accommodation to accommodation, and if you're planning a holiday which includes more people than are catered for by the main bedrooms you should check exactly how the extra sleeping arrangements are to be provided!

Charges

An indication of the tariff for each type of accommodation featured is also included, indicating the variance between the low and high season tariffs. However, given that many campsites have a large and often complex range of pricing options, incorporating special deals and various discounts, the charges we mention should be taken to be just an indication. We strongly recommend therefore that you confirm the actual cost when making a booking.

We also strongly recommend that you check with the campsite, when booking, what (if anything) will be provided by way of bed linen, blankets, pillows etc. Again, in our experience, this can vary widely from site to site.

On every campsite a fully refundable deposit (usually between 150 and 300 euros) is payable on arrival. There may also be an optional cleaning service for which a further charge is made. Other options may include sheet hire (typically 30 euros per unit) or baby pack hire (cot and high chair).

Low Cost Flights
An Inexpensive Way To Arrive At Your Campsite

Many campsites are conveniently served by a wide choice of low cost airlines. Cheap flights can be very easy to find and travellers increasingly find the regional airports often used to be smaller, quieter and generally a calmer, more pleasurable experience.

Low cost flights can make campsites in more distant regions a much more attractive option: quicker to reach, inexpensive flights, and simply more convenient.

Many campsites are seeing increased visitors using the low cost flights and are adapting their services to suit this clientele. An airport shuttle service is not uncommon, meaning you can take advantage of that cheap flight knowing you will be met at the other end and whisked to your campsite. No taxi queues or multiple drop-offs.

Obviously, these low cost flights are impractical when taking all your own camping gear but they do make a holiday in campsite owned accommodation much more straightforward. The low cost airline option makes mobile home holidays especially attractive: pack a suitcase and use bed linen and towels provided (which you will generally need to pre-book).

Pricing Tips

- Low cost airlines promote cheap flights but only a small percentage of seats are priced   at the cheapest price. Book early for the best prices (and of course you also get a better choice of campsite or mobile home)

- Child seats are usually the same costs as adults

- Full payment is required at the time of booking

- Changes and amendments can be costly with low cost airlines

- Peak dates can be expensive compared to other carriers

Car Hire

For maximum flexibility you will probably hire a car from a car rental agency. Car hire provides convenience but also will allow you access to off-site shops, beaches and tourist sights.

FR29010 Castel Camping le Ty-Nadan

▶ see report page 27

Route d'Arzano, F-29310 Locunolé (Finistère)

AR1 – IRM – Mobile Home

Sleeping: 2 bedrooms, sleeps 6: 1 double, 2 single beds, sofa bed, pillows & blankets provided

Living: living/kitchen area, heating, shower & wc

Eating: fitted kitchen with hobs, oven, fridge

Outside: table & chairs, 2 sun loungers, parasol

Pets: accepted

AR2 – CHALET – Chalet

Sleeping: 2 bedrooms, sleeps 6: 1 double, 2 single beds, sofa bed, pillows & blankets provided

Living: living/kitchen area, heating, shower & wc

Eating: fitted kitchen with hobs, fridge

Outside: table & chairs, 2 sun loungers, parasol

Pets: accepted

Other (AR1 and AR2): bed linen, cot and high chair for rent

Open: 3 April - 3 September

Weekly Charge	AR1	AR2
Low Season (from)	€ 324	€ 414
High Season (from)	€ 945	€ 1176

FR29050 Castel l'Orangerie de Lanniron

▶ see report page 29

Château de Lanniron, F-29336 Quimper (Finistère)

AR1 – ZEN – Mobile Home

Sleeping: 3 bedrooms, sleeps 6: 1 double, 2 single beds, bunkbed, pillows & blankets provided

Living: living/kitchen area, heating, air conditioning, shower & separate wc

Eating: fitted kitchen with hobs, microwave, coffee machine, fridge/freezer

Outside: table & chairs, 2 sun loungers, parasol, BBQ

Pets: not accepted

AR2 – CONFORT – Mobile Home

Sleeping: 2 bedrooms, sleeps 4/6: 1 double, 2 single beds, bunkbed, sofa bed, pillows & blankets provided

Living: living/kitchen area, heating, radio, shower & separate wc

Eating: fitted kitchen with hobs, microwave, coffee machine, fridge/freezer

Outside: table & chairs, 2 sun loungers, parasol, BBQ

Pets: not accepted

Other (AR1 and AR2): bed linen, cot and high chair for rent

Open: 1 April - 31 October

Weekly Charge	AR1	AR2
Low Season (from)	€ 455	€ 350
High Season (from)	€ 966	€ 840

FR29080 Camping le Panoramic

▶ see report page 32

Route de la Plage-Penker, F-29560 Telgruc-sur-Mer (Finistère)

AR1 – TRIGANO ELEGANTE 33 m² – Mobile Home

Sleeping: 3 bedrooms, sleeps 6: 1 double, 4 single beds, pillows & blankets provided

Living: living/kitchen area, heating, shower & wc

Eating: fitted kitchen with hobs, fridge

Outside: table & chairs, 2 sun loungers, parasol, BBQ

Pets: accepted

AR2 – TRIGANO ELEGANTE 25 m² – Mobile Home

Sleeping: 2 bedrooms, sleeps 4: 1 double, 2 single beds, sofa bed, pillows & blankets provided

Living: living/kitchen area, heating, shower & wc

Eating: fitted kitchen with hobs, fridge

Outside: table and chairs, sun lounger, parasol, BBQ

Pets: accepted

Open: 1 May -15 September

Weekly Charge	AR1	AR2
Low Season (from)	€ 300	€ 250
High Season (from)	€ 660	€ 580

FR29180 Camping les Embruns

▶ see report page 35

Rue du philosophe Alain, le Pouldu, F-29360 Clohars-Carnoët (Finistère)

AR1 – CAMPITEL – Chalet

Sleeping: 2 bedrooms, sleeps 4: 2 doubles, bunkbed, sofa bed

Living: living/kitchen area, heating, shower & wc

Eating: fitted kitchen with hobs, oven, coffee machine, fridge

Outside: table & chairs

Pets: accepted (with supplement)

AR2 – NAUTIQUE – Mobile Home

Sleeping: 3 bedrooms, sleeps 6: 1 double, 4 single beds, sofa bed

Living: living/kitchen area, heating, shower & wc

Eating: fitted kitchen with hobs, oven, coffee machine, fridge

Outside: table & chairs, parasol

Pets: accepted (with supplement)

Other (AR1 and AR2): cot and high chair for rent

Open: 3 April - 19 September

Weekly Charge	AR1	AR2
Low Season *(from)*	€ 320	€ 395
High Season *(from)*	€ 665	€ 690

FR44070 Camping Parc du Guibel

▶ see report page 52

Route de Kerdrien, F-44420 Piriac-sur-Mer (Loire-Atlantique)

AR1 – GALION – Mobile Home

Sleeping: 2 bedrooms, sleeps 4/6: 1 double, 1 single bed, sofa bed, pillows & blankets provided

Living: living/kitchen area, heating, fan, shower & separate wc

Eating: fitted kitchen with hobs, oven, grill, coffee machine, fridge/freezer

Outside: table & chairs, 2 sun loungers

Pets: accepted (with supplement)

AR2 – CHALET TYPE 2 – Chalet

Sleeping: 3 bedrooms, sleeps 6/8: 1 double, 1 single bed, bunkbed, sofa bed, pillows & blankets provided

Living: living/kitchen area, heating, fan, shower & separate wc

Eating: fitted kitchen with hobs, oven, grill, coffee machine, fridge/freezr

Outside: table & chairs, 2 sun loungers

Pets: accepted (with supplement)

Other (AR1 and AR2): bed linen, cot and high chair for rent

Open: 1 April - 30 September

Weekly Charge	AR1	AR2
Low Season *(from)*	€ 322	€ 364
High Season *(from)*	€ 700	€ 784

FR44090 Kawan Village du Deffay

▶ see report page 51

B.P. 18 Le Deffay, Sainte-Reine-de-Bretagne, F-44160 Pontchâteau (Loire-Atlantique)

AR1 – MOBILE HOME 5 – Mobile Home

Sleeping: 2 bedrooms, sleeps 5: 1 double, 1 single bed, bunkbed, pillows & blankets provided

Living: living/kitchen area, heating, radio, shower & separate wc

Eating: fitted kitchen with hobs, microwave, coffee machine, fridge/freezer

Outside: table & chairs, 2 sun loungers, parasol, BBQ

Pets: not accepted

AR2 – CHALET 4/6 PERSONS – Chalet

Sleeping: 2 bedrooms, sleeps 6: 1 double, 2 bunkbeds, sofa bed, pillows & blankets provided

Living: living/kitchen area, heating, radio, shower & wc

Eating: fitted kitchen with hobs, microwave, grill, dish washer, coffee machine, fridge/freezer

Outside: table & chairs, 2 sun loungers, parasol, BBQ

Pets: not accepted

Other (AR1 and AR2): bed linen, cot, high chair and baby bath for rent

Open: 1 April - 31 October

Weekly Charge	AR1	AR2
Low Season *(from)*	€ 239	€ 239
High Season *(from)*	€ 659	€ 699

FR44100 Camping le Patisseau

▶ see report page 49

29 rue du Patisseau, F-44210 Pornic (Loire-Atlantique)

AR1 – CHALET 6 – Chalet

Sleeping: 2 bedrooms, sleeps 6: 1 double, 2 single beds, sofa bed, pillows & blankets provided

Living: living/kitchen area, heating, shower & wc

Eating: fitted kitchen with hobs, microwave, fridge

Outside: table & chairs, parasol

Pets: not accepted

AR2 – MOBILE HOME CONFORT 6 – Mobile Home

Sleeping: 2 bedrooms, sleeps 6: 1 double, 2 single beds, sofa bed, pillows & blankets provided

Living: living/kitchen area, heating, shower & wc

Eating: fitted kitchen with hobs, microwave, fridge

Outside: table & chairs, parasol

Pets: not accepted

Open: 4 April - 11 November		
Weekly Charge	**AR1**	**AR2**
Low Season *(from)*	€ 455	€ 497
High Season *(from)*	€ 826	€ 868

FR44180 Camping de la Boutinardière

▶ see report page 54

Rue de la Plage de la Boutinardière, F-44210 Pornic (Loire-Atlantique)

AR1 – MOBILE HOME 5 PERSONS – Mobile Home

Sleeping: 2 bedrooms, sleeps 4/5: 1 double, 2 single beds, sofa bed, pillows & blankets provided

Living: living/kitchen area, heating, shower & wc

Eating: fitted kitchen with hobs, fridge

Outside: table & chairs, parasol

Pets: accepted (with supplement)

AR2 – MOBILE HOME 6 PERSONS – Mobile Home

Sleeping: 3 bedrooms, sleeps 6: 1 double, 4 single beds, pillows & blankets provided

Living: living/kitchen area, heating, shower & wc

Eating: fitted kitchen with hobs, fridge

Outside: table & chairs, parasol

Pets: accepted (with supplement)

Other (AR1 and AR2): bed linen, cot and high chair for rent

Open: 5 April - 4 October		
Weekly Charge	**AR1**	**AR2**
Low Season *(from)*	€ 370	€ 440
High Season *(from)*	€ 830	€ 900

FR44190 Camping le Fief

▶ see report page 57

57 chemin du Fief, F-44250 Saint Brévin-les-Pins (Loire-Atlantique)

AR1 – COTTAGE – Mobile Home

Sleeping: 3 bedrooms, sleeps 6: 1 double, 4 single beds

Living: living/kitchen area, shower & wc

Eating: fitted kitchen with hobs, microwave, fridge

Outside: table & chairs

Pets: accepted (with supplement)

AR2 – COTTAGE – Mobile Home

Sleeping: 2 bedrooms, sleeps 6: 1 double, 2 single beds

Living: living/kitchen area, shower & wc

Eating: fitted kitchen with hobs, microwave, fridge

Outside: table & chairs

Pets: accepted (with supplement)

Other (AR1 and AR2): bed linen, cot and high chair for rent

Open: 22 March - 5 October		
Weekly Charge	**AR1**	**AR2**
Low Season *(from)*	€ 434	€ 364
High Season *(from)*	€ 1043	€ 994

FR44210 Camping de l'Océan

▶ see report page 54

F-44490 Le Croisic (Loire-Atlantique)

AR1 – COTTAGE OCÉAN – Mobile Home

Sleeping: 2 bedrooms, sleeps 4/6: 1 double, 2 single beds, sofa bed, pillows & blankets provided

Living: living/kitchen area, heating, shower & wc

Eating: fitted kitchen with hobs, fridge

Outside: table & chairs, parasol

Pets: accepted (with supplement)

AR2 – OCEAN GRAND CONFORT FAMILLE – Mobile Home

Sleeping: 3 bedrooms, sleeps 6: 1 double, 4 single beds, pillows & blankets provided

Living: living/kitchen area, shower & wc

Eating: fitted kitchen with hobs, fridge

Outside: table & chairs, parasol

Pets: accepted (with supplement)

Other (AR1 and AR2): bed linen, cot and high chair for rent

Open: 4 April - 30 September

Weekly Charge	AR1	AR2
Low Season *(from)*	€ 390	€ 435
High Season *(from)*	€ 875	€ 1150

FR44220 Camping Parc de Léveno

▶ see report page 54

Route de Sandun, F-44350 Guérande (Loire-Atlantique)

AR1 – COTTAGE 2 – Mobile Home

Sleeping: 2 bedrooms, sleeps 6: 1 double, 2 single beds, sofa bed, pillows & blankets provided

Living: living/kitchen area, heating, shower & wc

Eating: fitted kitchen with hobs, fridge

Outside: table & chairs, parasol

Pets: accepted (with supplement)

AR2 – COTTAGE 3 BEDROOMS – Mobile Home

Sleeping: 3 bedrooms, sleeps 6: 1 double, 4 single beds, pillows & blankets provided

Living: living/kitchen area, shower & wc

Eating: fitted kitchen with hobs, fridge

Outside: table & chairs, parasol

Pets: accepted (with supplement)

Other (AR1 and AR2): bed linen, cot and high chair for rent

Open: 5 April - 30 September

Weekly Charge	AR1	AR2
Low Season *(from)*	€ 306	€ 323
High Season *(from)*	€ 780	€ 810

FR56280 Airotel les Sept Saints

▶ see report page 71

BP 14, F-56410 Erdeven (Morbihan)

AR1 – GRAND CONFORT – Mobile Home

Sleeping: 2 bedrooms, sleeps 4/6: 1 double, 2 single beds, sofa bed

Living: living/kitchen area, shower & wc

Eating: fitted kitchen with hobs, fridge

Outside: table & chairs, parasol, BBQ

Pets: accepted

AR2 – CHALET – Chalet

Sleeping: 2 bedrooms, sleeps 6: 1 double, 2 single beds, sofa bed

Living: living/kitchen area, heating, TV, shower & wc

Eating: fitted kitchen with hobs, fridge

Outside: table & chairs, parasol, BBQ

Pets: accepted

Other (AR1 and AR2): bed linen, cot and high chair for rent

Open: 31 March - 23 September

Weekly Charge	AR1	AR2
Low Season *(from)*	€ 300	€ 330
High Season *(from)*	€ 770	€ 800

FR14160 Camping Bellevue

▶ see report page 79

Route des Dives, F-14640 Villers-sur-Mer (Calvados)

AR1 – SAVANAH/RIVIERA – Mobile Home

Sleeping: 2 bedrooms, sleeps 5: 1 double, 2 single beds, sofa bed, pillows & blankets provided

Living: living/kitchen area, heating, shower & wc

Eating: fitted kitchen with hobs, microwave, coffee machine, fridge

Outside: table & chairs, parasol, BBQ

Pets: accepted

AR2 – TAMARIS – Mobile Home

Sleeping: 3 bedrooms, sleeps 6: 1 double, 4 single beds, pillows & blankets provided

Living: living/kitchen area, heating, shower & wc

Eating: fitted kitchen with hobs, microwave, coffee machine, fridge

Outside: table & chairs, parasol, BBQ

Pets: accepted

Other (AR1 and AR2): cot for rent

Open: 1 April - 31 October

Weekly Charge	AR1	AR2
Low Season *(from)*	€ 320	€ 380
High Season *(from)*	€ 595	€ 705

FR27070 Camping de l'Ile des Trois Rois

▶ see report page 83

1 rue Gilles Nicolle, F-27700 Andelys (Eure)

AR1 – MOBILE HOME – Mobile Home

Sleeping: 2 bedrooms, sleeps 4: 1 double, 2 single beds

Living: living/kitchen area, heating, shower & wc

Eating: fitted kitchen with hobs, fridge

Outside: table & chairs

Pets: not accepted

Open: 13 March - 14 November

Weekly Charge	AR1
Low Season *(from)*	€ 280
High Season *(from)*	€ 480

FR50030 Castel Camping le Château de lez Eaux

▶ see report page 85

Saint Aubin des Préaux, F-50380 Saint Pair-sur-Mer (Manche)

AR1 – CHALET 2 CHAMBRES – Chalet

Sleeping: 2 bedrooms, sleeps 5: 1 double, 2 singlebeds, sofa bed, pillows & blankets provided

Living: living/kitchen area, heating, shower & separate wc

Eating: fitted kitchen with hobs, microwave, coffee machine, fridge

Outside: table & chairs, parasol, BBQ

Pets: accepted

AR2 – CHALET 3 CHAMBRES – Chalet

Sleeping: 3 bedrooms, sleeps 6: 1 double, 4 single beds, sofa bed, pillows & blankets provided

Living: living/kitchen area, heating, shower & separate wc

Eating: fitted kitchen with hobs, microwave, coffee machine, fridge

Outside: table & chairs, 2 sun loungers, parasol, BBQ

Pets: accepted

Other (AR1 and AR2): bed linen, cot and high chair for rent

Open: 27 March - 26 september

Weekly Charge	AR1	AR2
Low Season *(from)*	€ 350	€ 560
High Season *(from)*	€ 700	€ 1015

FR80060 Camping le Val de Trie

▶ see report page 101

Rue des Sources, Bouillancourt-sous-Miannay, F-80870 Moyenneville (Somme)

AR1 – MORÉVA – Mobile Home

Sleeping: 2 bedrooms, sleeps 6: 1 double, 2 single beds, sofa bed, pillows & blankets provided

Living: living/kitchen area, heating, shower & separate wc

Eating: fitted kitchen with hobs, microwave, coffee machine, fridge/freezer

Outside: table & chairs, parasol, BBQ

Pets: not accepted

AR2 – PRIVILEGE ZEN – Mobile Home

Sleeping: 3 bedrooms, sleeps 6: 1 double, 2 single beds, bunkbed, pillows & blankets provided

Living: living/kitchen area, heating, radio, shower & separate wc

Eating: fitted kitchen with hobs, microwave, dishwasher, coffee machine, fridge/freezer

Outside: table & chairs, parasol, BBQ

Pets: not accepted

Other (AR1 and AR2): bed linen, cot and high chair for rent

Open: 1 April - 15 October		
Weekly Charge	AR1	AR2
Low Season (from)	€ 266	€ 365
High Season (from)	€ 595	€ 693

FR80070 Kawan Village la Ferme des Aulnes

▶ see report page 103

1 rue du Marais, Fresne-sur-Authie, F-80120 Nampont-Saint-Martin (Somme)

AR1 – CONFORT – Mobile Home

Sleeping: 2 bedrooms, sleeps 5: 1 double, 2 single beds, sofa bed, pillows & blankets provided

Living: living/kitchen area, heating, TV, shower & separate wc

Eating: fitted kitchen with hobs, microwave, coffee machine, fridge/freezer

Outside: table & chairs, parasol, BBQ

Pets: accepted (with supplement)

AR2 – PRIVILEGE – Mobile Home

Sleeping: 3 bedrooms, sleeps 6: 1 double, 2 single beds, pillows & blankets provided

Living: living/kitchen area, heating, safe, TV, DVD, CD, shower & separate wc

Eating: fitted kitchen with hobs, microwave, coffee machine, fridge/freezer

Outside: table & chairs, parasol, BBQ

Pets: accepted (with supplement)

Other (AR1 and AR2): bed linen for rent, cot and high chair for free

Open: 22 March - 3 November		
Weekly Charge	AR1	AR2
Low Season (from)	€ 490	€ 490
High Season (from)	€ 690	€ 690

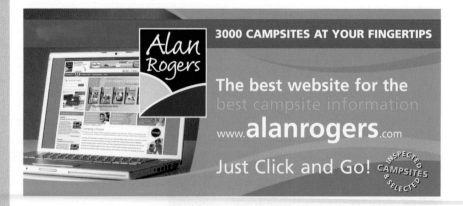

Alan Rogers

3000 CAMPSITES AT YOUR FINGERTIPS

The best website for the best campsite information

www.alanrogers.com

Just Click and Go!

INSPECTED CAMPSITES & SELECTED

`FR77020` Camping le Chêne Gris

▶ see report page 108

24 place de la Gare de Faremoutiers, F-77515 Pommeuse (Seine-et-Marne)

AR1 – BALI – Mobile Home

Sleeping: 2 bedrooms, sleeps 6: 1 double, 2 single beds, bunkbed, sofa bed, pillows & blankets provided

Living: living/kitchen area, heating, air conditioning, safe, shower & separate wc

Eating: fitted kitchen with hobs, microwave, coffee machine, fridge/freezer

Outside: table & chairs, parasol

Pets: not accepted

AR2 – TAHITI – Mobile Home

Sleeping: 2 bedrooms, sleeps 5: 1 double, 2 single beds, bunkbed, pillows & blankets provided

Living: living/kitchen area, heating, air conditioning, safe, 2 showers & 2 wcs

Eating: fitted kitchen with hobs, microwave, coffee machine, fridge/freezer

Outside: table & chairs, 2 sun loungers

Pets: not accepted

Other (AR1 and AR2): bed linen, cot and high chair for rent

Open: 25 April - 11 September		
Weekly Charge	AR1	AR2
Low Season (from)	€ 413	€ 441
High Season (from)	€ 763	€ 798

`FR77060` Le Parc de la Colline

▶ see report page 110

Route de Lagny, F-77200 Torcy (Seine-et-Marne)

AR1 – O'HARA – Mobile Home

Sleeping: 2 bedrooms, sleeps 6: 1 double, 2 single beds, sofa bed, pillows & blankets provided

Living: living/kitchen area, heating, shower & wc

Eating: fitted kitchen with hobs, fridge

Outside: table & chairs

Pets: accepted (with supplement)

AR2 – NEVA – Chalet

Sleeping: 2 bedrooms, sleeps 4: 1 double, 2 bunkbeds, pillows & blankets provided

Living: living/kitchen area, heating, shower & wc

Eating: fitted kitchen with hobs, fridge

Outside: table & chairs

Pets: accepted (with supplement)

Other (AR1 and AR2): cot and high chair for rent

Open: All year		
Weekly Charge	AR1	AR2
Low Season	€ 820	€ 730
High Season	€ 820	€ 730

`FR52030` Kawan Village Lac de la Liez

▶ see report page 120

Peigney, F-52200 Langres (Haute-Marne)

AR1 – COUNTRY LODGE – Chalet

Sleeping: 2 bedrooms, sleeps 6: 1 double, 2 single beds, sofa bed, bunkbed, pillows & blankets provided

Living: living/kitchen area, heating, shower & separate wc

Eating: fitted kitchen with hobs, microwave, coffee machine, fridge/freezer

Outside: table & chairs, 2 sun loungers, parasol

Pets: accepted (with supplement)

AR2 – ZEN – Mobile Home

Sleeping: 3 bedrooms, sleeps 6: 1 double, 4 single beds, pillows & blankets provided

Living: living/kitchen area, heating, radio, shower & separate wc

Eating: fitted kitchen with hobs, microwave, coffee machine, fridge/freezer

Outside: table & chairs, 2 sun loungers, parasol

Pets: accepted (with supplement)

Other (AR1 and AR2): bed linen, cot and high chair for rent

Open: 1 April - 15 October		
Weekly Charge	AR1	AR2
Low Season (from)	€ 350	€ 273
High Season (from)	€ 770	€ 630

FR17010 Camping Bois Soleil

▶ see report page 134

2 avenue de Suzac, F-17110 Saint-Georges-de-Didonne (Charente-Maritime)

AR1 – O'HARA COTTAGE CHARME – Mobile Home	AR2 – BURSTNER COTTAGE CONFORT – Mobile Home
Sleeping: 2 bedrooms, sleeps 4: 1 double, 2 single beds, pillows & blankets provided	**Sleeping:** 2 bedrooms, sleeps 5: 1 double, 3 single beds, pillows & blankets provided
Living: living/kitchen area, heating, shower & wc	**Living:** living/kitchen area, heating, shower & wc
Eating: fitted kitchen with hobs, microwave, fridge	**Eating:** fitted kitchen with hobs, microwave, fridge
Outside: table & chairs, parasol	**Outside:** table & chairs, parasol
Pets: not accepted	**Pets:** not accepted

Open: 3 April - 11 October

Weekly Charge	AR1	AR2
Low Season *(from)*	€ 400	€ 240
High Season *(from)*	€ 1000	€ 740

FR88040 Kawan Village Lac de Bouzey

▶ see report page 128

19 rue du Lac, F-88390 Sanchey (Vogezen)

AR1 – MOBILE HOME FLORES – Mobile Home	AR2 – ZEN – Mobile Home
Sleeping: 2 bedrooms, sleeps 4/6: 1 double, 2 single beds, sofa bed	**Sleeping:** 3 bedrooms, sleeps 6: 1 double, 4 single beds
Living: living/kitchen area, shower & wc	**Living:** living/kitchen area, shower & wc
Eating: fitted kitchen with hobs, microwave, fridge/freezer	**Eating:** fitted kitchen with hobs, microwave, fridge/freezer
Outside: table & chairs, 2 sun loungers, parasol, BBQ	**Outside:** table & chairs, 2 sun loungers, parasol, BBQ
Pets: accepted (on request)	**Pets:** accepted (on request)

Other (AR1 and AR2): cot for rent

Open: All year

Weekly Charge	AR1	AR2
Low Season *(from)*	€ 490	€ 560
High Season *(from)*	€ 770	€ 840

FR88130 Kawan Village Vanne de Pierre

▶ see report page 131

5 rue du camping, F-88100 Saint-Dié-des-Vosges (Vogezen)

AR1 – COUNTRY LODGE – Chalet	AR2 – ZEN – Mobile Home
Sleeping: 2 bedrooms, sleeps 4/6: 1 double, 2 single beds, sofa bed	**Sleeping:** 3 bedrooms, sleeps 6: 1 double, 4 single beds
Living: living/kitchen area, shower & separate wc	**Living:** living/kitchen area, heating, shower & separate wc
Eating: fitted kitchen with hobs, microwave, fridge	**Eating:** fitted kitchen with hobs, microwave, fridge
Outside: table & chairs, 2 sun loungers, parasol	**Outside:** table & chairs, 2 sun loungers, parasol
Pets: accepted (on request)	**Pets:** accepted (on request)

Open: All year

Weekly Charge	AR1	AR2
Low Season *(from)*	€ 560	€ 460
High Season *(from)*	€ 840	€ 770

Bois Soleil

Camping ★★★★
Charente-Maritime

Surrounded by pine trees and a sandy beach on the Atlantic Coast, with one direct access to the beach, Bois Soleil proposes to you many attractions like tennis, tabletennis, children playgrounds and entertainment. Shops, take-away and snack-bar with big TV screen.

Camping Qualité

Spring and Summer

2, avenue de Suzac - 17110 ST GEORGES DE DIDONNE
Tel: 0033 546 05 05 94 - Fax: 0033 546 06 27 43
www.bois-soleil.com / e-mail: camping.bois.soleil@wanadoo.fr

FR17070 Camping les Gros Joncs

see report page 138

850 route de Ponthezieres, F-17190 Saint Georges-d'Oléron (Charente-Maritime)

AR1 – O'HARA M36 – Bungalow

Sleeping: 2 bedrooms, sleeps 6: 1 double, 2 single beds, sofa bed

Living: living/kitchen area, TV, shower & separate wc

Eating: fitted kitchen with hobs, microwave, fridge/freezer

Outside: table & chairs

Pets: accepted

AR2 – PARADIS – Chalet

Sleeping: 3 bedrooms, sleeps 6/8: 1 double, 5 single beds

Living: living/kitchen area, TV, shower & separate wc

Eating: fitted kitchen with hobs, microwave, fridge/freezer

Outside: table & chairs

Pets: accepted

Other (AR1 and AR2): bed linen for rent

Open: All year

Weekly Charge	AR1	AR2
Low Season *(from)*	€ 435	€ 554
High Season *(from)*	€ 961	€ 1295

FR17280 Camping la Grainetière

see report page 144

Route de Saint-Martin, F-17630 La Flotte-en-Ré (Charente-Maritime)

AR1 – CONFORT – Chalet

Sleeping: 2 bedrooms, sleeps 4/5: 1 double, 2 single beds, sofa bed, pillows provided

Living: living/kitchen area, shower & separate wc

Eating: fitted kitchen with hobs, microwave, coffee machine, fridge

Outside: table & chairs, parasol

Pets: accepted (with supplement)

AR2 – LUXE – Mobile Home

Sleeping: 2 bedrooms, sleeps 4/5: 1 double, 2 single beds, sofa bed, pillows & blankets provided

Living: living/kitchen area, shower & separate wc

Eating: fitted kitchen with hobs, microwave, coffee machine, fridge

Outside: table & chairs, parasol

Pets: accepted (with supplement)

Other (AR1 and AR2): high chair for rent

Open: 4 april - 30 September

Weekly Charge	AR1	AR2
Low Season *(from)*	€ 220	€ 255
High Season *(from)*	€ 740	€ 790

FR85110 Camping l'Océan

see report page 150

Rue des Gabelous, F-85470 Brem-sur-Mer (Vendée)

AR1 – BIKINI – Mobile Home

Sleeping: 2 bedrooms, sleeps 4: 1 double, 2 single beds, pillows & blankets provided

Living: living/kitchen area, heating, shower & separate wc

Eating: fitted kitchen with hobs, microwave, fridge

Outside: table & chairs

Pets: accepted (with supplement)

AR2 – BERMUDES – Mobile Home

Sleeping: 3 bedrooms, sleeps 6: 1 double, 4 single beds, pillows & blankets provided

Living: living/kitchen area, heating, shower & separate wc

Eating: fitted kitchen with hobs, microwave, coffee machine, fridge

Outside: table & chairs

Pets: accepted (with supplement)

Other (AR1 and AR2): bed linen, cot and high chair for rent

Open: 1 April - 15 October

Weekly Charge	AR1	AR2
Low Season *(from)*	€ 390	€ 460
High Season *(from)*	€ 570	€ 630

FR85480 Camping Caravaning le Chaponnet

see report page 158

Rue du Chaponnet (N16), F-85470 Brem-sur-Mer (Vendée)

AR1 – CLASSIC – Mobile Home	AR2 – CHALET RESIDENTIEL – Chalet
Sleeping: 2 bedrooms, sleeps 6: 1 double, 2 single beds, sofa bed, pillows & blankets provided	**Sleeping:** 2 bedrooms, sleeps 7: 1 double, 1 single bed, bunkbed, sofa bed, pillows & blankets provided
Living: living/kitchen area, heating, shower & separate wc	**Living:** living/kitchen area, shower & separate wc
Eating: fitted kitchen with hobs, fridge	**Eating:** fitted kitchen with hobs, fridge
Outside: table & chairs, 2 sun loungers, parasol	**Outside:** table & chairs, 2 sun loungers, parasol
Pets: accepted (with supplement)	**Pets:** accepted (with supplement)

Open: April - September

Weekly Charge	AR1	AR2
Low Season (from)	€ 250	€ 275
High Season (from)	€ 740	€ 750

CAMPING LE CHAPONNET★★★★

Camping le Chaponnet ★★★★ • Rue du Chaponnet • F-85470 Brem sur Mer • France
T: [33] 2 51 90 55 56 • F: [33] 2 51 90 91 67 • campingchaponnet@wanadoo.fr
www.le-chaponnet.com

FR85150 Camping la Yole

see report page 152

Chemin des Bosses, Orouet, F-85160 Saint Jean-de-Monts (Vendée)

AR1 – LOUISIANE FLORÈS – Mobile Home	AR2 – LOUISIANE FLORÈS 2 – Mobile Home
Sleeping: 3 bedrooms, sleeps 6: 1 double, 4 single beds, pillows & blankets provided	**Sleeping:** 2 bedrooms, sleeps 6: 1 double, 2 single beds, sofa bed, pillows & blankets provided
Living: living/kitchen area, heating, shower & wc	**Living:** living/kitchen area, heating, shower & wc
Eating: fitted kitchen with hobs, microwave, fridge/freezer	**Eating:** fitted kitchen with hobs, microwave, fridge/freezer
Outside: table & chairs, 2 sun loungers, parasol	**Outside:** table & chairs, 2 sun loungers, parasol
Pets: not accepted	**Pets:** not accepted

Other (AR1 and AR2): bed linen, cot and high chair for rent

Open: 5 April - 26 September

Weekly Charge	AR1	AR2
Low Season (from)	€ 430	€ 395
High Season (from)	€ 810	€ 780

FR85210 Camping les Ecureuils

▶ see report page 153

Route des Goffineaux, F-85520 Jard-sur-Mer (Vendée)

AR1 – MOBILE HOME 4/6 PERSONS – Mobile Home

Sleeping: 2 bedrooms, sleeps 6: 1 double, 2 single beds, sofa bed, pillows & blankets provided

Living: living/kitchen area, heating, shower & separate wc

Eating: fitted kitchen with hobs, microwave, coffee machine, fridge

Outside: table & chairs, 2 sun loungers, parasol

Pets: not accepted

AR2 – MOBILE HOME 6 PERSONS – Mobile Home

Sleeping: 3 bedrooms, sleeps 6: 1 double, 4 single beds, pillows & blankets provided

Living: living/kitchen area, heating, shower & separate wc

Eating: fitted kitchen with hobs, microwave, coffee machine, fridge

Outside: table & chairs, 2 sun loungers, parasol

Pets: not accepted

Open: 4 April - 26 September

Weekly Charge	AR1	AR2
Low Season (from)	€ 460	€ 490
High Season (from)	€ 750	€ 800

FR85710 Camping le Bel Air

▶ see report page 150

6 chemin de Bel Air, F-85180 Château d'Olonne (Vendée)

AR1 – LOISIRS – Mobile Home

Sleeping: 2 bedrooms, sleeps 5: 1 double, 2 single beds, sofa bed, pillows & blankets provided

Living: living/kitchen area, heating, shower & separate wc

Eating: fitted kitchen with hobs, microwave, coffee machine, fridge

Outside: table & chairs

Pets: accepted (with supplement)

AR2 – PRESTIGE – Mobile Home

Sleeping: 3 bedrooms, sleeps 6/8: 1 double, 4 single beds, sofa bed, pillows & blankets provided

Living: living/kitchen area, heating, airco, shower & separate wc

Eating: fitted kitchen with hobs, microwave, oven, dish washer, coffee machine, fridge/freezer

Outside: table & chairs, 2 sun loungers

Pets: accepted (with supplement)

Other (AR1 and AR2): bed linen, cot and high chair for rent

Open: 15 March - 15 November

Weekly Charge	AR1	AR2
Low Season (from)	€ 240	€ 410
High Season (from)	€ 610	€ 980

FR37060 Kawan Village l'Arada Parc

▶ see report page 174

Rue de la Baratière, F-37360 Sonzay (Indre-et-Loire)

AR1 – SAMIBOIS – Chalet

Sleeping: 3 bedrooms, sleeps 6: 2 doubles, 1 bunkbed, pillows & blankets provided

Living: living/kitchen area, heating, shower & separate wc

Eating: fitted kitchen with hobs, microwave, coffee machine, fridge/freezer

Outside: table & chairs, BBQ

Pets: accepted (with supplement)

AR2 – O'HARA – Mobile Home

Sleeping: 2 bedrooms, sleeps 5: 1 double, 2 single beds, pillows & blankets provided

Living: living/kitchen area, heating, shower & separate wc

Eating: fitted kitchen with hobs, microwave, coffee machine, fridge

Outside: table & chairs, BBQ

Pets: accepted (with supplement)

Open: 28 March - 30 October

Weekly Charge	AR1	AR2
Low Season (from)	€ 345	€ 295
High Season (from)	€ 645	€ 595

FR41020 Castel Camping Château de la Grenouillère
▶ see report page 177

RN 152, F-41500 Suèvres (Loir-et-Cher)

AR1 – MOBILE HOME CONFORT – Mobile Home

Sleeping: 3 bedrooms, sleeps 6: 1 double, 4 single beds, sofa bed, pillows & blankets provided

Living: living/kitchen area, heating, shower & separate wc

Eating: fitted kitchen with hobs, fridge

Outside: table & chairs, parasol, BBQ

Pets: not accepted

AR2 – GITOTEL – Chalet

Sleeping: 2 bedrooms, sleeps 6: 2 doubles, bunkbed, pillows & blankets provided

Living: living/kitchen area, heating, shower & separate wc

Eating: fitted kitchen with hobs, fridge

Outside: table & chairs, parasol, BBQ

Pets: not accepted

Open: 25 April - 12 September

Weekly Charge	AR1	AR2
Low Season *(from)*	€ 385	€ 420
High Season *(from)*	€ 875	€ 910

FR41070 Kawan Village la Grande Tortue
▶ see report page 179

3 route de Pontlevoy, F-41120 Candé-sur-Beuvron (Loir-et-Cher)

AR1 – IRM SUPER MERCURE – Mobile Home

Sleeping: 2 bedrooms, sleeps 5: 1 double, 2 single beds, bunkbed, pillows & blankets provided

Living: living/kitchen area, heating, safe, shower & separate wc

Eating: fitted kitchen with hobs, microwave, coffee machine, fridge

Outside: table & chairs, 2 sun loungers

Pets: accepted (with supplement)

AR2 – LOUISIANE – Mobile Home

Sleeping: 3 bedrooms, sleeps 6: 1 double, 4 single beds, pillows & blankets provided

Living: living/kitchen area, heating, safe, shower & separate wc

Eating: fitted kitchen with hobs, microwave, coffee machine, fridge

Outside: table & chairs, 2 sun loungers

Pets: accepted (with supplement)

Other (AR1 and AR2): bed linen, cot, high chair and baby bath for rent

Open: 5 April - 20 September

Weekly Charge	AR1	AR2
Low Season *(from)*	€ 300	€ 420
High Season *(from)*	€ 665	€ 728

FR49040 Camping de l'Etang
▶ see report page 184

Route de Saint-Mathurin, F-49320 Brissac (Maine-et-Loire)

AR1 – WILLERBY – Mobile Home

Sleeping: 2 bedrooms, sleeps 6: 1 double, 2 single beds, bunkbed, sofa bed, pillows & blankets provided

Living: living/kitchen area, heating, shower & separate wc

Eating: fitted kitchen with hobs, fridge

Outside: table & chairs, sun lounger, parasol, BBQ

Pets: accepted (with supplement)

AR2 – CONCORDE – Mobile Home

Sleeping: 2 bedrooms, sleeps 5: 1 double, 2 single beds, bunkbed, sofa bed, pillows & blankets provided

Living: living/kitchen area, heating, shower & separate wc

Eating: fitted kitchen with hobs, fridge/freezer

Outside: table & chairs, sun loungers, parasol, BBQ

Pets: accepted (with supplement)

Open: 15 May - 15 September

Weekly Charge	AR1	AR2
Low Season *(from)*	€ 455	€ 385
High Season *(from)*	€ 685	€ 585

Mobile homes & chalets

FR71070 Kawan Village Château de l'Epervière

▶ see report page 202

F-71240 Gigny-sur-Saône (Saône-et-Loire)

AR1 – LOUISIANE ZEN – Mobile Home

Sleeping: 3 bedrooms, sleeps 6: 1 double, 2 single beds, bunkbed, pillows & blankets provided

Living: living/kitchen area, heating, TV, radio, shower & separate wc

Eating: fitted kitchen with hobs, microwave, coffee machine, fridge/freezer

Outside: table & chairs, 2 sun loungers, parasol

Pets: not accepted

AR2 – APARTMENT – Apartment

Sleeping: 2 bedrooms, sleeps 5: 1 double, 1 single, 1 bunkbed, pillows & blankets provided

Living: living/kitchen area, heating, TV, shower & separate wc

Eating: fitted kitchen with hobs, oven, dish washer, coffee machine, fridge/freezer

Outside: table & chairs

Pets: not accepted

Other (AR1 and AR2): bed linen, cot and high chair for rent

Open: 1 April - 30 September

Weekly Charge	AR1	AR2
Low Season *(from)*	€ 399	€ 429
High Season *(from)*	€ 829	€ 849

FR25080 Camping les Fuvettes

▶ see report page 209

F-25160 Malbuisson (Doubs)

AR1 – MOBILE HOME 800 – Mobile Home

Sleeping: 2 bedrooms, sleeps 4/5: 1 double, 2 single beds, sofa bed, pillows & blankets provided

Living: living/kitchen area, heating, shower & separate wc

Eating: fitted kitchen with hobs, microwave, coffee machine, fridge/freezer

Outside: table & chairs, parasol

Pets: accepted (with supplement)

AR2 – CHALET 4/5 PERSONS – Chalet

Sleeping: 2 bedrooms, sleeps 5: 1 double, 3 single beds, pillows & blankets provided

Living: living/kitchen area, heating, shower & wc

Eating: fitted kitchen with hobs, microwave, coffee machine, fridge

Outside: table & chairs

Pets: accepted (with supplement)

Open: 1 April - 1 October

Weekly Charge	AR1	AR2
Low Season *(from)*	€ 280	€ 300
High Season *(from)*	€ 590	€ 620

FR73030 Camping les Lanchettes

▶ see report page 224

F-73210 Peisey-Nancroix (Savoie)

AR1 – CHALET 1 – Chalet

Sleeping: 2 bedrooms, sleeps 4/5: 1 double, 2 single beds

Living: living/kitchen area, shower & wc

Eating: fitted kitchen with hobs, oven, dishwasher, fridge

Outside: table & chairs, parasol

Pets: not accepted

AR2 – CHARLAY BALLARIO – Chalet

Sleeping: 2 bedrooms, sleeps 4/6: 1 double, 4 single beds

Living: living/kitchen area, shower & separate wc

Eating: fitted kitchen with hobs, oven, fridge

Outside: table & chairs, parasol

Pets: not accepted

Open: 15 Dec. - 30 Sept.

Weekly Charge	AR1	AR2
Low Season *(from)*	€ 320	€ 320
High Season *(from)*	€ 600	€ 600

FR33110 Airotel Camping de la Côte d'Argent

▶ see report page 240

F-33990 Hourtin-Plage (Gironde)

AR1 – SAVANNAH – Mobile Home

Sleeping: 2 bedrooms, sleeps 4/6: 1 double, 2 single beds, sofa bed, pillows & blankets provided

Living: living/kitchen area, shower & wc

Eating: fitted kitchen with hobs, microwave, coffee machine, fridge/freezer

Outside: picnic table & benches, parasol

Pets: not accepted

AR2 – SUPER FAMILY – Mobile Home

Sleeping: 3 bedrooms, sleeps 6: 1 double, 4 single beds, pillows & blankets provided

Living: living/kitchen area shower & wc

Eating: fitted kitchen with hobs, microwave, coffee machine, fridge/freezer

Outside: picnic table & benches, parasol

Pets: not accepted

Open: 17 May - 14 September

Weekly Charge	AR1	AR2
Low Season *(from)*	€ 420	€ 504
High Season *(from)*	€ 945	€ 1015

FR33130 Yelloh! Village les Grands Pins

▶ see report page 243

Plage Nord, F-33680 Lacanau-Océan (Gironde)

AR1 – PREMIER – Mobile Home

Sleeping: 2 bedrooms, sleeps 4: 1 double, 2 single beds, pillows & blankets provided

Living: living/kitchen area, heating, shower & separate wc

Eating: fitted kitchen with hobs, microwave, coffee machine, fridge

Outside: table & chairs, 2 sun loungers

Pets: accepted

AR2 – SUNSET – Mobile Home

Sleeping: 3 bedrooms, sleeps 6: 1 double, 4 single beds, pillows & blankets provided

Living: living/kitchen area, heating, shower & separate wc

Eating: fitted kitchen with hobs, microwave, dishwasher, fridge/freezer

Outside: table & chairs, 2 sun loungers, parasol

Pets: accepted

Other (AR1 and AR2): bed linen, cot and high chair for rent

Open: 11 April - 26 September

Weekly Charge	AR1	AR2
Low Season *(from)*	€ 266	€ 448
High Season *(from)*	€ 903	€ 1218

FR40100 Camping du Domaine de la Rive

▶ see report page 254

Route de Bordeaux, F-40600 Biscarrosse (Landes)

AR1 – SAVANNAH – Mobile Home

Sleeping: 2 bedrooms, sleeps 6: 1 double, 2 single beds, sofa bed, pillows & blankets provided

Living: living/kitchen area, heating, shower & wc

Eating: fitted kitchen with hobs, microwave, fridge/freezer

Outside: table & chairs, 2 sun loungers, parasol

Pets: not accepted

AR2 – COTTAGE 3 – Mobile Home

Sleeping: 3 bedrooms, sleeps 6: 1 double, 4 single beds, pillows & blankets provided

Living: living/kitchen area, shower & wc

Eating: fitted kitchen with hobs, microwave, fridge/freezer

Outside: table & chairs, parasol

Pets: not accepted

Other (AR1 and AR2): bed linen for rent, cot and high chair for free

Open: 30 March - 30 September

Weekly Charge	AR1	AR2
Low Season *(from)*	€ 357	€ 392
High Season *(from)*	€ 1008	€ 1036

FR40140 Camping Caravaning Lou P'tit Poun

see report page 254

110 avenue du Quartier Neuf, F-40390 Saint Martin-de-Seignanx (Landes)

AR1 – FABRE REVE – Chalet

Sleeping: 2 bedrooms, sleeps 5: 1 double, 3 single beds

Living: living/kitchen area, shower & wc

Eating: fitted kitchen with hobs, fridge

Outside: table & chairs, 2 sun loungers

Pets: not accepted

AR2 – IRM MERCURE – Mobile Home

Sleeping: 2 bedrooms, sleeps 5: 1 double, 2 single beds, sofa bed

Living: living/kitchen area, shower & wc

Eating: fitted kitchen with hobs, fridge

Outside: table & chairs, 2 sun loungers

Pets: not accepted

Open: 1 June - 15 September

Weekly Charge	AR1	AR2
Low Season *(from)*	€ 285	€ 275
High Season *(from)*	€ 695	€ 675

FR40180 Camping le Vieux Port

see report page 257

Plage Sud, F-40660 Messanges (Landes)

AR1 – MOBILE HOME – Mobile Home

Sleeping: 2 bedrooms, sleeps 4: 1 double, 2 single beds, pillows & blankets provided

Living: living/kitchen area, heating, shower & wc

Eating: fitted kitchen with hobs, oven, fridge

Outside: table & chairs, parasol

Pets: not accepted

AR2 – CHALET – Chalet

Sleeping: 2 bedrooms, sleeps 4/5: 1 double, 3 single beds, pillows & blankets provided

Living: living/kitchen area, heating, shower & wc

Eating: fitted kitchen with hobs, oven, fridge/freezer

Outside: table & chairs, 2 sun loungers, parasol

Pets: not accepted

Other (AR1 and AR2): bed linen, cot and high chair for rent

Open: 1 April - 30 September

Weekly Charge	AR1	AR2
Low Season *(from)*	€ 385	€ 595
High Season *(from)*	€ 910	€ 1190

FR40190 Le Saint-Martin Airotel Camping

see report page 258

Avenue de l'Océan, F-40660 Moliets-Plage (Landes)

AR1 – DUO – Chalet

Sleeping: bedroom in living area, sleeps 3: 2 single beds, 1 cot, pillows & blankets provided

Living: living/kitchen area, heating, safe, shower & separate wc

Eating: fitted kitchen with hobs, microwave, coffee machine, fridge/freezer

Outside: table & chairs

Pets: accepted (with supplement)

AR2 – ZEPHYR – Chalet

Sleeping: 2 bedrooms, sleeps 5: 1 double, 2 single beds, sofa bed, pillows & blankets provided

Living: living/kitchen area, heating, safe, shower & separate wc

Eating: fitted kitchen with hobs, microwave, coffee machine, fridge/freezer

Outside: table & chairs, 2 sun loungers

Pets: accepted (with supplement)

Open: 4 April - 11 November

Weekly Charge	AR1	AR2
Low Season *(from)*	€ 185	€ 530
High Season *(from)*	€ 585	€ 1300

FR40250 Camping les Grands Pins

▶ see report page 260

1039 avenue de Losa, F-40460 Sanguinet (Landes)

AR1 – O'HARA OCÉANE – Mobile Home

Sleeping: 3 bedrooms, sleeps 6: 1 double, 4 single beds, pillows & blankets provided

Living: living/kitchen area, heating, shower & separate wc

Eating: fitted kitchen with hobs, microwave, coffee machine, fridge/freezer

Outside: table & chairs, 2 sun loungers, parasol

Pets: not accepted

AR2 – GITOTEL FABRE – Chalet

Sleeping: 2 bedrooms, sleeps 4: 1 double, 2 single beds, pillows & blankets provided

Living: living/kitchen area, heating, shower & wc

Eating: fitted kitchen with hobs, microwave, fridge

Outside: table & chairs, parasol

Pets: not accepted

Open: 1 April - 27 September		
Weekly Charge	**AR1**	**AR2**
Low Season *(from)*	€ 413	€ 357
High Season *(from)*	€ 938	€ 885

FR64110 Sunêlia Col d'Ibardin

▶ see report page 267

F-64122 Urrugne (Pyrénées-Atlantiques)

AR1 – O'HARA 4 – Mobile Home

Sleeping: 2 bedrooms, sleeps 4: 1 double, 2 single beds, pillows & blankets provided

Living: living/kitchen area, heating, shower & separate wc

Eating: fitted kitchen with hobs, microwave, coffee machine, fridge/freezer

Outside: table & chairs, parasol

Pets: not accepted

AR2 – O'HARA 6 – Mobile Home

Sleeping: 3 bedrooms, sleeps 6: 1 double, 4 single beds, pillows & blankets provided

Living: living/kitchen area, heating, shower & separate wc

Eating: fitted kitchen with hobs, microwave, coffee machine, fridge/freezer

Outside: table & chairs

Pets: not accepted

Other (AR1 and AR2): bed linen, cot and high chair for rent

Open: 1 April - 2 November		
Weekly Charge	**AR1**	**AR2**
Low Season *(from)*	€ 280	€ 385
High Season *(from)*	€ 623	€ 735

FR24020 Camping Caravaning les Granges

▶ see report page 283

F-24250 Groléjac-en-Périgord (Dordogne)

AR1 – RÊVE CONFORT – Mobile Home

Sleeping: 2 bedrooms, sleeps 4/5: 1 double, 2 single beds, sofa bed, pillows & blankets provided

Living: living/kitchen area, heating, shower & separate wc

Eating: fitted kitchen with hobs, microwave, coffee machine, fridge

Outside: table & chairs, 2 sun loungers, BBQ

Pets: accepted (with supplement)

AR2 – O'HARA – Mobile Home

Sleeping: 3 bedrooms, sleeps: 6, 1 double, 4 single beds, pillows & blankets provided

Living: living/kitchen area, heating, shower & separate wc

Eating: fitted kitchen with hobs, microwave, coffee machine, fridge

Outside: table & chairs, sun loungers, BBQ

Pets: accepted (with supplement)

Other (AR1 and AR2): bed linen, cot and high chair for rent

Open: 25 April - 13 September		
Weekly Charge	**AR1**	**AR2**
Low Season *(from)*	€ 313	€ 337
High Season *(from)*	€ 767	€ 861

FR24090 Domaine de Soleil Plage

▶ see report page 285

Caudon par Montfort, Vitrac, F-24200 Sarlat-la-Canéda (Dordogne)

AR1 – RÊVE – Chalet

Sleeping: 2 bedrooms, sleeps 5/7: 1 double, 2 single beds, bunkbed, pillows & blankets provided

Living: living/kitchen area, heating, TV, shower & wc

Eating: fitted kitchen with hobs, microwave, coffee machine, fridge

Outside: table & chairs, 2 sun loungers, parasol, BBQ

Pets: accepted (with supplement)

AR2 – SUPER MERCURE – Mobile Home

Sleeping: 2 bedrooms, sleeps 4/6: 1 double, 2 single beds, sofa bed, pillows & blankets provided

Living: living/kitchen area, heating, shower & separate wc

Eating: fitted kitchen with hobs, coffee machine, fridge

Outside: table & chairs, 2 sun loungers, parasol, BBQ

Pets: accepted (with supplement)

Other (AR1 and AR2): bed linen, cot and high chair for rent

Open: 3 April - 11 November

Weekly Charge	AR1	AR2
Low Season (from)	€ 310	€ 280
High Season (from)	€ 850	€ 780

FR24130 Camping les Grottes de Roffy

▶ see report page 289

Sainte Nathalène, F-24200 Sarlat-la-Canéda (Dordogne)

AR1 – O'HARA – Mobile Home

Sleeping: 2 bedrooms, sleeps 6/7: 1 double, 2 single beds, bunkbed, sofa bed, pillows & blankets provided

Living: living/kitchen area, heating, shower & separate wc

Eating: fitted kitchen with hobs, microwave, coffee machine, fridge/freezer

Outside: table & chairs, 2 sun loungers, parasol, BBQ

Pets: accepted

AR2 – O'HARA 3 BEDROOMS – Mobile Home

Sleeping: 3 bedrooms, sleeps 6/7: 1 double, 4 single beds, sofa bed, pillows & blankets provided

Living: living/kitchen area, shower & separate wc

Eating: fitted kitchen with hobs, microwave, coffee machine, fridge/freezer

Outside: table & chairs, 2 sun loungers, parasol, BBQ

Pets: accepted

Other (AR1 and AR2): bed linen and cot for rent

Open: 18 April - 19 September

Weekly Charge	AR1	AR2
Low Season (from)	€ 270	€ 280
High Season (from)	€ 812	€ 884

FR24160 Camping le Grand Dague

▶ see report page 292

Route du Grand Dague, Atur, F-24750 Périgueux (Dordogne)

AR1 – BALI – Mobile Home

Sleeping: 2 bedrooms, sleeps 6: 1 double, 2 single beds, bunkbed, sofa bed, pillows & blankets provided

Living: living/kitchen area, heating, shower & separate wc

Eating: fitted kitchen with hobs, microwave, fridge/freezer

Outside: table & chairs, 2 sun loungers, parasol

Pets: not accepted

AR2 – WAIKIKI – Mobile Home

Sleeping: 3 bedrooms, sleeps 6: 1 double, 4 single beds, sofa bed, pillows & blankets provided

Living: living/kitchen area, heating, air conditioning, shower & separate wc

Eating: fitted kitchen with hobs, microwave, fridge/freezer

Outside: table & chairs, 2 sun loungers, parasol

Pets: accepted

Open: 5 May - 28 September

Weekly Charge	AR1	AR2
Low Season (from)	€ 180	€ 234
High Season (from)	€ 336	€ 441

`FR24320` Camping les Peneyrals

▶ see report page 294

Le Poujol, F-24590 Saint Crépin-Carlucet (Dordogne)

AR1 – MERCURE – Mobile Home	**AR2 – EQUINOXE – Chalet**
Sleeping: 2 bedrooms, sleeps 4/5: 1 double, 2 single beds, sofa bed, pillows & blankets provided	**Sleeping:** 3 bedrooms, sleeps 6/7: 1 double, 4 single beds, sofa bed, pillows & blankets provided
Living: living/kitchen area, heating, shower & separate wc	**Living:** living/kitchen area, heating, TV, shower & separate wc
Eating: fitted kitchen with hobs, microwave, coffee machine, fridge	**Eating:** fitted kitchen with hobs, microwave, coffee machine, fridge
Outside: table & chairs, 2 sun loungers, parasol, BBQ	**Outside:** table & chairs, 2 sun loungers, parasol, BBQ
Pets: accepted (with supplement)	**Pets:** accepted (with supplement)

Other (AR1 and AR2): bed linen, cot and high chair for rent

Open: 14 May - 15 September

Weekly Charge	AR1	AR2
Low Season *(from)*	€ 300	€ 490
High Season *(from)*	€ 830	€ 830

`FR47010` Kawan Village Moulin du Périé

▶ see report page 311

F-47500 Sauveterre-la-Lemance (Lot-et-Garonne)

AR1 – IRM SUPER MERCURE – Mobile Home	**AR2 – FABRE RÊVE – Chalet**
Sleeping: 2 bedrooms, sleeps 6: 2 doubles, 2 single beds, pillows & blankets provided	**Sleeping:** 2 bedrooms, sleeps 7: 2 doubles, 2 single beds, bunkbed, pillows & blankets provided
Living: living/kitchen area, heating, shower & wc	**Living:** living/kitchen area, heating, shower & wc
Eating: fitted kitchen with hobs, fridge	**Eating:** fitted kitchen with hobs, fridge
Outside: table & chairs, parasol	**Outside:** table & chairs, parasol
Pets: not accepted	**Pets:** not accepted

Other (AR1 and AR2): bed linen, cot and high chair for rent

Open: 15 May - 18 September

Weekly Charge	AR1	AR2
Low Season *(from)*	€ 336	€ 392
High Season *(from)*	€ 658	€ 742

`FR23010` Castel Camping le Château de Poinsouze

▶ see report page 323

Route de la Châtre, B.P. 12, F-23600 Boussac-Bourg (Creuse)

AR1 – IRM SUPER MERCURE 29 m² – Mobile Home	**AR2 – COUNTRY LODGE – Chalet**
Sleeping: 2 bedrooms, sleeps 4/6: 1 double, 2 single beds, sofa bed	**Sleeping:** 2 bedrooms, sleeps 4/5: 1 double, 2 single beds, sofa bed
Living: living/kitchen area, shower & separate wc	**Living:** living/kitchen area, shower & separate wc
Eating: fitted kitchen with hobs, fridge	**Eating:** fitted kitchen with hobs, microwave, coffee machine, fridge
Outside: table & chairs, parasol, BBQ	**Outside:** table & chairs, 2 sun loungers, parasol, BBQ
Pets: not accepted	**Pets:** not accepted

Other (AR1 and AR2): bed linen, cot and high chair for rent

Open: 8 May - 13 September

Weekly Charge	AR1	AR2
Low Season *(from)*	€ 280	€ 330
High Season *(from)*	€ 570	€ 640

`FR07150` Camping Domaine de Gil

▶ see report page 342

Route de Vals-les-Bains, Ucel, F-07200 Aubenas (Ardèche)

AR1 – CONFORT – Mobile Home

Sleeping: 2 bedrooms, sleeps 4/5: 1 double, 2 single beds, sofa bed

Living: living/kitchen area, heating, shower & wc

Eating: fitted kitchen with hobs, coffee machine, fridge

Outside: table & chairs, parasol

Pets: not accepted

AR2 – GRAND LUXE – Mobile Home

Sleeping: 3 bedrooms, sleeps 7: 1 double, 4 single beds, sofa bed, pillows & blankets provided

Living: living/kitchen area, shower & separate wc

Eating: fitted kitchen with hobs, microwave, coffee machine, fridge

Outside: table & chairs, sun lounger, parasol

Pets: not accepted

Open: 14 April - 23 September		
Weekly Charge	AR1	AR2
Low Season (from)	€ 231	€ 315
High Season (from)	€ 630	€ 798

`FR26010` Domaine du Lac de Champos

▶ see report page 353

F-26260 Saint-Donat-sur-l'Herbasse (Drôme)

AR1 – ABEILLE MIMOSA – Chalet

Sleeping: 2 bedrooms, sleeps 6: 1 double, 3 single beds, sofa bed, pillows & blankets provided

Living: lliving/kitchen area, heating, shower & separate wc

Eating: fitted kitchen with hobs, coffee machine, fridge

Outside: table & chairs

Pets: accepted (with supplement)

AR2 – ABEILLE EDELWEISS – Chalet

Sleeping: 2 bedrooms, sleeps 6: 1 double, 4 single beds, sofa bed, pillows & blankets provided

Living: living/kitchen area, heating, shower & separate wc

Eating: fitted kitchen with hobs, coffee machine, fridge

Outside: table & chairs

Pets: accepted (with supplement)

Other (AR1 and AR2): bed linen, cot and high chair for rent

Open: Easter - 1 November		
Weekly Charge	AR1	AR2
Low Season (from)	€ 275	€ 290
High Season (from)	€ 485	€ 510

`FR26210` Camping les Bois du Chatelas

▶ see report page 355

Route de Dieulefit, F-26460 Bourdeaux (Drôme)

AR1 – GOELAND – Chalet

Sleeping: 2 bedrooms, sleeps 5/7: 1 double, 3 single beds, sofa bed, blankets provided

Living: living/kitchen area, heating, shower & separate wc

Eating: fitted kitchen with hobs, microwave, coffee machine, fridge/freezer

Outside: table & chairs

Pets: accepted

AR2 – TEXAS WATIPI – Mobile Home

Sleeping: 3 bedrooms, sleeps 7: 1 double, 4 single beds, sofa bed, blankets provided

Living: living/kitchen area, heating, shower & separate wc

Eating: fitted kitchen with hobs, microwave, coffee machine, fridge/freezer

Outside: table & chairs

Pets: accepted

Open: 12 April - 28 October		
Weekly Charge	AR1	AR2
Low Season (from)	€ 340	€ 300
High Season (from)	€ 755	€ 670

FR26290 Camping Château de Galaure

F-26330 Châteauneuf-de-Galaure (Drôme)

see report page 358

AR1 – BALI – Mobile Home

Sleeping: 2 bedrooms, sleeps 6: 1 double, 2 single beds, bunkbed, sofa bed, pillows & blankets provided

Living: living/kitchen area, heating, air conditioning, shower & separate wc

Eating: fitted kitchen with hobs, microwave, fridge/freezer

Outside: table & chairs, 2 sun loungers, parasol

Pets: not accepted

AR2 – WAIKIKI – Mobile Home

Sleeping: 3 bedrooms, sleeps 7: 1 double, 4 single beds, sofa bed, pillows & blankets provided

Living: living/kitchen area, heating, air conditioning, shower & separate wc

Eating: fitted kitchen with hobs, microwave, fridge/freezer

Outside: table & chairs, 2 sun loungers, parasol

Pets: not accepted

Other (AR1 and AR2): bed linen, cot and high chair for rent

Open: 25 April - 27 September		
Weekly Charge	**AR1**	**AR2**
Low Season *(from)*	€ 210	€ 258
High Season *(from)*	€ 446	€ 708

FR04010 Sunêlia Hippocampe

Route de Napoléon, F-04290 Volonne (Alpes-de-Haute-Provence)

see report page 362

AR1 – SUNELIA FAMILY – Mobile Home

Sleeping: 3 bedrooms, sleeps 6: 1 double, 2 single beds, pillows & blankets provided

Living: living/kitchen area, heating, shower & wc (air conditioning on request)

Eating: fitted kitchen with hobs, microwave, fridge/freezer

Outside: table & chairs, sun loungers, parasol

Pets: accepted

AR2 – SUNELIA GRAND CONFORT – Mobile Home

Sleeping: 2 bedrooms, sleeps 6: 1 double, 2 single beds, pillows & blankets provided

Living: living/kitchen area, heating, shower & wc

Eating: fitted kitchen with hobs, fridge

Outside: table & chairs, 2 sun loungers, parasol

Pets: accepted

Other (AR1 and AR2): bed linen, cot and high chair for rent

Open: 22 March - 30 September		
Weekly Charge	**AR1**	**AR2**
Low Season *(from)*	€ 336	€ 336
High Season *(from)*	€ 987	€ 938

FR04020 Castel Camping le Domaine du Verdon

Domaine du Verdon, F-04120 Castellane (Alpes-de-Haute-Provence)

see report page 363

AR1 – WATIPI – Mobile Home

Sleeping: 2 bedrooms, sleeps 4: 1 double, 2 single beds, pillows & blankets provided

Living: living/kitchen area, shower & wc

Eating: fitted kitchen with hobs, fridge

Outside: table & chairs, 2 sun loungers

Pets: accepted

AR2 – TITOM – Chalet

Sleeping: 2 bedrooms, sleeps 4: 1 double, 2 single beds, bunkbed, pillows & blankets provided

Living: living/kitchen area, shower & wc

Eating: fitted kitchen with hobs, fridge

Outside: table & chairs, 2 sun loungers

Pets: accepted

Other (AR1 and AR2): bed linen, cot and high chair for rent

Open: 15 May - 15 September		
Weekly Charge	**AR1**	**AR2**
Low Season *(from)*	€ 322	€ 364
High Season *(from)*	€ 672	€ 707

FR84020 Domaine Naturiste de Bélézy

see report page 479

F-84410 Bédoin (Vaucluse)

AR1 – NAUTILHOME – Mobile Home

Sleeping: 2 bedrooms, sleeps 5: 1 double, 2 single beds, sofa bed, pillows & blankets provided

Living: living/kitchen area, central heating, safe, shower & separate wc

Eating: fitted kitchen with hobs, microwave, coffee machine, fridge/freezer

Outside: table & chairs, 2 sun loungers, awning

Pets: not accepted

AR2 – BUNGALOW BOIS – Mobile Home

Sleeping: 2 bedrooms, sleeps 5: 1 double, 2 single beds, sofa bed, pillows & blankets provided

Living: living/kitchen area, heating, safe, shower & separate wc

Eating: fitted kitchen with hobs, microwave, dishwasher, coffee machine, fridge/freezer

Outside: table & chairs, 2 sun loungers

Pets: not accepted

Other (AR1 and AR2): bed linen, cot and high chair for rent

Open: 23 March - 2 October

Weekly Charge	AR1	AR2
Low Season (from)	€ 560	€ 539
High Season (from)	€ 938	€ 840

FR09020 Camping l'Arize

see report page 377

Lieu-dit Bourtol, F-09240 La Bastide-de-Sérou (Ariège)

AR1 – MH CONFORT 2 BEDROOMS – Mobile Home

Sleeping: 2 bedrooms, sleeps 6: 1 double, 2 single beds, sofa bed, pillows & blankets provided

Living: living/kitchen area, heating, shower & separate wc

Eating: fitted kitchen with hobs, fridge

Outside: table & chairs, parasol, BBQ

Pets: accepted (with supplement)

AR2 – WOODEN CHALET 3 BEDROOMS – Chalet

Sleeping: 3 bedrooms, sleeps 7: 1 double, 2 single beds, 2 bunkbeds, sofa bed, pillows & blankets provided

Living: living/kitchen area, heating, shower & separate wc

Eating: fitted kitchen with hobs, microwave, oven, grill, fridge

Outside: table & chairs, BBQ

Pets: accepted (with supplement)

Open: 30 January - 30 November

Weekly Charge	AR1	AR2
Low Season (from)	€ 287	€ 395
High Season (from)	€ 639	€ 754

FR32010 Kawan Village le Camp de Florence

see report page 379

Route Astaffort, F-32480 La Romieu (Gers)

AR1 – LOUISIANE ZEN – Mobile Home

Sleeping: 3 bedrooms, sleeps 6: 1 double, 2 single beds, bunkbed, pillows & blankets provided

Living: living/kitchen area, heating, shower & separate wc

Eating: fitted kitchen with hobs, microwave, fridge/freezer

Outside: table & chairs, 2 sun loungers

Pets: accepted

AR2 – IRM DELUXE – Mobile Home

Sleeping: 2 bedrooms, sleeps 6: 1 double, 2 single beds, sofa bed, pillows & blankets provided

Living: living/kitchen area, heating, shower & separate wc

Eating: fitted kitchen with hobs, microwave, fridge

Outside: table & chairs, 2 sun loungers

Pets: accepted

Open: 1 April - 11 October

Weekly Charge	AR1	AR2
Low Season (from)	€ 475	€ 430
High Season (from)	€ 850	€ 800

FR11070 Kawan Village les Mimosas

▶ see report page 393

Chaussée de Mandirac, F-11100 Narbonne (Aude)

AR1 – MOBILE HOME PLANCHA – Mobile Home

Sleeping: 2 bedrooms, sleeps 4: 1 double, 2 single beds, pillows & blankets provided

Living: living/kitchen area, shower & wc

Eating: fitted kitchen with hobs, microwave, coffee machine, fridge/freezer

Outside: table & chairs, 2 sun loungers, BBQ

Pets: not accepted

AR2 – FLORÈS – Mobile Home

Sleeping: 3 bedrooms, sleeps 6: 1 double, 4 single beds, pillows & blankets provided

Living: living/kitchen area, heating, air conditioning, shower & wc

Eating: fitted kitchen with hobs, microwave, coffee machine, fridge/freezer

Outside: table & chairs, 2 sun loungers

Pets: not accepted

Other (AR1 and AR2): bed linen, cot and high chair for rent

Open: 21 March - 1 November		
Weekly Charge	AR1	AR2
Low Season *(from)*	€ 273	€ 343
High Season *(from)*	€ 637	€ 833

FR11080 Camping la Nautique

▶ see report page 394

La Nautique, F-11100 Narbonne (Aude)

AR1 – TYPE VI – Mobile Home

Sleeping: 2 bedrooms, sleeps 6: 1 double, 2 single beds, sofa bed, pillows & blankets provided

Living: living/kitchen area, heating, radio, shower & separate wc

Eating: fitted kitchen with hobs, microwave or oven with grill, coffee machine, fridge/freezer

Outside: table & chairs, 2 sun loungers, parasol

Pets: accepted (with supplement)

AR2 – TYPE X – Mobile Home

Sleeping: 2 bedrooms, sleeps 6: 1 double, 2 single beds, sofa bed, pillows & blankets provided

Living: living/kitchen area, heating, radio, shower & separate wc

Eating: fitted kitchen with hobs, microwave or oven with grill, coffee machine, fridge/freezer

Outside: table & chairs, 2 sun loungers, parasol

Pets: accepted (with supplement)

Other (AR1 and AR2): bed linen, cot and high chair for rent

Open: 15 February - 15 November		
Weekly Charge	AR1	AR2
Low Season *(from)*	€ 250	€ 297
High Season *(from)*	€ 630	€ 805

FR34070 Yelloh! Village le Sérignan Plage

▶ see report page 408

Le Sérignan Plage, F-34410 Sérignan (Hérault)

AR1 – COTTAGE VIP – Mobile Home

Sleeping: 2 bedrooms, sleeps 4: 1 double, 2 single beds, pillows & blankets provided

Living: living/kitchen area, heating, fan, safe, shower & separate wc

Eating: fitted kitchen with hobs, microwave, coffee machine, fridge/freezer

Outside: table & chairs, 2 sun loungers, parasol

Pets: not accepted

AR2 – COTTAGE CABANE – Mobile Home

Sleeping: 3 bedrooms, sleeps 6: 1 double, 2 single beds, 2 bunkbeds, pillows & blankets provided

Living: living/kitchen area, heating, air conditioning, safe, shower & separate wc

Eating: fitted kitchen with hobs, microwave, dishwasher, coffee machine, fridge/freezer

Outside: table & chairs, 2 sun loungers, parasol

Pets: not accepted

Other (AR1 and AR2): bed linen, cot and high chair for rent

Open: 24 April - 27 September		
Weekly Charge	AR1	AR2
Low Season *(from)*	€ 203	€ 343
High Season *(from)*	€ 1134	€ 1813

`FR34110` Yelloh! Village le Club Farret

▶ see report page 407

F-34450 Vias-Plage (Hérault)

AR1 – BALI – Mobile Home

Sleeping: 3 bedrooms, sleeps 6: 1 double, 4 single beds, pillows provided

Living: living/kitchen area, heating, air conditioning, safe, shower & separate wc

Eating: fitted kitchen with hobs, microwave, coffee machine, fridge/freezer

Outside: table & chairs, 2 sun loungers, parasol

Pets: not accepted

AR2 – AFRICA – Mobile Home

Sleeping: 2 bedrooms, sleeps 4/6: 1 double, 2 single beds, sofa bed, pillows provided

Living: living/kitchen area, heating, shower & separate wc

Eating: fitted kitchen with hobs, microwave, coffee machine, fridge/freezer

Outside: table & chairs, 2 sun loungers, parasol

Pets: not accepted

Other (AR1 and AR2): bed linen, cot and high chair for rent

Open: 2 April - 26 September		
Weekly Charge	AR1	AR2
Low Season *(from)*	€ 301	€ 203
High Season *(from)*	€ 1253	€ 1043

`FR66070` Yelloh! Village le Brasilia

▶ see report page 421

B.P. 204, F-66141 Canet-en-Roussillon (Pyrénées-Orientales)

AR1 – OKAVANGO – Mobile Home

Sleeping: 2 bedrooms, sleeps 6: 1 double, 2 single beds, bunkbed, pillows & blankets provided

Living: living/kitchen area, heating, safe, shower & wc

Eating: fitted kitchen with hobs, microwave, grill, coffee machine, fridge/freezer

Outside: table & chairs, 2 sun loungers, parasol

Pets: accepted (with supplement)

AR2 – PINEDE – Bungalow

Sleeping: 2 bedrooms, sleeps 4: 1 double, 2 single beds, pillows & blankets provided

Living: living/kitchen area, heating, TV, shower & separate wc

Eating: fitted kitchen with hobs, microwave, grill, coffee machine, fridge/freezer

Outside: table & chairs, 2 sun loungers, parasol

Pets: accepted (with supplement)

Other (AR1 and AR2): bed linen, cot and high chair for rent

Open: 24 April - 26 September		
Weekly Charge	AR1	AR2
Low Season *(from)*	€ 259	€ 259
High Season *(from)*	€ 1015	€ 1015

`FR06080` Camping Caravaning les Cigales

▶ see report page 437

505 avenue de la Mer, F-06210 Mandelieu-la-Napoule (Alpes-Maritimes)

AR1 – O'HARA – Mobile Home

Sleeping: 2 bedrooms, sleeps 4: 1 double, 2 single beds, pillows & blankets provided

Living: living/kitchen area, heating, shower & wc

Eating: fitted kitchen with hobs, fridge

Outside: table & chairs, parasol

Pets: accepted (with supplement)

AR2 – OPTIMA – Mobile Home

Sleeping: 2 bedrooms, sleeps 6: 1 double, 2 single beds, sofa bed, pillows & blankets provided

Living: living/kitchen area, shower & wc

Eating: fitted kitchen with hobs, fridge

Outside: table & chairs, 2 sun loungers, parasol

Pets: accepted (with supplement)

Other (AR1 and AR2): bed linen for rent

Open: All year		
Weekly Charge	AR1	AR2
Low Season *(from)*	€ 380	€ 380
High Season *(from)*	€ 785	€ 785

FR83030 Camping Caravaning Leï Suves

Quartier du Blavet, F-83520 Roquebrune-sur-Argens (Var)

see report page 447

AR1 – TYPE D – Mobile Home

Sleeping: 2 bedrooms, sleeps 6: 1 double, 2 single beds, sofa bed

Living: living/kitchen area, shower & wc

Eating: fitted kitchen with hobs, oven, fridge

Outside: table & chairs

Pets: not accepted

Open: 1 April - 15 October	
Weekly Charge	AR1
Low Season *(from)*	€ 365
High Season *(from)*	€ 760

FR83050 Camping Résidence du Campeur

B.P. 12, D7, F-83371 Saint Aygulf (Var)

see report page 450

AR1 – MOBIL HOME 4/5 PERSONNES – Mobile Home

Sleeping: 2 bedrooms, sleeps 5: 1 double, 2 single beds, sofa bed, pillows & blankets provided

Living: living/kitchen area, heating, shower & separate wc

Eating: fitted kitchen with hobs, microwave, oven, grill, coffee machine, fridge/freezer

Outside: table & chairs, 2 sun loungers

Pets: accepted

AR2 – GRAND CONFORT B – Mobile Home

Sleeping: 2 bedrooms, sleeps 5: 1 double, 2 single beds, sofa bed, pillows & blankets provided

Living: living/kitchen area, heating shower & separate wc

Eating: fitted kitchen with hobs, microwave, oven, grill, coffee machine, fridge/freezer

Outside: table & chairs, 2 sun loungers

Pets: accepted

Other (AR1 and AR2): bed linen, cot and high chair for rent

Open: 28 March - 30 September		
Weekly Charge	AR1	AR2
Low Season *(from)*	€ 280	€ 490
High Season *(from)*	€ 760	€ 1170

FR83060 Camping Resort la Baume – la Palmeraie

Route de Bagnols, F-83618 Fréjus (Var)

see report page 448

AR1 – BASTIDON – Chalet

Sleeping: 3 bedrooms, sleeps 6/8: 1 double, 4 single beds, sofa bed

Living: living/kitchen area, shower & wc

Eating: fitted kitchen with hobs, microwave, fridge/freezer

Outside: table & chairs, 2 sun loungers

Pets: accepted

AR2 – PHOENIX – Mobile Home

Sleeping: 3 bedrooms, sleeps 6: 1 double, 4 single beds, sofa bed

Living: living/kitchen area, shower & wc

Eating: fitted kitchen with hobs, microwave, fridge/freezer

Outside: table & chairs, 2 sun loungers

Pets: accepted

Other (AR1 and AR2): bed linen, cot and high chair for rent

Open: 4 April - 26 September		
Weekly Charge	AR1	AR2
Low Season *(from)*	€ 469	€ 336
High Season *(from)*	€ 1386	€ 970

FR83190 Camping la Presqu'île de Giens

▶ see report page 455

153 route de la Madraque-Giens, F-83400 Hyères (Var)

AR1 – IRM EVASION – Mobile Home

Sleeping: 2 bedrooms, sleeps 4: 1 double, 2 single beds, pillows & blankets provided

Living: living/kitchen area, heating, shower & wc

Eating: fitted kitchen with hobs, microwave, coffee machine, fridge/freezer

Outside: table & chairs

Pets: accepted

AR2 – GITOTEL COTTAGE – Chalet

Sleeping: 3 bedrooms, sleeps 6: 2 doubles, 2 single beds, pillows & blankets provided

Living: living/kitchen area, heating, shower & wc

Eating: fitted kitchen with hobs, microwave, coffee machine, fridge/freezer

Outside: table & chairs

Pets: accepted

Open: 22 March - 5 October

Weekly Charge	AR1	AR2
Low Season *(from)*	€ 320	€ 370
High Season *(from)*	€ 680	€ 850

FR83200 Kawan Village les Pêcheurs

▶ see report page 457

F-83520 Roquebrune-sur-Argens (Var)

AR1 – SHELBOX PARADIS – Mobile Home

Sleeping: 2 bedrooms, sleeps 6: 1 double, 3 single beds, sofa bed, pillows & blankets provided

Living: living/kitchen area, heating, shower & separate wc

Eating: fitted kitchen with hobs, microwave, coffee machine, fridge/freezer

Outside: table & chairs, 2 sun loungers, parasol

Pets: accepted (with supplement)

AR2 – O'HARA O'PHEA 833 – Mobile Home

Sleeping: 2 bedrooms, sleeps 4/6: 1 double, 2 single beds, sofa bed, pillows & blankets provided

Living: living/kitchen area, heating, shower & separate wc

Eating: fitted kitchen with hobs, microwave, coffee machine, fridge/freezer

Outside: table & chairs, 2 sun loungers, parasol

Pets: accepted (with supplement)

Other (AR1 and AR2): bed linen, cot and high chair for rent

Open: 1 April - 30 September

Weekly Charge	AR1	AR2
Low Season *(from)*	€ 330	€ 400
High Season *(from)*	€ 765	€ 855

FR83220 Kawan Village Cros de Mouton

▶ see report page 459

B.P. 116, F-83240 Cavalaire-sur-Mer (Var)

AR1 – PRESTIGE – Mobile Home

Sleeping: 2 bedrooms, sleeps 6: 1 double, 2 single beds, sofa bed, pillows & blankets provided

Living: living/kitchen area, heating, shower & separate wc

Eating: fitted kitchen with hobs, microwave, fridge/freezer

Outside: table & chairs, parasol

Pets: accepted

AR2 – GITOTEL – Chalet

Sleeping: 2 bedrooms, sleeps 6: 2 doubles, 2 bunkbeds, pillows & blankets provided

Living: living/kitchen area, heating, shower & wc

Eating: fitted kitchen with hobs, microwave, fridge

Outside: table & chairs, parasol

Pets: accepted

Open: 15 March - 1 November

Weekly Charge	AR1	AR2
Low Season *(from)*	€ 440	€ 400
High Season *(from)*	€ 800	€ 720

FR83340 Camping Bonporteau

▶ see report page 460

B.P. 18 (RD559), F-83240 Cavalaire-sur-Mer (Var)

AR1 – EVASION – Mobile Home	AR2 – SUPER MERCURE – Mobile Home
Sleeping: 1 bedroom, sleeps 3: 1 double, 1 single bed, sofa bed, pillows & blankets provided	**Sleeping:** 2 bedrooms, sleeps 6: 2 doubles, 2 single beds, sofa bed, pillows & blankets provided
Living: living/kitchen area, heating, fan, shower & separate wc	**Living:** living/kitchen area, heating, fan, shower & separate wc
Eating: fitted kitchen with hobs, microwave, coffee machine, fridge	**Eating:** fitted kitchen with hobs, microwave, coffee machine, fridge
Outside: table & chairs, 2 sun loungers, parasol	**Outside:** table & chairs, 2 sun loungers, parasol
Pets: accepted	**Pets:** accepted

Other (AR1 and AR2): bed linen, cot and high chair for rent

Open: 15 March - 15 October

Weekly Charge	AR1	AR2
Low Season *(from)*	€ 294	€ 399
High Season *(from)*	€ 714	€ 924

FR20040 Riva Bella Nature Resort & Spa

▶ see report page 482

B.P. 21, F-20270 Alèria (Haute-Corse)

AR1 – CHALET 4 – Chalet	AR2 – CHALET 2 BEDROOMS – Chalet
Sleeping: 2 bedrooms, sleeps 5: 1 double, 2 single beds, bunkbed	**Sleeping:** 2 bedrooms, sleeps 4: 1 double, 2 bunkbeds, pillows & blankets provided
Living: living/kitchen area, heating, shower & wc	**Living:** living/kitchen area, heating, shower & wc
Eating: fitted kitchen with hobs, fridge	**Eating:** fitted kitchen with hobs, fridge
Outside: table & chairs, 2 sun loungers, parasol	**Outside:** table & chairs, 2 sun loungers, parasol
Pets: accepted (with supplement)	**Pets:** accepted (with supplement)

Open: 29 March - 1 November

Weekly Charge	AR1	AR2
Low Season *(from)*	€ 567	€ 329
High Season *(from)*	€ 1134	€ 763

FR20050 Village Naturiste la Chiappa

▶ see report page 482

F-20137 Porto-Vecchio (Corse-du-Sud)

AR1 – TYPE C – Bungalow	AR2 – TYPE B – Bungalow
Sleeping: 2 bedrooms, sleeps 4: 4 single beds, pillows & blankets provided	**Sleeping:** 1 bedroom, sleeps 2: 2 single beds
Living: living/kitchen area, shower & wc	**Living:** living/kitchen area, shower & wc
Eating: fitted kitchen with hobs, fridge	**Eating:** fitted kitchen with fridge
Outside: table & chairs	**Outside:** table & chairs
Pets: accepted	**Pets:** accepted

Open: 9 May - 10 October

Weekly Charge	AR1	AR2
Low Season *(from)*	€ 630	€ 420
High Season *(from)*	€ 1050	€ 700

Parcs Résidentiels de Loisirs

Recent years have seen a significant increase in the number of Parcs résidentiels de loisirs in France. In many ways, these parks resemble good campsites but with the important distinction that they do not have any touring pitches!

Amenities at the parks are invariably very impressive, often with top quality swimming pool complexes and fine restaurant facilities. However, all the pitches on these sites are occupied by either mobile homes or chalets, many of which are available for let.

These parks have been developed by their owners often with the expectation that their clients may be former campers or caravanners, or possibly those travelling from afar, with the common desire to combine the freedom of camping and caravanning with a high standard of home comforts.

We have chosen to include a small selection of the best parcs résidentiels, all of which are attractively located in popular regions of France. In every case, there will be a good choice of accommodation available for rent. We are, however, featuring 2 types of accommodation and give full details of what is provided in terms of living and sleeping accommodation, as well as an indication of the park's tariffs.

FR27060 Domaine de Marcilly

Route de Saint-Andre-de-l'Eure, F-27810 Marcilly-sur-Eure (Eure)
Tel: **02 37 48 45 42**. Email: **domainedemarcilly@wanadoo.fr**   www.alanrogers.com/FR27060

Just between Ile de France and Normandy, less than an hours drive from Paris, Domaine de Marcilly is beautifully located in a 15 hectare park, surrounded by pine, oak and birch trees. Although most pitches are dedicated to mobile homes, this park also welcomes motorcaravans and each pitch has a picnic table. Leisure facilities include a swimming pool and tennis courts. There are paths and cycle routes through the parkland and surrounding countryside, as well as riding and fishing. The site is well located for exploring the northern Loire Valley. Chartres and Paris are within easy reach.

Facilities

The sanitary block provides hot showers, washbasins, laundry room and facilities for disabled visitors. Washing machine. Motorcaravan service point. Heated swimming pool (1/6-30/9). Boules. Tennis. Internet point. TV room. Animation and entertainment during high season.
Off site: Local shops 900 m. Riding 3 km. Golf 10 km. Canoeing. Walking and cycling routes.

Directions

From Paris A13, A12 exit onto N12 for Houdan, take exit Goussainville, Havelu, Bu, then Marcilly. Site is on the D52 in the direction of St Andre.
GPS: N48:49.513 E01:19.422

AR1 – O'PHEA – Mobile Home

Sleeping: 2 bedrooms, sleeps 4/5: 1 double, 2 single beds, pillows & blankets provided

Living: living/kitchen area, heating, shower & wc

Eating: fitted kitchen with hobs, oven, microwave, fridge

Outside: table & chairs, BBQ

Pets: accepted

AR2 – O'PHEA – Mobile Home

Sleeping: 3 bedrooms, sleeps 6: 1 double, 2 single beds, sofa bed, pillows & blankets provided

Living: living/kitchen area, heating, shower & wc

Eating: fitted kitchen with hobs, oven, microwave, fridge

Outside: table & chairs, BBQ

Pets: accepted

Open: 1 April - 29 October

Weekly Charge	AR1	AR2
Low Season (from)	€ 300	€ 400
High Season (from)	€ 590	€ 660

★★★★

For weekends and holidays in Normandy
Come and discover the Domaine de Marcilly on
the borders of Ile de France and Normandy

Route de Saint-Andre de l'Eure - F-27810 Marcilly sur Eure - France
Tel.: 02 37 48 45 42 - Fax: 02 37 48 51 11
Email: domainedemarcilly@wanadoo.fr - www.domainedemarcilly.com

ancv

Runner up | FR33300 | Domaine Residentiel Naturiste la Jenny

F-33680 Le Porge (Gironde)
Tel: 05 56 26 56 90. Email: info@lajenny.fr

www.alanrogers.com/FR33300

Situated at the heart of Europe's largest forest, yet within walking distance of the Atlantic beaches through the forest, La Jenny is a naturist site providing 750 high quality chalets, of which 500 are let on behalf of the owners. This is an ideal spot for a quiet and peaceful holiday, yet with a great deal on offer for those seeking a more lively holiday. With four pools covering an area of 1,000 sq.m., a wide range of sports amenities, including golf, tennis and archery, there is always something to do.

Facilities

Supermarket. Boulangerie. Fish shop. Launderette. Restaurant. Pizzeria. Bar. Brasserie. Heated pool complex. Body care and fitness centres. Sauna. Yoga and aquagym. Children's club. Tennis. Golf. Bicycle hire. Pony club. Diving. Play area. Off site: Fishing 300 m. Riding 4 km.

Directions

From the Bordeaux ring road take exit 8 signed Lacanau. Follow D107 to Lacanau via Le Temple and La Porge, then towards Lege/Cap Ferret on the D3 to La Jenny (on the right). GPS: N44:50.660 W01:12.659

AR1 – LOUISIANE – Chalet

Sleeping: 3 bedrooms, sleeps 8: 2 doubles, bunkbed, sofa bed, pillows provided

Living: living/kitchen area, shower & separate wc

Eating: fitted kitchen with hobs, microwave, oven, dish washer, coffee machine, fridge

Outside: table & chairs

Pets: accepted (with supplement)

AR2 – TOURTERELLE – Chalet

Sleeping: 2 bedrooms, sleeps 6: 1 double, 2 single beds, sofa bed, pillows & blankets provided

Living: living/kitchen area, shower & separate wc

Eating: fitted kitchen with hobs, microwave, oven, coffee machine, fridge

Outside: table & chairs

Pets: accepted (with supplement)

Other (AR1 and AR2): bed linen, cot and high chair for rent

Open: 16 May - 12 September		
Weekly Charge	AR1	AR2
Low Season (from)	€ 1125	€ 830
High Season (from)	€ 1355	€ 1335

FR57090 | Parc Résidentiel de la Tensch

F-57670 Francaltroff (Moselle)
Tel: 03 87 01 79 04

www.alanrogers.com/FR57090

La Tensch is a large leisure park located south of St Avold in the Moselle département. The park has been developed around three lakes and fishing is understandably very popular here, although many watersports are also possible, including windsurfing, canoeing and jet skiing. Although there are a few touring pitches, this is primarily a 'parc résidentiel' with a large number of mobile homes and chalets for rent, as well as residential units. Many footpaths lead around the lakes.

Facilities

Shop. Bar/restaurant. Takeaway. Swimming pool. Children's pool. Pedaloes. Canoe hire. Bicycle hire. Tennis. Play area. Trampolines. Activity and entertainment programme. Games room. Mobile homes and chalets for rent. Off site: Riding. Fishing. Cycle and walking tracks.

Directions

Leave the A4 autoroute at exit 39 for St Avold and head south on D633 to St Avold. Continue south on D22 to Francaltroff and the site is clearly signed. GPS: N48:57.650 E06:46.467

AR1 – CHALET – Chalet

Sleeping: 2 bedrooms, sleeps 5: 1 double, 2 single beds, sofa bed, pillows & blankets provided

Living: living/kitchen area, heating, TV, shower & separate wc

Eating: fitted kitchen with hobs, microwave, oven, coffee machine, fridge/freezer

Outside: table & chairs

Pets: accepted (with supplement)

Other (AR1 and AR2): bed linen and cot for rent

Open: 6 May - 19 December	
Weekly Charge	AR1
Low Season (from)	€ 350
High Season (from)	€ 450

FR63000 Les Chalets du Hameau du Lac

Lieu dit le Pré Bad, le Lac Chambon, F-63790 Chambon-sur-Lac (Puy-de-Dôme)

Tel: **06 12 03 91 56**. Email: **auvergne-chalets-location@orange.fr**   www.alanrogers.com/FR63000

Hameau du Lac is a recently developed small complex of five modern, spacious, well equipped and insulated chalets with underfloor electric heating ideal for six people. It is situated on the banks of Lac Chambon (800 m altitude) in the heart of the beautiful Auvergne National Park. The site has access to the lake (300 m) and some chalets enjoy views across the lake and mountains. Although there are few amenities on site, a very wide range of leisure activities are on offer around the lake.

Facilities

Direct access to Lac Chambon. TV. Dishwasher. Electric barbecue. Central laundry facilities. Off site: Sailing, windsurfing, waterskiing, bathing beach on adjacent lake. Covered swimming pool in adjacent campsite. Cycle and walking trails. Murol 3 km. Super Besse and Mont Dore. Bicycle hire 1 km. Riding 3 km. Winter skiing 12 km.

Directions

Leave A75 south of Clermont Ferrand at exit 6 signed Champeix (D978). Join the N996, go through St Nectaire and Murol to Lac Chambon. Chalets on left at far end of lake just beyond car park. GPS: N45:34.434 E02:55.210

AR1 – CHALET – Chalet

Sleeping: 2 bedrooms, sleeps 6: 4 doubles, sofa bed, pillows & blankets provided

Living: living/kitchen area, heating, TV, shower & wc

Eating: fitted kitchen with hobs, oven, grill, microwave, dishwasher, coffee machine, fridge/freezer

Outside: table & chairs

Pets: accepted (under constant supervision)

Open: All year	
Weekly Charge	AR1
Low Season	€ 390
High Season	€ 680

FR66590 Camping le Bois du Valmarie

F-66702 Argelès-sur-Mer (Pyrénées-Orientales)

Tel: **04 68 81 04 61**. Email: **contact@camping-lasirene.fr**   www.alanrogers.com/FR66590

Le Bois de Valmarie is a member of the same group of sites as La Sirène (FR66560) and L'Hippocampe (FR66570). The site has 181 pitches, the majority of which are available for booking (none available for touring) and is located south of the port beside Racou beach. The site has a pleasant woodland location and a range of amenities including a large swimming pool complex with waterslides and a separate children's pool. The sea is just 50 m. from the site entrance with a sandy beach.

Facilities

Supermarket. Restaurant. Bar. Beach shop. Takeaway food. Swimming pool with waterslides and separate children's pool. Play area. Mobile homes for rent. Off site: Argelès town centre 3 km. Diving club. Blue Bear activity club. Emeraude Beach Club.

Directions

Leave autoroute at Perpignan Sud exit and join the N114 southbound toward Argelès. Take exit 13 and follow signs to Le Racou. Site is well signed from here. GPS: N42:32.270 E03:03.267

AR1 – SIRENE 2 – Mobile Home

Sleeping: 2 bedrooms, sleeps 4/6: 1 double, 2 single beds, sofa bed, pillows & blankets provided

Living: living/kitchen area, heating, air conditioning, shower & separate wc

Eating: fitted kitchen with hobs, microwave, oven, grill, coffee machine, fridge/freezer

Outside: table & chairs, 2 sun loungers, parasol, BBQ

Pets: not accepted

Open: 18 April - 27 September	
Weekly Charge	AR1
Low Season (from)	€ 248
High Season (from)	€ 973

FR65180 Village Cévéo de Luz

Quartier Maoubèze, F-65120 Luz Saint Sauveur (Hautes-Pyrénées)

Tel: **05 05 92 84 72**. Email: **luz@ceveo.com**   www.alanrogers.com/FR65180

Village de Luz is a holiday resort complex owned by the Cévéo group. The accommodation is chalet style (accessible by the disabled) and is located 500 m. from the village centre of Luz St Sauveur. The ski resort of Luz Ardiden is 14 km. distant. The complex here includes 2 restaurants (with breakfast available). Leisure facilities include a library and TV lounge, as well as clubs for toddlers, children and teenagers. During the winter season, ski lessons are organised.

Facilities	Directions
Restaurant. Bar. Lounge and TV room. Clubs for children and teenagers. Activity and entertainment programme. Off site: Cycle and walking tracks in the surrounding Pyrénées. Luz St Sauveur centre 500 m. Luz Ardiden (ski resort) 14 km.	Approaching from Lourdes use the D821 to Argelès Gazost and then the DD921 and D12 to Luz St Sauveur. The complex is clearly signed. GPS: N42:52.440 W0:00.480

AR1 – DEMI-PENSION – Rooms	AR2 – PENSION COMPLETE – Rooms
Sleeping: 1 bedroom, sleeps 2: 2 single beds, pillows & blankets provided	**Sleeping:** 1 bedroom, sleeps 2: 2 single beds, pillows & blankets provided
Living: living/kitchen area, heating, shower & separate wc	**Living:** living/kitchen area, heating, shower & separate wc
Pets: not accepted	**Pets:** not accepted

Other (AR1 and AR2): bed linen, cot and high chair for rent

Open: 31 May - 27 September		
Weekly Charge	AR1	AR2
Low Season *(from)*	€ 252	€ 308
High Season *(from)*	€ 301	€ 357

FR87040 Domaine Cévéo de Pierrefitte

Lac de Vassivière, F-87120 Beaumont du Lac (Haute-Vienne)

Tel: **05 55 69 15 88**. Email: **resa@ceveo.com**   www.alanrogers.com/FR87040

Domaine de Pierrefitte is an attractive holiday development belonging to the Cévéo group. There are a number of grassy pitches here, most with electrical connections (6A) as well as accommodation in either chalets, gites or mobile homes. There are also a number of teepees, with smaller, children's teepees adjacent. The site is located on the vast Lac de Vassivière, one of the largest lakes in France. Many sports activities are possible on the lake, including water skiing, sailing, canoeing and boat trips to the island of Vassivière. Fishing is also understandably popular.

Facilities	Directions
Bar. Restaurant. Covered swimming pool. Shop. Games room. Multisports terrain. Play area. Activity and entertainment programme. Off site: Cycle and walking tracks around the Lac de Vassivière.	Leave the A20 autoroute at exit 23 and head west on N145 to Puy-de-Lantais. Head south here on D912 to Bourganeuf. Here, continue south on D940 to Peyrat and then join the eastbound D222 to Pierrefitte. GPS: N45:47.180 E01:52.001

AR1 – PRESTIGE – Chalet	AR2 – GITE – Gipsy wagon
Sleeping: 3 bedrooms, sleeps 6: 4 single beds, bunkbed, pillows & blankets provided	**Sleeping:** 1 bedroom, sleeps 4: bunkbed, sofa bed, pillows & blankets provided
Living: living/kitchen area, heating, shower & wc	**Living:** living/kitchen area, heating, shower & separate wc
Eating: fitted kitchen with hobs, microwave, dishwasher, coffee machine, fridge	**Eating:** fitted kitchen with hobs, microwave, oven, coffee machine, fridge
Outside: table & chairs, parasol, BBQ	**Outside:** table & chairs, parasol, BBQ
Pets: accepted (with supplement)	**Pets:** accepted (with supplement)

Open: 4 April - 26 September		
Weekly Charge	AR1	AR2
Low Season *(from)*	€ 322	€ 266
High Season *(from)*	€ 609	€ 462

Villages et résidences de vacances

GREEN GLOBE
BENCHMARKED

BRONZE 2008
COMPANY

Animations Children's club Sport

Rent Full board Half- board

Flat Chalet Mobil home

Ocean Mountain Country

8 Destinations

La Baule
Saint-Rémy
Le Haut Bréda
Île de Ré
Pierrefitte
Le Pleynet
Mimizan
Luz

Cévéo
27, route du Cendre
63800 Cournon d'Auvergne
Tél : 33 (0)4 73 77 05 05
e-mail : resa@ceveo.com

www.ceveo.com

FR11020 Cottage Village Aux Hamacs

Route des Cabanes, F-11560 Fleury (Aude)

Tel: **04 68 33 22 22**. Email: **info@cottagevillage.fr**   www.alanrogers.com/FR11020

If you are looking for sun, sea and sand, Aux Hamacs is a good venue. It is situated adjacent to the Aude river with the attractive village of Fleury nearby and a good beach less than 2 km. away. It is also well located for exploring Cathar country with its amazing hilltop castles and attractions such as the Canal du Midi. Quietly situated amongst nature, the site is well away from the frenzy and rush associated with some of the resorts in this region, yet has all the amenities for an enjoyable stay.

Facilities	Directions
Shop, bar, restaurant and takeaway (all fully operational 27/6-15/9). Pool complex with three slides and paddling pool (27/6-15/9). Play areas. Activities and entertainment (high season). TV room. Games room. Internet (free). Fishing (no permit). Off site: Riding 5 km.	From A9 autoroute take exit 36 Beziers Ouest. Follow directions for Vendres Plage on the D64. At the fourth roundabout turn left to the river Aude and over the bridge, just a little up river from Grau de Venfres. GPS: N43:13.342 E03:13.009

AR1 – TYPE 1 – Mobile Home

Sleeping: 2 bedrooms, sleeps 4: 1 double, 2 single beds

Living: living/kitchen area, heating, shower & separate WC

Eating: fitted kitchen with hobs, microwave, coffee machine, fridge/freezer

Outside: table & chairs, 2 sun loungers, parasol

Pets: not accepted

AR2 – TYPE 2 – Mobile Home

Sleeping : 3 bedrooms, sleeps 6: 1 double, 4 single beds

Living: living/kitchen area, heating, shower & separate WC

Eating: fitted kitchen with hobs, microwave, coffee machine, fridge/freezer

Outside: table & chairs, 2 sun loungers, parasol

Pets: not accepted

Open: 1 April - 30 September

Weekly Charge	AR1	AR2
Low Season *(from)*	€ 308	€ 413
High Season *(from)*	€ 903	€ 987

Cottage Village *Where life is beautiful!*

Cottage Village Aux Hamacs*
Route des Cabanes - 11560 FLEURY (Aude)
Tel.: +33 (0)468 33 22 22

info@cottagevillage.fr - www.cottagevillage.fr

Need a low cost ferry?

It couldn't be simpler - just click, choose a ferry and book...

- Special deals for caravans and motorhomes
- View routes and compare prices
- Fully searchable by route and operator

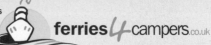 ferries4campers.co.uk

the Alan Rogers travel service

The best campsites for the best holidays

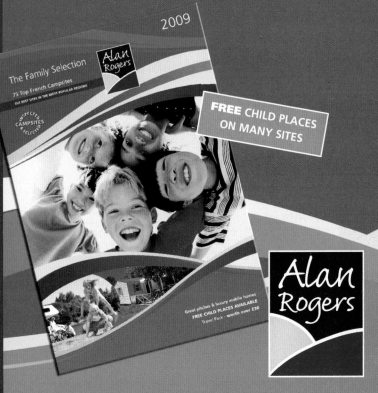

2009

The Family Selection
75 Top French Campsites
THE BEST SITES IN THE MOST POPULAR REGIONS

INSPECTED CAMPSITES & SELECTED

Alan Rogers

FREE CHILD PLACES ON MANY SITES

Great pitches & luxury mobile homes
FREE CHILD PLACES AVAILABLE
Travel Pack - worth over £30

The Family Selection
**PITCH AND MOBILE HOME BOOKINGS ON
A SELECTION OF FRANCE'S FINEST CAMPSITES**

- Expert, first-hand travel advice with 40 years experience
- Instant, no obligation quotations
- Personal travel advisor service
- Tailor-made holidays to suit you
- Leave the hassle to the experts
- Ferry-inclusive holidays ABTA bonded for your peace of mind

INSPECTED CAMPSITES & SELECTED

ABTA
ABTA No.W1610

FREE Brochure
Call **01580 214000**

www.**alanrogers**.com

Open All Year

The following sites are understood to accept caravanners and campers all year round. It is always wise to phone the site to check as the facilities available, for example, may be reduced.

Brittany
FR44320   Pierre Longue
FR56150   Haras
FR56210   Merlin l'Enchanteur

Normandy
FR27060   Marcilly
FR76090   Mun. Etennemare

Northern France
FR62120   Eté Indien

Paris & Ile de France
FR75020   Bois de Boulogne
FR77110   Parc de Paris
FR77060   Colline

Eastern France
FR88090   Lac de la Moselotte
FR88020   Belle Hutte
FR88040   Lac de Bouzey
FR88130   Vanne de Pierre
FR88050   Champé

Vendée & Charente
FR17070   Gros Joncs
FR85930   Forges
FR85890   Rouge-Gorge

Loire Valley
FR79020   Courte Vallée
FR45040   Hortus
FR41060   Dugny
FR49150   Thouet
FR53020   Malidor
FR86040   Futuriste

Burgundy
FR21060   Bouleaux
FR21090   Arquebuse
FR58030   Bezolle

Savoy & Dauphiny Alps
FR74230   Giffre

Atlantic Coast
FR33370   Montalivet
FR33350   Chez Gendron
FR33090   Pressoir
FR64040   Gaves

Dordogne & Aveyron
FR16040   Devezeau
FR16060   Marco de Bignac
FR24150   Deux Vallées
FR24480   Tailladis
FR46070   Plage (Saint-Cirq)
FR47150   Guillalmes
FR47110   Cabri

Limousin & Auvergne
FR19080   Vianon
FR63060   Clos Auroy
FR63000   Hameau du Lac

Rhône Valley
FR26110   4 Saisons
FR26290   Galaure
FR26100   Sagittaire
FR69010   Lyon

Provence
FR84160   Bagatelle

Midi-Pyrénées
FR09050   Mun. Prade (Sorgeat)
FR09120   Ascou la Forge
FR65130   Pyrenevasion
FR65080   Lavedan
FR65160   Monlôo

Mediterranean West
FR11110   Val d'Aleth
FR34490   Fondespierre
FR66490   Garenne

Mediterranean East
FR06080   Cigales
FR06050   Vieille Ferme
FR13130   Canet Plage
FR13120   Chantecler

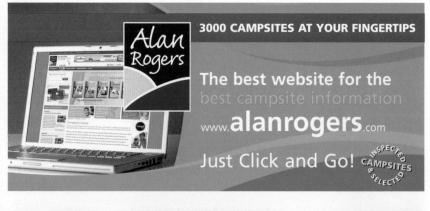

3000 CAMPSITES AT YOUR FINGERTIPS

Alan Rogers

The best website for the best campsite information

www.**alanrogers**.com

Just Click and Go!   INSPECTED CAMPSITES & SELECTED

Dogs

Since the introduction in 2000 of the Passports for Pets scheme many British campers and caravanners have been encouraged to take their pets with them on holiday. However, Pet Travel conditions are understandbly strict, the procedure is quite lengthy and complicated so we would advise you to check the current situation before travelling. The Passports for Pets website is: http://www.freespace.virgin.net/passports.forpets

For the benefit of those who want to take their dogs to France, we list here the sites which have indicated to us that they do not accept dogs or have certain restrictions. If you are planning to take your dog we do advise you to phone the site first to check – there may be limits on numbers, breeds, or times of the year when they are excluded.

Sites that do not accept dogs

FR14090	Brévedent	FR30390	Petits Camarguais	FR68080	Clair Vacances
FR16020	Gorges du Chambon	FR34560	Paradis	FR83320	Mogador
FR17010	Bois Soleil	FR40040	Paillotte	FR84020	Bélézy (Naturiste)
FR20030	Merendella	FR46040	Moulin de Laborde	FR85020	Jard
FR24040	Moulin du Roch	FR64060	Pavillon Royal	FR85210	Ecureuils
FR29140	Kerlann	FR66040	Soleil	FR85420	Bel
FR30160	Boucanet	FR66590	Bois du Valmarie		

Sites that accept dogs but with certain restrictions:

FR04110	Verdon Parc	FR29000	Mouettes	FR66290	Floride et
FR07630	Aluna	FR29380	Port de Plaisance		l'Embouchure
FR12040	Tours	FR30070	Boisson	FR66490	Garenne
FR12170	Caussanel	FR33080	Barbanne	FR74060	Colombière
FR17170	Charmilles	FR33210	Pointe du Medoc	FR83040	Bastiane
FR17210	Interlude	FR33290	Tedey	FR83120	Domaine
FR17290	Peupliers	FR34130	Neptune	FR83440	Malissonne
FR22210	Bellevue	FR35040	P'tit Bois	FR85000	Petit Rocher
FR23010	Château de	FR40250	Grands Pins	FR85030	Loubine
	Poinsouze	FR46190	Faurie	FR85150	Yole
FR24100	Moulinal	FR46310	Granges	FR85280	Places Dorées
FR24290	Moulin du Bleufond	FR63070	Pré Bas	FR85440	Brunelles
FR26030	Grand Lierne	FR64100	Etche Zahar	FR85770	Ferme du Latois
FR26200	Ecluse	FR66170	Mar I Sol	FR85870	Baie d'Aunis
FR28140	Senonches	FR66230	Romarin		

Golf

We understand that the following sites have facilities for playing golf. Where facilities are within easy reach and we have been given details, we have included this information in the individual site reports. However, we recommend that you contact the site to check that they meet your requirements.

FR29050	Orangerie de Lanniron
FR29470	Deux Fontaines
FR35020	Ormes
FR41030	Alicourts
FR33300	Jenny (Naturiste)

Travelling

When taking your car (and caravan, tent or trailer tent) or motorcaravan to the continent you do need to plan in advance and to find out as much as possible about driving in the countries you plan to visit. Whilst European harmonisation has eliminated many of the differences between one country and another, it is well worth reading the short notes we provide in the introduction to each country in this guide in addition to this more general summary.

Of course, the main difference from driving in the UK is that in mainland Europe you will need to drive on the right. Without taking extra time and care, especially at busy junctions and conversely when roads are empty, it is easy to forget to drive on the right. Remember that traffic approaching from the right usually has priority unless otherwise indicated by road markings and signs. Harmonisation also means that most (but not all) common road signs are the same in all countries.

Your vehicle

Book your vehicle in for a good service well before your intended departure date. This will lessen the chance of an expensive breakdown. Make sure your brakes are working efficiently and that your tyres have plenty of tread (3 mm. is recommended, particularly if you are undertaking a long journey).

Also make sure that your caravan or trailer is roadworthy and that its tyres are in good order and correctly inflated. Plan your packing and be careful not to overload your vehicle, caravan or trailer – this is unsafe and may well invalidate your insurance cover (it must not be more fully loaded than the kerb weight of the insured vehicle).

CHECK ALL THE FOLLOWING:

- GB sticker. If you do not display a sticker, you may risk an on-the-spot fine as this identifier is compulsory in all countries. Euro-plates are an acceptable alternative within the EU (but not outside). Remember to attach another sticker (or Euro-plate) to caravans or trailers. Only GB stickers (not England, Scotland, Wales or N. Ireland) stickers are valid in the EU.

- Headlights. As you will be driving on the right you must adjust your headlights so that the dipped beam does not dazzle oncoming drivers. Converter kits are readily available for most vehicle, although if your car is fitted with high intensity headlights, you should check with your motor dealer. Check that any planned extra loading does not affect the beam height.

- Seatbelts. Rules for the fitting and wearing of seatbelts throughout Europe are similar to those in the UK, but it is worth checking before you go. Rules for carrying children in the front of vehicles vary from country to country. It is best to plan not to do this if possible.

- Door/wing mirrors. To help with driving on the right, if your vehicle is not fitted with a mirror on the left hand side, we recommend you have one fitted.

- Fuel. Leaded and Lead Replacement petrol is increasingly difficult to find in Northern Europe.

Compulsory additional equipment

The driving laws of the countries of Europe still vary in what you are required to carry in your vehicle, although the consequences of not carrying a required piece of equipment are almost always an on-the-spot fine.

To meet these requirements we suggest that you carry the following:

- FIRE EXTINGUISHER

- BASIC TOOL KIT

- FIRST AID KIT

- SPARE BULBS

- TWO WARNING TRIANGLES – two are required in some countries at all times, and are compulsory in most countries when towing.

- HIGH VISIBILITY VEST – now compulsory in France, Spain, Italy and Austria (and likely to become compulsory throughout the EU) in case you need to walk on a motorway.

Insurance and Motoring Documents

Vehicle insurance

Contact your insurer well before you depart to check that your car insurance policy covers driving outside the UK. Most do, but many policies only provide minimum cover (so if you have an accident your insurance may only cover the cost of damage to the other person's property, with no cover for fire and theft).

To maintain the same level of cover abroad as you enjoy at home you need to tell your vehicle insurer. Some will automatically cover you abroad with no extra cost and no extra paperwork. Some will say you need a Green Card (which is neither green nor on card) but won't charge for it. Some will charge extra for the Green Card. Ideally you should contact your vehicle insurer 3-4 weeks before you set off, and confirm your conversation with them in writing.

Breakdown insurance

Arrange breakdown cover for your trip in good time so that if your vehicle breaks down or is involved in an accident it (and your caravan or trailer) can be repaired or returned to this country. This cover can usually be arranged as part of your travel insurance policy (see below).

Documents you must take with you

You may be asked to show your documents at any time so make sure that they are in order, up-to-date and easily accessible while you travel. These are what you need to take:

- Passports (you may also need a visa in some countries if you hold either a UK passport not issued in the UK or a passport that was issued outside the EU).

- Motor Insurance Certificate, including Green Card (or Continental Cover clause)

- DVLC Vehicle Registration Document plus, if not your own vehicle, the owner's written authority to drive.

- A full valid Driving Licence (not provisional). The new photo style licence is now mandatory in most European countries).

Personal Holiday insurance

Even though you are just travelling within Europe you must take out travel insurance. Few EU countries pay the full cost of medical treatment even under reciprocal health service arrangements. The first part of a holiday insurance policy covers people. It will include the cost of doctor, ambulance and hospital treatment if needed. If needed the better companies will even pay for English language speaking doctors and nurses and will bring a sick or injured holidaymaker home by air ambulance.

An important part of the insurance, often ignored, is cancellation (and curtailment) cover. Few things are as heartbreaking as having to cancel a holiday because a member of the family falls ill. Cancellation insurance can't take away the disappointment, but it makes sure you don't suffer financially as well. For this reason you should arrange your holiday insurance at least eight weeks before you set off.

Whichever insurance you choose we would advise reading very carefully the policies sold by the High Street travel trade. Whilst they may be good, they may not cover the specific needs of campers, caravanners and motorcaravanners.

Telephone 0870 405 4059 for a quote for our European Camping Holiday Insurance with cover arranged through Green Flag Motoring Assistance and Inter Group Assistance Services, one of the UK's largest assistance companies. Alternatively visit our website at www.insure4campers.com.

Travelling continued

European Health Insurance Card (EHIC)

Make sure you apply for your EHIC before travelling in Europe. Eligible travellers from the UK are entitled to receive free or reduced-cost medical care in many European countries on production of an EHIC. This free card is available by completing a form in the booklet 'Health Advice for Travellers' from local Post Offices. One should be completed for each family member. Alternatively visit www.dh.gov.uk/travellers and apply on-line. Please allow time to send your application off and have the EHIC returned to you.

The EHIC is valid in all European Community countries plus Iceland, Liechtenstein, Switzerland and Norway. If you or any of your dependants are suddenly taken ill or have an accident during a visit to any of these countries, free or reduced-cost emergency treatment is available - in most cases on production of a valid EHIC.

Only state-provided emergency treatment is covered, and you will receive treatment on the same terms as nationals of the country you are visiting. Private treatment is generally not covered, and state-provided treatment may not cover all of the things that you would expect to receive free of charge from the NHS.

Remember an EHIC does not cover you for all the medical costs that you can incur or for repatriation - it is not an alternative to travel insurance. You will still need appropriate insurance to ensure you are fully covered for all eventualities.

Travelling with children

Most countries in Europe are enforcing strict guidelines when you are travelling with children who are not your own. A minor (under the age of 18) must be accompanied by a parent or legal guardian or must carry a letter of authorisation from a parent or guardian. The letter should name the adult responsible for the minor during his or her stay. Similarly, a minor travelling with just one of his/her parents, must have a letter of authority to leave their home country from the parent staying behind. Full information is available at www.fco.gov.uk.

FRANCE
yes, you can

insure**4**campers.com

Personal travel insurance
European vehicle assistance insurance

Whatever form your camping or touring holiday may take, you'll need proper insurance for complete peace of mind. Our policies provide exactly the right cover for self-drive campsite-based holidays - at fantastic prices!

One call and you're covered

Visit www.**insure4campers.com**

or call us **NOW** for a no-obligation quote

01580 214006

Policies despatched within 24 hours

BROUGHT
TO YOU BY
ALAN ROGERS

Dover - France fares for less

Tel 0844 847 5007 **norfolkline.com**

You're better off booking with The Club!

As a member of Europe's Premier Club for touring caravanners, motor caravanners and trailer tenters, you'll enjoy an unrivalled range of services and benefits to ensure you make the most of your holiday.

- **Channel Crossing Booking Service** with special offers and discounts. You could 'save' more than your membership fee on your first trip alone.

- **European Site Booking Service** for over 200 inspected sites, including many from the Les Castels chain.

- **Red Pennant Insurance** - competitive, 'tailor-made' cover.

- **Camping Cheques** - 'go as you please' scheme for freedom of choice, now accepted by many Castels campsites.

- **Tours and Excursions** - themed holidays for the adventurous, first-timers and everyone in between.

- **Caravan Club Magazine** - free monthly and full of useful information and great holiday ideas.

To make sure you get the best deal when you book, call or visit our website to join or request an information pack.

0800 328 6635
www.caravanclub.co.uk

Quote ref. LC2009

THE CARAVAN CLUB

LES CASTELS

Superb 4-star touring sites in exceptional settings across France

LES ★★★★ CASTELS

Hôtellerie de Plein Air

Welcome to Les Castels where the grounds of stunning castles, beautiful manors and charming country houses provide unique natural settings for some of the finest touring sites in France, all created by owners with a passion for the simpler things in life. You will be assured of a warm and courteous welcome, tranquil surroundings, great services and a taste of authentic French "art de vivre".

• Courtesy, conviviality & hospitality
• Choice, comfort and 4-star quality
• Superb touring pitches
• Excellent services & facilities

LES CASTELS " PRIVILEGE CARD "
For special low-season rates contact us for details of the Les Castels "Privilège card"

Contact us for a brochure and discover a Castels site that matches your idea of a perfect holiday destination.

4 STARS AND A SOUL

www.les-castels.com

Les Castels - Manoir de Terre Rouge - 35270 Bonnemain - France
Tel. +33 02 23 16 03 20 / Fax +33 02 23 16 03 23

How can I
sail direct
to my holiday in France?

We know a way

Take one of our mile-saving routes from Portsmouth, Poole or Plymouth and arrive much closer to where you want to be.

With less time at the wheel, you'll have more time to holiday. And it's great value too, because with less driving you'll also be saving on fuel, tolls and overnight stops.

CORK

PLYMOUTH POOLE PORTSMOUTH

CHERBOURG

ROSCOFF CAEN

ST MALO

SANTANDER

brittanyferries.com 0871 244 1477

Brittany Ferries
— France & Spain —

Great magazines for touring, holidays and inspirational ideas!

For buying information, top tips and technical help, **Caravan, Motor Caravan Magazine** and **Park Home & Holiday Caravan** are all you need — every month!

SUBSCRIBE TODAY
AND SAVE 30%

☎ **0845 676 7778**

Lines are open seven days a week, 9am – 9pm. Closing date 31 December 2009
Quote code Caravan 44D or Motor Caravan 43M or
Park Home & Holiday Caravan 40F when calling

30% discount is by quarterly direct debit only.

TRY 3 ISSUES FOR JUST £3

GREAT SAVINGS!
Secure a 20% discount after your trial ends.

EXCLUSIVE OFFERS!
Get access to unique offers and discounts.

FREE DELIVERY!
Your copy direct to your door before it goes on sale in the shops.

OR

Practical Motorhome

- Touring inspiration and motor caravanning tips
- Common sense advice on maintaining and improving your motorhome
- In-depth motorhome reviews of all the latest models
- The complete motorhome magazine

Practical Caravan

- Holiday inspiration and travel guides for the UK and abroad
- Expert hints and tips to help you holiday better
- Buying advice and in-depth tests for towcars and caravans
- Britain's favourite caravan magazine for over 40 years

CALL **08456 777 812** now
or visit **www.themagazineshop.com/caravan09**
or **www.themagazineshop.com/motor09**
Please have your bank details ready and quote AR09

Campéole

CAMPSITES AND RENTED ACCOMMODATION

OVER 40 CAMPSITES

in France, Spain and Italy.

Seaside, mountain, countryside...

Pitches, mobile-home rental,

entertainment, swimming pool.....

INFORMATION AND BOOKING

www.campeole.co.uk

or **0 905 076 0240**

Calls cost £ 0.75 per minute plus network extras.

VACANCES
Andre Trigano.com
LE SPÉCIALISTE DU CAMPING

For the complete
Towing Experience

Towbars for most makes and models of cars and light commercial vehicles. Semi-automatic or automatic detachable swan neck systems and fixed flange ball Towbars.

A full range of accessories and spares including Couplings, Electrical Kits, Bumper Shields and Steps.

The award winning range of Towbar mounted Cycle Carriers will carry up to four cycles and can be fitted and removed in seconds.

FREE comprehensive catalogue with information and prices for over 1200 Towbars plus the locations of fitting centres nationwide.

i-FIT explains and guides you through the complexities of Towbar fitting. WEB-FIT lets you buy your Towbar and book an appointment with your local stockist to have it fitted - all online.

To view our full product range or to buy online, visit www.witter-towbars.co.uk
To find your nearest Witter stockist, visit the website, view our catalogue or see Yellow Pages or Yell.com

Towing solutions for a mobile world

WITTER
TOWBAR SYSTEMS

witter-towbars.co.uk

Witter Towbars Drome Road Deeside Industrial Park Deeside Flintshire CH5 2NY United Kingdom

Save up to 60% on your holiday

Camping Cheque ©

- Over 550 campsites – all just £11.95 per night
  (pitch +2 adults, inc electricity)
- Maximum flexibility - go as you please
- 24 Countries
- Fantastic Ferry Deals

Last year 250,000 people used nearly 1.6 million Camping Cheques and enjoyed half-price holidays around Europe. Make sure you don't miss out this year.

Fantastic Ferry Offers

CALL NOW for your **FREE** Holiday Savings

Guide

01580 214002

FOR FULL INFORMATION VISIT

www.campingcheque.co.uk

A SELECTION
OF CAMPSITES
FOR EXPLORING FRANCE
IN A WHOLE NEW WAY

SITES & PAYSAGES DE FRANCE,
A SELECTION OF QUALITY CAMPSITES COVERING
THE RICH DIVERSITY OF THE FRENCH REGIONS.

SITES & PAYSAGES de FRANCE offers campers and caravanners a carefully chosen selection of high quality, 3- and 4-star comfortable campsites across the country. Our campsites are situated in attractively landscaped, tree-shaded environments, with all the amenities for tents, caravans, camping-cars, mobile homes or chalet accommodation. All are laid out with 'room to breathe' and located in areas of great natural beauty, with masses to do and see, from on-site sport and leisure activities, to nearby heritage visits not forgetting the sublime joys of authentic local French cuisine.

**ASK US FOR
YOUR FREE
MAGAZINE**

information office:

tél. 00 33 820 20 46 46 - www.sitesetpaysages.com
E-mail us at: contact@sites-et-paysages.com

Off Peak Mobile Homes

from **£29.00** per night

Holiday Cheque gives you exclusive off peak access to quality mobile homes and chalets on over 100 of Europe's finest campsites. You'll find superb family facilities, including sensational pools, great value restaurants, friendly bars and real hospitality.

HOLIDAY CHEQUE

01580 214004

Call today for your **FREE** brochure

IT WILL SAVE YOU £££'S ON YOUR HOLIDAY

www.**holidaycheque**.co.uk

- ✓ Over 100 top campsites
- ✓ All from £29.00 per night
- ✓ High quality mobile homes
- ✓ Luxury high specification chalets
- ✓ Fully equipped - down to the corkscrew!
- ✓ Plus unbeatable ferry prices

COMPATIBLE WITH TOM TOM, GARMIN & MIO DEVICES

NEW from Alan Rogers

Sat Nav
To Your Campsite

Fed up with vague signs, indistinct directions and ambiguous road markings?

Navigating to continental campsites can be a complicated affair. That's why Alan Rogers have teamed up with MyPoi World to create a sure-fire solution.

Easily navigate to over 2,100 campsites in more than 30 European countries, including the UK. All campsites are 'inspected and selected' by Alan Rogers, giving you real peace of mind.

It's easy to use, with intuitive search criteria, making your journey a real pleasure.

- Select campsites by name, location or type of facilities
- Includes campsite phone number
- Identifies pet-friendly campsites
- Identifies presence of pool, shop, bar, restaurant etc
- Identifies if campsite is situated close to water

www.**alanrogers**.com

More information - and download option

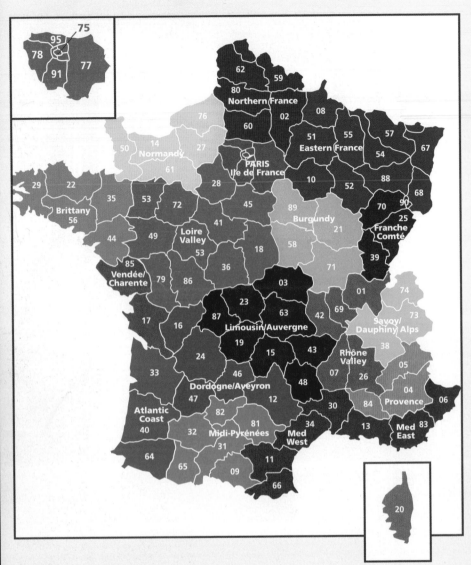

For administrative purposes France is actually divided into
23 official Regions covering the 95 départements (similar to our counties).

However, theses do not always coincide with the needs of tourists (for example,
the area we think of as the 'Dordogne' is split between two official regions.
We have, therefore, opted to feature our campsites within unofficial 'tourist' regions.

We use the departement numbers as the first two digits of our campsite numbers
so, for example, any site in the Manche departement will start with the number 50.

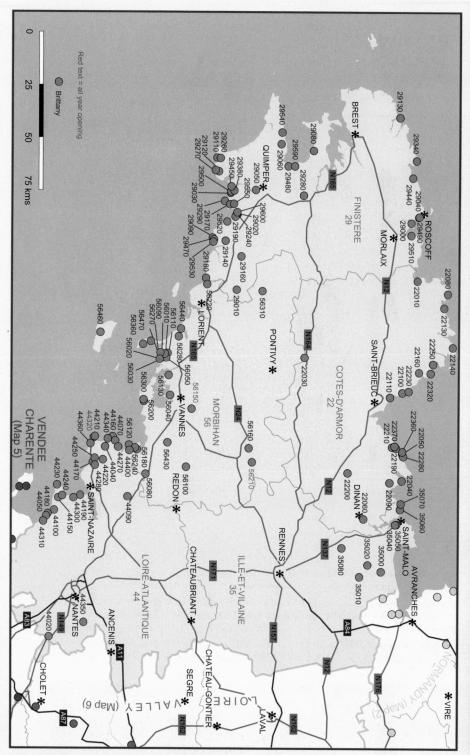

0   25   50   75 kms

Red text = all year opening

● Brittany

BREST ✱

29130

29340
29040
29440
29490
29000
29510
22010

ROSCOFF ✱

MORLAIX ✱

N12

FINISTERE
29

29540
29080
29590
29060
29480
29280

29260
29120
29110
29270
29380
29450
29550
29050
29030
29500
29170
29290
29520
29190
29240
29020
29090
29180
29470
29530
29140
29160
29010

QUIMPER ✱

56220

LORIENT ✱

56310

PONTIVY ✱

N165

N164

22030

SAINT-BRIEUC ✱

22080
22130
22140
22250
22160
22230
22100
22110
22320
22360
22050
22280
22370
22210
22190
22040
22090
35070
35060
35050
35040
35000
35020
35010
35080

DINAN ✱

SAINT-MALO

AVRANCHES ✱

COTES-D'ARMOR
22

22060
22200

N12

N137

N176

NORMANDY (Map 2)

VIRE ✱

56460
56470
56270
56090
56010
56110
56020
56360
56030
56440
56280
56050
56130
56300
56200
56040
56180
56080

MORBIHAN
56

56150
56430
56100
56210
56160

VANNES ✱

REDON ✱

RENNES ✱

N24

N157

N12

A84

ILLE-ET-VILAINE
35

44360
44320
44250
44170
44230
44240
44180
44050
44100
44310
44150
44300
44190
44040
44160
44340
44070
44120
44400
44270
44220
44280
44010
44090

SAINT-NAZAIRE ✱

CHATEAUBRIANT ✱

LOIRE-ATLANTIQUE
44

56240

N71

44350

NANTES ✱
N149
44020
A11
ANCENIS ✱

A83

CHOLET ✱
A87

VENDEE
CHARENTE
(Map 5)

SEGRE ✱

LAVAL ✱
N162

CHATEAU-GONTIER

LOIRE VALLEY (Map 6)

Sites on this map are featured on pages 17-74 of the guide.
Please refer to the numerical index (page 562) for exact campsite page references.

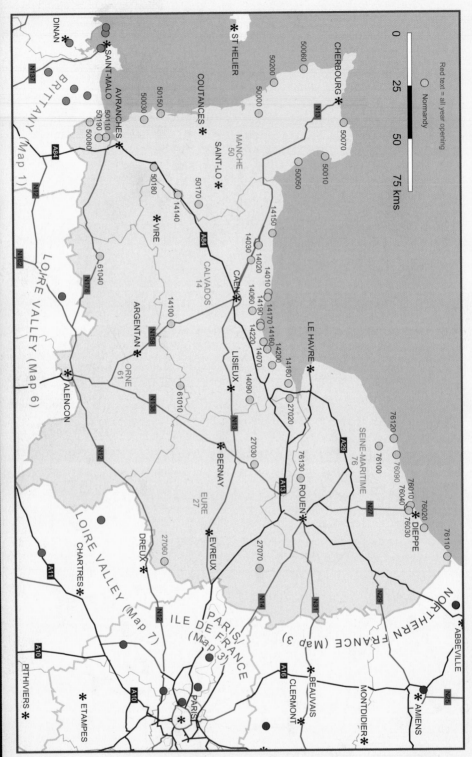

Red text = all year opening

○ Normandy

0   25   50   75 kms

DINAN *

BRITTANY (Map 1)

N137

SAINT-MALO *

AVRANCHES *

50200 ○

50060 ○

50150 ○

50030 ○

COUTANCES *

50110 ○
50190 ○
50080 ○

A84

N12

N162

LOIRE VALLEY (Map 6)

N176

61040 ○

50180 ○

VIRE *

14140 ○

A84

CALVADOS 14

14030 ○

14020 ○

ARGENTAN *

N158

14100 ○

ORNE 61

ALENCON *

N138

61010 ○

N12

DREUX *

27060 ○

A11

CHARTRES *

LOIRE VALLEY (Map 7)

N12

A10

PITHIVIERS *

ETAMPES *

A10

PARIS *

ILE DE FRANCE (Map 3)

N14

EVREUX *

EURE 27

27070 ○

27030 ○

BERNAY *

N13

LISIEUX *

14090 ○

27020 ○

14180 ○

14070 ○

14220 ○
14200 ○

14060 ○
14190 ○
14170 ○ 14160 ○

14010 ○

CAEN *

14050 ○

14150 ○

50170 ○

SAINT-LO *

MANCHE 50

50010 ○

50050 ○

50000 ○

50070 ○

CHERBOURG *

N13

ST HELIER *

LE HAVRE *

A13

ROUEN *

N27

76130 ○

SEINE-MARITIME 76

A29

76100 ○

76120 ○

76090 ○

76010 ○
76040 ○

DIEPPE *
76030 ○
76020 ○

76110 ○

N29

N31

BEAUVAIS *

A16

CLERMONT *

MONTDIDIER *

AMIENS *

N25

ABBEVILLE *

NORTHERN FRANCE (Map 3)

Sites on this map are featured on pages 75-94 of the guide.
Please refer to the numerical index (page 562) for exact campsite page references.

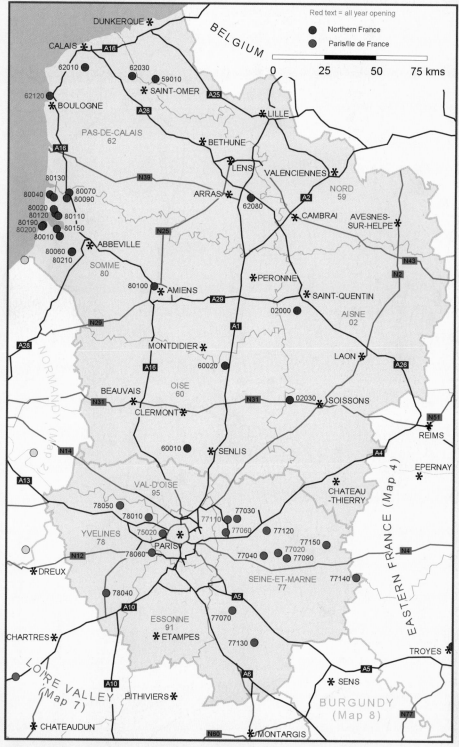

Red text = all year opening

● Northern France
● Paris/Ile de France

0   25   50   75 kms

DUNKERQUE ✳

BELGIUM

CALAIS ✳
A16

62010 ●

62030 ●
        59010 ●
✳ SAINT-OMER
A25

62120 ●

✳ BOULOGNE
A26

LILLE ✳

PAS-DE-CALAIS
62

✳ BETHUNE

A16

LENS ✳

VALENCIENNES ✳

80130 ●
N39

NORD
59

80040 ● ● 80070
          ● 80090

ARRAS ✳

62080 ●

A2

✳ CAMBRAI

AVESNES-
SUR-HELPE ✳

80020 ●
80120 ● ● 80110
80190 ●
80200 ● ● 80010 ● 80150

N25

N43

N2

✳ ABBEVILLE

80060 ●
80210 ●

SOMME
80

✳ PERONNE

✳ SAINT-QUENTIN

80100 ●
✳ AMIENS
A29

02000 ●

AISNE
02

N29

A1

A28

MONTDIDIER ✳

A16

60020 ●

LAON ✳
A26

BEAUVAIS
✳
N31

OISE
60

N31

02030 ●
✳ SOISSONS

NORMANDY (Map 2)

CLERMONT ✳

N51

REIMS

60010 ●
✳ SENLIS

A4

N14 ○

EPERNAY
✳

VAL-D'OISE
95

A13

CHATEAU-
THIERRY ✳

78050 ●

78010 ●
75020 ●
✳ PARIS

77030 ●
77110 ●
77060 ●

77120 ●

N4

YVELINES
78

77040 ●

77150 ●
77020 ●
77090 ●

EASTERN FRANCE (Map 4)

N12
78060 ●

○

✳ DREUX

SEINE-ET-MARNE
77

77140 ●

78040 ●

A10

A5

CHARTRES ✳

ESSONNE
91
✳ ETAMPES

77070 ●

77130 ●

TROYES ✳

LOIRE VALLEY
(Map 7)

A10

PITHIVIERS ✳

A6

✳ SENS

BURGUNDY
(Map 8)

N77

✳ CHATEAUDUN

N60

✳ MONTARGIS

Sites on this map are featured on pages 95-115 of the guide.
Please refer to the numerical index (page 562) for exact campsite page references.

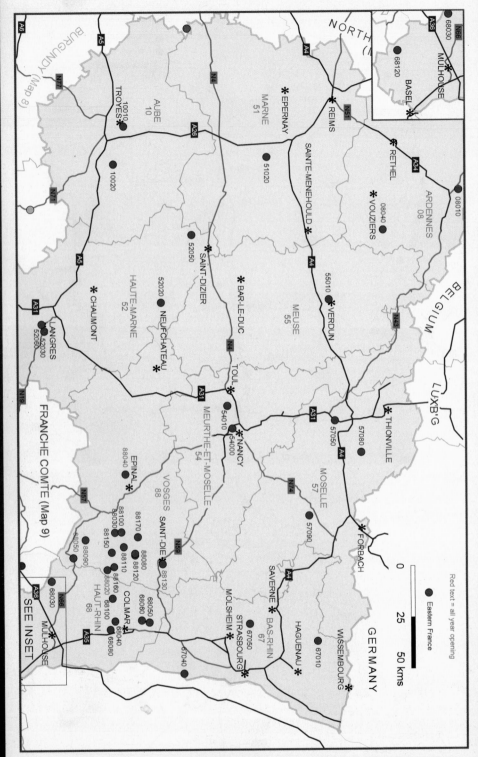

NORTH (1)

N66
68030
A36

68120

MULHOUSE
BASEL ✳

BURGUNDY (Map 8)

A5
N77
N4

10010
TROYES ✳
AUBE
10

10020

MARNE
51

EPERNAY ✳

SAINTE-MENEHOULD

REIMS ✳✳
N51

RETHEL ✳
A34

08040
VOUZIERS ✳
ARDENNES
08

08010

BELGIUM

51020

A26

52050
SAINT-DIZIER ✳

52020
NEUFCHATEAU ●
HAUTE-MARNE
52

CHAUMONT ✳

A31
LANGRES
52030
52060

N19

A5

A6

N19

FRANCHE COMTE (Map 9)

BAR-LE-DUC ✳

MEUSE
55

55010
VERDUN ✳

A4

TOUL ✳
N4

A31
54010
54000
NANCY ✳
MEURTHE-ET-MOSELLE
54

57050
57080
THIONVILLE ✳

A31
A4
N43

LUXB'G

88040
EPINAL ✳
N57

VOSGES
88

88100
88030
88170
88150
88050
88090
88080
88110
88020
88160
88120
88100
SAINT-DIE
N59
88130

MOSELLE
57

N74

57090

FORBACH ✳

SAVERNE
A4

HAGUENAU ●

WISSEMBOURG ✳

GERMANY

COLMAR ✳
68050
68060
68040
68080
HAUT-RHIN
68

MOLSHEIM ✳

67050
STRASBOURG ✳
BAS-RHIN
67

67010

A36
A35
N66
68030
MULHOUSE

SEE INSET

67040

0   25   50 kms

Red text = all year opening
● Eastern France

Sites on this map are featured on pages 116-132 of the guide.
Please refer to the numerical index (page 562) for exact campsite page references.

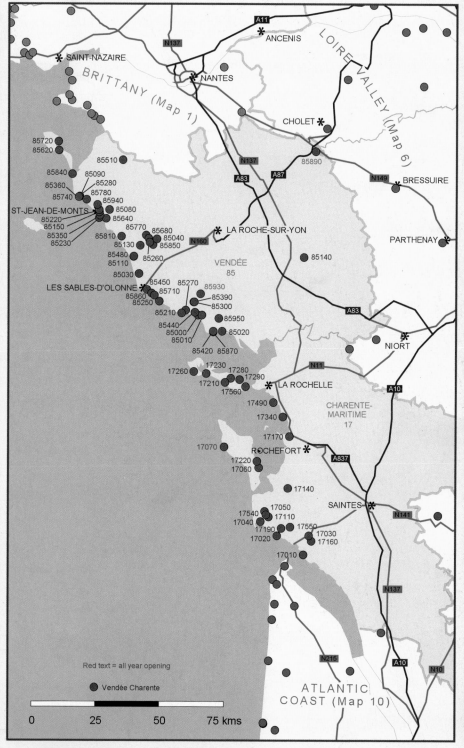

SAINT-NAZAIRE

BRITTANY (Map 1)

NANTES

A11
N137
ANCENIS

LOIRE VALLEY (Map 6)

CHOLET

85890

N137
A83
A87

85720
85620

85510

85840
85360
85740
85090
85280
85780
85940
85080
ST-JEAN-DE-MONTS
85220
85150
85350
85230
85810
85640
85770
85680
85040
85850
85130
85260
85480
85110
85030

N160
LA ROCHE-SUR-YON

VENDÉE
85

85140

N149
BRESSUIRE

PARTHENAY

A83

NIORT

LES SABLES-D'OLONNE
85450
85710
85860
85250
85210
85440
85000
85010
85270
85930
85390
85300
85950
85020
85420 85870

17260
17230
17210
17280
17290
17560

N11
LA ROCHELLE

A10

17490
17340

CHARENTE-MARITIME
17

17070
17170
ROCHEFORT

A837

17220
17060

17140

SAINTES

N141

17540
17040
17050
17110
17190
17020
17550
17030
17160

17010

N137

N215

A10

N10

Red text = all year opening

● Vendée Charente

ATLANTIC
COAST (Map 10)

0   25   50   75 kms

Sites on this map are featured on pages 133-168 of the guide.
Please refer to the numerical index (page 562) for exact campsite page references.

545

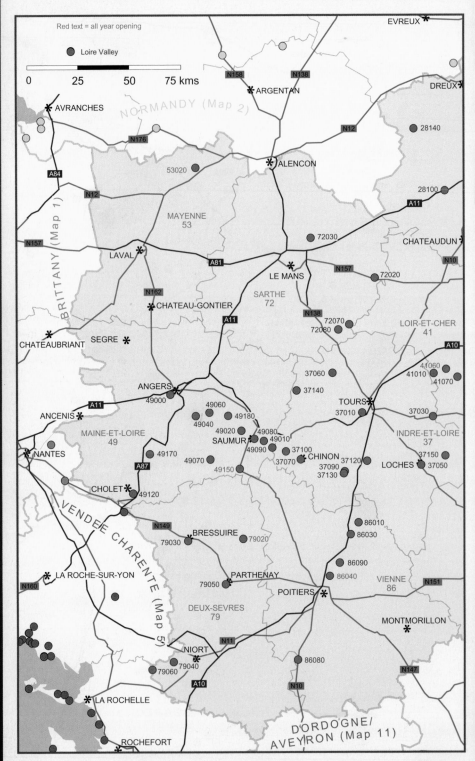

Red text = all year opening

● Loire Valley

0   25   50   75 kms

NORMANDY (Map 2)

EVREUX ✱

DREUX ✱

N158   N138

✱ ARGENTAN

AVRANCHES ✱

N176

● 28140

N12

A84

✱ ALENCON

28100 ●

N12

A11

53020

MAYENNE
53

CHATEAUDUN ✱

N157

BRITTANY (Map 1)

LAVAL ✱

A81

● 72030

N10

LE MANS ✱

N157

72020 ●

N162

SARTHE
72

✱ CHATEAU-GONTIER

A11

N138

72070 ●
72080 ●

LOIR-ET-CHER
41

CHATEAUBRIANT ✱   SEGRE ✱

37060 ●

A10

41060 ●
41010 ● ●
41070 ●

ANGERS ✱

● 37140

TOURS ✱

37030 ●

49000

37010 ●

ANCENIS ✱

A11

49060 ●
49040 ●   49180 ●
49020 ●   49080 ●
49010 ●

INDRE-ET-LOIRE
37

MAINE-ET-LOIRE
49

SAUMUR ✱

37150 ●

✱ NANTES

A87

49170 ●

49070 ●

49090 ●   37100 ●
37070 ●   CHINON   37120 ●
37090 ●
37130 ●

LOCHES ✱   37050 ●

49150 ●

CHOLET ✱
49120

VENDEE   (Map 5)

N149

✱ BRESSUIRE   79020 ●

86010 ●
86030 ●

79030 ●

CHARENTE

86090 ●
86040 ●

VIENNE
86

N151

✱ LA ROCHE-SUR-YON

PARTHENAY ✱

POITIERS ✱

N160

79050 ●

MONTMORILLON
✱

DEUX-SEVRES
79

N11

NIORT ✱

86080 ●

N147

79040 ●
79060 ●

A10

N10

✱ LA ROCHELLE

D'ORDOGNE/
AVEYRON (Map 11)

ROCHEFORT ✱

Sites on these maps are featured on pages 169-195 of the guide.
Please refer to the numerical index (page 562) for exact campsite page references.

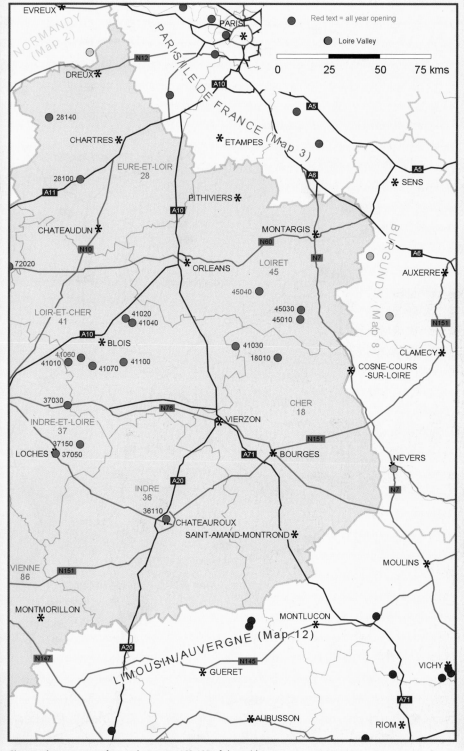

EVREUX

NORMANDY (Map 2)

N12

DREUX

28140

CHARTRES

PARIS ILE DE FRANCE (Map 3)

PARIS

Red text = all year opening

Loire Valley

0   25   50   75 kms

A10

A5

ETAMPES

A6

A5

SENS

28100

A11

EURE-ET-LOIR 28

PITHIVIERS

CHATEAUDUN

N10

72020

ORLEANS

MONTARGIS

N60

LOIRET 45

N7

BURGUNDY (Map 8)

A6

AUXERRE

45040

LOIR-ET-CHER 41

41020
41040

45030
45010

A10

BLOIS

41060
41010   41070   41100

41030

18010

CLAMECY

COSNE-COURS -SUR-LOIRE

37030

N76

CHER 18

INDRE-ET-LOIRE 37

VIERZON

N151

37150
LOCHES   37050

A71   BOURGES

NEVERS

A20

N7

INDRE 36

36110

CHATEAUROUX

SAINT-AMAND-MONTROND

VIENNE 86

N151

MOULINS

MONTMORILLON

MONTLUCON

A20

LIMOUSIN/AUVERGNE (Map 12)

N147

N145   GUERET

VICHY

A71

AUBUSSON

RIOM

Sites on these maps are featured on pages 169-195 of the guide.
Please refer to the numerical index (page 562) for exact campsite page references.

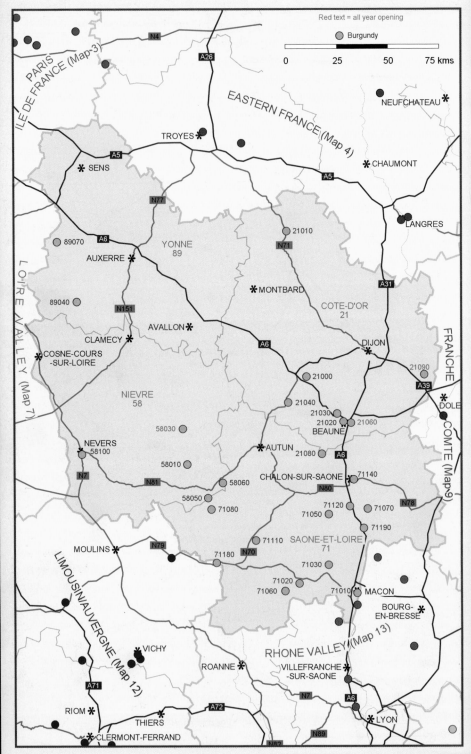

Red text = all year opening

Burgundy

0   25   50   75 kms

PARIS
ILE DE FRANCE (Map 3)

N4

A26

EASTERN FRANCE (Map 4)

NEUFCHATEAU ✳

TROYES ✳

✳ CHAUMONT

A5

✳ SENS

A5

LANGRES

N77

LOIRE VALLEY (Map 7)

A6

89070

YONNE
89

21010

N71

AUXERRE ✳

89040

N151

✳ MONTBARD

COTE-D'OR
21

A31

FRANCHE

AVALLON ✳

A6

DIJON

CLAMECY ✳

21090

COSNE-COURS
-SUR-LOIRE

A39

NIEVRE
58

21000

DOLE ✳

21040

58030

21030
21020   21060

COMTE (Map 9)

NEVERS
58100

58010

BEAUNE

21080

A6

N7

58060

N81

AUTUN ✳

CHALON-SUR-SAONE

71140

58050

N80

71120
71050

N78

71080

71070

71190

MOULINS ✳

N79

71110

SAONE-ET-LOIRE
71

71180   N70

71030

LIMOUSIN/AUVERGNE (Map 12)

71020
71060

71010 ✳ MACON

BOURG-
EN-BRESSE

✳ VICHY

RHONE VALLEY (Map 13)

A71

ROANNE ✳

VILLEFRANCHE
-SUR-SAONE ✳

RIOM ✳

THIERS ✳

A72

N7

A6

LYON

✳ CLERMONT-FERRAND

N89

N83

Sites on these maps are featured on pages 196-207 of the guide.
Please refer to the numerical index (page 562) for exact campsite page references.

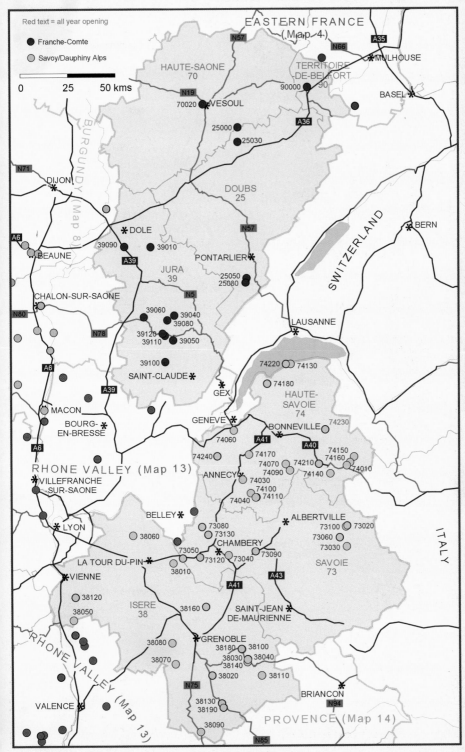

Red text = all year opening

● Franche-Comte
○ Savoy/Dauphiny Alps

0   25   50 kms

EASTERN FRANCE (Map 4)

HAUTE-SAONE 70

MULHOUSE

TERRITOIRE DE-BELFORT 90

90000

BASEL

N57

N66

A35

N19

70020 VESOUL

25000

25030

A36

DIJON

N71

BURGUNDY (Map 8)

DOUBS 25

SWITZERLAND

BERN

BEAUNE

A6

DOLE

39090   39010

A39

PONTARLIER

N57

JURA 39

25050
25080

LAUSANNE

CHALON-SUR-SAONE

N80

N78

N5

39060   39040
        39080
39120
39110   39050

39100

SAINT-CLAUDE

GEX

74220   74130

74180

HAUTE-SAVOIE 74

MACON

A6

A39

BOURG-EN-BRESSE

GENEVE

BONNEVILLE

74230

RHONE VALLEY (Map 13)

A6

VILLEFRANCHE-SUR-SAONE

LYON

74060

A41

74240

A40

74170
74070   74210
74090   74140
74030
74100
74110

74150
74160

74010

ANNECY

74040

BELLEY

73080
73130

ALBERTVILLE

73100   73020
73060
73030

38060

73050

CHAMBERY

73090

LA TOUR DU-PIN

73120   73040

SAVOIE 73

38010

VIENNE

A41

38120

ISERE 38

38160

SAINT-JEAN DE-MAURIENNE

A43

38050

38080

38070

GRENOBLE

38180   38100
38030   38040
38140
38020   38110

N75

RHONE VALLEY (Map 13)

BRIANCON

N94

VALENCE

38130
38190

38090

PROVENCE (Map 14)

N85

ITALY

Sites on these maps are featured on pages 208-235 of the guide.
Please refer to the numerical index (page 562) for exact campsite page references.

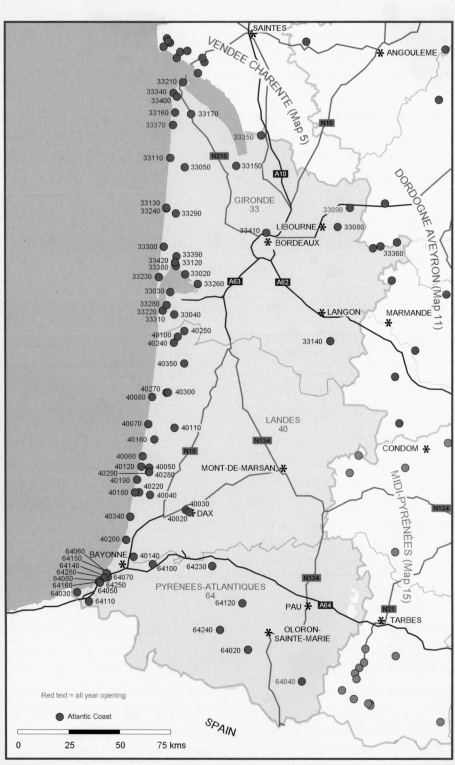

SAINTES

ANGOULEME

VENDEE CHARENTE (Map 5)

33210
33340
33400
33160   33170
33370
33350
N10
33110   N215
33050   33150
A10
GIRONDE
33
33130   33090
33240   33290   LIBOURNE   33080
33410
BORDEAUX   33360
33300
33420   33390
33380   33120
33230   33020
33030   33260   A63   A62
33280
33220   33040   LANGON
33310   MARMANDE
40100   40250
40240   33140
40350
40270
40080   40300
LANDES
40070   40110   40
40160   N134
40060   N10   CONDOM
40120   40050
40290   40280   MONT-DE-MARSAN
40190
40180   40220   40040
40340   40030
40200   40020   DAX   N124
BAYONNE
64060
64150
64140   64070   40140
64280   64100   64230
64080   64250
64160   64050
64030   64110   PYRENEES-ATLANTIQUES
64   64120
PAU   A64   N21
64240   OLORON-   TARBES
SAINTE-MARIE
64020
MIDI-PYRÉNÉES (Map 15)
DORDOGNE AVEYRON (Map 11)
N124
64040
SPAIN

Red text = all year opening

● Atlantic Coast

0   25   50   75 kms

Sites on these maps are featured on pages 236-270 of the guide.
Please refer to the numerical index (page 562) for exact campsite page references.

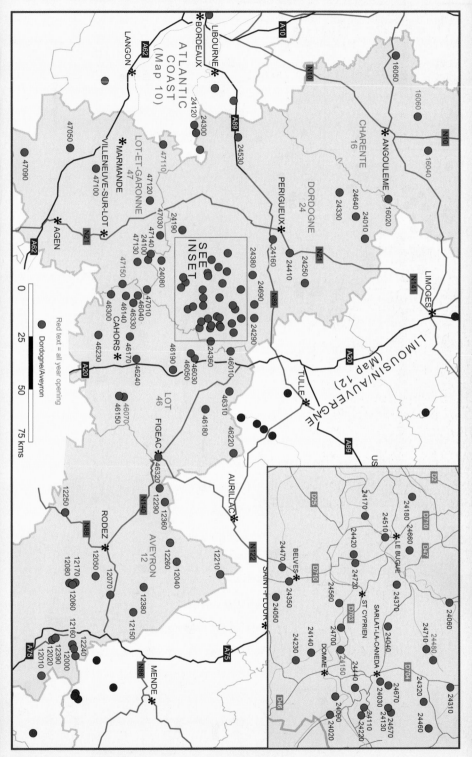

ATLANTIC
COAST
(Map 10)

CHARENTE
16

DORDOGNE
24

LOT-ET-GARONNE
47

LOT
46

AVEYRON
12

LIMOUSIN/AUVERGNE
(Map 12)

SEE
INSET

0
25
50
75 kms

Red text = all year opening

● Dordogne/Aveyron

Sites on these maps are featured on pages 271-314 of the guide.
Please refer to the numerical index (page 562) for exact campsite page references.

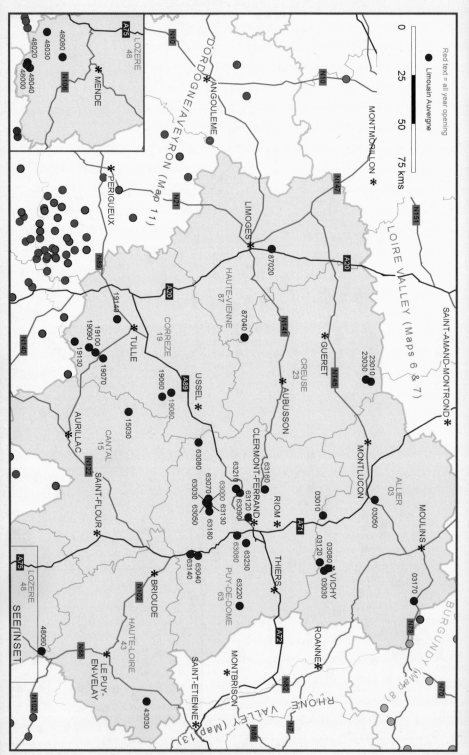

Sites on these maps are featured on pages 315-332 of the guide.
Please refer to the numerical index (page 562) for exact campsite page references.

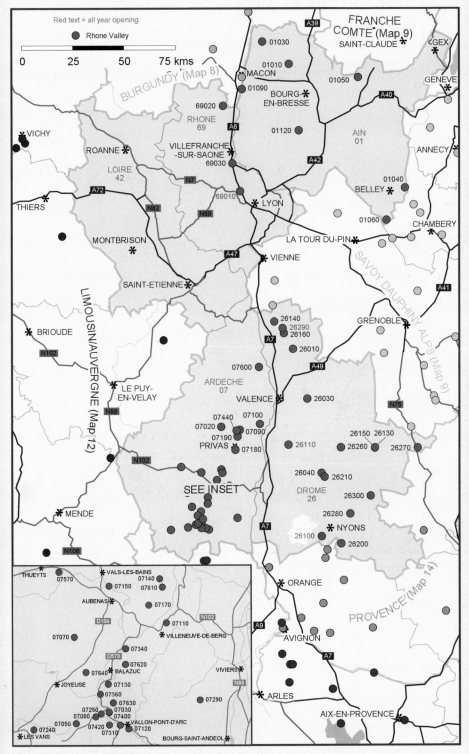

Red text = all year opening

● Rhone Valley

0   25   50   75 kms

BURGUNDY (Map 8)

01030
01010
MACON
01090
BOURG-
EN-BRESSE
69020
RHONE
69
VILLEFRANCHE
-SUR-SAONE
69030
69010
LYON

FRANCHE
COMTE (Map 9)
SAINT-CLAUDE ✳
GEX
01050
GENEVE
A39
A40
01040
BELLEY ✳
01060
ANNECY
AIN
01
01120
A42
A6
N7
N82
N89
N88
N102
N102
N106
A72
A47

VICHY
ROANNE ✳
LOIRE
42
THIERS ✳
MONTBRISON
SAINT-ETIENNE ✳

LA TOUR DU PIN ✳
VIENNE ✳
CHAMBERY

SAVOY DAUPHINY ALPS (Map 9)

BRIOUDE ✳

LIMOUSIN/AUVERGNE (Map 12)

LE PUY-
EN-VELAY

MENDE ✳

26140
26290
26160
26010
A7
07600
ARDECHE
07
VALENCE ✳
A49
26030
N75
GRENOBLE ✳
A41

07440 07100
07020   07090
07190
PRIVAS ✳
07180

26150 26130
26260   26270
26110
26040 26210
26300
26280
26100   ✳ NYONS
26200

DROME
26

SEE INSET

ORANGE ✳

PROVENCE (Map 14)

A9
A7
AVIGNON
ARLES ✳
AIX-EN-PROVENCE

THUEYTS ✳
07570
VALS-LES-BAINS ✳
07140
07150 07610
AUBENAS ✳
07170
D104
07110
N102
07070
VILLENEUVE-DE-BERG ✳
D579
07340
07620
07640
BALAZUC
JOYEUSE ✳
07130
07360
07630
07250 07030
07080   07400
07050 07420
07240   07120
LES VANS ✳ 07310
VALLON-PONT-D'ARC ✳
BOURG-SAINT-ANDEOL ✳
VIVIERS ✳
N86
07290

Sites on these maps are featured on pages 333-360 of the guide.
Please refer to the numerical index (page 562) for exact campsite page references.

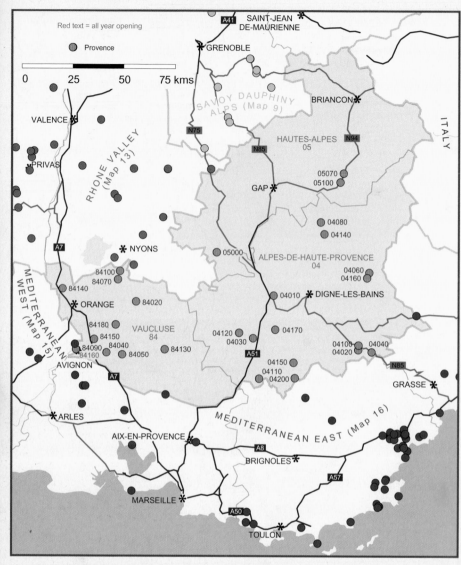

Red text = all year opening

⬤ Provence

0   25   50   75 kms

SAINT-JEAN
DE-MAURIENNE

A41

GRENOBLE

VALENCE

PRIVAS

RHONE VALLEY
(Map 13)

SAVOY DAUPHINY
ALPS (Map 9)

BRIANCON

HAUTES-ALPES
05

N75

N85

N94

05070
05100

GAP

04080

04140

N85

05000

ALPES-DE-HAUTE-PROVENCE
04

04060
04160

A7

NYONS

84100
84070

84140

ORANGE

84180
84150
84090
84160   84040
84050   84130

AVIGNON

A7

ARLES

84020

VAUCLUSE
84

04010   DIGNE-LES-BAINS

04120
04030

04170

04100   04040
04020

A51

04150
04110
04200

N85

GRASSE

MEDITERRANEAN
WEST (Map 15)

AIX-EN-PROVENCE

MEDITERRANEAN EAST (Map 16)

A8

BRIGNOLES

MARSEILLE

A50

A57

TOULON

ITALY

Sites on these maps are featured on pages 361-375 of the guide.
Please refer to the numerical index (page 562) for exact campsite page references.

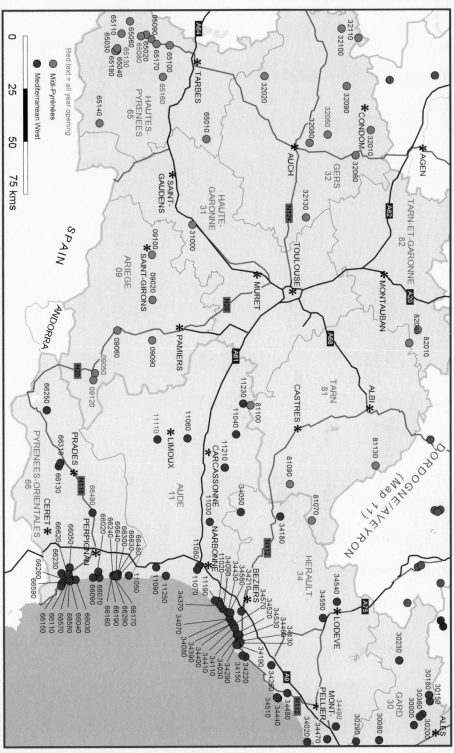

Sites on these maps are featured on pages 376-434 of the guide.
Please refer to the numerical index (page 562) for exact campsite page references.

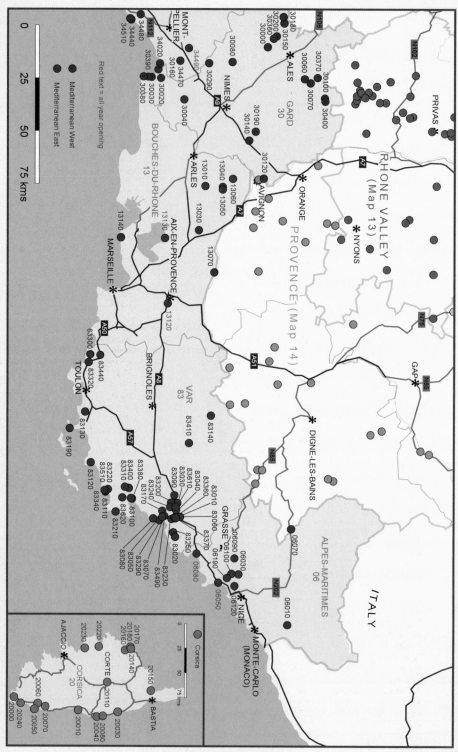

Red text = all year opening

Mediterranean West

Mediterranean East

0 25 50 75 kms

Corsica

0 25 50 75 kms

Sites on these maps are featured on pages 435-471 of the guide.
Please refer to the numerical index (page 562) for exact campsite page references.

Town and Village Index

Index - town and village

Index - town and village

Index - campsite number

Index by Campsite Region and Name

Index - campsite region and name

Widely regarded as the 'Bible' by site owners and readers alike, there is no better guide when it comes to forming an independent view of a campsite's quality. When you need to be confident in your choice of campsite, you need the Alan Rogers Guide.

☑ Sites only included on merit

☑ Sites cannot pay to be included

☑ Independently inspected, rigorously assessed

☑ Impartial reviews

☑ Over 40 years of expertise

INSPECTED CAMPSITES & SELECTED